Lecture Notes in Computer Science 16781

Advanced Research in Computing and Software Science

Subline of Lecture Notes in Computer Science

More information about this series at https://link.springer.com/bookseries/558

Massimo Torquati · Gabriele Mencagli ·
Valeria Cardellini · Alessia Antelmi ·
Doriana Medić
Editors

Euro-Par 2026: Parallel Processing

32nd European Conference on Parallel and Distributed Processing
Pisa, Italy, August 24–28, 2026
Proceedings, Part I

Springer

Editors
Massimo Torquati
University of Pisa
Pisa, Italy

Gabriele Mencagli
University of Pisa
Pisa, Italy

Valeria Cardellini
University of Rome Tor Vergata
Rome, Italy

Alessia Antelmi
University of Turin
Turin, Italy

Doriana Medić
University of Turin
Turin, Italy

ISSN 0302-9743 ISSN 1611-3349 (electronic)
Lecture Notes in Computer Science
ISBN 978-3-032-35247-7 ISBN 978-3-032-35248-4 (eBook)
https://doi.org/10.1007/978-3-032-35248-4

This Springer imprint is published by the registered company Springer Nature Switzerland AG
The registered company address is: Gewerbestrasse 11, 6330 Cham, Switzerland

Preface

This book is one of the two volumes comprising the proceedings of the 32nd International European Conference on Parallel and Distributed Computing (Euro-Par 2026), held in Pisa, Italy, from August 24 to 28, 2026. Euro-Par 2026 was organized by the Department of Computer Science of the University of Pisa.

Euro-Par is the premier European forum for all aspects of parallel and distributed computing. Building on more than three decades of scientific exchange, the conference covers the full spectrum of the field, from foundational algorithms to end-to-end applications, from low-power edge devices to exascale systems and cloud-to-edge computing continuums, and from architectural advances and compiler techniques to programming models, performance engineering, reproducibility, and sustainability.

Since its inception, Euro-Par has brought together researchers and practitioners from academia, research laboratories, and industry, providing a forum for the presentation and discussion of new results in parallel and distributed computing. Its organization into scientific tracks supports focused technical discussions while also fostering interaction across a broad and diverse community. In addition, Euro-Par provides a platform for workshops and satellite events addressing established, emerging, and interdisciplinary topics.

Previous conference editions were held in Stockholm, Lyon, Passau, Southampton, Toulouse, Munich, Manchester, Paderborn, Klagenfurt, Pisa, Lisbon, Dresden, Rennes, Las Palmas, Delft, Ischia, Bordeaux, Rhodes, Aachen, Porto, Vienna, Grenoble, Santiago de Compostela, Turin, Göttingen, Warsaw, Lisbon, Glasgow, Limassol, Madrid, and Dresden.

Euro-Par 2026 accepted papers were organized in the following six tracks:

- Track 1: Programming, Compilers, and Performance
- Track 2: Scheduling, Resource Management, Cloud, Edge Computing, and Workflows
- Track 3: Architectures and Accelerators
- Track 4: Scalable AI and Data Analytics
- Track 5: Theory and Algorithms
- Track 6: Domain-Specific and Applied Parallel and Distributed Computing

The scientific program was coordinated by the track chairs: Javier García-Blas and Paul Kelly for Track 1; Vana Kalogeraki and Guillaume Pierre for Track 2; Marco Danelutto and Ivy Peng for Track 3; Abhinav Bhatele and Robert Birke for Track 4; Anne Benoit and Geppino Pucci for Track 5; and Dalvan Griebler and Bertil Schmidt for Track 6.

A total of 332 papers were submitted to Euro-Par 2026. After an initial compliance check, 20 submissions were desk-rejected, and 312 papers entered the full single-blind reviewing process. The selection process was highly competitive and required the coordinated effort of the track chairs, 240 members of the program committee, and external reviewers. Altogether, 1187 reviews were produced, including 88 external reviews, corresponding to an average of 3.8 reviews per paper sent to full review.

Following the initial review phase, each track discussed the submitted papers and proposed sets of papers for acceptance, further discussion, or rejection. The papers from all tracks were then considered during the selection process, leading to the acceptance of 87 papers to be presented at the conference and published in these proceedings. This corresponds to an overall acceptance rate of 26.2%.

In addition, the following accepted papers were selected to be presented in a plenary session and to compete for the Euro-Par 2026 Best Paper Award, which was generously sponsored by Springer. The award winner was announced during the conference dinner.

1. Yi Miao and Stephen Jarvis. Constraint Driven Global Data Layout Optimization for Tensor Expressions
2. Romial Menra, Guillaume Rosinosky, Remous-Aris Koutsiamanis, Sébastien Bolle, and Jean-Marc Menaud. Understanding Power Limiting Mechanisms in Modern Processors: A Deep Dive into Intel RAPL and Turbo Boost Dynamics
3. Cristian Campos Ferrer, Angeles G. Navarro, and Sonia Gonzalez-Navarro. CASTM: An API for Accelerating Zero-Knowledge Proof Kernels on CGRA Architectures
4. Gianluca Mittone and Marco Aldinucci. Accelerating Sharded Data Parallelism at Scale with Federated Learning
5. Peter Sanders, Matthias Schimek, Tim Niklas Uhl, and Thomas Weidmann. Engineering Scalable Distributed List Ranking
6. Samuel Wiggins, Grace Zgheib, Mahesh A. Iyer, and Viktor Prasanna. Accelerating Multi-Agent Reinforcement Learning on Heterogeneous Platforms

To enhance the reproducibility of research published at Euro-Par, the conference encourages authors to submit artifacts, such as source code, datasets, scripts, and reproducibility instructions. Following the acceptance notification, authors of accepted papers were invited to submit artifacts for evaluation. A total of 23 artifacts were submitted in support of accepted papers and evaluated by the Artifact Evaluation Committee (AEC). The AEC accepted 20 artifacts. Papers with accepted artifacts are marked in the proceedings by a special badge, and the artifacts are made available online in the Euro-Par 2026 community on Zenodo (https://zenodo.org/communities/europar_2026/).

In addition to the technical program, we had the pleasure of hosting three distinguished *keynote* talks by:

- Michela Taufer, University of Tennessee, Knoxville, USA
- Anne-Marie Kermarrec, EPFL, Switzerland
- Luca Benini, ETH Zurich, Switzerland, and University of Bologna, Italy

Euro-Par 2026 was complemented by a rich program of workshops and satellite events. The workshops were held on August 24 and 25, preceding the main conference program, and provided focused venues for presenting and discussing research on specialized topics related to parallel and distributed computing. A selection of the papers presented at the workshops is published in separate Springer LNCS proceedings. The main conference program, held from August 26 to 28, also included the PhD Symposium, the poster track, and the Women in HPC session. These events provided additional opportunities for presenting ongoing work, discussing emerging research directions, and engaging with the wider parallel and distributed computing community. Contributions presented at the PhD Symposium, the poster track, and the Women in HPC session are published in the satellite-event proceedings.

The proceedings of Euro-Par 2026 are published in two Springer LNCS volumes. The first volume includes papers from the tracks Programming, Compilers, and Performance; Architectures and Accelerators; and Domain-Specific and Applied Parallel and Distributed Computing. The second volume includes papers from the tracks Scheduling, Resource Management, Cloud, Edge Computing, and Workflows; Scalable AI and Data Analytics; and Theory and Algorithms.

We would like to thank all authors, chairs, program committee members, external reviewers, artifact evaluators, and organizers of satellite events for their essential contributions to Euro-Par 2026. We are grateful to the Euro-Par Steering Committee for its guidance and support, and to the local organizing team at the Department of Computer Science of the University of Pisa for making the conference possible. We also thank our institutional and industrial sponsors for their support.

August 2026

Massimo Torquati
Gabriele Mencagli
Valeria Cardellini
Alessia Antelmi
Doriana Medić

Organization

General Chairs

Massimo Torquati	University of Pisa, Italy
Gabriele Mencagli	University of Pisa, Italy

Program Committee Chair

Valeria Cardellini	University of Rome Tor Vergata, Italy

Workshop Chairs

Biagio Cosenza	University of Salerno, Italy
Demetris Zeinalipour	University of Cyprus, Cyprus

Proceedings Chairs

Alessia Antelmi	University of Turin, Italy
Doriana Medić	University of Turin, Italy

PhD Symposium Chairs

Patrizio Dazzi	University of Pisa, Italy
Leonel Sousa	Universidade de Lisboa, Portugal

Poster Chairs

Tiziano De Matteis	Vrije Universiteit Amsterdam, The Netherlands
Iacopo Colonnelli	University of Turin, Italy

Women in HPC Chairs

Ayesha Afzal	University of Erlangen-Nürnberg, Germany
Marta Garcia-Gasulla	Barcelona Supercomputing Center, Spain
Diana Göhringer	TU Dresden, Germany

Publicity Chairs

Valerio Besozzi	University of Pisa, Italy
Xutong Liu	University of Washington, USA
Dalvan Griebler	Pontifical Catholic University of Rio Grande do Sul, Brazil

Web Chair

Barbara Cantalupo	University of Turin, Italy

Sponsor Chair

Marco Aldinucci	University of Turin, Italy

Steering Committee

Fernando Silva (SC Chair)	University of Porto, Portugal
Dora Blanco Heras (Vice-chair)	University of Santiago de Compostela, Spain
Anne Benoit	École Normale Supérieure de Lyon, France
Christos Kaklamanis	Computer Technology Institute, Patras, Greece
Demetris Zeinalipour (Workshops Chair)	University of Cyprus, Cyprus
Diana Göhringer	TU Dresden, Germany
Ewa Deelman	University of Southern California, USA
Felix Wolf (Web Chair)	Technical University of Darmstadt, Germany
George Papadopoulos	University of Cyprus, Cyprus
Henk Sips (Finances Chair)	Delft University of Technology, The Netherlands
Ivona Brandić	Technical University of Vienna, Austria
Jesus Carretero	University Carlos III of Madrid, Spain
Krzysztof Rzadca (Industrial Session Co-chair)	University of Warsaw, Poland

Leonel Sousa (PhD Symposium Co-chair)	University of Lisbon, Portugal
Maciej Malawski (Publicity Co-chair)	AGH University of Kraków, Poland
Marco Aldinucci (EU Strategy Chair)	University of Turin, Italy
Massimo Torquati (Artifacts Co-chair)	University of Pisa, Italy
Ramin Yahyapour	GWDG Göttingen, Germany
Rosa M. Badia	Barcelona Supercomputing Center, Spain
Tomàs Margalef	Universitat Autònoma de Barcelona, Spain
Wolfgang E. Nagel	TU Dresden, Germany

Honorary Members

Christian Lengauer	University of Passau, Germany
Luc Bougé	ENS Rennes, France
Ron Perrott	Oxford e-Research Centre, UK
Karl Dieter Reinartz	University of Erlangen-Nürnberg, Germany

Scientific Organization

Track 1: Programming, Compilers, and Performance

Chairs

Javier García-Blas	Universidad Carlos III de Madrid, Spain
Paul Kelly	Imperial College London, UK

Program Committee

Antonio Barbalace	University of Edinburgh, UK
Loris Belcastro	University of Calabria, Italy
Jean-Baptiste Besnard	Paratools SAS, France
Surendra Billa	Centre for Development of Advanced Computing, India
Walter Binder	University of Lugano, Switzerland
Christopher Brown	University of St Andrews, UK
João M.P. Cardoso	University of Porto, Portugal

Paul Carpenter	Barcelona Supercomputing Center, Spain
Sandra Catalan	Jaume I University, Spain
Serena Curzel	Politecnico di Milano, Italy
Pablo de Oliveira Castro	University of Versailles St-Quentin-en-Yvelines, France
Bernhard Egger	Seoul National University, South Korea
Dominik Göddeke	University of Stuttgart, Germany
Tsung-Wei Huang	University of Wisconsin at Madison, USA
Gabriel Iuhasz	West University of Timişoara, Romania
Seyong Lee	Oak Ridge National Laboratory, USA
Diego R. Llanos	University of Valladolid, Spain
Hector Martinez Perez	University of Córdoba, Spain
Lucas Mello Schnorr	Federal University of Rio Grande do Sul, Brazil
Raffaele Montella	University of Naples "Parthenope", Italy
Swann Perarnau	Argonne National Laboratory, USA
Mihail Popov	Inria Bordeaux, France
Ari Rasch	University of Münster, Germany
Jeremy Singer	University of Glasgow, UK
Miwako Tsuji	RIKEN Center for Computational Science, Japan
Ben van Werkhoven	Leiden University, The Netherlands
Wim Vanderbauwhede	University of Glasgow, UK
Chen Wang	Nanyang Technological University, Singapore
Zheng Wang	University of Leeds, UK
Jackson Woodruff	University of Edinburgh, UK
Sotirios Xydis	National Technical University of Athens, Greece

Track 2: Scheduling, Resource Management, Cloud, Edge Computing, and Workflows

Chairs

Vana Kalogeraki	Athens University of Economics and Business, Greece
Guillaume Pierre	University of Rennes, France

Program Committee

Cristina L. Abad	Escuela Superior Politécnica del Litoral, Ecuador
Ahmad Al-Shishtawy	Swedish Institute of Computer Science, Sweden
Ahmed Ali-Eldin Hassan	Chalmers University of Technology, Sweden

Christos Antonopoulos	University of the Peloponnese, Greece
Luciana Arantes	Sorbonne Université, France
Daniel Balouek	Inria, France
David Bermbach	TU Berlin, Germany
Monowar Bhuyan	Umeå University, Sweden
Luiz F. Bittencourt	University of Campinas, Brazil
Antony Chazapis	Foundation for Research and Technology - Hellas, Greece
Iacopo Colonnelli	University of Turin, Italy
Camille Coti	ÉTS Montréal, Canada
Hélène Coullon	IMT Atlantique, France
Tommaso Cucinotta	Scuola Superiore Sant'Anna, Italy
Alexandre da Silva Veith	Nokia Bell Labs, Belgium
Stéphane Delbruel	University of Bordeaux - LaBRI, France
Ciprian Dobre	Politehnica Bucharest, Romania
Stefano Forti	University of Pisa, Italy
Pantelis Frangoudis	TU Wien, Austria
Dimitra Giantsidi	Azure Research, UK
Aniruddha Gokhale	Vanderbilt University, USA
Vincenzo Gulisano	Chalmers University of Technology, Sweden
Konrad Iwanicki	University of Warsaw, Poland
Boris Koldehofe	TU Ilmenau, Germany
Ioannis Konstantinou	University of Thessaly, Greece
Spyros Lalis	University of Thessaly, Greece
Wes J. Lloyd	University of Washington, USA
Adrien Luxey-Bitri	University of Lille, France
Vania Marangozova	Grenoble Alpes University, France
Alessandro Margara	Politecnico di Milano, Italy
Anudipa Mondal	CNRS, France
Matteo Nardelli	Bank of Italy, Italy
Ana Oprescu	University of Amsterdam, The Netherlands
George Pallis	University of Cyprus, Cyprus
Nikela Papadopoulou	University of Glasgow, UK
Marina Papatriantafilou	Chalmers University of Technology, Sweden
Sungyong Park	Sogang University, South Korea
Marta Patiño-Martinez	Universidad Politécnica de Madrid, Spain
Florin Pop	Politehnica Bucharest, ICI Bucharest, Romania
Jan S. Rellermeyer	Hannover University, Germany
Etienne Rivière	UCLouvain, Belgium
Maria A. Rodriguez Sossa	University of Melbourne, Australia
Gabriele Russo Russo	University of Rome Tor Vergata, Italy
Krzysztof Rzadca	University of Warsaw and Google, Poland

Valerio Schiavoni	University of Neuchâtel, Switzerland
Abel Souza	University of California, Santa Cruz, USA
Javid Taheri	Queen's University Belfast, UK
Klervie Toczé	VU Amsterdam, The Netherlands
Dimitrios Tomaras	Athens University of Economics and Business, Greece
Luis Veiga	Technical University of Lisbon, Portugal
Monica Vitali	Politecnico di Milano, Italy
Roman Vitenberg	University of Oslo, Norway
Spyros Voulgaris	Athens University of Economics and Business, Greece
Sebastian Werner	TU Berlin, Germany

Track 3: Architectures and Accelerators

Chairs

Marco Danelutto	University of Pisa, Italy
Ivy Peng	KTH Royal Institute of Technology, Sweden

Program Committee

José L. Abellán	Universidad de Murcia, Spain
Boma Anantasatya Adhi	RIKEN Center for Computational Science, Japan
Jorge G. Barbosa	University of Porto, Portugal
Davide Bertozzi	University of Manchester, UK
Guillermo Botella Juan	Complutense University of Madrid, Spain
Xing Cai	Simula Research Laboratory, Norway
Juan M. Cebrian	University of Murcia, Spain
Teresa Cervero	Barcelona Supercomputing Center, Spain
Andreas Diavastos	Cyprus University of Technology, Cyprus
Manuel F. Dolz	Universitat Jaume I, Spain
Toshio Endo	Institute of Science Tokyo, Japan
Jesús Escudero-Sahuquillo	University of Castilla-La Mancha, Spain
Holger Fröning	Heidelberg University, Germany
Nicolas Gac	Université Paris-Saclay, France
Pedro Javier García	Universidad de Castilla-La Mancha, Spain
Vladimir Getov	University of Westminster, UK
Tanja Harbaum	ITIV, Karlsruhe Institute of Technology, Germany
Ian Karlin	Queen's University, Canada

Arjun Kashyap	NVIDIA, USA
Christoph Kessler	Linköping University, Sweden
Benjamin Klenk	NVIDIA, USA
Ryohei Kobayashi	Institute of Science Tokyo, Japan
Kazuhiko Komatsu	Tohoku University, Japan
Hatem Ltaief	King Abdullah University of Science and Technology, Saudi Arabia
George Michelogiannakis	KTH Royal Institute of Technology, Sweden
Agustín Navarro-Torres	University of Murcia, Spain
Mattias O'Nils	Mid Sweden University, Sweden
Marcus Paradies	LMU Munich, Germany
Laércio Pilla	LaBRI, France
Oscar Plata	University of Málaga, Spain
Dirk Pleiter	University of Groningen, The Netherlands
Christian Plessl	Paderborn University, Germany
Rohit Prasad	CEA, France
Julio Sahuquillo	Universitat Politècnica de València, Spain
Kazem Shekofteh	Heidelberg University, Germany
Shinji Sumimoto	University of Tokyo, Japan
Keita Teranishi	Oak Ridge National Laboratory, USA
Samuel Thibault	LaBRI, Université Bordeaux 1, France
Antonino Tumeo	Pacific Northwest National Laboratory, USA
Tomohiro Ueno	RIKEN, Japan
Roman Wyrzykowski	Częstochowa University of Technology, Poland
Yoshiki Yamaguchi	University of Tsukuba, Japan
Kazutomo Yoshii	Argonne National Laboratory, USA

Track 4: Scalable AI and Data Analytics

Chairs

Abhinav Bhatele	University of Maryland, College Park, USA
Robert Birke	University of Turin, Italy

Program Committee

Andreea Anghel	IBM Research, Switzerland
Francesco Antici	RIKEN Center for Computational Science, Japan
Achim Basermann	German Aerospace Center (DLR), Germany
Suren Byna	Ohio State University, USA

Sophie Cerf	Inria, France
Alexandru Costan	Inria, France
Ana Paula Couto da Silva	Universidade Federal de Minas Gerais, Brazil
Reza Farahani	University of Klagenfurt, Austria
Sukhpal Singh Gill	Queen Mary University of London, UK
Horacio González-Vélez	National College of Ireland, Ireland
Ligang He	University of Warwick, UK
Odej Kao	TU Berlin, Germany
Hideyuki Kawashima	Keio University, Japan
Youngjae Kim	Sogang University, South Korea
Zeynep Kiziltan	University of Bologna, Italy
Michael Kuhn	Otto von Guericke University Magdeburg, Germany
Preeti Malakar	IIT Kanpur, India
Manolis Marazakis	Institute of Computer Science, FORTH, Greece
Adriano Marques Garcia	Johannes Kepler University Linz, Austria
Gianluca Mittone	University of Turin, Italy
Daniel Nichols	Lawrence Livermore National Laboratory, USA
Jorji Nonaka	RIKEN Center for Computational Science, Japan
Ramon Nou	Barcelona Supercomputing Center, Spain
Dana Petcu	West University of Timişoara, Romania
M. Mustafa Rafique	Rochester Institute of Technology, USA
Jože M. Rožanec	Jožef Stefan Institute, Slovenia
Rizos Sakellariou	University of Manchester, UK
Siddharth Singh	NVIDIA, USA
Hari Subramoni	Ohio State University, USA
Osamu Tatebe	University of Tsukuba, Japan
Douglas Thain	University of Notre Dame, USA
Jeyan Thiyagalingam	Science and Technology Facilities Council, UK
Rafael Tolosana-Calasanz	University of Zaragoza, Spain
Yang Wang	Shenzhen Institutes of Advanced Technology, Chinese Academy of Sciences, China
Jidong Zhai	Tsinghua University, China
Huihuo Zheng	Argonne National Laboratory, USA
Keren Zhou	George Mason University, USA

Track 5: Theory and Algorithms

Chairs

Anne Benoit	École Normale Supérieure de Lyon, France
Geppino Pucci	University of Padua, Italy

Program Committee

Ruben Becker	Ca' Foscari University of Venice, Italy
Ioana Bercea	KTH Royal Institute of Technology, Sweden
Petra Berenbrink	University of Hamburg, Germany
Vittorio Bilò	University of Salento, Italy
Tiziana Calamoneri	Sapienza University of Rome, Italy
Matteo Ceccarello	University of Padua, Italy
Andrea Clementi	University of Rome Tor Vergata, Italy
Fabien Dufoulon	Lancaster University, UK
Lionel Eyraud-Dubois	LaBRI – Inria Bordeaux Sud-Ouest, France
Leszek Gąsieniec	University of Liverpool, UK
Christos Kaklamanis	University of Patras, Greece
Sayaka Kamei	University of Hiroshima, Japan
Loris Marchal	CNRS, France
Achour Mostéfaoui	Nantes Université, France
Yusuke Nagasaka	Fujitsu Limited, Japan
Sotiris Nikoletseas	Patras University, Greece
Manuel Penschuck	University of Southern Denmark, Denmark
Lucas Perotin	Inria, France
Ilie Sarpe	KTH Royal Institute of Technology, Sweden
Jonas Sauer	Karlsruhe Institute of Technology, Germany
Hongyang Sun	University of Kansas, USA
Jesper Träff	TU Wien, Austria
Bora Uçar	CNRS, France
Helen Xu	Georgia Tech, USA

Track 6: Domain-Specific and Applied Parallel and Distributed Computing

Chairs

Dalvan Griebler	Pontifical Catholic University of Rio Grande do Sul, Brazil
Bertil Schmidt	Johannes Gutenberg University Mainz, Germany

Program Committee

Salvador Abreu	NOVA-LINCS/University of Évora, Portugal
Nikolaos Alachiotis	University of Twente, The Netherlands
José A. Belloch	Universidad Carlos III de Madrid, Spain
Cristiana Bentes	State University of Rio de Janeiro, Brazil
Ramon Bertran	IBM Research, USA
Cristina Boeres	Universidade Federal Fluminense, Brazil
Benjamin Brock	University of California, Berkeley, USA
Álvaro Coutinho	Federal University of Rio de Janeiro, Brazil
Pasqua D'Ambra	Institute for Applied Computing-CNR, Italy
Schahram Dustdar	Vienna University of Technology, Austria
Luiz Fernandes	Pontifícia Universidade Católica do Rio Grande do Sul, Brazil
Tomás Fernández Pena	University of Santiago de Compostela, Spain
Umberto Ferraro Petrillo	Sapienza University of Rome, Italy
Stefka Fidanova	Institute of Information and Communication Technologies, Bulgaria
Basilio B. Fraguela	Universidade da Coruña, Spain
Balazs Gerofi	University of Tokyo, Japan
Diana Göhringer	TU Dresden, Germany
Jorge González Domínguez	Universidade da Coruña, Spain
Philipp Gschwandtner	University of Innsbruck, Austria
Juan F. R. Herrera	University of Edinburgh, UK
Andreas Hildebrandt	Johannes Gutenberg University Mainz, Germany
Vladislav Kashansky	Eteronix GmbH, Austria
Dragi Kimovski	University of Klagenfurt, Austria
Xiaorong Li	Singapore Institute of Technology, Singapore
Lu Liu	University of Leicester, UK
Weiguo Liu	Shandong University, China
Juan Á. Lorenzo Del Castillo	Inria Bordeaux, France
Arthur Lorenzon	Universidade Federal do Rio Grande do Sul, Brazil

Tze Meng Low	Carnegie Mellon University, USA
Santiago Marco-Sola	Barcelona Supercomputing Center, Spain
Fabrizio Marozzo	University of Calabria, Italy
Philippe Navaux	Universidade Federal do Rio Grande do Sul, Brazil
Virginia Niculescu	Babeş-Bolyai University of Cluj-Napoca, Romania
John Owens	University of California Davis, USA
Işıl Öz	Izmir Institute of Technology, Turkey
Yiannis Papadopoulos	AMD, USA
Juan Carlos Pichel Campos	University of Santiago de Compostela, Spain
Amir Raoofy	Technical University of Munich, Germany
István Reguly	Pázmány Péter Catholic University, Hungary
Juan Antonio Rico Gallego	Foundation for Computing and Advanced Technologies of Extremadura, Spain
Larry Rudolph	Two Sigma, USA
Claudio Schepke	Federal University of Pampa, Brazil
Felix Schuhknecht	Johannes Gutenberg University Mainz, Germany
Hermes Senger	University of São Paulo, Brazil
Jonas Thies	Delft University of Technology, The Netherlands
Paolo Trunfio	University of Calabria, Italy
Jessica Tseng	IBM Research, USA
Lars Wienbrandt	Kiel University, Germany
Steven Wright	University of York, UK
Zekun Yin	Shandong University, China

Artifact Evaluation Committee

Chairs

Daniele De Sensi	Sapienza University of Rome, Italy
Javier García-Blas	Universidad Carlos III de Madrid, Spain

Program Committee

Valerio Besozzi	Università di Pisa, Italy
Diego Camarmas-Alonso	Universidad Carlos III de Madrid, Spain
Adrián Castelló	Universitat Politècnica de València, Spain
Antonio De Caro	University of Salerno, Italy
Mahmoud Elshenawy	King Abdullah University of Science and Technology, Saudi Arabia

Giulio Malenza	University of Turin, Italy
Iker Martín-Álvarez	Universidad Jaume I, Spain
Panagiotis Mpakos	National Technical University of Athens, Greece
Ricardo Nobre	INESC-ID, Portugal
Lorenzo Piarulli	Sapienza University of Rome, Italy
Marco Edoardo Santimaria	University of Turin, Italy
Justin Wozniak	Argonne National Laboratory, USA

External Reviewers

Esmail Abdul Fattah	King Abdullah University of Science and Technology, Saudi Arabia
Alejandro Alonso-Marín	Barcelona Supercomputing Center, Spain
Tariq Alturkestani	King Abdullah University of Science and Technology, Saudi Arabia
Caaliph Andriamisaina	CEA, France
Mihail Asavoae	CEA, France
George Aziz	Curtin University, Australia
Luca Becchetti	Sapienza University of Rome, Italy
Adil Bin Bhutto	Umeå University, Sweden
Mohamed Bouaziz	King Abdullah University of Science and Technology, Saudi Arabia
Noé Chachignot	Inria, France
Tristan Coignion	Université de Lille, France
Thomas Collignon	Inria, France
Aurélien Delval	Université Paris-Saclay, France
Max Doblas	Barcelona Supercomputing Center, Spain
Nicolas Ducarton	Inria, France
Roman Erhardt	Karlsruhe Institute of Technology, Germany
Adrian Evans	CEA, France
William Fabre	CEA, France
Francescomaria Faticanti	Inria, France
Nicolás Fernández-Otero	University of Santiago de Compostela, Spain
Martin Galiwango	TU Delft, The Netherlands
Quentin Guilloteau	Inria, France
Alberto Gutiérrez Torre	Barcelona Supercomputing Center, Spain
Kurt Horvath	Alpen-Adria-Universität Klagenfurt, Austria
Shuhong Huang	Tsinghua University, China
Cristian Iñiguez	Barcelona Supercomputing Center, Spain
Tanjina Islam	University of Amsterdam, The Netherlands
Yasuaki Ito	Hiroshima University, Japan

Mathys Jam	Université Paris-Saclay, France
Fatma Jebali	CEA, France
Sai Krishna Deepak Kanneganti	Curtin University, Australia
Sebastian Koch	TU Berlin, Germany
Cristiano Künas	Universidade Federal do Rio Grande do Sul, Brazil
Kinman Lei	Tsinghua University, China
Stefano Leucci	University of L'Aquila, Italy
Yanchen Li	RIKEN, Japan
Jiaheng Liu	RIKEN, Japan
Júnior Löff	Università della Svizzera italiana, Switzerland
Iker Martín-Álvarez	Universitat Jaume I, Spain
Jose Mestre	Universitat Jaume I, Spain
Clement Mommessin	Inria, France
Alberto Mulone	University of Turin, Italy
Noelia Oliete-Escuín	Barcelona Supercomputing Center, Spain
Gerrit Pape	University of Paderborn, Germany
Francesco Pasquale	University of Rome Tor Vergata, Italy
Romain Pereira	Argonne National Laboratory, USA
Salvador Petit	Universitat Politècnica de València, Spain
Jolan Philippe	University of Orléans, France
César Piñeiro	University of Santiago de Compostela, Spain
Hiari Pizzini Cavagna	University of Bologna, Italy
Lucía Pons	Universitat Politècnica de València, Spain
Andrea Proia	University of Bologna, Italy
Vinod Rebello	Universidade Federal Fluminense, Brazil
Tim Christian Rese	TU Berlin, Germany
Atif Rizwan	Umeå University, Sweden
Andrea Rosà	Università della Svizzera italiana, Switzerland
Rinsai Rossetti	CY Cergy Paris University, France
Jacob Salvi	Università della Svizzera italiana, Switzerland
Werner Florian Samayoa	RIKEN, Japan
Jose Luis Sánchez	University of Castilla-La Mancha, Spain
Dolly Sapra	University of Amsterdam, The Netherlands
Filippo Schiavio	Università della Svizzera italiana, Switzerland
Trever Schirmer	TU Berlin, Germany
Luca Pepè Sciarria	University of Rome Tor Vergata, Italy
Masahiro Shibata	Kyushu Institute of Technology, Japan
Matthew Smith	University of York, UK
Philippe Swartvagher	Inria, France
Peter Thoman	University of Innsbruck, Austria
Cristian Urlea	University of Glasgow, UK

Alex Wiens	University of Paderborn, Germany
Bjarne Wintermann	University of Paderborn, Germany
Filip Wojcicki	Imperial College London, UK
Jacky Wong	Imperial College London, UK
Hao Wu	George Mason University, USA
Junyu Yin	George Mason University, USA
Obaidullah Zaland	Umeå University, Sweden
Mingshu Zhai	Tsinghua University, China
Xiaojun Zhai	University of Essex, UK
Qihao Zhang	Tsinghua University, China
Ziqi Zhao	Texas A&M University, USA

Contents

Architectures and Accelerators

Domain-Specific and Applied Parallel and Distributed Computing

Programming, Compilers, and Performance

Constraint Driven Global Data Layout Optimization for Tensor Expressions

Yi Miao[1(✉)] and Stephen Jarvis[2]

[1] School of Computer Science,
University of Birmingham, Birmingham, UK
yxm296@student.bham.ac.uk
[2] University of Surrey, Surrey, UK
s.jarvis@surrey.ac.uk

Abstract. Tensor contractions are a core computational primitive in scientific computing, machine learning, and quantum simulation. Achieving high performance for these operations on modern hardware requires not only selecting efficient computation kernels but also carefully orchestrating tensor memory layouts to match hardware-friendly formats. However, existing approaches such as Transpose–Transpose–GEMM–Transpose (TTGT) and GEMM-like Tensor–Tensor multiplication (GETT) either incur high data movement costs or sacrifice peak compute utilization. We present a compiler-based framework for optimizing tensor contraction expressions by systematically managing data layout to maximize throughput. At its core is an intermediate representation (IR) that explicitly separates transposition from computation and explicitly encodes associated layout constraints, enabling a two-phase optimization strategy: first, full expansion of the IR to expose all layout transformation opportunities; second, selective permutation fusion based on profile-guided optimization(PGO) to balance memory movement and compute efficiency. The optimized IR is lowered to high-performance backends, using BLAS to leverage hardware-accelerated matrix operation where beneficial, and fused GETT for bandwidth-sensitive cases. Experimental results on 24 binary contraction benchmarks and 8 tensor network expressions demonstrate substantial runtime improvements over state-of-the-art libraries, 2.42× speedup on CPU and 1.49× on GPU for tensor network expression. These results highlight the critical role of layout orchestration in unlocking the full potential of modern hardware tensor computation.

Keywords: Tensor Compiler · Einsum · Intermediate Representation · GPU

1 Introduction

Einsum notation has become a standard for expressing tensor contractions in domains such as machine learning [18,21], quantum computing [19,20], and

M. Torquati et al. (Eds.): Euro-Par 2026, LNCS 16781, pp. 3–16, 2027.
https://doi.org/10.1007/978-3-032-35248-4_1

protein structure prediction [11]. While it simplifies complex expressions, efficiently implementing einsum remains challenging. The key problem is analogous to matrix chain multiplication: finding an optimal contraction path to minimize FLOPs or intermediate sizes, then lowering each multiplication to efficient library calls.

Tools like opt_einsum [5] and cotengra [9] solve the path problem heuristically, and backends such as BLAS [2] or ATen [22] execute the resulting contractions. While BLAS efficiently supports 1D and 2D contractions, it does not extend naturally to higher-order tensors. Four strategies have emerged to bridge this gap: nested loop [1], Transpose–Transpose–GEMM–Transpose (TTGT) [8], decomposition into smaller GEMMs [7], and kernels that fuse transposition with computation, such as GETT and TBLIS [15,23]. These vary in generality, performance, and ability to utilize modern hardware.

To bridge the gap between multiple contraction path and each binary contraction optimization, Einsum Tree IR [3] extends contraction trees by distinguishing index ordering and child order. However, it assumes a single nested-loop-over-(packed)-GEMM (NLG) execution model for binary contractions and restricts layout transposition to input tensors. This design often produces small or skinny GEMMs with low arithmetic intensity and prevents exploration of alternative implementations such as direct GEMM, TTGT, or fused TTGT kernels. More fundamentally, Einsum IRs do not explicitly encode the layout requirements imposed by different contraction implementations, leaving an important optimization dimension unexplored.

To address these limitations, we propose the *Constraining-Tree Layout* (CTL) intermediate representation, which decouples computation from transposition and expresses layout requirements as explicit combinatorial constraints. Building on this representation, we introduce a two-phase optimization pipeline: an expansion phase that exposes layout opportunities using GEMM-based mappings, followed by a profile-guided phase that selectively fuses transpositions to balance data movement and compute throughput. Our compiler-based system targets high-performance libraries such as cuTENSOR, cuBLAS, TBLIS, and oneMKL. Across synthetic and real-world tensor network benchmarks, CTL achieves average speedups of 2.42× on CPU and 1.49× on GPU compared to state-of-the-art libraries. In summary, we make the following contributions.

1. We introduce the *Constraining-Tree Layout* (CTL) IR, which explicitly encodes layout constraints and implementation choices for each binary contraction, enabling joint reasoning over computation and memory layout.
2. We design a two-phase optimization pipeline that expands IR first and then fuses transpositions to improve backend efficiency while minimizing data movement.
3. We develop a lowering strategy targeting existing high-performance libraries, including TBLIS, Intel oneMKL, cuTENSOR, and cuBLAS.
4. We demonstrate consistent performance improvements across real-world tensor expression benchmarks on both CPU and GPU platforms.

2 Background

2.1 Einstein Summation, Contraction Tree and Einsum Tree

The Einstein summation convention provides a compact specification of tensor contractions widely used in scientific computing and tensor networks [14,24]. Given tensors $T_1, \ldots, T_r$, indices shared by multiple inputs but absent from the output are implicitly summed as $C^{k_1 \ldots k_p} = \sum_{i_1, i_2, \ldots \text{ not in } k_1, \ldots, k_p} T_1^{a_1 \cdots} \cdot T_2^{b_1 \cdots} \cdots T_r^{z_1 \cdots}$. While providing a declarative specification, its performance depends on how the contraction is implemented. Multi-tensor einsum expressions are typically lowered into a sequence of binary contractions following a *contraction path*, often optimized for FLOPs or intermediate sizes [5,9]. This partial order can be represented as a rooted binary *contraction tree*, where leaves denote inputs and internal nodes represent intermediate contractions. Transformations such as swapping children or permuting index strings preserve semantics because they maintain the same partial order (e.g., Figs. 1a–1b).

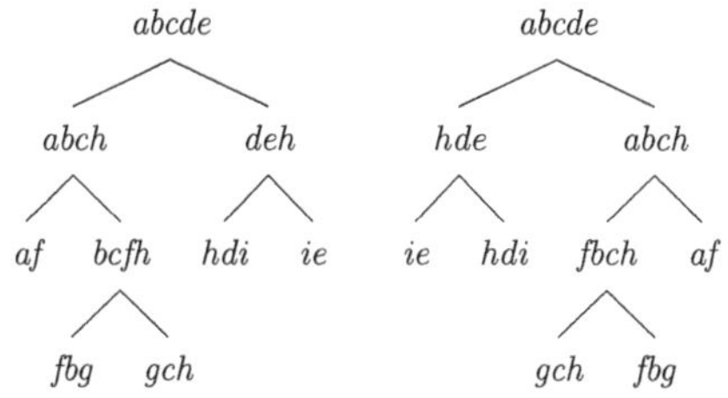

(a) Tree A (b) Tree B

Fig. 1. Tree representations of *"af,fbg,gch,hdi,ie → abcde"*, with contraction path `(1,2), (0,3), (0,1), (0,1)`, which is index 26 in Sect. 4.2. The two trees are same as contraction trees, but different as Einsum trees

To enable layout-aware optimization, the Einsum Tree IR [3] extends contraction trees by explicitly encoding tensor dimension ordering. Unlike contraction trees, swaps and permutations produce distinct Einsum Trees, allowing layout decisions to be modeled directly during compilation. Dimensions are categorized into five roles: M and N map to output dimensions, K denotes contraction dimensions, C denotes shared element-wise dimensions, and R denotes reducible dimensions. These categories guide lowering to tensor processing primitives such as transposition, GEMM (C[N][M] += A[K][M] * B[N][K]), and packed GEMM(C[N][M][C] += A[K][M][C] * B[N][K][C]).

Despite enabling layout reasoning, the Einsum Tree IR has several limitations: (1) It assumes a fixed NLG implementation for binary contractions. (2) Legal layout requirements are not explicitly encoded. (3) Transpositions are restricted to input tensors, limiting optimization of intermediates.

2.2 TTGT and Fused TTGT

A common implementation for binary contraction is TTGT, which transposes tensors into GEMM-friendly layouts, performs matrix multiplication, and transposes the result back [8,12]. While TTGT achieves high compute efficiency, explicit permutations may dominate runtime for bandwidth-bound contractions. Fused TTGT approaches reduce this overhead by integrating permutation with computation. GETT [23] and TBLIS [15] fuse layout transformation with GEMM-like kernels, minimizing data movement while retaining high performance.

For contractions with high arithmetic intensity, TTGT generally outperforms fused TTGT, even accounting for the cost of transpositions, due to its regular memory access patterns, which are better aligned with the architecture of modern high-throughput hardware. However, for contractions with low arithmetic intensity, transposition overhead becomes dominant, making fused TTGT a more favorable option.

3 Constraining-Tree Layout

3.1 Intermediate Representation

Consider a binary contraction of the form $A(acghbd), B(cdefgh) \rightarrow C(fbaegh)$, where tensor **A** has a set of dimensions indices $\{abcdgh\}$, **B** has $\{cdefgh\}$, and the result tensor **C** has $\{abefgh\}$. Suppose we aim to implement this contraction using the TTGT in which GEMM is of the NT (No-transpose–Transpose) configuration. In this setup, all three involved tensors must be transposed into specific layouts suitable for the GEMM kernel. Determining the appropriate layouts for the input and output tensors when using GEMM reduces to identifying suitable permutations of these index sets.

Definition 1 (Permutation). *Let U be a finite set with $|U| = n$. A* permutation *of U is a bijection $\pi : U \rightarrow \{1, 2, \ldots, n\}$.*

We adopt the categorization of dimensions from the Einsum Tree [3]. Specifically, the M and N dimensions correspond to $\{ab\}$ and $\{ef\}$, respectively; the K dimensions are $\{cd\}$; and the C (batched) dimensions are $\{gh\}$. In the GEMM API with the NT configuration, the input tensors are expected to follow a specific layout: the M/N dimensions must appear first, followed by the K dimensions, and finally the C dimensions. For the output tensor, it can be either *(MNC)* or *(NMC)*, which can be achieved by simply swapping input tensors. We formalize this requirement as follows:

Definition 2 (Block Precedence Constraints). *Let π be a permutation of a finite set U, and let $A, B \subseteq U$ be disjoint. We say that A* precedes *B* in *π, written $A \prec_\pi B$, if $\pi(x) < \pi(y)$ for all $x \in A,\ y \in B$. Let $\mathcal{P}(U)$ be the power set of U, A* block precedence constraint *in π is a binary relation $\prec \subseteq \mathcal{P}(U) \times \mathcal{P}(U)$ such that for all $(A, B) \in \prec$, $A \prec_\pi B$*

Additionally, the C dimensions must appear in the same order across all three tensors because they represent the batched dimensions. Similarly, the K dimensions must follow the same order in both A and B to ensure correct contraction behavior. We formalize these requirements with the following definitions:

Definition 3 (Order-Consistent Permutations). *Let $\mathcal{P}(U_1)$ and $\mathcal{P}(U_2)$ be power sets of U_1 and U_2, and let $\mathcal{S} \subseteq \mathcal{P}(U_1) \cap \mathcal{P}(U_2)$ be their shared subfamily. Let π_1 and π_2 be permutations of U_1 and U_2, respectively. We say that π_1 and π_2 are* order-consistent on $\mathcal{S}$ *if* $\forall X \in \mathcal{S} \forall a, b \in X: \quad \pi_1(a) < \pi_1(b) \iff \pi_2(a) < \pi_2(b)$.

Thus, we introduce two classes of constraints: *Block precedence constraints*, which define valid dimension block orderings within each tensor: P_α on **A**: $\{(\{ab\}, \{cd\}), (\{cd\}, \{gh\})\}$; P_β on **B**: $\{(\{ef\}, \{cd\}), (\{cd\}, \{gh\})\}$; P_γ on **C**: $\{(\{ab\}, \{gh\}), (\{ef\}, \{gh\})\}$. and *Order-consistency constraints*, which ensure compatible ordering of shared dimension blocks across tensors: O_α between **A** and **C**: $\{\{ab\}, \{gh\}\}$; O_β between **B** and **C**: $\{\{ef\}, \{gh\}\}$; O_γ between **A** and **B**: $\{\{cd\}, \{gh\}\}$;

Even a simple binary contraction can involve intricate layout constraints. This complexity increases significantly in the case of multi-tensor contractions, where the result of one contraction may serve as the input to another, introducing interdependent constraints across the contraction tree. To systematically capture both inter- and intra-contraction layout constraints, we propose the *Constraining-Tree Layout* (CTL) intermediate representation. CTL formalizes the implementation of einsum expression within a combinatorial framework. The core design principle of our IR is to decouple computation from transposition, allowing layout requirements of each contraction kernel to be expressed as explicit combinatorial constraints. As illustrated in Table 1, the CTL IR is composed of three interacting components: *computation*, *transposition*, and *constraints*.

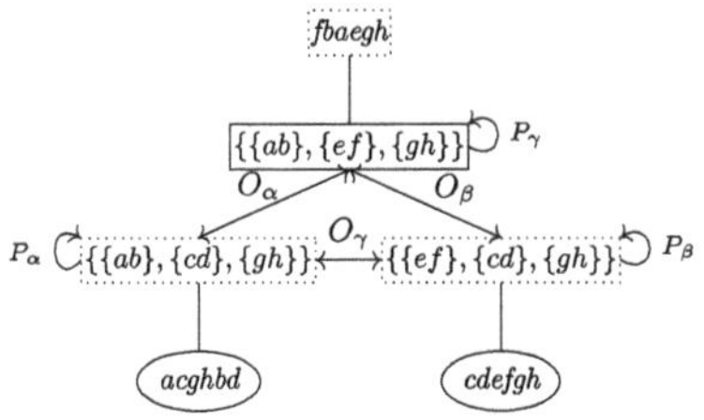

(a) Undetermined CTL

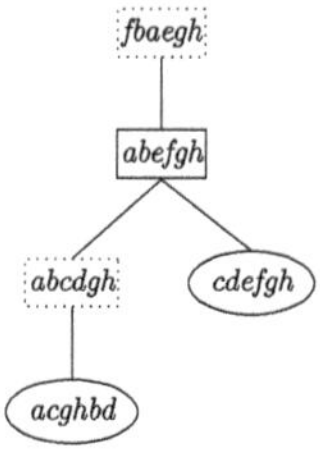

(b) Determined CTL.

Fig. 2. CTL of binary contraction of $acghbd, cdefgh \rightarrow fbaegh$.

Figure 2 shows the CTL instance of the constraints above. Each node in the CTL is classified as either *Determined* or *Undetermined*. A node is considered Undetermined if the permutation that satisfies all layout constraints has not yet

Table 1. Constraining-Tree Layout Primitives

Kind	Primitive	Description
Undetermined	$\{\{i_1...\}, \{i_2...\}...\}$	An **Undetermined** node appears in the form of a dimension family.
Determined	$i_1 i_2 i_3 ...$	An **Determined** node appears in the form of permutation of dimension indices.
Transposition	Transposition	**Transposition** of one tensor. Indices in node represent layout of result of transpositon, and transposed tensor is represented by child node.
Computation	GEMM	**GEMM** contraction of two tensors, which has constraints as shown in Fig. 2a
	Fused TTGT	**Fused TTGT** contraction of two tensors, which has no constraints on input and output tensots.
Constraint	$\longleftrightarrow$	Order-Consistency constraints
	———	Constraints have been satisfied, or no constraint.
	$\curvearrowright$ Node	Block precedence constraints that have to be satisfied.
	Node	Precedence constraints have been satisfied, or no such constraints need to be satisfied.
Input	Input	**Input** tensor, in which the layout is fixed

been found for the node. Given constraints represented in fig. 2a, determining whether a binary contraction can be implemented directly using GEMM without transposition reduces to checking whether the layouts (i.e., permutations of dimension indices) of tensors **A**, **B**, and **C** simultaneously satisfy block precedence, and order-consistency constraints. We formulate this as a satisfiability problem over permutations, where each tensor dimension is assigned an integer representing its position in the memory layout, which can be solved via an SMT solver (Z3) [6]. If the system is satisfiable, the resulting permutations for the input and output tensors conform to the GEMM interface. Otherwise, the contraction cannot be directly realized under the current kernel configuration without additional transpositions. As illustrated in Fig. 2b, Z3 determines that tensor B fits within the required constraints, so there are two transpositions in determined CTL, one fewer than the three typically introduced by standard TTGT.

3.2 Two-Phase Code Generation And Optimization

The motivation for this two-phase design stems from the difference between TTGT and fused TTGT [8,12,15,23]. TTGT transposes tensors into layouts compatible with high performance GEMM libraries, which may incur significant data movement overhead. In contrast, fused TTGT integrates computation and memory access over small tensor tiles, reducing data movement but potentially underutilizing modern hardware's computational capacity.

First Phase: Expansion. In this phase, we attempt to implement the entire contraction using only transposition and GEMM operations. We leverage the CTL representation to minimize the number of required transpositions. Consider the example contraction tree shown in Fig. 1. We first construct the initial, undetermined CTL tree, as depicted in Fig. 3a. We introduce a recursive algorithm, shown in Algorithm 1, which determines the CTL into its fully expanded form.

Algorithm 1: Recursive Determination of CTL Nodes

```
Function Determine(node):
    if node is Input then
        return
    if node is GEMM then
        foreach child c do
            Determine(c)
        if both children Determined then
            if order-consistent then
                solve layout from children;
            else
                insert Transposition for unsatisfied child;
        else
            jointly solve layouts for node and undetermined children;
    else if node is Transposition then
        Determine(child);
        if child layout satisfies disjointness & precedence then
            remove node and replace with child;
```

This recursive procedure ensures that, after traversal, each node in the CTL is assigned a valid layout, and unnecessary transpositions are eliminated based on constraint compatibility between adjacent GEMM operations (e.g., when the result of one GEMM serves as the input to another). The result of applying this expansion process to the initial CTL in Fig. 3a is shown in Fig. 3b.

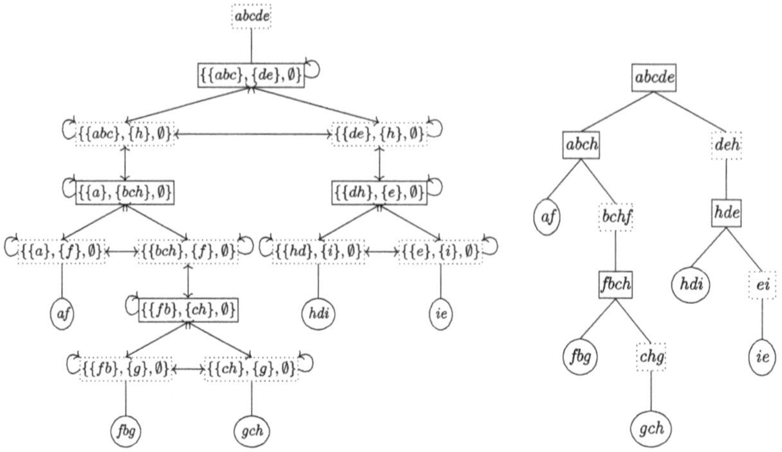

(a) Initial undetermined CTL Tree. To aid brevity, details of constraints are not listed. (b) Expanded CTL

Fig. 3. Bottom-Up approach to determine CTL into fully expanded form.

Second Phase: Fusion. After the first phase, all Contraction nodes are expanded into either GEMM or Transposition nodes. At this stage, each GEMM node has only two options: to remain as a standalone GEMM or to fuse with its surrounding transpositions into a fused TTGT (e.g., GETT/TBLIS). For an einsum expression with N input tensors, there are $N-1$ GEMMs, yielding an $O(N)$ decision space for fusion. To efficiently explore this space, we design a bottom-up fusing algorithm as shown in Algorithm 2 that evaluates each contraction and decides whether to fuse by profiling the execution time of the GEMM with adjacent transpositions and the fused TTGT. Since the decision complexity is linear, it is practical to adopt PGO in which fusion choices are guided by runtime profiling and the one-time compilation overhead is amortized over repeated executions of the same einsum expression on large datasets. Figure 4 illustrates how fusion with PGO works on the expanded CTL shown in Fig. 3b.

After applying the two-phase optimization process, the CTL is lowered to efficient backend libraries using Intel OneMKL or TBLIS on a CPU, and cuTENSOR(using GETT algorithm) or cuBLAS on a GPU. Transpositions are mapped directly to Permute operations provided by the TBLIS or cuTENSOR library.

4 Performance Evaluation

We evaluate our compiler-based tensor contraction framework on two benchmark suites: (1) 24 binary contractions from the TCCG benchmark by Springer and Bientinesi [23], covering diverse sizes and arithmetic intensities; and (2) one synthetic and seven real-world tensor network expressions from scientific computing papers, also used in Einsum IR [3]. For consistency, we adopt the same contraction paths as provided in [3].

Algorithm 2: Recursive Fusion Based on Profiling

```
Function FuseTransposition(node):
    if node is Input then
        return
    if node is Transposition then
        FuseTransposition(child);
        if child becomes fused TTGT then
            replace node with child in parent;
            return
    else if node is GEMM then
        foreach child c do
            FuseTransposition(c)
        if adjacent Transposition exists ∧ profiling improves then
            fuse with adjacent permutation nodes;
```

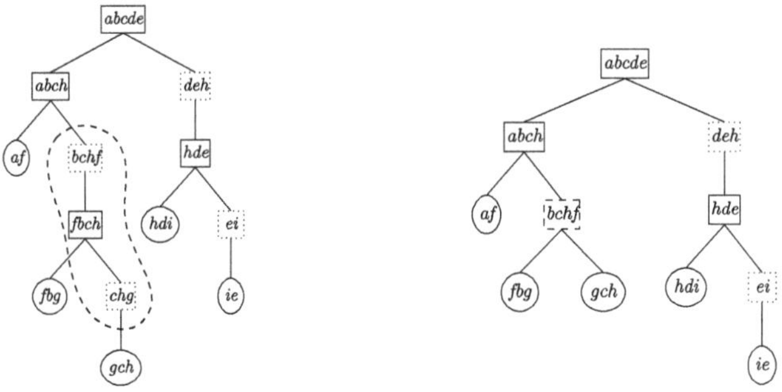

(a) Profiling detects profitable fusion chances. (b) Fused CTL.

Fig. 4. Fusion with PGO. This fusion examples are from experimenting on CPU.

CPU experiments were conducted on a 56-core Intel Xeon Platinum 8570, and GPU experiments on an NVIDIA A100-40GB (Ampere) running RHEL 8.8. Our implementation uses Intel OneMKL 2023.1, TBLIS v1.3.0, cuBLAS (CUDA 12.1.1), and cuTENSOR 2.2.0. We compare against Einsum IR (official build), cuTensorNet (cuQuantum 25.03.0), and opt_sum 3.4.0 with PyTorch 2.1.2 backend. On GPU, all methods use TF32 precision. Each result reports the mean runtime over 50 runs after one warm-up, shown as log-scaled speedup relative to opt_einsum (PyTorch backend) on both CPU and GPU.

We compare with:**ET-TPP**: Einsum Tree with libxsmm [10] (CPU); **ET-TBLIS**: Einsum Tree with TBLIS [15] (CPU);**cuTENSOR**: standalone cuTENSOR contractions (CUTENSOR_ALGO_DEFAULT_PATIENT); **cuTENSORNet**: contraction execution via cuQuantum (GPU);**OT**: opt_ einsum with PyTorch backend (CPU/GPU), used as the baseline.

4.1 Binary Tensor Contractions

As shown in Fig. 5a, CTL outperforms the baselines in most CPU cases. For IDs 1–7, it achieves substantial gains—up to 8× in case 5—while ET-TPP and ET-TBLIS frequently slow down relative to PyTorch. Since TCCG cases are ordered by arithmetic intensity [23], these results expose a key limitation of einsum trees: they perform poorly on bandwidth-bound contractions. As intensity increases (higher IDs), the performance gap narrows. In the highest-intensity cases, CTL avoids fusion and effectively reduces to TTGT, achieving performance comparable to OT, suggesting that PyTorch also relies on TTGT for binary contractions. The observed slowdowns of einsum trees align with our analysis in Sect. 1.

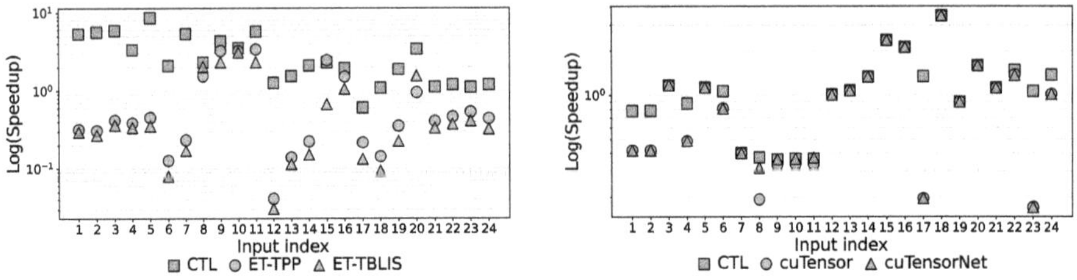

(a) CPU results. (b) GPU results.

Fig. 5. Speedup comparison of CTL for binary contractions.

Figure 5b shows that cuTENSOR and cuTENSORNet perform nearly identically, as the latter invokes cuTENSOR for binary contractions. For IDs 1–11, OT performs best, likely benefiting from optimized PyTorch routines. For higher-intensity cases (IDs 12–24), CTL and cuTENSOR deliver clear speedups. CTL remains consistently competitive with cuTENSOR and cuTENSORNet, and in cases 17 and 23 achieves up to 7× improvement. Overall, these results demonstrate the stability and efficiency of CTL across diverse binary contraction workloads.

4.2 Multiple Tensor Contractions

We evaluate CTL on eight multi-input einsum expressions previously used in Einsum IR [3], spanning tensor decompositions (TT [17,25], FCTN [28], TW [27]), quantum-inspired models (GETD [13], MERA [4], TRN [26]), and tensor-based inference (TNLM [4]). Unlike TCCG, these workloads involve multiple intermediate tensors and require deeper global orchestration.

Figure 6 reports runtime speedups on CPU and GPU. On CPU, CTL consistently outperforms ET-TPP and ET-TBLIS, which often generate many small GEMMs with rigid transposition handling. In contrast, CTL expands contractions into larger GEMMs when possible and selectively fuses permutations via

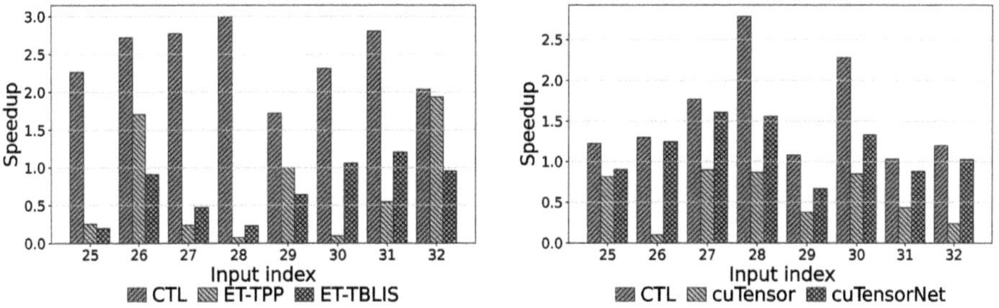

(a) CPU results.

(b) GPU results.

Fig. 6. Speedup comparison of CTL for multi-tensor contractions.

fused TTGT, reducing redundant data movement while maintaining high compute throughput. Compared to OT, CTL has achieved higher and more stable speedups across most cases.

On GPU, CTL also surpasses cuTENSOR and cuTENSORNet. cuTENSOR performs worst overall, even with `CUTENSOR_ALGO_DEFAULT_PATIENT`, because it optimizes binary contractions independently without global layout coordination. This can cause severe degradation in complex cases; for example, in case 26, CTL achieves up to a 12× speedup over cuTENSOR. cuTENSORNet improves over OT but still trails CTL despite sharing the same underlying backend, highlighting the benefit of CTL's global layout orchestration.

Table 2. Compilation time for CTL, Einsum Tree and opt_einsum. All measurements were in milliseconds.

ID	CTL_CPU	CTL_GPU	ET-TPP	ET-TBLIS	opt_einsum
25	30.412	98.981	50.138	1.359	0.204
26	230.091	100.674	52.092	1.260	0.203
27	40.487	61.973	43.742	0.911	0.176
28	31.687	90.221	52.610	0.993	0.197
29	110.231	109.847	55.967	0.861	0.196
30	78.897	90.341	74.321	0.942	0.302
31	290.323	670.215	214.135	2.391	0.832
32	17283.124	2274.298	351.363	2.805	1.452

Table 2 shows compilation times. As expected, CTL incurs higher compilation overhead than Einsum Tree mainly due to profile-guided fusion. However, this cost is amortized in practice, since einsum expressions are typically executed repeatedly and runtime dominates total cost.

Geometric mean speedups further confirm these results. On CPU, CTL achieves 2.42×, compared to 0.41× (ET-TPP) and 0.59× (ET-TBLIS). On GPU,

CTL achieves 1.49×, versus 0.46× (cuTENSOR) and 1.11× (cuTENSORNet). Overall, CTL consistently delivers strong gains across platforms, with particularly substantial improvements on CPU and meaningful acceleration on GPU.

4.3 Ablation Study

We evaluate the contribution of each optimization phase in CTL using three configurations: (i) *No Optimization*, which executes einsum expressions directly; (ii) *Expand Only*, which lowers expressions to GEMM and transposition nodes without fusion; and (iii) *Expand+Fuse*, the full pipeline combining expansion with selective fusion. This comparison isolates the impact of expansion and fusion on CPU and GPU backends.

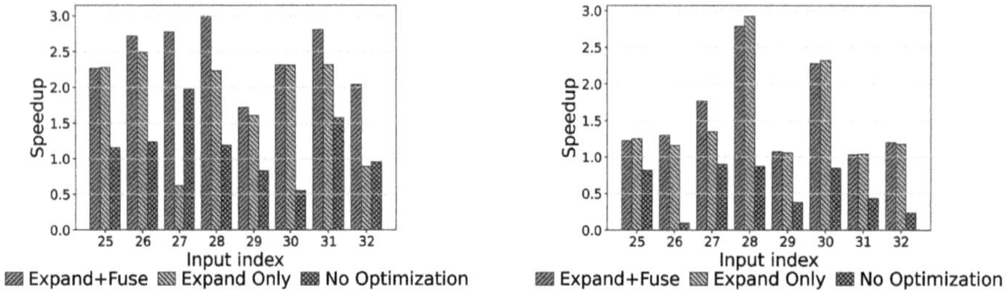

(a) CPU ablation results. (b) GPU ablation results.

Fig. 7. Ablation study of CTL on multi-tensor contractions.

Figure 7 reports runtime results. On both platforms, expansion yields substantial gains by exposing larger GEMMs. However, fusion is essential in cases where expansion alone increases data movement. For example, in case 27 on CPU, expansion produces three transpositions and three GEMMs, with transpositions dominating runtime. Fusion merges two transpositions with one GEMM into a TBLIS contraction, eliminating redundant transpositions and restoring performance. This demonstrates the complementary roles of expansion (increasing compute efficiency) and fusion (reducing data movement).

On GPU, the difference between *Expand Only* and *Expand+Fuse* is smaller. Even in case 27, expansion performs reasonably well, likely due to efficient transposition kernels in cuTENSOR or higher memory bandwidth. Nevertheless, fusion prevents worst-case slowdowns and ensures more stable performance.

Geometric mean speedups confirm this trend. On CPU, *Expand+Fuse*, *Expand Only*, and *No Optimization* achieve 2.42×, 1.67×, and 1.11×, respectively. On GPU, the corresponding speedups are 1.49×, 1.43×, and 0.46×. While expansion alone provides notable benefits, fusion is critical for consistent performance, particularly when layout transformations dominate.

Overall, these results validate our core premise: systematic layout orchestration through CTL enables hardware-efficient tensor contraction by balancing computation and data movement across diverse workloads.

5 Conclusion

We presented a compiler-based approach for optimizing tensor contractions through explicit memory layout orchestration. At the core of our approach is the CTL IR, which decouples transposition from computation and encodes layout constraints explicitly. Combined with a two-phase optimization pipeline, our method exposes large, backend-friendly GEMMs and minimizes redundant data movement. The result is a unified lowering strategy to BLAS and fused TTGT that achieves consistent speedups. While our system already demonstrates strong performance across benchmarks, future work will explore more hardware-aware scheduling, dynamic fusion decisions, fusion-aware contraction path selection and support for sparse and mixed-precision kernels. This work highlights the importance of layout as a first-class optimization target in modern tensor computation.

Data Availability Statement. The artifact is available in the Zenodo repository [16].

Disclosure of Interests. The authors have no competing interests to declare that are relevant to the content of this article.

References

1. Apra, E., Klemm, M., Kowalski, K.: Efficient implementation of many-body quantum chemical methods on the intel® xeon phi coprocessor. In: SC'14: Proceedings of the International Conference for High Performance Computing, Networking, Storage and Analysis, pp. 674–684. IEEE (2014)
2. Blackford, L.S., et al.: An updated set of basic linear algebra subprograms (BLAS). ACM Trans. Math. Softw. **28**(2), 135–151 (2002)
3. Breuer, A., et al.: Einsum trees: an abstraction for optimizing the execution of tensor expressions. In: Proceedings of the 30th ACM International Conference on Architectural Support for Programming Languages and Operating Systems, vol. 2, pp. 275–292. ASPLOS '25, Association for Computing Machinery, New York, NY, USA (2025). https://doi.org/10.1145/3676641.3716254
4. Breuer, A., et al.: Einsum trees: an abstraction for optimizing the execution of tensor expressions. In: Proceedings of the 30th ACM International Conference on Architectural Support for Programming Languages and Operating Systems, vol. 2, pp. 275–292 (2025)
5. Daniel, G., Gray, J., et al.: Opt_einsum-a python package for optimizing contraction order for einsum-like expressions. J. Open Source Softw. **3**(26), 753 (2018)
6. De Moura, L., Bjørner, N.: Z3: an efficient SMT solver. In: International Conference on Tools and Algorithms for the Construction and Analysis of Systems, pp. 337–340. Springer (2008)
7. Di Napoli, E., Fabregat-Traver, D., Quintana-Ortí, G., Bientinesi, P.: Towards an efficient use of the blas library for multilinear tensor contractions. Appl. Math. Comput. **235**, 454–468 (2014)
8. Epifanovsky, E., et al.: New implementation of high-level correlated methods using a general block tensor library for high-performance electronic structure calculations (2013)

9. Gray, J., Kourtis, S.: Hyper-optimized tensor network contraction. Quantum **5**, 410 (2021)
10. Heinecke, A., Henry, G., Hutchinson, M., Pabst, H.: LIBXSMM: accelerating small matrix multiplications by runtime code generation. In: SC '16: Proceedings of the International Conference for High Performance Computing, Networking, Storage and Analysis, pp. 981–991 (2016). https://doi.org/10.1109/SC.2016.83
11. Jumper, J., et al.: Highly accurate protein structure prediction with alphafold. Nature **596**(7873), 583–589 (2021)
12. Kolda, T.G., Bader, B.W.: Tensor decompositions and applications. SIAM Rev. **51**(3), 455–500 (2009)
13. Liu, Y., Yao, Q., Li, Y.: Generalizing tensor decomposition for n-ARY relational knowledge bases. In: Proceedings of the Web Conference 2020, pp. 1104–1114 (2020)
14. Markov, I.L., Shi, Y.: Simulating quantum computation by contracting tensor networks. SIAM J. Comput. **38**(3), 963–981 (2008)
15. Matthews, D.A.: High-performance tensor contraction without transposition. SIAM J. Sci. Comput. **40**(1), C1–C24 (2018)
16. Miao, Y., Jarvis, S.: Artifact of the paper:constraint driven global data layout optimization for tensor expressions (2026). https://doi.org/10.5281/zenodo.20515887
17. Nayar, S.: Columbia object image library (coil100) (1996). http://www1cs.columbia.edu/CAVE/software/softlib/coil-100.php
18. Novikov, A., Podoprikhin, D., Osokin, A., Vetrov, D.P.: Tensorizing neural networks. In: Advances in Neural Information Processing Systems, p. 28 (2015)
19. NVIDIA Corporation: cuquantum sdk: a high-performance library for accelerating quantum science (2025). https://docs.nvidia.com/cuda/cuquantum/24.11.0/. Accessed 20 May 2025
20. Orús, R.: Tensor networks for complex quantum systems. Nat. Rev. Phys. **1**(9), 538–550 (2019)
21. Peharz, R., et al.: Einsum networks: fast and scalable learning of tractable probabilistic circuits. In: International Conference on Machine Learning, pp. 7563–7574. PMLR (2020)
22. PyTorch Developers: ATen, PyTorch's tensor library (2025). https://github.com/pytorch/pytorch/tree/main/aten/src/ATen. Accessed 31 Mar 2025
23. Springer, P., Bientinesi, P.: Design of a high-performance gemm-like tensor-tensor multiplication. ACM Trans. Math. Softw. **44**(3) (2018). https://doi.org/10.1145/3157733
24. Stoudenmire, E., Schwab, D.J.: Supervised learning with tensor networks. Adv. Neural. Inf. Process. Syst. **29** (2016)
25. Usvyatsov, M., Ballester-Ripoll, R., Schindler, K.: tntorch: tensor network learning with pytorch (2022). https://arxiv.org/abs/2206.11128
26. Wang, W., Sun, Y., Eriksson, B., Wang, W., Aggarwal, V.: Wide compression: tensor ring nets. In: Proceedings of the IEEE Conference on Computer Vision and Pattern Recognition, pp. 9329–9338 (2018)
27. Wu, Z.C., Huang, T.Z., Deng, L.J., Dou, H.X., Meng, D.: Tensor wheel decomposition and its tensor completion application. Adv. Neural. Inf. Process. Syst. **35**, 27008–27020 (2022)
28. Zheng, Y.B., Huang, T.Z., Zhao, X.L., Zhao, Q., Jiang, T.X.: Fully-connected tensor network decomposition and its application to higher-order tensor completion. In: Proceedings of the AAAI Conference On Artificial Intelligence. vol. 35, pp. 11071–11078 (2021)

Evaluating the Parallelization Capabilities of State-of-the-Art Agentic Large Language Models

Peter Thoman[1(✉)] and Philipp Gschwandtner[2]

[1] Distributed and Parallel Computing Research Group, University of Innsbruck, 6020 Innsbruck, Austria
peter.thoman@uibk.ac.at

[2] Research Center High-performance Computing, University of Innsbruck, 6020 Innsbruck, Austria
philipp.gschwandtner@uibk.ac.at

Abstract. Advancements in large language models (LLMs), including base model improvements, various chain-of-thought approaches, and agentic tool use, have substantially increased their capacity for autonomous programming and software engineering. Their performance on such tasks is widely studied, tracked, and publicized; however, the majority of evaluations are based on Python, Java, or other high-level languages, with application domains in the web, business logic, or data analysis.

From the perspective of parallel language, programming interface (API), and systems research in the field of high-performance computing (HPC), the question arises whether these results translate to the capability of effectively parallelizing applications. In order to answer this question, we design and carry out a comprehensive study, tasking 8 state-of-the-art LLM agents with the parallelization of 11 small-to-medium-sized HPC benchmark applications. For each, we evaluate shared-memory, distributed memory, accelerator, and hybrid parallelization goals with appropriate APIs, and multiple agent invocations are performed for every data point to quantify random variance in outcome quality.

Our experimental setup includes validation in several steps, comprising semantic inspection, compilation, monitored execution, internal result checking, and external verification via known-good comparisons. For all valid programs, we also perform comparative performance benchmarking on a production supercomputer. We synthesize overall conclusions and quantify to what extent parallelization performance of LLMs correlates with time and tokens spent. All benchmark code, experiment and evaluation scripts, and generated data are fully available for analysis, replication and extension.

Keywords: LLM · Parallelization · OpenMP · MPI · CUDA

M. Torquati et al. (Eds.): Euro-Par 2026, LNCS 16781, pp. 17–31, 2027.
https://doi.org/10.1007/978-3-032-35248-4_2

1 Introduction

Over the past few years, large language models (LLMs) have changed the landscape of software development. Base model improvements, chain-of-thought reasoning, and agentic tool use–where the LLM autonomously invokes compilers, test suites, and shell commands–have pushed their capabilities from simple code completion to resolving real-world software engineering tasks [5,12]. These capabilities are widely benchmarked and publicized, with leaderboards tracking progress on an almost weekly basis.

However, the vast majority of these evaluations target Python, Java, or similar high-level languages, in general application domains. From the perspective of high-performance computing (HPC), this raises a natural question: *can state-of-the-art LLM agents effectively parallelize applications?* Parallelization–whether for shared-memory CPUs, distributed clusters, or GPU accelerators–requires a specialized understanding of data dependencies, synchronization, memory hierarchies, and communication patterns beyond what is tested in mainstream software engineering benchmarks. Existing work on LLMs for parallel code has begun to address parts of this question, as we discuss in Sect. 2. Yet no prior work has combined *agentic* tool use with coverage of various parallelization paradigms, application diversity, model variety, and end-to-end validation including performance benchmarking on production HPC hardware.

In this paper, we design and carry out such a study. We task 8 state-of-the-art LLM agents, all accessed through a common agentic interface, with the parallelization of 11 sequential C++ benchmark applications using four targets: OpenMP, MPI, CUDA, and hybrid parallelism. Results are validated in a five-stage pipeline–from semantic inspection through compilation, execution, internal checking, and external verification–and all valid programs are benchmarked on a supercomputer, deriving a final score on which we perform further analysis.

Our key findings are: (i) frontier LLM agents can successfully parallelize small-to-medium HPC applications, even for unseen code; (ii) result quality correlates with what human developers would find more or less difficult; (iii) OpenMP is the easiest target, hybrid the hardest, with MPI and CUDA in between; and (iv) more capable (and expensive) models, and more time spent, produce better parallelizations, but raw token expenditure does not predict quality. All benchmark code, experiment scripts, and generated data are publicly available for replication and extension[1].

2 Related Work

The evaluation of LLMs for code generation began with HumanEval [1], a Python benchmark measuring functional correctness via the pass@k metric. SWE-bench [5] evaluated LLMs on real GitHub issue resolution across large Python repositories, spawning variants such as SWE-bench Verified and Multimodal. In the agentic setting, SWE-agent [12] introduced specialized agent–computer interfaces for automated software engineering. These benchmarks are

[1] https://github.com/PeterTh/llm-eval-experiment.

exclusively Python-focused and test general-purpose software engineering rather than the performance-critical, low-level parallelization tasks central to HPC.

Nichols et al. [9] introduced ParEval, the first systematic benchmark for LLM-based parallel code generation, covering six execution models (serial, OpenMP, MPI, CUDA, Kokkos, and HIP) across 12 problem types. They found a significant gap between sequential and parallel code generation quality. The same group trained HPC-Coder [8], a fine-tuned model for HPC code that improves pass@k rates and OpenMP pragma labeling over general-purpose models. Mišić and Dodović [7] assessed ChatGPT and GitHub Copilot specifically for OpenMP parallelization of nine benchmark applications, comparing achieved speedups to manually optimized code. Diehl et al. [3] evaluated LLM-generated C++ and MPI+OpenMP code for Mandelbrot set computation, focusing on a single application. Valero-Lara et al. [11] presented ChatMPI, an LLM assistant targeting MPI parallelization of sequential C codes on six HPC kernels. On the GPU side, KernelBench [10] evaluates LLMs on writing efficient CUDA kernels for 250 PyTorch ML workloads. Cui et al. [2] provide a broad evaluation of LLMs for HPC performance optimization, comparing against traditional optimization tools.

In contrast to these works, our study is unique in several respects: we employ fully autonomous *agentic* tool use for end-to-end parallelization tasks rather than isolated code-completion prompts, we cover all four major parallelization paradigms (OpenMP, MPI, CUDA, and hybrid) uniformly across 11 applications and 8 state-of-the-art (as of February 2026) models, and we perform multi-stage validation and comparative performance benchmarking on production HPC hardware.

3 Experiment Design

3.1 Benchmark Selection

There are multiple, frequently conflicting design goals influencing benchmark selection. A fundamental decision for our study is to start from purely sequential benchmarks only, rather than e.g. having an agent attempt to parallelize an existing OpenMP program for clusters. This eliminates one compounding factor (going *from* any parallel language 'A' *to* any other 'B'). Similarly, we decided to stick to only one base language: C++. For our HPC target, while Fortran or plain C might also have been options, we use C++ as a uniform and common baseline.

Perhaps the most important axis for benchmark selection in this context is code size and the somewhat correlated metric of parallelization complexity. Our analysis is based on a set of small- to medium-sized benchmark applications with, generally, one to four computational kernels of significant algorithmic complexity which can in principle be efficiently parallelized. This choice makes the problem more tractable, but also prevents us from studying limitations which might surface in large-scale software engineering. Although it would be interesting to study how agents act when confronted with large, highly complex, or inherently sequential input applications, this was not the goal of this study.

Finally, while it is generally advantageous to evaluate performance of new parallel libraries, languages or systems on well-known benchmarks, in this particular case, we consider including at least some previously not widely publicized

Table 1. Benchmark Overview.

Benchmark	TLoC	Description
matmul	291	Simple dense matrix-matrix multiplication
floydwarshall	330	Floyd-Warshall all-pairs shortest path
stencil3d	348	Iterative 7-point stencil operation on a 3D grid
nbody	352	N-Body gravitational interaction simulation, direct algorithm
black-scholes	358	Black-Scholes European option pricing
cahn-hilliard	381	Phase separation dynamics simulation, Cahn-Hilliard equation
spmv	405	Sparse matrix-vector multiplication, CSR format
qtclustering	535	Grouping 2D points into clusters, Quality Threshold clustering
roomsim	1092	Room impulse response simulation, radiosity-based wave propagation, cross-correlation distance estimate
cholesky	2560	Cholesky decomposition of a symmetric positive definite matrix
unstructured	2664	Energy transfer simulation on an unstructured mesh represented as an arbitrary connectivity graph

applications to be crucial. These are much less likely to constitute a significant part of the LLM training set, and thus allow us to evaluate whether implementation quality is affected substantially when working on "unseen" targets.

Table 1 provides an overview of the benchmarks included in this study. Following the reasoning outlined above, all are presented to the agent as simple, minimally optimized, sequential implementations. The source code is now available[2], but these specific implementations were not public prior to this study. Benchmarks are sorted by total lines of code (TLoC), including all supporting files and headers. They range from very small, simple, and presumably very well-understood by the LLMs (e.g. *matmul*) to moderately sized, more specialized, and unseen (e.g. *roomsim*).

3.2 Model and Tool Selection

The selection of agentic coding tools and the underlying models they use, while separate and independent in principle, in practice is closely interrelated. Our goal for this work was to evaluate the capabilities of *state-of-the-art LLMs* in a scenario representing common real-world use.

Many companies training high-end models in the LLM space offer their own bespoke agentic development tools, such as Google's Antigravity[3], OpenAI's Codex[4], and Anthropic's Claude Code[5]. While these represent a best-case scenario for that particular provider's models, setting up our experiment with each of them individually would also unavoidably introduce variability in the tool use capabilities – in addition to and impossible to distinguish in its effect from the potential variability between the underlying LLMs which we want to observe.

Therefore, we chose *GitHub Copilot*, and more specifically its CLI interface[6], as the technology to base our evaluation on. This allows us to employ a variety of state-of-the-art models via a common interface, in a tool that is extremely widely used, with over 20 million unique users as of 2025 [6]. Model selection

[2] https://github.com/PeterTh/llm-eval-benchmarks.
[3] https://antigravity.google.
[4] https://developers.openai.com/codex/cli/.
[5] https://code.claude.com/docs/en/overview.
[6] https://github.com/features/copilot/cli.

follows a simple principle: for each model tier of each provider available within the GitHub Copilot CLI tool at the time of this study, we chose the most recent version. We then added the two freely available models to serve as a baseline. The resulting set is summarized in Table 2.

Here, the "Model" column contains the ID string for this model in Copilot CLI as of February 2026. "Cost" is the cost per API request for this model, relative to a baseline (currently set at 0.04 USD), and is interesting to note as a stand-in for the computational effort involved for inference on that particular model.

Table 2. Models included in this evaluation.

Provider	Model	Cost	Description
Google	gemini-3-pro-preview	1x	Google's flagship LLM
Anthropic	claude-opus-4.6	3x	Anthropic's flagship LLM
	claude-sonnet-4.5	1x	Anthropic's general purpose LLM
	claude-haiku-4.5	0.33x	Anthropic's low-cost LLM
OpenAI	gpt-5.2-codex	1x	OpenAI's coding-focused LLM
	gpt-5.2	1x	OpenAI's general-purpose LLM
	gpt-5-mini	0x	Free option 1 (baseline)
	gpt-4.1	0x	Free option 2 (baseline)

Readers might be surprised by the fact that claude *sonnet* and *haiku* are present in this study as version 4.5, while *opus* is present as version 4.6. This is consistent with the selection principle described above – at the point in time where this study was conducted, opus 4.6 was already deployed, but the others were not.

3.3 Prompting and Parallelization Targets

As one of our research goals is to establish whether the difficulty of different types of parallelization behaves similarly for LLM coding agents compared to human developers, we chose four different parallelization targets, distinguished by their respective prompt: shared memory CPU parallelism with OpenMP, local GPU parallelism with CUDA, distributed memory with MPI, and hybrid parallelism.

In order to allow the LLMs and tools as much freedom of choice as possible while adhering to the constraints imposed by the experiment setup, we chose a rather succinct prompt, with adjustments for each benchmark and parallelization target, but no variation across models. Figure 1 lists our prompt template. Here, the *Hybrid* option is intentionally vague, with the idea that the model should attempt to decide which strategy is most beneficial for which benchmark (phase). The latter part of the prompt serves to establish common ground rules that enable uniform analysis, validation, and benchmarking of the results produced.

Parallelize the ⟨*benchmark name*⟩ benchmark code found in ⟨*path*⟩

- OMP: with OpenMP for multicore CPU shared memory parallelism.
- CU: with CUDA for GPU parallelism.
- MPI: with MPI for distributed memory cluster parallelism.
- Hybrid: with a hybrid approach combining MPI, OpenMP, and CUDA as appropriate for the problem for maximum parallel performance on an accelerator cluster.

The program should be optimized for maximum performance and parallel scalability, while maintaining correctness and equivalent semantics to the original code. Change the code in the existing files only, and do not change the executable name; do not create new files. Update `CMakeLists` as needed. The resulting program should unconditionally use the specified parallelization approach. Use no new external dependencies.

Fig. 1. The prompt template used for all parallelization experiments.

Operating Environment. Ensuring safety is critical for any experiment involving autonomous LLM agents. We need to prevent the agent from damaging the experiment infrastructure, and also prevent it from "cheating" by accessing results of other runs or reference implementations. Our solution is to perform each agent invocation as a dedicated user, with data wiped clean before each run. This provides an ideal combination of agent freedom while ensuring safety at the level of a multi-user Linux environment.

4 Methodology

4.1 LLM Invocation

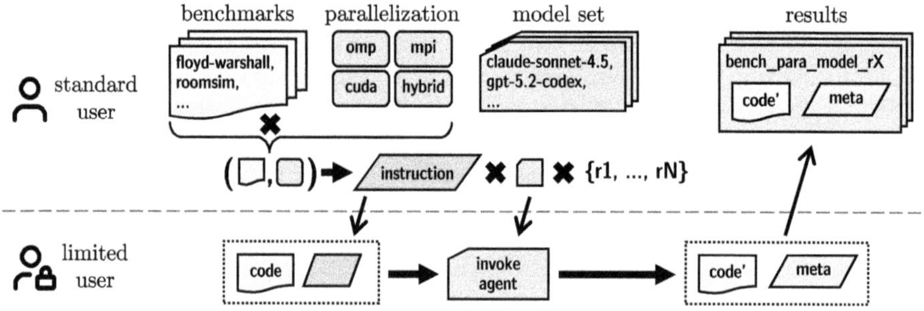

Fig. 2. Flowchart for LLM agent invocation during benchmark parallelization.

The first part of an experiment run requires the invocation of a given LLM agent for each combination of benchmarks and parallelization goals, with a pre-configured number of repetitions. Figure 2 illustrates the overall process carried out when an experiment is run with our infrastructure. Every experiment is defined by the following: (i) a set of benchmark applications (Sect. 3.1), which are each self-contained, (ii) a set of LLMs to evaluate (Sect. 3.2), and (iii) a set of parallelization targets (Sect. 3.3).

For each combination, a prompt is built following the template listed in Sect. 3.3, and it is packaged together with the benchmark source code and related files. These inputs are then transferred to a limited user account, which is wiped clean before each experiment. On this account, the agent is invoked, and is free to access the inputs and use any tools available to it.

Once the agent process completes, the resulting output code is transferred back to the enacting user for permanent storage and later analysis. Additionally, meta-information is collected and stored, including, (i) the total wall-clock time spent, (ii) the agent API time spent, (iii) the number of code line changes, and (iv) the number of LLM input, output and cached tokens consumed.

Resilience. As the goal of our study is not to evaluate the up-time or consistent quality of service of cloud AI providers, but instead the capabilities of the underlying models for parallelization, we re-run experiments in case of server-side or connection errors.

4.2 Validation

Once an LLM agent has created a code version, it is validated in a five-step validation pipeline, as summarized in Fig. 3.

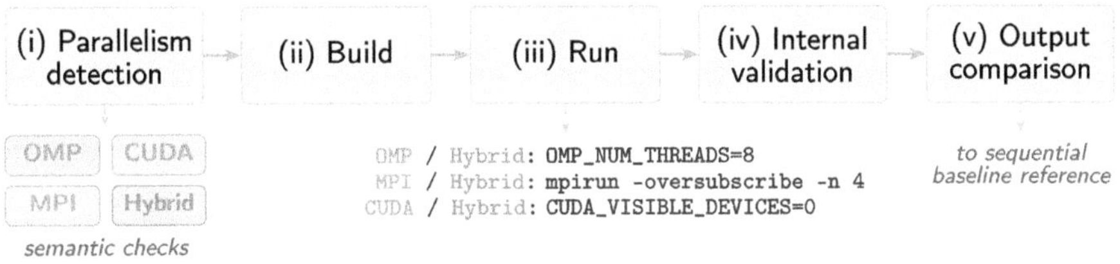

Fig. 3. Validation. Subsequent stages are only reached if all prior stages pass. Step (i) applies target-specific checks; (iii) injects runtime configuration.

The first stage applies basic semantic inspection to the generated source code, detecting patterns indicating the use of our target parallelization approaches. This entails detecting OpenMP pragmas, and/or the correct MPI initialization and finalization function calls, and/or CUDA kernel invocations. For *OMP*, *CUDA* and *MPI* targets, this validation stage is passed if the detected parallelization matches the target exactly. For *Hybrid*, any non-empty set of detected parallelizations is valid.

The second stage attempts to build the benchmark by first invoking `cmake` and then `make`. Successfully configuring and compiling passes this stage, otherwise the errors are logged. Subsequently, in the third stage, the resulting benchmark is invoked, with some additional configuration based on the target parallelization type. Here, we are only interested in validity, not yet performance, so a moderate problem size is chosen for each benchmark.

The fourth and fifth step perform actual result validation. Each benchmark in the experiment includes both an internal validation process, and an option for exporting results for external comparison-based validation. Internal validation is benchmark-specific, and might include options such as ensuring conservation of energy or basic result sanity checks. External validation compares the results against a known-good sequential baseline.

How likely it is for a proposed parallel implementation to pass internal validation but fail external validation varies across benchmarks. For some algorithms, even simple internal validation can detect most sources of errors introduced by parallelization, but this is not true in all cases.

5 Evaluation

For our evaluation, we instantiated the experiment described in the previous sections, with the 11 benchmark applications listed in Table 1, the 8 LLMs listed in Table 2, and the four parallelization targets described in Sect. 3.3. We performed 5 identical invocations for each of these data points in order to quantify agent consistency, for a total of 1760 agent invocations.

5.1 Hardware, Software, and Benchmark Configuration

Our experiment involved two systems: a local, dedicated system which was used to actually perform the agent runs and initial validation, and the Leonardo supercomputer[7] for performance evaluation.

The local system was configured with a dedicated, limited user for agent invocation as outlined in Sect. 4.1. This system features 2 sockets with an AMD EPYC 7763 64-Core processor each, 1 TB of system memory, and 4 NVIDIA GeForce RTX 3090 GPUs, and the agents had full access to this hardware. In terms of system software, it runs Ubuntu 24.04.1 LTS, with gcc 13.2.0 as the default compiler, CUDA 12.6, and OpenMPI 4.1.6. The total agent execution time on this system for the experiment was 168 h, with 16 total re-runs required due to server-side or infrastructure failures (0.9%).

For benchmarking on Leonardo, all OpenMP and CUDA programs were executed on a single, dedicated node with full access to its 32 CPU cores, and an NVIDIA A100 GPU for the CUDA versions. Both the MPI and Hybrid applications were executed across 4 nodes, with a total of 128 cores and 16 GPUs. The MPI version used 128 processes/ranks, while the hybrid version used 16 ranks – 4 per node – with 8 cores and one GPU assigned to each. We performed 5 repetitions of each benchmark and base our evaluation on the median result. Input parameters for the benchmarks were chosen to be sufficient to allow for meaningful parallelization on the given target and accurate measurement while keeping execution times as low as possible. Additionally, a timeout was set for

[7] Leonardo Top 500 listing with detailed specs: https://top500.org/system/180128.

each combination to prevent parallelization attempts with bad performance from needlessly consuming compute time. The full matrix of problem sizes and timeouts for each combination of benchmark and parallelization goal is available as part of the experiment repository[8].

5.2 Scoring

To enable the types of analysis we aim to perform, we require an overall measure of the *quality* of the result produced by a given LLM for a given benchmark and parallelization target. For this purpose, we have created a score metric which assigns a score from 0 to 10 (inclusive) to each generated program. Scores 0–4 indicate a specific validation failure each, 5 indicates successful validation, and 6 and above indicate increasing effectiveness in terms of execution speed. Table 3 summarizes this scoring scheme. The execution time boundaries for the benchmark tiers were purposefully set for each combination of application and parallelism target to distinguish substantial quality gaps, and are available in the experiment repository.

Table 3. Scoring System

0 : Requested parallelization not detected	
1 : Parallelization detected	**6** : Benchmark completed within time limit
2 : Successful build	**7** : Benchmark result in "OK" tier
3 : Successful execution	**8** : Benchmark result in "Good" tier
4 : Internal validation success	**9** : Benchmark result in "Top" tier
5 : Output comparison success	**10** : Best benchmark result for target

5.3 Results and Analysis

LLM-Focused. For our initial analysis, we want to focus on a comparison between the different models used by the coding agent, and their impact on the overall success across all benchmarks and parallelization targets. This information is summarized in Fig. 4.

It shows that there are very clear differences in model performance, with the freely available baseline models (GPT-4.1 and GPT-5 mini) demonstrating the lowest overall performance and most validation failures. Opus 4.6, which is the most expensive model to run per invocation, also performed best overall, remarkably with only 6 validation failures in total. The other Anthropic models, Sonnet and Haiku, perform in the expected order. General GPT-5.2 and its programming-focused Codex variant are quite close in overall performance, but with substantial differences in their respective result distribution. Codex shows more consistent success, but fewer good- to top-performing results compared to standard GPT-5.2. Gemini 3 performance is limited primarily due to a relatively large share of invalid results, although it did generate some top performers.

Overall, from this initial analysis it is clear that newer and more generally capable LLMs are also more successful as code parallelization agents.

[8] https://github.com/PeterTh/llm-eval-experiment/blob/52561bf6/benchmark.rb#L29-L80.

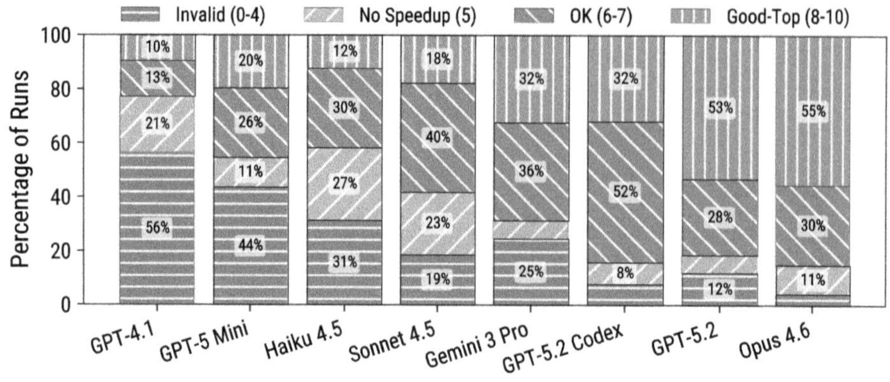

Fig. 4. Tiered success rates per LLM (models sorted by mean score).

Consistency. To quantify consistency, we analyze the variance in scores achieved by each model. Figure 5 shows the mean standard deviation across runs of identical benchmarks for each model and parallelization target. We find that all GPT models other than Codex are inconsistent with regards to their CUDA parallelization. Gemini 3 is generally inconsistent despite its absolute capabilities. Opus is both consistent and capable, and Sonnet 4.5 is remarkably consistent across the board, though at a lower absolute performance level.

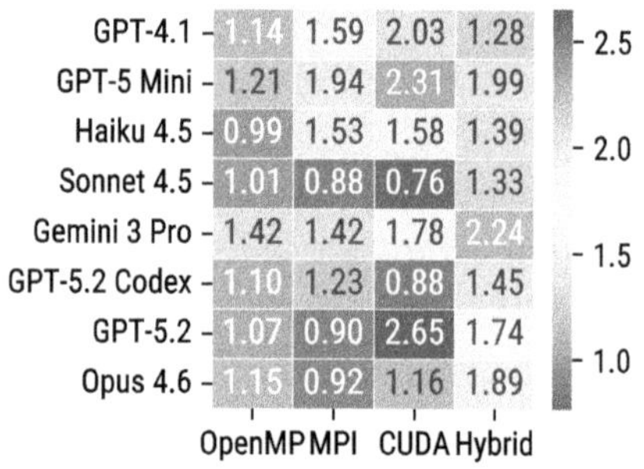

Fig. 5. Mean standard deviation of scores across repeated runs per model and parallelization target.

Relative Difficulty. Comparing score distributions by benchmark or by parallelization target provides insight into how challenging the parallelization process for that particular application or category is from the perspective of an LLM coding agent. A comparison between applications is visualized in Fig. 6a, and between parallelization targets in Fig. 6b.

Regarding the former comparison, we note the following: *cholesky*, *qtclustering*, and *roomsim* are the most challenging applications overall in this metric. They are also all relatively larger programs. However, size (in lines of code) is not, on its own, a good predictor for difficulty, as illustrated by *unstructured*. It is the largest code in the evaluation set, but parallelization is comparatively simple due to the core computational kernel only constituting a small part with straightforward data access patterns and transfers.

The fact that *black scholes* is the "easiest" application is unsurprising, as it is trivially parallelizable and requires no communication. This also results in the most top-heavy distribution function. Perhaps the most unexpected result

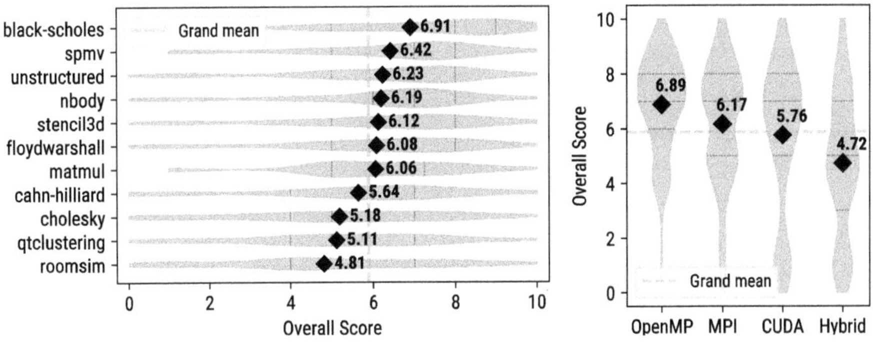

(a) Score distributions per application. (b) Per parallelization type.

Fig. 6. Quantifying relative difficulty of applications and parallelization targets.

in this analysis is the fact that *matmul* is found in the lower half of "more challenging" applications, despite the algorithmic simplicity and extremely common nature of DGEMM. Indeed, as the distribution visualization shows, *matmul* has exceedingly few failures; however, achieving even just good performance appears to be more challenging than for some stencil or simulation applications, resulting in a distribution that is very heavily clustered around the 5–6 score range.

The per-parallelization-type analysis in Fig. 6b reveals that parallelization for shared memory using OpenMP was the easiest target for the agents. MPI and CUDA are of similar difficulty, but with slightly different distributions. CUDA has a larger number of results in the lower half of invalid scores – a more detailed investigation reveals that some of the weaker models chose non-portable ways of setting up CUDA compilation which subsequently failed during validation. Hybrid parallelization is clearly the most challenging target, with its mean actually falling below the boundary score of 5 for valid (but potentially slow) results.

These observations are confirmed by pairwise Mann-Whitney U tests; the differences between all pairs of targets except for the MPI⇔CUDA pair are rated as statistically significant, but that one is not.

Detailed Results. Figure 7 provides the most detailed view of the results of our evaluation that is feasible to present within the limitations of this manuscript. The four per-parallelization-target heatmaps within the figure show the mean score achieved for each combination of LLM and benchmark application. In addition to supporting the conclusions drawn earlier regarding the relative quality of model output and difficulty of applications/parallelization targets, this also allows for some more precise insights.

Firstly, it is clearly necessary to include more complicated parallelization approaches and input programs to derive meaningful conclusions regarding model parallelization capabilities in 2026. If one were to e.g. only look at shared memory OpenMP parallelization for programs like *black scholes*, *spmv*, *unstructured*, and *nbody*, no substantial difference between models could be observed.

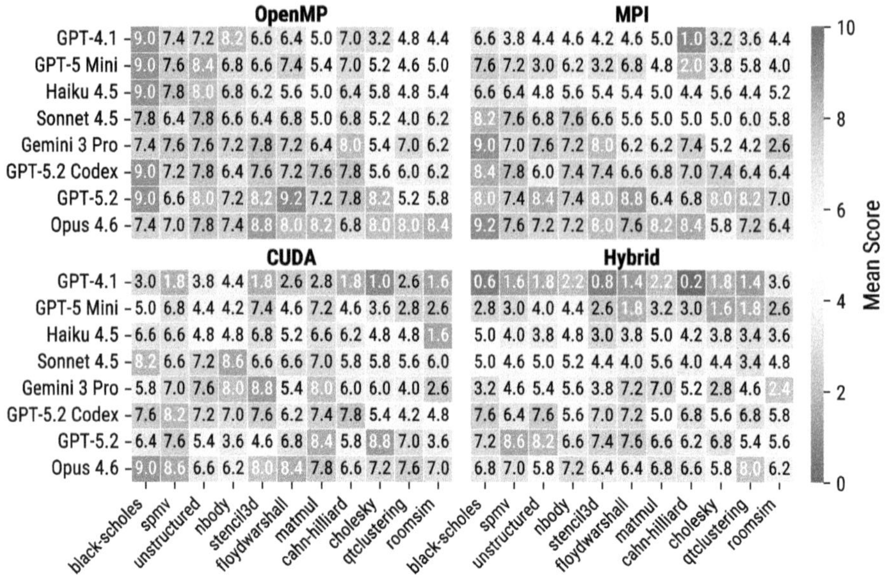

Fig. 7. Model performance across benchmarks and parallelization types.

Secondly, a few models show clear patterns of capability. GPT-4.1 is greatly let down by (primarily build-related) issues with CUDA parallelization, which also affect Hybrid results. Looking at only OpenMP and MPI, it would still be handily outperformed by newer models, but not nearly to the same absolute extent. Gemini 3 Pro is the most volatile model; its aggregate score is limited by some complete failures – e.g. in *roomsim* for any parallelization type other than OpenMP – but when it achieves a valid result it is frequently also a top performer. In general, we can identify "preferences" for specific application types per-model, where they outperform their average result quality, such as stencil-like applications for Gemini 3.

Model Efficiency. So far we have presented absolute performance independently of the resource consumption of each agent model. However, as outlined in Sect. 4.1, we also collected various metainformation for each agent invocation, including time spent and tokens used. The two plots in Fig. 8 present the relationship between these metrics and the average result quality of each model.

In terms of time spent (Fig. 8a), there is a positive correlation: more time spent on the task leads to better overall outcomes. Looking into individual logs, e.g. the Opus 4.6 agent spent more time running larger performance experiments compared to other LLMs. Haiku and Gemini are outliers: the former likely due to its overall weaker capabilities and different relationship with total tokens (as we will discuss soon), the latter due to its lack of consistency dragging down the mean score despite very competitive individual results, as noted previously.

Unlike for time, there is no statistically significant correlation between token count used and result quality across the experiment data set (Fig. 8b). GPT-5.2

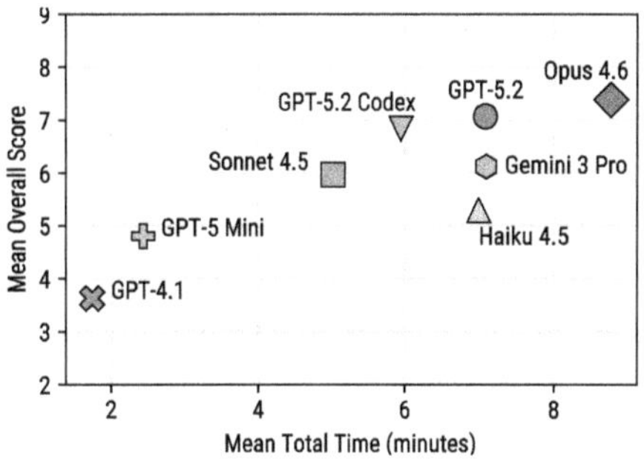

(a) Score vs. time spent per model.

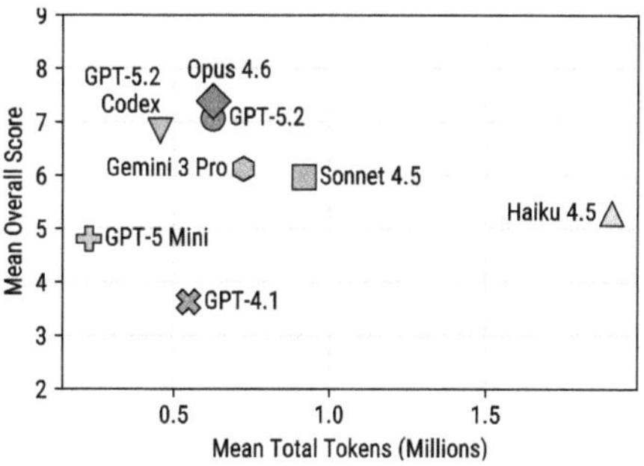

(b) Score vs. tokens used per model.

Fig. 8. Scatter plots quantifying mean model efficiency in time and tokens.

in its Codex variant and Opus 4.6 were the most token-efficient models, while Haiku 4.5 is an outlier, with roughly 3x as many tokens used compared to the average of the other agents. However, note that tokens spent do not directly correlate with computational effort across different model architectures: in particular, Haiku features a smaller core model which can spend more inference-time tokens at lower cost [4]. Our analysis does demonstrate that it is far less effective *per token* at parallelization tasks. Overall, this result suggests that more time spent on the problem can be advantageous, e.g. by allowing for more feedback cycles, but pure token expenditure can be inflated by ineffective iteration.

Threats to Validity. While we included a variety of application sizes and parallel patterns, even the largest and most difficult ones are still small compared to full-size applications. This was necessary to enable a broad analysis across a varied pool of applications, parallelization strategies, and LLMs, but does not allow for direct conclusions to be drawn regarding parallelization and optimization work on large applications. Similarly, we purposefully prepared simple, minimally optimized, sequential implementations of the input benchmark codes without external dependencies, which is a very different starting point than a scenario of working on an already parallel and optimized code.

In terms of execution environment, we have focused on what we consider to be the most practical approach: allowing an agent to access a relatively fast single node for development. There are options to be explored in either direction from this, such as blocking system access to quantify LLM capability without a feedback cycle, though this seems less relevant and was explored by prior work, or allowing access to the actual HPC resources. The latter would require more complex guardrails and budgeting, and also seems less applicable in practice. We have also only studied a single closed-source agentic tool, GitHub Copilot CLI, with one prompting template.

Finally, we have only focused on parallelization with the most common strategy for each target hardware type: OpenMP for shared memory, MPI for distributed memory, CUDA for GPUs, and a hybrid approach for heterogeneous clusters. It would be of particular interest to us to also evaluate less common languages, frameworks, and APIs, and perhaps derive a utility metric for these based on the outcome of such an experiment.

6 Conclusion

We have presented a novel, disciplined, comprehensive experiment design and implementation enabling the analysis of the parallelization capabilities of state-of-the-art agentic LLM coding tools in an HPC context, with full validation and benchmarking of the resulting applications on a supercomputer system.

Our experimental evaluation across 11 benchmarks, 4 parallelization targets, and 8 LLMs demonstrates the following: (i) current frontier agentic development tools are capable of parallelizing small-to-medium sized applications, even for unseen code and hybrid parallelization targets, with good performance results – though consistency varies; (ii) the mean quality of the results achieved per benchmark generally correlates with what human developers would find more or less difficult to accomplish, with trivially parallelizable applications allowing even weaker models to succeed, and applications with more complex communication requirements being more challenging; (iii) shared-memory parallelization for CPUs using OpenMP is the easiest parallelization target, MPI and CUDA are more challenging, but with different distributions, and Hybrid parallelization is clearly the most difficult; (iv) there is a positive correlation between overall time spent by an agent and output quality, but no such correlation exists between tokens consumed and the quality of the results generated.

Overall, we believe that future investigations can benefit from our work both by building on our methodology (supported by full source code and data availability), and by pre-selecting a subset of agents which has demonstrated the greatest aptitude for HPC-related work.

Disclosure of Interests. The authors have no competing interests to declare that are relevant to the content of this article.

References

1. Chen, M., et al.: Evaluating large language models trained on code. arXiv:2107.03374 arXiv preprint (2021)
2. Cui, B., Ramesh, T., Hernandez, O., Zhou, K.: Comprehensive evaluation of LLMs in HPC code performance optimization. In: Proceedings of the SC Workshops of the International Conference on High Performance Computing, Networking, Storage and Analysis (SC-W) (2025). https://doi.org/10.1145/3750720.3757280
3. Diehl, P., Nader, N., et al.: LLM-HPC++: evaluating LLM-generated modern C++ and MPI+OpenMP codes for scalable Mandelbrot set computation (2025)
4. Ghanta, V.S., Paladugu, P.S.L.: Matching frontier code agents with lightweight models via multi-model consultation (2026). https://ssrn.com/abstract=6065307
5. Jimenez, C.E., et al.: SWE-bench: can language models resolve real-world GitHub issues? In: The Twelfth International Conference on Learning Representations (2024)
6. Microsoft: Earnings fy25 q4 transcript, page 8 (2026). https://cdn-dynmedia-1.microsoft.com/is/content/microsoftcorp/TranscriptQandAFY25q4

7. Mišić, M., Dodović, S.: An assessment of large language models for OpenMP-based code parallelization: a user perspective. J. Big Data **11**(161) (2024). https://doi.org/10.1186/s40537-024-01019-z
8. Nichols, D., Davis, J.H., Bhatele, A.: HPC-Coder: modeling parallel programs using large language models (2023)
9. Nichols, D., Marathe, A., Menon, H., Gamblin, T., Bhatele, A.: HPC-coder: modeling parallel programs using large language models. In: ISC High Performance 2024 Research Paper Proceedings (39th International Conference), pp. 1–12 (2024)
10. Ouyang, A., Guo, S., Arora, S., Zhang, A.L., et al.: KernelBench: can LLMs write efficient GPU kernels? In: Proceedings of the 42nd International Conference on Machine Learning (ICML) (2025). https://arxiv.org/abs/2502.10517
11. Valero-Lara, P., Teranishi, K., Engelmann, C., Lee, S., Vetter, J.S.: ChatMPI: LLM-driven MPI code generation for HPC workloads. In: Proceedings of the Supercomputing Asia / International Conference on High Performance Computing in Asia-Pacific Region (HPC Asia) (2026).https://doi.org/10.1145/3773656.3773659
12. Yang, J., et al.: SWE-agent: agent-computer interfaces enable automated software engineering. In: The Thirty-eighth Annual Conference on Neural Information Processing Systems (2024). https://arxiv.org/abs/2405.15793

Velvet: Parallel Divide-and-Conquer in Safe Rust

Badia Liokouras(✉), Ben van Werkhoven, and Rob V. van Nieuwpoort

Leiden University, Leiden, The Netherlands
a.b.liokouras@liacs.leidenuniv.nl

Abstract. Parallel programming is essential yet error-prone, motivating the use of languages such as Rust that promise memory safety and data-race freedom by construction. However, the `unsafe` keyword, whose presence is amplified through transitive dependencies, leads to the majority of Rust programs not being provably safe in practice. This is also the case in widely reused parallel frameworks, raising the question of whether fully safe parallelism can be achieved, and if so, at what cost? To explore this, we present Velvet, a divide-and-conquer parallel programming model implemented entirely in safe Rust. Velvet adopts a Cilk-style spawn–sync abstraction with work-stealing scheduling, and integrates with the standard Rust toolchain without compiler modifications, preserving Rust's language-enforced safety guarantees. An evaluation with representative benchmarks shows that Velvet incurs minimal overhead despite its fully safe design. Furthermore, it achieves competitive performance and scalability with state-of-the-art Rust and C frameworks, namely Rayon, Cilk and OpenMP, on up to 128 cores. Based on our experience, we discuss the interplay between Rust's safety and performance, highlighting when both can be achieved simultaneously and where trade-offs emerge.

Keywords: Divide-and-conquer · Memory safety · Work-stealing · Rust

1 Introduction

Parallelization is a necessity to harness the power of modern computing systems, yet parallel programming is inherently complex and prone to errors such as data races and deadlocks. In shared-memory settings, mature frameworks such as Cilk [8,17] and OpenMP [6] provide effective programming abstractions and are widely used with C/C++ and Fortran, the traditional programming languages for performance-critical applications. However, these languages offer limited built-in guarantees for memory safety or data-race freedom, placing much of the burden of memory management and integrity on the programmer.

The lack of language-level memory safety has consequences beyond programmability, affecting reliability and security. In 2024, Google reported that

M. Torquati et al. (Eds.): Euro-Par 2026, LNCS 16781, pp. 32–46, 2027.
https://doi.org/10.1007/978-3-032-35248-4_3

roughly 70% of severe vulnerabilities in their codebases stemmed from memory mismanagement. This led them to advocate for memory-safe languages [16], echoing security agencies in Europe, North America and Oceania [1].

These developments motivate parallel programming models that combine high performance with language-enforced memory safety. Rust offers a compelling foundation for exploring such models, being a modern programming language with strong type and memory safety at its core. Safety in Rust is enforced largely at compile time via zero-cost abstractions such as *ownership* and *lifetimes* [10]. These mechanisms ensure that every value is dropped exactly once, references always outlive their referents, and aliasing and mutability are mutually exclusive. Together, such properties guarantee that well-typed programs are free from undefined behavior stemming from common memory bugs such as dangling pointers, use-after-free, double-free and data races [3]. This distinguishes Rust from traditional systems languages where weak or absent enforcement of memory invariants makes such errors pervasive and difficult to detect [18].

Granted, Rust's safety checks can be selectively bypassed using the `unsafe` keyword, which is necessary in certain low-level scenarios. However, the use of `unsafe` fundamentally weakens Rust's core value proposition, as it shifts responsibility for memory safety from mechanized checks to informal reasoning. **In this work, we use "safe" to refer specifically to code that contains no `unsafe` blocks**, without assertions beyond what the Rust compiler enforces.

Empirical studies show that memory and concurrency bugs in Rust codebases primarily originate in `unsafe` blocks, which are often concealed behind safe APIs that hide unchecked invariants from callers [15]. Moreover, Evans et al. [7] demonstrate the extent to which `unsafe` propagates through dependencies: while a minority of Rust codes explicitly use `unsafe`, transitive dependency chains amplify its presence such that the majority of all Rust libraries and applications are not guaranteed to be memory-safe and data-race free. These findings highlight that avoiding `unsafe` is not merely a matter of local correctness or code style, but a prerequisite for auditability and for preserving Rust's global safety guarantees, especially for widely reused frameworks.

This becomes particularly salient for parallel programming, where reusable frameworks are widespread. Rayon[1] is regarded as the de facto standard for shared-memory parallelism in Rust [14]. While ergonomic and performant, Rayon internals rely extensively on `unsafe`. For example, parallel tasks are abstracted as `unsafe` type-erased raw pointers, and lock-free work-queues are implemented with manually managed memory buffers. This reliance on `unsafe` reflects the difficulty of expressing efficient parallelism using only the safe fragment of Rust, and highlights that fully safe parallel frameworks remain an open challenge.

To meet this challenge, we present *Velvet*,[2] a high-level programming model for divide-and-conquer (D&C) parallelism. By restricting expressiveness to this well-established paradigm, Velvet automates much of the parallelization of user

[1] https://crates.io/crates/rayon.

[2] https://github.com/liokouras/velvet.

programs while abstracting away low-level scheduling and synchronization. Velvet adopts a Cilk-style spawn–sync model with work-stealing scheduling [8] and is implemented **entirely in safe Rust**. It requires no modifications to the language or compiler and is compatible with the standard Rust toolchain. Concretely, this work makes the following contributions:

- A demonstration of a fully safe parallel D&C programming model and work-stealing runtime, implemented in standard Rust without compiler or language modifications. (Sect. 2).
- An evaluation using representative D&C benchmarks, showing that our safety-oriented design incurs minimal overhead and achieves competitive performance and scalability with the state of the art in both Rust and C (Sect. 3).
- A discussion on the interplay between safety and performance, identifying when the two are mutually achievable and when they compete (Sect. 4).

After presenting the main contributions, the paper turns to a survey of related work (Sect. 5), and conclusions and future directions (Sect. 6).

2 Design and Implementation of Velvet

This section presents an overview of Velvet's design and implementation. Velvet exposes a simple macro-based API and features a work-stealing runtime. In what follows, we highlight how this is realized within the safe segment of Rust.
Velvet is intended for task-parallelism expressed in a D&C manner. In this paradigm, a problem is split into independent subproblems until they are sufficiently small to compute directly, after which their solutions are combined. This is naturally expressed through recursion; for example, Listing 1.1 illustrates a recursive D&C implementation of calculating the nth Fibonacci number.

Programmers use Velvet to parallelize recursive D&C functions by annotating them with Velvet's `spawnable` macro, as on Line 1. Observe also the use of a `THRESHOLD` value on Line 3. This is typical in parallel D&C to limit task creation and execute smaller subproblems directly, often using a more efficient serial algorithm. Programmers may use such serial thresholds explicitly in their `spawnable` functions, but it is not strictly necessary; Lines 3 to 5 could also be replaced with the recursive base-case: `if n < 2 { return n; }`.

```
1 #[spawnable]
2 fn fib(n: u64) -> u64 {
3   if n < THRESHOLD {
4     return fib_fast(n);
5   }
6   let r1 = fib(n-1);
7   let r2 = fib(n-2);
8   return r1 + r2;
9 }
```

Listing 1.1. D&C Fibonacci

At compile-time, functions annotated with `spawnable` are transformed for parallel execution. Recursive calls are replaced with `spawn`-operations, which create tasks that may execute in parallel with the current computation. These tasks are enqueued in a local work-queue, making them available for stealing. The recursive calls on Lines 6 and 7 are transformed into `spawns`.

Because `spawns` are non-blocking, their completion can only be guaranteed after synchronization. This is achieved using `sync`-operations, which are **automatically placed** where necessary to ensure correctness and respect data dependencies, namely before a `spawned` task's result is read, or before the enclosing function returns. Conceptually, each `spawn` is paired with its own `sync`, although multiple `spawns` may be `synced` at the same program location. This allows for more fine-grained parallelism than in, for example, Cilk, where a single `sync` acts as a monolithic local barrier. `syncs` are placed after Line 7, before the return values of the two `spawned` tasks are read on Line 8.

While Velvet automatically resolves local data dependencies, more complex scenarios involving shared state require explicit programmer hints. If a `spawned` task modifies shared state that is subsequently read by the parent task, or if the parent task calls functions that read from such state, the programmer must provide the variable or function names as arguments to the `spawnable` macro. This allows Velvet to identify dependencies outside the function's local scope and to ensure that the necessary `sync`-operations execute in time.

The abstraction used for parallel tasks created during a `spawn` operation is key to Velvet's design. Tasks encapsulate the function call's input arguments and, if applicable, a thread-safe location for returning the result. The latter is necessary in case a task is stolen, because the return value must be communicated back to the worker that `spawned` the task. Implementing an efficient parallel task abstraction that upholds memory safety is challenging. Rayon, for example, uses type-erased task handles that encapsulate stack-allocated closures and raw pointers to parent stack frames. This is efficient, as it avoids the overhead of heap allocation and dynamic dispatch, but requires `unsafe`. Velvet takes a different approach, and uses information available at compile-time to generate a concrete, application-specific task `enum`. The type is generated as part of the build process via a Cargo build script,[3] preserving compatibility with the standard Rust toolchain and remaining subject to all compiler safety checks. By using a concrete `enum`, the Velvet runtime can match and execute tasks without the overhead of dynamic dispatch or the risks of raw pointer manipulation.

The resolution of these tasks occurs during synchronization. When a worker executes a `sync`-operation, it dequeues a task from its local work-queue. Encoded in the task type is whether the task has been stolen or not. If it has not, the worker executes the task directly. If it has been stolen, the worker must wait for the task to complete and its result becomes available. Although logically blocked, the worker does not idle. Instead, it begins work-stealing.

Velvet employs a traditional work-stealing strategy. A worker operates at the **tail** of its own local queue, following a last-in first-out (LIFO) execution strategy. Conversely, thieves steal tasks from the **head** of other workers' queues, in a first-in first-out (FIFO) manner. This combination of LIFO local execution and FIFO stealing follows established work-stealing principles and is well suited for D&C workloads. Prioritizing most-recently-`spawned` local work improves cache local-

[3] Cargo is Rust's standard build system and package manager, and Cargo build scripts are Rust programs that execute during package compilation.

ity, while FIFO stealing prioritizes older and typically larger tasks (a property of D&C), lowering stealing overhead [19].

To realize these double-ended access patterns, Velvet implements work-queues as Arc<Mutex<VecDeque<Task>>>.[4] The entire queue is protected by a single lock, disallowing concurrent accesses. Although this upholds safety in a way that the Rust compiler can statically guarantee, it is conservative. Since thieves and queue-owners operate at opposite ends of the queue, it is desirable to allow concurrent accesses, which is achieved in, for example, Rayon (using `unsafe`). By remaining in the safe segment of Rust, Velvet's queue design prioritizes compiler-verified thread-safety over fine-grained concurrency. As shown in Sect. 3, this does not prevent the runtime from scaling effectively.

3 Performance Evaluation

We evaluate Velvet on seven D&C benchmarks, demonstrating that it generates safe code that compiles and executes correctly and efficiently. Section 3.1 describes the experimental setup and Sect. 3.2 introduces the benchmarks. In Sect. 3.3 we measure Velvet's overhead and in Sect. 3.4 we assess Velvet's parallel performance by comparing it to that of Rayon, Rust's de facto standard shared-memory parallelization framework, and to Cilk and OpenMP, which are similar frameworks for C.

3.1 Experimental Setup

We perform our experiments on a dual-socket node equipped with two AMD EPYC 7702 processors running at 2.00 GHz, for a total of 128 physical cores. All Rust benchmarks are compiled with rustc 1.93.1 (stable) in release mode (`--release`). The Rayon versions use Rayon 1.11.0. The C benchmarks are compiled with Clang 20.1.8 at optimization level `-O3`, and we parallelize using OpenMP 5.1 and OpenCilk 2.1 [17]. All reported experimental results are an average of five runs, following an initial untimed warm-up. For all serial and parallel executions, threads are pinned to cores to prevent migration.

3.2 Benchmark Applications

We have selected seven D&C algorithms for our evaluation. With the exception of one alternative Merge Sort implementation, all benchmarks are written in safe Rust. Each benchmark has a Velvet version parallelized using the `spawnable` macro, and at least one Rayon version. Rayon's programming model is based on parallel iterators and the binary `join()` operator, which does not always map naturally onto the D&C paradigm when the number of recursive calls, or *branch*

[4] `Arc` (*Atomically Reference Counted*) is a thread-safe reference-counting pointer, `Mutex` is a mutually-exclusive lock, and `VecDeque` is a doubly-ended queue. All are offered by the Rust standard library and are thus considered safe.

factor, is greater than two. Nevertheless, we wrote the Rayon versions idiomatically to reflect common usage. For the C comparison, we have written an equivalent C program for each benchmark and parallelized it with `cilk_spawn` and `cilk_sync` in Cilk and `task` and `taskwait` in OpenMP. The following describes each benchmark and presents the settings used in our experiments.

Fibonacci (*fib*). Although the naive recursive algorithm is not efficient, it is a valuable microbenchmark for measuring framework overhead. Each recursive call only performs one integer addition, resulting in minimal computation.

Adaptive Integration (*adapint*). This benchmark computes $\int_a^b f(x)\,dx$ using adaptive trapezoidal integration. The adaptivity of the algorithm lies in the dynamic partitioning into subintervals. In our experiments, $f(x) = 0.1x\sin(x)$. The branch factor is two, so the Rayon version uses the `join()` primitive.

Traveling Salesperson (*tsp*). This branch-and-bound algorithm finds the shortest Hamiltonian path through a set of cities, using a shared `glob_min` value for pruning. The branch factor varies dynamically with the number of remaining cities, so the Rayon version uses a parallel iterator over candidate cities.

N-Queens (*nqueen*). This algorithm counts all valid arrangements of n-many queens on an $n \times n$ chessboard using recursive backtracking with pruning. The branch factor varies dynamically, so the Rayon version uses a parallel iterator over candidate column positions and a sum reduction of the solution counts.

Barnes-Hut (*bh*). This $O(N \log N)$ N-body algorithm [4] organizes bodies in a quad-tree, where the force-update step consists of an "outer"' traversal to select the target body and an "inner" traversal to compute the forces acting on it. The inner traversal approximates bodies in distant nodes as a single mass and recursively explores nearby nodes. We report specifically on the performance of the force-update step as it dominates runtime. We implement three Rayon variants: *TreeIter* parallelizes a custom quad-tree iterator with Rayon's `par_bridge()`, thus using a single parallel iterator for the outer traversal. *ChildIter* iterates over each internal node's children, thus using multiple small parallel iterators for the outer traversal. *BodyIter* replaces the outer traversal with a parallel iteration over the array of bodies. We include this to test whether Rayon's affinity for flat structures outweighs the benefits of tree-based selection.

Matrix Multiplication (*matmul*). We implement a D&C algorithm where each matrix is represented as a hierarchical tree of quadrants. Because this has a branch factor of eight, our Rayon implementation uses a custom `join8()` function which combines four calls to the binary `join()` primitive. The official Rayon demo includes two different matrix multiplication benchmarks,[5] so we also include those in our comparison.

Merge Sort (*sort*). This is a canonical D&C sorting algorithm, however parallelizing the merge-step safely in Rust is challenging. Although the algorithm ensures disjoint writes the output array, the compiler cannot statically verify

[5] https://github.com/rayon-rs/rayon/blob/main/rayon-demo/src/matmul/mod.rs.

this, so it requires explicit synchronization. Our safe implementation thus uses an array of atomic integers, and every read and write of array elements requires atomic operations. To quantify the performance loss of this over-synchronization, we also wrote a version that uses `unsafe`. Specifically, we define a manually managed buffer that uses `unsafe` pointer-based memory operations. The buffer also `unsafe`ly implements the `Send` and `Sync` *marker traits*, which tell the compiler whether a type may be safely moved and shared across threads.[6] Our unsafe application uses this custom buffer for the array to be sorted. *We emphasize that this does not affect the safety of the Velvet framework itself, and that* `unsafe` *is confined to the application level.* The branch factor of both the partition-step and the merge-step is two, so the Rayon version uses the `join()` primitive for both. An `unsafe` version is unnecessary for Rayon, since its internals already use `unsafe` and allow for concurrent writes to unsynchronized data structures. We return to this matter in Sect. 4.

The serial implementation of the sorting step (applied after reaching the serial threshold) uses Rust's standard `slice.sort()`. To maintain algorithmic consistency, the serial base case in the C implementations also invoke `slice.sort()` through a Rust foreign-function interface. This ensures that any performance differences reflect parallel orchestration overheads rather than differences in the underlying sorting algorithm. We use the Rust base-case because we found that the standard Rust implementation performed better than native C sorting implementations. As such, we are favoring the fastest option across the languages.

Table 1. Problem sizes, serial thresholds and runtime metrics for each benchmark, including the pure serial runtime, given these inputs. The reported number of stolen jobs are an average when executed with Velvet on 64 threads.

Benchmark	Problem size	Serial threshold	Serial run-time (s)	Nr. `spawns`	Nr. steals	Time per `spawn` (ms)
fib	$n = 52$	$n = 25$	138.32	$8.3 \cdot 10^5$	1,838	0.1669
adapint	$[a, b] = [-10^4, 4.0 \cdot 10^6]$ $\epsilon = 10^{-4}$	Diff. = 1500	199.94	$9.1 \cdot 10^6$	1,976	0.0220
tsp	Nr. cities: 25	Rem. cities: 18	167.25	$8.1 \cdot 10^6$	4,902	0.0205
nqueen	$N = 16$	Rem. rows: 11	199.39	$5.0 \cdot 10^6$	2,949	0.0382
bh	Nr. bodies: $4 \cdot 10^6$	Nr. bodies: 500	129.76	$8.8 \cdot 10^4$	9,132	1.6094
matmul	Mat. dim.: 8192×8192 64×64	Mat. dim.:	183.86	$2.1 \cdot 10^6$	2,607	0.0930
sort	Array size: $2 \cdot 10^9$	Array size; Sorting: 2^{21} Merging: $2 \cdot 2^{21}$	135.59	5,120	3,764	27.7587

6 These traits are derived automatically when a type is composed entirely of other `Send`/`Sync` types. Manual and `unsafe` implementation is required here because the buffer relies on raw pointers, which the compiler cannot guarantee to be thread-safe.

Benchmark Settings. As explained in Sect. 2, parallel algorithms often use serial thresholds, which programmers can integrate into `spawnable` functions. Table 1 lists the thresholds and inputs we use for each benchmark, as well as the runtime of the pure serial baseline corresponding to a conventional sequential implementation without any parallel constructs. This is used to compute the speedups reported in Sect. 3.4.

3.3 Framework Overhead

This section evaluates Velvet's overhead, both at compile-time and run-time.

Compile-time. Since Velvet generates parallel code at compile time, it is expected to introduce compile-time overhead. We quantify this by comparing compilation times of Velvet programs to equivalent handwritten parallel codes for both clean builds and incremental builds after small edits. In the worst case, clean builds are 1.7× slower with Velvet, while incremental builds show at most 1.1× slowdown and, in the best case, no measured difference. The absolute differences are on the order of milliseconds, which is negligible compared to the effort of manual parallelization, and to the run-time gains achieved from parallelization.

Table 2. Velvet's work overhead (**WO**). For *fib*, *adapint* and *tsp*, t_s is the same as the serial baseline reported in Table 1. For the benchmarks marked with an asterisk (*), t_s is different because the parallel implementation differs from the serial one.

	fib, no threshold	*fib*	*adapint*	*tsp*	*nqueen**	*bh**	*matmul**	*sort**
t_s	138.32	138.32	199.94	167.25	193.59	142.23	193.61	142.16
$t_{1,no}$	3208.48	138.97	199.45	166.54	191.26	142.74	195.02	141.72
$\mathbf{WO}_{no}$	**23.20**	**1.00**	**1.00**	**1.00**	**0.99**	**1.00**	**1.01**	**1.00**
$t_{1,opt}$	1778.12	138.89	199.71	171.12	194.46	142.22	195.12	142.12
$\mathbf{WO}_{opt}$	**12.86**	**1.00**	**1.00**	**1.02**	**1.00**	**1.00**	**1.01**	**1.00**

Run-time (Work Overhead). *Work overhead* [8] measures the cost of parallel orchestration and arises from creating, enqueueing and dequeueing parallel tasks. This overhead is paid when `spawn`ed tasks are executed on the same worker that initiated the `spawn`, which is the common case in D&C. As shown in Table 1, only a small fraction of `spawn`ed tasks tend to be stolen. This execution pattern motivates the *work-first principle* [8], which aims to minimize overhead on the common, non-stolen execution path. A key consequence of this principle is that, rather than always enqueueing all parallel tasks to make them available for stealing, one task is executed directly by the current worker. In Velvet, this optimization takes the form of *direct recursion*: when the branch factor is statically known, the final recursive call is executed directly. For cases with dynamic branching (e.g., *tsp* and *nqueen*), the optimization is not applied automatically, as it would require dynamic checks for the final recursive call.

Work overhead is measured by comparing the runtime of the *serial elision* (t_s) with that of the single-threaded Velvet execution (t_1). The serial elision is the program containing annotated `spawnable` functions, but not re-written by Velvet. This is sometimes the same as the baseline serial program, but if there are changes in the parallel implementation, for example added synchronization of shared data structures, the serial elision includes these changes. The ratio t_1/t_s isolates the overhead introduced by Velvet's parallel orchestration; a value of 1.00 indicates serial-equivalent performance.

Results are shown in Table 2. Besides the benchmarks listed in Table 1, we include a version of *fib* without a serial threshold to illustrate worst-case overhead. The metrics $t_{1,no}$ and WO_{no} correspond to executions without direct recursion on the final call, while $t_{1,opt}$ and WO_{opt} apply the optimization. In the worst case (*fib*, no serial threshold), Velvet has substantial work overhead, and applying the direct recursion optimization almost halves it. For the benchmarks with a serial threshold, the overhead factor is around 1, and the direct recursion optimization has minimal additional impact. For *tsp* and *nqueen*, the optimization is detrimental due to the dynamic checks for detecting the last recursive call.

3.4 Parallel Performance

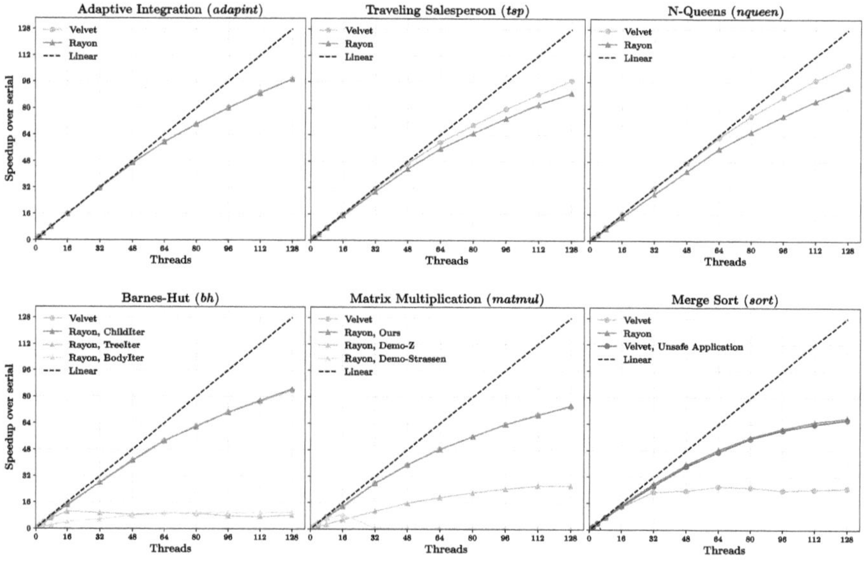

Fig. 1. Parallel speedup of six benchmarks, parallelized with Velvet and Rayon.

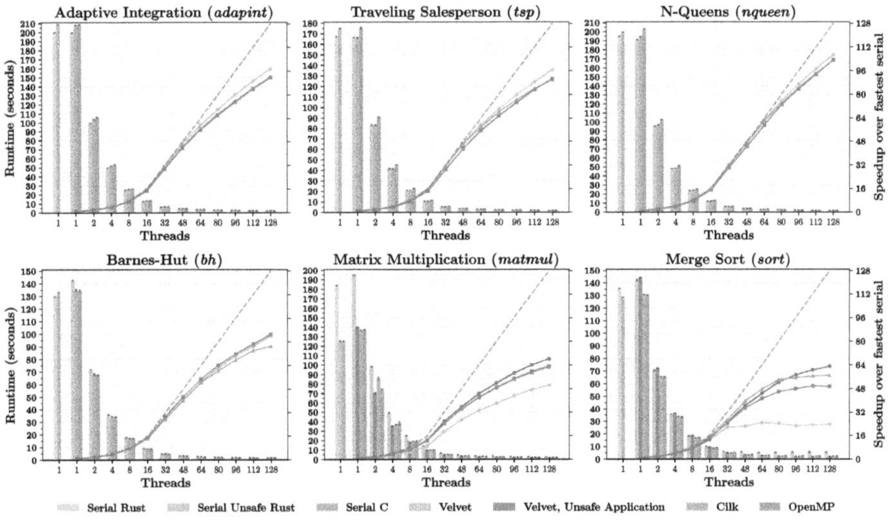

Fig. 2. Runtimes (bars) and parallel speedups (lines) of six benchmarks, parallelized with Velvet, Cilk and OpenMP.

We evaluate the parallel performance of Velvet in two stages. We first compare it with that of Rayon, to assess how Velvet performs within its own language ecosystem. We then broaden the comparison to Cilk and OpenMP, situating Velvet relative to mature C-based frameworks. Here, we exclude *fib*, which primarily serves as a microbenchmark and does not reflect a realistic D&C workload.

Figure 1 shows the parallel speedup of the benchmarks achieved with Velvet and Rayon, relative to the corresponding serial baseline reported in Table 1. The diagonal dashed lines represent ideal linear scaling.

For the benchmarks in the top row, both Velvet and Rayon scale nearly linearly on up to 64 threads, after which they slow down. On the other hand, the benchmarks in the bottom row slow to sub-linear speedup at around 32 threads. The top three benchmarks are compute-bound and involve minimal data, whereas the bottom three are relatively more data-intensive. We therefore attribute this difference in scalability to memory bandwidth effects; as thread count grows, the data-intensive workloads place increasing pressure on the shared memory hierarchy and memory bus.

In general, Velvet's scalability is competitive with Rayon's. We observe that Velvet scales better than Rayon when Rayon uses a top-level parallel iterator (*tsp*, *nqueen*). When Rayon uses many small parallel iterators (*bh*-ChildIter) or `join()`-based logic (*adapint*, *sort*, our *matmul*), it scales identically to Velvet, although for *sort*, this is only the case for the unsafe application. We further observe that for *bh*, the custom Rayon iterator (TreeIter) does not scale. Neither does the variant that selects bodies by iterating over the body array (BodyIter), validating tree-based traversal as the appropriate strategy for body selection.

For *sort*, Rayon outperforms Velvet with the fully safe application. However, the version that uses `unsafe` to sidestep over-synchronization scales on par with Rayon. In this case, **Velvet itself is entirely safe**, meaning the slowdown observed in the safe application is due to synchronization overhead at the application level, rather than being due to the parallelization framework itself.

Figure 2 presents the execution times (bars) of the benchmarks parallelized with Velvet, Cilk and OpenMP, alongside the serial Rust and C baselines. It also shows the parallel speedups achieved with each framework (lines), computed relative to the fastest serial baseline for each benchmark.

There is a noticeable discrepancy in the serial runtimes for *matmul*, where C outperforms Rust despite implementing identical algorithms. This performance gap is due to Rust's runtime array-bounds checks, which are automatically inserted by the compiler and which require `unsafe` to disable. To confirm this, we implement a version of *matmul* with `unsafe` in the recursive base case to bypass bounds checking and mirror C's raw pointer arithmetic. This is the pink **Serial Unsafe Rust** bar, and it indeed matches the runtime of serial C. We also parallelize this unsafe application with Velvet.

For all benchmarks, Velvet's scalability is competitive with that of the C frameworks, and in many cases it is better at the highest threadcounts. Granted, for *matmul* and *sort*, this is only the case for the unsafe applications, which exclude runtime bounds checks (*matmul*) and over-synchronization (*sort*) which are also absent in the C versions.

4 Discussion

The experience of implementing and evaluating Velvet highlights several tradeoffs inherent in safe parallelism. This section presents a discussion of these tradeoffs, and of the limitations that define the scope of the framework.

Safety Trade-Offs. Our results support two main observations. First, that a parallel D&C programming model and runtime *can* be implemented entirely in safe Rust. Second, that this *may* have a bearing on expressiveness and performance. Despite the design constraints imposed by safe Rust, particularly in the work-queue implementation, our evaluation shows that Velvet's runtime has minimal overhead and achieves parallel scalability comparable to Rayon, Cilk and OpenMP. This means that for D&C workloads, eliminating `unsafe` at the runtime level does not entail measurable performance penalties and, importantly, that users are not required to have hidden `unsafe` code in their software stack.

Granted, the presence of `unsafe` in the runtime can affect how applications are expressed. Velvet's source code transformations introduce no `unsafe`, and the resulting program remains fully subject to the compiler's safety analyses. This means that Velvet preserves Rust's existing safety guarantees without weakening or extending them. In contrast, Rayon internally relies on `unsafe` abstractions to enable application-level patterns that would otherwise violate Rust's aliasing rules, such as holding multiple mutable references to the same data structure. A representative pattern where this difference surfaces is when parallel updates are made to the same data structure, but mutual exclusion and correctness are guaranteed by the algorithm rather than by synchronization in the data structure itself. The *sort* benchmark in Sect. 3 is an instance of this pattern, and strictly adhering to safe Rust demands unnecessary synchronization. Rayon circumvents this by being internally `unsafe`, while the version parallelized with Velvet requires explicit application-level `unsafe` to achieve comparable performance.

This distinction reflects two philosophies within Rust's ecosystem. Frameworks such as Rayon use `unsafe` internally but provide *apparently* safe APIs. Velvet maintains a strict alignment with Rust's static guarantees: operations that cannot be verified by the compiler must be made explicit and justified by the programmer. RayonâĂŹs approach can improve expressiveness and performance at the application level, but the presence of `unsafe` in the software stack is non-negotiable; it is there regardless of whether the application calls for it. Velvet instead gives the programmer agency and prioritizes auditability, even if this requires additional synchronization or user-visible `unsafe`. We argue that *both* are valid approaches. For applications that do not require `unsafe`, Velvet imposes no additional burden. Where `unsafe` is warranted, the preferred choice depends on whether ergonomics or explicit safety reasoning take priority.

Beyond framework-level design choices, our evaluation also highlights a general manifestation of the safety–performance trade-off. While Rust is celebrated for its zero-cost abstractions, safety is not always free, even in serial programs. In the *matmul* benchmark, the Rust compiler's insertion of runtime bounds checks introduced a measurable penalty compared to C. Because these checks prevent out-of-bounds memory access, they represent a persistent "real-cost abstraction". While Velvet has minimal parallelization overhead, it remains subject to these fundamental language-level safety costs, and matching C's performance may require `unsafe` in the application.

Limitations and Scope. From the programmer's perspective, Velvet requires little more than annotating recursive functions with a macro. While this hides much boilerplate, it also hides code transformations that can make it harder for programmers to reason about their application. For example, the automatic `sync`-placement is transparent, potentially making it difficult to reason about performance and parallel semantics. Furthermore, debugging may become challenging, since runtime behavior depends on generated code that the programmer does not directly write. This points to a broader discussion about programming models and finding effective levels of abstraction. To alleviate some of these challenges while keeping the high level of abstraction, IDE tooling could be developed to, for example, visualize `sync` placements.

Velvet currently requires that `spawnable` functions have a recursive structure. This restriction allows for a lightweight framework that automates `spawn` and `sync` insertion without much programmer input. However, it naturally limits applicability. Supporting more general task-parallelism is a viable extension, but it would likely require more explicit programmer guidance for `spawn`-insertion.

Finally, Velvet does not target data-parallel patterns such as parallel iteration over collections, for which iterator-based frameworks like Rayon are more appropriate. For this reason, our empirical comparison with Rayon should not be interpreted as an argument for Velvet to replace Rayon in all contexts. Instead, Velvet occupies a complementary point in the design space, targeting applications where parallelism arises dynamically as a function of recursive structure. Rayon is nevertheless our primary baseline because it is the most widely used Rust-native parallel programming framework, and thus represents the current standard against which new approaches are evaluated.

5 Related Work

Velvet builds on the tradition established by Cilk's spawn–sync model [8,17] and its use of work-stealing for efficient scheduling [20]. This approach is widely adopted by systems such as Satin for distributed Java [19] and the task-based paradigm in OpenMP [6]. While these systems typically require modified compilers or language extensions, Velvet achieves similar results through a library-based approach using standard Rust tools. In this regard, Velvet is conceptually aligned with algorithmic skeletons [9] that provide high-level abstractions such as divide-and-conquer, but unlike opaque skeleton callbacks, Velvet transforms provided source code directly. Language-enforced safe parallelism is well-studied in functional languages [12,13], though these rely on pervasive immutability rather than ownership. Velvet differentiates itself by targeting systems programming under Rust's memory safety model.

Several parallelization frameworks exist in the Rust ecosystem, but they target different paradigms and rely on `unsafe` code blocks to various degrees. Rayon[7] focuses on data-parallel iterators, Tokio[8] is designed for asynchronous and I/O-bound workloads, while PPL [5] and Rust-SSP [14] focus on pipeline parallelism and data-stream processing. In contrast, Velvet targets recursive task parallelism, and is designed to avoid hidden `unsafe` code altogether.

On the interaction of safety and parallel performance in Rust, Abdi et al. [2] evaluate Rust's claim of "fearless concurrency" across various parallel patterns, finding that regular data accesses are safe while irregular read–write patterns require `unsafe`. Their study takes the parallelization framework for granted, using Rayon or manually managed threads. In contrast, we target the parallelization framework itself. We show that a work-stealing D&C scheduler can be implemented entirely in safe Rust, and examine how eliminating `unsafe` in the framework reshapes the safety–performance trade-off at the application level.

6 Conclusion

We presented Velvet, a parallel framework for divide-and-conquer programs implemented entirely in safe Rust. Featuring a macro-based interface, users annotate recursive functions to be transformed into parallel code, with the resulting

[7] https://crates.io/crates/rayon.
[8] https://crates.io/crates/tokio.

program remaining subject to the Rust compiler's characteristic safety checks. At runtime, work is distributed via decentralized work-stealing. Unlike existing frameworks which tend to rely on `unsafe` internals, Velvet explores a distinct design point by employing conservative but safe runtime structures and statically generated task representations to uphold strong typing.

Our evaluation across multiple benchmarks on up to 128 cores demonstrates that Velvet incurs negligible overhead and achieves performance competitive with Rayon, the current standard for shared-memory parallelism in Rust, and Cilk and OpenMP in C. These results demonstrate that safety and performance are not *necessarily* at odds in parallel programming frameworks. Nevertheless, the *matmul* and *sort* benchmarks exemplify two scenarios where safety and performance *do* compete. For *matmul*, this manifested as runtime boundary checks inserted by the Rust compiler, even for the serial implementation. For *sort*, Rust's safety guarantees force us to over-synchronize in the parallel implementation, or to explicitly use `unsafe` at the application level.

Our evaluation thus far has focused on small- and mid-scale workloads. Applying Velvet to large-scale, real-world applications is a natural next step to validate its practicality. Velvet can also be extended to support general task-parallelism, and further optimizations can be explored. For example, implementing adaptive or non-uniform memory access (NUMA)-aware strategies in the work-stealing mechanism. More broadly, the combination of source code generation and compiler-enforced safety that Velvet uses to construct safe and efficient abstractions may translate to other domains such as accelerated computing, distributed systems and databases, pointing to interesting opportunities at the intersection of programming languages and systems research.

Data Availability Statement. The artifact is available in the Zenodo repository [11].

Disclosure of Interests. The authors have no competing interests to declare.

References

1. The case for memory safe roadmaps. Tech. rep., Cybersecurity and Infrastructure Security Agency (CISA), National Security Agency (NSA), Federal Bureau of Investigation (FBI), Australian Cyber Security Centre (ACSC), Canadian Centre for Cyber Security (CCCS), National Cyber Security Centre–United Kingdom (NCSC-UK), and New Zealand National Cyber Security Centre (NCSC-NZ) (2023)
2. Abdi, J., Posluns, G., et al.: When is parallelism fearless and zero-cost with rust? In: Symposium on Parallelism in Algorithms and Architectures (SPAA) (2024)
3. Astrauskas, V., Müller, P.: Leveraging rust types for modular specification and verification. Programming Languages (2019)
4. Barnes, J., Hut, P.: A hierarchical O(N log N) force-calculation algorithm. Nature (1986)
5. Besozzi, V.: Ppl: Structured parallel programming meets rust. In: Parallel, Distributed and Network-Based Processing (PDP) (2024)
6. Dagum, L., Menon, R.: Openmp: an industry standard API for shared-memory programming. IEEE Comput. Sci. Eng. (1998)

7. Evans, A.N., Campbell, B.: Is rust used safely by software developers? In: International Conference on Software Engineering (ICSE) (2020)
8. Frigo, M., Leiserson, C.E.: The implementation of the cilk-5 multithreaded language. In: Programming Language Design and Implementation (PLDI) (1998)
9. González-Vélez, H., Leyton, M.: A survey of algorithmic skeleton frameworks. Softw. Pract. Exp. (2010)
10. Jung, R., Jourdan, J.: Rustbelt: securing the foundations of the rust programming language. Programming Languages (2017)
11. Liokouras, B., van Werkhoven, B., et al.: Artifact of the paper: velvet: parallel divide-and-conquer in safe rust (2026). https://doi.org/10.5281/zenodo.20507828
12. Marlow, S., Newton, R.: A monad for deterministic parallelism. In: Symposium on Haskell (2011)
13. Marlow, S., Peyton Jones, S., et al.: Runtime support for multicore haskell. In: International Conference on Functional Programming (ICFP) (2009)
14. Pieper, R., Löff, J.: High-level and efficient structured stream parallelism for rust on multi-cores. J. Comput. Lang. (2021)
15. Qin, B., Chen, Y.: Understanding memory and thread safety practices and issues in real-world rust programs. In: Programming Language Design and Implementation (PLDI) (2020)
16. Rebert, A., Kern, C.: Secure by design: Google's perspective on memory safety. Tech. rep, Google Security Engineering (2024)
17. Schardl, T.B., Lee, I.A.: Opencilk: a modular and extensible software infrastructure for fast task-parallel code. In: Principles and Practice of Parallel Programming (PPoPP) (2023)
18. Szekeres, L., Payer, M.: Sok: eternal war in memory. In: Symposium on Security and Privacy (2013)
19. Van Nieuwpoort, R.V., Wrzesińska, G.: Satin: a high-level and efficient grid programming model. Trans. Program. Lang. Syst. (2010)
20. Yang, J., He, Q.: Scheduling parallel computations by work stealing: a survey. Int. J. Parallel Prog. (2018)

Communication Offloading on SmartNIC DPUs: A Quantitative Approach

Jacob Wahlgren[1], Andong Hu[1], Roger Pearce[2], Maya Gokhale[2], and Ivy Peng[1(✉)]

[1] KTH Royal Institute of Technology, Stockholm, Sweden
{jacobwah,andonghu,ivybopeng}@kth.se
[2] Lawrence Livermore National Laboratory, Livermore, USA
{pearce7,gokhale2}@llnl.gov

Abstract. SmartNIC Data Processing Units (DPUs) offer a promising solution for saving high-end CPU resources by offloading tasks to programmable cores near the network interface. In this work, we explore the feasibility of SmartNIC DPUs in supporting an asynchronous communication model called "fire-and-forget", particularly its core message routing service. We design a communication offloading engine called Buddy that decouples communication tasks from the application process. Buddy runs flexibly on SmartNIC DPUs such as the Nvidia BlueField-3 DPU and generic x86 CPUs. Our evaluation results in five applications identify the memory-to-communication ratio as a key predictor of the offloading performance. Host-dominated workloads, such as Quicksilver and Sparse Matrix Transpose, achieved up to 1.55x speedup with communication offloaded to the DPU. We further identify a 625x increase in DRAM traffic due to the absence of Direct Cache Access support on the DPU, highlighting a critical need in future SmartNIC designs.

Keywords: DPU · BlueField · Communication Offloading

1 Introduction

Data center networking is undergoing a transformation in the increasing adoption of SmartNICs to reduce resource cost and improve energy efficiency [14]. Unlike traditional passive Network Interface Cards (NICs), these emerging devices integrate fully-featured programmable CPUs, such as ARM and RISC-V cores, directly into the network interface, known as a Data Processing Unit (DPU). On-path SmartNICs feature embedded processors integrated directly in the network data path. In contrast, off-path SmartNICs offer decoupled, general-purpose processing, enabling offloading infrastructure tasks from the host CPU, freeing high-performance CPU cores to focus on application computation. This was previous demonstrated in MPI communication [2,13], and workloads such as weather simulation [15], graph processing [17] and molecular dynamics [7].

This work explores the feasibility of SmartNIC DPUs in supporting an asynchronous communication model called "fire-and-forget" [3,5,10,12]. This model

M. Torquati et al. (Eds.): Euro-Par 2026, LNCS 16781, pp. 47–61, 2027.
https://doi.org/10.1007/978-3-032-35248-4_4

aims to maximize parallelism in communication by relaxing message ordering and software aggregation and routing to bundle application-level messages into network-efficient packets. Traditionally, this routing service would co-run with application processes and share the compute and memory resources that could otherwise be used by the application. In this work, we explore offloading the communication routing service to SmartNIC DPUs, identify key application metrics useful for configuring offloading, and draw design insights for future SmartNIC designs to support communication offloading efficiently.

To quantitatively study offloading the routing service needed in the "fire-and-forget" model, we design *Buddy*,[1] a communication library that supports sending messages of arbitrary sizes asynchronously without involving the receiver. Buddy can either co-run on the host or be offloaded to the BlueField DPUs. When offloading message routing to the DPU, Buddy decouples communication management from application logic to reduce the resource usage on the host CPU. We use Buddy to quantitatively study key factors of communication offloading performance, such as task partitioning between DPU and CPU, aggregation of fine-grained messages to network-efficient packets, and SmartNIC architectural aspects.

In summary, the main contributions of this work are:

- Design, implement, and optimize Buddy, a communication routing offloading library for "fire-and-forget" model suitable for SmartNIC DPUs and generic hosts.
- Evaluate performance in five applications: Single Source Shortest Path (SSSP), Triangle Counting, Histogram, Sparse Matrix Transpose, and Quicksilver. Quicksilver, Sparse Matrix Transpose, and Histogram achieve speedup from 1.13× to 1.55×, with the memory-to-communication ratio as an effective indicator.
- Identify key optimization factors: transfer granularity, pipelining, and multi-threading, contributing to 9.5×, 12.4×, and 6.2× improvement.
- Compare the BlueField-3 DPU against an x86 CPU for an offloading target and find the lack of DCA support as the main performance limitation for communication offloading.

2 Background

SmartNICs and DPUs. SmartNICs and DPUs have emerged to address challenges in performance and efficiency. A SmartNIC extends the capability of a NIC by integrating programmable logic (e.g. ASIC/FPGA) on the data path, enabling host-side workloads to be offloaded to the NIC. Data Processing Units (DPUs) go one step further, featuring general-purpose CPUs and a standalone Linux software stack. Several vendors provide commercial DPU solutions with ARM cores, including AMD Pensando, Intel IPU, and Nvidia BlueField. In this

[1] https://github.com/KTH-ScaLab/buddy.

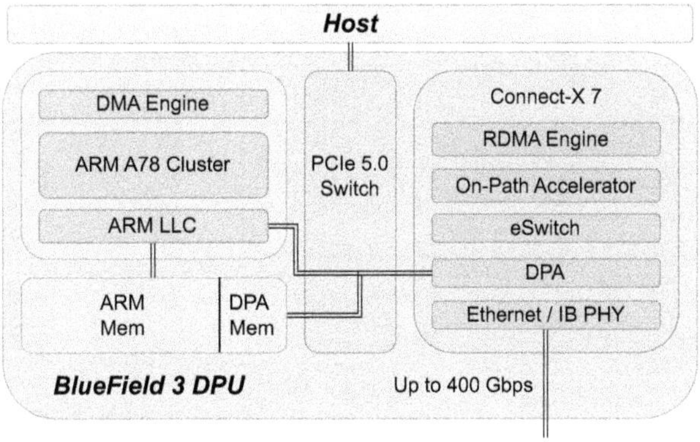

Fig. 1. An overview of Nvidia BlueField-3 DPU architecture.

work, we focus on the BlueField-3. Figure 1 illustrates the overall architecture. BlueField-3 combines a Connect-X 7 NIC with an ARM A78 CPU that consists of 8 to 16 cores. Compared to its predecessor BlueField-2, its memory system is upgraded to dual-channel 32 GiB LPDDR5 memory. The programming environment for BlueField is provided by Nvidia's Data-Center-on-a-Chip Architecture (DOCA) framework, which offers a set of libraries, drivers, and APIs that abstract low-level hardware resources such as DMA and RDMA engines.

High-Performance Networking. High-performance I/O devices generally use Direct Memory Access (DMA) to read and write directly to the main memory without involving CPU. In networking, this concept is extended to Remote Direct Memory Access (RDMA). With RDMA, nodes in a cluster can exchange data without CPU involvement. With one-sided RDMA, the initiator can READ or WRITE to specific memory addresses, while two-sided RDMA enables the specific addresses to be determined by the recipient with the SEND operation. As each operation incurs an overhead both in the NIC and the network switches, larger messages generally improve the throughput. Direct Cache Access (DCA), also known as cache injection, is a technique to improve I/O performance beyond DMA [8]. DCA enables network devices to directly inject data into the CPU's caches, bypassing the main memory [4,18].

3 Buddy Design

Overview. Frequent irregular communication is a challenge in HPC systems since it leads to many small inefficient messages across the network. Message aggregation combined with multi-hop routing, a core component for enabling the "fire-and-forget" model, provides higher throughput by a trade-off with latency [12]. The design goal of Buddy is to decouple message routing from the application, and reduce the burden on the host processor by offloading it to the DPU. Message routing services are memory-bound, and thus may pollute cache and stall CPU cores for the core application work. Offloading routing

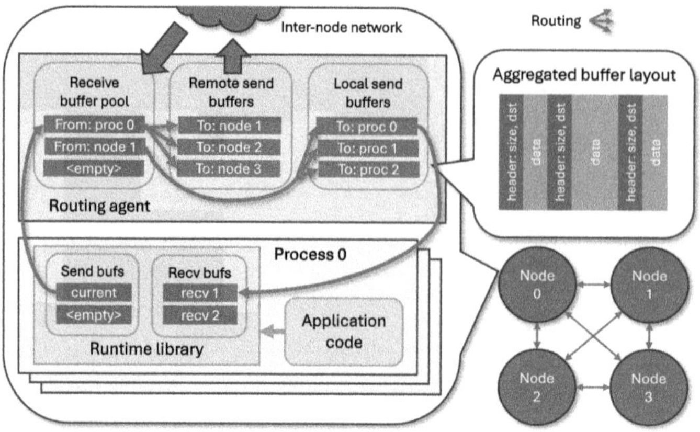

Fig. 2. An overview of the Buddy design, where the routing agent interfaces between local processes and remote nodes to aggregate individual messages.

services to DPUs frees the host processor to focus on the core application work instead of communication. Buddy targets distributed applications that exhibit the following characteristics:

- Small and arbitrary messages. Processes communicate with messages significantly smaller than the link MTU.
- Fire-and-forget. Messages can be delivered asynchronously without requiring explicit confirmation from the receiver to the sender.
- Throughput-oriented. Application performance is limited by throughput rather than the latency of individual messages.
- Relaxed message ordering. Messages may be delivered out of order, enabling optimized routing and avoiding head-of-line blocking.

Our design is illustrated by Fig. 2 and consists of two major components: the *runtime library* and the *routing agent*. The runtime library offers an API for applications to interact with Buddy to send and receive messages, while the routing agent is a separate service handling the routing of incoming and outgoing messages between local application processes and remote cluster nodes. The routing agent can either co-run on the same CPU as the application, or be offloaded to another processor, e.g., a DPU. Figure 2 shows the different communication buffers and operations involved in sending and receiving messages. On the routing agent, three groups of communication buffers are used: receive buffers, remote send buffers, and local send buffers. These components make extensive use of zero-copy RDMA to avoid overheads.

Message aggregation happens at each hop in the design. First, the runtime library aggregates all outgoing messages, which could be of arbitrary sizes, from the application to ensure efficient transfer to the routing agent. Next, the local routing agent on the sending side aggregates all messages destined to the same

Algorithm 1 Routing kernel.

```
function ROUTE(array of aggregated messages)
    for message m do
        total_size = sizeof(header) + m.payload_size
        next = routing_table[m.dst]
        send_buf = get_buf(next, total_size)
        if send_buf then
            memcpy(send_buf.tail, m)
            send_buf.tail += total_size
        else
            return false
    return true
```

remote node. Similarly, the routing agent on the receiving side aggregates incoming messages to the same local rank (i.e., Local send buffers in Fig. 2). Finally, it delivers a set of aggregated messages from different sources to the destination process.

Routing Agent. The routing agent receives messages from local processes on the node and from remote nodes. As messages are received, the routing agent parses the message headers and routes them to their destination. The aggregated send buffers are flushed once they are full or a timeout is reached to avoid stale communication. To ensure that all messages are eventually delivered, the routing agent employs an idle timeout. If no messages are received for a certain time, the routing agent flushes all outstanding send buffers, even if they are not full.

The routing kernel is the key performance-critical operation in the agent. A simplified version is shown in Algorithm 1. The kernel is applied to all incoming message bundles, both from local processes and from remote nodes. The time complexity of the routing algorithm is $O(n+m)$ for n messages and m total bytes, which is independent of the number of endpoints. We precompute the next-hop routing table at initialization. During routing, if no send buffer is available, the kernel exits prematurely, and the remaining messages are put on a blocklist. Once an outstanding send is completed, the kernel is applied to the entries of the blocklist. Multiple threads are used in message routing to leverage the full hardware performance. Locks or atomics would lead to significant contention in each loop iteration. Instead, separate send buffers are allocated per thread.

Runtime Library. The runtime library offers support for applications to send and receive arbitrary sized messages with Buddy. It provides the necessary interfaces to bootstrap Buddy communications and manage aggregated send and receive buffers. All runtime library functions are non-blocking, enabling applications to maximize the time for useful computation. Furthermore, the runtime library leverages multiple send and receive buffers to enable pipelining of application compute with communication in a similar fashion to the routing agent. The low-level API consists of functions for sending or receiving aggregated message buffers and a call to poll for completions.

Communication Protocol. Buddy communication travels two different data paths: intra-node between the runtime library and the routing agent, and inter-node between routing agents on different nodes. For inter-node communication, based on our characterization results on the testbed, RDMA is used for low-latency and high-bandwidth data movement for simplicity, portability, and flexibility. This enables the routing agent to be able to run both on a DPU or on any generic host cores. The RDMA protocol is based on SEND/RECV operations for its high performance since it avoids the need for distributed bookkeeping. Note that we also considered the DPU's DMA API, but benchmarking revealed no performance advantage over standard RDMA on the testbed. Message aggregation is implemented by concatenating multiple small messages in each RDMA request. Each message is encoded as an 8-byte header containing the payload size and destination rank, followed by the payload data. This format enables flexibility in the application as arbitrary-sized messages can be mixed freely.

Implementation. We implement the Buddy routing agent and runtime library in C++. Communication is bootstrapped using MPI, where we use MPI ranks as addresses of application processes. RDMA communication is implemented with the *ibverbs* library. All communication buffers are pre-allocated at initialization time to avoid the overhead of memory registration during runtime. In the routing agent, multi-threading is implemented by using OpenMP threads and a shared receive queue.

4 Experimental Setup

Our first testbed has two nodes equipped with BlueField-3 DPUs. The hosts have dual-socket Intel Xeon Gold 6326 CPUs, 16 cores each, and 512 GiB DDR4 memory. The DPUs have 8 ARM cores and 16 GiB LPDDR5 memory. The NIC is capable of 100 Gbps InfiniBand or RoCE link. The connection between hosts and DPUs is PCIe 4×16, which has a maximum unidirectional bandwidth of 31.5 GB/s. Both of the hosts and DPUs are running Linux 5.15 with DOCA version 2.7.0085. On this testbed, we used up to 8 threads for routing in all scenarios, which is the number of DPU cores. For scalability demonstration, we employ another testbed with 8 BlueField-3 nodes. The hosts have an AMD EPYC 9454 CPU with 48 cores and 770 GiB DDR5 memory. The DPUs have 16 ARM cores and 32 GiB LPDDR5 memory. This system also runs Linux 5.15 but has DOCA version 3.2.1.

We use a set of five applications to evaluate communication offloading. They come from a variety of domains and feature different communication patterns as shown in Table 1. Each of the applications features irregular communication patterns as they send fine-grained asynchronous messages in an unstructured fashion. The Histogram, Sparse Transpose, Triangle Counting, and SSSP (Single Source Shortest Path) benchmarks are based on [10] for which we developed a compatability layer. For these applications, we use randomized inputs and set the problem size to 100x the host's last-level cache. Quicksilver is a proxy

Table 1. Tested benchmarks and applications.

Application	Domain	Comm. pattern
Histogram	Data Analysis	Data-dependent
Sparse Transpose	Linear Algebra	All-to-all
Triangle Counting	Graph Analysis	Topology-dependent
SSSP	Graph Analysis	Topology-dependent
QuickSilver	Physics	3D neighborhood

application that solves a dynamic Monte Carlo particle transport problem. We ported it to the low-level API with around 200 inserted and 400 deleted lines. For the experiments, we use the CTS2 benchmark problem with a reduced number of steps.

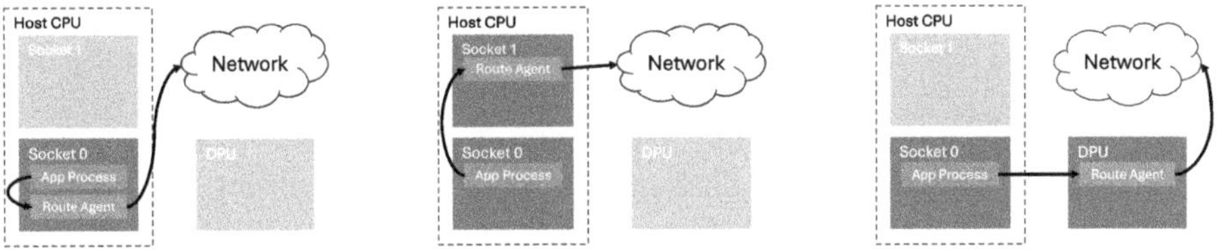

(a) None (b) x86 (c) Dpu

Fig. 3. Three offloading scenarios with arrows representing RDMA data transfer.

We compare three offloading scenarios in this work, as illustrated by Fig. 3. Since Buddy enables communication offloading using a generic infrastructure that is portable to different environments, this enables us to compare the routing offloading performance with the routing agent deployed on different hardware. The first non-offloading scenario does not decouple the routing component from application. The second and third scenarios decouple the routing agent either to a separate socket or the SmartNIC DPU.

- None: The application process and routing agent both run on the same host cores (with simultaneous multi-threading) as a performance baseline.
- x86: The routing agent is offloaded to a separate socket with a powerful host CPU, as an upper bound on communication offloading performance.
- Dpu: The routing agent is offloaded to low-power cores on the SmartNIC.

5 Application Performance

Offloading Performance. A comparison of the application-level performance in the different offloading scenarios is shown in Fig. 4. The plot shows the mean

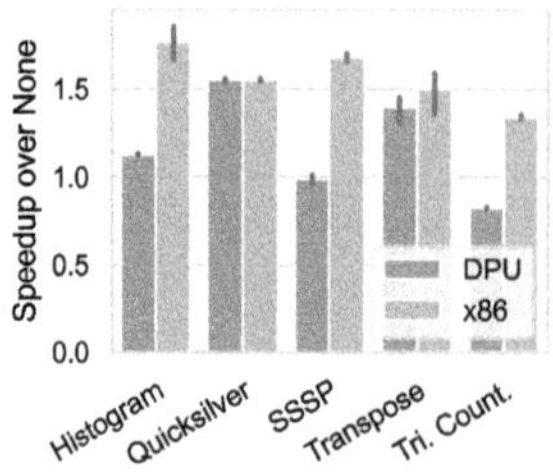

Fig. 4. Speedup compared to no offloading.

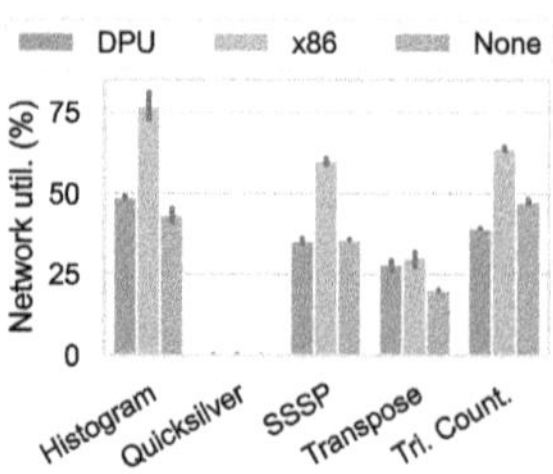

Fig. 5. Network utilization in different scenarios.

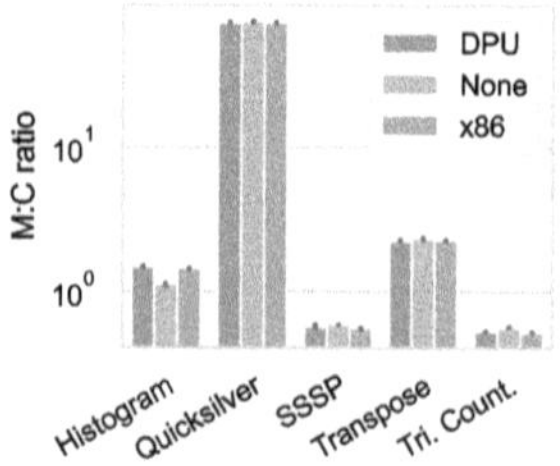

Fig. 6. M:C ratio in different scenarios (log scale).

performance of five runs. In all applications, X86 offloading improved performance compared to the non-offloading baseline, from a mean of 1.35× speedup in Triangle Counting to 1.77× in Histogram. DPU offloading improved performance in three applications, with 1.13× speedup in Histogram, 1.40× in Sparse Transpose, and 1.55× in Quicksilver. The performance was not improved in SSSP and Triangle Counting, with 0.99× and 0.83× speedup, respectively.

To explain the performance difference between the applications, we employed additional profiling metrics. First, we measured the network utilization, shown in Fig. 5. We calculate it as the inter-node communication throughput of Buddy over the theoretical link speed. In the X86 scenario, Histogram reached a high network utilization of 77%. SSSP and Triangle Counting also achieved high utilizations with 60% and 64%, respectively. These applications also had the largest difference between the X86 and DPU performance. Evidently, they can benefit from communication offloading, but DPU offloading is limited by bottlenecks in the DPU hardware, i.e., weaker cores and memory. Two applications had a lower network utilization, with 30% for Sparse Transpose and only 0.1% for Quicksilver. They have more local work relative to the amount of communication, and therefore benefit from offloading as it frees up resources for local computation work. Offloading to x86 cores is more beneficial because it suffers less from the weaker DPU system compared to X86.

While tasks such as Sparse Transpose contain no floating-point computations, traversing the sparse structure incurs many cache misses and constitutes the major local work in the benchmark. We measured the ratio of memory accesses to communication (M:C ratio) in the applications to characterize the balance of local work to communication. The total amount of memory accessed is measured as the number of LLC cache misses times the cache line size (with HPCToolkit), while the amount of communication is measured as the number of bytes routed by the routing agent. For instance, a ratio of 2 means that the application loads 2 bytes from memory for each 1 byte it communicates with Buddy. The M:C ratios are shown in Fig. 6. They are largely consistent across the offloading scenarios, although it deviates slightly for NONE in Histogram. Quicksilver has by far the highest ratio around 72, explaining the low network utilization we observed, followed by Sparse Transpose with 2.3 and Histogram with 1.5. SSSP and Triangle Counting have more communication than memory traffic with ratios of 0.56 and 0.53, respectively.

Table 2. Summary of application offloading results.

Application	Speedup x86	Speedup DPU	Net. util.	M:C ratio	Category
Histogram	✓ (1.77)	✓ (1.13)	77%	1.5	Balanced
Quicksilver	✓ (1.55)	✓ (1.55)	0.1%	72	Host-dominated
SSSP	✓ (1.68)	✗ (0.99)	60%	0.56	Comm-dominated
Transpose	✓ (1.51)	✓ (1.40)	30%	2.3	Host-dominated
Tri. Count	✓ (1.35)	✗ (0.83)	64%	0.53	Comm-dominated

We summarize the results in Table 2. Based on the M:C ratio, we categorize the applications into three groups. Quicksilver and Sparse Transpose have a high degree of local work (M:C ratio > 2) and are therefore *host-dominated*. SSSP and Triangle Counting have a high degree of communication (M:C ratio < 1) and are therefore *communication-dominated*. Histogram lies in between, we consider it *balanced*. The host-dominated applications see a significant speedup (1.40–1.55) from DPU offloading, while the communication-dominated applications see no benefit. The balanced Histogram has a modest speedup of 1.13.

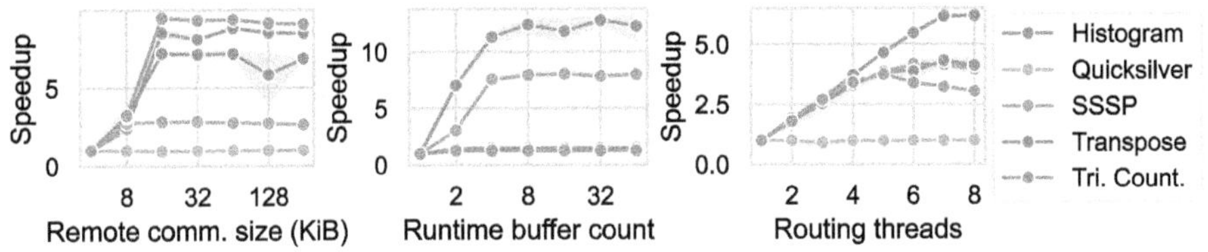

Fig. 7. Impact of tuning and optimizations on application performance.

Optimizations. We studied the impact of tuning and optimizations on communication offloading performance by measuring application performance with varied Buddy configurations in DPU mode. Remote communication size is the size of buffers for routing-agent to routing-agent traffic over the network, with 4 KiB (i.e. the link MTU) as the baseline. Runtime buffer count is the number of send and receive buffers in the runtime library. Routing threads is the number of OpenMP threads in the routing agent. The speedup is shown in Fig. 7.

In most cases, increasing the communication size to 8 KiB results in a 2–3x speedup, reaching a plateau around 16–32 KiB, with up to 9.5x in Triangle

Counting, due to increased communication efficiency. The performance impact on Quicksilver is negligible, as it is strongly host-dominated. Increasing the runtime buffers enables communication pipelining and better overlap. The performance of SSSP and Transpose was significantly improved, reaching a plateau around 8 buffers with 8.0x and 12.4x, respectively, while other applications were not significantly affected.Utilizing multiple threads in the routing agent improves performance for most applications, with up to 6.2x speedup at 7 or 8 threads in Histogram. Triangle Counting peaks at 5 threads with 3.7x speedup, while SSSP and Tranpose peak at 7 threads with 4.2x and 4.3x, respectively. These results show that communication granularity, pipelining, and multi-threaded DPU services are key optimizations for communication offloading.

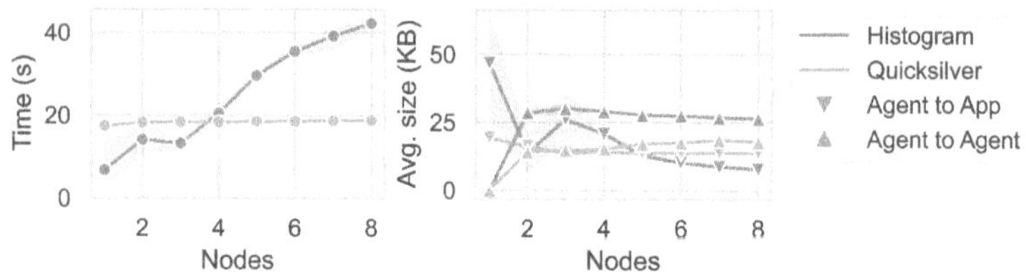

Fig. 8. Performance of scaling Histogram and Quicksilver with DPU offloading up to 8 nodes and the average transfer sizes.

Scalability. We evaluated the scalability of Buddy communication offloading on the 8-node cluster by performing a weak scaling test of Histogram and Quicksilver with DPU offloading. In Histogram, we scale both the size of the distributed table and the total number of updates, and in Quicksilver, we scale both the number of mesh elements and the number of particles. The routing agent uses 16 threads. The execution time and average transfer size per run across 5 runs are shown in Fig. 8.

Quicksilver achieves close to ideal weak scaling with almost constant execution time regardless of the number of nodes. This is in line with our finding that Quicksilver is host-dominated. In Histogram, the execution time is fastest with 1 node, as there is no cost for inter-node data transfer. With 2 and 3 nodes, the time is similar. From 3 to 5 nodes, the time scales linearly, after which the growth rate decreases slightly.

The average transfer size highlights a factor limiting the scalability of Histogram. While the average agent-to-agent (i.e. cross-node) transfer size remains in the range 26–30 KB (for nodes > 1), the average agent-to-application (i.e. intra-node) transfer size decreases from 26 KB at 3 nodes to 8 KB at 8 nodes. On the other hand, the transfer size in Quicksilver remains in the range 14–19 KB for all distributed cases. These findings indicate that Buddy's scalability on balanced or communication-dominated workloads could be improved by further tuning buffer sizes and idle timeouts for agent-to-application transfers on multiple nodes.

6 DPU Bottleneck Analysis

BlueField-3. To understand how DPU design can be enhanced to support communication offloading, we analyze the system bottlenecks. In the previous section, we observed that DPU offloading is weaker than X86 offloading, which could be explained by weaker cores, memory subsystem, or higher data transfer costs in the DPU scenario. However, we cannot tell from these experiments which system component is the bottleneck.

We investigate two potential bottlenecks by injecting interference and measuring the relative performance of Buddy. As a baseline case, we use DPU offloading with 7 threads. To inject DPU memory interference, we concurrently execute a memory-intensive workload on the 8th core. To inject interference into the link between the host and DPU, we concurrently execute a communication-intensive workload on the 8th core and a free core on the host. The memory-intensive workload is a vector addition with a working set of 32 MB (more than 2x the last-level cache capacity). The communication-intensive workload is the `ib_send_bw` RDMA benchmark in bidirectional mode with 64 KB message size. For these experiments, we use the Histogram application, which has a large disparity between X86 and DPU performance, and repeat experiments five times.

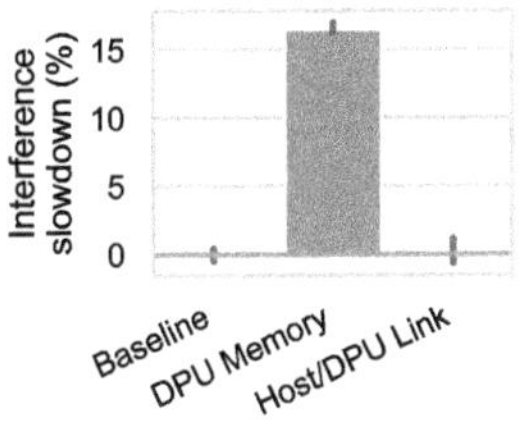

Fig. 9. Performance of DPU offloading with different kinds of interference.

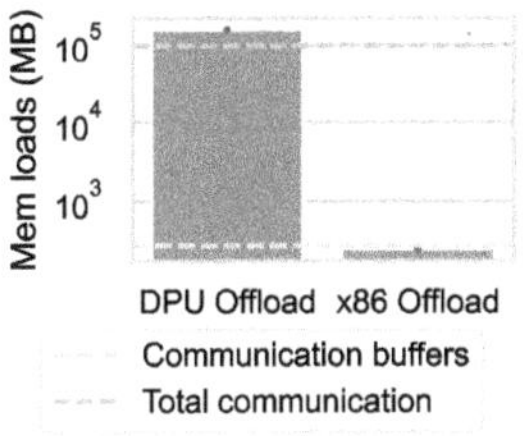

Fig. 10. Amount of data loaded from DRAM in the routing agent (log scale).

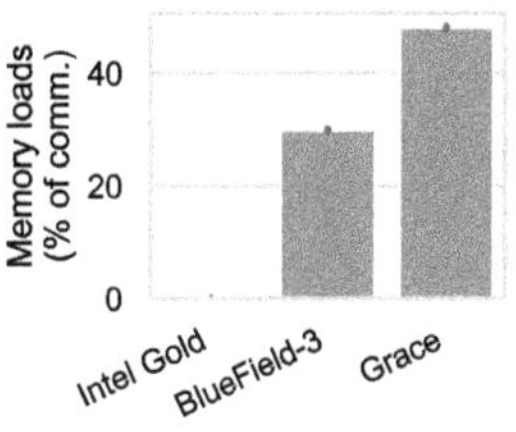

Fig. 11. LLC misses fraction of total network traffic in micro-benchmark.

Figure 9 presents the slowdown of the application with different sources of interference. Communication interference does not significantly impact the performance of DPU offloading. However, DPU memory interference decreases the performance by 17%, indicating that the DPU's main memory is the performance bottleneck for DPU offloading. Furthermore, we profile LLC misses in the routing agent using `perf` to compare the frequency of DRAM accesses in DPU and X86 offloading, as shown in Fig. 10. The total L3 cache misses correspond to 249 MiB and 153 GiB of data loaded from memory in X86 and DPU, respectively. The value for X86 roughly corresponds to reading all of the communication buffers a single time (272 MiB), while the value for DPU is 1.6x the total communicated data volume (95 GiB). The ratio of cache misses corresponds to a 625x increase in main memory demand loads with DPU offloading compared to x86 offloading. The low memory traffic in x86 can be explained by the fact that the CPU supports Intel DDIO, and thus utilizes DCA to place arriving data directly into the cache without going through main memory. While ARM has a DCA feature called Cache Stashing, the larger memory traffic in DPU indicates that it is not supported or not enabled on the BlueField-3 ARM cores.

In conclusion, the DPU memory is the bottleneck in Buddy applications with DPU offloading. Memory traffic is significantly higher in DPU than x86 because the DPU does not leverage DCA.

Future SmartNICs. Addressing the identified bottleneck in future SmartNICs would enable DPU-based communication processing, such as the software routing, closer to the underlying network speed, benefiting high-throughput DPU applications. At the time of writing, Nvidia recently announced its next-generation SmartNIC BlueField-4. We note that the BlueField-4 will leverage the Nvidia Grace CPU for the ARM cores of the DPU and a more powerful memory system, which could address the identified limitations of weak CPU and memory in the previous generations of BlueField DPUs for enabling efficient routing offloading needed for the "fire-and-forget" model.

To inform expectations for the future SmartNIC DPU on the DCA capabilities, we designed an experiment to test on the Grace CPU. We utilized the `ib_send_bw` benchmark from perftest, with a small modification to read each byte of received data on the main CPU thread instead of just discarding it. To test the DCA capabilities of a system, we execute the benchmark and measure the total number of LLC misses using `perf stat`, and calculate the total cache misses as a fraction of the total amount of data received. Specifically, we set the message size to 64 KiB and the number of iterations to 10,000, giving a total of 625 MiB data, and scale the cache misses by the cache line size (64 B). We execute the benchmark in loopback mode.

We execute the benchmark on a system with an Nvidia Grace CPU and an Nvidia ConnectX-7 NIC. Our Grace system features 72 ARM Neoverse V2 cores and 480 GiB of LPDDR5X memory. For comparison, we also execute the benchmark on Intel Gold and BlueField-3, corresponding to the x86 and DPU offloading scenarios. The results from three runs are shown in Fig. 11. As expected, the Intel system has essentially no cache misses, while the BlueField-3 system has a significant amount with 30%. Interestingly, the Grace system has an even larger amount of misses at 48%. This indicates that the Grace system, like the BlueField-3, is not utilizing DCA. We hypothesize that CPU prefetching is the reason total cache misses on BlueField-3 and Grace remain below 100%. These results show that DCA does not come "for free" by upgrading the CPU. To enable high-throughput communication offloading, future SmartNIC architects should consider DCA as a critical feature.

7 Related Works

In HPC, SmartNICs have been used both for communication and as general-purpose coprocessors. In [2,13], the MPI progress engine is offloaded to enable computation overlap while PEDAL [9] offloads in-flight compression and decompression in MPICH Works such as [7] offload specific application kernels, while ODOS [15,16] enables general-purpose offloading with OpenMP. Outside the SmartNIC area, SDT [11] enhances CPU architecture with specialized Simultaneous Data-delivery Threads to co-run application threads and communication threads with performance isolation.

Previous works have shown the benefits of software aggregation and routing in irregular communication without leveraging SmartNIC offloading. Garg and Sabharwal [5] studied the HPCC RandomAccess benchmark and demonstrated how message aggregation and software routing improved the performance by 2x on the Blue Gene/L supercomputer. Subsequent works have proposed libraries and multiple routing and aggregation schemes, including BCL [3], Conveyors [10], and YGM [12].

One previous work claimed that DCA is already supported in BlueField-2 DPU [6]. The authors draw this conclusion from the fact that the `ib_write_bw` benchmark can achieve a bandwidth higher than the STREAM benchmark on the DPU. However, we believe that the conclusion is incorrect. Without modifying the benchmark, as we did in Sect. 6, the CPU does not access the data at all, and the benchmark's throughput is limited only by the NIC's DMA capabilities rather than the CPU's memory bottleneck.

Other recent works on DCA only focus on Intel DDIO. Farshin et al. [4] dissected the implementation of DDIO, proposed a set of optimization guidelines for performance isolation, and demonstrated DDIO fine-tuning. Alian et al. [1] presented a gem5 simulator model for DDIO and characterized its impact on memory utilization and performance on storage and network processing benchmarks. Wang et al. [18] further studied the architectural details of DDIO to develop analytical models to diagnose performance issues, tune configurations, and inspire future hardware designs.

8 Conclusion

In this work, we explored the prospects of offloading communication routing with SmartNICs, a key component for enabling the "fire-and-forget" model. To this end, we developed a prototype offloading engine called Buddy and evaluated it on Nvidia BlueField-3. We found that DPU offloading efficiency depends on the amount of local work in the application. Specifically, the memory-to-communication ratio is a key indicator of DPU offloading performance, with host-dominated workloads gaining the most from offloading. Secondly, we identified the absence of Direct Cache Access (DCA) for network packets as an architectural bottleneck in the DPU, causing a 625x increase in memory traffic compared to an x86-based scenario with DCA, which highlights an important consideration for future SmartNIC designs.

Acknowledgment. This work was performed under the auspices of the U.S. Department of Energy by Lawrence Livermore National Laboratory under Contract DE-AC52-07NA27344 under LDRD Project 24-ERD-047. LLNL-CONF-2019409.

Disclosures. The authors have no competing interests to declare.

References

1. Alian, M., Yuan, Y., Zhang, J., Wang, R., Jung, M., Kim, N.S.: Data direct I/O characterization for future I/O system exploration. In: 2020 IEEE International Symposium on Performance Analysis of Systems and Software (ISPASS) (2020)
2. Bayatpour, M., Sarkauskas, N., Subramoni, H., Maqbool Hashmi, J., Panda, D.K.: BluesMPI: efficient MPI non-blocking Alltoall offloading designs on modern BlueField smart NICs. In: International Conference on High Performance Computing (2021)
3. Brock, B., Buluç, A., Yelick, K.: BCL: a cross-platform distributed data structures library. In: Proceedings of the 48th International Conference on Parallel Processing (2019)
4. Farshin, A., Roozbeh, A., Maguire Jr, G.Q., Kostić, D.: Reexamining direct cache access to optimize I/O intensive applications for multi-hundred-gigabit networks. In: 2020 USENIX Annual Technical Conference (USENIX ATC 20) (2020)
5. Garg, R., Sabharwal, Y.: Software routing and aggregation of messages to optimize the performance of HPCC Randomaccess benchmark. In: Proceedings of the 2006 ACM/IEEE Conference on Supercomputing (2006)
6. Gu, T., Fei, J., Canini, M.: OmNICCL: Zero-cost sparse AllReduce with direct cache access and SmartNICs. In: Proceedings of the 2024 SIGCOMM Workshop on Networks for AI Computing (2024)
7. Karamati, S., et al.: "Smarter" NICs for faster molecular dynamics: a case study. In: 2022 IEEE International Parallel and Distributed Processing Symposium (IPDPS) (2022)
8. León, E.A., Ferreira, K.B., Maccabe, A.B.: Reducing the impact of the memory wall for I/O using cache injection. In: 15th Annual IEEE Symposium on High-Performance Interconnects (HOTI 2007) (2007)
9. Li, Y., Kashyap, A., Chen, W., Guo, Y., Lu, X.: Accelerating lossy and lossless compression on emerging bluefield DPU architectures. In: 2024 IEEE International Parallel and Distributed Processing Symposium (IPDPS), pp. 373–385 (2024)
10. Maley, F.M., DeVinney, J.G.: Conveyors for streaming many-to-many communication. In: 2019 IEEE/ACM 9th Workshop on Irregular Applications: Architectures and Algorithms (IA3) (2019)
11. Mamandipoor, A., Tran, H.D., Alian, M.: SDT: cutting datacenter tax through simultaneous data-delivery threads. IEEE Comput. Archit. Lett. (2025)
12. Steil, T., Reza, T., Priest, B., Pearce, R.: Embracing irregular parallelism in HPC with YGM. In: Proceedings of the International Conference for High Performance Computing, Networking, Storage and Analysis (2023)
13. Suresh, K.K., et al.: A novel framework for efficient offloading of communication operations to BlueField SmartNICs. In: 2023 IEEE International Parallel and Distributed Processing Symposium (IPDPS) (2023)
14. Tibbetts, N., Ibtisum, S., Puri, S.: A survey on heterogeneous computing using SmartNICs and emerging data processing units. Futur. Gener. Comput. Syst. (2025)

15. Usman, M., Benito, M., Iserte, S., Peña, A.J.: ODOS-MPI: HPC-friendly SmartNIC offloading of computation/communication kernels. In: Proceedings of the International Conference for High Performance Computing, Networking, Storage and Analysis (2025)
16. Usman, M., Iserte, S., Ferrer, R., Peña, A.J.: DPU offloading programming with the OpenMP API. In: Proceedings of the SC'23 Workshops of The International Conference on High Performance Computing, Network, Storage, and Analysis (2023)
17. Wahlgren, J., Schieffer, G., Gokhale, M., Pearce, R., Peng, I.: Disaggregated memory with smartnic offloading: a case study on graph processing. In: 2024 IEEE 36th International Symposium on Computer Architecture and High Performance Computing (SBAC-PAD), pp. 159–169. IEEE (2024)
18. Wang, M., Xu, M., Wu, J.: Understanding I/O direct cache access performance for end host networking. Proc. ACM Measur. Anal. Comput. Syst. **6**(1) (2022)

MemBridge: Bridging the Static-Dynamic Semantic Gap in Memory Profiling via Variable-Centric Instrumentation

Wentao Feng, Shaowen Li, Ziyi Song, Shizhe Shang, Kuiying Ban, Zhongyu Yu, Jiaxing Qi, Zhongzhi Luan(✉), Hailong Yang, and Depei Qian

Beihang University, Haidian Qu100191, Beijing Shi, China
{went_feng,lishaowen,songziyi,shangshizhe,bankuiying,yzy1207, jiaxingqi,luan.zhongzhi,hailong.yang,depeiq}@buaa.edu.cn

Abstract. Fine-grained memory profiling is critical for optimizing software on modern hierarchical memory systems, yet it is fundamentally limited by the static–dynamic semantic gap: compilation discards source-level information, leaving low-level memory accesses anonymous. Existing tools either impose prohibitive overhead or lack automated attribution, especially for heap objects and multi-level pointers. We present **MemBridge**, a lightweight, cross-architecture profiling framework that bridges this gap through variable-centric instrumentation. By fusing compile-time semantics with a DBI pipeline, MemBridge automatically and precisely attributes runtime memory accesses to source-level variables including complex heap-allocated data, while selective instrumentation and loop-aware sampling keep average overhead to $\sim$ **1.4**×. MemBridge provides architecture-agnostic plugin APIs (e.g., a false-sharing detector in $\sim$ 300 lines) and supports iterative optimization workflows. Evaluation on NPB and SPEC CPU2006 shows MemBridge outperforms existing tools (e.g., Gleipnir fails to terminate within 48 h) and, when used to guide false-sharing fixes, delivers over 4× speedup in large-scale applications. MemBridge thus offers a practical, portable, and semantically rich solution for memory tracing and performance analysis.

Keywords: Memory Profiling Framework · HPC · Variable Centric · Static-Dynamic Semantic Gap · Low Overhead

1 Introduction

The relentless growth of the processor–memory performance gap has made memory access efficiency a primary determinant of application performance. Optimizing software for deep memory hierarchies demands fine-grained insights into how data structures are accessed at runtime [9,12,17,18]. Specifically, the ability to map low-level memory operations (loads and stores on raw addresses) back to high-level program semantics such as variables, struct members, or array elements. However, this mapping is fundamentally hindered by the **static-dynamic semantic gap**: the loss of compile-time information (names, types,

M. Torquati et al. (Eds.): Euro-Par 2026, LNCS 16781, pp. 62–76, 2027.
https://doi.org/10.1007/978-3-032-35248-4_5

allocation contexts, pointer relationships) during execution, which leaves runtime operations as anonymous addresses.

Existing profiling tools exacerbate this gap through two systemic challenges. First, **ecosystem fragmentation**: many specialized tools are architecture-specific (e.g., x86-only false sharing detectors [8,11]) or OS-dependent [2], limiting cross-platform adoption. Second, the **granularity–overhead trade-off**: coarse-grained profilers (e.g., HPCToolkit [1], Perf) identify hot functions but lack variable-level attribution, while fine-grained tools (e.g., DINAMITE [13]) impose prohibitive slowdowns (100×+) and generate massive, semantically sparse traces, rendering them impractical for iterative optimization on large-scale applications.

To address these challenges, we present **MemBridge**, a lightweight, cross-architecture profiling framework that bridges the static–dynamic semantic gap through **variable-centric instrumentation**. By integrating compiler-derived static information into a dynamic binary instrumentation pipeline (DynamoRIO), MemBridge enables automated source-level attribution of runtime memory accesses, including heap-allocated data accessed via multi-level pointers. MemBridge adopts an **annotation-driven, selective profiling model**: developers annotate key variables with `TRACKED`, focusing instrumentation on critical data structures within hot regions. This design avoids the prohibitive overhead (>100×) of whole-program tracing tools like DINAMITE or Gleipnir while retaining fine-grained semantic attribution—a trade-off aligned with standard iterative optimization workflows where developers first identify hotspots via coarse-grained profilers (e.g., Perf, HPCToolkit). MemBridge further provides architecture-agnostic plugin APIs (e.g., `MemBridge_ResolveAddress`) for online analyzers (false sharing, cache misses, lock contention) in approximately 300 lines of code, insulating developers from hardware complexities.

Our core contributions are: (1) formalizing the static-dynamic semantic gap and proposing a method to bridge it via automated source-level attribution; (2) introducing a variable-centric instrumentation model that makes fine-grained memory profiling practical and iterative; (3) implementing MemBridge as a cross-architecture framework and demonstrating its low overhead and effectiveness through comprehensive evaluation on real-world benchmarks.

The rest of this article is organized as follows. Section 2 reviews related work and design motivations. Section 3 describes the MemBridge architecture and implementation. Section 4 presents our experimental evaluation.

2 Related Work and Motivation

Fine-grained memory profiling is hindered by the static–dynamic semantic gap: the loss of source-level information (variable names, types, structures) at runtime, leaving only raw memory addresses. Instrumentation-based tools attempt to bridge this gap but face inherent trade-offs. Static Binary Instrumentation (SBI) [4,6,19,20] offers low overhead but lacks runtime visibility; Dynamic

Table 1. Memory Profiling Tools Comparison

Feature	Gleipnir	DINAMITE	MemTrace	PROMPT	**MemBridge**
Automated Heap Track	×	✓	×	✓	✓
Multi-level pointer Track	×	×	×	×	✓
Nested Struct Track	×	✓	×	×	✓
Scope & Lifetime Track	×	×	×	×	✓
Selective Instrumentation	✓	×	×	✓	✓
On-the-fly Analysis	×	×	×	×	✓
Overhead	$> 100\times$	$> 500\times$	$\sim 2\times$	$\sim 10\times$	$\sim 1.4\times$
x86	✓	✓	✓	✓	✓
ARM	✓	✓	×	×	✓

Binary Instrumentation (DBI) [5,10,14] captures execution details but loses high-level semantics and incurs significant overhead. Hybrid approaches combine static information with dynamic analysis, yet existing works remain limited.

Notable tools such as Gleipnir [7], DINAMITE [13], MemTrace [15], and PROMPT [22] each attempt source-level attribution but suffer from common shortcomings: they either impose prohibitive overhead (often >100×), fail to automatically track heap objects or multi-level pointers, lack selective instrumentation, or are tied to specific architectures/compilers. Table 1 summarizes these deficiencies, highlighting that no existing tool simultaneously provides automated heap tracking, multi-level pointer support, nested structure resolution, scope awareness, selective instrumentation, on-the-fly analysis, and cross-architecture portability with low overhead.

To systematically address these shortcomings, we first identify the fundamental discrepancies between static program structure and dynamic execution. Table 2 enumerates eight key semantic gaps that existing tools fail to bridge, especially those involving heap objects, multi-level pointers, and nested structures (gaps highlighted in blue are inadequately addressed by tools surveyed in Table 1). These gaps motivate the need for a new approach.

MemBridge directly tackles these limitations through a tightly integrated static–dynamic methodology, enabling precise, low-overhead source-level attribution across diverse architectures—fully automatically, even for heap objects and multi-level pointers. The following section details its design.

Table 2. Semantic Gap Addressed by MemBridge

#	Static Info	Dynamic Info
Gap 1	variable name	runtime address
Gap 2	scope/lifetime	tracing range
Gap 3	struct nesting path	absolute offset
Gap 4	pointer identifier	address interpretation
Gap 5	pointer level	final target region
Gap 6	pointer allocation semantic	allocation size & address
Gap 7	propagation semantic	memory region bounds
Gap 8	source code line number	instrumentation range

3 MemBridge

MemBridge is a lightweight, cross-architecture profiling framework that bridges the static–dynamic gap via variable-centric instrumentation. It injects compile-time semantics into a DynamoRIO pipeline to automate source-level attribution of all memory accesses, supports all data types (built-in, structs, multi-level pointers), and provides architecture-agnostic APIs for online analysis plugins.

3.1 Overview

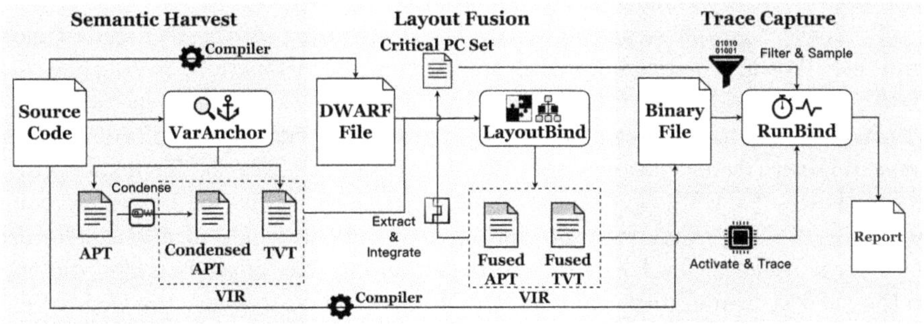

Fig. 1. The overview of MemBridge's workflow.

MemBridge's workflow is structured as a three-stage pipeline (Fig. 1), realized by three tightly integrated subtools: **VarAnchor**, **LayoutBind**, and **RunBind**. Together, they address the eight semantic gaps enumerated in Table 2.

- **Semantic Harvest (VarAnchor)**: Static analysis of source code and developer annotations extracts high-level attributes (names, types, structural paths) for user-specified variables, constructing a Variable Information Repository (VIR) in JSON format. This defines the logical scope of profiling, bridging Gap 1 & 2 .
- **Layout Fusion (LayoutBind)**: By integrating DWARF debug information, this phase resolves the concrete memory layout of each anchored variable—offsets, alignments, and size—and captures static instruction metadata (e.g., PC values). The enriched mapping bridges Gap 3 & 4 & 5 .
- **Trace Capture (RunBind)**: At runtime, RunBind leverages the resolved layout to guide selective instrumentation via DynamoRIO. It monitors memory accesses, correlates addresses with anchored variables in real time, and applies filtering and sampling. Dynamic allocation events (Gap 6) and pointer propagation (Gap 7) are tracked, and source-line-level attribution (Gap 8) is performed. The result is a structured behavioral profile that integrates static semantics with execution traces.

The methodology follows the C/C++ type system: we first establish core mechanisms for built-in types (Sect. 3.2), then extend them to structured types (Sect. 3.3) and derived types (pointers, arrays; Sect. 3.4), demonstrating how the unified pipeline enables precise, variable-centric tracing across the type hierarchy. Finally, Sect. 3.5 presents targeted optimizations that ensure practical efficiency.

3.2 Runtime Variable Semantic Reconstruction

Recovering source-level variable semantics at runtime is essential, yet compilation reduces them to indistinguishable memory addresses in the binary. This information loss (Gap 1) makes it difficult to associate runtime memory accesses with their corresponding source-level variables.

To recover variable semantics at runtime, we adopt a **static–dynamic fused** approach. We first address **spatial semantics** reconstruction: recovering concrete memory addresses. The static phase extracts source-level metadata via **VarAnchor** (names, types, scope) and augments it with debug information via **LayoutBind** (frame bases, offsets, PC intervals) to form the **Tracked Variables Table (TVT)**. The dynamic phase then computes addresses by combining TVT offsets with runtime context. For built-in types, local variables are resolved as follows: for **FP/SP-based** addressing, the offset is added directly to the current frame/stack pointer; for **CFA-based** addressing, the CFA rule is evaluated first, then the offset is applied. This two-stage pipeline establishes the core mechanism, later extended to structured and derived types.

Beyond spatial reconstruction, accurate tracking also requires **temporal semantics**: variable lifetimes and lexical scopes to check the validation of a memory region, which compilation removes (Gap 2). To reconstruct runtime lifetimes and scopes, we introduce a **semantic-scope management mechanism** that maintains a simulated call stack for key functions—functions containing tracked variables (Fig. 2(a)). Upon function invocation, a call-frame with its variable metadata is pushed; upon return, it is popped.

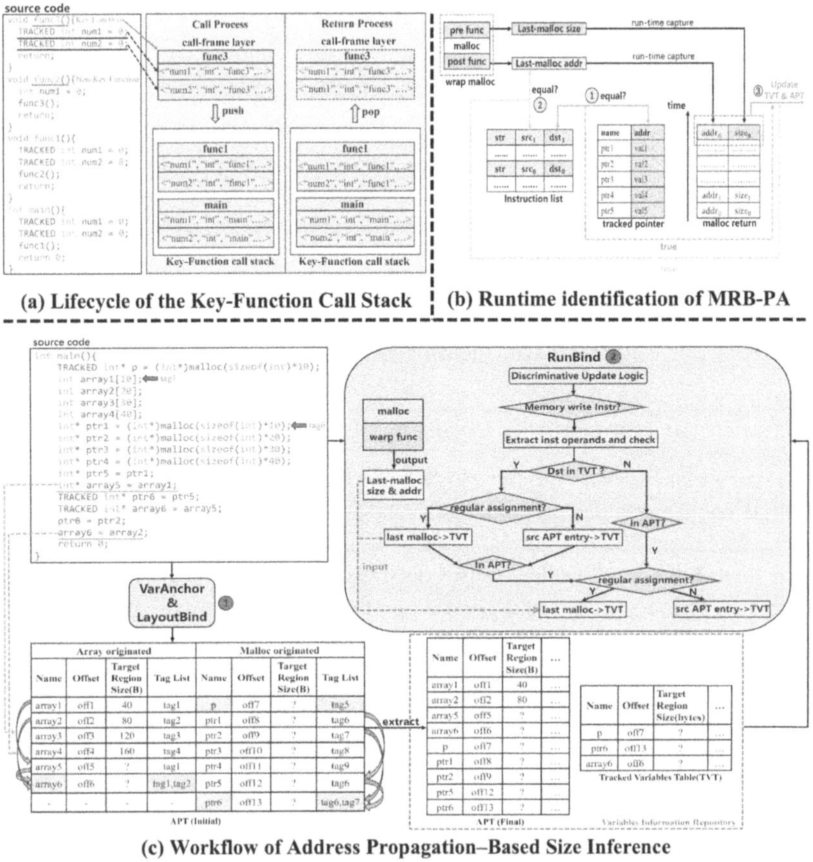

Fig. 2. Workflow of three key strategies. (a)Simulated call stack. (b) (1) Check `dst = addr`? (2) Check `src = last-malloc-addr`? (3) If both hold, update TVT and APT with `last_malloc_size` and `last_malloc_addr`. (c)The initial APT is built via source-level analysis (1) and then refined through tag-based pruning to retain only entries relevant to tracked variables (highlighted in blue). Both APT and TVT are subsequently updated during execution according to the discriminative update logic in RunBind (2).

This simulated call stack provides two key benefits. **(1) Efficient address matching:** metadata lookup starts from the top frame, avoiding a full scan of all variables. **(2) Reduced address-reuse interference:** by restricting matches to the current temporal and structural context, stale stack-frame regions are not misidentified as active variables.

3.3 Hierarchical Expansion of Structured Types

Structured types introduce additional complexity due to their hierarchical composition. When tracked variables reside within nested members, identifying target fields and computing their runtime offsets requires careful handling.

This difficulty stems from Semantic Gap 3 : compilation flattens struct hierarchies, making member fields with identical names indistinguishable in the binary. To bridge this gap, we develop two complementary mechanisms. We first resolve member ambiguity by recording the full nesting path of each tracked variable, which uniquely identifies fields during DWARF parsing. To compute absolute offsets, we recursively traverse nested struct definitions and cumulatively sum the offsets along this path, yielding the variable's final absolute offset.

3.4 Temporal Coupling in Pointer Accesses

Pointer variables present unique challenges for semantic reconstruction due to their dual nature: they represent both the pointer itself and the memory location it references. Consequently, pointer semantics cannot be recovered from isolated memory accesses. Critically, compilation removes the temporal coupling between reading a pointer and accessing its target. This loss gives rise to the pointer-specific semantic challenges summarized in Gap 4 – 7 . To address these, we treat this temporal coupling as a key semantic feature and design runtime tracking strategies that reconstruct this linkage during execution, enabling precise pointer tracking.

Strategy 1 (Gap 4): Unified Representation of Pointer and Referent. Pointer variables involve both the pointer value and the memory region they reference, which are accessed with tight temporal coupling at runtime. To capture this relationship, we represent all variables using a unified data structure that stores each variable's address together with an optional referent field. A pointer flag derived from static analysis determines whether the referent field is active. During execution, accesses to tracked variables update their entries, while accesses to referenced memory regions are recorded through the associated pointer entry. This unified representation preserves the intrinsic linkage between pointers and their referents without requiring separate pointer-specific data structures.

Strategy 2 (Gap 5): Resolving Multi-level Pointer Targets. Multi-level pointers exhibit hybrid semantics: their level of indirection is statically fixed, but the concrete address at each level is resolved only at runtime. To bridge this gap, we statically record pointer depth via AST analysis and dynamically resolve the final target by iterative dereferencing during execution. For instance, a variable declared as `int** p` is identified as a double pointer; its ultimate referenced address is obtained by performing two memory dereferences at runtime.

Strategy 3 (Gap 6): Malloc-Return–Based Pointer Assignment Tracking (MRB-PA). We classify pointer assignments as **regular** or **irregular**. Regular assignments arise when a pointer captures the return value of a dynamic memory allocation function; irregular assignments encompass all other cases. Only regular assignments directly reveal the size of the referenced memory.

Regular assignments follow a consistent **temporal pattern** at the assembly level: the return value of an allocation call is typically stored immediately into a pointer variable. Leveraging this property, we design a **lightweight runtime mechanism** (Fig. 2(b)) that records the most recent allocation's address and size, then compares them with the source operand of pointer store instructions. Upon a match, the assignment is marked as regular and the corresponding pointer metadata is updated.

Strategy 4 (Gap 7): Inferring Memory Bounds for Irregular Pointer Assignments. Irregular assignments derive pointer values from existing variables rather than allocation calls, obscuring the memory bounds of the referenced region. To address this, we introduce an **address-propagation chain** that tracks how addresses and their associated sizes propagate across variables through successive assignments.

As illustrated in Fig. 2(c), static analysis first constructs an **Address Propagation Table (APT)** that records propagation relationships among variables, pruning irrelevant entries via a tag-based strategy. At runtime, both the tracked-variable table and the APT are updated upon assignments. Regular assignments obtain size information directly from allocation records; irregular assignments infer bounds through propagation relationships or fall back to static type information when necessary.

Together, these strategies reconstruct both the temporal coupling between pointer and pointee accesses and the memory bounds of referenced regions, enabling comprehensive runtime tracking of pointer semantics.

3.5 Performance Optimization Strategies

To bridge the semantic gap between source code locations and dynamic instrumentation (Gap 8) while ensuring low overhead without compromising core analytical capabilities, MemBridge employs two key strategies that use static information to precisely guide runtime instrumentation.

(1) Variable-Centric Instrumentation. This PC-filtering method instruments only instructions that access user-specified variables. **VarAnchor** records source lines where marked variables are accessed. **LayoutBind** maps these lines to concrete program counters (PCs) via debug info, producing a set of *critical PCs*. At runtime, **RunBind** checks each instruction's PC and triggers a `clean call` only if it belongs to this set, eliminating instrumentation of irrelevant code.

(2) Loop-Aware Sampling. To handle repetitive loop patterns without excessive overhead, MemBridge identifies loops containing *critical PCs* during static analysis. At runtime, it injects a lightweight per-loop iteration counter. Only every N-th iteration (e.g., every 100th) fully instruments the critical PCs within that iteration; others are skipped. This sampling drastically reduces expensive `clean calls` while still capturing dominant memory access behavior.

4 Evaluation

This section presents a comprehensive evaluation of MemBridge's performance, scalability, and practical utility. In particular, we compare the effectiveness of Variable-Centric Instrumentation and Loop-Aware Sampling, and illustrate their impact on overhead reduction. Two case studies further demonstrate the tool's practicality: the first illustrates its usage and report interpretation; the second showcases how MemBridge guides iterative optimization for large-scale parallel programs, including a direct comparison with Gleipnir that highlights MemBridge's advantages in automated heap tracking and online analysis capabilities.

4.1 Exerimental Setup

All experiments are conducted on a server running Kylin Linux Advanced Server release V10 (Sword), equipped with a 128-core Phytium S2500 processor based on the AArch64 architecture. The system was configured with 256 GB of DDR4 memory, along with a three-level cache hierarchy consisting of 32 KB L1 cache per core, 2 MB of shared L2 cache, and 8 MB of shared L3 cache.

We evaluate MemBridge's performance overhead and scalability using the NPB [3] and SPEC CPU 2006 v1.0.1 [21] benchmarks. For each C/C++ application, we track one key variable—examples include built-in types, structured types (e.g., `MAIN_Param.nTimeSteps` in `treeup.c` of `mcf`), and derived types such as `node→pred→basic_arc→tail` in `main.h` of `lbm`. These variables primarily govern loop execution, track iteration progress, determine termination conditions, and update program state.

The NPB applications are executed using the Class A input size, while the SPEC CPU 2006 benchmarks utilize the `ref` input set. All benchmarks are compiled with `gcc 7.3.0(clang 10.0.1` also supported) using `-g` flags.

4.2 Variable-Centric Instrumentation

Time Overhead: Figure 3 compares the runtime overhead of Instrument-Everything and our Variable-Centric Instrumentation against a native baseline. Full instrumentation introduces prohibitive slowdowns (115× ∼ 242×), whereas our selective approach reduces overhead to near-native levels for most benchmarks (1.02× ∼ 2.01×)—an improvement of over two orders of magnitude. While the current evaluation tracks one variable per benchmark, MemBridge's overhead scales with the aggregate access frequency of tracked variables, not their count, because each variable has an independent PC-filter set. Five benchmarks (`ep`, `mcf`, `milc`, `namd`, and `hmmer`) exhibit higher overhead (15.18× ∼ 40.15×), despite a 3 ∼ 8× reduction relative to full instrumentation. This is because their tracked variables reside in extremely tight, high-frequency loops, causing selective probes to be invoked repeatedly. Hence, while variable-centric instrumentation achieves near-native overhead for moderately accessed variables, it remains sensitive to those accessed at high rates.

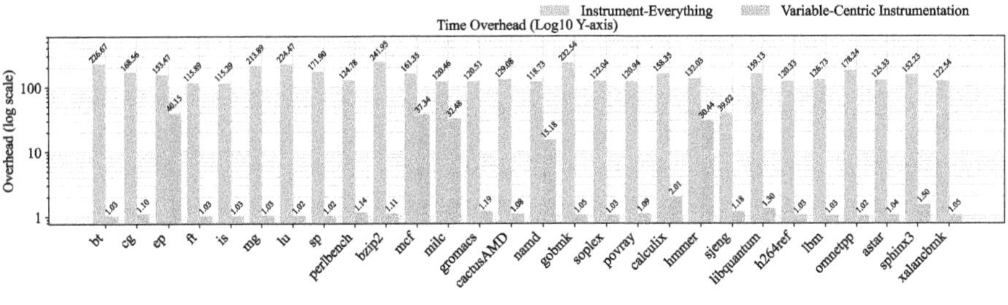

Fig. 3. Normalized runtime overhead of Instr.-Everything and Var-Centric Instr.

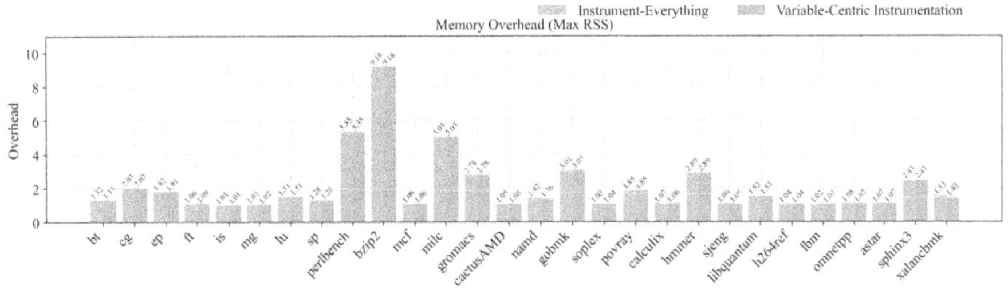

Fig. 4. Normalized memory overhead of Instr.-Everything and Var-Centric Instr.

Memory Overhead: Figure 4 presents the normalized memory overhead for two instrumentation configurations. Variable-Centric Instrumentation maintains a low memory footprint for most programs, typically within $1.01\times \sim 1.09\times$ of the native baseline (e.g., `ft`, `is`, `mg`). Three benchmarks exhibit elevated overhead ($> 5\times$): `perlbench`, `bzip2`, and `milc`.

The high overheads of `perlbench`, `bzip2`, and `milc` stem from distinct pathological behaviors: dynamic runtime features (indirect branches, JIT, short-lived basic blocks), low compute-to-memory ratios with random access, and complex control flow with frequent calls, respectively. All three induce severe code-cache fragmentation and metadata inflation, reflecting pathological interactions with the instrumentation framework rather than fundamental scalability limitations.

Comparison with Gleipnir: In contrast, Gleipnir failed to complete any of the evaluated benchmarks within 48 h, exhibiting a minimum slowdown exceeding $250\times$. Moreover, its generated trace files were impractically large—even the smallest exceeded 100GB. Deploying Gleipnir also required substantial manual effort, including adapting Valgrind versions and porting to ARM architectures. These difficulties underscore MemBridge's decisive advantages in cross-architecture support, overhead control, and practical usability.

4.3 Loop-Aware Sampling

Figure 5 evaluates loop-aware sampling (at a rate of 1/100) on the five high-overhead benchmarks (`ep`, `mcf`, `milc`, `namd`, `hmmer`). Pure variable-centric instrumentation incurs 15.18×–40.15× overhead due to frequent accesses in hot loops; adding sampling reduces this to 1.78×–1.90×, well below 2×. This demonstrates that lightweight sampling decouples observation cost from access frequency while preserving essential behavioral insight. With sampling enabled, the average overhead across all evaluated benchmarks drops to ∼ **1.4**×, making the combined approach both scalable and practical for production-level profiling.

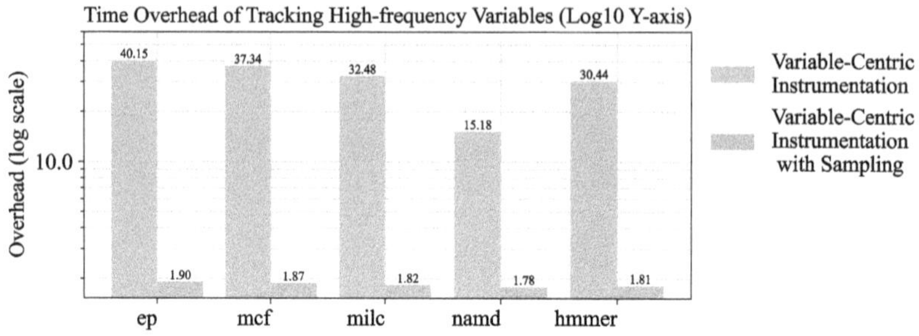

Fig. 5. Effectiveness of Loop-Aware Sampling. With Loop-Aware Sampling enabled, the average time overhead across all programs is reduced to about **1.4x**.

4.4 Scalability

Time: Figure 6-left evaluates the time-overhead scalability of MemBridge across six NPB benchmarks as core counts increase from 1 to 32. The framework maintains consistently low overhead, demonstrating strong scalability. Two kernels exhibit distinct behaviors: `cg` shows a gradual rise from 1.06× to 1.26×, attributable to contention on shared instrumentation structures in this communication- intensive workload; `ep` sustains the highest overhead (1.75×–1.82×) due to tracing a high-frequency variable, yet overhead slightly decreases with more cores as probe operations are largely parallel and amortized across threads.

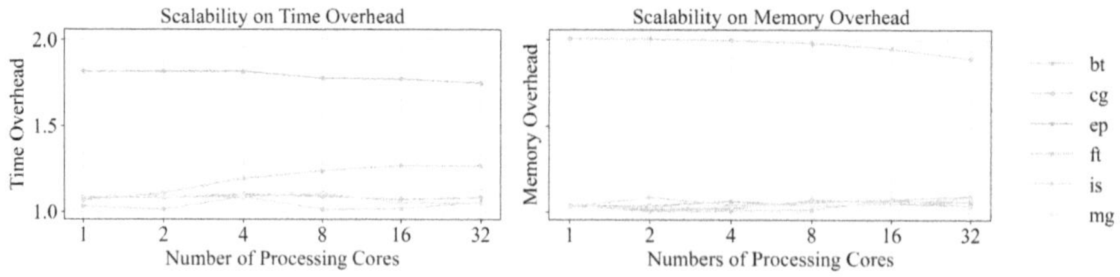

Fig. 6. Scalability on Time Performance(left) and Memory Performance(right).

Memory: Figure 6-right depicts memory-overhead scalability. Overhead remains largely flat across core counts, confirming that memory consumption is dominated by fixed per-process metadata rather than per-thread allocations. For most kernels, overhead stays near 1.0× from 4 to 32 cores. `cg` again stands out with an initial $\sim 2\times$ overhead that gradually declines, indicating that its shared data structures incur an upfront cost later amortized across threads.

Overall, MemBridge exhibits excellent scalability in both time and memory, incurring only marginal additional cost as parallelism increases.

4.5 Use Cases

This section demonstrates MemBridge's practical workflow and analytical capabilities through two scenarios. First, we outline its usage and report generation. Second, we apply a built-in analysis tool to identify, diagnose, and iteratively optimize performance issues, comparing its output against Gleipnir.

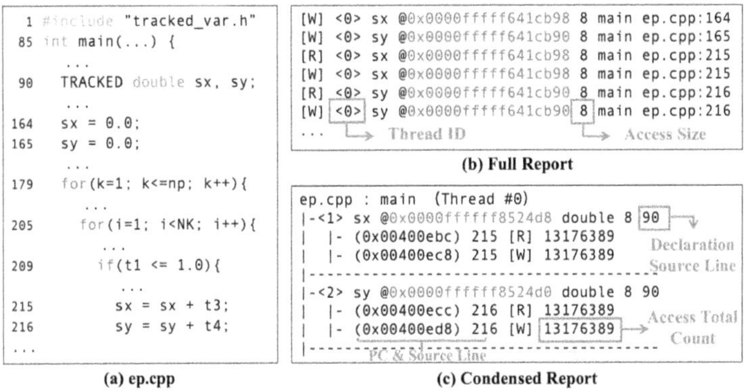

Fig. 7. Source code and corresponding reports. Compared with MemBridge, **DINAMITE lacks support** for variable-centric instrumentation of variables.

1) A User's Guide: Using MemBridge and Interpreting Reports. In practice, developers can identify candidate variables using coarse-grained profilers (e.g. HPCToolkit or Perf) to locate hot data structures, then apply `TRACKED` annotations for MemBridge-level diagnosis (Fig. 7(a)). Two helper scripts streamline the process: `./run_clean.sh` removes previous outputs, and `./run_path.sh` launches the analysis with the syntax: `./run_path.sh <source_paths> [...] <executable_path> [-<args>] <F/C> [sampling_rate]`. The `<F|C>` argument selects the report format: **Full** (`F`) outputs every memory access event with thread ID, code location, and access details; **Condensed** (`C`) aggregates accesses by function and thread for higher-level overviews (Fig. 7(b)(c)). An optional `sampling_rate` (default $\frac{1}{100}$) enables loop-aware sampling to reduce overhead.

2) False Sharing Detection and Iterative Optimization. We demonstrate the practical application of a false-sharing detector implemented using MemBridge's plugin APIs: `MemBridge_ResolveAddress(addr, var_info_t*)`, `MemBridge_Callback(event_t, callback)`, `MemBridge_GetThreadId()`, in approximately 300 lines of code. Through two concrete case studies, we illustrate a complete iterative workflow—from detection and localization to optimization, verification, and performance comparison—showcasing how the framework enables evidence-based performance tuning.

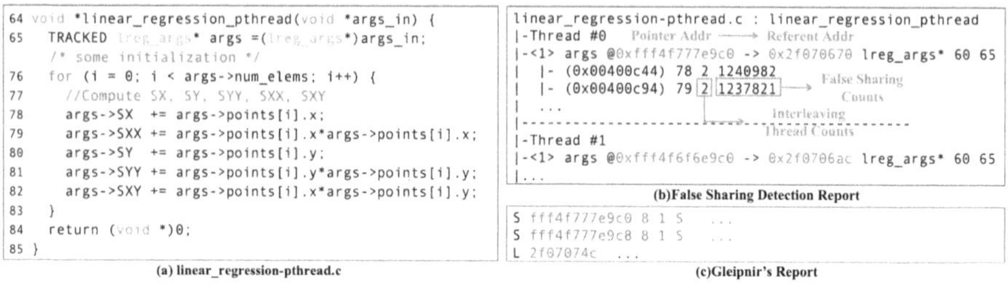

Fig. 8. Source code and false sharing reports. Compared with MemBridge, **Gleipnir does not** support tracking of heap-allocated complex struct pointers, **nor** does it provide APIs for developing online analysis plugins.

Case 1: Phoenix linear_ regression. Initial profiling with MemBridge immediately raised a false-sharing alarm for Phoenix `linear_regression` [16], as shown in Fig. 8(b). The detector pinpointed contention to a shared array of aggregate structs (`lreg_args` in Fig. 8(a)), where threads frequently updated distinct fields that happen to be on the same cache line. In contrast, **Gleipnir failed** to report this issue (Fig. 8(c)) due to its inability to automatically track heap-allocated complex structures and its lack of online analysis plugin support, underscoring MemBridge's advantage in automated, semantic-aware detection. Three standard optimizations were then applied and re-evaluated using the detector: (i) **Padding** the struct to cache-line size, (ii) **Thread-local privatization** of accumulators, and (iii) **Cache-line aligned array partitioning**.

All three eliminated false-sharing alerts, yet their speedups differed: thread-local privatization achieved the highest acceleration (4×), as it most effectively avoids inter-thread write contention for this benchmark's fine-grained update pattern. This case highlights the tool's role in rapidly verifying fixes and identifying the most effective optimization.

Case 2: SPLASH-3 OCEAN (ncp). MemBridge also detected false sharing in `OCEAN (ncp)`, arising from concurrent updates to the shared array `q_multi`. Padding the array eliminated false sharing and improved parallel speedup by 25%, but expanded the working set, increasing absolute execution time by 50%, rendering the fix impractical. Thread-local privatization could in principle avoid this trade-off, but would require substantial program restructuring. The detailed memory trace provided by MemBridge thus offers critical insight for designing more tailored optimizations.

Collectively, these case studies demonstrate that MemBridge's lightweight plugin APIs (enabling custom analyzers like the false-sharing detector in around 300 lines of code) combined with its low-overhead profiling framework supports an efficient, iterative optimization workflow for large-scale parallel programs.

5 Conclusion

This paper presented **MemBridge**, a lightweight cross-architecture profiler that bridges the static–dynamic semantic gap. By injecting compile-time semantics into DynamoRIO, it enables automatic source-level attribution of runtime accesses—including complex heap objects via multi-level pointers—while maintaining only **1.4**× overhead through variable-centric instrumentation and loop-aware sampling.

MemBridge mitigates ecosystem fragmentation via architecture-agnostic APIs (e.g., `MemBridge_ResolveAddress`), enabling portable online analyzers in ∼300 lines of code, and resolves the granularity–overhead trade-off through selective, region-guided instrumentation. Evaluations on NPB and SPEC CPU2006 demonstrate scalable, low-footprint performance, outperforming Gleipnir which failed to complete within 48 h and required substantial manual porting effort. Beyond profiling, the semantic-rich traces support profile-guided optimization and ML-based tuning as future work. By combining semantic awareness with portability and low overhead, MemBridge thus provides a production-ready solution for memory tracing and performance analysis in complex C/C++ applications.

Disclosure of Interests. The authors have no competing interests to declare that are relevant to the content of this article.

References

1. Adhianto, L., et al.: Hpctoolkit: tools for performance analysis of optimized parallel programs. Concurr. Comput. Pract. Exper. **22**(6), 685–701 (2010)
2. Alam, M.M.U., Liu, T., Zeng, G., Muzahid, A.: Syncperf: categorizing, detecting, and diagnosing synchronization performance bugs. In: Proceedings of the Twelfth European Conference on Computer Systems, pp. 298–313 (2017)
3. Bailey, D.H., et al.: The NAS parallel benchmarks—summary and preliminary results. In: Proceedings of the 1991 ACM/IEEE Conference on Supercomputing, pp. 158–165 (1991)
4. Brandner, F., Hepp, S., Jordan, A.: Criticality: static profiling for real-time programs. Real-Time Syst. **50**(3), 377–410 (2014)
5. Bruening, D., Amarasinghe, S.: Efficient, transparent, and comprehensive runtime code manipulation (2004)
6. Gorgovan, C., d'Antras, A., Luján, M.: Mambo: a low-overhead dynamic binary modification tool for arm. ACM Trans. Architect. Code Optimization (TACO) **13**(1), 1–26 (2016)

7. Janjusic, T., Kavi, K.: Gleipnir: a memory profiling and tracing tool. ACM SIGARCH Comput. Architect. News **41**(4), 8–12 (2013)
8. Liu, T., Berger, E.D.: Sheriff: precise detection and automatic mitigation of false sharing. In: Proceedings of the 2011 ACM International Conference on Object Oriented Programming Systems Languages and Applications, pp. 3–18 (2011)
9. Liu, T., Liu, X.: Cheetah: detecting false sharing efficiently and effectively. In: Proceedings of the 2016 International Symposium on Code Generation and Optimization, pp. 1–11 (2016)
10. Luk, C.K., et al.: Pin: building customized program analysis tools with dynamic instrumentation. ACM Sigplan Notices **40**(6), 190–200 (2005)
11. Luo, L., et al.: Laser: light, accurate sharing detection and repair. In: 2016 IEEE International Symposium on High Performance Computer Architecture (HPCA), pp. 261–273. IEEE (2016)
12. Makor, L., Kloibhofer, S., Hofer, P., Leopoldseder, D., Mössenböck, H.: Automated profile-guided replacement of data structures to reduce memory allocation. arXiv:2502.20536 arXiv preprint (2025)
13. Miucin, S., Brady, C., Fedorova, A.: End-to-end memory behavior profiling with dinamite. In: Proceedings of the 2016 24th ACM SIGSOFT International Symposium on Foundations of Software Engineering, pp. 1042–1046 (2016)
14. Nethercote, N., Seward, J.: Valgrind: a framework for heavyweight dynamic binary instrumentation. ACM Sigplan Notices **42**(6), 89–100 (2007)
15. Payer, M., Kravina, E., Gross, T.R.: Lightweight memory tracing. In: USENIX Annual Technical Conference (USENIX ATC 13), pp. 115–126 (2013)
16. Ranger, C., Raghuraman, R., Penmetsa, A., Bradski, G., Kozyrakis, C.: Evaluating mapreduce for multi-core and multiprocessor systems. In: IEEE 13th International Symposium on High Performance Computer Architecture, pp. 13–24. IEEE (2007)
17. Roy, P., Liu, X.: Structslim: a lightweight profiler to guide structure splitting. In: Proceedings of the 2016 International Symposium on Code Generation and Optimization, pp. 36–46 (2016)
18. Roy, P., Song, S.L., Krishnamoorthy, S., Liu, X.: Lightweight detection of cache conflicts. In: Proceedings of the 2018 International Symposium on Code Generation and Optimization, pp. 200–213(2018)
19. Schubert, P.D., Hermann, B., Bodden, E.: Phasar: an inter-procedural static analysis framework for c/c. In: International Conference on Tools and Algorithms for the Construction and Analysis of Systems, pp. 393–410. Springer (2019)
20. Solanki, R.K.: C analyzer: a static program analysis tool for c programs. arXiv:2403.12973 arXiv preprint (2024)
21. Spradling, C.D.: Spec cpu2006 benchmark tools. ACM SIGARCH Comput. Architect. News **35**(1), 130–134 (2007)
22. Xu, Z., et al.: Prompt: a fast and extensible memory profiling framework. Proc. ACM Program. Lang. **8**(OOPSLA1), 449–473 (2024)

TBF: A Tunable Blocking-and-Fusion Algorithm for Efficient GPU Symmetric Rank-2K Updates

Lijuan Hu[1], Xinzhe Chen[1,2], Haowei Li[1,2], Hongyaoxing Gu[1,2], Wenjing Ma[1,3], Fangfang Liu[1,3](✉), Cui Wang[1], and Yuwen Zhao[1]

[1] Institute of Software Chinese Academy of Sciences, Beijing, China
fangfang@iscas.ac.cn
[2] University of Chinese Academy of Sciences, Beijing, China
[3] Key Laboratory of System Software, Chinese Academy of Sciences, Beijing, China

Abstract. Symmetric rank-2k update (SYR2K) is a core BLAS-3 routine but remains hard to optimize on GPUs because only triangular output is valid. However, few existing methods pay enough attention to the triangular characteristics of the output matrix, reducing memory access efficiency and computational performance. We present *TBF*, a tunable blocking-and-fusion framework that treats off-diagonal and diagonal regions differently: fused GEMM-like kernels for off-diagonal blocks and shape-aware batched SYR2K kernels for diagonal blocks. *TBF* includes joint Batch-K flattened tiling, dual-term shared-tile buffering, and cross-platform parameter tuning. On NVIDIA A100, A800, AMD MI210, and HYGON Z100, *TBF* achieves up to 1.4× over cuBLAS and up to 1.7× over rocBLAS on regular sizes, with larger gains on short-wide cases.

Keywords: SYR2K · Kernel Fusion · BLAS · Tiling · Tuning

1 Introduction

The symmetric rank-2k update (SYR2K) computes $C \leftarrow \alpha AB^T + \alpha BA^T + \beta C$, where C is symmetric and only its lower (or upper) triangle is stored [1,2]. SYR2K is a core Level-3 BLAS routine that appears as a building block in tiled Cholesky factorization, symmetric eigenvalue solvers, and other dense linear algebra algorithms that maintain symmetric intermediate results. Because these algorithms are widely used in scientific simulation, machine learning and data analysis, the efficiency of SYR2K directly affects the end-to-end performance of many large-scale workloads on modern GPU accelerators.

Despite the importance of SYR2K, optimizing it on SIMT-based GPUs is fundamentally harder than optimizing GEMM. The triangular output semantics introduce three specific difficulties at the hardware level. First, the guard condition $row \geq col$ required for each output element causes warp divergence at diagonal block boundaries: threads whose assigned elements fall outside the

M. Torquati et al. (Eds.): Euro-Par 2026, LNCS 16781, pp. 77–91, 2027.
https://doi.org/10.1007/978-3-032-35248-4_6

triangle are masked, wasting execution slots. Second, diagonal thread blocks perform roughly half the work of off-diagonal blocks of the same dimension, leading to load imbalance across the GPU's streaming multiprocessors. Third, triangular write-back patterns break the natural alignment expected by the memory subsystem, degrading write coalescing and increasing the number of memory transactions per warp. These three effects compound when the problem is decomposed into small blocks, making the diagonal path disproportionately expensive relative to its share of floating-point operations. The standard mitigation, first systematized by Kågström et al. [18], is to reformulate Level-3 symmetric BLAS operations in terms of GEMM. Under this approach the output matrix is partitioned into $n_b \times n_b$ blocks: off-diagonal blocks are computed as pairs of standard GEMMs, which can leverage the highly tuned GEMM paths in template libraries [3,14–16]. Diagonal blocks, however, must still respect the triangular guard and are handled by dedicated SYR2K kernels operating on an $n_b \times k$ input with small n_b but potentially large k. This short-wide shape yields low arithmetic intensity and memory-bound regime.

Despite extensive research on batched BLAS routines for GPUs [8,10], the batched short-wide SYR2K kernel on diagonal blocks has received little dedicated optimization effort. Meanwhile, autotuning methodologies have proven effective for GEMM kernel selection [6,17], but have not been applied to the distinct parameter space of the diagonal SYR2K kernel. Moreover, the rapid cadence of GPU architecture releases renders hand-tuned kernels obsolete within a single product cycle, making cross-platform tunability not merely convenient but essential for sustainable performance portability. Therefore, an effective solution must *jointly* address all challenges mentioned through a coordinated kernel design and tuning framework. This gap motivates our work. This work addresses two questions: (1) how to block and fuse SYR2K while respecting triangular semantics and efficiently utilizing GPU resources, and (2) how to make the design tunable across heterogeneous architectures without rewriting kernels per platform. We present *TBF*, a tunable blocking-and-fusion framework that treats off-diagonal and diagonal regions with distinct strategies. On four target platforms, *TBF* achieves up to 1.4× speedup over cuBLAS and Magma [17] on NVIDIA A800-80G and A100-40G, up to 1.7× over rocBLAS on AMD MI210, and up to 1.6× on HYGON Z100 for regular sizes ($n = k$), with gains exceeding 60× in extreme short-wide settings ($k \gg n$). To our knowledge, TBF is the first framework that jointly optimizes diagonal and off-diagonal paths of SYR2K with cross-platform auto-tuning, which exploits SYR2K's algebraic structure and generalizes to other operations. Our main contributions are:

- **Coordinated blocking-and-fusion for SYR2K.** We decompose SYR2K into diagonal and off-diagonal paths and map them to batched SYR2K and fused GEMM-style kernels, respectively. An adaptive dispatcher selects between optimal library GEMM, batched GEMM, and dynamic diagonal kernels according to problem shape and architecture-specific thresholds.
- **Diagonal-kernel optimizations for short-wide inputs.** We design joint Batch-K flattened tiling to increase parallelism, dual-term shared-tile buffer-

ing to halve traffic, and bidirectional vectorization to improve coalescing under mixed transpose and non-transpose cases—together raising effective arithmetic intensity by up to 2× on the memory-bound diagonal path.
- **Cross-platform autotuning and validation.** We build a template-based tuning workflow over an eight-dimensional parameter space and demonstrate robust speedups on A100-40G, A800-80G, MI210, and Z100 across FP32, FP64, and complex FP64 precisions, including strong gains when $k \gg n$.

2 Background

2.1 GPU and DCU Architecture

CUDA, ROCm and DTK follow similar SIMT execution principles but differ in scheduling granularity, memory hierarchy details, and library/runtime behavior [4,7]. In this paper we target NVIDIA A100/A800, AMD MI210, and HYGON Z100 (DCU), all of which provide high-bandwidth memory and on-chip scratchpad/register resources, but expose different trade-offs between occupancy, bandwidth utilization, and kernel launch overhead. These differences motivate a tunable rather than fixed SYR2K design.

2.2 SYR2K on Hardware Accelerators

SYR2K updates a symmetric matrix as $C = \alpha AB^T + \alpha BA^T + \beta C$ [1,2]. Only the lower (or upper) triangular portion of C is stored and updated. This triangular semantics creates irregular parallelism and weak write coalescing compared with dense GEMM. In practice, the diagonal path is often memory-bound and becomes the main bottleneck. MAGMA [17] relies on generic square GEMM calls for SYR2K, causing redundant updates to the unused triangular region without algorithmic specialization. Alternatively, Algorithm 1 details the rocBLAS baseline [15], illustrating its diagonal kernel structure: a two-pass tile accumulation that loads A/B tiles into shared memory and computes AB^T and BA^T sequentially. This design does not meet the requirements for high performance.

2.3 Related Work

Batched BLAS. Batched BLAS routines have been extensively studied for small-matrix workloads on GPUs [8–10]. These works demonstrate that grouping many small operations into a single kernel launch can saturate GPU parallelism. However, compared with batched GEMM/TRSM and batched factorizations, batched SYR2K has been less systematically optimized in mainstream GPU BLAS stacks, and practical implementations often rely on GEMM-based reformulations or specialized kernels to handle the triangular storage and diagonal updates efficiently.

Autotuning for GPU Kernels. ATLAS [19] pioneered empirical autotuning for BLAS, and subsequent systems such as CLTune [21] and kernel tuning toolkit [22] extended this to GPU kernels. Charara et al. [24] proposed a

Algorithm 1: Baseline diagonal kernel (rocBLAS-style)

```
/* Define shared memory buffers                                  */
__shared__ T sh_A[BK][BK], sh_B[BK][BK];
/* Two-pass accumulation: AB^T then BA^T                         */
for (P, Q) ∈ {(A, B), (B, A)} do
    TileAccumulate(P, Q, C, α, K, BK);
    __syncthreads();

Procedure TileAccumulate(P, Q, C, α, K, BK):
    for k ← 0 to K − 1 step BK do
        sh_A[][] = P[],    sh_B[][] = Q[];
        __syncthreads();
        if from ≤ to then
            T sum = T(0);
            for i ← 0 to BK − 1 do
                sum += sh_A[][] * sh_B[][];
            C[] += α * sum;
```

recursive TRMM/TRSM formulation, using a tunable base-case size for cross-GPU portability. BLIS [20] provides a layered BLAS framework amenable to architecture-specific micro-kernel tuning. Our work applies a similar template-and-search methodology, but targets the SYR2K-specific parameter space where triangular output semantics, short-wide input shape, and cross-platform architectural diversity must be addressed jointly—a combination absent from prior autotuning studies.

3 Optimization Design

The core design principle of *TBF* is that the challenges identified in Sect. 1 must be resolved through a *coordinated* rather than piecemeal approach. We first partition the output matrix via blocking to decompose diagonal and off-diagonal regions into tasks with distinct optimization targets. Both regions are aggressively fused into larger computational units to maximize GPU utilization. For the memory-bound diagonal blocks, we exploit the intrinsic symmetry(AB^T and BA^T reusing the tiles) to devise novel thread-mapping schemes and dynamic tiling algorithms that restructure data movement patterns for substantial performance gains. All optimizations are parameterized by architecture-specific tuning knobs, ensuring portability without sacrificing per-platform efficiency.

3.1 Overall Blocking and Fusion Design

Based on the SYR2K triangular structure [5], we partition the computation according to the symmetric output matrix. We define a minimal global block

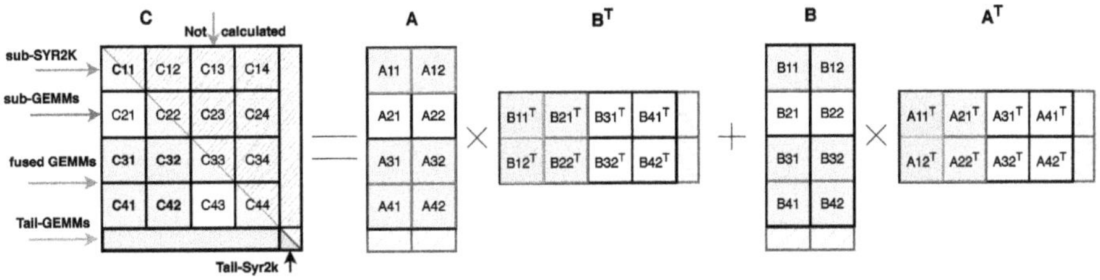

Fig. 1. Overall blocking design for the output matrix with non-power-of-two dimension.

Algorithm 2: Overall design for SYR2K with minimal global block n_b

---

Input: Input matrices $A(n, k)$ and $B(n, k)$
Input: Output matrix $C(n, n)$
Output: $C \leftarrow \alpha AB^T + \alpha BA^T + \beta C$
/* Block, batch and compute the diagonal parts */
C_diag += BatchedSYR2K(A, B, C, n_b, k);
/* Process the tail diagonal parts */
if $n \bmod n_b \neq 0$ **then**
    C_diag_t += TailSYR2K(A, B, C, n%n_b, k);
i = 1;
while $\frac{n}{n_b \cdot i \cdot 2} \geq 1$ **do**
    /* Block, fuse and compute the off-diagonal parts */
    ldda=i*n_b,lddc=(1+ldc)*2*n_b;
    C_offD1 += BatchedGEMM(A + ldda, B^T, C + lddc, ldda, ldda, k);
    C_offD2 += BatchedGEMM(B + ldda, A^T, C + lddc, ldda, ldda, k);
    rem = (n - (i+1)*n_b) % (2*ldda);
    if *rem* $\neq 0$ **then**
        /* Process the tail off-diagonal parts */
        C_offD1_t += GEMM(A+ldda, B^T, C+lddc, rem, ldda, k);
        C_offD2_t += GEMM(B+ldda, A^T, C+lddc, rem, ldda, k);
    i = i * 2;

---

size n_b (e.g., $n_b = 32$ for a 32×32 sub-block), partition the domain into $n_b \times n_b$ blocks, and handle boundary remainders separately [13]. For **diagonal blocks**, the triangular shape requires decomposition into batched SYR2K sub-blocks. Contiguous sub-blocks along rows and columns are fused into a single batched call; tail blocks that cannot be batched are processed separately. For **off-diagonal blocks**, we decompose the computation into GEMM sub-blocks. The fusion strategy selects between a single large GEMM or batched sub-GEMMs depending on sub-block adjacency. The mathematical foundation is as follows. Diagonal blocks are partitioned into independent triangular SYR2K subproblems and fused into batched calls when subblocks are contiguous in memory. Off-diagonal blocks are grouped into larger GEMM-equivalent updates so that multiple neighboring blocks can be computed by two fused matrix products (AB^T

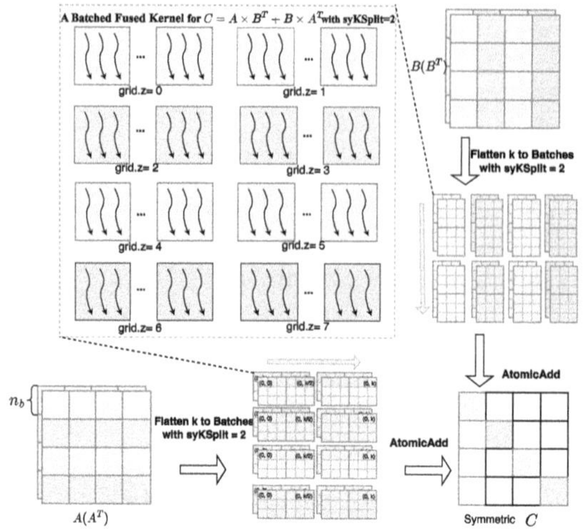

Fig. 2. Dynamic JointBatch-K Flattened Tiling: the workload is flattened and dispatched to more blocks by tuning parameters.

and BA^T). Tail blocks are handled by the same decomposition with boundary-aware dimensions. Algorithm 2 presents the overall procedure (Fig. 1).

3.2 Batched Short-Wide Kernel Design

As Algorithm 2 reveals, all off-diagonal blocks can be reformulated as highly optimized GEMM-like operations [3,6]. In contrast, diagonal blocks cannot be directly substituted with analogous kernels due to their triangular structure. Moreover, vendor BLAS libraries lack native high-performance batched-SYR2K support [8,9], and neither NVIDIA nor AMD architectures expose high-precision (e.g., FP64) tensor core interfaces suitable for such computation [11,12]. Consequently, optimizing diagonal block computation is the critical bottleneck. We propose several targeted strategies below, supporting both upper and lower cases. Complex-conjugate types are handled in-kernel with minimal overhead.

Insight on Special Diagonal Input Size. Supposing the output size is $n \times k$, diagonal batched SYR2K operates on $n_b \times k$ inputs with small n_b and often large k, i.e., short-wide shape. For this regime, arithmetic intensity is

$$\mathrm{AI} = \frac{n_b k}{4(2k + n_b)} \approx \frac{n_b}{8} \quad (k \gg n_b), \tag{1}$$

which indicates a memory-bound kernel when n_b is modest. This analysis motivates an *inner-product* formulation that accumulates partial results in registers and writes each triangular output entry exactly once. Compared to outer-product tiling that flushes each C tile per K-block, our approach reduces C stores by

Algorithm 3: Dynamic Joint Batch-K Flattened Tiling

```
Procedure syr2k_dispatch(int n, int k, T* A, T* B, T* C, int
  batch):
    /* Grid with syKSplit over k dimension                        */
    bx = (n + syBLKDimX - 1) / syBLKDimX;
    by = (n + syBLKDimY - 1) / syBLKDimY;
    gridDimZ = batch * syKSplit;
    maxZ = DeviceMaxGridDimZ();
    dim3 threads(syBLKDimX, syBLKDimY);
    /* Loop for very-large-k corner cases                         */
    for i ← 0 to gridDimZ − 1 step maxZ do
        ib = min(maxZ, gridDimZ - i);
        kernel_dispatch<<<dim3(bx,by,ib), threads>>> (...);

Procedure kernel_dispatch(...):
    /* Dispatch after syKSplit over k                             */
    k_per = ceil(k / syKSplit);
    z_id = (blockIdx.z + i) / syKSplit;
    part = (blockIdx.z + i) % syKSplit;
    syr2k_device_compute(A, B, C, part, k_per, ...);
```

$\approx \lceil k/nb \rceil$, enhances locality via register accumulation, and maps naturally to per-thread, full-k independent output computation.

Dynamic Joint Batch-*K* Flattened Tiling. Given that $k \gg n_b$ in most diagonal kernel invocations, we apply a dynamic Joint Batch-K flattened tiling algorithm to overcome the memory-bound limit. Conventionally, batched operations tile along m, n, and batch dimensions, with grid-z mapped to batch indices. However, this partitioning imposes excessive per-block computational load when $k \gg n_b$, causing severe register pressure that degrades both occupancy and thread-level parallelism (TLP). Moreover, prior blocking schemes tied the number of thread blocks to the batch size (batch $= n/n_b$), which—when n is small—can leave many SMs idle. We therefore flatten the K dimension and tile over the joint (batch, K) space, yielding a tiling strategy that (a) enables dynamic tuning of launch geometry to saturate the GPU, and (b) mitigates per-block register pressure from long K-loops, thereby improving occupancy. The key control knob is *syKSplit*, which partitions k along grid-z. This increases parallelism when $k \gg n_b$ and limits per-block register pressure. Partial sums from different k partitions are merged with lightweight atomic accumulation; in practice, moderate *syKSplit* values (4–32) provide the best trade-off between parallelism and atomic overhead. Figure 2 illustrates this strategy. As *syKSplit* increases, more thread blocks are launched with shorter k-loops, improving SM utilization at the cost of additional atomic reductions. Table 1 summarizes the full tunable parameter space.

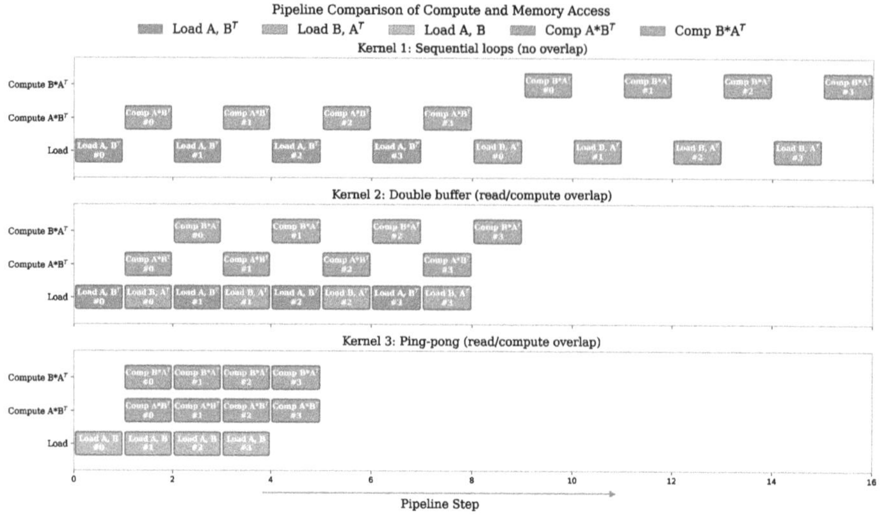

Fig. 3. Pipeline comparison across three configurations: (a) serialized baseline without optimization; (b) used double-buffer to overlap the next tile load with the current computation; and (c) *TBF*, computation overlapped and redundant loads eliminated.

Fused Computation with Dual-Term Shared-Tile Buffering. Using two independent shared-memory buffers for the AB^T and BA^T passes is expensive. We instead reuse the same staged tiles and pipeline global-load, shared-memory, and register-compute phases. The key insight is that SYR2K computes both $A_i B_j^T$ and $B_i A_j^T$ from the *same* pair of tiles, so a single load of A and B supports both symmetric terms:

$$C_{t_x,t_y} \leftarrow C_{t_x,t_y} + \sum_{k_i=k_{\text{sub}}}^{k_{\text{end}}-1} \sum_{j=0}^{s-1} \left(A_{b,\kappa,t_x} B_{b,\kappa,t_y} + B_{b,\kappa,t_x} A_{b,\kappa,t_y} \right) \tag{2}$$

where $\kappa = k_i \cdot s + j$, $s =$ `syStride`, and $b =$ `block_id`. This design halves shared-memory traffic for the symmetric pair and improves latency hiding through double-buffered overlap. Empirically, it raises effective arithmetic intensity by 1.5–2× and sustains higher occupancy across target platforms. The double-buffering pipeline proceeds as follows: while tiles in buffer 0 are consumed by the compute phase (FMA accumulation of both AB^T and BA^T terms), the next iteration's tiles are asynchronously loaded into buffer 1. Shared-memory bank conflicts are avoided by allocating odd-shaped tiles with the extra column/row padding eliminating 4-byte-stride conflicts on architectures. For portability, `syKTile` and `syNTile` are tuned per architecture to balance register pressure, shared-memory usage, and occupancy. Figure 3 illustrates the progression from the fully serialized baseline to our optimized pipeline.

Table 1. Tunable parameters

Parameter	Description
`minOptNb`	Global minimum n_b
`syBlkDimX`	`blockDim.x` for diag-part
`syBlkDimY`	`blockDim.y` for diag-part
`syNTile`	Shared-mem size along n
`syKTile`	Shared-mem size along k
`sykSplit`	Split number over k
`syStride`	Computation stride
`vecStep`	Vectorized-Load stride

Table 2. Tunable parameter examples

Set	Parameter values
`set1`	{8, 8, 8, 8, 16, 16, 2, 2}
`set2`	{16, 16, 16, 16, 16, 16, 2, 2}
`set3`	{32, 32, 32, 32, 32, 16, 4, 2}

Note: The parameter order follows Table 1: {`minOptNb`, `syBlkDimX`, `syBlkDimY`, `syNTile`, `syKTile`, `syKSplit`, `syStride`, `vecStep`}.

Bidirectional Memory Vectorization. To further improve bandwidth efficiency, we employ bidirectional vectorized loads for both A and B. *Bidirection* can be regarded as a vectorization scheme that unifies the treatment of transposed and non-transposed operands. Because the matrices are stored in column-major order, vectorized loading of the transposed view is better aligned with contiguous memory locations. We therefore load A^T and B^T from global memory in a transpose-oriented manner, and then access them from shared memory in a non-transposed manner for the computation phase when A or B is required. This design matches the global-memory access pattern to the storage layout while preserving efficient vectorized reuse in shared memory. Alignment-aware dispatch selects a vector path (e.g., `double2`) when legal and falls back to masked scalar loads at boundaries, maintaining correctness while improving effective bandwidth across all three target platforms.

3.3 Overall Dispatcher and Tuning Design

We implement *TBF* with C++ templates and a runtime dispatcher. The dispatcher chooses among different library GEMM, batched GEMM, and diagonal SYR2K kernels according to problem size and tuned thresholds (e.g., *minOptNb*). This design separates algorithm logic from hardware-specific parameter choices. Offline, we generate and benchmark candidate kernel configurations; online, we select the best precompiled variant by shape and datatype via index lookup, with negligible overhead. The tuned parameter space is summarized in Table 1.

4 Performance Evaluation

4.1 Experimental Setup

We evaluate *TBF* on four platforms: (1) NVIDIA A100-SXM4-40GB (40 GB HBM2, 1.56 TB/s bandwidth, 19.5 TFLOPS FP64 Tensor Core)/ NVIDIA A800-SXM4-80GB (80 GB HBM2e, 2.04 TB/s bandwidth, 19.5 TFLOPS FP64 Tensor Core), (2) AMD MI210 (64 GB HBM2e, 1.6 TB/s, 22.6 TFLOPS FP64), and (3) HYGON Z100 (16 GB HBM2, 1 TB/s, 6.9 TFLOPS FP64). For Nvidia, the main comparison results were obtained on an NVIDIA A100 40GB GPU. To further demonstrate the applicability of our method to a higher-bandwidth platform, we additionally carried out supplementary experiments on an NVIDIA A800 80GB GPU. Software stacks are cuBLAS 12.8, cuBLAS 13.3, rocBLAS 4.0, dcuBLAS 25.04, and Magma 2.10. All experiments use random inputs and results were validated against authoritative BLAS libraries, such as cuBLAS, and successfully passed all correctness tests. Each measurement is **averaged** report with 95% confidence intervals over 30 runs after 3 warm-up iterations. We report both regular ($n = k$) and irregular ($k \gg n$) shapes on different platforms.

4.2 Ablation Studies

We isolate diagonal-kernel improvements on A100 using the ported rocBLAS diagonal part (Algorithm 1) as baseline. Three cumulative variants are evaluated: ❶$mc1$: add reused shared-memory and computation overlapping (Sect. 3.2); ❷$mc2$: add bidirectional vectorization to $mc1$ (Sect. 3.2); ❸$mc3$: add Dynamic Join gBatch-K Flattened Tiling to $mc2$ (Sect. 3.2).

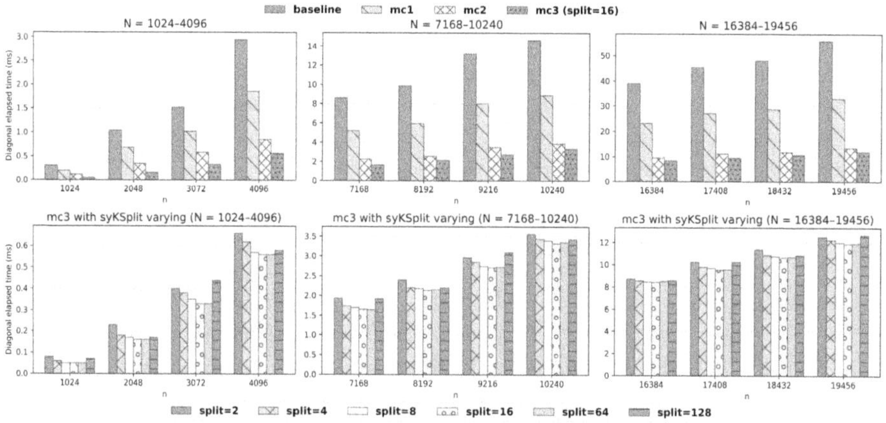

Fig. 4. Ablation studies of the TBF diagonal kernel optimizations on A100.

Across 12 matrix sizes (1024–19456), Fig. 4 shows consistent runtime reduction at each stage. The measured execution time corresponds exclusively to the diagonal block computations within the full SYR2K kernel runtime. The top row of bar charts depicts the execution time of the baseline and method combinations $mc1, mc2, mc3$. We observe that the combined optimization of $mc1, mc2, mc3$ consistently reduces execution time across all problem dimensions, where $mc1$ achieves an average 1.7× speed up over the baseline, $mc2$ attains 1.4× acceleration over $mc1$, and $mc3$ delivers 1.165× speed up over $mc2$. The bottom row illustrates the performance impact of dynamic flattened-k batch tiling technique

Table 3. Speedup of *TBF* over cuBLAS 13.3 on A800 ($k \gg n$)

k	n=16	n=32	n=64	n=128
1024	27.70	2.71	4.78	3.79
2048	38.65	4.59	7.85	4.83
4096	51.78	6.96	9.77	5.62
8192	63.03	9.36	11.12	5.91
16384	69.53	12.48	11.15	6.00

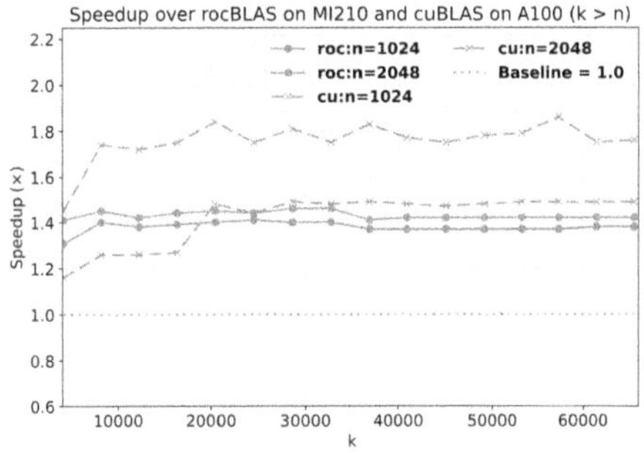

Fig. 5. Speedups over rocBLAS and cuBLAS 12.8 with $k > n$.

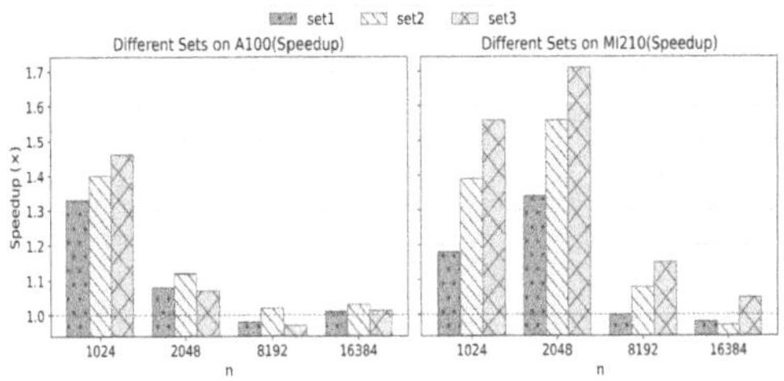

Fig. 6. Speedups over rocBLAS and cuBLAS with different parameter sets.

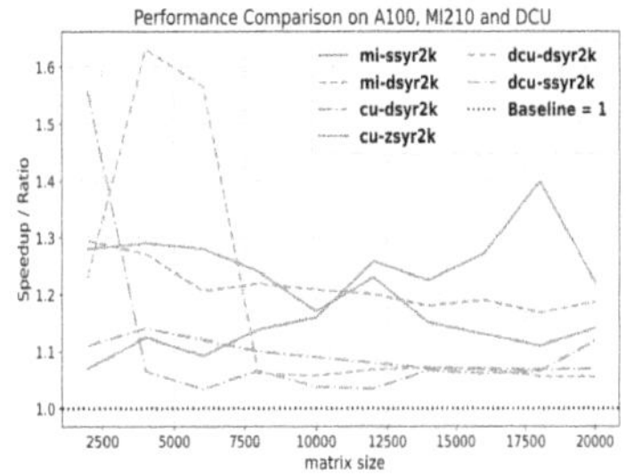

Fig. 7. *TBF* performance on A100, MI210, and Z across FP32, FP64, and complex FP64.

under varying degrees of dimension flattening. Results indicate that a moderate split factor achieves the highest acceleration ratio.

4.3 Irregular Shape Performance ($k > n$)

The diagonal path dominates when $k > n$, so this regime highlights the benefit of our design. In the extreme case $k \gg n$ on A800 (Table 3), *TBF* achieves speedups up to 69× at $n = 16$, $k = 16384$. The gains are most pronounced for very small n where cuBLAS diagonal kernels are severely underutilized. As n grows, the off-diagonal GEMM fraction increases and the overall speedup converges to the GEMM-limited regime. For non-extreme $k > n$ cases (Fig. 5), we test $n \in \{1024, 2048\}$ and $k \in [4096, 65535]$. Average speedups are 1.38× (rocBLAS) and 1.76× (cuBLAS 12.8) at $n = 1024$, and 1.43×/1.42× at $n = 2048$. These results confirm robust gains beyond corner cases.

4.4 Parameter Sensitivity

We evaluate parameter sensitivity on A100 and MI210 using the three parameter sets from Table 2. The best set varies with both architecture and problem size:

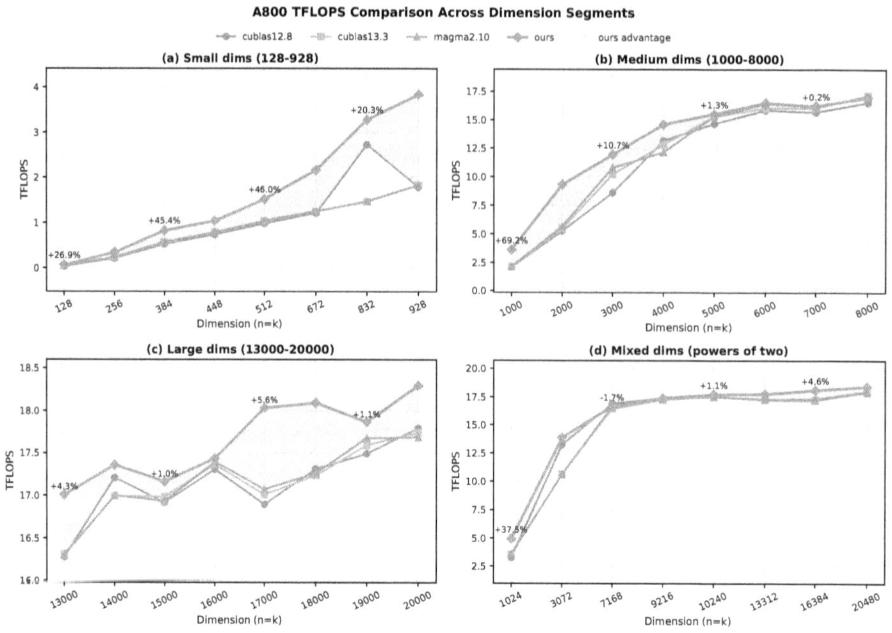

Fig. 8. TFLOPS comparison on A800 (n=k, FP64). *TBF* achieves the largest gains at small-to-moderate dimensions where diagonal blocks dominate runtime; all methods converge toward the hardware roofline (~18 TFLOPS) at large n.

set_1 favors small matrices on A100, set_3 works best for large problems on MI210, while set_2 provides a reasonable default. This confirms the necessity of offline autotuning rather than a fixed configuration (Fig. 6).

4.5 Cross-Platform Performance

Across FP32, FP64, and complex FP64 precisions (Fig. 7), *TBF* consistently outperforms vendor libraries on all three platforms. On regular sizes ($n = k$), average gains are 1.14× over cuBLAS 12.8 (A100), 1.18× over rocBLAS (MI210), and 1.14× over dcuBLAS. Smaller problems show larger gains because diagonal work contributes a larger fraction of total runtime. Moreover, Fig. 8 repeats this trend on A800: *TBF* delivers up to 2.1× higher throughput than cuBLAS 13.3 at $n \leq 1000$, narrows to 1.7× at $n = 2000$, and converges within 5% of the hardware roofline for $n \geq 8000$. These results highlight TBF's advantage in small-to-moderate regimes where vendor libraries underutilize GPUs. Consistent cross-architecture gains validate our template-based design, which adapts to diverse hardware via tuning alone, eliminating architecture-specific SYR2K code paths.

4.6 Discussion

TBF is most effective when diagonal blocks account for a meaningful fraction of runtime, which occurs at small-to-moderate n or when $k \gg n$. For very large n (e.g., $n > 16384$ with moderate k), off-diagonal GEMM dominates, so *TBF*'s gains approach vendor-library performance because cuBLAS and rocBLAS already provide highly optimized GEMM paths. The flattened-k tiling also relies on atomic accumulation across k partitions; overly aggressive *syKSplit* values (e.g., > 32) can introduce contention that offsets the benefit of increased parallelism. In practice, our autotuning selects moderate values (4–32) to balance these effects. Runtime adaptation to dynamically changing problem sizes remains future work. Nevertheless, *TBF* delivers consistent gains in the key regime of small-to-moderate n with large k, which often dominates wall-clock time in algorithms such as tiled Cholesky factorization. Beyond traditional scientific computing, *TBF*'s optimization principles are also relevant to AI workloads. Symmetric matrix updates with triangular structure appear in natural-gradient methods such as K-FAC [23], Gaussian-process kernel computation, and covariance estimation in variational inference. These workloads often perform SYR2K-like operations on moderate-sized blocks, and the short-wide diagonal shape ($n_b \ll k$) targeted by *TBF* matches scenarios where feature dimension k exceeds the per-layer parameter block size. Adapting *TBF*'s fused diagonal kernel and cross-platform tuning to these AI primitives is a natural extension.

5 Conclusion

We presented *TBF*, a tunable blocking-and-fusion SYR2K framework that separates off-diagonal compute-efficient fusion from diagonal memory-efficient kernels. By combining flattened-k tiling, reusable buffering, bidirectional vectorization, and architecture-aware dispatch, *TBF* delivers portable gains across three GPU architectures. Our key insight is that the diagonal path of SYR2K—despite contributing a small fraction of total FLOPs—dominates wall-clock time due to its memory-bound, short-wide input shape, and that targeted optimizations on this path yield disproportionate end-to-end speedups. Experiments on NVIDIA A100, A800, AMD MI210, and HYGON Z100 show up to 1.4$\times$ over cuBLAS, up to 1.7$\times$ over rocBLAS, and up to 1.6$\times$ on Z100 for regular sizes, with gains exceeding 64$\times$ in extreme short-wide settings ($k \gg n$). An ablation study confirms that each optimization contributes measurably and that cross-platform autotuning is essential to realize the full benefit.

Acknowledgments. This work was supported by the Strategic Priority Research Program (Category B) of the Chinese Academy of Sciences (Grant No. XDB0500100).

Disclosure of Interests. The authors have no competing interests to declare that are relevant to the content of this article.

References

1. Dongarra, J.J., Du Croz, J., Hammarling, S., Duff, I.S.: A set of level 3 basic linear algebra subprograms. ACM Trans. Math. Softw. **16**(1), 1–17 (1990)
2. Blackford, L.S., Demmel, J., Dongarra, J., Duff, I., Hammarling, S., Henry, G., et al.: An updated set of basic linear algebra subprograms (BLAS). ACM Trans. Math. Softw. **28**(2), 135–151 (2002)
3. Goto, K., van de Geijn, R.A.: Anatomy of high-performance matrix multiplication. ACM Trans. Math. Softw. **34**(3), 12 (2008)
4. Volkov, V., Demmel, J.W.: Benchmarking GPUs to tune dense linear algebra. In: Proceedings of the 2008 ACM/IEEE Conference on Supercomputing (SC'08), pp. 1–11. IEEE, Piscataway (2008)
5. Gustavson, F.G.: Recursion leads to automatic variable blocking for dense linear-algebra algorithms. IBM J. Res. Dev. **41**(6), 737–756 (1997)
6. Kurzak, J., Tomov, S., Dongarra, J.: Autotuning GEMM kernels for the Fermi GPU. IEEE Trans. Parallel Distrib. Syst. **23**(11), 2045–2057 (2012)
7. Jia, Z., Maggioni, M., Staiger, B., Scarpazza, D.P.: Dissecting the NVIDIA Volta GPU architecture via microbenchmarking. In: Proceedings of the 11th Workshop on General Purpose GPU Computing (GPGPU-11), pp. 52–61. ACM, New York (2018)
8. Abdelfattah, A., Haidar, A., Tomov, S., Dongarra, J.: Novel HPC techniques to batch execution of many variable size BLAS computations on GPUs. In: Proceedings of the 2017 International Conference on Supercomputing (ICS'17), pp. 1–10. ACM, New York (2017)
9. Abdelfattah, A., Tomov, S., Dongarra, J.: Matrix multiplication on batches of small matrices in half and half-complex precisions. J. Parallel Distrib. Comput. **145**, 188–201 (2020)
10. Abdelfattah, A., Costa, T., Dongarra, J., Gates, M., Haidar, A., Hammarling, S., et al.: A set of batched basic linear algebra subprograms and LAPACK routines. ACM Trans. Math. Softw. **47**(3), 21 (2021)
11. Haidar, A., Tomov, S., Dongarra, J., Higham, N.J.: Harnessing GPU tensor cores for fast FP16 arithmetic to speed up mixed-precision iterative refinement solvers. In: Proceedings of International Conference on High Perform. Comput. Netw. Storage Anal. (SC'18), pp. 603–613. IEEE, Piscataway (2018)
12. Huang, J., Yu, C.D., van de Geijn, R.A.: Implementing Strassen's algorithm with CUTLASS on NVIDIA Volta GPUs. arXiv:1808.07984 [cs.MS] (2018). https://arxiv.org/abs/1808.07984, Accessed 12 Mar 2026
13. Li, X., Liang, Y., Yan, S., Jia, L., Li, Y.: A coordinated tiling and batching framework for efficient GEMM on GPUs. In: Proceedings of the 24th ACM SIGPLAN Symposium on Principles and Practice of Parallel Programming (PPoPP '19), pp. 229–241. ACM, New York (2019)
14. NVIDIA: cuBLAS Library User Guide. NVIDIA Corporation, Santa Clara (2026). https://docs.nvidia.com/cuda/cublas/, Accessed 12 Mar 2026
15. AMD: rocBLAS Documentation. Advanced Micro Devices, Inc., Santa Clara (2026). https://rocm.docs.amd.com/projects/rocBLAS/en/latest/, Accessed 12 Mar 2026
16. NVIDIA: CUTLASS: CUDA Templates for Linear Algebra Subroutines and Solvers, v3.5.0. Software library. NVIDIA Corporation, Santa Clara (2024). https://github.com/NVIDIA/cutlass, Accessed 12 Mar 2026

17. Heroux, M., Abdelfattah, A., Beams, N., Carson, R., Ghysels, P., Kolev, T., et al.: MAGMA: Enabling exascale performance with accelerated BLAS and LAPACK for diverse GPU architectures. Int. J. High Perform. Comput. Appl. **38**(5), 468–490 (2024)
18. Kågström, B., Ling, P., Van Loan, C.: GEMM-based level 3 BLAS: high-performance model implementations and performance evaluation benchmark. ACM Trans. Math. Softw. **24**(3), 268–302 (1998)
19. Whaley, R.C., Dongarra, J.J.: Automatically tuned linear algebra software. In: Proceedings of the 1998 ACM/IEEE Conference on Supercomputing (SC'98), p. 38. IEEE, Piscataway (1998)
20. Van Zee, F.G., van de Geijn, R.A.: BLIS: A framework for rapidly instantiating BLAS functionality. ACM Trans. Math. Softw. **41**(3), 14 (2015)
21. Nugteren, C., Codreanu, V.: CLTune: A generic auto-tuner for OpenCL kernels. In: Proceedings of the 2015 IEEE 9th International Symposium on Embedded Multicore/Many-core Systems-on-Chip (MCSoC'15), pp. 195–202. IEEE, Piscataway (2015)
22. van Werkhoven, B.: Kernel Tuner: A search-optimizing GPU code auto-tuner. Future Gener. Comput. Syst. **90**, 347–358 (2019)
23. Martens, J., Grosse, R.: Optimizing neural networks with Kronecker-factored approximate curvature. In: Bach, F., Blei, D. (eds.) Proceedings of the 32nd International Conference on Machine Learning (ICML 2015). PMLR, vol. 37, pp. 2408–2417. JMLR.org, Lille (2015)
24. Charara, A., Ltaief, H., Keyes, D.: Redesigning Triangular Dense Matrix Computations on GPUs. In: Dutot, P.-F., Trystram, D. (eds.) Euro-Par 2016. LNCS, vol. 9833, pp. 477–489. Springer, Cham (2016). https://doi.org/10.1007/978-3-319-43659-3_35

Abstraction at What Cost? Evaluating Python DSLs for Transformer GPU Kernel Primitives on Nvidia Blackwell

Tanmay Nandanikar(✉) and Bartosz Sawicki

Warsaw University of Technology, Warsaw, Poland
{tanmay.nandanikar.dokt, bartosz.sawicki}@pw.edu.pl

Abstract. Writing high-performance GPU kernels for transformer workloads remains a significant engineering challenge. Nvidia's cuTile library, introduced in December 2025, offers a tile-centric programming model that aims to simplify kernel authoring while retaining near-expert performance. In this work, we evaluate cuTile against Triton, Nvidia Warp, and optimized baselines (PyTorch) across three representative transformer primitives: general matrix multiplication (GEMM), Flash Attention, and Paged Attention. Various batch sizes and sequence lengths were compared for GEMM, and Flash Attention respectively. All experiments are conducted on an Nvidia Blackwell GPUs (Blackwell sm_120) and profiled with Nvidia Nsight Systems. We find that cuTile delivers competitive kernel-level performance on GEMM and Flash Attention, but needs careful optimization to close the gap with Triton on Paged Attention. Optimizations include compile-time index tiling, disabling gather bounds checking, memory latency hints, target architecture selection, optimization hints, and changes in math expressions. Our results suggest that cuTile's tile abstraction is well-suited for regular, compute-bound kernels but faces challenges on memory-bound workloads. We discuss the implications for GPU kernel productivity and outline directions for improvement.

Keywords: GPU kernels · transformer inference · CUDA · Triton · cuTile · performance benchmarking · Blackwell architecture

1 Introduction

For two decades, the Single-Instruction Multiple-Thread (SIMT) model has defined the GPU programming landscape, forcing developers to micromanage thousands of threads, explicit synchronization barriers, and brittle shared memory layouts. However, as silicon complexity scales (culminating in the Nvidia Blackwell architecture (B200/B300) and its specialized Tensor Cores) the burden of manual thread-level orchestration has become a fundamental bottleneck to both developer productivity and peak hardware utilization. We are witnessing a mandatory strategic shift toward tile-based abstractions. In this paradigm,

M. Torquati et al. (Eds.): Euro-Par 2026, LNCS 16781, pp. 92–105, 2027.
https://doi.org/10.1007/978-3-032-35248-4_7

computation is expressed as operations on multidimensional data blocks (tiles) rather than scalar threads. This transition is essential for abstracting hardware intricacies, allowing the compiler and runtime to handle resource allocation while ensuring that kernels remain forward-compatible across evolving architectural generations.

The transformer architecture [1] underpins modern large language models (LLMs) and vision transformers. As models scale to billions of parameters, the latency of individual GPU kernels (matrix multiplications, attention mechanisms, and KV-cache management) becomes a critical bottleneck. Writing efficient CUDA kernels requires deep expertise in shared memory tiling, warp-level primitives, register pressure management, and occupancy tuning.

Several Python-embedded domain-specific languages (DSLs) lower this barrier. OpenAI's Triton [2] provides a block-level programming model with automatic memory coalescing. Nvidia Warp [6] offers a tile-based API for simulation and general GPU computation. Most recently, Nvidia introduced `cuda.tile` (cuTile) [6] in December 2025: a tile-centric Python DSL that wraps CUDA's Cooperative Groups and Tensor Memory Accelerator (TMA) hardware. CuTile's `ct.load`/`ct.store`/`ct.mma` primitives abstract away memory staging and tensor core invocation, while `ct.gather` provides indirect memory access. This raises a natural question: *does this abstraction sacrifice performance, and if so, where?*

We present one of the early independent evaluations of cuTile alongside Triton, Warp (for GEMM), and baseline implementations (cuBLAS/PyTorch SDPA) across three transformer primitives on Blackwell hardware. `GEMM`: the compute backbone of all transformer layers. `Flash Attention` [3]: fused, memory-efficient self-attention for prefill `Paged Attention` [5]: KV-cache attention with non-contiguous memory pages for autoregressive decoding. Our contributions are:

- A head-to-head comparison of cuTile, Triton, Warp (only for GEMM), and PyTorch across three transformer primitives at multiple problem sizes on Blackwell.
- A follow-up cuTile variant study showing that the original Paged Attention kernel is not performance-representative: compile-time index generation, disabled gather bounds checks, and occupancy hints improve BF16 latency at CTX=4096 from 5,517 µs to 609 µs, within 3.3% of Triton.
- A specialized indirect tile-extraction microbenchmark showing that cuTile `ct.gather` remains 1.16× slower than Triton's block-pointer/TMA path on random 32×32 block extraction, indicating residual overhead for irregular access even after the larger Paged Attention gap is removed.
- A cross-precision analysis showing that the *baseline* cuTile Paged Attention kernel scales much more weakly from FP32 to BF16 than Triton, motivating the variant study and highlighting the sensitivity of memory-bound kernels to implementation details.

2 Background and Related Work

Evolution of GPU DSLs. To abstract the complexities of modern GPU hardware, several domain-specific languages (DSLs) and compilers have been developed. Early frameworks like Halide [9] focused on image processing pipelines, while TVM [8] introduced automated end-to-end compilation for deep learning tensors. For dense linear algebra, low-level template libraries such as CUTLASS [6] provide high performance but require deep C++ expertise. Recently, Python-embedded DSLs have emerged to bridge the gap between high-level framework usability and low-level hardware utilization.

Triton. Triton [2] is an open-source Python DSL and compiler for GPU programming. Programs specify operations on fixed-size blocks; the compiler handles memory coalescing, shared memory allocation, and warp scheduling via an MLIR-based backend. Triton is the default kernel backend in PyTorch 2.x through `torch.compile`.

Nvidia Warp. Warp [6] provides `tile_load`/`tile_matmul`/`tile_store` with a kernel-per-thread model extended by cooperative tile primitives. It targets differentiable simulation but supports general GPU computation. Warp does not support BF16.

cuTile (`cuda.tile`). CuTile [6], released December 2025, wraps TMA hardware and tensor cores in a high-level tile API. It provides `ct.load`/`ct.store` for contiguous tile I/O routed through TMA, `ct.mma` for tensor-core GEMM, and `ct.gather` for indirect memory access. Nvidia's TileGym [6] repository provides reference cuTile kernels for GEMM, Flash Attention, and contiguous decode attention. They notably do not provide a Paged Attention implementation with non-contiguous KV caches. The GEMM and Flash Attention reference kernels are partially adapted from the TileGym repository.

GPU Benchmarking Studies for Deep Learning. Historically, GPU benchmarking focused on raw hardware microbenchmarks [10,11] or end-to-end suites like MLPerf [12], which obscure kernel-level DSL overheads. While early Triton evaluations [2,14] demonstrated near-cuBLAS performance for compute-dense operations on Volta and Ampere, generative AI has fundamentally shifted bottleneck profiles. Prior literature lacks a systematic evaluation of how high-level tile abstractions perform on Hopper and Blackwell's asynchronous hardware (TMA) when handling the highly irregular, memory-bound access patterns that dominate modern LLM inference. This work directly addresses that gap.

Transformer Inference Primitives. Modern transformer models [1] rely on three critical kernel primitives that serve as primary targets for DSL benchmarks. GEMM and FlashAttention [3,16] are heavily compute-bound, testing a DSL's ability to maximize Tensor Core occupancy and hide memory latency. Conversely, autoregressive decoding relies on Paged Attention [5], which stores Key-Value (KV) caches in non-contiguous physical memory pages to manage dynamic sequences. This transforms attention into a severely memory-bandwidth-bound operation with indirect, irregular memory accesses. While libraries like FlashInfer [17] optimize these patterns using specialized C++, evaluating how Python DSLs handle such indirect accesses (via cuTile's `ct.gather` or Triton's pointer arithmetic) remains an open challenge that forms the core of our evaluation.

3 Evaluation

We evaluate cuTile on three representative GPU workloads: dense matrix multiplication (GEMM), Flash Attention, and Paged Attention with irregular memory access.

3.1 Experimental Setup

All experiments run on an Nvidia GeForce RTX 5070 Ti (Blackwell, GB203, sm_120) with 70 SMs, 16 GB GDDR7 (896 GB/s bandwidth), and 48 MB L2 cache. The software stack consists of PyTorch 2.10.0, Triton 3.6.0, `cuda-tile` 1.1.0, Warp 1.11.1, and CUDA Toolkit 13.1. GEMM and Flash Attention kernels were adapted from Nvidia TileGym [6] reference implementations, while the Paged Attention kernels and their optimized variants were authored from scratch for this study.

Kernel Implementations. We implement custom kernels in cuTile, Triton, and Warp where applicable, while PyTorch dispatches to vendor libraries (cuBLAS or SDPA). Unless otherwise noted, kernels operate on FP16 inputs and follow standard warmup and benchmarking procedures.

Benchmarking Protocol and Correctness. Performance is measured via Nsight Systems ($n \geq 5$ invocations) and CUDA events, following standard warmup iterations. Each configuration is run three times to confirm reproducibility (cross-run variability <1.2%, coefficient of variation < 1.1%). All kernels are validated against a PyTorch reference. In FP32, cuTile and Triton produce bitwise-identical outputs for Paged Attention; in BF16, maximum absolute differences are $\leq 7.8 \times 10^{-3}$, consistent with BF16 rounding.

3.2 GEMM

We evaluate square $N \times N$ FP16 dense matrices. CuTile uses tile sizes $(64, 64, 32)$; Triton uses $(128, 256, 64)$; Warp uses $(64, 64, 32)$. PyTorch dispatches to cuBLAS.

Table 1 presents FP16 GEMM latencies. CuTile consistently outperforms both Triton and Warp, remaining within 1.3× of cuBLAS. At N=4096, cuTile achieves 1,809 µs versus cuBLAS's 1,407 µs (1.29×), while Triton requires 4,639 µs (3.29×) and Warp 5,617 µs (3.99×). CuTile's `ct.mma` maps directly to TMA-based data movement and tensor core execution, adding negligible overhead over the vendor library for this regular, compute-bound workload.

Table 1. GEMM kernel latency (µs, mean ± σ) on FP16 square matrices (n=5).

N	cuBLAS	cuTile	Triton	Warp
512	4.5 ± 0.1	5.4 ± 0.04	64.7 ± 0.5	19.6 ± 0.1
1024	26.7 ± 0.2	35.1 ± 0.2	126.0 ± 0.9	106.1 ± 0.1
2048	183 ± 1.6	238.7 ± 0.4	586 ± 3.9	731 ± 0.6
4096	$1{,}407 \pm 4.2$	$1{,}809 \pm 1.5$	$4{,}639 \pm 18$	$5{,}617 \pm 2.6$
8192	$11{,}171 \pm 10$	$14{,}132 \pm 15$	$35{,}077 \pm 34$	$46{,}070 \pm 51$

3.3 Flash Attention

Inputs are shaped (B=2, H=8, S, D=64) in FP16. CuTile uses tiles (64, 32); Triton uses blocks (128, 64). PyTorch dispatches to its vendor Flash Attention backend.

Table 2 reports Flash Attention latencies in µs (Nsight Systems kernel time). PyTorch SDPA, dispatching to a vendor-optimized kernel, is fastest at all sequence lengths. Sequence length is referred to as S henceforth. CuTile and Triton perform within 7% of each other, with the gap to SDPA widening at longer sequences (1.26× at S=8192). This is expected: SDPA uses architecture-specific tile shapes and software pipelining. CuTile is faster than Triton at S=512 (19.7 vs. 21.9 µs), suggesting that cuTile's lower launch overhead or smaller block size is advantageous for short sequences.

Table 2. Flash Attention latency (µs, mean ± σ) at various sequence lengths (B=2, H=8, D=64, FP16, n=25).

Seq Len	PyTorch SDPA	cuTile	Triton
512	15.8 ± 0.0	19.7 ± 0.1	21.9 ± 0.0
1024	54.3 ± 0.1	69.8 ± 0.2	65.4 ± 0.4
2048	204.7 ± 0.2	262.0 ± 0.4	245.4 ± 0.6
4096	802.0 ± 0.6	956.8 ± 0.7	944.0 ± 0.9
8192	$2{,}990 \pm 3.2$	$3{,}775 \pm 4.5$	$3{,}489 \pm 2.9$

BF16 Flash Attention latencies are within 0.1% of the FP16 numbers for all frameworks, consistent with the compute-bound nature of this workload: halving the data width does not change tensor-core throughput.

3.4 Paged Attention

We use B=16, H=16, D=128, block size 16, and context lengths from 512 to 16,384. Benchmarks are performed in FP32 and BF16. BF16 was selected for

Paged Attention as it is the standard precision for modern LLM inference and shares the same memory bandwidth footprint as FP16.

The baseline cuTile kernel uses `ct.gather` for indirect KV-cache access, whereas Triton performs equivalent access via pointer arithmetic. PyTorch iterates over batch elements in Python.

Table 3 and Fig. 1 show the behavior of the *baseline* cuTile Paged Attention kernel. In FP32, Triton outperforms this baseline by 5.2–5.5× across all context lengths, while baseline cuTile is only marginally faster than the unfused PyTorch reference. At CTX=4096, Triton achieves 1,212 ± 2.2 µs, baseline cuTile 6,665 ± 3.7 µs, and PyTorch 7,015 µs. The stability of this gap initially suggests a severe problem on the cuTile path, motivating the follow-up variant study in Table 4. All fused-kernel measurements have coefficient of variation $< 0.3\%$ (n=1,011).

Table 3. Paged Attention latency (µs, mean ± σ) in FP32 for the *baseline* cuTile kernel (B=16, H=16, D=128; n=1,011 for fused kernels).

CTX	PyTorch (Ref)†	cuTile	Triton
512	1,235	852 ± 1.2	154 ± 0.4
1024	2,221	1,717 ± 1.5	305 ± 0.7
2048	3,600	3,372 ± 2.9	610 ± 1.1
4096	7,015	6,665 ± 3.7	1,212 ± 2.2
8192	14,047	13,329 ± 5.7	2,479 ± 4.1
16384	28,037	26,693 ± 7.3	5,090 ± 10.1

†PyTorch unfused: σ unavailable (per-iteration timing aggregates ∼161K sub-kernel launches); cross-run variability <1.2%.

Paged Attention Optimized Variants. Table 4 revisits Paged Attention at a representative operating point (CTX=4096, BF16). The tuned cuTile variant removes auxiliary index-tensor loads by generating index tiles in-kernel using compile-time ranges, eliminates gather bounds checks when indices are known valid, and introduces explicit latency hints on memory operations to better overlap DRAM accesses with computation. These changes remove unnecessary global-memory traffic and reduce indexing overhead in the inner loop.

The aggressive variant keeps the same paged, non-contiguous KV-cache layout but further adds explicit kernel configuration hints (target occupancy and compiler optimization level) together with refined latency annotations for key loads and stores, improving scheduling and memory-level parallelism on Blackwell GPUs.

Together these changes reduce cuTile latency from 5,517 µs to 1,114 µs (tuned) and then to 609 µs (aggressive), a 9.05× improvement over the original

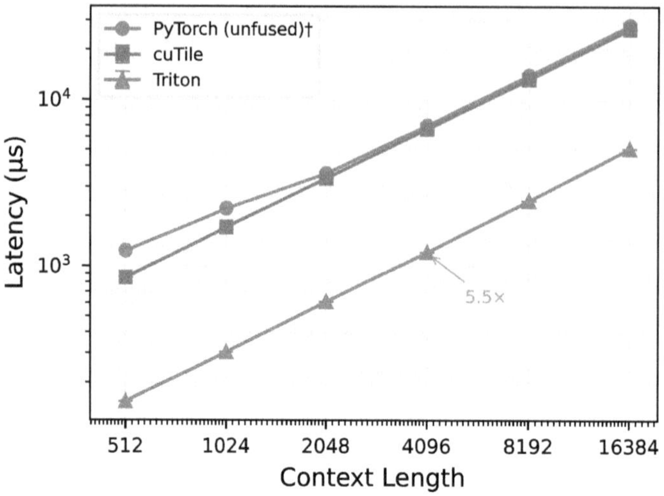

Fig. 1. Paged Attention latency vs. context length (FP32, log scale). Error bars show $\pm 1\sigma$ (n=1,011); bars are smaller than markers. †PyTorch unfused. per-iteration σ unavailable.

kernel and within 3.3% of Triton. Because the data structure and access pattern remain paged, this result shows that the original gap was not an intrinsic consequence of non-contiguous KV-cache access.

Table 4. Representative BF16 Paged Attention variant study at CTX=4096 (B=16, H=16, D=128).

Kernel	Latency (µs)	Max Diff vs. PyTorch
PyTorch (Ref.)	3,291.54	—
cuTile (old)	5,517.06	1.465×10^{-3}
cuTile (tuned)	1,113.90	2.075×10^{-3}
cuTile (aggressive)	609.44	2.075×10^{-3}
Triton	589.84	1.465×10^{-3}

3.5 Specialized Indirect Tile Extraction

To isolate irregular block selection outside the softmax/reduction pipeline, we extract 16,384 random 32×32 tiles from an 8192×8192 matrix. Table 5 shows that Triton's block-pointer/TMA kernel remains faster than cuTile's `ct.gather` version, but only by 1.16×. This is a meaningful difference, yet far smaller than the original baseline Paged Attention gap, indicating that indirect access overhead remains real but does not by itself explain the earlier 5×–9× disparity.

Table 5. Specialized indirect tile-extraction benchmark (16,384 random 32×32 tiles from an 8192×8192 FP16 matrix).

Kernel	Latency (μs)
cuTile (`ct.gather`)	136.62
Triton (block pointer / TMA)	117.40

4 Analysis

In this section, we investigate the underlying hardware and software factors driving the performance differences observed in our evaluation. Select experiments with interesting results are presented. We use the roofline model to classify workloads, analyze kernel occupancy to explain the `ct.gather` bottleneck, examine cross-precision scaling behavior, and highlight the overheads of dynamic kernel selection and dispatch in unfused baselines.

4.1 Roofline Model

The roofline model [7] bounds performance by the minimum of peak compute throughput π and memory bandwidth β scaled by operational intensity I (FLOPs/byte). The ridge point $I^* = \pi/\beta$ separates memory-bound ($I < I^*$) from compute-bound ($I > I^*$) regimes. Based on our hardware specifications and the peak cuBLAS GEMM result, the RTX 5070 Ti achieves an observed FP16 throughput of $\pi = 98.4$ TFLOPS. With $\beta = 896$ GB/s, the ridge point is $I^* \approx 110$ FLOPs/byte.

At a representative problem size of 4096, both FP16 GEMM ($I_{\text{GEMM}} = N/3 \approx 1{,}365$) and Flash Attention ($I_{\text{Flash}} = S/2 = 2{,}048$) operate far to the right of the ridge point ($> 12 \times I^*$), making them heavily compute-bound. In contrast, decoding a single query token in Paged Attention yields a constant operational intensity of $I_{\text{Paged}} = 2/b$ (where b is the element byte width). This results in $I = 0.5$ for FP32 and $I = 1.0$ for BF16—over 100× below the ridge point, placing Paged Attention firmly in the memory-bound regime.

Results on the Roofline. Figure 2 plots the achieved performance of each framework against the roofline at representative size 4096. GEMM and Flash Attention cluster in the compute-bound region: cuBLAS reaches 97.7 TFLOPS (99% of the observed peak) and all DSLs exceed 29 TFLOPS. The *baseline* Paged Attention kernels occupy the opposite extreme. Triton's fused kernel achieves 443 GFLOPS at I=0.5 (FP32), which is 98.9% of the memory-bandwidth ceiling ($\beta \cdot I = 448$ GFLOPS)—an optimally bandwidth-utilized memory-bound kernel. In BF16, Triton reaches 901 GFLOPS at I=1.0 (ceiling: 896 GFLOPS), confirming near-ideal scaling with reduced element width. This exceeds the theoretical memory bandwidth ceiling (901 GFLOPS vs. 896 GFLOPS), and could likely be driven by L2 cache hits and L2 multicasting, which reduce physical DRAM traffic below the algorithmic data volume assumed by the roofline model. It might also be due to measurement error. The baseline cuTile kernel, by contrast, achieves only 80.7 GFLOPS in FP32 (18.0% of the ceiling) and 95.8 GFLOPS in BF16 (10.7%), showing that the original implementation leaves most of the available bandwidth unused. Importantly, the follow-up variant study in Table 4 demonstrates that this shortfall is not an inherent roofline limit of cuTile itself, but of a particular paged-attention formulation.

This roofline classification provides a unifying lens for our results: cuTile's tile abstraction is effective for compute-bound kernels that lie far to the right of the ridge point, where tensor-core utilization is the dominant performance factor. For memory-bound kernels to the left of the ridge point, where efficient global-memory access patterns determine throughput, performance becomes much more sensitive to auxiliary staging, index handling, and scheduling choices on the `ct.gather` path.

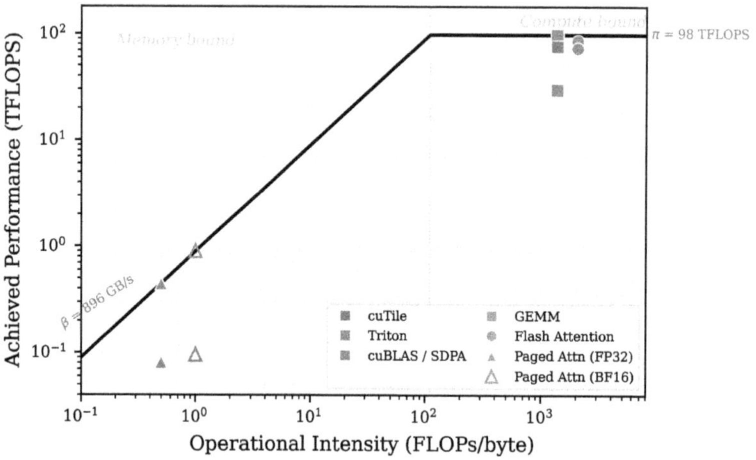

Fig. 2. Roofline analysis on the RTX 5070 Ti (π=98.4 TFLOPS, β=896 GB/s). Filled markers denote FP16/FP32; open markers denote BF16. GEMM and Flash Attention are compute-bound ($I \gg I^*$). Paged Attention is deeply memory-bound ($I \ll I^*$): Triton reaches 99% of the bandwidth ceiling, while cuTile reaches only 18%.

4.2 Occupancy and the `ct.gather` Bottleneck

Table 6 presents per-kernel resource consumption at a representative size of 4096. For GEMM and Flash Attention, all frameworks use high register counts (255 registers/thread), yielding modest occupancy (8–17%). Performance is still competitive because these workloads are compute-bound: tensor cores stay busy even at low occupancy.

Paged Attention tells a different story. The baseline cuTile kernel uses 168 registers/thread and 75 KB of shared memory per block, limiting each SM to a

Table 6. Kernel resource usage and estimated occupancy at size 4096.

Bench.	Kernel	Regs	Thr.	Warps	Smem	Occ.
GEMM	cuTile	255	256	8	41 KB	16.7%
	Triton	255	128	4	96 KB	8.3%
	cuBLAS	96	128	4	49 KB	16.7%
	Warp	128	128	4	25 KB	16.7%
Flash	cuTile	255	256	8	33 KB	16.7%
	Triton	255	128	4	49 KB	8.3%
	SDPA	255	128	4	49 KB	8.3%
Paged	cuTile	168	384	12	75 KB	25.0%
	Triton	56	128	4	512 B	75.0%

single resident block (25% occupancy). Triton uses only 56 registers and 512 bytes of shared memory, fitting ~9 blocks per SM (75% occupancy)—a 3× occupancy advantage.

These numbers implicate the original `ct.gather`-based formulation, but the follow-up variant study shows that `ct.gather` alone is not the full explanation. The baseline kernel also loads auxiliary index tensors from memory and gives the compiler no gather bounds or occupancy hints. Removing those overheads and adding explicit occupancy guidance reduces CTX=4096 BF16 latency from 5,517 µs to 609 µs while preserving the same paged, non-contiguous KV-cache layout. Thus the original result should be read as a warning about naive implementations of cuTile on irregular workloads, not proof that paged attention is fundamentally beyond the programming model.

TileGym's [6] reference decode-attention kernels still provide an important clue: they use `ct.load` with `allow_tma=True` on contiguous KV caches, whereas the paged variant must rely on `ct.gather`. The specialized indirect-access benchmark in Table 5 shows that this gather path remains somewhat costlier than Triton's block-pointer/TMA route even in isolation, but only by 16%.

4.3 Cross-Precision Scaling: FP32 vs. BF16

To further diagnose the bottleneck, we benchmark Paged Attention in BF16. For a memory-bandwidth-bound kernel, halving the data width from 32-bit to 16-bit should yield ~2× speedup. Table 7 and Fig. 3 reveal three distinct scaling regimes.

Triton: ~2× (expected). Triton's Paged Attention kernel is memory-bandwidth-bound: it loads Q, K, V from global memory via pointer arithmetic. Halving the data width from FP32 to BF16 halves the memory traffic, yielding speedups of 1.98–2.37× across context lengths. This is the textbook result for a bandwidth-limited kernel.

Table 7. Paged Attention latency (µs, mean ± σ) in BF16 (B=16, H=16, D=128; n=1,011 for fused kernels).

CTX	PyTorch (Ref)†	cuTile	Triton
512	2,202	706 ± 0.8	64 ± 0.7
1024	2,191	1,422 ± 1.6	153 ± 0.7
2048	2,206	2,819 ± 2.0	297 ± 1.0
4096	3,357	5,603 ± 2.6	596 ± 1.7
8192	7,163	11,231 ± 3.8	1,219 ± 3.7
16384	14,184	22,590 ± 7.5	2,488 ± 4.3

† See Table 3 footnote.

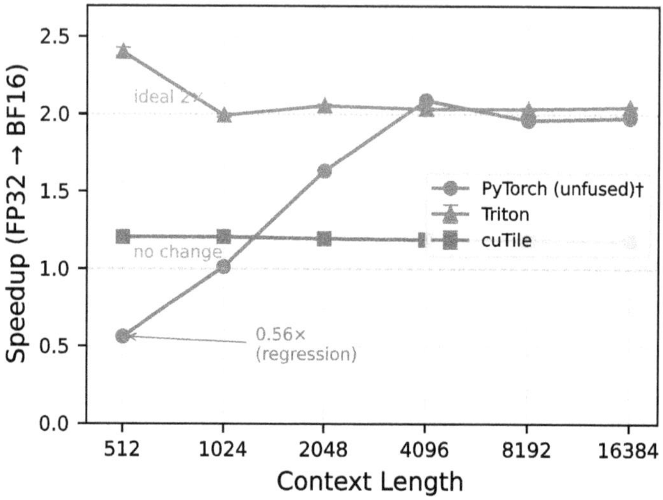

Fig. 3. Speedup from FP32 to BF16 for Paged Attention.

cuTile: ∼1.2× (baseline, limited). The *baseline* cuTile kernel plateaus at 1.18–1.21×, remarkably consistent across all context lengths. The shared-memory staging and index-management overhead on the original `ct.gather` path is largely precision-independent: these costs dominate over the data-movement savings. This confirms our occupancy-based diagnosis for the baseline kernel. Critically, in BF16 this baseline cuTile implementation is *slower* than the unfused PyTorch reference at CTX $\geq$ 2048 (e.g., 5,603 ± 2.6 vs. 3,357 µs at CTX=4096), reversing the FP32 ordering. However, the optimized BF16 variants in Table 4 show that this limited scaling characterizes the original kernel rather than an unavoidable property of cuTile.

PyTorch: regression at small context. PyTorch's unfused implementation shows an anomalous regression at small context lengths: at CTX=512, BF16 is 1.8× *slower* than FP32 (2,202 vs. 1,235 µs). The PyTorch BF16 latency plateaus at ~2,200 µs for CTX ≤ 2048 before recovering the expected ~2× scaling at large context. This plateau arises because each of the ~16,000 per-iteration sub-operations (matmul, softmax, elementwise) dispatches through cuBLAS, which selects suboptimal WMMA kernels for BF16 at small matrix sizes.

4.4 Productivity and Implementation Complexity

Triton and cuTile represent *pointer-centric* and *tensor-centric* programming respectively. While both DSLs reside in Python, the cognitive load required to code and maintain the kernels differs based on how they handle memory layout and hardware acceleration.

Authoring vs. Tuning. Triton requires manual management of memory offsets and strides (e.g., `Q + q_offset + offs_m * stride_qm`); an error in this logic leads to memory corruption. Conversely, cuTile abstracts away strides, allowing interaction with tensors via multi-dimensional indices. On Blackwell, these high-level calls automatically configure the TMA hardware. However, Paged Attention reveals a trade-off: while cuTile reduces the logic of non-contiguous access through `ct.gather`, achieving performance parity requires developers to manually inject hardware-level hints (latency and occupancy). As shown in Table 8, cuTile simplifies the path to a correct kernel but shifts the engineering effort from pointer arithmetic to fine-grained compiler guidance.

Table 8. Comparison of implementation complexity for Flash Attention.

Metric	Triton	cuTile
Model	1D Pointer Arithmetic	ND Tensor Indexing
Memory	Manual Strides/Offsets (~12 LoC)	Automatic/Logical (~2 LoC)
Control	Implicit/Block Pointers	Explicit Latency/Occupancy Hints

5 Discussion

Our results reveal a clear divide between cuTile's behavior on regular kernels and the fragility of untuned irregular kernels. CuTile's tile abstraction maps naturally to TMA-based contiguous loads and tensor-core execution, making it effective for *regular, compute-bound* kernels: it matches cuBLAS within 1.3× on GEMM and stays close to Triton on Flash Attention. For these workloads, the abstraction cost is negligible.

The optimized Paged Attention results substantially change the interpretation of the original negative result. The baseline cuTile kernel interacts poorly with `ct.gather`, auxiliary index-tensor loads, and conservative scheduling, producing the large gap shown in Tables 3 and 7. Yet a tuned kernel that eliminates those extra costs is 4.95× faster than the original at CTX=4096 in BF16, and adding occupancy hints reduces the remaining gap to just 3.3% versus Triton. Because the optimized kernel still operates on the same paged, non-contiguous KV-cache layout, the baseline result cannot be interpreted as an intrinsic limitation of cuTile. Instead, the evidence points to a more nuanced conclusion: irregular kernels in cuTile are highly sensitive to implementation style and compiler guidance. To be more specific, achieving peak performance on irregular paths requires developers to manually minimize global memory traffic by generating indices on-the-fly and disabling safety checks. Providing explicit occupancy and latency hints is essential to help the compiler manage register pressure and overlap non-contiguous DRAM lookups with computation. Ultimately, while cuTile provides a high-level API, it still demands low-level hardware awareness to ensure that memory-bound kernels saturate the available bandwidth

The specialized irregular-access benchmark shows that cuTile `ct.gather` is still slower than Triton's block-pointer/TMA path, but only by 1.16×. This suggests that indirect access is a real sensitivity point, not a categorical blocker.

Warp's Position. Warp trails cuTile and cuBLAS by 3–4× on GEMM and does not support BF16. Its primary strength is differentiable simulation; our results confirm it is not competitive for transformer inference.

Threats to Validity. All experiments use a single consumer GPU. Data-center Blackwell GPUs (B100/B200) with more SMs could shift occupancy-sensitive results. We do not evaluate multi-GPU configurations or batch sizes representative of production serving. All reported measurements exhibit coefficients of variation below 1.1%, with the majority below 0.3%, indicating high reproducibility on our hardware.

6 Conclusion

We have presented one of the early comparative evaluations of Nvidia's cuTile against Triton, Warp, and PyTorch across three transformer kernel primitives on Blackwell hardware. CuTile achieves within 1.3× of cuBLAS on GEMM and stays close to Triton on Flash Attention, demonstrating that its tile abstraction incurs little overhead for regular, compute-bound workloads. For Paged Attention, the baseline cuTile kernel underperforms badly, but the optimized variant study shows that this is not the final takeaway: a tuned cuTile implementation improves BF16 latency at CTX=4096 by 9.05× over the original and comes within 3.3% of Triton while preserving the same paged, non-contiguous KV-cache layout. A specialized indirect tile-extraction benchmark still leaves cuTile `ct.gather` 1.16× slower than Triton's block-pointer/TMA path, indicating that irregular access remains a real but manageable sensitivity. The key lesson is therefore more nuanced than our initial baseline suggested: fair evaluation of cuTile on irregular workloads requires representative, tuned kernels rather than naive first implementations.

Disclosure of Interests and Artifact Availability. The authors have no competing interests to declare that are relevant to the content of this article. The artifact supporting this work is available in the Zenodo repository [18].

References

1. Vaswani, A., et al.: Attention is all you need. In: Advances in Neural Information Processing Systems, vol. 30 (2017)
2. Tillet, P., Kung, H.T., Cox, D.: Triton: An intermediate language and compiler for tiled neural network computations. In: Proceedings of the 3rd MLSys Conference (2019)
3. Dao, T., Fu, D.Y., Ermon, S., Rudra, A., Ré, C.: FlashAttention: Fast and memory-efficient exact attention with IO-awareness. In: Advances in Neural Information Processing Systems, vol. 35, (2022)
4. Dao, T.: FlashAttention-2: Faster attention with better parallelism and work partitioning. In: International Conference on Learning Representations (2024)
5. Kwon, W., et al.: Efficient memory management for large language model serving with PagedAttention. In: Proceedings of the 29th Symposium on Operating Systems Principles, pp. 611–626 (2023)
6. Nvidia repositories: Warp, TileGym, cutlass, cutle-python. https://github.com/NVIDIA/
7. Williams, S., Waterman, A., Patterson, D.: Roofline: an insightful visual performance model for multicore architectures. Commun. ACM **52**(4), 65–76 (2009)
8. Chen, T., et al.: TVM: An automated end-to-end optimizing compiler for deep learning. In: Proceedings of the 13th USENIX Symposium on Operating Systems Design and Implementation (OSDI), pp. 578–594 (2018)
9. Ragan-Kelley, J., Barnes, C., Adams, A., Paris, S., Durand, F., Amarasinghe, S.: Halide: A language and compiler for optimizing image processing pipelines. In: ACM SIGPLAN Notices, vol. 48, no. 6, pp. 519–530 (2013)
10. Jia, Z., Maggioni, M., Staiger, B., Scarpazza, D.P.: Dissecting the NVIDIA Volta GPU architecture via microbenchmarking. arXiv preprint arXiv:1804.06826 (2018)
11. Jia, Z., Maggioni, M., Smith, J., Scarpazza, D.P.: Dissecting the NVIDIA Ampere architecture via microbenchmarking. arXiv preprint arXiv:2107.08569 (2021)
12. Reddi, V.J., Cheng, C., Kanter, D., Mattson, P., Schmuelling, G., Wu, C.J., et al.: MLPerf inference benchmark. In: 2020 ACM/IEEE 47th Annual International Symposium on Computer Architecture (ISCA), pp. 446–459. IEEE (2020)
13. Roesch, J., et al.: Relay: A new IR for machine learning frameworks. In: Proceedings of the 2nd ACM SIGPLAN International Workshop on Machine Learning and Programming Languages (MAPL), pp. 58–68 (2018)
14. Dao, T., Gu, A., et al.: Simplifying GPU programming with Triton. IEEE Micro **42**(4), 64–72 (2022)
15. Aminabadi, R.Y., Black, S., Ammar, T., Metz, L.: DeepSpeed-Inference: Enabling highly efficient generative applications. arXiv preprint arXiv:2207.00032 (2022)
16. Shah, J., Dao, T.: FlashAttention-3: Fast and accurate attention with asynchrony and low-precision. arXiv preprint arXiv:2407.08608 (2024)
17. Ye, Z.: FlashInfer: Fast large language model inference on GPUs. arXiv preprint arXiv:2403.00800 (2024)
18. Nandanikar, T., Sawicki, B.: Artifact of the paper: Abstraction at what cost? Evaluating Python DSLs for transformer GPU kernel primitives on Nvidia Blackwell. Zenodo (2026). https://doi.org/10.5281/zenodo.20507933

Closer in the Gap: Towards Portable Performance on RISC-V Vector Processors

Ruimin Shi[1], Maya Gokhale[2], Pei-Hung Lin[2], Xavier Teruel[3], and Ivy Peng[1](✉)

[1] KTH Royal Institute of Technology, Stockholm, Sweden
{ruimins,ivybopeng}@kth.se
[2] Lawrence Livermore National Laboratory, Livermore, USA
{gokhale2,lin32}@llnl.gov
[3] Barcelona Supercomputing Center, Barcelona, Spain
xavier.teruel@bsc.es

Abstract. The RISC-V Vector Extension (RVV) is a cornerstone for sustaining compute throughout in scientific and machine learning workloads. However, compiler support and performance monitoring on RVV 1.0 hardware remain actively evolving. In this work, we design a suite of assembly microbenchmarks to calibrate performance counters on the BananaPi-F3 RVV hardware. Using the benchmarks, we find that predication overhead and stride load pose performance bottlenecks that current compiler cost models do not yet fully capture. Evaluating GCC 15 and Clang 21 across six scientific and ML applications, GCC 15 produces more stable and efficient code generation, outperforming Clang 21 in four of six benchmarks. Clang 21 achieves superior performance only in SGEMM and DGEMM, attributable to more aggressive instruction reduction as confirmed by our validated perf counters. Default LMUL selection proves near-optimal in most cases, though GCC 15 shows greater potential for performance gains through larger LMUL tuning than Clang 21. Finally, we contribute an RVV backend for Google's Qsim quantum circuit simulator implemented using RVV intrinsics, where GCC 15 again outperforms LLVM 21 on this complex, real-world workload.

1 Introduction

The RISC-V Instruction Set Architecture (ISA) has attracted increasing interest from both industry and academia for its open, modular design and suitability for workload-specific customization [5,10,13,15]. A cornerstone of RISC-V's relevance to High-Performance Computing is the *RISC-V Vector Extension* (RVV). Many HPC workloads, including ML training and inference, scientific simulations, and signal processing, are built around data-parallel algorithms that benefit directly from wide vector execution. Unlike traditional SIMD with fixed vector lengths in ISA, RVV adopts a *Vector-Length-Agnostic* (VLA) model where the active vector length can be determined at runtime. Another popular VLA realization is ARM's scalable vector extension (SVE), which was first implemented

M. Torquati et al. (Eds.): Euro-Par 2026, LNCS 16781, pp. 106–120, 2027.
https://doi.org/10.1007/978-3-032-35248-4_8

in Fujitsu's A64FX processor powering the Fugaku supercomputer, and widely adopted in recent NVIDIA Grace and AWS Graviton processors [16].

For achieving portable performance on various RVV hardware, compiler support and performance profiling are both important. Auto-vectorization compiler support is the key enabler for portable performance on broad RVV hardware. At the fast pace of new RVV hardware emerging, compiler support allows applications to harness different vector hardware without rewriting applications. However, compared to vector length-specific SIMD, RVV's VLA model imposes new challenges on the compiler support for auto-vectorization. One particular challenge is that under uncertainty about the hardware vector width at compilation time, a compiler must generate correct `vsetvl` sequences that set active vector length at runtime, select an appropriate value for the vector length multiplier (LMUL), and handle tail elements and masks. Addressing these difficulties, GNU and LLVM are both under active development to ramp up RVV support.

Prior works have characterized compiler support for RVV, including comparative evaluations of GCC 14 and LLVM 19 on ratified RVV 1.0 hardware [1,6,10]. However, both compilers have since undergone substantial RVV-specific development. For instance, GCC 15 introduced early-break loop vectorization, corrected memory misaligned access, and dynamic LMUL selection. LLVM 21 added multiple hardware-specific scheduling models for recent RVV hardware. An up-to-date evaluation of these compiler advances is therefore timely and necessary. Meanwhile, performance monitoring on RISC-V hardware remains significantly less mature than on x86 or AArch64 [3]. The RISC-V specification mandates only two HPM counters, `cycle` and `instruction`, leaving other events to custom-specific implementation. Therefore, validating the availability and reliability of performance monitoring counters remains necessary for optimizing performance on RVV hardware. In this paper, we make the following contributions:

- We design a suite of assembly microbenchmarks targeting key RVV 1.0 arithmetic and data access operations, and validate RVV-specific hardware performance events in *perf* on RVV hardware.
- We evaluate the enhanced support for RVV autovectorization in GCC15 and LLVM21 in six HPC and ML proxy applications on two RVV1.0 hardware.
- We quantify that predication masks introduce 35% overhead w.r.t unmasked `vsetvl` for tailing elements, and strided vector ld/st instructions incur up to $4\times$ the cost of unit-stride equivalents
- We contribute an RVV backend for a production quantum circuit simulator Qsim using RVV intrinsics and find that GCC 15 outperforms LLVM 21 on this complex, real-world workload.

2 Background

RVV Processors and VLA. The RVV version v1.0 [2] was ratified in 2021 and since then, hardware implementation has gained traction in vendors and undergone active development [13]. RVV supports the VLA programming model, similar to ARM scalable vector extension (SVE). Different from vector length specific (VLS), such as x86 AVX and ARM NEON, which require the vector length known at compilation time, VLA allows the same binary to be portable across RVV hardware with different vector length (VLEN). RVV defines 32 VLEN-bit long vector registers. Recent implementations support VLEN from 128 up to 16384 [13]. Through dynamic register typing, RVV tag data element types and size to vector registers instead of instructions, to enable a fixed ISA supporting growing VLEN. The active vector length (VL) is determined at runtime via the `vsetvl` instruction and depends on the memory allocated to vector registers in hardware implementation, the number of activated vector registers, and the selected element width (SEW). LMUL is a multiplier of values 1/8, 1/4, 1/2, 1, 2, 4, or 8, which groups multiple vector registers into one 'logical' vector so that when LMUL is larger than 1, more elements can be executed in one instruction. Combining these architectural parameters, the theoretical maximum number of elements that can be operated on with a single vector instruction is $VL = \frac{LMUL * VLEN}{SEW}$. RVV also provides the masking mechanism to support predicated vector execution and non-unit stride and indexed gather/scatter operations for irregular loop patterns.

Compiler Support for VLA Model. RVV intrinsics and autovectorization are the primary mechanisms to translate RVV's architectural portability into practical performance portability in applications. Both GCC and LLVM have offered code generation compliant with RVV 1.0 specification. A capable compiler can generate code that automatically adapts to the underlying vector hardware at runtime, removing the need for platform-specific hand tuning required by VLS. Both GCC and LLVM have invested heavily in RVV 1.0 support.

The RVV 1.0 C intrinsics provide developers with direct access to individual vector instructions from the C/C++ source code, including control over SEW, LMUL, VL and masks. Intrinsics thus represent the performance ceiling against which compiler-generated autovectorized outcomes can be measured. For irregular access patterns, hand-written intrinsic code consistently outperforms compiler-generated code in earlier LLVM Clang releases. [1].

Compiler autovectorization transforms scalar loops into vector code automatically, selecting appropriate LMUL values, emitting `vsetvl` instructions [6]. GCC 14 and Clang 19 were the first GNU and LLVM releases with production-quality RVV autovectorization and full C intrinsics. GCC 15 extends this with saturating arithmetic(`vssubu.vv`, `vnclipu.wi`), early-break vectorization (loops with conditional `break` statements), and an improved `-O2` cost model. LLVM's RISC-V backend has received intensive investment since then, in areas including VL tail folding and split register allocation between the RVV and scalar register files. LLVM 21 advances by extending the RISC-V backend to support a rich set of CPU models, including the SpacemiT scheduling model.

3 Methodology

We develop a set of hand-written RVV 1.0 assembly microbenchmarks[1] for assessing key RVV 1.0 instructions and for verifying *perf* performance profiling counters. Leverage those validated *perf* counters, we compare and analyze the performance difference of GCC 15 and Clang 21 in autovectorizing six representative proxy applications from HPC and ML domains on two RVV 1.0 testbeds.

Assembly Microbenchmarks. Since compiler-generated code may conflate micro-architectural behaviors with compiler decisions, we use a set of assembly microbenchmarks that issue precisely controlled sequences of RVV 1.0 instructions with explicit control of operand types and register configurations. We leverage the assembly codes to establish the performance ceiling in terms of raw throughput on the target testbed. Each assembly benchmark consists of a hand-written inner loop repeating a target RVV instruction for 10^8 times. The operands are pre-staged in vector registers to eliminate cold-start effects. Dependency among successive instructions is broken to expose peak issue throughput. If VL<VLEN or mask operations are used, `vta` and `vma`, configured by `vsetvli`, will control the behavior of destination tail elements and inactive masked-off elements, respectively. We opt for the agnostic policy when preserving the tail/masked-off elements in the destination vector register is not required.

The first set of benchmarks targets memory instructions to support common access patterns. Unit-stride loads and stores (`vle`N`.v` / `vse`N`.v vd, (rs1)`) are used for sequential access patterns. Non-uniform access patterns are realized through two options: (1) strided loads and store (`vlse`N`.v` / `vsse`N`.v vd, (rs1)`), and (2) through masked vector loads (`vle`N`.v` / `vse`N`.v vd, (rs1), v0.t`) with an alternating mask pattern `1010...` stored in `v0.t`. Indexed gather and scatter operations (`vluxei`/ `vsuxei`) are not evaluated because they have the same access behavior as `vlse`/`vsse` in the fixed-stride case, but introduce the additional index register and are seldom selected by the compiler auto-vectorization. The second set of benchmarks targets floating-point and integer arithmetic instructions. Assembly codes target vector addition (`vfadd.vv`), multiplication (`vfmul.vv`), fused multiply-add (`vfmacc.vv`), and division (`vfdiv.vv`) in FP16 (`e16`), FP32 (`e32`), and FP64 (`e64`), and their integer counterpart instructions at 8-bit, 16-bit, 32-bit, and 64-bit element widths.

Performance Counter Calibration with Assembly Benchmarks. Unlike mature architectures such as x86 or AArch64, where performance counters are thoroughly documented, the hardware performance counters on RVV hardware through the Linux `perf` subsystem are implementation-defined [3]. Therefore, before using counter-derived metrics for analyzing RVV vectorization efficiency, we calibrate which events are reliable on this specific microarchitecture. In particular, we collect seven `perf` events: total retired instruction, vector instruction,

[1] https://github.com/KTH-ScaLab/rvv-evaluation.

vector ld/st instruction, FP ld/st instruction, and FP instruction. Table 1 summarizes the measurement of these events in 10 assembly benchmarks, where the target instruction sequences are known from assembly codes and their counts are presented in *Ref ins.* Take the `vfadd.vv` benchmark for example, a loop issuing N `vfadd.vv` must retire N vector FP instructions and a small number of extra scalar loop-control instructions. Thus, the total retired instructions as reported in *Retired ins.* should be close to but slightly higher than *Ref ins.*

A counter is deemed reliable if its reported value approximates the reference within a tolerance of 5% across five independent runs. This threshold is chosen to accommodate minor perturbations from interrupt handling and context-switch overhead, a known limitation in RVV performance monitoring [3]. The retired instruction achieves 98.4–99% accuracy on all 10 benchmarks. Similarly, vector ld/st and FP ld/st instructions only show $< 10^{-5}\%$ error. Counters whose reported values are beyond the tolerance are unreliable and thus excluded in the profiling analysis in Sects. 5. Vector instruction, which records all vector instructions, is expected to be close to 0 in `fadd` and `fmadd` benchmark, shows an error of approximately 50%. A similar issue appears in FP instructions `vfadd.vv` and `vmacc.vv`, where the expected value is also near zero, but the real value shows an error of 100%.

Table 1. Perf event statistics for different assembly instructions.

Assembly bench.	Ref #ins.	Retired ins.	Vec. ld ins.	Vec. st ins.	Vec. ins.	FP ld ins.	FP st ins.	FP ins.
flw	1.28×10^{10}	1.31×10^{10}	16	16	55	$\mathbf{1.28 \times 10^{10}}$	696	1.28×10^{10}
lw	1.28×10^{10}	1.31×10^{10}	16	16	53	736	855	1613
vle.vv	1.28×10^{10}	1.31×10^{10}	$\mathbf{1.28 \times 10^{10}}$	17	$\mathbf{1.28 \times 10^{10}}$	662	738	2443
fsw	1.28×10^{10}	1.31×10^{10}	16	16	55	601	$\mathbf{1.28 \times 10^{10}}$	1.28×10^{10}
sw	1.28×10^{10}	1.31×10^{10}	16	16	53	736	855	1613
vse.vv	1.28×10^{10}	1.32×10^{10}	1108	$\mathbf{1.28 \times 10^{10}}$	$\mathbf{1.28 \times 10^{10}}$	662	738	2443
vfadd.vv	1.28×10^{10}	1.30×10^{10}	124	17	$\mathbf{1.28 \times 10^{10}}$	652	726	2.56×10^{10}
vmacc.vv	1.28×10^{10}	1.30×10^{10}	144	17	$\mathbf{1.28 \times 10^{10}}$	632	723	2.56×10^{10}
fadd	1.28×10^{10}	1.30×10^{10}	16	16	6.40×10^{9}	770	856	1.28×10^{10}
fmadd	1.28×10^{10}	1.30×10^{10}	16	16	6.40×10^{9}	770	856	1.28×10^{10}

Application Benchmarks. To evaluate auto-vectorization performance under realistic workload conditions, we select six proxy applications representative of dominant computational and memory patterns in scientific and ML workloads. Stream measures sustained memory bandwidth through simple element-wise kernels. SpMV exhibits irregular memory access via sparse matrix-vector multiplication, where indirect indexing and poor spatial locality make it latency-bound. DGEMM and SGEMM implement double- and single-precision dense matrix multiplication, respectively, whose loop structure is regular and compute-bound, representing ideal cases for autovectorization. YOLOv3 and AlexNet represent CNN inference workloads that mix regular convolution with non-linear activations and pooling. Together, these applications cover diverse patterns and exercise the various data precision characterized in the assembly microbenchmarks. Further, we evaluate a production-level application for simulating quantum computers developed by Google, called QSIM, to investigate the RVV compiler support for both auto-vectorization and RVV intrinsics. For this, we also provide a manually ported QSIM using RVV intrinsics for comparison[2].

Compiler and Testbed Setup. GCC15.1.0 and Clang21.1.1 are used. All compiler configurations are augmented with "-O3/-Ofast -fopenmp". The first version of compilation, *non-vec*, uses flag "-march=rv64gc -fno-tree-vectorize" in GCC15 and "-mllvm -scalable-vectorization=off" in Clang21, to disable the vectorization. The second version, *auto-vec*, uses flag "-march=rv64gcv_zfh_zvfh" in GCC15 and "-march=rv64gcv_zfh_zvfh -mllvm -scalable-vectorization=on" in Clang21. This version enables the autovectorization and uses the default `LMUL` setting in each compiler. In a variant, we also specify `LMUL`, using "-mrvv-max-lmul" in GCC15 and "-mllvm -riscv-v-register-bit-width-lmul" in Clang21.

The testbeds consist of Milk-V Jupiter and BananaPi BPI-F3, both are based on the Spacemit(R) X60 CPU with 8 cores implementing 2 × 256-bit RVV1.0 support, running at 1.6 GHz (BananaPi) and 1.8 GHz (Jupiter) frequency. The memory hierarchy includes 32 KB L1 instruction and 32 KB L1 data caches per core, and a shared 2 × 512 KB L2 caches. The systems are equipped with 16 GB of LPDDR4X (Milk-V Jupiter) and LPDDR4 (BPI-F3) main memory. We use the perf in Linux kernel 6.1.15 and kernel 6.6.63 on the BSC testbed.

4 Understanding Basic RVV Instructions

We start our evaluation with two categories of vector instructions, i.e., data access instructions and arithmetic instructions. For ld/st instructions, we investigate three access patterns, covering sequential, non-unit, and tailing elements. While the sequential ld/st can be achieved with the `vle/vse` instructions, non-unit and tailing elements can be achieved in different ways, as illustrated in Fig. 1. Thus, we design the assembly benchmark for each variant to identify the recommended choice for programmers.

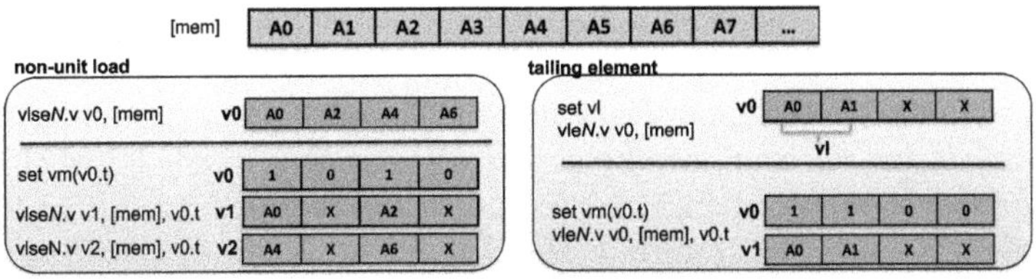

Fig. 1. The diagram of non-unit and tailing vector load.

[2] https://github.com/KTH-ScaLab/qsim_rvv.

For a sequential load pattern, unit-stride load `vle8` achieves the highest throughput of 28.4 Gops/s on Jupiter (25.2 Gops/s on BPI-F3), and its `16|32|64`-bit variants scale the throughput proportionally to 14.2,7.1,3.55 Gops/s, respectively. This throughput approaches the hardware's theoretical peak closely.

For non-unit load patterns, we focus on the stride access patterns. For instance, for stride = 2, `mem[0]`, `mem[2]`, `mem[4]`, $\cdots$, `mem[2*i]` should be accessed, shown in Fig. 1. We design three benchmarks to compare different instructions to achieve the same access pattern. In the first benchmark, vector stride load instruction `vlse` is used to gather elements from memory with a stride of 2 into a vector register. The second benchmark uses united load `vle` to access contiguous elements from `mem` and a mask register (1010) to only enables the corresponding positions of required elements `0, 2, 4,` $\cdots$ in the destination vector register. To load the same number of elements as a single `vlse`, this method requires two masked `vle` instructions. Moreover, the configuration instructions to generate masks are added at initialization stage. All additional overheads are included in the throughput measurements. Finally, the third benchmark adds a reference to a scalar implementation, where scalar loads are used to read elements with a constant stride from memory to scalar registers.

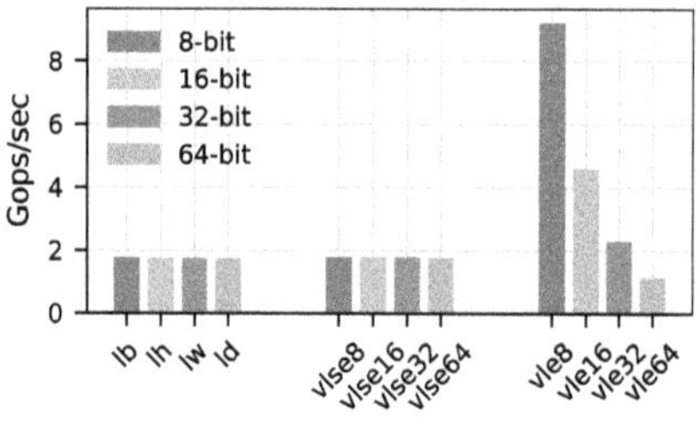

Fig. 2. The peak throughput of non-uniform load instructions on Jupiter.

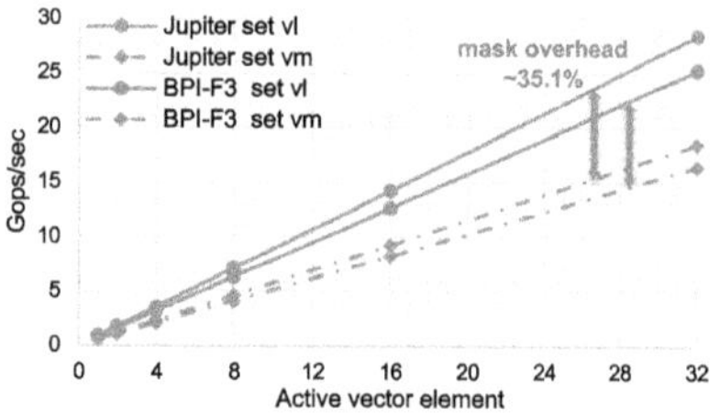

Fig. 3. Compare the performance of tailing elements via setvl and mask operations on BPI-F3 and Jupiter.

Figure 2 presents the results of the three benchmarks for stride loads on Jupiter. The results show `vlse` and scalar are consistent at 1.78 Gops/s in any variants. `vle` with mask achieves the best performance of 9.2 Gops/s at 8-bit precision and the throughput scales up with reduced data precision. In 64-bit data precision, the throughput of the `vle` with mask is 0.65× lower than `vlse`. Store has identical performance as load at all instructions, except `vsse32` only achieving 1.2 Gops/s, thus omitted from Fig. 2.

RVV provides a unique way of handling tail elements by setting its active vector length VL, in addition to the masked predicate operations. To guide the selection between these two options, we design two assembly benchmarks to compare these two ways of handling irregular vector lengths. Shown in Fig. 1(b), we load vl elements with useless tail element in destination vector register, where vl< VLMAX. The first benchmark uses the vset{i}vl{i} instruction to change the VL. The second benchmark achieves the same goal by setting the mask register v0.t. Figure 3 presents the performance comparison of these two methods. Setting vl reaches about 28.4 Gops/s and 25.2 Gops/s at 32 active elements, whereas mask achieves only 18.5 Gops/s and 16.4 Gops/s on Jupiter and BPI-F3, respectively. A constant 35.1% performance loss in masked operations at any active vector elements. The mask configuration introduces negligible cost, as only three additional instructions are required in initialization. The observed overhead mainly comes from vector execution, representing the inefficiency in executing the masked vector instructions in vector units.

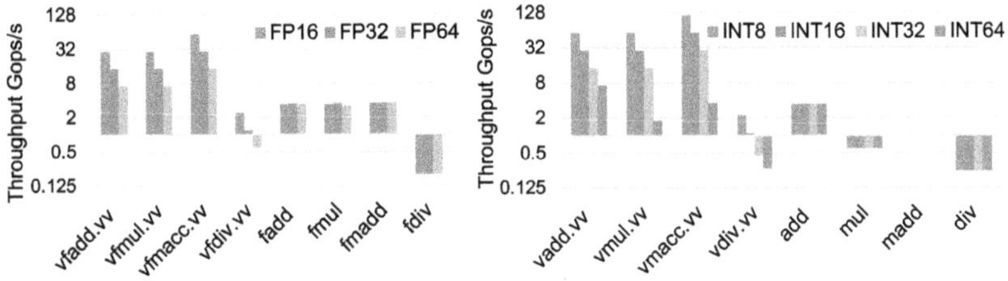

Fig. 4. The peak throughput of selected vector and scalar arithmetic instructions in FP16/32/64 and INT8/16/32/64 on Jupiter.

Evaluating peak arithmetic throughput is essential to establish the performance ceiling and determine whether the 2×256-bit vector pipelines deliver the theoretical throughput across different element sizes. In this evaluation, we focus on floating-point (FP16|32|64) and integer (INT8|16|32|64) operations important for scientific and machine learning workloads. We design each microbenchmark consisting of a tight, dependency-free loop of a single RVV 1.0 instruction, e.g., (v(f)add.vv, v(f)mul.vv, v(f)macc.vv, v(f)div.vv), issued at different LMUL. The benchmark preloads operands into vector registers to eliminate memory latency and repeats 4×32 instructions with v0-v32 as destination per iteration and 10^8 iterations to reach steady operation throughput. We also measure the scalar counterparts ((f)add, (f)mul, (f)madd) identically to provide the baseline for quantifying the vector speedup. Figure 4 summarizes the measured throughput.

The result reveals that the fused multiply-add vector operation achieves the highest throughput of all measured instructions, with FP16 reaching 57.5 Gops/s, 28.7 Gops/s for FP32, and 14.4 Gops/s for FP64, consistent with the expected doubling of element count per vector register as precision is halved. The fused multiply-add vfmacc.vv at FP32 nearly matches the throughput of vfadd.vv and vfmul.vv, demonstrating that the hardware can issue fused operations at full vector throughput. This is favourable for BLAS-like kernels that are dominated by DAXPY and GEMM patterns. The scalar counterparts, fadd, `fmul`, and `fmadd` instructions achieve only 3.1-3.5 Gops/s regardless of precision, indicating 16× throughput advantage of the vector variants for FP16. For INT arithmetic instructions, `vmul.vv` scales proportionally 51.1, 25.6, 12.8 Gops/s with INT8-32 and only 1.6 Gops/s for INT64, while scalar `mul` only achieves a constant at 0.53 Gops/s, even worse than `fmul`, indicating the inefficient scalar multiplier support in ALU. Both `vdiv.vv` and scalar `div` show very low throughput (0.22- 1.97 Gops/s), reflecting the high latency of the divider. This encourages the programmers and compiler optimization to replace division with shift or multiplication if possible.

5 GCC15 and Clang21 Support in Proxy Apps

While the assembly benchmark helps understand performance ceiling, evaluating proxy applications from scientific and ML workloads is necessary to assess whether autovectorization translates into application level speedups. We evaluate six proxy applications compiled with GCC 15 and Clang 21 into non-vectorized and autovectorized binaries. We report all speedups normalized against the non-vectorized GCC 15 baseline. We evaluate performance on both BPI-F3 and Jupiter and observe consistent conclusions across the two platforms. Therefore, unless otherwise stated, the following results presented are from Jupiter.

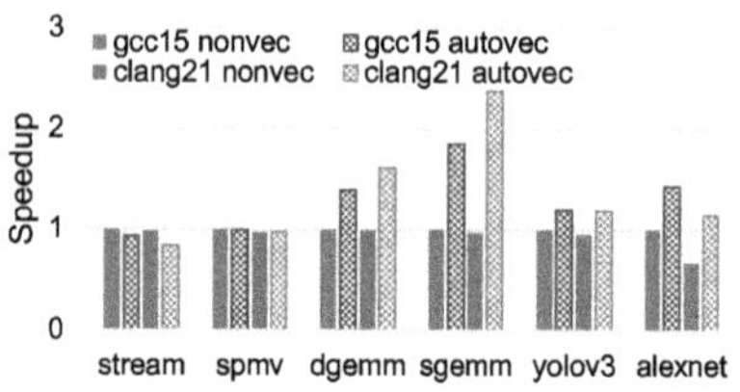

(a) Runtime speedup

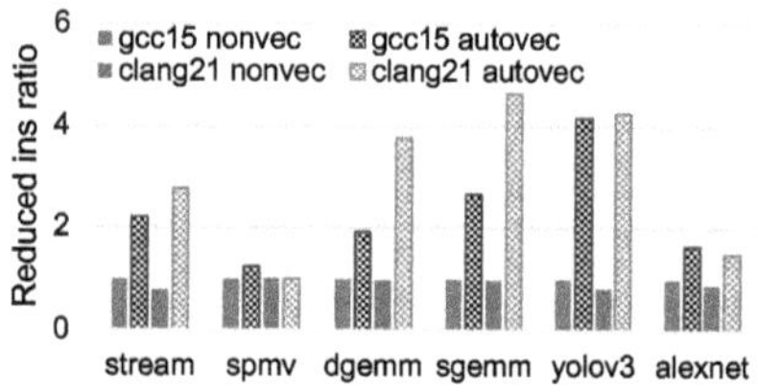

(b) Reduced instruction ratio

Fig. 5. The performance by GCC 15 and Clang 21 autovectorization across six proxy apps on Jupiter, normalized by the GCC 15 nonvec baseline.

Figure 5a presents an overview of achieved speedup by GCC15 and Clang21 on Milk-V Jupiter. The autovectorization benefits are highly application-dependent. Clang 21 achieves more speedup than GCC 15 in sgemm and dgemm, where sgemm gains approximately 2.4× speedup with Clang 21 and around 1.85× with GCC 15. While both compilers can effectively vectorize gemm's regular inner loop, Clang 21 yields better speedup probably because of its SpacemiT X60 specific instruction scheduling model and LMUL selection. In the YOLOv3 and AlexNet benchmarks, GCC 15 achieves better speedup than Clang 21. For instance, AlexNet shows approximately 1.45× speedup with GCC 15 but only 1.2× speedup with Clang 21. Stream and SpMV, two memory-bound benchmarks, show no autovectorization benefit from both compilers. While GCC 15 achieves the same performance as the non-vectorized version, Clang 21 even decreases the performance to be worse than the non-vectorized version in stream, i.e., the Clang 21 vectorized stream is about 20% slower than Clang 21 non-vectorized version. A notable observation from comparing the non-vectorized baseline is that Clang 21 is consistently slightly below 1.0, suggesting that GCC 15 generates better scalar codes. Figure 5b reveals that instruction reduction ratio is a strong predictor of speedup, but the relationship is application-dependent. SGEMM and YOLOv3 show the largest reductions in instructions, with Clang 21 autovec, retiring 4.7× and 4.3× fewer instructions, respectively than the GCC 15 scalar baseline. While the reduction in instructions in SGEMM and YOLOv3 confirms that wide vector operations successfully amortize computation across multiple elements, stream also exhibits a large instruction reduction (2.2× for GCC 15 and 2.8× for Clang 21) but without a corresponding speedup, which is as expected for its memory-bandwidth nature. The DGEMM and AlexNet reductions are moderate, i.e., approximately 2.0× and 1.6× for GCC 15 autovec. They correlate with their moderate speedups.

SpMV shows nearly no instruction reduction under either compiler in RVV. For comparison, we evaluate the same kernel on another VLA architecture, ARM SVE, where a 1.99× instruction reduction by GCC auto-vectorization is observed on a 128-bit SVE Neoverse V2 core. This discrepancy suggests that the automatic vectorization support for RVV remains less mature and requires further improvements in the compiler toolchains.

Comparing the two compilers, Clang 21 consistently reduces more instructions than GCC 15 across all vectorized applications, but this advantage is most effectively converted into speedup when the application is compute-bound. For memory-bound workloads, the instruction savings go largely unrealized as the LPDDR4X channel memory subsystem becomes the bottleneck.

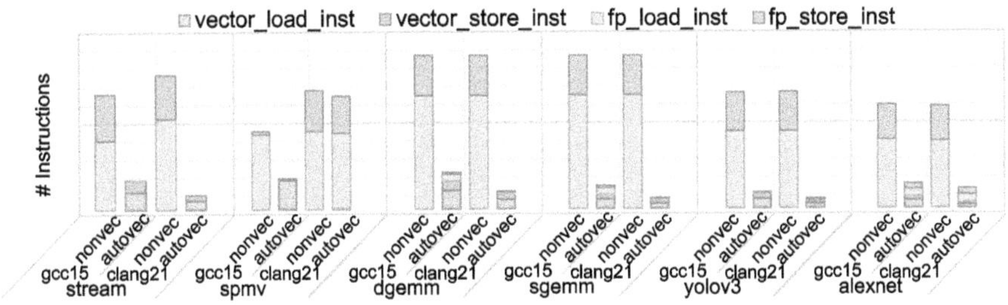

Fig. 6. The breakdown load/store instructions in BPI-F3.

Profiling Analysis. In this section, we leverage those reliable performance counters to decompose the retired instruction mix into vector load and store, floating-point load and store events to compare the instruction breakdown in different compiler-vectorized versions. The profiling result present in Fig. 6 reveals that autovectorization dramatically reduces the total number of memory access instructions across all six applications, with the most reductions occurring in DGEMM and SGEMM.

In SGEMM, the non-vectorized baseline is dominated by a large portion of FP ld/st instructions, which collapse to a small fraction under autovectorization, as each vector load can replace multiple scalar FP loads, indicating both GCC 15 and Clang 21 can effectively recognize such patterns. In Stream, the autovectorized version successfully eliminates most scalar load/store to a small residual of vector load and store instructions. However, although Clang 21 achieves a larger instruction reduction for STREAM, the observed performance is worse, likely caused by unsuitable memory access order after vectorization. As an in-order CPU model, the performance of Spacemit(R) X60 is sensitive to the static instruction scheduling by compilers. SpMV is the notable exception: both non-vectorized and autovectorized versions retain a similar instruction mix with a dominant FP load component and negligible vector memory instructions in Clang 21. Although vector load dominates in GCC 15 and obviously reduces the FP ld/st instructions, the total instructions are almost not reduced according to Fig. 5b. Further analyzing the compiler vectorized report, for the indexing memory access `vector[colIndex[col]]`, Clang 21 can not identify array bounds in SPMV, avoiding any parallelization optimization techniques. GCC 15 can vectorize part of the code using variable-length unit vector load, but additional missed optimizations associated with statement clobbers memory, avoiding further vectorization in fused-multiply-add.

Comparing GCC 15 and Clang 21, Clang 21 without vectorization generates more scalar memory instructions, likely due to differences in scalar loop unrolling and scheduling policies. Under autovectorization, however, Clang 21 reduces its instruction stack more aggressively than GCC 15 in DGEMM, SGEMM, and the ML workloads. The autovectorized Clang 21 bar for SGEMM approaches the smallest total instruction count of any configuration, consistent with its larger instruction-reduction ratio and higher speedup. For YOLOv3 and AlexNet, GCC 15 autovec and Clang 21 autovec produce nearly identical instruction mixes, which explains why their speedups converge for these workloads despite the larger scalar-code difference between the two compilers.

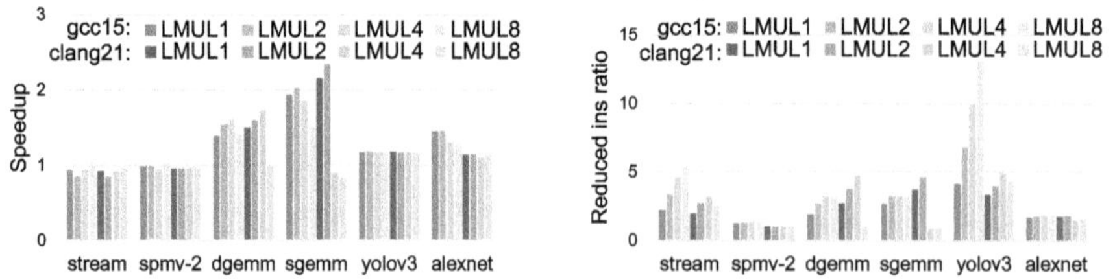

(a) runtime speedup (b) Reduced instruction ratio

Fig. 7. The impact of LMULs selection on Jupiter, normalized by GCC 15 nonvec.

Impact of LMUL in GCC15 and Clang21. Although autovectorization defaults to a compiler-chosen LMUL value, the choice of LMUL is known to affect performance profoundly by trading register count against element throughput per instruction [6,10]. Higher LMUL values process more elements per cycle but reduce the number of available architectural vector registers from 32 (at LMUL = 1) down to just 4 (at LMUL = 8), trading off between instruction-level parallelism and register pressure. Therefore, we sweep LMUL in these proxy applications to determine whether the compiler's default LMUL selection is optimal for each workload and to guide users toward performance-portable choices when targeting the SpacemiT microarchitecture.

Figure 7 shows that the optimal LMUL setting is application- and compiler-dependent for performance. For SGEMM, Clang 21 at LMUL = 2 achieves the highest speedup, approximately 2.35×. However, the performance degrades sharply at LMUL = 8, to around 0.85×, below scalar performance, due to the high risk of register spilling. GCC 15 on SGEMM and DGEMM benefits from increasing LMUL up to $LMUL = 4$, reaching approximately 2.0× and 1.6× respectively. One hypothesis is that the conservative unrolled and vectorized loop strategy in GCC 15 allows it to better tolerate the higher register pressure caused by larger LMUL. Stream and SpMV remain near or below 1.0× across all LMUL values for both compilers. This is expected because their bottlenecks at memory bandwidth and irregular memory access latency, respectively, could be even exacerbated by widening vector register groups. For most applications, selecting LMUL = 1 or LMUL = 2 provides better performance. Larger LMUL values increase register pressure and may trigger register spilling, which significantly degrades performance. This observation suggests that the compiler's default LMUL selection strategy is close to the optimal, and tuning the larger LMUL in GCC 15 can get more performance gains than Clang 21.

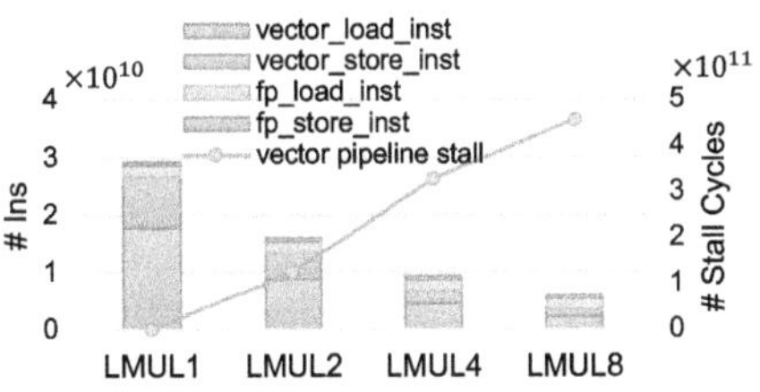

Fig. 8. Yolov3 profiling analysis on the impact of LMULs.

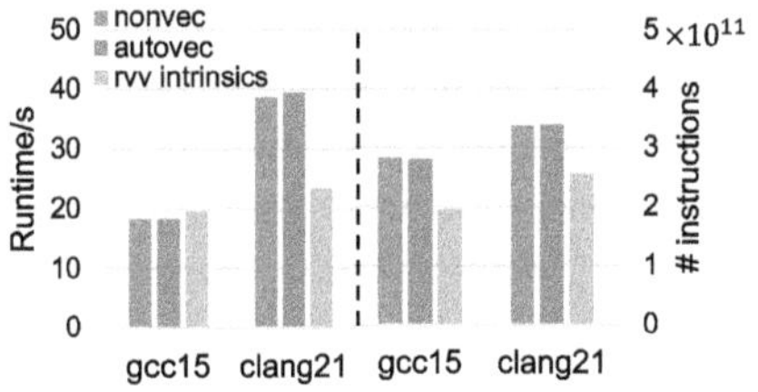

Fig. 9. The comparison of Qsim across 3 versions using 8 cores.

Instruction reduction does not always translate into performance speedup, for example, YOLOv3 by GCC shows a proportional instruction reduction ratio with LMUL (13.1× at LMUL = 8), closer to the theoretical value. However, the speedup of YOLOv3 and AlexNet is insensitive to LMUL for both compilers, remaining 1.2×, implying that their performance is constrained by some other factors other than VL. To understand the execution bottleneck of YOLOv3 in larger LMUL, we further break down its profiling results. We profile the instruction composition to verify the effectiveness of vectorization, shown in Fig. 8. The profiling results show that scalar load/store instructions are largely replaced by vector load/store instructions, indicating that the kernel has been effectively vectorized. However, despite the reduction in total instruction and ld/st instructions, no speedup benefit is observed. To investigate the bottleneck, we profile the vector pipeline behavior. Figure 8 reflects that the vector store pipeline cycles increase linearly with larger LMUL, rising from 2.3×10^8 at LMUL1 to 4.6×10^{11} at LMUL8. This indicates that aggressive vector register grouping increases pressure on the vector pipeline, eventually exceeding its peak throughput. Consequently, instructions must wait for available vector pipeline resources to execute and commit, resulting in pipeline stalls.

6 Qsim Quantum Circuit Simulator

Google's Qsim [14] is a Schrodinger full state-vector simulator, which is highly optimized for FP32 arithmetic. Previous porting on ARM SVE backends achieves high performance [17]. Qsim uses interleaving layout to store the real and imaginary parts of the complex value for each state vector. The interleaved memory access pattern in Qsim makes compiler auto-vectorization difficult. To enable effective vectorization on RISC-V platforms, we port the implementation using RVV intrinsics via VLEN-adaptive memory layout adjustment and fine-grained vectorized loop by setting proper masks in operation to disable useless elements per vector instructions.

The autovec version shows nearly identical runtime to the nonvec version in GCC 15 (18.3 s) and Clang 21 (39.4 s) in Fig. 9 and no instruction reduction is observed, indicating that the compiler fails to effectively vectorize Qsim. The RVV intrinsics implementation significantly reduces the instruction count on both compilers, achieving around 1.4 × reduction ratio with GCC 15 and 1.3 × with Clang 21. However, the runtime with GCC 15 is even slightly longer than nonvec version, whereas Clang 21 achieves 1.6 × speedup compared to its own nonvec version. Despite the improvement from RVV intrinsics in Clang 21, its absolute runtime remains about 1.2 × slower than GCC 15, and the generated instructions is 1.2-1.3 × higher. Qsim results highlight the limitations of current compiler auto-vectorization for applications with complex memory access patterns as Qsim. GCC 15 performs better than Clang 21 in this real-world workload. Manual RVV intrinsics can effectively reduce instruction counts, but the achieved performance is strongly dependent on compiler code generation quality, requiring further optimization and compiler support for VLA architectures.

7 Related Work

Understanding and profiling the performance of RVV processors is critical for both architectural design and software optimization. Previous studies evaluated and analyzed the performance of a set of RISC-V processors equipped with RVV, ranging from high-performance computing [5,10] to machine learning [7,8] workloads. For the feasibility and maturity of compiler support for auto-vectorization, several works evaluated the performance comparison between the GNU and LLVM compiler toolchains for RISC-V RVV across TSVC scientific loops and real applications [6,9]. Adit et al. [1] emphasized a significant performance gap between auto-vectorized and hand-optimized code for the RVV extension by examining LLVM's support for both RVV and VLS-style Intel AVX and ARM Neon. Peccia et al. [12] auto-tuned the vector instructions for AI workloads by integrating the scheduler into the TVM compiler.

Several studies explored the performance on specific RVV hardware via rewriting assembly and intrinsics [4,11]. Since high-end RVV hardware is still emerging, evaluating on the cycle-accurate simulators such as GEM5 [8,15] is used to profile the detailed vector activities and explore the RVV design space. Ref [3,18] compare three instrumentation methods: inline assembly CSR reads, Linux perf, and PAPI and proposed a Linux 6.10 kernel patch to toggle between perf-managed and direct CSR-based counter access.

8 Conclusion

In this work, we first developed assembly benchmarks to calibrate vector-related *perf* events on BananaPi RVV hardware. Evaluating the latest GCC 15 and Clang 21 support for RVV 1.0 auto-vectorization and intrinsics across six scientific and ML applications, we find that GCC 15 produces more stable and efficient code generation than Clang 21. Default LMUL selection proves near-optimal in most cases, though GCC 15 shows greater potential for performance gains through larger LMUL tuning than Clang 21. We further developed an RVV backend for Google's Qsim quantum circuit simulator using RVV intrinsics, where GCC 15 again outperforms LLVM 21 on this complex, real-world workload. Nevertheless, compared to mature compiler support for ARM SVE, both compilers require continued development to fully realize the performance potential of RVV 1.0.

Acknowledgments. This work was performed under the auspices of the U.S. Department of Energy by Lawrence Livermore National Laboratory under Contract DE-AC52-07NA27344 under LDRD Project 24-ERD-047. This research is supported by the European Commission under the Horizon project HIGHER (101189612). This research is supported by the RISC-V ExCALIBUR project at EPCC.

Disclosure of Interests. The authors have no competing interests to declare that are relevant to the content of this article.

References

1. Adit, N., Sampson, A.: Performance left on the table: an evaluation of compiler autovectorization for RISC-V. IEEE Micro **42**(5), 41–48 (2022)

2. Asanovic., K.: https://github.com/riscv/riscv-v-spec/releases/tag/v1.0 (2021)
3. Banchelli, F.: RISC-V in HPC: a look into tools for performance monitoring. In: International Conference on High Performance Computing, pp. 562–575 (2025)
4. Bernstein, O.: RISC-V Vector benchmark. https://github.com/camel-cdr/rvv-bench
5. Brown, N.: Is RISC-V ready for HPC prime-time: evaluating the 64-core sophon SG2042 RISC-V CPU. In: Proceedings of the SC'23 Workshops, pp. 1566–1574 (2023)
6. Carpentieri: A performance analysis of autovectorization on RVV RISC-V boards. In: Proceedings of the PDP, pp. 129–136 (2025)
7. Garcia, A.M.: Inference performance of large language models on a 64-core RISC-V CPU with silicon-enabled vectors. Future Gener. Comput. Syst. 108242 (2025)
8. Gupta, S.R.: Accelerating CNN inference on long vector architectures via co-design. In: 2023 IEEE International Parallel and Distributed Processing Symposium, pp. 145–155. IEEE (2023)
9. Lai, H.M.: RISC-V vectorization coverage for HPC: a TSVC-based analysis. In: Proceedings of the SC'25 Workshops, pp. 1676–1683 (2025)
10. Lee, J.K.: Test-driving RISC-V vector hardware for HPC. In: Bienz, A., Weiland, M., Baboulin, M., Kruse, C. (eds.) International Conference on High Performance Computing, pp. 419–432. Springer, Cham (2023). https://doi.org/10.1007/978-3-031-40843-4_31
11. Lin, J.K.: Rewriting and optimizing vector length agnostic intrinsics from arm SVE to RVV. In: Proceedings of the 53rd ICPP Workshops, pp. 38–47 (2024)
12. Peccia, F.N., Haxel, F., Bringmann, O.: Tensor program optimization for the RISC-V vector extension using probabilistic programs. In: 2025 IEEE/ACM International Conference On Computer Aided Design (ICCAD), pp. 1–9. IEEE (2025)
13. Perotti, M., et al.: A "new ara" for vector computing: an open source highly efficient RISC-V V 1.0 vector processor design. In: ASAP. IEEE (2022)
14. Quantum AI team: QSIM (2025). https://doi.org/10.5281/zenodo.4067237
15. Ramírez, C., et al.: A RISC-V simulator and benchmark suite for designing and evaluating vector architectures. TACO **17**(4), 1–30 (2020)
16. Shi, R., Schieffer, G., Gokhale, M., Lin, P.H., Patel, H., Peng, I. : ARM SVE unleashed: performance and insights across HPC applications on nvidia grace. In: Nagel, W.E., Goehringer, D., Diniz, P.C. (eds.) European Conference on Parallel Processing, pp. 33–47. Springer, Cham (2025). https://doi.org/10.1007/978-3-031-99857-7_3
17. Shi, R., et al.: High-performance vector-length agnostic quantum circuit simulations on arm processors. In: International Parallel and Distributed Processing Symposium. IEEE (2026)
18. Vizcaino, P., et al.: Designing a QEMU plugin to profile multicore long vector RISC-V architectures: rave. Future Gener. Comput. Syst. 108100 (2025)

Performance Portable BLAS3 Micro-Kernel Generator

Stepan Nassyr[1(✉)], Daniel Seibel[1], Prateek Chawla[1], Jayesh Badwaik[1], Andreas Herten[1], and Dirk Pleiter[2]

[1] Jülich Supercomputing Centre - Forschungszentrum Jülich GmbH, Jülich, Germany
s.nassyr@fz-juelich.de

[2] Bernoulli Institute, University of Groningen, Groningen, The Netherlands

Abstract. Dense matrix operations are among the few numerical tasks where modern processor architectures can achieve throughput near the peak of floating-point operations. Implementations of commonly utilized mathematical library functions such as the general matrix multiply function (GEMM) necessitate advanced optimization adhering to recognized implementation strategies, like hierarchical building blocks with performance-critical microkernels in the lowest layer. The most difficult aspect continues to be this microkernel. To achieve optimal performance on a specific processor solution, the microkernel must be meticulously optimized, considering various aspects of the processor's micro-architecture and L1 data cache design. Due to the necessity for strict control over the used instructions and their scheduling, it remains prevalent to depend on implementations of these microkernels crafted in assembly language.

Currently, an increasingly diverse set of processor solutions is available in the market. This renders the conventional method of manually-crafted micro-kernels progressively less viable. To address this limitation, we propose an assembly generator utilizing suitable abstractions to enable the generation of high-performance code for various processor solutions across diverse instruction set architectures. The software framework facilitates the semi-automatic generation of microkernels that can be incorporated into existing libraries, like the BLAS implementation BLIS. This paper presents results for the GEMM function of BLIS on a diverse array of processors that support x86, ARM, and RISC-V SIMD and vector instruction sets. The results indicate that the throughput attained is comparable to, and in certain instances surpasses, the performance of open-source or vendor-supplied BLAS libraries.

Keywords: Assembly generator · dense matrix-matrix multiplication · SIMD/vector instructions · processor microarchitectures · x86/Arm/RISC-V ISA

1 Introduction

Despite advancements in compiler technologies and enhanced processor microarchitectures, the optimal utilization of hardware capabilities for diverse mathe-

M. Torquati et al. (Eds.): Euro-Par 2026, LNCS 16781, pp. 121–135, 2027.
https://doi.org/10.1007/978-3-032-35248-4_9

matical functions remains challenging. This observation specifically pertains to the general matrix multiply (GEMM) function, which is a performance-critical operation in numerous machine-learning applications. A recognized method exists for achieving high-performance implementations of matrix-matrix multiplications on a single processor core, grounded in architectural design patterns prevalent in virtually all contemporary processor architectures [1]. This methodology is exemplified by various open-source implementations of libraries featuring linear algebra functions, such as OpenBLAS or BLIS[1] [2]. It anticipates several nested loops, with the innermost loop executing a microkernel. To achieve near-optimal performance, this microkernel must be carefully tailored to specific hardware architectures. In practice, as tight control over code generation is required, the microkernel is often implemented in assembly, which means performance depends on non-negligible efforts of a skilled software developer.

Despite the established nature of this approach, the expanding diversity of Instruction Set Architectures (ISAs), along with numerous processor architectures, renders it progressively less economical. In the area of high-performance computing (HPC), processors from Intel and AMD based on the x86 ISA are dominating, according to recent editions of the TOP500 list[2]. However, this is challenged by systems with Arm-based processors. Moreover, various efforts towards high-performance processors based on RISC-V ISA are pursued. Diversity is amplified by implementation details of individual processor designs, by various SIMD and vector instruction extensions, and now also matrix extensions such as Arm's Scalable Matrix Extension (SME) are emerging.

To address this challenge, we propose a novel multi-stage methodology for generating adaptable and high-performance microkernels. To enable performance portability, the proposed method is based on abstractions suitable for expressing the operations that need to be performed by the microkernel. This approach provides the necessary flexibility to adapt to different processor microarchitectures and generate highly efficient code for different ISAs.

We implemented our methodology in a tool called `ukrgen` for generating microkernels. Moreover, we developed the tool `blisgen` to generate a new configuration for the BLIS library and populate it with one of the generated microkernel. To test the tools, customised versions of the BLIS library have been created for a diversity of processors supporting different ISAs including x86, Arm, and RISC-V. The choice of processors includes both high-end solutions and solutions with a small power envelope targeting an embedded processor market.

In this paper, we focus on the performance evaluation of the microkernel itself using a custom benchmark. Utilizing this benchmark, we can demonstrate nearly equivalent performance in comparison to vendor-provided microkernels, where such options are available. Where vendors do not provide microkernels, those generated using `ukrgen` consistently show superior performance compared to available implementations.

With this paper, we make the following contributions:

---

[1] https://github.com/flame/blis.

[2] https://top500.org/.

1. A novel methodology for producing microkernels for general matrix multiplication and analogous implementations in a performance-portable manner is presented.
2. This method is implemented in the code generator `ukrgen` that supports various ISAs including different SIMD and vector instruction extensions.
3. A collection of performance measurements for a set of vastly different processors is shown, supporting our claim of performance portability.

This paper is organised as follows: After presenting related work in Sect. 2, we document details of the proposed methodology in Sect. 3. Implementation details are presented in Sect. 4. Next, we document our test setup and performance results in Sect. 5. Finally, the content of the paper is summarised in Sect. 6, which also comprises our conclusions.

2 Related Work

The quest for efficient implementations of general matrix multiply (GEMM) functions has been addressed in numerous publications. Today, many of them are based on the implementation structure described in [1]. While this is a good basis for efficient implementations, careful tuning for different processor microarchitectures remains necessary. Performance portability, therefore, remains an open challenge. In the past, it has been proposed to address this challenge through auto-tuning techniques [3] (a more recent example is the TVM framework [4]). Others argued that it is more efficient using performance models to tune implementation parameters for specific processor architectures [5]. But this argument only holds for large matrices.

For the specific challenge of generating microkernels, various efforts have been made to ease code generation. One approach is to design or leverage domain-specific languages like Exo 2, which was used for generating GEMM microkernels [6]. An earlier version of the code generator presented in this work, called `asmgen-gemm`, was designed for being able to generate microkernels for a very large variety of microarchitecture models for simulations using gem5 [7].

There exists another motivation for automatising generation of the code of GEMM implementations. For small and/or skewed matrices, the optimal code selection also becomes problem size dependent. Since it is not efficient to create libraries with many different implementations of the GEMMM function, just-in-time (JIT) compilation techniques started to be used. LIBXSMM is an early example for this approach [8], which, however, does support only a single ISA. This limitation also concerns autoGEMM [9], which is, however, an interesting approach as it combines a tiling scheme similar to this work, autotuning techniques based on TVM, and automatised code generation for Arm architectures.

3 Methodology

In this section, we present our methodology behind the abstractions in our `ukrgen` generator, as well as our approach to benchmarking and optimization.

3.1 Abstraction Methodology

Set of Tile Operations. The GEMM function implements the following computational task:

$$C \leftarrow \alpha \cdot A \cdot B + \beta \cdot C, \tag{1}$$

where A, B, and C are matrices of size $M \times K$, $K \times N$, and $M \times N$, respectively. α and β are scalars.

A GEMM microkernel implements the same operation on a partial $M_r \times N_r$ tile of the C matrix, multiplying K_r micropanels from A and B and accumulating the results. Typically it's implemented in such a way that it contains a loop over a larger block size K_C with K_r as the unroll factor.

The computational task can be decomposed by decomposing the matrices into 2-dimensional tiles. Based on this decomposition, we introduce the *Set of Tile Operations* (STO) as an abstraction such that we can express the computational task in terms of STOs. The two dimensions of the tiles have a dimension type, which can be fixed or variable and a size. The tiles can contain sub-tiles, in which case the dimension sizes indicate how many subtiles are repeated in the tile in each dimension. A tile with sub-tiles represents a microkernel structure, its' dimension sizes multiplied with the dimension sizes of the subtiles determine the M_r, N_r and K_r dimensions. A tile without sub-tiles represents a *data atom* (for example, a register). An operation is a *computational atom* (for example, an instruction) of the target architecture. A microkernel for a computational problem is represented by an STO. A program that takes an operation and a tile with sub-tiles as an input to generate an STO is called a generator. An STO comprises L tiles, L 2-dimensional indices, L subindices, and an operation.

For any processors architectures, we can derive both the possible data atoms and computational atoms from the supported ISA by identifying the relevant instructions and what kind of registers those instructions operate on. For example a vector register in RVV or SVE can be represented with a tile that has one fixed dimension with size 1 and one variable dimension with size 1 (since those ISAs are vector-length-agnostic, while an AVX512 register containing double-precision floating point elements would be a tile with one fixed dimension of size 1 and one fixed dimension of size 8. At this point, we limit ourselves to 4 possible operations: fused-multiply-add, fused-dot-product-add, fused-outer-product-add and fused-matrix-multiply-add. For matrix multiplications, all 4 operations can represent a partial matrix multiplication. Figure 1 shows a visual representation of each operation in the context of a larger matrix multiplication.

For a GEMM kernel, 3 STOs are required: One STO for the matrix-multiplication and accumulation and two STOs for the scalar multiplications with α and β together with the final accumulation. Parameters of the GEMM STO generator determine the shape and size of the microkernel (M_r and N_r), as well as the unroll factor (K_r).

Load-Store CPU Execution Model. Lowering the STO down to actual code requires an execution model. As we target conventional processor architecture,

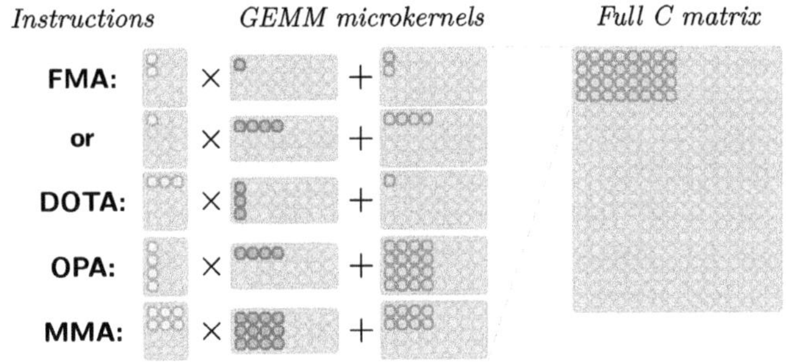

Fig. 1. Visual representation of microkernels made with 4 common arithmetic operations encoded as instructions in modern SIMD and vector ISAs.

we defined a *Load-Store CPU* (LSC) execution. The model uses a small set of virtual instructions, which can be interpreted as an intermediate representation (IR). The STOs are mapped onto multiple blocks of LSC instructions. The structure of a resulting GEMM kernel is shown in Fig. 2.

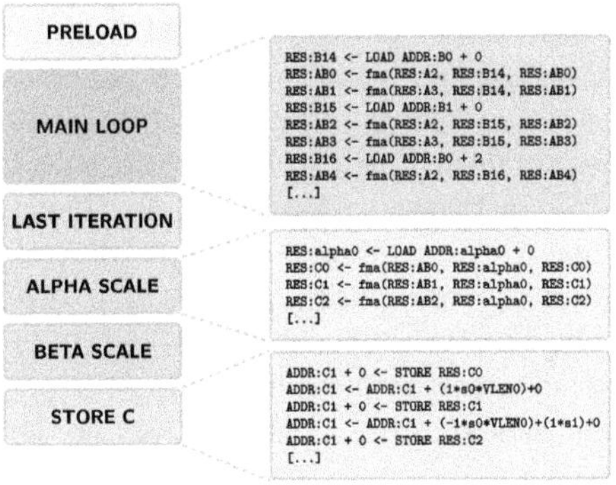

Fig. 2. LSC blocks for a GEMM kernel

For each operation for an STO, the model allocates virtual data registers for the components its tiles are mapped to and resolves the required data into them. This involves mapping the 2-dimensional tile indices to a memory address space and generating load instructions. To support vector-length-agnostic operations and allow for arbitrary row and column strides, the offset data structure in the LSC IR contains multiples of products between vector lengths and strides – the complete offset being the sum of those – this enables resolution of the offsets at runtime. When the data is resolved, a transformation instruction is inserted, corresponding to the operation in the STO.

Load and store instructions operate on virtual address registers. As the model progresses through the STO to create an LSC block, it keeps an internal state of its registers. The necessary data for an operation is resolved in a way that results in the required load being inserted right before the transformation instruction. In case a load instruction using the address register and offset is not valid, an addition instruction is inserted to advance the address register by the offset. To enable preloading, a trick is employed by mapping the STO twice and keeping only the specified number of load instruction for the preload LSC block and using the register state after those instructions for the second mapping, resulting in the loads to not be inserted.

Since the model tracks the register state, the alpha-scale LSC block uses the data registers containing the accumulated tile without inserting load instructions. The beta-scale LSC block then loads the values for C, scales them with beta and adds the accumulated tile to them. Finally, a block of store instructions for the C tile is generated.

The model is parameterized, enabling control over the number of data and address registers to use per component and how many registers to preload.

ISA Abstraction. The abstraction over different ISAs is handled by the `asmgen` library. The library implements a limited set of assembly instructions for multiple ISAs. It currently supports AVX2+FMA (128,256 bit), AVX512, NEON, SVE, SME, RVV 0.7.1 and RVV 1.0 SIMD ISAs, as well as a subset of instructions from their respective base ISAs (x86_64, AArch64, RISCV64) that is necessary for the kernel generation. `ukrgen` includes logic to populate the valid parameter space and to choose a code path based on which instructions are available in `asmgen` for an ISA, i.e. emulating strided loads with lane-loads in NEON.

Generating assembler instructions from the LSC IR happens in two stages – a *pre-specialization stage* that modifies the IR to reflect the actual instructions available in the ISA and the *specialization stage* that directly transforms LSC instructions to assembly. The two steps are kept separate to allow for an optional software re-scheduling and register renaming during the pre-specialization stage. All virtual registers are allocated from ISA registers at the specialization stage.

3.2 Benchmarking Methodology

To evaluate how the generated microkernels perform, we perform two types of benchmarks – a full GEMM benchmark comparing the BLIS library populated with `ukrgen`-generated GEMM microkernels using the BLIS-internal GEMM benchmark, which keeps the highest per-size performance out of 3 iterations, and a standalone microkernel benchmark, which executes the microkernel with varying K_C on one core over a an amount of bytes corresponding to $10 \times K_{C,max}$ for statistical significance, with the actual memory region truncated to the investigated K_C. The second benchmark allows judging the microkernel performance independently of the rest of the BLIS library, as full optimization usually also involves packing kernels and block size optimization, which is not handled by `ukrgen`.

We measure the elapsed time using the C++ `std::chrono` library. To ensure the accuracy of the results, we always pin the threads to the same cores with either OpenMP (full GEMM benchmark) or `numactl` (standalone microkernel benchmark). Additionally, we ensure enough iterations are performed between measurements to minimize measurement overhead and perform multiple measurements to gather statistical data for each benchmark case. We also measure `perf_event` performance counters for cycle counts and cache misses to verify our findings and ensure the standalone benchmark is set up correctly to keep the microkernel in different cache levels.

3.3 Optimization Methodology

Our optimization strategy is deeply intertwined with the parameterization of the generator as the parameters that enable control over the code structure are chosen based on architecture knowledge, performance models, observations from micro-benchmarking and expert insight. It is important to note that `ukrgen` itself does not automate microkernel optimization, instead it allows optimization of the microkernel through its parameters.

We have used both performance models and prior experience with the systems to select the parameter values. When the source of a known high-performing microkernel was available or its structure known, we generated a kernel with the parameters chosen to match that kernel as closely as possible, while also additionally benchmarking other configurations for comparison.

Apart from the kernel configuration itself, an important part of ensuring a high-performing blocked GEMM, as it is implemented in BLIS, is the optimization of block sizes K_C, M_C and N_C to efficiently exploit the memory/cache hierarchy. A performance model for choosing the block sizes has been introduced in [5]. Additionally, to block sizes calculated using this performance model, we also performed a simple scan of the 3-dimensional parameters space and chose the best performing combination.

4 Implementation

In this section, we present selected details of the implementation of the code generator (`ukrgen`) and the tool for integrating the generated microkernels into the BLIS framework (`blisgen`)

STO. At the level of STOs, components are assigned to tiles. For GEMM, these are `A`, `B`, `C`, `alpha` and `beta`, which correspond to microtiles/-panels form matrices A, B, C and the scalars α, β, respectively. An additional component, `AB`, is used as accumulator tile for multiplying A and B.

LSC Execution Model. When transforming the STOs into LSC blocks, the model allocates virtual registers per-component. The number of registers to allocate for input and accumulator components, and the number of registers to preload data for input components is user-configurable. The register type to use (vector/tile/scalar) is automatically determined from the tile shape in the STO. Registers are represented by their component name and an index, i.e. `A0`, `B2`, `AB14`, etc.

Minimize-Register-Use Scheduler. In the specialization stage, the unlimited number of virtual registers are mapped onto the actually available ISA registers. Though not directly affecting performance, without register reuse, the possible microkernel sizes are limited. To reduce the number of required architected registers, we implemented a *Minimize-Register-Use (MRU) scheduler*, which modifies the LSC IR before the specialization stage and comprises the following steps:

- Dependent instructions are moved as close together as possible to reduce register lifetime.
- The LSC IR blocks are analysed to identify registers that are not being reused such that they could be reallocated.
- This analysis is also performed throughout the to-reschedule block to track which registers become free.
- Virtual registers that would be newly allocated in the LSC IR are replaced with reallocated previously used free registers.

Dependency Scheduler. On some architectures, it can be observed that proper reordering of instructions can have a significant performance impact. We implemented a simple instruction scheduler that can enforce a certain distance between dependent instructions by placing independent instructions between them. The distance is configurable and can be specified differently depending on the type of instruction dependence (e.g., read-after-write), register, or instruction.

Full GEMM. We implemented the tool `blisgen` that is capable of creating a custom BLIS source populated with `ukrgen`-generated kernels and a new configuration that uses them. The tool takes the original BLIS source code and the configurations files for the single precision (SGEMM) and double-precision version (DGEMM) of the GEMM kernels. This source can then be compiled in a typical BLIS fashion. This enables evaluation of the generated kernels in a full framework.

Packing. Currently, `ukrgen` doesn't yet generate packing kernels, but we describe some aspects of the in-the-works implementation: Specific packing kernels for each GEMM microkernel are not required. Packing uses chunk size ($cdim$), chunk count (n), and memory strides ($inca$, lda, ldp). Chunks are "contiguous-vectorized" when $cdim = N \times VLEN$, and "transpose-vectorized" (lda as stride and $inca$ as leading dimension) along n otherwise (masked contiguous vectorization is an alternative). We intend to pre-generate accelerated kernels for $cdim \in \{1 \ldots N_c\} \times VLEN$ and $cdim \in \{1 \ldots N_t\}$, dispatching via a wrapper. For an $m_r \times n_r$ GEMM microkernel, packing invocations typically use $cdim \in \{m_r, n_r\}$, and would hit these fast code paths provided the dimensions do not exceed the N_c or N_t thresholds.

5 Evaluation

This section comprises documentation and analysis of the performance results. Table 1 shows the platforms we evaluated generated kernels on and their architectural details.

Table 1. Processor Architecture and Performance Comparison

Processor	Arch.	#Cores	SIMD ISA	#SIMD	Peak FP64/core	Freq.	ROB	Frontend
Xeon 8168	Skylake-SP	24	AVX-512	2 (512b)	86.4 GFLOP/s	2.7 GHz	224	4-way OoO
Ryzen 9950X	Zen5	16	AVX-512	2 (512b)	182.4 GFLOP/s	4.3 GHz	448	2 × 4-way OoO
Kunpeng 920	TaiShan v110	64	NEON	2 (128b)	10.4 GFLOP/s	2.6 GHz	128	4-way OoO
NVIDIA Grace	Neoverse V2	72	NEON/SVE2	4 (128b)	39.2 GFLOP/s	3.2 GHz	320	8-way OoO
SpacemiT K1	X60	8	RVV 1.0	1 (256b)	12.8 GFLOP/s	1.6 GHz	0	2-way iO
BCM2837	Cortex-A53	4	NEON	1 (128b)	4.8 GFLOP/s	1.2 GHz	0	2-way iO

Some details aren't easily conveyed through the table, e.g. the TaiShan v110 can do 2 FP32 FMAs per cycle, but only 1 FP64 FMA and on the SpacemiT K1, vector loads/stores share resources with vector FMAs, limiting peak performance.

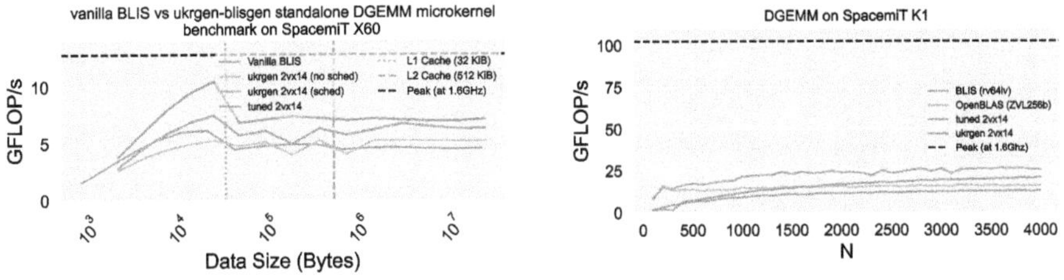

(a) Standalone (b) Full DGEMM (8c)

Fig. 3. Standalone and full DGEMM on SpacemiT K1 (RVV 1.0).

SpacemiT does not offer an optimized BLAS library for the K1. However, a tuned BLIS version has been earlier implemented. The GEMM microkernel in this version is a 2vx14 kernel and has been tuned both by hand and with the help of a scheduling tool. Figure 3a shows the results of the standalone microkernel benchmark for the tuned version, the upstream BLIS version, which uses a 4vx4 microkernel, and two versions of the 2vx14 microkernel generated by `ukrgen` – one without and one with scheduling enabled.

The first notable observation is that the naively expected peak performance of 12.8 GFLOP/s is not reached. This is due to the processor architecture where vector load instructions share resources with vector FMA instructions. Taking this into account, the actual theoretical peak performance for a 2vx14 kernel is $(8\,\text{FLOP/cycle}) \cdot (28/(28+2)) \cdot (1.6\,\text{GHz}) = 11.95\,\text{GFLOP/s}$ and for a 4vx4 microkernel it is $(8\,\text{FLOP/cycle}) \cdot (16/(16+4)) \cdot (1.6\,\text{GHz}) = 10.24\,\text{GFLOP/s}$. The K1 is also an in-order architecture, which explains performance differences between 3 kernels with essentially the same instructions. The `ukrgen` microkernel with scheduling disabled performs the loads of the data into vector registers immediately before they are used, which causes the VFPU pipelines to stall until the data becomes available. The microkernel scheduling enabled improves the performance by guaranteeing a certain number of independent instructions to be issued in between. The earlier developed tuned microkernel has been optimized using a genetic algorithm that slightly mutated the instruction scheduling and kept the best performing kernels for multiple hundreds of thousands of generations. It indicates that the scheduler performance model that works with only distances between dependencies cannot fully exploit the performance potential of the K1. This leaves room for better performing scheduling algorithms.

Figure 3b shows the GEMM benchmark on the SpacemiT K1. Despite tuning efforts, no implementation we tested is able to come close to the peak performance, as the chips' cache design is unable to provide the necessary bandwidth to the compute units. We can, however, observe that our `ukrgen` generated BLIS version outperforms the upstream RVV BLIS configuration and beats OpenBLAS for larger matrix sizes.

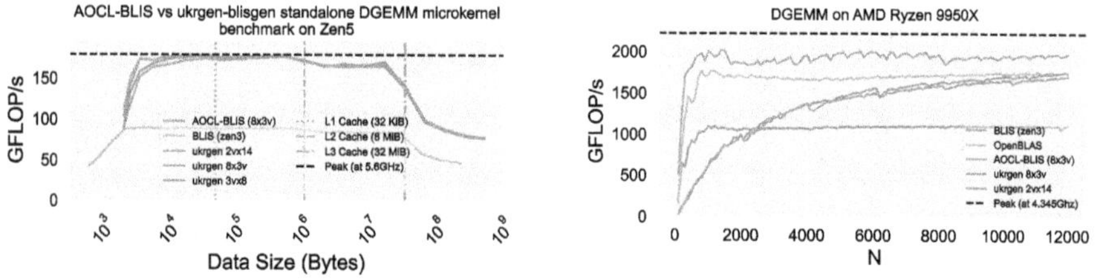

(a) Standalone (b) Full DGEMM (16c)

Fig. 4. Standalone and full DGEMM on Ryzen 9950X (AVX-512).

Standalone microkernel benchmarks for Zen5 in Fig. 4a show that the `ukrgen`-generated microkernels behave nearly identical to the AOCL-BLIS microkernel from AMD. It also indicates that all kernels are capable of achieving close-to-peak performance. It is beneficial when a microkernel can reach the peak performance already at smaller data sizes, since block sizes are typically chosen to keep the execution of the microkernel in L1D Cache. Moreover, enhanced performance at reduced matrix sizes is anticipated. In Zen5, the AOCL-BLIS 8×3v and the ukrgen 2vx14 microkernels exhibit marginally superior performance for small data sizes. Upstream BLIS configurations for AMD processors are exclusively available for Zen3 and are based on AVX2 kernels. Using AVX2 instructions, it is not possible to achieve a similarly high performance as for AVX512. In the Full GEMM benchmark illustrated in Fig. 4b, we demonstrate that the performance of our ukrgen-based BLIS library progressively improves with increasing problem size, whereas OpenBLAS, AOCL-BLIS, and upstream BLIS swiftly attain a performance plateau. The standalone benchmark demonstrates that the microkernels attain near-peak performance, suggesting that overall performance is constrained by insufficient memory/cache access optimization, as ukrgen is not currently generating packed microkernels or prefetch instructions.

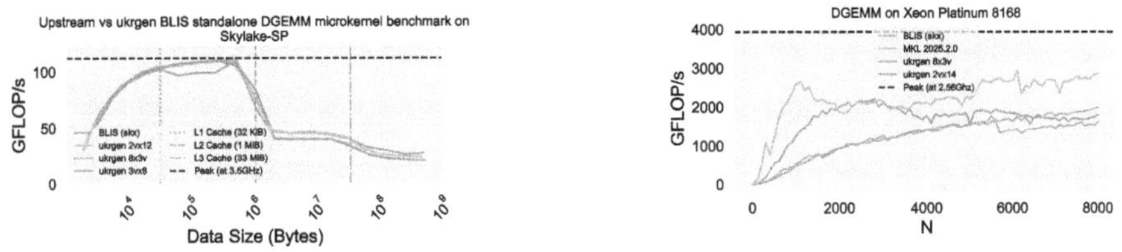

(a) Standalone (b) Full DGEMM (48c)

Fig. 5. Standalone and full DGEMM on Xeon Platinum 8168 (AVX-512).

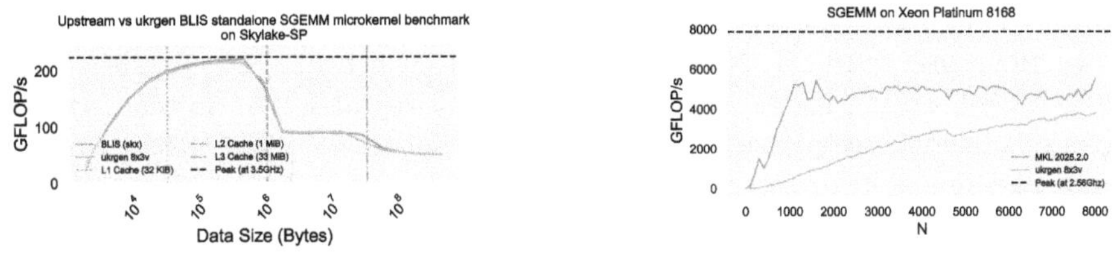

(a) Standalone (b) Full SGEMM (48c)

Fig. 6. Standalone and full SGEMM on Xeon Platinum 8168 (AVX-512).

Upstream BLIS has a configuration skx for Skylake-SP processors, which uses a 2vx14 microkernel for DGEMM, which leverages software prefetching techniques. In Fig. 5a we compare standalone benchmarks of ukrgen-generated microkernels and the skx microkernel. We observe very similar performance behaviour for all tested microkernels. The skx microkernel shows a dip when performing out of the L2 cache, as the software prefetch instructions clash with the standalone benchmark setup. Figure 5b shows full GEMM benchmarks results of two ukrgen configurations in comparison with the MKL library, as well as BLIS using the **skx** configuration. We observe again a slow but steady climb of performance with problem size for the generated kernels. BLIS **skx** shows an area of maximum performance around $N = 2500$, performing en-par with MKL, as the prefetch strategy becomes favourable in this region. The **ukrgen** microkernel with the same structure as the **skx** version shows a performance drop above $N = 5500$, which does not occur with the 8×3v variant, which was our best performer. **ukrgen** microkernels again show good standalone performance and a slow climb with full problem size due to the lack of packing and prefetching. We chose the Xeon system to showcase in Fig. 6 that the FP32 performance behaviour of **ukrgen** microkernels doesn't differ significantly from FP64.

(a) Standalone (b) Full DGEMM (128c)

Fig. 7. Standalone and full DGEMM on Kunpeng920 (NEON).

Figure 7a shows standalone benchmarks on the Kunpeng 920 processor. We have discovered that the BLIS `firestorm` configuration, originally targeting Apple Silicon chips, performs outstandingly well on this architecture, reaching over 99.5% of peak. The code of this microkernel makes heavy use of lane-FMA instructions like `fmla v0.2d, v1.2d, v2.d[0]`, which **ukrgen** currently cannot generate, opting for broadcast-loads and full vector-FMAs instead. It also includes packing and software prefetching. This causes more load instructions to be emitted and is the likely cause of the generated kernels falling behind, reaching only up to 79.3%. For the full GEMM benchmark on 2 sockets (128 cores), as seen in Fig. 7b, the `firestorm` configuration was able to reach 90.5% efficiency after re-tuning blocksizes for this processor Arm's library ArmPL does not optimize for this processor and is outperformed both by the modified `firestorm` configuration and our **ukrgen**-generated BLIS, reaching only 46.6% of peak, while our best generated kernel achieves 66.7%.

Standalone benchmarks for NVIDIA Grace are shown in Fig. 8a. Since the SVE units on the processor were configured for 128 bit, we tested both NEON and SVE microkernels. The upstream `firestorm` microkernel again shows good performance. Our equivalent 8×3v NEON microkernel is unable to achieve the same performance, highlighting the importance of lane-fmas and prefetching on this architecture. The SVE version of the generated 8×3v microkernel however was our best performer. The upstream and **ukrgen** 2vx10 kernels show the same performance behaviour. For the Full GEMM benchmarks in Fig. 8b we continue

(a) Standalone

(b) Full DGEMM (72c)

Fig. 8. Standalone and full DGEMM on NVIDIA Grace (NEON/SVE).

to observe the gradual climb with problem size for **ukrgen** BLIS, while libraries with packing microkernels and prefetching reach their peak quickly (Fig. 9).

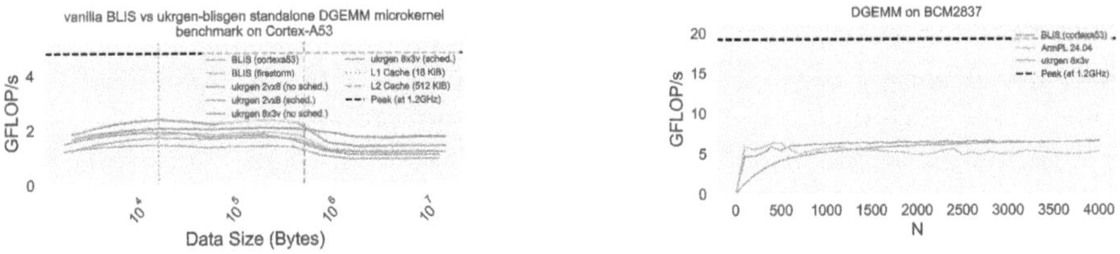

(a) Standalone

(b) Full DGEMM (4c)

Fig. 9. Standalone and full DGEMM on BCM2837 (NEON).

Similarly to our observations for the in-order K1, software scheduled microkernels perform better on the BCM2837 with the Cortex-A53, showing that scheduling has high impact on in-order architectures. The scheduled 8×3v variant outperformed the upstream BLIS `cortexa53` microkernel. In the Full GEMM benchmark we see the **ukrgen** reach the same performance as the `cortexa53` configuration for larger matrix sizes, with the latter reaching a plateau faster due to software prefetching. ArmPL is outperformed by the other configurations for larger matrices, but shows the strongest small matrix performance. Close-to-peak performance is not reached on the Cortex-A53 due to limitations in both the frontend and cache hierarchy.

6 Summary and Conclusions

In this paper, we presented a methodology for generating code for GEMM kernels in a performance portable manner. The methodology has been implemented in the new code generation tool **ukrgen**. The tool supports the generation of microkernel codes for multiple ISAs, including relevant extensions. The initial support of scheduling algorithms show that significant performance benefits can be achieved on in-order processor architectures. The second tool, `blisgen`, automatises the integration of these microkernels into the open-source BLIS library.

We tested both standalone microkernels and the generated BLIS libraries for a diverse set of processor architectures across various market segments, ranging from embedded solutions to HPC systems. As shown in our study, the measured performance was en-par with available tuned solutions in many cases, including vendor-provided libraries. For cases, where such libraries do not exist, the observed performance was good compared to the theoretically expected performance. It could thus be shown that with our tools it is possible to generate tuned GEMM implementations with very limited effort and, therefore, fill gaps caused by the increasing number of available processor solutions. Tuned variants of libraries such as BLIS can be provided for a significantly broader range of processor architectures.

Various opportunities for improvement of the current solution have been identified. This includes, among others, the support of packing kernels, emerging matrix extensions like SME, and the support of other scheduling algorithms.

For the future, we are also exploring the support of the 'fused-in packing' technique proposed in [10]. This would enable the generation of code that can achieve high performance for both small and large problem sizes.

Irregular matrices entail complex generation capabilities with non-trivial performance results. it will be a core direction of research which we will follow in the future to further extend our methodology and implementation.

Acknowledgments and Disclosure of Interests. Funding for parts of this work has been received from EuroHPC's project DARE SGA 1 under Grant Agreement No. 101202459 and the project EUPILOT under Grant Agreement No. 101034126. We want to thank the Open Edge and HPC Initiative for access to an Arm-based development environment through the HAICGU cluster at the Goethe University of Frankfurt. The authors have no competing interests to declare relevant to this article.

References

1. Goto, K., Geijn, R.A.V.D.: Anatomy of high-performance matrix multiplication. ACM Trans. Math. Softw. (TOMS) **34**(3), 1–25 (2008)
2. Van Zee, F.G., van de Geijn, R.A.: BLIS: a framework for rapidly instantiating BLAS functionality. ACM Trans. Math. Softw. **41**(3), 6 (2015)
3. Whaley, R.C., Petitet, A.: Minimizing development and maintenance costs in supporting persistently optimized BLAS. Softw. Pract. Exp. **35**(2), 101–121 (2005)
4. Chen, T., et al.: TVM: an automated end-to-end optimizing compiler for deep learning. In: 13th USENIX Symposium (OSDI 18), vol. 10, pp. 578–594. USENIX Association, Carlsbad (2018)
5. Low, T.M., Igual, F.D., Smith, T.M., Quintana-Orti, E.S.: Analytical modeling is enough for high-performance BLIS. ACM Trans. Math. Softw. **43**(2), 8 (2016)
6. Castelló, A., Bellavita, J., Dinh, G., Ikarashi, Y., Martínez, H.: Tackling the matrix multiplication micro-kernel generation with exo. In: Proceedings of CGO '24, pp. 182–192. IEEE Press (2024)

7. Nassyr, S., Pleiter, D.: Exploring processor micro-architectures optimised for BLAS3 micro-kernels. In: Euro-Par 2024: Parallel Processing, pp. 47–61. Springer, Cham (2024). https://doi.org/10.1007/978-3-031-69766-1_4
8. Heinecke, A., Henry, G., Hutchinson, M., Pabst, H.: LIBXSMM: accelerating small matrix multiplications by runtime code generation. In: SC '16, pp. 981–991 (2016)
9. Wu, D., et al.: autoGEMM: pushing the limits of irregular matrix multiplication on arm architectures. In: SC '24, vol. 11, pp. 1–15. IEEE Computer Society, Los Alamitos (2024)
10. Xu, R.G., Van Zee, F.G., van de Geijn, R.A.: Towards a unified implementation of GEMM in BLIS. In: ISC '23, pp. 111–121. Association for Computing Machinery, New York (2023)

CoDA: Constraint-Based Distance Adjustment Optimization for Distance-Based ISAs

Shu Sugita(✉), Masumi Aoki, Junichiro Kadomoto, and Hidetsugu Irie

The University of Tokyo, Tokyo, Japan
{sugita,aoki,kadomoto,irie}@mtl.t.u-tokyo.ac.jp

Abstract. Distance-based ISA is a class of architectures that specify operands using relative distances between instructions instead of register indices. This unique operand specification enables out-of-order execution without conventional register renaming, a critical bottleneck in scaling up wide-frontend processors. The practical efficiency of this hardware-software co-design relies heavily on Distance Adjustment (DA), which is a specialized compilation process that ensures consistency of reference distances across different branch paths. However, existing DA optimization methods cannot guarantee feasibility under all required constraints, leading to frequent fallbacks to inefficient baseline algorithms. This paper proposes Constraint-Based Distance Adjustment (CoDA), a novel approach that formulates the DA task as a constraint optimization problem. By incorporating previously unaddressed constraints into a mathematical model, CoDA provides a mathematical guarantee of solution feasibility, thereby eliminating optimization uncertainty. Evaluation results using the STRAIGHT ISA demonstrate that while the state-of-the-art method incurs fallbacks in 16.7% of cases on average, CoDA consistently achieves successful adjustment without any fallbacks. Furthermore, CoDA reduces additional MOVE instructions by 13.2% and total instructions by 3.8%, achieving up to 9.8% cycle reduction per benchmark and 2.2–2.9% on average. Energy consumption is also reduced by 1.4–2.5%, with CoDA-optimized STRAIGHT outperforming RISC-V by up to 9.2% on a future wide-frontend processor design.

Keywords: Distance-Based ISA · Hardware-Software Co-Design · Compiler Optimization · Constraint Optimization

1 Introduction

Distance-Based ISA (DBI) is an emerging architectural paradigm designed to overcome the scalability limitations of modern high-performance processors [2, 4]. Unlike traditional ISAs that specify operands using register indices, DBI specifies operands using inter-instruction distances. This design eliminates false dependencies at the architecture and hardware levels, inherently obviating the

M. Torquati et al. (Eds.): Euro-Par 2026, LNCS 16781, pp. 136–150, 2027.
https://doi.org/10.1007/978-3-032-35248-4_10

need for complex renaming logic. By removing this scalability bottleneck, DBI offers a promising path toward wider frontend capabilities and improved power efficiency.

While this new instruction format simplifies the hardware, it requires specialized compilation techniques. Among them, the most critical process for code quality is Distance Adjustment (DA) [14]. DA is a process that makes the distance to each operand consistent regardless of branch direction. This adjustment is performed using MOVE instructions that copy values and RPINC instructions that advance destination allocation positions. However, excessive insertion of these adjustment instructions leads to reduced execution efficiency and increased power consumption. Therefore, the optimization of DA is essential to maximize the benefits of DBI.

The main challenge in the existing DA optimization [5] is its inability to guarantee a valid solution under strict architectural constraints. This method derives solutions in two stages: (i) ordering adjustment using MOVEs and (ii) distance alignment using RPINCs. However, depending on the placement determined by the first-stage optimization, distance alignment in the subsequent stage may become impossible. In such cases, the method must fall back to an inefficient baseline algorithm, resulting in degraded execution performance.

This paper proposes Constraint-Based DA (CoDA), which formulates DA as a constraint optimization problem. CoDA adopts the same two-stage optimization as existing methods, but incorporates the feasibility condition for distance alignment as a constraint in the first stage, guaranteeing a feasible solution. We additionally introduce the first RPINC optimization in Phase II, formulating it as a constraint optimization problem based on the determined MOVE placement.

We evaluated CoDA by implementing it within the compiler for STRAIGHT ISA [2]. Our evaluation focuses on compilation reliability and execution efficiency. CoDA eliminated all fallbacks in DA, while the state-of-the-art method [5] incurred fallbacks in 16.7% of cases on average. Cycle-accurate simulation showed that CoDA reduced additional MOVEs by an average of 13.2% and the total instruction count by 3.8%, achieving up to 9.8% cycle reduction per benchmark and 2.2–2.9% on average, with energy reductions of 1.4–2.5%.

The main contributions of this paper are as follows:

- We identify two unaddressed constraints in the existing DA methods, the fixed-placement constraint and the inter-path interference constraint, and formally model them as feasibility conditions.
- We propose CoDA, which incorporates these conditions into Phase I as a constraint optimization problem, providing a mathematical guarantee of solution feasibility.
- We introduce the first dedicated optimization for RPINC instructions in Phase II, which computes the RPINC-minimal placement conditional on the MOVE placement fixed in Phase I. By reformulating placement as interval capacity management, the problem is decoupled from instruction-order dependencies, substantially reducing formulation complexity.

- Evaluations show that CoDA eliminates all compilation fallbacks, reduces additional MOVEs by 13.2%, and achieves 2.2–2.9% cycle and 1.4–2.5% energy reductions on average over the state-of-the-art method.

2 Background

2.1 Target Architecture

DBI has two core characteristics: (i) implicit destination writing determination by instruction fetch order and (ii) operand specification by distance. These are implemented by the Register Pointer (RP). The RP points to the index of the instruction destination and increments automatically for each instruction. This allows the register file to function logically as a circular buffer. The RP of the source register referenced by an instruction is calculated by subtracting the distance from its own RP. Due to instruction encoding constraints, there is an upper limit (Max Reference Distance; MRD) on the distance that can be specified.

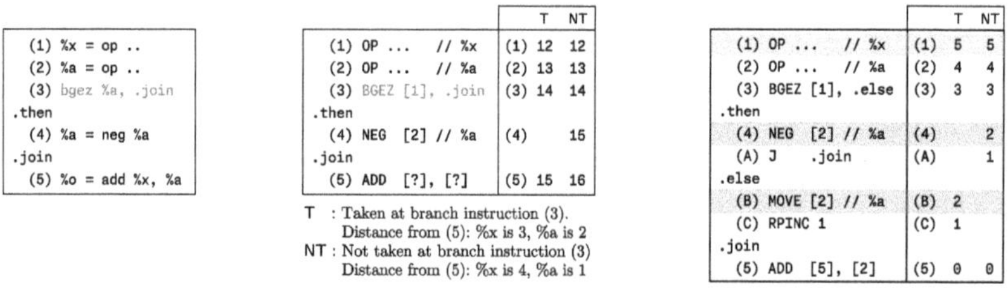

(a) Example Code (b) RP Progression (c) Adjustment Result

Fig. 1. RP progression and distance adjustment in DBI. For the code fragment shown in (a), (b) illustrates the RP progression in a naively translated instruction sequence, and (c) presents the adjusted operand distances and the resulting code.

In DBI, RP progression depends on the execution path. Figure 1 (a), (b) show an example of a code segment with branches and the behavior of RP during execution. Therefore, to ensure that the program operates correctly regardless of branch direction, the instruction sequence must be adjusted to match distances at each merge point. This adjustment is called Distance Adjustment (DA).

2.2 Distance Adjustment

DA is the process of matching the distance of each data across all incoming paths at merge points of control flow. This ensures that all instructions can specify correct references without depending on the execution path. Figure 1 (c) shows an example of DA for the program in Fig. 1 (b). The notation [x] in assembly represents distance x.

DA requires the insertion of MOVEs and RPINCs. MOVE is an instruction that copies the value of a register to another register. RPINC is an instruction that advances the RP by an arbitrary value. Program efficiency is thus determined by how much these adjustment instructions can be suppressed.

Compilers typically perform this adjustment precisely at the insertion points of SSA phi-functions. The phi-function has the role of integrating operands arriving from different paths at control flow merge points. In other words, the main purpose of DA is to match the distances of *phi-producers*, the producer instructions for each operand of the phi-function. Note that in DBI, even the identical operand may have different distances across paths, so phi-functions with the same operand must also be considered for DA.

2.3 Existing DA Approaches

Existing DA methods include two main approaches: (i) basic algorithm [2] that is reliable but inefficient, and (ii) graph-based algorithm [5] that is efficient but uncertain. These DA methods assume that critical edges have been removed from the control flow graph. This ensures that regions for inserting adjustment instructions are reserved.

The basic algorithm [2] inserts MOVEs at a fixed order at the end of each incoming path. This forces the replication of all operands to the same physical register position. This method significantly increases the number of execution instructions. However, it can reliably achieve DA as long as appropriate register spilling is performed in advance [14]. Therefore, it serves as a guaranteed baseline for achieving DA.

The graph-based method [5] is a state-of-the-art DA method that optimizes MOVEs using graph algorithms. This method adopts a fix-and-optimize strategy that performs MOVE and RPINC insertion separately. In the first step, a constraint graph for the execution order of phi-producers on each path is created, and the optimal MOVE insertion to align their execution order is determined. This optimization is reduced to the minimum feedback arc set problem. Based on the MOVE insertion determined in the first step, the second step inserts RPINC between instructions to align the distance of phi-producers.

2.4 Limitations of DA Optimization

Although the graph-based method is highly efficient compared to the basic algorithm, it suffers from distance adjustment failures under specific conditions. We have identified that the root cause lies in two unaddressed constraints: the *fixed-placement constraint* and the *inter-path interference constraint*. The graph-based method fails to account for these constraints during the first phase; thus, it cannot guarantee a placement that satisfies distance alignment requirements.

The fixed-placement constraint requires that an instruction be placed at a specific position within a block. This constraint arises when the placement of an instruction has already been determined for another merge point, or when fixed placement constraints exist, such as for function arguments. Existing methods

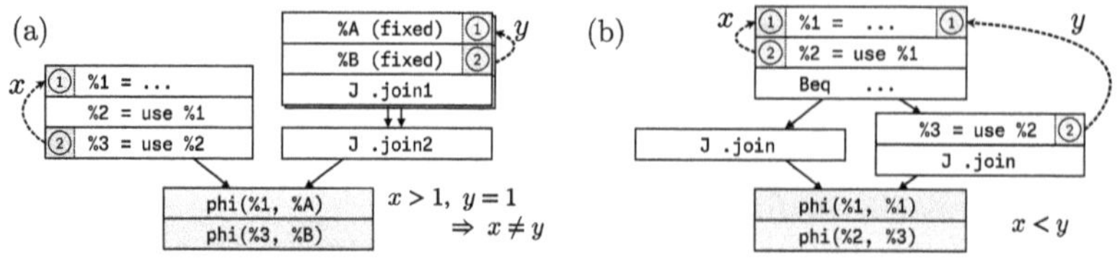

Fig. 2. Limitations of existing DA methods. (a) Fixed-placement constraint, (b) Inter-path interference constraint. In both cases, the order of phi-producers is the same between paths, but the distances cannot be aligned.

consider only execution order adjustment in the first step, and thus there may be cases where no valid placement with matching distances exists (Fig. 2 (a)).

The inter-path interference constraint applies to instructions shared across multiple paths. While the positions of instructions on mutually independent paths can independently determine distances by inserting RPINC, adjusting instructions common to multiple paths causes adjustments in one path to affect the distances in other paths. Consequently, there may be cases where distances of multiple phi-functions cannot be matched simultaneously (Fig. 2 (b)).

Failure to satisfy these constraints forces a fallback to the basic algorithm, thereby degrading performance. To address this, CoDA explicitly handles them to simultaneously achieve high performance and guaranteed feasibility.

3 CoDA: Problem Statement

CoDA applies DA independently to each merge point, as defined below.

Definition 1 (DA Scope and Objective). DA is applied to each merge point. The adjustment scope for a single DA instance extends from the merge point backwards along each path, terminating at either a preceding merge point or the function call site. The objective of DA is to align the distances to the phi-producers at the merge point across paths ensuring that the aligned distance remains within MRD.

This definition follows [5]. CoDA also adopts the same approach for aspects beyond this definition, including the application order of merge points and MRD constraints on instructions other than phi-producers.

To naturally express the fixed-placement and inter-path interference constraints, we introduce two key concepts in our formulation: *fixed/free segments* and *local/global offsets.*

Definition 2 (Fixed and Free Segment). Instructions within a block are categorized based on whether their position and execution order are fixed. By partitioning the block according to this property, we define a subsequence with fixed attributes as a *fixed segment*, and one with flexible attributes as a *free segment.*

This distinction allows us to explicitly identify the presence of fixed-placement constraints. Furthermore, as established in Sect. 2.3, our DA formulation assumes a control flow graph with critical edges removed; thus, the terminal segments of merge paths are always free segments.

Definition 3 (Local and Global Offset). The *local offset* of an instruction is defined as the distance from the bottom of its segment to the instruction itself, corresponding to the RP movement amount. The *global offset* is the distance from the merge point to the instruction along a specific path.

These concepts address the inter-path interference constraint by computing the global offset from the local offset, which remains constant regardless of path. This ensures correct adjustment even when insertions affect multiple paths.

Finally, we define the DA problem using these definitions.

Definition 4 (DA Problem). For a merge point that is the target of DA, let the set of segments within the adjustment range be S. Let the set of merging paths be P. A path $p \in P$ is a sequence of segments contained in S. Let the set of phi-functions existing at the merge point be F. Each $f \in F$ has the original producer $\mathsf{orig}(f, p)$ to be referenced for each path $p \in P$.

For this definition, DA performs the following two operations. (i) Insert $\mathsf{move}(f, p)$ that copies $\mathsf{orig}(f, p)$ into a free segment in path p for each $(f, p) \in F \times P$. (ii) Rearrange the instruction order within each free segment arbitrarily and insert RPINCs at arbitrary positions.

The objective of DA is to align the global offset of the target value (orig or move) for all $f \in F$ regardless of path $p \in P$ through these operations and keep the distance within MRD.

4 CoDA Phase I: Move Placement

This phase optimizes MOVE instructions, which require a register read and write and thus have higher execution costs than RPINC instructions, which only advance the RP. The model proposed in this section expresses all fundamental constraints of DA to ensure the feasibility of Phase II. Therefore, it can be adapted for simultaneous optimization in a single phase.

Segment-Level Definition For a segment $s \in S$, let the set of instructions contained therein be I_s. For an instruction $i \in I_s$, let $l[i]$ denote its local offset. Also, let $w[s]$ denote the total movement of the RP advancing within segment s.

If s is a fixed segment, these variables are constants. However, the handling of results from phi functions of preceding merge points is as follows: if that merge point has already been adjusted, we use the adjusted value. Otherwise, the local offset is set to infinity. This ensures that instructions before adjustment will always have one MOVE inserted into a free segment.

Conversely, if s is a free segment, these variables become optimization targets. Let $i \prec j$ denote that instruction i must be executed prior to instruction j. Under this definition, a valid schedule must satisfy the following constraints:

$$\forall i \in I_s, \quad 1 \leq l[i] \leq |I_s| + \mathsf{MRD} \tag{1}$$

$$\mathsf{all\text{-}different}(\{l[i] \mid i \in I_s\}) \tag{2}$$

$$\forall i, j \in I_s \text{ s.t. } i \prec j, \quad l[i] > l[j] \tag{3}$$

$$\max(\{l[i] \mid i \in I_s\} \cup \{0\}) \leq w[s] \leq |I_s| + \mathsf{MRD} \tag{4}$$

Note that the local offsets $l[i]$ do not need to be continuous. The empty slots between instructions correspond to positions reserved for inserted MOVEs or RPINCs. The MRD term in Eq. (1) and (4) bounds the additional slots for inserted adjustment instructions, since the global offset of every phi-producer must not exceed MRD.

Path-Level Definition For an instruction i, let $\mathsf{seg}(i)$ be the segment containing i. For a path p, the global offset $g[p, i]$ is its local offset $l[i]$ plus the total width of segments executed after $\mathsf{seg}(i)$:

$$g[p, i] = l[i] + \sum_{s \in p, \mathsf{seg}(i) \prec s} w[s] \tag{5}$$

If no such segment exists, the sum is 0.

Phi-Level Definition For each phi-function $f \in F$, let $\phi[f]$ be the aligned global offset. We assume all $f \in F$ are distinct and require $1 \leq \phi[f] \leq \mathsf{MRD}$:

$$\forall f \in F, \quad 1 \leq \phi[f] \leq \mathsf{MRD} \tag{6}$$

$$\mathsf{all\text{-}different}(\{\phi[f] \mid f \in F\}). \tag{7}$$

For a path $p \in P$, if $\phi[f] \neq g[p, \mathsf{orig}(f, p)]$, a MOVE at offset $\phi[f]$ on p is necessary. For efficiency, we constrain MOVE insertion to the segment immediately preceding the merge point, as execution frequency decreases toward path ends[1].

Incorporating this restriction, the adjustment by the MOVE insertion is expressed by the following equation:

$$\forall (f, p) \in F \times P, \quad \phi[f] \neq g[p, \mathsf{orig}(f, p)] \implies \begin{cases} \bigwedge_{i \in I_{\mathsf{pred}(p)}} \phi[f] \neq l[i] \\ \wedge\, \phi[f] < g[p, \mathsf{orig}(f, p)] \\ \wedge\, \phi[f] \leq w[\mathsf{pred}(p)] \end{cases} \tag{8}$$

Here, $\mathsf{pred}(p)$ denotes the segment immediately preceding path p. The three equations in the consequent part represent the constraints that the inserted MOVE must satisfy within the segment, corresponding to Eq. (2)–(4).

[1] Since the adjustment scope consists only of branches, the execution frequency decreases as the position approaches the end of each path.

Objective We adopt an execution frequency-based cost function as the objective, aligning with existing DA methods. The cost function C_{I} for Phase I is defined as follows, where $\mathsf{freq}(s)$ denotes the execution frequency of segment s:

$$C_{\mathrm{I}} = \sum_{p \in P} \mathsf{freq}(\mathsf{pred}(p)) \sum_{f \in F} \left[\phi[f] \neq g[p, \mathsf{orig}(f, p)] \right]. \tag{9}$$

Here, $[\cdot]$ denotes Iverson's bracket, which evaluates to 1 if the enclosed expression is true and 0 otherwise. Note that incorporating RPINC costs would enable a single-phase optimization. However, since RPINC counts depend on the placement of both instructions and MOVEs, this combined approach tightly couples RPINC variables with all placement constraints, substantially increasing solver complexity. This motivates the two-phase design.

Solution and Feasibility From the solution of decision variables $\{l[i], w[s], \phi[f]\}$ obtained via this formulation, a concrete schedule can be reconstructed through the following procedure. First, for each segment s, we reserve $w[s]$ instruction slots and position each instruction $i \in I_s$ at the location corresponding to its local offset $l[i]$. Next, for any pair (f, p) where $\phi[f] \neq g[p, \mathsf{orig}(f, p)]$, a MOVE is inserted at the position where the global offset equals $\phi[f]$. Finally, any consecutive empty slots generated between instructions are filled with RPINCs.

The feasible solution space of this formulation encompasses the results produced by the basic algorithm [2]. Consequently, CoDA inherently maintains the same level of robustness as the basic algorithm, guaranteeing a valid solution.

5 CoDA Phase II: Distance Alignment

Overview. Since Phase I optimizes MOVE placement without considering RPINC costs, the resulting segment may require RPINC insertions at many intervals.

In this phase, we optimize the placement and quantity of RPINCs based on the solution obtained in Phase I, while fixing the following two elements: (i) The instructions referenced by phi-functions, including MOVE instructions inserted in Phase I. We refer to these as *adjustment targets*. (ii) The static execution order of these adjustment targets within each segment.

By fixing these elements, each segment can be redefined as a sequence of *intervals* delimited by the adjustment targets. In this phase, we model the RPINC optimization by treating the number of general instructions and the immediate values of the inserted RPINCs within each interval as decision variables.

Definition 5 (Segment Partitioning). A segment s containing n_s adjustment targets $\{a_1, \ldots, a_{n_s}\}$ (ordered by reverse execution) is partitioned into $n_s + 1$ intervals. We introduce the boundaries a_0 and a_{n_s+1} at the beginning and end of the segment, with local offsets $l[a_0] = 0$ and $l[a_{n_s+1}] = w[s] + 1$. Each interval

$j \in [0, n_s]$ between a_j and a_{j+1} is characterized by m_j (general instructions) and r_j (RP increment from RPINCs). The local offset $l[a_i]$ is thus determined as:

$$l[a_i] = \sum_{j=0}^{i-1}(m_j + r_j + 1), \quad w[s] = \sum_{j=0}^{n_s}(m_j + r_j + 1) - 1. \tag{10}$$

Modeling Assignments. The decision variables $\{r_j\}$ can be freely chosen, while $\{m_j\}$ must satisfy instruction dependencies. To model these constraints without exhaustive scheduling, we introduce the concept of a *feasible range.*

Definition 6 (Feasible Range). Due to dependencies on the adjustment targets, the placement of any general instruction i is restricted to a specific continuous interval. If this interval lies between target instructions a_s and a_t (where $0 \leq s < t \leq n_s + 1$), we define $[s, t)$ as the *feasible range* of instruction i. The boundaries s, t are determined by $s = \max\{j \mid a_j \succ i\}$ and $t = \min\{j \mid i \succ a_j\}$. By the definition of a_0 and a_{n_s+1}, any instruction i satisfies $a_0 \succ i \succ a_{n_s+1}$.

This concept has two key properties that facilitate efficient modeling.

Theorem 1. Let $\mathcal{M}$ denote the set of valid non-negative integer assignments $\{m_i\}$ for which a placement satisfying all execution order constraints exists. Let $\mathcal{M}'$ denote the set of non-negative integer assignments $\{m_i\}$ arising from assigning each instruction to an arbitrary interval within its feasible range, ignoring execution order constraints. Then, $\mathcal{M} = \mathcal{M}'$.

Proof. The inclusion $\mathcal{M} \subseteq \mathcal{M}'$ holds trivially since $\mathcal{M}'$ relaxes the order constraints of $\mathcal{M}$. To prove $\mathcal{M}' \subseteq \mathcal{M}$, we construct a valid schedule for any $\{m_i\} \in \mathcal{M}'$ using the following greedy algorithm:

- Iterate through intervals $k = 0, \ldots, n$. In each interval k, select m_k instructions from the unplaced instructions eligible for that interval (i.e., whose feasible range $[s_u, t_u)$ contains k).
- The priority of instruction u is given by the tuple $P(u) = (t_u, s_u, \mathsf{loff}[u])$ under lexicographic ordering, where $[s_u, t_u)$ is the feasible range of u and $\mathsf{loff}[u]$ is the local offset determined in Phase I.

This greedy strategy satisfies three key properties:

1. Slot Sufficiency: This strategy resembles the Earliest Deadline First (EDF) scheduling algorithm. Since execution order constraints are disregarded in $\mathcal{M}'$, all required slot counts m_k can always be filled across the intervals.
2. Candidate Listing Order: For any pair $i \prec j$, transitivity implies $s_j \leq s_i$. Thus, j does not become eligible in any interval before i is placed, so j is never selected before i is a candidate.
3. Candidate Selection Order: Similarly, $i \prec j$ implies $t_j \leq t_i$, and loff breaks ties when feasible ranges coincide. Hence, i always has strictly higher priority than j, ensuring i is selected first.

Property 1 ensures that the algorithm never runs out of eligible instructions at any interval. Properties 2 and 3 together guarantee that i is always selected before j whenever $i \prec j$, regardless of whether they are simultaneously eligible. Thus, any $\{m_i\} \in \mathcal{M}'$ corresponds to a valid schedule, proving $\mathcal{M}' \subseteq \mathcal{M}$. □

Theorem 2. Let $N_{s,t}$ denote the number of instructions whose feasible range is $[s, t)$. A non-negative integer assignment $\{m_i\}$ belongs to $\mathcal{M}'$ if and only if the following inequality holds for every interval $[i, j) \subseteq [0, n+1)$:

$$\sum_{[s,t)\subseteq[i,j)} N_{s,t} \leq \sum_{k\in[i,j)} m_k \leq \sum_{[s,t)\cap[i,j)\neq\emptyset} N_{s,t} \tag{11}$$

Proof. We model the assignment of instructions to intervals as a bipartite matching problem. Applying Hall's theorem to this bipartite graph, a valid assignment exists if and only if every instruction can be matched to a feasible interval, which is equivalent to the inequality holding for every contiguous interval subset. □

Leveraging these properties, Phase II optimization is decoupled from dependencies on individual instruction orders. Our method reduces the optimization scope to managing the capacity of each interval, thereby yielding a substantially more compact formulation. Since this formulation covers all valid placements by Theorem 1, the solver is guaranteed to find an optimal solution given the Phase I solution.

The model for Phase II can be derived from the Phase I formulation by applying the following two modifications: (i) For each segment, instead of Eqs. (1)–(4), we use the constraints of Eqs. (10) and (11). (ii) Since the MOVEs required for adjustment are assumed to be already placed, we use the constraint that the global offset of f's adjustment targets is equal to $\phi[f]$, instead of Eq. (8).

In Phase II, the cost function C_{II} is defined as follows:

$$C_{\text{II}} = \sum_{s\in S} \mathsf{freq}(s) \sum_{0\leq i\leq n_s} [r_i \neq 0]. \tag{12}$$

Since RPINC advances the RP by an arbitrary immediate value in a single instruction, each interval requires at most one RPINC; thus $[r_i \neq 0]$ directly counts the number of inserted RPINC instructions.

Since the solution from Phase I satisfies all constraints in this formulation, a feasible solution is guaranteed to exist. From the solution, a valid schedule for each segment can be deterministically constructed using the greedy algorithm described in the proof of Theorem 1.

6 Experiments

6.1 Evaluation Setup

Table 1. Processor Parameters.

Parameter	10-wide	16-wide
Frontend Width	10	16
Scheduler	256	512
ROB (R)	768	1536
LSQ	LQ: 192, SQ: 128	LQ: 384, SQ: 256
Frontend Latency	RISC-V: 7, STRAIGHT: 5	
Execution Units {10-wide, 16-wide}	Int × {8, 12}, iMul × {2, 3}, Load × {3, 5}, Store × {2, 4}, Float × 4, iDiv × 1, fDiv × 1	
Phys. Reg.	RISC-V: Unified × R, STRAIGHT: Unified × $R + 127$	
Branch Pred.	64 KiB TAGE	
BTB	4-way, 8192 entries	
RAS	16 entries	
Mem. Dep. Pred.	PHAST [3]	
L1I/D Cache	128 KiB, 8-way, 3 cycles	
L2 Cache	8 MiB, 16-way, 12 cycles	
Prefetcher	Stream prefetcher at L2	
Main memory	100 cycles	

Table 2. Fallback Rate

		# of Fallback Cases	
Bench.	# of Cases	Graph-Based [5]	CoDA
mcf_s	210	35 (16.7 %)	0
lbm_s	48	9 (18.8 %)	0
xz_s	802	235 (29.3 %)	0
cjpeg	607	85 (14.0 %)	0
core	179	18 (10.1 %)	0
linear	186	14 (7.5 %)	0
loops	434	37 (8.5 %)	0
nnet	189	19 (10.1 %)	0
parser	261	28 (10.7 %)	0
radix	152	13 (8.6 %)	0
sha	93	11 (11.8 %)	0
zip	512	110 (21.5 %)	0
Total	3673	614 (16.7 %)	0

We evaluate CoDA in terms of compiler performance (fallback rate and solving time) and code quality (executed instructions, cycles, and energy consumption). We use 12 benchmarks: all nine CoreMark-PRO benchmarks and three benchmarks (mcf_s, lbm_s, xz_s) from SPEC CPU 2017. For SPEC benchmarks, we measure representative regions consistent with prior work [5].

Processor parameters are summarized in Table 1. We set the 10-wide configuration based on modern high-performance processors [7,13] and the 16-wide configuration to model a larger future frontend. We use the STRAIGHT cycle-accurate simulator [6] for simulation and McPAT [8] for power estimation.

We implement CoDA with the CP-SAT solver [12]. We integrate it into the STRAIGHT compiler based on LLVM 19.1.7. The execution frequency freq is computed using BranchProbabilityInfo in LLVM. We compare CoDA with two baselines: RISC-V and the graph-based method [5]. To ensure a fair comparison, all methods share the same compiler infrastructure. When the graph-based method cannot satisfy distance alignment, it falls back to its basic algorithm.

6.2 Evaluation Results

Compiler Performance. Table 2 shows fallback rates without a time limit. In this evaluation, we exclude C libraries to avoid double counting. The graph-based method fell back in 16.7% of cases due to fixed-placement and inter-path interference constraints. In contrast, CoDA achieved 0% fallback.

Table 3 shows CoDA's compilation-time overhead on a Ryzen 9 9950X. We use a single worker and impose a 15 s time limit per merge point. Most merge

Table 3. Compilation Overhead of CoDA (single worker, 15-second limit)

Bench.	Status S	Status F	Status U	Time [s] Phase I	Time [s] Phase II
mcf_s	210	0	0	1.803	0.287
lbm_s	48	0	0	0.860	0.153
xz_s	800	1	1	137.427	2.021
cjpeg	606	1	0	22.566	0.691
core	179	0	0	0.787	0.216
linear	186	0	0	1.021	0.224
loops	434	0	0	3.287	0.535
nnet	189	0	0	3.618	0.222
parser	261	0	0	1.114	0.283
radix	152	0	0	0.899	0.165
sha	93	0	0	0.519	0.100
zip	511	1	0	42.863	0.948

points solve in under 10 ms; however, one merge point in xz_s times out due to a large switch-loop with many phi-functions and merge paths. We leave code transformations for such cases to future work. Phase II is consistently faster than Phase I across all benchmarks. This result indicates that the interval-level model is more tractable than instruction-level modeling.

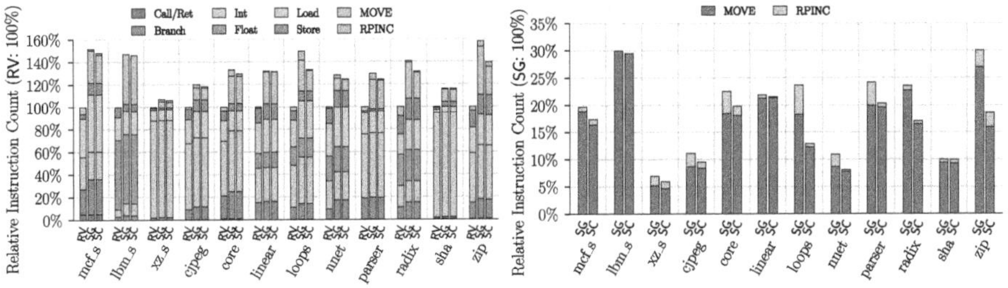

(a) Instruction Count Distribution (b) Comparison of MOVE and RPINC

Fig. 3. Executed Instructions (RV: RISC-V, SG: Graph-Based, SC: CoDA).

Code Quality. Figure 3 (a) shows instruction counts normalized to RISC-V. Most of the gap between RISC-V and STRAIGHT is due to MOVEs and RPINCs inserted by distance alignment. Figure 3 (b) compares the two STRAIGHT methods for MOVE and RPINC only. CoDA reduces executed instructions by 3.8% on average compared to the graph-based method. The reduction in executed MOVEs accounts for 13.2% of executed additional MOVEs. Moreover, RPINC counts in CoDA are comparable to or lower than those of the graph-based method. Fewer MOVEs impose stricter placement constraints on adjustment targets, increasing the demand for RPINC-based adjustment. Phase II absorbs this pressure and prevents RPINC overhead from offsetting the gains from Phase I.

Figure 4 shows executed cycles and energy consumption. Relative to the graph-based method, CoDA reduces executed cycles by 2.9% in 10-wide and 2.2% in 16-wide. Cycle reductions are largest in the following benchmarks: xz_s

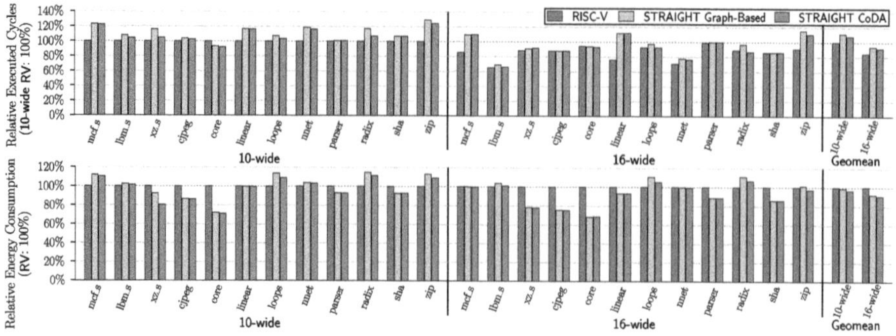

Fig. 4. Executed Cycles and Energy Consumption (Normalized to RISC-V).

(9.8%), radix (8.5%), zip (3.8%), loops (3.6%), and lbm_s (3.3%). For xz_s and zip, the graph-based method suffers from a high fallback rate, which leads to unoptimized MOVE placement. By eliminating these fallbacks, CoDA directly contributes to cycle reduction.

Energy consumption was reduced by 2.5% in 10-wide and 1.4% in 16-wide configurations compared to the graph-based method. Furthermore, CoDA outperformed RISC-V in both 10-wide (-3.5%) and 16-wide (-9.2%) configurations. This result indicates that the elimination of renaming logic in STRAIGHT reduces power consumption sufficiently to offset the instruction overhead from DA, whereas executed cycles reflect this overhead directly. CoDA's instruction reductions further enhance this energy advantage over RISC-V.

7 Related Work

Distance-Based ISAs. STRAIGHT ISA [2], used as the evaluation target in this study, represents the simplest and most typical instance of a DBI. It employs a single RP to manage a circular-buffer register file. Other DBI architectures have extended this fundamental concept in different directions. Clockhands [4] utilizes multiple RPs, each paired with a dedicated register file. Since each RP advances at a different speed, this mechanism allows for flexible management of register values with varying lifetimes. TURBULENCE [11] adopts a hybrid design that combines traditional numbered registers with distance-specified registers. Instructions writing to the latter group can execute out-of-order without special hardware mechanisms. Leveraging this, TURBULENCE introduces partial out-of-order execution to GPUs.

These architectures introduce further complexity to DA, but matching distances at merge points is a universal requirement for DBI. Therefore, by adjusting the local order for each RP, our formulation can be naturally extended to multiple RP and hybrid designs.

Related Classical Backend Optimizations. DA is analogous to the composite optimization of register allocation and instruction scheduling in traditional architectures. This similarity arises because, in DBI, determining the destination register of an instruction is equivalent to determining its execution order.

Constraint-based approaches have been explored in traditional composite optimizations [1,10]. The primary distinction lies in problem dimensionality; traditional methods require separate variable sets for execution order and register assignment [9], whereas DBI's one-to-one correspondence reduces these to a single variable set. This substantially reduces both variable count and constraint complexity, enabling a more compact formulation.

8 Conclusion

This paper proposes CoDA, a constraint-based formulation of distance adjustment (DA), the critical compilation step that determines the efficiency of DBI. By modeling previously unaddressed constraints as formal feasibility conditions, CoDA eliminates the optimization uncertainty inherent in existing methods.

Evaluation results show that CoDA eliminated all fallbacks, ensuring reliable and optimized DA in every case, whereas the state-of-the-art method incurred fallbacks in 16.7% of cases. CoDA reduced additional MOVEs by 13.2% and total instructions by 3.8%, achieving 2.2–2.9% cycle reduction and 1.4–2.5% energy reduction over the graph-based method. CoDA-optimized STRAIGHT also outperformed RISC-V in energy consumption by up to 9.2%, demonstrating that the architectural advantage of DBI is fully realized only with reliable DA.

The proposed formulation establishes a principled basis for DBI compiler research, and its generalizable structure provides a foundation for future optimizations that fully exploit DBI's potential in wide-frontend processor designs.

Acknowledgments. This work was supported by JSPS KAKENHI Grant Numbers JP23K28050 and Premo Inc.

Disclosure of Interests. The authors have no competing interests to declare that are relevant to the content of this article.

References

1. Domagała, L., van Amstel, D., Rastello, F., Sadayappan, P.: Register allocation and promotion through combined instruction scheduling and loop unrolling. In: Proceedings of the 25th International Conference on Compiler Construction, pp. 143–151 (2016)
2. Irie, H., et al.: STRAIGHT: hazardless processor architecture without register renaming. In: 2018 51st Annual IEEE/ACM International Symposium on Microarchitecture (MICRO), pp. 121–133 (2018)
3. Kim, S., Ros, A.: Effective context-sensitive memory dependence prediction. In: 2024 IEEE International Symposium on High-Performance Computer Architecture (HPCA), pp. 515–527 (2024)

4. Koizumi, T., Shioya, R., Sugita, S., Amano, T., Degawa, Y., Kadomoto, J., Irie, H., Sakai, S.: ClockHands: rename-free instruction set architecture for out-of-order processors. In: Proceedings of the 56th Annual IEEE/ACM International Symposium on Microarchitecture, pp. 1–16 (2023)
5. Koizumi, T., Sugita, S., Shioya, R., Kadomoto, J., Irie, H., Sakai, S.: Compiling and optimizing real-world programs for STRAIGHT ISA. In: 2021 IEEE 39th International Conference on Computer Design (ICCD), pp. 400–408 (2021)
6. Koizumi, T., et al.: straight-dev/env (2022). https://github.com/straight-dev/env/
7. Lam, C.: Lion Cove: Intel's P-Core Roars (2024). https://chipsandcheese.com/p/lion-cove-intels-p-core-roars
8. Li, S., Ahn, J.H., Strong, R.D., Brockman, J.B., Tullsen, D.M., Jouppi, N.P.: McPAT: an integrated power, area, and timing modeling framework for multicore and manycore architectures. In: Proceedings of the 42nd Annual IEEE/ACM International Symposium on Microarchitecture, pp. 469–480 (2009)
9. Lozano, R.C., Carlsson, M., Blindell, G.H., Schulte, C.: Combinatorial register allocation and instruction scheduling. ACM Trans. Program. Lang. Syst. **41**(3) (2019)
10. Lozano, R.C., Schulte, C.: Survey on combinatorial register allocation and instruction scheduling. ACM Comput. Surv. **52**(3) (2019)
11. Matsuo, R., Koizumi, T., Irie, H., Sakai, S., Shioya, R.: Enhancing GPU performance through complexity-effective out-of-order execution using distance-based ISA. IEICE Trans. Info. Syst. **E108.D**(6), 558–569 (2025)
12. Perron, L., Didier, F.: CP-SAT (2026). https://developers.google.com/optimization/cp/cp_solver
13. Schor, D.: Arm Launches Next-Gen Flagship Cortex-X925 (2024). https://fuse.wikichip.org/news/7761/arm-launches-next-gen-flagship-cortex-x925/
14. Sugita, S., Koizumi, T., Shioya, R., Irie, H., Sakai, S.: A sound and complete algorithm for code generation in distance-based ISA. In: Proceedings of the 32nd ACM SIGPLAN International Conference on Compiler Construction, pp. 73–84 (2023)

Assessing the Performance Impact of Data Layouts: a Benchmarking Approach

Jolly Chen[1,2(✉)], Ana Lucia Varbanescu[1], and Axel Naumann[2]

[1] University of Twente, Enschede, The Netherlands
{jolly.chen,a.l.varbanescu}@utwente.nl
[2] CERN, Geneva, Switzerland
{jolly.chen,axel.naumann}@cern.ch

Abstract. Data layouts can significantly impact application performance. However, choosing the best-performing layout for a given application, especially one using complex data structures, remains a challenge: how the data-layout performance depends on factors such as the data access pattern and machine parameters is not sufficiently understood.

In this paper, we present a *2D design space exploration (DSE)* approach to systematically study the performance impact of data layouts. Starting from a given array of (complex) data structures and a set of representative C++ kernels that read the array, our approach (1) generates all possible data layouts for the input array via structure splitting and data member reordering, (2) generates and executes the kernels with each layout, and (3) collects performance data. Through exhaustive testing, we empirically quantify the impact of different layouts and observe patterns that can help develop data layout selection guidelines.

To demonstrate our approach, we apply it to a set of kernels representing common high-energy physics computations and a particle structure with 7 data members. We generate and measure over 37500 versions of each kernel for 4 different architectures (2 Intel and 2 AMD CPUs), and collect over 6 million data points. Our results indicate that data layouts do have a significant impact on runtime performance when the input is sufficiently large. We identify several causes for the large performance gaps (up to 67%) between layouts and, based on these observations, suggest empirical guidelines for (semi-)automated data layout refactoring.

Keywords: Data Layouts · Benchmarking · Optimisation Guidelines

1 Introduction

The organisation of data in memory (i.e., the *data layout*) strongly affects an application's memory access pattern, thereby impacting overall performance [5]. Consequently, data layout transformations have been shown to be an effective optimisation technique. For arrays of structured data, common techniques include *array regrouping* and *structure splitting*, where different arrays are

M. Torquati et al. (Eds.): Euro-Par 2026, LNCS 16781, pp. 151–165, 2027.
https://doi.org/10.1007/978-3-032-35248-4_11

grouped into a single array of structures or the structure's data members are split into separate arrays, respectively [4,12]. The two most prominent layouts that result from these techniques are the *Array-of-Structures (AoS)*, where the structures in the array are stored contiguously in memory, and the *Structure-of-Arrays (SoA)* layout, where the elements of each data member are stored contiguously in memory. Another technique is to reorder data members within the data structure [11].

Quantifying the true performance impact of data layouts on applications is challenging: benchmarking different layouts *in-situ* is challenging due to the necessary-yet-expensive code rewrites and the combined effects of multiple data structures, while accurate modelling is not feasible due to the increased complexity of processors and compilers. Instead, we propose to quantify the data layout performance using a *2D design space exploration (DSE)* approach that combines representative kernels with a *data-layout generator*. The generator controls data layout complexity, and the chosen workloads let us isolate and study individual (data layout, access pattern) combinations.

In this paper, we present our C++ DSE framework that, (1) given a complex data structure (DS) and a set of n C++ kernels ($K_i, i = 1..n$) that access an array A of DS instances using different patterns ($AP_i, i = 1..n$), (2) generates all possible data-layouts ($DL_j(A, j = 1..m)$) for the input array A through structure splitting and data member reordering, and (3) benchmarks all $n \times m$ combinations on p different machines ($M_k, k = 1..p$), collecting runtime information and hardware counter data. By exhaustively benchmarking all possible layouts, we empirically determine an upper bound for the performance gap between the best- and worst-performing layouts. Moreover, analysing the collected benchmarking data, we make general observations and provide developers with guidelines for selecting well-performing layouts.

The contributions of our work are as follows:

- We provide a data-layout generator that enables systematic studies on the performance impact of data layouts of complex data structures.
- We showcase the DSE in action for a large design space, combining $n = 2$ access patterns representative for high-energy physics computations on CPUs, $m = 37633$ data layouts, and $p = 4$ different systems (AMD Zen 2, AMD Zen 4, Intel Haswell, and Intel Skylake), and formulate five key observations.
- We formulate three empirical guidelines for choosing a well-performing layout - i.e., a layout likely within 38% of the best-performing one.

2 *DS*E: Creating the Design-Space

In this section, we describe the two components of our DSE framework: the kernels used to vary memory access patterns and the method devised to generate different layouts. The code is available on GitHub[1].

[1] https://github.com/jolly-chen/data-layout-benchmarks

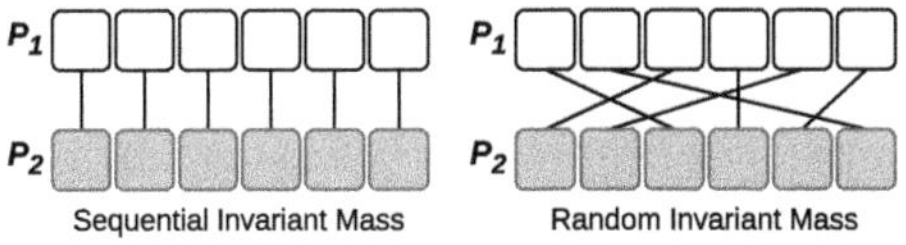

Fig. 1. Particle pairs used by (left) SIM and (right) RIM using $\mathbf{P}_1$ and $\mathbf{P}_2$ of size 6.

```
struct Particle {
    int id;
    double pt, eta, phi, e;
    char charge;
    std::array<std::array<double, 3>, 3> posCovMatrix; };
```

Listing 1. Default particle structure

2.1 Kernels

We select two kernels that represent common operations in High Energy Physics. In each kernel, we compute the invariant mass of two particles at a time from the two particle arrays, $\mathbf{P}_1$ and $\mathbf{P}_2$. A particle object represents a physics object with properties such as momentum and energy. The invariant mass computation involves additions, multiplications, and trigonometric functions. The results of the computations are written to a circular buffer of maximum 2^{16} double-precision values, $\mathbf{D}_{res}$, to prevent the compiler from optimising the computation away. Figure 1 illustrates how we combine elements from the arrays in different ways to capture distinct access patterns. The two kernels are:

- *Sequential Invariant Mass (SIM)* iterates sequentially over both P_1 and P_2 and computes the invariant mass element-wise (i.e., between particles with the same index in both arrays).
- *Random Invariant Mass (RIM)* iterates sequentially over P_1 and computes the invariant mass of the current particle in P_1 with a random particle in P_2.

Kernels are executed with *small arrays* (fitting in L1 cache) and *large arrays* (exceeding all cache levels), with particle counts determined by: $|\mathbf{P}^{small}| < \lfloor \frac{\text{L1 size in bytes}}{\text{sizeof}(p_i)\times 3} \rfloor$ and $|\mathbf{P}^{large}| > \lceil \frac{\text{L3 size in bytes}}{\text{sizeof}(p_i)} \rceil$ respectively, where $\text{sizeof}(p_i)$ is the size of one particle in bytes. For the small arrays, the factor 3 ensures that all input three arrays $(\mathbf{P}_1, \mathbf{P}_2, \mathbf{D}_{res})$ fit within the L1 cache.

2.2 Data Layout Generator

The default particle data structure used in the kernels is shown in Listing 1 . The Invariant Mass kernels access data members `pt, eta, phi`, and `e`. In C++, the order in which data members are declared directly determines the order in which they are allocated in memory.

To change the data layout of the default particle data structure, we use a *split-merge* strategy, illustrated in Fig. 2 for a simplified structure `S`. Given `S` with three data members, we can *split* S into two sub-structures, where each sub-structure contains a subset of the data members of the original S. For example, the split operation denoted as ({0}, {2,1}) puts the first data member of S into a sub-structure and puts the second and third data members into a second sub-structure. Note that the declaration order of the second and third data members has changed from the original structure.

Once the original structure has been split into sub-structures, we can merge a new structure, `PartitionedContainer`, that places sub-structures into separate containers. In Fig. 2, this changes the data layout from `xyzxyzxyz...` to `xxx...yzyzyz...`. Note that placing all data members in the same sub-structure results in an AoS (Array-of-Structures) layout, while placing all data members in separate sub-structures results in an SoA (Structure-of-Arrays) layout.

To avoid having to change the kernel code when the layout changes, we define an index operator in `PartitionedContainer` that returns a *proxy* structure with the same data members as the original structure, but with reference data types that point to the elements in the sub-structure arrays. For example, if we have an array of the structure S named s and a `PartitionedContainer` with an array of a sub-structure named subs0 that contains the first member of S, as shown in Fig. 2, the proxy would allow us to access the data with the original syntax `s[0].x` instead of `s.subs0[0].x`. Assembly inspection confirmed that the proxy is optimised away by the compiler, incurring no runtime overhead.

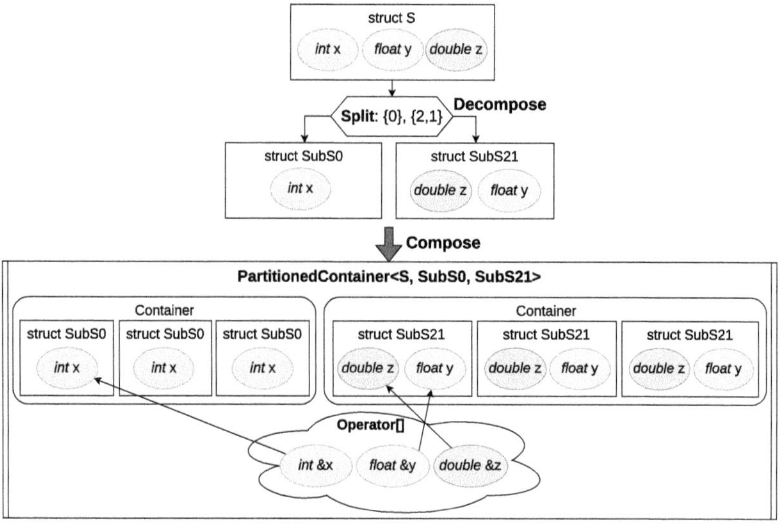

Fig. 2. Splitting a structure S into sub-structures and merging them into a partitioned array of structures.

We use a Python script to generate the implementation of the sub-structures and partitioned containers. We generate all possible sub-substructures and their

```
struct SubParticle4321 { double e, phi, eta, pt; };
struct SubParticle056 {
  int id;
  char charge;
  std::array<std::array<double, 3>, 3> posCovMatrix; };

struct ParticleRef {
  int &id;
  double &pt, &eta, &phi, &e;
  char &charge;
  std::array<std::array<double, 3>, 3> &posCovMatrix; };

struct PartitionedContainer4321_056 {
  SubParticle4321 *p1;
  SubParticle056 *p2;

  ParticleRef operator[](size_t idx) {
    return ParticleRef{
      p2[idx].id,  p1[idx].pt, p1[idx].eta, p1[idx].phi,
      p1[idx].e,   p2[idx].charge, p2[idx].posCovMatrix };}};
```

Listing 2. Example of transformed Particle after the split (`{4,3,2,1}, {0,5,6}`)

combinations to merge into a `PartitionedContainer`. Listing 2 shows an example of what code is generated for the split (`{4,3,2,1}, {0,5,6}`) on the particle structure. Note that we do not reorder the sub-structure containers within the `PartitionedContainer`. This is because they are allocated in different memory locations, so we assume that reordering the containers would not affect performance.

The total number of ways to split a structure with n members into $1..n$ sub-structures, N_n, where the members in each sub-structure are ordered, can be computed using the recursive formula: $N_n = 2{\cdot}(n-1){\cdot}N_{n-1} - (n-1){\cdot}(n-2){\cdot}N_{n-2}$ with $N_0 = N_1 = 1$ [7]. For our particle structure with 7 data members, we obtain 37633 different layouts, of which $7! = 5040$ are categorised as AoS and 1 as SoA.

3 DS*E*: Exploration Setup

We run all benchmarking on four CPUs (details in Table 1) with different micro-architectures: AMD Zen 2, AMD Zen 4, Intel Haswell, and Intel Skylake.

We use the latest compiler available on the machine to compile the code with the `-O3 -std=c++26 -march=native -ftree-vectorize -ffast-math` flags. Compilation on the AMD Zen 4 machine took 8.5 h and required 135 GB of RAM. Due to memory limitations on the other machines, we generate, compile, and run the layouts in batches. All our benchmarks use a single core. To avoid thread migration overheads, we pin the thread using `likwid-pin`[2].

For each kernel and layout combination, one "warmup" iteration is performed (the kernel is executed but not measured), followed by 10 repetitions during which the runtime is measured. In addition, we use PAPI 7.2.0[3] to collect hardware counters data. The input arrays are initialised to the same values for each layout before the timer starts.

[2] https://github.com/RRZE-HPC/likwid/wiki/Likwid-Pin

[3] https://github.com/icl-utk-edu/papi

Table 1. Systems used to run all benchmarks.

	AMD Zen 2	AMD Zen 4	Intel Haswell	Intel Skylake
CPU model	EPYC 7402P	EPYC 9534	Xeon E5-2630v3	Core i9-9900K
L1 Cache	32 KB	32 KB	32 KB	32 KB
L2 Cache	512 KB	1 MB	256 KB	256 KB
L3 Cache	16 MB	32 MB	20 MB	16 MB
System:	DAS-5[a]	CERN NGT[b]	DAS-6[c]	local machine[d]
Small Arrays [elem]	91	91	91	91
Large Arrays [elem]	139,810	279,620	174,762	139,810
Compiler	GCC 14.2.0	Clang 20.1.8	GCC 14.2.0	GCC 14.2.1

[a] https://www.cs.vu.nl/das5/home.shtml
[b] https://ngt.docs.cern.ch/
[c] https://www.cs.vu.nl/das/
[d] Without other programs running, and the frequency scaling governor is set to performance mode.

4 *DSE*: Results and Analysis

Our design-space exploration generates substantial amounts of data. We propose a top-down approach to analyse the results:

1). Analyse the overall performance of all layouts to determine the gap between the best and worst cases.
2). Analyse performance-counter data for all layouts to determine whether there is a correlation with overall performance.
3). Investigate in detail the root causes for the observed performance of several outliers, including the best- and worst-performing layouts and layouts with specific features (e.g., "fully" AoS or SoA).

We collected performance data for more than 37500 data layouts. In the following sections, we refer to a specific layout with an encoded notation, such as `4321_056`, for the transformation in Listing 2, where the digits correspond to the data members of the original particle structure (`0-6`), and the underscore indicates an array separation.

4.1 Overall Performance

Table 2 presents the best and worst measured runtime (averaged over 10 runs) for all combinations of kernels, problem sizes, and platforms. We observe that the performance gap between the best and worst layout (per-platform) is, on average, around 50%, but can reach up to $\frac{|0.01-0.03|}{0.01} \approx 67\%$ for the small problem size and $\frac{|29.5-72.25|}{29.5} \approx 59\%$ for the large problem size. Thus, selecting the right data layout does significantly impact performance.

Table 2. Best- and worst-case measured kernel runtime (averaged over 10 runs) for all combinations of kernels, dataset sizes, and platforms.

		AMD Zen 2		AMD Zen 4		Intel Haswell		Intel Skylake	
	Arrays	Best	Worst	Best	Worst	Best	Worst	Best	Worst
SIM	Small	0.01464	0.03199	0.01054	0.01844	0.01942	0.04834	0.01210	0.02479
		0_25416_3	324506_1	132540_6	4350216	6410253	2064_351	013624_5	01_54236
	Large	25.93	50.20	39.47	44.46	41.13	52.55	20.21	35.28
		30_241_5_6	1043652	240531_6	3645201	0234_1_56	24103_65	06_2314_5	01_56423
RIM	Small	0.01473	0.03134	0.01055	0.02656	0.01960	0.05887	0.01194	0.02145
		0_4312_5_6	05_26341	42013_65	40152_63	12043_56	52430_61	206451_3	01_46523
	Large	29.50	72.25	56.96	119.5	44.70	106.3	21.82	46.50
		60_1_2_3_4_5	0164532	0_124_3_5_6	20153_64	0_421_3_65	0125364	605_1234	510_234_6

Key Observation 1: The largest observed performance gap between the best and worst data layout can be as high as 67%.

To visualise the performance gap between different layouts, we plot the distribution of average runtime across all layouts in Fig. 3. Due to space constraints, we only present the histogram for the newest architecture, AMD Zen 4, but the other histograms exhibit similar shapes. All collected data is made available on Zenodo [2]. We do label the figure with the positions of the best and worst layouts for the other architectures to show the similarity in performance.

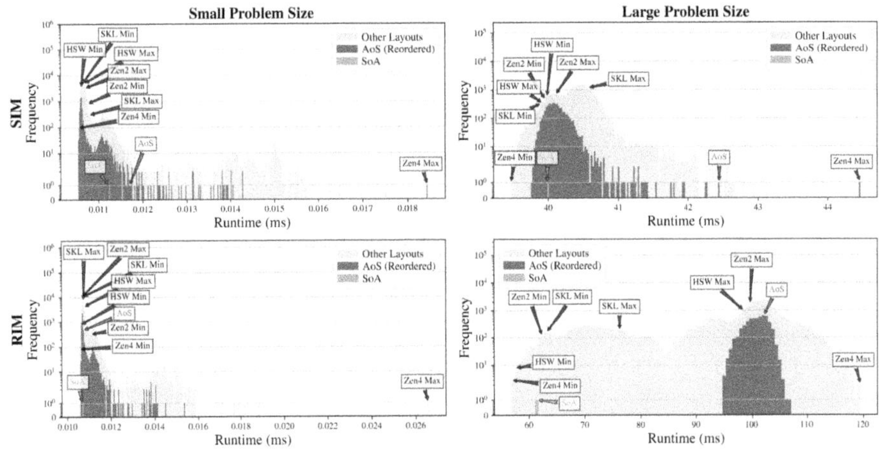

Fig. 3. Distribution of the measured average runtime over 10 runs per kernel (rows) and problem size (columns) on AMD Zen 4. The red bars cover all 5040 AoS layouts, the orange bar covers the SoA layout, and the blue bars cover all other layouts. (Color figure online)

We observe that, for the small problem size, the majority of layouts perform close to the best one, with a few outliers; for the large problem size, a wide spread in runtime is visible. Interestingly, the RIM kernel exhibits a bimodal distribution across all tested architectures, suggesting the presence of two groups: 'good' and 'bad' layouts. Moreover, we found that the best-performing layouts in kernels with large arrays for one architecture fall within the better half of the observed runtimes on other architectures, suggesting that while results vary across architectures, good layouts remain relatively performant.

Key Observation 2: The performance of a data layout depends on the architecture, but the best-performing layout on one architecture stays within the top 50% on alternative (similar) architectures.

For the RIM kernel on large problem sizes, where performance differences are most pronounced, the best layouts separate the used data members (indices 1–4) from the unused ones. This matches the intuition that grouping relevant data improves spatial locality and reduces unnecessary loads. In contrast, for the SIM kernel, the best layouts group the used data members with unused integer and char members.

We also examine the performance of the AoS and SoA layouts in Table 3, which are common choices for (human) developers. The relatively poor performance of the AoS layout `0123456`, which preserves the original particle structure, shows how easy it is to end up with subpar performance. The spread of AoS layouts with different data-member orderings in Fig. 3 further shows that data-member ordering strongly affects performance. In contrast, SoA performs close to the best layout (within 7%). However, the SIM kernel results in Fig. 3 show that SoA does not always outperform the best AoS layout, so switching from AoS to SoA does not guarantee better performance.

Key Observation 3: SoA generally performs better than AoS, but an AoS with a customised ordering of data members can outperform SoA.

Table 3. Summary of measured average runtime in milliseconds of the AoS (`0123456`) and SoA (`0_1_2_3_4_5_6`) layouts.

		AMD Zen 2		AMD Zen 4		Intel Haswell		Intel Skylake	
Kernel	Arrays	AoS	SoA	AoS	SoA	AoS	SoA	AoS	SoA
SIM	Small	0.02768	0.01477	0.01170	0.01124	0.02242	0.01996	0.01226	0.01227
	Large	26.57	26.28	42.45	39.99	43.29	41.72	21.16	20.46
RIM	Small	0.02784	0.01519	0.01072	0.01068	0.02208	0.02002	0.01218	0.01208
	Large	48.46	29.74	102.1	61.45	97.12	46.44	30.47	22.98

Figure 4 plots the average runtime for each data layout and kernel with the large problem size, with standard deviation error bars. For the SIM kernel with slower layouts, we see large runtime variance (up to 10 ms) for the same layout, despite unchanged input data and executable. This behaviour is not machine-specific; the same large variance appears on other architectures.

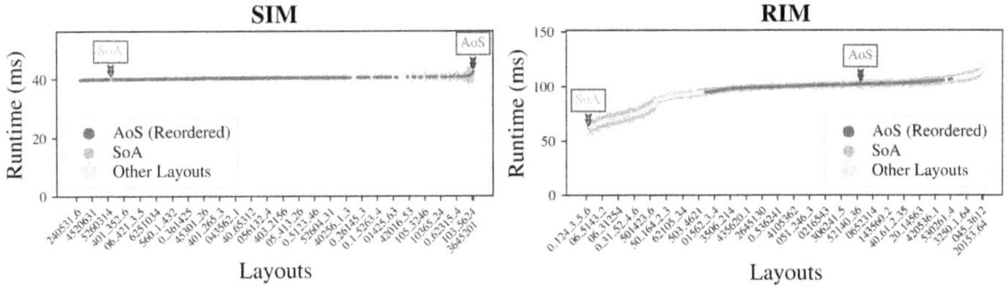

Fig. 4. Scatter plot of average runtime for all layouts with the large problem size, sorted in increasing order from left to right. To keep the x-axis readable, we label the best, worst, and intermediate layouts at intervals of 1500.

4.2 Memory Performance

To analyse memory performance, we collect performance-counter data for "L1 fills", i.e., the number of requests to fill the L1 cache from any source (L2, L3, or DRAM). Figure 5 shows L1 fills for each layout, sorted by increasing runtime (as in Fig. 4). In the first third of the layouts for SIM, we see lower counts for non-AoS, indicating fewer L1 misses and potentially explaining their better performance. However, AoS layouts at the left end have nearly as many L1 fills as the poorly performing layouts. For the RIM kernel, we again initially observe fewer L1 fills for better layouts, but in the middle region, where runtime in Fig. 4 stagnates, L1 fills no longer appear to correlate with overall performance.

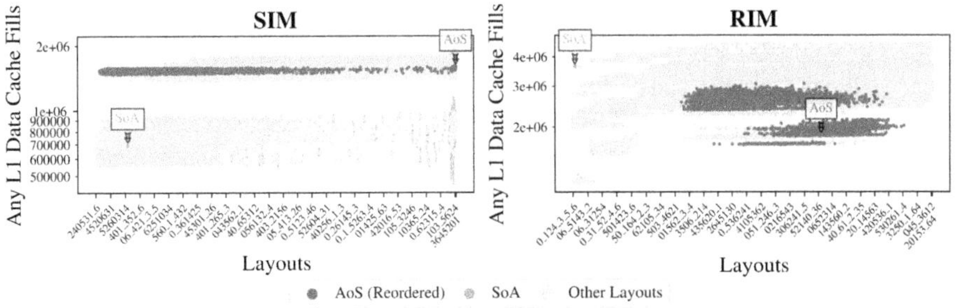

Fig. 5. L1 fills per layout sorted by runtime, as in Fig. 4.

Table 4 shows "L1 fills" per data source for the best, SoA, AoS, and worst layouts. The data is collected by rerunning the kernels with the selected layouts, counting only L1-fill events. It shows that the worst-performing layouts incur high memory transfer costs due to cache line retrievals from lower memory hierarchy levels. Notably, in the RIM kernel, causes more L1 fills than the worst layout, yet performs better because most requests are to the faster L2/L3 caches rather than DRAM. This highlights that L1 miss count alone is insufficient to predict layout performance, as different misses carry different penalties depending on where they are resolved. This makes it extremely difficult to predict the best-performing layout since it is non-trivial to estimate at which level an L1 miss will be resolved.

Table 4. L1 fills per data source, sorted by increasing memory transfer cost from left to right. In an AMD Zen 4 CPU, each core has its own L1 and L2 caches, and the L3 cache is shared across a Core Complex (CCX) unit (a group of 8 cores) [1].

Kernel	Layout	Local L2	L3 or another L2 in the same CCX	Cache from another CCX	DRAM	Cache from another CCX, different NUMA node	DRAM, different NUMA node
SIM	Best	642841.8	5243.2	0.0	9715.8	0.0	1.2
	SoA	713719.8	5590.6	2.4	9934.6	0.0	1.2
	AoS	1528529.0	5034.4	8.2	32799.0	0.2	1.2
	Worst	1518203.4	5254.0	0.4	17661.2	0.2	0.8
RIM	Best	880837.4	1020692.4	1.0	182844.0	0.0	3.0
	SoA	1418318.8	1975601.0	2.2	206154.4	0.4	4.8
	AoS	1045308.4	128166.4	25.0	690576.4	0.0	5.0
	Worst	1525977.4	504130.4	25.2	971536.0	0.0	6.2

Key Observation 4: Cache misses impact the performance of a data layout, but the scale of the impact is also determined by the *different costs* associated with these misses.

4.3 Instruction Mix

To better understand the cause of the performance variation unaccounted for in the L1 analysis, we also analyse hardware-counters data for retired instructions[4]. Figure 6 shows the total number of retired instructions for each layout, sorted in increasing order. The data reveals several plateaus, suggesting that different layouts yield distinct instruction mixes after compilation. Additionally, the runtime plot for the RIM kernel indicates that within each plateau (except the lowest), there is substantial runtime variance.

To check whether layouts with equal instruction counts share the same instruction mix, we inspect the assembly count of the RIM kernel for the AoS, SoA, best, and worst layouts, as well as the best and worst layouts that have been labelled in Fig. 6 for the first, sixth, eighth, and tenth plateaus. Table 5 shows that the assembly operation counts fluctuate within the same group, with

[4] We also collected information about retired vector instructions, but found no vectorisation is taking place.

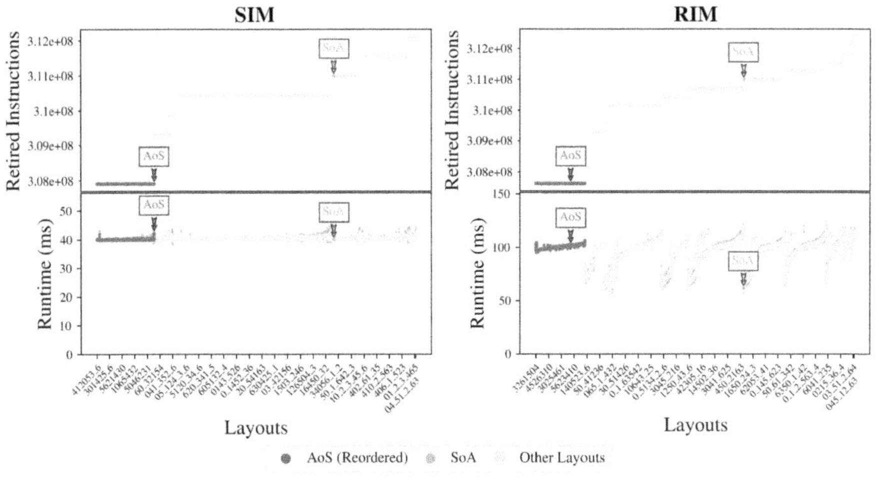

Fig. 6. Total number of retired instructions and average runtime for all layouts, sorted by number of instructions with the large problem size.

differences arising not in arithmetic operations but in the number of move operations needed to resolve data member addresses. We speculate that the runtime variance for the same instruction count stems from differing move operation latencies depending on the target address. This subtle yet impactful difference further suggests that statically determining the best-performing layout is infeasible.

Table 5. Number of assembly operations in the RIM kernel.

Group 1			Group 6		Group 8			Group 10		Group 14
Worst	AoS	`5623410`	`065_1_432`	`10643_25`	`42305_16`	`450_2613`	SoA	`50_61_342`	`0_1_2_564_4`	Best
237	235	243	246	240	249	249	253	249	262	254

Key Observation 5: The data layout alone may lead the compiler to choose a different instruction mix for the exact same computation, due to the complex calculation of the accessed members' memory addresses/offsets.

Key Observation 6: Even for data layouts with the same instruction mix, significant performance variations may appear due to (some) instruction latencies being context-dependent (i.e., due to different scheduling, pipelining, and caching).

5 Discussion

The analysis of our DSE's results (2 kernels × 37633 layouts × 4 architectures) has led to six key observations, illustrating how to extract value from such a detailed dataset. In this section, we present the guidelines we derived from the observations to support programmers in selecting a *well-performing* data layout, and discuss the generalisation and limitations of our approach.

5.1 Guidelines

We derive three rules to guide the selection of better-performing layouts. We name the rules as follows: *Used Together*, *Used Not Mixed with Unused*, and *SoA of Used Members*. In Fig. 7, we present the runtime histograms of our DSE experiments on all four architectures, and highlight the layouts that meet each rule (also leading to colour-based "nicknames" for the guidelines).

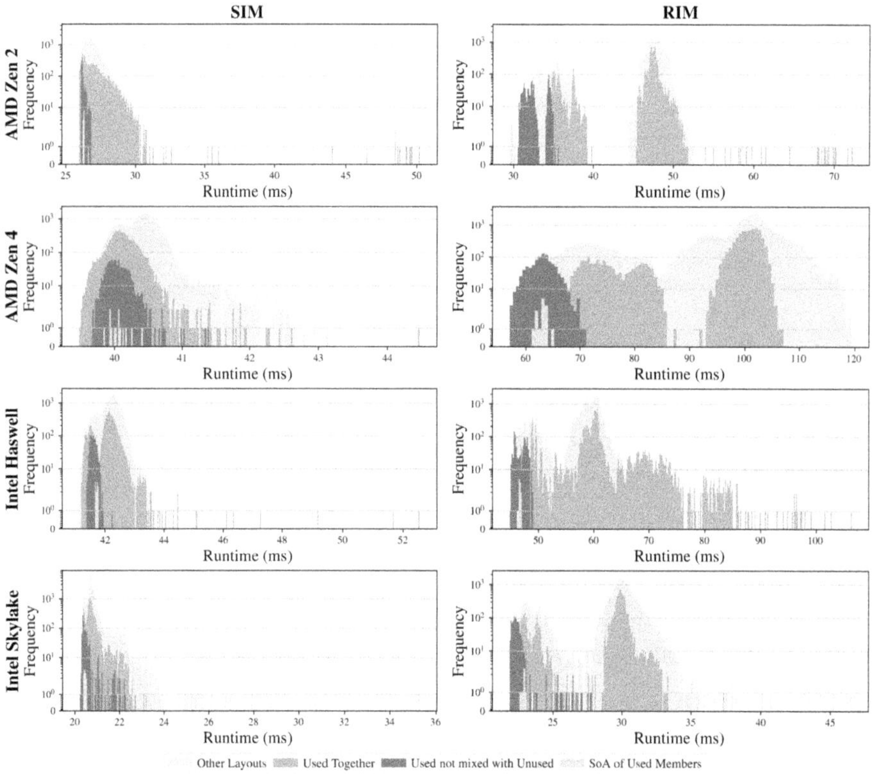

Fig. 7. Layout distribution by guideline, per architecture (rows) and kernel (columns).

(Dark Blue) Used Together: group the used data members into a single array, possibly including unused members. For example, `0_1234_56` and `012345_6` meet this rule, but not `0_12_34_56`. This rule is based on our observation that most of the best-performing layouts have in common that all the used data members are grouped together in Table 2. In Fig. 7, we observe that this rule is highly unstable as the layouts under consideration cover a wide runtime range.

(Purple) Used Not Mixed With Unused: used data members are not in the same array as unused data members, and the used data members are not necessarily in the same array. This, for example, includes `0_1234_56` and `0_12_34_56`, but not `012345_6`. Figure 7 shows that this rule has a 95% chance of yielding a layout in the top 38% (except for SIM on Skylake, where it is 91%) and a 50% chance of ending up in the top 11%.

(Yellow) SoA Of Used Members: each used data member is in its own array, e.g., `0_1_2_3_4_5_6` and `1_2_3_4_560`, but not `0_12_34_56`. This is a more restrictive version of the previous rule, and Fig. 7 shows that it results in a 95% chance of finding a top-36% layout (again, except for the 96% SIM on Skylake) and a 50% chance of finding a top-15% layout.

5.2 Generalization and Limitations

While these guidelines help select a layout likely within the top 38% of observed performance, identifying the best layout remains difficult. As Fig. 7 shows, a layout meeting the "Yellow" rule can outperform all "Purple" layouts, but may also underperform them. Results also show architectural dependence: on AMD Zen 2, the "Yellow" rule yields the best layout for the RIM kernel, while on Intel Skylake, the "Purple" rule does. Finally, we cannot guarantee these rules generalise beyond the tested kernels and architectures. Although exhaustively benchmarking all layouts demands significant compilation and compute time, our DSE approach with automated layout generation makes extending the analysis to new configurations as straightforward as possible.

6 Related Work

That data layouts impact performance is well known, yet rarely systematically quantified. Prior work on arrays of structured data typically examines only a limited number of layouts, with a substantial body dedicated to comparing AoS with SoA [5,6]. Beyond these coarse-grained layouts, numerous studies explored finer-grained data layout transformation techniques, such as array regrouping, structure splitting, and data member reordering. These studies use various metrics, such as reference affinity [11,12] and the estimated cache efficiency [4,9,10], to guide the transformation. However, these studies compare only the recommended layout against a baseline, rather than exploring the full design space. Notably, array regrouping appears under various names in literature, e.g., *array interleaving* [10], *instance interleaving* [11], or *inter-array data regrouping* [4].

In the context of heterogeneous systems, [8] systematically explores a multi-dimensional space of alternative code variants using a synthetic microbenchmark and different data layouts. While the setup resembles ours, there are notable differences in target architecture and data structure complexity. Thus, to the best of our knowledge, ours is the first work to systematically quantify the impact of data layouts on CPU performance using complex data structures.

7 Conclusion

Programming for high performance requires optimising every aspect of one's code. In this work, we focus on data-layout selection, a challenge even for simple codes using complex data structures and CPUs with deep cache hierarchies. To this end, we present a design-space exploration (DSE) approach to quantify the performance impact of data layouts in applications using (complex) arrays of data structures. Our DSE combines: realistic kernels written with varied access patterns (see Sect. 2.1), a data-layout generator (see Sect. 2.2) that systematically enumerates all possible layouts, and comprehensive benchmarking, to execute all kernels × all layouts, collecting runtime and hardware-counter data. A top-down analysis, evaluating all layouts before focusing on key ones, can help identify performance-influencing factors and derive layout-selection guidelines.

We demonstrate the DSE approach using two kernels representative of common high-energy physics computations, with 7-member particle structures across 4 CPU micro-architectures, analysing over 37500 automatically generated data layouts. We observe significant performance gaps of up to 67% between the best- and worst-performing layouts, with structure-of-arrays generally approaching the best. While predicting the best-performing layout is challenging due to complex interactions across the memory hierarchy, isolating used from unused data members likely yields a layout within the top 38% of observed performance (for the tested systems). Though these findings cannot be directly generalised, our automated DSE simplifies reassessment for new architectures and kernels.

Future work will focus on expanding the root-cause analysis of layout-specific runtime variance, broadening the study to kernels with varying arithmetic intensity and additional architectures, and refining the proposed guidelines into comprehensive and generalisable programming/compiling rules.

Acknowledgments and Artifact Availability. This work was funded by the Eric & Wendy Schmidt Fund for Strategic Innovation through the CERN Next Generation Triggers project (grant SIF-2023-004). The artifact is available in Zenodo [3].

Disclosure of Interests. The authors declare no relevant competing interests.

References

1. AMD: Processor Programming Reference (PPR) for AMD Family 19h Model 10h-1fh, Revision A1 Processors (PUB) (55901). https://docs.amd.com/v/u/en-US/55901

2. Chen, J.: Results for all systems. https://doi.org/10.5281/zenodo.20269809
3. Chen, J., Varbanescu, A.L., Naumann, A.: Artifact of the paper: Assessing the performance impact of data layouts: a benchmarking approach (2026). https://doi.org/10.5281/zenodo.20511012
4. Ding, C., Kennedy, K.: Inter-array data regrouping. In: Carter, L., Ferrante, J. (eds.) LCPC 1999. LNCS, vol. 1863, pp. 149–163. Springer, Heidelberg (2000). https://doi.org/10.1007/3-540-44905-1_10
5. Faria, N., Silva, R., Sobral, J.L.: Impact of data structure layout on performance. In: Euromicro 2013 (2013). https://doi.org/10.1109/PDP.2013.24
6. Homann, H., Laenen, F.: SoAx: A generic C++ structure of arrays for handling particles in HPC codes. Comput. Phys. Commun. **224**, 325–332 (2018). https://doi.org/10.1016/j.cpc.2017.11.015
7. OEIS Foundation Inc.: Entry A000262. https://oeis.org/A000262
8. Qasem, A., Aji, A.M., Rodgers, G.: Characterizing data organization effects on heterogeneous memory architectures. In: IEEE/ACM CGO 2017, pp. 160–170 (2017). https://doi.org/10.1109/CGO.2017.7863737
9. Sharma, K., Karlin, I., Keasler, J., McGraw, J.R., Sarkar, V.: Data layout optimization for portable performance. In: Euro-Par 2015 (2000). https://doi.org/10.1007/978-3-662-48096-0_20
10. Sharma, N., Panda, P.R., Catthoor, F., Raghavan, P., Aa, T.V.: Array interleaving—an energy-efficient data layout transformation. ACM Trans. Des. Autom. Electron. Syst. **20**(3) (2015). https://doi.org/10.1145/2747875
11. Truong, D., Bodin, F., Seznec, A.: Improving cache behavior of dynamically allocated data structures. In: PACT 1998, pp. 322–329 (1998). https://doi.org/10.1109/PACT.1998.727268
12. Zhong, Y., Orlovich, M., Shen, X., Ding, C.: Array regrouping and structure splitting using whole-program reference affinity. ACM SIGPLAN Not. **39**(6), 255–266 (2004). https://doi.org/10.1145/996893.996872

Adaptive Data Augmentation with Bayesian Optimization for Basic Block Throughput Prediction

Xiabing Hu[1], Xuezheng Xu[2], Deheng Yang[2], Bowen Liu[2], Chun Huang[1], and Qiong Li[2(✉)]

[1] National University of Defense Technology, Changsha, People's Republic of China
{huxiabing,chunhuang}@nudt.edu.cn
[2] Academy of Military Sciences, Beijing, People's Republic of China
qiong.li@nanhulab.ac.cn

Abstract. Accurate prediction of basic block throughput is essential for compiler optimization and microarchitectural performance analysis. However, existing data-driven approaches rely on large labeled datasets that are costly to collect and often fail on rare yet performance-critical instruction patterns. This paper presents BADA, an adaptive data augmentation with Bayesian optimization for basic block throughput prediction. BADA first constructs a feature representation to quantify the characteristics of basic block patterns, then applies Bayesian optimization to efficiently locate informative vectors, and finally employs a constraint-aware generator to map the selected vectors into executable basic blocks. We evaluate BADA on three representative RISC-V microarchitectures with two deep learning models. Experimental results show that BADA achieves 13.5%23.1% relative reduction in Mean Absolute Percentage Error (MAPE) under the same data scale. Remarkably, it reaches comparable or better MAPE using only one-fourth of the original data while preserving high cross-architecture generalization.

Keywords: Performance prediction · Bayesian optimization · Data augmentation · Basic block throughput

1 Introduction

Accurate performance prediction has become a cornerstone of modern compiler optimization and system-level performance analysis [18,24,27]. It enables compilers to estimate execution cost without relying on time-consuming hardware testing, thereby guiding optimization decisions such as instruction scheduling [21], register allocation [9], and phase ordering [17]. Among various code representations, a basic block [5] serves as the most fundamental unit for such analysis. Accurately predicting the throughput of basic blocks is thus essential as the basis

M. Torquati et al. (Eds.): Euro-Par 2026, LNCS 16781, pp. 166–180, 2027.
https://doi.org/10.1007/978-3-032-35248-4_12

for efficient and automated performance optimization in performance-critical tasks, from compiler heuristic learning to microarchitectural design exploration.

Problem Statement. This work targets the problem of predicting the throughput of basic blocks. Specifically, we aim to predict the number of processor cycles required for execution, which is the inverse of throughput. Formally, we model it as a supervised learning task that learns a mapping from instruction sequences to their measured throughput.

Existing Work. Existing methods for basic block throughput prediction can be broadly categorized into two types: rule-based analytical models and data-driven machine learning models. Analytical models such as LLVM Machine Code Analyzer (LLVM-MCA) [8] and Intel Architecture Code Analyzer (IACA) [16] rely on detailed microarchitectural knowledge to simulate instruction execution and estimate performance. They typically construct mathematical abstractions of the processor pipeline and use parameters such as instruction latency and resource utilization to estimate execution time. In contrast, data-driven approaches, such as Ithemal [23] and DeepPM [26], directly learn the mapping between assembly sequences and throughput from empirical measurements collected on target hardware.

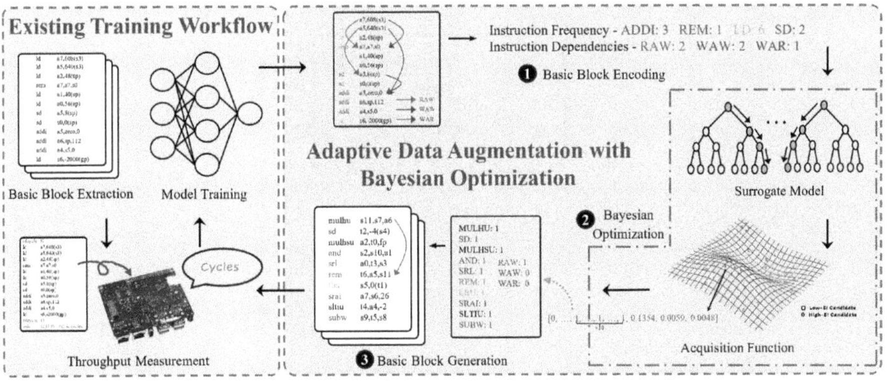

Fig. 1. Overview of the adaptive data augmentation with BO (BADA).

Limitations. Although analytical models provide interpretable results, their development and maintenance demand detailed microarchitectural knowledge and per-architecture calibration, making them impractical for rapidly evolving processors. Consequently, recent studies have turned to data-driven approaches for throughput prediction. As illustrated in the left part of Fig. 1, such approaches generally follow a standard workflow of basic block extraction, throughput measurement, and model training. However, these data-driven predictors show limited generalization when applied to unseen instruction patterns or new microarchitectures. For example, prior studies [23] collected 1.42M basic blocks from several benchmark suites. We adopt the same methodology and re-measure the dataset on RISC-V, resulting in a total of approximately two million lines of C code and three million basic blocks. Despite this considerable scale, the data distribution remains highly skewed. As shown in Fig. 2, we trained an LSTM-based throughput model [23] on the same dataset used in prior studies and found that the instruction frequencies exhibit a long-tailed distribution, where rare instruction types not only account for fewer than a thousand samples but also suffer from significantly higher prediction errors–up to 17 times greater than those of frequent instructions. These results indicate that existing datasets lack sufficient diversity, making it difficult for models to generalize. A naive approach to improve accuracy is to simply enlarge the dataset, but exhaustive data collection is impractical–profiling millions of basic blocks takes weeks even on hardware, and would be far slower in pre-silicon environments. With the advancement of chip agile development technologies, the iteration cycles of modern CPUs, such as those based on the RISC-V architecture [13,29], are becoming increasingly shorter, and the barriers to entry are continuously lowering. This trend creates a demand for rapid iteration of compilers. However, the cost of model training, which can take several weeks, is prohibitively high. If this training were conducted during the pre-silicon phase, the cost would increase by several times further.

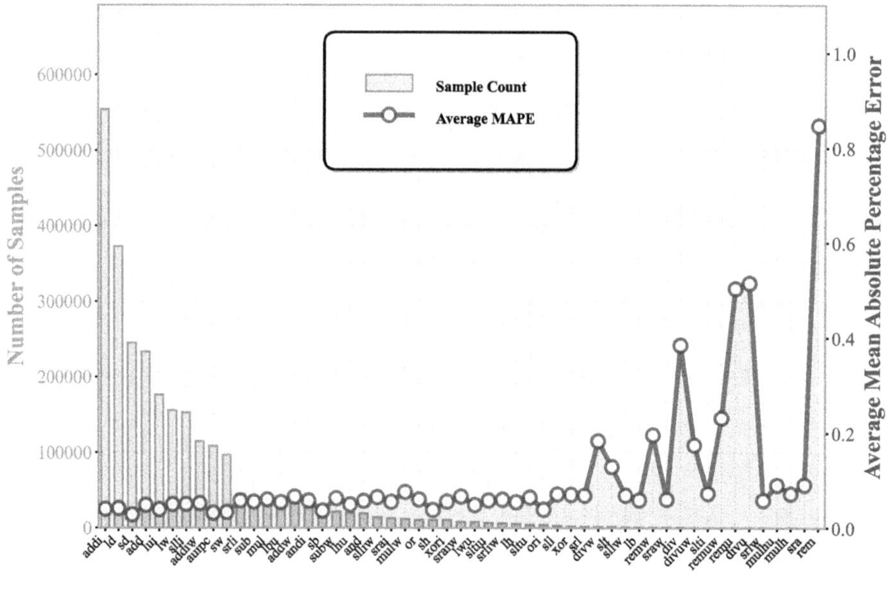

Fig. 2. Instruction distribution and per-instruction MAPE of the LSTM Model [23] on the RISC-V code.

Challenges. We aim to build a small yet representative dataset that captures critical instruction patterns efficiently. However, there are three main challenges that make traditional random or heuristic augmentation strategies insufficient to fully exploit available data, thereby limiting model improvement.

- **Quantifying data diversity.** It is non-trivial to measure how well a dataset covers diverse instruction patterns without a quantitative feature representation of basic blocks.
- **Efficient discovery of informative samples.** Manually collecting high-loss basic blocks in real-world programs outside the dataset for data augmentation is prohibitively inefficient.
- **Architecture-specific adaptability.** Different microarchitectures exhibit distinct pipeline behaviors, requiring the data distribution to adapt dynamically rather than relying on a fixed, generic dataset.

Our Solution. To address these challenges, we propose BADA, an adaptive data augmentation framework leveraging Bayesian optimization. The overall workflow of BADA is depicted in Fig. 1. First, to quantify data diversity, we encode basic blocks into vector representations by incorporating key performance factors, such as instruction types and data dependencies. This encoding enables a quantitative analysis of instruction pattern distributions and facilitates the identification of sparse regions within the extensive input basic blocks. Based on this representation, we formulate the search for informative samples as a global optimization problem. Bayesian optimization is employed to actively explore regions of high uncertainty, thereby guiding the discovery of meaningful data points. Subsequently, to bridge the abstract feature vectors and executable basic blocks, a constraint-aware generator synthesizes basic blocks from the optimized representations. Through this iterative process, BADA adaptively generates informative basic blocks tailored to different microarchitectures.

In summary, this paper makes four primary contributions:

- We present an adaptive data augmentation approach to basic block throughput prediction with Bayesian optimization.
- We present a feature representation for basic blocks that enables identification of high-loss regions.
- We present a constraint-aware basic block generator that maps selected candidates to executable RISC-V basic blocks.
- We demonstrate through extensive experiments on three RISC-V microarchitectures that BADA achieves 13.5%–23.1% relative reduction in MAPE under the same data scale and that augmented datasets surpass baselines trained with four times more data.

2 Methodology

In this section, we present the methodology of BADA, which consists of three core phases: basic block encoding, Bayesian-guided candidate selection, and basic block generation.

2.1 Basic Block Encoding

To facilitate a quantitative optimization process, we first define a rigorous feature representation for a basic block. Specifically, we transform a basic block into a hybrid feature vector $\mathbf{x}$, which comprises two types of features: instruction frequency and instruction dependency.

Instruction Frequency. The frequency of various instruction types provides a direct reflection of the performance characteristics of a basic block. For instance, division instructions are more time-consuming compared to addition instructions. Let T represent the total number of unique instruction types in the Instruction Set Architecture (ISA). The first T elements in $\mathbf{x}$ represent the frequencies of each instruction type within the basic block.

Instruction Dependencies. Dependencies between instructions impact pipeline efficiency and consequently affect the performance of a basic block. We focus on three typical data dependencies, including read-after-write (RAW), write-after-read (WAR), and write-after-write (WAW). The last three elements of $\mathbf{x}$ are the density of dependencies, which is defined as the number of dependencies divided by the length of the basic block.

2.2 Bayesian Optimization

Bayesian optimization (BO) [12,25] has emerged as a powerful approach for optimizing complex black-box functions. It builds a surrogate model to approximate the unknown objective and uses an acquisition function to decide where to sample next. By balancing exploration and exploitation, BO efficiently identifies promising regions in the search space with only a limited number of evaluations. This property makes it particularly suitable for our setting, where profiling new basic blocks is time-consuming.

Surrogate Model. One primary element of an efficient BO algorithm is an accurate surrogate model that estimates the loss for any given feature vector $\mathbf{x}$. We adopt a Random Forest (RF) [25] regressor rather than Gaussian Processes (GP) [12,25] because RFs offer better scalability and robustness in high-dimensional, non-smooth loss landscapes where instruction patterns exhibit discrete and categorical-like behaviors. Feature vectors are standardized before training, and duplicate samples are aggregated using median loss for stability.

Acquisition Function. The acquisition function is a policy that uses the surrogate model's outputs to decide which feature vector $\mathbf{x}$ to sample next. We adopt the Expected Improvement (EI) [12,25] acquisition function, which naturally balances exploitation and exploration. Compared with the Probability of Improvement (PI) [25] or Upper Confidence Bound (UCB) [25], EI not only identifies regions with high predicted loss but also prioritizes points in previously underexplored areas where improvement is most likely. The process of acquiring the next samples consists of two steps.

Candidate Generation. To efficiently explore the high-dimensional feature space, we employ Latin Hypercube Sampling (LHS) [22], which ensures uniform and stratified coverage across all dimensions. Such uniform sampling provides representative candidates and thereby avoids the clustering effects common in purely random sampling, leading to a more comprehensive exploration of the design space.

For the instruction frequency features, we sample from a Multinomial distribution parameterized by the LHS point, which creates a realistic combination of instruction counts.

Candidate Selection. We form a combined evaluation set that contains both the existing training samples and the new LHS-generated candidates. The acquisition function is then evaluated for every point $\mathbf{x}$ in this set. Using the surrogate's predictive mean $\mu(\mathbf{x})$ and standard deviation $\sigma(\mathbf{x})$, and denoting the current best observed loss as y_{best}, the EI for each candidate $\mathbf{x}$ is computed as

$$\text{EI}(\mathbf{x}) = \sigma(\mathbf{x}) \cdot (\xi \Phi(\xi) + \phi(\xi)) \tag{1}$$

$$\xi = \frac{\mu(\mathbf{x}) - y_{\text{best}}}{\sigma(\mathbf{x})} \tag{2}$$

where Φ and ϕ are the Cumulative Distribution Function (CDF) and Probability Density Function (PDF) of the standard normal distribution, respectively. Finally, the top-k candidates with the highest EI values are selected for synthesis and measurement.

2.3 Basic Block Generation

The constraint-aware generator constructs a syntactically valid basic block matching the target feature vector $\mathbf{x}$ by satisfying instruction frequency and dependency constraints. We utilize a structure called a Dependency Kernel (hereafter referred to as a kernel), where a sequence of instructions shares a single register to generate deterministic counts of RAW, WAR, and WAW dependencies. This formulation treats dependency generation as a combinatorial optimization problem of selecting optimal kernel sizes.

We employ a greedy strategy to iteratively select kernel sizes. However, a simple greedy approach risks overshooting the target for one dependency type, thereby consuming instruction slots required for others. To prevent this, we design a utility function that balances satisfaction progress against resource contention. Specifically, we define the utility of a kernel size as the difference between the effective gain and the overflow penalty. The effective gain is the number of generated dependencies capped by the remaining budget, encouraging progress toward the target. Simultaneously, the overflow penalty accounts for any dependencies generated in excess of the budget. Since basic block length is limited, different dependency types compete for the same finite instruction slots. Generating dependencies beyond the target yields no value for feature matching but wastefully occupies slots needed for other types. By subtracting this penalty, our algorithm avoids local optima where one constraint is satisfied at the expense of others. Driven by this utility definition, the optimization objective at each step is to select the kernel size that maximizes the aggregate utility across all dependency types. The algorithm repeats this selection process, iteratively updating the remaining budgets until the targets are met or the instruction limit is reached.

Finally, instruction types are sampled according to the frequency distribution in $\mathbf{x}$, and registers are allocated to enforce the planned kernel structures. To ensure semantic correctness and prevent unintended dependency collisions, we employ a strict register allocation policy that utilizes disjoint registers for non-dependent instructions and avoids illegal memory accesses or state corruption.

3 Experiment Setup

3.1 Dataset

Following prior studies [23], we constructed a comprehensive dataset of basic blocks extracted from diverse real-world applications and benchmark suites that covers a wide range of workloads, including performance-critical compiler benchmarks, general-purpose applications and so on.

Basic blocks were extracted from disassembled binaries compiled with the `O2` optimization flag using custom scripts that follow the standard definition, restricted to the RV64IM subset, excluding CSR, branch/jump instructions, and system calls. Redundant entries from duplicated compilation units were removed through feature-level deduplication, yielding 898,072 unique basic blocks.

3.2 Performance Profiling

BADA is orthogonal to both the underlying neural network architecture and the performance measurement methodology. Our study focuses on enhancing data efficiency rather than designing better predictors or measurement tools. Therefore, all experiments compare models trained with and without our augmentation method under identical configurations, isolating the improvement brought solely by data generation.

To validate the platform-independence of our approach, we evaluate BADA on both real hardware and LLVM-MCA simulator across three RISC-V platforms with varying microarchitectural complexity:

- **StarFive VisionFive 2** (Hardware): Quad-core U74-MC SoC @ 1.5 GHz.
- **SiFive-U74** (Simulator): Dual-issue in-order pipeline.
- **XiangShan-Nanhu** (Simulator): Six-issue out-of-order pipeline.

Simulators enable rapid and reproducible profiling of the full dataset, whereas hardware measurements were conducted by adapting the BHive benchmark framework [11] from x86 to RISC-V, executing each basic block in isolation under a fixed CPU frequency. In our setup, simulator profiling proceeds at about 27 s per 1000 samples, while hardware profiling takes roughly 400 s for the same workload, underscoring the high cost of data collection. The time overhead of BADA is negligible compared to the process of collecting basic blocks from real-world programs and subsequently measuring their throughput. For example, BADA can generate, on average, 1200 basic blocks per second.

3.3 Experimental Configuration

We evaluated BADA using two representative throughput prediction models: the LSTM-based *Ithemal* [23] and the Transformer-based *DeepPM* [26]. All models were implemented following their original configurations.

Following prior studies [23,26], we adopt the MAPE as the primary metric to evaluate the effectiveness of our method. The dataset was randomly divided into three sets: 800k training samples, 50k validation samples and 48k test samples, ensuring representative coverage of diverse instruction and dependency patterns.

Experiments were conducted on an Ubuntu 24.04.2 LTS workstation equipped with a 12th Gen Intel Core i5-12400 CPU, 32 GB RAM, and an NVIDIA GeForce RTX 3090 GPU with 24 GB VRAM. To address implementation transparency, BADA was developed using PyTorch 2.5.1 for model training, scikit-learn 1.5.1 for the Random Forest surrogate model, and SciPy 1.14.1 for Latin Hypercube Sampling.

4 Evaluation

4.1 Efficiency

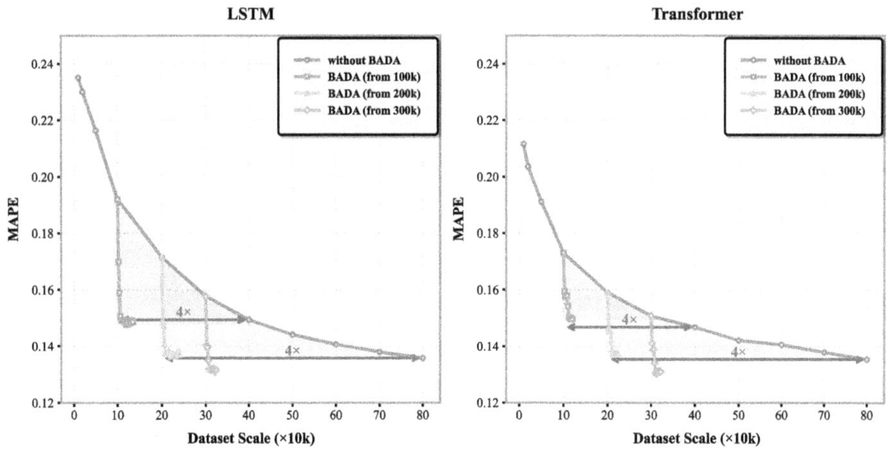

Fig. 3. MAPE trajectories of models trained with and without BADA at different initial dataset scales on StarFive VisionFive 2.

To comprehensively assess the efficiency of BADA, we evaluate it on the StarFive VisionFive 2 hardware platform, employing both LSTM and Transformer architectures. We begin the training process from three distinct initial dataset scales, with incremental steps of $2,000$ samples. Figure 3 illustrates the MAPE trajectories between training without BADA and incremental learning with BADA across models, showing consistent MAPE decreases with significantly reduced data requirements.

Table 1. MAPE with BADA from different initial data scales on StarFive VisionFive 2.

Model architecture	Initial Size	Base MAPE	Best MAPE	Δ%
LSTM	100k	0.192020	0.147658	23.1%
	200k	0.171541	0.136397	20.5%
	300k	0.157755	0.130858	17.0%
Transformer	100k	0.173015	0.149599	13.5%
	200k	0.159004	0.136973	13.9%
	300k	0.150804	0.130439	13.5%

Table 1 summarizes the quantitative results. For the LSTM model, the MAPE obtained with BADA shows a notable decrease compared to that obtained without it, achieving relative reductions ranging from 17.0% to 23.1%. The Transformer model exhibits similarly stable improvements across all configurations, with relative reductions in MAPE ranging from 13.5% to 13.9%, demonstrating strong generalization and robustness.

More importantly, the model trained on the augmented 100k dataset surpasses the accuracy of the model trained on the original 400k dataset. Similarly, the model trained on the augmented 200k dataset outperforms the model trained on the original 800k dataset. This indicates that, with the proposed targeted data augmentation in BADA, only 25% of the original data volume is required to achieve or exceed the same MAPE. In real hardware, this amounts to a roughly 70% reduction in the end-to-end data collection and training cycle, substantially lowering the overall modeling cost and turnaround time.

Overall, these results confirm that BADA effectively reduces MAPE and enhances data efficiency across different model architectures while maintaining high predictive accuracy in real hardware environments.

4.2 Portability

To evaluate the portability of BADA across different microarchitectures and measurement environments, we conducted comparative experiments using 100k samples as the initial dataset scales on three representative RISC-V platforms: StarFive VisionFive 2, SiFive-U74, and XiangShan-Nanhu. These platforms span

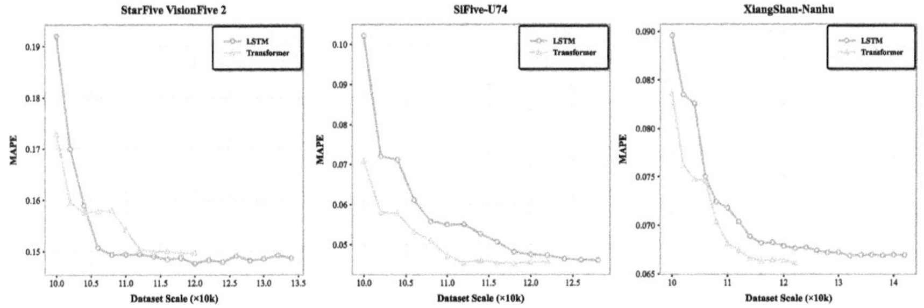

Fig. 4. MAPE trajectories of models trained with BADA across three microarchitectures.

a wide spectrum of pipeline complexities, providing a diverse testbed for verifying the stability of BADA under different execution models.

Table 2. MAPE with BADA from 100k initial data scales across different microarchitectures.

Platform	Model	Base MAPE	Best MAPE	Δ%
StarFive VisionFive 2	LSTM	0.192020	0.147658	23.1%
	Transformer	0.173015	0.149599	13.5%
SiFive-U74	LSTM	0.102164	0.046104	54.9%
	Transformer	0.069896	0.045394	35.1%
XiangShan-Nanhu	LSTM	0.089579	0.066870	25.4%
	Transformer	0.083647	0.066139	20.9%

As shown in Fig. 4, BADA consistently reduces MAPE and achieves faster convergence with fewer samples across all platforms, demonstrating effectiveness in both simulated and real hardware settings. The quantitative results in Table 2 show that on StarFive VisionFive 2, relative reductions reach 23.1% and 13.5%, respectively, representing slightly smaller but significant improvements. On the in-order SiFive-U74, the relative reductions increase to 54.9% and 35.1%, showing the most pronounced improvement. On the out-of-order XiangShan-Nanhu, LSTM and Transformer achieve relative reductions of 25.4% and 20.9%.

Overall, the trend reveals that BADA benefits more from deterministic execution environments and simpler pipelines. Under the same microarchitecture, simulation-based measurements show larger gains due to their determinism and repeatability. In contrast, hardware runs are affected by cache interference, OS scheduling, thermal drift, and measurement noise, which reduce the net gain of individual augmented samples. Under the same measurement condition, in-order pipelines with predictable execution benefit more from BADA, while out-of-order designs introduce dynamic reordering, leading to smaller but consistent gains.

In summary, BADA achieves stable improvements across different microarchitectures and measurement environments, demonstrating strong microarchitecture-agnostic adaptability and broad applicability across diverse hardware platforms.

4.3 Case Study

To illustrate BADA's efficiency on underrepresented instruction patterns, we examine a concrete example of targeted augmentation.

```
ld      a7,608(s3)
ld      a5,640(s3)
ld      a2,48(sp)
rem     a7,a7,s0
ld      a1,40(sp)
ld      a0,56(sp)
sd      a5,8(sp)
sd      s0,0(sp)
addi    a5,zero,0
addi    a6,sp,112
addi    a4,s5,0
ld      s6,-2000(gp)
```

(a) Original basic block

```
mulhu   s11,s7,a6
sd      t2,-4(s4)
mulhsu  a2,t0,fp
and     s2,s10,a1
srl     a0,t3,s3
rem     t6,a5,s11
lbu     s5,0(t1)
srai    a7,s6,26
sltiu   t4,a4,-2
subw    s9,t5,s8
```

(b) BADA-generated basic block

Fig. 5. A case study on rare `rem` patterns.

Figure 5a shows a basic block containing a rare `rem` instruction, for which the original LSTM model predicts 12.16 cycles against the actual 73 cycles, resulting in a MAPE of 82.25%. This represents a typical failure case on rare patterns: the `rem` instruction appears in fewer than 0.1% of training samples. BADA identifies this pattern as high-loss through RF surrogate. The framework then generates synthetic samples containing `rem` along with other underrepresented instructions (`mulhu`, `mulhsu`, `sltiu`), as shown in Fig. 5b.

After retraining with BADA-generated samples, the enhanced model predicts 68.51 cycles for the original block, achieving a MAPE of 6.55% and a 92.04% relative reduction. This demonstrates BADA's ability to identify and address model weaknesses on rare instruction patterns with minimal additional data.

4.4 Threats to Validity

First, our experimental evaluation primarily focused on the RISC-V architecture, driven by its significant relevance to the compiler community's need for rapid iteration. Although our core method is architecture-agnostic, its porting to other architectures (e.g., ARM) would principally involve reimplementing the instruction mapping component for basic block encoding and generation. We have open-sourced BADA to facilitate further investigation and extension.

Second, our evaluation utilized two established models for basic block throughput prediction, namely Transformer and LSTM. We deliberately limited our experiments to these models and did not include larger-scale LLMs at this stage. The primary consideration is the critical constraint of inference speed in practical compilation scenarios, where we hypothesize that current LLMs may not satisfy the low-latency requirements for frequent invocations within a compiler pass. Whether LLMs can achieve higher precision with less data remains an interesting yet separate research direction beyond the scope of this study.

5 Related Work

Static Throughput Prediction. Existing throughput estimation methods fall into two categories: analytical and learned models. Analytical models [3,16] such as llvm-mca [8], OSACA [20],and uiCA [1,2] estimate basic block throughput based on microarchitectural rules and scheduling constraints, achieving sub-1% accuracy after careful calibration. Data-driven approaches [4,6,7,19,28], exemplified by Ithemal [23] and DeepPM [26], learn execution behavior directly from measured data using neural models. While removing the need for hardware-specific modeling, they require large labeled datasets that are costly to collect and remain sensitive to rare instruction patterns.
Bayesian Optimization. Bayesian Optimization is widely used for AutoML [25], compiler autotuning [10], and design space exploration [14], offering sample-efficient optimization of expensive black-box objectives. Existing BO-based frameworks primarily focus on hyperparameter or configuration tuning rather than data generation. In contrast, this work leverages BO to guide targeted data augmentation for throughput prediction, enabling systematic exploration of underrepresented instruction regions and improving model generalization across microarchitectures.

6 Conclusion

This paper presents BADA, an adaptive data augmentation framework with Bayesian optimization for basic block throughput prediction. BADA systematically identifies underrepresented instruction patterns and synthesizes informative samples to enhance model generalization. It can be seamlessly integrated with existing learning-based predictors.

Acknowledgements and Artifact Availability. This work was supported by the National Key Research and Development Program of China (Grant No.2023YFB3001600) and the National Natural Science Foundation of China (Grant No. 62402515). The artifact is available in the Zenodo repository [15].

Disclosure of Interests. The authors have no competing interests to declare that are relevant to the content of this article.

References

1. Abel, A., Reineke, J.: uops.info: characterizing latency, throughput, and port usage of instructions on intel microarchitectures. In: Proceedings of the Twenty-Fourth International Conference on Architectural Support for Programming Languages and Operating Systems, pp. 673–686. ASPLOS '19, New York, NY, USA (2019). https://doi.org/10.1145/3297858.3304062
2. Abel, A., Reineke, J.: uiCA: accurate throughput prediction of basic blocks on recent intel microarchitectures. In: Proceedings of the 36th ACM International Conference on Supercomputing. ICS '22, New York, NY, USA (2022). https://doi.org/10.1145/3524059.3532396
3. Abel, A., Sharma, S., Reineke, J.: Facile: fast, accurate, and interpretable basic-block throughput prediction. In: 2023 IEEE International Symposium on Workload Characterization (IISWC), pp. 87–99 (2023). https://doi.org/10.1109/IISWC59245.2023.00023
4. Adams, A., Ma, K., Anderson, L., et al.: Learning to optimize halide with tree search and random programs. ACM Trans. Graph. **38**(4) (2019). https://doi.org/10.1145/3306346.3322967
5. Alfred, V.A., Monica, S.L., Jeffrey, D.U.: Compilers Principles, Techniques & Tools (2007)
6. Amalou, A.N., Fromont, E., Puaut, I.: Catreen: context-aware code timing estimation with stacked recurrent networks. In: 2022 IEEE 34th International Conference on Tools with Artificial Intelligence (ICTAI), pp. 571–576 (2022). https://doi.org/10.1109/ICTAI56018.2022.00090
7. Amalou, A.N., Fromont, E., Puaut, I.: Fast and accurate context-aware basic block timing prediction using transformers, pp. 227–237. CC 2024, New York, NY, USA (2024). https://doi.org/10.1145/3640537.3641572
8. Biagio, A.D., Davis, M.: LLVM machine code analyzer (2018). available: https://llvm.org/docs/CommandGuide/llvm-mca.html. [Accessed 10 Sep 2025]
9. Castañeda Lozano, R., Carlsson, M., Drejhammar, F., et al.: Constraint-based register allocation and instruction scheduling. In: Eighteenth International Conference on Principles and Practice of Constraint Programming. vol. 7514, pp. 750–766. Québec City, Canada (2012). https://doi.org/10.1007/978-3-642-33558-7_54
10. Chen, J., Xu, N., Chen, P., Zhang, H.: Efficient compiler autotuning via Bayesian optimization. In: 2021 IEEE/ACM 43rd International Conference on Software Engineering (ICSE), pp. 1198–1209 (2021). https://doi.org/10.1109/ICSE43902.2021.00110
11. Chen, Y., Brahmakshatriya, A., Mendis, C., et al.: BHive: a benchmark suite and measurement framework for validating x86-64 basic block performance models. In: 2019 IEEE International Symposium on Workload Characterization (IISWC), pp. 167–177 (2019). https://doi.org/10.1109/IISWC47752.2019.9042166
12. Frazier, P.: A tutorial on Bayesian optimization. ArXiv **abs/1807.02811** (2018)
13. Fu, Z., Tedeschi, R., Ottavi, G., et al.: Ramping up open-source Risc-v cores: assessing the energy efficiency of superscalar, out-of-order execution. In: Proceedings of the 22nd ACM International Conference on Computing Frontiers, pp. 12–20. CF '25, New York, NY, USA (2025). https://doi.org/10.1145/3719276.3725186
14. Hellsten, E.O., Souza, A., Lenfers, J., et al.: BACO: a fast and portable Bayesian compiler optimization framework. In: Proceedings of the 28th ACM International Conference on Architectural Support for Programming Languages and Operating Systems, vol. 4, pp. 19–42. ASPLOS '23, New York, NY, USA (2024). https://doi.org/10.1145/3623278.3624770

15. Hu, X., Xu, X., Yang, D., Liu, B., Huang, C., Li, Q.: Artifact of the paper: adaptive data augmentation with Bayesian optimization for basic block throughput prediction (2026). https://doi.org/10.5281/zenodo.20501352, https://doi.org/10.5281/zenodo.20501352
16. Intel Corporation: Intel architecture code analyzer. [Online] (2019). available: https://software.intel.com/content/www/us/en/develop/articles/intel-architecture-code-analyzer.html. [Accessed: Sep. 10, 2025]
17. Jain, S., Andaluri, Y., VenkataKeerthy, S., et al.: POSET-RL: phase ordering for optimizing size and execution time using reinforcement learning. In: 2022 IEEE International Symposium on Performance Analysis of Systems and Software (ISPASS), pp. 121–131 (2022). https://doi.org/10.1109/ISPASS55109.2022.00012
18. Jia, Z., Thomas, J., Warszawski, T., et al.: Optimizing DNN computation with relaxed graph substitutions. In: Proceedings of Machine Learning and Systems, vol. 1, pp. 27–39 (2019)
19. Kaufman, S., Phothilimthana, P., Zhou, Y., et al.: A learned performance model for tensor processing units. In: Proceedings of Machine Learning and Systems, vol. 3, pp. 387–400 (2021)
20. Laukemann, J., Hammer, J., Hofmann, J., et al.: Automated instruction stream throughput prediction for intel and AMD microarchitectures. In: 2018 IEEE/ACM Performance Modeling, Benchmarking and Simulation of High Performance Computer Systems (PMBS), pp. 121–131 (2018). https://doi.org/10.1109/PMBS.2018.8641578
21. McGovern, A., Moss, J.: Scheduling straight-line code using reinforcement learning and rollouts. In: Advances in Neural Information Processing Systems, vol. 11 (1998)
22. McKay, M.D., Beckman, R.J., Conover, W.J.: A comparison of three methods for selecting values of input variables in the analysis of output from a computer code. Technometrics **42**(1), 55–61 (2000)
23. Mendis, C., Renda, A., Amarasinghe, D., et al.: IThemal: accurate, portable and fast basic block throughput estimation using deep neural networks. In: Proceedings of the 36th International Conference on Machine Learning. Proceedings of Machine Learning Research, vol. 97, pp. 4505–4515 (2019)
24. Narayanan, D., Harlap, A., Phanishayee, A., et al.: PipeDream: generalized pipeline parallelism for DNN training. In: ACM Symposium on Operating Systems Principles (SOSP 2019) (2019)
25. Shahriari, B., Swersky, K., Wang, Z., et al.: Taking the human out of the loop: a review of Bayesian optimization. Proc. IEEE **104**(1), 148–175 (2016). https://doi.org/10.1109/JPROC.2015.2494218
26. Shim, J.S., Han, B., Kim, Y., Kim, J.: DeepPM: transformer-based power and performance prediction for energy-aware software. In: 2022 Design, Automation & Test in Europe Conference & Exhibition (DATE), pp. 1491–1496 (2022). https://doi.org/10.23919/DATE54114.2022.9774589
27. Stephenson, M., Amarasinghe, S., Martin, M., et al.: Meta optimization: improving compiler heuristics with machine learning. SIGPLAN Not. **38**(5), 77–90 (2003). https://doi.org/10.1145/780822.781141

28. Sýkora, O., Phothilimthana, P.M., Mendis, C., Yazdanbakhsh, A.: Granite: A graph neural network model for basic block throughput estimation. In: 2022 IEEE International Symposium on Workload Characterization (IISWC), pp. 14–26 (2022). https://doi.org/10.1109/IISWC55918.2022.00012
29. Xu, Y., Yu, Z., Tang, D., et al.: Towards developing high performance RISC-V processors using agile methodology. In: 2022 55th IEEE/ACM International Symposium on Microarchitecture (MICRO), pp. 1178–1199 (2022). https://doi.org/10.1109/MICRO56248.2022.00080

A Compiler-Assisted Workflow for Efficiency-Guided Selective Tracing

Sebastian Kreutzer[1(✉)], Valentin Seitz[2], Joan Vinyals[2], Tim Heldmann[1], Christian Iwainsky[1], Marta Garcia[2], Jesus Labarta[2], and Christian Bischof[1]

[1] Technische Universität Darmstadt, Darmstadt, Germany
sebastian.kreutzer@tu-darmstadt.de
[2] Barcelona Supercomputing Center, Barcelona, Spain

Abstract. Traces are essential for HPC root-cause analysis, but full tracing at scale without countermeasures incurs prohibitive overheads and data volume. Selective tracing is one approach to combat this issue, by restricting trace collection on a structural and temporal level. Configuring such selective tracing typically requires iterative profiling, source code modifications and often recompilation. We present a process for systematic selective tracing that combines static whole-program analysis with insightful efficiency metrics. At compile time, it extracts an annotated call graph and embeds runtime-reconfigurable instrumentation based on LLVM XRay. At runtime, a low overhead profiling identifies performance-critical regions, while a lightweight validation mechanisms resolve statically unresolvable call-graph issues caused by dynamic function calls. Analysts can then derive a selective tracing configuration according to analysis requirements without the need to rebuild the application. This enables targeted tracing with reduced overheads and trace sizes. A case study using this workflow on Vlasiator, reduced initial profiling overhead from 300% to 17%. The generated traces maintained critical insight, while reducing trace size by 10× compared to the default tracing approach.

Keywords: Selective tracing · Compiler-assisted performance analysis · Runtime-configurable instrumentation · High-Performance Computing · LLVM XRay · Call Graph Analysis

1 Introduction

Traces provide the analyst with a detailed timeline of the program's execution, and have long been established as an essential tool for HPC performance analysis. They allow to reason about temporal behavior and causal dependencies of parallel applications, which are often hidden in flat call profiles.

However, the ongoing growth of HPC systems has rendered generating traces for large-scale runs time- and resource-consuming. Such runs can yield extremely

M. Torquati et al. (Eds.): Euro-Par 2026, LNCS 16781, pp. 181–194, 2027.
https://doi.org/10.1007/978-3-032-35248-4_13

Table 1. Comparison of selective tracing axes across HPC performance tools.

Tool	Structural Axis	Temporal Axis	Detail Axis
Score-P [5]	Compiler instrumentation (via filter files), source annotations	Configurable invocation ranges	On/off
TAU [12]	Compiler/dynamic instrumentation (via filter files), source annotations	Source code API	On/off
Extrae [10]	Source annotations, dynamic instrumentation	Source code API	On/off, burst mode

large trace sizes, often exceeding hundreds of gigabytes. Post-processing and analyzing such traces requires extensive compute and memory resources and can constitute a significant bottleneck in the analysis workflow.

In a typical analysis, however, the high level of detail offered by traces is only really needed for a few code regions of interest. Moreover, it might be sufficient to record only a handful of occurrences of these regions, provided there is no significant change in behavior or performance over time.

Significant size reduction is, therefore, achievable by limiting trace collection to relevant execution windows, a concept referred to as *selective tracing*. This motivates a selection process across three axes: *structural* selection, defining the code regions of interest within the application's structure, *temporal* selection, deciding when to record a region, and *measurement detail*, determining the kinds of performance data (e.g., MPI and OpenMP events, hardware perf. counters, etc.) to capture within its scope. Table 1 displays a comparison of selective tracing features in established HPC performance tools.[1] While structural selection is well-supported via configurable compiler or dynamic binary instrumentation, there is less support on the temporal axis. In TAU and Extrae, this is only possible via source-level API calls, with Score-P allowing the user to configure active ranges in a file. Similarly, Score-P and TAU allow toggling between full detail and disabling measurement. Extrae provides a less-detailed burst mode that records summary metrics collected inside a programmable time window.

In general, however, there is a distinct lack of tool support for combining these features in practical tracing workflows. The analyst must decide on a set of selected regions, a range of active invocations and their associated measurement detail level. While initial profiling results can guide this process, this still requires a manual selection, and switching between different configurations is arduous, requiring source modifications for TAU and Extrae. Furthermore, fully disabling recording outside of regions of interest creates a visibility gap, making it impossible to detect performance drift or sporadic degradations that occur outside this window.

This paper presents a novel end-to-end performance analysis toolchain for configurable selective tracing on the structural and temporal level. We introduce the following features to mitigate the aforementioned issues:

[1] Sampling-based tools are not considered, as they provide no structured program view to base selective features on.

- A runtime-configurable instrumentation method that allows a single build to be used across all phases of the analysis, requiring zero source modifications.
- User-guided instrumentation selection aided by static whole-program call graph analysis, coupled with a runtime filtering mechanism, allowing for customizable instrumentation selection without the need for manual refinement.
- Semi-automated creation of trace configurations based on parallel performance metrics.
- A runtime system that enables a high level of temporal tracing control, including support for multiple levels of measurement detail.

We implement these features in a toolchain that automates the build process using an LLVM-based compiler wrapper. This wrapper integrates XRay [2] (LLVM's runtime-configurable instrumentation mechanism), extracts and annotates the call graph during link-time optimization (LTO), and links the runtime libraries, providing the foundation for our analysis workflow. On a conceptual level, this workflow is divided into two measurement phases, each preceded by a tool-assisted selection stage. This process is illustrated in Fig. 1.

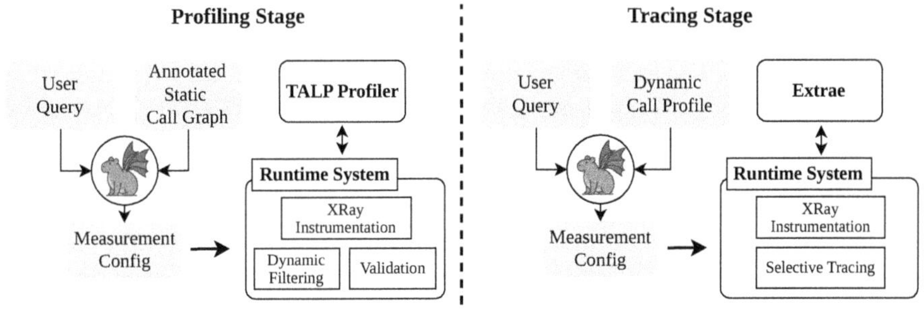

Fig. 1. Stages of the proposed tracing workflow.

The resulting instrumented binary is then executed to generate tailored tracing configurations in a two-stage approach. The initial *profiling* stage collects performance metrics that can be used to generate trace configurations. As full instrumentation is typically much too expensive, we employ the selective instrumentation tool CaPI [6] to generate a suitable low-overhead measurement configuration based on static call graph analysis. During the subsequent execution, TALP [8] is used to collect parallel efficiency metrics for the selected regions, using dynamic filtering as an additional overhead limiter. The performance metrics generated by TALP are then merged with the existing static information to create an annotated dynamic call graph.

In the *tracing* stage, the analyst queries this annotated call graph to generate a trace configuration according to the current measurement objective. For an initial overview trace, for example, the analyst may focus on regions with low overall parallel efficiency and restrict full measurement detail to a few invocations. We provide a GUI to simplify this process, including a profile visualizer, a query editor and on-the-fly trace size estimation for the current configuration. Using the same initial binary, the target application is executed using Extrae as a tracing back-end, recording a trace according to the given configuration.

We make the following key contributions:

- A tracing infrastructure based on a multi-fidelity selective tracing model
- A selective instrumentation approach combining static analysis and runtime filtering, using LLVM XRay for dynamic adaptability with a single application binary.
- A analysis workflow driven by parallel performance metrics, automating the creation of storage-optimized trace configurations.

2 Related Work

The challenge of managing trace data volume in the era of exascale computing has led to several distinct research directions. We categorize these efforts into data compression and automated analysis.

Compression and Structural Abstraction. One major approach to mitigating trace volume is reducing the size of the recorded data through structural compression. Methods such as *ScalaTrace* [9], *CYPRESS* [16] and *PALLAS* [3] utilize pattern-matching algorithms to identify repetitive execution streams, representing them as compressed loops. *Folding* [11] takes a different approach, aggregating coarse-grained sampling over repetitive structures to capture them in high detail, while limiting the amount of collected data. While effective at reducing storage requirements, such techniques often rely on structural regularity, which can obscure sporadic performance anomalies. Our selective tracing approach is orthogonal to these approaches, and could in principle be used in combination with them.

Automated Analysis. To reduce the manual effort of navigating large traces, *Scalasca* [14] performs automated searches for performance bottlenecks, such as wait states and communication inefficiencies. This reduces the burden on the analyst, but still requires an initial full trace. Recent trends have also explored in-situ analysis frameworks like *SOSflow* [15], which process performance data in memory as it is generated. While these minimize disk I/O, they do not allow for retrospective full-detail analysis.

3 Toolchain

This section gives an overview of the different parts of the toolchain, divided into compile-time and run-time components.

3.1 Compilation and Instrumentation

Our workflow requires the program binary to be used throughout both measurement phases, to be adaptable to different measurement objectives, and supporting multiple tool back-ends. To achieve this, we heavily modify the target's build process, introducing the following features:

1. Reconfigurable instrumentation with XRay
2. Static whole-program call graph extraction and embedding
3. Integration of runtime management and tool abstraction libraries

An overview of the components of the built binaries is shown in Fig. 2.

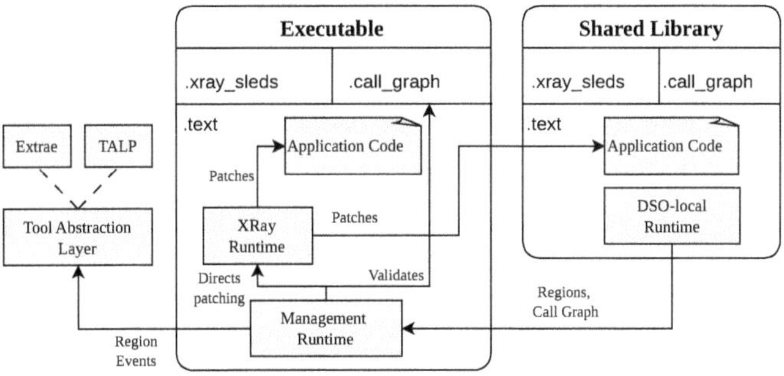

Fig. 2. Overview of the components of the final executable and shared library binaries (multiple libraries are possible).

Call graph extraction and embedding. We rely on an annotated whole-program call graph for the initial low-overhead instrumentation selection and as auxiliary information in the later tracing phase. To this end, we employ the *CaGe* call graph generator from the *MetaCG* project. This tool was developed for the purpose of extracting a whole-program call graph at link-time and annotating it with static code metrics. This call graph is then embedded into a custom ELF section, making it available to extract and analyze both statically and, for validation purposes, at runtime. The executable and every built shared library (DSO) provide their own embedded graph, which can be merged for a complete program representation.

Instrumentation. We use XRay for general-purpose function instrumentation and custom events. Since XRay is fully integrated into LLVM, inserting the binary sleds and linking the necessary runtime libraries is handled automatically with a set of XRay-specific flags. An additional compiler pass is run to insert custom XRay events, e.g. to notify the runtime about `MPI_Init/Finalize` calls[2]. Additionally, we instrument unresolved indirect

[2] Note that we cannot rely on interception with PMPI, as this is typically already used by the respective profiling/tracing backend.

calls, e.g., resulting from function pointers in C and C++. This enables the runtime to catch calls that may be missing in the static call graph and evaluate their impact on overall profile coverage.

Build Orchestration. To hide the complexity of modifying many aspects of the build process, we provide a prefixing compiler wrapper called `capicc`. Placed before the regular compiler invocation, it (1) directs Clang to run in LTO mode with the flags required for XRay, (2) registers custom instrumentation and call graph analysis passes and (3) links in the main runtime and tool abstraction libraries. For better integration with CMake-based projects, we provide a wrapper generator that creates a drop-in replacement for a specific compiler binary.

3.2 Runtime Behavior

The central runtime library fulfills a variety of functions:

- Interacting with the XRay runtime to identify patchable functions, to apply filtering, and to implement instrumention.
- Keeping track of and instrumenting dynamically loaded DSOs.
- Passing region enter/exit events to the chosen profiling/tracing tool.
- Dynamic filtering to further enable overhead reduction.
- Ensuring consistency of the call stack in the presence of exceptions.
- Validating completeness of the static call graph.

The following paragraphs describe noteworthy aspects in more detail:

Dynamic Filtering. The static filtering approach allows the analyst to filter out functions that are known to be irrelevant a priori (e.g., standard library calls or specific parts of the codebase), as well as those deemed unimportant based on heuristics. Purely static approaches, however, are limited by the fact that they cannot predict runtime behavior accurately, which may lead to the inclusion of functions with high overhead potential. Instrumenting short-running functions with extremely high call counts can drastically increase measurement overhead.11 1 To mitigate this issue, we augment the static filter with a dynamic approach to catch such instances, based on the *throttling* feature introduced in TAU [12]. This system disables further measurements of a function after a set number of recorded invocations, if the runtime per call is below a given configurable threshold. In contrast to TAU, where the profiling call is still invoked during each function invocation, XRay allows us to dynamically unpatch such measurement points, thus eliminating any residual overhead during the rest of the execution entirely.

Call Graph Validation. Most applications contain a number of indirect calls, i.e., calls to a dynamic address rather than a pre-defined symbol. While some instances can be resolved via *points-to* analysis (PTA), statically determining a minimal set of call targets is generally not possible. Such cases lead to missing edges in the static call graph and may affect downstream analyses.

In prior work, we investigated the use of state-of-the-art PTA in combination with minimal, targeted instrumentation in order to minimize and, if unresolvable, detect such defects at runtime [7]. Here, we adopt this approach to validate the static call graph at runtime and to assess the impact missing edges have on profile coverage. To this end, we first instrument unresolvable calls to notify the runtime library of the known parent function and the dynamic call address. The runtime library then resolves the target symbol and inserts a corresponding edge into a *patch graph* it maintains. At the end of execution, the patch graph is merged into the embedded static call graph and saved for later use. To assess the impact of missing edges, the underlying selection query (stored in the measurement configuration) is re-evaluated, reporting the difference in the final selection set. If there is little deviation, the analyst can be sure that the generated profile accurately covers the execution and may proceed with the results. In the case of significant differences, however, the analyst may choose to repeat the profiling step, now using the adapted selection based on the patched call graph.

4 Selective Tracing Model

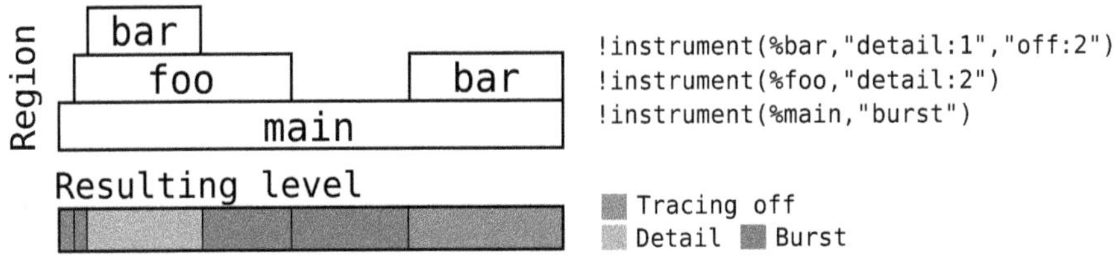

Fig. 3. Example of the selective tracing model for three regions

Each measurement level carries a fidelity value, and levels are totally ordered by these values. When the runtime registers a new region, it applies a *max*() rule: the effective fidelity can only increase relative to the current state. Figure 3 illustrates this for three regions, assuming `off` has the highest fidelity value in this example.

This ensures that once a parent region is marked for high-fidelity tracing, all nested invocations inherit at least that level of detail, preserving the integrity of the trace while allowing for fine-grained temporal and structural pruning.

In our implementation, we support the following measurement levels with Extrae as a tracing backend, ordered from lowest to highest: `off` fully disables tracing, `annotate` records only function entry/exit time stamps, `burst` records programming models in burst mode, `full` records all events, and `forceoff` forces the `off` mode. We added the `forceoff` level to always retain the ability to completely disable tracing, regardless of the current call stack.

5 Workflow

This section elaborates the proposed workflow and corresponding tools for creating highly scalable trace configurations.

As illustrated in Fig. 1, this workflow is divided into a preparational profiling and a tracing phase, each preceded by a selection step.

5.1 Selection and Analysis Utilities

The CaPI instrumentation selection tool serves as the basis for both selection steps. It was built as a means to create highly configurable selection pipelines operating on an annotated static call graph. Using CaPI's concise selection DSL, the user can parameterize and combine pre-defined selector modules to accurately adapt to the chosen target application and measurement objective. This allows combining powerful selection heuristics, using the static code metrics attached to the call graph, with application-specific knowledge.

For this work, CaPI was extended to support selection based on dynamic profile data. To achieve this, we provide a tool that combines the static call graph with recorded performance metrics, creating a context-sensitive call tree. A variety of new selectors were added that allow to filter the recorded functions based on these metrics. We also introduced a GUI to improve the user-experience. Central features are:

- Loading and visualization of both static and dynamic call graphs and associated metadata.
- A flame graph view of the profile data.
- A query editor to help create and interactively run selection queries.
- Visualization of selection results, including trace size estimation.

5.2 Workflow Phases

Starting out with the instrumented target binary, the workflow is structured in four phases: *Static Selection*, *Profiling*, *Trace Configuration* and *Tracing*.

Static Selection. First, the analyst runs a static selection query using either the GUI or CLI tool. We found selection based on *inclusive statement count* [4] to be effective for a general-purpose profile. For a function F, this metric is defined as the sum of the number of instructions over all functions in the subgraph reachable from F. Functions are selected, if their inclusive instruction count surpasses a threshold value k. If desired, this can be refined using a variety of other methods, such as MPI call path selection and function-level code metrics, e.g. loop information or static FLOP counts.

Profiling. Given the initial selection, the application is run in profiling mode. This generates a JSON file containing a context-sensitive call profile with associated efficiency metrics. In a post-processing step, these results are then combined with the static call graph, annotating functions that have been dynamically filtered. Additionally, the analyst is notified with the call graph validation results.

Trace Selection. The analyst loads the profile into the GUI, using the provided visualization methods to inspect the results. Depending on the current focus of analysis, the analyst creates a query based on performance metrics, static information, and if desired, manual selection of individual functions. For a given selection, the analyst can specify the tracing behavior for a set of invocation ranges, as modelled in Sect. 4.

Tracing. Finally, the application is executed in tracing mode using the measurement configuration created in the preceding step. The chosen tracing back-end produces a trace file, which the analyst can investigate using the tool's regular infrastructure for trace analysis and visualization. In a typical analysis workflow, the analyst then chooses a new focus of analysis and may return to the *Trace Configuration* step to adjust the configuration accordingly.

6 Case Study

We demonstrate the effectiveness of the presented tooling infrastructure by running a case study on Vlasiator [13], a space plasma simulation code employing hybrid MPI/OpenMP parallelism. All experiments were run on the general purpose partition of the Mare Nostrum 5 general purpose partition [1], consisting of two Intel Sapphire Rapids 8480+ processors and 256GB main memory per node.

6.1 Call Graph Generation and Static Selection

We build `vlasiator` using the `capicc` wrapper, generating and embedding the static call graph inside the XRay-instrumented executable. The call graph consists of 2371 function nodes and contains no cycles. For this case study, we run a general-purpose instrumentation selection query based on the inclusive instruction count metric, requiring no specific knowledge of the target code's architecture. This models a typical first analysis pass, in which the analyst is tasked with evaluating an application previously unknown to them. If desired, additional selection mechanism can be added to capture application-specific aspects, such as a focusing on call paths relevant for MPI or OpenMP, or specific code sections of interest.

In Fig. 4 we evaluate the impact of the inclusive instruction threshold k on the number of selected functions. This yields an approximately linear decline on the log-log scale, indicating a power law relationship between threshold and selection size. While there is no clear optimal choice for this threshold, we found that values for $k \in [1000, 10000]$ are effective in producing profiles with reasonable call granularity.

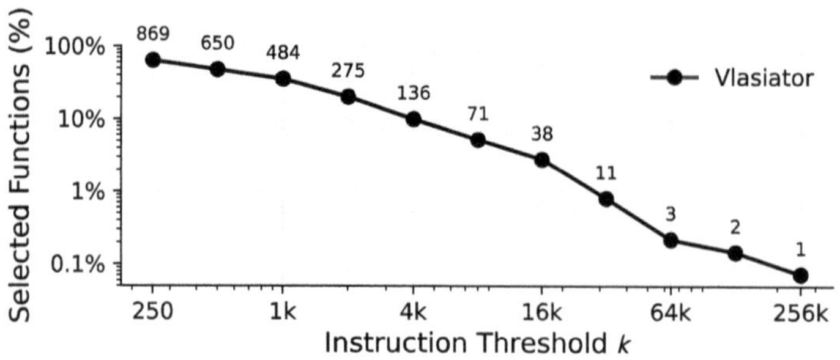

Fig. 4. Percentage of total functions selected using the inclusive instruction count metric. Absolute values are annotated.

6.2 Profiling and Validation

We use the configuration created with $k = 1000$ to generate the profile. This produces the context-sensitive call profile with attached TALP efficiency metrics.

We compare the runtime results for a small run with 4 nodes in Marenostrum 5 with two Score-P profiling runs using Score-P 9.2 (llvm-plugin variant): one without any explicit filtering, and one that uses a dynamic filter generated by the `scorep-score` utility based on the initial run. We also measure a TAU variant (version 2.35.1), using the LLVM instrumentation plugin and a static filter excluding all functions with less than 1000 instructions, and runtime throttling enabled. We use an identical minimum function runtime threshold of $10\mu s$ for the dynamic filtering in the CaPI runtime, TAU throttling settings, and the `scorep-score` filter. Additionally, we measure the TALP profiler without CaPI region instrumentation, collecting only global efficiency metrics. The results are shown in Fig. 5a. Our tool displays an overhead of 17.1% over the vanilla runtime, similar to running TALP without instrumentation (15.7%). This compares to a 3× overhead observed with an unfiltered Score-P instrumentation, offering the highest detail level, but skewing the results significantly. After applying the `scorep-score` filter, Score-P's overhead drops to 66%. In the this configuration, TAU yields similar overheads to CaPI, but is limited to a flat profile.

The runtime call graph validation system records 39 indirect call edges. Running the original query with these added edges results in the selection of 14 additional functions, equating to an increase of 2.9% in the size of the selection set. Due to the small number of added functions, of which 9 are related to I/O, we proceed with the obtained profile.

6.3 Efficiency-Guided Selection and Tracing

The resulting profile from the 500 node Vlasiator run can now be explored in the GUI and queried with CaPI to generate selective trace configurations. We generate a configuration that targets functions with sub-par parallel efficiency, using the following query in Listing 1.1 written in CaPI's selection DSL.

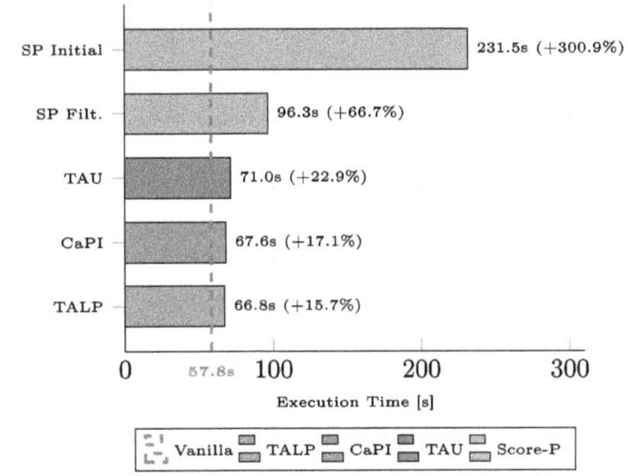

(a) Profiling runtime comparison. The red dashed line indicates the non-instrumented vanilla execution.

TALP Efficiency metrics	
Parallel eff.	0.39
MPI Parallel eff.	0.85
MPI Communication eff.	0.93
MPI Load balance	0.91
OpenMP Parallel eff.	0.54
OpenMP Scheduling eff.	1.00
OpenMP Load balance	1.00
OpenMP Serialization eff.	0.54
Useful IPC	0.43
Average Freq. [GHz]	2.97
Useful instruction	5.55e+12
Useful cycles	1.31e+13
Invocations	50
MPI calls	27022560

(b) Efficiency metrics of the **calculateSpatialTranslation** function, as generated by a 4 node profiling run.

Fig. 5. Profiling results with Vlasiator.

```
talp_fns     = has_talp_metrics()
bad_par_eff  = %talp_fns |> talp_parallel_efficiency("<=", 0.4)
                         |> talp_elapsed_time(">", 2e9)
filtered     = %talp_fns |> talp_dyn_filtered()
init_fns     = by_name(".*init.*")
init_phase   = %init_fn  |> on_call_path_from()
relevant     = ((%bad_par_eff - %filtered - %init_phase)
                         |> on_call_path_to())
!instrument(%relevant, "annotate:1-3", "detail:4", "burst:5")
!instrument(%relevant, "burst:1-3,5", "detail:4")
!instrument(%init_fn, "burst")
```

Listing 1.1. CaPI query for selective tracing on Vlasiator.

The resulting configuration traces the initialization phase in burst mode, one invocation of the relevant kernels in full detail, and only annotating function names for the rest.

6.4 Tracing

With the tracing configuration done, we execute the second step of the workflow and trace the application with Extrae version 4.2.12 both naively without compiler regions and no selective tracing and with the prepared tracing configuration. In both cases we intercept both MPI and OpenMP programming model calls and read two hardware performance counters per event. In the burst mode, we collect MPI and OpenMP statistics using a window of 100ms.

For the naive approach we report an immediate trace size of around 990GB. Note, that this trace only contains the programming model interceptions and hardware counter information. No source code related information is available in this trace. Using the tracing profile generated, we report an immediate trace

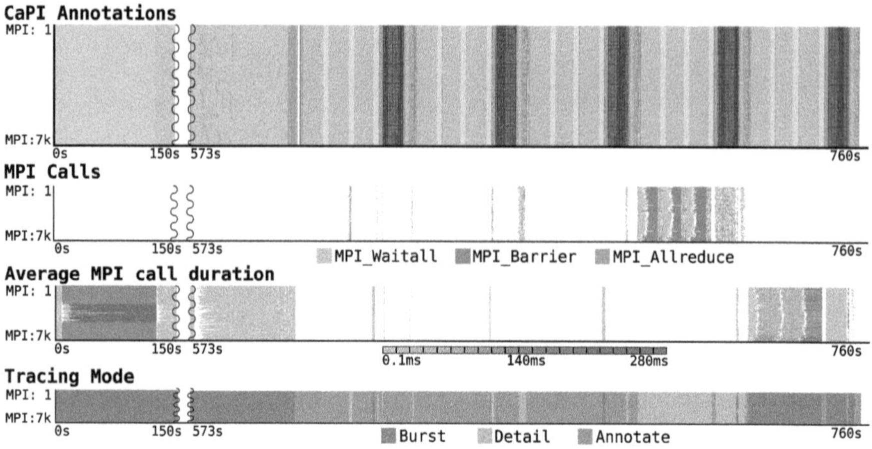

Fig. 6. Selective trace visualized with Paraver. The Y-axis depicts processors, while the X-axis is time. The CaPI annotations legend and large parts of the initialization timeline have been omitted for space reasons.

size of around 90GB. While this is still quite big, it is still within the envelope of being analyzable. It additionally contains the region annotations, that allow the analyst to trace performance problems more easily back to the source code. Figure 6 shows the trace visualization of the 500 node run. While the MPI calls information is only available in the `detail` tracing mode, `burst` metrics like average MPI call duration still can provide valuable insight into the application behavior at a reduced fidelity.

7 Conclusion

Full tracing of large-scale HPC applications provides essential detail, but often incurs prohibitive runtime overhead, trace volume, and analysis cost. In this paper, we presented a tool-assisted workflow, for guided selective tracing that combines static call graph analysis, runtime-configurable instrumentation, and dynamic performance data collected in a low-overhead profiling phase. Our approach enables analysts to derive selective tracing configurations from a single instrumented binary, without the need of manual source-code modifications or recompilation between profiling and tracing stages. To improve robustness in real-world applications, we introduced a lightweight runtime call graph validation mechanism that detects and repairs missing edges caused by indirect calls.

In the Vlasiator case study, the workflow produced a trace configuration that enabled focused traces with detailed information while reaching a 10× trace size reduction. Future work will focus on broader backend support, further automation of trace-configuration generation, and more extensive evaluation of trace-size reduction, scalability, and diagnostic utility across additional HPC applications.

Acknowledgments. This work was in part supported by the Federal Ministry of Education and Research (BMBF) and the states of Hesse as part of the NHR program. The authors gratefully acknowledge the computing time provided to them on the high-performance computer Lichtenberg II. This work also received funding from the European High-Performance Computing Joint Undertaking (JU) under grant agreement No 101093261 (Plasma-PEPSC project). The Plasma-PEPSC project (PCI2022-135050-2) is also co-funded by MICIU/AEI/10.13039/501100011033 and by the UE NextGenerationEU/PRTR.

Disclosure of Interests. The authors have no competing interests to declare that are relevant to the content of this article.

Reproducibility. The repository containing the reproducibility artifacts is available under: https://github.com/sebastiankreutzer/europar26-artifact/

References

1. Banchelli, F., et al.: Introducing marenostrum5: a European pre-exascale energy-efficient system designed to serve a broad spectrum of scientific workloads. Fut. Gener. Comput. Syst. **176**, 108125 (2026). https://doi.org/10.1016/j.future.2025.108125
2. Berris, D.M., Veitch, A., Heintze, N., Anderson, E., Wang, N.: Xray: a function call tracing system. Tech. rep. (2016). a white paper on XRay, a function call tracing system developed at Google
3. Guelque, C., Honoré, V., Swartvagher, P., Thomas, G., Trahay, F.: PALLAS: a generic trace format for large HPC trace analysis. In: 2025 IEEE International Parallel and Distributed Processing Symposium (IPDPS), pp. 273–284 (2025). https://doi.org/10.1109/IPDPS64566.2025.00032
4. Iwainsky, C., Bischof, C.: Calltree-controlled instrumentation for low-overhead survey measurements. In: 2016 IEEE International Parallel and Distributed Processing Symposium Workshops (IPDPSW), pp. 1668–1677 (2016). https://doi.org/10.1109/IPDPSW.2016.54
5. Knüpfer, A., et al.: Score-P: a joint performance measurement run-time infrastructure for periscope,scalasca, tau, and Vampir. In: Tools for High Performance Computing 2011, pp. 79–91. Springer Berlin Heidelberg, Berlin, Heidelberg (2012). https://doi.org/10.1007/978-3-642-31476-6_7
6. Kreutzer, S., Iwainsky, C., Lehr, J.P., Bischof, C.: Compiler-assisted instrumentation selection for large-scale C++ codes. In: Anzt, H., Bienz, A., Luszczek, P., Baboulin, M. (eds.) High Performance Computing. ISC High Performance 2022 International Workshops. pp. 5–19. Springer International Publishing, Cham (2022). https://doi.org/10.1007/978-3-031-23220-6_1
7. Kreutzer, S., Martens, S., Arzt, P., Heldmann, T., Bischof, C.: CGPatch: streamlining static call graph validation using selective instrumentation. In: Neuwirth, S., Paul, A.K., Weinzierl, T., Carson, E.C. (eds.) High Performance Computing, pp. 287–299. Springer Nature Switzerland, Cham (2026). https://doi.org/10.1007/978-3-032-07612-0_22

8. Lopez, V., Ramirez Miranda, G., Garcia-Gasulla, M.: TALP: a lightweight tool to unveil parallel efficiency of large-scale executions. In: Proceedings of the 2021 on Performance EngineeRing, Modelling, Analysis, and VisualizatiOn STrategy, pp. 3–10. PERMAVOST '21, Association for Computing Machinery, New York, NY, USA (2021). https://doi.org/10.1145/3452412.3462753
9. Noeth, M., Ratn, P., Mueller, F., Schulz, M., de Supinski, B.R.: ScalaTrace: scalable compression and replay of communication traces for high-performance computing. Journal of Parallel and Distributed Computing **69**(8), 696–710 (2009). https://doi.org/10.1016/j.jpdc.2008.09.001
10. Servat, H., Llort, G., Huck, K., Giménez, J., Labarta, J.: Framework for a productive performance optimization. Parallel Comput. **39**(8), 336–353 (2013). https://doi.org/10.1016/j.parco.2013.05.004
11. Servat, H., Llort, G., Giménez, J., Huck, K., Labarta, J.: Folding: detailed analysis with coarse sampling. In: Brunst, H., Müller, M.S., Nagel, W.E., Resch, M.M. (eds.) Tools for High Performance Computing 2011. pp. 105–118. Springer, Berlin, Heidelberg (2012). https://doi.org/10.1007/978-3-642-31476-6_9
12. Shende, S.S., Malony, A.D.: The tau parallel performance system. Int. J. High Perf. Comput. Appl. **20**(2), 287–311 (2006). https://doi.org/10.1177/1094342006064482
13. von Alfthan, S., et al.: Vlasiator: first global hybrid-Vlasov simulations of earth's foreshock and magnetosheath. J. Atmos. Solar Terr. Phys. **120**, 24–35 (2014). https://doi.org/10.1016/j.jastp.2014.08.012
14. Wolf, F., et al.: Usage of the SCALASCA toolset for scalable performance analysis of large-scale parallel applications. In: Resch, M., Keller, R., Himmler, V., Krammer, B., Schulz, A. (eds.) Tools for High Performance Computing, pp. 157–167. Springer, Berlin, Heidelberg (2008). https://doi.org/10.1007/978-3-540-68564-7_10
15. Wood, C., et al.: Projecting performance data over simulation geometry using SOSflow and alpine. In: Bhatele, A., Boehme, D., Levine, J.A., Malony, A.D., Schulz, M. (eds.) Programming and Performance Visualization Tools, pp. 201–218. Springer International Publishing, Cham (2019). https://doi.org/10.1007/978-3-030-17872-7_12
16. Zhai, J., Hu, J., Tang, X., Ma, X., Chen, W.: CYPRESS: combining static and dynamic analysis for top-down communication trace compression. In: SC '14: Proceedings of the International Conference for High Performance Computing, Networking, Storage and Analysis, pp. 143–153 (2014). https://doi.org/10.1109/SC.2014.17, iSSN: 2167-4337

How Efficient are the Efficient Cores?—An Experimental Evaluation of Energy Efficiency in Asymmetric Multicore Processors

Hana Shatri Ahmeti(✉), Matthias Korch, Tim Werner, and Thomas Rauber

University of Bayreuth, Bayreuth, Germany
{hana.shatri,matthias.korch,tim.werner,thomas.rauber}@uni-bayreuth.de

Abstract. Modern multi-core processors increasingly combine cores of different sizes to balance performance and power. However, when energy efficiency is the primary objective, selecting the optimal core types, number of cores, and operating frequencies for a given workload is not always straightforward. In this study, we experimentally evaluate eight hybrid processors from Intel's Alder Lake, Raptor Lake, and Arrow Lake architectures, as well as AMD's Zen 4 and Zen 5 platforms. We conduct our experiments across three bottleneck-oriented workloads, compute-bound, bandwidth-bound, and latency-bound, measuring energy consumption and performance while varying the number of active cores and the operating frequencies. To provide practical guidance, we compare performance and energy-efficient cores across these different configurations. Our results highlight how energy consumption differs across successive processor generations under different workloads, providing a practical classification between core types for modern hybrid processors. Additionally, we examine how energy efficiency scales with respect to die area.

Keywords: Asymmetric multicore processors · Energy efficiency · Workload characterization

1 Introduction

The new processor architectures increasingly include cores of different sizes, combining within the same die performance-cores that can operate at higher frequencies but consume more power with efficient-cores that operate at lower frequencies and consume less power. Although the presence of different core types offers greater flexibility by providing more execution options, finding the most optimal configuration when searching for a balanced performance- and energy-efficient execution is not straightforward. Due to variations in performance and power consumption of the cores in these so-called asymmetric multicore processors (AMPs), different workload types might behave differently. In addition to

M. Torquati et al. (Eds.): Euro-Par 2026, LNCS 16781, pp. 195–209, 2027.
https://doi.org/10.1007/978-3-032-35248-4_14

architectural differences of the cores, the choice of parameters such as frequency and core count influence power and performance.

In this work, we analyze energy efficiency trade-offs between performance- and efficient-cores across eight asymmetric processors from Intel's Alder Lake, Raptor Lake and Arrow Lake architectures, as well as AMD's Zen 4 and Zen 5 hybrid platforms. Beyond a cross-architectural comparison and generational transition analysis, our goal is to investigate whether, and under which conditions, modern energy-efficient cores can truly surpass performance-cores in terms of energy-efficiency. Hence, we derive insights into optimal energy-efficient configurations with respect to core type, core count, operating frequency, and workload characteristics. The main contributions of this paper are:

- An experimental comparison of performance- and efficient-cores across eight AMPs, evaluating power, performance, and energy-efficiency under three bottleneck-oriented workloads with varying frequencies and core counts.
- A die-area-normalized comparison of energy-efficiency between performance- and efficient-cores.
- A practical classification indicating when performance- and efficient-cores are more favorable depending on workload characterization.

2 Experimental Methodology

Since parallel applications are potentially limited by a mixture of bottlenecks, we consider three bottleneck-oriented workloads to investigate boundary cases of the performance and energy-efficiency ranges of asymmetric CPUs.

2.1 Evaluated Platforms

We evaluate eight modern asymmetric processors from different generations and platforms, some of which support simultaneous multithreading (SMT). The platforms with their mircroarchitecture codenames and chip designs are summarized in Table 1. Intel refers to performance-cores (P-cores) and efficient-cores (E-cores) to distinguish between high-performance and energy-efficient cores. Alder Lake and Raptor Lake use the same E-core microarchitecture (Gracemont), whereas Arrow Lake E-core (Skymont) has changed significantly. While Intel uses different microarchitectures for P- and E-cores, AMD accompanies their regular Zen cores with compact ('c') cores of the same microarchitecture, optimized for density and power efficiency [1], e.g., by decreasing the maximum clock frequency. For consistency, we therefore also refer to AMD's cores as P- and E-cores. On Intel architectures, only P-cores have a private L2 cache, while E-cores are arranged in clusters of 4 with a shared L2 cache. In contrast, the L2 cache on AMD architectures is always private per P- and E- core.

The systems used are summarized in Table 2. There, $\mathbf{n_P}$ and $\mathbf{n_E}$ denote the number of P- and E-cores, respectively. The clock rates of P- and E-cores ($\mathbf{f_P}$

Table 1. Microarchitecture code names and chip design.

Platform	Abbreviation	Manufacturer	P-core	E-core	SMT	Design
Alder Lake	Ald	Intel	Golden Cove	Gracemont	P-cores	monolithic
Raptor Lake	Rpl	Intel	Raptor Cove	Gracemont	P-cores	monolithic
Arrow Lake	Arl	Intel	Lion Cove	Skymont	–	tile-based
Zen 4	Z4	AMD	Zen 4	Zen 4c	P- & E-cores	monolithic
Zen 5	Z5	AMD	Zen 5	Zen 5c	P- & E-cores	monolithic

Table 2. Evaluated systems.

CPU	Arch	n_P	n_E	f_P [GHz]	f_E [GHz]	P_{CPU} [W]	$L2_P$ [MB]	$L2_E$ [MB]	L3 [MB]	f_{mem} [GHZ]
Core i9-12900K	Ald	8	8	3.2–5.2	2.4–3.9	125–241	1.25	2	30	2.4
Core i7-13700K	Rpl	8	8	3.4–5.3	2.5–4.2	125–253	2	4	30	2.8
Core Ultra 9 285K	Arl	8	16	3.7–5.7	3.2–4.6	125–250	3	4	36	3.2
Core Ultra 7 265	Arl	8	12	2.4–5.3	1.8–4.6	65–182	3	4	30	3.2
Core Ultra 7 265T	Arl	8	12	1.5–5.3	1.2–4.6	35–112	3	4	30	3.2
Core Ultra 7 255H	Arl	6	8	2.0–5.1	1.5–4.4	28–115	3	4	24	4.2
Ryzen 5 PRO 8500G	Z4	2	4	4.1–4.0	3.3–3.7	46–65	1	1	16	2.6
Ryzen AI 5 PRO 340	Z5	3	3	2.0–4.8	2.0–3.4	15–54	1	1	16	2.8

and $\mathbf{f_E}$) are shown as base–turbo ranges, and the power consumption of the CPU $\mathbf{P_{CPU}}$ is shown as the range between processor base power and maximum turbo power. The L2 cache capacity for P-cores and E-cores ($\mathbf{L2_P}$ and $\mathbf{L2_E}$) is listed as per-core capacity or, when applicable, as per-E-cluster capacity. The L3 cache is shared among all cores and is listed as its total capacity. The memory clock frequency to which our systems have been configured is listed as $\mathbf{f_{mem}}$.

2.2 Workloads

We use three different workloads for characterizing different execution behaviors:

Compute-Bound: Our compute-bound benchmark performs a series of AVX-2 FMA and MUL vector operations with a 2:1 ratio in double precision. To increase the utilization of the SIMD units, it operates entirely on `ymm` registers using mostly independent instructions. The computations are based on the logistic equation, so that the instructions operate on seemingly random data, because operations on NANs or zeros would consume significantly less energy. The benchmark is parallelized with OpenMP and provides dynamic load balancing.

Bandwidth-Bound: As a bandwidth-bound workload, we use the STREAM triad [8], which is parallelized with OpenMP and vectorized with AVX-2. By adjusting the array sizes, we can measure L2, L3, or memory bandwidth.

Latency-Bound: The latency-bound workload performs a configurable amount of independent pointer chases simultaneously. While within a single pointer chase each memory access is depending on the previous one, which prevents a core from pipelining those accesses, the core can still pipeline the memory accesses of independent pointer chases. Thus, by configuring the amount of concurrent pointer chases, we can simulate a varying degree of instruction level parallelism (ILP) for the memory accesses. The pointers are stored in an array and initialized so that there is only a single cycle which has the length of the array size. By varying the pointer-array size, we can simulate different working sets. To disable hardware prefetchers, the pointers also seemingly reference each other randomly.

2.3 Experimental Setup

We designed a fully automated workflow to execute all experiments consistently, facilitating the reproducibility of the results. In this work, we compare the energy efficiency between P- and E-cores. For each workload, measurements are collected at each predefined frequency level, while incrementally increasing the number of active cores, from one core up to the maximum number of cores of each type.

Frequency Control: To ensure a deterministic performance measurement, we fix CPU frequencies by setting minimum and maximum to the same value using the Linux `sysfs` interface. To analyze energy behavior across different frequencies, we vary it from the minimum value (0.8 GHz), and increase it in 0.2 GHz increments up to the maximum supported frequency for each core type.

Core Isolation: To pin the execution exclusively to either E-cores or P-cores, thus preventing thread migration across asymmetric core types, we enforced core affinity using `taskset` in combination with setting the number of OpenMP threads to the desired core count.

Performance and Energy Measurement: For performance and energy consumption measurements, we used Linux `perf` and `turbostat`. For each experiment, `turbostat` runs as a background monitor, while the benchmark is executed under `perf stat`. Using `perf`, we collect performance counters such as *instructions*, *cycles*, *cache-references*, *cache-misses*, as well as package and core energy measurements from *power/energy-pkg/* and *power/energy-core(s)/*. `turbostat` samples every 2 s, also monitoring core and uncore frequencies, package temperature, and CPU busy time throughout execution. Upon completion of the benchmark, the monitoring is terminated and all logs are aggregated into a single file, used to generate the corresponding performance and energy plots.

3 Results

In this section, we present the energy characteristics of P-cores and E-cores for compute-bound, bandwidth-bound, and latency-bound workloads. Our analysis considers the impact of frequency scaling and core count. For each workload, we consider the energy per unit of work while comparing the optimal P-core and E-core configurations. Figure 1 shows the energy-frequency scaling across all machines and workloads at their global optimal energy-efficient core counts.

In addition, we assess the energy efficiency relative to die area, providing a comprehensive view of architectural trade-offs. Figure 2 presents the energy efficiency density (EED) metric EED $= \frac{\text{Speedup}\cdot\text{Energy Reduction}}{\text{Area Overhead}}$ [7]. For Intel architectures, we evaluate EED by comparing 1 P-core vs. 1–4 E-cores, and 2 P-cores vs. 5–8 E-cores, reflecting $\approx 1:0.25$ die-area ratio between E- and P-cores [6]. For AMD, we compare 1 Zen 4/5 core vs. 1-2 Zen 4c/5c cores and 2 Zen 4/5 cores vs. 2–3 Zen 4c/5c cores, based on die-area ratios of $\approx 1:0.65$ (Zen 4) and of $\approx 1:0.75$ (Zen 5) [2]. This metric captures the performance-energy-area trade-offs, where $EED > 1$ indicates higher efficiency of E-core configurations per die area relative to the P-core baseline. In both figures, bandwidth- and latency-bound workloads are shown only for their respective memory-bound sizes.

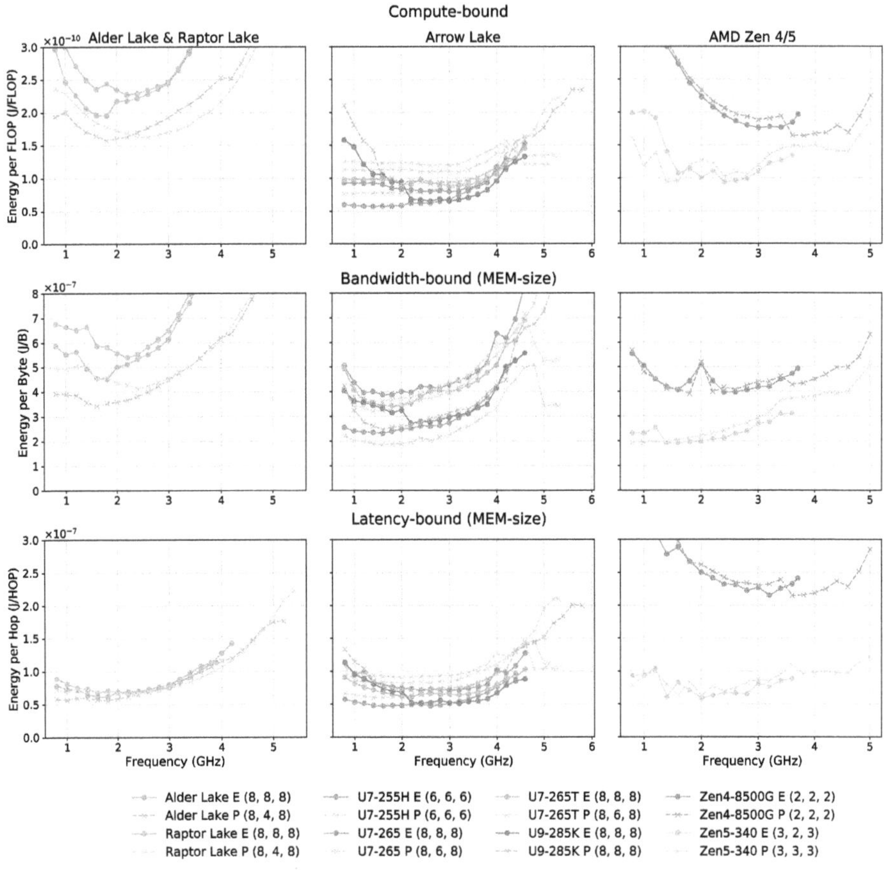

Fig. 1. Energy efficiency evaluation across workloads at optimal core counts. In the legend, the numbers in parentheses denote the optimal number of cores for the compute-bound, memory-bound, and latency-bound workload, respectively.

3.1 Compute-Bound Workload

P-core vs. E-core. The Alder Lake and Raptor Lake systems favor P-cores for the compute-bound case, with P-cores achieving about 1.23× higher energy efficiency on Alder Lake and 1.39× on Raptor Lake in the optimal configurations. The global optimum occurs at 8 cores and reduced clock frequency, indicating that voltage-frequency scaling degrades energy efficiency at higher frequencies. As shown in Fig. 1, the optimal energy efficiency shifts from ≈ 1.8 GHz in Alder Lake to ≈ 2.4 GHz in Raptor Lake, reflecting the steeper power slope in Alder Lake and thus resulting in energy-optimal operating point at lower frequency.

In contrast, Arrow Lake machines alter this pattern with E-cores being ≈ 1.34–1.46× more energy efficient. Within a common core count range of E- and P- cores, the global optimum remains at the maximum number of cores. However, since power increases only sub-linearly with core count across all architectures (i.e., doubling the number of cores does not double power-consumption), then well-scaling workloads can further increase the energy efficiency gains by adding additional cores to their execution. Therefore, this case further benefits from additional E-cores when present.

The optimal frequency range is 1.6–3.2 GHz, which is higher than Alder Lake and Raptor Lake due to a slower power-frequency scaling (see Fig. 1). For Ultra 7 machines, above ≈ 80 °C, thermal throttling sharply lowers core/uncore frequency, reducing power at higher frequencies. This produces the sudden drop in energy in Fig. 1 for P-cores of U7-255H and U7-265T for all workloads.

In AMD machines, the difference in energy efficiency between optimal configurations within the common core-count range is minimal, with the global optimum at 1.4–3.8 GHz. However, also for Zen 4, energy-efficiency further improves when the number of E-cores exceeds the maximum number of P-cores.

Die area Differences. When evaluated using EED, it highlights another generational transition, with Arrow Lake E-cores demonstrating a superior area-energy-efficiency. As shown in Fig. 2, Alder Lake, Raptor Lake, and AMD machines show a modest area-efficiency of E-cores compared to P-cores. In contrast, Arrow Lake maintains a substantially higher EED across E-core counts.

3.2 Bandwidth-Bound Workload

P-core vs. E-core. For this workload, P-cores in Alder Lake and Raptor Lake are consistently more energy efficient across all configurations and sizes. In Alder Lake, P-cores outperform E-cores by ≈ 1.49×, 1.6×, 1.3× for L2-, L3-, and memory-bound workloads, respectively. Raptor Lake shows similar behavior (≈ 1.3×, 2.3×, 1.3×). For both architectures, the optimal core count depends on workload size: 2–4 cores for L2 and memory-bound cases, and 7–8 cores for L3, likely due to L2-cache and main-memory saturation.

In Arrow Lake, E-cores are only ≈ 1.02–1.11× more energy-efficient for L2-workloads. However, P-cores surpass E-cores starting from L3-size, with gaps of ≈ 1.6–2.2×, which decrease to ≈ 1.06–1.14× once main memory bandwidth dominates. The optimal core count for L2-size remains at 2–3 cores, but increases for the other two cases. However, on systems with more E- than P-cores, scaling E-core count can match P-core energy efficiency in memory-bound scenarios.

On AMD systems, core-type differences regarding energy-efficiency are small within common core count comparison, with Zen 5 favoring E-cores by at most $\approx 1.14\times$ (L3) and Zen-4 favoring P-cores by at most $\approx 1.05\times$ (L2). This difference becomes negligible once the main-memory becomes the bottleneck. On Zen 4, however, increasing E-core count outperform P-cores by $\approx 1.4\times$ for L2 and L3, but the difference remains minimal for the memory-bound case.

For all the machines, the optimal frequency compared across all configurations decreases with increasing workload size.

Die Area Differences. For bandwidth-bound workload, EED shows different scaling behavior. On Alder Lake and Raptor Lake, E-cores exhibit a lower area-energy-efficiency than P-cores, with EED exceeding the P-core baseline only at small E-core counts before dropping below it. On AMD systems, the compact cores maintain minimal area-efficiency over the larger cores across all cache levels. In contrast, on Arrow Lake, EED gains for L2- and L3-sized workloads are more pronounced, and E-cores remain more efficient even for memory-bound workloads. This indicates that bandwidth limits reduce the area-normalized energy-efficiency, however, Arrow Lake and AMD E-cores still maintain advantage.

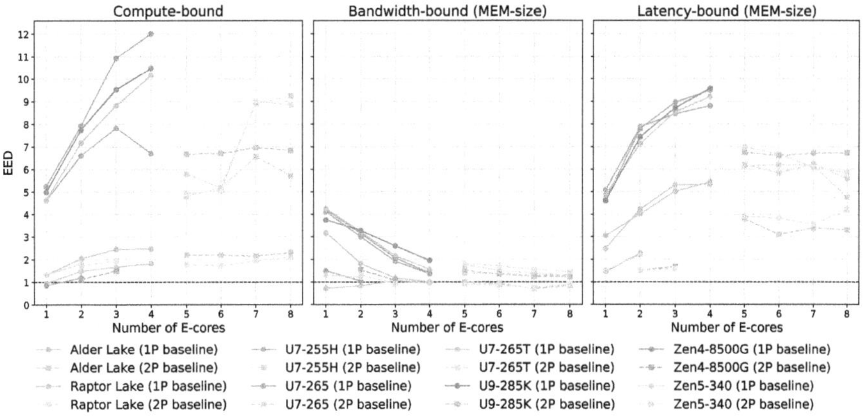

Fig. 2. Energy Efficiency Density (EED) of E-cores across workloads.

3.3 Latency-Bound Workload

P-core vs. E-core. For L2-sized workload, P-cores are more energy efficient than E-cores on all Intel machines when compared at their respective optimal configurations ($\approx 1.9\times$ in Alder Lake, $\approx 1.6\times$ in Raptor Lake, and ≈ 1.8–$2.4\times$ in

Arrow Lake). On AMD machines, differences are smaller, with compact cores leading by at most $\approx 1.1\times$.

For L3-sized workload, P-cores remain more energy efficient on Alder Lake and Raptor Lake systems. However, the energy-efficiency gap between the optimal P-core and E-core configurations narrows to $\approx 1.3\times$ and $\approx 1.1\times$, respectively, operating at 0.8 GHz. In contrast, on Arrow Lake, E-cores become more energy-efficient by $\approx$ 1.08–1.27$\times$, with the global optimum occurring at 1.4–2.6 GHz. On AMD systems, the difference is further reduced.

For the main-memory latency-bound case, where the problem size exceeds all cache levels, Alder Lake remains P-cores dominant, with global optimum at 7–8 cores and 1.8 GHz. On Raptor Lake, the gap between E- and P-core configurations narrows to $\approx 1.007\times$, with optimal settings at 7–8 cores and 2.2 GHz (E-cores) and 2.4 GHz (P-cores). On Arrow Lake, E-cores continue to dominate by $\approx 1.3\times$, with the global optimum occurring at 6–8 cores and 1.6–3.2 GHz, while on AMD systems, P- and E-core configurations have a less than 1.07$\times$ difference. However, since Zen 4 provides more E-cores than P-cores, scaling beyond P-core count consistently makes E-core configurations more energy-efficient.

Die Area Differences. For the latency-bound workload, area-normalized efficiency varies with workload size. For the L2-sized workload, Alder Lake and Raptor Lake E-cores show moderately higher area-efficiency compared to P-cores, while on Arrow Lake machines EED falls below 1 at higher E-core counts. This behavior changes for the L3-sized workload where Alder Lake E-cores show no area-efficiency compared to P-cores, while Raptor Lake still favors E-cores. In contrast, Arrow Lake EED improves, maintaining a higher area-efficiency. For memory-bound workloads, E-cores outperform P-cores on all Intel machines, with significantly higher improvements for Arrow Lake. AMD compact cores consistently maintain an area-energy-efficiency advantage over larger cores across the memory hierarchy, with no significant variations across cache levels.

4 Discussion

4.1 Intra-architecture Power and Performance Comparison

From the experiments, we observe a very important generational transition, with the new E-cores actually becoming more energy efficient than P-cores. In the older architectures (Alder Lake and Raptor Lake), the throughput differences between the Gracemont E-cores and the Golden Cove or Raptor Cove P-cores strongly influence energy efficiency. These differences largely stem from the architectural limitations of these E-cores, which deliver substantially lower computational throughput ($\approx 1.9\times$ lower FLOPs per cycle), lower cache and memory bandwidth ($\approx 2\times$ lower for L2-sized workload, $\approx 3\times$ for L3-sized, and $\approx 2\times$ again for bandwidth-bound workload), and they sustain lower accesses per second ($\approx 2\times$ lower for L2-sized and $\approx 1.4\times$ lower for L3-sized to strongly memory-bound cases). Consequently, although they are more power-efficient than P-cores

(≈ 1.3× on average), their architectural constraints limit their achievable performance, leading to lower energy efficiency across all types and sizes of workloads.

In contrast, the architectural enhancements made in Arrow Lake not only boost the performance of Lion Cove P-cores compared to the older Golden Cove and Raptor Cove architectures, but also deliver a substantial improvement in Skymont E-core performance. P-cores benefit from consistent improvement, such as wider decode, bigger micro-op caches, FMA units, and increased L2 caches, while Skymont E-cores feature as well wider decode, larger micro-op cache, expanded load/store queue, and larger ROBs compared to previous generation. These improvements of the Skymont E-cores also narrow the performance gap with Lion Cove P-cores and enable higher energy efficiency.

Along with lower power consumption (≈ 1.26× on average), Skymont E-cores show a slight throughput advantage over P-cores (≈ 1.1× higher FLOPs per cycle), making them more energy efficient for compute-bound workloads. In addition, they show only ≈ 1.2× lower L2 bandwidth for the stream triad, still achieving better energy efficiency due to their reduced power consumption. The bandwidth gap from P-cores widens to ≈ 2.2× for L3-sized workloads, then narrows again to ≈ 1.3× for the strongly memory-bandwidth-bound cases, making them less efficient for these cases. In the latency bound scenarios, E-cores initially show lower energy efficiency for L2-sized workload, due to their ≈ 2.8× lower access rate compared to P-cores. This trend changes for larger problem sizes, where although E-cores access rate per second remains lower by ≈ 1.17×,

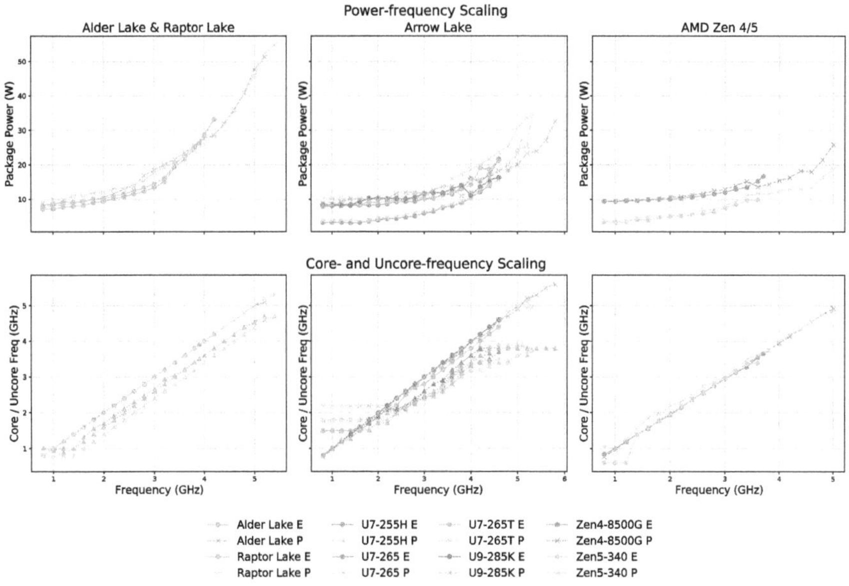

Fig. 3. Two-core compute-bound workload under fixed min/max frequencies (x-axis): (top) power vs. frequency; (bottom) core (circle) and uncore (triangle) vs. frequency.

their reduced power consumption compensates for the performance difference, resulting in a slight energy efficiency domination.

AMD systems show very similar performance between larger Zen 4/5 and compact Zen 4c/5c cores, with small variations in power consumption. As a result, energy efficiency differences are primarily driven by the variations in power consumption rather than performance capabilities.

4.2 Cross-Architectural Power and Performance Comparison

Power Transitions. As shown in Fig. 3, another important transition is the notable difference in power-frequency scaling across the architectures. The older generations, Alder Lake and Raptor Lake architectures show the highest overall power consumption. Although their power trend is comparable to other architectures up to $\approx$ 2.4 GHz, it increases sharply for higher frequencies. In contrast, Arrow Lake and AMD machines demonstrate a more gradual increase in power with frequency, suggesting a more favorable power-frequency scaling. Due to this, when the target is energy-efficiency, the optimal frequency range remains lower for older architectures, while it increases for newer ones.

As shown in Fig. 3, the observed power correlates with core and uncore frequency. The second row of the figure shows the fixed minimum and maximum

Table 3. Workload-to-Core mapping for energy-efficient execution. *CB, BB, LB: compute-, bandwidth-, and latency-bound; t: core type; n: number of cores; f: frequency; m_e: max number of E-cores.*

WL			Alder Lake	Raptor Lake	Arrow Lake	Zen 4	Zen 5
		t	P-core	P-core	E-core	E/P-core	E/P-core
CB	–	**n**	8	8	6-8 ($\mathbf{m_e}$)	2 ($\mathbf{m_e}$)/2	3
		f	1.8	2.4	1.6–3.2	3.0/3.8	1.4/2.4
		t	P-core	P-core	E-core	E/P-core	E-core
	L2	**n**	3	2	2-3	2($\mathbf{m_e}$)/2	3
BB		**f**	2.0	2.8	2.0–3.4	2.8–3.2/3.6	1.4
		t	P-core	P-core	P-core	E/P-core	E-core
	L3	**n**	7	8	6–8	2($\mathbf{m_e}$)/2	3
		f	2.0	2.6–3.0	1.6–3.2	2.6/3.6	1.4
		t	P-core	P-core	P-core	E/P-core	E/P-core
	MEM	**n**	4	4	6–8	2(3)/2	2/3
		f	1.6	2.4	1.4–1.6	1.8	1.4/0.8
		t	P-core	P-core	P-core	E-core	E/P-core
	L2	**n**	8	8	6–8	2($\mathbf{m_e}$)	3
LB		**f**	1.8	2.6	1.6–3.0	2.8–3.6	1.6
		t	P-core	P-core	E-core	E/P-core	E/P-core
	L3	**n**	8	8	6–8 ($\mathbf{m_e}$)	2($\mathbf{m_e}$)/2	3/3
		f	0.8	0.8	1.4–2.6	2.4/3.6	1.6/2.0
		t	P-core	E/P-core	E-core	E/P-core	E/P-core
	MEM	**n**	7–8	7–8	6–8 ($\mathbf{m_e}$)	2($\mathbf{m_e}$)/2	3
		f	1.8	2.2/2.4	1.6–3.2	2.8/3.6	2.0

core clock frequencies on the x-axis, while on the y-axis it shows the corresponding core and uncore frequencies that were measured during executions. As it can be seen for older architectures, the uncore frequency tracks the core frequency, while in Arrow Lake the core-uncore ratio widens at higher frequencies, limiting uncore to ≈ 3.8 GHz and preventing a sharp rise in power.

Implications of Power and Performance in Systems Ranking. Performance varies across workloads and architectures. For compute-bound workload, AMD Zen 4/4c achieve the highest FLOPs per cycle, followed by Arrow Lake E/P-cores, while Gracemont E-cores deliver the lowest throughput. For bandwidth-bound workloads, AMD Zen 5/5c and Raptor Lake P-cores generally achieve the highest throughput for L2-size, while Arrow Lake P-cores lead once the workload becomes strongly memory bound. Lastly, for latency bound workloads, Arrow Lake P-cores perform best for L2-sized problems, while Alder Lake and Raptor Lake P-cores outperform the other architectures once the problem size exceeds the last-level cache, indicating that monolithic die designs can provide an advantage for latency sensitive workloads since they avoid inter tile communication latency.

However, despite not delivering the highest performance throughput, the most power efficient machines, the Ultra 7 255H mobile CPU and AMD Zen 5 system emerge as the most energy-efficient machines overall, with both their E- and P-cores. This emphasizes the great impact of aggressive power optimization in modern architectures. Ultra 9 285K on the other hand, follows, due to its especially improved performance, while Ultra 7 265 variants and AMD Zen 4 form a middle tier comparable behavior. In contrast, although Alder Lake and Raptor Lake P-cores deliver the highest throughput for e.g., the latency bound case, they still are penalized due to their higher power consumption and therefore not placed as the most energy-efficient in any of the cases, with their Gracemont E-cores typically remaining the least efficient overall.

Table 4. Comparison with respect to die area.

	WL size	Alder Lake	Raptor Lake	Arrow Lake	Zen 4/5
Compute-bound	–	E-core	E-core	E-core	E-core
Bandwidth-bound	L2	P-core	P-core	E-core	E-core
	L3	P-core	P-core	E-core	E-core
	MEM	P-core	P-core	E-core	E-core
Latency-bound	L2	E/P-core	E/P-core	P-core	E-core
	L3	P-core	E/P-core	E-core	E-core
	MEM	E-core	E-core	E-core	E-core

5 Workload-to-Core Mapping Guidelines

Table 3 summarizes our observations and gives practical guidance on whether P- or E-core execution yields better energy efficiency for each architecture and workload, including favorable core counts and frequency ranges. $\mathbf{m_e}$ indicates that when systems provide more E-cores than P-cores, scaling to the maximum number of E-cores outperforms P-core configurations in energy efficiency. Table 4 summarizes energy efficiency related to die area.

For Alder Lake and Raptor Lake, their Gracemont E-cores exhibit significantly lower performance than their Golden Cove and Raptor Cove P-cores. Consequently, despite their lower power consumption, they are not more energy efficient. However, when compared with respect to die area, they are preferred for the compute-bound case, as collectively they can provide increased throughput, as well as for the strongly memory-latency bound case where performance is limited by memory access latency rather than core performance. Since accesses across cores are independent, their aggregated throughput can exceed that of one P-core. For L2- and L3-sized workloads, the difference in area efficiency is reduced, but neither core type is clearly favored.

For Arrow Lake architectures, the performance of their Skymont E-cores is significantly improved. Hence, their slightly higher throughput and lower power consumption makes them favorable for compute bound cases. In addition, due to their comparable performance to Lion Cove P-cores, they are also advantageous for some certain bandwidth-bound and latency-bound workload sizes. Although they deliver slightly lower bandwidth and access rate, their lower power consumption makes them more energy efficient in those cases overall. For classification with respect to die area, Skymont E-cores compared to P-cores show a clearly better area efficiency in all cases except L2-sized latency-bound workload, while also showing a significant improvement over the previous generation of E-cores.

For AMD Zen 4/5 and Zen 4c/5c, performance is similar, so energy differences mainly come from differences in power consumption. As a result, it is generally difficult to favor one core type over the other. However, due to their similar per-core performance, the compact cores achieve higher aggregated throughput for all the workloads when considered with respect to die area, therefore achieving better area-energy-efficiency.

6 Related Work

While early considerations of emulated AMPs, e.g. [4], concluded that CPU-bound programs should be mapped to fast cores and memory-intensive programs to slow cores, later case studies on AMP products observed a multifaceted scene. Intel reported that Alder Lake's fixed-frequency performance of a P-core is generally higher than that of an E-core for the SPEC CPU 2017 benchmarks [12]. This was confirmed by [17] who proposed microarchitectural improvements targeting performance and power to better fit either high or low instruction per cycle (IPC) applications. [14] compared P- and E-cores of Raptor Lake Refresh using database workloads and found that E-cores obtain better performance per watt for analytical and, in particular, for transactional workloads. [18] analyzed energy efficiency on Alder Lake and Raptor Lake for π computation, Linux kernel compilation, file compression and file encryption. They observed that energy efficiency of E-cores was higher for memory-intensive tasks, whereas P-cores were more energy efficient for floating point tasks, in particular when the difference in performance was large. [5] evaluated the asymmetric M1–M4 Apple CPUs using HPC workloads (STREAM and GEMM), but did not compare P- and E-core efficiency. Similarly, [11] considered LU decomposition in Java on Alder Lake and M4, but also did not compare P- and E-cores.

To guide the operating system on thread mapping, Intel provides the *Thread Director*, which has been investigated in [13]. Improved runtime techniques based on monitoring performance counters have been proposed in [3], which focus on performance but not energy. The work in [10] proposes an online tuning approach that dynamically adjusts the number of threads for each parallel region of OpenMP applications, focusing on the reduction of the energy delay product (EDP). [9] takes an offline approach to tune the number of threads and the clock frequency by a genetic algorithm. [16] combines a user-space resource manager with a runtime library, allowing application and resource manager to interact. The core allocation aims to optimize energy-utility cost, a metric adapted from EDP. Frequency-scaling is still considered for future work.

7 Conclusion

In this work, we experimentally investigated the energy efficiency of eight AMPs with P- and E-cores using three bottleneck-oriented workloads. Our analysis shows a clear difference in the power-frequency scaling trend across generations for both core types. While older generations show a steeper rise in power consumption, the newer architectures maintain a more gradual increase. Consequently, energy efficiency degrades more slowly with increasing frequency, allowing for energy-optimal operating points at higher frequencies.

To emphasize the great impact of aggressive power optimization, the Ultra 7 255H mobile CPU and AMD's Zen 5 system emerge as the most energy-efficient machines overall, despite not delivering the highest performance throughput.

When comparing within the E-core and P-core configurations among different core and frequency scalings, we can see another generational shift with the newer Skymont E-cores achieving higher energy efficiency than the Lion Cove P-cores for some of the workloads, while also outperforming them in nearly all area-energy-efficiency comparisons. Similarly, AMD compact cores maintain higher area-energy-efficiency. Thus, suggesting that newer E-cores emerge as strong competitors to P-cores when energy efficiency is the primary goal.

While this work provides a practical workload-to-core configuration mapping, applying these results to real applications remains challenging. Our analysis highlights the impact of bottleneck workload characteristics, microarchitectural features and power-frequency scaling, however, additional factors can further affect efficiency in real applications. In addition, real applications often exhibit a mixture of different workload characteristics, making the selection of the most energy-efficient configuration non-trivial. In future work, we plan to extend this analysis to mixed workloads and investigate the impact of additional system factors to develop a more comprehensive energy-model for hybrid architectures.

Artifact Availability. The artifact is available in the Zenodo repository [15].

Disclosure of Interests. The authors have no competing interests to declare that are relevant to the content of this article.

References

1. Advanced Micro Devices, Inc.: 5th Gen AMD EPYC Processor Architecture, 1st edn. (2025). White paper
2. Alcorn, P.: AMD dishes out more Zen 5 details – compact core is 25% smaller than the normal core, new SoC and chip architecture with dual CCXs. Tom's Hardware (2024). https://www.tomshardware.com/pc-components/cpus/amd-dishes-more-zen-5-details-compact-core-is-25-smaller-than-the-normal-core-new-soc-architecture-disclosed
3. Bilbao, C., Saez, J.C., Prieto-Matias, M.: Flexible system software scheduling for asymmetric multicore systems with PMCSched: a case for Intel Alder Lake. Concurr. Comput. Pract. Exp. **35**(25) (2023). https://doi.org/10.1002/cpe.7814
4. Fedorova, A., Saez, J.C., Shelepov, D., Prieto, M.: Maximizing power efficiency with asymmetric multicore systems. Commun. ACM **52**(12), 48–57 (2009). https://doi.org/10.1145/1610252.1610270
5. Hübner, P., Hu, A., Peng, I., Markidis, S.: Apple vs. oranges: evaluating the Apple silicon M-series SoCs for HPC performance and efficiency. In: 2025 IEEE International Parallel and Distributed Processing Symposium Workshops (IPDPSW), pp. 45–54 (2025). https://doi.org/10.1109/IPDPSW66978.2025.00013
6. Intel Technology: 12th gen performance hybrid architecture explained. YouTube video (2021). https://www.youtube.com/watch?v=YthL9raFx_s
7. Lian, H., et al.: Uni-STC: unified sparse tensor core. In: 2026 IEEE International Symposium on High Performance Computer Architecture (HPCA) (2026). https://doi.org/10.1109/HPCA68181.2026.11408500
8. McCalpin, J.D.: Stream: sustainable memory bandwidth in high performance computers. https://www.cs.virginia.edu/stream/
9. Moori, M.K., Rocha, H.M.G.D.A., Beck, A.C.S.: Energy-efficient execution of parallel regions on heterogeneous multi-cores. In: 2025 38th SBC/SBMicro/IEEE Symposium on Integrated Circuits and Systems Design (SBCCI) (2025). https://doi.org/10.1109/SBCCI66862.2025.11218680
10. Moori, M.K., Rocha, H.M.G.D.A., Lorenzon, A.F., Beck, A.C.S.: Efficient thread tuning for asymmetric multicores. In: 2024 37th SBC/SBMicro/IEEE Symposium on Integrated Circuits and Systems Design (SBCCI), pp. 1–5 (2024). https://doi.org/10.1109/SBCCI62366.2024.10703981
11. Rosa, F.J., de la Torre, J.C., Aragón-Jurado, J.M., Valderas-González, A., Dorronsoro, B.: Energy–performance trade-offs of LU matrix decomposition in java across heterogeneous hardware and operating systems. Appl. Sci. **16**(2) (2026). https://doi.org/10.3390/app16021002

12. Rotem, E., et al.: Intel Alder Lake CPU architectures. IEEE Micro **42**(3), 13–19 (2022). https://doi.org/10.1109/MM.2022.3164338
13. Saez, J.C., Prieto-Matias, M.: Evaluation of the Intel thread director technology on an Alder Lake processor. In: Proceedings of the 13th ACM SIGOPS Asia-Pacific Workshop on Systems (APSys 2022), pp. 61–67. ACM (2022). https://doi.org/10.1145/3546591.3547532
14. Sen, R.: Performance or efficiency? A tale of two cores for DB workloads. In: Proceedings of the 20th International Workshop on Data Management on New Hardware (DaMoN 2024). ACM (2024). https://doi.org/10.1145/3662010.3663444
15. Shatri Ahmeti, H., Korch, M., Werner, T., Rauber, T.: How efficient are the efficient cores? - an experimental evaluation of energy efficiency in asymmetric multicore processors (2026). https://doi.org/10.5281/zenodo.20527175
16. Smejkal, T., Khasanov, R., Castrillon, J., Härtig, H.: HARP: energy-aware and adaptive management of heterogeneous processors. In: Proceedings of the 26th International Middleware Conference (Middleware 2025), pp. 270–284. ACM (2025). https://doi.org/10.1145/3721462.3770774
17. Yue, A., Mehta, S.: An application-oriented approach to designing hybrid CPU architectures. In: 2023 IEEE International Symposium on Performance Analysis of Systems and Software (ISPASS), pp. 92–102 (2023). https://doi.org/10.1109/ISPASS57527.2023.00018
18. Żytko, D., Badurowicz, M.: Analysis of performance and energy efficiency of processors with hybrid architecture. J. Comput. Sci. Inst. **34**, 54–59 (2025). https://doi.org/10.35784/jcsi.6690

Architectures and Accelerators

Characterizing Needleman-Wunsch Sequence Alignment on the Graphcore IPU: Memory Trade-Offs and Optimization Strategies

S.-Kazem Shekofteh(✉), Nils Kochendörfer, and Holger Fröning

Hardware and Artificial Intelligence (HAWAII) Lab, Heidelberg University, Heidelberg, Germany
{kazem.shekofteh,holger.froening}@ziti.uni-heidelberg.de,
nils.kochendoerfer@stud.uni-heidelberg.de

Abstract. The Needleman-Wunsch (NW) algorithm, essential for DNA and protein sequence alignment, faces unique challenges when implemented on Graphcore's Intelligence Processing Unit (IPU). This work presents the first detailed characterization of full-matrix NW alignment on the IPU, exploring memory optimization strategies within the platform's 900 MB on-chip SRAM architecture. We develop multiple implementation variants with dynamic workload distribution across 8,832 threads (1,472 tiles × 6 threads). Our benchmarks on the GC200 IPU demonstrate performance of 3–7 GCUPS for realistic workloads and up to 36 GCUPS for sustained diagonal computations, exceeding a GPU baseline (15 GCUPS on NVIDIA A30) by 2.4×. Memory optimization, reducing per-vertex data from seven variables to one, achieves 45% reduction in exchange code and 60% reduction in vertex instances. However, Poplar's static compilation overhead limits maximum sequence lengths to approximately 9,000 elements. We identify critical trade-offs between vertex granularity, memory footprint, and parallelism, providing practical guidelines for mapping wavefront algorithms to this emerging architecture.

Keywords: Needleman-Wunsch · Intelligence Processing Unit · Sequence Alignment · Memory Optimization · Wavefront Parallelism

1 Introduction

The computational biology community increasingly relies on specialized hardware to handle massive sequencing data. Human chromosomes contain 50–260 million nucleotide base pairs, and comparing such sequences is fundamental for understanding evolutionary relationships and diagnosing genetic disorders. While GPUs have become standard for accelerating bioinformatics, emerging architectures offer unique characteristics worth investigating.

M. Torquati et al. (Eds.): Euro-Par 2026, LNCS 16781, pp. 213–226, 2027.
https://doi.org/10.1007/978-3-032-35248-4_15

Graphcore's Intelligence Processing Unit (IPU) places 918 MB of SRAM directly on-chip across 1,472 independent tiles, achieving 46.9 TB/s aggregate memory bandwidth. This trades total capacity for bandwidth, eliminating the memory wall for workloads that fit on-chip. We previously investigated IPUs for irregular HPC workloads [14], butterfly factorizations for vision transformers [15], and memory optimization in ML applications [13].

The Needleman-Wunsch (NW) algorithm [11], a fundamental dynamic programming approach for global sequence alignment, creates variable parallelism via its wavefront dependency pattern. Implementing NW on the IPU exposes fundamental questions about how static compilation, per-tile memory limits, and Bulk-Synchronous Parallel (BSP) execution interact with irregular algorithms. In the IPU's Poplar programming model, computation is expressed through *vertices* as small computational kernels assigned to tiles, whose per-instance metadata and inter-tile communication overhead become a dominant memory concern, as we show in this work.

This work makes the following contributions:

- The first detailed characterization of full-matrix NW alignment on the Graphcore IPU, with a quantitative breakdown of memory footprint components (control code, exchange code, vertex instances, and data) and their impact on maximum sequence lengths.
- Vertex data reduction techniques: from seven to one parameter per vertex, yielding 45% exchange code and 60% vertex instance savings.
- A three-phase implementation with adaptive frame sizing and dynamic workload distribution enabling sequences up to 9,400 elements on a single IPU.
- Practical guidelines for mapping wavefront algorithms to the IPU.

2 Background

2.1 IPU Architecture

The Graphcore GC200 IPU is organized hierarchically across three levels, as shown in Fig. 1. At the system level (Fig. 1, top-left), the M2000 chassis houses four GC200 IPUs interconnected via a low-latency IPU-Fabric, with DDR4 DRAM accessible as external storage. At the processor level (Fig. 1, top-right), each GC200 integrates 1,472 independent tiles with 900 MB of In-Processor-Memory providing 47.5 TB/s aggregate bandwidth, connected through a non-blocking 8 TB/s all-to-all IPU-Exchange, and linked externally via PCIe Gen4 (64 GB/s) and 10 IPU-Links (320 GB/s chip-to-chip). At the tile level (Fig. 1, bottom), each tile contains a multi-threaded processor with six worker threads and one supervisor thread, scheduled round-robin to hide memory latency—unlike GPU warps that operate in SIMT lockstep, each IPU tile executes its own independent instruction stream.

Each tile has 624 KB of local SRAM (208 KB non-interleaved, 416 KB interleaved supporting 128-bit loads). Total on-chip memory is 918 MB per IPU. Off-chip DDR4 DRAM is accessible via *data streams* (host-driven, 2.5–3.2 GB/s) or

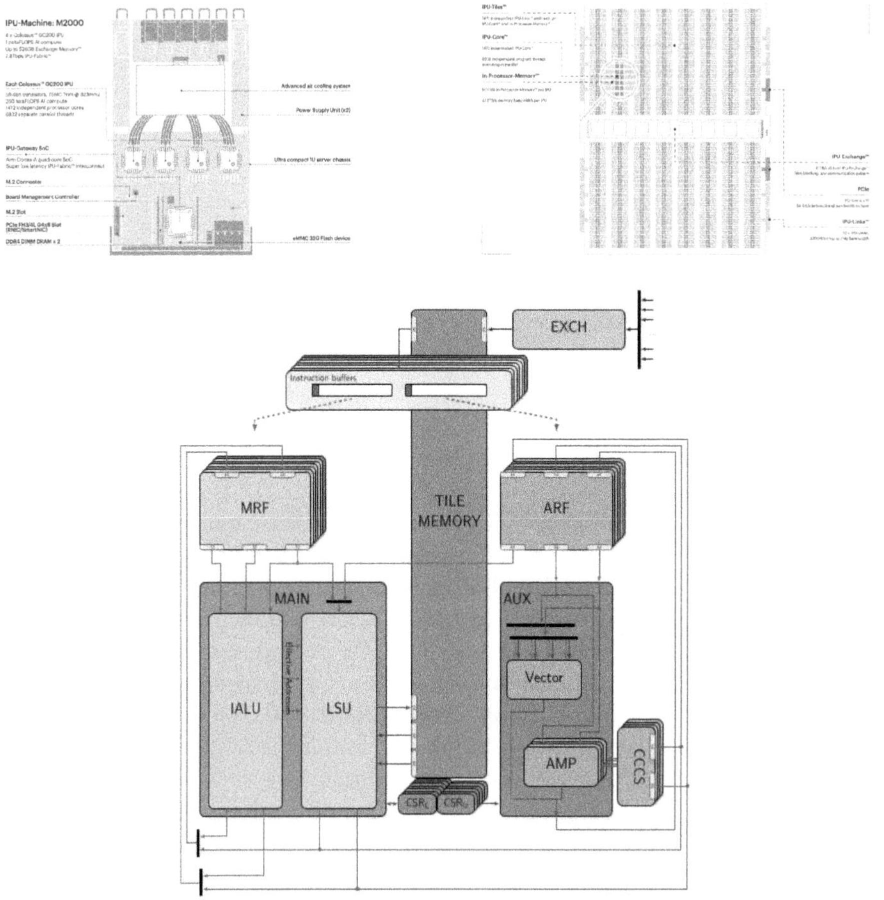

Fig. 1. IPU architecture at three levels of detail. Top-left: Graphcore M2000 system containing four GC200 IPUs with DDR4 DRAM and IPU-Fabric interconnect [4]. Top-right: GC200 processor die layout showing 1,472 IPU-Tiles with In-Processor-Memory (900 MB, 47.5 TB/s), IPU-Exchange (8 TB/s all-to-all), PCIe Gen4 host interface, and 10 IPU-Links for chip-to-chip communication [6]. Bottom: Internal structure of a single tile, showing the MAIN pipeline (IALU, LSU for integer and memory operations), AUX pipeline (floating-point and vector unit), tile-local SRAM, instruction buffers for 7 hardware contexts (1 supervisor + 6 workers), and the exchange interface [5].

remote buffers (device-driven, 4.5–5.5 GB/s). Graphcore's successor processor, *Bow*, applies wafer-on-wafer stacking to deliver higher per-tile clock rates and bandwidth while retaining the same Poplar programming model and on-chip-only memory philosophy [6]; the qualitative trade-offs analyzed in this paper therefore carry over to Bow. Table 1 compares the GC200 and NVIDIA A30.

Poplar Programming Model. The Poplar SDK's C++ API requires explicit graph construction. A *vertex* is a small C++ class with a `compute()` method

Table 1. Architectural comparison: GC200 IPU vs. NVIDIA A30 GPU.

Feature	GC200 IPU	NVIDIA A30
Processing units	1,472 tiles	3,584 CUDA cores
Max threads	8,832	229,376
On-chip SRAM	918 MB	10.75 MB
Off-chip DRAM	256 GB (host)	24 GB (HBM2e)
FP32 peak	62.5 TFlops/s	10.3 TFlops/s
Power	150 W	165 W
Execution model	MIMD (BSP)	SIMT

and fixed input/output ports; each vertex *instance* is statically bound to one tile at graph-build time and reads/writes only memory the host has mapped to that tile. A *compute set* is a barrier-synchronized batch of vertex instances fired together, followed by an explicit data-exchange phase—analogous to a CUDA kernel launch, but with each vertex pinned to a tile rather than scheduled dynamically across SMs. The six worker threads on a tile pick instances from the active compute set in round-robin order, providing latency hiding rather than a separate axis of parallelism inside a vertex. The IPU follows the Bulk-Synchronous Parallel (BSP) model: local compute, global sync, exchange. All code and data are statically compiled into a graph, creating overhead in four buckets: *control code* (program flow), *vertex code* (compiled logic), *vertex instances* (per-instance metadata: port descriptors, stack frames), and *exchange code* (inter-tile communication routines). For programs with millions of vertices, this overhead can *exceed* actual problem data. The `poplar_start` variable (program entry point) must reside on one tile and can grow to 60–220 KB, consuming up to 35% of a tile's capacity.

2.2 Needleman-Wunsch Algorithm

The NW algorithm [11] computes optimal global alignment via dynamic programming. Given sequences $A = a_1 \dots a_m$ and $B = b_1 \dots b_n$ over alphabet Σ (e.g., $\{A, C, G, T\}$ for DNA), it constructs score matrix $M \in \mathbb{R}^{(m+1)\times(n+1)}$:

Initialization: $M(0,0) = 0$, $M(i,0) = i \cdot \delta$, $M(0,j) = j \cdot \delta$, where $\delta < 0$ is the gap penalty.

Matrix Fill: Each cell depends on three neighbors:

$$M(i,j) = \max \begin{cases} M(i-1,j-1) + s(a_i,b_j) & \text{(diagonal: match/mismatch)} \\ M(i-1,j) + \delta & \text{(top: deletion)} \\ M(i,j-1) + \delta & \text{(left: insertion)} \end{cases} \quad (1)$$

where $s(a_i, b_j) = \sigma_{\text{match}}$ if $a_i = b_j$, else σ_{mismatch}. We use $\sigma_{\text{match}} = +1$, $\sigma_{\text{mismatch}} = -1$, $\delta = -1$.

Traceback: Starting from $M(m,n)$, optimal choices are traced back to reconstruct the alignment.

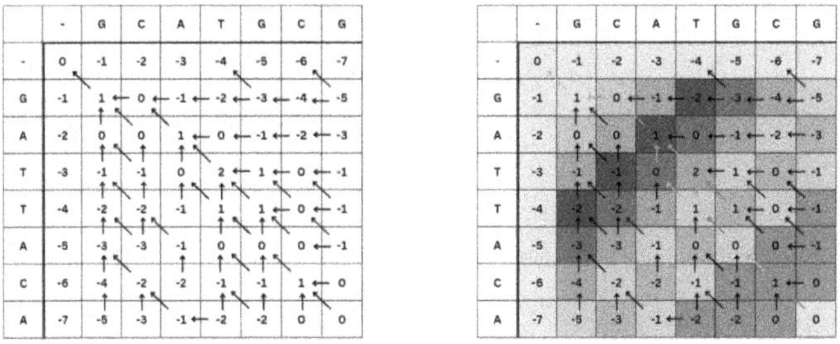

Fig. 2. Left: NW score matrix for GCATGCG vs. GATTACA ($\sigma_{\mathrm{match}} = +1$, $\sigma_{\mathrm{mismatch}} = -1$, $\delta = -1$). Arrows show cell dependencies: each $M(i,j)$ depends on its top, left, and top-left neighbors. Right: Diagonal parallelization—same-colored cells are independent and computed simultaneously. Diagonal lengths vary from 1 (corners) to $\min(m,n)+1$ (center).

Diagonal Wavefront Parallelism. All cells on anti-diagonal $D_d = \{(i,j) \mid i+j=d\}$ are independent (Fig. 2, right), with diagonal length varying from 1 to $\min(m,n)+1$ and back. This creates three phases—*build-up*, *saturated*, and *culmination*—whose variable parallelism challenges architectures that benefit from uniform workloads. Total complexity is $O(mn)$.

3 Related Work

GPU Implementations. Chaudhary et al. [3] achieve 6× CPU speedup using diagonal skewing with inter-block barriers. Kurt et al. [8] use CUDA cooperative groups for grid-level synchronization. Blocked diagonal approaches show ∼3× speedup over element-wise implementations [9]. Commercial tools like NVIDIA Parabricks [17] optimize for many short sequences.

FPGA and PIM Approaches. NW's wavefront maps naturally to spatial architectures: systolic arrays demonstrated linear-time alignment in hardware, and FPGA implementations [12] instantiate processing elements mirroring the wavefront with dedicated dependency interconnect. The IPU shares this spatial distribution of computation and memory but trades hardwired dataflow for programmability at the cost of software overhead. Processing-in-Memory architectures like GenASM [2] address the memory bandwidth bottleneck via near-data computation.

IPU for HPC and Bioinformatics. Jia et al. [7] find nearly 2× single-precision throughput vs. V100. Louw and McIntosh-Smith [10] demonstrate GPU-competitive stencil performance. Most relevant, X-Drop [1] achieves up

Table 2. Comparison with related sequence alignment implementations.

Work	Platform	Problem	Max Len.	Perf.	Strategy
Chaudhary [3]	GPU	Single	14k	6× CPU	Barrier sync.
Kurt [8]	GPU	Single	55k	15 GCUPS	Coop. groups
Lee [9]	GPU	Single	3M	3× naive	Blocked diag.
Oliver [12]	FPGA	Many	—	High thru.	Systolic array
X-Drop [1]	IPU	Many	n/a	10× GPU	Adaptive band
iPuma [16]	IPU (64)	Many	n/a	1.7× GPU	Multi-IPU
This work	**IPU (1)**	**Single**	**9,400**	**36 GCUPS*** **3–7†**	**Adaptive frame**

*Optimal diagonal; †Realistic three-phase.

to 10× GPU speedup using an adaptive band heuristic that prunes the score matrix, and iPuma [16] scales to 64 IPUs with a load-balancing driver—but both target *many short sequences*, where each alignment fits in one tile and the challenge is throughput across pairs rather than per-pair memory footprint. Neither addresses what happens when one alignment must span many tiles: the wavefront synchronization, exchange-code growth, and `poplar_start` pressure analyzed here. Our work complements theirs by characterizing *single large sequence* alignment with the full $O(mn)$ matrix retained (Table 2).

4 Methodology

4.1 Mapping NW to the IPU

Per-Vertex Compute Kernel. Each NW vertex owning cell (i, j) on anti-diagonal D_d receives pointers to a window of the previous two diagonals (Sect. 4.2) and writes one output cell as

$$out = \max\bigl(prev2 + s(a_i, b_j),\ prev1_{\text{up}} + \delta,\ prev1_{\text{left}} + \delta\bigr), \tag{2}$$

where $s(\cdot, \cdot)$ and δ are compile-time constants baked into the vertex code, and a_i, b_j are looked up in per-tile sequence buffers. For frame size k, this kernel is looped over k output cells and the dependency window grows to $k{+}3$ values from D_{d-1} and $k{+}2$ values from D_{d-2}.

Single-Tile Baseline. We first implement NW on a single tile, mapping the full $m \times n$ score matrix to tile zero, and test four variants. **V1 (FP single-thread row-wise):** one worker iterates the matrix row by row in single-precision FP, with sequences and scoring constants passed at runtime. **V2 (FP, constant-embedded scores):** identical to V1 but with σ_{match}, σ_{mismatch}, δ baked into the vertex code; the score matrix cannot be made constant, so savings are limited to the scalars and V2 overlaps V1 in the plot. **V3 (integer single-thread):** V1's row-wise structure but with 32-bit integer scores, routing through the IALU on the MAIN pipeline instead of the AUX-pipeline FP unit. **V4 (FP six-thread diagonal):** replaces the row-wise scan with a diagonal sweep in which the six workers cooperatively process each anti-diagonal as a compute set, with intra-tile barriers between diagonals (Fig. 3, left and center); the only variant that exploits intra-tile worker parallelism.

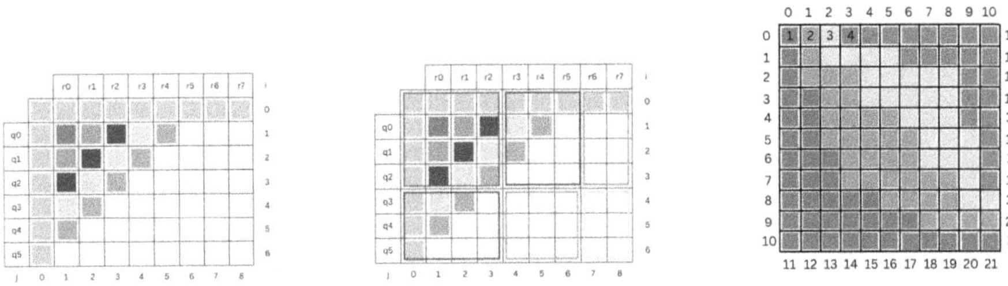

Fig. 3. Left: Single-tile diagonal approach; colors are successive anti-diagonals (compute sets). Center: Six-thread tiled distribution; colored frames are compute sets: purple (1st), blue (2nd), green (3rd), yellow (4th). Right: Dynamic workload distribution across full IPU; colors represent threads. In the saturated phase, each vertex computes multiple consecutive elements. (Color figure online)

Full-IPU Diagonal. Extending to all 1,472 tiles, each anti-diagonal becomes one compute set with one vertex per element; initialization vertices are folded into the same compute sets, eliminating a separate phase. A vertex computing one element runs on one of six worker threads per tile—threads provide latency hiding via round-robin scheduling, not extra intra-vertex parallelism—so maximum parallelism requires $\geq 8{,}832$ vertices per compute set.

4.2 Vertex Data Reduction

Initially, each vertex receives seven parameters: position (i, j), three dependency values, and scoring constants $(\sigma_{\text{match}}, \sigma_{\text{mismatch}}, \delta)$. With 2.25M vertices for length-1,500 sequences, this creates 200 MB exchange code and 124 MB vertex instances—far exceeding the 27 MB for actual data (Table 3).

We exploit diagonal dependency structure: computing consecutive elements i through $i+k$ on diagonal d requires elements $i-1$ through $i+k+1$ from diagonal $d-1$ (only $k+3$ values, not $3(k+1)$, due to overlap). By allocating contiguous dependency arrays and passing each vertex a *single reference* to the relevant segment, per-vertex data drops from seven to one variable. Score constants are embedded in vertex code (this increases vertex code by 753 KB but decreases instances by 547 KB—negligible net difference).

This single optimization saves over 165 MB for 2.25M vertices: *minimizing per-vertex state is paramount for IPU programming.*

Table 3. Impact of vertex data reduction (length 1,500; memory across all 1,472 tiles).

Config.	Exchange Code	Vertex Inst.	Control	Total Overhead
7 variables	200.4 MB	124 MB	86.5 MB	410.9 MB
1 variable	115 MB	51.6 MB	79 MB	245.6 MB
Reduction	**42.6%**	**58.4%**	**8.7%**	**40.2%**

Table 4. Frame size trade-offs. Vertex count is for length 1,500.

Frame	Peak GCUPS	Max Length	Vertices (len. 1500)
1	1.25	~2,000	3.6M
10	1.6	~3,500	360K
50	0.25	~9,400	72K

4.3 Frame Size Optimization

Frame size—the number of consecutive diagonal elements per vertex—is a compile-time decision trading parallelism for memory. Frame size 1 maximizes parallelism but caps sequences at ~2,000 elements via overhead pressure; frame size 50 reduces vertices 50×, enabling sequences up to 9,400 elements at reduced throughput (Table 4).

4.4 Dynamic Workload Distribution

Complementing compile-time frame sizing, *dynamic workload distribution* is a runtime scheme for the saturated phase. The threshold 8,832 = 1,472 tiles × 6 workers is the maximum useful concurrency on a GC200: additional instances time-multiplex onto the same workers and add no parallelism while still paying full per-instance metadata, exchange-code, and `poplar_start` cost. We therefore fix vertex count at 8,832 and have each compute $\lceil d/8832 \rceil$ elements for diagonal length d; the first (d mod 8832) vertices handle one extra element for load balancing (Fig. 3, right).

4.5 Three-Phase Implementation

The full implementation combines these techniques:

Build-up (diagonals 1 to 8,832): One vertex per element, thread count growing per diagonal. Partitioned into nine program launches due to memory constraints.

Saturated (diagonals 8,832 to $m+n-8{,}832$): Fixed 8,832 vertices with dynamic distribution. Our experiments fit 637 diagonals per launch, achieving 6.5 GCUPS at 67.6% memory utilization.

Culmination: Mirrors build-up in reverse with nine program launches.

4.6 Remote Buffer Strategies

To extend beyond on-chip limits, we explore two streaming strategies:

Squared Sub-matrix: The score matrix is partitioned into 1,500 × 1,500 sub-matrices processed sequentially via remote buffers. This enables up to 22,500-element sequences (225 iterations) but at ~0.6 GCUPS due to copy overhead. Beyond 225 iterations, interconnect deadlocks prevent further scaling.

Diagonal Streaming: Only three diagonals reside in memory (two dependencies + result). Shows continuously increasing performance up to the memory limit, but also encounters interconnect stability issues after hundreds of remote buffer operations.

5 Results

5.1 Experimental Setup

Hardware: Graphcore M2000 (one GC200 IPU used); NVIDIA A30 GPU (selected for similar 165 W vs. 150 W power envelope). **Software:** Poplar SDK, C++, `-O3`; PopVision Graph Analyzer for memory profiling. **Data:** pairs of synthetic DNA sequences drawn independently and uniformly at random over $\{A, C, G, T\}$, lengths 500–36M, with no enforced identity or divergence. NW's matrix-fill cost depends only on lengths and the scoring scheme, not on content, so random inputs are representative for performance and memory-footprint characterization. Scoring: $+1/-1/-1$. Each configuration runs 10,000 iterations (1,000 for >500 MB); std. dev. <2%.

5.2 Single-Tile Baseline

Figure 4 (left) shows V1–V4 of Sect. 4. V1 and V2 both reach ~5.5 MCUPS (V2's compile-time folding affects only scoring scalars, so its line overlaps V1). V4 reaches 7.5 MCUPS (1.4× over V1); V3 reaches 4.25 MCUPS, confirming that the AUX-pipeline FP unit outperforms the IALU. Maximum single-tile length: 780 elements (600 KB of 624 KB).

Running the same program independently on every one of the 1,472 tiles—each tile solving its own complete NW problem with no inter-tile communication—establishes a throughput baseline of 1,472 simultaneous alignments (Fig. 4, right). It yields 10.75 GCUPS for V4 and 7.25 GCUPS for V1: near-linear scaling, isolating coordination cost from computation cost.

5.3 Frame Size Trade-Offs

Figure 5 (left) shows full-IPU diagonal performance vs. data size for several frame sizes. Performance increases with data size (the IPU needs sufficient parallelism); smaller frames give higher GCUPS at comparable sizes, while larger frames enable dramatically longer sequences. Frame 10 achieves the highest absolute

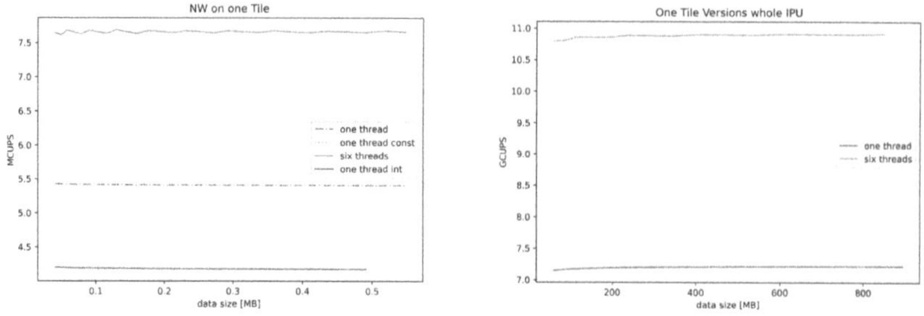

Fig. 4. Left: Single-tile performance for the four variants of Sect. 4—V4 FP six-thread diagonal (7.5 MCUPS), V1 FP single-thread row-wise and V2 FP single-thread with constant-embedded scores (visually overlapping at ~5.5 MCUPS—V2's compile-time folding affects only the small scoring scalars, below plot resolution), and V3 integer single-thread (4.25 MCUPS). Right: Throughput baseline obtained by replicating the same NW problem independently on every one of the 1,472 tiles with no inter-tile communication, isolating coordination cost from computation cost; near-linear scaling to 10.75 GCUPS (V4) and 7.25 GCUPS (V1).

GCUPS (1.6) by running at sizes where frame 1 cannot. Table 5 gives the underlying memory breakdown: for frame 1 (length 1,900) overhead totals ~637 MB vs. only 27 MB of data—a 23× ratio—which frame 50 (length 9,100) improves to 1.3×, though exchange code (393 MB) still dominates because each vertex transfers larger segments.

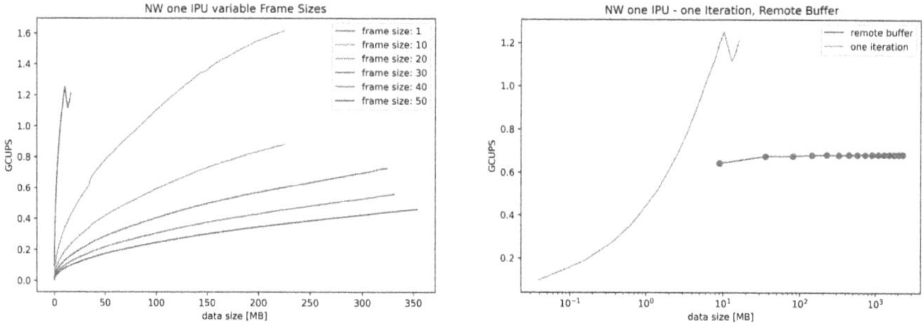

Fig. 5. Left: frame size impact on full-IPU diagonal performance—smaller frames yield higher GCUPS, larger frames enable longer sequences. Right: remote-buffer baseline (solid: on-chip; dotted: multi-iteration sub-matrix); processable data grows but GCUPS drops to ~0.6.

5.4 Remote Buffer Implementations

Figure 5 (right) shows the squared sub-matrix approach: processable data scales from 2,000 to 22,500-element sequences but throughput drops to ~0.6 GCUPS. The diagonal-streaming variant shows similar scaling but is also limited by interconnect deadlocks after hundreds of remote-buffer operations.

Table 5. Memory breakdown: frame 1 (length 1,900) vs. frame 50 (length 9,100).

Component	Frame 1	Frame 50
Variables (data)	26.8 MB	330 MB
Control code	137 MB	10.2 MB
Vertex code	2.2 MB	6.1 MB
Exchange code	258 MB	393 MB
Vertex instances	236 MB	8.3 MB
Other (descriptors, stack)	4 MB	10 MB
Total	**~664 MB**	**~768 MB**

5.5 Optimal Diagonal Performance

Single-diagonal benchmarks isolate the saturated phase from the build-up/culmination tails, representing a best-case uniform workload. Figure 6 (left): one-element-per-vertex achieves 15–30 GCUPS up to 550K elements, beyond which per-vertex overhead exhausts on-chip capacity. Figure 6 (right): the dynamic-workload-distribution variant (Sect. 4.4) with a constant 8,832 instances reaches 29–36 GCUPS for 550K–36M elements, exceeding our GPU baseline. Program-launch overhead is minimal: 1–1,000 launches sustain ~32 GCUPS.

Fig. 6. Optimal single-diagonal performance. Left: one element per vertex, 15–30 GCUPS, limited to 550K elements by vertex memory overhead. Right: dynamic distribution with 8,832 constant threads, 29–36 GCUPS for 550K–36M elements.

5.6 GPU Baseline and Comparison

We benchmark two GPU implementations on the NVIDIA A30. The barrier synchronization approach [3] achieves only 0.2 GCUPS (constant across sizes, failing beyond 30K elements). The cooperative groups approach [8] achieves 5–15 GCUPS for 10K–50K elements but fails beyond 55K (requires compute capability 9.0; A30 supports 8.0). Figure 7 shows both GPU baselines alongside the original GTX 1650 results from [8] for reference. The GTX 1650 Super outperforms the A30 at all sequence lengths due to better cooperative groups support; the A30 was selected for its comparable power envelope to the IPU (165 W vs. 150 W).

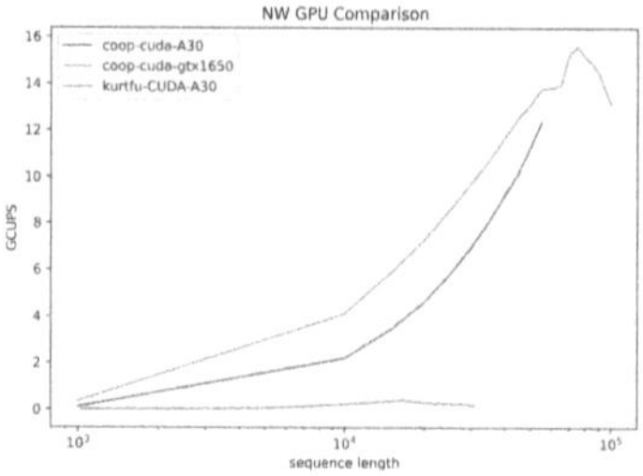

Fig. 7. GPU baseline performance on NVIDIA A30: cooperative groups (coop-cuda-A30, up to 12 GCUPS) vs. barrier synchronization (kurtfu-CUDA-A30, ~0.2 GCUPS). The GTX 1650 reference (coop-cuda-gtx1650) reaches 15 GCUPS due to better cooperative groups support.

Comparative Summary. The IPU achieves 36 GCUPS on the single-diagonal best-case workload (2.4× the GPU's 15 GCUPS). Realistic three-phase IPU implementations average 3–7 GCUPS—comparable to the GPU's 5–12 GCUPS but with a much shorter maximum sequence length (9,400 vs. 55,000); the GPU's 24 GB DRAM advantage enables longer sequences. The three-phase build-up and culmination achieve 1.25–3.0 GCUPS (nine launches each; `poplar_start` grows to 63 KB), and the saturated phase reaches 6.5 GCUPS—roughly 1/6 of optimal diagonal performance, reflecting multi-phase overhead.

6 Discussion

Memory Dominates Computation. Poplar's static compilation overhead—not computational capacity—is the primary bottleneck. Despite 62.5 TFlops/s theoretical performance, program metadata consumes 10–20× more memory than problem data. The `poplar_start` bottleneck (up to 220 KB on one tile) is invisible in the programming model. This contrasts with GPUs, where bottlenecks typically involve data capacity rather than program metadata.

The Parallelism–Memory Trade-off is specific to the IPU: fine-grained parallelism (frame size 1) achieves 36 GCUPS but limits sequences to 2,000 elements, while coarse-grained parallelism (frame size 50) enables 9,400 elements at roughly 80% reduced throughput. On GPUs, by contrast, increasing problem size generally *improves* utilization without explicit memory management.

Practical Guidelines. The IPU sits between FPGAs (spatial dataflow) and GPUs (programmability), eliminating the memory wall for on-chip data at the cost of severely limited capacity. From this work: target 8,832–50,000 vertices,

10–100 elements per vertex, minimize per-vertex data, prioritize workload uniformity, and profile with PopVision early. The IPU suits *database search* (many short alignments) over single large sequences, consistent with X-Drop and iPuma.

Architectural Requirements and Limitations. For chromosome-scale alignment, IPU-class architectures would need runtime-resolved vertex collections, non-uniform remote-buffer transfers with bounded queueing, and distributed `poplar_start` control state—without these, on-chip-only architectures remain best suited to many-short-sequence regimes (X-Drop, iPuma). Concrete limitations of this study: maximum length (~9K) is far below genomic requirements, multi-IPU scaling is unexplored due to interconnect issues, and the GPU comparison uses two implementations.

7 Conclusion

We present the first detailed characterization of full-matrix NW alignment on the Graphcore IPU, reaching 36 GCUPS on uniform workloads (2.4× GPU baseline) and 3–7 GCUPS for realistic three-phase implementations with sequences capped at ~9,000 elements. Findings generalize beyond NW: program metadata can dominate data by an order of magnitude on the IPU; reducing per-vertex state yields substantial savings (45% exchange code, 60% vertex instances); and the IPU excels with uniform workloads but struggles with the variable parallelism inherent to wavefront algorithms. **Future work** includes hybrid CPU+IPU pipelines that stream matrix tiles through bounded remote-buffer queues to escape the on-chip cap, composing our vertex data-reduction with the many-pair regime of X-Drop [1] and iPuma [16] on identical hardware, re-running our memory breakdown on the Bow processor to isolate model-intrinsic bottlenecks from GC200-specific ones, and extending the analysis to Smith–Waterman and gap-affine schemes (Gotoh, WFA) and to multi-IPU scaling once the IPU-Link path stabilizes for streaming workloads.

Disclosure of Interests. The authors have no competing interests to declare that are relevant to the content of this article.

References

1. Burchard, L., Zhao, M.X., Langguth, J., Buluç, A., Guidi, G.: Space efficient sequence alignment for SRAM-based computing: X-Drop on the Graphcore IPU. In: SC 2023 (2023). https://doi.org/10.1145/3581784.3607094
2. Cali, D.S.: GenASM: a high-performance, low-power approximate string matching acceleration framework for genome sequence analysis. In: MICRO 2053, pp. 951–966 (2020)
3. Chaudhary, A., Kagathara, D., Patel, V.: A GPU based implementation of Needleman-Wunsch algorithm using skewing transformation. In: IC3 2015, pp. 498–502 (2015). https://doi.org/10.1109/IC3.2015.7346733

4. Graphcore: IPU overview – M2000 hardware (2022). https://docs.graphcore.ai/projects/ipu-overview/
5. Graphcore: Tile vertex ISA (2022). https://docs.graphcore.ai/projects/tiles-and-vertex-isa/
6. Graphcore: IPU processor – products (2024). https://www.graphcore.ai/products/ipu
7. Jia, Z., Tillman, B., Maggioni, M., Scarpazza, D.P.: Dissecting the graphcore IPU architecture via microbenchmarking (2019). https://arxiv.org/abs/1912.03413
8. Kurt, F., Altilar, D.T., Metin, A.Y.: Implementations of the Needleman-Wunsch algorithm for GPU architectures. In: 7th National High Performance Computing Conference, Istanbul, Turkey (2022)
9. Lee, Y.S., Kim, Y.S., Uy, R.L.: Serial and parallel implementation of Needleman-Wunsch algorithm. Int. J. Adv. Intell. Inform. **6**(1), 97–108 (2020). https://doi.org/10.26555/ijain.v6i1.361
10. Louw, T., McIntosh-Smith, S.: Using the graphcore IPU for traditional HPC applications. In: 3rd Workshop on Accelerated Machine Learning (AccML) (2021)
11. Needleman, S.B., Wunsch, C.D.: A general method applicable to the search for similarities in the amino acid sequence of two proteins. J. Mol. Biol. **48**(3), 443–453 (1970). https://doi.org/10.1016/0022-2836(70)90057-4
12. Oliver, T., Schmidt, B., Maskell, D.: Reconfigurable architectures for bio-sequence database scanning on FPGAs. IEEE Trans. Circuits Syst. II **52**(12), 851–855 (2005)
13. Shekofteh, S.K., Alles, C., Fröning, H.: Reducing memory requirements for the IPU using butterfly factorizations. In: SC-W 2023, pp. 1255–1263 (2023). https://doi.org/10.1145/3624062.3624196
14. Shekofteh, S.K., Alles, C., Kochendörfer, N., Fröning, H.: On performance analysis of graphcore IPUs: analyzing squared and skewed matrix multiplication (2023). https://arxiv.org/abs/2310.00256
15. Shekofteh, S.K., Bogacz, D., Alles, C., Fröning, H.: Butterfly factorization for vision transformers on multi-IPU systems. Parallel Comput. **127**, 103165 (2026). https://doi.org/10.1016/j.parco.2025.103165
16. Zhao, M., Burchard, L., Schroeder, D.T., Langguth, J., Cai, X.: iPuma: high-performance sequence alignment on the Graphcore IPU. In: ISC High Performance 2024, pp. 1–11 (2024). https://doi.org/10.23919/ISC.2024.10528941
17. Zhu, T., Vats, P., et al.: Parabricks: GPU accelerated universal pan-instrument genomics analysis software suite. bioRxiv (2025). https://doi.org/10.1101/2025.07.23.666378

Backend Code Generation for Graph DSLs Targeting Diverse Accelerator Platforms

Ashwina Kumar[1](✉), M. Venkata Krishna[2], Prasanna Bartakke[1], Mathew Thomas[1], Rahul Kumar[1], Rajesh Pandian M[1], Nibedita Behera[1], and Rupesh Nasre[1]

[1] Indian Institute of Technology Madras, Chennai, India
ashwinakumar825@gmail.com
[2] PSG Tech, Coimbatore, India

Abstract. Sparse graphs are ubiquitous in real and virtual worlds. With the phenomenal growth in semi-structured and unstructured data, sizes of the underlying graphs have witnessed a rapid growth over the years. Analyzing such large structures necessitates parallel processing, which is challenged by the intrinsic irregularity of sparse computation, memory access, and communication. It would be ideal if programmers and domain-experts get to focus only on the sequential computation and a compiler takes care of auto-generating the parallel code. On the other side, there is a variety in the number of target hardware devices, and achieving optimal performance often demands coding in specific languages or frameworks. Our goal in this work is to focus on a graph DSL which allows the domain-experts to write almost-sequential code, and generate parallel code for different accelerators from the same algorithmic specification. In particular, we illustrate code generation from the StarPlat graph DSL for NVIDIA, AMD, and Intel GPUs using CUDA, OpenCL, SYCL, HIP, and OpenACC programming languages. Using a suite of ten large representative graphs and four popular algorithms, we present the efficacy of StarPlat's versatile code generator.

Keywords: Parallel Computing · GPUs · Accelerator · Graph Processing and Large-Scale Graph Analytics

1 Introduction

Graphs [15] naturally model several real-world phenomena such as social networks, road networks and biological systems. To deal with such a scale [10], it is natural to employ farms of parallel machines housing powerful accelerators. We continue to witness various architecture designers and vendors proposing new hardware to enable us process huge data fast.

To accelerate our algorithms [12] and applications optimally on a certain hardware, currently, the domain expert (such as a biologist) needs to program in a certain language or a framework geared towards the hardware. For instance,

M. Torquati et al. (Eds.): Euro-Par 2026, LNCS 16781, pp. 227–240, 2027.
https://doi.org/10.1007/978-3-032-35248-4_16

NVIDIA GPUs are tied closely with CUDA, Intel GPUs expect SYCL, while AMD GPUs need HIP for extracting the best performance. This is clearly not ideal, as it demands a domain-expert to continue learning new parallel languages rather than focusing on domain-specific algorithmic innovations. To address this, we have been moving towards common computing languages such as OpenCL, Sycl, and OpenACC, which are supposed to be platform portable. Unfortunately, their support is currently limited, and sometimes driven by vendor competition.

In this work, we focus on the domain of graph algorithms [5] and accelerators, and help domain-experts generate parallel code for multiple accelerators from the same algorithmic specification. In this endeavor, we employ a recently proposed domain-specific language for graph algorithms named StarPlat [2], which supports three backends: OpenMP, MPI, and CUDA. We augment its compiler to support multiple accelerator backends: CUDA, OpenCL, SYCL, HIP, and OpenACC. This paper makes the following contributions.

- A code generator which builds upon the intermediate representation (AST) of StarPlat to support NVIDIA, Intel, and AMD GPUs. This relieves the domain-expert from learning new languages to write parallel code.
- Custom processing per accelerator for optimized computation. This allows StarPlat to, for instance, optimize data-clause around loops in OpenACC, while optimize a reduction operation for the SYCL backend.
- An extensive experimental evaluation of the generated codes against library-based Gunrock and manually-optimized LonestarGPU on ten large graphs and four popular graph algorithms (betweenness centrality, page rank, single-source shortest paths, and triangle counting), illustrating StarPlat's ability to be competitive with library-based and hand-crafted codes.
- Portability-performance tradeoffs across multiple hardware platforms.

2 StarPlat Language Design

We briefly describe StarPlat [2] in this section. StarPlat is a domain-specific language for graph algorithms. It supports three backends: OpenMP, MPI, and CUDA. In this work, we build support for a variety of accelerators via various parallel languages. Listing 1.1 presents the algorithmic specification for computing single-source shortest paths (SSSP) in StarPlat. The example indicates how a graph algorithm looks in StarPlat. Due to its high-level nature, it permits us to focus on the algorithm without worrying about the architectural nuances.

Example. The function computeSSSP takes four arguments: a graph g, propNode dist, propEdge weight, and source vertex src. Statement 2 declares a variable modified of type propNode. propNode<bool> marks modified as bool type attribute associated with each vertex. Statement 3 creates a bool type vertex attribute modified_nxt. The function attachNodeProperty associates the three attributes with each vertex of g, and initializes the property values of

```
1  function computeSSSP (Graph g, propNode<int> dist, propEdge<int>
       weight, node src) {
2      propNode<bool> modified;
3      propNode<bool> modified_nxt;
4      g.attachNodeProperty(dist = INF, modified = False,
           modified_nxt = False);
5      src.modified = True;
6      src.dist=0;
7      bool finished = False;
8      fixedPoint until (finished: !modified) {
9          forall (v in g.nodes().filter(modified == True)) {
10             forall (nbr in g.neighbors(v)) {
11                 edge e = g.get_edge(v, nbr);
12                 <nbr.dist, nbr.modified_nxt> = <Min(nbr.dist,
                       v.dist + e.weight), True>;
13             }
14         }
15     modified = modified_nxt;
16     g.attachNodeProperty(modified_nxt = False);
17     }
18 }
```

Listing 1.1. Single Source Shortest Paths (SSSP) specification in StarPlat

dist to infinity (`INT_MAX`), modified to false and modified_nxt to false as aggregate operations in Statement 4. In Statements 5–6 the distance of src is set to zero, and the vertex is also marked as modified. Statement 8 is a **`fixedPoint`** construct which makes sure the iterative procedure executes until the variable finished becomes true. Each iteration updates the variable finished, which determines if another iteration is required. If no vertices are changed, a fixed-point is reached. This is achieved by or-ing the modified attribute of each node and assigning to finished. Statement 9 defines parallel iteration over the graph nodes using the iteration construct forall. Furthermore, processing a subset of the vertices that satisfy a condition is made possible by the optional filter clause. In Statement 10, the forall construct indicates that all of the neighbors of vertex `v` are iterated over in parallel, and that the corresponding edge is relaxed for each neighbor nbr (Statements 11–12). A good illustration of the abstraction offered by the DSL's constructions is the multiple assignment construct in Statement 12, which executes multiple tasks (taken from Green-Marl [8]). The rvalue **`Min(nbr.dist, v.dist + e.weight)`** is assigned to the dist attribute of **`nbr`** with the sum of **`v.dist`** and **`e.weight`** based on whether the alternative distance via v is smaller than the existing distance of **`nbr`**. If **`nbr.dist`** is updated, the modified_nxt attribute of **`nbr`** is set. Further modified_nxt is assigned to modified in Statement 15 and attachNodeProperty makes modified_nxt to false in Statement 16.

```
__global__ void computeSSSP (...) {
  unsigned id = blockIdx.x * blockDim.x + threadIdx.x;
  ...
  for (int ee = gpu_OA[id]; ee < gpu_OA[id+1]; ee++) {
    int nbr = g.gpu_edgeList[ee];
    ...
}...}...
computeSSSP<<<nblocks, blocksize>>>(...);
cudaDeviceSynchronize();
```

Listing 1.2. CUDA code generated for neighborhood iteration (HIP is similar)

3 Code Generation for Multiple Accelerators

A code generator takes the AST and the symbol table as an input, and generates C++ code for that particular backend. We augment StarPlat's code generator to support CUDA, OpenCL, SYCL, HIP, and OpenACC. In this section, we discuss key design decisions and the challenges faced during code generation.

Graph Representation. To have a common representation across accelerators and CPU too, we use an array-based compressed sparse row (CSR) format.

Neighborhood Iteration. Listing 1.2 illustrates it for NVIDIA GPUs. A challenge in CUDA [14] is that the kernel launch and the kernel function are separate. This demands a split-code generation, unlike other backends. This is non-trivial because the StarPlat source code uses simply a `forall` loop. The CUDA code generator needs to identify the variables used in the kernel, transfer those to the device (`cudaMemcpy`) and pass those as parameters to the kernel. The kernel uses the CSR representation (offset array `gpu_OA`) to traverse through the neighbors. Neighborhood iteration in HIP follows the same process as in CUDA, with the primary difference being the use of the HIP APIs such as `hipMemcpy` and `hipDeviceSynchronize` instead of their CUDA counterparts. Listing 1.3 shows neighbor iteration in OpenACC using `#pragma acc` annotations. The code generator does not need to create a separate kernel, but faces a non-triviality different from that in CUDA: the variables used within the loop need to be *promoted* up to a `data copyin` clause. Without this promotion, the variables would be repeatedly copied across the two devices (e.g., edge weights, vertex attributes). Listing 1.4 shows neighbor iteration in SYCL expressed as a data-parallel kernel using the `parallel_for` function. The function allows the body to be executed by multiple threads (on CPU or GPU). Sycl uses a queue (Q) to process various tasks, and is associated with a device (CPU or GPU or FPGA). The final `wait` function acts as a join with the caller (in this case CPU). The body of `parallel_for` consists of a nested loop to iterate through vertices and their neighbors, similar to the CUDA, HIP, and OpenACC codes, and the outer loop is parallelized. Finally, Listing 1.5 shows neighbor iteration in OpenCL, which, similar to CUDA, has a separate kernel and host processing, with a different syntax. Apart from the boilerplate code to setup the environment (not shown),

```
#pragma acc data copyin(g)
{
  #pragma acc data copyin( g.edgeList[0:g.num_edges()],
      g.indexofNodes[:g.num_nodes()+1], weight[0:
      g.num_edges()], modified[0: g.num_nodes()],
      modified_nxt[0:g.num_nodes()]) copy(dist[0:g.num_nodes()])
  { ...
    #pragma acc parallel loop
    for(int v=0; v<g.num_nodes(); v++) {
        for (int ee = g.indexofNodes[v]; ee<g.indexofNodes[v+1];
            ee++) {
          int nbr = g.edgeList[ee];
          ...
    }...} ...
} }
```

Listing 1.3. OpenACC code generated for neighborhood iteration

```
Q.submit([&](handler &h){
  h.parallel_for(NUM_THREADS, [=](id<1> v){
    for (; v < V; v += NUM_THREADS){
     ...
     for(int ee=g.gpu_indexOfNodes[v];
           ee<g.gpu_indexOfNodes[v+1];ee++) {
          int nbr = g.gpu_edgeList[ee];
          ...
    }...} ...
}); }).wait()
```

Listing 1.4. SYCL code generated for neighborhood iteration

the function `clEnqueueNDRangeKernel` enqueus the kernel into the command-queue, from which the GPU driver dequeues and executes the task.

Reductions. StarPlat triggers a reduction when combined-operators are used. Reductions help synchronize for correctness, and may also improve performance (e.g., when implemented in a hierarchical fashion). We discuss accelerator-specific code generation for reduction below. Due to restrictions on the number of *resident thread-blocks* [9] that might block the kernel, the situation in CUDA becomes challenging. Thus, a reduction needs to be carefully implemented. One way to combat this is by utilizing host-side reduction operation as a distinct kernel (for example, using `thrust::reduce`). However, doing so necessitates ending the kernel, leaving the GPU, coming back to the host, calling the reduction kernel, returning to the host, and then starting a new kernel to complete the remaining tasks in the `forall` loop. In addition to complicating code production, this makes processing as a whole, ineffective. Therefore, we rely on CUDA's [7] atomic instructions to generate the functionally equivalent code (e.g., using the function `atomicAdd` as shown in Listing 1.6 for operator $+=$ as used in the tri-

```
__kernel void computeSSSP(...){
    unsigned id = get_global_id(0);
    ...
    for(int ee = gpu_OA[id]; ee < gpu_OA[id+1]; ee++){
        int nbr = gpu_edgeList[ee];
        ...
    } ...
} ...
// from host
status = clEnqueueNDRangeKernel(command_queue, computeSSSP, 1,
    NULL, global_work_size, local_work_size, 0, NULL, &event);
clWaitForEvents(1, &event);
```

Listing 1.5. OpenCL code generated for neighborhood iteration

```
int nbr = gpu_edgeList[edge];
int e = edge;
int dist_new = gpu_dist[v] + gpu_weight[e];
if (gpu_dist[nbr] > dist_new) {
    atomicMin(&gpu_dist[nbr], dist_new);
    gpu_modified_next[nbr] = true;
    gpu_finished[0] = false;
}
```

Listing 1.6. CUDA and HIP code generated for reduction / `Min` construct

angle counting algorithm). HIP also utilizes a similar approach. In the case of OpenACC, the loops with a reduction operation are marked with a `reduction pragma`. The reduction clause in OpenACC is helpful in parallelizing such situations to avoid data races. An example of OpenACC's reduction clause is shown in Listing 1.7.

```
#pragma acc parallel loop reduction(+:diff)
for (int v = 0; v < g.num_nodes(); v++) {
  float sum = 0.0;
  for (int ee = g.rev_indexofNodes[v]; ee <
      g.rev_indexofNodes[v+1]; ee++) {
    int nbr = g.srcList[ee] ;
    sum = sum + pageRank[nbr] / (g.indexofNodes[nbr+1] -
        g.indexofNodes[nbr]);
  }
  float val = (1 - delta) / num_nodes + delta * sum;
  diff = diff + val - pageRank[v];
  pageRank_nxt[v] = val;
}
```

Listing 1.7. OpenACC reduction code generated for PageRank (PR)

fixedPoint Construct. The `fixedPoint` construct translates to a while loop conditioned on the fixed-point variable provided in the construct. Typically, the convergence is based on a node property, but it can be an arbitrary computation. This code is generated on the host, so it is similar in template for all the five backends. CUDA code updates a copy of the `finished` flag on the GPU, which is `cudaMemcpy`'ed to the host (as shown in Listing 1.8).

```
while (!finished) {
    finished = true;
    if (...) { // Min-construct expansion
        ...
        finished = false; // fixedPoint identifier updation
} }
```

Listing 1.8. Code generated for the `fixedPoint` construct

4 Backend Optimizations

[CUDA, HIP, OpenCL] Optimized Host-Device Data Transfer. We run a standard program analysis on the AST to determine which variables must be transmitted between devices. For instance, since a graph is static, its copy from the GPU to the CPU at the conclusion of the kernel is not necessary. The updated vertex attributes, however, need to be returned. Similar to this, during a fixed-point processing, the `finished` flag is set on the CPU, conditionally set on the GPU, and read on the CPU once again. The variable must therefore be moved back and forth the two devices. Device-only variables are generated for the `forall`-local variables.

[CUDA, HIP, OpenCL] Memory Optimization in OR-Reduction. When we write the `fixedPoint` construct, the fixed-point is computed using the `modified` attribute. If any of the vertices' `modified` flags are set, another iteration is fundamentally required. StarPlat makes use of this, which is essentially a logical-OR operation, to create a single flag variable that is set by multiple threads concurrently (with a reliance on hardware atomicity for primitive types). In terms of time and memory, managing this flag is less expensive than moving arrays of the `modified` flags across devices.

5 Experimental Evaluation

Algorithms. Using StarPlat, we developed four algorithms: Betweenness Centrality (BC), PageRank (PR), Single Source Shortest Path (SSSP), and Triangle Counting (TC), for benchmarking and for comparing with other frameworks and graph libraries. With this small specification, a domain-expert can generate the implementations for these algorithms in different accelerator forms: CUDA, OpenCL, SYCL, HIP, and OpenACC. Ignoring the header files, the compiler generates around 150, 120, 125, and 75 lines for BC, PR, SSSP, and TC respectively for the CUDA and HIP backends. The numbers increase by 50% and 100% for SYCL and OpenCL, and reduce by about 33% for OpenACC.

Graphs. We use ten large graphs in our experiments, which are a mix of different types. Six of these are social networks exhibiting the small-world property, two are road networks having large diameters and small vertex degrees, while two are synthetically generated. One synthetic graph has a uniform random distribution (generated using Green-Marl's graph generator [8]), while the other one has a skewed degree distribution following the recursive-matrix format (generated using SNAP's RMAT generator with parameters a = 0.57, b = 0.19, c = 0.19, d = 0.05) [13]. They are listed in Table 1, sorted on the number of edges in each category. For unweighted graphs, we assign edge-weights selected uniformly at random in the range [1,100] (for SSSP).

Table 1. Input graphs (Δ indicates degree).

Graph	Short name	$\|V\|$ $\times 10^6$	$\|E\|$ $\times 10^6$	Avg. Δ	Max. Δ
twitter-2010	TW	21.2	265.0	12.0	302,779
soc-sinaweibo	SW	58.6	261.0	4.0	4,000
orkut	OK	3.0	234.3	76.3	33,313
wikipedia-ru	WK	3.3	93.3	55.4	283,929
livejournal	LJ	4.8	69.0	28.3	22,887
soc-pokec	PK	1.6	30.6	37.5	20,518
usaroad	US	24.0	28.9	2.0	9
germany-osm	GR	11.5	12.4	2.0	13
rmat876	RM	16.7	87.6	5.0	128,332
uniform-random	UR	10.0	80.0	8.0	27

Machine Configurations. We ran our CUDA, OpenCL, and OpenACC experiments on a compute node, whose configuration is as follows: Intel Xeon Gold 6248 CPU with 40 hardware threads spread over two sockets, 2.50 GHz clock, and 192 GB memory running RHEL 7.6 OS. All the codes in C++ are compiled with GCC 9.2, with optimization flag -O3. Various backends have the following versions: OpenACC version 20.7-0, OpenCL version 2.0, CUDA version 10.1.243 and run on Nvidia Tesla V100-PCIE GPU with 5120 CUDA cores spread uniformly across 80 SMs clocked at 1.38 GHz with 32 GB global memory and 48 KB shared memory per thread-block. Since SYCL code can run on both CPU and GPU, we ran it on the CPU (with the configuration mentioned above, with 40 threads). However, since the machine does not house Intel GPUs and is not configured to work with its V100 GPUs, we ran it on Intel DevCloud GPU UHD Graphics [0x9a60] and also on another NVIDIA GPU GeForce RTX 2080 Ti.

We ran our experiments for HIP on a node with the following configuration: an Intel Core i9-10980XE CPU paired with 64 GB memory and an AMD RX6900 GPU with 16 GB of video memory and a memory bandwidth of 512 Gbps. The GPU contains 5120 stream processors and has a peak single precision compute performance of 23.04 TFLOPs. Compilation and execution was done on Ubuntu 22.04.2 LTS running HIP version 5.4.22804.

Table 2. StarPlat's CUDA code performance comparison against LonestarGPU and Gunrock v1.2. All times are in seconds. The number in the second column for BC is the number of iterations executed. LonestarGPU does not have BC implemented and fails to load the largest graph TW (OOM == out of memory)

Algo.		Framework	TW	SW	OK	WK	LJ	PK	US	GR	RM	UR	Total
BC	1	LonestarGPU	-	-	-	-	-	-	-	-	-	-	-
	1	Gunrock v1.2	2.122	4.237	0.525	0.535	0.548	0.317	**2.811**	**1.750**	1.238	0.944	15.027
	1	StarPlat	**0.002**	**0.004**	**0.149**	**0.153**	**0.078**	**0.029**	17.656	6.359	**0.225**	**0.079**	24.734
	20	StarPlat	6.992	2.279	2.762	3.014	1.298	0.534	369.701	126.485	2.949	1.593	517.607
	80		28.179	9.332	11.331	12.050	4.886	1.907	1444.656	518.968	6.509	6.372	2044.189
	150		55.548	OOM	21.241	27.271	9.609	3.794	2636.453	978.758	9.912	11.957	—
PR		LonestarGPU	-	**0.240**	0.363	**0.104**	**0.225**	**0.240**	**0.832**	**0.294**	**0.240**	**0.240**	—
		Gunrock v1.2	15.230	36.910	2.430	2.460	2.952	1.085	13.345	6.499	9.170	5.487	95.568
		StarPlat	**4.081**	7.112	**0.256**	1.780	1.300	0.257	3.420	0.679	0.891	0.257	20.033
SSSP		LonestarGPU	-	0.077	0.217	0.058	0.084	0.037	**0.162**	**0.091**	0.129	0.183	—
		Gunrock v1.2	2.272	4.057	0.616	0.556	0.562	0.311	1.283	1.140	1.034	0.915	12.746
		StarPlat	**0.001**	**0.002**	**0.078**	**0.044**	**0.027**	**0.012**	1.667	0.695	**0.120**	**0.028**	2.674
TC		LonestarGPU	-	31.990	2.998	2.771	**0.110**	**0.039**	11.874	5.695	**1.270**	0.499	—
		Gunrock v1.2	**67.718**	7.369	**0.843**	**0.997**	0.850	0.404	1.490	0.712	3.200	1.040	84.623
		StarPlat	10540.002	**1.410**	46.700	4.009	3.006	0.655	**0.001**	**0.001**	824.620	**0.034**	11420.430

Baselines. We compare StarPlat-generated accelerator codes against the following two hand-crafted baselines, which also implement the same set of algorithms (except for BC). While the original papers are dated, the software has been updated. Both the baselines use the latest releases developed by the authors and maintained by their groups.

- Gunrock [16] provides data-centric abstractions to apply a graph operator on vertices or edges to compute the next frontier using the following three functions to be supplied by the user: `filter`, `compute`, and `advance`. It supports the CUDA backend.
- LonestarGPU [4] is a collection of hand-optimized CUDA programs [6], with varied optimizations applied for data-driven and topology-driven computations [14].

5.1 Comparison Across Frameworks

Our goal is to match the performance of the hand-crafted code. Table 2 presents the absolute running times of the four algorithms on our ten graphs for the three frameworks: LonestarGPU, Gunrock, and StarPlat. The running times include CPU-GPU data transfer (since we will be comparing these times against the CPU-only times as well).

Betweenness Centrality. BC involves running forward and backward shortest paths from various source vertices. Since Brandes algorithm [3] is time-consuming, literature often compares time for a few iterations, spanning a few source vertices (otherwise, it can take several days to complete BC on large graphs). The number of iterations is shown against BC in the second column in Table 2. LonestarGPU does not have BC as part of its collection. Compared to Gunrock, StarPlat-generated code outperforms on eight out of the ten graphs. Both the graphs for which Gunrock outperforms are road networks, having large diameters. Gunrock relies heavily on bulk-synchronous processing and its three API are very well optimized.

PageRank. We observe that the three frameworks have consistent relative performance, with hand-crafted LonestarGPU codes outperforming the other two and StarPlat outperforming Gunrock. StarPlat exploits the double buffering approach to read the current PR values and generate those for the next iteration (see Listing 1.7). This separation reduces synchronization requirement during the update but necessitates a barrier [17] across iterations. LonestarGPU uses an in-place update of the PR values and converges faster.

Single-Source Shortest Paths. Gunrock uses Dijkstra's algorithm for computing the shortest paths using a two-level priority queue. We have coded a variant of the Bellman-Ford algorithm in StarPlat. Hence, the comparison may not be most appropriate. But we compare the two only from the application perspective – computing the shortest paths from a source in the least amount of time. LonestarGPU and StarPlat outperform Gunrock on all ten graphs. Between LonestarGPU and StarPlat, there is no clear winner. They, in fact, have competitive execution times across graphs.

Triangle Counting. Unlike the other three algorithms, TC is not a propagation-based algorithm. In addition, it is characterized by a doubly-nested loop inside the kernel (to iterate through neighbors of neighbors). Another iteration is required for checking edge, which can be implemented linearly or using binary search if the neighbors are sorted in the CSR representation. Due to this variation in the innermost loop, the time difference across various implementations can be pronounced, which we observe across the three frameworks.

5.2 Comparison Across Accelerators

Almost all the work in literature in this domain involves CUDA. We did not find any published and open-source framework, library, or benchmark to compare against for HIP, SYCL, OpenCL, and OpenACC backends. Technically, it is inappropriate to compare across different hardware with different software architectures. Nonetheless, we delve into this comparison from the end-users perspectives who want their algorithmic code to complete execution as fast as possible. Table 3 compares the performance of the four algorithms across various accelerator codes generated by StarPlat. To our knowledge, this is the first study comparing various accelerators and their languages for graph algorithms.

Table 3. Performance (seconds) of StarPlat-generated code on different accelerators. Second column for BC indicates the number of iterations executed. (OOT == one hour timeout on Intel DevCloud) A value of 0.00 means time is less than 10 milliseconds.

Algo.		Framework	TW	SW	OK	WK	LJ	PK	US	GR	RM	UR	Total
	1	CUDA	**0.01**	**0.01**	0.15	0.15	0.08	0.03	17.66	6.36	**0.23**	0.08	24.73
	1	OpenACC (Nvidia GPU)	0.76	1.64	0.57	0.63	0.60	0.12	58.77	21.30	4.29	0.79	89.47
	1	OpenACC (Intel CPU)	0.46	1.66	45.15	29.01	76.79	14.06	1670.08	608.26	103.65	59.13	2608.25
	1	OpenCL (Nvidia GPU)	**0.01**	**0.01**	0.17	**0.07**	0.08	0.03	3.73	1.37	0.30	0.07	5.83
	1	SYCL (Intel CPU)	0.45	0.51	1.29	1.08	0.78	0.58	71.40	31.09	2.15	1.25	110.58
	1	SYCL (Intel GPU)	0.21	0.29	0.86	0.67	0.35	0.22	57.37	21.22	1.11	1.05	79.35
	1	SYCL (Nvidia GPU)	**0.01**	**0.01**	0.15	0.09	0.07	0.03	**3.02**	**1.31**	0.56	0.10	**5.34**
	1	HIP (AMD GPU)	1.22	0.03	**0.1**	0.33	**0.06**	**0.02**	3.48	1.38	0.53	**0.03**	8.18
	20	CUDA	6.99	2.28	2.76	3.01	1.30	0.53	369.70	126.49	2.95	1.59	517.61
	20	OpenACC (Nvidia GPU)	16.608	32.6	11.83	12.3	6.42	2.3	1600.2	928.71	86.5	10.81	2708.278
	20	OpenACC (Intel CPU)	8.84	84.5	983.61	748.49	1597.88	249.00	30692.97	13267.05	1778.04	1455.57	50865.95
	20	OpenCL (Nvidia GPU)	**0.05**	0.60	2.12	**0.96**	1.40	**0.16**	84.42	27.55	**2.28**	1.33	120.87
	20	SYCL (Intel CPU)	7.69	1.95	14.76	12.33	7.14	3.1	1611.54	578.56	32.68	16.35	2286.11
	20	SYCL (Intel GPU)	2.40	4.60	13.60	10.98	5.13	2.37	1,122.09	384.42	20.74	18.44	1584.77
	20	SYCL (Nvidia GPU)	0.10	**0.16**	3.06	1.44	**1.11**	0.51	**56.69**	**23.41**	12.22	1.92	**100.60**
	20	HIP (AMD GPU)	5.25	0.62	**1.89**	8.32	1.15	0.39	72.4	27.5	4.26	**0.58**	142.36
BC	80	CUDA	28.179	9.332	11.331	12.050	4.886	1.907	1444.656	518.968	**6.509**	6.372	2044.189
	80	OpenACC (Nvidia GPU)	63.78	148.28	**0.35**	51.91	371.58	9.23	7783.67	5644.65	258.06	36.01	14367.52
	80	OpenACC (Intel CPU)	51.93	547.75	982.17	3166.13	2730.46	1087.26	96859.19	51268.69	4318.54	10101.74	171113.86
	80	OpenCL (Nvidia GPU)	**0.15**	2.39	8.81	**3.64**	5.22	**0.83**	322.60	111.83	13.54	5.31	474.32
	80	SYCL (Intel CPU)	24.18	7.26	58.70	45.62	28.21	11.97	5398.65	2354.16	112.75	59.84	10455.99
	80	SYCL (Intel GPU)	9.12	18.36	50.14	39.63	20.73	8.48	4196.69	1487.65	79.45	62.26	5972.51
	80	SYCL (Nvidia GPU)	0.37	**0.68**	11.43	6.07	**4.38**	1.87	**206.52**	**98.62**	47.89	7.37	**385.2**
	80	HIP (AMD GPU)	20.74	2.49	7.82	33.44	4.68	1.37	283.52	113.18	12.05	**2.3**	561.59
		CUDA	4.08	7.11	**0.26**	1.78	1.30	0.26	3.42	0.68	0.89	**0.26**	20.03
		OpenACC (Nvidia GPU)	**0.83**	1.18	0.63	**0.45**	0.44	0.36	**0.63**	**0.45**	**0.57**	0.70	**6.24**
		OpenACC (Intel CPU)	27.60	344.60	4.52	2.60	2.22	0.53	0.95	0.96	7.75	3.11	394.84
PR		OpenCL (Nvidia GPU)	345.59	4.50	33.37	54.13	55.87	19.78	204.97	58.91	439.45	131.88	1357.43
		SYCL (Intel CPU)	70.22	39.91	25.92	13.57	52.95	21.02	347.02	197.28	33.96	47.05	848.90
		SYCL (Intel GPU)	14.57	30.72	4.37	3.28	7.04	2.76	43.38	23.53	7.56	5.69	142.89
		SYCL (Nvidia GPU)	2.70	4.00	1.26	1.19	**0.35**	**0.15**	1.08	0.55	1.20	0.30	12.78
		HIP (AMD GPU)	17.05	**0.67**	2.72	5.73	3.98	3.24	12.23	3.31	13.79	14.3	77.02
		CUDA	**0.00**	**0.00**	0.08	**0.04**	**0.03**	**0.01**	1.67	0.70	**0.12**	**0.03**	**2.67**
		OpenACC (Nvidia GPU)	0.72	0.90	0.65	0.42	0.36	0.27	2.8	1.24	0.96	0.48	8.8
SSSP		OpenCL (Nvidia GPU)	**0.00**	**0.00**	0.08	0.05	**0.03**	**0.01**	3.72	1.36	**0.12**	**0.03**	5.41
		SYCL (Intel CPU)	2.95	0.73	2.17	1.03	1.28	0.75	53.64	12.15	2.01	1.93	78.63
		SYCL (Intel GPU)	0.82	0.02	0.32	0.12	0.11	0.05	**0.18**	1.24	0.38	0.18	79.39
		SYCL (Nvidia GPU)	4.08	7.11	0.26	1.78	1.30	0.26	3.42	**0.68**	0.89	0.26	6.55
		HIP (AMD GPU)	**0.00**	**0.00**	**0.04**	0.09	**0.03**	**0.01**	2.53	1.08	0.16	**0.03**	3.97
		CUDA	10540.00	1.41	46.70	**4.01**	3.01	0.66	**0.00**	**0.00**	824.62	**0.03**	11420.43
		OpenACC (Nvidia GPU)	15522.84	3.23	62.00	6.10	4.98	1.32	0.40	0.35	10770.25	0.45	31625.92
		OpenACC (Intel CPU)	20776.85	42.10	3300.97	545.79	225.29	31.58	1.38	0.58	10299.78	15.24	35239.56
TC		OpenCL (Nvidia)	10162.17	1.38	48.05	**4.01**	3.08	0.67	**0.00**	**0.00**	791.78	0.04	**11011.17**
		SYCL (Intel CPU)	OOT	21.29	108.86	OOT	11.56	2.21	0.25	0.19	1585.90	0.82	–
		SYCL (Intel GPU)	OOT	11.58	75.12	OOT	8.76	2.89	0.13	0.09	902.38	0.49	–
		SYCL (Nvidia GPU)	OOT	**0.99**	**40.81**	4.04	**2.37**	**0.00**	**0.00**	0.68	**0.89**	0.26	–
		HIP (AMD GPU)	**7198.63**	1.47	50.21	6982.21	5.96	0.71	**0.00**	**0.00**	2729.31	**0.03**	16968.53

Betweenness Centrality. We observe that overall SYCL on NVIDIA GPUs performs the best among the backends with OpenCL on NVIDIA GPUs being a close second. On NVIDIA GPUs, OpenACC performs poorly compared to CUDA, OpenCL, and SYCL. SYCL on NVIDIA GPU outperforms SYCL on Intel GPU. Unlike CUDA, SYCL's implementation does not depend upon `grid.synchronization()`, resulting in better performance on road networks. OpenACC's pragma-based implementation on NVIDIA GPU performs comparable to SYCL on Intel GPU. But on Intel CPU, OpenACC performs poorly compared to SYCL. We also observed that for short diameter graphs, the BC time scales linearly with the number of sources across the backends.

PageRank. Unlike in BC, OpenACC on NVIDIA GPUs outperforms the other backends for PR. SYCL on NVIDIA GPUs is a close second, followed by CUDA. OpenCL on NVIDIA GPUs is the slowest (other than on graph GR). On Intel CPU, OpenACC outperforms SYCL on all but one graph (SW). SYCL on Intel GPU outperforms the Intel CPU versions.

Single-Source Shortest Paths. Similar to BC, CUDA outperforms other backends for SSSP. On NVIDIA GPUs, CUDA is followed by OpenCL, then SYCL, and then OpenACC (ignoring two graphs SW and UR for which our generated OpenCL code did not produce the correct results). We also observed that in our setup OpenACC on multi-core did not produce correct results for SSSP. We nailed it down to the usage of atomics, which we are discussing with NVIDIA.

Triangle Counting. Although only a few lines in the DSL, TC is a time-consuming algorithm. This is evident from SYCL going out of time (one hour timeout on DevCloud) on two graphs (TW and OK). Otherwise, SYCL performs well on almost all the graphs. On NVIDIA GPUs, CUDA and OpenCL perform similarly, while OpenACC is twice as slow. On Intel CPU, SYCL considerably outperforms OpenACC. SYCL on Intel GPU is comparable to that on Intel CPU. Among all the graphs, TW and RM stand-out for extremely high running times. This is due to (i) a large number of triangles in them, and (ii) their skewed degree distribution.

6 Related Work

On accelerators, graph algorithms have been primarily explored in CUDA. Gunrock [16] is a graph library which uses data-centric abstractions to perform operations on edge and vertex frontiers. LonestarGPU [4] is a collection of graph analytic CUDA programs. It employs multiple techniques related to computation, memory, and synchronization to improve the performance of the underlying graph algorithms. We quantitatively compare StarPlat against Gunrock and LonestarGPU. Medusa [19] is a software framework which eases the work of GPU computation tasks. It exploits the BSP model, and proposes a new model EVM (Edge Message Vertex). GraphIt [18] provides a novel DSL for graph computations that distinguishes between the computation (algorithm) and the computation process (schedule). CuSha [11] is a graph processing framework that uses two graph representations: G-Shards and Concatenated Windows (CW). In order to increase GPU utilization for processing sparse graphs, CW is a new format that improves the use of shards.

7 Conclusion

We illustrated that it is feasible to generate efficient parallel code for multiple accelerators from the same algorithmic specification in a graph DSL. This is not only viable, but is also a desirable approach especially for domain-experts who are currently forced to learn multiple languages for accelerating their scientific computation. We acknowledge that the necessary hardware needs to be available, and the corresponding compiler should be present. In future, we would like to support dynamic graph processing in StarPlat.

Artifact Availability. The artifact is available in the Zenodo repository [1].

Disclosure of Interests. The authors have no competing interests to declare that are relevant to the content of this article.

References

1. Ashwina, K., et al.: Artifact of the paper: backend code generation for graph DSLS targeting diverse accelerator platforms (2026). https://doi.org/10.5281/zenodo.20519221
2. Behera, N., Kumar, A., Nitish, S., Pandian, R., Nasre, R.: StarPlat: a versatile DSL for graph analytics. J. Parallel Distrib. Comput. **194**, 104967 (2024). https://doi.org/10.1016/j.jpdc.2024.104967. https://www.sciencedirect.com/science/article/pii/S074373152400131X
3. Brandes, U.: A faster algorithm for betweenness centrality. J. Math. Sociol. **25**, 163–177 (2001)
4. Burtscher, M., Nasre, R., Pingali, K.: A quantitative study of irregular programs on GPUs. In: Proceedings of the 2012 IEEE International Symposium on Workload Characterization, IISWC 2012, La Jolla, CA, USA, 4–6 November 2012, pp. 141–151. IEEE Computer Society, New York, NY, USA (2012). https://doi.org/10.1109/IISWC.2012.6402918
5. Gogoi, B., Cheramangalath, U., Nasre, R.: Custom code generation for a graph DSL. In: GPGPU 2020, pp. 51–60. Association for Computing Machinery, New York, NY, USA (2020). https://doi.org/10.1145/3366428.3380772
6. Gupta, K., Stuart, J.A., Owens, J.D.: A study of persistent threads style GPU programming for GPGPU workloads. IEEE (2012)
7. Harris, M.: Optimizing parallel reduction in CUDA
8. Hong, S., Chafi, H., Sedlar, E., Olukotun, K.: Green-Marl: a DSL for easy and efficient graph analysis. SIGPLAN Not. **47**(4), 349–362 (2012). https://doi.org/10.1145/2248487.2151013
9. Hong, S., Kim, S.K., Oguntebi, T., Olukotun, K.: Accelerating CUDA graph algorithms at maximum warp. In: PPoPP 2011, pp. 267–276. Association for Computing Machinery, New York, NY, USA (2011). https://doi.org/10.1145/1941553.1941590
10. Hong, S., Salihoglu, S., Widom, J., Olukotun, K.: Simplifying scalable graph processing with a domain-specific language. In: Proceedings of Annual IEEE/ACM International Symposium on Code Generation and Optimization. In: CGO 2014, pp. 208–218. Association for Computing Machinery, New York, NY, USA (2014). https://doi.org/10.1145/2581122.2544162

11. Khorasani, F., Vora, K., Gupta, R., Bhuyan, L.N.: Cusha: vertex-centric graph processing on GPUs. In: Proceedings of the 23rd International Symposium on High-Performance Parallel and Distributed Computing. In: HPDC 2014, pp. 239–252. Association for Computing Machinery, New York, NY, USA (2014). https://doi.org/10.1145/2600212.2600227
12. Kulkarni, M., Burtscher, M., Inkulu, R., Pingali, K., Casçaval, C.: How much parallelism is there in irregular applications? In: Proceedings of the 14th ACM SIGPLAN Symposium on Principles and Practice of Parallel Programming. In: PPoPP 2009, pp. 3–14. Association for Computing Machinery, New York, NY, USA (2009). https://doi.org/10.1145/1504176.1504181
13. Leskovec, J., Sosič, R.: SNAP: a general-purpose network analysis and graph-mining library. ACM Trans. Intell. Syst. Technol. (TIST) **8**(1), 1 (2016)
14. Nasre, R., Burtscher, M., Pingali, K.: Data-driven versus topology-driven irregular computations on GPUs. In: 2013 IEEE 27th International Symposium on Parallel and Distributed Processing, pp. 463–474. IEEE, New York (2013). https://doi.org/10.1109/IPDPS.2013.28
15. Shi, X., et al.: Graph processing on GPUs: a survey. ACM Comput. Surv. **50**(6) (2018). https://doi.org/10.1145/3128571
16. Wang, Y., Davidson, A.A., Pan, Y., Wu, Y., Riffel, A., Owens, J.D.: Gunrock: a high-performance graph processing library on the GPU. In: Asenjo, R., Harris, T. (eds.) Proceedings of the 21st ACM SIGPLAN Symposium on Principles and Practice of Parallel Programming, PPoPP 2016, Barcelona, Spain, 12–16 March 2016, pp. 11:1–11:12. ACM, Barcelona, Spain (2016). https://doi.org/10.1145/2851141.2851145
17. Xiao, S., Feng, W.C.: Inter-block GPU communication via fast barrier synchronization. In: 2010 IEEE International Symposium on Parallel & Distributed Processing (IPDPS), pp. 1–12 (2010). https://doi.org/10.1109/IPDPS.2010.5470477
18. Zhang, Y., Yang, M., Baghdadi, R., Kamil, S., Shun, J., Amarasinghe, S.: Graphit: a high-performance graph DSL. Proc. ACM Program. Lang. **2**(OOPSLA) (2018). https://doi.org/10.1145/3276491
19. Zhong, J., He, B.: Medusa: simplified graph processing on GPUs. IEEE Trans. Parallel Distrib. Syst. **25**(6), 1543–1552 (2014). https://doi.org/10.1109/TPDS.2013.111

SMEAtten: Fast and Memory-Efficient Outer Product-Based Attention on ARMv9 CPUs with SME

Tengyang Zheng, Han Huang, Junru Chen, Xianwei Zhang(✉), and Yutong Lu(✉)

School of Computer Science and Engineering, Sun Yat-sen University, Guangzhou, China
{zhengty26,huangh367,chenjr97}@mail2.sysu.edu.cn, {zhangxw79,luyutong}@mail.sysu.edu.cn

Abstract. Transformer-based models are widely used in modern artificial intelligence, and the attention mechanism is a major determinant of their runtime efficiency. To accelerate matrix-intensive workloads, such as attention, ARMv9 introduces the Scalable Matrix Extension (SME) to enhance matrix processing capabilities on ARM CPUs. However, efficiently accelerating attention with SME remains challenging because of suboptimal compute-unit utilization, inefficient memory access, and limited task-level parallelism. To address these challenges, we present SMEAtten, a fast and memory-efficient attention design for ARMv9 CPUs with SME. SMEAtten incorporates three key techniques: throughput-driven interleaved matrix-vector attention kernels, an SME-adapted data layout and access scheme based on blocking, packing, buffering, and access-compute overlap, and inter-task parallelism exploitation. Experimental results show that SMEAtten delivers an average speedup of 13.62× over state-of-the-art baselines and achieves up to 56.09× acceleration in PyTorch integration evaluations. SMEAtten also supports efficient execution on different ARMv9 platforms, including LX2 and Apple M4.

Keywords: Attention · ARMv9 · Scalable Matrix Extension

1 Intoduction

Transformers have driven significant advances in natural language processing (NLP), powering highly effective models such as BERT [9] and GPT [21]. At the core of these models is the self-attention mechanism, which captures dependencies among tokens in a sequence [10,24]. A single attention computation over a **QKV** (query–key–value) triplet forms an **individual task**, and practical deployments typically execute many such tasks concurrently. Each task further consists of several **kernel-level operations**, such as the $QK^\top$ matrix multiplication and softmax normalization, which together contribute substantially to the

M. Torquati et al. (Eds.): Euro-Par 2026, LNCS 16781, pp. 241–255, 2027.
https://doi.org/10.1007/978-3-032-35248-4_17

overall execution cost [17]. As a result, attention computation is highly resource-intensive, accounting for approximately 70% of the total runtime on average [10] and becoming the primary performance bottleneck in Transformer-based systems [7,18,19,23].

As Transformer workloads continue to spread across both everyday applications and large-scale services, ARMv9 is becoming an increasingly attractive platform for efficient Transformer execution [17]. ARM-based processors are now widely deployed across diverse systems, ranging from edge devices such as Apple M4 [2] and ARM C1 [5] to high-performance servers such as LX2 [14] and NVIDIA Grace [6]. To improve matrix-processing capability on ARM CPUs, ARMv9 introduces the Scalable Matrix Extension (SME) [25], which has been adopted by modern processors including LX2 and Apple M4. The fundamental outer-product instruction in SME extends the traditional one-dimensional SIMD computation model into a two-dimensional computation paradigm, improving performance by as much as 4× [22]. These features make ARMv9 with SME a promising substrate for accelerating Transformer attention, and SME-based acceleration has already attracted growing interest [14] [15].

Although ARMv9 CPUs with SME provide substantial matrix-computation capability, efficiently accelerating attention on them remains challenging. SME follows an outer-product-based execution model that differs fundamentally from both traditional vector units and inner-product-based matrix units [20]. Existing library-style optimizations [3,4,13] often introduce extra overheads and cannot efficiently coordinate the mixed matrix-dominant and light-weight vector operations in attention. Moreover, SME-based execution must adapt to different hardware organizations across ARMv9 CPUs, which further complicates efficient and scalable deployment. As a result, existing attention optimization techniques [8,11,12,16] do not fully match SME, which calls for a dedicated architectural design.

To address these issues, efficient attention on CPUs with SME must resolve three key challenges: 1) Suboptimal kernel performance, due to pipeline stalls and insufficient exploitation of SME-specific computational features. 2) Inefficient memory access, often caused by fixed partitioning or platform-specific memory layouts [11]. 3) Limited task parallelism, as the task distribution is typically based only on input size rather than available compute capacity or system topology [1,13,26]. To overcome these limitations, we propose **SMEAtten**, an efficient attention design optimized for modern ARMv9 CPUs equipped with Scalable Matrix Extension [25]. At the **kernel** level, we implement attention kernels using interleaved SVE/SME instructions under a careful instruction scheduling strategy. Within **a single task**, we employ an SME-adapted data layout and access scheme to improve data locality and reduce memory overhead. Across **multiple tasks**, we account for the underlying core topology and dynamically distribute tasks to maximize parallel efficiency.

In summary, our contributions are as follows:

- We identify three key limitations that hinder attention execution on SME-enabled CPUs: unnecessary memory waste, low utilization of SME units, and poor task-level parallelism. These limitations explain why existing attention implementations fail to effectively leverage SME architectures.

- We propose an SME-oriented attention design. Our design incorporates interleaved matrix-vector micro kernels and an SME-adapted data layout to improve matrix units utilization and reduce memory overhead. It also introduces an inter-task parallelism strategy that accounts for the core clusters in modern ARMv9 processors.
- We implement SMEAtten in a lightweight and practical way using *ARM C Language Extensions* for SME/SVE kernels and *Pthreads* for the parallel execution runtime. Evaluation shows that SMEAtten delivers substantial performance improvements across both LX2 and Apple M4 CPUs, demonstrating high efficiency and portability.

2 Background Motivation

2.1 ARMv9 Architecture

With the growing interest in AI workloads, ARMv9 introduces the Scalable Matrix Extension (SME) to enhance matrix-processing capability. Centered around the ZA (Z-Array) tiles, SME provides the Matrix Outer Product Add (MOPA) instruction, which takes two SVE vectors as input and accumulates the results into the ZA tiles. Compared with the traditional one-dimensional vector computation model, SME exposes a two-dimensional matrix-oriented paradigm with higher throughput for matrix-intensive workloads.

SME also introduces streaming execution and specialized load/store behaviors that affect instruction scheduling, data access, and cache utilization. Although different ARMv9 processors may expose different SME implementations, they share the same matrix-oriented execution foundation, which makes SME promising for attention acceleration while introducing new optimization challenges compared with conventional SIMD-based execution (Fig. 1).

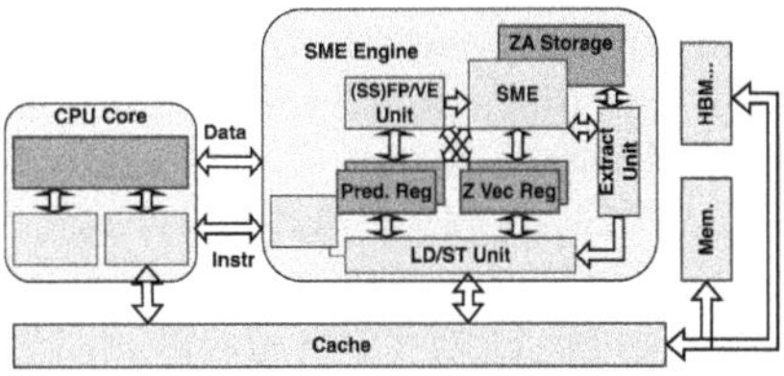

Fig. 1. ARMv9 micro architecture.

2.2 Outer Product-Based Attention

Mainstream attention implementations [11,23] typically follow a GEMM-centric workflow, where the QK^T and SV multiplications dominate the computation.

When mapped onto CPUs with SME, this workflow leads to the structure shown in Fig. 2. It consists of **intra-MM**, which includes two batched matrix multiplications and three point-wise operations (*scale*, *mask*, and *softmax*), and **inter-MM**, which repeats this process $batch_{size} \times h$ times. To exploit high-performance GEMM libraries such as KBLAS and Accelerate, previous works partition the input matrices into blocks. Under this design, the SME engine executes $S \leftarrow Q \times K^T$ and $O \leftarrow S \times V$, while SVE vectors handle the point-wise operations.

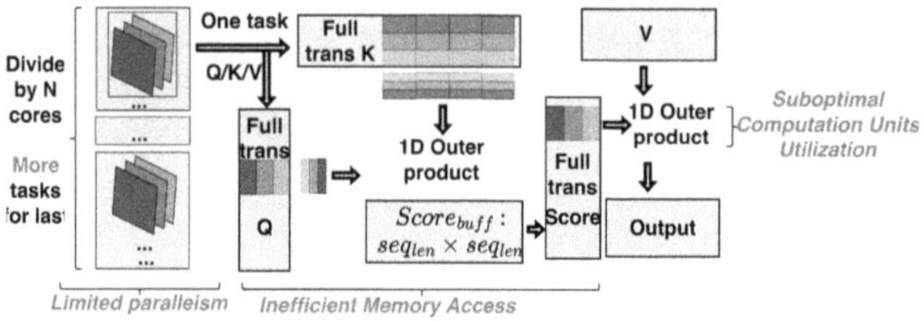

Fig. 2. Typical outer product-based attention.

2.3 Motivation and Related Work

Although SME opens new opportunities for accelerating attention computation, it also creates several performance challenges when transitioning from a vector-centric to a matrix-centric compute paradigm. These challenges manifest primarily as: a) suboptimal utilization of computational units, b) inefficient memory access, and c) limited task parallelism. Prior attention optimizations on GPUs, conventional ARM CPUs, and general matrix or SDPA libraries address some of these issues, but they do not directly align with SME's outer-product-based computation and mixed SVE/SME execution.

Suboptimal Computation Units Utilization: Existing attention kernels are typically designed for either vector units or inner-product-based matrix units [11,12], and therefore cannot fully exploit SME's execution model. On SME-enabled CPUs, attention combines matrix-dominant and light-weight vector operations, which require different instruction mappings on SME and SME2. Moreover, the interaction between SVE and SME execution introduces additional opportunities for instruction-level overlap, calling for a tailored kernel and scheduling design. A recent ARM CPU attention implementation, MEATTEN [11], exploits data reuse with NEON-based kernels. As shown in Fig. 3, MEATTEN achieves only a small fraction of the compute capability available on SME-enabled CPUs across sequence lengths. This large utilization gap suggests that a vector-centric implementation cannot effectively exploit SME, and leaves substantial room for architecture-aware kernel mapping and instruction scheduling.

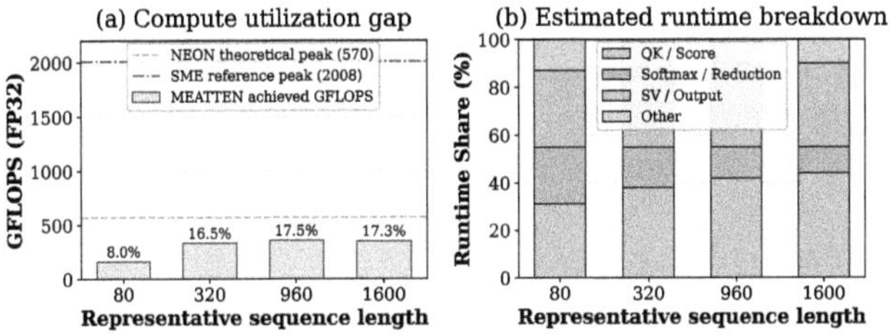

Fig. 3. Compute utilization and runtime breakdown of MEATTEN on ARMv9.

Inefficient Memory Access: Existing attention implementations often optimize locality for vector or inner-product-based matrix units [8,11,16,23]. However, these designs do not match SME's outer-product execution model. Directly migrating them either increases memory overhead, such as storing fully transposed intermediates in Fig. 2, or leads to non-contiguous accesses within blocks. Therefore, attention on SME requires a dedicated data layout and access scheme. The runtime breakdown in Fig. 3 further indicates that the dominant attention phases remain the major contributors to execution time, which makes memory access efficiency within these phases particularly important (Fig. 4).

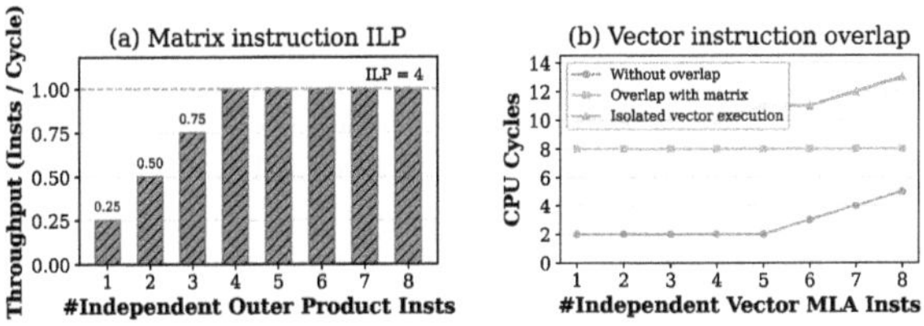

Fig. 4. Illustration of matrix instruction ILP and vector instruction overlap on ARMv9.

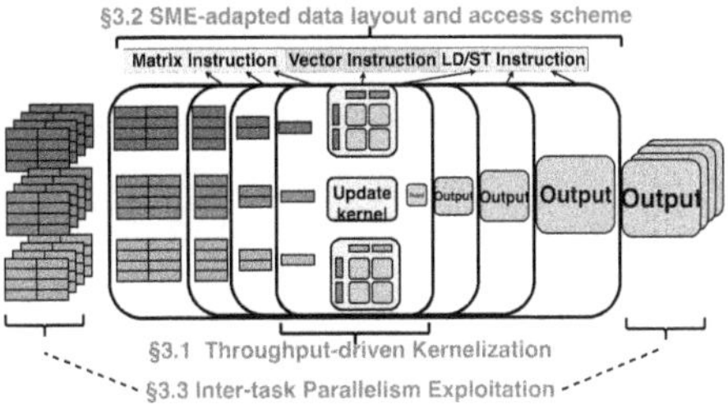

Fig. 5. Overview of SMEAtten. SMEAtten improves attention execution on ARMv9 CPUs with SME through kernelization, data layout optimization, and inter-task parallelism.

Limited Task Parallelism: The parallelism of attention varies with both seq_{len} and $batch_{size}$ [11], while existing task-partition strategies are usually designed for vector-centric or inner-product-based implementations [1,13,26]. As a result, they cannot effectively adapt to SME-based execution or to the topology differences across ARMv9 CPUs, such as the shared SME engine on Apple M4 and the per-core SME engines on LX2. This calls for an architecture-aware task allocation mechanism.

These challenges motivate an architecture-aware design that jointly improves compute utilization, memory access, and task scheduling on SME-enabled CPUs.

3 Design

In this section, we present *SMEAtten*, a novel design for accelerating attention computations on CPUs with SME. As shown in Fig. 5, *SMEAtten* comprises three core components:

- Integrated matrix-vector **micro kernels** in Sect. 3.1 that leverage matrix and vector units and schedule instructions based on attention characteristics to enhance computation throughput.
- SME-adapted **data layout and access scheme for a single task** in Sect. 3.2, which organizes blocking, packing, buffering, and access-compute overlap to improve locality and reduce memory overhead.
- **Inter-Task parallelism** exploitation in Sect. 3.3 to execute in different micro architectures with SME, which partitions and distributes tasks, and identifies the architecture features for task-thread mapping.

3.1 Throughput-Driven Kernelization

Efficient attention on SME-enabled CPUs requires high utilization of both matrix and vector resources. At the block level, SMEAtten organizes attention into three kernels, namely **Score**, **Update**, and **Output**, where **Score** computes block scores $S = Q \times K^T$, **Update** maintains the row-wise softmax states across blocks, and **Output** accumulates the output from the normalized scores and V. Among them, **Score** and **Output** are matrix-dominant and compute-intensive, while **Update** mainly performs light-weight vector operations for softmax-state maintenance. Accordingly, we focus on the compute-centric design first, while the memory-centric optimizations are presented in Sect. 3.2.

2D Outer-Product Kernel. SMEAtten selects two vectors from Q_b and two vectors from K_b, arranges them into a 2×2 grid, and accumulates all pairwise combinations directly into four ZA tiles. In FP32 mode, SME naturally exposes four parallel accumulation regions, and the 2×2 mapping aligns with this four-way structure, allowing four outer products to proceed concurrently. Compared with asymmetric groupings such as 1×4 and 4×1, the 2×2 mapping requires

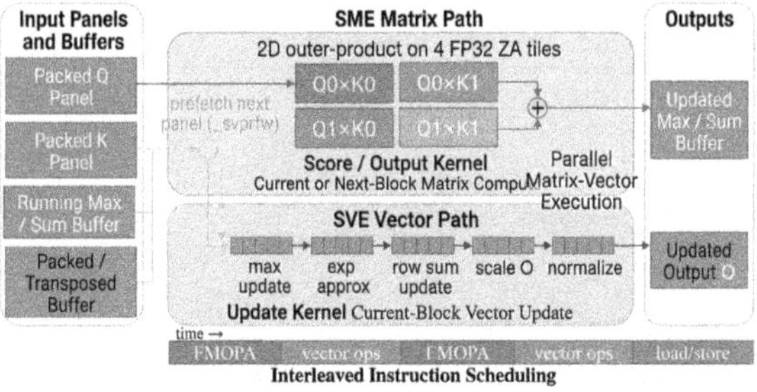

Fig. 6. Block-level cooperative SME/SVE execution in SMEAtten.

fewer live operand registers and yields a better compute-to-memory ratio. Overall, this mapping better matches SME's execution model, increases tile-level parallelism, and reduces instruction count by up to 20%.

Vector Operations. Besides the matrix-dominant **Score** and **Output** kernels, attention also requires several light-weight vector operations, as shown by the SVE vector path in Fig. 6. These operations include maximum update, exponential approximation, row-sum update, partial-output scaling, and normalization. Since they are dominated by element-wise transformation and row-wise state maintenance rather than outer-product accumulation, SMEAtten maps them to the **Update** kernel on the SVE path. This vector-side organization efficiently maintains the running softmax states across blocks while leaving the SME path to focus on the matrix-heavy computation.

For architecture-specific tuning, SMEAtten further selects different instruction variants on SME and SME2 for these vector-side operations. In the **Update** kernel, we use higher-throughput SME2 instructions such as *svtbl2* and *svsel* to accelerate vector lookup and selection during state update. In addition, SME2 also allows us to further optimize the matrix-side pipeline by merging the *max* and *store* operations in the **Score** kernel through multi-vector instructions.

Matrix-Vector Cooperative Execution. In the SME architecture, the SME instructions can only take up to one of the two issue ports of the SME units. Thus, there leaves a chance to overlap the matrix instructions with vector instructions, as described in (ILP tests in sec2). Since a 2D outer-product update uses only part of the architectural vector registers as SME inputs, the unused SVE registers are assigned to an independent vector path for extra inner-product-style accumulation on independent fragments. In this way, SME handles the main matrix-dominant computation, while SVE opportunistically processes additional vector work in parallel. This cooperation also guides execution across kernels, as shown in Algorithm 1. In the **Update** kernel, the vector path becomes dominant, while SME can simultaneously start the matrix multiplication of the next block.

Algorithm 1: Interleaved SME/SVE execution in SMEAtten

Input: current-block states $m_{j-1}, m_j, s_{j-1}, O_{old}$; next-block packed panels Q_{b+1}, K_{b+1}

initialize ZA tiles for next-block Score;
for $t \leftarrow 0$ **to** i_{end} ***step*** vl **do**
  $m_{new} \leftarrow \max(m_{j-1}[t], m_j[t])$, $\Delta \leftarrow m_{j-1}[t] - m_{new}$;
  update s using SME/SME2 vector lookup and select operations;
  $s \leftarrow$ *poly_corr*(s, Δ);
  $s_{j-1}[t] \leftarrow s_{j-1}[t] \times s$, $O_{old}[t : t + vl] \leftarrow O_{old}[t : t + vl] \times s$;
  if *next block exists* **then**
    prefetch next packed panels with *_svprfw*;
    load q_0, q_1 from Q_{b+1} and k_0, k_1 from K_{b+1};
    issue *FMOPA*$(ZA_0 \ldots ZA_3, \{q_0, q_1\}, \{k_0, k_1\})$;

3.2 SME-Adapted Data Layout and Access Scheme

Attention execution on SME-enabled CPUs is highly sensitive to data movement due to repeated accesses to tiled $Q/K/V$ data and intermediate *Score* buffers. To improve locality and reduce data access overhead, SMEAtten adopts an SME-adapted data layout and access scheme based on blocking, packing, buffering, and access-compute overlap, as shown in Fig. 7 and constrained by Eqs. 1–4.

L2 Cache Blocking. SMEAtten applies **blocking** at the L2-cache level to bound the working set of each attention task. We divide $Q/K/V/O$ into blocks and process one Q block together with the corresponding K and V blocks. This loop ordering improves temporal locality across the *Score* and *Output* kernels. We constrain the block sizes using Eq. 1 so that the main working set remains cache-resident.

L1 Cache Packing. Within each block, SMEAtten performs **packing** to reconstruct the accessed panels into contiguous layouts that are friendly to SME outer-product execution. The packed panels are streamed into registers for the micro kernels, reducing irregular accesses and L1 cache misses during both the *Score* and *Output* kernels. We use Eq. 2 and Eq. 3 to constrain the panel sizes within the L1 cache, and set p_1 and p_2 to 32 according to the micro-kernel configuration.

Memory Buffer. SMEAtten preallocates a fixed-size **buffer pool** for packed and transposed operands consumed by the compute kernels. The total buffering footprint is bounded by Eq. 4, where H_{task} denotes the memory capacity assigned to each attention task. Since the buffering memory can differ from the original input location, SMEAtten places the pool in high-bandwidth memory when available, so that packed panels and transposed operands can be supplied with lower access cost.

Finally, SMEAtten overlaps memory access with computation through **instruction reordering**. While the current panel is being consumed by the SME/SVE micro kernels, the next packed or transposed panel is prefetched into cache using _*svprfw* in line 8. This access-compute overlap partially hides data movement behind ongoing computation and helps sustain throughput across blocks and panels.

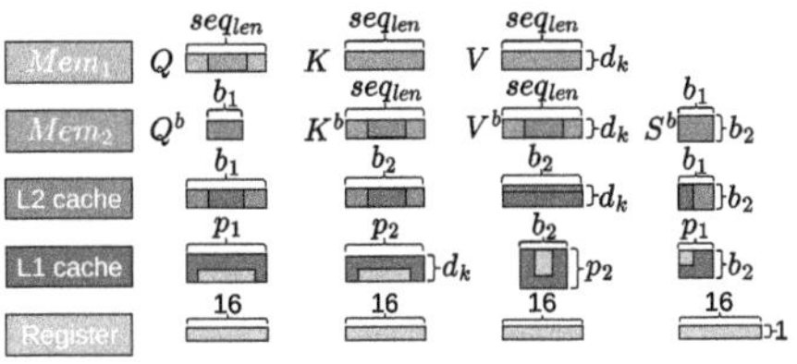

$$b_1 \times b_2 + b_1 \times d + b_2 \times d < \mathrm{CL}_2 \quad (1)$$

$$p_1 \times d + d \times b_2 + p_1 \times b_2 < \mathrm{CL}_1 \quad (2)$$

$$p_1 \times b_2 + p_2 \times b_2 + p_1 \times d < \mathrm{CL}_1 \quad (3)$$

$$b_1 \times d + b_1 \times b_2 + s \times d \times 2 < \mathrm{H}_{task} \quad (4)$$

Fig. 7. ARMv9-aware packing, blocking, buffering, and prefetching strategy. Mem_1/Mem_2 denote low/high speed memory on ARMv9 platforms.

3.3 Inter-Task Parallelism Exploitation

The designs above could only enhance performance within a single task. To execute efficiently on **multicore**, SMEAtten partitions and distributes tasks carefully, and then maps threads to cores depending on microarchitecture, to exploit parallelism.

To adapt to different sizes of inputs for a single task, we utilize data padding and then migrate our SME-adapted data layout and access scheme. Matrices smaller than a block are padded to match the block size, whereas for matrices exceeding one block, padding is applied solely to the last panel to complete the final block. During computing at the panel level, we utilize the *mask* registers in SME to avoid wrong calculations.

To reasonably divide and distribute tasks, SMEAtten follows the Algorithm 2 that identifies architecture features and computation characteristics. Considering the expensive transposition operation, we partition $batch_{size} \times h$ tasks at the task level rather than within tasks. Depending on the number of threads T, SMEAtten follows the line 1 in Algorithm 2 to divide the tasks. Based on the computing capabilities of the SME and SVE units, we aggregate the core performance within each cluster and sort the clusters in descending order, as shown from line 2 to line 4 in Algorithm 2. Then, according to the thread identifier, we determine the mapped core and the range of task indices assigned to it, as shown at line 5. We bind threads to the cores in a one-to-one manner. As for the remaining tasks, we dynamically push them to free threads, each time a single task. Based on our mapping method, SMEAtten maintains the continuity of data among adjacent cores, ensuring efficient parallelism.

3.4 Portable Implementation

SMEAtten also remains portable across ARMv9 CPUs with different SME organizations. Using LX2 and Apple M4 as examples, at the **kernel** level, SMEAtten

Algorithm 2: TASKALLOC function with thread-core mapping.

Input: Number of threads T, thread identifier $thread_{id}$, total number of tasks N, SME/SVE GFLOPS G^{SME}/G^{SVE}

Output: Assigned task indices $task_s$, $task_e$ and corresponding CPU cores

Step 0: Compute $q = \lfloor N/T \rfloor$ and remainder tasks $R = N \bmod T$. Store the R extra tasks into an array $\mathcal{R}$.

Step 1: Collect SME/SVE units' GFLOPS (G^{SME}/G^{SVE}), and the SME–SVE mapping relation $\mathcal{M}$.

Step 2: Construct an array $\mathcal{A}$ of size $|\mathcal{M}|$, where each element is

$$\mathcal{A}[i] = G_i^{SME} + 2 \cdot \sum_{j \in \mathcal{M}(i)} G_j^{SVE},$$

and another array $\mathcal{B}$ where $\mathcal{B}[i] = |\mathcal{M}(i)|$.

Step 3: Sort $\mathcal{A}$ and $\mathcal{B}$ jointly in descending order of $\mathcal{A}$.

Step 4: For a given $thread\_id$:

- Determine the SME group index by subtracting $\mathcal{B}[i]$ sequentially until $thread\_id < \mathcal{B}[i]$.
- Within that group, map the residual index to the corresponding SVE core, and get $Core_{map}$.
- Compute the task range as $[thread\_id \times q, \ (thread\_id + 1) \times q)$

return $task_s$, $task_e$ *and* $Core_{map}$.

implements both SME and SME2 kernels through ARM C Language Extensions and selects the appropriate version according to the target microarchitecture. Within **a single task**, SMEAtten places inputs and buffers according to the memory hierarchy, e.g., using unified LPDDR5x on Apple M4 and DDR/HBM on LX2. Across **multiple tasks**, portability is supported by the `TASKALLOC` function in Algorithm 2, which adapts to both the P/E-core clusters of Apple M4 and the single-core clusters of LX2 based on the SME-SVE mapping relation.

4 Evaluation

4.1 Experiment Setups

We conduct tests on the LX2 CPU and Apple M4 CPU. The hardware configurations and comparison methods are summarized in Table 1. We set the batch size to 64, the number of attention heads to 12, and the head dimension to 64. We vary the sequence length from 160 to 1600, use FP32, and keep the same input configurations and thread counts across methods on each platform. We report performance in GFLOPS, computed as the total floating-point operations of the two matrix multiplications in attention divided by execution time. All methods are evaluated with the same input configurations, precision, and thread counts on each platform, while execution is measured through each implementation's available operator path.

4.2 Performance Improvement

In this experiment, we evaluate the parallel performance of the SDPA operator using 32 cores on LX2 and 4 performance cores on M4. As shown in

Table 1. Experimental setup.

Hardware platforms				
CPU	L1 Cache	L2 Cache	Memory	Core Cluster
LX2	64 KB	512 KB	32/4 GB DDR/HBM	32 cores/NUMA node
Apple M4	320 KB	4096 KB	16 GB LPDDR5x	4P+6E cores
Comparison methods				
XNNPACK fused SDPA operator [1]				XNN_F
XNNPACK non-fused SDPA (individual routines) [1]				XNN_NF
MEATTEN (ARMv8, NEON-optimized) [11]				MEATTEN
SMEAtten (Our work)				SMEAtten

Fig. 8, SMEAtten outperforms XNN_NF, XNN_F and MEATTEN across sequence lengths 160–1600. Compared to MEATTEN, SMEAtten achieves average speedups of **4.11**× on M4 and **13.62**× on LX2. The highest speedup appears at $seq_{len} = 960$, where dynamic parallelism mitigates load imbalance for large inputs; at $seq_{len} = 160$, SMEAtten still reaches **3.94**× on M4 and **5.80**× on LX2.

Moreover, all competing methods encounter out-of-memory errors when $seq_{len} > 960$. These OOM cases mainly come from intermediate score and other temporary buffers whose memory footprint grows rapidly with sequence length. In contrast, SMEAtten still maintains strong performance and scales well at larger sequence lengths by reusing bounded packed panels and buffer space, as discussed in Sect. 3.2.

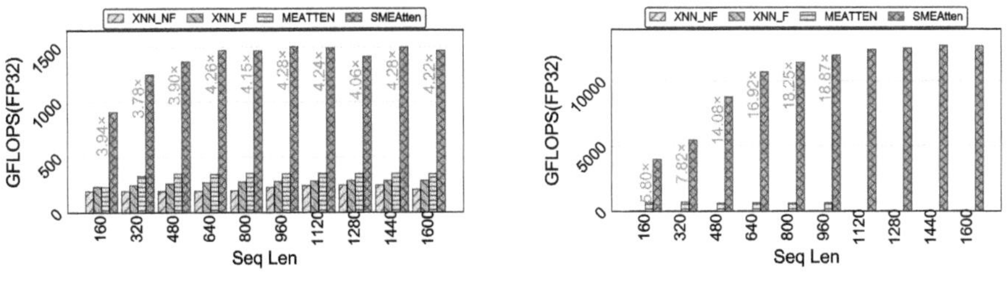

(a) M4, 4 threads

(b) LX2, 32 threads

Fig. 8. Performance improvement on M4 and LX2.

4.3 Performance Breakdown

To evaluate the effectiveness of SMEAtten, we analyze the contribution of each design component in Fig. 9. Starting from a baseline implementation without SMEAtten-specific optimizations, we incrementally evaluate the kernelized

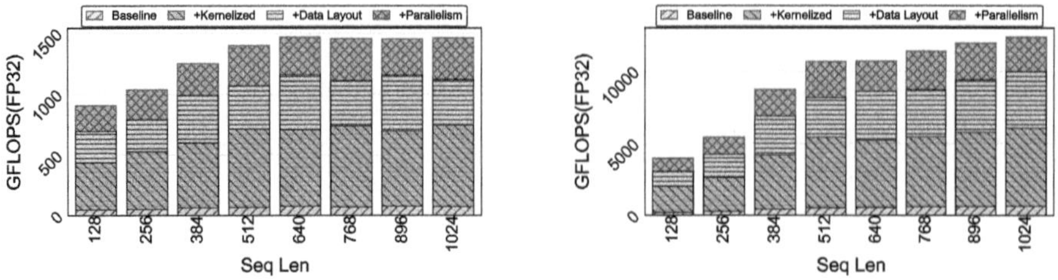

(a) M4, 4 threads (b) LX2, 32 threads

Fig. 9. Performance breakdown of SMEAtten on M4 and LX2.

implementation, the kernelized implementation with the SME-adapted data layout and access scheme, and the full SMEAtten system with inter-task parallelism.

- Enabling the integrated matrix–vector micro-kernels directly improves SME throughput, reaching up to **10.63**× on M4 and **10.47**× on LX2 at seq_{len} = 512.
- Adding the SME-adapted data layout and access scheme improves memory management and the L1 cache hit rate, yielding average speedups of **1.57**× on M4 and **1.60**× on LX2 over the kernelized implementation.
- Finally, adding the inter-task parallelism mechanism further improves long-sequence performance, with additional average speedups of **1.29**× on M4 and **1.28**× on LX2.

4.4 Cache and Memory Utilization

To demonstrate the feasibility of our SME-adapted data layout and access scheme, we evaluate MEATTEN and SMEAtten with different seq_{len} to collect their L1 cache hit rates and HBM usage in Table 2 on LX2. Our strategy is tailor-made for outer-product matrix units, deserving a higher cache hit rate, which is discussed in detail in Sect. 3.2. The results, shown in Table 2, are consistent match our expectations: SMEAtten delivers an average of **7.64%** hit rate improvement over MEATTEN, up to **9.78%**. The larger improvement of L1 cache hit rates for larger inputs indicates the advantages of our data layout and tiling strategy. MEATTEN fails to execute when the sequence length is 1024 and 2048, resulting in an out-of-memory error. On the contrast, SMEAtten still maintains low HBM Usage, saving **3.9** GB HBM at least. Additionally, SMEAtten increases the HBM usage at a rate lower than linear, starting from a modest baseline footprint and scaling gradually with sequence length.

4.5 Scalability and Portability Analysis

We conduct the scaling and portability experiments on LX2 and Apple M4, as shown in Fig. 10. SMEAtten reaches average performance of **111.82** GFLOPS

Table 2. L1 hit rates and HBM usage on LX2. MA denotes MEATTEN, and SA denotes SMEAtten.

Seq.	L1 Hit (%)		HBM (MB)		Seq.	L1 Hit (%)		HBM (MB)	
Len.	MA	SA	MA	SA	Len.	MA	SA	MA	SA
256	66.76	71.73	405.01	17.55	1024	48.21	57.12	OOM	32.84
512	63.44	70.35	1212.68	22.65	2048	45.90	55.68	OOM	53.23

on M4 and **385.48** GFLOPS on LX2, corresponding to **36.77**×, **25.59**×, and **19.00**× the performance of XNN_NF, XNN_F, and MEATTEN on LX2. SMEAtten also exhibits a steeper growth curve than other methods, indicating that our parallel mechanism scales well across SME-enabled architectures. Owing to the subnuma design within a NUMA node, SMEAtten experiences a sudden decrease in scalability around 20 cores on LX2.

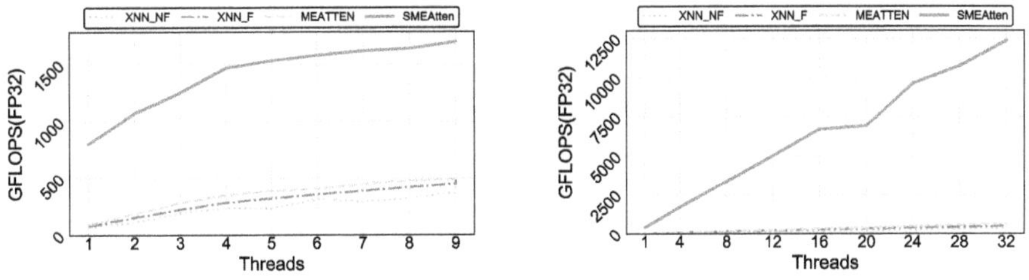

(a) M4 scalability

(b) LX2 scalability

Fig. 10. Thread scalability on M4 and LX2 ($seq_{len} = 1120$).

4.6 PyTorch Integration Case Studies

In Fig. 11, we replace only the SDPA computation in PyTorch with SMEAtten and evaluate the resulting attention module against PyTorch's native implemen-

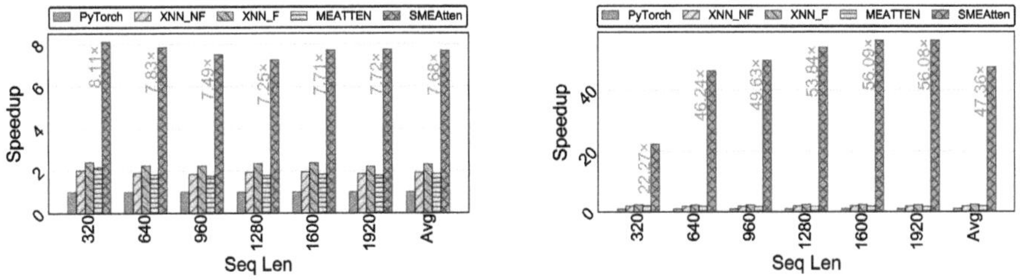

(a) M4 PyTorch integration

(b) LX2 PyTorch integration

Fig. 11. PyTorch integration results on M4 and LX2, using PyTorch's native implementation as the baseline.

tation. SMEAtten reaches up to **8.11**× speedup on M4 and **56.09**× on LX2, while MEATTEN remains slower because of less effective memory allocation and task distribution in its PyTorch integration.

5 Conclusion

Attention computation serves as a critical component in Transformer-based models and a key determinant of overall performance. In this study, we present SMEAtten, the first practical attention computation framework designed to fully exploit the capabilities of the Scalable Matrix Extension on modern CPUs. Experiments on both LX2 and Apple M4 show that SMEAtten achieves substantial performance gains while remaining portable across SME-enabled CPUs.

Acknowledgments. We sincerely thank the anonymous reviewers for their constructive comments and suggestions. Tengyang Zheng and Han Huang contributed equally to this work. This work is supported by the Guangdong S&T Program under Grant NO. 2024B0101040005, NSFC Grant #62461146204 / #62472462.

Disclosure of Interests. The authors have no competing interests to declare that are relevant to the content of this article.

References

1. Google XNNPack. https://github.com/google/xnnpack (2023)
2. Apple introduces M4 pro and M4 max. https://www.apple.com/newsroom/2024/10/apple-introduces-m4-pro-and-m4-max/ (2024). [Accessed 12-Feb-2025]
3. Hpc kit download (2024). https://www.hikunpeng.cn/developer/hpc/hpckit-download, [.Accessed 12-Feb-2025]
4. Accelerate (2025). https://developer.apple.com/documentation/accelerate. [Accessed 12-Feb-2025]
5. ARM C1-premium. https://www.arm.com/products/silicon-ip-cpu/c1-premium (2025). [Accessed 12-Feb-2025]
6. Nvidia GB200 NVL72: HPC & AI GPU for data centers. https://www.nvidia.com/en-in/data-center/gb200-nvl72/ (2025). [Accessed 12-Feb-2025]
7. Abdelfattah, A., et al.: A set of batched basic linear algebra subprograms and lapack routines. ACM Trans. Math. Softw.(TOMS) **47**(3), 1–23 (2021)
8. Chen, H., et al.: KTransformers: unleashing the full potential of CPU/GPU hybrid inference for MOE models. In: Proceedings of the ACM SIGOPS 31st Symposium on Operating Systems Principles (2025)
9. Devlin, J., Chang, M.W., Lee, K., Toutanova, K.: BERT: pre-training of deep bidirectional transformers for language understanding. In: Proceedings of the 2019 Conference of the North American chapter of the Association for Computational Linguistics: Human Language Technologies, vol. 1 (long and short papers), pp. 4171–4186 (2019)
10. Du, J., Jiang, J., You, Y., Huang, D., Lu, Y.: Handling heavy-tailed input of transformer inference on GPUs. In: Proceedings of the 36th ACM International Conference on Supercomputing, pp. 1–11 (2022)

11. Fu, X., Yang, W., Dong, D., Su, X.: Optimizing attention by exploiting data reuse on arm multi-core CPUs. In: Proceedings of the 38th ACM International Conference on Supercomputing, pp. 137–149 (2024)
12. Gao, X., Lin, X., Liu, R.: Comparable GPU: optimizing the BERT model with AMX feature. In: 2023 IEEE 3rd International Conference on Computer Communication and Artificial Intelligence (CCAI), pp. 158–162. IEEE (2023)
13. Heinecke, A., Henry, G., Hutchinson, M., Pabst, H.: LibXSMM: accelerating small matrix multiplications by runtime code generation. In: SC'16: Proceedings of the International Conference for High Performance Computing, Networking, Storage and Analysis, pp. 981–991. IEEE (2016)
14. Huang, H., et al.: HStencil: matrix-vector stencil computation with interleaved outer product and MLA. In: The International Conference for High Performance Computing, Networking, Storage, and Analysis (SC), St. louis, MO, United States (2025)
15. Huang, L., Huang, H., Chen, Z., Lu, Y.: KirbyMM: outer-product based matrix multiplication on ARMv9 processor
16. Intel Corporation: intel-extension-for-PyTorch (2025). https://deepwiki.com/intel/intel-extension-for-pytorch/5.2-attention-mechanism-optimizations
17. Jiang, J., Du, J., Huang, D., Li, D., Zheng, J., Lu, Y.: Characterizing and optimizing transformer inference on arm many-core processor. In: Proceedings of the 51st International Conference on Parallel Processing, pp. 1–11 (2022)
18. Kim, H., Ye, G., Wang, N., Yazdanbakhsh, A., Kim, N.S.: Exploiting intel® advanced matrix extensions (AMX) for large language model inference. IEEE Comput. Archit. Lett. (2024)
19. Li, X., Liang, Y., Yan, S., Jia, L., Li, Y.: A coordinated tiling and batching framework for efficient GEMM on GPUs. In: Proceedings of the 24th Symposium on Principles and Practice of Parallel Programming, pp. 229–241 (2019)
20. Markidis, S., Der Chien, S.W., Laure, E., Peng, I.B., Vetter, J.S.: Nvidia tensor core programmability, performance & precision. In: IEEE IPDPSW, pp. 522–531 (2018)
21. Radford, A., Narasimhan, K., Salimans, T., Sutskever, I.: Improving language understanding by generative pre-training (2018)
22. Remke, S., Breuer, A.: Hello SME! Generating fast matrix multiplication kernels using the scalable matrix extension. In: SC24-W: Workshops of the International Conference for High Performance Computing, Networking, Storage and Analysis, pp. 1443–1454. IEEE (2024)
23. Shah, J., Bikshandi, G., Zhang, Y., Thakkar, V., Ramani, P., Dao, T.: FlashAttention-3: fast and accurate attention with asynchrony and low-precision. Adv. Neural. Inf. Process. Syst. **37**, 68658–68685 (2024)
24. Vaswani, A., et al.: Attention is all you need. Adv. Neural Info. Process. Syst. **30** (2017)
25. Wilkinson, F., McIntosh-Smith, S.: An initial evaluation of arm's scalable matrix extension. In: 2022 IEEE/ACM International Workshop on Performance Modeling, Benchmarking and Simulation of High Performance Computer Systems (PMBS), pp. 135–140. IEEE (2022)
26. Yang, W., Fang, J., Dong, D., Su, X., Wang, Z.: Optimizing full-spectrum matrix multiplications on armv8 multi-core CPUs. IEEE Trans. Parallel Distrib. Syst. **35**(3), 439–454 (2024)

RWIP: Region-Level Write-Intensity Prediction for GPU L2 Cache Based on Hybrid-Retention STT-MRAM

Yujie Pu[1], Chen Zhao[1(✉)], Jianfeng An[1], Wenzhe Zhao[2], and Pengju Ren[2]

[1] Northwestern Polytechnical University, Xi'an, China
yujiepu@mail.nwpu.edu.cn, chenzhao@nwpu.edu.cn
[2] Xi'an Jiaotong University, Xi'an, China

Abstract. Spin-transfer torque MRAM (STT-MRAM) is a promising technology for scaling GPU L2 caches thanks to its high density and near-zero leakage power. However, its high write latency and energy make simply replacing SRAM with STT-MRAM unattractive under the massive write traffic and concurrency of modern GPUs. This work observes that GPU writes exhibit strong coarse-grained spatial locality, such that cache blocks mapped to the same region tend to share similar write intensity. Motivated by this insight, we propose Region-Level Write-Intensity Prediction (RWIP) for GPU L2 cache based on hybrid-retention STT-MRAM. The L2 cache is partitioned into a low-retention (LR) region for write-intensive data and a high-retention (HR) region for read-dominant and long-lived data. RWIP instantiates a lightweight per-subpartition Region Predictor Table (RPT), which is accessed only after a write miss in both the LR and HR regions. RWIP leverages early region-level write activity to predict the write intensity of incoming cache blocks, thereby proactively allocating write-intensive blocks into the LR region. On average, compared to baseline GPU with SRAM-based L2 cache and the prior typical work, RWIP improves instructions per cycle (IPC) by 19% and 6%, respectively, and reduces L2 dynamic power by 20% and 14%, respectively. Moreover, the high density of STT-MRAM allows RWIP to provision a larger L2 cache under an equal on-chip area, reducing DRAM power by 54% on average relative to the baseline.

Keywords: GPU L2 cache · STT-MRAM · Cache management · Region prediction

1 Introduction

Graphics Processing Units (GPUs) have emerged as the indispensable computational engines powering the artificial intelligence era. In early GPU memory architectures, the L2 cache capacity was relatively small compared to register files, L1 cache, and shared memory. However, as shown in Fig. 1, starting with

M. Torquati et al. (Eds.): Euro-Par 2026, LNCS 16781, pp. 256–270, 2027.
https://doi.org/10.1007/978-3-032-35248-4_18

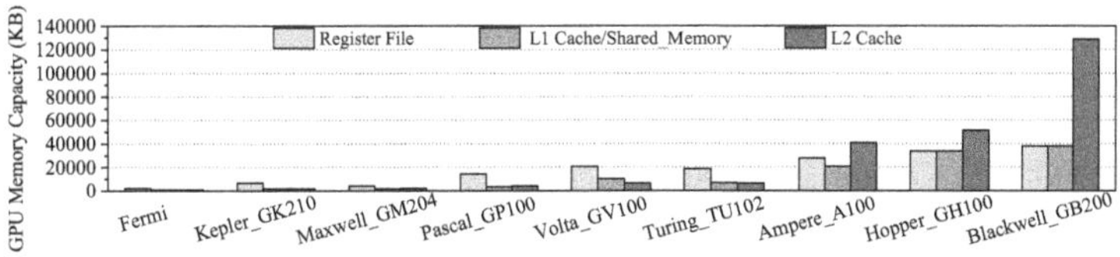

Fig. 1. Evolution of GPU memory hierarchy capacity (KB) across NVIDIA GPU architectures [1–9].

the Ampere architecture, NVIDIA has substantially increased L2 cache capacity, reaching 50 MB in Hopper and 126 MB in Blackwell [7–9].

A large-capacity L2 cache is highly beneficial to overall GPU performance. Prior studies indicate that off-chip memory accesses can significantly impact the performance and energy efficiency of many memory-bound GPU workloads due to both latency and bandwidth constraints [10]. Although expanding the L2 cache effectively reduces off-chip memory traffic, such straightforward capacity scaling significantly increases on-chip area pressure and power consumption.

While an increasingly large L2 cache has become a prevalent trend in modern GPUs, traditional SRAM arrays face severe leakage and scalability bottlenecks as process technology advances into deep-nanometer nodes [11]. Unlike logic, SRAM bitcell scaling has significantly decelerated due to fundamental layout and device constraints, exacerbating the on-chip area pressure for large caches [25,26]. Consequently, spin-transfer torque MRAM (STT-MRAM) [12] is a compelling alternative for GPU L2 caches, offering near-zero leakage and approximately 4× higher density than SRAM. However, STT-MRAM suffers from inherently high write latency and energy consumption, which leads to severe performance degradation and energy inefficiency if it is directly used as an L2 cache replacement.

While prior studies successfully integrate STT-MRAM into CPU caches [27–29], their reliance on fine-grained metadata creates severe bottlenecks under the massive concurrency of GPU architectures. Existing GPU-specific STT-MRAM management schemes also exhibit significant limitations. Block-level approaches [19] track writes per cache line, incurring storage overheads that scale poorly with L2 capacity. Program-counter-based (PC-based) predictors [10] guide cache allocation using program counters, demanding complex hardware to track dynamic instruction footprints. Crucially, by evaluating write intensity as an isolated, fine-grained metric, these approaches fail to exploit the strong spatial locality inherent in GPU workloads. This granular approach overlooks the potential for more scalable, region-aware prediction mechanisms that can be efficiently integrated into GPU L2 cache.

In this work, GPU write behavior is observed to exhibit spatial locality at a coarse granularity. Specifically, cache blocks mapped to the same region in the L2 cache tend to show similar write intensity. Motivated by this observation, Region-Level Write-Intensity Prediction (RWIP) is proposed for GPU L2 cache based on hybrid-retention STT-MRAM. RWIP combines a lightweight region predictor table (RPT) with a hybrid STT-MRAM cache organization that consists of a low-retention (LR) region and a high-retention (HR) region. By placing write-intensive data into the LR region based on region-level prediction, RWIP reduces STT-MRAM write latency and energy. The main contributions of this work are summarized as follows:

- The GPU L2 write behavior is characterized at a coarse granularity, and the results show that region-level information can reliably capture write-intensive blocks across diverse workloads.
- RWIP is proposed for GPU L2 cache based on hybrid-retention STT-MRAM, employing a lightweight RPT to classify regions as write-hot or write-cold with minimal overhead. Based on the predicted region hotness, RWIP preferentially allocates write-intensive data to the LR region.
- RWIP is implemented and evaluated on GPGPU-Sim. Compared to baseline GPU with SRAM-based L2 cache and the prior typical work [19], RWIP improves IPC by 19% and 6%, respectively, and reduces L2 dynamic power by 20% and 14%, respectively.

2 Background

2.1 STT-MRAM

STT-MRAM offers roughly a 4× density improvement and minimal static power compared to traditional SRAM [10]. As shown in Fig. 2, an STT-MRAM cell utilizes a magnetic tunnel junction (MTJ) to store data through relative magnetization orientations. Switching this magnetic state requires a polarized current, inherently causing high write latency and energy. As shown in Table 1, STT-MRAM exhibits a fundamental trade-off between retention time and write overhead, where cells with lower retention times require significantly less write energy but need frequent refreshes to prevent data loss. Prior studies indicate that GPU cache blocks frequently experience rewrites within a very short time

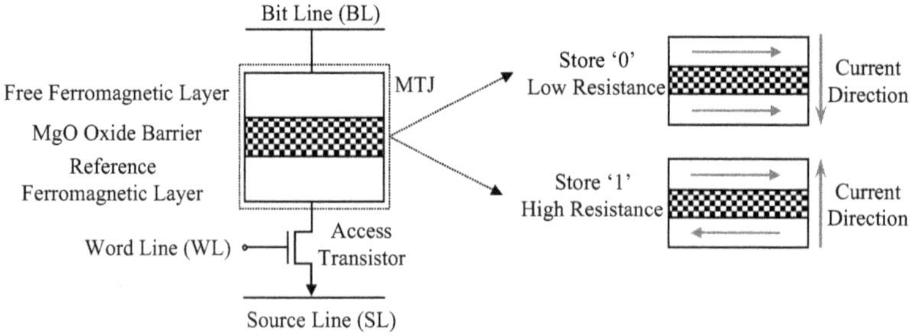

Fig. 2. STT-MRAM cell structure. An MTJ is composed of a free ferromagnetic layer, an MgO oxide barrier, and a reference ferromagnetic layer.

window (e.g., 100 µs) and that a retention time of 40 ms is sufficient to accommodate over 90% of cache write operations [19]. Therefore, preferentially allocating write-intensive data to low-retention STT-MRAM cells effectively reduces write latency and energy.

Table 1. STT-MRAM cell parameters under different magnetization stability heights Δ, including retention time (R.T), write latency (W.L) and write energy (W.E) [19].

Δ	R.T	W.L(ns)	W.E(nJ)
40.29	10 year	10	1.158
17.50	40 ms	2	0.161
11.51	100 us	0.8	0.070

2.2 Related Work

While STT-MRAM adoption has been extensively explored in CPU cache [27–29] and deeply studied for constructing GPU register files [30–33], these methods cannot be directly applied to GPU L2 cache due to their massive capacity and complex access patterns. At the GPU cache hierarchy level, existing STT-MRAM management schemes generally rely on PC-based predictors for L1 cache [10], or line-level tracking, such as multi-retention L2 designs that steer frequently rewritten blocks using per-line write counters [19]. However, PC-based schemes require additional hardware to track dynamic instruction footprints, while their effectiveness at the L2 level may be reduced because many memory requests are filtered by the L1 cache hierarchy. Meanwhile, block-level tracking incurs hardware overheads proportional to cache capacity, making it difficult to scale with large L2 caches. In contrast, this work leverages coarse-grained spatial locality to accurately predict block write intensity with minimal hardware overhead.

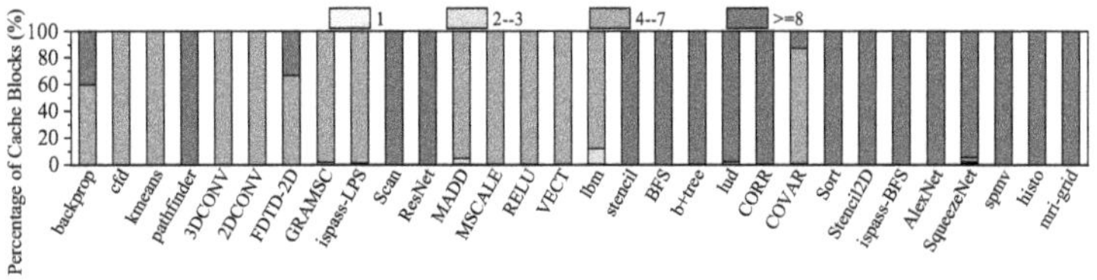

Fig. 3. Block-level write count distribution. All cache blocks are categorized into four distinct bins based on their final write count (wc).

3 Motivation

3.1 GPGPU Application Write Characterization

GPU configuration is summarized in Table 2. Table 3 summarizes the benchmarks evaluated to characterize the write behavior of the GPU L2 cache. Figure 3 shows that the fraction of single-write blocks (wc=1) is small, and the majority of blocks are concentrated in high write-intensity bins (wc≥8 and wc=4–7), indicating that write-intensive behavior is common and persistent. Therefore, promptly identifying write-intensive blocks and proactively steering them to the LR region can mitigate the high write latency and energy cost of STT-MRAM.

Table 2. GPU configuration

SM config	80 SMs, 4 warp schedulers/SM
L1D and shared memory	L1D 32 KB/SM, shared memory 96 KB/SM
L2 cache	384 KB per memory sub-partition, 18MB HR region and 6MB LR region, 24 MB total
DRAM organization	32 memory channels, FR-FCFS scheduler

3.2 Region-Level Write-Intensity Characteristics

Benchmarks are classified into uniform and non-uniform based on whether the write intensity of data blocks within a region is uniform. Δwc denotes the difference between the maximum and minimum write counts among different blocks within the same region, and $P(\Delta wc \leq 3)$ is the fraction of regions satisfying $\Delta wc \leq 3$. A benchmark is labeled uniform if $P(\Delta wc \leq 3)$ is at least 90% for all four region sizes; otherwise, it is labeled non-uniform. The benchmark classification is summarized in Table 3.

Table 3. Benchmark classification.

Suite	Benchmark	Category	Suite	Benchmark	Category	Suite	Benchmark	Category
[15]	backprop	Uniform	[24]	ResNet	Uniform	[18]	CORR	Non-Uniform
[15]	cfd	Uniform	[23]	MADD	Uniform	[18]	COVAR	Non-Uniform
[15]	kmeans	Uniform	[23]	MSCALE	Uniform	[16]	Sort	Non-Uniform
[15]	pathfinder	Uniform	[23]	RELU	Uniform	[16]	Stencil2D	Non-Uniform
[18]	3DCONV	Uniform	[23]	VECT	Uniform	[13]	ispass-BFS	Non-Uniform
[18]	2DCONV	Uniform	[17]	lbm	Uniform	[24]	AlexNet	Non-Uniform
[18]	FDTD-2D	Uniform	[17]	stencil	Uniform	[24]	SqueezeNet	Non-Uniform
[18]	GRAMSC	Uniform	[15]	BFS	Non-Uniform	[17]	spmv	Non-Uniform
[13]	ispass-LPS	Uniform	[15]	b+tree	Non-Uniform	[17]	histo	Non-Uniform
[16]	Scan	Uniform	[15]	lud	Non-Uniform	[17]	mri-grid	Non-Uniform

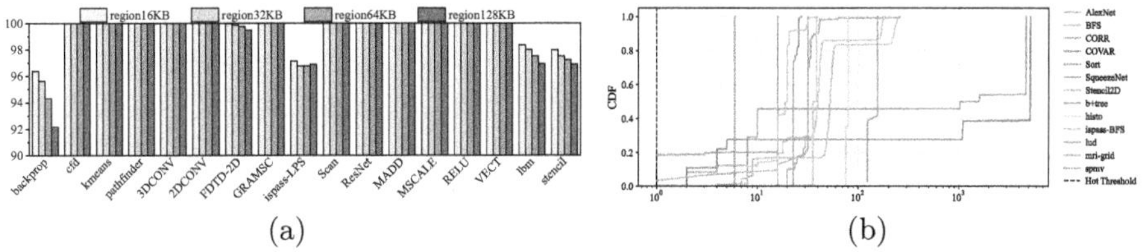

Fig. 4. Region-level write-intensity characteristics. (a) $P(\Delta wc \leq 3)$ under different region sizes. (b) For non-uniform benchmarks, the cumulative distribution function (CDF) of the minimum final write count within each 64 KB region on a logarithmic scale, where the vertical dashed line indicates the hotness threshold T_H.

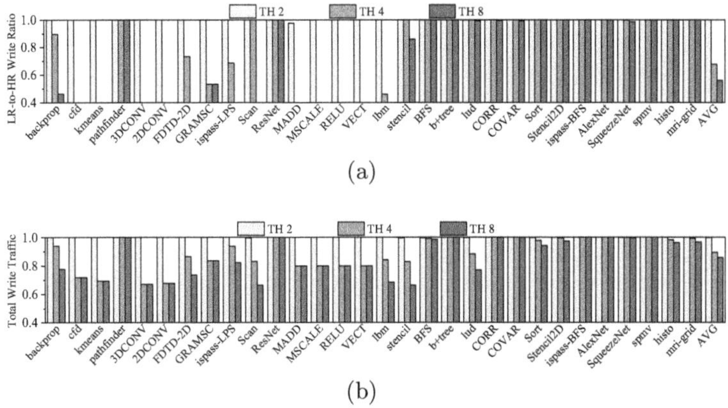

Fig. 5. Sensitivity to hotness threshold T_H, normalized to T_H=1. (a) Normalized LR-to-HR write ratio. (b) Normalized total write traffic.

As shown in Fig. 4(a), $P(\Delta wc \leq 3)$ remains high across 16–128 KB region sizes, indicating that blocks within the same region tend to exhibit similar write intensity. A non-uniform pattern is also observed, where some blocks within a region exhibit much higher write intensity than others, yet this variation does not undermine the region's overall write-intensive behavior. As shown in Fig. 4(b), even the minimum write count within these regions typically exceeds the hotness threshold T_H, ensuring the entire region is effectively classified as write-hot.

3.3 Threshold Sensitivity

A cache block is considered write-intensive when its write count exceeds the hotness threshold T_H. To determine the optimal identification timing for write-intensive data blocks, the impact of T_H on LR region utilization and total write traffic is evaluated.

Figure 5(a) shows that as T_H increases, the fraction of writes from write-intensive blocks directed to the LR region drops markedly across many benchmarks. This indicates that write-intensive blocks are placed into the LR region later, which fundamentally weakens the benefit of the hybrid architecture. Figure 5(b) shows that increasing T_H slightly reduces total write traffic for some workloads, but the reduction is modest in the common case. Overall, larger thresholds provide only limited traffic reduction while substantially undermining LR region utilization. Therefore, a threshold of T_H=1 maximizes the early steering of write-intensive blocks while maintaining a write traffic overhead close to the baseline.

Based on the above discussion and Sect. 3.2, extending the small-threshold strategy to the region level avoids per-block counters while enabling early identification of write-intensive data.

4 RWIP

4.1 Overview

Figure 6(a) illustrates the overall design of RWIP, consisting of three key components. First, the controller (A) coordinates the access flow within each subpartition and performs write-related placement and migration control. The partitioned cache (B) consists of LR and HR regions and maintains retention counters (RCs) to track block refresh timing. LR region targets write-intensive blocks to reduce write latency and energy, while HR region mainly stores read-dominant and longer-lived data. The final component, the region predictor table (RPT) (C) maintains a lightweight per-subpartition table that records region-level hotness and predicts the write intensity of incoming cache blocks.

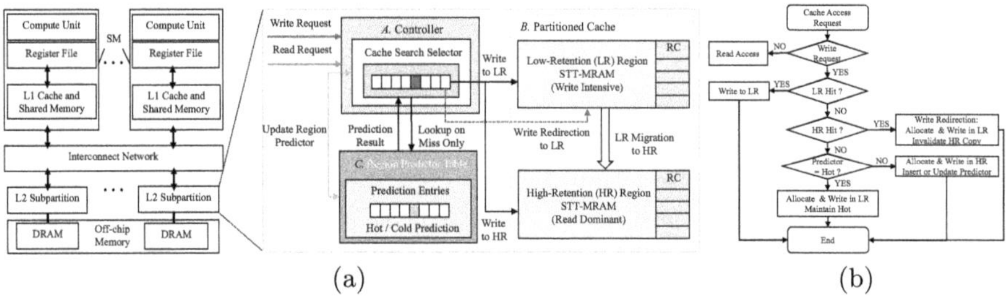

Fig. 6. (a) Overview of RWIP architecture: Controller (A), Partitioned Cache with Retention Counters (RC) (B), and Region Predictor Table (C). (b) The L2 cache access and allocation flowchart.

4.2 Controller

The controller aims to select appropriate cache management actions for each cache block and actively manage block residency across the LR and HR regions.

As illustrated in Fig. 6(b), upon receiving a cache access request, the controller first identifies the request type. Read accesses do not require RPT access and are handled according to the default cache policy. For a write request, the controller first checks the LR region. On a hit in the LR region, the write is performed directly in the LR region without predictor access. On a write hit in the HR region, write redirection is applied by allocating and updating the block in the LR region and invalidating the HR region copy. This maintains a one-copy invariant across the LR and HR regions. The RC state is updated consistently with the valid copy to preserve refresh consistency. When a write misses in both the LR and HR regions, the RPT is consulted to determine the placement of the incoming block. If the region entry exists and is predicted to be hot, the block is allocated in the LR region. Otherwise, the block is allocated in the HR region, while the RPT is modified by either updating the state bits or inserting a new entry. When the LR region needs space, a block evicted from the LR region is migrated to the HR region instead of being immediately discarded. If the HR region is full, replacement follows the default L2 cache replacement rule.

4.3 Partitioned Cache

As shown in Fig. 6(a), each L2 subpartition is partitioned into LR and HR regions, with each region maintaining RC arrays associated with cache blocks. The RC track the retention time of each block, enabling refresh management within the subpartition. Due to the shorter retention time of the LR region, blocks in the LR region use a 4-bit RC to support a more precise refresh mechanism, whereas blocks in the HR region use a 2-bit RC due to the longer retention time. Specifically, when a block in the LR region approaches its retention time, it is migrated to the HR region via a buffer to prevent bit decay. In contrast, an expiring block in the HR region is simply invalidated if clean, or forcibly written back if dirty, to guarantee execution correctness. To avoid the latency and power overhead of parallel lookups, a sequential lookup policy is adopted. Similar to [19], this mechanism is implemented using a cache search selector. Write requests search LR region first then HR region, while read requests search HR region first then LR region. This asymmetric ordering prioritizes the region more likely to contain the requested data.

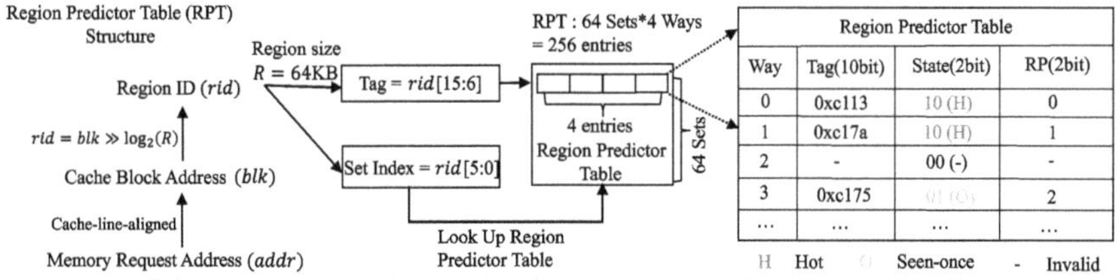

Fig. 7. Detailed structure of the RPT, where each entry consists of a region tag, a hotness state, and replacement field (RP).

4.4 Region Predictor Table

The RPT is a predictor that captures region-level write hotness and guides block placement decisions on write misses. Instantiating a RPT for each L2 subpartition eliminates centralized predictors and cross-subpartition coordination. Figure 7 illustrates the RPT structure.

The RPT is implemented as a small set-associative tag table with 256 entries organized as 64 sets × 4 ways. The set index is derived from the low 6 bits of *rid* (i.e., $set = rid[5:0]$), while each way stores the remaining higher bits as the region tag. With a 64 KB region size, *rid* is a 16-bit quantity, and thus the tag corresponds to $rid[15:6]$. Each RPT entry consists of a 10-bit region tag, a 2-bit hotness state, and a 2-bit replacement field (RP). The hotness field has the following states:

- *invalid*: entry not allocated;
- *seen-once*: the region has been observed to generate the first write evidence but is not yet considered hot;
- *hot*: the region is classified as write-hot.

The RPT lookup is performed only after a write request misses in both LR and HR regions, ensuring that the predictor is not on the cache-hit critical path. On the first insertion, the entry is initialized to *seen-once*; when a subsequent write miss hits the same region entry, it transitions to *hot*. This simple state transition naturally implements the hotness threshold T_H=1 identified in Sect. 3.3 without requiring explicit per-region hardware counters. Once promoted, the entry remains sticky-hot while resident in the RPT, reducing oscillations and update traffic while enabling timely write steering. When the target RPT set is full, an entry to be replaced is selected using the 2-bit RP field.

Table 4. The detailed experimental configurations

Baseline L2 cache(SRAM)	96KB/sub-partition, 6MB in total
STT L2 cache(STT-MRAM)	384KB/sub-partition, 24MB in total, Read: 1 cycle, Write: 5 cycles
STT-DAC and RWIP L2 cache(STT-MRAM)	384KB/sub-partition, 18MB 36-way HR region, Read: 1 cycle, Write: 5 cycles; 6MB 12-way LR region, Read: 1 cycle, Write: 1 cycle
SRAM Read/Write Energy	0.64/0.77 nJ/access [19–21]
STT-MRAM Read/LR Write/HR Write Energy	0.16/0.89/1.54 nJ/access [19–21]

5 Experiment and Evaluation

5.1 Experimental Environment and Configuration

RWIP was implemented on GPGPU-Sim 4.2.1 [13], and GPU power consumption was evaluated using AccelWattch [20]. The detailed experimental configuration is summarized in Table 4. Four methods are evaluated:

1. **Baseline**: a conventional SRAM-based GPU L2 cache.
2. **STT-L2**: an STT-MRAM L2 cache with four times the baseline capacity under an equal on-chip area.
3. **STT-DAC**: the prior design in [19] is implemented by adopting an organization partitioned into LR and HR regions and maintaining a per-block write counter in the L2 cache to monitor write intensity.
4. **RWIP**: the proposed method implemented on top of the STT-L2 configuration. The default RWIP configuration uses a 256-entry RPT and a 64 KB region size.

5.2 Performance

IPC. As shown in Fig. 8, RWIP improves average IPC by 19%, 29%, and 6% over baseline, STT-L2, and STT-DAC, respectively. STT-L2 suffers an 8% performance degradation relative to the baseline due to the high STT-MRAM write latency.

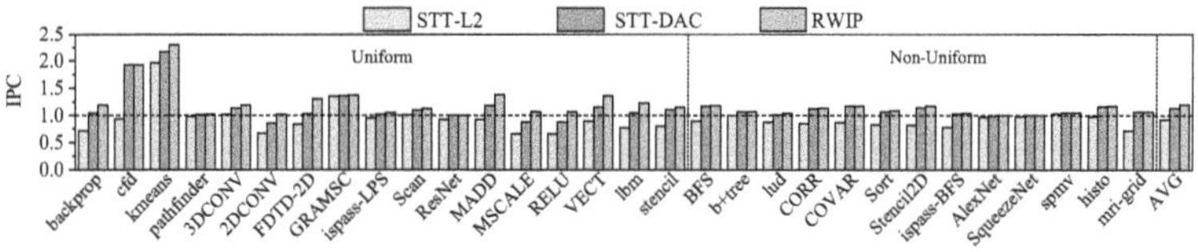

Fig. 8. IPC normalized to baseline

STT-DAC relies on static region assignment and reactive migrations, fundamentally limiting its ability to dynamically and promptly steer write-intensive blocks to the LR region. In contrast, RWIP uses the RPT to proactively allocate write-intensive blocks to the LR region. This predictive placement not only minimizes costly writes to the HR region but also effectively eliminates the extra overhead incurred by write-induced migrations from the HR to the LR region. Consequently, RWIP significantly reduces overall access latency, particularly for write-intensive GPU workloads.

L2 Dynamic Power. As shown in Fig. 9, RWIP reduces the average L2 dynamic power to 0.80×, achieving a 20%, 26%, and 14% reduction compared to the baseline, STT-L2, and STT-DAC, respectively. STT-L2 incurs increased energy consumption due to the high write energy of STT-MRAM. The reactive management policy and additional data migration overheads of STT-DAC intrinsically limit its energy efficiency. In contrast, RWIP allocates write-intensive blocks directly to the LR region, thereby reducing high-energy writes to the HR region and mitigating the redundant write migration overheads in STT-DAC.

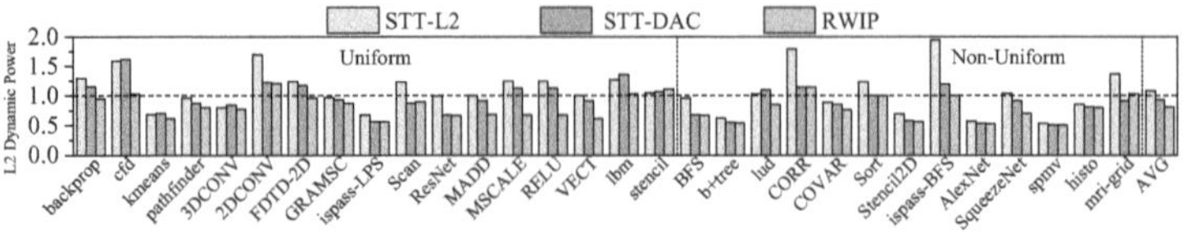

Fig. 9. L2 dynamic power normalized to baseline

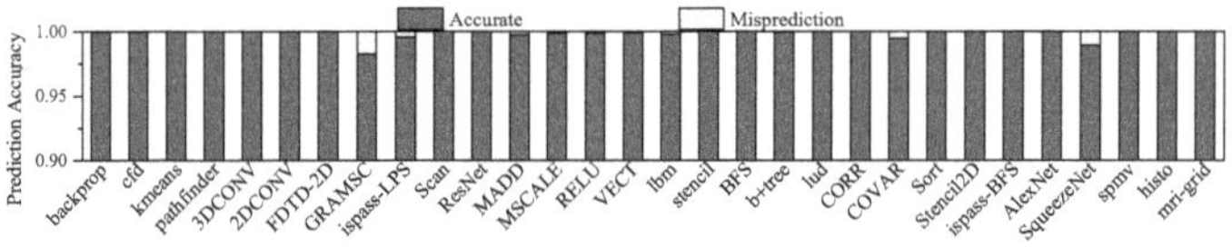

Fig. 10. The prediction accuracy of RPT

Region Predictor Accuracy. A prediction is considered accurate when a write-intensive block is allocated to the LR region or a low-write block is allocated to the HR region. Conversely, a misprediction occurs when a low-write block is erroneously allocated to the LR region or a write-intensive block is misdirected to the HR region. As shown in Fig. 10, the RPT maintains a consistently high prediction accuracy across almost all workloads, indicating that region-level prediction can infer the true write intensity of blocks without maintaining per-block counters. Therefore, RWIP can place write-intensive blocks into the LR region as early as possible.

DRAM Power. As shown in Fig. 11(a), RWIP reduces average DRAM power by 54% compared to the baseline, primarily because the enlarged L2 cache reduces off-chip memory transactions for capacity-sensitive workloads. Notably, RWIP and STT-DAC exhibit very similar DRAM power because they preserve the same global L2 access behavior and differ mainly in the timing of write-intensive block placement. STT-DAC initially allocates lines to the HR region and gradually migrates them to the LR region, whereas RWIP directly steers lines to the LR region upon classification. This internal L2 management difference produces minimal variations in off-chip DRAM traffic.

L2 Hit Rate. As shown in Fig. 11(b), RWIP improves the hit rate compared to the baseline, benefiting from the enlarged L2 cache capacity. The difference

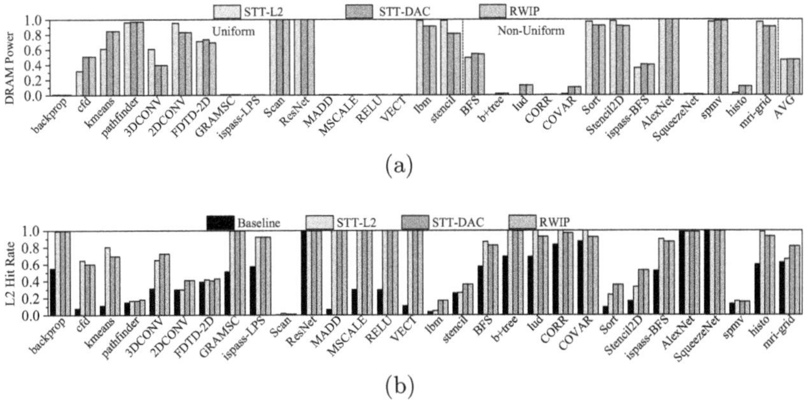

Fig. 11. (a) DRAM power normalized to baseline. (b) L2 hit rate.

between STT-DAC and RWIP remains small across most workloads, as the region-based predictor solely adjusts the placement timing of cache lines between the HR and LR regions. Furthermore, RWIP achieves a marginally higher hit rate than STT-L2 in specific benchmarks because isolating the HR and LR regions optimizes replacement decisions and mitigates write-induced pollution.

5.3 Sensitivity Analysis

As shown in Fig. 12(a), IPC generally improves with larger region sizes, but these performance gains exhibit diminishing returns beyond 64 KB. The initial improvement occurs because expanding the region granularity reduces RPT contention and enhances overall cache coverage of memory requests. However, excessively large regions degrade intra-region write-intensity uniformity and increase the risk of mispredictions. The 64 KB region strikes an optimal balance among performance, effective capacity, and prediction accuracy.

As shown in Fig. 12(b), L2 dynamic power decreases monotonically as the region size increases, eventually reaching saturation. Fine-grained regions incur significant energy overheads due to frequent RPT accesses, state transitions, and complex internal control operations. Enlarging the region size effectively mitigates these management overheads and lowers the RPT replacement frequency, thereby reducing L2 dynamic power.

5.4 Hardware Cost

As shown in Table 5, RWIP and STT-DAC have comparable total hardware cost. Each RPT entry in RWIP consists of a 10-bit region tag, a 2-bit hotness state, and a 2-bit replacement field, resulting in a total RPT overhead of about 28 KB. The RC counters contribute about 60 KB in total, and a 10-line LR$\rightarrow$HR migration buffer is included. STT-DAC requires a per-block 1-bit write counter, identical RC counters, and two 10-line migration buffers. Although STT-DAC appears

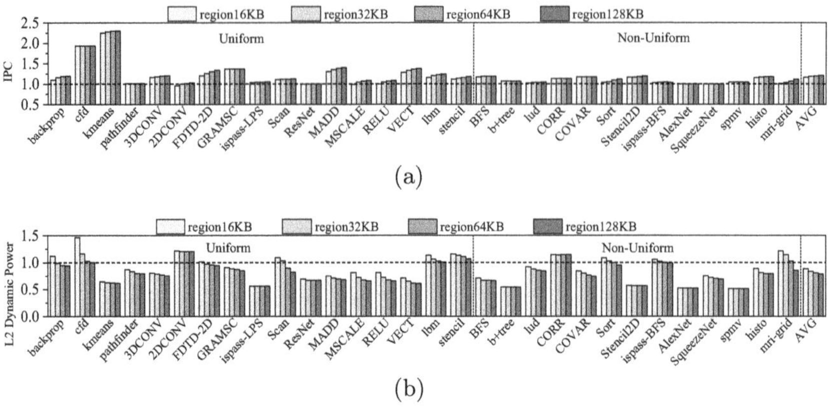

Fig. 12. Sensitivity analysis normalized to baseline. (a) IPC. (b) L2 dynamic power.

slightly smaller in raw storage, its write counter grows linearly with cache capacity and its access is more likely to be coupled with the L2 access pipeline. In contrast, RWIP replaces per-line write counter tracking with a lightweight RPT and restricts predictor access to write-miss events, making it more scalable to larger-capacity GPU L2 cache. The additional control logic in RWIP is simple and localized, adding limited complexity to the cache controller.

Table 5. The hardware cost comparison between RWIP and STT-DAC.

Component	RWIP	STT-DAC
RPT / Write counter	28 KB	24 KB
Per-block RC counters	60 KB	60 KB
Migration buffer(s)	1.25 KB	2.5 KB
Total hardware cost (vs. 24 MB L2)	89.25 KB (0.36%)	86.5 KB (0.35%)

6 Conclusion

This paper proposed RWIP, which partitions the L2 cache into LR and HR regions and uses a lightweight RPT. The additional hardware overhead of RWIP is only about 0.36% of a 24MB L2 capacity. On average, RWIP improves IPC by 19% over the baseline and 6% over the design in [19], while reducing L2 dynamic power by 20% and 14%, respectively. The significant performance gain achieved with low hardware overhead demonstrates the effectiveness of RWIP.

Acknowledgments. This work was supported in part by the National Key Research and Development Program of China under Grant 2024YFB4303700; in part by the STI2030-Major Project under Grant 2022ZD0208805.

Disclosure of Interests. The authors have no competing interests to declare that are relevant to the content of this article.

References

1. NVIDIA: NVIDIA Fermi Compute Architecture Whitepaper (2009)
2. NVIDIA: NVIDIA Kepler GK110/GK210 Architecture Whitepaper (2014)
3. NVIDIA: NVIDIA Maxwell GM204 GPU Architecture Whitepaper (2014)
4. NVIDIA: NVIDIA Tesla P100 Architecture Whitepaper (2016)
5. NVIDIA: NVIDIA Tesla V100 GPU Architecture Whitepaper (2017)
6. NVIDIA: NVIDIA Turing GPU Architecture Whitepaper (2018)
7. NVIDIA: NVIDIA A100 Tensor Core GPU Architecture Whitepaper (2020)
8. NVIDIA: NVIDIA H100 Tensor Core GPU Architecture Whitepaper (2022)
9. NVIDIA: NVIDIA Blackwell Architecture Technical Brief (2024)
10. Zhang, J., Jung, M., Kandemir, M.: FUSE: fusing STT-MRAM into GPUs to alleviate off-chip memory access overheads. In: 2019 IEEE International Symposium on High Performance Computer Architecture (HPCA), pp. 426–439 (2019)
11. Kirtania, S.G., Phadke, O., Sarker, E.: Amorphous indium oxide channel FEFETs with write voltage of 0.9 V and endurance $>10^{12}$ for refresh-free embedded memory. IEEE Trans. Electron Devices **72**(5), 2691–2699 (2025)
12. Dong, X., Wu, X., Sun, G.: Circuit and microarchitecture evaluation of 3D stacking magnetic RAM (MRAM) as a universal memory replacement. In: 45th ACM/IEEE Design Automation Conference (DAC), pp. 554–559 (2008)
13. Bakhoda, A., Yuan, G.L., Fung, W.W.L.: Analyzing CUDA workloads using a detailed GPU simulator. In: IEEE International Symposium on Performance Analysis of Systems and Software (ISPASS), pp. 163–174 (2009)
14. Bishnoi, R., Ebrahimi, M., Oboril, F., et al.: Improving write performance for STT-MRAM. IEEE Trans. Magn. **52**(8), 1–11 (2016)
15. Che, S., Boyer, M., Meng, J.: Rodinia: A benchmark suite for heterogeneous computing. In: IEEE International Symposium on Workload Characterization (IISWC), pp. 44–54 (2009)
16. Danalis, A., Marin, G., McCurdy, C., et al.: The scalable heterogeneous computing (SHOC) benchmark suite. In: Proceedings of the 3rd Workshop on General Purpose Processing Using GPUs (GPGPU), pp. 63–74 (2010)
17. Stratton, J.A., Rodrigues, C., Sung, I.-J.: ParBoil: a revised benchmark suite for scientific and commercial throughput computing. Center for Reliable and High-Performance Computing, vol. 127 (2012)
18. Pouchet, L.-N.: PolyBench: The polyhedral benchmark suite (2012). https://www.cs.colostate.edu/~pouchet/software/polybench/. Accessed 12 Mar 2026
19. Samavatian, M.H., Abbasitabar, H., Arjomand, M.: An efficient STT-RAM last level cache architecture for GPUs. In: 51st ACM/EDAC/IEEE Design Automation Conference (DAC), pp. 1–6 (2014)
20. Kandiah, V., Peverelle, S., Khairy, M.: AccelWattch: A power modeling framework for modern GPUs. In: 54th Annual IEEE/ACM International Symposium on Microarchitecture (MICRO), pp. 738–753 (2021)
21. Liu, X., Mao, M., Bi, X., et al.: Exploring applications of STT-RAM in GPU architectures. IEEE Trans. Circuits Syst. I Regul. Pap. **68**(1), 238–249 (2021)
22. Lee, J., Kim, H.: TAP: a TLP-aware cache management policy for a CPU-GPU heterogeneous architecture. In: 2012 IEEE International Symposium on High-Performance Computer Architecture (HPCA), pp. 1–12 (2012)

23. linjames0: Transformer-CUDA (2023). https://github.com/linjames0/Transformer-CUDA. Accessed 11 Mar 2026
24. Karki, A., Keshava, C.P., Shivakumar, S.M.: Detailed characterization of deep neural networks on GPUs and FPGAs. In: Proceedings of the 12th Workshop on General Purpose Processing Using GPUs (GPGPU), pp. 12–21 (2019)
25. Yeap, G., Lin, S.S., Shang, H.L.: 2NM platform technology featuring energy-efficient nanosheet transistors and interconnects co-optimized with 3DIC for AI, HPC and mobile SoC applications. In: 2024 IEEE International Electron Devices Meeting (IEDM), pp. 1–4 (2024)
26. Hu, J.R., Liu, L., Liu, S., et al.: Co-Optimization of GPU AI chip from technology, design, system and algorithms. In: 2024 IEEE International Electron Devices Meeting (IEDM), pp. 1–4 (2024)
27. Mohammadi, A., Cheshmikhani, E., Asadi, H.: A reliability-aware replacement policy for STT-MRAM caches in server-class processors. IEEE Trans. Reliab. **74**(4), 4915–4929 (2025)
28. Gajaria, D., Gomez, K.A., Adegbija, T.: STT-RAM-based hierarchical in-memory computing. IEEE Trans. Parallel Distrib. Syst. **35**(9), 1615–1629 (2024)
29. Hassan, N., Min, B., Jung, C.: WarmCache: exploiting STT-RAM cache for low-power intermittent systems. In: Proceedings of the 52nd Annual International Symposium on Computer Architecture (ISCA), pp. 586–600 (2025)
30. Li, G., Chen, X., Sun, G.: A STT-RAM-based low-power hybrid register file for GPGPUs. In: 52nd ACM/EDAC/IEEE Design Automation Conference (DAC), pp. 1–6 (2015)
31. Deng, Q., Zhang, Y., Zhao, Z., et al.: FRF: toward warp-scheduler friendly STT-RAM/SRAM fine-grained hybrid GPGPU register file design. IEEE Trans. Comput. Aided Des. Integr. Circuits Syst. **39**(10), 2396–2409 (2020)
32. Jeong, I., Oh, Y., Ro, W.W., et al.: TEA-RC: thread context-aware register cache for GPUs. IEEE Access **10**, 82049–82062 (2022)
33. Jeong, E., Park, E.S., Koo, G., et al.: Conflict-aware compiler for hierarchical register file on GPUs. J. Syst. Architect. **149**, 103099 (2024)

HGNNMap: Heterogeneous Graph Neural Network-Based Mapping for Spatial Accelerators

Shengzhong Tang[1,2], Zhihua Fan[1(✉)], Tianyu Liu[1,2], Xuejun An[1], Xiaochun Ye[1], and Wenming Li[1]

[1] SKLP, Institute of Computing Technology, Chinese Academy of Sciences, Beijing, China

[2] University of Chinese Academy of Sciences, Beijing, China

Abstract. Spatial accelerators are critical for achieving high performance and energy efficiency in domain-specific computing, but fully exploiting their potential requires efficient compiler support. Recent reinforcement learning (RL)-based mappers have shown promising results; however, state-of-the-art approaches typically employ dual-GNN encoders that model mapping-state components using isolated graphs. This structural separation creates an information barrier that limits the extraction of higher-order cross-graph relationships and severely degrades the semantic representation of partial mapping information. To address this limitation, this paper presents HGNNMap, a heterogeneous graph neural network (HGNN)-based framework that unifies the dataflow graph, hardware abstraction graph, and partial mapping into a single Heterogeneous Mapping State Graph (HMSG) and learns their joint representations. Experimental results show that HGNNMap achieves average compilation speedups of 9.35× on ADRES and 2.77× on HyCUBE over state-of-the-art dual-GNN-based mappers, demonstrating the effectiveness of introducing HGNNs into spatial accelerator mapping.

Keywords: Spatial accelerator · CGRA · Mapping · Heterogeneous Graph Neural Network

1 Introduction

Spatial accelerators, including modern neural network engines [4,5] and Coarse-Grained Reconfigurable Arrays (CGRAs) [7,14], have emerged as a dominant paradigm for domain-specific computing. By processing data spatially across an interconnected array of processing elements, these architectures deliver exceptional performance and energy efficiency. However, because they explicitly expose low-level distributed hardware resources to software, fully realizing their theoretical potential depends heavily on sophisticated compiler support.

At the core of this compilation process lies the mapping problem. Given an application represented as a dataflow graph (DFG), where nodes denote computational operations and edges denote data dependencies, mapping involves

M. Torquati et al. (Eds.): Euro-Par 2026, LNCS 16781, pp. 271–285, 2027.
https://doi.org/10.1007/978-3-032-35248-4_19

assigning operations to physical hardware resources and determining feasible routing paths. Because resource management is delegated entirely to the compiler, the resulting spatial arrangement fundamentally determines the program's execution performance.

Mapping is inherently challenging due to its combinatorial nature and the tight coupling between placement and routing decisions. Traditional exact and heuristic approaches either scale poorly or compromise mapping quality, motivating recent interest in learning-based methods that aim to explore the mapping space more effectively. Among these, reinforcement learning (RL)-based mappers have emerged as the dominant paradigm because the mapping process can be naturally formulated as a sequence of decisions. Existing RL-based mappers can be broadly categorized into two classes: multi-step methods [8,10,11,18], which make incremental placement decisions, and one-step methods [12,26], which predict the complete mapping in a single step. This work focuses on the former formulation.

In multi-step RL-based mappers, the agent selects a placement for one DFG node at each step. To make this decision, the agent must understand the *mapping state*, which consists of four components: (1) the hardware abstraction graph (HAG), (2) the DFG, (3) the current partial mapping, which is dynamically generated by the agent's historical placement decisions and the environment's subsequent routing steps, and (4) the current DFG node to be placed. The encoder is responsible for extracting compact representations from these components, making it critical to the agent's performance. Early RL-based mappers employed convolution-based encoders [11], whereas recent approaches favor graph neural networks (GNNs) [8,12,18,26] because both the DFG and HAG are naturally represented as graphs.

State-of-the-art mappers [8,18] specifically employ a dual-GNN encoder (illustrated in Fig. 1) that processes the DFG and HAG independently. Partial mapping information is incorporated through a "mapped node ID" feature associated with both HAG and DFG nodes, while the embedding of the current DFG node is concatenated after a linear transformation.

Although such encoders are effective at capturing intra-graph structures, they separate the mapping-state components into two isolated graphs and provide no explicit mechanism for cross-graph message passing. This separation creates an information barrier during GNN propagation and introduces two fundamental bottlenecks in representation learning. First, it limits interactions among mapping-state components, preventing the extraction of higher-order cross-graph combinatorial information that are critical for placement decisions. Second, dual-GNN encoders fail to capture the full relational semantics of the partial mapping, resulting in severe information loss. As discussed in Sect. 3.1, this structural deficiency produces ambiguous representations that force the agent to rely on inefficient trial-and-error search behaviors, significantly increasing compilation time.

To address these limitations and systematically eliminate the cross-graph information barrier, we propose HGNNMap, the first spatial-accelerator mapper

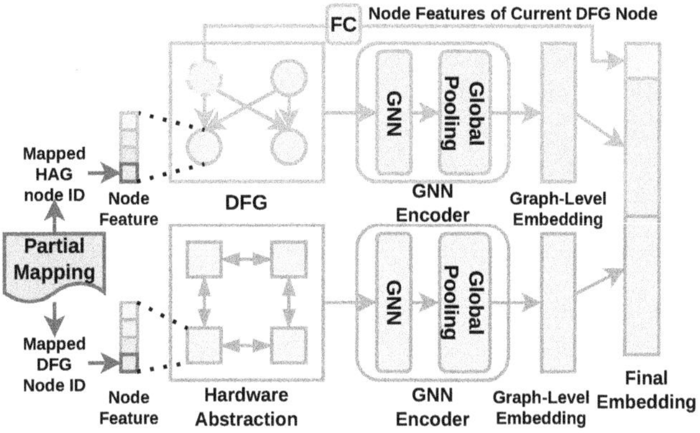

Fig. 1. Typical dual-GNN encoder.

to formulate the complete mapping state as a unified Heterogeneous Mapping State Graph (HMSG). By integrating the DFG, HAG, partial mapping, and current DFG node into a single graph topology and employing a heterogeneous GNN (HGNN) encoder, the framework explicitly enables relation-aware interactions through mapping edges. Consequently, HGNNMap learns richer and more semantically aligned representations of the mapping state and seamlessly integrates them into a multi-step RL framework.

Our key contributions are summarized as follows:

1. We identify fundamental representational bottlenecks in dual-GNN encoders, highlighting their inability to capture higher-order cross-graph relational dependencies and the severe state aliasing induced by decoupled partial-mapping representations.
2. We propose HGNNMap, the first HGNN-based mapper, which introduces a unified Heterogeneous Mapping State Graph (HMSG) to enable explicit DFG–HAG interactions and relation-aware message passing.
3. We demonstrate substantial performance gains: compared to state-of-the-art dual-GNN baselines, HGNNMap nearly doubles the mapping success rate on unseen DFGs (from 32.48% to 60.49%) and achieves average compilation speedups of 9.35× on ADRES and 2.77× on HyCUBE for real-world kernels.

2 Background

2.1 Heterogeneous Graph

A heterogeneous graph (HetG) [23] is a graph in which each node and edge is associated with a type. Unlike homogeneous graphs, where all nodes and edges are of the same type, heterogeneous graphs are designed to model complex systems involving diverse entities and relationships. Formally, a heterogeneous graph is defined as follows.

Definition 1 (Heterogeneous Graph). *A heterogeneous graph is defined as* $G = (V, E, \tau, \phi)$*, where* V *and* E *denote the node set and edge set, respectively. Each node* $v \in V$ *and each edge* $e \in E$ *is associated with a type, defined by the mapping functions* $\tau : V \rightarrow T_v$ *and* $\phi : E \rightarrow T_e$*, respectively, where* T_v *and* T_e *denote the sets of node types and edge types.*

2.2 Heterogeneous Graph Neural Network

A Heterogeneous Graph Neural Network (HGNN) aims to learn low-dimensional embeddings of heterogeneous graphs while preserving their structural and semantic information. Since heterogeneous graphs contain multiple node and edge types, HGNNs incorporate relation-aware message-passing mechanisms that enable type-specific transformation functions for different nodes and edges. This design supports more expressive representation learning on graphs with complex relational structures.

Compared to traditional Graph Convolutional Networks (GCNs), HGNN architectures—such as Relational GCN (R-GCN) [19]—extend standard graph convolutions by associating each relation type with a dedicated transformation matrix. By applying relation-specific weight matrices during neighborhood aggregation, these models effectively capture the distinct structural semantics of different edge types, thereby significantly improving expressiveness on multi-relational graphs.

3 Motivation and Analysis

3.1 Limitations of Dual-GNN Encoders

Insight 1. *Understanding the mapping state fundamentally requires capturing higher-order cross-graph combinatorial information along explicit cross-graph relational paths.*

Mapping decisions inherently depend on interactions among all components of the mapping state. When placing a DFG node, the agent must consider:

1. dependencies to already-mapped DFG neighbors of the current DFG node,
2. the mapped hardware locations of these neighbors via the partial mapping,
3. hardware connectivity and resource availability around those mapped locations.

This reasoning relies on all four components of the mapping state and follows multi-hop relational chains such as: current DFG node → (DFG dependency) → DFG node → (partial mapping) → HAG node → (HAG adjacency) → HAG node → ... We refer to this structural chain as a **Cross-Graph Relational Path**. Such paths capture **higher-order cross-graph combinatorial information**, which is essential for accurate placement decisions.

However, in dual-GNN encoders, the DFG, HAG, and partial mapping are modeled and learned in two isolated graphs. Moreover, information about the current DFG node is excluded from GNN message passing. As a result, these multi-hop cross-graph relational paths are not represented as valid message-passing routes, preventing explicit propagation of cross-graph dependencies. Consequently, the agent must infer such dependencies implicitly from concatenated embeddings.

Insight 2. *Partial mapping is a binary DFG–HAG relation whose semantics cannot be preserved under dual-GNN encoders with separated representations.*

A partial mapping does not describe properties of DFG or HAG nodes in isolation; instead, it defines a relationship between them. Its semantics emerge only when interpreted jointly across both graphs.

However, dual-GNN encoders represent this information in a decoupled manner, breaking the relational context and causing severe information loss. Importantly, this loss is not merely an accuracy degradation but reflects a fundamental identifiability issue in the mapping problem. Once critical cross-graph semantics are discarded, distinct mapping states can collapse into similar embeddings (i.e., state aliasing), even though they require different placement actions. In such cases, the policy is forced into a guess-and-check behavior: it cannot reliably distinguish good actions from bad ones and must rely on repeated trial-and-error to recover. This directly increases the number of failed placement attempts and restarts, thereby expanding the effective search budget and overall compilation time. Therefore, eliminating this structural information loss is a necessary condition for scalable learned mapping, rather than an incremental optimization.

3.2 Experimental Analysis of Dual-GNN Encoders

While the analysis of Insight 2 highlights the structural limitation of dual-GNN encoders, we further investigate whether this limitation also manifests empirically. To isolate encoder representation capability from the complexity of RL and routing, we introduce a lightweight proxy task-*mappability prediction*—that evaluates a single question: can an encoder jointly model the DFG, HAG, and partial mapping?

Definition 2 (Mappability Prediction Problem). *Let* $D = (V_D, E_D)$ *denote the DFG of a program, and* $M = (V_M, E_M)$ *the HAG of a spatial accelerator. A* partial mapping *is a function* $P : V'_M \to V'_D$ *from a subset of HAG nodes* $V'_M \subseteq V_M$ *to a subset of DFG nodes* $V'_D \subseteq V_D$. *The* ***mappability prediction problem*** *is to predict, given* (D, M, P), *whether there exists a valid* full mapping $F : V_M \to V_D$ *such that* $\forall v \in V'_M,\ F(v) = P(v)$.

We consider two configurations. The "dual-GNN" follows the design of MapZero, while "dual-GNN-Mapped" replaces the "mapped DFG/HAG node ID" feature with a "mapped flag", which provides lossy information about the partial mapping. For further implementation details, readers may refer to Sect. 5.4.

Figure 6 shows the training results. Interestingly, we make the following observations:

1. A dual-GNN using full mapping information as node features performs worse than a dual-GNN using lossy mapping information (i.e., only a mapped flag).
2. The training curves indicate that providing more detailed mapping information does not improve representation quality; instead, it hinders convergence.

These counterintuitive results suggest that the dual-GNN architecture cannot effectively exploit the structural information contained in the partial mapping. When encoded as node features, this information becomes noisy and leads to representation collapse.

3.3 Motivation for Introducing HGNN

To address the above limitations, we introduce a heterogeneous graph neural network (HGNN) encoder and reformulate the mapping state as a Heterogeneous Mapping State Graph (HMSG), where: (1) DFG nodes and HAG nodes correspond to different node types; (2) DFG dependencies, hardware adjacencies, and partial-mapping relations correspond to different edge types; and (3) the partial mapping itself is modeled as explicit, typed bidirectional edges connecting DFG and hardware nodes.

By representing the partial mapping as *mapped-to* and *mapped-by* edges, we elevate DFG–HAG interactions to first-class elements in the graph and enable explicit cross-graph information exchange. By unifying all information into a single graph, the HGNN can fully exploit interactions among all mapping-state components. Moreover, the relation-specific transformations in HGNNs, which naturally align with the heterogeneous structure of the mapping problem, further improve model expressiveness and generalization.

4 Methodology

This section describes HGNNMap, a multi-step RL-based mapper built on the proposed HGNN encoder. We first present graph embedding generation, including the Heterogeneous Mapping State Graph (HMSG) formulation and the HGNN architecture, which constitutes our main contribution. We then introduce the RL framework. Throughout, we use the Modulo Routing Resource Graph (MRRG) [15] as the hardware abstraction graph (HAG) because it provides a high-fidelity, port-level resource representation. The MRRG contains two node types: function nodes and routing nodes.

4.1 Graph Embedding Generation

The goal of graph embedding generation is to distill the mapping state into a structured, low-dimensional representation for downstream decision-making. We represent the entire mapping state as a single Heterogeneous Mapping State Graph (HMSG) and apply the HGNN encoder directly to it. The current DFG node information is embedded as part of its node features within the HMSG.

Node Feature Design. Specifically, the **DFG node features** include (1) in-degree, (2) out-degree, (3) opcode, (4) ASAP value, (5) ALAP value, (6) self-loop flag, (7) mapped flag, and (8) **current node flag**. The **MRRG node features** include (1) in-degree, (2) out-degree, (3) node type, (4) cycle, (5) latency, (6) coordinate, and (7) mapped flag.

Unlike previous dual-GNN encoders, the **current node flag** explicitly marks the current DFG node within the HMSG, allowing the HGNN to consider it during message passing and learn more relevant representations for placement decisions. By contrast, prior dual-GNN encoders incorporate the feature of the current node only after GNN propagation, limiting their ability to model interactions with other mapping-state components.

Heterogeneous Mapping State Graph. As described in Sect. 2.1, the HMSG is defined as $H = (V, E, \tau, \phi)$, where V and E include nodes and edges from both the DFG and MRRG. Additionally, E includes *partial-mapping edges*, which we describe below. The node type set T_v is {DFG Node, (MRRG) Function Node, (MRRG) Routing Node}, and the edge type set T_e is {dependency, adjacent-to, mapped-to, mapped-by}.

Given a DFG $D = (V_d, E_d)$, an MRRG $M = (V_m, E_m)$, and a partial mapping $\rho : V_m \rightarrow V_d$, the HMSG H is constructed in two steps:

1. Set $V = V_d \cup V_m$ and $E = E_d \cup E_m$. Each node is assigned a type from T_v according to its category. All DFG edges are labeled as *dependency*, and MRRG edges are labeled as *adjacent-to*.
2. For each mapped pair $\rho(u) = v$, add bidirectional partial-mapping edges (u, v) and (v, u) to E, labeling (u, v) as *mapped-by* and (v, u) as *mapped-to*.

The resulting HMSG integrates all information from D, M, and ρ. After feature encoding, the current DFG node information is additionally incorporated into the HMSG representation. Figure 2 provides an illustrative example. Due to the large number of MRRG routing nodes, Fig. 2b shows only the hardware topology, while Fig. 2d omits most routing nodes for clarity. The dashed lines in Fig. 2d represent partial-mapping edges, each corresponding to a pair of *mapped-to* and *mapped-by* edges.

In summary, the HMSG contains eight explicit relation types: DFG dependency relation ($r_1 = \langle$DFG Node, dependency, DFG Node$\rangle$), three MRRG adjacency relations ($r_{2-4} = \langle$Function/Routing Node, adjacent-to, Function/Routing Node$\rangle$), and four partial mapping relations ($r_{5-6} = \langle$DFG Node, mapped-to, Function/Routing Node$\rangle$ and their inverse mapped-by relations r_{7-8}).

HGNN Encoder Architecture. Figure 3 illustrates the architecture of the HGNN encoder. The encoder takes the HMSG as input and produces a compact embedding for the downstream RL policy. It first applies three HGNN blocks to propagate and update node features over the heterogeneous graph. Node

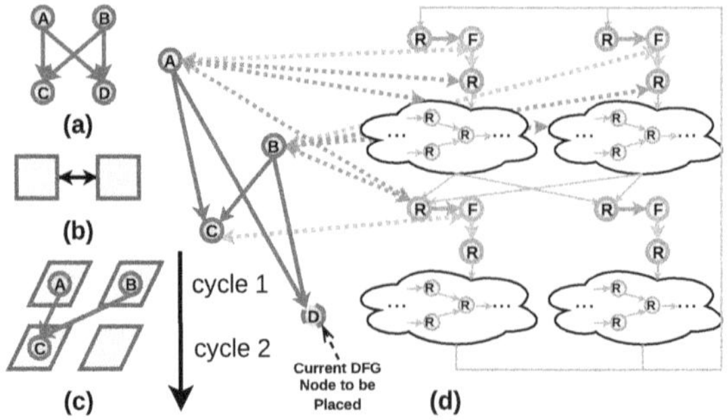

Fig. 2. An example of Heterogeneous Mapping State Graph. (a) The DFG, (b) the target spatial accelerator, (c) current partial mapping, (d) the HMSG that integrates the information of a-c and the current DFG node information.

embeddings are then aggregated separately for each node type using max pooling to obtain type-level embeddings. Finally, the transformed embedding of the current DFG node B is concatenated with these type-level embeddings. Unlike state-of-the-art dual-GNNs that rely on raw node embeddings, this transformed representation provides richer structural and semantic information.

Each HGNN block consists of a Heterogeneous Graph Attention Network (HGAT) layer, a GraphNorm layer [3], a ReLU activation [1], and a dropout layer [22]. The HGAT layer is the core component, enabling node-to-node message passing conditioned on relation types. HGAT extends the relational GCN (R-GCN) [19] with multi-head graph attention (GAT) mechanisms [25], allowing the encoder to capture the varying importance of heterogeneous neighbors during message passing.

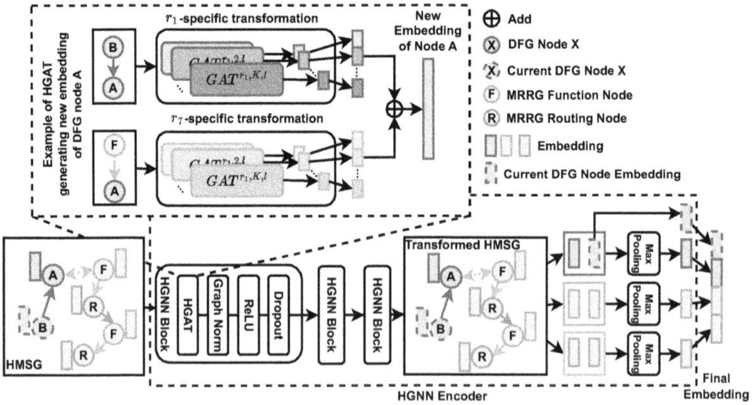

Fig. 3. The HGNN encoder network architecture overview.

Figure 3 also illustrates how HGAT generates the updated embedding of DFG node A. Since node A is connected only through two incoming relation types (r_1 and r_7), only the corresponding r_1-specific and r_7-specific transformations are applied. Messages for each relation type are processed by its corresponding multi-head GAT, concatenated across attention heads, and then aggregated across relation types via summation to produce the updated embedding of node A.

4.2 RL Framework

RL Formulation. We model mapping as a multi-step reinforcement learning (RL) problem formulated as a tuple $\langle S, A, R, T \rangle$. At each step, the agent places one DFG node, while Dijkstra's algorithm determines the corresponding routing. DFG nodes are processed in a randomized order. The state S corresponds exactly to the mapping state, which is represented by the HMSG. The action space A comprises all available MRRG function nodes, with occupied nodes masked to exclude invalid actions. During the transition T, the environment routes the new connection using Dijkstra's algorithm and updates the HMSG with the updated partial mapping and the next DFG node. Finally, we adopt a sparse AlphaZero-style [21] reward R, assigning a reward of 1 upon successful completion of a full mapping and -1 when no valid MRRG node remains.

Agent Network. We adopt an actor–critic architecture [24] similar to MapZero. The network consists of the proposed HGNN encoder, followed by a policy network and a value network. Both heads are implemented as three-layer fully connected (FC) networks that take the HGNN embedding as input. The policy network outputs a vector of size $|A|$, while the value network outputs a scalar estimating the value of the current state. Although the value network is not used during inference, it is critical for training stability and convergence.

Training. We use Proximal Policy Optimization (PPO) [20] as the training algorithm. To generate realistic DFGs, we extract node and edge distributions from real-world benchmarks to synthesize random graphs, and filter for legal and mappable instances, yielding a dataset of 3,000 DFGs. To accelerate convergence and stabilize training, we adopt curriculum learning [2], starting from small DFGs and gradually increasing their size. The dataset is split into training and test sets with an 8:2 ratio. The training process runs for 400 epochs, with each epoch sampling 4,096 steps from the training set. The batch size is 64.

5 Evaluation

5.1 Experimental Setup

HGNNMap is implemented on top of CGRA-ME 2.0 [17], which provides both kernel DFGs and MRRGs. We evaluate all mappers on ADRES [14] and HyCUBE [7], each configured as a 4×4 PE array. Thirteen real-world kernels are selected from Microbench [17] and PolyBench [16], as summarized in Table 1. The MII(A,H) column reports the minimum initiation interval (MII) [9] on ADRES and HyCUBE, respectively. For brevity, we use *acc* to denote *accumulate* and *matmul* to denote *matrix multiplication*.

Table 1. Kernel Statistics

Kernels	Nodes/Edges	MII (A, H)	Kernels	Nodes/Edges	MII (A, H)	Kernels	Nodes/Edges	MII (A, H)
mac	23/26	1,1	simple	34/39	1,1	conv2	27/31	1,1
matmul	32/34	1,1	acc	32/37	1,1	mults1	44/52	3,3
atax	28/30	1,1	durbin	28/30	1,1	gemm	34/36	2,1
gemver	37/40	2,2	cholesky	31/35	2,1	syrk	47/52	2,1
doitgen	36/38	2,1						

Our primary baselines are state-of-the-art dual-GNN mappers, namely MapZero-M and SmartMap-M (where "-M" denotes disabling Monte Carlo Tree Search). To verify whether the findings in Sect. 3.2 generalize to RL-based mapping, we further evaluate MapZero-Mapped, a variant of MapZero-M that uses the simplified "mapped flag" feature. All baselines follow the same actor–critic architecture as HGNNMap, but replace the HGAT layer with a standard GAT layer, substitute the "mapped DFG/function node ID" feature with a "mapped flag" (except for MapZero-Mapped), and omit the "current node flag". Through a comprehensive hyperparameter search, we set the hidden dimension to 64 for HGNNMap and 128 for all other learning-based mappers.

Although HGNNMap is compatible with MCTS, we explicitly disable MCTS for all evaluated methods for three reasons. First, MCTS is a powerful general-purpose search algorithm that would confound the evaluation of the encoder's representation capability. Isolating policy performance via pure RL sampling provides a controlled setting for fair comparison. Second, incorporating MCTS during training on our dataset is computationally prohibitive; expanding 100–200 nodes per step (as in MapZero) would require hundreds of days of computation on our hardware, and reducing the dataset size leads to severe overfitting. Finally, since MCTS does not address the underlying cross-graph representation bottleneck, demonstrating the superiority of HGNN as a neural prior already provides strong evidence that an MCTS-augmented HGNNMap would yield an even stronger overall system.

We also compare our approach against an exact ILP-based mapper (ILPMapper) [6]. All experiments are conducted on a server equipped with dual Intel Xeon 6334 CPUs, one NVIDIA H100 GPU, and 1 TB of memory, with a per-run time limit of two hours.

5.2 Performance on Dataset

We first evaluate model performance on the dataset during training using the *success rate*, defined as $\frac{N_{\text{succ}}}{N_{\text{total}}}$, where N_{succ} denotes the number of successful episodes and N_{total} denotes the total number of sampled episodes. Each episode corresponds to one interaction sequence between the agent and the environment, terminating when mapping succeeds or fails. The success rate is measured every epoch on the training set and every five epochs on the test set. We omit average reward curves, as the reward can be simplified to $\frac{N_{\text{succ}}-N_{\text{fail}}}{N_{\text{total}}} = 2\cdot\text{success\_rate}-1$.

As shown in Fig. 4 and Table 2, HGNNMap significantly outperforms all baselines, achieving peak success rates of 92.21% on the training set and 60.49% on the test set, compared to MapZero-M's 48.56% and 32.48%, respectively. MapZero-Mapped performs in between, consistent with the observations in Sect. 3.2. SmartMap-M exhibits slightly weaker generalization than MapZero-M, likely due to the overhead introduced by its scalability-oriented state-action design. Overall, HGNNMap's improved representation learning translates into substantially higher mapping success rates on both seen and unseen DFGs.

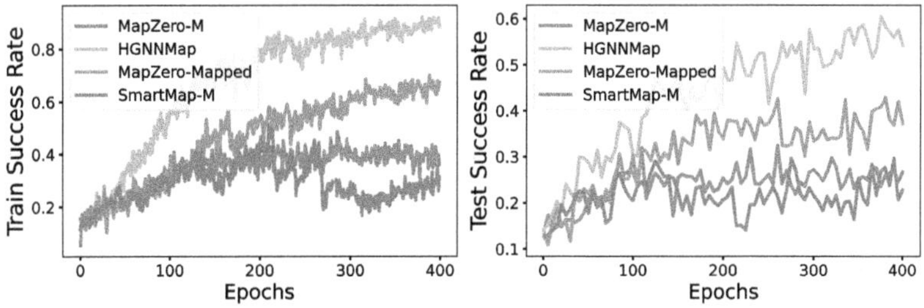

Fig. 4. Success rates of different methods over the train set and the test set.

5.3 Performance on Real-World Kernels

Since MapZero-M, MapZero-Mapped, and HGNNMap are trained on a large-scale dataset, we evaluate them by sampling actions and restarting upon failure until valid mappings are obtained. For all kernels, MRRGs are sized according to their MII. RL-based methods report results averaged over five runs.

Regarding mapping quality, all learning-based mappers achieve optimal throughput by converging to the theoretical MII within the time limit. In contrast, the exact ILPMapper incurs the longest compilation time and fails to map the complex *mults1* kernel within the time limit. Furthermore, Table 2 reports normalized routing resource usage, measured by the number of utilized critical routing nodes (e.g., registers and routing PEs). HGNNMap consistently consumes the fewest resources, whereas ILPMapper requires significantly more. This efficiency suggests that HGNNMap's improved representation learning produces more compact and well-optimized mappings, thereby accelerating convergence and improving success rates.

As shown in Table 2 and Fig. 5, HGNNMap achieves substantial compilation speedups over all baselines, including 9.35× on ADRES and 2.77× on HyCUBE compared to MapZero-M. This acceleration is primarily driven by its higher success rate, which significantly reduces the number of required exploration trials. As expected, speedups on HyCUBE are smaller because its more abundant routing resources reduce mapping difficulty, diminishing the relative advantage of HGNNMap's stronger representations. Additionally, for simpler kernels, some baselines narrow the performance gap due to their lower inference overhead (discussed in Sect. 5.5). However, on more complex kernels such as acc, where expressive representations are critical, HGNNMap achieves up to a 51.2× speedup over MapZero-M.

Overall, HGNNMap consistently outperforms all baselines, particularly on resource-constrained architectures and complex kernels. Furthermore, the superior performance of MapZero-Mapped over MapZero-M further supports our analysis in Sect. 3.2.

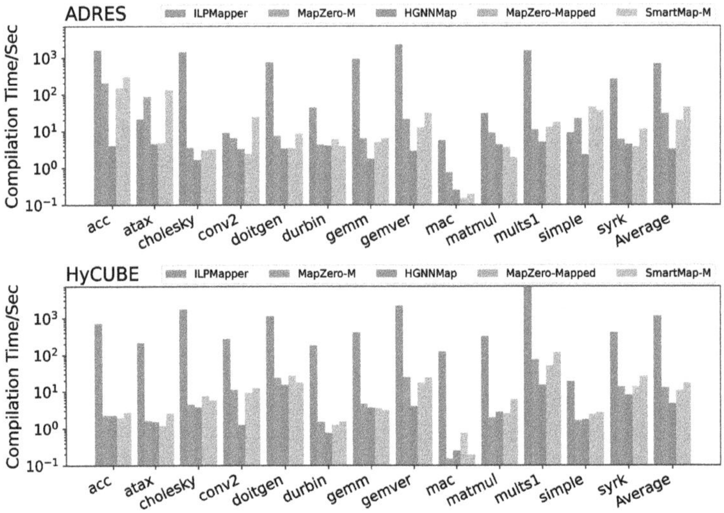

Fig. 5. Compilation time comparison on ADRES and HyCUBE.

5.4 Learned Representation on Mappability Prediction Problem

To more directly assess representation quality, we evaluate three encoder configurations (namely, HGNN, dual-GNN, and dual-GNN-Mapped) on the mappability prediction task, which requires joint reasoning over the DFG, HAG, and partial mapping. As a classification task, mappability prediction enables direct

Table 2. Performance Comparison of Different Mappers

Metric	ILPMapper	SmartMap-M	MapZero-M	MapZero-Mapped	HGNNMap
Best Train Success Rate	–	51.29%	48.56%	70.11%	92.21%
Best Test Success Rate	–	29.69%	32.48%	42.99%	60.49%
Routing Resources Usage (ADRES)	1.37×	1.14×	1.20×	1.18×	1.00×
Routing Resources Usage (HyCUBE)	3.07×	1.10×	1.15×	1.23×	1.00×
HGNNMap Speedup (ADRES)	213.72×	13.96×	9.35×	6.08×	1.00×
HGNNMap Speedup (HyCUBE)	247.23×	3.69×	2.77×	2.28×	1.00×

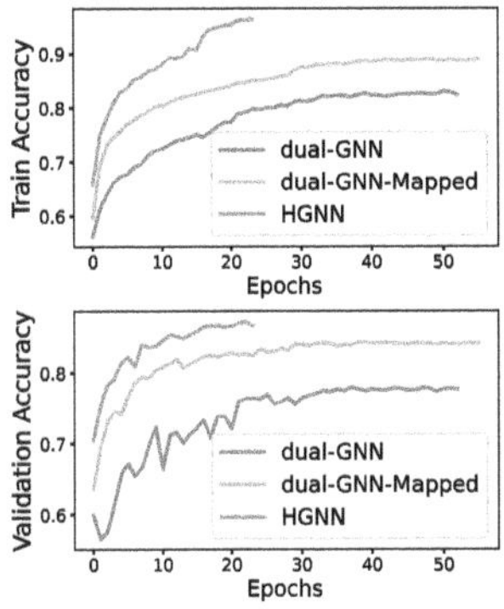

Fig. 6. Training results on the mappability prediction task.

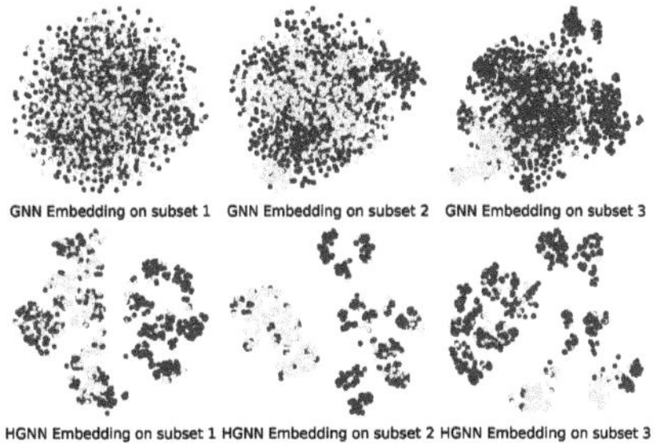

Fig. 7. Representation visualization via t-SNE.

visualization of learned representations and provides more intuitive insights into model behavior. The dataset contains 20,000 randomly generated samples.

The HGNN and dual-GNN configurations reuse their respective encoders from previous experiments, followed by a three-layer fully connected (FC) classifier. The final layer outputs a two-dimensional vector representing the probabilities of the positive and negative classes. The dual-GNN-Mapped setup follows Sect. 3.2.

As shown in Fig. 6, the HGNN achieves both the fastest convergence and the highest accuracy, reaching 97.6% on the training set and 89.6% on the validation set. To qualitatively evaluate the learned representations, we apply t-SNE [13] to visualize embeddings from three randomly selected subsets of the data. As illustrated in Fig. 7, the HGNN produces embeddings with clear inter-class separation, whereas dual-GNN embeddings exhibit substantial overlap. This contrast strongly suggests that HGNN effectively extracts highly discriminative and semantically meaningful features by jointly reasoning over the DFG, HAG, and partial mapping.

5.5 Overheads

Table 3 compares the overheads of HGNNMap and MapZero-M (other baselines exhibit similar profiles to MapZero-M). Despite incurring 1.7× higher infer-

Table 3. Overhead and Performance Trade-off Comparison

Model	Params	Rel. Inf. Time	Test Succ. Rate	ADRES Speedup	HyCUBE Speedup
MapZero-M	∼0.24M	1.0×	32.48%	1.0×	1.0×
HGNNMap	∼1.24M	1.7×	60.49%	9.35×	2.77×

ence latency and 2.2× longer training time, HGNNMap's approximately twofold improvement in success rate substantially reduces the number of search restarts. Consequently, overall compilation is significantly accelerated, achieving speedups of 9.35× on ADRES and 2.77× on HyCUBE. These results indicate that end-to-end mapping efficiency is primarily bottlenecked by state identifiability rather than raw network throughput.

6 Conclusion

This paper addresses the representational bottlenecks of existing dual-GNN encoders by proposing HGNNMap, a heterogeneous graph-based RL framework for spatial-accelerator mapping. By formulating the mapping state as a single HMSG and enabling relation-aware message passing, HGNNMap explicitly captures cross-graph interactions while preserving partial-mapping semantics. Experimental results demonstrate that HGNNMap significantly improves mapping success rates and reduces compilation time on realistic architectures, highlighting the strong potential of heterogeneous graph modeling for learned mapping.

Acknowledgments. This work was supported by National Key R&D Program of China (Grant No. 2023YFB4503500), National Natural Science Foundation of China (Grant No. 62502498), Beijing Natural Science Foundation (Grant No. L234078).

Disclosure of Interests. The authors declare that there is no competing interest.

References

1. Agarap, A.F.: Deep Learning using Rectified Linear Units (ReLU) (2019)
2. Bengio, Y., et al.: Curriculum learning. In: ICML, pp. 41–48 (2009)
3. Cai, T., et al.: GraphNorm: a principled approach to accelerating graph neural network training. In: ICML, pp. 1204–1215 (2021)
4. Chen, T., et al.: DianNao: a small-footprint high-throughput accelerator for ubiquitous machine-learning. In: ASPLOS, pp. 269–284 (2014)
5. Chen, Y.H., et al.: Eyeriss: a spatial architecture for energy-efficient dataflow for convolutional neural networks. In: ISCA, pp. 367–379 (2016)
6. Chin, S.A., et al.: An architecture-agnostic integer linear programming approach to CGRA mapping. In: DAC, pp. 1–6 (2018)
7. Karunaratne, M., et al.: HyCUBE: a CGRA with reconfigurable single-cycle multi-hop interconnect. In: DAC, pp. 1–6 (2017)

8. Kong, X., et al.: MapZero: mapping for coarse-grained reconfigurable architectures with reinforcement learning and Monte-Carlo tree search. In: ISCA, pp. 1–14 (2023)
9. Lam, M.: Software pipelining: an effective scheduling technique for VLIW machines. In: PLDI, pp. 318–328 (1988)
10. Li, J., et al.: TransMap: an efficient CGRA mapping framework via transformer and deep reinforcement learning. In: IPDPSW, pp. 626–633 (2024)
11. Liu, D., et al.: Data-flow graph mapping optimization for CGRA with deep reinforcement learning. TCAD **38**(12), 2271–2283 (2019)
12. Liu, D., et al.: E2EMap: end-to-end reinforcement learning for CGRA compilation via reverse mapping. In: HPCA, pp. 46–60 (2024)
13. van der Maaten, L., et al.: Visualizing data using t-SNE. JMLR **9**, 2579–2605 (2008)
14. Mei, B., et al.: ADRES: an architecture with tightly coupled VLIW processor and coarse-grained reconfigurable matrix. In: FPL, pp. 61–70 (2003)
15. Mei, B., et al.: Exploiting loop-level parallelism on coarse-grained reconfigurable architectures using modulo scheduling. In: DATE, p. 10296 (2003)
16. Pouchet, L.N.: PolyBench/C – Homepage of Louis-Noël Pouchet. https://www.cs.colostate.edu/~pouchet/software/polybench/
17. Ragheb, O., et al.: CGRA-ME 2.0: a research framework for next-generation CGRA architectures and CAD. In: IPDPSW, pp. 642–649 (2024)
18. Ramos, F.T., et al.: SmartMap: architecture-agnostic CGRA mapping using graph traversal and reinforcement learning. In: DATE, pp. 1–7 (2025)
19. Schlichtkrull, M., et al.: Modeling Relational Data with Graph Convolutional Networks (2017)
20. Schulman, J., et al.: Proximal Policy Optimization Algorithms (2017)
21. Silver, D., et al.: Mastering the game of Go without human knowledge. Nature **550**(7676), 354–359 (2017)
22. Srivastava, N., et al.: Dropout: a simple way to prevent neural networks from overfitting. J. Mach. Learn. Res. **15**(1), 1929–1958 (2014)
23. Sun, Y., et al.: Mining heterogeneous information networks: a structural analysis approach. SIGKDD Explor. Newsl. **14**(2), 20–28 (2013)
24. Sutton, R.S., et al.: Reinforcement Learning: An Introduction, vol. 1 (1998)
25. Veličković, P., et al.: Graph attention networks. In: ICLR (2018)
26. Zhuang, Y., et al.: Towards high-quality CGRA mapping with graph neural networks and reinforcement learning. In: ICCAD, pp. 1–9 (2022)

Characterizing GPU Warm-Up Beyond Data Transfers

Julien Tixier[1(✉)], Dominique Houzet[1], and Virginie Burnaz-Fresse[2]

[1] Univ. Grenoble Alpes, CNRS, Grenoble INP, GIPSA-lab, 38000 Grenoble, France
{julien.tixier,dominique.houzet}@gipsa-lab.grenoble-inp.fr
[2] Laboratoire Hubert Curien, Université Jean Monnet, 42000 Saint-Étienne, France
virginie.fresse@univ-st-etienne.fr

Abstract. GPUs have become central to high-performance computing and machine learning, yet efficiently using their full capabilities requires a thorough understanding of low-level runtime behaviors, many of which remain insufficiently documented. Among those, the *data transfer warm-up*, an initialization overhead usually associated with the first `cudaMemcpy` in a CUDA program, is commonly acknowledged yet poorly understood in the literature. In this paper, we revisit this phenomenon and present three contributions. First, we demonstrate that the warm-up is not a fixed overhead bound to `cudaMemcpy` but rather a *floating overhead* that attaches to different CUDA operations depending on the program context. Second, we show that this overhead can be measured even in programs that perform no `cudaMemcpy` at all, decoupling it from the transfer mechanism. Third, we report that interleaving CPU computation between GPU operations causes abnormal inflation of profiled GPU durations, even when the profiler confirms no temporal overlap. All experiments were performed on an NVIDIA RTX 4080 Super using CUDA 12.9 and profiled with NVIDIA Nsight Systems 2025.1.3. These findings challenge common assumptions about GPU initialization costs and expose limitations in conventional benchmarking practices.

Keywords: GPU · Warm-up · Data transfer · Memory allocations · Profiling

1 Introduction

Graphics Processing Units have evolved from specialized rendering hardware into general-purpose parallel accelerators that take over many of today's most demanding workloads. Deep learning has driven an unprecedented increase in the use of GPUs, such as with modern large language models that routinely require thousands of GPU-hours for training [1,12]. Beyond machine learning, GPUs are central to scientific computing [9], computational fluid dynamics [5], and molecular dynamics [2], where efficient GPU utilization directly impacts both time-to-solution and energy consumption.

M. Torquati et al. (Eds.): Euro-Par 2026, LNCS 16781, pp. 286–299, 2027.
https://doi.org/10.1007/978-3-032-35248-4_20

As GPU adoption grows, so does the interest in accurate performance characterization at the runtime level [3,14]. Among the subtle overheads that affect GPU benchmarking, the *data transfer warm-up*, an initialization cost observed as an inflation of the first data transfer, is widely acknowledged yet poorly understood. Building on our prior work [11], which established that the warm-up correlates with allocated GPU memory and can recur across data transfers, this paper makes three contributions that fundamentally recharacterize the phenomenon.

To investigate these behaviors, we design experiments that isolate memory allocation, data transfer, and synchronization into controlled sequences.

2 Related Work

This section reviews the current state of the art and highlights the gaps that motivate our study.

The GPU computing community has long recognized that early iterations of a program behave differently from steady state. Some papers [13] show that naive benchmarks produce misleading results, and practical guides [10] recommend discarding the first few executions to avoid initialization artifacts. Yet this advice remains purely empirical: no prior work has investigated *why* the warm-up occurs, what triggers it, or under which conditions it recurs.

The most common explanation attributes the overhead to CUDA's lazy context initialization (i.e., driver loading and device selection, all deferred to the first CUDA API call) [6]. However, the warm-up we observe behaves differently: it scales with allocation size, recurs across transfers, and attaches to different operations depending on the synchronization context, none of which are consistent with a one-time context setup.

Recent advances in GPU virtual memory management provide indirect evidence for an alternative explanation. CUDA 10.2 introduced fine-grained control over address spaces [8], and some papers [4] demonstrate that page table operations carry non-trivial costs. The CUDA Programming Guide [6] documents that `cudaMalloc` triggers internal GPU-side operations, including page table setup, memory commitment, and buffer zeroing, some of which are performed asynchronously, reinforcing the idea that `cudaMalloc` is a source of warm-ups.

Accurately measuring these effects is further complicated by the profiling tools themselves. Instrumentation-based profilers such as Nsight Systems [7] are based on statistical sampling, making them subject to the *probe effect*, whereby measurement perturbs the system under observation. While this is typically understood as added overhead, our findings reveal that CPU-side activity alters the results.

Our earlier work [11] was the first to systematically characterize the data transfer warm-up, establishing that it correlates with allocated device memory and can recur when the largest allocation grows. That study, however, treated the warm-up as inherent to `cudaMemcpy` and left its true origin open. The present paper closes this gap by showing that the overhead is generated by `cudaMalloc`, floats across synchronization boundaries, and persists even in programs that perform no data transfer at all.

3 Experimental Methodology

All experiments were implemented in CUDA and executed on an NVIDIA GeForce RTX 4080 Super and profiled with NVIDIA Nsight Systems version 2025.1.3. For better reproducibility, our source code is available at our repository[1].

3.1 Reference Code Structures

We designed two reference codes that serve as controlled baselines for all experimental variants: each variant modifies a single aspect (synchronization, transfers, or CPU activity) while keeping the rest unchanged. The two codes differ only in the temporal separation between memory allocations, transfers, and deallocations. Both operate on 20 progressively growing allocations (doubling from 4 KB to 2048 MB) to systematically trigger warm-up conditions [11], and both use the default synchronous CUDA instructions: `cudaMalloc` (to allocate memory), `cudaMemcpy` (to transfer data from host to device) and `cudaFree` (to deallocate memory).

Pseudo-code* 1*: Single-Loop Structure. All operations are interleaved in a single loop: each iteration performs one `cudaMalloc` (growing in size each iteration), two 4 KB `cudaMemcpy` calls, and one `cudaFree`. Because each allocation is twice the size of the previous one, each iteration triggers a new warm-up [11].

Pseudo-code 1 Allocations, transfers, and deallocations in a single loop

```
for i = 1 to 20 do
    cudaMalloc {Growing size: 4 KB to 2048 MB}
    cudaMemcpy {4 KB}
    cudaMemcpy {4 KB}
    cudaFree
end for
```

Pseudo-code* 2*: Separate-Loops Structure. Operations are isolated into three dedicated loops (all mallocs, then all memcpys, then all frees). Preallocating all memory before any transfer ensures the largest contiguous allocation is established at the first `cudaMemcpy`, which should, under the conventional model, produce at most a single warm-up [11].

Two deliberate choices underlie both structures: 4 KB transfers make transfer duration negligible relative to warm-up overhead, and *two* consecutive transfers per iteration account for the warm-up sometimes attaching to the *second* `cudaMemcpy` [11].

[1] https://gricad-gitlab.univ-grenoble-alpes.fr/tixierju/gpu-warmup-characterization.

Pseudo-code 2 Allocations, transfers, and deallocations in separate loops

```
for i = 1 to 20 do
  cudaMalloc {Growing size: 4 KB to 2048 MB}
end for

for i = 1 to 20 do
  cudaMemcpy {4 KB}
  cudaMemcpy {4 KB}
end for

for i = 1 to 20 do
  cudaFree
end for
```

3.2 Reference Measurements

Figure 1 depicts the profiled `cudaMemcpy` durations for both base pseudo-codes when executed without explicit synchronization.

Figure (a) (associated to pseudo-code 1) depicts a longer duration on the second `cudaMemcpy` of each iteration, which, as established earlier, carries the warm-up. The figure depicts how the warm-up durations vary from ≈ 112 µs for the first warm-ups to ≈ 41 ms for the last (which reminds of the previously established relation between memory allocation and data warm-up duration).

Figure (b) (associated to pseudo-code 2) depicts a unique peak of ≈ 69 ms on the second `cudaMemcpy` of the very first iteration, which, as established earlier, carries a unique cumulated warm-up that accounts for all previous allocations.

4 Contribution 1: The Warm-Up as a Floating Overhead

Prior work [11] and the surrounding literature consistently attribute the warm-up to `cudaMemcpy`, interpreting the inflated duration of the first or second transfer as evidence that the overhead originates in the transfer mechanism. We demonstrate that this artifact is an incorrect attribution of the measurement methodology. The warm-up is an asynchronous overhead generated by `cudaMalloc` that *floats* to whichever synchronization boundary first forces the CPU to wait for it.

4.1 Experimental Variants

To isolate the role of synchronization, we add two synchronized variants to the unsynchronized
Brut baseline: **EventSync** inserts `cudaEventSynchronize` immediately after each CUDA call;**DeviceSync** inserts `cudaDeviceSynchronize` instead. In both variants the GPU is fully idle before the next API call; only the synchronization primitive differs.

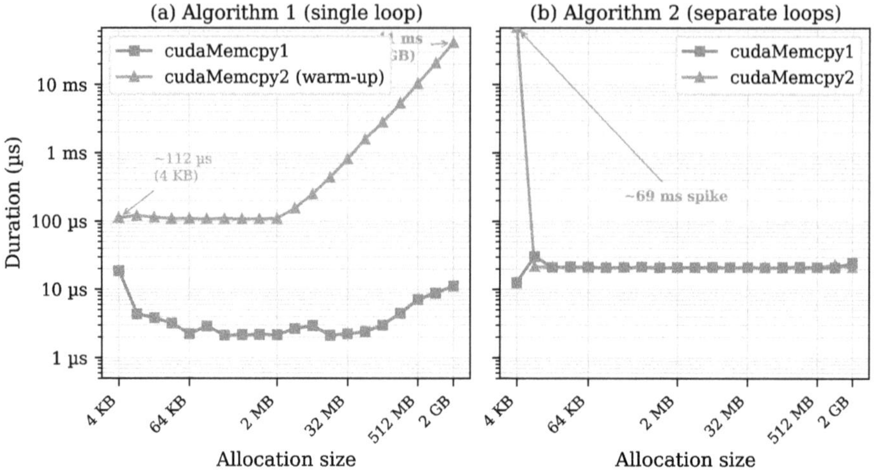

Fig. 1. Baseline `cudaMemcpy` durations without synchronization. (a) pseudo-code 1: warm-up spike on `cudaMemcpy2` at every iteration, growing from 110 µs (4 KB) to 41 ms (2 GB). (b) pseudo-code 2: single 68.8 ms spike at iteration 1; all subsequent transfers at 21 µs.

4.2 Same Overhead, Different Operation: Pseudo-code 1

Figure 2 depicts per-iteration synchronization durations for pseudo-code 1 under EventSync (panel a) and DeviceSync (panel b). Table 1 gives mean values for iterations 1–10 (4 KB to 2 MB), where the per-iteration warm-up is approximately constant at ~100 µs.

Table 1. Mean synchronization duration per sync point for pseudo-code 1, iterations 1–10 (mean ± std, 10 runs). Bold values carry the ~107 µs warm-up; the overhead migrates between operations depending on the synchronization primitive.

Sync point	EventSync (µs)	DeviceSync (µs)
After `cudaMalloc`	**107.4** (±6.7)	0.4 (±0.1)
After `cudaMemcpy1`	19.2 (±1.1)	**108.5** (±8.0)
After `cudaMemcpy2`	18.6 (±0.6)	20.7 (±2.4)
After `cudaFree`	15.5 (±1.3)	0.6 (±0.3)

Under **EventSync**, the warm-up appears on the `cudaEventSynchronize` after `cudaMalloc` (107.4 µs vs. a 15.5 µs post-free baseline) only; syncs after `cudaMemcpy` calls remain uninflated. Under **DeviceSync**, the picture inverts: the sync after `cudaMalloc` is negligible (0.4 µs) while the sync after `cudaMemcpy1` carries the full ~108.5 µs overhead. The total warm-up cost per iteration is identical; only its location in the profiler trace has changed.

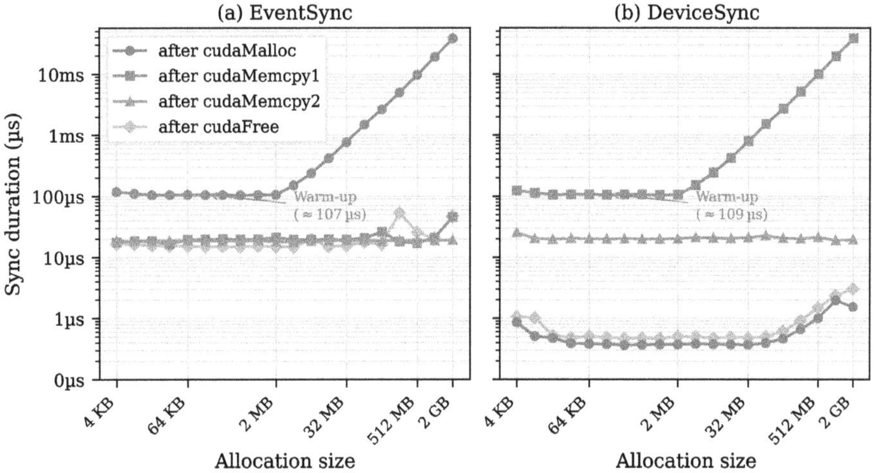

Fig. 2. Floating warm-up in pseudo-code 1. The same ~107 µs overhead appears after `cudaMalloc` under EventSync (a) but shifts to after `cudaMemcpy1` under DeviceSync (b), demonstrating that the warm-up attaches to whichever synchronization barrier first drains it.

Why this asymmetry arises. `cudaEventSynchronize` blocks until all queued work on the main stream completes, so the warm-up drains before `cudaMemcpy` begins. The `cudaDeviceSynchronize` after `cudaMalloc` returns in ~0.4 µs, indicating it does not wait for the internal asynchronous work generated by the allocation; this deferred work is eventually caught by the next synchronous barrier, the `cudaDeviceSynchronize` after `cudaMemcpy1`.

4.3 Cumulated vs. Distributed Overhead: Pseudo-code 2

Pseudo-code 2 separates all 20 allocations from all transfers. Without synchronization, all 20 `cudaMalloc` calls execute before any `cudaMemcpy`, so their asynchronous GPU-side work accumulates without being drained, creating a natural experiment in which the same total cost shows up in three different forms (Fig. 3):

Brut: the full 68,793 µs drains on `cudaMemcpy2` of iteration 1 [11]; all subsequent transfers are normal (~26 µs).
DeviceSync: the same 68,772 µs spike shifts to the sync after `cudaMemcpy1`; syncs after mallocs remain near-zero (~0.3 µs).
EventSync: the total is *distributed* across 20 individual post-malloc syncs, ranging from 108 µs (4 KB) to 39,007 µs (2 GB); no `cudaMemcpy` is inflated.

These three outcomes are not three different behaviors of the GPU, but three different measurement projections of the same underlying asynchronous cost. The warm-up is not a property of `cudaMemcpy`, it is the accumulated asynchronous GPU-side work from `cudaMalloc` calls, draining at whatever synchronization boundary it first encounters.

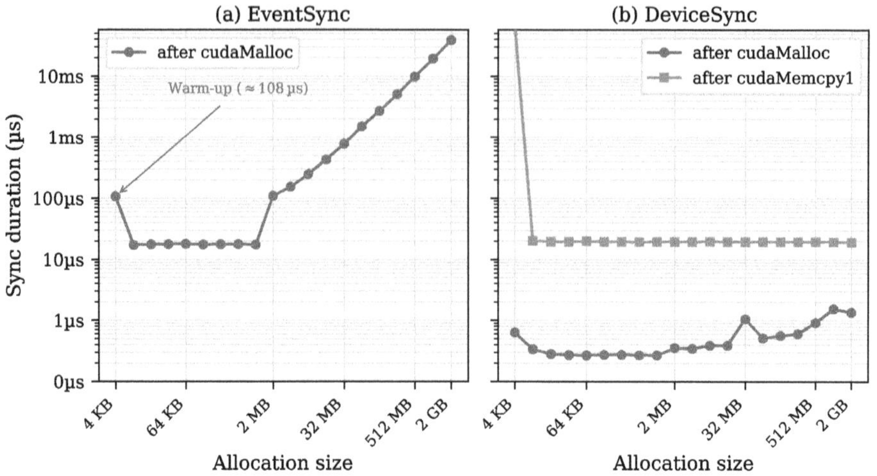

Fig. 3. Cumulated vs. distributed warm-up in pseudo-code 2. (a) DeviceSync: the accumulated 69 ms overhead drains as a single spike after `cudaMemcpy1`. (b) EventSync: the same total cost is distributed across 20 individual syncs after each `cudaMalloc`.

4.4 Warm-Up Floating to `cudaFree`

To probe how far the overhead can float, we test **NoMemcpy+DeviceSync**: no `cudaMemcpy` calls, with `cudaDeviceSynchronize` after each `cudaMalloc` and `cudaFree`. As established above, `cudaDeviceSynchronize` does not drain the malloc work; with no `cudaMemcpy` available either, the overhead travels further and lands on `cudaFree` (which is the first operation that internally synchronizes with the device when no other blocking primitive is present, making it the natural sink for deferred GPU work).

Table 2 confirms this: the sync after `cudaMalloc` stays at ∼0.4 µs throughout, leaving `cudaFree` as the sole operation to drain the warm-up, growing from 117 µs to 49 620 µs in 20 iterations (even though `cudaFree` is normally very fast, normally lasting a few µs). Furthermore, this behavior exactly follows the observed warm-up curves depicted in Figs. 1 and 2).

Table 2. Warm-up absorbed by `cudaFree` in pseudo-code 1 (NoMemcpy+DeviceSync, median over 10 runs).

Iter	Size	DS post-Malloc (µs)	`cudaFree` (µs)	DS post-Free (µs)
1	4 KB	0.7	117	1.1
10	2 MB	0.4	111	0.5
15	64 MB	0.4	1,546	1.7
19	1 GB	1.8	24,605	2.6
20	2 GB	1.7	49,620	4.8

4.5 Discussion

These results decisively rule out `cudaMemcpy` as the source of the warm-up and demonstrate that the phenomenon is inherent to GPU memory allocation, not data movement. The common warm-up mitigation strategy of issuing a preliminary small transfer provides no benefit if the overhead does not attach to `cudaMemcpy` under the program's synchronization regime. Any profiling study attributing a latency spike to a specific CUDA operation without controlling for synchronization may be reporting an incorrect attribution caused by the interplay between asynchronous GPU work and synchronization semantics.

5 Contribution 2: Warm-Up Without Data Transfers

The previous section showed, as an extreme case of floating overhead, that the warm-up propagates all the way to `cudaFree` when `cudaMemcpy` is removed from pseudo-code 1 under DeviceSync. We now test this systematically across all four combinations, both pseudo-codes and both synchronization variants, with *no* *`cudaMemcpy`* in any of them. If warm-up originates from `cudaMalloc`, it must still appear; if it were a property of the data-transfer mechanism, it should vanish.

5.1 NoMemcpy Variants

Four configurations are derived by removing all `cudaMemcpy` calls from the base pseudo-codes, retaining only `cudaMalloc`, `cudaFree`, and synchronization: pseudo-code 1 $\times$ {DeviceSync, EventSync} and pseudo-code 2$\times${DeviceSync, EventSync}. No data is transferred in any variant; any anomalous overhead must originate from memory management alone.

5.2 Pseudo-code 1: Warm-Up on `cudaFree` and EventSync

Table 2 already documents the DeviceSync case: `cudaFree` carries a $\sim$110 µs overhead for small allocations (4 KB–2 MB), identical in magnitude to the warm-up previously observed on `cudaMemcpy` 1 and on `cudaMalloc` 3 (figure b). Under EventSync (Fig. 4a), the same mass appears instead on `cudaEventSynchronize` post-`cudaMalloc`: $\sim$106 µs for all small allocations, while `cudaFree` returns to its $\sim$15 µs baseline (as confirmed by EventSync post-`cudaFree` durations). As in Contribution 1, the total warm-up cost is conserved; only its location in the profiler trace has changed.

5.3 Pseudo-code 2: Catastrophic Drain on `cudaFree`

The pre-allocated structure provides the most dramatic demonstration. With 20 `cudaMalloc` calls separated from 20 `cudaFree` calls and *no* *`cudaMemcpy`* at all, the warm-up from all allocations accumulates silently during the first loop.

Figure 4b and Table 3 detail the DeviceSync results:

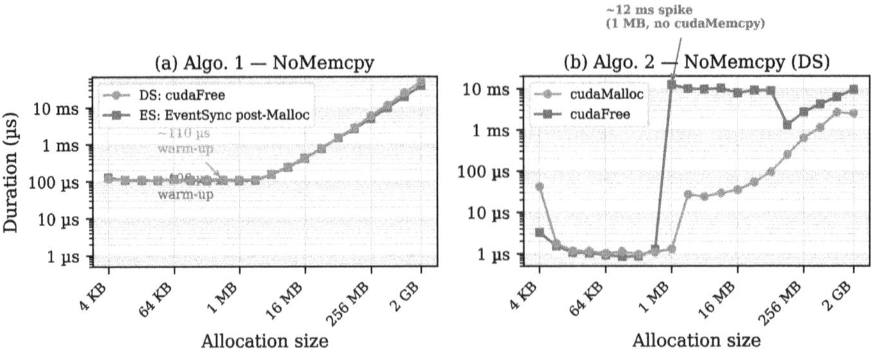

Fig. 4. Warm-up persists without any `cudaMemcpy`. (a) Pseudo-code 1: the ∼107 µs overhead appears on `cudaFree` (DeviceSync) or post-`cudaMalloc` sync (EventSync). (b) Pseudo-code 2 (DeviceSync): accumulated overhead drains on `cudaFree` with a 12 ms spike at iteration 9.

Table 3. Pseudo-code 2 (NoMemcpy+DeviceSync): `cudaMalloc` and `cudaFree` durations. Iterations 1–8 show no anomaly; the accumulated warm-up drains abruptly on `cudaFree` at iteration 9 (12,412 µs). † Iteration 1 elevated due to CUDA context initialization.

Iter	Size	`cudaMalloc` (µs)	`cudaFree` (µs)
1 †	4 KB	42.2	3.3
2	8 KB	1.8	1.5
8	512 KB	1.1	1.3
9	1 MB	1.3	**12,412**
10	2 MB	27.1	**9,984**
15	64 MB	94.4	**8,946**
20	2 GB	2,501	**9,465**

- **Iterations 1–8** (4 KB–512 KB): `cudaMalloc` ∼1 µs; `cudaFree` ∼1 µs—no anomaly.
- **Iteration 9** (1 MB): `cudaMalloc` = 1.3 µs; `cudaFree` = **12,412 µs**—an overhead factor of ×11,513.
- **Iterations 10–15** (2 MB–64 MB): `cudaFree` sustains ∼8,000–10,000 µs across six consecutive iterations.
- **Iterations 16–20** (128 MB–2 GB); `cudaFree` shows an *instability* with a tenfold drop in duration, followed by a linear increase on the log-log plot, with the duration growing by a factor of 10 over the 5 next calls (from 256 MB to 2 GB).

The ∼12 ms spike on `cudaFree` at iteration 9 arises with no `cudaMemcpy` ever called. The accumulated GPU-side work from all 20 `cudaMalloc` calls travels past the small-allocation frees (iterations 1–8, which resolve quickly and do not trigger a sync with the pending GPU work) and drains at the first "large-allocation" `cudaFree`, at the 1 MB threshold (we consider 1 MB to be a threshold for large-allocations because of this phenomenon). This size-dependent triggering is consistent with the allocation-size dependence documented in [11].

Under EventSync (not shown), the spike is smaller but still substantial: `cudaFree` at iteration 9 reaches ∼357 µs (×211), because EventSync after each `cudaMalloc` drains a fraction of the accumulated work throughout the first loop.

5.4 Discussion

Across all four NoMemcpy configurations, an anomalous overhead (∼106 µs to ∼12 ms) appears on operations with zero data transfer, thus confirming that the `cudaMemcpy` instruction is neither the source nor the necessary carrier of the warm-up. The overhead originates from `cudaMalloc`-triggered asynchronous GPU-side work, deferred to the next CPU-blocking call regardless of whether that call involves a data transfer. The common mitigation strategy of issuing a preliminary `cudaMemcpy` provides no fundamental benefit when the overhead does not naturally land on a memory-copy under the program's synchronization regime.

6 Contribution 3: Phantom Inflation from CPU Activity

While investigating the warm-up phenomenon, we encountered an unexpected interaction between CPU-side activity and the profiled durations of GPU memory operations. When CPU work is interleaved between CUDA operations, the profiler reports substantially inflated GPU durations despite confirming no temporal overlap between CPU and GPU activity. We refer to this as *phantom inflation*.

6.1 Experimental Design

We modified both pseudo-code 1 and pseudo-code 2 by inserting CPU work (500 ms) immediately after each CUDA operation, testing two types: **active computation** (nested arithmetic loops) and **explicit sleep** (`std::this_thread ::sleep_for`). Variants with `cudaEventSynchronize` after each CUDA call were also tested. In all cases, the profiler timeline confirms GPU operations complete before any CPU activity begins [6].

6.2 Profiling Results

Table 4 summarizes cumulated durations over 20 iterations, averaged over 10 executions; Fig. 5 depicts inflation percentages for NoSync conditions.

`cudaFree` is consistently the most inflated operation: +487% and +958% (Compute and Sleep) for pseudo-code 1, and +350% and +819% for pseudo-code 2, which can be explained because the operation is known to perform

Table 4. Phantom inflation: cumulated CUDA operation durations (µs) under CPU activity scenarios (sum over 20 iterations, mean of 10 runs).

Condition	cudaMalloc	cudaMemcpy1	cudaMemcpy2	cudaFree	Total
Pseudo-code 1 (single loop)					
Baseline (no CPU)	4,021	91	84,417	18,157	106,686
Baseline (EventSync)	4,175	78	33	17,882	102,468*
CPU Compute (NoSync)	5,274	643	11,735	106,584	124,236
CPU Compute (EventSync)	6,027	480	295	93,868	412,562*
CPU Sleep (NoSync)	32,023	1,725	15,305	192,155	241,208
CPU Sleep (EventSync)	33,188	1,743	1,775	190,609	569,570*
Pseudo-code 2 (separate loops)					
Baseline (no CPU)	7,591	428	69,198	17,627	94,845
Baseline (EventSync)	4,678	42	31	17,567	103,094*
CPU Compute (NoSync)	4,556	9,670	10,776	79,273	104,276
CPU Compute (EventSync)	5,102	327	315	75,544	387,152*
CPU Sleep (NoSync)	27,374	12,780	14,272	162,066	216,492
CPU Sleep (EventSync)	28,389	1,846	1,812	158,655	520,365*

*EventSync totals include `cudaEventSynchronize` overhead.

device-side cleanup and implicitly synchronize with the device, making it particularly sensitive to timing distortions introduced by CPU-side activity. `cudaMalloc` also inflates substantially under sleep (+696% and +261%). Crucially, inflation occurs even with pure CPU computation, ruling out OS scheduler wake-up costs as the sole explanation. The EventSync variants confirm the effect persists with synchronization (totals up +303% and +276% over EventSync baselines). Notably, `cudaMemcpy2` shows *reduced* durations under CPU occupation, the warm-up redistributes when CPU activity is present, consistent with Contribution 1.

6.3 Gap Between Computation and Sleep

The measured overhead is consistently larger (up to 6 times longer) in sleep mode than during computation. While further testing would be needed to confirm it, this additional gap can plausibly be attributed to OS scheduler wake-up costs: since the scheduler has already been ruled out as the cause of the baseline overhead observed during computation, it remains a credible explanation for the extra cost specifically incurred when the thread is sleeping.

6.4 Ruling Out Common Hypotheses

Three alternative explanations were tested. **(1) Disguised synchronization:** all operations are documented as synchronous [6] and the profiler timeline shows

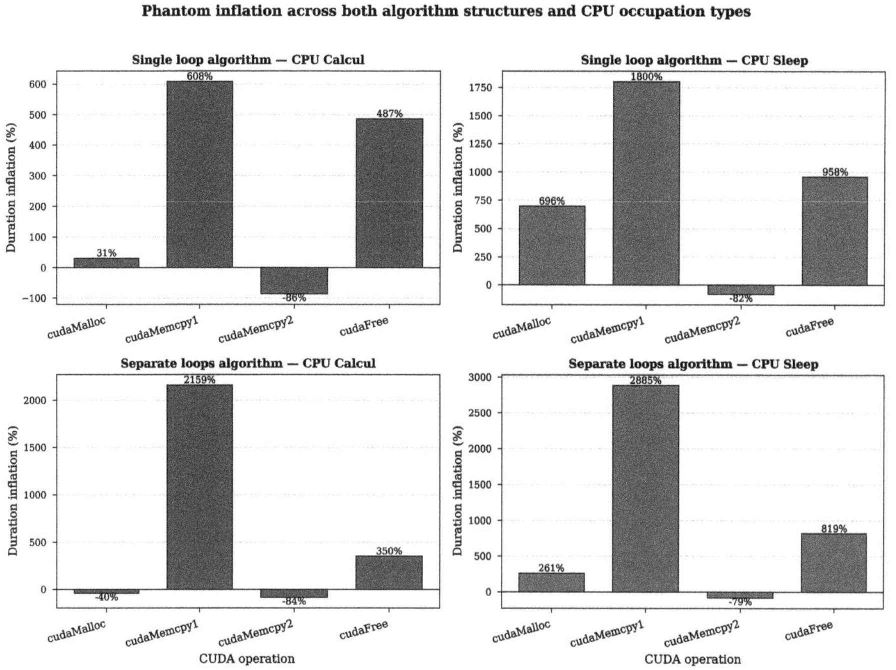

Fig. 5. Phantom inflation rates relative to baseline (NoSync). `cudaFree` is the most inflated operation (+958% under sleep); negative values for `cudaMemcpy2` reflect warm-up redistribution (the shifts of warm-ups between operations depending on synchronization talked about in the first contribution).

no CPU-GPU overlap. **(2) Profiler CPU-tracing overhead:** disabling CPU profiling did not eliminate the inflation. **(3) Run-to-run variability:** the same inflated durations are reproduced consistently across 10 executions.

6.5 Implications

Developers profiling GPU operations in mixed CPU-GPU workloads may obtain measurements inflated by up to an order of magnitude.

Since real applications always involve CPU-GPU interleaving, profiled durations may not reflect actual GPU-side costs, complicating performance analysis and warm-up characterization. This calls into question the validity of profiling results obtained under realistic workloads, where CPU-GPU interleaving is unavoidable. The consistent inflation across all variants suggests that the CUDA runtime's internal timing or bookkeeping interacts with the host thread's execution state, even in the absence of overlap. We recommend that future profiling studies carefully control and report CPU-side conditions.

7 Conclusion

This paper has revisited the GPU warm-up phenomenon and shown that its conventional interpretation, a fixed, one-time cost tied to the first `cudaMemcpy`, fundamentally misrepresents its nature.

Contribution 1 established that the warm-up is a *floating overhead* generated asynchronously by `cudaMalloc`: it attaches to whichever CPU-blocking synchronization boundary it first encounters, so the same overhead appears on entirely different operations depending on the synchronization context. **Contribution 2** showed that this overhead persists in programs performing *no data transfer at all*, definitively dissociating it from `cudaMemcpy` and locating its origin in GPU internal memory management. **Contribution 3** documented a *phantom inflation* effect: interleaved CPU activity inflates profiled CUDA durations by up to 10× despite the profiler confirming no temporal overlap, ruling out OS wake-up costs as the sole explanation.

These results invalidate a common assumption: that issuing a preliminary `cudaMemcpy` reliably absorbs the warm-up. We extend a previous study [11] that observed similar behavior on both an RTX 2060 Super and an RTX 4080; only the RTX 4080 was available here, and we encourage further experiments across architectures, drivers, and CUDA toolkits. Future profiling work should explicitly report the synchronization strategy, control CPU-side conditions, and avoid attributing latencies to specific CUDA calls without validating that the attribution holds under different measurement conditions.

Acknowledgments. This work received no specific funding.

Disclosure of Interests. The authors have no competing interests to declare that are relevant to the content of this article.

References

1. Brown, T., et al.: Language models are few-shot learners. In: Advances in Neural Information Processing Systems (NeurIPS), vol. 33, pp. 1877–1901 (2020)
2. Eastman, P., et al.: OpenMM 7: rapid development of high performance algorithms for molecular dynamics. PLoS Comput. Biol. **13**(7), e1005659 (2017). https://doi.org/10.1371/journal.pcbi.1005659
3. Hao, Y., Jain, N., Van der Wijngaart, R., Saxena, N., Fan, Y., Liu, X.: DrGPU: a top-down profiler for GPU applications. In: Proceedings of the 2023 ACM/SPEC International Conference on Performance Engineering (ICPE), pp. 43–54 (2023). https://doi.org/10.1145/3578244.3583736
4. Kehne, J., Metter, J., Bellosa, F.: GPUswap: enabling oversubscription of GPU memory through transparent swapping. In: Proceedings of the 11th ACM SIGPLAN/SIGOPS International Conference on Virtual Execution Environments (VEE), pp. 65–77 (2015). https://doi.org/10.1145/2731186.2731192
5. Niemeyer, K.E., Sung, C.-J.: Recent progress and challenges in exploiting graphics processors in computational fluid dynamics. J. Supercomput. **67**(2), 528–564 (2013). https://doi.org/10.1007/s11227-013-1015-7

6. NVIDIA Corporation: CUDA C++ programming guide, release 12.x. https://docs.nvidia.com/cuda/cuda-c-programming-guide/. Accessed 09 Mar 2026
7. NVIDIA Corporation: Nsight systems user guide. https://docs.nvidia.com/nsight-systems/UserGuide/. Accessed 09 Mar 2026
8. NVIDIA Corporation: Virtual memory management — CUDA C++ programming guide, release 12.x. https://docs.nvidia.com/cuda/cuda-c-programming-guide/index.html#virtual-memory-management. Accessed 09 Mar 2026
9. Owens, J., et al.: GPU computing. Proc. IEEE **96**(5), 879–899 (2008). https://doi.org/10.1109/JPROC.2008.917757
10. Sanchez Brizuela, G.: How to benchmark CUDA kernels. https://guillesanbri.com/CUDA-Benchmarks/. Accessed 09 Mar 2026
11. Tixier, J., Fresse, V., Houzet, D.: Analysis of warm-up effects in GPU memory management. In: Workshop Proceedings of the 54th International Conference on Parallel Processing (ICPP Workshops), pp. 193–194 (2025). https://doi.org/10.1145/3750720.3757299
12. Touvron, H., et al.: LLaMA: open and efficient foundation language models. In: Proceedings of the 40th International Conference on Machine Learning (ICML), vol. 202, pp. 34844–34863. PMLR (2023)
13. Volkov, V., Demmel, J.: Benchmarking GPUs to tune dense linear algebra. In: Proceedings of the 2008 ACM/IEEE Conference on Supercomputing (SC), pp. 1–11 (2008). https://doi.org/10.1109/SC.2008.5214359
14. Yang, Z., Adamek, K., Armour, W.: Accurate and convenient energy measurements for GPUs: a detailed study of NVIDIA GPU's built-in power sensor. In: Proceedings of the International Conference for High Performance Computing, Networking, Storage and Analysis (SC), pp. 307–323 (2024). https://doi.org/10.1109/SC41406.2024.00028

Repurposing the Cross-Segment Space on Sunway SW26010Pro for MC-Balanced Bigshare Execution

Qixin Chang[1], Lifeng Yan[1], Hailong Liu[2], Weiguo Liu[1], and Xiaohui Duan[1(✉)]

[1] Shandong University, Jinan, China
{cqx,lifeng.yan}@mail.sdu.edu.cn, {weiguo.liu,sunrise.duan}@sdu.edu.cn
[2] Laoshan Laboratory, Qingdao, China
hlliu2@qnlm.ac

Abstract. The SW26010Pro processor in the next-generation Sunway system introduces bigshare mode, in which a single process spans multiple Core Groups (CGs) and accesses an aggregated memory space larger than that of the conventional one-process-per-CG model. However, programs in bigshare mode often underperform. Our analysis suggests that a primary cause is asymmetric execution-image placement: the execution image is placed in memory associated with a single CG, concentrating accesses on one memory controller (MC), increasing instruction-fetch latency, and limiting effective bandwidth. To address this issue, we repurpose the cross-segment space—originally designed for sharing data across CGs—as an execution space for execution images. The space is system-defined and interleaved across all six CGs at a fixed 256 B granularity. We implement swcrun, a loader that enables this placement without modifying application source code. Compared with the default bigshare mode, swcrun achieves average speedups of 1.64× on the swRodinia benchmark suite and 1.83× on SWBWA. We further analyze its implications in multi-node communication.

Keywords: Sunway SW26010Pro processor · Bigshare parallel mode · Cross-segment space · Memory-controller contention

1 Introduction

SW26010Pro, the successor to the SW26010 processor deployed in the Sunway TaihuLight supercomputer [1–3], has been adopted in the next-generation Sunway system [4–6]. Each processor integrates six Core Groups (CGs), each containing one Management Processing Element (MPE) and 64 Compute Processing Elements (CPEs). Compared with SW26010, SW26010Pro delivers approximately 4× the peak computational performance. Beyond the performance gains, it introduces a new parallel execution model.

On SW26010, each process is bound to one MPE, manages the 64 CPEs within its CG, and accesses only the memory local to that CG. This execution

M. Torquati et al. (Eds.): Euro-Par 2026, LNCS 16781, pp. 300–313, 2027.
https://doi.org/10.1007/978-3-032-35248-4_21

model is referred to as the normal mode. In addition to supporting normal mode, SW26010Pro introduces bigshare mode, in which a process manages all 384 CPEs across the processor and can access the aggregated memory resources of all CGs. The bigshare mode provides several advantages. First, it enables a single process to access a much larger memory space, which is important for memory-intensive applications. Second, it reduces the number of processes required for a given workload, thereby lowering inter-process communication overhead. Third, because a single process manages all CPEs, work partitioning can be handled within one process, which simplifies implementation and makes load balancing across CGs easier. Its main drawback is that fewer MPEs are utilized. Nevertheless, this trade-off is often acceptable because approximately 98.5% of the processor's peak computational capability is provided by the CPEs.

However, empirical results show that programs running in bigshare mode often suffer performance degradation. For the same workload, per-CPE performance can be lower than that in normal mode. Profiling with performance monitoring unit (PMU) counters reveals that this degradation is largely attributable to increased CPE instruction-fetch latency and reduced effective memory bandwidth available to the CPEs. A closer look at the memory subsystem provides further insight. Each CG integrates a dedicated memory controller (MC) serving both the MPE and its associated CPEs. In bigshare mode, several MC-related performance counters increase substantially compared with normal mode, indicating increased pressure on the MCs and intensified contention in the memory subsystem.

To the best of our knowledge, neither the detailed microarchitectural design of the MCs nor the program-loading mechanism of SW26010Pro has been publicly documented. Moreover, MC selection is transparent to software, and no architectural interface is exposed to inspect, control, or modify it. We therefore do not claim direct visibility into how the default loader places the execution image in the memory system. Instead, our analysis is based on black-box experimental evidence. The observed behavior is most consistent with asymmetric execution-image placement in bigshare mode: the process appears to be launched on the MPE of one CG, with the execution image correspondingly placed in the memory associated with that CG. As a result, CPEs in other CGs are more likely to access the execution image via inter-CG paths, which provides a plausible explanation for the elevated instruction-fetch latency, increased MC-side pressure, and reduced effective memory bandwidth observed in bigshare mode.

To further validate this hypothesis, we conduct a controlled experiment in which each CPE is assigned an identical workload. When only the 64 CPEs within a single CG are used under bigshare mode, per-CPE performance matches that of normal mode. In contrast, when all 384 CPEs are used, per-CPE performance decreases noticeably. These results support our inference that cross-CG memory accesses, rather than increased parallelism itself, are primarily responsible for the observed performance degradation.

Based on the above analysis and our hypothesis, we next consider what an effective solution should achieve. The key requirement is to ensure that all six

MCs are effectively utilized. However, the architecture does not provide explicit mechanisms for controlling the MCs, leaving them completely transparent to the program. For example, there is no way to control how the program is placed in memory served by specific MCs or how to allocate a memory buffer in memory associated with a particular MC. Fortunately, the architecture provides a system-defined shared address region, referred to as the cross-segment space, which is inherently interleaved across all six MCs at a fixed granularity of 256 B. This region was originally designed to support data sharing among CGs within a processor, rather than to serve as an execution space for programs. We observe, however, that its intrinsic interleaving property is exactly what is needed to balance MC utilization. Based on this insight, we repurpose the cross-segment space as a program loading and execution space for bigshare mode.

To ensure the correct program loading and execution from the cross-segment space, we implement a new loader, `swcrun`, for bigshare mode. Instead of loading the execution image in the memory associated with a single CG, swcrun loads the execution image into the cross-segment space, leveraging its inherent MC-level interleaving. By doing so, instruction-fetch and data-access traffic is distributed across all six MCs, reducing memory contention in bigshare mode without requiring modifications to application source code.

The main contributions of this work are as follows:

- We analyze the performance degradation in bigshare mode through PMU-based profiling and controlled experiments.
- We propose cross-segment execution, repurposing the cross-segment space for execution image placement in bigshare mode, and analyze its impact on instruction-fetch latency, data-access latency, memory bandwidth, and overall performance.
- We design and implement swcrun, a loader that enables cross-segment execution on SW26010Pro, achieving this optimization without requiring modifications to application source code.
- We characterize the program loading pipeline on SW26010Pro and provide practical guidance for system software and application developers.

2 Background

2.1 SW26010Pro Processor

Figure 1 depicts the hardware architecture of SW26010Pro. Each processor consists of six CGs, each containing one MPE, 64 CPEs, and one MC, with 16 GB of DDR4 memory accessible by both the MPE and CPEs. In bigshare mode, a single process can access up to 96 GB of memory per processor (6×16 GB). The processors communicate through a Network-on-Chip (NoC).

The MPE is a full-featured 64-bit RISC core responsible for I/O, communication, and CPE management. In contrast, each CPE is a simplified 64-bit RISC core designed for computational tasks. Each CPE has 256 KiB of user-controlled on-chip local data memory (LDM), which can be partitioned into an implicit data cache (D-cache) and an explicitly addressable scratchpad. The D-cache can be configured to 0 KiB, 32 KiB, or 128 KiB for data caching. The explicit scratchpad can hold global/static data, stacks, and other software-defined buffers. Transfers between LDM and main memory are handled by direct memory access (DMA).

Even though the D-cache can be configured up to 128 KiB, each CPE has only a 32 KiB instruction cache (I-cache), with no L2 or L3 I-cache. Compared with other heterogeneous accelerators, such as GPUs, a CPE functions as an independent general-purpose core for coarse-grained tasks. Performance optimizations, including explicit DMA/LDM operations and loop unrolling, expand the instruction working set, which exacerbates the I-cache constraint and increases I-cache miss rates.

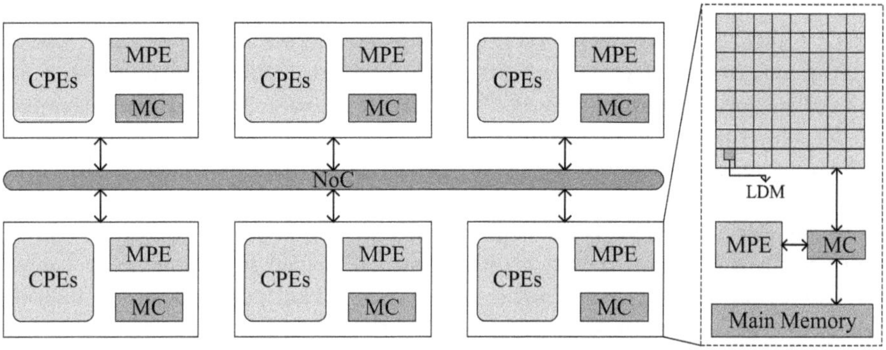

Fig. 1. The hardware architecture of the SW26010Pro processor.

2.2 Process Address Space

In bigshare mode, the process memory address space is divided into several regions, each with distinct visibility and usage semantics.

- Private-segment space: Mapped as read-write; visible only to the owning CPE; used for per-CPE private data.
- Read-only shared-segment space: Mapped as read-execute; visible to the MPE and CPEs of the associated CG and, in bigshare mode, to the MPE and all CPEs on the processor; stores MPE code, CPE code, and read-only data.
- Read-write shared-segment space: Mapped as read-write; has the same visibility as the read-only shared-segment space; stores writable shared data (i.e., the data segment).
- Cross-segment space: Mapped as read-write; visible to all MPEs and CPEs on the processor; intended for data requiring synchronization and sharing across CGs. This space is formed by interleaving portions of the DRAM regions associated with the six CGs, with a fixed interleave size of 256 B (a system-defined parameter that is not configurable from user space).

The base addresses of these spaces are system-defined and immutable, whereas their sizes are specified through job-submission parameters and interpreted by the loader. After job submission, the loader maps the program sections into their corresponding process spaces. Among these regions, the cross-segment space uniquely combines processor-wide visibility with fixed MC-level interleaving, making it an ideal candidate for addressing the MC imbalance observed in bigshare mode.

2.3 Related Work

Memory placement is a well-established concept in multi–MC architectures. Tools such as [7] and applications like [8,9] primarily control data-page placement at runtime, while [10] discusses replicating read-only code (e.g., OS kernel text) across multi-MC systems. However, in bigshare mode, user-level software cannot control how the execution image is placed across MCs, nor can it obtain a contiguous mapping within a target CG. Therefore, these runtime placement and replication techniques are not directly applicable. Instead, we repurpose the hardware-defined cross-segment space into an MC-balanced execution space, performing mapping redirection during program loading. This remaps the entire execution image to mitigate the single-MC bottleneck. While the general principle of memory placement is known, we demonstrate how to realize it in practice under SW26010Pro constraints to address the observed performance anomaly.

A link-time solution is infeasible because execution permissions are unavailable in the cross-segment space, which would require some code to remain in executable regions while placing other parts in the cross-segment space. This results in a large address distance between the two parts, leading to link-time errors. Run-time relocation is also infeasible, because some relocation information is hard-coded in the program. Working around this issue would require source-code modifications, making the solution non-universal. As shown in Sect. 3, both instruction fetches and data accesses contribute to the performance degradation. Therefore, the entire execution image should be placed in the cross-segment space. A loader-based solution naturally supports this requirement.

3 Microarchitectural Effects of Cross-Segment Execution

3.1 Experimental Methodology

This section characterizes cross-segment execution using instruction-fetch latency, data-access latency, and effective memory bandwidth. It also provides black-box evidence for our hypothesis that the performance degradation of bigshare mode is associated with increased MC-side pressure caused by asymmetric execution-image placement.

When programs are loaded using swcrun, the lower-order virtual address bits of program segments remain unchanged, so the I-cache and D-cache behavior matches that of the default loader. PMU measurements further show identical I-cache and D-cache miss ratios for the default loader and swcrun across all experiments. Thus, performance differences cannot be attributed to cache mapping effects. The cross-segment space enforces a fixed 256 B interleaving across six MCs, whose impact on latency and bandwidth remains unclear. We therefore use three microbenchmarks to measure instruction-fetch latency, data-access latency, and memory bandwidth under three configurations: normal mode, default bigshare mode, and bigshare mode with swcrun. In all cases, each CPE executes an identical workload, and results are averaged over multiple runs unless otherwise specified.

3.2 Latency

Instruction Fetch Latency. We measure the impact of cross-segment execution on instruction-fetch latency using a PMU counter that measures `I-cache miss time` (i.e., the cycles spent fetching instructions after I-cache misses). We synthesize code footprints with 2K–32K instructions (8–128 KiB, as each Sunway instruction is 4 B). Each footprint consists of functions containing only `mov` instructions that write constants to the zero register. Function lengths are randomly chosen in the range of 1–512 instructions. For each footprint, we generate a random sequence of 1024 function calls and repeatedly invoke it to obtain stable PMU measurements, characterizing steady-state instruction-fetch behavior.

Figure 2 shows the normalized `I-cache miss time` (normal mode = 1.0). With swcrun, the value remains close to 1.0 across all code footprints (ranging from 0.97 to 1.09). In contrast, bigshare mode consistently shows higher `I-cache miss time`, even when the footprint fits within the I-cache. At 8K instructions, the footprint approaches the CPE I-cache capacity, leaving little room for replacement. Under the randomized function-call pattern, many fetched instruction blocks may be evicted before reuse, substantially reducing the effectiveness of the I-cache. This is reflected in the PMU-reported `I-cache miss count`, where misses increase much more sharply from 4K to 8K ($\approx 19\times$) than from 8K to 16K ($\approx 8\times$).

Data Access Latency. To quantify the impact of cross-segment execution on data-access latency, we construct a microbenchmark that accesses a large array allocated in the cross-segment space. The array is aligned to 256 B, matching the interleaving granularity, so the serving MC can be determined from the address mapping. For a given CPE in one CG, we compare accesses to addresses mapped to its local CG with accesses to addresses mapped to each of the other five CGs. Accesses are issued in a random order using a pre-generated index sequence. To isolate raw memory-access latency, we disable the CPE's D-cache by setting `cache_size=0`. Latency is measured by dividing the total access cycles by the number of accesses.

We evaluate the five remote-CG cases separately and report the minimum and maximum latency, as well as the local-access latency. Compared to normal mode, the latency for accessing data mapped to the local CG remains unchanged, indicating that cross-segment execution does not increase local data-access latency. For remote-CG accesses, the latency increase varies by target CG, with increases

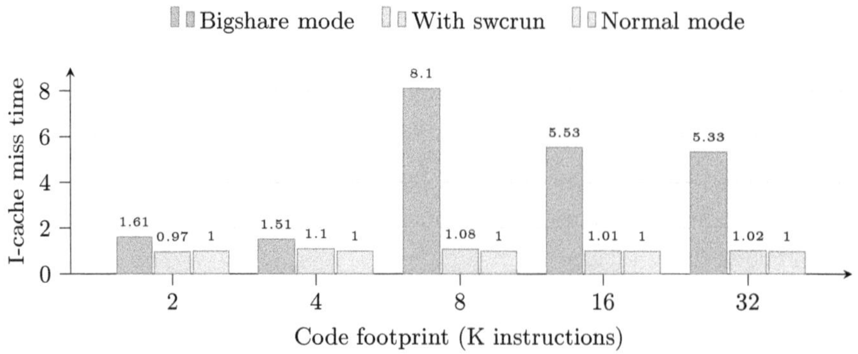

Fig. 2. Normalized I-cache miss time (normal mode = 1.0) versus code footprint (2K–32K instructions) for normal mode, bigshare mode, and bigshare mode with swcrun. The 32 KiB CPE I-cache capacity corresponds to 8K instructions.

ranging from 0% to about 10% relative to local accesses. A noticeable pattern in latency between MCs suggests that latency is influenced by the interconnect topology, but further discussion is outside the scope of this paper due to the lack of publicly available information on the MC interconnect structure. Nevertheless, the overall impact of cross-segment execution on data-access latency remains limited.

3.3 Bandwidth

We evaluate bandwidth by transferring data from main memory to each CPE's LDM via DMA, using a transfer size of 1024 B to achieve near-optimal bandwidth utilization [11]. The results of this experiment show that, in bigshare mode, the bandwidth initially matches that of normal mode, although it does not scale with the aggregate bandwidth of all six MCs as expected. After applying swcrun, the bandwidth increases sixfold as expected.

We further analyze the PMU data, using the `CH0_R8B` counter as an example. This counter represents the number of cycles required to read 8 B of data. In bigshare mode, only one MC shows significant activity for this metric, while the others remain close to zero. The value for the active MC was about 12× higher than that in normal mode. After applying swcrun, this metric appeared across all MCs, and the average value became comparable to that in normal mode, suggesting a more balanced distribution of memory access load.

4 Implementation

4.1 Design

Our goal is to enable correct program loading and execution in the cross-segment space, thereby addressing the performance problems in bigshare mode. In the standard configuration, the cross-segment space is non-executable because it is designed for cross-CG data sharing. Moreover, correct execution requires more than simply enabling execute permission: the loader must also update internal state and runtime metadata to preserve mapping, relocation, and startup semantics after remapping. Therefore, we design and implement swcrun, a new loader for cross-segment space execution. This approach requires no source-code modification or recompilation of individual source files; users only relink the program with the new linker script and launch the resulting executable with swcrun.

Because Sunway program loading is not publicly documented in sufficient detail, we derived swcrun by analyzing the default loader through debugging and system-call tracing, with documented loaders on other architectures as references. Our analysis shows that the Sunway loader is responsible not only for mapping program segments, but also for initializing the runtime environment and configuring CPE resources before execution. We next describe the implementation of swcrun, focusing on CPE device setup, program loading, and Sunway-specific segment handling.

4.2 Implementation of Swcrun

CPE Device Initialization and Configuration. On SW26010Pro, CPEs are exposed to user space via a device file and controlled through a combination of `ioctl()` operations and memory-mapped control/status registers. swcrun first opens the CPE device and obtains the corresponding file descriptor. For each CG, it issues an `ioctl()` to map the CPE control space into the process address space. Subsequent control and status operations are then performed through direct register accesses, thereby avoiding repeated system-call overhead. swcrun next initializes the execution context, queries CPE availability, selects the target CPEs, and configures them for execution. This configuration includes parameters such as the D-cache size and the amount of LDM reserved for cross-CPE sharing. Finally, swcrun sets the sizes of each segment space, resolves the entry address of the CPE start routine, and launches CPE execution. These steps preserve the runtime and CPE setup semantics expected by the default execution model while enabling execution from the cross-segment space.

Program Loading. Sunway programs use an ELF-compatible format. Accordingly, swcrun parses the program image and maps each segment to the appropriate virtual region. To enable execution from the cross-segment space, swcrun must configure execute permissions on both the MPE and CPE sides. On the MPE side, this is achieved with `mprotect()`, which updates page-level protection attributes. On the CPE side, access control follows a segment-based model, so the corresponding execute-permission bits must also be updated. Beyond segment mapping and permission setup, program loading on Sunway also involves runtime initialization. In particular, some runtime and library interfaces are dispatched through function pointers resolved at load time, and compiler-injected symbols (e.g., CPE identifiers and related runtime variables) must be resolved and patched after remapping.

Sunway-Specific Handling. Several architecture-specific components require explicit handling during startup. First, each CPE has a private-segment space for thread-local storage (TLS), created during CPE configuration. Accesses to TLS variables are implemented by reading a control and status register (CSR) to obtain the base address of the private segment and then adding a fixed offset. Although TLS contents can be initialized by copying values into each CPE's private segment, we found that a hardware-level address translation exists between the CSR-reported base address and the actual storage location. This prevents remapping TLS to the cross-segment space, so TLS remains in the private-segment space. Second, to support dynamic allocation from the cross-segment space, we implement a cross-segment allocator and wrap the CPE-side `malloc()`, so that heap allocations requested by CPE code are served from the cross-segment space. Third, in addition to functioning as a D-cache, LDM also hosts CPE data and stack. Because LDM is an on-chip scratchpad distinct from main memory, objects placed in LDM must be materialized by copying their initial values into each CPE's LDM at startup. When LDM is used as a stack, its placement must be carefully determined to ensure proper alignment, growth direction, and the absence of conflicts with other LDM-resident objects. Finally, because CPEs cannot issue system calls directly, Sunway forwards such requests to the MPE via signals. swcrun therefore installs the required signal handlers in the loader so that CPE-side requests, such as output operations, can be handled correctly and execution can resume afterward.

5 Evaluation

We evaluate swcrun using the swRodinia benchmark suite and SWBWA, a production bioinformatics application, and further examine its impact on multi-node communication. All experiments are conducted on nodes of the next-generation Sunway supercomputer. Unless otherwise stated, all configurations use the same software environment, runtime settings, and input datasets. Each experiment is repeated multiple times, and we report the mean performance.

5.1 SwRodinia

Rodinia [12] is a widely used benchmark suite for parallel and heterogeneous computing. Because it is not directly supported on Sunway, we use swRodinia [13], a Sunway port of Rodinia, and further adapt it to support execution in bigshare mode. Unless otherwise specified, each application is run with one MPE and 384 CPEs (one node), using swRodinia's default inputs and configuration except for enabling bigshare mode. Table 1 summarizes the evaluated applications. We also report the corresponding Berkeley Dwarf class [14,15], which characterizes applications by their dominant computation and communication patterns. We compare the default bigshare mode against bigshare mode with swcrun, and use the default bigshare configuration as the baseline. Correctness is verified by comparing the outputs with those produced by the baseline configuration.

Table 1. Application information.

Application	Dwarf	Description
backprop	Unstructured Grid	Machine-learning algorithm
bfs	Graph Traversal	Breadth-first search
hotspot3D	Structured Grid	3D thermal diffusion
jacobi	Sparse Linear Algebra	Iteratively solve $Ax = b$
kmeans	Dense Linear Algebra	Lloyd's k-means clustering
nn	Dense Linear Algebra	K-nearest neighbor search
nw	Dynamic Programming	Global sequence alignment
pathfinder	Dynamic Programming	Minimum-cost path in a grid
stencil	Structured Grid	7-point stencil computation

Figure 3 shows the resulting speedups, with baseline execution times ranging from milliseconds to seconds across the benchmarks. The benefit of swcrun is workload-dependent and can be explained by two dominant mechanisms: improved memory bandwidth and reduced instruction-fetch pressure. For memory-intensive kernels, the dominant benefit comes from improved memory bandwidth through more balanced MC utilization. This is illustrated by `backprop`: while swcrun improves performance by 5.04×, manually placing the working data in the cross-segment space reduces the additional benefit of swcrun to only 1.1×, indicating that most of the original gain comes from improved memory bandwidth. For kernels with relatively larger instruction footprints, such as `kmeans`, the dominant benefit comes from reduced instruction-fetch pressure. This interpretation is supported by the corresponding reduction in `I-cache miss time`. In contrast, kernels that exhibit neither strong data-bandwidth pressure nor substantial instruction-fetch pressure derive limited benefit. Overall, this workload-dependent interpretation explains the performance variation across applications in Fig. 3, and no slowdowns are observed in this set of experiments.

5.2 SWBWA

SWBWA [16] is a sequence-alignment tool designed for the Sunway platform. It relies on bigshare mode because its memory demand can exceed the per-process memory capacity available in normal mode. In addition, SWBWA produces a single output file; under normal mode, generating this file would require MPI-based result aggregation, increasing implementation complexity and potentially reducing efficiency.

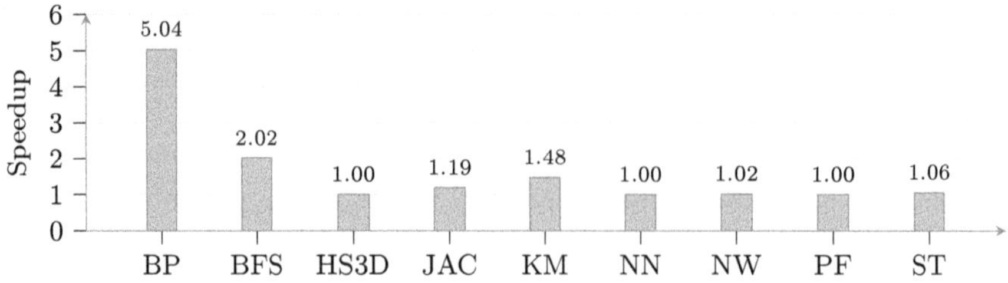

Fig. 3. Speedup of swcrun over the bigshare baseline for the evaluated swRodinia kernels (baseline = bigshare without swcrun). Abbreviations: BP = backprop, HS3D = hotspot3D, JAC = jacobi, KM = kmeans, PF = pathfinder, and ST = stencil

We evaluate swcrun on three datasets from NCBI, where read length is reported in base pairs (bp): D1 (SRR2496709, 12M reads, 100 bp, DNA targeted sequencing), D2 (SRR12131337, 20M reads, 141 bp, RNA sequencing), and D3 (ERR1203383, 15M reads, 75 bp, whole-exome sequencing), covering different sources, sequencing technologies, read lengths, and sequence counts, in order to assess performance across diverse input characteristics. To enable a direct comparison across execution modes, we use datasets small enough for SWBWA to run as a single process. We use the single-process runtime as the baseline and compare it against three configurations: (i) MPI with six processes (one per CG), each using 64 CPEs; (ii) default bigshare mode; and (iii) bigshare mode with swcrun.

Figure 4 reports speedups relative to the single-process baseline. Although bigshare mode activates all CPEs, its average speedup is only 2.89×, indicating substantial efficiency loss and further confirming the performance issues observed in bigshare mode. Our analysis suggests that instruction fetching on the CPEs is a major bottleneck for SWBWA: the application has a large CPE instruction footprint and frequent control-flow changes, both of which likely increase I-cache miss pressure and instruction-fetch latency. With swcrun, the average speedup increases to 5.29×, suggesting that cross-segment execution effectively alleviates this bottleneck.

The observed performance difference between swcrun and the MPI configuration can be explained by their different work partitioning strategies. In the MPI configuration, SWBWA uses static file-based partitioning to reduce communication overhead. In bigshare mode, however, SWBWA uses an atomic counter to assign reads dynamically to CPEs. When read lengths are similar, static partitioning typically achieves good load balance, in which case swcrun may incur extra overhead from dynamic scheduling. When static partitioning becomes imbalanced, however, swcrun can achieve better performance because dynamic assignment balances work more effectively. The comparison with MPI is also influenced by output handling. In our current setup, each MPI rank writes its own output file, so inter-process communication is limited and result aggregation is avoided. Supporting a single output file would require additional aggregation and coordinated I/O across ranks, which SWBWA does not include in the current implementation. Bigshare mode naturally supports the single-process output model, allowing SWBWA to produce a single output file within one process.

5.3 Multi-node Communication

We use IMB-MPI1 from the Intel MPI Benchmarks (IMB) suite [17] to evaluate MPI communication performance. It covers representative blocking and non-blocking point-to-point operations, as well as collective operations, each evaluated over a predefined range of message sizes. We compare communication performance with swcrun against the default bigshare mode, using 2, 4, and 8 nodes.

In the point-to-point tests, swcrun exhibits size-dependent performance behavior. For messages smaller than 1 KiB, performance is comparable to, or up to about 8% slower than, the default bigshare mode. This behavior depends on whether the message buffer resides on the local CG and is consistent with the results in Sect. 3.2: cross-CG accesses incur additional access latency, which becomes more visible when the communication is dominated by per-message overhead. As message sizes increase, communication becomes increasingly bandwidth-bound, allowing the higher effective bandwidth enabled by swcrun to take effect. For example, for a 4 MiB message, swcrun achieves about 30% higher performance. Some collective operations, such as Allgather and Bcast, show a similar pattern: slightly worse performance (up to 8%) for small messages and better performance (about 7%) for large messages.

However, swcrun performs worse for certain collective operations, such as Allreduce and Barrier. For example, Barrier shows an average slowdown of 10.6%. We speculate that these operations involve frequent accesses to communication buffers or synchronization variables, making them more sensitive to cross-CG access latency.

This issue can be mitigated with additional engineering efforts. For operations such as Allreduce, where users can pass buffer pointers explicitly, placing the relevant data in the shared-segment space reduces cross-CG access overhead. In a preliminary implementation, we verified that this optimization can recover performance to the level of the default bigshare mode. For Barrier, whose synchronization state is managed internally, addressing the issue would likely require modifications to the MPI implementation. We leave these optimizations to future work.

6 Conclusion

This work demonstrates that the performance degradation of bigshare mode on the Sunway SW26010Pro processor can be plausibly explained by asymmetric execution-image placement, which concentrates instruction and data traffic on a single MC. By repurposing the architecture-defined cross-segment space for program execution, swcrun restores balanced MC utilization and translates

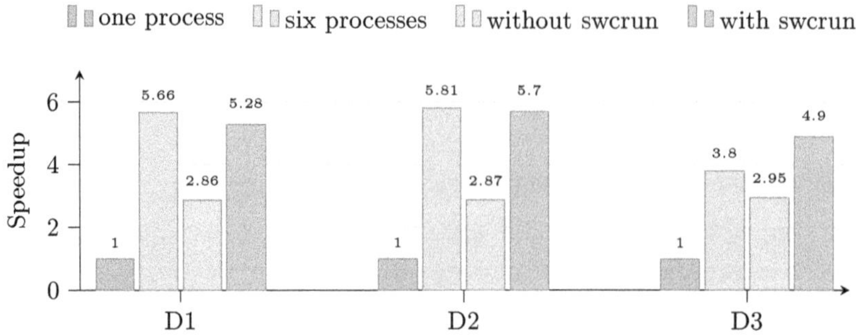

Fig. 4. Speedup of SWBWA under different execution modes on three datasets (baseline: one-process execution).

this architectural opportunity into practical performance gains without requiring source-code modifications.

Our experiments indicate that swcrun is particularly effective for single-node bigshare workloads. In practice, a noticeable performance drop of a single CPE under bigshare mode relative to normal mode may indicate asymmetric execution-image placement, for which swcrun provides an effective, low-intrusion solution. swcrun can be adopted without recompilation, requiring only relinking and execution with the new loader. For multi-node execution, however, the benefit depends on whether communication is more bandwidth-bound or latency-bound, and collective operations such as `Allreduce` may require additional optimizations to fully realize the benefit of swcrun. As future work, we plan to introduce an MPI wrapper layer to better control communication buffer placement and optimize collective operations in multi-node execution.

Disclosure of Interests. The authors have no competing interests to declare that are relevant to the content of this article.

References

1. Fu, H., et al.: The sunway taihulight supercomputer: system and applications. SCIENCE CHINA Inf. Sci. **59**, 1–16 (2016)
2. Chen, Y., Li, K., Yang, W., Xiao, G., Xie, X., Li, T.: Performance-aware model for sparse matrix-matrix multiplication on the sunway taihulight supercomputer. IEEE Trans. Parallel Distrib. Syst. **30**(4), 923–938 (2018)
3. Ao, Y., Yang, C., Liu, F., Yin, W., Jiang, L., Sun, Q.: Performance optimization of the HPCG benchmark on the sunway taihulight supercomputer. ACM Trans. Archit. Code Optim. (TACO) **15**(1), 1–20 (2018)
4. Liu, Y., et al.: Closing the "quantum supremacy" gap: achieving real-time simulation of a random quantum circuit using a new sunway supercomputer. In: Proceedings of the International Conference for High Performance Computing, Networking, Storage and Analysis, pp. 1–12 (2021)

5. Fu, Y., et al.: Towards exascale computation for turbomachinery flows. In: SC23: International Conference for High Performance Computing, Networking, Storage and Analysis, pp. 1–12. IEEE Computer Society (2023)
6. Wei, J., et al.: A performance-portable kilometer-scale global ocean model on orise and new sunway heterogeneous supercomputers. In: SC24: International Conference for High Performance Computing, Networking, Storage and Analysis, pp. 1–12. IEEE (2024)
7. numactl contributors: numactl: NUMA support for Linux (2024). https://github.com/numactl/numactl. Accessed 05 Mar 2026
8. Zhang, K., Chen, R., Chen, H.: Numa-aware graph-structured analytics. In: Proceedings of the 20th ACM SIGPLAN Symposium on Principles and Practice of Parallel Programming, pp. 183–193 (2015)
9. Psaroudakis, I., Scheuer, T., May, N., Sellami, A., Ailamaki, A.: Adaptive NUMA-aware data placement and task scheduling for analytical workloads in main-memory column-stores. Proc. VLDB Endow. **10**(2), 37–48 (2016)
10. Corbet, J.: Kernel-text replication on NUMA systems. LWN.net (2024). https://lwn.net/Articles/956900/. Accessed 05 Mar 2026
11. Zhu, Q., Luo, H., Yang, C., Ding, M., Yin, W., Yuan, X.: Enabling and scaling the HPCG benchmark on the newest generation sunway supercomputer with 42 million heterogeneous cores. In: Proceedings of the International Conference for High Performance Computing, Networking, Storage and Analysis, pp. 1–13 (2021)
12. Che, S., et al.: Rodinia: a benchmark suite for heterogeneous computing. In: 2009 IEEE International Symposium on Workload Characterization (IISWC), pp. 44–54. IEEE (2009)
13. Chen, B., et al.: *swRodinia*: a benchmark suite for exploiting architecture properties of sunway processor. In: Wolf, F., Gao, W. (eds.) Bench 2020. LNCS, vol. 12614, pp. 22–38. Springer, Cham (2021). https://doi.org/10.1007/978-3-030-71058-3_2
14. Asanovic, K., et al.: The landscape of parallel computing research: a view from Berkeley, EECS department. University of California, Berkeley, pp. 2006–183 (2006)
15. Asanovic, K., et al.: A view of the parallel computing landscape. Commun. ACM **52**(10), 56–67 (2009)
16. Yan, L., et al.: Swbwa: a highly efficient NGS aligner on the new sunway architecture. In: European Conference on Parallel Processing, pp. 183–196. Springer (2025)
17. Intel® MPI Benchmarks User Guide, Intel Corporation (2021), version 2021.2. https://cdrdv2-public.intel.com/766173/mpi-library_user-guide-benchmarks_2021.2-766171-766173.pdf

Taking the Leap: Efficient and Reliable Fine-Grained NUMA Migration in User-Space

Felix Schuhknecht(✉) and Nick Rassau

Johannes Gutenberg-University Mainz, 55122 Mainz, Germany
{schuhknecht,rassau}@uni-mainz.de

Abstract. Modern multi-socket architectures offer a single virtual address space, but physically divide main-memory across multiple regions, where each region is attached to a CPU and its cores. While this simplifies the usage, developers must be aware of non-uniform memory access (NUMA), where an access by a thread running on a core-local NUMA region is significantly cheaper than an access from a core-remote region. For example, if the query answering within a database system is parallelized across the cores of multiple regions, then the portion of the database on which the query is operating should be distributed across the same regions to ensure local accesses. As the present data placement might not fit this, migrating pages from one NUMA region to another can be performed to improve the situation. To do so, different options exist: One option is to rely on automatic NUMA balancing integrated in Linux, which is steered by the observed access patterns and frequency. Another option is to actively trigger migration via the system call `move_pages()`. Unfortunately, both variants have significant downsides in terms of their feature set and performance. As an alternative, we propose a new user-space migration method called `page_leap()` that can perform page migration asynchronously at a high performance by exploiting features of the virtual memory subsystem. The method is (a) actively triggered by the user, (b) ensures that all pages are eventually migrated, (c) handles concurrent writes correctly, (d) supports pooled memory, (e) adaptively adjusts its migration granularity based on the workload, and (f) supports both small pages and huge pages.

Keywords: Memory migration · Non-uniform memory access (NUMA) · Virtual Memory · Data management

1 Introduction

Multi-socket server architectures offer a single virtual address space, but physically divide main-memory across multiple regions, where each region is attached to a CPU and its cores. While this single virtual address space simplifies development, programmers must still be cautious: If a thread accesses physical memory

M. Torquati et al. (Eds.): Euro-Par 2026, LNCS 16781, pp. 314–328, 2027.
https://doi.org/10.1007/978-3-032-35248-4_22

on a NUMA region that is different from the one of the core on which it currently runs, then this *remote access* is significantly more expensive than a *local access*. Consequently, these so-called *non-uniform memory accesses (NUMA)* [4] must be taken into account when aiming for high performance. For example, in database management systems (DBMSs), if query answering is parallelized across the cores of multiple regions, then the portion of the database on which the query is operating should be distributed across the same regions to ensure local accesses. Unfortunately, the current data placement might not fit this parallelization. To improve upon the situation, individual physical memory pages can be *migrated* from one NUMA region to another at runtime to bring them closer to the worker thread and thus speed up future accesses.

To perform migration, there are two different options: (1) To rely on the *implicit page migration* mechanism of the OS, which is carried out automatically and transparently by the kernel. The core concept is that the OS monitors the number of accesses and access patterns on allocated memory regions at a certain frequency. If it observes a sufficient amount of remote accesses, it might decide to migrate pages to a different region. Of course, migrating pages is costly, but it might pay off in the future, so the heuristic aims at balancing this tradeoff. Linux calls the concept of implicit page migration *auto NUMA balancing* [5], which on many distributions is activated by default (`/proc/sys/kernel/numa_balancing` set to `1`) and works for anonymous memory allocations backed by small pages and transparent huge pages, e.g., as created by `mmap()`. While automatic NUMA balancing works transparently, it has two downsides: (a) The user does not have any control over when page migration happens and whether it happens at all. As our evaluation will show, frequent concurrent modifications, as they are common in DBMSs facing transactional workloads, make auto NUMA balancing often "wait" for times of little load to do the migration, which might actually never come. This leads to continuous stream of unnecessary remote accesses. Also, (b) the migration is performed into freshly allocated memory and does not allow migration into already allocated, pooled memory. This causes costly page faults, rendering the migration unnecessarily expensive if the application anyways pools memory, like DBMSs often do. These problems lead us to the second type of page migration mechanism, namely (2) *explicit page migration* methods. In this case, the migration of pages is actively triggered by the programmer by calling a corresponding function and by specifying the pages to migrate. In Linux, this migration function is the ancient `move_pages()` system call, which is wrapped by the `numa_move_pages()` method [9] from `libnuma`. It allows to migrate a specified subset of the currently allocated pages from user-space. While this system call provides control over the migration, it unfortunately also comes with problems: (a) There is no option to adjust the migration granularity; it always happens at page size. If a large number of pages must be migrated, this can heavily penalize the calling thread. (b) There is still no guarantee that the page migration of all pages is performed. If a page is currently busy (i.e. the subsystem is holding a reference to the page) or the page became dirty during migration, it could simply not migrate it. (c) Just like auto NUMA balancing, it does not allow migration into pooled memory and hence suffers from page faults.

1.1 User-Space Remapping: page_leap()

Ideally, we would like to have a migration method that is controllable from user-space, migrates all requested pages with certainty, and supports migration into pooled memory. Further, the method should be thread-safe and tolerate concurrent modifications. In the following, we propose exactly such a method, which we call `page_leap()`. The core concept is based on the technique of memory rewiring [17] by which the mapping from virtual to physical memory can be manipulated from user-space at runtime. To perform a page migration, we carry out two steps: one on the physical level and one on the virtual level. On the physical level, the page content is non-atomically copied from the source NUMA region to the destination NUMA region, potentially into already-pooled memory. On the virtual level, the virtual page is then atomically remapped to the physical page of the destination region, rendering it "active". To detect and handle concurrent writes that would invalidate an ongoing page migration, we use a segmentation fault handler that invalidates the migration of the page and triggers a new migration attempt until eventually all pages have been migrated. Our approach also supports different migration granularities that are adaptively adjusted based on the observed workload. Table 1 summarizes the features of `page_leap()` in comparison with auto NUMA balancing and `move_pages()`.

Table 1. Feature comparison of auto NUMA balancing, `move_pages()`, and our proposed method `page_leap()`.

Method	Pooling	Controlled	Reliable	Adaptive
Auto NUMA	×	×	×	×
`move_pages()`	×	✓	×	×
`page_leap()` (ours)	✓	✓	✓	✓

2 Understanding the Problem

Let us first analyze the impact of NUMA placement and the current solution for manual page migration.

2.1 Experimental Environment and Setup

For the upcoming experimental evaluation, we use a two-socket server equipped with two Intel Xeon Gold 6326 CPUs running Alma Linux with a vanilla kernel

5.14. Each NUMA region has 128 GB of RAM, resulting in 256 GB in total. Auto NUMA balancing is activated by setting `/proc/sys/kernel/numa_balancing` to `1`) The code, which is available at https://gitlab.rlp.net/fschuhkn/efficient_numa_page_migration, is compiled with g++11.4 on optimization level O3. All reported runtimes are the average of five runs, although we observe little to no variance across runs. For all upcoming experiments, we pin the main thread of the process, which performs all measured accesses to the memory, to the first core of NUMA region 1 using the `taskset -c 1` command [10]. This means that NUMA region 0 will be the remote region, while NUMA region 1 will be the local region in the following. To use huge pages for `page_leap()`, a `hugetlbfs` filesystem must be mounted and a sufficient number of huge pages on each NUMA region must be pre-allocated. The same holds for `move_pages()`, which we extended accordingly. Auto NUMA balancing relies on transparent huge pages, as it does not support migrating `hugetlbfs` huge pages.

2.2 Local Accesses vs Remote Accesses

We start by analyzing how much more expensive remote accesses actually are over local accesses on the present machine. To do so, we allocate a memory area of 4 GB on NUMA region 0 (remote) respectively NUMA region 1 (local) using the `mbind()` method which permanently binds the memory to the corresponding region. This is also the setup used for all following experiments. After initializing the memory with random integers, we perform a set of accesses on the region from our main thread running on NUMA region 1. We test four different access patterns (sequential read/writes and random read/writes) to see whether the pattern has an impact on the cost. For sequential reads/writes, we simply access each byte from the start of the area to the end, resulting in around 4.2 billion sequential accesses in total. For random reads/writes, we access 10M randomly selected bytes. Figure 1 shows the results for both small pages and huge pages. We can observe that for all access patterns, remote accesses are indeed significantly more expensive than local accesses, justifying the need for local accesses and hence efficient NUMA migration. Interestingly, the difference between remote and local accesses is for sequential accesses as pronounces as for random accesses, indicating that prefetching under a sequential access pattern cannot hide the cost of remote accesses.

2.3 Page Migration Using `move_pages()`

We next evaluate `move_pages()` for explicit page migration. To asses the overhead of `move_pages()`, we first compare it against simply copying the content of all pages from one NUMA region to the other via traditional `memcpy()`. As every migration method has at least to physically copy the content of all pages, this baseline should be the optimum any migration method can reach. Here, we differentiate between copying into fresh memory, i.e., the copying is the first access to the memory triggering page-faults, and copying into pooled and hence already page-faulted memory. Note that `memcpy()` is no proper replacement for

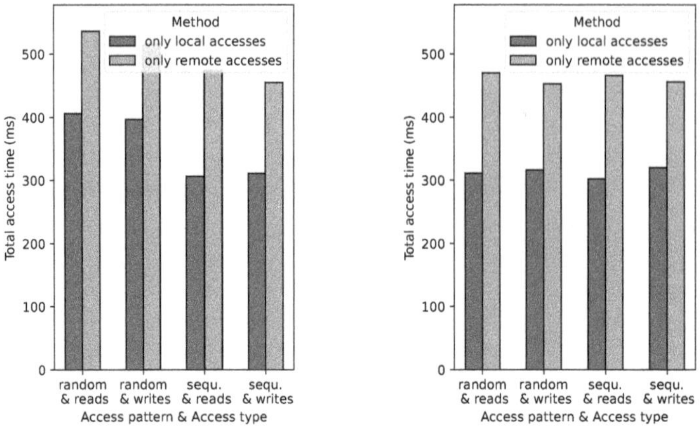

(a) Small pages. (b) Huge pages.

Fig. 1. Local accesses vs remote accesses under different access patterns for small pages and huge pages.

`move_pages()` or any other migration method due to two limitations: (1) It results in a new virtual location of the data. Hence, all components using the memory must update their references. In contrast, using a migration method, the migration is completely transparent. (2) Concurrent writes by another thread to the "old" page during the `memcpy()` would violate correctness. Figure 2 shows the results for both small pages and huge pages. We can see that `move_pages()` is ×1.39 faster than `memcpy()` into fresh memory for small pages and ×2.31 faster for huge pages. This changes, when `memcpy()` targets into page-faulted memory. In that case `memcpy()` peaks at ×7.24 for small pages and ×2.41 for huge pages. This can be explained by the fact that `memcpy()`, which runs in user-space, receives fresh memory that must be zeroed by the OS, while `move_pages()`, which runs in kernel-space, can skip this step (this is safe as it overwrites the claimed memory entirely during migration). Overall, this shows that for both small pages and huge pages, there is clearly something to gain over `move_pages()` when using pooled memory.

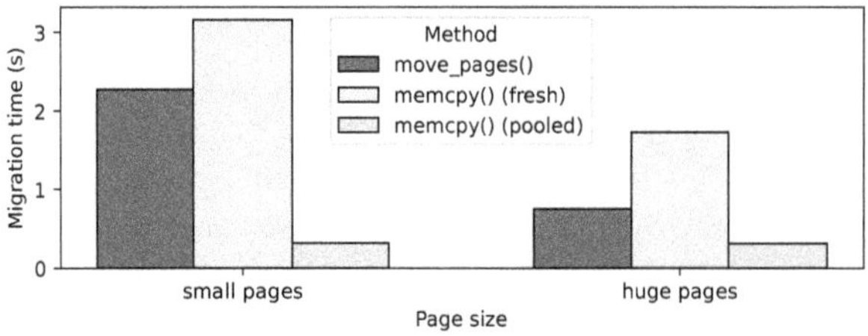

Fig. 2. Migration time of `move_pages()` vs `memcpy()` from one NUMA region to the other for small and huge pages.

3 page_leap() Architecture

The core concept of page migration in `page_leap()` exploits the separation of virtual memory from physical memory in user-space and has been implemented in a few hundred lines of C++ code. If the virtual page `vpage0` currently maps to a physical page `ppage0` that is allocated on NUMA region 0, we essentially perform two simple steps to migrate: First, we allocate a physical page `ppage1` on NUMA region 1 from the pool of that region and copy the content from the source physical page to this target physical page using `memcpy()`. Second, after copying, we remap the virtual page `vpage0` to the physical page `ppage1` automatically using `mmap()`, such that subsequent accesses will hit `ppage1` on NUMA region 1.

To be able to perform such a remapping in the first place, we utilize a technique called memory rewiring [15,17,18], which introduces a handle to physical memory in user-space in the form of so-called main-memory files. Using `mmap()`, virtual pages can be (re)mapped to offsets in the main-memory file, which hence allows to freely adjust the mapping between virtual and physical memory at runtime. A nice side-effect of this technique is that the remapping can happen at the granularity of multiple neighboring pages, reducing the number of performed `mmap()` calls for areas that are a multiple of the page size.

3.1 Correctly Handling Concurrent Writes

So far, if a write is performed to a portion of the source physical page that has already been copied then after remapping to the target physical page, the write would be lost. To handle this situation, we must (a) detect any write to an area that is currently under copying. If detected, (b) we must invalidate the copied area and retry the migration. To achieve (a) without forcing the user to actively delegate all writes through a special interface, we use signal handling to do the job. Precisely, we set the protection of the area to migrate to read-only using the `mprotect()` system call, as shown in Fig. 3a for the page `v2`. By this, a write attempt to the area triggers a segmentation fault, which we can then catch with a custom segmentation fault handler [14,19]. This handler is a pre-registered, but otherwise normal user-space function that is called by the OS when the segmentation occurs, and which receives the virtual memory address of the attempted write. In this handler, we then mark the area as *dirty* in a helper structure, reset its protection to writable, and return to retry the write attempt, which now succeeds. To take care of (b), when the copying of a area has been performed and is about to become real via remapping, we first check whether it became dirty or not, as shown in Fig. 3b. Only if it did not become dirty, we perform the remapping. Otherwise, we insert the dirty area into a queue to retry the migration, where we can adaptively split the area to increase its chance of migration-success as explained in the next section. The process terminates as soon as all pages have been migrated or a specified timeout is reached. Note that this is an advantage over `move_pages()`, which does not guarantee that all pages are migrated.

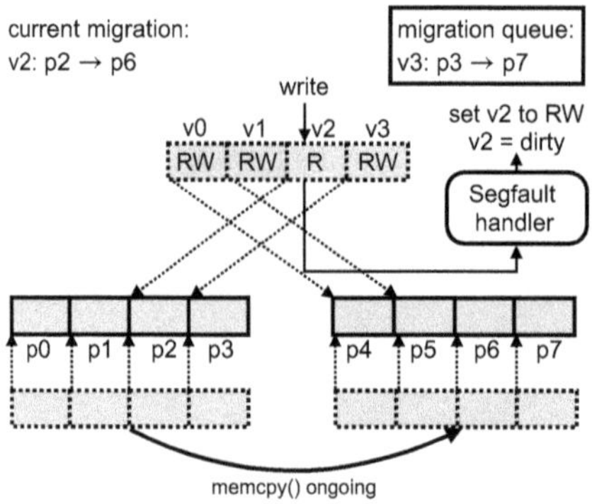

(a) A write to area **v2** is happening that is currently being copied via **memcpy()**. This triggers a segmentation fault, which is caught by our custom handler. This flags the area as dirty.

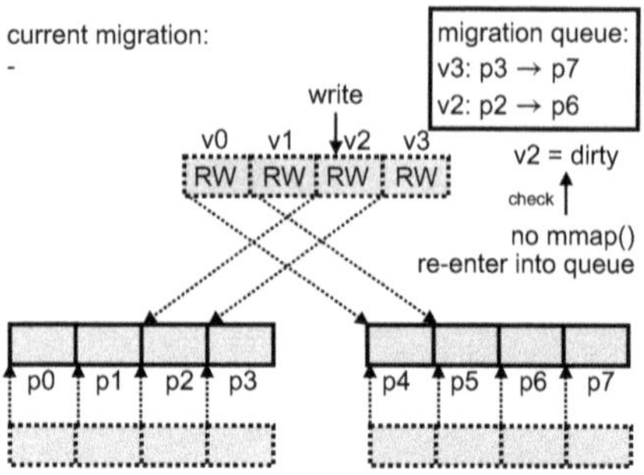

(b) Before the remapping is performed, it is checked whether the area became dirty in the meantime. This is the case, so no remapping is performed, and the area is re-queued for a later migration.

Fig. 3. Correctly handling concurrent writes for four pages, where the third page is currently under migration.

3.2 Adaptive Area Size

As `page_leap()` can migrate at arbitrary area sizes that are a multiple of the page size, a question is how to choose the area size: A size too small might cause unnecessary overhead due to repetitive required system calls, whereas a size too large increases the likelihood of areas becoming dirty, causing retries. To handle the problem without requiring knowledge about the workload and its pressure in terms of modifications, `page_leap()` implements an adaptive solution: The user must only select an initial area size to start from—in the experimental evaluation, we will identify such a suitable initial size. Then, during migration, if an area becomes dirty and must be retried, `page_leap()` splits the area into multiple smaller areas based on a reduction factor to increase the chance of success. By this, `page_leap()` automatically adjusts its area size and hence migration granularity to the pressure of the workload. Additionally, skewed modifications on subsets of the dataset will reduce the area size only for the areas under pressure.

4 Migration Without Concurrent Writes

In Fig. 4, we start by evaluating the migration time of `page_leap()` against `move_pages()` for small pages and huge pages without any concurrent accesses happening, resembling the best case for both methods. For both methods, we report the time until the migration is fully completed. For `page_leap()`, we test for small pages eleven different initial area sizes (4 KB to 256 MB) and for huge pages seven sizes (2 MB to 256 MB). Note that area sizes larger than 256 MB did not show any further improvement but only increase the chance of retries. As no concurrent accesses are happening in this experiment, no retries are happening and hence no adaptive adjustment of area sizes takes places here. Auto NUMA balancing is not included in this comparison, as there are no accesses that could trigger a migration – we will include and discuss it in Sect. 5. As a baseline, we show the migration time of raw `memcpy()` as the theoretical optimum.

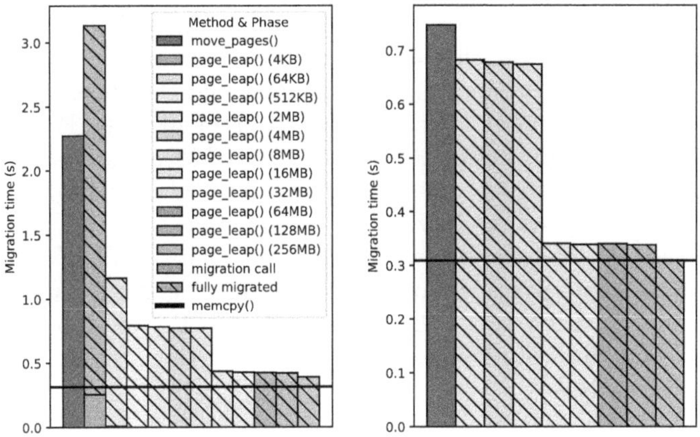

(a) Small pages (pooled). (b) Huge pages (pooled).

Fig. 4. `move_pages()` vs `page_leap()` without concurrent accesses for different granularities and page sizes. `memcpy()` resembles the theoretical optimum.

We can see that for both pages sizes, `page_leap()` is able to outperform `move_pages()` in nearly all configurations. Only for the 4 KB area size, the system call overhead becomes too dominant. For area sizes of 64 KB and 16 MB for small pages and huge pages respectively, `page_leap()` outperforms `move_pages()` already by a factor of two or more, demonstrating the superiority of `page_leap()` for migration without concurrent accesses. We can also observe plateaus within each plot, showing improvement jumps at 512 KB, and 16 MB. This indicates that these area sizes are very good candidates for the initial area sizes to start from under adaptive splitting. Also, we can observe that `page_leap()` reaches the optimum of `memcpy()` for both page sizes at an area size of 16 MB already, showing that `page_leap()` becomes dominated by the copying phase.

5 Migration Under Concurrent Writes

Next, we inspect the performance under concurrent writes, where for `page_leap()`, potential additional costs from signal handling and retrying migrations comes into play. For each method, we asynchronously perform the migration while we fire a continuous burst of uniformly selected random writes on the memory, specified at a requested throughput in writes/s. As representatives for a low, high, and extreme pressure case, we test 10 K, 100 K, and 10M (small pages) respectively 100M (huge pages) writes/s. Additionally, we include a skewed workload where out of 100 K writes/s, 75% concentrate only on 128 MB (3.125%) of the memory. Firing the burst serves two purposes: First, we see how the migration of each method is negatively affected by the concurrent burst, i.e., by slowing down migration, increasing the number of retries, or even leaving pages un-migrated. Second, we see whether the migration also negatively impacts the write burst and at which point the requested throughput cannot be sustained anymore. Note that as soon as the migration finishes or a timeout occurs after 10 s, the write burst also terminates and the experiment ends. We then also report the current location or error status of all pages. For `page_leap()`, we again show for completeness all previously tested area sizes, but focus on the most promising previously identified sizes of 512 KB and 16 MB, where the stated area sizes are now *initial* area sizes – in combination with the used reduction factor of 2, the retry of an area now automatically splits it in half and retries the migration of the two halves. For auto NUMA balancing, since it does not signal its start or finish in any way, we check every 100 ms whether all pages have been migrated already and stop the measurement if yes. Otherwise, we continue until the timeout is reached.

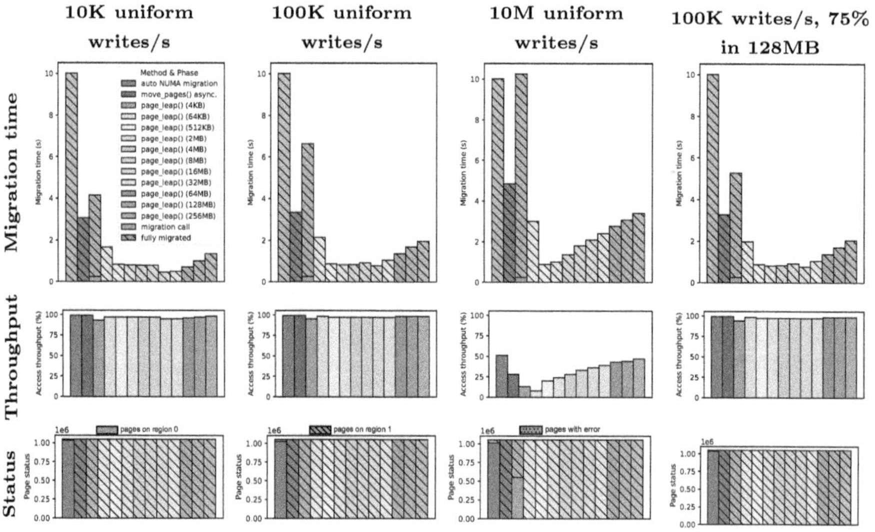

Fig. 5. Migration under concurrent writes for small pages and a reduction factor 2 for `page_leap()`.

We first look at the results for small pages in Fig. 5, where we report the migration time, the actually achieved throughput as a percentage of the requested throughput, and the page status. When comparing the migration time first, we can see that for all workloads, `page_leap()` manages to significantly outperform both `move_pages()` and auto NUMA balancing for a large number of initial area sizes. The previously determined 16 MB clearly performs best for the 10 K and 100 K writes/s cases, whereas for the extreme case of 10M requested writes/s, an initial area size of 512 KB performs best. For the skewed case, both area sizes perform equally well. Hence, for small pages, we recommend to generally run `page_leap()` with an initial area size of 16 MB to hit the sweet spot—under normal pressure, we then exploit the effectiveness of larger copies and fewer remappings, while under extreme pressure, the method is still able to quickly enough adapt to smaller area sizes to still outperform the alternatives. When inspecting the achieved throughput of writes, we can see that all methods handle the low and high pressure cases well and stay close to 100%. Only under extreme pressure, the throughput cannot be sustained anymore. Regarding the page status, `page_leap()` (for reasonable initial area sizes) and `move_pages()` always manage to migrate all pages before the timeout occurs. Auto NUMA balancing performs poorly for all workloads, as it migrates only a small portion of the pages. For huge pages in Fig. 6, we can see that for the low pressure, high pressure, and skewed case, `page_leap()` for an initial area size of 16MB still outperforms `move_pages()` by up to 2x, but the advantage is overall smaller. Due to the larger underlying page size, all methods now operate closer to the theoretical copying optimum. We have to admit that `move_pages()` shows a more robust performance for the extreme case—however, it also achieves a lower throughput. Also, although that auto NUMA balancing times out, at the end, all pages have been migrated. This shows that for huge pages, where a smaller number of pages is in use, auto NUMA balancing utilizes the "pause" after the write burst has ended and actually migrates the pages. Still, it again shows its unpredictability in terms of when and if at all the migration actually happens.

Next, in Table 2, we quantify the actual overhead of `page_leap()` under concurrent writes for the case of 100 K writes/s. To do so, we first measure for different area sizes the total amount of memory `page_leap()` actually has to copy, including the memory additionally copied during retries. Then, we measure how long it takes to copy the same amount of memory via `memcpy()` from one region to the other. Here, we make sure to also copy areas individually. We then report the difference in time, which essentially resembles the overhead of `page_leap()` for everything that happens on top of the raw copying. Table 2 shows the memory overhead and time overhead for both page sizes, where we include the (impractical) extremes of 4 KB and 256 MB as well as the recommended initial area sizes of 512 KB and 16 MB. For the 4 KB case, we can clearly see that the system call overhead is the bottleneck, as no retries are happening at all. For 256 MB, around 420% are additionally copied, leading to a 27.5% respectively 18.3% time overhead. The recommended sizes, however, keep both memory and time overhead at most around 50% over `memcpy()`, demonstrating the efficiency of `page_leap()` for reasonably chosen initial area sizes.

So far, we have analyzed the access throughput purely while the migration is happening by stopping the fired burst as soon as the migration has ended (or the

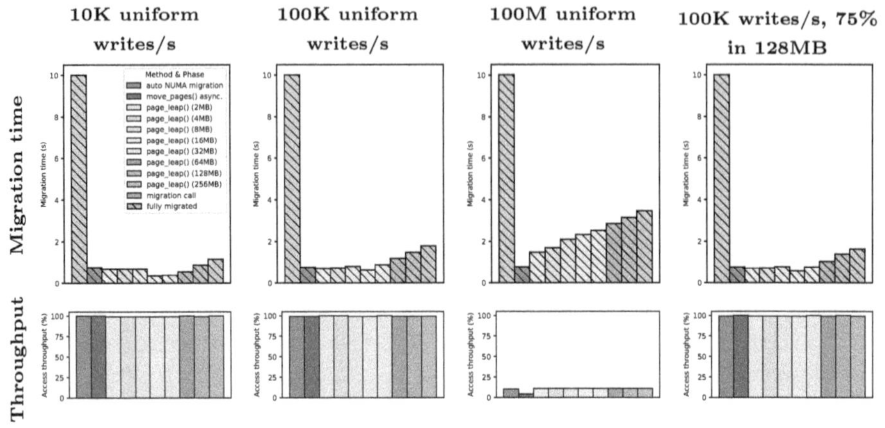

Fig. 6. Migration under concurrent writes for huge pages and a reduction factor 2 for `page_leap()`. The page status is omitted here as all methods fully migrated all pages in all cases (100% on region 1).

Table 2. Time overhead and memory overhead over `memcpy()`

Area	Small pages		Huge pages	
	Memory	Time	Memory	Time
4 KB	0 MB (0.0%)	5635 ms (659%)	–	–
512 KB	**5.5 MB (0.13%)**	**210 ms (31.3%)**	–	–
2 MB	42 MB (1.02%)	155 ms (22.9%)	66 MB (1.61%)	34 ms (5.1%)
16 MB	**2.1 GB (52.5%)**	**245 ms (47.5%)**	**1.8 GB (45%)**	**135 ms (28.4%)**
256 MB	17.1 GB (427.5%)	437 ms (27.5%)	16.80 GB (420%)	274 ms (18.3%)

timeout occurs). To now also measure the positive impact of a fast migration, namely being able to perform local accesses earlier, we adjust the experiment to fire the write burst for the whole 10 s, independent of when the migration finishes. Figure 7 shows the results for small pages while varying the requested throughput. We can see that when increasing the requested throughput, `page_leap()` is able to sustain it significantly longer than both baselines and constantly performs best: For instance, at 6M requested writes/s, `page_leap()` can still fully sustain the throughput, while auto NUMA balancing achieves only 65% of it. This shows that migrating as fast as possible significantly pays off as less remote accesses happen over the total duration.

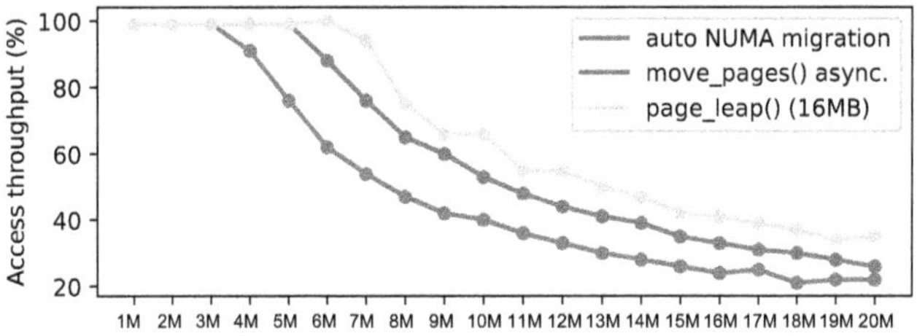

Fig. 7. Achieved write/s throughput for a run of 10 s.

6 Handling Database Workloads

Finally, let us evaluate how **page_leap()** handles actual database workloads. We evaluate a scenario as it could occur in a morsel-driven database engine [1] that semantically partitions its database across two NUMA regions, where a thread of one region is currently idling, while all morsels that still need to be processed are located on the other region. In this situation, the thread can migrate the morsels over to region 1 to speed up the query processing.

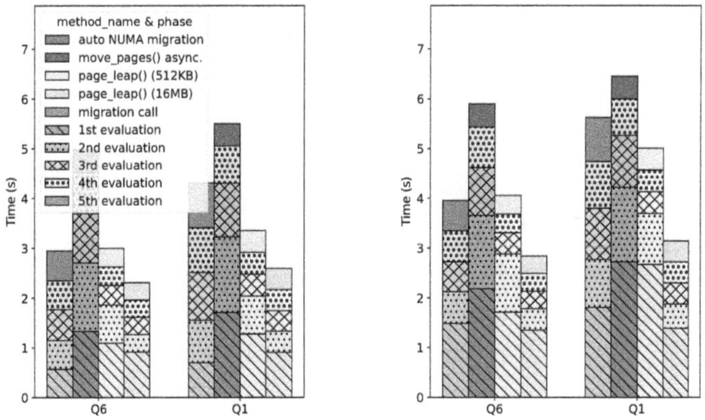

(a) Without concurrent writes. (b) With concurrent writes.

Fig. 8. TPC-H workloads.

To analyze this scenario, we allocate a set of morsels of a total size of 1 GB of the TPC-H `lineitem` table on NUMA region 0. We then migrate the morsels over via `move_pages()` respectively `page_leap()` into pooled memory before query answering. Additionally, we include auto NUMA balancing. As queries, we evaluate hand-written variants of TPC-H Q1 and Q6, as they operate on `lineitem` only and study their performance with and without concurrent writes fired without delay, which are carried out by a separate thread that performs $10M$ writes into the L_ORDERKEY field of uniformly selected rows. As L_ORDERKEY is neither used by Q1 nor Q6, this does not impact the query result, but still penalizes the migration procedures. Figure 8 shows the time for the asynchronous migration call (for page_leap() and move_pages()) followed by a sequence of five executions of the respective query. We can observe that page_leap() again clearly outperforms move_pages(), where page_leap() pays off over move_pages() already from the second query on for both recommended area sizes. This shows that page_leap() can also operate effectively in the context of database workloads.

7 Related Work

Before concluding, we discuss the related work in the field. First, in terms of general-purpose techniques for NUMA migration, other built-in methods are worth mentioning: One representative is numactl, a command-line tool by which page migration can be triggered as well. However, as it cannot be comfortably used from *within the process* like the remaining methods, we did not consider it as a baseline here. Also, there exists the system call migrate_pages() from libnuma. However, in contrast to move_pages(), it is not able to migrate only a subset of pages of the process, but always migrates all pages, which is typically not flexible enough. Hence, it does not provide a fine-grained way of page migration. Related to move_pages() is also the recent work of [13], which presents a faster version of the system called move_pages2(). However, as this requires modifying the kernel while page_leap() works out-of-the-box on a vanilla kernel, we did not consider it as a baseline here. In the database context, NUMA-aware algorithms and data structures have been a topic of interest for many years. These works operate around efficient data placement [12] and scheduling [11] on NUMA systems, NUMA-aware joins [6], and NUMA-aware execution engines from a holistic perspective [7]. In terms of memory rewiring, numerous other works also exist that exploit it. These range from data structures, such as linked lists [17], packed memory arrays [8], resizable hash tables schemes [16], and radix trees [3] to algorithms such as out-of-place partitioning [17] and snapshotting [14,19].

8 Conclusion

Conclusion. In this paper, we analyzed the weaknesses of the built-in implicit and explicit page migration mechanisms, auto NUMA balancing, and move_pages(), and proposed a practical alternative that works in user-space on a vanilla Linux kernel. We experimentally demonstrated that our alternative significantly reduces migration overhead while ensuring correctness under concurrent writes and providing a guarantee to migrate eventually, if desired. Further, our method supports the migration into pooled memory, which offers a significant advantage over the baseline methods.

Acknowledgments and Artifact Availability. We are grateful to the anonymous reviewers for their comments and suggestions on this paper. The artifact (source code) is available in the Zenodo repository [2].

Disclosure of Interests. The authors have no competing interests to declare that are relevant to the content of this article.

References

1. Dursun, K., Binnig, C., Çetintemel, U., Swart, G., Gong, W.: A morsel-driven query execution engine for heterogeneous multi-cores. Proc. VLDB Endow. **12**(12), 2218–2229 (2019). https://doi.org/10.14778/3352063.3352137
2. Felix Schuhknecht, N.R.: Artifact of the paper: taking the leap: efficient and reliable fine-grained NUMA migration in user- space (2026). https://doi.org/10.5281/zenodo.20507798
3. Fent, P., Jungmair, M., Kipf, A., Neumann, T.: START - self-tuning adaptive radix tree. In: 36th IEEE International Conference on Data Engineering Workshops, ICDE Workshops 2020, Dallas, TX, USA, 20–24 April 2020, pp. 147–153. IEEE (2020). https://doi.org/10.1109/ICDEW49219.2020.00015
4. Gawade, M., Kersten, M.L.: NUMA obliviousness through memory mapping. In: Pandis, I., Kersten, M.L. (eds.) Proceedings of the 11th International Workshop on Data Management on New Hardware, DaMoN 2015, Melbourne, VIC, Australia, May 31 - June 04, 2015, pp. 4:1–4:7. ACM (2015)
5. Hat, R.: Automatic NUMA balancing (2025). https://docs.redhat.com/en/documentation/red_hat_enterprise_linux/7/html/virtualization_tuning_and_optimization_guide/sect-virtualization_tuning_optimization_guide-numa-auto_numa_balancing
6. Lang, H., Leis, V., Albutiu, M.-C., Neumann, T., Kemper, A.: Massively parallel NUMA-aware hash joins. In: Jagatheesan, A., Levandoski, J., Neumann, T., Pavlo, A. (eds.) IMDM 2013-2014. LNCS, vol. 8921, pp. 3–14. Springer, Cham (2015). https://doi.org/10.1007/978-3-319-13960-9_1
7. Leis, V., Boncz, P.A., Kemper, A., Neumann, T.: Morsel-driven parallelism: a NUMA-aware query evaluation framework for the many-core age. In: Dyreson, C.E., Li, F., Özsu, M.T. (eds.) International Conference on Management of Data, SIGMOD 2014, Snowbird, UT, USA, 22–27 June 2014, pp. 743–754. ACM (2014). https://doi.org/10.1145/2588555.2610507
8. Leo, D.D., Boncz, P.A.: Packed memory arrays - rewired. In: 35th IEEE International Conference on Data Engineering, ICDE 2019, Macao, China, 8–11 April 2019, pp. 830–841. IEEE (2019). https://doi.org/10.1109/ICDE.2019.00079
9. Linux manual page: move_pages() (2025). https://man7.org/linux/man-pages/man2/move_pages.2.html
10. Linux manual page: Taskset (2025). https://www.man7.org/linux/man-pages/man1/taskset.1.html
11. Psaroudakis, I., Scheuer, T., May, N., Sellami, A., Ailamaki, A.: Scaling up concurrent main-memory column-store scans: towards adaptive NUMA-aware data and task placement. Proc. VLDB Endow. **8**(12), 1442–1453 (2015). https://doi.org/10.14778/2824032.2824043
12. Psaroudakis, I., Scheuer, T., May, N., Sellami, A., Ailamaki, A.: Adaptive NUMA-aware data placement and task scheduling for analytical workloads in main-memory column-stores. Proc. VLDB Endow. **10**(2), 37–48 (2016). https://doi.org/10.14778/3015274.3015275
13. Rayhan, Y., Aref, W.G.: Revisiting page migration for main-memory database systems. CoRR **abs/2503.17685** (2025). https://doi.org/10.48550/ARXIV.2503.17685

14. Salkhordeh, R., Schuhknecht, F.M., Asadi, H., Eiden, S., Brinkmann, A.: No time to halt: in-situ analysis for large-scale data processing via virtual snapshotting. In: Simitsis, A., Kemme, B., Queralt, A., Romero, O., Jovanovic, P. (eds.) Proceedings 28th International Conference on Extending Database Technology, EDBT 2025, Barcelona, Spain, 25–28 March 2025, pp. 438–450. OpenProceedings.org (2025). https://doi.org/10.48786/EDBT.2025.35
15. Schuhknecht, F., Henneberg, J.: Accelerating main-memory table scans with partial virtual views. In: May, N., Tatbul, N. (eds.) Proceedings of the 19th International Workshop on Data Management on New Hardware, DaMoN 2023, Seattle, WA, USA, 18–23 June 2023, pp. 89–93. ACM (2023). https://doi.org/10.1145/3592980.3595315
16. Schuhknecht, F.M.: Taking the shortcut: actively incorporating the virtual memory index of the OS to hardware-accelerate database indexing. In: 14th Conference on Innovative Data Systems Research, CIDR 2024, Chaminade, HI, USA, 14–17 January 2024. www.cidrdb.org (2024)
17. Schuhknecht, F.M., Dittrich, J., Sharma, A.: RUMA has it: rewired user-space memory access is possible! Proc. VLDB Endow. **9**(10), 768–779 (2016). https://doi.org/10.14778/2977797.2977803
18. Schuhknecht, F.M., Henneberg, J.: Towards adaptive storage views in virtual memory. In: 13th Conference on Innovative Data Systems Research, CIDR 2023, Amsterdam, The Netherlands, 8–11 January 2023. www.cidrdb.org (2023). https://doi.org/10.48550/arXiv.2209.01635
19. Schuhknecht, F.M., Priesterroth, A., Henneberg, J., Salkhordeh, R.: AnyOLAP: analytical processing of arbitrary data-intensive applications without ETL. Proc. VLDB Endow. **14**(12), 2823–2826 (2021). https://doi.org/10.14778/3476311.3476354

NeuroRing: Scaling Spiking Neural Networks via Multi-FPGA Bidirectional Ring Topologies and Stream-Dataflow Architectures

Muhammad Ihsan Al Hafiz(✉) and Artur Podobas

KTH Royal Institute of Technology, Stockholm, Sweden
{miahafiz,podobas}@kth.se

Abstract. Spiking neural networks (SNNs) are a promising paradigm for energy-efficient event-driven computation, but large-scale SNN execution remains challenging because sparse spike communication and synchronization can dominate runtime. Existing solutions across CPU, GPU, ASIC, and FPGA platforms offer different trade-offs between programmability, efficiency, and scalability. To address this gap, we present NeuroRing, a modular and scalable SNN accelerator based on a stream-dataflow architecture and a bidirectional ring topology, implemented in High-Level Synthesis (HLS) on FPGAs. NeuroRing supports modular single- and multi-FPGA deployment and is compatible with existing SNN workflows through integration with the NEST simulator. We evaluate NeuroRing on the cortical microcircuit benchmark and a Sudoku constraint-satisfaction workload. Results show that NeuroRing preserves the key activity statistics of the NEST reference model, achieves faster-than-real-time execution of the full-scale cortical microcircuit with a real-time factor (RTF) of 0.83, exhibits meaningful strong and weak scaling, and provides competitive energy efficiency on two programmable FPGAs. These results position NeuroRing as a flexible and scalable platform for both neuroscience simulation and broader event-driven applications.

Keywords: SNN · Accelerator · FPGA · Stream · Dataflow · Ring Topology

1 Introduction

Spiking Neural Networks (SNNs) are a promising model for energy-efficient event-driven computation and biologically realistic brain simulation, and are used in applications ranging from computational neuroscience [8] and constraint-satisfaction problems [10] to computer vision [1]. SNNs are energy-efficient because of sparse spike-based communication, where neurons exchange information only when events occur. However, large-scale SNN workloads remain challenging, particularly for networks with high connection density, such as the cortical microcircuit model [11]. In such workloads, spike communication and

M. Torquati et al. (Eds.): Euro-Par 2026, LNCS 16781, pp. 329–343, 2027.
https://doi.org/10.1007/978-3-032-35248-4_23

synchronization can dominate execution cost, requiring specialized architectures that exploit the characteristics of event-driven computation.

A broad range of systems has been developed to accelerate large-scale SNN simulation, each with different trade-offs. Specialized neuromorphic hardware, such as SpiNNaker, has demonstrated real-time simulation of the full cortical microcircuit at biological time scales [12], but such platforms are less accessible than commodity Central Processing Unit (CPU) and Graphics Processing Unit (GPU) systems. GPU-based approaches have also achieved near-real-time performance on similar workloads [5], while High-Performance Computing (HPC) deployments of the NEST simulator [2] have demonstrated strong performance and straightforward scaling across compute nodes [8]. Reconfigurable hardware offers another attractive option: Field Programmable Gate Array (FPGA)-based systems have shown strong energy efficiency and flexibility [13], from single-node devices [9] to large FPGA clusters [6,7]. However, existing FPGA-based SNN accelerators are often optimized for specific workloads, hardware organizations, or deployment settings. As a result, there remains a need for architectures that combine modularity, scalable multi-FPGA execution, backend-agnostic integration, and practical portability, while remaining suitable for high-performance large-scale SNN simulation.

In this work, we propose NeuroRing, a stream-dataflow SNN architecture with a bidirectional ring topology and modular High-Level Synthesis (HLS) kernels for multi-FPGA scaling. The main contributions are as follows:

1. We design and implement NeuroRing as a modular SNN accelerator that supports both single- and multi-FPGA deployment via stream-based communication and bidirectional ring routing.
2. We integrate NeuroRing with the NEST simulator through a Python-based workflow and evaluate it on two representative workloads: the cortical microcircuit for neuroscience and a Sudoku solver for constraint satisfaction.
3. We analyze the architectural trade-offs of NeuroRing through design-space exploration and evaluate its scalability under strong and weak scaling.
4. We compare NeuroRing with the Dardel supercomputer baseline, showing competitive strong-scaling performance with substantially lower power and energy consumption.

2 Spiking Neural Networks

SNNs are the third generation of artificial neural networks that encode information in the timing of spikes [3]. These networks are inspired by biological neurons, which use action potentials called spikes, to encode temporal information in their signals [14]. This mechanism for transferring information can lead to energy savings in hardware implementation because it transmits and processes sparse spike events only when activity occurs, as in the human brain.

The dynamics of spiking neurons can be described through different – more or less biologically plausible – models. The neuron model represents the mathematical formulation of the behavior of the neural membrane potential and ion channel conductances [3]. Examples of neuron models include the Leaky Integrate-and-Fire (LIF) model, the Izhikevich model, and the Hodgkin-Huxley model. The LIF model is a common neural model popular for its simplicity and ability to represent what is observed in vitro. Formally, the LIF is composed of two Ordinary Differential Equations (ODEs) with a spike-generation event condition:

$$\text{LIF}\begin{cases} \dfrac{dV}{dt} = \begin{cases} 0,\ V = V_{\text{reset}}, & t - t_{\text{last}} < \tau_{\text{ref}}, \\ \dfrac{-(V - E_{\text{L}}) + (I_{\text{syn}} + I_{\text{DC}})R}{\tau_m}, & t - t_{\text{last}} \geq \tau_{\text{ref}}, \end{cases} \\ \dfrac{dI_{\text{syn}}}{dt} = -\dfrac{I_{\text{syn}}}{\tau_{\text{syn}}} + \sum_j w_j \delta(t - t^j), \\ \text{if } V(t^-) > V_{\text{th}} : \text{emit\_spike}(),\ V(t^+) = V_{\text{reset}},\ t_{\text{last}} = t. \end{cases} \quad (1)$$

The LIF model integrates input current over time and emits a spike when the membrane potential reaches a threshold. The neuron dynamics are represented by Eq. 1 [12]. The membrane potential V evolves with time constant τ_m relative to the leak reversal potential (resting potential) E_{L}, driven by the synaptic current I_{syn}, direct current I_{DC}, and membrane resistance R. The synaptic current decays with time constant τ_{syn} and increases upon spike arrival, where $\delta(t - t^j)$ denotes an incoming spike at time t^j, and w_j is the synaptic weight associated with that spike, determining the magnitude and sign of its contribution to I_{syn}. Positive and negative weights correspond to excitatory and inhibitory contributions, respectively. When V exceeds the threshold potential V_{th}, the neuron emits a spike, resets to V_{reset}, and updates the last spike time t_{last}. During the refractory period τ_{ref}, i.e., when $t - t_{\text{last}} < \tau_{\text{ref}}$, the membrane potential is clamped at V_{reset} and does not respond to synaptic input, while the synaptic current continues to follow its decay dynamics. Example networks using LIF in this paper are the cortical microcircuit [11] and the Sudoku solver [4].

3 Related Work

A wide range of SNN accelerators has been proposed across ASIC, CPU, GPU, and FPGA platforms to improve simulation speed and energy efficiency. A common, non-trivial benchmark used to quantify accelerator performance is the cortical microcircuit model [11], which has a dense (and realistic) connection density [7]. The cortical microcircuit benchmark is particularly challenging because its relatively large synaptic fanout makes spike communication and distribution a major design concern, unlike more structured computer-science workloads with smaller connection fanout.

In 2019, Rhodes et al. [12] demonstrated real-time simulation of the cortical microcircuit on SpiNNaker, a specialized neuromorphic platform. Subsequent work explored more accessible platforms. Golosio et al. [5] used a GPU-based approach and achieved near-real-time performance on a similar workload. Kurth et al. [8] later mapped the microcircuit model built in the NEST simulator to

HPC compute nodes, achieving performance beyond biological real time while also enabling straightforward scaling across supercomputer nodes.

Reconfigurable hardware has further improved the balance between flexibility and energy efficiency. Heittmann et al. [6] used a large FPGA cluster of 432 Xilinx Z7045 devices and achieved a Real-Time Factor (RTF) of 0.25, at an energy cost of 783 nJ per synaptic event. Kauth et al. [7] reduced the platform scale to 35 NetFPGA SUME devices and reported an RTF of 0.05 with 48 nJ per synaptic event. More recently, Lindqvist et al. [9] used a single-node Agilex 7 FPGA and achieved an RTF of 0.79 with 21 nJ per synaptic event.

These studies show that FPGAs are attractive for scalable SNN simulation, but they also highlight a remaining challenge: building modular architectures that are scalable across single- and multi-device deployments and flexible with respect to both the simulator backend and the workload domain. NeuroRing addresses this gap through a stream-dataflow architecture and a bidirectional ring topology that supports modular deployment, backend-agnostic integration, and the execution of workloads from both neuroscience and constraint satisfaction.

4 The NeuroRing Architecture

4.1 Stream-Dataflow Processing Core

The NeuroRing processing core is built from the *NeuroRing* and *SynapseRouter* kernels, which follow a stream-dataflow design. These kernels are instantiated as compute units and paired to form one NeuroRing core. Most on-chip communication is stream-based, allowing the compute units to execute concurrently and overlap computation with communication. As shown in Fig. 1, one NeuroRing core consists of two Compute Units (CUs): the *NeuroRing* CU, and the *SynapseRouter* CU. The NeuroRing CU contains three main processes: the Neuron Processing Unit (NPU), synapse-list fetch, and spike recorder. The NPU performs the neuron-state update and spike generation. *NeuroRing* supports the LIF neuron model and Poisson generator, although other neuron models can be integrated by modifying the NPU code. The NPU uses an 8-lane pipelined architecture, where eight 32-bit floating-point synaptic weights are processed in parallel from a packed 256-bit input stream. Neuron-state variables, such as membrane potential and synaptic current, are stored in on-chip memory and partitioned by a factor of 8 to sustain parallel access by the processing lanes.

The NPU outputs spike events, which are passed to the synapse-list fetch process. For each emitted spike, the corresponding outgoing synapse list is fetched from High Bandwidth Memory (HBM). Each synapse entry is encoded as a 64-bit packet containing a 32-bit synaptic weight, a 2-bit synchronization field, a 22-bit destination field, and an 8-bit delay field. These entries are transferred via 256-bit Advanced eXtensible Interface (AXI) burst accesses, corresponding to four synapse packets per transaction. To reduce routing latency, the synapse list is sorted according to destination-core proximity, so that locally consumed and nearest-neighbor packets are generated first. The fetched packets are then

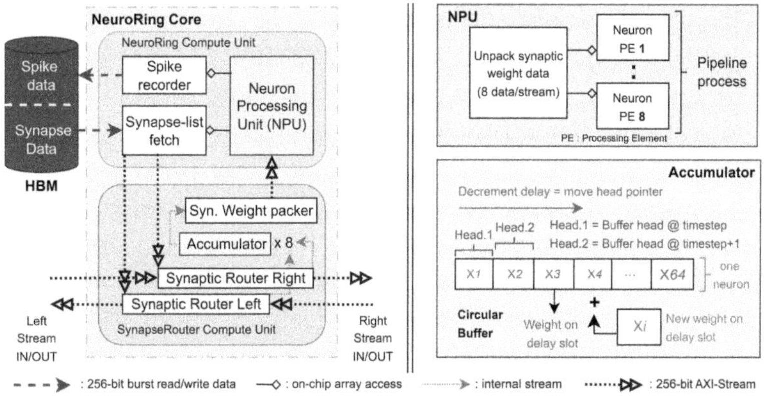

Fig. 1. Architecture of the proposed NeuroRing core, showing **(left)** the overarching core architecture, and **(right)** details of the NPU and the accumulator structure.

dispatched to either the left or right ring stream based on the shorter route to the destination core, with routing determined by the destination core ID. After the synapse list of each spiking neuron has been emitted, a local synchronization token is inserted to ensure that all packets associated with the current spike are propagated before the next neuron is processed, helping prevent ring congestion and deadlock. After all spikes in the current timestep have been emitted, the NPU generates a global synchronization token that propagates through the right ring to signal the timestep's completion across all cores. During this period, the spike recorder writes spike traces back to HBM. The HBM interface uses one AXI4 master interface, which can be mapped to one or more HBM channels depending on the required memory capacity. The HBM address space is divided into a spike-recording region and a synapse-list region.

The SynapseRouter is an independent CU and runs concurrently with the NeuroRing CU. It is activated by incoming AXI-stream packets and internal streams. Each router receives packets from two sources: the local NeuroRing CU and the neighboring core. Packets addressed to the current core are consumed locally and sent to the accumulator, while packets for other destinations are forwarded to the next core in the ring. Incoming packets from neighboring cores are prioritized to preserve ring progress and avoid deadlock under backpressure. Eight accumulators operate in parallel to process packets delivered by the left and right routers. Each accumulator is assigned a destination-address range based on the core capacity and core ID. Synaptic weights are accumulated in a circular buffer with 8-bit delay indexing. Although this supports up to 256 delay positions, the current implementation allocates 64 delay slots per neuron, which is sufficient for the evaluated workloads and reduces memory usage. The accumulator data are stored in UltraRAM (URAM); since each URAM word can hold 72 bits, two 32-bit synaptic weights are packed into a single URAM word to improve storage efficiency. At timestep completion, each accumulator releases the synaptic-weight value scheduled for the next timestep, packs it into the input stream, and forwards it to the NPU to start the next timestep cycle.

4.2 Bidirectional Ring Topology

A bidirectional ring topology is adopted to support scalable development within and across FPGAs. Because our design is modular, NeuroRing cores can be replicated and connected to neighboring cores via their left and right AXI-stream ports. Within a single device, these connections form a closed bidirectional ring. Across devices, the ring is extended through high-speed serial links.

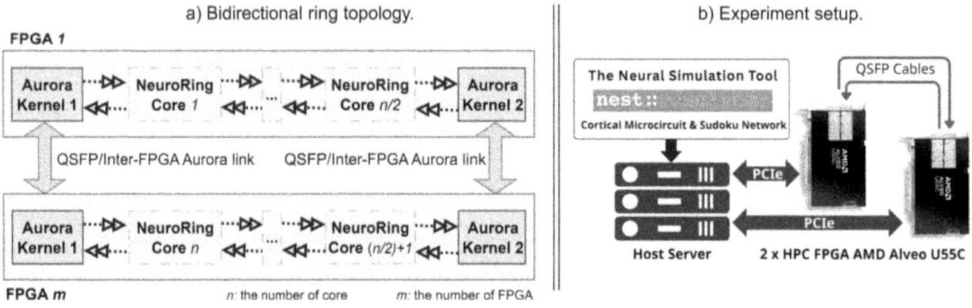

Fig. 2. Bidirectional ring topology and experiment setup.

Figure 2a shows the system-level organization. Each device contains multiple NeuroRing cores and two Aurora kernels located at the ring boundaries. The Aurora kernels provide inter-FPGA serial communication and extend the ring across devices via full-duplex QSFP links. This organization preserves the same left/right routing semantics used within a single FPGA while enabling multi-device scaling. Each core is assigned a unique core ID used to determine packet routing and destination matching.

In the Vitis flow, scaling is realized by replicating NeuroRing-core instances and specifying their stream connections in the connectivity configuration file. Aurora kernels are only required for multi-FPGA deployments. Because all target devices use the same kernel image, the generated bitstream can be reused across FPGAs. This makes the architecture straightforward to extend from a single-device implementation to a multi-FPGA deployment.

4.3 Hardware Generalization

NeuroRing is designed as a modular and backend-agnostic architecture for event-driven neural simulation. Rather than assuming a simulator-specific backend, it operates on a flattened synapse-list representation, in which each neuron stores its outgoing synaptic connections as a list of destination, delay, and synaptic weight entries. This abstraction allows NeuroRing to support different network-generation flows, provided that they can export compatible connectivity data and a supported neuron model. In this work, the network is generated using the NEST simulator [2], after which the synaptic connections are extracted and converted into the synapse-list representation required by NeuroRing.

The architecture can be configured for different neuron capacities per core, synapse-list sizes, and timestep settings. The number of replicated cores is limited by the available hardware resources of the target FPGA. In addition, the neuron model can be modified by adapting the HLS implementation of the NPU, allowing the same architecture to support different neuron dynamics.

5 Experimental Setup

NeuroRing is implemented in C++ using AMD Vitis HLS and synthesized with the Vitis 2025.1 flow for the AMD/Xilinx Alveo U55C FPGA. Experiments were conducted on a host server equipped with two U55C cards installed via Peripheral Component Interconnect Express (PCIe). Inter-FPGA communication was realized through Aurora links over two QSFP cables, as shown in Fig. 2b. The code is publicly available at https://github.com/ihsanalhafiz/NeuroRing.

Neural workloads were generated using NEST v3.9.0, and the host runtime was implemented in Python 3.10.19 using `pyxrt` to transfer network data, launch FPGA kernels, and retrieve results. After constructing the model in the NEST simulator, we extracted the connection data using the `GetConnections` and `GetStatus` methods. The extracted connection information includes the source neuron, target neuron, synaptic weight, and synaptic delay. Synaptic weights and all neuron-state computations are represented using 32-bit floating-point precision. As a software baseline for strong scaling, we used the CPU partition of the Dardel supercomputer to run a half-scale cortical microcircuit using the same Python reference implementation. Latency was measured on the host side; it is the wall-clock simulation time unless stated otherwise. FPGA power was obtained from the average board power reported by `xrt-smi examine`, sampled during kernel execution, while CPU power on Dardel was collected using `pat_run` and `pat_report`. Performance is reported using the RTF, defined as wall-clock simulation time divided by biological simulation time [7,9]. To evaluate performance and scalability, NeuroRing is compiled with neuron capacities of 2048, 4096, 5632, and 8192 neurons/core. Depending on the workload, the number of deployed cores ranges from 1 to 20, and both single-FPGA and two-FPGA configurations are evaluated.

5.1 Case Studies

The Cortical Microcircuit is a model of a unit cell of early mammalian sensory cortex that covers 1 mm^2 of cortical surface in a spiking network. The full-scale network consists of 77,169 neurons that are organized into four layers of inhibitory and excitatory populations, denoted by 2/3E, 2/3I, 4E, 4I, 5E, 5I, 6E, and 6I [11]. Neuron connections are encoded using population-specific probabilities, with a total of $\sim$0.3 billion synapses. The model can be driven by DC or Poisson-distributed external input. In this work, we use DC input for the evaluated NeuroRing and NEST reference runs. The model has become widely adopted by the computational neuroscience community for benchmarking neuroscience simulators because it involves a realistic number of connections with realistic probabilities [7]. The synaptic fan-out averages 3,873 connections per neuron, with a maximum of 6,749. This high fan-out poses challenges for spike communication and memory bandwidth in hardware. It is simulated with a timestep of 0.1 ms, and all simulation parameters are obtained from [11]. The cortical microcircuit is tested at Full, Half, and Quarter neuron scales with a synaptic scale factor of 1, corresponding to 77,169, 38,586, and 19,292 neurons, respectively. The simulation time is 10 s for performance evaluation.

The Sudoku workload is derived from the NEST example network [4] with adjusted parameters and implements a winner-takes-all formulation, with each Sudoku digit represented by five neurons. Digit neurons are connected to neurons representing conflicting digits in the same row, column, and 3×3 subgrid. The resulting 9×9 Sudoku network contains 3645 neurons. In addition to the recurrent constraint connections, the network includes Poisson stimulation and background noise sources. Three easy Sudoku benchmark instances are used.

Table 1. Hardware utilization and operating frequency of the NeuroRing architecture

No	Core Capacity	Use Case	Cores	Setup	Freq. (MHz)	LUT (%)	Reg (%)	BRAM (%)	URAM (%)	DSP (%)
1	2048	Half CM[b]	20	2 FPGAs	268.3[a]	49.26[a]	37.04[a]	44.54[a]	26.04[a]	18.88[a]
2	4096	Quarter CM[b]	5	1 FPGA	304.1	29.45	22.07	20.49	21.88	9.46
3	4096	Half CM[b]	10	1 FPGA	203.5	49.81	37.94	31.25	43.75	18.88
4	4096	Full CM[b]	20	2 FPGAs	272.4[a]	50.24[a]	38.46[a]	45.29[a]	42.71[a]	18.88[a]
5	5632	Full CM[b]	14	2 FPGAs	198.7[a]	38.59[a]	29.26[a]	66.67[a]	41.25[a]	14.01[a]
6	8192	Full CM[b]	10	2 FPGAs	260.0[a]	31.13[a]	22.87[a]	54.71[a]	37.50[a]	9.46[a]
7	4096	Sudoku	1[c]	1 FPGA	302.1	15.72	10.82	26.69	9.38	2.22

[a]Resource utilization reported per FPGA (dual-FPGA systems use identical boards).
[b]CM = cortical microcircuit benchmark.
[c]One compute core and one Poisson spike generator.

6 Results and Discussion

6.1 Hardware Utilization

All kernels are synthesized with a target frequency of 300 MHz. Table 1 reports the achieved frequency and hardware utilization for the evaluated NeuroRing configurations. Larger designs generally show higher utilization and lower operating frequency, reflecting a timing-closure trade-off. Smaller neuron capacities per core also raise utilization because more cores are required for the same workload. DSP usage remains relatively low because the current implementation uses the LIF neuron model, which is less arithmetic-intensive than models such as the Izhikevich or Hodgkin–Huxley models [13]. The Sudoku configuration has the lowest utilization, as it uses only one NeuroRing compute core and one Poisson spike-generator core.

6.2 Correctness

Correctness is evaluated against NEST, used here as the software reference. The comparison uses the full-scale cortical microcircuit mapped to a NeuroRing configuration with 4096 neurons/core, 20 cores, and 2 FPGAs. Validation is based on three standard spike-train statistics: firing rate, coefficient of variation (CV) of inter-spike intervals, and Pearson correlation [6,7,9]. Figure 3 shows that NeuroRing closely matches the NEST reference across layers L23, L4, L5, and L6 for firing rate, CV of inter-spike intervals, and Pearson correlation. The overall agreement indicates that NeuroRing preserves both the irregular spiking behavior and the correlation structure of the cortical microcircuit. Small differences remain in some tails and peak shapes, likely due to implementation-level numerical and synchronization effects. Overall, the close match in layer-wise statistics confirms that NeuroRing reproduces the essential dynamics of the NEST baseline.

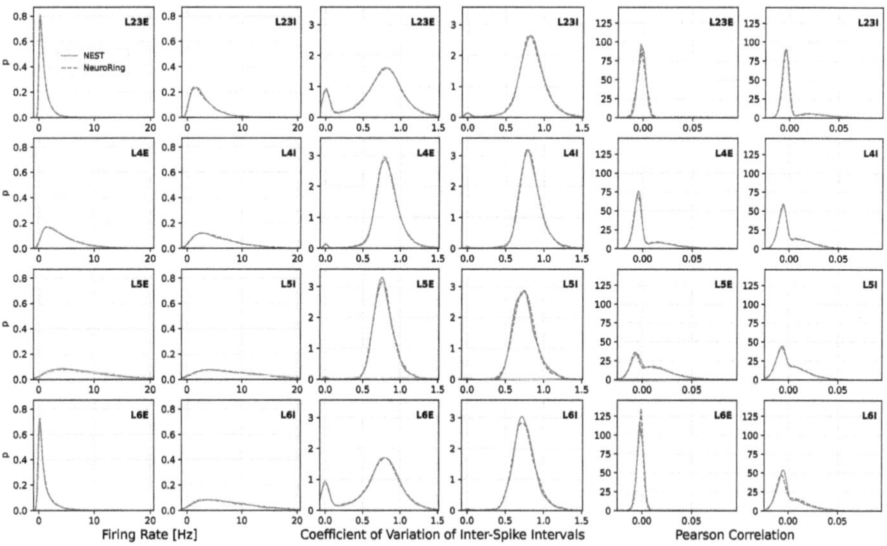

Fig. 3. Layer-wise statistical comparison for the full-size cortical microcircuit.

6.3 Architectural Design Space Exploration

This experiment evaluates how neuron capacity per core affects RTF, power, and energy efficiency for the full-size cortical microcircuit on two FPGAs. As shown in Fig. 4a, reducing the capacity from 8192 to 4096 neurons/core improves the RTF from 1.11 to 0.83 because the workload is distributed over more cores. The 5632-neuron/core case deviates from a linear trend due to its lower post-implementation frequency of 198.7 MHz. Figure 4b shows that total power remains around 70 W for the 8192- and 5632-neuron/core cases, and increases to 83.08 W for the 4096-neuron/core case, where more cores are instantiated. However, the energy per synaptic event decreases from 82 nJ to 73 nJ. Overall, these results show that reducing the neuron capacity per core improves both real-time performance and energy per synaptic event, at the cost of increased total power. These results suggest that, for this workload and platform, smaller core capacities are favorable when the primary objective is real-time performance and energy per synaptic event, provided that sufficient hardware resources are available.

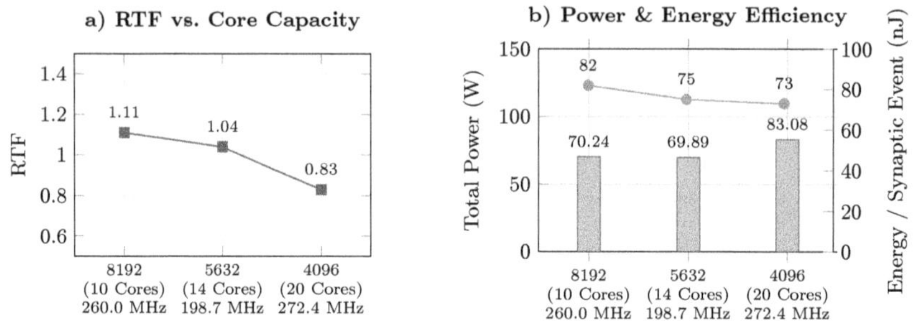

Fig. 4. Impact of core capacity variation on RTF, Power, and Energy.

6.4 System Scalability

Strong Scaling evaluates how performance changes when a fixed workload is distributed over more hardware resources. Here, the half-size cortical microcircuit is used as the fixed workload and executed on both the NeuroRing and the Dardel CPU platform under single-unit and dual-unit configurations. For NeuroRing, the single-unit configuration uses 10 cores with 4096 neurons/core on 1 FPGA, while the dual-unit configuration uses 20 cores with 2048 neurons/core on 2 FPGAs. For Dardel, the single-unit and dual-unit configurations use 1 and 2 CPU nodes, respectively, with 2 ntasks per node and 32 CPUs per task.

Figure 5a shows that scaling NeuroRing from a single-unit to a dual-unit configuration reduces the RTF from 0.73 to 0.51, or a speedup of about 1.43×. For Dardel, the RTF decreases from 0.43 to 0.36, giving a smaller speedup of about 1.19×. In both cases, the speedup is sublinear, indicating that communication and synchronization overhead limit ideal strong scaling. For NeuroRing, this overhead mainly comes from the longer ring and inter-FPGA communication, while for Dardel, it is associated with inter-node MPI communication.

Figures 5b and 5c show that the reduction in runtime is accompanied by higher power and energy cost on both platforms. For NeuroRing, total power increases from 32.71 W to 79.17 W, and energy per synaptic event rises from 49 nJ to 84 nJ. Dardel shows the same trend, increasing from 314.1 W to 587.6 W

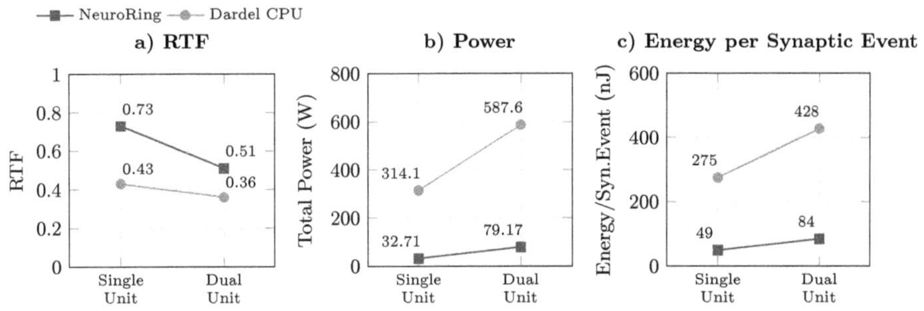

Fig. 5. Strong-scaling comparison for the Half cortical microcircuit between NeuroRing and the Dardel CPU system.

and from 275 nJ to 428 nJ. Although Dardel achieves lower absolute RTF in this half-size experiment, NeuroRing provides a comparable scaling trend at substantially lower power and energy, highlighting its potential as an energy-efficient platform.

Weak Scaling evaluates performance when workload size and resources increase proportionally. Using 4096 neurons/core, the Quarter, Half, and Full cortical microcircuit workloads are mapped to 5, 10, and 20 cores.

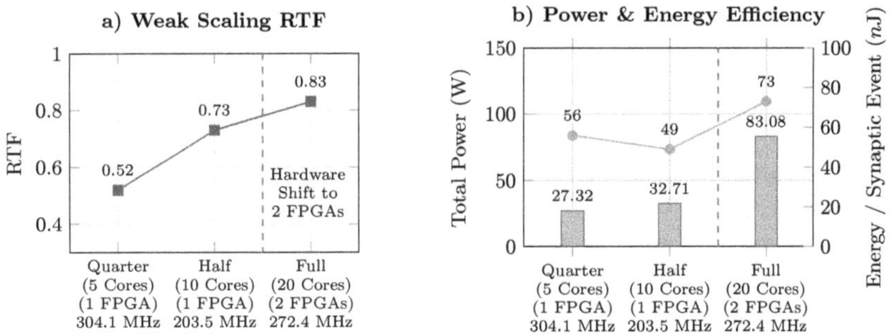

Fig. 6. Weak-scaling performance of the NeuroRing architecture (4096 neurons/core).

Ideally, the RTF would remain constant. Instead, Fig. 6a shows that the RTF increases from 0.52 for the Quarter workload to 0.73 for the Half workload and 0.83 for the Full workload, indicating a deviation from ideal weak scaling. The degradation from Quarter to Half occurs even within a single FPGA and is likely influenced by the lower post-implementation frequency of the Half configuration (203.5 MHz) compared with the Quarter configuration (304.1 MHz). The Full configuration reaches a higher frequency (272.4 MHz), but its execution is distributed across two FPGAs, which introduces additional inter-FPGA communication and synchronization overhead. As a result, the larger configuration still shows a higher RTF. Figure 6b shows that total power increases with scale, rising from 27.32 W for Quarter to 32.71 W for Half and 83.08 W for Full. The increase is particularly pronounced when moving to the two-FPGA configuration. In terms of energy per synaptic event, the Half configuration gives the best result at 49 nJ, compared with 56 nJ for Quarter and 73 nJ for Full. Overall, proportional resource growth is applied, but weak-scaling efficiency degrades due to lower frequency and inter-FPGA overhead.

6.5 State-of-the-Art Comparison

To position NeuroRing with respect to prior SNN simulation platforms, Table 2 compares the full-size cortical microcircuit use case across FPGA, GPU, CPU, and ASIC-based systems. For NeuroRing, we report the configuration with 20 cores, 4096 neurons/core, deployed on 2 AMD/Xilinx Alveo U55C FPGAs.

Table 2. State-of-the-art Comparison for the full-size cortical microcircuit use case.

System	Hardware	Platform	RTF	Energy/Syn.Ev.(nJ)
Fast SNN FPGA [9]	1 Agilex 7	FPGA	0.79	21
neuroAIx [7]	35 NetFPGA SUME	FPGA	0.05	48
IBM INC-3000 [6]	432 Xilinx XCZ7045	FPGA	0.25	783
NeuronGPU [5]	1 GeForce RTX 2080 Ti	GPU	1.06	180
NEST [8]	2 AMD EPYC Rome	CPU	0.53	480
SpiNNaker [12]	318 SpiNNaker chips	ASIC	1.00	600
NeuroRing (4096)	2 AMD/Xilinx Alveo U55C	FPGA	0.83	73

Table 2 compares NeuroRing with prior full-size cortical microcircuit implementations across FPGA, GPU, CPU, and ASIC platforms. NeuroRing achieves faster-than-real-time execution with an RTF of 0.83 using two AMD/Xilinx Alveo U55C FPGAs. Although it does not provide the lowest reported energy per synaptic event among FPGA systems, it is more energy-efficient than the listed GPU and CPU baselines and improves upon the large SpiNNaker [12] and IBM INC-3000 systems [6] in energy per synaptic event. NeuroRing's main distinction is its modular HLS-based implementation on commercial data-center FPGAs, together with a Python/NEST workflow that enables existing NEST models to be mapped to the FPGA backend after model construction. Overall, NeuroRing is positioned as a programmable and scalable FPGA-based SNN simulation platform that balances real-time performance, energy efficiency, and architectural flexibility.

6.6 Beyond Neuroscience: Constraint Satisfaction Problem

To demonstrate applicability beyond neuroscience, NeuroRing is evaluated on three Sudoku puzzles formulated as SNN winner-takes-all networks, following the NEST example in Sect. 5.1. All instances use one NeuroRing compute core with 4096 neurons/core and one auxiliary Poisson spike generator core. The same parameter set is used for all three instances, including 200 Hz stimulus and noise rates, inhibitory weight −100, stimulus/noise weights 200, synaptic delay 1.0 ms, and LIF neuron parameters $dt = 0.1$ ms, $C_m = 250$ pF, $I_e = 200$ pA, $\tau_m = 20$ ms, $t_{ref} = 2$ ms, $\tau_{syn,ex} = \tau_{syn,in} = 5$ ms, $V_{reset} = -70$ mV, $E_L = -65$ mV, $V_{th} = -50$ mV, and $V_m \sim \mathcal{U}(-65, -55)$ mV. Different puzzles may require retuning input-rate and synaptic-weight parameters; we leave systematic transferability analysis to future work. The solution is decoded from the digit population with the highest spike count in each cell.

Sudoku 1

6	**5**	**8**	9	**3**	1	4	**2**	7
4	3	**2**	6	7	8	**9**	1	**5**
9	1	**7**	2	4	5	**6**	**8**	3
2	**9**	6	3	**5**	**4**	8	**7**	1
5	8	1	7	**6**	**2**	3	4	9
7	4	**3**	**8**	**1**	9	**2**	**5**	6
1	2	**9**	5	8	**3**	7	**6**	**4**
8	**6**	**5**	**4**	**9**	7	**1**	**3**	2
3	**7**	4	1	2	**6**	5	9	8

Sudoku 2

2	**5**	4	6	8	3	**1**	**9**	7
6	8	7	9	1	5	3	**4**	**2**
9	**1**	3	4	**2**	**7**	**5**	**6**	**8**
3	**4**	**5**	8	7	**1**	**9**	2	**6**
7	2	6	**3**	**4**	9	8	5	1
8	**9**	1	**2**	5	**6**	4	7	**3**
5	3	**8**	**7**	6	4	**2**	**1**	9
1	**6**	2	5	9	**8**	7	3	**4**
4	7	9	**1**	3	2	**6**	**8**	**5**

Sudoku 3

4	9	**6**	7	1	5	**8**	3	**2**
7	5	3	**4**	**2**	**8**	1	**9**	**6**
2	**1**	8	6	**3**	9	**7**	4	**5**
5	**3**	**1**	2	6	7	**9**	**8**	4
6	4	9	**1**	8	3	2	5	**7**
8	**2**	7	**9**	**5**	4	6	1	**3**
3	7	4	8	9	**2**	5	**6**	1
1	**8**	**5**	3	**7**	**6**	4	2	9
9	6	**2**	**5**	4	**1**	**3**	7	**8**

Performance summary: Sim.Time = 0.5 s, End-to-End Latency = 0.53–0.57 s, SNN Exec. Latency = 0.06–0.07 s, Power ≈ 20.8 W, Energy = 109–110 nJ/synaptic event.

Fig. 7. Three Sudoku benchmarks. Gray cells: given puzzle. Blue cells: solver solution. (Color figure online)

Figure 7 shows that all three puzzles are solved correctly. The results show stable performance across the instances, with end-to-end latency of 0.53–0.57 s, SNN execution latency of 0.06–0.07 s, and power of about 20.8 W. The higher energy per synaptic event compared with the cortical microcircuit case is due to the smaller number of synaptic events, so the fixed platform power is distributed over fewer spike-processing events. These results show that NeuroRing can support constraint satisfaction problems beyond neuroscience benchmarks on a compact single-FPGA configuration.

7 Conclusion

This paper presented NeuroRing, a modular and scalable multi-FPGA architecture for spiking neural network simulation based on a bidirectional ring topology and stream-dataflow execution in HLS. NeuroRing supports configurable neuron capacity per core, scales across single- and multi-FPGA deployments, and preserves the key statistics of the NEST reference model. Results showed faster-than-real-time execution of the full-size cortical microcircuit, meaningful strong and weak scaling, and competitive energy efficiency using only two programmable FPGAs. The Sudoku case study further demonstrated NeuroRing's applicability to constraint-satisfaction workloads beyond neuroscience. These results highlight the potential of NeuroRing as a flexible and efficient architecture for scalable SNN simulation and related event-driven workloads. Future work will focus on extending NeuroRing with reconfigurable neuron models and on-chip learning capabilities, enabling support for more diverse SNN workloads and adaptive neural dynamics.

Acknowledgments. This work was funded by the European Commission Directorate-General for Communications Networks, Content and Technology, grant no. 101135809 (EXTRA-BRAIN), the Swedish Research Council grant no. 2021-04579 (Building Digital Brains), and the Swedish e-Science Research Centre (SeRC). The computations were enabled by resources provided by the National Academic Infrastructure for Supercomputing in Sweden (NAISS), partially funded by the Swedish Research Council through grant agreement no. 2022-06725.

Disclosure of Interests. The authors have no competing interests to declare that are relevant to the content of this article.

References

1. Agarwal, R., Ghosal, P., Murmu, N., Nandi, D.: Spiking neural network in computer vision: techniques, tools and trends. In: Borah, S., Gandhi, T.K., Piuri, V. (eds.) Advanced Computational and Communication Paradigms, pp. 201–209. Springer, Singapore (2023)
2. Gewaltig, M.O., Diesmann, M.: NEST (neural simulation tool). Scholarpedia **2**(4), 1430 (2007). https://doi.org/10.4249/scholarpedia.1430
3. Ghosh-Dastidar, S., Adeli, H.: Spiking neural networks. Int. J. Neural Syst. **19**(04), 295–308 (2009). https://doi.org/10.1142/S0129065709002002
4. Gille, J., Furber, S., Rowley, A.: Script controlling the simulation of a single game of Sudoku — NEST simulator documentation. https://nest-simulator.readthedocs.io/en/v3.9/auto_examples/sudoku/sudoku_solver.html. Accessed 17 Feb 2026
5. Golosio, B., Tiddia, G., De Luca, C., Pastorelli, E., Simula, F., Paolucci, P.S.: Fast simulations of highly-connected spiking cortical models using GPUs. Front. Comput. Neurosci. **15** (2021). https://doi.org/10.3389/fncom.2021.627620
6. Heittmann, A., et al.: Simulating the cortical microcircuit significantly faster than real time on the IBM INC-3000 neural supercomputer. Front. Neurosci. **15** (2022). https://doi.org/10.3389/fnins.2021.728460
7. Kauth, K., Stadtmann, T., Sobhani, V., Gemmeke, T.: neuroAIx-Framework: design of future neuroscience simulation systems exhibiting execution of the cortical microcircuit model 20× faster than biological real-time. Front. Comput. Neurosci. **17** (2023). https://doi.org/10.3389/fncom.2023.1144143
8. Kurth, A.C., Senk, J., Terhorst, D., Finnerty, J., Diesmann, M.: Sub-realtime simulation of a neuronal network of natural density. Neuromorphic Comput. Eng. **2**(2), 021001 (2022). https://doi.org/10.1088/2634-4386/ac55fc
9. Lindqvist, B.A., Podobas, A.: Algorithms for fast spiking neural network simulation on FPGAs. IEEE Access **12**, 150334–150353 (2024). https://doi.org/10.1109/ACCESS.2024.3479933

10. Pignari, R., Fra, V., Macii, E., Urgese, G.: Efficient solution validation of constraint satisfaction problems on neuromorphic hardware: the case of Sudoku puzzles. IEEE Trans. Artif. Intell. **6**(8), 2061–2072 (2025). https://doi.org/10.1109/TAI.2025.3536428
11. Potjans, T.C., Diesmann, M.: The cell-type specific cortical microcircuit: relating structure and activity in a full-scale spiking network model. Cerebral Cortex (New York, NY) **24**(3), 785–806 (2014). https://doi.org/10.1093/cercor/bhs358
12. Rhodes, O., et al.: Real-time cortical simulation on neuromorphic hardware. Philos. Trans. Royal Soc. A Math. Phys. Eng. Sci. **378**(2164), 20190160 (2019). https://doi.org/10.1098/rsta.2019.0160
13. Szczerek, W.J., Podobas, A.: A quarter of a century of neuromorphic architectures on FPGAs – an overview (2025). https://arxiv.org/abs/2502.20415v3
14. Vreeken, J.: Spiking neural networks, an introduction (2003). https://webdoc.sub.gwdg.de/ebook/serien/ah/UU-CS/2003-008.pdf. Accessed 19 Jan 2026

CASTM: An API for Accelerating Zero-Knowledge Proof Kernels on CGRA Architectures

Cristian Campos Ferrer(✉), Angeles G. Navarro, and Sonia Gonzalez-Navarro

University of Malaga, Malaga, Spain
{cricamfe,angeles,sonia}@ac.uma.es

Abstract. Wearable biomedical devices increasingly require on-device privacy guarantees through Zero-Knowledge Proofs (ZKPs), yet the underlying cryptographic kernels, based on modular exponentiation over prime fields, far exceed what low-power microcontrollers can deliver. Coarse-Grained Reconfigurable Arrays (CGRAs) offer near-ASIC efficiency with the reprogrammability needed to track evolving ZKP standards, but programming them requires manual, cycle-by-cycle scheduling across a spatial processing-element mesh. We present CASTM, a *CGRA API & Spatial Temporal Mapper* for the OpenEdgeCGRA architecture. CASTM preserves explicit spatial-temporal control while raising the abstraction level through structured abstractions and architecture-aware operators that encapsulate recurring modular-arithmetic idioms. For the S-box layer, a key component of the popular ZKP-friendly hash function Poseidon2, CASTM achieves 1.26× speedup w.r.t. the hand-optimized version while reducing source code by approximately 6.0×. We also identify that for long ZKP kernels multi-batch configuration reload is the dominant bottleneck, and show that increasing the Configuration Register File from 32 to 512 entries (+4.5% FPGA area) allows us to deploy the full Poseidon2 kernel on the CGRA, achieving 1.33× speedup and 33.7% energy savings over an ultra-low power RISC-V CPU core.

Keywords: OpenEdgeCGRA · Zero-Knowledge Proofs · Poseidon2

1 Introduction

Wearable biomedical devices—continuous glucose monitors, cardiac rhythm analyzers, inertial fall predictors—generate vast amounts of physiological data transmitted wirelessly to cloud platforms [6]. Regulatory frameworks (HIPAA, GDPR) impose strict requirements on data provenance, yet current device architectures lack mechanisms for the device itself to *prove* that a measurement is authentic without revealing raw signals. Zero-Knowledge Proofs (ZKPs) [8,11] resolve this tension: a prover (the sensor) convinces a verifier

M. Torquati et al. (Eds.): Euro-Par 2026, LNCS 16781, pp. 344–358, 2027.
https://doi.org/10.1007/978-3-032-35248-4_24

(a server) that a statement holds—e.g., that a glucose trajectory was computed correctly—without disclosing the underlying data. Elliptic Curve Cryptography (ECC) [13] underpins the most compact constructions, keeping proof sizes small for bandwidth-constrained links. However, power requirements of ZKP cryptographic kernels far exceed what low-power microcontrollers can deliver [1].

Deploying ZKP on hardware demands *reconfigurability*. Different proof systems (Groth16 [11], PLONK [8], STARKs [4]) use different prime fields (31-bit BabyBear, 64-bit Goldilocks, 256-bit BN254), S-box exponents ($d \in \{3, 5, 7\}$), and elliptic curves. Plonky3 [16] introduced BabyBear only in 2024, replacing the Goldilocks field of Plonky2. An ASIC designed for one configuration becomes obsolete when the next proof system changes parameters. Coarse-Grained Reconfigurable Arrays (CGRAs) occupy the right design point: unlike FPGAs, they reconfigure at the instruction level with microsecond latency; unlike ASICs, they remain fully reprogrammable [15]. In our research, we target the X-HEEP framework [14], an extensible RISC-V based SoC designed for ultra low power edge computing, capable of interfacing with custom peripherals like accelerators. In particular, applications of the X-HEEP framework, such as HEEPocrates and HEEPsilon, feature a CGRA integrated via the Extendible Accelerator Interface (XAIF): the OpenEdgeCGRA [17], a 4×4 PE mesh with a 32-bit datapath, which we consider in this paper.

The computational bottleneck in ZKP is the hash function. We focus our research on the Poseidon2 framework [10], which implements a hash that minimizes finite-field multiplications per permutation, making it highly suitable for our data privacy use case (a biomedical wearable). Its main computational kernel is the S-box layer—$x^d \bmod p$—which accounts for over 90% of computation on a CGRA with 32-bit datapath. For 31-bit BabyBear ($p = 2^{31} - 2^{27} + 1$, $d = 7$), each S-box requires two modular squarings and two modular multiplications, each involving Barrett reduction [3] with 62-bit intermediates decomposed across 32-bit PEs. Yet programming the CGRA is the real challenge: the developer must specify, for each of the $N \times M$ PEs and each clock cycle, the exact instruction, registers, and neighbor links. For the S-box layer this spans 2,030 lines, took two weeks of expert effort, and a single misplaced operand produces silent errors detectable only through full simulation. Automatic compilers [7,20] avoid this burden but cannot express cross-PE carry chains, toroidal routing, or branchless conditional selects that are essential for modular arithmetic.

In this paper we present CASTM (CGRA API & Spatial Temporal Mapper) a domain-specific API, which occupies the middle ground: the programmer retains explicit control over *which PE* executes *which instruction* at *which cycle*, but through parametric functions, loops, labeled subroutines, and architecture-aware operators instead of raw CSV encodings. A four-stage deterministic compilation flow produces simulator-native CSV with structured error diagnostics. More precisely, we make the following contributions: **(C1)** We introduce CASTM, the first API targeting spatial-temporal CGRA programming for a class of cryptographic kernels based on arithmetization operating on finite fields (Sect. 3). **(C2)** We map the S-box layer ($x^7 \bmod p$, BabyBear) onto OpenEdgeCGRA and validate the resulting flow against independent C/C++ references (Sect. 3.3). **(C3)** We show CASTM reduces source code by approximately 6.0× vs. manual CSV while achieving 20.5% fewer clock cycles on the S-box kernel (Sect. 4.1). **(C4)** We identify multi-batch configuration reload as the dominant bottleneck and evaluate increasing Configuration Register File –CRF– capacity to enable full Poseidon2 deployment on CGRA (Sect. 4.2). **(C5)** We show that throughput and energy favor different deployments of Poseidon2 on the CPU and the CGRA (Sect. 4.3).

2 Background and Related Work

2.1 OpenEdgeCGRA Architecture

Coarse Grained Reconfigurable Arrays (CGRAs) are primarily composed of an array of interconnected PEs (or Reconfigurable Cells –RCs–) that can be configured dynamically to implement a variety of computational tasks. The PEs are connected through a fixed interconnect, executing in lockstep under a configuration bitstream loaded before kernel execution [15]. Each PE contains a word-width ALU, a small register file, and neighbor connections. Unlike FPGAs (bit-level reconfiguration, high overhead), CGRAs reconfigure at the instruction level with microsecond latency.

OpenEdgeCGRA [17] provides: *(i)* a 4×4 toroidal mesh of PEs (i.e., 16 PEs), where column 3 wraps to column 0 and row 3 to row 0, giving maximum distance of 4 hops between any two PEs; *(ii)* per-PE resources including a 32-bit ALU (1 clock cycle), 32×32 multiplier (3 clock cycles), four registers (R0–R3), output register ROUT visible to neighbors, and branchless select instructions (BSFA/BZFA); *(iii)* shared scratchpad SRAM with 2-cycle latency (one access/column/cycle) organized as 4 interleaved banks; and *(iv)* tight coupling with a RISC-V host core (X-HEEP [14]). At SoC level, we consider two host-to-memory organizations. The simpler one-to-many path (*OneToM*) forces host and accelerator traffic to share a common route to memory, whereas the richer *N:M* crossbar sustains more parallel access to the interleaved SRAM banks. As a result, *OneToM* incurs more serialization and contention, while *N:M* reduces memory-induced stalls.

Configuration and Execution Model. A kernel is encoded as a sequence of 32-bit *configuration words*—one per PE per cycle—stored in a Configuration Register File (CRF) with D entries per column—32 entries in our baseline CGRA. Before dispatch, the host CPU writes configuration words into an SRAM backing store called the *Context Memory* (CMEM) via memory-mapped I/O (MMIO). During execution, each column's program counter advances through CRF entries in lockstep, dispatching one instruction per PE. When a kernel exceeds the CRF capacity, the host must reload the CMEM with the next batch of instructions before the CGRA can resume—a transparent but costly operation whose implications are analyzed in Sect. 4.2.

2.2 CGRA Programming: Limitations for ZKP Workloads

Manual scheduling requires placing instructions among NB bundles of PE slots, satisfying data dependencies, multi-cycle latencies, memory-port arbitration, and register pressure—producing CSV files of ~4,750 lines for our main kernel, with errors detectable only through simulation.
Automatic compilers (Compigra [7], Wang et al. [20]) accept C code and use heuristic placement, working well for regular DSP kernels but encountering structural limitations for cryptographic modular arithmetic (our use case): (1) multi-precision limb decomposition is invisible at the C level; (2) toroidal routing patterns have no C-level representation; (3) architectural primitives like BSFA (*Branch/Select on Flag A*, a branchless correction needed in our main kernel) are inaccessible; and (4) heuristic scheduling forfeits cycle-count predictability needed for real-time ZKP functions.

2.3 Poseidon2 S-Box Exponentiation

Poseidon2 [10] is a ZKP-friendly hash function engineered to minimize finite-field multiplications per permutation, since each multiplication translates directly to proof-generation cost. Figure 1 shows its round structure: it operates on a state $s = (s_0, s_1, s_2, \ldots, s_{t-1})$ of t field elements through $R_F/2$ full rounds, then R_P partial rounds for cell s_0, and next $R_F/2$ full rounds again on s. Full rounds apply a round-constant addition ($+c_i$), a S-box layer ($x \mapsto x^d \bmod p$) to all state elements, and a linear *Maximum Distance Separable* layer (MDS, a $t \times t$ matrix used to provide maximum diffusion); in partial rounds, the round constant and S-box apply only to s_0, followed by the internal matrix MI. For a typical parameterization ($t = 16$, $R_F = 8$, $R_P = 13$), Poseidon2 invokes $8 \times 16 + 13 = 141$ S-box evaluations, making the S-box layer over 90% of total computation on a 32-bit CGRA.

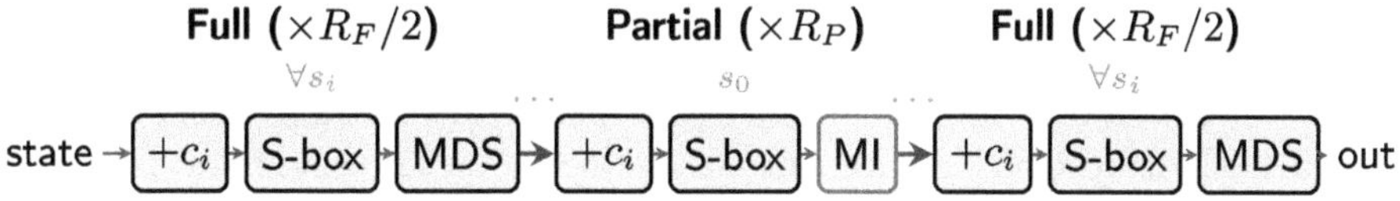

Fig. 1. Poseidon2 permutation structure. The S-box ($x^d \bmod p$) dominates cost.

2.4 Related Work

Table 1 positions our contribution relative to existing ZKP hardware accelerators. PipeZK [21] proposes an ASIC pipeline for MSM (*Multi-Scalar Multiplication*) and NTT (*Number Theoretic Transform*), which are the two most time-consuming computational primitives for generating Zero-Knowledge Proofs (zk-SNARKs), but it does not address ZK-friendly hashing. AMAZE [1] implements

MiMC (a ZK-friendly hash function) on FPGA with fixed RTL, achieving 13× over CPU. HashEmAll [18] provides FPGA-optimized cores for Rescue-Prime, Griffin, and Reinforced Concrete (up to 23× over CPU on BN254), yet it targets different hash families than Poseidon2. TRIDENT [5] accelerates the original Poseidon [9] on FPGA for BLS12-381 (Filecoin).

Although FPGAs are inherently reprogrammable platforms, the accelerators listed above implement their arithmetic pipelines as fixed RTL designs optimized for a specific prime field and hash function. Adapting them to a different field (e.g., from BLS12-381 to BabyBear) or a different hash (e.g., from MiMC to Poseidon2) would require modifying the HDL source, re-running synthesis and place-and-route, and generating a new bitstream—a process that takes minutes to hours and demands hardware design expertise. In principle, an FPGA design *could* be parameterized to support multiple fields, but none of the cited works adopt this approach, as field-specific optimization yields higher throughput. A CGRA operates at a different abstraction level: the hardware (ALUs, registers, interconnect) remains fixed, and switching to a new kernel amounts to loading a new instruction configuration via DMA, completing in microseconds with no hardware re-synthesis. This distinction is particularly relevant for wearable ZKP devices, where the proof system may evolve (new field, new exponent, new hash) and the device must adapt through a software update rather than FPGA re-flashing.

Separately, on the CGRA programming side, efficient CGRA compilers must support both spatially configured and time-multiplexed tasks. Spatially configured CGRAs employ pipelined dataflows with persistent runtime configurations, ideal for highly parallel tasks with predictable memory patterns, while time-multiplexed CGRAs offer flexible interconnections suitable for dynamic resource sharing and complex control flow. Compigra [7] and Wang et al. [20] provide automatic C-to-CGRA compilation tools that represent the state-of-the-art and consider some of the mentioned spatial-temporal challenges. However, they target general-purpose kernels and lack mechanisms for multi-precision spatial arithmetic, toroidal routing, or branchless correction—features essential for ZKP workloads.

To our knowledge, no prior work has mapped the Poseidon2 hash function onto a CGRA, designed an API for spatial-temporal cryptographic programming, or analyzed Configuration Register File capacity pressure for ZKP-class workloads.

3 The CASTM API

CASTM[1] can be seen as a deterministic C-like Domain Specific Language (DSL) whose design principle is *explicit spatial-temporal control with structured abstraction*: the programmer specifies what executes on which PE at which cycle, but through high-level constructs instead of raw encodings.

[1] Available at https://github.com/PhDCristian/CASTM.

Table 1. Comparison with related ZKP hardware accelerators. The "Reprogrammability" column reflects the cost of switching to a different hash or field.

Work	Platform	Primitive	Field	Reprogrammability
PipeZK [21]	ASIC	MSM+NTT	BN254	Fabrication
AMAZE [1]	FPGA	MiMC	BN254	RTL re-synthesis
HashEmAll [18]	FPGA	Rescue/Griffin	BN254	RTL re-synthesis
TRIDENT [5]	FPGA	Poseidon	BLS12-381	RTL re-synthesis
This work	**CGRA**	**Poseidon2**	**BabyBear**	**DMA load (μs)**

3.1 API Design

A CASTM program declares a *target profile*, a *build configuration*, and one or more *kernel* definitions. Table 2 organizes the constructs into three layers: spatial-temporal statements (instruction placement), structured abstractions (functions, loops, labels), and architecture-aware operators for modular arithmetic idioms.

Table 2. CASTM API constructs by abstraction layer.

Layer	Construct	Semantics
Spatial-temporal statements	`bundle { ...}`	Groups instructions into one bundle
	`@r,c: instr;`	Single-PE placement at (row, col)
	`at @r..r,c..c: instr;`	Range placement across PE sub-grid
	`at all: instr;`	Broadcasts instruction to all PEs
	`R0 = R1 + R2;`	C-like expression → ALU opcode
	`LWI / SWI R0, 40;`	Memory load/store (13-bit imm.)
	`BSFA R3,R0,R2,SELF;`	Branchless select on ALU sign flag
Structured abstractions	`function f(a,b) {...}`	Parametric macro, expanded at call site
	`for c in range(N)`	For loop
	`goto label; / goto R3;`	Direct or register-indirect jump
Arch.-aware operators	`std::extract_bytes`	Parallel byte extraction across row/col
	`std::carry_chain`	Multi-limb carry propag. across PEs
	`std::broadcast`	Wave distribution to all PEs via mesh
	`std::normalize`	Limb normalization with carry folding
	`std::reduce`	Collective accumul. across PE subset

The *spatial-temporal statements* layer provides direct control over instruction placement: every statement maps one-to-one to a CSV entry. The *structured abstractions* layer reduces repetition without scheduling opacity: `function` expands the function body at the call site by default (parametric macro expansion) but can be compiled to shared subroutines under the `jump-reuse` expansion mode, which emits each function body once and links calls through a register-based return convention. The *architecture-aware operators* layer encapsulates multi-instruction CGRA idioms for modular arithmetic, each expanding to a fixed, documented sequence.

To illustrate the contrast with manual CSV, consider broadcasting a memory load to all 16 PEs. In CSV, this requires 16 identical entries per cycle (each encoding opcode, mux selects, register indices, and immediate as 7 numeric fields): `29,0,0,0,1,0,0` repeated 16 times. In CASTM, the same operation is `bundle { at all: LWI R0, 0; }` –a single line that the compiler expands to 16 entries, eliminating an entire class of copy-and-paste errors.

3.2 Compilation Pipeline

The compiler performs a four-stage deterministic pipeline: **Parse** (tokenize, syntax validate) → **Analyze** (semantic checks, function expansion, constant resolution) → **Lower** (operator expansion, loop, flat IR generation) → **Emit** (per-PE CSV encoding). Each stage is a pure transformation with no heuristic decisions. The compiler rejects ambiguous scheduling (e.g., two instructions on the same PE in the same cycle) with diagnostics reporting source location, PE coordinate, and cycle number.

CASTM combines three properties no prior CGRA tool provides simultaneously: *deterministic compilation with explicit placement* (cycle count predictable at authoring time), *architecture-aware operators* and *transparent expansion* (every construct has a documented, predictable expansion to CSV).

3.3 S-Box Kernel Walkthrough

Figure 2 illustrates how our S-box kernel decomposes $x^7 \bmod p$ into four (modular) phases: 1) x^2 (`subrC` –squaring–); 2) $x^3 = x^2 \cdot x$ (`subrB` –general multiplication–); 3) $x^4 = (x^2)^2$ (`subrC`); and 4) $x^7 = x^4 \cdot x^3$ (`subrB`). Each phase performs a Barrett modular multiplication that consists of a base multiplication (`subrB`/`subrC`) followed by a Barrett modular reduction (`subrA`).

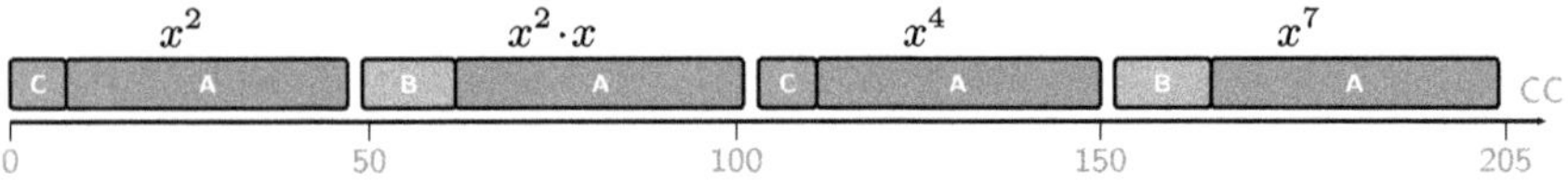

Fig. 2. Temporal breakdown of the S-box kernel (205 CC). Barrett modular reduction (`subrA`) consumes 76% of execution.

Figure 3 shows how Barrett multiplication [3] is decomposed into four algorithmic stages mapped to specific CGRA hardware capabilities. Step 1 represents the base product (`subrB`/`subrC`) while steps 2–4 correspond to the Barrett modular reduction (`subrA`). Step 1 is implemented as a parallel convolution: 32-bit operands decomposed into four 8-bit limbs, producing 16 partial products on the 4×4 PE mesh in our CGRA. Step 2 represents the quotient estimation and is mapped as a toroidal accumulation via nearest-neighbor routing; Step 3, the modular subtraction, avoids expensive division via subtraction and AND masking; then step 4 performs the final modular correction via branchless conditional `BSFA` (a single-cycle register select based on the ALU sign flag).

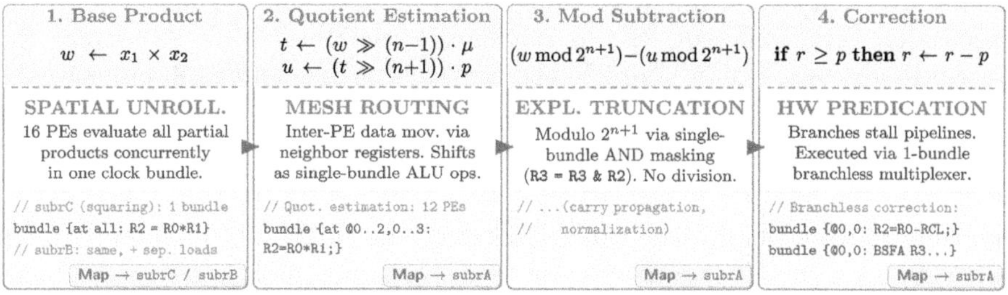

Fig. 3. Barrett multiplication mapped onto the CGRA. Each box shows the mathematical operation (top), hardware strategy (middle), and CASTM code excerpt (bottom).

```
kernel "SBox" {
    // PEs initialization
    bundle { @0,1: goto subrC; @3,0: R3 = ZERO + ret1; }
    ret1:
    bundle { @0,0: SWI R3, 720; @0,1: goto subrB;
             @3,0: R3 = ZERO + ret3; } // ▷ triple merge: SWI+goto+SADD in 1 bundle
    ...
    // Subroutine C: squaring (8 bundles)
    subrC:
    extract_bytes_col(R0, R1); // ▷ 4 PEs extract bytes in parallel
    extract_bytes_row(R0, R0);
    bundle { at all: R2 = R0 * R1; } // ▷ 16 partial products simultaneously
    // Toroidal accumulation (4 bundles via RCR/RCT/RCB)
    bundle { @3,0: goto subrA; }
    // Subroutine A: Barrett reduction (39 bundles)
    subrA:
    bundle { @0,0: R1 = RCR; @0,1: R0 = RCB; @0,2: R1 = RCB;}
    // Quotient estimation: 12 PEs compute qhat limbs
    bundle { at @0..2,0..3: R2 = R0 * R1; }
    // ... (carry propagation, normalization)
    // Branchless correction:
    bundle { @0,0: R2 = R0 - RCL; }
    bundle { @0,0: BSFA R3, R0, R2, SELF; } // ▷ if (r-p)<0: keep r; else: r-p
    bundle { @3,0: goto R3; }      // ▷ return via register-indirect jump
}
```

Listing 1.1. S-box kernel for $x^7 \bmod p$, in CASTM (key excerpts for `subrC` and `subrA`). `RCR/RCL/RCT/RCB` represent *Read Cell Right, Left, Top, Bottom*, respectively.

Listing 1.1 shows key excerpts of the S-box kernel. The kernel structure reveals several design decisions enabled by CASTM:

Jump-Reuse Subroutines. All calls to subroutines are performed via register-indirect jumps. The Barrett modular reduction phase (`subrA`, 39 bundles) is shared across all four modular operations through a simple calling convention: the caller stores a return-address label in R3 (`R3 = ZERO + retN`, line 3, line 6), and the subroutine returns with `goto R3` (line 24). This avoids duplicating 39 bundles × 4 calls = 156 wasted bundles, reducing total kernel size from ∼700 to 73 bundles (see Sect. 4.1). In CASTM, this pattern is expressed naturally with labels and `goto`; in manual CSV, the developer must compute absolute addresses for every jump target.

Triple Instruction Merging. At label `ret1`, three independent operations execute on three different PEs in the same cycle (lines 5–6): `SWI` stores the intermediate result, `goto` jumps to the next subroutine, and `SADD` prepares the return address. The `bundle{}` statement makes this spatial parallelism explicit and verifiable; in CSV, it is easy to accidentally place two instructions on the same PE, causing a silent overwrite.

Systolic Convolution. The `subrC` uses the 4 × 4 mesh as a spatial multiplier (lines 10–14): `extract_bytes` operators decompose operands into byte-size limbs distributed across columns and rows, then `at all: R2 = R0 * R1` computes all 16 partial products simultaneously. Toroidal accumulation converges results in 4 cycles via neighbor reads (RCR, RCT, RCB). All 16 PEs compute their partial product simultaneously; for squaring, the symmetric pairs are folded via in-place doubling during the subsequent accumulation phase, reducing it from 13 to 8 bundles compared to `subrB` that accumulates all the partial results explicitly.

Branchless Correction. The final BSFA instruction (line 23) selects between r and $r - p$ based on the sign flag, completing modular reduction in a single cycle without branching—avoiding control divergence across the PE mesh.

The jump-reuse feature imposes a residency constraint: all 73 bundles of the kernel must remain simultaneously resident in the Configuration Register File –CRF– so that register-indirect control flow can execute without fragmentation. When the kernel no longer fits, it must be partitioned into multiple dispatchable segments, sacrificing subroutine sharing and introducing reload overhead. Section 4.2 quantifies this S-box-specific CRF-pressure trade-off and shows why it becomes a first-order architectural constraint for the full Poseidon2 evaluation.

4 Experimental Results

All CGRA cycle counts in Sect. 4.1 are obtained from the ESL-CGRA simulator [2] (deterministic mode). Section 4.3 reports steady-state RTL measurements from Verilator cycle-accurate simulation of the HEEPsilon SoC (ultra-low power CV32E20 host, RV32IMC, single-issue in-order, without cryptography support). CPU-only time is derived at 250 MHz, whereas CGRA deployments on the OpenEdgeCGRA 4 × 4, 32-bit datapath use 100 MHz. CPU energy follows a fixed CV32E20 reference model of 2.5 mW applied to active-cycle counts; CGRA energy comes from the ESL simulator replay of the deployed kernels. The full Poseidon2 RTL data additionally includes a canonical-state replay with exact agreement to the reference.

4.1 S-Box Kernel Comparison

We evaluate three approaches to mapping the S-box kernel onto the CGRA: (1) a hand-optimized schedule (Manual), which represents our best expert effort schedule in this study, (2) the Compigra compiler [7], and (3) CASTM, our approach. Table 3 summarizes the ESL-measured results; Fig. 4 presents a visual comparison along with the estimated energy per invocation [2].

Table 3. S-box kernel: comparison of compilation approaches under ESL-CGRA simulation. NB: number of compiled bundles; CC: clock cycles including stalls; Disp.: number of CGRA dispatches; Idle (%): idle-PE ratio, summarized as a bundle-wise geometric mean.

Approach	NB	CC	Disp.	Idle (%)
Manual	406	678	1	64.3%
Compigra	2,564	3,544	244	89.9%
CASTM	**73**	**539**	1	**41.7%**

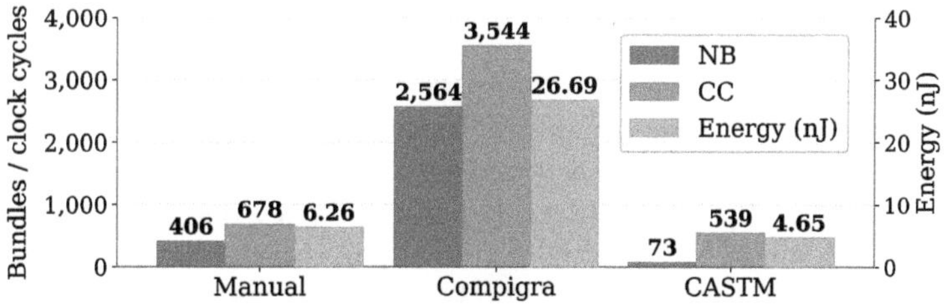

Fig. 4. Comparison of the S-box kernel mappings produced by Manual, Compigra, and CASTM on the CGRA. Blue and green bars use the left axis and report the number of compiled bundles (NB) and clock cycles (CC), respectively; orange bars use the right axis and report energy (nJ) per invocation.

Energy per invocation combines the ESL-reported execution energy with the fixed dead-time cost incurred at each CGRA dispatch. This normalization is necessary because the three mappings differ not only in cycle count but also in execution granularity: without accounting for dispatch overhead, a fragmented schedule would understate the system-level cost of repeatedly launching and draining the accelerator. Idle (%) in Table 3 is reported as a bundle-wise geometric mean over per-bundle idle-PE ratios.

Compigra Cannot Map S-Box Directly. The automatic compiler's scheduling heuristic fails on the S-box kernel because Barrett reduction requires cross-PE carry chains and branchless conditional selects that exceed its mapping capabilities. The workaround is to manually decompose $x^7 \bmod p$ into sub-kernels and iteratively subdivide when compilation fails—a trial-and-error process that weakens the "automatic" premise. The result is 244 dispatches with 89.9% Idle and 0.0% of SMUL utilization: the hardware multiplier is never used, and the CGRA spends most cycles idle while data is shuffled between dispatches.

CASTM Achieves the Lowest Cycle Count. The 73 compiled bundles (vs. 406 for the Manual schedule) reflect jump-reuse subroutines that share Barrett reduction across the four modular multiplications (x^2, x^3, x^4, x^7). The resulting 539 CC (vs. 678 CC for Manual) represents a 20.5% cycle reduction attributable to better PE utilization: 41.7% Idle (vs. 64.3%) and active use of the hardware multiplier (4.1% SMUL). Under the energy model, CASTM also remains the most efficient mapping at 4.65 nJ, below Manual at 6.26 nJ and far below Compigra at 26.69 nJ. The gap is architecturally coherent with the schedules themselves: Compigra expands the kernel into 244 dispatches, so its higher energy reflects not only a longer execution (3,544 CC) but also repeated launch and quiescent overheads that are largely avoided by the single-dispatch in the CASTM schedule.

Productivity. The Manual approach requires 2,030 lines; CASTM requires 340 lines—an approximately 6.0× reduction. This gap is structural: CASTM's parameterized functions and loops express the kernel once, whereas the handwritten schedule must spell out each PE-cycle placement explicitly, making coding slower and substantially more error-prone.

Code Complexity. Table 4 quantifies complexity using Halstead active volume metric, $V_{\text{act}} = N \log_2 \eta$, where N counts active (non-NOP) tokens [12]. We do not report Halstead effort because, for low-vocabulary ISA-level code, it can produce anomalous scaling [19]. Owing to explicit per-PE-per-cycle encoding, the Manual schedule reaches 64.5× the `C++` baseline. By absorbing spatial placement and NOP scheduling into the compiler, CASTM reduces this to 6.4×, corresponding to a 10.10× compression factor relative to the Manual schedule. Ideally, Compigra could reduce this complexity to 2.4× the `C++` baseline, although at the cost of 6.58× more cycles than CASTM due to inefficient PE utilization as previously explained.

Table 4. Halstead metrics for the S-box kernel. LOC: physical source lines; $\eta = n_1 + n_2$: unique vocabulary; $N = N_1 + N_2$: active token length (NOP excluded); $V_{\text{act}} = N \log_2 \eta$: active volume [12]; Ratio is V_{act} normalized to `C++ (Ref.)`.

Approach	LOC	η	N	V_{act}	Ratio
C++ (Ref.)	25	39	104	550	1.0×
Compigra C++	47	53	227	1,300	2.4×
Manual CSV	2,030	48	6,348	35,453	64.5×
CASTM (**Ours**)	**340**	**55**	**607**	**3,509**	**6.4×**

4.2 S-Box Configuration Register Pressure

The S-box kernel also allows us to conduct a controlled sensitivity study for configuration residency. Two implementations bracket the design space: the *Manual* kernel (406 bundles, flat layout) and the *CASTM* kernel (73 bundles, jump-reuse with shared subroutines). Because the Manual kernel uses only sequential control flow, it can be split into independent sub-kernels at any CRF depth. The CASTM kernel cannot: its register-indirect returns (`JUMP R3`) require all 73 bundles to be simultaneously resident in the CRF.

When a kernel of NB bundles exceeds the CRF depth D, it must be partitioned into $K = \lceil NB/D \rceil$ sub-kernels. In HEEPsilon's default CMEM organization, each sub-kernel fills an entire memory bank, so every transition between sub-kernels forces the host to reload all configuration data. The overhead decomposes as:

$$T_{\text{ovh}} = \underbrace{\textstyle\sum_i (s_i + 1)}_{\text{CRF load}} + \underbrace{4(K-1)}_{\text{controller}} + \underbrace{(K-1)(16D+16)}_{\text{CMEM reload}}$$

where the sum runs over the $K-1$ transitions (s_i is the size of each reloaded sub-kernel). The first two terms—streaming instructions into the CRF and controller handshake cycles—are small. The CMEM reload term dominates: it transfers the full bank contents via MMIO, costing approximately $16NB$ cycles for a large K, nearly *constant* regardless of D.

At the default $D = 32$, the Manual kernel loses 91% of its cycles due to reload overhead ($K = 13$); doubling or quadrupling D barely helps because the total data volume stays proportional to NB. Overhead only vanishes when the entire kernel fits ($K = 1$): this happens for $D = 512$ in Manual, and $D = 128$ in CASTM. The 5.6× bundle compression from Manual to CASTM (406→73) now translates into a 4× reduction in CRF requirement, at the cost of 0.9% additional area for $D = 128$ vs. 4.5% for $D = 512$ (i.e. +49,152 flip-flops vs. +245,760 flip-flops on Artix-7 XC7A200T [14])[2]. However, this comes with a rigidity constraint: for any $D < 73$, the CASTM kernel cannot execute at all.

4.3 Poseidon2: RTL Validation

The S-box CRF-pressure analysis above showed that, for long ZKP kernels, configuration fragmentation and reload overhead dominate before arithmetic throughput can become visible. The full Poseidon2 kernel (366 bundles) requires $D = 512$ to fit without partitioning. Under that condition, we analyze three deployment options when running a batch of Poseidon2 hashes: a *CPU-only* reference that executes all the hashes on the CPU, a *CGRA-only* version that offloads all the hashes to the CGRA, and a *CPU+CGRA* implementation, which evenly launches the hashes concurrently on the CPU and the CGRA. Both *CGRA-only* and *CPU+CGRA* keep the full Poseidon2 kernel on the accelerator (Table 5).

[2] These figures are FPGA synthesis results, not an ASIC or wearable-SoC cost model; power overhead of the larger CRF is not reported here.

Table 5. Poseidon2: comparison of RTL metrics. T: Time (μs); Th: Throughput (hashes per sec.); Sp: Speedup; E: Energy (μJ); ES: Energy Savings (%).

Configuration	T_{CPU}	T_{CGRA}	T_{tot}	Th	Sp	E_{CPU}	E_{CGRA}	E_{tot}	ES
CPU-only	733.4	—	733.4	1,363	1.00	4.584	—	4.584	0
CGRA-only	7.4	543.5	550.8	1,816	1.33	0.047	2.993	**3.039**	**33.7**
CPU+CGRA	358.3	290.8	**358.3**	**2,791**	**2.05**	2.240	1.596	3.836	16.3

The throughput ranking is straightforward. T_{CPU} and T_{CGRA} report the time per-hash (full Poseidon2) for which the host CPU and the accelerator are active, with T_{tot} being the total time per-hash. From this last metric we see that *CPU+CGRA* is the fastest because both devices work in parallel reaching 358.3 µs/hash, the highest throughput, 2,791 hashes/sec., and up to 2.05× speedup over the *CPU-only*. Interestingly, there is room for improvement for this hybrid deployment because as we see from the T_{CPU} and T_{CGRA} times, the workload is currently not balanced between devices. A more advanced scheduling strategy aware of the computational power of each device could be used, but this issue is beyond the scope of this paper, and we leave it for future work. *CGRA-only* also outperforms *CPU-only* at 550.8 µs/hash and 1.33× speedup.

Energy favors a different organization. E_{CPU} and E_{CGRA} represent the energy per-hash consumed by the CPU and CGRA, respectively, while E_{tot} is the total energy and ES is the energy savings with respect to *CPU-only*. Now, *CGRA-only* reduces the total energy to 3.039 µJ/hash, a 33.7% reduction relative to *CPU-only*, whereas *CPU+CGRA* reaches 3.836 µJ/hash, or 16.3% reduction. In the hybrid deployment, the E_{CGRA} component is the minimum, but the less efficient E_{CPU} contribution increases because the CPU computes part of the hashes, which ultimately degrades the total energy.

From the T_{CPU} (E_{CPU}) metric in the *CGRA-only* case, we can infer the overhead due to kernel dispatch (input parameter setting + kernel launching + output reading). As we see, this overhead is very low, around 1.3% of total time and 1.5% of total energy.

In our study, we have found that memory stalls are the most significant source of overhead for this CGRA kernel, representing 23.5% of active cycles. These memory access stalls are mainly due to memory bank conflicts that are even more relevant if other memory subsystem design choices are considered. For instance, replacing the more flexible host-to-memory crossbar *N:M* that we have considered in this analysis, with the simpler shared path *OneToM*, degrades the *CGRA-only* performance from 56,416 CC to 68,643 CC and reduces speedup from 1.33× to 1.06×.

4.4 Lessons Learned

Our results provide some interesting architectural lessons. Firstly, CRF configuration capacity is a primary tuning knob: before fragmentation is removed, system behavior is dominated by reload traffic rather than arithmetic execution. Thus, kernels should be designed to fit the CRF as a single unit. Once this requisite is satisfied, throughput and energy do not necessarily favor the same organization of kernels: a hybrid deployment as *CPU+CGRA* provides the highest throughput, whereas *CGRA-only* minimizes total energy consumption. The next optimization step lies less in creating finer-grain offload variants than in reducing the cost of delivering data to an already efficient accelerator by minimizing memory bank conflicts. Also for hybrid deployments, load-balancing scheduling strategies must be considered.

5 Conclusions

In this paper, we have presented CASTM, the first API targeting the spatial-temporal programming model of CGRA architectures for a class of cryptographic kernels based on arithmetization operating on finite fields. Specifically, for the BabyBear S-box layer on the OpenEdgeCGRA architecture, CASTM achieves a 20.5% cycle reduction over hand-optimized CSV (539 CC vs. 678 CC), while reducing source code by approximately 6.0×.

RTL validation of the full Poseidon2 hash function on the ultra-low power HEEPsilon SoC gives us some system lessons. The Configuration Register File capacity is the enabling condition: once the kernel fits in the CRF the running times are no longer masked by reload fragmentation. Under that condition, offloading the full kernel to the CGRA (*CGRA-only*) minimizes the total energy at 3.039 μJ/hash (33.7% energy savings), whereas a hybrid deployment that computes hashes on the CPU and the accelerator (*CPU+CGRA*) offers the highest throughput at 358.3 μs/hash and 2.05× speedup.

In summary, we have shown that it is possible to enable privacy-preserving verification on wearable biomedical devices through Zero-Knowledge Proofs, on hardware that is both energy-efficient and reprogrammable, allowing it to track the rapid evolution of ZKP systems.

Future Work. Two directions follow: (1) dual-port SRAM or DMA burst modes to reduce the memory stalls that now represent the main source of overhead; and (2) evaluation on alternative ZKP fields (Goldilocks, BN254) and post-quantum workloads to test the generality of CASTM's API.

Disclosure of Interests. The authors have no competing interests to declare that are relevant to the content of this article.

References

1. Ahmed, A., et al.: AMAZE: accelerated MiMC hardware architecture for zero-knowledge applications on the edge. In: Proceedings of the 43rd IEEE/ACM International Conference on Computer-Aided Design (ICCAD 2024), pp. 1–9. ACM (2024)

2. Aspros, M.H., et al.: A flexible framework for early power and timing comparison of time-multiplexed CGRA kernel executions. In: Proceedings of the 22nd ACM International Conference on Computing Frontiers, pp. 62–65. ACM (2025)
3. Barrett, P.: Implementing the Rivest Shamir and Adleman public key encryption algorithm on a standard digital signal processor. In: Odlyzko, A.M. (ed.) CRYPTO 1986. LNCS, vol. 263, pp. 311–323. Springer, Heidelberg (1987). https://doi.org/10.1007/3-540-47721-7_24
4. Ben-Sasson, E., et al.: Scalable, transparent, and post-quantum secure computational integrity. IACR Cryptology ePrint Archive (2018)
5. DatenLord: TRIDENT: a hardware-implemented Poseidon hasher (2022). https://github.com/datenlord/TRIDENT. zPrize 2022 entry; Xilinx Varium C1100
6. Dias, D., Paulo Silva Cunha, J.: Wearable health devices—vital sign monitoring, systems and technologies. Sensors **18**(8), 2414 (2018)
7. Embedded Systems Laboratory, EPFL: Compigra: Open-source C/C++-to-CGRA compilation toolchain (2026). https://github.com/esl-epfl/Compigra
8. Gabizon, A., Williamson, Z.J., Ciobotaru, O.: PLONK: permutations over Lagrange-bases for oecumenical noninteractive arguments of knowledge. In: IACR Cryptology ePrint Archive (2019)
9. Grassi, L., et al.: Poseidon: a new hash function for zero-knowledge proof systems. In: 30th USENIX Security Symposium (USENIX Security 2021), pp. 519–535 (2021)
10. Grassi, L., et al.: Poseidon2: a faster version of the poseidon hash function. In: Progress in Cryptology - AFRICACRYPT 2023, pp. 177–203. Springer (2023)
11. Groth, J.: On the size of pairing-based non-interactive arguments. In: Fischlin, M., Coron, J.-S. (eds.) EUROCRYPT 2016. LNCS, vol. 9666, pp. 305–326. Springer, Heidelberg (2016). https://doi.org/10.1007/978-3-662-49896-5_11
12. Halstead, M.H.: Elements of Software Science. Elsevier North-Holland, NY (1977)
13. Liu, Z., et al.: Efficient implementation of NIST-compliant elliptic curve cryptography for 8-bit AVR-based sensor nodes. IEEE Trans. Inf. Forensics Secur. **11**(7), 1385–1397 (2016)
14. OpenHW Group and University of Bologna: X-heep documentation (2026). https://x-heep.readthedocs.io/en/latest/index.html
15. Podobas, A., et al.: A survey on coarse-grained reconfigurable architectures from a performance perspective. IEEE Access **8**, 146719–146743 (2020)
16. Polygon Zero Team: Plonky3: a high-performance ZK proving system. Technical report and project documentation (2024)
17. Rodríguez Álvarez, R., et al.: An open-hardware coarse-grained reconfigurable array for edge computing. In: Proceedings of the 20th ACM International Conference on Computing Frontiers, pp. 391–392. ACM, New York (2023)
18. Sheybani, N., et al.: Gotta hash 'em All! Accelerating hash functions for zero-knowledge proof applications. In: IEEE International Symposium on Hardware Oriented Security and Trust (HOST) (2025)
19. Sinha, B.P., Srikanthan, T.: A software complexity measure for reconfigurable computing. In: IEEE International Symposium on VLSI Design, Automation and Test (VLSI-DAT), pp. 1–4 (2011)
20. Wang, Y., et al.: An MLIR-based compilation framework for control flow management on coarse grained reconfigurable arrays (2025)
21. Zhang, Y., et al.: PipeZK: accelerating zero-knowledge proof with a pipelined architecture. In: 48th ACM/IEEE International Symposium on Computer Architecture (ISCA), pp. 416–428 (2021)

SISA: A Scale-In Systolic Array for GEMM Acceleration

Luigi Altamura(✉), Alessio Cicero, Mateo Vázquez Maceiras, Mohammad Ali Maleki, and Pedro Trancoso

Department of Computer Science and Engineering, Chalmers University of Technology and University of Gothenburg, SE-41296 Gothenburg, Sweden
{altamura,alessio.cicero,maceiras,mohammad.ali.maleki,ppedro}@chalmers.se

Abstract. The currently dominant AI/ML workloads, such as Large Language Models (LLMs), rely on the efficient execution of General Matrix-Matrix Multiplication (GEMM) operations. Thus, most systems are equipped with dedicated matrix hardware accelerators built on square Systolic Arrays (SAs) of Processing Elements (PEs). While this organization was effective for traditional Deep Neural Networks (DNNs), LLMs introduce input-dependent and highly skewed matrices, leading to underutilized SA resources.

To address this challenge, we propose SISA (Scale-In Systolic Array), a novel SA architecture that partitions the traditional square array into horizontal rectangular slabs. With minimal overhead, SISA exposes parallelism through independently scheduled slabs for efficient execution of small or skewed matrix shapes, while retaining full-array operation for large GEMMs. SISA achieves up to 8.52× speedup and 93% energy-delay-product (EDP) reduction for representative LLMs compared to a state-of-the-art monolithic SA with the same number of PEs.

Keywords: systolic array · GEMM · LLM · accelerator · adaptive architecture

1 Introduction

In recent years, the use of AI-based applications has increased rapidly. Large Language Models (LLMs), which form the backbone of widely deployed interactive systems such as ChatGPT, are quite demanding on the computing systems. LLM inference consists of two distinct phases: *prefill* and *decode*, each with fundamentally different characteristics. During prefill, the model processes the entire input prompt using dense General Matrix-Matrix Multiplications (GEMMs), which are compute-bound. In contrast, decode generates tokens sequentially using General Matrix-Vector Multiplications (GEMVs), making it predominantly memory-bandwidth bound. In addition to GEMVs, the decode also repeatedly accesses the key–value (KV) cache, which increases in size at each decode step.

M. Torquati et al. (Eds.): Euro-Par 2026, LNCS 16781, pp. 359–372, 2027.
https://doi.org/10.1007/978-3-032-35248-4_25

These characteristics naturally map the phases to different architectural primitives. Prefill benefits from Systolic Array (SA)-based accelerators that maximize throughput for large GEMMs, whereas decode is better suited to Vector Processing Units (VPUs) that efficiently handle GEMVs. However, for LLM systems serving multiple concurrent requests, batching can increase arithmetic intensity and amortize memory traffic [1,2]. This introduces GEMM operations in the decode phase as well, making SA-based accelerators a primary architecture for LLMs. Consequently, many modern AI accelerators incorporate SAs. The best-known example is the Google TPU, which integrates a large square SA (e.g., 128×128 and 256×256 PEs) [11] that efficiently executes the large GEMMs common in LLMs and, more generally, Deep Learning (DL) workloads.

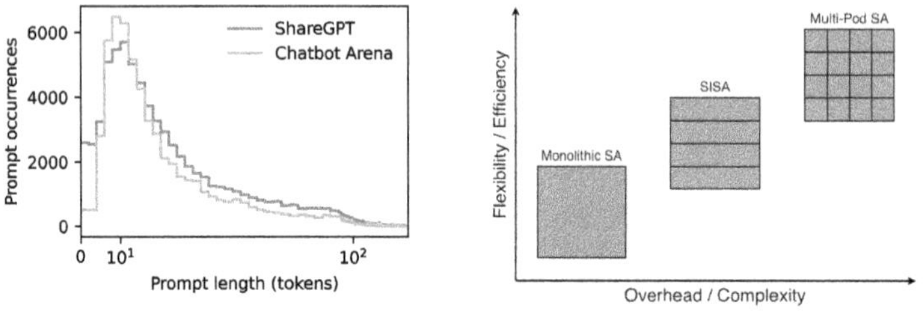

(a) (b)

Fig. 1. (a) Prompt length derived from interactive chatbot requests and (b) alternative SA designs.

Nevertheless, when matrices are highly-skewed or smaller than the SA size, a significant fraction of PEs remain idle. Previous works have shown that such SA-matrix shape mismatches lead to considerable under-utilization [4], and these mismatches are common in practice. Figure 1a shows that real-world chatbot prompts are typically short (mean 41.8, median 12 tokens) [17], leading to skewed GEMMs during the LLM prefill phase. Consequently, the LLM prefill phase often involves skewed matrices (e.g., (12, 8192) for a 12-token prompt in Llama3.2-3B). In addition, the number of tokens per prompt varies across requests. When multi-batching is not possible or when latency-sensitive prefill is required, matrix shapes remain highly skewed, since increasing batching may degrade Quality-of-Service by increasing the Time To First Token (TTFT).

When decode requests are batched to amortize memory access costs in a GEMM-based LLM decode phase, the resulting matrix shapes depend on the batch size, with small batches yielding highly skewed matrices. However, two factors prevent aggressively large batching (e.g., decode batch sizes beyond 32–64). First, larger batch sizes increase response time, so batching is kept moderate to balance QoS and efficiency. Second, the decode phase accesses the KV cache, which can become large depending on the request. Since each request maintains its own KV cache, batching requires multiple such structures to be stored simultaneously in memory, further limiting the batch size.

In order to address these and other mismatch issues between SAs and GEMM shapes of matrices, researchers have proposed different architectures that can adapt the arrangement of available PEs to better accommodate the shapes of the matrices [5,7,9,10,12,13,15,19,20]. In Fig. 1b we show the tradeoff between flexibility/efficiency and overhead/complexity. Monolithic SA accelerators serves as the baseline, whereas flexible accelerators such as the multi-pod SA offers more flexibility at the cost of increased buffer and interconnection network overheads.

To address this challenge, we propose SISA, a new SA architecture that extends the traditional $n \times n$ square design with a *scale-in* mechanism that partitions the array into horizontal smaller rectangular sub-arrays, referred to as slabs, capable of parallel, independently scheduled execution. This slab-level parallelism enables SISA to efficiently process highly skewed matrix shapes by increasing effective parallelism relative to a monolithic array. When full-array execution is advantageous, SISA seamlessly operates as a conventional systolic array, preserving peak GEMM performance while incurring only minimal additional on-chip buffering overhead. This design point is represented in Fig. 1b.

The main contributions of this work are:

- A novel SA architecture that operates either as a unified array or partitioned into slabs that better accommodate to skewed matrix shapes.
- A scheduling and tiling mechanism that exploits parallelism across slabs.
- An instance of SISA with 128×128 PEs and its evaluation using state-of-the-art (SOTA) LLM models.

We have evaluated SISA with GEMM operations from LLMs, and observed a speedup of up to 8.52× and a reduction in energy-delay-product (EDP) up to 93% when compared to a TPU with the same amount of compute and memory resources. In the worst case, SISA achieves comparable performance to the TPU with only an 8.47% higher EDP. When compared to alternative SOTA flexible SA architectures, SISA performs better in most cases, achieving speedups up to 2.61× while also exhibiting lower area overhead.

2 Related Work

To meet the computational requirements of LLMs, SAs appear as a fitting architecture to build ML accelerators. SAs are architectures composed by a set of interconnected PEs. Thanks to their regular structure and communication patterns, SAs can offer high computational capabilities for GEMM while keeping energy consumption efficient compared to other architectures: in SAs, results are fed directly to the next computational unit without intermediate storage, following a systolic wavefront.

However, while monolithic SAs are a matching architecture for computing GEMM, multiple variations have been presented in recent works. These variations of SAs aim to better match the characteristics and requirements of different workloads like LLMs. In this section, we present the most relevant proposals, which are summarized in Table 1.

Table 1. Comparison of SAs across key design requirements. For relative requirements, like the area overhead, we take as reference an equivalent monolithic SA.

Architecture	Fine-Grained Array/Pods Reconfigurability	Low Area Overhead	Low Data Movement
TPU [11]	X	✓	✓
Gemmini [6]	X	✓	✓
SOSA [20]	✓	X	X
SAVector [5]	✓	✓	X
Planaria [7]	X	✓	✓
FlexSA [12]	✓	X	✓
HALO [19]	✓	X	✓
DyNNamic [10]	✓	X	✓
SARA [15]	✓	X	✓
ReDas [9]	✓	X	✓
SISA (this work)	✓	✓	✓

Monolithic Arrays. Early DL accelerators adopted large, fixed-size SAs to maximize GEMM throughput, like Google's TPU [11] and Gemmini [6]. Scaling up a single array provides high compute density and high throughput for large workloads, but it suffers from substantial under-utilization for small or irregular matrices, where many PEs remain idle due to poor alignment between workload shape and array dimensions [4].

Multi-Pod Systolic Architectures. To improve utilization, one approach is to build architectures based on smaller SAs, named pods, and distribute computation across them. Example of this approach are Scale-Out Systolic Arrays (SOSA) [20] and Vectored Systolic Arrays (SAVector) [5]. Overall, multi-pod systolic architectures enhance parallel tile-level processing but inherently increase data movement and off-chip memory access due to duplicated tile loads across pods. In addition, their fixed pod granularity limits utilization on large GEMMs where a unified array would provide higher data reuse. These architectures increase flexibility but introduce redundant data movement and elevated memory traffic, resulting in a reduction of the overall efficiency.

Reconfigurable Systolic Arrays. To be able to provide efficient execution of small, medium, and large GEMMs, reconfigurable SAs support runtime reconfiguration of large SAs into smaller tiles, increasing utilization while retaining the performance of monolithic SAs for large GEMMs. However, this reconfigurability comes at a cost, which depends on the specific approach followed. Planaria [7], which targets multi-workload execution, is limited to coarse-grained reconfiguration, i.e., not flexible enough, and thus still suffers from under-utilization issues. Works like FlexSA [12], HALO [19], DyNNamic [10], and SARA [15] support finer reconfigurability, but that comes with an increased area overhead. ReDas aims to solve this problem to some extend, but does it so at the cost of not being able to use all PEs in multiple configurations [9].

This Work. Contrary to existing works, SISA provides a SA architecture that (1) exhibits the compute density of a large SA for big GEMM operations, (2) enables more flexible execution modes that mitigate under-utilization, and (3) does so with low area overhead.

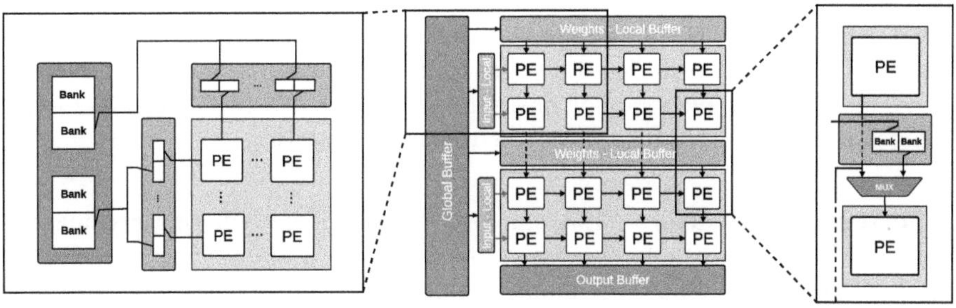

Fig. 2. Overview of the SISA architecture with detailed views of the memory hierarchy and slab fusion mechanism.

3 Scale-In Systolic Array

3.1 Architecture

At a high level, SISA consists of a fixed pool of PEs organized as a logical two-dimensional SA and horizontally partitioned into rectangular slabs to efficiently process skewed matrices. Each slab forms an independently controllable systolic unit with local buffers for activations and weights. Through multiplexing and power-gating, slabs can be fused into larger logical arrays or operated independently to exploit parallelism within a GEMM. Unused slabs can be power-gated to reduce idle energy. SISA operates as a CPU-hosted accelerator with access to external memory. Figure 2 provides an overview of the architecture.

Slab Structure and Dataflow. Each slab has a rectangular organization, spanning the full width of the SA while occupying a fraction of its height since LLM workloads are typically narrow in one dimension but wide in the other. As described earlier, each slab includes local buffers for activations and weights, while output values are written directly to the global output buffer. SISA employs an Output-Stationary (OS) dataflow. Under this dataflow, each PE is responsible for a unique output element and maintains the corresponding accumulator locally for the duration of the GEMM processing. As a result, partial sums do not traverse inter-PE interconnects; only activations and weights are streamed through the array. This property simplifies slab composition and enables modular and scalable execution across fused and independent slabs. The OS dataflow is particularly effective when the SA matches, even partially, the output tensor dimensions of the GEMM.

Slab Fusion Mechanism. Slabs can be fused along the height dimension of the SA to form larger logical slabs. As shown in Fig. 2, this is enabled through a simple buffer bypass implemented with multiplexers, forwarding the weights from one slab to the next while bypassing redundant slab-local weight buffers. When fused, adjacent slabs execute a single tile as a larger logical SA. Multiple fused slab groups may operate concurrently, each executing a different tile of the same GEMM. The selected configuration remains static during tile execution and is updated only between tiles. Its setup overhead, which is limited to selecting bypass multiplexers and enabling or disabling slab-local buffers and power gates, is therefore negligible compared to tile execution time [18].

Buffering Organization. SISA employs a hierarchical buffering organization composed of a global buffer, slab-local buffers, and a global output buffer. As shown in Fig. 2, all buffers use double buffering to overlap data movement with computation. The global buffer stores activations and weights, while the output buffer collects slab results before they are written back to memory.

Global Buffer Organization. The global buffer is implemented as a collection of partitioned SRAM banks. Each bank is dedicated to providing activations or weights to a specific set of local slab buffers. Thanks to the regular data access patterns of SA-based GEMM execution, this organization enables building larger SRAM capacity while maintaining bounded access latency. Each bank has a port width of multiple elements, allowing it to write to several local buffers per cycle and increasing effective bandwidth with limited latency overhead.

Output Buffer Organization. A multi-banked output buffer collects the results produced by the slabs and supports both independent and fused slab execution.

Local Slab Buffers. Each slab contains small local buffers for input activations and weights placed next to the array boundary to directly feed the PEs. Each upper-boundary PE of the slab receives data from a dedicated pair of banks.

Power-Gating. Power management in SISA is performed at the granularity of individual slabs. Slab-local buffers can be selectively disabled, and entire slabs can be power-gated when not required for execution. This coarse-grain power-gating strategy minimizes idle energy consumption.

3.2 Tiling and Scheduling

SISA decomposes each GEMM into tiles that map naturally onto slab configurations. Given $C[M, N] = A[M, K] \times B[K, N]$, SISA tiles the M, N, and K dimensions to satisfy on-chip storage constraints while maximizing data reuse and SA utilization. Tiles are statically scheduled across slabs (or fused slab groups), enabling concurrent execution when resources are available. When tiling along K is required, partial tiles are processed sequentially and accumulated before advancing to the next output tile. Figure 3 illustrates the execution strategies across different GEMM shapes.

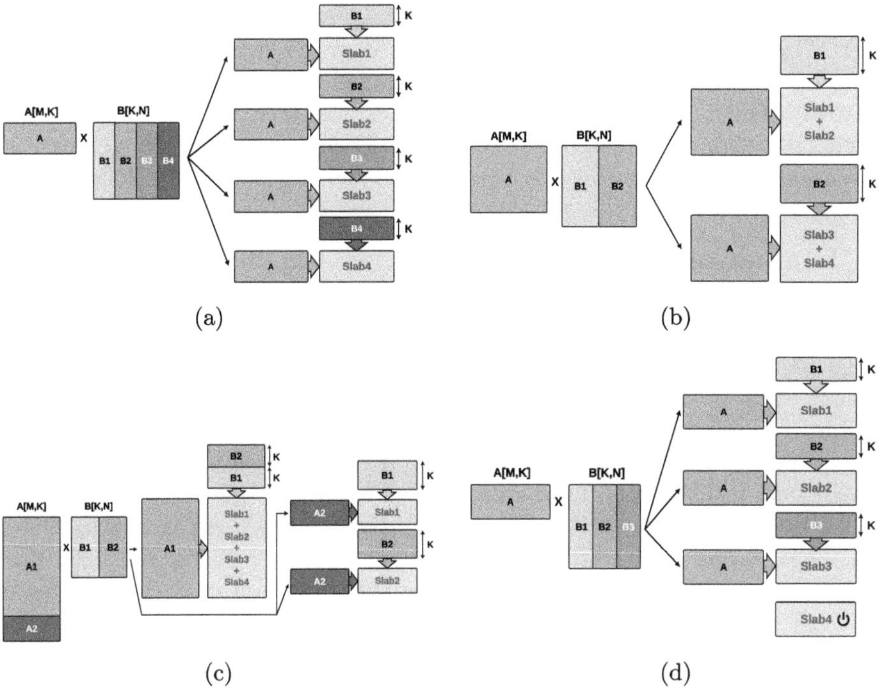

Fig. 3. Tiling and execution strategies in SISA for different GEMM shapes. (a) Independent slab execution for small-M GEMMs, distributing tiles across slabs along N. (b) Slab fusion for intermediate-M GEMMs, forming larger logical SAs matching tile height. (c) Monolithic execution for large-M GEMMs using the full array. (d) Slab-level power-gating disables slabs when parallelism is limited.

M $\leq$ Slab Height. When M is smaller than the slab height, SISA distributes computation along the N dimension, as shown in Fig. 3a. The input matrix A is loaded once into on-chip memory and reused across tiles, while the weight matrix B is partitioned along N into tiles matching the slab width. Each B tile is assigned to a slab, allowing multiple tiles to execute in parallel. If the number of tiles is smaller than the available slabs, unused slabs are power-gated, as illustrated in Fig. 3d. If tiles exceed on-chip storage capacity, SISA further partitions the computation along K while keeping A resident to maximize reuse.

Slab Height < M $\leq$ Array Height. When M exceeds the slab height but remains smaller than the full systolic array height, SISA fuses multiple slabs along M to form a taller logical slab, illustrated in Fig. 3b. The fused slabs execute tiles whose M dimension matches the fused height. After determining the fusion configuration, SISA applies the same tiling strategy along N. Each fused slab group processes one tile, enabling parallel execution across groups. Because fusion reduces the number of independent slab groups, fewer tiles may execute concurrently and remaining tiles are processed in subsequent iterations.

M > Array Height. When M exceeds the full array height, SISA executes the GEMM using a fully fused configuration equivalent to a monolithic systolic array, shown in Fig. 3c. The computation is decomposed into a main tile spanning the full array height. After completing this tile, residual tiles are executed using the appropriate slab configuration, either by fusing slabs to match the residual M dimension or by distributing the computation across independent slabs.

4 Evaluation

4.1 Experimental Setup

For area and energy evaluation, we model SISA using RTL synthesis and SRAM estimation tools. The design is synthesized with Cadence Genus 18.14 targeting a 28 nm technology node with the ASAP7 cell library [16] at 1 GHz. On-chip buffers are modeled using CACTI [3]. For performance evaluation, we extend SCALE-Sim [14] to support the architectural features required by our design.

We compare SISA against two representative SA baselines: Google's TPUv4 [11], representing a monolithic SA, and ReDas [9], a reconfigurable SA that reports improvements over prior SOTA designs discussed in Sect. 2. All baselines are modeled according to their published configurations using the same RTL+CACTI methodology to ensure fairness. CACTI-based SRAM estimations were validated against the detailed memory area numbers reported in ReDas, obtained using TSMC's 28 nm memory compiler. The relative error is only 0.27%.

SISA is evaluated using a 128×128 SA, consistent with the configurations adopted in TPUv4 and ReDas. We do not model the roundabout interconnect overhead in ReDas, which benefits this baseline. Further architectural details of the evaluated designs are provided in Sect. 4.2.

Table 2. Dimensions of unique GEMM operations across models, reported as triples (M, N, K). m denotes the sequence length in the prefill phase or batch size in the decode phase.

ID	Qwen2.5-0.5B	Qwen2.5-1.5B	Llama3.2-3B	Qwen2.5-7B
0	(m,896,896)	(m,1536,1536)	(m,3072,3072)	(m,3584,3584)
1	(m,128,896)	(m,356,1536)	(m,1024,3072)	(m,512,3584)
2	(m,4864,896)	(m,8960,1536)	(m,8192,3072)	(m,3584,18944)
3	(m,896,4864)	(m,1536,8960)	(m,3072,8192)	(m,18944,3584)
4	(m,151936,896)	(m,151936,1536)	(m,128256,3072)	(m,152064,3584)

As GEMM is the dominant operation in LLM execution [1] and since SISA is an architecture to optimize GEMM, we perform this evaluation on the GEMM operations present in modern relevant LLMs of different size: Qwen2.5[1] 0.5B,

[1] https://huggingface.co/collections/Qwen/qwen25.

1.5B, and 7B, as well as Llama3.2 3B[2]. We extracted the model information from the pre-trained models available in HuggingFace. Although these models contain many layers, they are largely composed of repeated computational blocks. Larger models typically preserve the same underlying GEMM patterns while scaling the matrix dimensions, and are therefore unlikely to change the observed performance and energy trends of SISA. Table 2 reports the unique GEMM sizes considered as triples (M, N, K).

Table 3. SISA Configuration, Area, and Per-Cycle Static Energy (1 GHz)

Parameter	Value	Area	Energy/Cycle (nJ)
SA Size	128×128	192.91 mm^2	21.60
Global Buffer Size	8 MB	22.45 mm^2	5.22
Slabs Buffer Sizes	8 KB, 64 KB	0.30 mm^2	0.12
Output Buffer Size	2 MB	5.61 mm^2	1.25
Total	–	**221.27 mm^2**	**28.19nJ**

4.2 Designing a 128×128 PE 8-Slab SISA

Slabs. The slab height of 16 is primarily chosen to match practical off-chip bandwidth limits. With eight slabs operating in parallel, concurrently streaming activations and weights at BF16 precision requires approximately 2.3 TB/s, already close to the bandwidth of a state-of-the-art HBM4 stack (> 2.8 TB/s [8]). Finer-grain partitioning would require higher off-chip memory bandwidth, whereas coarser-grain partitioning would reduce parallelism. Therefore we focus on the evaluated configuration, which already exhibits low overhead.

Memory Organization. For a fair comparison, we allocate the same total on-chip memory capacity across TPU, ReDas, and SISA, organized according to each architecture. The TPU-like baseline employs two 4 MB buffers (activation and weight) and one 2 MB output buffer. ReDas distributes four 2.5 MB buffers around the SA, following its multi-mode organization. SISA preserves the same total memory budget using 8 MB global activation and weight buffer and 2 MB of output buffer.

Area and Energy Breakdown. Table 3 reports the post-synthesis area and per-cycle static energy of SISA at 1 GHz. The 128×128 BF16 SA dominates both area (192.91 mm^2) and energy (21.60 nJ/cycle), while the memory hierarchy contributes 6.59 nJ/cycle from leakage. Dynamic energy of SRAM and DRAM are modeled separately using per-access energy parameters and are accounted for during workload execution.

[2] https://huggingface.co/meta-llama/Llama-3.2-3B-Instruct.

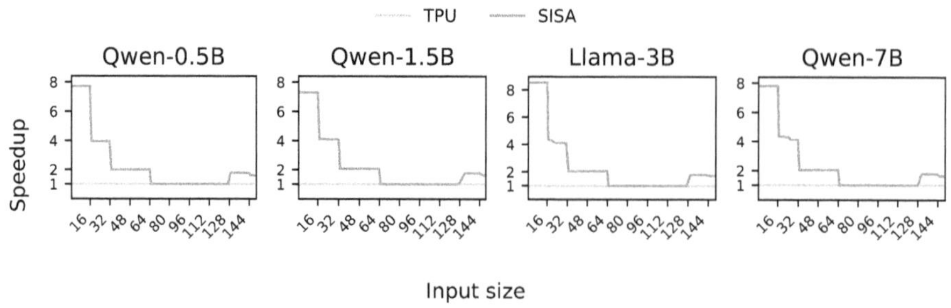

Fig. 4. Speedup of SISA compared to TPU. Higher is better.

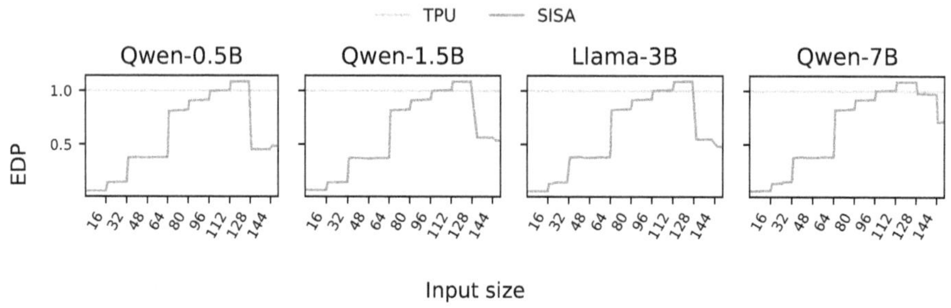

Fig. 5. Normalized EDP of SISA compared to TPU. Lower is better.

4.3 SISA Evaluation

Figures 4 and 5 report the speedup and normalized EDP of SISA over a monolithic TPU-like systolic array for sequence lengths m from 1 to 150, covering the different operating modes of SISA and their trade-offs. Each point aggregates the execution of the linear layers listed in Table 2, scaled by the number of times each layer appears in the model. In the prefill phase, this corresponds to all GEMMs required to process a prompt of length m, while in the decode phase it corresponds to all GEMMs required to generate one token with batch size m.

Small Sequence Lengths ($m \leq 16$). For small m dimensions, SISA executes slabs independently, exposing fine-grain parallelism and improving PE utilization. In this regime, SISA achieves up to 8.52× speedup and reduces EDP by up to 93% compared to TPU. This improvement comes from eliminating the severe under-utilization of monolithic arrays when mapping skewed GEMMs. The speedup slightly exceeds the 8× parallelism provided by the eight slabs because a monolithic 128-PE array must drain outputs across the full array height even when the output dimension is small. In contrast, slab-level execution avoids this overhead and writes results directly to the global buffer.

Intermediate Sequence Lengths ($16 < m \leq 64$). As m increases, SISA progressively fuses slabs into larger logical arrays (32×128 and 64×128), trading parallelism for improved data reuse. In these configurations, SISA achieves up to 4.12× and 2.06× speedup, with EDP reductions of up to 85% and 65%, respectively, as performance gradually approaches that of a monolithic array.

Large Sequence Lengths ($m > 64$). For $64 < m \leq 128$, both architectures operate as a fully fused array and achieve comparable performance. In this range, SISA enables slab-level power gating when the effective M dimension is underutilized, reducing EDP by up to 18%. When the array is fully utilized ($112 < m \leq 128$), SISA incurs an 8.47% EDP overhead due to its distributed memory hierarchy and additional local buffers and multiplexers. For $m > 128$, after the full 128×128 tile, SISA processes the remaining partial tiles using independent slabs, yielding up to 1.79× additional speedup and 46% EDP reduction.

Area Comparison. Table 3 shows that the systolic array dominates total chip area. Relative to a BF16 TPU with the same 128×128 array, SISA introduces a 3% PE-array overhead for slab-level power gating [18], corresponding to 2.7% of total chip area. Using different bank sizes, wider port widths, and slab-local buffers slightly increases SRAM area compared to the TPU design, contributing an additional 2.74% of total area. Overall, SISA increases total chip area by about 5.44%.

In summary, SISA delivers substantial gains in the under-utilized regime while maintaining comparable performance to monolithic arrays at large sequence lengths, with only modest area overhead.

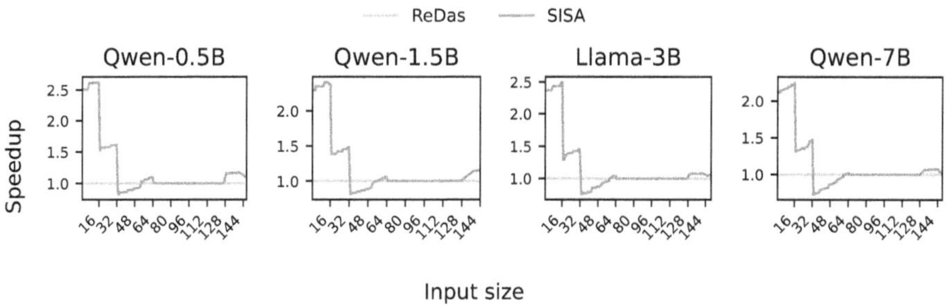

Fig. 6. Speedup of SISA compared to ReDas.

4.4 SISA Versus Alternative Reconfigurable SA

Figure 6 shows SISA speedup over ReDas across the same sequence-length sweep. We compare performance against ReDas using an extended version of SCALE-Sim, as described in Sect. 4.1. This abstraction favors ReDas in latency by providing optimistic estimates. Applying it to energy would instead underestimate ReDas consumption and yield unreliable EDP values. Therefore, we restrict the ReDas comparison to latency/performance. The relative area and energy overheads of the two designs are analyzed later in this section.

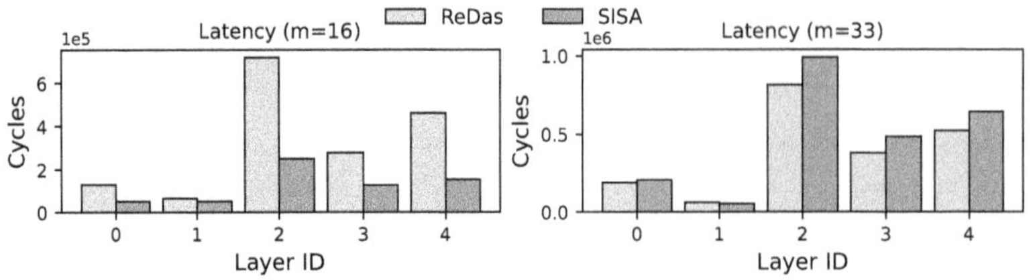

Fig. 7. Latency of Qwen2.5-0.5B linear layers at $m = 16$ (best case) and $m = 33$ (worst case) for SISA, weighted by layer occurrence. Lower is better.

Small Sequence Lengths ($1 \leq m \leq 32$)**.** In this regime, SISA outperforms ReDas. Operating in independent slab mode, SISA maximizes PE utilization and achieves up to 2.61× and 1.61× speedup in the 16×128 and 32×128 configurations, respectively. Although ReDas reshapes its array, its coarse granularity limits effective PE activation for skewed GEMMs, resulting in lower utilization.

Large Sequence Lengths ($m \geq 33$)**.** As m increases, ReDas performs best in the mid-range ($m \approx 33$–50) across all models, where its reshaping aligns well with the workload. Beyond $m \approx 50$, SISA regains advantage for Qwen2.5-0.5B and Qwen2.5-1.5B, whose layer dimensions better match slab sizes, reducing residual-tile overhead that continues to affect ReDas. For larger models, the higher compute volume amortizes residual tiles, allowing ReDas to maintain a modest advantage, although SISA underperforms by at most 1.36×. At $m =$ 64, SISA slightly recovers despite using the same PE budget: ReDas forms a 64×256 array, while SISA operates as two 64×128 slabs, reducing fill-and-drain overhead. For $64 \leq m \leq 128$, both architectures operate in effectively monolithic configurations and achieve comparable performance. Beyond $m > 128$, SISA again benefits from slab-level execution when processing residual tiles, achieving up to 1.17× speedup over ReDas.

Per-Layer Analysis: Qwen2.5-0.5B ($m = 16$ **vs.** $m = 33$)**.** As shown in Fig. 6, SISA outperforms ReDas for most input sizes in the 1–150 range, with limited losses in the few unfavorable cases. To illustrate these trends, we analyze two representative points: the best-case configuration ($m = 16$) and the worst-case configuration ($m = 33$). Table 2 lists the linear layers of Qwen2.5-0.5B, and Fig. 7 shows their latency in cycles weighted by layer occurrence for these two cases. The overall results are presented earlier in this section.

For $m = 16$, SISA operates in an $8 \times (16 \times 128)$ configuration, while ReDas forms a 16×448 array. In this setting, SISA achieves higher utilization and reduced tail inefficiencies. Additionally, 44% of execution occurs with one or more slabs power-gated, improving energy efficiency without affecting latency. Although smaller than the final projection layer, Layer 2 ($M = 16$, $N = 4864$, $K = 896$) is repeated 48 times per block and dominates the total latency.

At $m = 33$, SISA transitions to a fused $2 \times 64 \times 128$ configuration, while ReDas reshapes into a 32×384 array, activating more PEs and achieving its peak advantage. For Layer 1 ($M = 33$, $N = 896$, $K = 896$), SISA still attains slightly higher utilization due to better slab alignment, partially offsetting the additional PE availability of ReDas.

Area and Energy Comparison. ReDas has a slightly lower memory overhead, with SRAM accounting for about 0.4% less of the total chip area than in SISA. However, its PE-array incurs a 70% per-PE area overhead and a 2.49× power increase for INT8. When scaling the design from INT8 to BF16, the PE area increases due to the wider datapath. In our design, the PE array dominates chip area (87.2%), while on-chip SRAM accounts for 12.8%. Therefore, increasing PE complexity has a much larger impact on total area and energy. Although the relative overhead of ReDas may decrease in BF16, it still introduces additional logic inside each PE. In contrast, SISA preserves a simple PE design and concentrates overhead in the memory hierarchy, resulting in only a 5.44% total chip area increase and a lower overall overhead than ReDas.

Overall, SISA achieves higher performance in most regimes and comparable performance otherwise, while incurring lower area and energy overhead.

5 Conclusion

In this work we proposed SISA, a new SA architecture based on slabs of PEs that achieves higher speedup and better EDP than SOTA flexible and monolithic SA architectures for highly skewed matrices. SISA is particularly effective for small- to medium-batch decoding and latency-sensitive prefill workloads common in interactive LLM applications. With minimal area overhead over TPUv4, SISA delivers up to 8.52× speedup and 93% EDP reduction, while in the worst case maintaining comparable performance with only 8.47% higher EDP. Compared to the best alternative SOTA design, SISA achieves up to 2.61× higher speedup with lower area overhead.

Acknowledgments. This work was supported in part by the Swedish Foundation for Strategic Research (SSF) under grant numbers SIP21-0087, FUS21-0063, CHI19-0048 and by the European High-Performance Computing Joint Undertaking (JU) under grant agreement number 101202459 (DARE SGA1).

Disclosure of Interests. The authors have no competing interests to declare that are relevant to the content of this article.

References

1. Agrawal, A., et al.: Taming throughput-latency tradeoff in LLM inference with Sarathi-serve (2024). https://arxiv.org/abs/2403.02310
2. Aminabadi, R.Y., et al.: Deepspeed inference: enabling efficient inference of transformer models at unprecedented scale (2022). https://arxiv.org/abs/2207.00032
3. Balasubramonian, R., Kahng, A.B., Muralimanohar, N., Shafiee, A., Srinivas, V.: Cacti 7: new tools for interconnect exploration in innovative off-chip memories. ACM TACO **14**(2), 1–25 (2017)

4. Boroumand, A., et al.: Google neural network models for edge devices: analyzing and mitigating machine learning inference bottlenecks. In: 2021 30th International Conference on PACT, pp. 159–172. IEEE (2021)
5. Choi, S., et al.: Savector: vectored systolic arrays. IEEE Access **12**, 44446–44461 (2024)
6. Genc, H., et al.: Gemmini: enabling systematic deep-learning architecture evaluation via full-stack integration, pp. 769–774. IEEE Press (2022). https://doi.org/10.1109/DAC18074.2021.9586216
7. Ghodrati, S., et al.: Planaria: dynamic architecture fission for spatial multi-tenant acceleration of deep neural networks. In: 2020 53rd Annual IEEE/ACM MICRO, pp. 681–697 (2020)
8. Gosalia, V.: Building AI, region by region: why memory and storage define the next decade (2025). https://www.micron.com/about/blog/applications/ai/building-ai-region-by-region-why-memory-and-storage-define-the-next-decade
9. Han, M., et al.: ReDas: a lightweight architecture for supporting fine-grained reshaping and multiple dataflows on systolic array. IEEE Trans. Comput. **73**(08), 1997–2011
10. Hanson, E., Li, S., Qian, X., Li, H.H., Chen, Y.: Dynamic: dynamically reshaping, high data-reuse accelerator for compact DNNs. IEEE Trans. Comput. **72**(3), 880–892 (2023)
11. Jouppi, N.P., et al.: Ten lessons from three generations shaped Google's TPUv4i: industrial product. In: 2021 ACM/IEEE 48th Annual ISCA, pp. 1–14 (2021)
12. Lym, S., Erez, M.: FlexSA: flexible systolic array architecture for efficient pruned DNN model training (2020). https://arxiv.org/abs/2004.13027
13. Martínez, H., Castelló, A., Igual, F.D., Quintana-Ortí, E.S.: The Cambrian explosion of mixed-precision matrix multiplication for quantized deep learning inference. Futur. Gener. Comput. Syst. **177**, 108231 (2026)
14. Raj, R., et al.: Scale-SIM V3: a modular cycle-accurate systolic accelerator simulator for end-to-end system analysis. In: 2025 IEEE ISPASS, pp. 186–200 (2025)
15. Samajdar, A., Qin, E., Pellauer, M., Krishna, T.: Self adaptive reconfigurable arrays (SARA): learning flexible GEMM accelerator configuration and mapping-space using ML. In: Proceedings of the 59th ACM/IEEE DAC, pp. 583–588
16. Vashishtha, V., Vangala, M., Clark, L.T.: ASAP7 predictive design kit development and cell design technology co-optimization. In: 2017 IEEE/ACM ICCAD (2017)
17. Wang, M., Ye, Y., Zhou, Z.: LLM serving optimization with variable prefill and decode lengths (2025). https://arxiv.org/abs/2508.06133
18. Xue, Y., Huang, J.: Regate: enabling power gating in neural processing units. In: Proceedings of the 58th IEEE/ACM International Symposium on Microarchitecture, pp. 1160–1177 (2025)
19. Yi, J.Y., et al.: HALO: hybrid systolic arrays via logical partitioning for acceleration of complex-valued neural networks. In: 2025 IEEE IISWC, pp. 206–218 (2025)
20. Yüzügüler, A.C., Sönmez, C., Drumond, M., Oh, Y., Falsafi, B., Frossard, P.: Scale-out systolic arrays. ACM TACO **20**(2) (2023)

Realizable N:M Sparse Transformer Inference via Search–Kernel Co-design

Yiming Liu[1], Wenqi Lou[2(✉)], Zhiguang Wang[3], Zhiwei Ke[1], Fengrui Zuo[1], Chao Wang[1], and Xuehai Zhou[1]

[1] University of Science and Technology of China, Hefei, China
liuyiming9974@mail.ustc.edu.cn , cswang@ustc.edu.cn
[2] Suzhou Institute of Advanced Research, University of Science and Technology of China, Suzhou, China
louwenqi@ustc.edu.cn
[3] National Key Laboratory of Modeling and Simulation for Complex Systems, Beijing, China

Abstract. Vision Transformers (ViTs) achieve strong accuracy but incur high inference latency. Semi-structured N:M sparsity can reduce arithmetic cost, yet its theoretical savings often fail to translate into proportional end-to-end speedups on modern GPUs. This mismatch arises because deployment latency depends not only on arithmetic reduction but also on execution regularity and hardware scheduling under sparsity. Achieving practical acceleration, therefore, requires coordinated design across sparse execution and sparsity configuration. To this end, we propose a hardware-software co-design framework for N:M sparse ViT inference. On the hardware side, we design MD-SpMM, an N:M sparse CUDA kernel that reorganizes sparse GEMM into micro-dense, Tensor-Core-aligned dataflow and uses inference-aware adaptive parallelism to sustain utilization. On the software side, we perform layer-wise sparsity search under explicit end-to-end latency budgets using a three-stage heuristic search with constraint relaxation to avoid premature convergence and enable deployment-aware sparsity allocation. Experiments on multiple ViT/Swin models and GPU platforms show that the framework achieves over 2.2× latency speedup while maintaining comparable accuracy and delivering superior accuracy under the same latency constraint. The code will be publicly released.

Keywords: Semi-structured sparsity · Hardware–software co-design · Vision Transformer · CUDA kernels

1 Introduction

Vision Transformers (ViTs) leverage self-attention to capture long-range dependencies and achieve strong performance in tasks such as image classification and semantic segmentation [20]. However, this benefit comes with high inference cost:

M. Torquati et al. (Eds.): Euro-Par 2026, LNCS 16781, pp. 373–387, 2027.
https://doi.org/10.1007/978-3-032-35248-4_26

ViTs rely heavily on matrix multiplications in projection and feed-forward layers, imposing substantial compute and memory demands that make deployment on real hardware increasingly challenging [16,24].

Model compression, especially pruning, has been widely studied to mitigate this burden by removing redundant parameters while preserving accuracy [2]. Among pruning schemes, semi-structured N:M sparsity has emerged as a practical compromise between accuracy preservation and hardware regularity, and has been adopted across CNNs, ViTs, and related accelerators [9,10,12,25].

Despite this progress, the theoretical savings of N:M sparsity often fail to translate into proportional end-to-end latency gains in real inference, especially under INT8 deployment, as evidenced by the experimental comparisons in Sect. 6. In this regime, latency depends not only on arithmetic reduction but also on execution regularity, memory behavior, and scheduling effects under sparsity. This reveals a persistent gap between theoretical efficiency and practical performance. The gap is often misinterpreted as sparsity being "ineffective", whereas it is more accurately attributed to the difficulty of realizing sparsity efficiently on current deployment stacks.

We therefore focus on *realizable acceleration*: whether N:M sparsity can deliver a target end-to-end latency reduction on a real deployment stack, rather than merely improving proxy metrics such as FLOPs, global sparsity, or isolated operator speedups [4,18,23]. From a system perspective, realizable acceleration requires satisfying two tightly coupled conditions. First, sparse computation must be *execution-realizable*: sparse operators should deliver stable and efficient execution on real hardware instead of exhibiting irregular behavior that prevents consistent latency reduction [10]. Second, sparsity assignment must be *latency-grounded*: when N:M sparsity is applied in a layer-wise manner, per-layer ratios should be selected under explicit deployment-level latency constraints rather than abstract sparsity or FLOPs-based objectives that poorly reflect end-to-end cost [8]. Violating either condition leads to unrealizable speedups in practice, even when theoretical computation reduction is significant. Yet existing approaches often optimize only one side [7,9,10,13], motivating an end-to-end co-design framework that couples execution-realizable sparse kernels with latency-grounded layer-wise configuration and lightweight candidate evaluation.

To this end, we propose a hardware-software co-design framework for realizable N:M sparse inference acceleration. On the hardware side, we design MD-SpMM, an N:M sparse CUDA kernel that restructures sparse computation into Tensor-Core-aligned execution through micro-dense restructuring and adaptive parallelism. On the software side, we introduce a latency-grounded layer-wise search pipeline that combines a profiling-based latency predictor and a feasible-region-aware evolutionary solver to evaluate candidates efficiently. By integrating execution-realizable kernels with latency-grounded sparsity search, the framework consistently translates sparsity-induced computation reduction into end-to-end latency improvement on real deployment stacks.

In summary, this work makes the following contributions:

- We present a **search–kernel co-design framework** for *realizable* N:M sparse Transformer acceleration, built on execution realizability and configuration realizability under deployment latency constraints, and enabling more accurate and reliable acceleration under the same target speedup.
- We design **MD-SpMM**, an execution-realizable Tensor-Core-native N:M sparse kernel that converts sparse computation into regular MMA-centric execution with scalable inference parallelism. Across diverse matrix multiplication shapes and sparsity levels, it delivers 2.0× average speedup over cuBLAS dense GEMM and 1.6×–4.0× speedup over nmSPARSE [10].
- We propose a latency-grounded layer-wise N:M search pipeline that integrates a calibrated LUT-based latency predictor with a feasible-region-aware evolutionary solver to efficiently discover high-quality sparse configurations. With our hardware–software co-design, the resulting solutions achieve over 2.2× latency reduction while delivering higher accuracy, yielding up to +1.4% Top-1 accuracy on ImageNet-1K and consistently outperforming prior methods across ViT and Swin inference settings.

2 Background and Motivation

2.1 Vision Transformers and Layer-Wise N:M Configuration

Vision Transformers (ViTs) process an image as a sequence of patch embeddings and forward it through a stack of Transformer blocks. In practice, inference is dominated by the Q/K/V projections, the attention output projection, and the two FFN linear layers. For common vision workloads, these matrix-heavy operators account for most of the end-to-end inference time, making them the primary targets for sparsification [24].

N:M sparsity constrains each group of M weights to retain N nonzeros. In ViTs, it is often applied uniformly across all Transformer blocks, as illustrated in Fig. 1. However, despite their similar block structure, layers at different depths contribute unequally to model accuracy and inference latency due to their depth-dependent roles [5,8,18]. This leads to heterogeneous sparsity sensitivity across blocks, making a single global N:M ratio suboptimal. Consequently, ViT sparsification is more naturally formulated as a layer-wise N:M configuration problem.

2.2 The Lack of Efficient Sparse Execution Mechanisms

Although N:M sparsity reduces multiply-accumulate operations, it does not directly yield efficient execution on modern Tensor Core GPUs. This mismatch is especially pronounced for INT8 inference, where dense GEMM already achieves high efficiency through regular dataflow, predictable control flow, and high MMA utilization [1,14,15]. In this regime, sparse speedup depends not only on arithmetic reduction but also on whether execution remains compatible with the hardware execution model. Existing sparse kernels often rely on metadata handling, runtime decoding, and irregular memory accesses, which disrupt Tensor Core dataflow and reduce utilization [6,10,22].

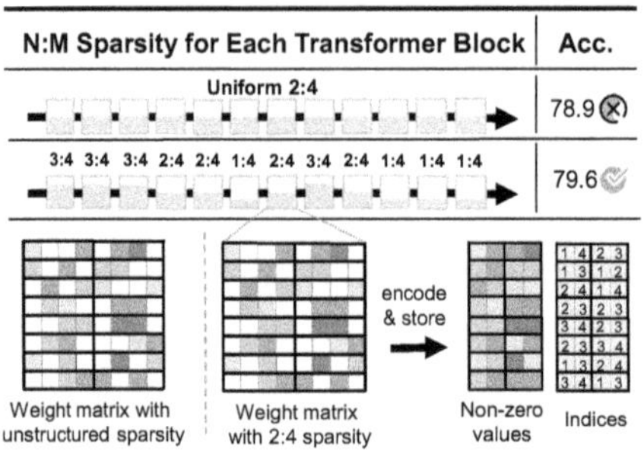

Fig. 1: N:M sparsity and uniform vs. layer-wise configurations in ViTs.

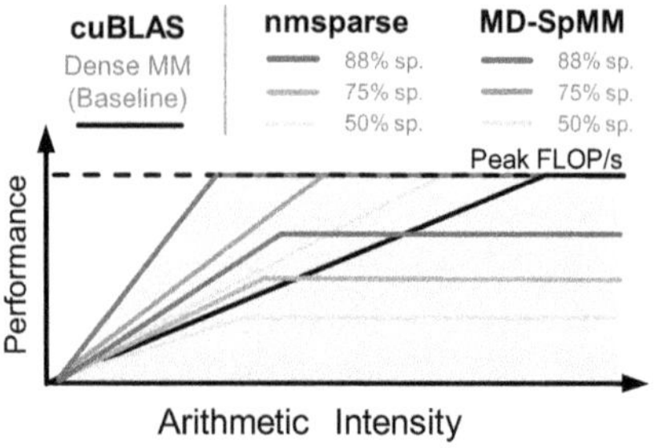

Fig. 2: Roofline analysis of N:M sparse INT8 inference on GPUs.

As illustrated by the Roofline analysis in Fig. 2, existing approaches exhibit a clear execution trade-off. nmSPARSE [10] follows sparse decoding and irregular access patterns, leading to low arithmetic intensity and limited utilization, whereas cuBLAS sustains high efficiency with dense GEMM but cannot exploit N:M structure. This gap highlights the need for sparse execution mechanisms that preserve Tensor-Core-friendly regularity while exposing the arithmetic benefit of N:M sparsity.

2.3 The Need for Latency-Grounded Layer-Wise Configuration

Introducing latency constraints into sparse configuration search is necessary but challenging, since meeting a target latency requires different sparsity levels across models, layers, and deployment environments. Traditional methods that optimize proxy metrics such as sparsity ratio or FLOPs often fail to capture real deployment behavior. Even with similar overall sparsity, different layer-wise assignments can lead to substantially different end-to-end latencies. Moreover, enforcing latency constraints fragments the feasible space by discarding invalid configurations, weakening search-space connectivity and making exploration prone to narrow feasible regions.

To address this issue, sparse configuration optimization must incorporate deployment-level latency semantics. In particular, latency models built on the target hardware and deployment stack are needed to guide the search toward configurations that both satisfy latency constraints and enable realizable end-to-end acceleration. This mitigates the mismatch between abstract optimization objectives and real hardware behavior [3,4,19].

3 Problem Formulation and Method Overview

Given a Transformer model and a target end-to-end latency budget, the problem is to realize N:M sparse inference that preserves model quality while delivering actual speedup on the target hardware.

As shown in Fig. 3, we address this problem through two coordinated components. At the execution level, we design MD-SpMM, a sparse kernel that realizes N:M sparsity through Tensor-Core-aligned execution. At the configuration level, we build a latency-grounded layer-wise search pipeline, in which a calibrated LUT-based latency predictor enforces deployment feasibility and a hardware-aware search strategy explores the fragmented feasible region under explicit latency constraints.

Together, these components instantiate the two requirements of realizable acceleration introduced in Sect. 1. MD-SpMM addresses execution realizability, while the latency-grounded search addresses configuration realizability by identifying layer-wise N:M assignments aligned with end-to-end deployment behavior. In this sense, realizable acceleration is achieved only when sparse execution and sparsity configuration are jointly optimized.

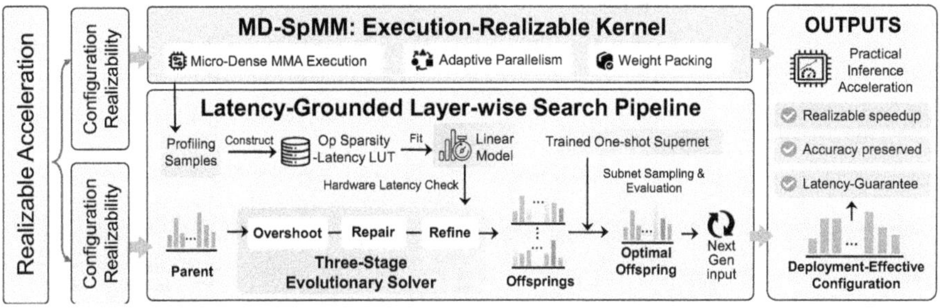

Fig. 3: Overview of the search-kernel co-design framework for N:M sparse Transformer acceleration.

4 MD-SpMM: Dataflow-Centric N:M Sparse Kernels

4.1 Design Methodology

From the perspective of execution realizability, INT8 inference with N:M sparsity depends not only on reduced arithmetic but also on whether sparse execution matches the hardware execution model. We identify two first-order requirements: (i) *dataflow regularity* to sustain Tensor Core MMA utilization, and (ii) *inference-scale parallelism* to maintain high SM occupancy across varying operator shapes. Violating either requirement by introducing index-driven control, irregular memory access, or insufficient thread-block parallelism can erase theoretical sparsity gains in end-to-end latency. As shown in Fig. 4, MD-SpMM uses three mechanisms: (1) Weight Packing for decode-friendly sparse storage, (2) Micro-Dense Execution for MMA-centric regular tiles, and (3) Adaptive Parallelism to improve occupancy while bounding reduction overhead.

4.2 Micro-Dense: From N:M Sparsity to Tensor Core Dataflow

To make N:M sparsity compatible with Tensor Core execution, we introduce *Micro-Dense*, which reformulates N:M SpMM as an MMA-centric regular dataflow. Under N:M sparsity, each window of size M contains N nonzeros. Rather than exposing them to the compute stage as irregular sparse operands, Micro-Dense materializes only these N nonzeros into fixed MMA-compatible dense tiles aligned with Tensor Core fragment shapes, so Tensor Cores still operate on regular dense fragments and runtime computation remains entirely MMA-based.

This design shifts sparsity irregularity out of the MMA compute path and into the loading-and-decoding stage. To keep the resulting overhead low, we adopt a decode-friendly packed representation (`B_pack`) that jointly encodes nonzero values and their positions within each N:M window. This removes separate index loads and enables lightweight decoding, which is overlapped with shared-memory placement and MMA issuance.

Therefore, Micro-Dense confines sparsity handling to packed loading and lightweight decoding, allowing runtime computation to operate directly on MMA-aligned tiles. Overall, it establishes a clear execution mapping: N:M sparsity → Micro-Dense tiles → Tensor Core dataflow.

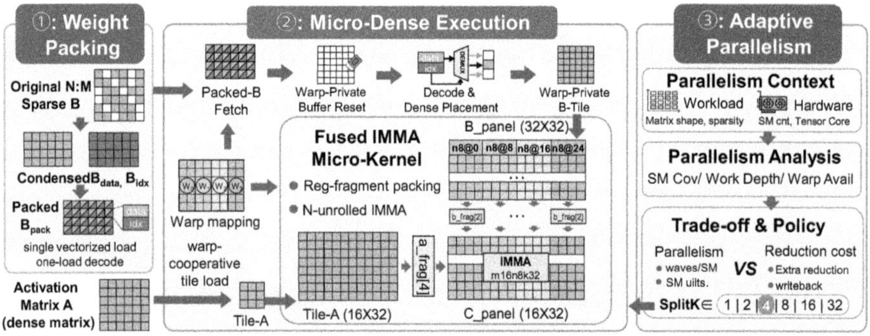

Fig. 4: Overview of the MD-SpMM kernel design.

4.3 Adaptive Parallelism: Split-K for Inference-Scale SpMM

Micro-Dense improves per-block Tensor Core efficiency, but inference can still suffer from *under-occupancy* when operator shapes expose limited parallel work. End-to-end performance therefore depends not only on efficient single-block execution, but also on scalable and predictable parallelism across workloads.

We address this with split-K parallelism, which partitions the reduction dimension so multiple thread blocks compute partial sums in parallel, expanding the parallel space from the output dimensions (M, N) to $(M, N, splitK)$. Split-K boosts occupancy but introduces reduction and extra write-back overhead, so its benefit must be controlled.

We therefore adopt a rule-driven splitK selection strategy. First, **parallelism priority**: splitK is increased until the number of blocks is sufficient to fully schedule SMs. Second, **controlled reduction**: splitK is restricted to a small discrete candidate set so that K-splits remain aligned with Tensor Core granularity and reduction overhead stays predictable. When K is small or reduction dominates, the strategy reverts to a smaller splitK.

In this approach, all splits share the same compute template and partial sums are merged only in the final stage, avoiding additional control complexity. Combined with Micro-Dense, this adaptive parallelism enables consistent speedup across deployment scenarios.

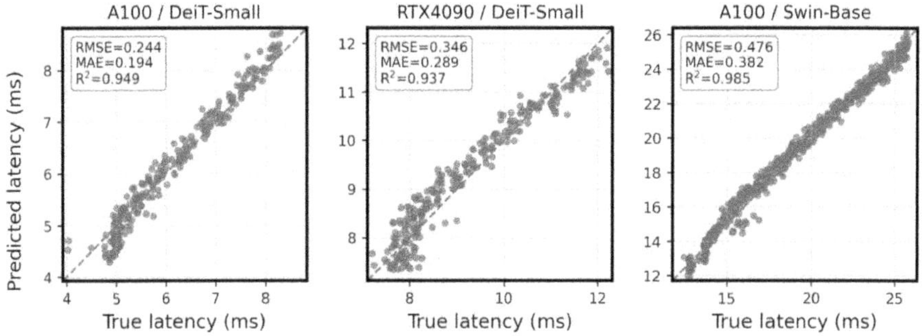

Fig. 5: Predicted vs. measured end-to-end latency on platforms and architectures.

5 Latency-Grounded Layer-Wise Sparsity Search

While MD-SpMM makes N:M sparsity execution-realizable, determining an effective layer-wise sparsity configuration remains challenging, since accuracy alone is insufficient and the end-to-end latency impact of sparsity is strongly deployment-dependent. We therefore develop a latency-grounded search strategy that explicitly incorporates latency constraints to guide the search toward higher-quality and deployment-feasible configurations.

5.1 Lookup Table-Based Latency Modeling

Accuracy ranking alone is insufficient, since the search must also satisfy an end-to-end latency budget. Because measuring full-model latency for every candidate is too costly, we build a lightweight predictor for feasibility checks [3,5,11,21].

Under a fixed hardware–software stack, we profile MD-SpMM operators and build an operator-level sparsity–latency lookup table (LUT). For each operator

Algorithm 1: HW-aware heuristic search algorithm

Input: Model M; latency budget $\mathcal{T}_{\text{target}}$; number of generations $\mathcal{G}$; number of offspring λ; //define: parent x; child y.

Initialization: $candidate$ = `UniSparGen`($\mathcal{T}_{target}, M$);
x_1 = `Rand_Spar`($candidate$, $toward = \mathcal{T}_{target}$);
Search: for g ***in*** $[1, \mathcal{G}]$ **do**
    $offsprings = []$;
    3Stage-OffspringGen: for i ***in*** $[1, \lambda]$ **do**
        $y_i = x_g$;
        for l ***in*** `Random_K`($\{ l \mid y_i[l] < 8 \}$) **do**
            $y_i[l] = N + 1$; //Densify the l-th layer of y_i (e.g., 4:8 to 5:8), keeping other layers unchanged.
        while $Latency(y_i) > \mathcal{T}_{target}$ **do**
            l = `Random_1`($\{ l \mid y_i[l] > 1 \}$);
            $y_i[l] = N - 1$; //Sparsify the l-th layer of y_i
        $D := \{ l \mid (y_i[l] < 8) \wedge \Delta\texttt{Fitness}_l \geq 0 \}$; //layers whose densification yields a fitness gain.
        while $D \neq \emptyset$ **do**
            y_i[`Random_1`(D)]$=N+1$; //Random densify one layer
            $D := \{ l \mid (y_i[l] < 8) \wedge \Delta\texttt{Fitness}_l \geq 0 \}$; //Update
        $offsprings.append(y_i)$;
    Selection: x_{g+1} = `MAX_Fitness`($offsprings$);
return $x_{\mathcal{G}+1}$; (final sparse configuration)

shape and candidate N:M ratio, we benchmark sparse matrix multiplication latency (average repeated runs). Empirically, the latency is largely determined by operator shape and sparsity level, yielding a LUT indexed by (*shape*, *sparsity*). Since ViT-family models reuse only a small set of operator shapes, the LUT can be rebuilt offline within seconds when the deployment environment changes.

To predict end-to-end latency, we fit a first-order linear model on top of the LUT. Let $t_\ell(s_\ell)$ denote the LUT latency of layer ℓ under sparsity setting s_ℓ, then

$$T_{\text{pred}} = \sum_{\ell=1}^{L} \gamma_\ell \, t_\ell(s_\ell) + b, \tag{1}$$

where $\gamma_\ell \geq 0$ and $b \geq 0$ are calibrated by non-negative least squares (NNLS) using a small number of full-model measurements. This calibration absorbs graph-level scheduling, runtime overhead, and compiler optimizations beyond single-operator profiling. After calibration, the predictor enables constant-time feasibility checks during search with within-5% error (Fig. 5), grounding layer-wise sparsity decisions in deployment latency rather than abstract sparsity metrics.

5.2 Hardware-Aware Layer-Wise Sparsity Search

Given the latency predictor, we search for a layer-wise N:M configuration that maximizes model quality under a target latency budget. Let M denote the model, and let $s = [s_1, \ldots, s_L]$ denote the layer-wise N:M configuration, where each s_ℓ is selected from a discrete set of hardware-supported N:M ratios. We solve

$$\max_{s} \; Acc(\mathcal{M}(s)) \quad \text{s.t.} \quad \mathcal{T}_{\text{pred}}(\mathcal{M}(s)) \leq \mathcal{T}_{\text{target}}, \tag{2}$$

where $Acc(\cdot)$ denotes the Top-1 accuracy on ImageNet-1K and $\mathcal{T}_{\text{target}}$ is the target end-to-end latency budget.

This problem is challenging because, under layer-wise N:M sparsity, the mapping from sparsity configuration to deployment latency is highly nonlinear. The latency constraint therefore partitions the search space into multiple disconnected feasible regions. As a result, prior local-perturbation-based methods [17] tend to get trapped on small "feasibility islands", causing the search to stagnate.

To address this, we adopt a feasible-region-aware $(1 + \lambda)$ evolutionary search that follows an *overshoot–repair–refine* procedure, enabling effective transitions across fragmented feasible regions in the sparsity–latency landscape. The overall pipeline is summarized in Algorithm 1. The search is instantiated within the standard one-shot sparsity search framework [8], where the supernet training stage remains unchanged and each candidate configuration is scored by its inherited accuracy under the trained supernet.

During initialization, we first construct several latency-feasible configurations with approximately uniform sparsity distributions and select the one with the highest `fitness` score (Eq. 3) as the initial parent. We then repeatedly invoke **3Stage-OffspringGen** to produce λ offspring via the following three stages:

$$\texttt{Fitness}(\mathcal{S}) = \begin{cases} \texttt{Acc}_{\text{Inherit}}(\mathcal{M}(s)), & \mathcal{T}_{\text{pred}}(\mathcal{M}(s)) \leq \mathcal{T}_{\text{target}}, \\ -\infty, & \text{otherwise.} \end{cases} \tag{3}$$

1) *Overshoot* (Lines 7–8) adopts a "relax-first" strategy: a small random subset of layers is moved to the next denser sparsity level, deliberately violating the latency budget. This avoids the vanishing effect (noise-level score variations) of conventional 1:1 "sparsify-dens" perturbations near the feasibility boundary.

2) *Repair* (Lines 9–11) then restores feasibility by increasing sparsity on randomly sampled layers until the latency constraint is met, avoiding the directional bias of greedy, latency-guided repair and encouraging diverse search trajectories.

3) *Refine* (Lines 12–15) then explores the feasible boundary by gradually densifying the model while retaining only latency-valid updates. Candidate configurations with non-decreasing `fitness` are accepted, allowing the search to advance along the feasible boundary iteratively.

Throughout the search, the latency predictor provides constant-time feasibility checks, and the final configuration is selected through offspring competition under the latency constraint. Overall, this design enables more effective exploration of the fragmented feasible space and improves the quality of deployment-feasible layer-wise N:M configurations.

6 Experiments

6.1 MD-SpMM Kernel Evaluation

Benchmark. We evaluate MD-SpMM using a benchmark across matrix shapes and sparsity levels. The matrices are defined by the dimensions M, N, and K for matrix multiplication, where M is the number of rows, and N and K are the number of columns in the input and output matrices, respectively. We consider sparsity levels of 50%, 75%, and 87.5%, with $M \in \{64, 128, 256, 512\}$ and $N, K \in \{128, 256, 512, 1024\}$. Experiments are performed on A100, RTX 4060, and RTX 4090 GPUs using Ubuntu 22.04 and CUDA 12.2, with C++/CUDA kernel implementation compiled using `nvcc`. We report latency excluding one-time offline weight packing, since `B_pack` construction is performed once before deployment. All runtime costs during inference are included, including decoding overhead, data movement, and MMA computation. Thus, both kernel latency and end-to-end latency correspond to pure inference-time execution.

Baselines. We compare MD-SpMM against state-of-the-art dense and sparse baselines: cuBLAS, NVIDIA's highly optimized dense GEMM library representing the vendor-optimized upper bound, and nmSPARSE [10], a representative library for N:M sparse matrix multiplication.

Table 1: Adaptive parallel strategy across platforms and sparsity levels.

Platform	A100			RTX 4090			RTX 4060		
Sparsity	50%	75%	87.5%	50%	75%	87.5%	50%	75%	87.5%
Top-1 Hit Rate	0.813	0.875	0.827	0.799	0.711	0.690	0.720	0.763	0.714
Avg. Norm. Perf.	0.990	0.990	0.990	0.983	0.965	0.958	0.972	0.968	0.960
Worst Norm. Perf.	0.818	0.774	0.803	0.786	0.746	0.739	0.773	0.694	0.696

Results. We first evaluate the adaptive parallel strategy against fixed Split-K settings. For each shape–sparsity pair, we test multiple Split-K candidates and use the lowest latency as the oracle optimum. Table 1 summarizes the Top-1 hit rate, average normalized performance, and worst-case normalized performance. The adaptive strategy selects the oracle-optimal configuration in most cases and remains close to optimal even in non-hit cases, while also maintaining strong worst-case robustness. Compared with a fixed parallel setting, it improves overall kernel performance by more than 50%.

Figure 6 reports the kernel speedup of MD-SpMM and nmSPARSE over dense cuBLAS across matrix shapes under different N:M sparsity levels. The vertical axis shows speedup normalized to dense cuBLAS, while the horizontal axis indexes different matrix shapes; speedups above 4 are truncated for clarity.

MD-SpMM consistently outperforms nmSPARSE and delivers stable acceleration across platforms. On A100, it achieves around 2.0× average speedup over cuBLAS and 1.6×–4.0× speedup over nmSPARSE [10]. Similar trends are

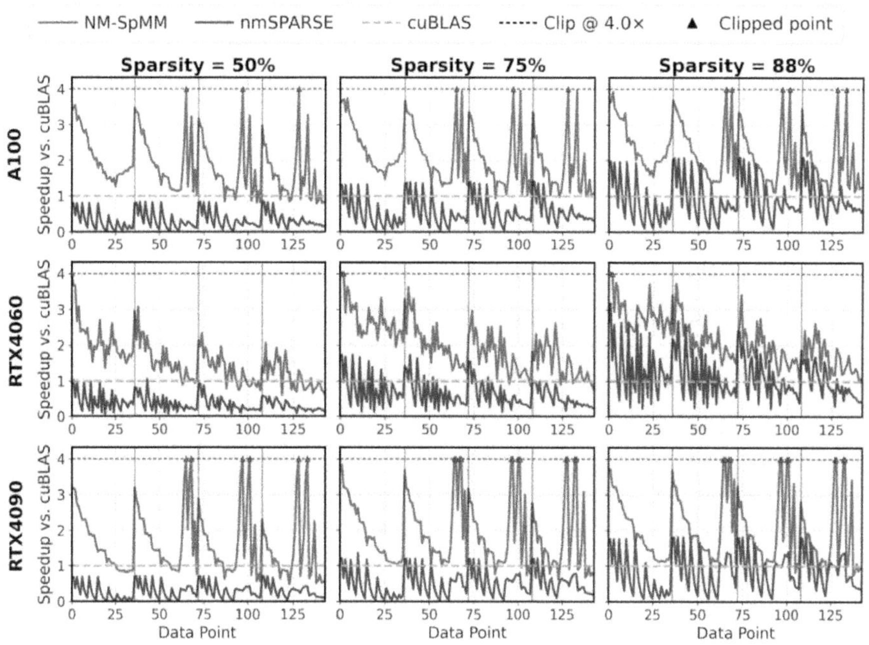

Fig. 6: Speedup over cuBLAS across matrix shapes under different sparsity levels.

observed on RTX 4060 and RTX 4090, with absolute gains varying due to hardware characteristics such as compute capability and memory bandwidth.

These results show that practical N:M sparse acceleration requires not only arithmetic reduction, but also regularized Tensor-Core-friendly execution together with shape-aware parallel adaptation. Overall, MD-SpMM substantially improves the execution realizability of N:M sparsity under deployment-relevant conditions.

6.2 Feasible-Region-Aware Search Validation

Benchmark: We evaluate the proposed search strategy on DeiT-Small, DeiT-Base, and Swin-Small under 1.5×, 2.0×, and 2.5× target speedups on A100, RTX 4060 and RTX 4090 GPUs. To improve efficiency, search is conducted on ImageNet-300, a subset of ImageNet-1K with 300 classes, 500 training images, and 50 validation images per class. We find that it preserves the search trends and final configurations observed on full ImageNet-1K while substantially reducing search cost.

Baseline: We instantiate our method within the standard one-shot layer-wise sparsity search framework, keeping supernet training unchanged and replacing only the post-training search stage with our latency-grounded search algorithm. We compare against Evo-Press [17], a representative evolutionary method for

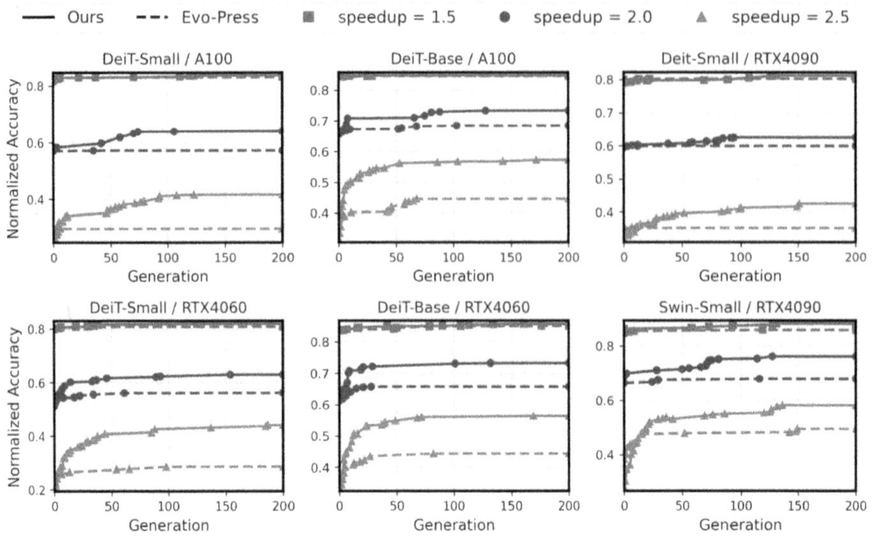

Fig. 7: Comparison of search trajectories between Evo-Press and our method across models and speedup settings.

layer-wise sparsity search, under the same one-shot framework and latency prediction setup. Under this setting, the dominant cost still comes from supernet training; the full pipeline with 200 search generations takes about 10 h on three A100 GPUs.

Results: Figure 7 shows the search trajectories of our method and Evo-Press across different models and target speedups. Our method exhibits more stable convergence and consistently reaches better final solutions, while Evo-Press more often stagnates near inferior local regions. In many cases, our method overtakes Evo-Press as early as the 20th–30th generation, and the gap further widens under higher speedup targets, where the feasible region becomes more constrained and fragmented. Moreover, the search typically converges within about 100 generations, indicating good search efficiency in practice. These results demonstrate that explicitly incorporating latency constraints into the search process improves both search quality and robustness under practical deployment budgets.

6.3 Overall Evaluation

Benchmark. To evaluate the end-to-end effectiveness of the proposed search-kernel co-design framework, we conduct INT8 sparse inference experiments on DeiT-Small and DeiT-Base using an NVIDIA A100 GPU. All methods are tested under the same inference stack and deployment setting.

Baselines. We compare different combinations of sparsity configuration strategies and execution backends. On the search side, we consider uniform N:M sparsity, EvoPress [17], and our latency-grounded layer-wise search. On the execution side, we compare nmSPARSE [10] and MD-SpMM as sparse execution backends, while cuBLAS serves as the dense reference. This allows us to isolate the effect of search, kernel, and their combination under the same deployment constraint.

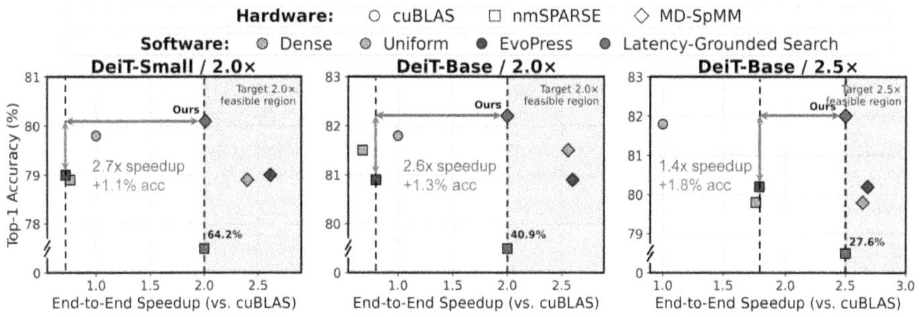

Fig. 8: Accuracy-speedup trade-offs across search and kernel combinations.

Results: Figure 8 summarizes the resulting accuracy–speedup trade-offs, where the shaded feasible region denotes configurations satisfying the target speedup. Improving sparse execution alone is insufficient if sparsity allocation remains weak or latency-unaware. When deploying N:M sparse models with nmSPARSE, irregular execution overhead often offsets arithmetic savings, so more aggressive sparsity is required to meet the target speedup, which in turn causes noticeable accuracy degradation. Conversely, improving sparsity allocation alone is also insufficient without a realizable sparse backend. Uniform N:M sparsity and proxy-driven approaches, such as EvoPress, optimize abstract objectives that are misaligned with deployment latency, often over-pruning latency-critical layers or producing configurations that fail to satisfy the latency constraint. Together, these results show that practical sparse acceleration requires both realizable sparse execution and latency-aligned layer-wise sparsity search.

By contrast, the proposed framework achieves the best overall result by coupling latency-grounded search with MD-SpMM. The former allocates layer-wise sparsity according to deployment behavior, while the latter ensures that these allocations translate into realizable end-to-end speedup on hardware. As a result, compared with conventional strategy combinations, our method consistently delivers better accuracy–speedup trade-offs across all evaluated settings, with an average 2.2× speedup gain and 1.4% accuracy improvement.

Overall, these results highlight a key principle for practical N:M acceleration: neither sparsity search nor sparse execution alone is sufficient. Favorable accuracy–speedup trade-offs require jointly optimizing layer-wise sparsity configuration and hardware-realizable sparse execution, so that algorithmic sparsity decisions remain aligned with deployment performance.

7 Conclusion

This paper argues that practical N:M sparse Transformer acceleration is a search-kernel co-design problem. MD-SpMM makes sparse execution more realizable on Tensor-Core GPUs, while the proposed latency-grounded layer-wise search pipeline allocates sparsity by deployment behavior rather than abstract sparsity objectives. Together, they turn N:M sparsity into a more stable and deployment-effective acceleration mechanism under explicit latency targets.

Acknowledgments. This work was supported in part by the Strategic Priority Research Program of the Chinese Academy of Sciences, Grant Nos. XDB0660101, XDB0660000, and XDB0660100, in part by the National Natural Science Foundation of China under Grant No. 62502489, in part by Jiangsu Provincial Natural Science Foundation under Grants BK20241818 and BK20250479.

Disclosure of Interests. The authors have no competing interests to declare that are relevant to the content of this article.

References

1. Chen, Z.: Efficient tensor core-based gpu kernels for structured sparsity under reduced precision. SC, 1–14 (2021)
2. Deng, L., et al.: Model compression and hardware acceleration for neural networks: a comprehensive survey. Proc. IEEE **108**(4), 485–532 (2020)
3. Feng, C.: LitePred: transferable and scalable latency prediction for hardware-aware neural architecture search. In: Proc. NSDI, pp. 1463–1477 (2024)
4. Frantar, E.: Spdy: accurate pruning with speedup guarantees. In: Proc. ICML, pp. 6726–6743 (2022)
5. Fu, W.: Unicos: a unified neural and accelerator co-search framework for cnns and vits. In: DAC pp, 1–6 (2025)
6. Gale, T.: Sparse gpu kernels for deep learning. In: Proc. SC, pp. 1–14 (2020)
7. He, Y., Lin, J., Liu, Z., Wang, H., Li, L.-J., Han, S.: AMC: AutoML for model compression and acceleration on mobile devices. In: Ferrari, V., Hebert, M., Sminchisescu, C., Weiss, Y. (eds.) ECCV 2018. LNCS, vol. 11211, pp. 815–832. Springer, Cham (2018). https://doi.org/10.1007/978-3-030-01234-2_48
8. Huang, N.C.: Elsa: exploiting layer-wise n: m sparsity for vision transformer acceleration. In: Proc. CVPR, pp. 8006–8015 (2024)
9. Kang, X.: Suarch: accelerating layer-wise n: M sparse pattern with a unified architecture for deep-learning edge device. In: Proc. ASP-DAC, pp. 700–705 (2025)
10. Lin, B.: Efficient gpu kernels for n: m-sparse weights in deep learning. In: Proc. MLSys, pp. 513–525 (2023)
11. Liu, W.: Arch2end: two-stage unified system-level modeling for heterogeneous intelligent devices. IEEE Trans. Comput.-Aided Des. Integr. Circuits Syst **43**(11), 4154–4165 (2024)
12. Liu, Z.G.: S2ta: exploiting structured sparsity for energy-efficient mobile cnn acceleration. In: Proc. HPCA, pp. 573–586 (2022)
13. Lou, W.: Unleashing network/accelerator co-exploration potential on fpgas: a deeper joint search. IEEE Trans. Comput.-Aided Des. Integr. Circuits Syst **43**(10), 3041–3054 (2024)

14. Mishra, A.: Accelerating sparse deep neural networks. arXiv (2021)
15. NVIDIA: NVIDIA A100 Tensor Core GPU Architecture, Whitepaper (2020)
16. Qin, Y.: Enhancing long sequence input processing in fpga-based transformer accelerators through attention fusion. In: Proc. GVLSI, pp. 599–603 (2024)
17. Sieberling, O.: Evopress: towards optimal dynamic model compression via evolutionary search. In: ICML (2024)
18. Sun, W., et al.: Dominosearch: find layer-wise fine-grained n: M sparse schemes from dense neural networks. Adv. Neural. Inf. Process. Syst. **34**, 20721–20732 (2021)
19. Tang, C.: CloserToMe: a unified framework for accurate and transferable latency prediction across heterogeneous devices. In: Proc. AAAI, pp. 25805–25813 (2026)
20. Touvron, H., et al.: Training data-efficient image transformers & distillation through attention. In: Proc. ICML, pp. 10347–10357 (2021)
21. Wang, Z., et al.: UniCoX: a unified cost model for tensorized program tuning across ubiquitous accelerators. IEEE Trans. Comput. **75**(1), 305–319 (2025)
22. Wang, Z., et al.: UniSparTa: a unified sparse tensor program tuning framework. IEEE Trans. Comput.-Aided Des. Integr. Circ. Syst. (2025)
23. Yang, T.-J., et al.: NetAdapt: platform-aware neural network adaptation for mobile applications. In: Ferrari, V., Hebert, M., Sminchisescu, C., Weiss, Y. (eds.) ECCV 2018. LNCS, vol. 11214, pp. 289–304. Springer, Cham (2018). https://doi.org/10.1007/978-3-030-01249-6_18
24. You, H.: Vitcod: vision transformer acceleration via dedicated algorithm and accelerator co-design. In: Proc. HPCA, pp. 273–286 (2023)
25. Zhou, A.: Learning n: m fine-grained structured sparse neural networks from scratch. In: Proc. ICLR (2021)

Performance Analysis of Hardware-Accelerated Compressed Memory Swap

Eunyeong Sim and Woongki Baek(✉)

UNIST, Ulsan, Republic of Korea
{simey1128,wbaek}@unist.ac.kr

Abstract. With the widespread deployment of data-intensive applications such as big data and machine learning, hardware-accelerated compressed memory swap (CMS-H) is emerging as a promising solution to build high-performance and cost-efficient tiered-memory systems. However, prior works on CMS-H lack a performance comparison of CMS-H with various swap backends and detailed performance analysis of CMS-H based on a production-quality OS and commodity CPUs with support for Intel In-Memory Analytics Accelerator (IAA). To bridge this gap, this work compares the performance of CMS-H with representative swap backends including the one with the state-of-the-art NVM Express (NVMe) SSD technology, presents an in-depth performance analysis of CMS-H, and identifies its inefficiencies. Guided by the characterization results, we propose three optimization techniques (i.e., parallel page compression and decompression, zero-copy page decompression, and eager zspage allocation) for CMS-H.

1 Introduction

As data-intensive applications such as big data and machine learning are widely deployed, memory demands in datacenters are rapidly growing. Further, there have been a slowdown in DRAM device scaling [11,13] and large fluctuations in DRAM prices [21]. Consequently, DRAM has become one of the most crucial hardware components in datacenters in terms of costs [21].

Compressed memory swap (CMS) is a widely-used technique to build high-performance and cost-efficient tiered-memory systems [10]. With CMS, victim pages are compressed and swapped out to memory instead of disks. By eliminating slow disk I/Os, CMS provides higher performance than disk-based swap.

There are mainly two variants of CMS – (1) software-based CMS (CMS-S) and hardware-accelerated CMS (CMS-H). CMS-S implements the key operations (i.e., page compression and decompression) of CMS in software. In contrast, CMS-H offloads the key operations to the hardware accelerator.

Since CMS-S requires no hardware support, it can run on various CPUs including old-generation CPUs. However, as quantified in this work, it incurs

M. Torquati et al. (Eds.): Euro-Par 2026, LNCS 16781, pp. 388–402, 2027.
https://doi.org/10.1007/978-3-032-35248-4_27

significant performance overheads because it performs page compression and decompression using CPU cores, which are unoptimized for such operations.

CMS-H is a practical solution that addresses the performance issues of CMS-S through hardware acceleration and widely supported by production-quality OS and commodity CPUs. For example, the mainline Linux kernel supports CMS-H on Intel CPUs using hardware accelerators (i.e., IAA) [5,17,18].

Prior works have conducted a high-level performance analysis of CMS-H [17,18] and explored the feasibility of using hardware accelerators (e.g., Intel QuickAssist Technology (QAT) [22], FPGA [7], and SmartNIC [6]) other than IAA. However, they lack an in-depth analysis of CMS-H based on a production-quality OS and commodity CPUs equipped with IAA, which is crucial for identifying its performance bottlenecks and investigating feasible optimizations.

To bridge this gap, this work makes the following contributions:

- We present a performance comparison of CMS-H with representative swap backends including disk-based swap with a PCIe Gen 5 NVMe SSD.
- We provide an in-depth performance analysis of CMS-H and identify its performance inefficiencies.
- We present three performance optimization techniques (i.e., parallel page compression and decompression, zero-copy page decompression, and eager zspage allocation) for CMS-H and discuss their estimated performance impact.

2 Background

Compressed Memory Swap: When high memory usage is detected, the OS reclaims memory by swapping out pages stored in memory to the swap space. Swap-out operations are typically performed in an asynchronous manner in that OS-level memory reclaim threads swap out pages in background when the memory usage is higher than a threshold. In contrast, swap-in operations are synchronously performed in that a process that tries to access a page currently stored in the swap space is blocked until the OS swaps the page into memory.

With disk-based swap (DBS), the OS evicts victim pages to the swap space in the disk. Since DBS performs expensive disk I/Os for page transfers, it incurs considerable performance overheads.

Compressed memory swap (CMS) addresses the performance issues of DBS by evicting victim pages to the swap space in memory. To ensure that memory is reclaimed by swapping out pages, the CMS compresses victim pages before storing them in the in-memory swap space. When the OS swaps a page into memory, it first decompresses the page and stores the decompressed page in memory.

A variety of production-quality OSes (e.g., zswap (Linux) [24], compressed memory (macOS) [16], memory compression (Windows) [14]) provide support for CMS. In this work, we focus on zswap in Linux because it is open-sourced (which is one of the highly-crucial factors for in-depth performance analysis) and widely used.

There are mainly two variants of CMS – (1) software-based and (2) hardware-accelerated CMS. The software-based CMS (CMS-S) uses conventional CPUs to compress and decompress pages. While CMS-S can be used in old-generation CPUs without hardware support, it incurs significant performance overheads as quantified in this work.

In contrast, the hardware-accelerated CMS (CMS-H) employs an on-chip [17, 18,22] or off-chip [6,7,22] accelerator to compress and decompress pages. As quantified in this work, CMS-H significantly reduces the performance overheads for page compression/decompression.

Various compression/decompression algorithms and memory pool management techniques are used for CMS. In this work, we focus on the Deflate algorithm [2], which is supported by CMS-S and CMS-H.

In addition, we use zsmalloc [23], which is the memory pool manager of Linux kernel for CMS. zsmalloc exhibits low memory fragmentation by allowing an arbitrary number of compressed memory objects to be stored in a zspage (as long as they fit in a single zspage) and classifying zspages into size classes, each of which accommodates compressed memory objects with similar sizes.

Intel In-Memory Analytics Accelerator: Intel CPUs with IAA include one or more IAA devices [8]. Each IAA device has 8 work queues and 8 engines. Each IAA device also includes a set of analytics pipes that are capable of performing decompression and other operations (e.g., SQL filtering) and compression pipes.

Each work queue stores descriptors submitted by software. Each descriptor encodes the information on the associated job such as the operation type (e.g., compression or decompression) and the addresses and sizes of the input and output.

Engines fetch descriptors from the work queues and submit them to the corresponding pipes (i.e., the analytics or compression pipes) based on the operation type through the arbiter. The arbiter selects descriptors to be submitted to the pipes in a QoS- and fairness-aware manner. Engines also manage data transfers between the host memory and the pipes. Data transfers are performed through DMA and can be overlapped with the computations performed by the pipes.

3 Experimental Methodology

System Configuration: To quantify the performance of various swap backends, we use a server that includes two 16-core Intel 8444H CPUs, 128-GB DDR5 DRAM (16 GB $\times$ 8), a 2-TB PCIe Gen 4 NVMe SSD (Samsung 990 PRO), and a 2-TB PCIe Gen 5 NVMe SSD (Samsung 9100 PRO). Each CPU includes four IAA devices. Each IAA device has eight IAA engines, eight analytics pipes for decompression, and two compression pipes. Ubuntu 24.04 and Linux kernel 6.18.7 are installed on the evaluated server.

We analyze the performance of four swap backends (i.e., disk-based swap on a PCIe Gen 4 NVMe SSD (DBS-4), disk-based swap on a PCIe Gen 5 NVMe SSD (DBS-5), software-based compressed memory swap (CMS-S), and hardware-accelerated compressed memory swap (CMS-H)). As for CMS-S and CMS-H, we use the Deflate algorithm for page compression and decompression, which is the algorithm supported by the two swap backends, and zsmalloc to manage the memory pool of CMS. In addition, as for CMS-H, we configure IAA to utilize all the available devices and engines and two work queues per device.

To investigate the NUMA impact on the performance of the four swap backends, we configure the server in two modes – (1) NUMA local access mode and (2) NUMA remote access mode. In the NUMA local access mode, we only employ the CPU 0 and install all the DRAM modules and NVMe SSDs in the local slots of the CPU 0.

In contrast, in the NUMA remote access mode, we only employ the CPU 0 and install all the DRAM modules and NVMe SSDs in the local slots of the CPU 1. Since the evaluated server lacks local M.2 slots for the CPU 1, we install NVMe SSDs in the local U.2 slots of the CPU 1 using M.2-to-U.2 adapters.

Microbenchmark: To quantify the performance of the four swap backends, we design and implement a microbenchmark based on the code used in the prior work [15,17]. The microbenchmark supports random memory accesses and multiple processes.

The microbenchmark employs two datasets (i.e., Silesia [19] and Defconfig [15]). The two datasets show different characteristics in terms of the compression ratio and the portion of zero pages. Specifically, the Defconfig dataset exhibits a higher compression ratio (e.g., 3.81 with CMS-H) and a higher portion (6.66%) of zero pages than those (e.g., 1.91 with CMS-H and 0.21%) of the Silesia dataset.

The microbenchmark consists of four phases – the (1) buffer initialization, (2) swap-out, (3) swap-cache eviction (for DBS-4 and DBS-5), and (4) swap-in phases. During the buffer initialization phase, the microbenchmark allocates a memory buffer (i.e., an one-dimensional array) with a configurable size (e.g., 8 GB). The microbenchmark is configurable to use one of the two aforementioned datasets. It fills the buffer by repeatedly writing the values read from the selected dataset. We ensure that the buffer remains in memory after completing the buffer initialization phase by configuring the buffer size to be significantly smaller than the DRAM capacity of the evaluated server.

During the swap-out phase, the microbenchmark operates in an iterative manner. In each iteration, the microbenchmark randomly chooses a 4-KB page from the memory buffer and invokes the `madvise` system call to trigger a swap-out operation for the page.[1] The microbenchmark repeats this step until it triggers a swap-out operation for every page in the buffer.

Even after the swap-out phase, some pages of the buffer may still exist in the swap cache that holds a subset of pages that have recently been evicted from memory when DBS-4 or DBS-5 is used. If a page is in the swap cache, the swap-in operation loads the page not from the swap backend but from memory. We aim to investigate the performance differences of various swap backends by measuring

---

[1] Since using the `madvise` system call is a feasible way to trigger a swap-out operation without incurring a concurrent swap-in operation, we employ this approach. The performance overhead of the `madvise` system call is small (e.g., 6.52% of the swap-out latency with CMS-H) and our performance data collection tool excludes the code of the `madvise` system call when measuring the latencies.

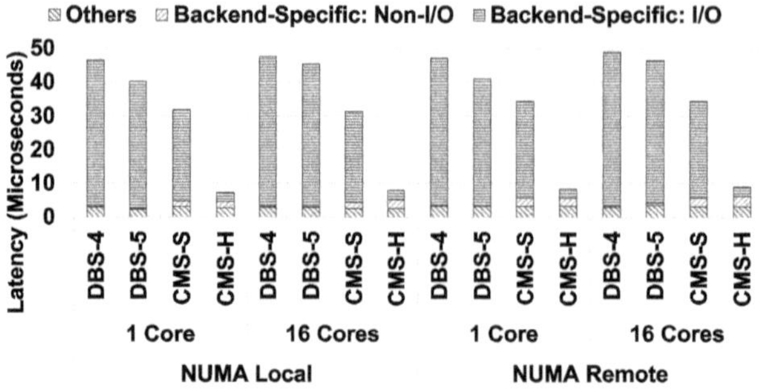

Fig. 1. Swap-in latency of various backends with the Silesia dataset

and analyzing the time spent for loading a page from the swap backend to memory.

To this end, during the swap-cache eviction phase (for DBS-4 and DBS-5), the microbenchmark evicts (almost) all the entries in the swap cache. Specifically, the microbenchmark allocates a dummy memory object whose size is slightly larger than the physical memory capacity of the server and accesses the dummy object. This ensures that the physical memory is mostly filled with the dummy object and the swap cache contains no (or very few, if any) pages of the buffer. After the completion of the swap-out and swap-cache eviction phases, most of the pages of the buffer are stored in the swap space.

During the swap-in phase, the microbenchmark triggers a swap-in operation for every 4-KB page in the buffer in a random order by loading the first byte data from every page. Since most of the pages of the buffer are stored in the swap space after the swap-out phase, each load instruction executed during the swap-in phase is highly likely to trigger a swap-in operation.

Performance Data Collection: We use bpftrace to collect the latencies of the swap-in and swap-out operations [1]. Specifically, we employ bpftrace to dynamically add instrumentation code at the beginning and end of a code region (e.g., a function in Linux kernel) of interest. The instrumented code samples the current time stamp values at the beginning and end of the code region and computes the difference between the time stamp values to measure the latency. All the latency data reported in this work is the average of 2,097,152 (i.e., $\frac{8\text{GB}}{4\text{KB}} = 2^{21}$) samples.

We only instrument one code region at a time to keep the performance data collection overhead as small as possible. The performance data collection overhead is 2.68% on average.

4 Performance Analysis of Swap Backends

This section investigates the performance of the four swap backends. Figures 1, 2, 3 and 4 show the swap-in and swap-out latencies of the swap backends. We vary the core count (i.e., 1 and 16 cores), the NUMA configuration (i.e., NUMA local and NUMA remote access modes), and the datasets (i.e., Silesia and Defconfig) to investigate their performance impact.

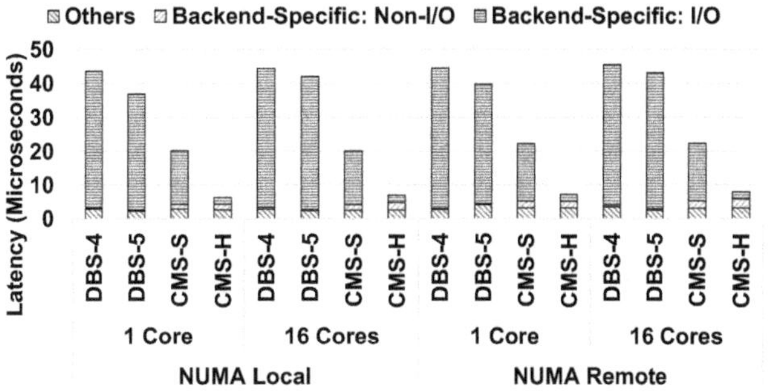

Fig. 2. Swap-in latency of various backends with the Defconfig dataset

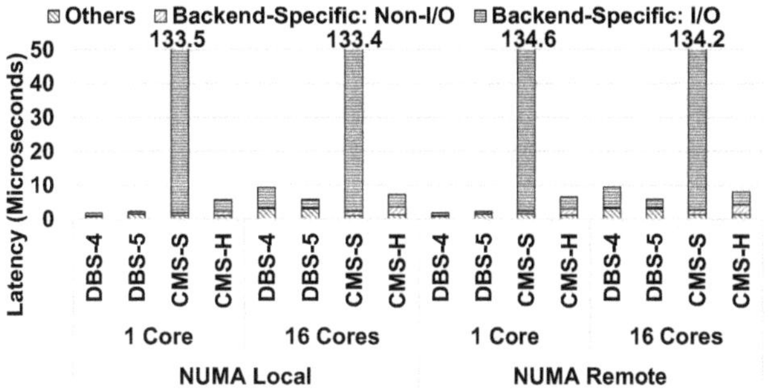

Fig. 3. Swap-out latency of various backends with the Silesia dataset

Each bar in Figs. 1, 2, 3, and 4 consists of three segments. The "Backend-Specific: I/O" and "Backend-Specific: Non-I/O" segments show the times spent for the I/O operations (i.e., disk I/O with DBS-4 and DBS-5 and page compression and decompression with CMS-S and CMS-H) to swap in/out a page from/to the swap space and the rest of the swap backend-specific code.[2] The "Others" segment reports the time spent for the rest of the swap-in or swap-out operation.

4.1 Single-Core Performance Analysis

We first analyze the performance of the four backends with the configuration of 1 core, the NUMA local access mode, and the Silesia dataset. Figure 1 shows the swap-in latencies. We observe the following data trends.

First, DBS-4 (6.39×), DBS-5 (5.51×), and CMS-S (4.37×) incur significantly higher swap-in latencies than CMS-H. This is mainly because the I/O time with DBS-4, DBS-5, and CMS-S is excessively longer than CMS-H.

DBS-4 exhibits the highest swap-in latency because of the high read latency of the PCIe Gen 4 NVMe SSD. While DBS-5 delivers considerably lower swap-in latency than DBS-4, it is significantly outperformed by CMS-H.

[2] Note that no disk I/Os are performed during the execution of the swap-in and swap-out operations with CMS-S and CMS-H. For consistency, we use the term "I/O" across the four swap backends.

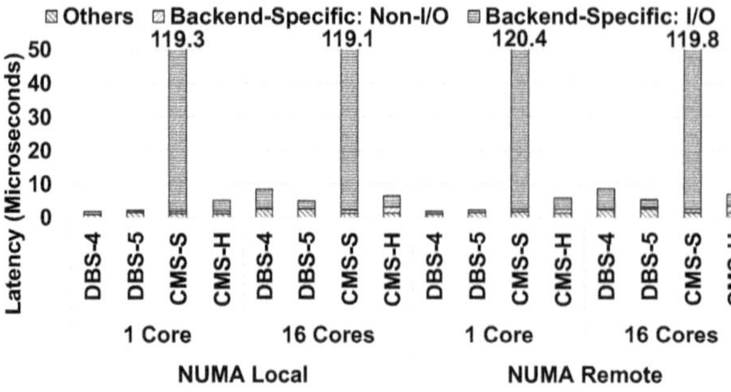

Fig. 4. Swap-out latency of various backends with the Defconfig dataset

CMS-S considerably outperforms DBS-4 and DBS-5 by eliminating the expensive disk I/Os. However, it exhibits significantly higher latency than CMS-H due to the performance overheads for decompressing a page using a CPU core, which is unoptimized for page decompression.

CMS-H achieves the lowest swap-in latency through the elimination of time-consuming disk I/Os and hardware-accelerated page decompression. In addition, unlike the other backends, the time spent for the non-I/O part accounts for a significant portion (26.71%) of the swap-in latency, motivating the need for in-depth performance analysis of CMS-H (Sect. 5).

Figure 3 reports the swap-out latencies of the four swap backends. DBS-4 and DBS-5 exhibit significantly lower swap-out latencies than CMS-S and CMS-H. For example, the swap-out latencies of DBS-4 and DBS-5 are 3.20 and 2.52 times lower than CMS-H. This is mainly because DBS-4 and DBS-5 are implemented to perform disk I/Os in an asynchronous manner in that the swap-out handler issues a disk I/O and immediately returns without waiting for the completion of the issued disk I/O.

In contrast, CMS-S and CMS-H incur higher swap-out latencies. This is mainly because they are implemented to perform I/Os in a synchronous manner in that the swap-out handler is blocked until the victim page is compressed and stored in the in-memory swap space. Especially, CMS-S exhibit excessively high swap-out latency because compressing a page using a CPU core takes a significant amount of time.

CMS-H delivers considerably lower swap-out latency than CMS-S by accelerating page compression through hardware. In addition, similarly to the case with the swap-in operation, the time spent for the non-I/O part accounts for a considerable amount of the swap-out latency, which will further be investigated in Sect. 5.

4.2 Sensitivity to the Core Count

We investigate the performance sensitivity of the four swap backends to the core count. Figure 1 shows the swap-in latencies with the configuration of 16 cores, the NUMA local access mode, and the Silesia dataset.

First, DBS-4 (2.18%) and DBS-5 (12.81%) incur slightly higher swap-in latency with 16 cores than 1 core. This is mainly because of the increased I/O time. Since 16 processes running on 16 cores concurrently trigger swap-in operations, I/O requests are generated more frequently with 16 cores than 1 core, which incur contention on the underlying storage system. However, the bandwidths of the evaluated PCIe Gen 4 and Gen 5 NVMe SSDs are sufficiently high to keep the increase in the I/O time moderate.

Second, CMS-S exhibits similar swap-in latency with 16 cores to that with 1 core. Especially, the I/O time, which accounts for a dominant portion (84.95%) of the swap-in latency with CMS-S, remains unaffected. While 16 processes concurrently trigger swap-in operations, a sufficient number of cores (i.e., 16 cores) are allocated to perform page decompression and memory bandwidth is sufficiently high, preventing them from being the performance bottleneck.

Third, CMS-H incurs slightly higher (9.43%) swap-in latency with 16 cores. The I/O time remains unaffected because of the high computational capability of IAA and memory bandwidth. However, the overall swap-in latency increases due to the increase in the time spent for the non-I/O part increases with 16 cores, which will be discussed in Sects. 5.1 and 5.3.

Figure 3 reports the swap-out latencies with the configuration of 16 cores, the NUMA local access mode, and the Silesia dataset. We observe similar data trends to those of the swap-in latencies.

4.3 Sensitivity to NUMA

We analyze the performance sensitivity of the four swap backends to the NUMA configuration. Figures 1, 2, 3, and 4 report the swap-in and swap-out latencies of the swap backends in both the NUMA local and NUMA remote access modes.

First, DBS-4 and DBS-5 exhibit small performance differences in terms of the swap-in and swap-out latencies with different NUMA configurations. This is mainly because the additional NUMA latency (e.g., 84.91 nanoseconds for a 64-byte load) is significantly lower than the disk latency and the bandwidth of the UPI link (e.g., the peak bandwidth of 143.20 GB/s) is significantly higher than the disk bandwidth.

Second, CMS-S deliver similar swap-in and swap-out latencies with different NUMA configurations. With CMS-S, swap-in and swap-out operations are compute-intensive because CPU cores execute a large number of arithmetic instructions to compress and decompress a page. Therefore, the additional latency due to NUMA remote memory accesses have insignificant performance impact.

Third, the performance sensitivity of CMS-H to the NUMA configuration is low. The times spent for compressing and decompressing a page are significantly reduced through hardware-accelerated page compression and decompression. Therefore, swap-in and swap-out operations with CMS-H are more memory intensive than CMS-S, which could potentially make them more performance sensitive to the NUMA configuration. However, since IAA is capable of overlapping computations and data transfers through DMA, it effectively hides additional latency incurred by NUMA remote memory accesses. Hence, CMS-H exhibits low performance sensitivity to the NUMA configuration.

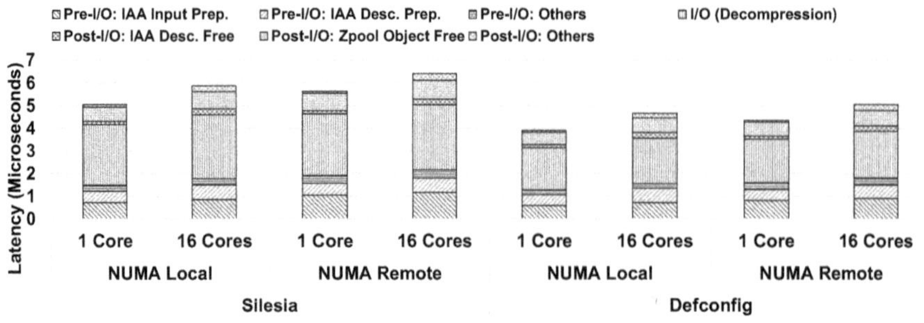

Fig. 5. Swap-in latency of CMS-H

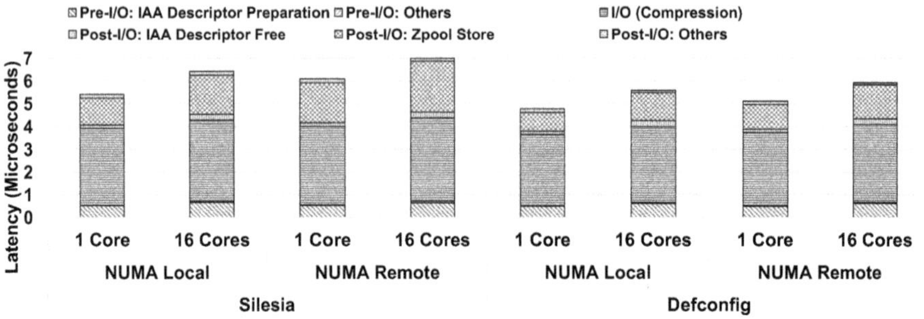

Fig. 6. Swap-out latency of CMS-H

4.4 Sensitivity to the Dataset

We investigate the performance sensitivity of the four swap backends to the dataset. Figures 2 and 4 show the swap-in and swap-out latencies with the Defconfig dataset.

The four swap backends exhibit similar performance trends with the Defconfig dataset to those with the Silesia dataset. One noticeable difference is that the I/O time of the four swap backends is reduced with the Defconfig dataset. The Defconfig dataset contains more zero pages than the Silesia dataset. Since zero pages incur no actual I/Os during the swap-in/out operations, the average I/O time decreases with the four swap backends.

In addition, the compression ratio (e.g., 3.81 with CMS-H) of the Defconfig dataset is higher than that (e.g., 1.91 with CMS-H) of the Silesia dataset. Therefore, the I/O time with CMS-S and CMS-H decreases with the reduced amount of data transfers (due to smaller compressed pages).

5 In-Depth Performance Analysis of CMS-H

This section presents an in-depth performance analysis of hardware-accelerated compressed memory swap (CMS-H) to identify performance inefficiencies existing in the current implementation. Figures 5 and 6 show the times spent for the backend-specific parts of the swap-in and swap-out operations with CMS-H.

We decompose swap-in and swap-out operations into three phases – the (1) pre-I/O, (2) I/O (i.e., decompression or compression), and (3) post-I/O phases. Each bar in Figs. 5 and 6 consists of multiple segments, each of which indicates the time spent for performing a major activity in the pre-I/O, I/O, and post-I/O phases.

5.1 Pre-I/O Phase

We first analyze the performance of the pre-I/O phase of the swap-in operation with CMS-H. As shown in Fig. 5, the pre-I/O phase of the swap-in operation consists of three segments – (1) IAA input preparation, (2) IAA descriptor preparation, and (3) others.

The IAA input preparation segment includes the time spent for accessing the zpool to retrieve a zspage that contains the compressed page and accounts for a considerable portion (16.61%) of the swap-in latency. If the compressed page is stored in two physical pages in the zspage, CMS-H is implemented in a way to copy the two chunks of the compressed page into a single contiguous buffer. In addition, since the zpool is protected using a lock for thread safety, it can cause lock contention with 16 cores.

The IAA descriptor preparation segment includes the time spent for allocating and configuring the descriptor that is submitted to IAA for page decompression. Since CMS-H performs time-consuming activities such as accessing the IAA work queues, selecting an IAA work queue, and retrieving one of the available IAA descriptors from the selected work queue, the IAA descriptor allocation takes a considerable amount of time. In addition, since the IAA descriptor allocation requires a lock to access the work queue, we conjecture that it increases the swap-in latency with 16 cores.

Figure 6 shows that the pre-I/O phase of the swap-out operation with CMS-H consists of two segments – (1) IAA descriptor preparation and (2) others. The IAA descriptor preparation time accounts for the time spent for preparing an IAA descriptor to request page compression to IAA and exhibits similar data trends to those with the swap-in operation.

5.2 I/O Phase

As shown in Figs. 5 and 6, the I/O time accounts for the largest portion (52.85%) of the swap-in and swap-out latencies. While CPUs with hardware support for page compression and decompression are equipped with multiple IAA devices, the current implementation of CMS-H has a limitation in that it lacks the capability of parallelizing page compression and decompression using multiple IAA devices.

5.3 Post-I/O Phase

Figure 5 shows that the post-I/O phase of the swap-in operation consists of three segments – (1) IAA descriptor free, (2) zpool object free, and (3) others. Among the three segments, the zpool object free segment accounts for the largest portion (13.35%) of the swap-in latency because CMS-H executes the code to access the data structure used to manage the zpool and deallocate the memory allocated for the zpool object. The IAA descriptor free and zpool object free times increase with 16 cores. We conjecture that this is mainly due to the contention on the locks that protect the work queue and the data structure.

We analyze the performance of the post-I/O phase of the swap-out operation. As shown in Fig. 6, the post-I/O phase of the swap-out operation consists of three segments – (1) IAA descriptor free, (2) zpool store, and (3) others. Among the three segments, the zpool store segment accounts for the largest portion (24.31%) of the swap-out latency. The current implementation of CMS-H allocates a zspage in a lazy manner when there is no free zspage to store the compressed page. While the zspage allocation occurs only when no free zspage is available, the zspage allocation time is long (e.g., 3.09 microseconds with the Silesia dataset) and accounts for a significant portion (33.53%) of the zpool store segment.

6 Performance Optimizations

Guided by the characterization results, we present three optimization techniques (i.e., parallel page compression and decompression, zero-copy page decompression, and eager zspage allocation) for hardware-accelerated compressed memory swap (CMS-H). We also discuss their estimated performance impact (with the configuration of 1 core, the NUMA local access mode, and the Silesia dataset).

6.1 Parallel Page Compression and Decompression

One of the major inefficiencies of the current implementation of CMS-H is that it only employs a single IAA device to compress and decompress a page despite that each CPU is equipped with multiple IAA devices. The page compression and decompression times, which account for significant portions (60.15% and 36.90%) of the swap-out and swap-in times as quantified in Sects. 4 and 5 can considerably be reduced through parallel page compression and decompression.

To improve the performance of CMS-H, we propose the parallel page compression and decompression techniques. For brevity, we focus on the case in which the parallel page compression technique divides a page into two sub-pages, each of which has the half size of the page. It compresses two sub-pages with two IAA devices in a fully parallel manner. It then creates two zpool objects and stores the two compressed sub-pages into the two zpool objects.

The parallel page decompression technique simultaneously decompresses the two sub-pages using two IAA devices. Since the sub-page size (i.e., the half size of a page) is known in advance (before completing the decompression of the first sub-page), each IAA device can write the decompressed sub-page in a fully parallel manner with the output address computed by adding the address of the newly swapped-in page and the offset of 0 (i.e., the first sub-page) or the half size of a page (i.e., the second sub-page).

The parallel page compression and decompression techniques can improve the performance of the swap-out and swap-in operations by reducing the I/O times. Specifically, the estimated reductions in the I/O times with the parallel page compression and decompression techniques are 1.34 microseconds for the swap-in operation and 1.69 microseconds for the swap-out operation. However, since they use additional zpool object and IAA descriptor, the code for managing the zpool and IAA descriptor needs to be optimized in order to maximize the performance gains of the parallel page compression and decompression techniques.

6.2 Zero-Copy Page Decompression

Another inefficiency of the current implementation of CMS-H is that, when a compressed page is stored in two physical pages in a zspage, CMS-H copies two chunks into a single contiguous buffer before decompressing it using IAA. Since IAA is capable of decompressing a single logical stream that is physically stored in multiple non-contiguous buffers, the aforementioned memory copy is unnecessary and increases latency and memory traffic.

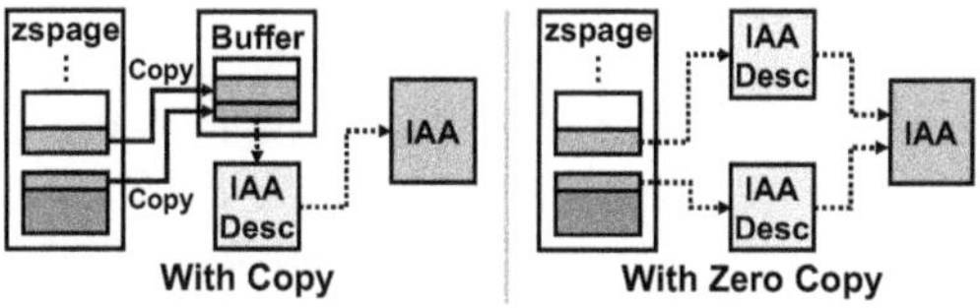

Fig. 7. Zero-copy page decompression

To eliminate the overhead incurred by the unnecessary memory copy, we propose the zero-copy page decompression technique (Fig. 7). When a compressed page spanning two physical pages in a zspage needs to be swapped in memory, the zero-copy page decompression technique provides the pointers to the two IAA descriptors, each of which contains information on each chunk, instead of copying the two chunks to a single buffer. The zero-copy page decompression technique eliminates the memory copy overheads in terms of time (0.51 microseconds) and memory traffic.

The zero-copy page decompression technique requires an additional IAA descriptor for the second chunk. However, the overheads (e.g., IAA descriptor preparation time) related to the additional IAA descriptor can significantly be reduced (or completely eliminated) by overlapping the IAA descriptor preparation of the second chunk with the decompression of the first chunk.

6.3 Eager Zspage Allocation

During the execution of the swap-out operation, the current implementation of CMS-H allocates a zspage in a lazy manner when there is no available zspage. While the zspage allocation occurs relatively infrequently, it takes a significant amount of time, considerably increasing the swap-out latency.

To address the performance issue of lazy zspage allocation, we propose the eager zspage allocation technique. The key idea of the eager zspage allocation technique is to pre-allocate a sufficient number of free zspages to eliminate the time spent for zspage allocation during the execution of the swap-out operation.

Specifically, the eager zspage allocation technique employs a threshold for each size class. When a number of available free zspages of a class becomes lower than the threshold, it proactively allocates new zspage(s).

To hide the latency of allocating new zspage(s), the eager zspage allocation technique overlaps the zspage allocation with the page compression. The zspage allocation and page compression can simultaneously be performed by a CPU core and an IAA device, respectively. Therefore, the latency for allocating new zspage(s) can effectively be hidden. The eager zspage allocation technique is expected to reduce the swap-out latency by eliminating the time spent for allocating a new zspage, which accounts for 9.37% of the swap-out latency.

7 Related Work

Prior works have conducted high-level performance analysis of hardware-accelerated memory swap (CMS-H) [17,18]. While insightful, the prior works focus on measuring the performance differences between CMS-H and software-based compressed memory swap (CMS-S) and lacks the investigation of performance inefficiencies of CMS-H. Our work significantly differs in that it presents a performance comparison of CMS-H with various swap backends including the disk-based swap with the state-of-the-art NVMe SSD technology, provides an in-depth performance analysis of CMS-H and identifies its performance inefficiencies, and proposes three optimization techniques (i.e., parallel page compression and decompression, zero-copy page decompression, and eager zspage allocation).

Prior works have investigated techniques to improve the performance of compressed memory swap using hardware components other than IAA such as QAT [22], FPGA [7], and SmartNIC [6]. Our work is considerably different from the prior works in that it presents an in-depth performance of CMS-H that is based on a production-quality OS (i.e., the mainline Linux kernel) and commodity CPUs with support for IAA and is widely deployed and used in real datacenters and proposes performance optimization techniques for CMS-H based on the in-depth characterization results.

Prior works have explored system software techniques to effectively utilize CMS-S in various domains such as embedded and cloud computing [3,4,9,10,12,20,21]. Our work significantly differs in that it focuses on the performance analysis and optimization of CMS-H.

8 Conclusions

In this work, we present a performance comparison of hardware-accelerated memory swap (CMS-H) with various swap backends including the one with high-performance NVMe SSD technology and an in-depth performance analysis of CMS-H. Our performance analysis demonstrates that, while CMS-H significantly outperforms other swap backends including the disk-based swap with a PCIe Gen 5 NVMe SSD and software-based compressed memory swap, it also has performance inefficiencies such as sequential page compression and decompression and unnecessary memory copy. In addition, we propose three optimization techniques (i.e., parallel page compression and decompression, zero-copy page decompression, and eager zspage allocation) for CMS-H.

Acknowledgments. This research was partly supported by NRF (RS-2026-25483165, 60%) and IITP-ITRC (IITP-2026-RS-2021-II211817, 40%).

Disclosure of Interests. The authors have no competing interests to declare that are relevant to the content of this article.

References

1. bpftrace: dynamic tracing for Linux. https://bpftrace.org/. Accessed 13 May 2026
2. Deutsch, L.P.: DEFLATE Compressed Data Format Specification version 1.3. RFC 1951 (1996)
3. Han, M., Park, E., Shin, Y., Oh, D.-J., Cho, Y., Baek, W.: COSMOS: coordinated management of cores, memory, and compressed memory swap for QoS-aware and efficient workload consolidation for memory-intensive application. IEEE Access (2023)
4. Hwang, J., Jeong, J., Kim, H., Choi, J., Lee, J.: Compressed memory swap for QoS of virtualized embedded systems. IEEE Trans. Consumer Electr. (2012)
5. IAA Compression Accelerator Crypto Driver. https://docs.kernel.org/driver-api/crypto/iaa/iaa-crypto.html. Accessed 13 May 2026
6. Ji, H., et al.: STYX: exploiting SmartNIC capability to reduce datacenter memory tax. In: USENIX Annual Technical Conference (USENIX ATC 23), USENIX ATC 2023 (2023)
7. Ji, H., et al.: Demystifying a CXL Type-2 device: a heterogeneous cooperative computing perspective. In: Proceedings of the 2024 57th IEEE/ACM International Symposium on Microarchitecture. MICRO 2024 (2024)
8. Kang, J., Xia, Q., Jeong, I., Park, Y., Kim, N.S.: Intel® in-memory analytics accelerator: performance characterization and guidelines. In: IEEE International Symposium on Performance Analysis of Systems and Software (ISPASS), ISPASS 2025 (2025)
9. Kim, J., Kim, C., Seo, E.: *ezswap*: enhanced compressed swap scheme for mobile devices. IEEE Access (2019)
10. Lagar-Cavilla, A., et al.: Software-defined far memory in warehouse-scale computers. In: Proceedings of the Twenty-Fourth International Conference on Architectural Support for Programming Languages and Operating Systems. ASPLOS 2019 (2019)
11. Lee, S.-H.: Technology scaling challenges and opportunities of memory devices. In: IEEE International Electron Devices Meeting (IEDM), IEDM 2016 (2016)
12. Li, C., Shi, L., Liang, Y., Xue, C. J.: SEAL: user experience-aware two-level swap for mobile devices. In: IEEE Transactions on Computer-Aided Design of Integrated Circuits and Systems (2020)
13. Mack, C.A.: Fifty Years of Moore's Law. IEEE Trans. Semicond. Manuf. (2011)
14. Memory Compression in Windows 10 RTM. https://learn.microsoft.com/en-us/shows/seth-juarez/memory-compression-in-windows-10-rtm. Accessed 2026/05/13
15. memory-usage-analyzer. https://github.com/intel/memory-usage-analyzer/tree/main/tests/madvise. Accessed 13 May 2026
16. OS X Mavericks Core Technologies Overview. https://images.apple.com/media/us/osx/2013/docs/OSX_Mavericks_Core_Technology_Overview.pdf. Accessed 13 May 2026

17. Ravindran, B., Seshasayee, B., Sridhar, K., Al-Fahad, R., Gopal, V., P.G., Chowdhury, M.: Memory-tiering with intel® in-memory analytics accelerator (Intel® IAA). Addressing Memory Challenges: Enhancing Data Center Efficiency with zswap and Intel IAA
18. Ravindran, B., Sridhar, K., Al-Fahad, R., Gopal, V.: Memory-Tiering with Intel® In-Memory Analytics Accelerator. Improve Effective Memory Capacity with Efficient In-Memory Compression using Zswap and IAA
19. Silesia Corpus. https://wanos.co/docs/docs/frequently-asked-questions/silesia-corpus/. Accessed 13 May 2026
20. Song, T., Kim, M., Lee, G., Kim, Y.: Prediction-guided performance improvement on compressed memory swap. In: IEEE International Conference on Consumer Electronics (ICCE), ICCE 2022 (2022)
21. Weiner, J., et al.: TMO: transparent memory offloading in datacenters. In: Proceedings of the 27th ACM International Conference on Architectural Support for Programming Languages and Operating Systems, ASPLOS 2022 (2022)
22. Xia, Q., Ji, H., Zhou, Y., Kim, N.S.: Hardware-accelerated kernel-space memory compression using intel QAT. IEEE Comput. Architecture Lett. (2025)
23. zsmalloc. https://docs.kernel.org/mm/zsmalloc.html. Accessed 13 May 2026
24. zswap. https://docs.kernel.org/admin-guide/mm/zswap.html. Accessed 13 May 2026

When Faster Kernels Do Not Mean Faster Applications in Exascale GPU Systems

Mariana T. Costa[1], Antigoni Georgiadou[2], James B. White III[2], Woong Shin[2], Bruno V. Alvarez[3], Jordà Polo[3], Karl Schulz[3], Philippe Navaux[1], Bronson Messer[2], and Arthur Lorenzon[1](✉)

[1] Institute of Informatics, Federal University of Rio Grande do Sul, Rio Grande do Sul, Brazil
{mariana.costa,navaux,aflorenzon}@inf.ufrgs.br
[2] Oak Ridge National Laboratory, Oak Ridge, USA
{georgiadoua,whiteiiijb,shinw,bronson}@ornl.gov
[3] Advanced Micro Devices, Santa Clara, USA
{Bruno.VillasenorAlvarez,Jorda.Polo,Karl.Schulz}@amd.com

Abstract. Power management methods such as power capping or dynamic frequency capping have long been considered primary mechanisms for addressing the power constraints of exascale computing and beyond. However, their effectiveness in GPU-accelerated HPC applications is not straightforward, as they are inherently multi-kernel and exhibit heterogeneous computational and memory behavior across execution phases. As a result, improvements observed at the kernel level may not translate into better application-level performance. In this work, we investigate how device-level power capping and frequency capping affect the performance–energy behavior of GPU applications on the Frontier exascale supercomputer. We evaluate multiple power and frequency configurations across three representative applications (*Cholla*, *Pennant*, and *HACC*) to identify those that deliver the best performance–energy trade-offs. Using these configurations, we perform an intra-kernel analysis combining GPU hardware counters with runtime profiling to examine how power management policies influence kernel execution and distributed runtime behavior. Our results show that faster kernels do not necessarily lead to faster applications. For example, in *Pennant* running across 32 nodes, the dominant kernel executes up to 20% faster under power capping, yet these gains are partially offset by higher communication costs and load imbalance across MPI calls. Similarly, in *Cholla*, synchronization imbalance increases from 30.6% to 39.8% and communication imbalance from 5.8% to 16.6%, leading to longer MPI wait times despite faster kernel execution.

Keywords: Exascale Systems · Energy Efficiency · Performance · Power Management

M. Torquati et al. (Eds.): Euro-Par 2026, LNCS 16781, pp. 403–417, 2027.
https://doi.org/10.1007/978-3-032-35248-4_28

1 Introduction

With the widespread deployment of exascale systems, applications from diverse scientific and engineering domains are increasingly executed on large-scale GPU-accelerated platforms [3]. These applications are inherently multi-kernel, combining computational phases with different arithmetic intensity, memory access patterns, and synchronization requirements within a single execution. As a result, their performance and power consumption vary significantly across kernels and execution phases. In this scenario, hardware constraints may influence different parts of the execution in distinct ways, making kernel-level behavior a key factor shaping the application's overall runtime and energy profile.

Because applications running on GPUs are diverse and operate under strict thermal and power constraints, modern architectures provide hardware mechanisms that cater to different performance and energy consumption requirements during execution. Two commonly exposed mechanisms are device-level power capping [9] and frequency capping [11]. Although both aim to control energy usage or enforce power budgets, they constrain hardware operation through different control strategies. Power capping limits total device power by dynamically adjusting voltage and frequency, whereas frequency capping imposes a fixed upper bound on the clock frequency. These mechanisms therefore create different operating conditions that affect compute throughput, memory subsystem activity, and pipeline behavior during kernel execution.

The effectiveness of these controls depends on how individual kernels use hardware resources. Kernels dominated by arithmetic operations may be strongly affected by frequency limits, whereas memory-bound kernels may exhibit lower sensitivity to clock frequency but stronger dependence on the memory subsystem. In multi-kernel applications, where execution phases place distinct demands on the hardware, these mechanisms may affect each kernel differently. Moreover, as applications scale across multiple nodes, the effects of power management mechanisms extend beyond kernel execution and interact with communication and synchronization phases. Under these conditions, improvements observed in individual kernels do not necessarily translate into better application-level performance, since load imbalance and MPI overheads can offset kernel-level gains.

These interactions make it difficult to interpret the behavior of power management policies when observed only at the application level. Despite this complexity, most existing studies evaluate power management strategies primarily using aggregate metrics such as total runtime or energy-to-solution [1,2,8,14,15]. While these metrics provide useful high-level insights, they do not reveal which kernels benefit from specific power management policies or how hardware-level behavior interacts with distributed execution dynamics. As a result, application-level observations often obscure the mechanisms that determine performance–energy trade-offs in multi-kernel HPC workloads.

To address this gap, the main contribution of this work is a detailed analysis of how power and frequency capping influence the performance and energy behavior of GPU-accelerated applications in exascale systems. We perform an extensive evaluation of multiple power and frequency capping configurations across three representative scientific applications (*Cholla*, *Pennant*, and *HACC*) on the Frontier supercomputer, across different node counts and GPUs, analyzing their impact on performance and energy consumption to identify the configurations that provide the best performance–energy trade-offs. Using these configurations, we then conduct an intra-kernel analysis, combining GPU hardware performance counters with runtime profiling to examine how the selected power and frequency settings influence kernel execution.

By correlating kernel-level metrics with synchronization and MPI communication costs, we demonstrate that improvements in kernel execution efficiency do not necessarily translate into better application-level performance. For example, in *Pennant* running across 32 nodes, the dominant kernel executes up to 20% faster under the power-capped configuration, which provides the best performance–energy trade-off, compared to the corresponding frequency-capped configuration. However, these kernel-level gains are partially offset by higher communication overheads and increased load imbalance across MPI calls, which reduce the overall performance benefit at scale. A similar behavior is observed in *Cholla*, where the dominant kernels run slightly faster under power capping, yet synchronization and communication imbalances increase from 30.6% to 39.8% and from 5.8% to 16.6%, respectively, leading to longer MPI wait times and favoring the frequency-capped configuration in multi-node executions.

2 Background

2.1 GPU Power Management

Modern GPUs provide hardware mechanisms to regulate performance and power under thermal and electrical constraints. Two common controls are frequency capping and device-level power capping.

Frequency Capping operates over a discrete set of performance states (P-states), each defined by a specific clock frequency and associated supply voltage [11]. Selecting a lower P-state reduces the maximum allowable clock frequency of the device and, in some architectures, the memory subsystem. Because dynamic power in CMOS circuits is proportional to $C \cdot V^2 \cdot f$, reducing frequency, typically accompanied by voltage reduction, decreases switching activity and overall power consumption. When a frequency cap is applied, the upper bound of the available P-states is restricted. The hardware prevents the clock from exceeding the configured clock limit, regardless of workload demand. The control is open-loop with respect to instantaneous power draw: the frequency ceiling remains fixed unless reconfigured by software. Frequency transitions are managed by on-chip controllers that coordinate voltage rails and clock domains.

Power Capping enforces an upper limit on total device power consumption, typically specified in watts [9]. This mechanism relies on a closed-loop feedback controller integrated into the GPU power management unit. On-chip sensors measure voltage and current across multiple power rails, and the resulting power estimate is continuously compared against the configured limit. When the measured power approaches or exceeds the cap, the controller reduces consumption by adjusting performance-related parameters, including clock frequencies and supply voltages. Under power capping, the operating frequency is not fixed. Instead, it varies according to workload characteristics and instantaneous resource utilization. Compute-intensive kernels with high switching activity are more likely to reach the power ceiling, triggering sustained frequency throttling. Kernels limited by memory bandwidth or latency may operate below the power threshold and maintain higher effective frequencies. The resulting execution behavior depends on the interactions among workload demand, architectural bottlenecks, and the responsiveness of the hardware control loop.

2.2 Related Work

Recent work on energy efficiency in GPU-accelerated HPC has explored power and frequency capping strategies, evolving from application-level evaluations to system-level optimization frameworks. Early studies compared the effectiveness of different capping mechanisms. Kryzwaniak et al. [10] proposed DEPO, a runtime system that dynamically adjusts GPU power limits based on application behavior. Similarly, Simmendinger et al. [15] introduced a phase-aware capping mechanism to reduce power consumption. Using operational telemetry from the Frontier supercomputer, Karimi et al. [8] projected energy savings of up to 8.5%, corresponding to more than 1,400 MWh in potential reductions. Application-focused analyses also demonstrated the benefits of capping strategies [1] and multi-objective optimization of GPU power limits on the GH200 platform [14].

More recently, intelligent control mechanisms have been explored. Yiming et al. [17] proposed DRLCap, a reinforcement learning approach that dynamically adjusts GPU frequency caps during program execution. Angelelli et al. [2] introduced an Eco-Mode, in which users voluntarily opt into power-capped execution. Finally, predictive approaches based on job characteristics are emerging. Antici et al. [5] developed a machine-learning model to predict CPU power consumption for workloads on the Fugaku supercomputer. In the GPU domain, Lorenzon et al. [12] introduced V-FORGE, a frequency-aware scheduling framework evaluated on 400 AMD MI250X GPUs.

Our Contributions. This study provides a detailed and extensive empirical analysis of power and frequency capping mechanisms for GPU-accelerated scientific applications running on the Frontier supercomputer. Instead of proposing new runtime frameworks or optimization techniques, our goal is to examine how these mechanisms influence application behavior at both the kernel and runtime levels. In particular, we analyze how each capping strategy affects kernel execution, GPU hardware-level metrics, and application-level behavior, including synchronization and communication overheads across MPI processes. By correlating low-level hardware activity with runtime behavior, the analysis clarifies how power management policies interact with the computational and communication characteristics of large-scale HPC workloads. This work builds upon our previous study [4] by extending the analysis to kernel-level behavior and by examining how hardware metrics relate to performance differences observed under power and frequency constraints.

3 Methodology

3.1 Applications

We evaluate three representative GPU-accelerated applications from computational astrophysics and scientific simulation workloads: *Cholla*, *Pennant*, and *HACC*. These applications exhibit distinct computational and memory-access characteristics, as depicted in Table 1. **Cholla** is a multidimensional hydrodynamics code that solves the Euler equations using the Piecewise Parabolic Method (PPM) [16]. Its workload is primarily composed of GPU kernels performing stencil-based computations over structured three-dimensional grids. **Pennant** is a proxy application for Lagrangian hydrodynamics that models shock hydrodynamics on unstructured meshes. The application demonstrates complex memory access patterns and sensitivity to both compute throughput and memory-hierarchy performance [6]. **HACC** (Hardware Accelerated Cosmology Code) is a large-scale cosmology application used to simulate the formation of cosmic structure [7]. Its workload combines compute-intensive kernels with phases that involve particle updates, grid projections, and data reordering.

Table 1. Characteristics of each application, averaged over GPU kernels.

	FLOPs/byte	FLOPs/s	L2Cache Hit (%)
Cholla	0.62	6.58E+11	37.51
Pennant	0.67	5.57E+11	45.11
HACC	215.04	4.67E+12	84.02

3.2 Testbed System

All experiments were conducted on the **Frontier** supercomputer at the Oak Ridge Leadership Computing Facility [3]. Each compute node comprises a 64-core AMD EPYC 7763 processor with 512 GB of DDR4 memory and four AMD Instinct MI250X accelerators. Each MI250X contains two Graphics Compute Dies (GCDs) per node, for a total of eight GCDs per node. Since each GCD operates independently, we treated each GCD as a separate GPU, yielding a total of eight MPI processes per node. To evaluate scalability effects, applications were executed under two configurations: (*i*) a single-node setup using all 8 GCDs, and (*ii*) a multi-node configuration spanning 32 nodes (256 GCDs). The MI250X accelerator has a thermal design power of 560 W and supports dynamic frequency scaling from 500 MHz to 1700 MHz. For the frequency-capping study, we evaluated 31 discrete frequency levels at 40 MHz increments across this range. For power capping, 21 power limits were tested, from 140 W to 560 W in 20 W increments. All frequency and power caps were statically configured prior to execution using ROCm management utilities.

Applications were compiled with ROCm 6.2.4 using `hipcc` and targeting the MI250X architecture via `-offload-arch=gfx90a`. The Frontier runtime environment included the modules `craype-accel-amd-gfx90a` and `rocm/6.2.4`, ensuring reproducibility across experiments. Each experiment was performed 10 times, and the reported results correspond to the average. Across all runs, the observed standard deviation remained below 2%, resulting in narrow 95% confidence intervals.

3.3 Evaluated Metrics

To collect power, energy, and other system-level metrics, we used Omnistat, an open-source monitoring tool designed for low-overhead data collection [13]. Omnistat was developed to gather runtime statistics from AMD Instinct™ GPUs[1], including the MI250X GPUs deployed in the Frontier supercomputer. For our experiments on Frontier, the tool was configured through a runtime control file that enables the collection of GPU metrics via the system management interface. During each experiment, Omnistat aggregated the collected metrics per Slurm job across all compute nodes allocated to the job.

To analyze runtime behavior and MPI activity, we used the Cray Performance Analysis Tool (*CrayPat*). It provides detailed information on the execution timeline, including time spent in individual kernels, MPI functions, and synchronization routines, as well as metrics on load imbalance across processes. With that, one can quantify communication and synchronization costs. At the hardware level, GPU metrics were collected using `rocprofv3`, part of the ROCm profiling suite. The collected performance monitoring counters include metrics related to compute activity (e.g., number of waves and instruction issue behavior), memory subsystem utilization (e.g., cache accesses and latency-related counters), stall cycles and pipeline back-pressure indicators (e.g., SPI and memory-related stalls), and kernel execution characteristics (e.g., workgroup size and register usage).

4 Evaluation

In this section, we evaluate the impact of the GPU power-management mechanisms on the performance and energy of the studied applications. We first analyze each workload's behavior using a Pareto-front methodology to identify operating points that offer different trade-offs between execution time and energy consumption. Based on this analysis, we select the best-performing energy-balanced

[1] AMD, the AMD Arrow logo and combinations thereof are trademarks of Advanced Micro Devices, Inc.

configurations for each application and examine them in more detail through an intra-kernel investigation focusing on the most-representative kernels of each workload. Finally, we present a discussion of the main findings.

4.1 Performance–Energy Trade-Off

Figure 1 shows the results for *Cholla*, *Pennant*, and *HACC* running on 1 node (8 GCDs) and 32 nodes (256 GCDs). Each plot includes all evaluated configurations, enabling the identification of the Pareto front in the performance–energy space on the Frontier system. Each point represents a configuration: power-capping settings are shown as blue circles and frequency-capping settings as red triangles, with color intensity indicating the cap magnitude, meaning darker shades correspond to higher cap values. The *x-axis* reports execution time, and the *y-axis* reports total energy consumption. Configurations closer to the lower-left region combine shorter runtime with lower energy consumption. The default (uncapped) configuration is highlighted, along with the operating points that provide the best performance–energy trade-off for each mechanism. To identify these points, we first determine the Pareto-optimal set, that is, configurations where no other setting achieves both lower runtime and lower energy. Among these, we selected the one with the smallest Euclidean distance to the origin $(0, 0)$, computed as $d = \sqrt{T^2 + E^2}$, where T is execution time in seconds and E is total energy consumption in joules.

Figure 1 shows that multiple configurations lie on the Pareto front for all applications and node counts. This indicates that several operating points provide comparable performance–energy trade-offs. For example, in *Cholla* running on 32 nodes, several frequency-capping configurations between 1330 MHz and 1700 MHz achieve nearly identical execution times but differ in energy consumption. In this region of the front, lower frequencies reduce energy consumption with negligible impact on runtime, showing that similar performance can be achieved at different energy costs.

To better understand how these trade-offs manifest in practice, we now examine each application individually. For *Cholla*, the behavior differs between the 1-node and 32-node executions. The results show that the default configuration does not provide the best trade-off between performance and energy, regardless of the number of nodes used. In the 1-node configuration, power-capping at 320 W achieves the best execution time, while frequency-capping at 940 MHz results in the lowest energy consumption (22.5% lower than the default). This suggests that reducing the power limit can preserve performance, whereas moderate frequency reductions are more effective at lowering energy usage. The behavior changes in the 32-node configuration, where the best execution times are observed under frequency-capping settings.

In contrast to *Cholla*, *Pennant* exhibits more stable behavior across the evaluated configurations. In the 1-node scenario, most power- and frequency-capping settings lie on the Pareto front, indicating that the application is relatively insensitive to moderate changes in GPU operating conditions. The best performance–energy trade-off is achieved with configurations below the default operating point, such as 420 W or 1220 MHz, which reduce energy consumption by about 10–13% while maintaining comparable execution times. When scaling to 32 nodes, the behavior changes slightly. Although several power-capping configurations deliver execution times comparable to those obtained with frequency capping, they generally consume more energy and therefore do not appear on the Pareto front. In practice, only the 540 W configuration remains on the front, providing the fastest execution time among the evaluated settings, albeit at a higher energy cost. In contrast, frequency-capping configurations occupy the more energy-efficient region of the front. In particular, the configuration at 1620 MHz achieves the best performance–energy trade-off, reducing energy consumption by 4.5% compared to the 540 W power-capped configuration while increasing execution time by only about 2%.

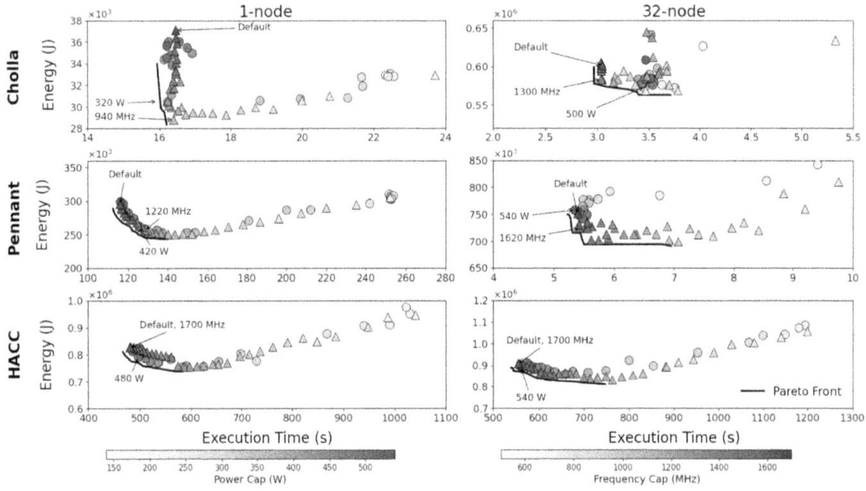

Fig. 1. Performance–energy trade-offs under power and frequency capping for *Cholla*, *Pennant*, and *HACC*. Annotated markers highlight the default configuration and the best capping results.

HACC exhibits a behavior that partially resembles *Pennant* in the 1-node scenario but differs when scaling to multiple nodes. For the 1-node execution, the best performance–energy trade-off is achieved at 480 W, reducing energy consumption by about 4% relative to the default while maintaining similar performance. However, stronger power limits (e.g., below 260 W) significantly increase execution time, offsetting any potential energy savings. A similar trend is observed with frequency capping; configurations approaching the default frequency (1700 MHz) produce results close to the baseline. As a result, most configurations above 340 W or 1400 MHz lie on the Pareto front, offering different trade-offs between execution time and energy consumption. When scaling to 32 nodes, the behavior becomes more stable than in the other applications. This stability is explained by the weak-scaling configuration used for *HACC*, where the workload per node remains constant as the system size increases. Under these conditions, the Pareto front is mainly composed of configurations near the default operating point, while stronger caps degrade performance without providing sufficient energy savings to remain competitive.

4.2 Intra-kernel Analysis

To explain the performance–energy trade-offs identified in the previous analysis, we now examine the behavior of the applications at the kernel level. Specifically, we perform an intra-kernel investigation using the power- and frequency-capping configurations that provided the best performance–energy balance for each workload. The goal is to understand how these configurations affect the execution of the most-representative kernels, as well as the communication and synchronization phases that contribute to overall runtime. To this end, we combine GPU hardware performance metrics collected with *rocprofv3* and runtime profiling information obtained with *CrayPat*. While *rocprofv3* provides low-level GPU hardware counters that characterize kernel behavior, *CrayPat* enables detailed runtime analysis, including kernel execution time, MPI communication overheads, synchronization costs, and load imbalance across processes.

Figure 2 summarizes this analysis by presenting the execution time of the four most-representative kernels in each application (selected based on their contribution to total execution time and collectively accounting for 80% to 90% of the total application runtime) together with the time spent in synchronization (*Sync*) and communication (*Comm*) phases. All values are normalized to the power-capped configuration, such that values below 1.0 indicate that frequency capping results in faster execution for that component. In the following subsections, we examine each application's behavior in detail.

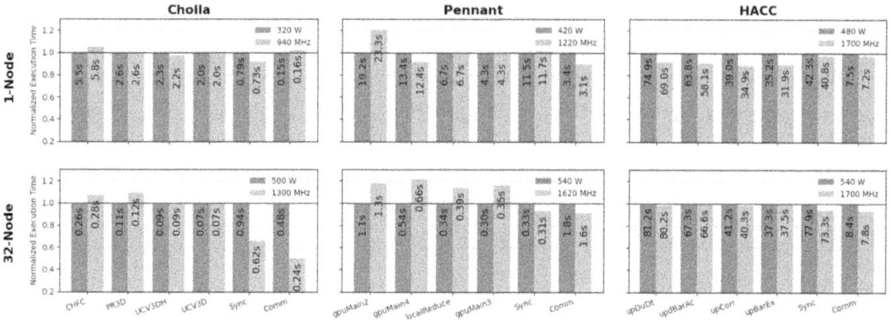

Fig. 2. Normalized execution time of the best performance–energy trade-off for the most-representative kernels of each application, as identified in Fig. 1.

Cholla. We begin with *Cholla*, whose behavior changes significantly with the system scale. In the 1-node case, the power-capped configuration (320 W) achieves about 5% better performance on the most-representative kernel (*CHFC*), while the remaining kernels exhibit only minor differences between the two configurations. Although the frequency-capped configuration slightly reduces the time spent in MPI synchronization (e.g., `MPI_Barrier` and `MPI_Waitall`), these phases contribute only a small fraction of the total runtime. Consequently, the faster execution of the *CHFC* kernel under power capping dominates the runtime.

When scaling to 32-nodes, the power-capped setting (500 W) still provides better performance for the most-representative kernels (*CHFC* and *PR3D*). To understand this behavior, we analyze the hardware metrics of the dominant *CHFC* kernel, shown in Fig. 3. The `TD_SPI_STALL` metric, which measures the fraction of cycles where waves stall in the instruction issue pipeline, is slightly higher under power capping, indicating increased waiting before instruction dispatch. However, this configuration also exhibits a significantly higher `TCC_BUSY` rate (about 20%), indicating stronger activity in the cache and memory subsystems. At the same time, `VALUBusy`, representing the utilization of the vector arithmetic units, is about 10% lower than in the 1300 MHz configuration. Together, these metrics indicate that *CHFC* is primarily constrained by data movement rather than arithmetic throughput. The increased cache activity under power capping improves data availability to the compute units, allowing each kernel invocation to complete slightly faster, as reflected in the histogram of call durations, despite the higher instruction issue stalls.

Although these effects improve kernel execution, the impact on overall application performance becomes dominated by communication and synchronization when the application scales to multiple nodes. In practice, the power-capped configuration spends substantially more time in MPI operations: 2× higher in communication and 1.51× larger in synchronization. A key factor behind this behavior is the higher load imbalance across MPI ranks, which amplifies these waiting periods. As shown in Table 2, load imbalance increases substantially under power capping, with synchronization imbalance rising from 30.6% to 39.8% and communication imbalance from 5.8% to 16.6%. These higher imbalance levels indicate that processes reach communication points at increasingly different times, causing earlier ranks to wait longer during MPI operations. Consequently, even though the compute kernels execute faster under power capping, the additional waiting time during synchronization and communication offsets these gains, allowing the frequency-capped configuration (1300 MHz), which exhibits lower imbalance across MPI calls, to achieve a lower overall execution time.

Pennant. For *Pennant*, the overall behavior is similar, but the factors influencing performance differ. In the 1-node case, the most-representative kernel (*gpuMain2*) executes about 20% faster under the power-capped configuration, while the remaining kernels show only minor differences between configurations. However, part of this advantage is offset by the time spent in communication

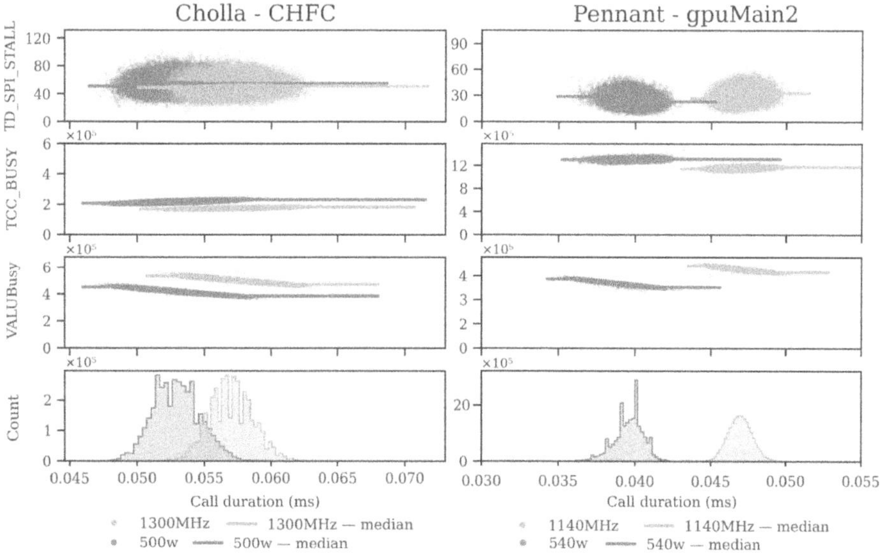

Fig. 3. Distribution of GPU hardware-counter values per kernel invocation for the dominant kernels of *Cholla* and *Pennant*, as identified in Fig. 2.

phases, which slightly favors the frequency-capped configuration. Furthermore, as shown in Table 2, the load imbalance across MPI calls is similar between the two configurations, indicating that communication effects are not yet dominant at this scale.

When scaling to 32 nodes, the four most-representative kernels execute faster under the power-capped configuration (540 W) than under frequency capping (1620 MHz). A key reason for this behavior is that the power cap allows the GPU to dynamically reach higher operating frequencies when the power budget permits. Figure 4 illustrates this effect by showing a snapshot of the GPU frequency during execution under both configurations. The hardware metrics collected for the dominant *gpuMain2* kernel, shown in Fig. 3, help explain how these higher frequencies translate into faster kernel execution. The `TD_SPI_STALL` metric remains similar for both configurations, indicating comparable pressure on the instruction issue pipeline. However, the power-capped configuration exhibits a higher `TCC_BUSY` rate (about 10–15%), reflecting stronger activity in the cache and memory subsystem. Together with the higher attainable operating frequency, this increased memory subsystem activity enables the kernel to sustain more efficient data movement through the memory hierarchy while maintaining high computational throughput.

Despite improvements in kernel execution, communication phases become 12% more expensive under power capping. Table 2 also shows that load imbalance across MPI calls increases in this configuration, particularly for communication, which rises from 82.9% to 89.4%. This indicates that the faster kernel execution under power capping does not occur uniformly across processes. As some ranks complete their compute phases earlier than others, execution-time variability increases, causing processes to reach communication points at different times. As distributed data exchanges already account for a significant portion of runtime, as shown in Fig. 2 (1.8 s and 1.6 s for 540 W and 1620 MHz, respectively), this variability amplifies waiting times during communication phases. Consequently, although the compute kernels benefit from the higher operating frequency enabled by the power cap, the additional communication overhead limits the impact of these improvements on the total application runtime.

Table 2. Load Imbalance across MPI operations reported by *CrayPat*.

	Cholla				Pennant				HACC			
	1-Node		*32-Node*		*1-Node*		*32-Node*		*1-Node*		*32-Node*	
	320 W	940 MHz	500 W	1300 MHz	480 W	1220 MHz	540 W	1620 MHz	480 W	1700 MHz	540 W	1700 MHz
Sync.	40.5%	42.2%	39.8%	30.6%	94.1%	95.7%	77.3%	76.4%	70.2%	69.8%	21.4%	20.8%
Comm.	38.1%	30.5%	16.6%	5.8%	46.6%	48.8%	89.4%	82.9%	66.8%	65.9%	57.1%	56.2%

HACC. For *HACC*, the behavior differs from the previous applications because the performance of its dominant kernels is more strongly influenced by the GPU operating frequency. In the 1-node scenario, the kernels run 15% faster under the frequency-capped configuration (1700 MHz, the system's default) than under the 480 W power cap. This difference is primarily explained by the higher sustained clock frequency achieved under the 1700 MHz configuration, as shown by the authors in [4]. Since the main compute phases of *HACC* are compute-intensive, higher operating frequencies directly translate into faster kernel execution. In this configuration, communication and synchronization account for a small portion of the total runtime, and the load imbalance across MPI calls remains similar across configurations, as shown in Table 2. As a result, the runtime differences are mainly determined by the execution speed of the compute kernels.

When scaling to 32 nodes, the gap between configurations becomes smaller. The best power-capped configuration increases to 540 W, allowing the GPU to operate closer to the maximum frequency and therefore reducing the difference relative to the 1700 MHz configuration during kernel execution. However, as the application scales, the communication and synchronization phases become more visible in the overall execution time. Also, Table 2 shows that the power-capped configuration exhibits slightly higher load imbalance across MPI calls, with synchronization imbalance increasing from 20.8% to 21.4% and communication imbalance from 56.2% to 57.1%. Although these variations are smaller than those observed in other applications, they still introduce additional waiting time during MPI operations. Consequently, while the compute kernels exhibit similar performance across both configurations, the increase in communication overhead under power capping reduces their advantage in the multi-node scenario.

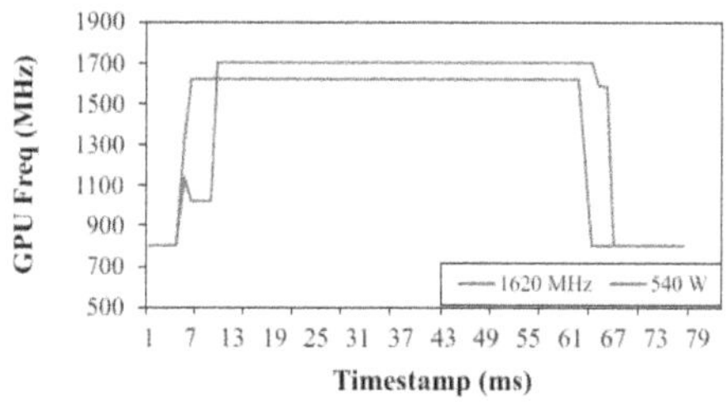

Fig. 4. Snapshot of the average GPU-frequency behavior of Pennant with 32 nodes under frequency capping (1620 MHz) and power capping (540 W).

4.3 Discussion

The results show that power and frequency capping cannot be fully characterized by application-level metrics alone. In several cases, power-capped configurations improved dominant kernel execution by shifting the balance between compute throughput and memory subsystem utilization, with increased cache activity and opportunistic behavior. Frequency boosts contributed to kernel efficiency.

However, improvements observed at the kernel level do not necessarily translate into application-level gains. As the number of nodes increases, the communication and synchronization phases become increasingly influential on overall runtime. In such scenarios, load imbalance across MPI calls may offset the benefits obtained during kernel execution. This behavior is rooted in the difference between the two control mechanisms. Frequency capping forces all GCDs to operate below the same clock, producing uniform execution times across ranks. In contrast, power capping allows each GCD to independently adjust its operating frequency based on instantaneous power. This per-GCD frequency variability introduces execution-time differences across ranks, which are amplified at synchronization points as faster ranks wait for slower ones. The results observed for *Cholla* and *Pennant* illustrate this behavior, where faster kernel execution under power capping is partially negated by increased waiting time during MPI communication and synchronization. From a system perspective, the benefits obtained through power management can be limited by the communication subsystem when kernel execution becomes uneven across processes.

These observations suggest that power and frequency capping should be considered together with communication behavior when optimizing large-scale GPU applications. In workloads where communication dominates or where synchronization phases are frequent, selecting configurations that reduce execution variability across ranks may be more beneficial than maximizing individual kernel performance. For example, moderate frequency caps can provide more predictable execution times across GPUs, helping reduce process skew at synchronization points. Similarly, phase-aware power management policies that apply different caps during compute and communication phases could help preserve kernel efficiency while limiting imbalance during distributed operations.

From a practical standpoint, these results indicate that effective performance–energy optimization in GPU-based HPC systems requires coordinated tuning across compute and communication layers. Application developers may benefit from analyzing kernel-level metrics together with MPI behavior to identify phases where aggressive power management may introduce imbalance. At the system level, runtime systems and job schedulers could leverage this information to select power or frequency settings that balance kernel efficiency with communication stability, particularly for large-scale distributed workloads.

5 Conclusion

Power management has become a critical aspect of operating GPU-accelerated exascale systems, yet its impact on multi-kernel HPC applications remains difficult to interpret using only application-level metrics. In this work, we performed an extensive evaluation of power- and frequency-capping configurations for three representative applications (*Cholla*, *Pennant*, and *HACC*) on the Frontier supercomputer and analyzed their behavior at the kernel and runtime levels. Our results show that improvements in kernel execution efficiency do not necessarily translate into better application-level performance. For instance, in *Pennant*, the dominant kernel executes up to 20% faster under the power-capped configuration that delivers the best performance–energy trade-off, yet these gains are partially offset by increased communication costs and load imbalance across MPI calls. Similarly, in *Cholla*, synchronization imbalance increases from 30.6% to 39.8% and communication imbalance from 5.8% to 16.6% under power capping, leading to longer MPI wait times despite faster kernel execution. Future work will extend this analysis to additional applications and architectures and will explore adaptive runtime mechanisms that dynamically select power-management policies based on kernel behavior and communication patterns.

Acknowledgments. This research used resources of the Oak Ridge Leadership Computing Facility at the Oak Ridge National Laboratory, which is supported by the Office of Science of the US Department of Energy (DOE) under Contract No. DE-AC05-00OR22725. This manuscript has been authored by UT-Battelle, LLC, under contract DE-AC05-00OR22725 with the DOE. The publisher acknowledges the US government license to provide public access under the DOE Public Access Plan (http://energy.gov/downloads/doe-public-access-plan). This study was financed in part by CAPES (Finance Code 001), FAPERGS, and CNPq.

Disclosure of Interests. The authors have no competing interests to declare that are relevant to the content of this article.

References

1. Acun, F., Zhao, Z., Austin, B., Coskun, A.K., Wright, N.J.: Analysis of power consumption and GPU power capping for MILC. In: SC24 Workshops, pp. 1856–1861 (2024)

2. Angelelli, L., Carastan-Santos, D., Dutot, P.F.: Run your HPC jobs in eco-mode: revealing the potential of user-assisted power capping in supercomputing systems. In: Klusáček, D., Corbalán, J., Rodrigo, G.P. (eds.) JSSPP 2024. LNCS, vol. 14591, pp. 181–196. Springer, Cham (2024). https://doi.org/10.1007/978-3-031-74430-3_10
3. Atchley, S., et al.: Frontier: exploring exascale. In: SC23. Association for Computing Machinery, New York, NY, USA (2023)
4. Costa, M.T., et al.: Characterizing the impact of GPU power management on an exascale system. In: Proceedings of the SC '25 Workshops of the International Conference for High Performance Computing, Networking, Storage and Analysis. SC25 Workshops, pp. 1524–1533. ACM, New York, NY, USA (2025)
5. Ding, N., et al.: Maximizing power-constrained supercomputing throughput. In: ISC High Performance, pp. 1–13 (2025)
6. Ferenbaugh, C.R.: PENNANT: an unstructured mesh mini-app for advanced architecture research. Concurr. Comput.: Pract. Exper. **27**(17), 4555–4572 (2015)
7. Habib, S., Morozov, V., Frontiere, N., Finkel, H., Pope, A., Heitmann, K.: HACC: extreme scaling and performance across diverse architectures. In: SC13, pp. 1–10 (2013)
8. Karimi, A.M., Maiterth, M., Shin, W., Sattar, N.S., Lu, H., Wang, F.: Exploring the frontiers of energy efficiency using power management at system scale. In: SC24 Workshops. SC24-W, pp. 1835–1844. IEEE Press (2025)
9. Komoda, T., Hayashi, S., Nakada, T., Miwa, S., Nakamura, H.: Power capping of CPU-GPU heterogeneous systems through coordinating DVFS and task mapping. In: IEEE ICCD, pp. 349–356 (2013)
10. Krzywaniak, A., Czarnul, P., Proficz, J.: Dynamic GPU power capping with online performance tracing for energy efficient GPU computing using DEPO tool. Future Gener. Comput. Syst. **145** (2023)
11. Sueur, L., Heiser, E.G.: Dynamic voltage and frequency scaling: the laws of diminishing returns. In: Proceedings of the 2010 International Conference on Power Aware Computing and Systems, pp. 1–8 (2010)
12. Lorenzon, A.F., Beck, A.C.S., Navaux, P.O.A., Messer, B.: Energy-efficient GPU allocation and frequency management in exascale computing systems. In: ISC High Performance, pp. 1–11 (2025)
13. Omnistat: Omnistat: scale-out cluster telemetry (2026). https://github.com/ROCm/omnistat. Accessed 20 Feb 2026
14. Patrou, M., et al.: Power-capping metric evaluation for improving energy efficiency in HPC applications (2025). https://arxiv.org/abs/2505.21758
15. Simmendinger, C., Marquardt, M., Mäder, J., Schneider, R.: PowerSched—managing power consumption in overprovisioned systems. In: CLUSTER Workshops, pp. 1–8 (2024)
16. Villasenor, B., et al.: cholla-hydro/cholla: A GPU-based hydro code (2025). https://github.com/cholla-hydro/cholla
17. Yiming, W., et al.: DRLCap: runtime GPU frequency capping with deep reinforcement learning. IEEE Trans. Sustain. Comput. **PP**, 1–15 (2024). https://doi.org/10.1109/TSUSC.2024.3362697

Optimizing SpMV Kernel for Banded Matrices on FPGAs Using High-Level Synthesis

Federico Favaro[1(✉)], Ernesto Dufrechou[2], Juan P. Oliver[1], and Pablo Ezzatti[2]

[1] Instituto de Ingeniería Eléctrica, Montevideo, Uruguay
{ffavaro,jpo}@fing.edu.uy
[2] Instituto de Computación, Facultad de Ingeniería Universidad de la República, Montevideo, Uruguay
{edufrechou,pezzatti}@fing.edu.uy

Abstract. Sparse Matrix-Vector Multiplication (SpMV) is a key kernel in numerical linear algebra, and its performance depends strongly on the distribution of nonzero elements. When nonzeros are concentrated near a few diagonals, the matrix can be stored efficiently in DIA form. We present a band-specialized DIA-style SpMV kernel using High-Level Synthesis (HLS) for High Bandwidth Memory (HBM)-equipped FPGAs and compare it with AMD's Vitis SpMV kernel. On densely banded matrices, our design achieves geometric-mean gains from 9.5× to 1.2× in GFLOPS and from 9.5× to 1.5× in GFLOPS/W. On sparse-banded matrices derived from SuiteSparse, the advantage decreases as the band widens due to zero padding, but remains strong for narrow bands, reaching 9.5× at band size 8. Against a multithreaded OpenMP DIA baseline on a Xeon Silver 4208, the FPGA achieves up to 4.08× higher GFLOPS and up to 6.39× higher GFLOPS/W. Overall, the proposed throughput-oriented banded kernel consistently outperforms a general-purpose HLS SpMV design for small and moderate band sizes, with clear energy-efficiency gains.

Keywords: SpMV · Banded matrices · FPGA · High-Level Synthesis

1 Introduction

Sparse Matrix-Vector Multiplication (SpMV) is a fundamental kernel in sparse numerical linear algebra and appears in many scientific and engineering applications. Its performance depends strongly on the distribution of nonzero elements, since this determines memory-access regularity, data reuse, and load balance. On conventional processors, SpMV is often memory-bound because sparse formats introduce irregular accesses and limited reuse of the input vector. When nonzeros are concentrated near a limited number of diagonals, however, the matrix can be stored efficiently in Diagonal (DIA) form, keeping only the diagonal values and their offsets from the main diagonal. This structure is common in problems

M. Torquati et al. (Eds.): Euro-Par 2026, LNCS 16781, pp. 418–432, 2027.
https://doi.org/10.1007/978-3-032-35248-4_29

arising from discretized partial differential equations [11], and is particularly attractive for throughput-oriented hardware implementations.

At the same time, energy consumption has become a major concern in high-performance computing [5], motivating the search for more efficient hardware platforms. In this context, FPGAs are appealing because they allow the datapath to be tailored to the matrix structure, exposing fine-grained parallelism and enabling efficient streaming architectures with good energy efficiency. Recent high-end devices also provide large external-memory bandwidth through multi-bank HBM, while High-Level Synthesis (HLS) tools have made FPGA development more accessible by enabling hardware generation from C/C++ descriptions.

In this work, we focus on matrices with nonzeros concentrated near the main diagonal; a band-specialized kernel can exploit this regularity to reduce control overhead and improve throughput. We target HBM-equipped FPGAs and compare our design against the SpMV kernel from AMD's Vitis SPARSE library, which provides a relevant baseline as a general-purpose HLS implementation.

In this context, our contributions are:

- **Band-specialized HLS kernel with throughput-oriented dataflow.** We implement a DIA-style SpMV kernel for HBM-equipped FPGAs using packetized lanes and N_{ch} parallel channels, sustaining an initiation interval (II) of 1. Key optimizations include a single load of the dense vector followed by forwarding across channels, register-level alignment for diagonal offsets, fully unrolled packet MAC, and row-interleaved reductions to hide adder latency.
- **Comprehensive evaluation against FPGA and CPU baselines.** Across dense- and sparse-banded datasets and multiple band sizes, our kernel achieves higher GFLOPS and GFLOPS/W than the Vitis SpMV kernel, with the largest gains at small and moderate band sizes. We also compare against a multithreaded CPU DIA baseline, where the FPGA delivers higher performance and energy efficiency across representative cases.

2 Context

When the nonzero elements are concentrated around a limited set of diagonals, the matrix can be represented more effectively using a diagonal-oriented format. In this representation, each stored diagonal is identified by its offset with respect to the main diagonal, and its coefficients are laid out contiguously in memory. Such an organization is particularly well suited to SpMV, as it regularizes both matrix accesses and the corresponding accesses to the dense vector. Consequently, diagonal (DIA) storage is a natural choice for banded matrices, as well as for hybrid schemes that isolate a banded component from a more general sparse matrix.

By contrast, CSR-like traversals involve irregular row lengths and indirect vector accesses, which on FPGAs translate into load imbalance, irregular memory behavior, and additional control overhead.

Diagonal and banded matrices arise in several important applications, including structured-grid discretizations of PDEs, cubic spline interpolation, and batch formulations of Kalman smoothing [11]. In these cases, the resulting systems are often tridiagonal, banded, or block-tridiagonal, making them natural targets for specialized storage formats and accelerators.

As a reference implementation, this work considers the SpMV kernel from the Vitis SPARSE library [15], a highly optimized HLS-based design targeting HBM-equipped Alveo devices. Prior work has shown that this kernel constitutes a strong baseline for general sparse matrices, but that its performance degrades on matrices with relatively few nonzero elements per row, as is the case for sparse banded matrices [6]. This observation motivates the design of a specialized FPGA kernel tailored to banded sparsity patterns.

3 Related Work

The irregular memory access patterns of SpMV have motivated numerous FPGA-based accelerators. Jain et al. [8] combine HLS and RTL techniques to optimize SpMV on AMD devices, and Elkurdi et al. [4] build a deeply pipelined RTL kernel that exploits banded sparsity for FEM matrices on DDR-bandwidth-limited devices.

More recent work has emphasized HLS and HBM-equipped devices. Hosseinabady et al. [7] propose a streaming CSR-based dataflow engine, HiSparse [3] presents an HLS-based SpMV accelerator for FPGA-HBM platforms, Serpens [12] introduces a general-purpose HBM-based design for arbitrary sparse matrices, and Oliver et al. [9] propose a block-row compressed format with a task-based FPGA implementation. The AMD Vitis Sparse Library [15] also provides a high-performance vendor-supported SpMV implementation optimized for modern Alveo platforms.

The most recent works continue to push general SpMV efficiency on the same Alveo U280 platform. HiHiSpMV [13] uses hierarchical row reductions across all 32 HBM pseudo-channels in 512-bit mode to reach 98 GFLOPS peak under a fully HLS-based design. HiSpMV [10] targets imbalanced matrices via hybrid row distribution and vector buffering across HBM pseudo-channels. SPASM [14] takes a pattern-aware approach, composing 4×4 local structure tiles to synthesize Vitis HLS hardware per matrix; it can represent banded matrices as a special case, but within a general, preprocessing-dependent framework.

None of these recent HBM/HLS designs exploits DIA-format band storage. The closest dedicated prior work is Elkurdi et al. [4], whose RTL kernel predates HBM and HLS. Our design differs on three axes: (i) 20 HBM2 pseudo-channels (16 for matrix streams) provide far higher bandwidth than DDR; (ii) single-load forwarding, 8-wide FMA datapaths, and ping-pong accumulators sustain II=1; and (iii) the design is fully HLS-based. HiHiSpMV [13] exceeds our aggregate throughput by using all 32 HBM pseudo-channels, but on dense banded inputs our kernel achieves comparable per-channel efficiency with fewer channels and lower resources, making it attractive when banded structure is known a priori.

4 Proposal

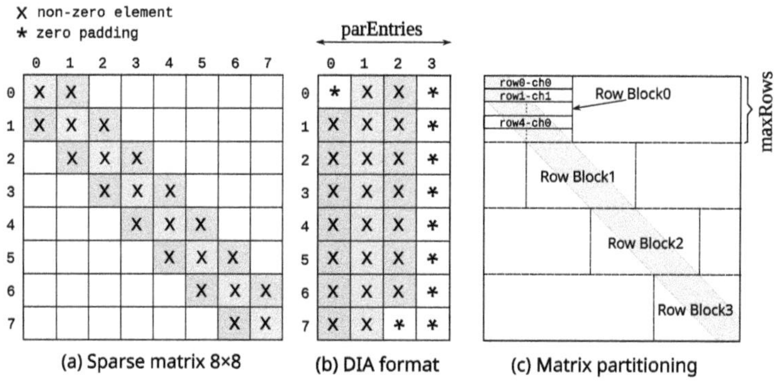

Fig. 1. Matrix representation format for diagonal kernels. (a) shows the banded matrix, and (b) its corresponding diagonal storage format. The width is padded to a multiple of $t_{\text{ParEntries}}$ to accommodate the data path width of the kernel. In (c), rows are interleaved across 16 channels (two groups of 8) so each channel processes every 16-th row; $t_{\text{ParEntries}}$ is the data path width, and **maxRows** is the row block size used for partitioning. In our implementation, $t_{\text{ParEntries}}$ =8 and **maxRows** =1024.

We propose a SpMV kernel optimized for banded matrices represented in DIA-style storage. This section describes the representation format, preprocessing, and kernel architecture. For a sparse matrix $A \in \mathbb{R}^{n \times n}$, input vector $x \in \mathbb{R}^n$, and output vector $y \in \mathbb{R}^n$, the kernel computes $y = A \cdot x$.

4.1 Representation Format

When nonzeros are concentrated on a small set of diagonals, the matrix can be stored in DIA form, keeping only the diagonal values and their offsets from the main diagonal. Our representation extends DIA with a partitioning scheme tailored to blockwise SpMV on banded matrices. Figure 1 illustrates the adopted format.

In preprocessing, the diagonals are stored as columns of a new matrix of dimensions $n \times \text{bw}$, where n is the number of rows and bw is the bandwidth (number of stored diagonals). Sub-diagonals are padded to the row size: diagonals below the main diagonal receive leading zeros, while diagonals above it receive trailing zeros. The rows are then padded to a multiple of the block size (**maxRows**), and the columns to a multiple of the kernel datapath width ($t_{\text{ParEntries}}$). For each block, rows are grouped according to the number of compute channels (N_{ch}), since the channels read and process different rows in parallel.

Coefficients are stored by interleaving rows across channels, so each channel processes every N_{ch}-th row. This improves reuse of vector x because consecutive rows share overlapping input elements. Within each block, coefficients are ordered by rows and then by columns, so the kernel processes all elements of one band (a group of $t_{\text{ParEntries}}$ consecutive diagonals) before moving to the next.

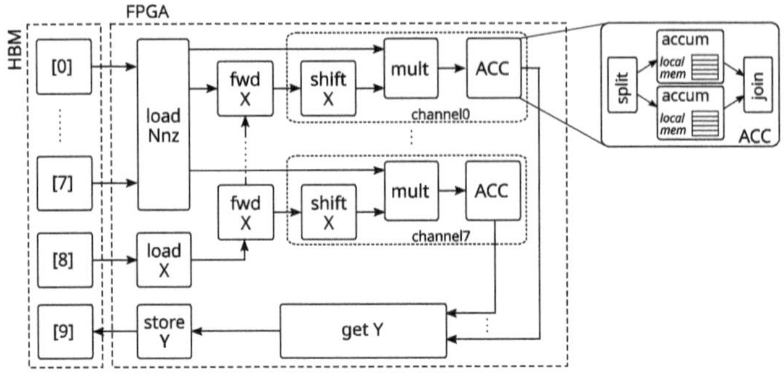

Fig. 2. Architecture of one 8-channel group of the DIA-banded SpMV kernel. The full design instantiates two groups.

4.2 Implemented Kernel

We developed an HBM-based kernel for parallel SpMV in AMD HLS C++ and compiled it with Vitis 2022.2 for the Alveo U280. All operations use single precision. The kernel is parameterized by three values fixed at compile time: N_{ch} = 16 (compute channels), $t_{\text{ParEntries}} = 8$ (FP32 elements per cycle per channel), and `maxRows` = 1024 (row-block size, set empirically to maximize performance within BRAM constraints). $t_{\text{ParEntries}}$ is dictated by the 256-bit AXI width and N_{ch} by the HBM allocation; no per-application tuning is needed since performance depends primarily on band width, which is known before execution.

Figure 2 shows the kernel architecture. It comprises 16 streaming compute channels organized as two groups of 8, each processing one half of the matrix. Each channel reads coefficients from a dedicated HBM bank, and each group shares a dedicated block to read the required elements of vector x.

For banded matrices, the x values required for one row can be obtained from those of the previous row by shifting the access window by one position. Exploiting this regularity, the kernel reads packets of $t_{\text{ParEntries}}$ consecutive elements of x, streams them through the compute channels in systolic fashion, and shifts them according to the assigned rows. Because of the regular matrix structure and the chosen values of N_{ch} and $t_{\text{ParEntries}}$, each channel always applies the same fixed shift.

Each compute block receives a packet of coefficients and aligned x values, performs the dot product, and generates one partial result per cycle, which is forwarded to the accumulation blocks.

Each compute block writes its partial results to a local accumulation block responsible for a subset of rows within each row block. Because floating-point addition has latency L, directly accumulating one row per cycle creates loop-carried dependencies. We avoid this by interleaving the accumulation of M rows, with $M > L$.

After accumulation, the local memory must be drained and the results forwarded to the gather block and then to external memory. Since this drain phase takes $\texttt{maxRows}/(N_{\text{ch}} \cdot t_{\text{ParEntries}})$ cycles, each channel uses two reduction blocks in ping-pong fashion: while one drains its results, the other processes the next row block.

4.3 Kernel Optimizations and Dataflow

We implement a fully streaming, packetized dataflow with initiation interval (II) 1 throughout. The kernel uses $N_{\text{ch}} = 16$ channels organized as an $8 + 8$ topology and packets of $t_{\text{ParEntries}}$ elements. The following optimizations sustain frequency and throughput:

- Diagonals are stored in diagonal-major layout and strip-mined across the N_{ch} HBM pseudo-channels. Each channel uses a dedicated AXI master and FIFO (depth 16), allowing burst transfers to overlap with compute.
- We load x once from HBM and forward it through a lightweight chain so all channels receive a local copy without re-reading memory, avoiding HBM contention and sustaining II = 1.
- For diagonal offset d, the required x entries are shifted by d positions. A register-level network combines the previous and current packets to produce, each cycle, a $t_{\text{ParEntries}}$-lane vector aligned to the required offset.
- For each packet, $t_{\text{ParEntries}}$ element-wise multiply-accumulate operations are performed in parallel. The lane loop is fully unrolled and the outer packet loop is pipelined with II = 1, sustaining one packet per cycle per channel.
- Partial products stream into per-channel accumulators and are interleaved across rows to hide adder latency. Each lane updates a different row, avoiding conflicts and maintaining II = 1.

Since all pipelines achieve II = 1, each lane sustains one multiply–add operation per cycle. Therefore, the theoretical peak performance is:

$$\text{GFLOPS} = 2 \times N_{\text{ch}} \times t_{\text{ParEntries}} \times F_{\text{clk}}/10^9.$$

5 Experimental Evaluation

We evaluate the proposed diagonal kernel on two datasets and compare it against the SpMV kernel from the Vitis SPARSE library. First, we use artificially generated densely banded matrices to measure performance under conditions favorable to our design. Second, we use sparse-banded matrices derived from SuiteSparse inputs to assess whether the proposed kernel remains advantageous when the band contains zeros.

5.1 Evaluated Datasets

We selected 33 square matrices from the SuiteSparse Matrix Collection [2] with dimensions and nonzero counts that fit the memory capacity of the Alveo U280. The selection includes matrices from structural, PDE, circuit, and optimization problems, with dimensions from 3,000 to 55,000 and nonzero counts from 45,000 to 16,000,000. We intentionally retained matrices with different degrees of concentration near the main diagonal so that the sparse-band experiments include both favorable and unfavorable cases for the proposed format. Table 1 reports both the original NNZ and the NNZ retained inside representative bands.

For the first dataset, we generated artificial densely banded matrices with random coefficients and band sizes from 8 to 136 in steps of 16. Their dimensions match those of the SuiteSparse matrices.

For the second dataset, we derived sparse-banded matrices by zeroing all elements outside a fixed band in the SuiteSparse inputs. Our kernel processes the full band, including zeros, whereas the Vitis kernel processes only the retained sparse entries within the band, subject to its own padding scheme. This allows us to evaluate whether the proposed kernel remains advantageous on real sparse matrices whose nonzeros are concentrated near the main diagonal.

5.2 Measurement Setup

Both kernels were compiled with Vitis 2022.2 and evaluated on an Alveo U280 accelerator card. Table 2 reports post-implementation resource utilization and clock frequency. Both designs run at similar frequency (333 MHz for Vitis, 314 MHz for banded), use 20 of 32 HBM pseudo-channels, and employ single-precision floating-point arithmetic. The banded kernel uses fewer LUTs, registers, and on-chip memory, with a similar DSP count.

Kernel runtime was measured by enclosing the top-level kernel in a sequential loop and averaging over 2,000 in-hardware iterations, thus avoiding host launch overhead.

The Vitis kernel was adapted to use single precision, doubling datapath parallelism, and its row partition size was tuned for matrices with few nonzeros per row [6]. The tuning procedure in [6] performs a grid search over all exposed parameters of the Vitis kernel; we report results for the best-performing configuration for each matrix.

We report kernel-only runtime, excluding PCIe transfers, since both designs are compared on the same FPGA platform.

Board power was sampled at 1 Hz using vendor-provided sensor readings. Each point consists of one warm-up epoch followed by a run of at least 60 s; we report median steady-state power and compute GFLOPS/W as GFLOPS divided by board power. Measurements were automated with PMLIB [1].

5.3 Results for Densely Banded Matrices

Figure 3 shows GFLOPS for three representative densely banded matrices. The proposed kernel outperforms Vitis in all cases, with the advantage being largest

Table 1. Dimensions and nonzero counts (NNZ) of the 33 SuiteSparse matrices. Columns 4–6 report the NNZ retained within bands of sizes 8, 72, and 136.

Matrix	Rows	NNZ			
		Orig mat	band size 8	band size 72	band size 136
nasa2910	2910	174296	16932	76639	91842
ex9	3363	99471	24295	48323	60928
bcsstk24	3562	159910	26754	59262	60930
bcsstk15	3948	117816	18945	49278	53325
bcsstk28	4410	219024	32128	82937	91948
s2rmq4m1	5489	263351	38359	87785	87785
nd3k	9000	3279690	71567	455247	512714
ted_B	10605	144579	28177	132579	144579
ted_B_uns	10605	144579	28177	132579	144579
msc10848	10848	1229776	69373	225684	257070
vibrobox	12328	301700	30173	56456	63624
sme3Da	12504	874887	18627	28982	33216
cbuckle	13681	676515	98162	225593	225593
olafu	16146	1015156	113561	404679	439191
gyro_k	17361	1021159	101421	248043	310967
bodyy4	17546	121550	52428	53126	56004
nd6k	18000	6897316	143071	904757	1000660
bodyy6	19366	134208	57796	59459	62937
raefsky4	19779	1316789	134069	439294	575148
qpband	20000	45000	20000	20000	20000
chipcool0	20082	281150	25203	41910	55805
TS162	20374	812749	20850	41062	41289
Zd_Jac3	22835	1915726	22865	23178	23786
bcsstk36	23052	1143140	170344	506905	720100
msc23052	23052	1142686	138413	256911	263475
net75	23120	1489200	23120	23120	23120
TS2052	25626	6761100	27292	27718	27795
smt	25710	3749582	165107	902334	1381243
TS300	28338	2943887	29127	29532	29593
thread	29736	4444880	207313	776415	946133
TS2383	38120	16171169	41304	42933	43693
ct20stif	52329	2600295	350332	1015869	1224325
nasasrb	54870	2677324	301602	900848	906041

Table 2. Resource utilization (post-implementation reports) for the two FPGA kernels on the target device (Alveo U280).

Resource	Used	Fixed	Available	Util [%]
Vitis SpMV kernel				
CLB LUTs	328533	107629	1303680	25
CLB Registers	503370	136086	2607360	19
Block RAM Tile	351	0	2016	17
URAM	112	0	960	12
DSPs	712	4	9024	8
HBM banks	20	0	32	63
FCLK	333 MHz			
banded kernel (ours)				
CLB LUTs	233277	107629	1303680	18
CLB Registers	348963	136086	2607360	13
Block RAM Tile	312	0	2016	15
URAM	0	0	960	0
DSPs	749	4	9024	8
HBM banks	20	0	32	63
FCLK	314 MHz			

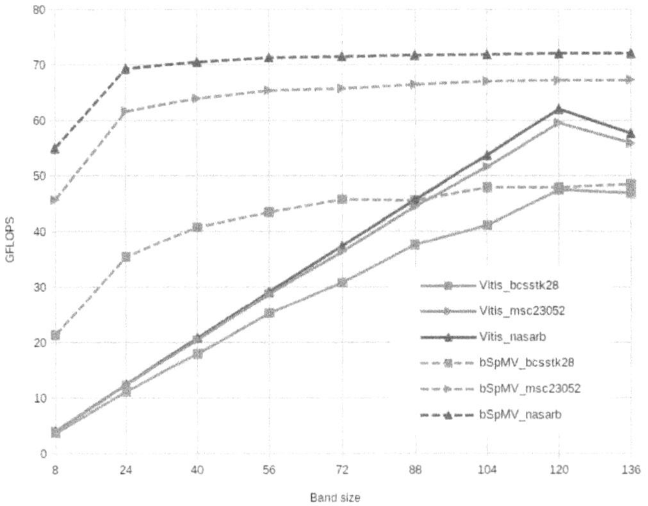

Fig. 3. GFLOPS of banded vs. Vitis kernel for densely banded matrices with band sizes ranging from 8 to 136. Example for three matrix dimensions: 4K (bcsstk28), 23K (msc23052), and 54K (nasasrb).

for small bands. As the band size increases the difference gradually diminishes, with performance becoming comparable at size 136—showing no improvement for the smallest matrix and 1.2× speedup for the medium and large matrices.

Table 3. Densely banded matrices: geometric mean ± standard deviation across 33 inputs per band (board power).

band	Vitis kernel		banded kernel	
	GFLOPS	Power (W)	GFLOPS	Power (W)
8	4.1 ± 0.2	39.4 ± 0.2	38.4 ± 10.4	39.3 ± 1.6
24	12.2 ± 0.5	40.5 ± 0.2	55.5 ± 10.2	41.5 ± 1.3
40	19.9 ± 1.1	44.0 ± 0.4	59.1 ± 9.1	42.0 ± 1.0
56	27.9 ± 1.6	45.0 ± 0.5	61.5 ± 8.0	42.3 ± 0.9
72	35.0 ± 2.4	48.5 ± 0.9	62.7 ± 7.4	42.4 ± 0.8
88	42.8 ± 2.9	49.4 ± 0.9	63.3 ± 7.2	42.5 ± 0.7
104	49.3 ± 4.2	52.2 ± 1.4	64.1 ± 6.8	42.6 ± 0.6
120	56.9 ± 4.8	53.2 ± 1.4	64.5 ± 6.6	42.6 ± 0.6
136	54.0 ± 3.5	53.3 ± 1.1	64.8 ± 6.5	42.6 ± 0.5

Table 3 reports the geometric mean and standard deviation of GFLOPS and board power across the 33 matrices. Vitis performance increases with band size because its runtime remains nearly constant while the operation count grows. This confirms its limited efficiency on matrices with few elements per row. In contrast, the proposed kernel sustains relatively stable throughput across band sizes, except at band size 8, where reduction overhead becomes comparatively more significant.

Both kernels share similar theoretical peak throughput (same HBM pseudo-channels, datapath width, and DSP count), yet the proposed kernel performs better on banded inputs by exploiting DIA structure. With $N_{\mathrm{ch}} = 16$, $t_{\mathtt{ParEntries}} = 8$, and $F_{\mathrm{clk}} = 314$ MHz, the theoretical peak is 80.4 GFLOPS. The measured geometric-mean reaches 38.4 GFLOPS (48% of peak) at band 8 and 64.8 GFLOPS (81%) at band 136; the gap reflects block-level overheads and reduction draining that are progressively amortized as the band widens. In terms of power, Vitis increases from about 39 W to 53 W as band size grows, whereas the proposed kernel remains nearly constant at about 42 W.

5.4 Results for Sparse-Banded Matrices

We next evaluate sparse-banded matrices obtained by trimming the SuiteSparse inputs to band sizes from 8 to 136. Figure 4 shows results for three representative matrices. GFLOPS is computed using only the nonzeros retained within the band. For medium and large matrices, the proposed kernel outperforms Vitis for

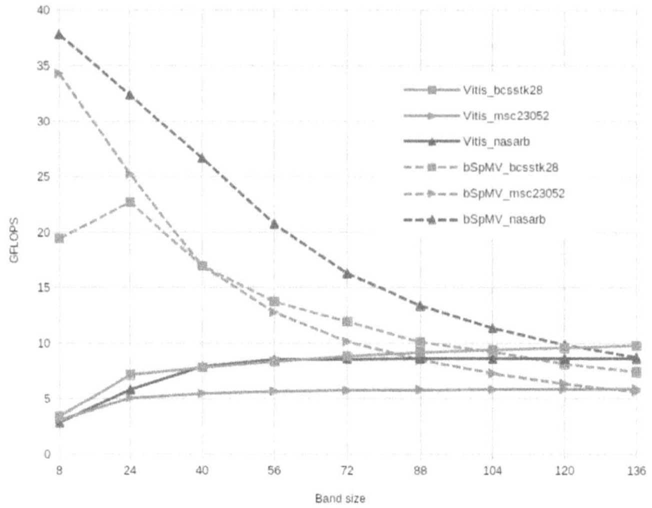

Fig. 4. GFLOPS of banded vs. Vitis kernel for sparse-banded matrices with band sizes ranging from 8 to 136. Example for three matrix dimensions: 4K (bcsstk28), 23K (msc23052), and 54K (nasasrb).

most band sizes, while for smaller matrices the advantage is limited to narrower bands.

Table 4 reports the geometric mean and standard deviation across the 33 matrices. In this setting, Vitis performance grows only slightly with band size because the retained NNZ grows more slowly than in the dense-band case. The proposed kernel, on the other hand, degrades as the band widens because it always processes the full band, including padded zeros; for most matrices, the effective band density decreases with band size. Beyond zero-padding, lower band density means more wasted computation and more HBM reads per useful result, reducing useful throughput. This could be mitigated by skipping empty diagonals in the DIA format, or by switching to a general-purpose SpMV kernel when band density falls below a threshold.

Even so, the proposed kernel achieves substantial gains for narrow bands: 9.5× at band size 8, 4.6× at 24, and 2.9× at 40 (Table 5). The advantage then narrows, reaching 1.7× at band size 72, 1.2× at 104, and 0.9× at 136. Energy-efficiency gains follow the same trend, from 9.3× at band size 8 to 1.6× at 72, 1.2× at 104, and 0.9× at 136.

5.5 Comparison Against Multicore CPU

As an additional reference, we compare the proposed FPGA kernel against a C++ OpenMP+SIMD implementation of blocked DIA SpMV compiled with g++. The matrix is stored in packed DIA form and processed in row blocks of size

Table 4. Sparse-band matrices: geometric mean ± standard deviation across 33 inputs per band (board power).

band	Vitis kernel		banded kernel	
	GFLOPS	Power (W)	GFLOPS	Power (W)
8	1.8 ± 1.3	38.8 ± 0.5	17.1 ± 14.1	39.3 ± 1.6
24	3.0 ± 3.6	39.2 ± 0.8	13.8 ± 16.9	41.5 ± 1.3
40	3.6 ± 5.1	39.6 ± 1.4	10.4 ± 15.6	42.0 ± 1.0
56	3.9 ± 6.2	39.9 ± 1.7	8.5 ± 13.9	42.3 ± 0.9
72	4.1 ± 6.6	40.1 ± 1.9	7.1 ± 11.8	42.4 ± 0.8
88	4.3 ± 6.9	40.3 ± 2.0	6.1 ± 10.2	42.5 ± 0.7
104	4.4 ± 7.3	40.4 ± 2.2	5.3 ± 9.2	42.6 ± 0.6
120	4.5 ± 7.7	40.5 ± 2.3	4.8 ± 8.4	42.6 ± 0.6
136	4.6 ± 8.0	40.6 ± 2.4	4.3 ± 7.8	42.6 ± 0.5

Table 5. Per-band geometric-mean ratios over 33 matrices: values > 1 favor our banded FPGA kernel over Vitis SpMV.

	8	24	40	56	72	88	104	120	136
Performance ratio [GFLOPS] (banded/Vitis)									
Dense bands	9.5	4.6	3.0	2.2	1.8	1.5	1.3	1.1	1.2
Sparse bands	9.5	4.6	2.9	2.2	1.7	1.4	1.2	1.1	0.9
Efficiency ratio [GFLOPS/W] (banded/Vitis)									
Dense bands	9.5	4.5	3.1	2.3	2.0	1.7	1.6	1.4	1.5
Sparse bands	9.3	4.3	2.8	2.0	1.6	1.3	1.2	1.0	0.9

B, with each thread accumulating into a private buffer before writing back to y. For each diagonal, the implementation intersects the current tile with the valid row range implied by the diagonal offset, thereby skipping off-matrix padded entries. The inner row loop is vectorized with `#pragma omp simd`, reading matrix and vector data contiguously and accumulating into the thread-local buffer.

Experiments were run on an Intel Xeon Silver 4208 (8 cores, SMT enabled) with DDR4 memory under Ubuntu 20.04, MKL oneAPI 2023.2, and OpenMP 201511. After sweeping thread counts $t \in \{1, 2, 4, 8, 16\}$, we found 8 threads to be the best setting. MKL's banded routine (`cblas_sgbmv`) did not scale beyond a single thread; the OpenMP+SIMD kernel consistently outperformed it and is used as the CPU baseline. We report median GFLOPS and GFLOPS/W over multiple runs. Energy was measured with RAPL (CPU package + DRAM) over a 60 s steady-state window using PMLIB [1].

We evaluated matrices of sizes 3K, 12K, and 48K using the same band sizes as before. Across the 27 cases, the FPGA achieves a median speedup of 1.84× over the 8-thread CPU and a median energy-efficiency gain of 2.40× (Table 6).

These CPU comparisons are kernel-only; PCIe transfer time is excluded. In iterative solvers (e.g., CG, GMRES), the matrix is typically transferred once while SpMV is called many times, so PCIe cost can be amortized when vector data also remains on the device.

Table 6. CPU (OMP 8t) vs FPGA results (single precision). CPU: Xeon Silver 4208; FPGA: proposed banded kernel on Alveo U280.

n	band	GFLOPS ↑		speedup	GFLOPS/W ↑		Eff. ratio
		CPU	FPGA	FPGA/CPU	CPU	FPGA	(FPGA/CPU)
3000	8	6.39	17.30	2.71	0.135	0.460	3.41
3000	24	10.32	31.75	3.08	0.218	0.979	4.49
3000	40	11.76	37.22	3.16	0.247	1.261	5.11
3000	56	12.04	41.20	3.42	0.251	1.098	4.38
3000	72	12.57	43.52	3.46	0.262	1.508	5.76
3000	88	12.94	44.59	3.45	0.266	0.907	3.41
3000	104	12.36	46.39	3.75	0.253	1.425	5.63
3000	120	12.19	46.92	3.85	0.248	1.585	6.39
3000	136	11.69	47.70	4.08	0.237	1.271	5.36
12000	8	22.35	37.82	1.69	0.455	1.179	2.59
12000	24	41.26	55.46	1.34	0.790	1.201	1.52
12000	40	47.06	59.31	1.26	0.887	1.577	1.78
12000	56	50.07	61.66	1.23	0.936	1.493	1.59
12000	72	50.29	62.87	1.25	0.931	1.067	1.15
12000	88	51.76	63.50	1.23	0.945	1.505	1.59
12000	104	50.53	64.29	1.27	0.896	1.622	1.81
12000	120	47.90	64.59	1.35	0.835	1.354	1.62
12000	136	46.06	64.97	1.41	0.782	1.520	1.94
48000	8	42.07	53.74	1.28	0.795	0.994	1.25
48000	24	69.22	68.19	0.98	1.254	1.599	1.28
48000	40	65.02	69.65	1.07	1.102	1.629	1.48
48000	56	50.07	70.39	1.41	0.803	1.524	1.90
48000	72	41.53	70.73	1.70	0.664	1.133	1.71
48000	88	36.09	71.02	1.97	0.573	1.374	2.40
48000	104	31.84	71.15	2.23	0.495	1.533	3.10
48000	120	29.31	71.30	2.43	0.456	1.616	3.54
48000	136	27.02	71.43	2.64	0.424	1.639	3.86

6 Conclusions

In this article, we presented and evaluated an SpMV kernel optimized for banded matrices represented in DIA-style storage, implemented in HLS for FPGAs using single-precision arithmetic. The kernel processes banded matrices in a block-based manner using 16 computation channels in parallel, each connected to an independent HBM channel.

For densely banded matrices, our kernel consistently outperformed the Vitis SpMV kernel, with the largest gains at small band sizes. In particular, it achieved a median speedup of 9.5× for band size 8, while the advantage narrowed to 1.2× in GFLOPS and 1.5× in GFLOPS/W at band size 136.

For sparse-banded matrices derived from SuiteSparse, our kernel also outperformed Vitis for most band sizes, especially for narrow bands, with speedups of 9.5×, 4.6×, and 2.9× for band sizes 8, 24, and 40, respectively. As the band size increased, performance decreased because the kernel processes the full band, including padded zeros; at band size 136, Vitis performed better on average.

Compared with a multithreaded CPU DIA baseline (8 threads on Xeon Silver 4208), the FPGA achieved a median speedup of 1.84×, with a maximum speedup of 4.08×, and a median energy-efficiency gain of 2.40×, with a maximum gain of 6.39×. Overall, these results show that the banded kernel is particularly effective for matrices with small to moderate band sizes, providing substantial performance and energy-efficiency gains over both FPGA and CPU baselines. The banded kernel is preferable across all tested dense-band configurations and remains advantageous for sparse bands up to roughly 104–120 diagonals, depending on whether performance or energy efficiency is prioritized. Table 5 provides a quantitative boundary for kernel selection.

As future work, we plan to explore a hybrid SpMV approach that splits the input matrix into a banded region processed by the banded kernel and a remaining sparse region handled by a conventional sparse kernel, which could improve overall parallelization efficiency depending on the nonzero distribution.

Disclosure of Interests. The authors have no competing interests to declare that are relevant to the content of this article.

References

1. Barrachina, S., et al.: An integrated framework for power-performance analysis of parallel scientific workloads. Energy, 114–119 (2013)
2. Davis, T.A., Hu, Y.: The University of Florida sparse matrix collection. ACM Trans. Math. Softw. **38**(1), 1:1–1:25 (2011)
3. Du, Y., Hu, Y., Zhou, Z., Zhang, Z.: High-performance sparse linear algebra on HBM-equipped FPGAs using HLS: a case study on SpMV. In: Proceedings of the 2022 ACM/SIGDA International Symposium on Field-Programmable Gate Arrays. FPGA '22, pp. 54–64. Association for Computing Machinery, New York, NY, USA (2022). https://doi.org/10.1145/3490422.3502368

4. Elkurdi, Y., Fernández, D., Souleimanov, E., Giannacopoulos, D., Gross, W.J.: FPGA architecture and implementation of sparse matrix–vector multiplication for the finite element method. Comput. Phys. Commun. **178**(8), 558–570 (2008). https://doi.org/10.1016/j.cpc.2007.11.014
5. Ezzatti, P., Quintana-Ortí, E.S., Remón, A., Saak, J.: Power-aware computing. Concurr. Comput. Pract. Exp. **31**(6), e5034 (2019). https://doi.org/10.1002/cpe.5034, e5034 cpe.5034
6. Favaro, F., Dufrechou, E., Oliver, J.P., Ezzatti, P.: Tuning high-level synthesis SpMV kernels in Alveo FPGAs. Microprocess. Microsyst. **110**, 105104 (2024)
7. Hosseinabady, M., Nunez-Yanez, J.L.: A streaming dataflow engine for sparse matrix-vector multiplication using high-level synthesis. IEEE Trans. Comput. Aided Des. Integr. Circuits Syst. **39**(6), 1272–1285 (2020). https://doi.org/10.1109/TCAD.2019.2912923
8. Jain, A.K., Omidian, H., Fraisse, H., Benipal, M., Liu, L., Gaitonde, D.: A domain-specific architecture for accelerating sparse matrix vector multiplication on FPGAs. In: Mentens, N., Sousa, L., Trancoso, P., Pericàs, M., Sourdis, I. (eds.) 30th International Conference on Field-Programmable Logic and Applications, FPL 2020, Gothenburg, Sweden, 31 August–4 September 2020, pp. 127–132. IEEE (2020). https://doi.org/10.1109/FPL50879.2020.00031
9. Oliver, J., Álvarez, C., Cervero, T., Martorell, X., Davis, J.D., Ayguadé, E.: Accelerating SPMV on FPGAs through block-row compress: a task-based approach. In: 2023 33rd International Conference on Field-Programmable Logic and Applications (FPL), pp. 151–158 (2023). https://doi.org/10.1109/FPL60245.2023.00029
10. Rajashekar, M.B., Tian, X., Fang, Z.: HiSpMV: hybrid row distribution and vector buffering for imbalanced SpMV acceleration on FPGAs. In: Proceedings of the 2024 ACM/SIGDA International Symposium on Field Programmable Gate Arrays. FPGA '24, pp. 154–164. Association for Computing Machinery, New York, NY, USA (2024). https://doi.org/10.1145/3626202.3637557
11. Saad, Y.: Iterative Methods for Sparse Linear Systems, 2nd edn. Society for Industrial and Applied Mathematics, Philadelphia, PA, USA (2003)
12. Song, L., Chi, Y., Guo, L., Cong, J.: Serpens: a high bandwidth memory based accelerator for general-purpose sparse matrix-vector multiplication. In: Proceedings of the 59th ACM/IEEE Design Automation Conference (DAC '22), pp. 211–216 (2022). https://doi.org/10.1145/3489517.3530420
13. Tareen, A.R., Meyer, M., Plessl, C., Kenter, T.: HiHiSpMV: sparse matrix vector multiplication with hierarchical row reductions on FPGAs with high bandwidth memory. In: 2024 IEEE 32nd Annual International Symposium on Field-Programmable Custom Computing Machines (FCCM), pp. 32–42 (2024). https://doi.org/10.1109/FCCM60383.2024.00014
14. Wu, Z., Wang, M., So, H.K.H.: A hardware-software design framework for SpMV acceleration with flexible access pattern portfolio. In: 2025 IEEE International Symposium on High Performance Computer Architecture (HPCA), pp. 836–848 (2025). https://doi.org/10.1109/HPCA61900.2025.00068
15. Xilinx Inc.: Vitis sparse library (2022). https://xilinx.github.io/Vitis_Libraries/sparse/2022.2/index.html. Accessed 01 Mar 2023

OmniZK: A Versatile Accelerator Architecture for Zero-Knowledge Proofs

Zhengbang Yang[1,2], Lutan Zhao[1(✉)], Han Liu[1,2], Kai Li[1,2], and Rui Hou[1]

[1] State Key Laboratory of Cyberspace Security Defense, Institute of Information Engineering, CAS, Beijing, China
{yangzhengbang,zhaolutan,liuhan,likai,hourui}@iie.ac.cn

[2] School of Cyber Security, University of Chinese Academy of Sciences, Beijing, China

Abstract. Zero-knowledge proofs (ZKPs) have emerged as powerful privacy-preserving protocols with broad applications. However, the immense computational overhead of proof generation remains a critical obstacle. Existing hardware accelerators are tightly coupled to specific ZKP protocols, lacking the adaptability to support diverse protocols with varying computation kernels and arithmetic bit-widths. This paper presents OmniZK, a versatile accelerator architecture designed to efficiently support a broad spectrum of ZKP protocols. OmniZK employs homogeneous arrays of Unified Processing Elements (UPEs) interconnected via flexible mesh networks as its hardware substrate. It abstracts and maps heterogeneous ZKP computation kernels, including polynomial operations, multi-scalar multiplication, and Merkle tree construction, onto this unified finite-field arithmetic layer. Each UPE utilizes a hardware-efficient divide-and-conquer strategy to dynamically support arithmetic bit-widths ranging from 64 to 768 bits. Furthermore, OmniZK introduces optimized kernel mapping strategies that exploit multiple levels of parallelism to eliminate pipeline stalls, alongside a fast batched inversion method that substantially reduces vector inversion latency. Experimental results show that OmniZK achieves average speedups of 3.93× and 1.69× over the state-of-the-art elliptic-curve-based accelerator LegoZK and hash-based accelerator UniZK, respectively.

Keywords: Zero-Knowledge Proof · Cryptography · Accelerator

1 Introduction

Zero-knowledge proofs (ZKPs) have emerged as powerful privacy-preserving protocols that have attracted increasing attention from both academia and industry [4,5,7,9,14,16,22,24]. They enable a prover to demonstrate the correctness of a computation without revealing sensitive information, offering transformative potential for privacy-critical applications such as financial systems [3,6], databases [20,30], and verifiable machine learning [8,13]. However, the immense computational overhead of proof generation remains a critical obstacle to its

M. Torquati et al. (Eds.): Euro-Par 2026, LNCS 16781, pp. 433–447, 2027.
https://doi.org/10.1007/978-3-032-35248-4_30

widespread deployment. To accelerate this process, recent works have proposed various hardware accelerators [11,12,17,18,21,25,27–29] targeting specific ZKP computation kernels, such as Multi-Scalar Multiplication (MSM), Polynomial Operations (POLY), and Merkle Tree Construction (MTC). While these custom hardware solutions offer significant speedups, their rigid, protocol-coupled designs severely limit their adaptability.

The fundamental limitation of existing accelerators stems from the diverse and rapidly evolving landscape of ZKP protocols. For instance, Groth16, an elliptic-curve-based protocol widely deployed owing to its compact proof size and low verification overhead, is heavily bottlenecked by the large-bit-width (256–768 bits) MSM kernel. In contrast, modern hash-based protocols like Plonky2 abandon elliptic curves entirely, shifting the computational burden to 64-bit POLY and MTC kernels. This order-of-magnitude discrepancy in arithmetic bit-widths and the shift in dominant kernels mean that an accelerator tailored for Groth16 is virtually unusable for Plonky2, and vice versa. As ZKP applications diversify, redesigning ASICs for each new protocol or cryptographic primitive is an unsustainable hardware paradigm.

To break this hardware fragmentation, we identify a crucial convergence: despite the macroscopic heterogeneity in data types (elliptic curve points vs. hash blocks) and arithmetic bit-widths, the underlying execution of all major ZKP kernels ultimately reduces to fundamental finite-field arithmetic (addition, subtraction, and multiplication). Furthermore, these kernels exhibit abundant, highly regular parallel computation patterns. This inherent parallelism and computational convergence provide the theoretical foundation for extracting a unified, spatial hardware substrate capable of accelerating different ZKP protocols.

Building upon these insights, we propose OmniZK, a versatile ZKP accelerator architecture designed to efficiently support a broad spectrum of protocols. Instead of employing dedicated modules for different kernels, OmniZK utilizes homogeneous arrays of Unified Processing Elements (UPEs) interconnected via flexible mesh networks. To accommodate the extreme variance in arithmetic bit-widths (from 64 to 768 bits), the UPEs employ a hardware-efficient divide-and-conquer strategy to process arithmetic operations. Furthermore, we tightly integrate the architecture with optimized mapping strategies to exploit massive parallelism, and propose a novel fast batched inversion method to reduce the latency of vector inversions.

The main contributions of this paper are summarized as follows:

- This paper presents OmniZK, a versatile architecture capable of supporting a wide spectrum of ZKP protocols. By leveraging arrays of Unified Processing Elements (UPEs) as its core substrate, OmniZK abstracts and maps heterogeneous ZKP computation kernels onto a unified finite-field arithmetic layer to enable highly efficient acceleration for different ZKP protocols.
- This paper proposes optimized mapping strategies that exploit multiple levels of parallelism inherent in ZKP kernels. By expanding the scheduling window and reordering independent operations, our design effectively elimi-

nates dependency-induced pipeline stalls, thereby maximizing computational throughput and reducing overall latency.
- This paper proposes a fast batched inversion method. The method transforms a large number of inversions into cumulative multiplications and exponentiations, and reduces the quantity of computation by storing and reusing intermediate results, thereby significantly improving the performance of vector inversion.
- This paper presents a complete RTL implementation of OmniZK synthesized in the TSMC 7 nm process, occupying an area of 57.44 mm^2 and consuming 47.69 W of power. Experimental evaluations demonstrate that OmniZK achieves average speedups of 3.93× and 1.69× over the state-of-the-art elliptic-curve-based and hash-based ZKP ASIC accelerators, LegoZK and UniZK, respectively.

2 Background

2.1 ZKP Proof Generation Process

The ZKP proof generation process typically involves three stages: polynomial generation (PG), polynomial interactive oracle proof (PIOP), and polynomial commitment (PC). First, the target application is compiled into a constraint system, from which the PG stage generates polynomials via interpolation based on the execution trace. The PIOP stage then performs finite-field arithmetic on these polynomials using random challenges. Finally, the PC stage leverages cryptographic primitives, typically elliptic curves or hash functions, to evaluate the polynomials at random points, ensuring computational integrity and privacy.

2.2 Computation Kernels in ZKP

The aforementioned process relies on three primary computation kernels: Polynomial Operations (POLY), Multi-Scalar Multiplication (MSM), and Merkle Tree Construction (MTC).

Polynomial Operations involve finite-field number theoretic transforms (NTTs), Inverse NTTs (INTTs), and element-wise arithmetic (e.g., additions, subtractions, multiplications, and inversions). Costly finite-field inversions are typically computed via Fermat's Little Theorem ($a^{-1} = a^{P-2} \bmod P$), reducing them to $O(\log P)$ multiplications by fast exponentiation.

Multi-scalar Multiplication computes the inner product of a scalar vector and an elliptic curve point vector. It is typically implemented using the Pippenger algorithm [23]. This algorithm transforms the core computation from expensive scalar-point multiplications into significantly cheaper point additions. Furthermore, elliptic curve points are typically represented in projective coordinates. This representation allows point additions to be executed entirely through finite-field additions, subtractions, and multiplications, thereby circumventing costly inversion operations.

Merkle Tree Construction heavily relies on hash functions. The Poseidon Hash [15] is a widely adopted, zero-knowledge-friendly implementation in modern ZKP protocols. Its core execution simply involves finite-field vector additions, matrix-vector multiplications, and element-wise exponentiations on a state vector and a set of round constant vectors and matrices.

Table 1 summarizes the characteristics of these computation kernels. Crucially, the operations within all these kernels can be decomposed into finite-field additions, subtractions, and multiplications. This computational convergence serves as the foundational premise for OmniZK to accelerate heterogeneous ZKP kernels using unified processing elements. Additionally, under different cryptographic primitive configurations, the arithmetic bit-widths required by these kernels vary drastically. Specifically, for the Groth16 protocol based on different elliptic curves (e.g., MNT4-753, BLS12-381, BN128), the arithmetic bit-width ranges from 256 to 768 bits. Conversely, the Plonky2 protocol, which relies on the Poseidon hash, operates on a mere 64-bit arithmetic bit-width. This extreme variance mandates that OmniZK's unified processing elements provide highly efficient support for multiple, flexible arithmetic bit-widths.

Table 1. Characteristics of computation kernels in different ZKP protocols.

Protocols	Kernels	Operators	Arithmetic Bit-width		
Groth16 (EC-based)	POLY	Vector Add, Sub, Mult, Inv and (I)NTT	MNT4-753	BLS12-381	BN128
			768 bits	256 bits	256 bits
	MSM	Point Addition	MNT4-753	BLS12-381	BN128
			768 bits	384 bits	256 bits
Plonky2 (hash-based)	POLY	Vector Add, Sub, Mult, Inv and (I)NTT	64 bits		
	MTC	Poseidon Hash	64 bits		

3 OmniZK Architecture

OmniZK utilizes homogeneous arrays of Unified Processing Elements (UPEs) interconnected via flexible mesh networks as its core computational substrate. This section details its overall architecture, the organization of UPE arrays, and the divide-and-conquer strategy for flexible bit-width support.

3.1 Architecture Overview

Figure 1 illustrates the overall architecture of OmniZK, which comprises five primary components: the UPE arrays, a scratchpad memory, an on-chip fabric, an HBM controller, and a central controller. The UPE arrays serve as the computational core, executing all finite-field arithmetic operations. The scratchpad is an 8 MB on-chip buffer divided into 16 banks to support concurrent accesses, effectively decoupling off-chip memory accesses from on-chip computations. The on-chip fabric routes data between the scratchpad and the UPE arrays. The HBM controller manages off-chip memory accesses to two HBM stacks, providing an aggregate memory bandwidth of 1 TB/s. The central controller orchestrates resource allocation, data transfer scheduling, and computation configurations.

During execution, data loaded from the HBM is buffered in the scratchpad and dispatched to the UPE arrays. Results are stored in the scratchpad or selectively evicted to the HBM to reclaim on-chip capacity. To hide memory access latency, the central controller leverages the multi-bank scratchpad for double buffering, partitioning on-chip storage into computation and prefetch regions to overlap execution with data fetching.

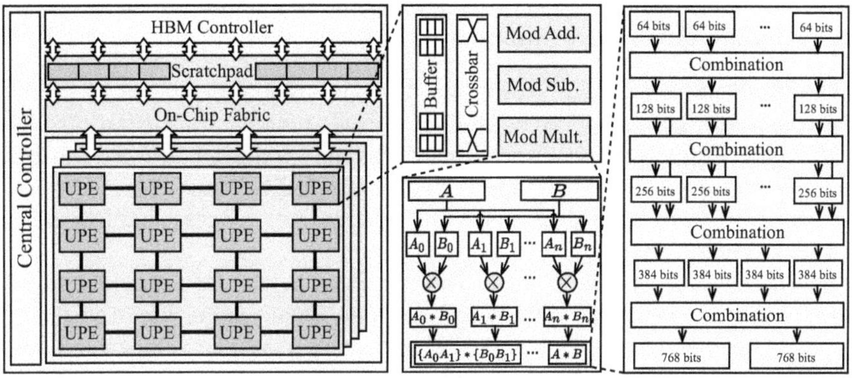

Fig. 1. OmniZK Architecture.

3.2 Unified Processing Element (UPE) Arrays

The computational core consists of multiple UPEs interconnected via flexible mesh networks. The current implementation of OmniZK integrates four UPE arrays, with each array containing a 4×4 grid of UPEs. The mesh networks support the dynamic configuration of data flow paths between UPEs, enabling multiple UPEs to be flexibly combined into deep pipelines tailored for different computation kernels. During pipeline execution, a given UPE may receive input operands from various upstream UPEs. Because these upstream UPEs may have varying computational path lengths, the arrival times of these operands can differ. Therefore, each UPE features an internal buffer to temporarily store early-arriving operands. Computation is triggered only when all required operands are ready, ensuring strict data synchronization across all pipeline stages. This buffer comprises four banks, each with a depth of 256. This capacity allows OmniZK to support pipelines up to 256 stages deep, satisfying the requirements of all major ZKP computation kernels.

As illustrated in Fig. 1, each UPE integrates three arithmetic units: a modular adder (Mod Add), a modular subtractor (Mod Sub), and a modular multiplier (Mod Mult). Each arithmetic unit employs a fully pipelined design, capable of completing one corresponding finite-field operation per clock cycle. Internally, a crossbar establishes flexible datapaths among the internal buffer and the arithmetic units. Through this crossbar, operands can be sourced either from the buffer or from the outputs of other units, while computation results can be written back to the buffer or forwarded directly to subsequent units. These configurable intra-UPE datapaths enable arbitrary combinations of additions, subtractions, and multiplications, flexibly realizing the complex finite-field operation sequences required by diverse ZKP kernels.

3.3 Flexible Bit-Width Support

As discussed in Sect. 2, the arithmetic bit-width requirements for finite fields vary drastically across different ZKP protocols, ranging from 64 to 768 bits. To efficiently support these diverse bit-widths on a unified hardware substrate, the UPE employs a 768-bit datapath and utilizes a divide-and-conquer strategy to decompose wide-bit-width operations into narrower ones, enabling flexible bit-width configurations from 64 up to 768 bits.

Specifically, for operands with a bit-width of S, the UPE partitions them into multiple segments of width w, where each segment executes the required operation independently. Under a w-bit arithmetic configuration, the results of each segment directly constitute the final output, providing a parallelism degree of $\frac{S}{w}$. Under a $2w$-bit configuration, the $2w$-bit result is recombined from the w-bit intermediate results, yielding a parallelism degree of $\frac{S}{2w}$. For additions and subtractions, the $2w$-bit result is reconstructed from two w-bit results by properly propagating carries or borrows. For multiplications, the $2w$-bit result is reconstructed from partial products and cross-products of w-bit sub-words. By applying the Karatsuba algorithm [19], OmniZK reduces the required multiplications from four to three, reusing intermediate results to minimize hardware overhead. By recursively applying this decomposition strategy, the UPE can flexibly parse input operands into various bit-width combinations (such as 768, 384, 256, 128, and 64 bits) and provide parallel execution, perfectly satisfying the diverse arithmetic bit-width requirements of modern ZKP protocols.

4 Kernel Mapping

Orchestrated by the central controller, OmniZK decomposes the ZKP proof generation into heterogeneous computation kernels and maps them onto the UPE arrays using optimized strategies that exploit kernel parallelism. In practice, a lightweight software runtime translates these high-level kernel configurations into static UPE instruction streams and network routing tables, which are subsequently dispatched by the central controller.

4.1 Polynomial Operations

Polynomial operations form the computational backbone of many ZKP protocols, exhibiting massive and regular data-level parallelism. OmniZK capitalizes on this characteristic by employing flexible vector blocking and hardware-friendly decomposition strategies, efficiently mapping them onto the UPE arrays.

Vector Arithmetic. Vector addition, subtraction, and multiplication are element-wise operations with independence among elements. OmniZK partitions the vectors into blocks and distributes them across different UPEs for parallel execution, where each UPE processes a sub-vector in a pipelined manner. Multiple UPE arrays can simultaneously process different vector blocks, exploiting both intra-array and inter-array parallelism to maximize computational throughput.

Number Theoretic Transform. Due to the massive scale, complex data dependencies, and irregular memory accesses of NTTs in ZKP, OmniZK employs a well-established NTT decomposition method [10,26,29]. It transforms a large-scale NTT into multiple smaller-scale NTTs, interleaved with element-wise twiddle factor multiplications. OmniZK maps these small-scale NTTs onto fully pipelined modules constructed by cascading multiple UPEs via the mesh network. By instantiating these NTT modules across different UPE arrays, OmniZK effectively accelerates the decomposed NTTs in parallel.

Fast Batched Inversion. Because the finite-field modulus P used in ZKP is typically large (with $\log P$ reaching tens or even hundreds), the latency of vector inversion is significant. To amortize this immense inversion overhead, OmniZK employs batched inversion, transforming the inversion of N elements into a single inversion alongside multiple finite-field multiplications. Specifically, this method first computes the product of all elements and inverts it. It then computes the corresponding partial product for each element (i.e., the product of all elements except itself) and multiplies it by the inverted total product to obtain the inverse of each element. Calculating these partial products is the most computationally intensive step in batched inversion. The naive approach computes the product of the remaining $N-1$ elements independently for each element, resulting in a complexity of $O(N^2)$.

To overcome this bottleneck, we propose a fast partial product algorithm that reduces the complexity to $O(N \log N)$. The core insight of this algorithm is that there is a massive amount of reusable intermediate multiplication results between the partial product computation and the total product computation. Based on this observation, the fast partial product algorithm constructs

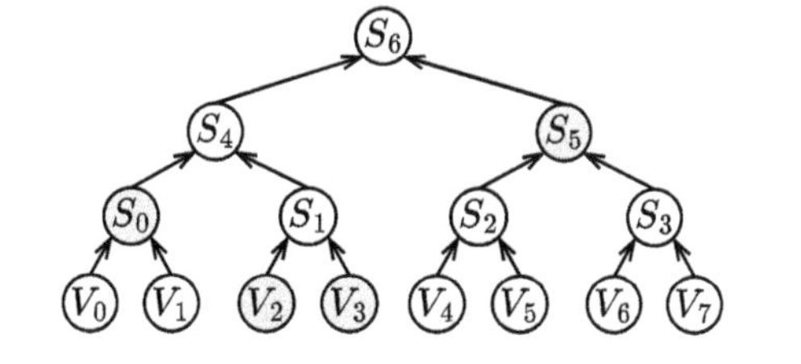

$$\prod_{i \neq 2} V_i = V_3 \times S_0 \times S_5 \qquad V_2^{-1} = \prod_{i \neq 2} V_i \times S_6^{-1}$$

Fig. 2. A multiplication binary tree storing intermediate results in the product of all leaf nodes.

a multiplication binary tree to store all intermediate results generated during the total product computation, as illustrated in Fig. 2. For any leaf node in the tree, its corresponding partial product can be expressed as the product of at most $\log N$ nodes.

The key to mapping vector inversion onto the UPE arrays lies in constructing the multiplication binary tree shown in Fig. 2, which is essentially a sequence of vector multiplications with lengths halving at each successive level. The operations at each level of the tree correspond to a vector multiplication, where the two input vectors are extracted from the even-indexed and odd-indexed elements of the input nodes at that level, respectively. OmniZK sequentially maps these vector multiplications onto the UPE arrays for execution, writing the intermediate results of each level back to the scratchpad for reuse in subsequent steps.

4.2 Multi-scalar Multiplication

To enhance MSM performance, OmniZK fully exploits the four levels of parallelism inherent in the Pippenger algorithm and maps them onto the hardware, as depicted in Fig. 3.

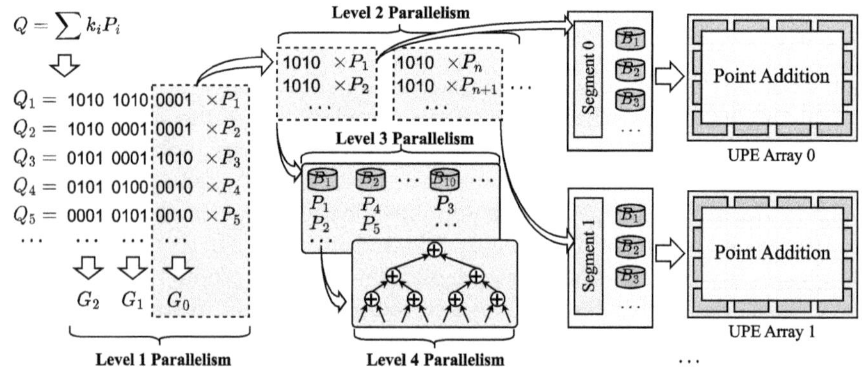

Fig. 3. Four levels of parallelism in multi-scalar multiplication (MSM) using the Pippenger algorithm and the mapping strategy for MSM.

The first level of parallelism stems from the mutual independence among sub-scalar vectors. The second level arises from the segmented processing of a single vector inner product, where each segment can be independently computed for a local inner product before aggregation. OmniZK partitions these sub-scalar vectors into multiple segments and dispatches them to different UPE arrays. These arrays compute the inner products between the segments and their corresponding point vectors in parallel, leveraging these two levels of parallelism to maximize the computational throughput. The third level of parallelism originates from the independence among accumulation operations for different buckets. The fourth level is derived from the data independence among point additions within the same level of the addition tree during the reduction of a single bucket. OmniZK uniformly dispatches the point additions involved in both bucket accumulations and addition tree reductions to the UPE arrays for pipelined execution.

Notably, inherent data dependency chains exist within the point addition operations. When processing the upper-level nodes of the addition tree, the UPE pipeline is prone to stalls due to the limited number of independent point additions available for parallel execution. To address this limitation, OmniZK interleaves the scheduling of independent point addition operations from different buckets (leveraging the third and fourth levels of parallelism) to continuously feed the pipeline. This effectively eliminates pipeline stalls caused by data dependencies, thereby fully unleashing the computational throughput of the UPEs.

4.3 Merkle Tree Construction

Merkle Tree Construction exhibits a highly parallel-friendly nature. Along the Merkle Tree, the hash computations for nodes within the same level of the tree are mutually independent, allowing for massive parallel execution. Within a single hash, the Poseidon Hash primarily involves operations on the state vector and the round constant vectors/matrices, which similarly present abundant parallel opportunities.

Prior to execution, OmniZK evenly distributes the round constant vectors and matrices required by the Poseidon Hash into the buffers of the respective UPEs, avoiding repetitive loading overheads during runtime. During execution, OmniZK parses the input data blocks of each hash instance into a state vector comprising finite-field elements and dispatches it to the corresponding UPEs for computation. For operations necessitating multiple sequential arithmetic steps, such as matrix-vector multiplications and vector exponentiations, OmniZK schedules the data to flow through multiple UPEs via the mesh network, executing them in a pipelined manner. Because the inter-level dependencies of the Merkle Tree are highly regular and predictable (i.e., the input of level l depends on the output of level $l-1$), OmniZK stores computation results for each level in the scratchpad to allow data reuse during level transitions, preserving data locality and avoiding frequent HBM accesses.

Furthermore, tight data dependencies exist among the multiple rounds of vector operations within a single Poseidon Hash; each round of operations must wait for the completion of the previous round before initiating. This leads to frequent UPE pipeline stalls, severely degrading computational throughput. To mitigate this inefficiency, OmniZK expands the scheduling window to encompass multiple hash instances within the same level of the Merkle Tree. By reordering the vector operations, OmniZK inserts operations from other hashes between two

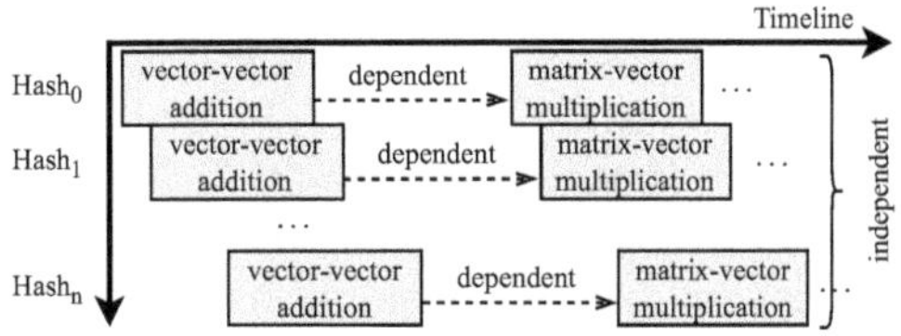

Fig. 4. Operation scheduling for parallel hash computations in a Merkle Tree.

dependent vector operations within a single hash, as illustrated in Fig. 4. This operation scheduling methodology effectively eliminates pipeline stalls induced by data dependencies, significantly reducing the overall latency.

5 Evaluation

5.1 Experimental Setup

Table 2. Area and Power breakdown of OmniZK.

Component	Area (mm^2)	Power (W)
UPE Array (×4)	22.39	13.72
NoC	0.23	0.81
Scratchpad (8 MB)	4.88	0.92
Controller	0.17	0.44
HBM Controller	29.8	31.8
Total	57.44	47.69

We implement the complete OmniZK architecture in RTL and synthesize it using Synopsys Design Compiler in the TSMC 7 nm process, achieving a frequency of 1 GHz. Table 2 presents a detailed breakdown of the area and power consumption of each OmniZK component. In total, OmniZK occupies 57.44 mm^2 of area and consumes 47.69 W of power.

We compare OmniZK against two state-of-the-art ZKP ASIC accelerators, LegoZK [28] and UniZK [27]. LegoZK targets the elliptic-curve-based Groth16 protocol [16], focusing on accelerating Polynomial Operations and Multi-Scalar Multiplication. UniZK targets the hash-based Plonky2 protocol [24], accelerating Polynomial Operations and Merkle Tree Construction. To further characterize OmniZK's efficiency on individual computation kernels, we evaluate the performance of Vector Inversion, NTT, MSM, and MTC, comparing them against CPU baselines. The CPU implementations are built upon open-source libraries [1,2] and run on an Intel Xeon Platinum 8592V processor with 128 hardware threads.

5.2 Overall Performance

Table 3 presents the end-to-end performance of OmniZK across different ZKP protocols, together with speedups relative to the elliptic-curve-based accelerator LegoZK and the hash-based accelerator UniZK.

For elliptic-curve-based protocol instances, both OmniZK and LegoZK use the MNT4-753 curve over a 768-bit finite field. OmniZK achieves an average speedup of 3.93× over LegoZK. This improvement is primarily attributed to OmniZK's exploitation of multiple levels of parallelism across diverse computation kernels, combined with efficient scheduling strategies that fully unleash the parallel and pipelined computational capabilities of the UPE arrays.

For hash-based protocol instances, both OmniZK and UniZK operate over a 64-bit finite field. Under this configuration, each 768-bit arithmetic unit in OmniZK supports up to 12 parallel 64-bit operations. OmniZK achieves an average speedup of 1.69× over UniZK. This speedup is smaller than that achieved over LegoZK, primarily because UniZK exploits the special properties of the Goldilocks field, where modular reduction requires only a few additions, subtractions, and bit shifts, thereby substantially reducing the arithmetic overhead.

OmniZK deliberately forgoes this field-specific optimization, as it is tightly coupled to a particular field choice and cannot be generalized across the diverse finite fields used in different ZKP protocols. This design decision reflects OmniZK's core objective of versatility: maintaining consistent efficiency across both elliptic-curve-based and hash-based protocols without sacrificing generality.

Table 3. Overall performance of OmniZK and comparison with LegoZK(elliptic-curve-based) and UniZK(hash-based).

Application	LegoZK (EC-based)	OmniZK	Speedup
AES	0.011 s	0.003 s	3.67×
SHA	0.009 s	0.002 s	4.50×
RSA-Enc	0.019 s	0.005 s	3.80×
RSA-SHA	0.021 s	0.005 s	4.20×
Merkle Tree	0.039 s	0.011 s	3.55×
Auction	0.054 s	0.014 s	3.86×
Application	**UniZK (hash-based)**	**OmniZK**	**Speedup**
Factorial	0.828 s	0.454 s	1.82×
Fibonacci	0.023 s	0.015 s	1.53×
ECDSA	0.065 s	0.039 s	1.67×
SHA-256	0.908 s	0.487 s	1.86×
Image Crop	0.373 s	0.209 s	1.79×
MVM	0.320 s	0.219 s	1.46×

5.3 Breakdown Analysis

This section presents the performance of individual ZKP computation kernels on OmniZK and their speedups over CPU implementations. The evaluated kernels include Vector Inversion, NTT, MSM, and MTC, with input vector lengths ranging from 2^{24} to 2^{32}. Since ZKP protocols based on different cryptographic primitives require different arithmetic bit-widths, we evaluate OmniZK under multiple bit-width configurations to demonstrate its broad adaptability. Detailed results are shown in Fig. 5.

For Vector Inversion, OmniZK achieves average speedups of approximately 659×, 279×, and 123× over the CPU implementations under 768-bit, 256-bit, and 64-bit configurations, respectively. As bit-width increases, CPU computational cost grows significantly, while OmniZK's highly parallel architecture maintains efficiency, resulting in increasingly pronounced speedups.

For NTT, OmniZK achieves average speedups of approximately 1635×, 705×, and 279× under the three configurations. The complex data dependencies and irregular memory access patterns of NTT make it difficult for CPU implementations to effectively exploit caches and computation resources. OmniZK

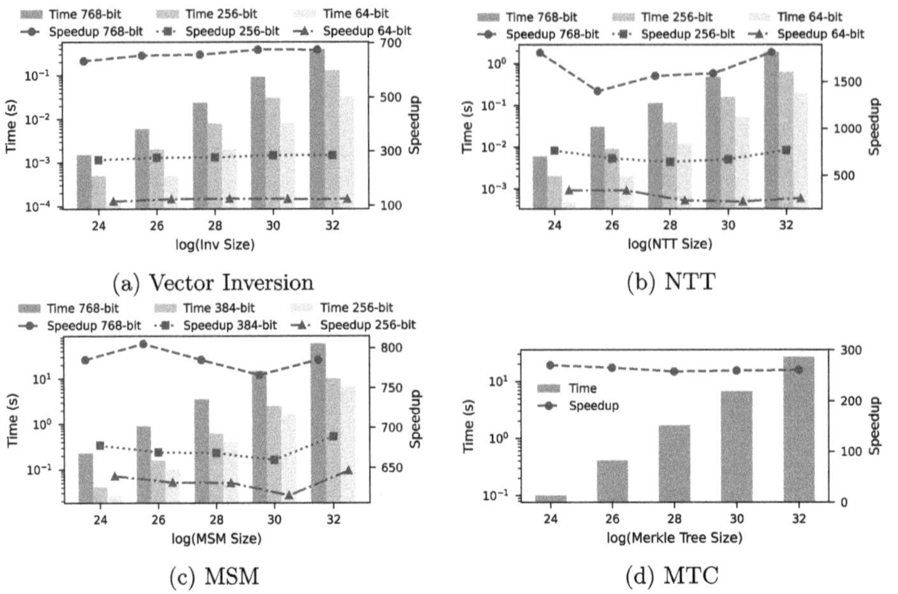

Fig. 5. Performance of different ZKP computation kernels on OmniZK, and their speedups over CPU implementations.

addresses this through a hardware-friendly NTT decomposition strategy and a fully pipelined, highly parallel execution architecture, yielding substantial performance gains.

For MSM, OmniZK achieves average speedups of approximately 785×, 673×, and 633× under the 768-bit, 384-bit, and 256-bit configurations. This scaling trend highlights OmniZK's architectural advantage in comprehensively exploiting the four levels of parallelism inherent in the Pippenger algorithm. Larger bit-widths expose substantially more independent operations across these parallelism levels, enabling the interleaved scheduling to effectively eliminate pipeline stalls and maximize computational throughput.

For MTC, OmniZK achieves an average speedup of approximately 263×. The high intra-layer parallelism and regular inter-layer dependencies of Merkle Tree Construction make it well-suited for hardware acceleration. OmniZK's operation reordering strategy enables the parallel, pipelined execution of vector operations across multiple hash instances on the UPE arrays, delivering significant performance enhancement.

5.4 Scalability

To evaluate the scalability of OmniZK, we measure its normalized latency and area cost under configurations with different UPE counts and memory bandwidths, as shown in Fig. 6. As expected, increasing either the UPE count or the memory bandwidth improves performance at the cost of larger chip area. Moreover, the balance between these two resources significantly impacts overall efficiency. For instance, the configuration with 128 UPEs and 512 GB/s bandwidth incurs higher area overhead than that with 64 UPEs and 1 TB/s bandwidth, yet delivers worse performance due to memory becoming the bottleneck. Therefore, to balance performance and hardware cost, we select the configuration with 64 UPEs and 1 TB/s memory bandwidth for OmniZK in this work.

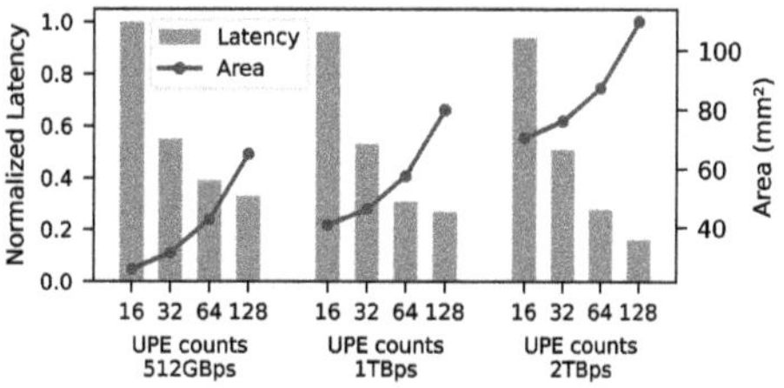

Fig. 6. Normalized latency and area cost of OmniZK under different UPE counts and memory bandwidths.

6 Related Work

PipeZK [29] and LegoZK [28] are ASIC accelerators designed for the elliptic-curve-based Groth16 protocol [16]. While PipeZK accelerates specific kernels like NTT and MSM, it offloads a portion of the computations to the CPU, severely limiting end-to-end performance. LegoZK addresses this inefficiency by proposing a reconfigurable architecture. Conversely, UniZK [27] targets the hash-based Plonky2 protocol [24], mapping its computation kernels onto a systolic array architecture. However, these existing accelerators remain rigidly coupled to specific cryptographic primitives, and cannot accommodate the diverse spectrum of modern ZKP systems. In contrast, OmniZK unifies support for different ZKP protocols at the fundamental finite-field arithmetic layer, contributing novel kernel mapping and scheduling strategies to efficiently execute a wide variety of kernels on the unified hardware substrate.

7 Conclusion

This paper presents OmniZK, a versatile hardware architecture designed to accelerate a broad spectrum of ZKP protocols. OmniZK unifies the execution of heterogeneous ZKP computation kernels onto arrays of Unified Processing Elements (UPEs). Furthermore, by employing optimized kernel mapping strategies, OmniZK maximizes computational throughput without sacrificing generality. Evaluations demonstrate that OmniZK achieves average speedups of 3.93× and 1.69× over the state-of-the-art ZKP accelerators, LegoZK and UniZK, respectively. OmniZK presents a conscious trade-off between versatility and performance. By eliminating the prohibitive redesign costs of dedicated silicon, it offers a more sustainable hardware paradigm for the rapidly evolving ZKP landscape.

Acknowledgements. This work is supported by the National Key R&D Program of China (Grant No. 2023YFB4503200 and 2023YFB4503201), the Strategic Priority Research Program of Chinese Academy of Sciences (Grant No. XDB0690100), the National Natural Science Foundation of China for Distinguished Young Scholars (Grant No. 62125208), and National Natural Science Foundation of China (Grant No. 62427809). Lutan Zhao is the corresponding author.

Disclosure of Interests. The authors have no competing interests to declare that are relevant to the content of this article.

References

1. https://github.com/scipr-lab/libsnark (2014)
2. https://github.com/0xpolygonzero/plonky2 (2020)
3. Ben-Sasson, E.: Zerocash: decentralized anonymous payments from bitcoin. In: Symposium on Security and Privacy, pp. 459–474 (2014)
4. Ben-Sasson, E., et al.: Scalable, transparent, and post-quantum secure computational integrity. Cryptology ePrint Archive, Paper 2018/046 (2018)
5. Ben-Sasson, E., Chiesa, A., Riabzev, M., Spooner, N., Virza, M., Ward, N.P.: Aurora: transparent succinct arguments for R1CS. In: Ishai, Y., Rijmen, V. (eds.) EUROCRYPT 2019. LNCS, vol. 11476, pp. 103–128. Springer, Cham (2019). https://doi.org/10.1007/978-3-030-17653-2_4
6. Bonneau, J.: Coda: decentralized cryptocurrency at scale. Cryptology ePrint Archive (2020)
7. Campanelli, M., Faonio, A., Fiore, D., Querol, A., Rodríguez, H.: Lunar: a toolbox for more efficient universal and updatable zkSNARKs and commit-and-prove extensions. In: Tibouchi, M., Wang, H. (eds.) ASIACRYPT 2021. LNCS, vol. 13092, pp. 3–33. Springer, Cham (2021). https://doi.org/10.1007/978-3-030-92078-4_1
8. Chen, B.J.: ZKML: an optimizing system for ml inference in zero-knowledge proofs. In: EuroSys, pp. 560–574 (2024)
9. Chiesa, A., Hu, Y., Maller, M., Mishra, P., Vesely, N., Ward, N.: Marlin: preprocessing zkSNARKs with universal and updatable SRS. In: Canteaut, A., Ishai, Y. (eds.) EUROCRYPT 2020. LNCS, vol. 12105, pp. 738–768. Springer, Cham (2020). https://doi.org/10.1007/978-3-030-45721-1_26
10. Chu, E., George, A.: Inside the FFT black box: serial and parallel fast Fourier transform algorithms (2019)
11. Daftardar, A.: SZKP: a scalable accelerator architecture for zero-knowledge proofs. In: PACT, pp. 271–283 (2024)
12. Daftardar, A., et al.: Need for zkSpeed: accelerating hyperplonk for zero-knowledge proofs. In: ISCA, pp. 1986–2001 (2025)
13. Feng, B.: ZENO: a type-based optimization framework for zero knowledge neural network inference. In: ASPLOS, pp, 450–464 (2024)
14. Gabizon, A., et al.: PLONK: permutations over Lagrange-bases for oecumenical noninteractive arguments of knowledge. IACR Cryptology ePrint Archive, p. 953 (2019)
15. Grassi, L.: Poseidon: a new hash function for zero-knowledge proof systems. In: USENIX Security 21, pp. 519–535 (2021)

16. Groth, J.: On the size of pairing-based non-interactive arguments. In: Fischlin, M., Coron, J.-S. (eds.) EUROCRYPT 2016. LNCS, vol. 9666, pp. 305–326. Springer, Heidelberg (2016). https://doi.org/10.1007/978-3-662-49896-5_11
17. Ji, Z.: Accelerating multi-scalar multiplication for efficient zero knowledge proofs with multi-GPU systems. In: ASPLOS, pp. 57–70 (2024)
18. Ji, Z.: Accelerating number theoretic transform with multi-GPU systems for efficient zero knowledge proof. In: ASPLOS pp. 1–14 (2025)
19. Karatsuba, A.A.: Multiplication of many-digital numbers by automatic computers. Dokl. Akad. Nauk SSSR **145**, 293–294 (1962)
20. Li, X., et al.: ZKSQL: verifiable and efficient query evaluation with zero-knowledge proofs. Proc. VLDB Endow. **16**(8), 1804–1816 (2023)
21. Ma, W.: GZKP: a GPU accelerated zero-knowledge proof system. In: ASPLOS, pp. 340–353 (2023)
22. Maller, M.: Sonic: Zero-knowledge snarks from linear-size universal and updatable structured reference strings. In: CCS, pp. 2111–2128 (2019)
23. Pippenger, N.: On the evaluation of powers and related problems. In: 17th Annual Symposium on Foundations of Computer Science (SFCS 1976), pp. 258–263 (1976)
24. PolygonZero: Plonky2: fast recursive arguments with plonk and fri (2022)
25. Samardzic, N.: Accelerating zero-knowledge proofs through hardware-algorithm co-design. In: MICRO, pp. 366–379 (2024)
26. Wang, C., Gao, M.: SAM: a scalable accelerator for number theoretic transform using multi-dimensional decomposition. In: ICCAD, pp. 1–9 (2023)
27. Wang, C., Gao, M.: UniZK: accelerating zero-knowledge proof with unified hardware and flexible kernel mapping. In: ASPLOS, pp. 1101–1117 (2025)
28. Yang, Z.: LegoZK: a dynamically reconfigurable accelerator for zero-knowledge proof. In: HPCA, pp. 113–126 (2025)
29. Zhang, Y.: PipeZK: accelerating zero-knowledge proof with a pipelined architecture. In: ISCA, pp. 416–428 (2021)
30. Zhang, Y.: VSQL: verifying arbitrary SQL queries over dynamic outsourced databases. In: Symposium on Security and Privacy, pp. 863–880 (2017)

Domain-Specific and Applied Parallel and Distributed Computing

Hierarchical Recursive Precision for Accelerating Symmetric Linear Solves on MXUs

Vicki Carrica[1(✉)], Rabab Alomairy[1,2], Evelyne Ringoot[1], and Alan Edelman[1]

[1] CS and AI Laboratories, Massachusetts Institute of Technology, Cambridge, MA, USA
{vickicar,rabab.alomairy,eringoot,edelman}@mit.edu
[2] Computer, Electrical and Mathematical Sciences and Engineering Division, King Abdullah University of Science and Technology (KAUST), Thuwal, Kingdom of Saudi Arabia
rabab.omairy@kaust.edu.sa

Abstract. Symmetric positive-definite system solvers based on Cholesky factorization are fundamental to many scientific applications, such as climate modeling. We present a portable, nested recursive mixed-precision solver designed for Matrix Processing Units (MXUs), including NVIDIA Tensor Cores (H200) and AMD Matrix Cores (MI300X), that assigns low-precision FP16 arithmetic to large off-diagonal blocks, while preserving high precision on diagonal blocks to ensure numerical stability. The solver is implemented in Julia, providing a high-level, hardware-agnostic interface. We demonstrate up to a 5.07× speedup relative to the diagonal-precision vendor baseline, with 100× better accuracy than pure half precision on H200, providing higher accuracy than low-precision at higher speed than high-precision. Positive performance trends are also observed on MI300X, demonstrating broad applicability across GPUs.

Keywords: Cholesky decomposition · mixed precision · recursive algorithms · GPU acceleration · TRSM · SYRK · tensor cores · matrix processing units (MXUs) · Julia language · quantization

1 Introduction

Symmetric linear systems are a critical performance bottleneck in large simulations, for example, computational fluid dynamics [30], climate modeling [3], and Gaussian process regression [23]. Direct solution methods of such symmetric linear systems involve calculating their Cholesky decomposition, which relies on triangular solve (TRSM) and symmetric rank-k update (SYRK). These systems have traditionally been solved in uniform high precision, creating a computational bottleneck on modern AI accelerators. While modern lower-precision Matrix Processing Units (MXUs), such as NVIDIA Tensor Cores and

M. Torquati et al. (Eds.): Euro-Par 2026, LNCS 16781, pp. 451–465, 2027.
https://doi.org/10.1007/978-3-032-35248-4_31

AMD Matrix Cores [13], deliver high throughput for low precision operations, Cholesky requires numerical stability to prevent divergence. Because scientific computing demands high-accuracy results, standard uniform-precision solvers cannot safely exploit these fast MXUs. Deploying these hardware capabilities in scientific computing therefore requires a mixed-precision approach where high accuracy and improved speed are combined. In this work, we demonstrate that integrating mixed-precision into the well-known multi-stage recursive subdivision algorithm enables leveraging the capabilities of MXUs and results in significant speed-ups while maintaining higher accuracy than low-precision solutions. *Recursive subdivision* [6,11,20] is a well-known strategy to enhance data locality and parallelism in Cholesky factorization through introducing matrix-multiplies. While prior recursive formulations typically apply only to the diagonal POTRF operation—leaving off-diagonal updates (TRSM and SYRK) in standard blocked form—we extend this into a fully *nested recursive formulation*. In our approach, the decomposition tree recursively subdivides not only POTRF but also TRSM and SYRK, further increasing the granularity of GEMM operations [14]. We integrate this in a *tree-structured mixed-precision hierarchy* that assigns low precision (FP16) to large off-diagonal blocks and progressively higher precision (FP32 or FP64) to recursively refined diagonal regions. This mixed-precision strategy aligns better with the recursive subdivision algorithm than prior mixed-precision approaches, which either focus on iterative refinement [16,27] or apply uniform low precision to predefined matrix partitions [29,33]. We focus in this work on diagonally dominant problems, for which this is a reasonable strategy. For non-diagonally dominant problems, other mixed-precision strategies need to be considered. The solver is implemented as a layered mixed-precision scheme in Julia.

The main contribution of this work is the integration of a tree-based mixed-precision scheme into a multi-stage recursive subdivision strategy in a unified portable data structure, demonstrating significant speedups of mixed-precision approaches over high-precision vendor libraries on a single GPU, while maintaining higher accuracy than low precision. On NVIDIA H200 GPUs, our solver achieves a 5.32× speedup over FP64 cuSOLVER, and a 5.07× speedup against cuSOLVER FP32, with 100× better accuracy than pure FP16 and 88% of Pure FP16's peak throughput. Similar trends are observed on AMD MI300X, showcasing the cross-platform scalability and practicality of our approach.

2 Related Work

2.1 Recursive Decomposition

Recursive formulations have long been studied as a strategy to improve data locality and expose parallelism in dense linear algebra. Dense linear algebra algorithms such as the Cholesky decomposition are often bounded by communication cost, rather than arithmetic cost, motivating the development of communication-avoiding Cholesky implementations [9]. Early efforts in dense matrix settings—such as [6,20]—proposed recursive blocked factorizations, and recursive formulations for hierarchical low-rank solvers [19,25], where recursion is limited to the diagonal factorization, with off-diagonal updates computed via standard blocked methods following LAPACK-style parallelism [7]. More recently, optimizing task granularity in hybrid CPU-GPU environments has been done through recursive task graphs [21,22,31]. For GPU hardware, Charara et al. [17] introduced a recursive triangular solver (TRSM) designed to exploit data locality and task decomposition on GPU architectures, which Carrica et al. [14] implemented as a recursive GPU TRSM in Julia, demonstrating its benefits on tensor-core hardware. While existing approaches thus leverage standard blocked updates [18], to the best of our knowledge, they typically do not extend the recursive approach across all three phases—POTRF, TRSM, and SYRK. Our approach evaluates a *recursive GPU-based SYRK* extending across all three phases, along with a mixed-precision variant that strategically exploits low-precision GEMM acceleration, demonstrating it results in performance benefits over non-nested approaches, hereby addressing the linear solve bottleneck in scientific computing by accelerating this phase.

2.2 Mixed-Precision Linear Algebra

Mixed-precision techniques have gained significant attention as a means to accelerate numerical algorithms while reducing energy consumption. Higham et al. [27], along with others [2,8,12,15,16,26] studied mixed-precision iterative refinement for dense and sparse systems. More recently, task-based and batched GPU solvers have explored integrating low-precision arithmetic at the kernel level [3,4,29,33], often relying on uniform block-level precision assignment. Other approaches apply precision dynamically based on sub-matrix norms [3] or use non-uniform thresholds for block low-rank LU factorization [5]. These strategies are not directly aligned with the algorithmic recursion of the Cholesky factorization. In our approach for diagonally dominant matrices, FP16 precision is assigned to large off-diagonal blocks and higher precision (FP32 or FP64) to recursively refined diagonal region, aligning a *tree-structured precision hierarchy* with the recursive subdivision strategy. This enables controlled use of MXU-accelerated low-precision GEMM operations without compromising stability. Our approach also integrates lightweight per-block quantization and dequantization [28], ensuring robustness when operating near FP16's dynamic range limits (Sect. 3.4). To our knowledge, this is the first work to unify recursive decomposition and layered mixed-precision execution in a hardware-portable solver framework.

3 Methods

3.1 Julia Language Abstractions

The implementation of a recursive mixed-precision Cholesky solver is facilitated by the Julia programming language [10]. Julia's multiple dispatch and type inference with compile-time specialization permits writing single hardware-agnostic calls to specialized core operations—`POTRF`, `TRSM`, `SYRK`, and `GEMM`—which the compiler then resolves and optimizes automatically based on data type (e.g., FP16, FP32, FP64), enabling a unified mixed-precision recursive solver framework, combining portability and high performance [1,24,32]. In previous work, a full-cycle low-level implementation of TRSM and TRMM, directly compiled to GPU machine language, was demonstrated to provide performance on par with vendor-optimized functions [14]. In the current work, we focus on the recursive implementation of Cholesky, and lean on low-level vendor library implementation of POTRF, TRSM, SYRK, and GEMM through multiple dispatch for the base cases. This algorithm could in the future be a critical building block towards the performant low-level hardware-agnostic implementation of Cholesky decomposition for small and large data sizes for all GPU hardware.

3.2 Nested Recursive Algorithm Design

We implement a nested recursive Cholesky algorithm that decomposes symmetric positive-definite (SPD) matrices by hierarchically breaking down all three core computational phases: POTRF (Cholesky factorization), TRSM (triangular solve), and SYRK (symmetric rank-k update). By replacing standard TRSM and SYRK updates with their recursive counterparts, we expose more parallelism and achieve deeper task granularity. This structure increases arithmetic intensity and enables greater utilization of BLAS-3 routines, particularly GEMM, which are highly optimized on modern GPU architectures with MXUs. The nested recursive structure allows for greater memory hierarchy utilization. By recursively dividing the problem until blocks fit within the L2 cache, it enhances data locality and maximizes cache reuse compared to standard flat algorithms.

For TRSM, this form of recursion was first introduced for GPUs in [18], and its portable Julia implementation was recently explored in [14].

Algorithm 1. Tree-POTRF$_L(A, b)$: Nested-recursive Cholesky (lower)

Require: $A \in \mathbb{R}^{n \times n}$ SPD; leaf size b
1: **if** $n \leq b$ **then**
2: $\quad A \leftarrow \text{POTRF}_L(A)$
3: $\quad$ **return**
4: **end if**
5: Choose n_1 (e.g. $n_1 = \lfloor n/2 \rfloor$); $n_2 = n - n_1$
6: Partition $A = \begin{bmatrix} A_{11} & 0 \\ A_{21} & A_{22} \end{bmatrix}$
7: Tree-POTRF$_L(A_{11},\ b)$ $\quad\triangleright\ A_{11} \leftarrow L_{11}L_{11}^{\top}$
8: Tree-TRSM$_{R,L,T}(A_{21},\ L_{11},\ b)$ $\quad\triangleright\ A_{21} \leftarrow A_{21}L_{11}^{-\top}$
9: Tree-SYRK$_L(A_{22},\ A_{21},\ \alpha = -1,\ \beta = 1,\ b)$ $\quad\triangleright\ A_{22} \leftarrow A_{22} - A_{21}A_{21}^{\top}$
10: Tree-POTRF$_L(A_{22},\ b)$

Algorithm 1 outlines the recursive Cholesky factorization for an SPD matrix A (see Fig. 1). At each level, the matrix is split into a diagonal block A_{11} and a trailing submatrix A_{22}. The decomposition proceeds through four recursive stages: (1) diagonal POTRF on A_{11} (line 7), (2) triangular solve (TRSM) on the off-diagonal block (line 8), (3) symmetric rank-k update (SYRK) on the

Algorithm 2. Tree-TRSM$_{R,L,T}(B, L, b)$

Require: $B \in \mathbb{R}^{m \times n}$, $L \in \mathbb{R}^{n \times n}$ lower-tri; leaf b

```
1: if min(m, n) ≤ b then
2:     B ← TRSM(...; L, B)
3:     return
4: end if
5: n1 = ⌊n/2⌋, Split L = [L11 0; L21 L22], B = [B1 | B2]
6: TREE-TRSM(B1, L11, b)
7: B2 ← B2 − B1 L21^T
8: TREE-TRSM(B2, L22, b)
```

Algorithm 3. Tree-SYRK$_L(C, A, \alpha, \beta, b)$

Require: $C \in \mathbb{R}^{n \times n}$ sym.; $A \in \mathbb{R}^{n \times k}$; leaf b

```
1: if n ≤ b then
2:     C ← SYRK(...; α, A, β, C)
3:     return
4: end if
5: n1 = ⌊n/2⌋, Split A = [A1; A2], C = [C11 0; C21 C22]
6: TREE-SYRK(C11, A1, α, β, b)
7: C21 ← βC21 + αA2 A1^T
8: TREE-SYRK(C22, A2, α, β, b)
```

trailing submatrix A_{22} (line 9), and (4) recursive POTRF on the updated A_{22} (line 10). Algorithm 2 applies TRSM recursively to solve $B \leftarrow BL^{-T}$ for a lower-triangular matrix L. If the matrix size falls below the threshold b, a standard TRSM kernel is used (line 2). Otherwise, L and B are split, and the update $B_2 \leftarrow B_2 - B_1 L_{21}^T$ is computed using GEMM (line 7). Similarly, Algorithm 3 performs the SYRK update $C \leftarrow \beta C + \alpha AA^T$ recursively. The off-diagonal contribution $C_{21} \leftarrow \beta C_{21} + \alpha A_2 A_1^T$ is explicitly computed via GEMM (line 7), while the diagonal blocks are handled recursively.

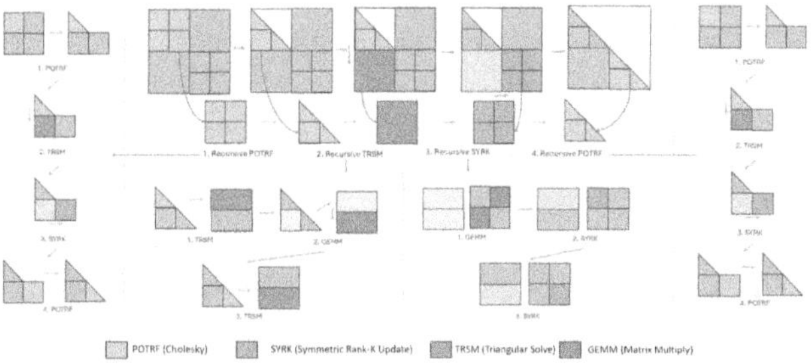

Fig. 1. Nested Recursive Cholesky Decomposition Tree.

3.3 Hierarchical Mixed Precision on the Recursion Structure

This hierarchical recursion naturally supports our *layered mixed-precision scheme* integrated into our recursive Cholesky algorithm.

Specifically, we assign: (i) **Low precision (e.g., FP16)** to large, off-diagonal blocks that dominate the computation but are less sensitive to numerical error. These are typically updated using GEMM during TRSM and SYRK phases. (ii) **Higher precision (e.g., FP32 or FP64)** to diagonal blocks, which undergo POTRF and are more susceptible to round-off errors. These blocks contribute directly to the factorization's stability and accuracy.

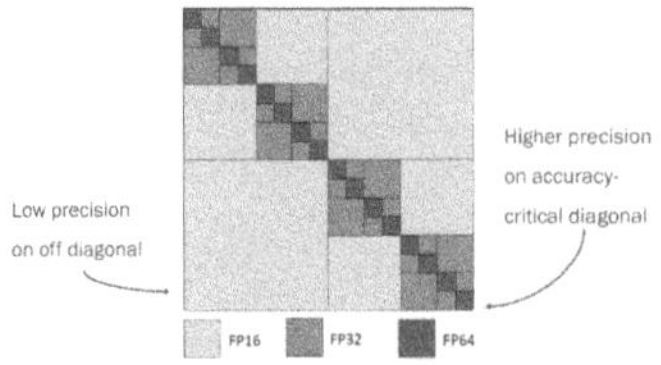

Fig. 2. Recursive data structure enabling layered mixed precision.

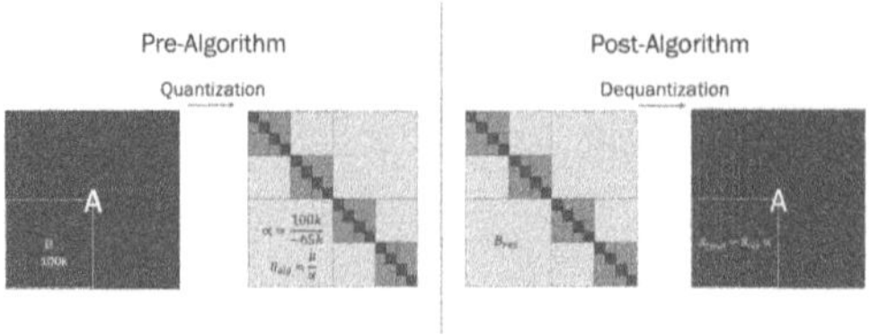

Fig. 3. Blockwise quantization and dequantization workflow.

This layered precision design (Fig. 2) maximizes performance while preserving overall stability. In the context of Cholesky, this assignment is particularly effective because the diagonally dominant matrices we target have the most numerically sensitive operations near the diagonal.

Our method is based on a custom recursive data structure implemented in Julia, which represents a symmetric matrix A as a tree of submatrices. In terms of memory usage, this algorithm requires no additional memory during computation. The hierarchical data structure relies entirely on matrix views to partition the data, and the recursive solver updates these blocks strictly in-place.

3.4 Layered Quantization and Dequantization Strategy

To mitigate FP16's limited dynamic range and avoid numerical overflow, we introduce a lightweight, per-block quantization and dequantization step at each level of the recursive tree. Prior to each low-precision GEMM operation, matrix blocks are rescaled into a dynamic range appropriate for FP16 execution, and then scaled back after the operation completes. Figure 3 illustrates this process.

Let A be the symmetric positive definite matrix to factorize, and B an associated data block (e.g., right-hand side or update block) with large dynamic range. To prevent overflow when operating in low precision, we explicitly manage the dynamic range relative to $R_{\max}$, the maximum representable finite value of the target format We compute a scaling factor α as $\alpha = \max\left(1, \frac{\|B\|_\infty}{R_{\max}}\right)$.

Prior to the algorithm, if the values in B exceed the range (i.e., $\frac{\|B\|_\infty}{R_{\max}} > 1$), this scaling compresses B_{alg} into the safe range $[-R_{\max}, R_{\max}]$. If the values are already within range, α remains 1, and B_{alg} preserves the original scale. Upon algorithm completion on B_{alg}, we obtain an intermediate result B_{res}, which is dequantized: $B_{\text{final}} = B_{\text{res}} \cdot \alpha$. This quantization–dequantization process is embedded at each level of the recursive solver and is applied only to off-diagonal blocks. Combined with our tree-structured precision layering, this enables high throughput on MXUs while preserving numerical stability. In practice, the quantization and dequantization of blocks take up negligible computation time.

4 Results

4.1 Hardware and Software Specifications

We evaluated our implementation on two high-end GPU platforms: the NVIDIA H200 and the AMD MI300X. In the current work, we focus on single-GPU evaluation only. The NVIDIA H200 features 141 GB of HBM3e memory and 4.8 TB/s of memory bandwidth. The AMD MI300X provides 192 GB of HBM3 memory with 5.3 TB/s of peak bandwidth, 304 compute units, and 256 MB of L3 cache. All benchmarks were conducted using Julia 1.12.0, with GPU support enabled via CUDA.jl (v5.9.5), AMDGPU.jl (v2.1.4), KernelAbstractions.jl (v0.9.39), and GPUArrays.jl (v11.3.1). Our Julia-based implementation is fully portable across vendors, with performance-critical kernels dispatching to either NVIDIA's cuBLAS/cuSOLVER or AMD's rocBLAS/hipSOLVER backends, depending on the target device.

For our benchmarks, we generated dense, symmetric positive-definite matrices with random uniform entries. To ensure positive definiteness and robust conditioning, we added n to the diagonal elements of the matrix. These well-conditioned synthetic matrices were chosen to evaluate the maximum throughput and baseline stability of our recursive mixed-precision solver. This setup isolates algorithmic performance from data-induced instabilities, while our real-world matrix evaluation (Sect. 4.5) assess practical applicability and limitations.

4.2 Results Analysis on NVIDIA H200

We denote precision configurations as ordered lists from the outermost (largest off-diagonal) to the innermost (diagonal) recursion level. For instance, `[FP16, FP32]` assigns FP16 to the off-diagonal block and FP32 to the diagonal blocks.

SYRK Performance. Figure 4 (left) reports the speedup of our Julia-based nested recursive implementation on the H200, normalized against cuBLAS `SYRK` in FP64. As the matrix size increases, our recursive kernel consistently outperforms cuBLAS across all precision configurations. The FP64 variant already achieves up to a 14× speedup at $n = 65{,}536$, benefiting from increased concurrency and improved reuse of tile-local data. The `Pure F16` configuration exposes the hardware's peak throughput, reaching a 69.5× speedup relative to the FP32 baseline. By selectively exploiting this low-precision performance, mixed-precision layouts such as `[FP16, FP16, FP32]` achieve over 9× acceleration against their respective diagonal precision baseline, while the five-layer configuration `[FP16, FP16, FP16, FP16, FP32]` delivers up to a 12.5× speedup with practical accuracy.

TRSM Performance. Figure 4 (right) shows the speedup of our Julia-based recursive implementation on the H200, normalized to `cuBLAS TRSM` in `FP64`. For smaller matrices, all precision configurations perform similarly to the FP64. As the matrix size increases, our recursive and mixed-precision variants begin to clearly outperform cuBLAS. The `Pure F16` implementation achieves the highest throughput, reaching up to a 5.7× speedup against the FP32 baseline at $n = 65{,}536$. Layered mixed-precision hierarchies such as `[F16, F16, F16, F16, F32]` still provide substantial gains, delivering up to 4.9× acceleration relative to their diagonal precision baseline, offering better numerical robustness than pure FP16.

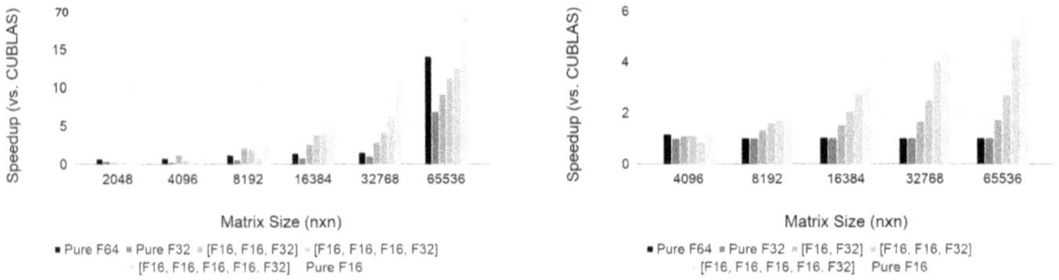

Fig. 4. Speedup of Recursive SYRK (left) and TRSM (right) on H200. Mixed-precision is normalized to diagonal precision baselines; pure FP16 uses the FP32 baseline.

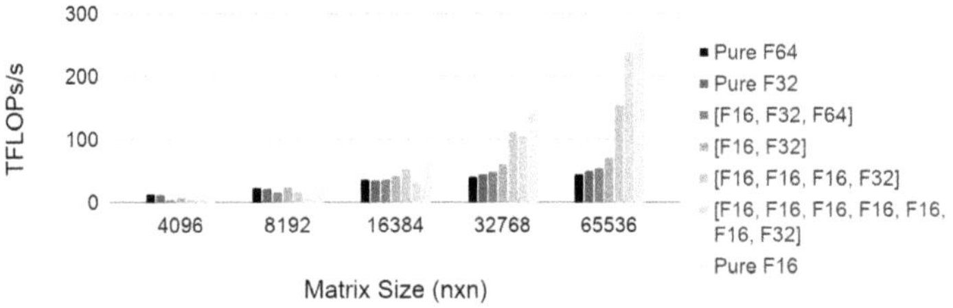

Fig. 5. Cholesky Throughput on NVIDIA H200. Effective TFLOPs across matrix sizes.

Cholesky Throughput. Figure 5 reports the Cholesky throughput on the H200. For large problems (e.g., $n = 65{,}536$), the FP64 and FP32 recursive variants already match or slightly exceed the cuSOLVER FP64 throughput. The triple-precision `[F16, F32, F64]` configuration provides an intermediate boost, reaching roughly 54 TFLOP/s. Meanwhile, the deep mixed-precision configuration `[F16, F16, F16, F16, F16, F32]` reaches more than 5× the FP64 cuSOLVER rate. The `Pure F16` implementation attains the highest raw throughput overall, approaching 6× the FP64 baseline, demonstrating how hierarchical mixed precision can fully exploit the H200's MXUs for Cholesky. At the same matrix size, both cuSOLVER FP64 and our recursive FP64 achieve roughly 65% of the peak FP64 Tensor Core performance, whereas `Pure F16` reaches about 30% of the theoretical FP16 peak. This drop in efficiency at lower precision reflects a shift in the bottleneck: as computation becomes cheaper, the algorithm increasingly becomes limited by memory bandwidth and data movement overhead rather than flops. The large off-diagonal FP16 GEMMs are compute-bound and the POTRF base cases and smaller block updates are memory-bound. In this regime, our deepest mixed-precision configuration `[F16, F16, F16, F16, F16, F16, F16, F32]` sustains about 22% of the FP16 peak, yet remains roughly two orders of magnitude more accurate than `Pure F16`. Together, these results highlight that peak utilization alone is not the right objective: carefully layered mixed precision can trade a modest reduction in hardware efficiency for dramatically improved accuracy while still delivering multi× speedup over the standard high-precision solver.

Cholesky Performance. Our performance evaluation of Cholesky factorization on the H200 GPU (Fig. 6, left) highlights the benefit of precision-aware recursion. Speedups for mixed-precision configurations are normalized against the cuSOLVER baseline corresponding to their diagonal precision. Shallow configurations `[F16, F32]` yield modest speedups against cuSOLVER FP32, and the `[F16, F32, F64]` configuration overcomes initial small-matrix overhead to reach a 1.21× speedup against cuSOLVER FP64. Deeper mixed-precision hierarchies, such as `[F16, F16, F16, F32]` and `[F16, F16, F16, F16, F16, F16, F32]`, show progressively higher gains-reaching up to 3.29× and 5.07× speedups respectively relative to their FP32 diagonal for large matrices ($n = 65{,}536$). Due to the absence of a vendor FP16 solver, the deepest configuration (`Pure F16`) is evaluated against the FP32 baseline, achieving a 5.75× acceleration, highlighting the synergy between low-precision arithmetic and our recursive implementation. These gains stem from the aggressive use of fast `FP16` compute and efficient tiling strategies that exploit the H200's high memory bandwidth and ample L2 cache.

We can break down the execution time of the full FP64 recursive solver at $n = 65{,}536$, which has a runtime of 2,141 ms. The recursive TRSM and SYRK updates account for roughly 788 ms (37%) and 514 ms (24%) of the total runtime, respectively. The remaining 839 ms (39%) is spent in the POTRF base cases and recursive overhead. Because the TRSM and SYRK off-diagonal updates account for over 60% of the execution time, accelerating the performance of these specific routines via low-precision is what drives the speedups observed in large matrices.

Cholesky Accuracy. Figure 6 (right) reports the accuracy of our mixed-precision Cholesky on the H200 GPU. It shows the relative error norm between the Cholesky factor computed using each mixed-precision configuration and the baseline FP64 result, plotted across matrix sizes. Note that we report the factorization error ($||A - LL^T||/||A||$) rather than the residual error of a solved system, as it provides a more conservative measure of numerical stability. As expected, `Pure F64` attains the highest accuracy, with more than 15 correct digits. The configuration `[F32, F32, F32, F64]` remains very close, preserving roughly 12 digits and outperforming `Pure F32`, which yields about 8 digits. Introducing FP16 at the lower levels (`[F16, F32]`) still maintains single-precisionlike accuracy (around 78 digits), while delivering substantial speedups in our performance results. For applications requiring strict reliability, adding a top layer of FP64 (`[F16, F32, F64]`) tightly tracks the `Pure F64` baseline accuracy while still offering performance gains. Deeper hierarchies with more FP16 (`[F16, F16, F16, F32]` and `[F16, F16, F16, F16, F16, F32]`) gradually reduce accuracy to about 56 digits, yet remain more accurate than `Pure F16`, which drops below 4 digits. Overall, this illustrates a clear trade-off: the deepest configuration (`[F16, F16, F16, F16, F16, F16, F32]`) achieves a 5.07× speedup but retains only 56 digits of accuracy, whereas the `[F16, F32, F64]` configuration reaches roughly 9 digits of accuracy but with a more modest 1.21× speedup.

4.3 Results Analysis on AMD MI300X

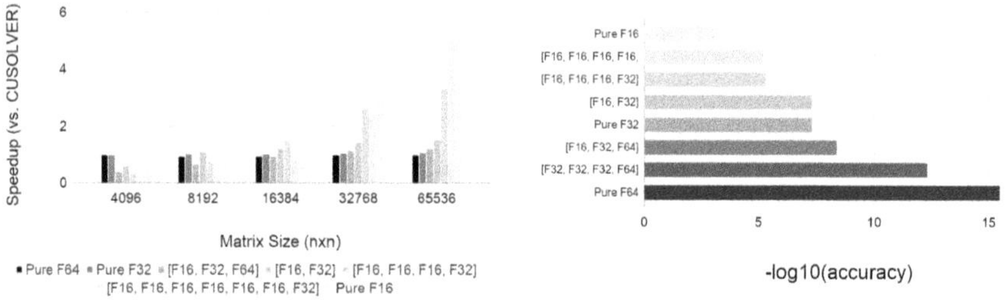

Fig. 6. Cholesky Speedup (left) and Accuracy (right) on H200. Left shows speedup normalized to diagonal precision, while right displays relative error norms ($-\log_{10}$).

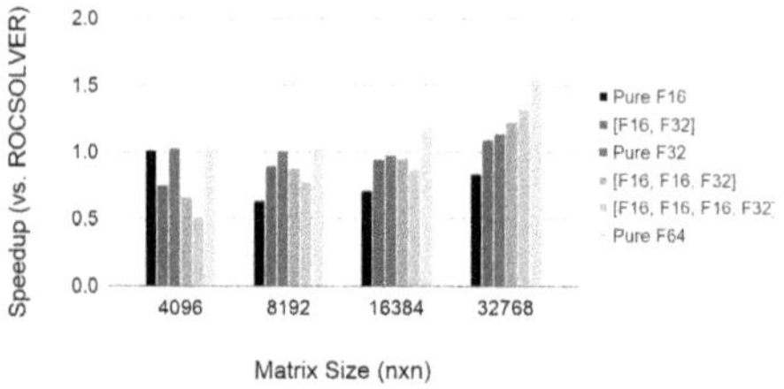

Fig. 7. Cholesky Speedup on AMD MI300X. Speedups are normalized against the `rocSOLVER` baseline corresponding to their diagonal precision.

We evaluate our recursive Cholesky solver on the MI300X. To ensure a fair evaluation, speedups for mixed-precision configurations are normalized against the vendor-optimized `rocSOLVER` baseline corresponding to their diagonal precision. Figure 7 shows the relative speedup across matrix sizes.

Our `Pure F64` recursive solver achieves up to a 1.54× speedup over `rocSOLVER` FP64 at $n = 32{,}768$, benefiting from recursive blocking and improved cache reuse on the MI300X. The `Pure F32` variant yields a 1.14× speedup over `rocSOLVER` FP32. Mixed-precision variants with increasing layering depth provide further gains relative to their diagonal baselines. For instance, the `[F16, F16, F32]` configuration reaches a 1.23× speedup against the FP32 baseline, while our deepest evaluated layout on this architecture, `[F16, F16, F16, F32]`, achieves up to a 1.32× speedup. Due to the absence of a vendor FP16 solver, the `Pure F16` configuration is evaluated against the FP32 baseline, yielding a 0.84× speedup (indicating a performance drop). These results confirm that our recursive, mixed-precision solver outperforms `rocSOLVER` for large matrices, though the overall gains on AMD are more modest than on NVIDIA due to the current lack of mixed-precision matrix multiplication (`GemmEx`) support in Julia AMD.

4.4 Effect of Recursive Depth and Matrix Scale

One of the key advantages of utilizing a nested recursive formulation is the ability to tune the performance and accuracy by changing the number of levels of recursion. The speedup of the best mixed-precision configuration scales linearly with matrix size (Fig. 9), reaching a peak of 5.07× relative to its diagonal precision baseline at n = 65,536. This trend is driven by the fact that larger matrices allow for deeper recursion hierarchies while maintaining leaf block sizes large enough to run efficiently on hardware. At these larger scales, increasing the recursive depth maximizes the proportion of floating-point operations that occur in the off-diagonal blocks, which are computed with FP16 GEMM operations. However, this strategy is less effective on smaller matrices; if the recursion is too deep relative to the matrix size, the blocks become too small, and the overhead of managing many tiny tasks outweighs the computational benefits. The exact point where MXU acceleration overtakes recursive overhead is hardware-dependent: on the H200, mixed-precision configurations become advantageous at $n = 8192$, whereas on the MI300X, the threshold is n = 32,768.

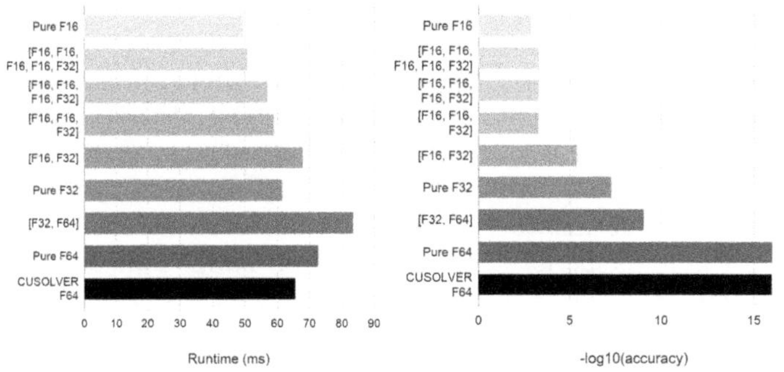

Fig. 8. Runtime (left) and accuracy (right) of mixed-precision on `bodyy5` matrix.

4.5 Results on Real-World Matrices and Limitations

We evaluated our mixed-precision nested recursive Cholesky algorithm on real-world matrices using datasets from the SuiteSparse Matrix Collection, accessed via the Julia `MatrixDepot` package on an NVIDIA GPU. One key matrix we evaluated was `Pothen/bodyy5`, a sparse, symmetric positive-definite matrix derived from NASA structural engineering data ($n = 18{,}589$). As shown in Fig. 8, mixed precision retains high accuracy for moderately conditioned matrices like `bodyy5`. Our blockwise quantization effectively scales the values to prevent immediate overflow. We notice that as the precision increases from FP16 $\rightarrow$ FP32 $\rightarrow$ FP64, the runtime correspondingly increases because higher precision arithmetic requires more computational resources and memory bandwidth. Mixed-precision configurations such as [F16, F32] and [F16, F16, F32] provide an intermediate performance point, achieving substantial speedups compared to pure FP64 while maintaining greater numerical stability than pure FP16.

However, the solver is not well-suited for small matrices or matrices with a large dynamic range. For small matrices ($n < 8192$)(Figure 9)the type conversion overhead outweighs the MXU acceleration benefits, and performance is reduced. Best results are obtained for diagonally dominant matrices. Furthermore, matrices that possess extreme dynamic ranges lose positive definiteness in the process. For example, `Simon/raefsky4` ($n = 19{,}779$) has a dynamic range exceeding 10^{11}: where the quantization process compresses the lower values to zero, destroys the positive definiteness of the sub-blocks, and causes division by zero and `NaN` propagation. Specifically, numerical errors introduced in the off-diagonal blocks can easily lead to a loss of positive definiteness in the Schur complement, even if the subsequent diagonal block is computed in high precision. Therefore, static blockwise quantization is insufficient for these cases, and future work should explore more dynamic quantization schemes.

4.6 Portability and Impact of Hardware

Figure 10 shows the runtime of the fastest mixed-precision scenarios at each data size for the H200 and MI300X GPUs, demonstrating the portability of our implementation: with a single high-level algorithmic implementation, we cover all GPU hardware backends by using multi-dispatch to direct the base case functions to the optimized vendor library implementations. Several factors contribute to the lower performance observed on AMD compared to NVIDIA hardware, including the performance of the optimized base cases and the inclusion of mixed-precision matrix multiplication (`GemmEx`). For this benchmark, we included mixed-precision matrix multiplication for NVIDIA, but not for AMD hardware, due to its unavailability at the time in Julia. Future work into fully hardware-agnostic mixed-precision `GEMM` operations could address this and render the entire algorithm lifecycle hardware-agnostic, potentially unlocking new levels of performance not only on AMD hardware, but also on Apple GPUs.

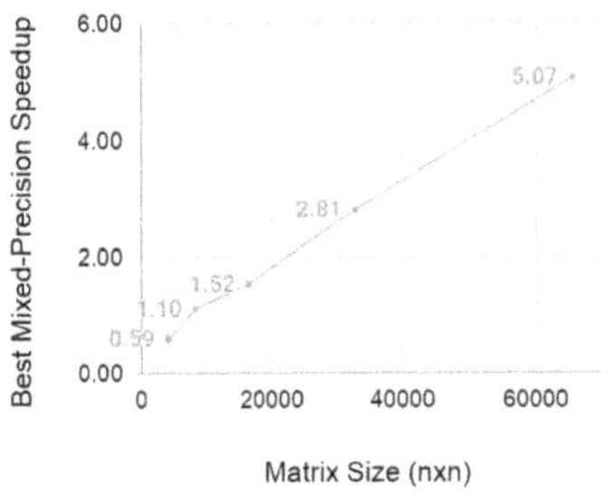

Fig. 9. Speedup Scaling with Matrix Size on NVIDIA hardware. Performance gains improve as size grows, allowing deeper recursion.

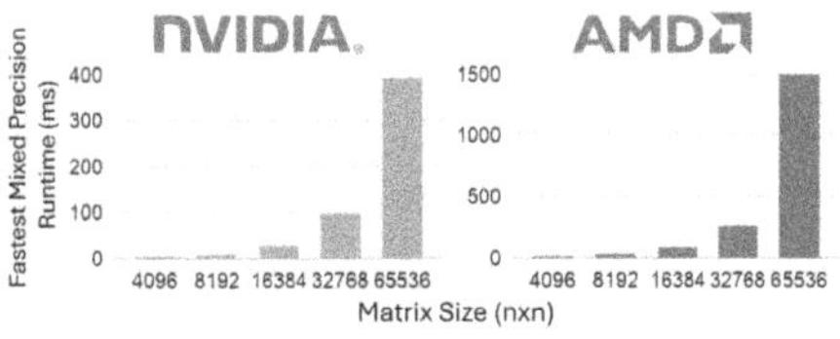

Fig. 10. Cross-Platform Portability. Best mixed-precision runtime (ms) on NVIDIA H200 and AMD MI300X.

5 Conclusion and Future Work

We presented a portable, mixed-precision solver for symmetric linear systems based on a nested recursive Cholesky decomposition. By uniformly applying recursion across the POTRF, TRSM, and SYRK phases—including the first recursive GPU implementation of SYRK—this formulation exposes a rich hierarchy of GEMM operations that maps efficiently onto MXUs. Our Julia implementation realizes over a 5× speedup relative to diagonal-precision baselines on the H200 and exhibits consistent improvements on the MI300X, though currently constrained by Julia's AMD `GemmEx` support.

The strategy proposed in this work is best suited for matrices that are diagonally dominant, with limited dynamic range, and are sufficiently large (e.g., $n \geq 8192$), where the computational gains of reduced-precision arithmetic outweigh the recursive overhead. Future work will explore dynamic quantization schemes and extend this strategy to broader classes of problems, such as block-sparse, banded systems, and $\mathrm{LDL}^{\top}$ factorizations.

Acknowledgments. We thank the members of the Julia Lab. R.A. acknowledges the KAUST Ibn Rushd post-doctoral fellowship. The authors acknowledge the MIT ORCD, TACC at UT Austin (TG-CIS250776, allocation CIS250776 through ACCESS, supported by U.S. NSF 2138259, 2138286, 2138307, 2137603, and 2138296), and the AMD University Program. This material is based upon work supported by the US NSF (CNS-2346520, RISE-2425761, DMS-2325184, OAC-2103804, OSI-2029670), DARPA (HR00112490488), USAFR (FA8750-19-2-1000), and DoE NNSA (DE-NA0004266). The U.S. Government, its agencies and employees do not make any warranty, do not assume any liability or responsibility, do not make any endorsement for anything in this report, and do not represent that its use would not infringe privately owned rights. The views and opinions of authors expressed herein are those of the authors alone.

Disclosure of Interests. The authors have no competing interests to declare that are relevant to the content of this article.

References

1. Alomairy, R.: Dynamic task scheduling with data dependency awareness using Julia. In: Proceedings of HPEC, pp. 1–7 (2024)
2. Alomairy, R.: Scalable Hamming distance computation using accelerated matrix transformations. In: Proceedings of ISC High Perform, pp. 1–13 (2025)
3. Alomairy, R.: Sustainably modeling a sustainable future climate. In: Proceedings of HPEC, pp. 1–8 (2025)
4. Alomairy, R.M.: High-performance scientific applications using mixed precision and low-rank approximation powered by task-based runtime systems. Ph.D. thesis, KAUST (2022)
5. Amestoy, P.R., et al.: Mixed precision low-rank approximations and their application to block low-rank LU factorization. IMA J. Numer. Anal. (2023)
6. Andersen, B.S., et al.: A recursive formulation of Cholesky factorization of a matrix in packed storage. ACM Trans. Math. Softw. **27**(2), 214–244 (2001)
7. Anderson, E.: LAPACK Users' Guide. SIAM (1999)
8. Baboulin, M., et al.: Accelerating scientific computations with mixed precision algorithms. Comput. Phys. Commun. **180**(12), 2526–2533 (2009)
9. Ballard, G.: Communication-optimal parallel and sequential Cholesky decomposition. In: Proceedings of SPAA '09, pp. 245–252 (2009)
10. Bezanson, J., et al.: Julia: A fresh approach to numerical computing. SIAM Rev. **59**(1), 65–98 (2017)
11. Bosilca, G., Ltaief, H., Dongarra, J.: Power profiling of Cholesky and QR factorizations on distributed memory systems. Comput. Sci. Res. Dev. **29**(2) (2014)
12. Buttari, A., et al.: Mixed precision iterative refinement techniques for the solution of dense linear systems. Int. J. High Perform. Comput. Appl. **21**(4), 457–466 (2007)
13. Carrica, V.: Accelerating linear solve with mixed precision nested recursive subdivision on AI hardware (2025). sC25 Poster
14. Carrica, V.: Toward portable GPU performance: Julia recursive implementation of TRMM and TRSM. arXiv preprint arXiv:2504.13821 (2025)
15. Carson, E., Higham, N.J.: A new analysis of iterative refinement and its application to accurate solution of ill-conditioned sparse linear systems. SIAM J. Sci. Comput. **39**(6), A2834–A2856 (2017)
16. Carson, E., Higham, N.J.: Accelerating the solution of linear systems by iterative refinement in three precisions. SIAM J. Sci. Comput. **40**(2), A817–A847 (2018)
17. Charara, A., Keyes, D., Ltaief, H.: A framework for dense triangular matrix kernels on various manycore architectures. Concurrency Computat. Pract. Exper. **29**(15), e4187 (2017)
18. Charara, A., Keyes, D., Ltaief, H.: Batched triangular dense linear algebra kernels for very small matrix sizes on GPUs. ACM Trans. Math. Softw. (2019)
19. Chen, C., Martinsson, P.G.: Solving linear systems on a GPU with hierarchically off-diagonal low-rank approximations. In: Proceedings of SC22, pp. 1–15 (2022)
20. Eliahu, D., et al.: Frpa: A framework for recursive parallel algorithms. Tech. rep. EECS, UC Berkeley (2015)
21. Faverge, M., et al.: Programming heterogeneous architectures using hierarchical tasks. Concurrency Computat. Pract. Exper. **35**(25), e7811 (2023)
22. Furmento, N., et al.: Optimizing parallel heterogeneous system efficiency: Dynamic task graph adaptation with recursive tasks. J. Parallel Distrib. Comput. **205**, 105157 (2025)

23. Gardner, J.: GPyTorch: Blackbox matrix-matrix Gaussian process inference with GPU acceleration. NeurIPS **31** (2018)
24. Giordano, M.: Productivity meets performance: Julia on A64FX. In: Proceedings of IEEE CLUSTER, pp. 549–555 (2022)
25. Grasedyck, L., Kriemann, R., Le Borne, S.: Domain decomposition based H-LU preconditioning. Numer. Math. **112**(4), 565–600 (2009)
26. Haidar, A.: Harnessing GPU tensor cores for fast FP16 arithmetic to speed up mixed-precision iterative refinement solvers. In: Proceedings of SC18, pp. 603–613 (2018)
27. Higham, N.J., Mary, T.: Mixed precision algorithms in numerical linear algebra. Acta Numer. **31**, 347–414 (2022)
28. Lang, J.: A comprehensive study on quantization techniques for large language models. In: Proceedings of ICAIRC, pp. 224–231 (2024)
29. Ltaief, H.: Toward capturing genetic epistasis from multivariate genome-wide association studies using mixed-precision kernel ridge regression. In: Proceedings of SC24, pp. 1–12 (2024)
30. Piscaglia, F., Ghioldi, F.: GPU acceleration of CFD simulations in OpenFOAM. Aerospace **10**(9), 792 (2023)
31. Ren, J.: Accelerating mixed-precision out-of-core cholesky factorization with static task scheduling. In: Proceedings of ISC High Performance, pp. 1–12 (2025)
32. Ringoot, E.: A GPU-resident memory-aware algorithm for accelerating bidiagonalization of banded matrices. arXiv preprint arXiv:2510.12705 (2025)
33. Zhang, Q.: Leveraging hardware-aware computation in mixed-precision matrix multiply: A tile-centric approach. In: Proceedings of WAMTA, pp. 174–185 (2025)

Thunder: Efficient Multi-node FHE Acceleration Framework via In-Transit Computation

Kai Li[1,2], Lutan Zhao[1,2(✉)], Qingyun Niu[1,2], Yinhang Zheng[1,2], Zhengbang Yang[1,2], Boyan Zhao[1], Lu Gao[1,2], and Rui Hou[1,2]

[1] State Key Laboratory of Cyberspace Security Defense, Institute of Information Engineering, CAS, Beijing, China
{likai,zhaolutan,niuqingyun,zhengyinhang,yangzhengbang,zhaoboyan,gaolu,hourui}@iie.ac.cn

[2] School of Cyber Security, University of Chinese Academy of Sciences, Beijing, China

Abstract. Despite its ability to compute directly on encrypted data, Fully Homomorphic Encryption (FHE) is severely hindered by computational overhead. Leveraging multi-node hardware accelerators with fine-grained parallelism can alleviate this bottleneck, but introduces significant communication overhead. In this paper, we propose Thunder, an efficient multi-node FHE acceleration framework that reduces communication overhead through in-transit computation, thereby improving FHE performance. At the algorithm level, we propose a streaming Base Conversion (BConv) algorithm. It eliminates global data dependencies in BConv computation, thereby hiding communication latency. At the architecture level, we migrate BConv computation units from the compute nodes to the fabric, the communication hub of the multi-node hardware accelerators. This migration eliminates global data synchronization and reduces inter-node data traffic. Together, the algorithm-architecture co-design reduces communication overhead by up to 92.7%. Thunder is implemented on both FPGA and ASIC platforms. Compared to single-node FPGA accelerators, FPGA-based Thunder achieves up to 10.05× speedup; against state-of-the-art multi-node accelerators, Thunder delivers 2.09× (FPGA) and 1.33×–2.92× (ASIC) performance improvements.

Keywords: Fully Homomorphic Encryption · Parallelism · Accelerators

1 Introduction

Fully Homomorphic Encryption (FHE) enables direct computation on encrypted data, ensuring data confidentiality throughout the computational process. However, the significant computational overhead of FHE limits its widespread adoption. To address this, prior works propose single-node accelerators based on

M. Torquati et al. (Eds.): Euro-Par 2026, LNCS 16781, pp. 466–480, 2027.
https://doi.org/10.1007/978-3-032-35248-4_32

FPGA [2,24,25], ASIC [10,13–16,20,21], and GPU [9,23,27] platforms to accelerate FHE. Yet, single-node accelerators still fall short of the performance demanded by practical FHE deployment, and scaling them further is hindered by memory bandwidth and chip area constraints. As a result, multi-node accelerators [1,2,12,26] emerge as a promising solution to achieve substantial performance gains.

Multi-node FHE accelerators support two parallel modes: coarse-grained ciphertext-wise parallelism and fine-grained limb-wise parallelism. In the ciphertext-wise mode, the number of parallelizable ciphertexts is limited. This is because bootstrapping, the performance bottleneck of FHE, is inherently sequential [1]. Moreover, message packing strategies [8,17,19] further limit the number of ciphertexts available for parallel execution. Consequently, these limitations restrict the overall performance improvement to 1.27×-1.77×. In contrast, in the limb-wise mode, a single ciphertext is decomposed into multiple data-independent limbs. These limbs are distributed across multiple nodes to execute bootstrapping in parallel, thereby achieving a significantly higher speedup.

However, in limb-wise mode, classical multi-node architectures [2,12] introduce substantial communication overhead, which becomes a new performance bottleneck. This overhead mainly stems from the key computation pattern in bootstrapping, $INTT \rightarrow BConv \rightarrow NTT$, as shown in Fig. 1(a). In these architectures, each node is equipped with dedicated functional units, where the NTTU and BConvU handle INTT/NTT and BConv computations, respectively. Since BConv depends on the INTT results of all limbs, each BConvU must wait for global data synchronization to aggregate all INTT results before proceeding, as illustrated in Fig. 1(b). This generates significant cross-node communication overhead, which offsets the performance gains enabled by limb-wise parallelism. Therefore, reducing communication overhead in the limb-wise mode is the key to further improving FHE performance on multi-node accelerators.

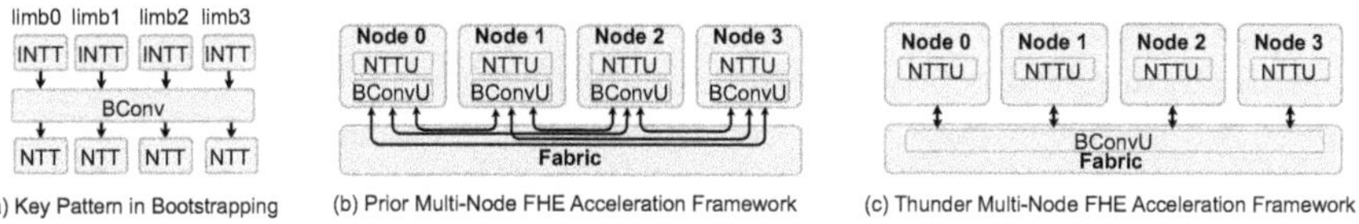

Fig. 1. (a) The $INTT \rightarrow BConv \rightarrow NTT$ computation pattern in limb-wise mode: BConv has a global data dependency on all limbs. (b) Prior accelerators require global data synchronization before BConv computation. (c) Thunder migrates BConvU into the fabric, eliminating global data synchronization.

In this paper, we propose Thunder, an efficient multi-node FHE acceleration framework that leverages in-transit computation to significantly reduce inter-node communication overhead. The key idea leverages algorithm-architecture co-design to offload the BConv operation to the fabric, the communication hub of the multi-node accelerator. This eliminates global data synchronization across nodes and reduces communication traffic, as shown in Fig. 1(c). As a result, Thunder reduces the overall communication overhead by up to 92.7%. Specifically, our contributions are summarized as follows:

- At the algorithm level, we propose a streaming BConv algorithm. It decouples the global limb dependency in the classical BConv algorithm into partial data dependencies. Specifically, BConv computation is decomposed into sub-operations, each of which depends only on the data currently received from the network. This hides communication latency within the BConv computation. As a result, the BConv units can process already-received limbs while simultaneously receiving the remaining ones.
- At the architecture level, we propose migrating BConvU from compute nodes to the fabric, eliminating global data synchronization across nodes and reducing inter-node data traffic. We design a streaming BConv tile, a dedicated computation unit for the locally dependent sub-operations proposed at the algorithm level. The BConv tile is mapped onto the fabric in the form of a weight-stationary systolic array. In this design, the INTT/NTT operators in the $INTT \rightarrow BConv \rightarrow NTT$ pattern are computed on each node. Each node only needs to send its INTT results to the fabric for centralized BConv computation.
- We develop an FPGA prototype (FPGA-Thunder) using Xilinx FPGAs and build an ASIC simulator (ASIC-Thunder). Under the same 8-node configuration, FPGA-Thunder achieves 2.09× speedup over FAB-2, the state-of-the-art multi-node FPGA accelerator using coarse-grained parallelism. With 64 nodes, FPGA-Thunder achieves 10.05× speedup over the single-node FPGA accelerator FAB. ASIC-Thunder achieves 1.33×–2.92× speedup over Cinnamon, the state-of-the-art multi-node ASIC accelerator.

2 Background and Motivation

Our target FHE scheme is CKKS [7], which supports approximate arithmetic and is widely adopted in privacy-preserving applications. Multi-node accelerators employ two parallel modes to accelerate CKKS: (1) Ciphertext-wise parallelism is a coarse-grained mode that processes multiple ciphertexts in parallel. (2) Limb-wise parallelism is a fine-grained mode that decomposes a single ciphertext into multiple limbs for parallel computation, supporting up to 35 limbs in this work.

The choice between these two parallel modes is determined by the characteristics of bootstrapping, which dominates FHE computation (56.3% in HELR [19], 78.6% in ResNet-20 [17]). However, it is inherently sequential at the ciphertext level [1], limiting ciphertext-wise parallelism to only 1.27×–1.77× speedup. Therefore, this paper focuses on limb-wise parallelism. We analyze HELR [19], ResNet-20 [17], and LSTM [18] using Cinnamon [12]'s architecture (configurations in Sect. 7) and make the following observations:

Observation 1: The global data synchronization overhead of BConv scales with the number of nodes, becoming the core bottleneck limiting the scalability of multi-node architectures. This overhead stems from

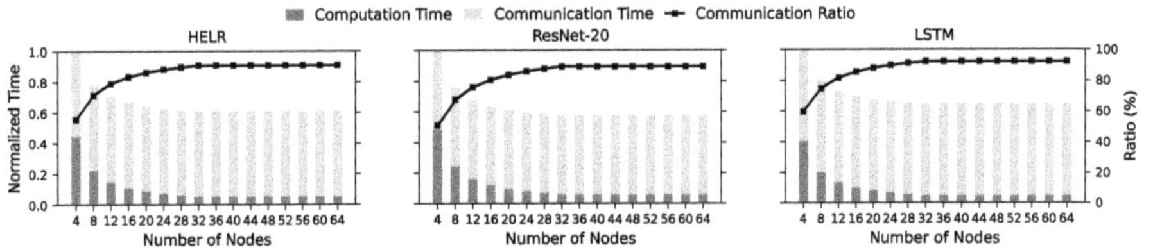

Fig. 2. Normalized execution time (computation and communication) of HELR, ResNet-20, and LSTM across different node configurations, normalized to 4 nodes and the communication overhead ratio.

the core computation pattern in bootstrapping, $INTT \rightarrow BConv \rightarrow NTT$, which accounts for over 80% of the total bootstrapping execution time [13]. Since the BConv algorithm depends on the INTT results of all limbs, each node must complete global data synchronization before BConv computation. As the number of nodes increases, the per-node computation overhead is continuously amortized. However, the cross-node data traffic introduced by global data synchronization does not decrease accordingly. This causes communication overhead to gradually dominate the overall execution time. As shown in Fig. 2, as nodes scale from 4 to 64, the communication overhead ratio increases from around 50% to over 90%, limiting overall speedup to 1.54×–1.74×.

Observation 2: Global data dependency prevents computation-communication overlap, making it difficult to hide communication overhead. The BConv algorithm switches the RNS moduli of limbs in a ciphertext (e.g., from $Q = \{q_i\}, 0 \leq i < L$ to $P = \{p_j\}, 0 \leq j < K$). It consists of two steps, as shown in Equations (1) and (2). The root of BConv's global data dependency lies in Equation (2): each output limb $[C]_{p_j}$ depends on all limbs $[C']_{q_i} (0 \leq i < L)$ in the ciphertext $[C']_Q$. In multi-node accelerators, each node handles the INTT computation of different limbs. Therefore, BConv must stall until all nodes complete their INTT computation and exchange data globally. This synchronization barrier forces communication and computation to execute sequentially rather than overlapping in parallel.

$$[C']_{q_i} = [C]_{q_i} \cdot \hat{q_i}^{-1} \bmod q_i, 0 \leq i < L \tag{1}$$

$$[C]_{p_j} = \sum_{i=0}^{L-1} [C']_{q_i} \cdot \hat{q_i} \bmod p_j, 0 \leq j < K \tag{2}$$

Observation 3: Network congestion caused by global data synchronization limits the benefit of increasing communication bandwidth. During global data synchronization, multiple nodes send data to the same destination simultaneously, as shown in Fig. 1(b). This triggers resource contention on the receiving port, leading to network congestion. Our analysis reveals that in classical multi-node architectures, congestion dominates the overall communication overhead, as shown in Fig. 3. Increasing bandwidth only reduces the non-congestion portion of communication overhead. It does not resolve the congestion caused by global data synchronization. Therefore, even doubling the bandwidth reduces communication overhead by only 13.0%-17.7%.

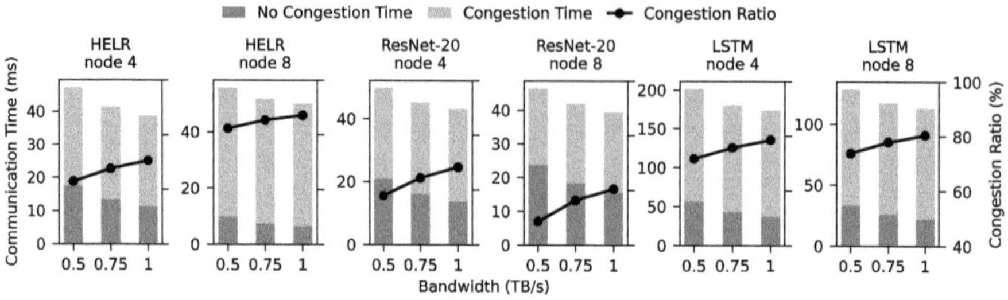

Fig. 3. Impact of increased bandwidth on communication overhead reduction under different node configurations.

Motivations. Based on the above three observations, eliminating BConv's global data dependency and global data synchronization is the key to reducing communication overhead and improving the performance of multi-node FHE accelerators. The in-transit computation mechanism is a natural fit for this goal: by executing computation concurrently as data transfers to the fabric, it hides communication latency and eliminates global data synchronization among multiple nodes.

Therefore, we propose an algorithm-architecture co-design to realize in-transit computation. At the algorithm level, we decompose BConv into sub-operations each depending only on data received in a single transmission, allowing BConv to compute concurrently with data transmission (Sect. 4). At the architecture level, we migrate BConv computation to the fabric as a systolic array, eliminating global data synchronization and avoiding network congestion (Sect. 5). This co-design enables BConv to execute in a streaming manner during data transmission to the fabric, requiring no global data synchronization. It hides communication latency and reduces overall data traffic, significantly improving FHE performance on multi-node accelerators.

3 Design Overview

We propose Thunder, a multi-node FHE acceleration framework that supports in-transit computation. The framework consists of multiple compute nodes and a fabric equipped with BConv computation capability. Figure 4(a) shows an example of Thunder with four nodes.

The compute node design is compatible with existing accelerator architectures [2,13,14,21], consisting of computation units for NTT, automorphism, modular multiplication, and modular addition, along with HBM off-chip memory

Algorithm 1. Streaming Base Conversion

Require: $[C]_Q = \{[C]_{q_i}\}$, $Q^{-1} = \{q_i^{-1}\}$, precomputed base table $B = \hat{q}_i \bmod p_j$, $0 \leq i < L$, $0 \leq j < K$
Ensure: $[C]_P = \{[C]_{p_j}\}$, $0 \leq j < K$

$b \leftarrow$ hardware transfer granularity per node per cycle
$c \leftarrow$ number of nodes in limb-wise parallelism
// *Step 1: Element-wise scaling;*
for all $n \in [0, N)_b$, $l \in [0, L)_c$ **do**
    $[C']_Q[l : l{+}c,\ n : n{+}b] \leftarrow \text{ModMult}([C]_{q_l}[n : n{+}b],\ Q^{-1}[l : l{+}c])$
end for
// *Step 2: Decomposed matrix multiplication;*
for all $k \in [0, K)$, $b_1 \in [0, b)$ **do**
    for all $n \in [0, N)_b$, $l \in [0, L)_c$ **do**
        $[C]_P[k,\ n{+}b_1] \mathrel{+}= \text{InnerProduct}(B[k][l : l{+}c],\ [C']_Q[l : l{+}c,\ n{+}b_1])$
    end for
    $[C]_P[k,\ n{+}b_1] \leftarrow \text{HybridMod}([C]_P[k,\ n{+}b_1],\ p_k)$
end for

and on-chip register files. To support interaction with the fabric, each compute node is augmented with a synchronization module (sync) and a communication module (network PHY). Each compute node sends its INTT results directly to the fabric via the network PHY. The fabric consists of a switch, a network PHY, and a BConv unit. The BConv unit is tightly coupled with the switch, forwarding incoming data directly for computation without broadcasting or waiting.

4 Streaming BConv Algorithm

To eliminate the global data dependency, we decompose the BConv algorithm into sub-limb-level sub-operations. In CKKS, each limb is treated as a vector of N coefficients. Equation (2) in the BConv algorithm is essentially a matrix multiplication between a $K \times L$ constant basis table B (with elements $\hat{q}_i \bmod p_j$) and an $L \times N$ matrix $[C^{'}]_Q$. We exploit the decomposability of matrix multiplication to divide BConv into independent sub-operations. Since each sub-operation targets only a subset of limbs, it completely eliminates the global data dependency.

Specifically, we achieve this by partitioning the matrix multiplication according to the network transmission granularity. Suppose the multi-node accelerator contains c compute nodes. Each node transmits b coefficients to the fabric per transfer. In each transmission cycle, the fabric simultaneously receives data from all c nodes, forming a $c \times b$ sub-data matrix. Based on this transmission pattern, the original $K \times L$ and $L \times N$ matrix multiplication is partitioned into $\lceil \frac{L}{c} \rceil \cdot \lceil \frac{N}{b} \rceil$ smaller $K \times c$ and $c \times b$ matrix multiplications. This allows BConv to start computation immediately upon receiving the first $c \times b$ data block in the fabric, while continuing to receive subsequent data. Algorithm 1 presents the optimized streaming BConv algorithm.

5 Microarchitecture of Streaming BConv Unit in Fabric

The BConv Unit is designed to support in-transit computation. It consists of four modules: computation, modular reduction, and scheduling and synchronization, as shown in Fig. 4(b). The BConv unit computation module consists of two submodules: ModMults and BConv tile systolic array. They are responsible for step 1 and step 2 of the BConv algorithm in Algorithm 1, respectively.

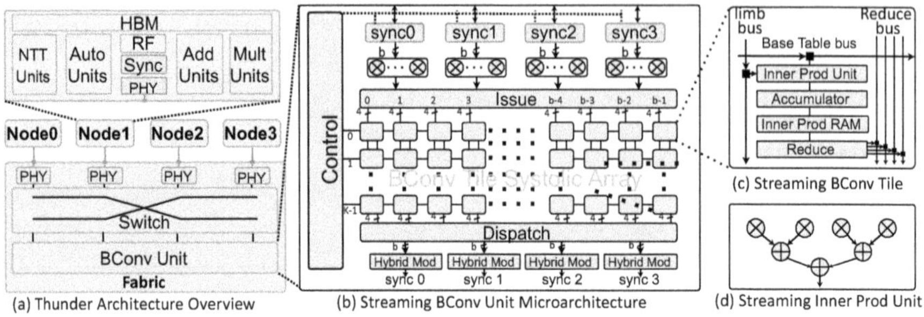

Fig. 4. (a) Illustration of Thunder multi-node architecture. (b) Streaming *BConv Unit* microarchitecture featuring a systolic *BConv Tile* array. (c) *BConv Tile* Microarchitecture. (d) *Inner Prod Unit* with tree-based structure.

ModMults. The BConv unit deploys c groups of streaming modular multipliers. Each group contains b modular multipliers. They specifically process the limb data $[C]_{q_i}$ sent by specific compute nodes. The parameter $\hat{q_i}^{-1}$ is preconfigured before computation. This allows each ModMult group to start computation immediately upon receiving $[C]_{q_i}$, overlapping with data transmission.

BConv Tile Systolic Array. We organize these *BConv tiles* as a weight-stationary systolic array. Before computation, the base table B is preloaded into each *BConv Tile*. Consequently, computations trigger immediately upon receiving the limb data $[C']_{q_i}$. The j-th row of *BConv tiles* computes the limb $[C]_{p_j}$. It stores both the intermediate and final results. Different *BConv tiles* in the same row compute and store different coefficients of the limb $[C]_{p_j}$.

BConv Tile Microarchitecture. As shown in Fig. 4(c), each *BConv tile* consists of an *Inner Prod Unit*, an *Accumulator*, an *Inner Prod RAM*, and a *Reduce* module. The *Inner Prod Unit* executes a length-c inner product. Figure 4(d) illustrates its microarchitecture. The *Accumulator* adds the new inner product result to the accumulated value in the *Inner Prod RAM* and writes it back. After computation, the *Reduce* module outputs the result to the *Reduce Bus.*

BConv Tile Streaming Execution. Before BConv computation, the *Base Table Bus* distributes the base table B to all *BConv tiles.* The *Issue* module then broadcasts the incoming limbs $[C']_{q_i}$ to all *BConv tiles* via the *limb bus.* Upon receiving $[C']_{q_i}$, each *BConv tile* immediately executes the inner product between the base table B and $[C']_{q_i}$. It accumulates the result and saves it to the *Inner Prod RAM.* After $\lceil \frac{L}{c} \rceil \cdot \lceil \frac{N}{b} \rceil$ accumulations, the *Reduce Bus* transmits the final results to the *Dispatch* module and routes them back to the corresponding nodes.

The read-add-write addresses increment circularly, ensuring adjacent operations never conflict and avoiding RAW hazards for continuous streaming execution.

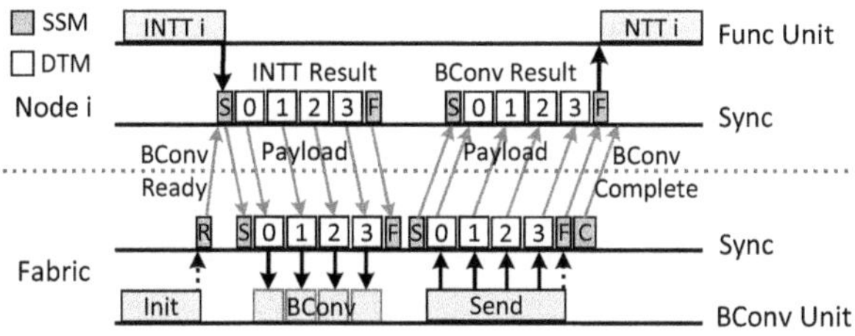

Fig. 5. Workflow of $INTT \rightarrow BConv \rightarrow NTT$ computation collaboratively performed by node and fabric using message-passing synchronization. status synchronization messages(SSM) and data transfer messages(DTM).

5.1 Modular Reduction Optimization

To reduce the resource overhead of the BConv Unit, Thunder adopts two optimizations: lazy reduction and hybrid mod.

Lazy Reduction. Deploying modular reduction inside each BConv Tile introduces significant logic resource overhead. Therefore, Thunder adopts a lazy reduction strategy: each BConv Tile only computes and stores the raw inner product results. Modular reduction is moved out of the BConv Tiles and deferred until the data returns to the compute nodes, where multiple BConv Tiles share a common modular reduction unit. Compared to performing modular reduction inside each BConv Tile, this strategy reduces the logic resource and register overhead of the BConv Unit by 49.8% and 50.9%, respectively.

Hybrid Mod. Lazy reduction reduces resource overhead but introduces a new problem. Without intermediate modular reduction, inner product results are accumulated directly, causing the values to exceed the square of the modulus, the input range of the Barrett algorithm. The classical shift-and-subtract method can compress values into the valid range, but consumes significant logic and register resources. To address this, we propose hybrid mod, which efficiently performs pre-reduction via multiplication. We split the input x into a low l-bit part x_l and a high h-bit part x_h, where $l + h = |x|$. Thus, $x \bmod q = (x_h \cdot (2^l \bmod q) + x_l) \bmod q$. We set $\frac{q_{\min}^2}{4} \leq x_l < \frac{q_{\min}^2}{2}$ and $x_h < \frac{q}{2}$. We precompute the constant $C = 2^l \bmod q$. Under these conditions, $x_h \cdot C < \frac{q^2}{2}$. In hardware, we only add one multiplier and one adder to compute $x_h \cdot C + x_l$. This result is strictly less than q^2, satisfying the input requirement of the Barrett algorithm. Evaluation on our FPGA prototype shows that compared to the shift-and-subtract method, Hybrid Mod reduces the logic resource and register overhead of modular reduction by 71.2% and 58.2%, respectively.

5.2 Scheduling and Synchronization

To ensure strict execution ordering between the compute nodes and the fabric, Thunder introduces a scheduling module *control* and a synchronization module *sync* in the fabric. They coordinate the execution of nodes and the fabric via a message-passing mechanism.

The instruction-driven *control* module orchestrates the BConv Unit, issuing an initialization instruction to configure B and $\hat{q_i}^{-1}$ before computation. During computation, it interconnects with all *sync* modules to track the data transmission progress of each node and the computation status of the BConv unit.

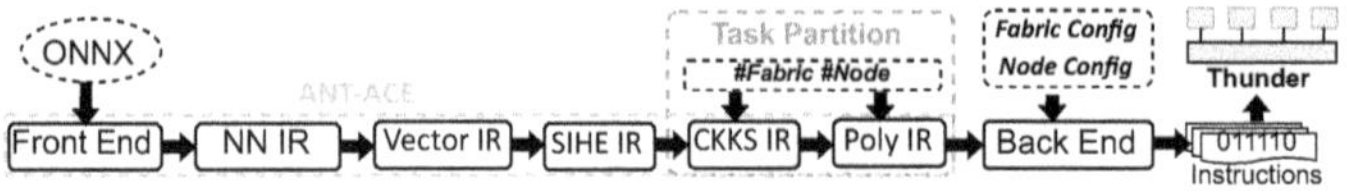

Fig. 6. The workflow of mapping applications to Thunder.

The *sync* module is responsible for state synchronization and data transfer between the nodes and the Fabric. Each *sync* module incorporates message queues to manage message exchange. Messages are categorized into status synchronization messages (SSM) for exchanging computation and transfer status, and data transfer messages (DTM) for transmitting INTT results and BConv outputs. Figure 5 illustrates the coordinated execution flow of the $INTT \rightarrow BConv \rightarrow NTT$ pattern using this message-passing mechanism.

6 Instruction Set Architecture and Software Support

To support in-transit computation, we introduce new instructions and corresponding software support. We extend the FHE instruction set with two types of instructions: First, **communication instructions** (*send*, *receive*, *broadcast*) enable data transfer and synchronization between nodes and the fabric. The *control* module decodes these instructions and coordinates their execution through the *sync* modules via the message-passing mechanism. Second, **BConv-related instructions** handle parameter initialization and computation: the fabric first configures parameters via *initialization* and synchronizes them across all nodes, and upon receiving each node's INTT results, it initiates *BConv* computation.

We build upon the open-source FHE compiler ANT-ACE [5] for task mapping. As shown in Fig 6, tasks are partitioned at the CKKS IR and Poly IR levels according to Thunder's configuration. A dedicated backend allocates resources and generates instruction sequences for direct execution on Thunder.

7 Implementation and Evaluation

We implement Thunder at the RTL level and evaluate Thunder on both FPGA and ASIC platforms.

FPGA-Thunder. We prototype Thunder on AMD Xilinx FPGAs, mapping nodes to Alveo U280 and fabrics to HTG-930-13P, deployed on dual Intel Xeon 8592 hosts. Synthesis and implementation are performed using Vivado 2022.2, with post place-and-route results summarized in Fig. 7. FPGA-Thunder consists of eight nodes and two fabrics. Each node integrates 256 parallel functional units at 300 MHz, and each fabric integrates 8×35 BConv tiles at 400 MHz. Each node is connected to two fabrics via dual 100 Gbps QSFP28 links. At 400 MHz, each 100 Gbps QSFP28 port transfers 8 36-bit words per cycle.

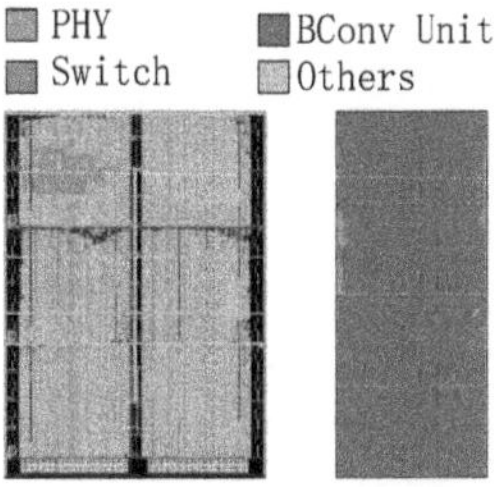

Node layout on U280 Fabric layout on 13P

Node (U280)	LUT	FF	BRAM	URAM	DSP
PHY	1.6K	6.5K	12	0	0
Others	868.4K	641.5K	636	640	4225
Total	66.80%	24.88%	31.55%	66.67%	46.82%

Fabric(13P)	LUT	FF	BRAM	URAM	DSP
BConvUnit	1007K	2194K	1224	560	9216
Switch	0.8K	35	0	0	0
PHY	10.7K	50.5K	96	0	0
Others	31.5K	37.5K	67	0	0
Total	60.81%	66.05%	51.60%	43.75%	75.00%

Resource utilization on U280 and HTG-930-13P

Fig. 7. Implementation result of FPGA-Thunder.

ASIC-Thunder comprises 12 nodes (1024-way parallelism, 1 GHz) interconnected by four fabrics, same as SOTA multi-node accelerator Cinnamon [12]. Each node is equipped with four 256GB/s Network PHYs, individually connected to the four fabrics. Each fabric integrates 92×35 *BConv Tiles*. At 1 GHz, each 256 GB/s Network PHY transfers 92 36-bit words per cycle. Using the TSMC 7 nm PDK, the *BConv Unit* area and power are estimated as 22.6 mm^2 and 36.3 W. Performance is evaluated using a cycle-accurate simulator whose parameters (e.g., latency) are derived from RTL implementation and cross-verified with the FPGA-Thunder design.

Benchmark. Thunder adopts 128-bit secure parameters aligned with prior work [14]: $N = 2^{16}$, $n = 2^{15}$, $L = 35$, $L_{eff} = 8$, $\alpha = 12$, dnum $= 3$, and 36-bit moduli q_i. **Full-packed bootstrapping** [6] employs DS scaling [3] with `fftIters`=3, consuming 26 levels and retaining 8 effective levels. **HELR** [19] performs encrypted MNIST classification with 30 iterations (batch size 1024, 196 features); **ResNet-20** [17] conducts inference on a single encrypted CIFAR-10 image. **LSTM** [18] executes private RNN inference on encrypted IMDb using 128-word $\times$ 128-dimension ciphertext vectors.

Baseline. For the FPGA platform, FAB-2 serves as the state-of-the-art multi-node baseline, consisting of 8 compute nodes with a parallelism of 256, running at 300MHz. For the ASIC platform, Cinnamon-12 serves as the state-of-the-art multi-node baseline, consisting of 12 compute nodes with a parallelism of 1024, running at 1 GHz.

Performance. Table 1 compares Thunder with state-of-the-art accelerators. For FPGA, FAB-2's fabric is used solely for communication, while FPGA-Thunder achieves 2.09× speedup over FAB-2 on HELR. For ASIC, Thunder achieves 1.38×–3.96× speedup over single-node ASIC-FAST [10] and 1.33×2.92× speedup over multi-node Cinnamon under the same 1024 GBps bandwidth. We also compared with the single-node FPGA-FAST [24], which does not employ double-prime scaling. Under the same parameter settings, FPGA-Thunder outperforms FAST by 1.44× and 2.98× on HELR and ResNet, respectively.

Table 1. Benchmark Performance

Platform	Work	Number of Nodes	Bandwidth	Bootstrapping ($T_{A.S.}(\mu s)$)	HELR (ms)	Resnet20(ms)	LSTM (ms)
FPGA	**FAB** [2]	1	-	-/0.477	103.00	-	-
	FAB-2 [2]	8	100Gbps	-	81.00	-	-
	Poseidon [25]	1	-	127.45/-	72.89	2661.57	1848.49
	FPGA-Thunder	8	200Gbps	**34.00/0.119**	**38.73**	**1030.23**	**1366.98**
ASIC	**F1+** [20]	1	-	58.30/-	19.97	2693.00	2573.00
	Craterlake [21]	1	-	3.91/-	3.81	249.45	138.00
	ARK [13]	1	-	-/0.014	7.42	125.00	-
	BTS [15]	1	-	-/0.045	39.90	1910.00	-
	SHARP [14]	1	-	3.12/-	2.53	99.00	-
	ASIC-FAST [10]	1	-	1.38/-	1.33	68.59	-
	CIFHER [16]	1	-	5.58/-	3.34	189	-
	Cinnamon-12 [12]	12	512GBps	1.63/-	1.52	70.57	-
			1024GBps	1.45/-	1.28	50.52	-
	ASIC-Thunder	12	1024GBps	**0.75/0.002**	**0.96**	**17.32**	**23.85**

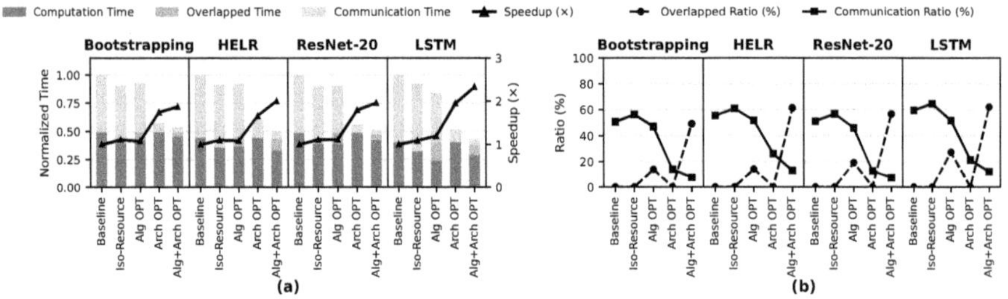

Fig. 8. (a) Execution time and speedup of bootstrapping, HELR, ResNet-20, and LSTM on FPGA-Thunder. (b) Overlapped communication ratio and communication overhead ratio. **Baseline**: eight nodes, no optimizations. **Iso-Resource**: all FPGA resources allocated to compute nodes. **Alg OPT**: Baseline with Algorithm 1 applied. **Arch OPT**: BConv computation migrated to the fabric.

7.1 Ablation Experiments

Impact of Algorithmic and Architectural Co-design. Thunder reduces the communication overhead of fine-grained parallelism through algorithmic and architectural co-design. As shown in Fig. 8(a), the ablation study shows that combining both optimizations achieves 1.87×–2.33× speedup, with the architectural optimization contributing the most. Specifically, Fig. 8(b) illustrates the exact breakdown. The algorithmic optimization (Alg OPT) hides 13.8% to 27.2% of the communication time compared to the Baseline. The architectural optimization (Arch OPT) reduces the communication data volume by 71.7% to 86.6%. Ultimately, the co-design (Alg+Arch OPT) reduces the total communication overhead by a massive 88.3% to 92.7% (Fig. 9).

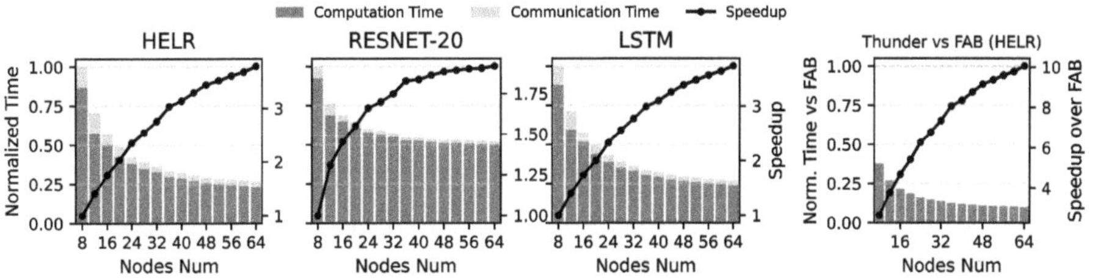

Fig. 9. The first three subfigures are normalized to the 8-node FPGA-Thunder on HELR, ResNet-20, and LSTM, respectively. The fourth subfigure is normalized to the execution time of FAB on HELR.

Iso-Resource Performance Analysis. To justify the resource allocation of our in-transit architecture, we conduct an iso-resource evaluation. We reconfigure the fabric resources used for in-transit computation as additional compute nodes, forming a homogeneous 10-node accelerator. As shown in Fig. 8(a), this configuration achieves only 1.09×–1.11× speedup over the 8-node baseline. This is far below the 1.87×–2.33× improvement delivered by Thunder's in-transit computation. Simply adding compute nodes only amortizes computation overhead. It does not alleviate the global data synchronization overhead caused by BConv, leaving communication as the dominant bottleneck.

7.2 Scalability and Security Analysis

Scalability Analysis. To further evaluate Thunder's scalability, we conduct larger-scale tests on FPGA-Thunder. Real hardware experiments provide the results for configurations up to 16 nodes. A cycle-accurate simulator generates the remaining results. Figure 9 illustrates the performance of HELR, ResNet-20, and LSTM across different node counts. The 64-node FPGA-Thunder achieves a 1.92× to 3.78× speedup over the 8-node baseline. Furthermore, the 64-node FPGA-Thunder accelerates HELR by 10.05× compared to the single-node FAB accelerator, surpassing the 1.27× performance ceiling imposed by ciphertext-wise parallelism. We observe continuous overall performance improvements as the node count increases. This is primarily driven by the limb-wise parallelism in bootstrapping, which scales well with additional nodes. However, the marginal gains gradually diminish with larger node counts. The number of limbs in a ciphertext strictly caps at 35. Consequently, hardware utilization inevitably drops when the number of compute nodes exceeds this threshold.

Security Analysis. Thunder adopts the same 128-bit security parameters as prior works [13,14,21]. At the algorithm level, Thunder optimizes BConv for hardware efficiency while remaining strictly mathematically equivalent to the original, preserving CKKS security guarantees. At the architecture level, all node-fabric communication and in-fabric BConv computation operate exclusively in the ciphertext domain, introducing no side-channel vulnerabilities. Therefore, Thunder provides the same security guarantees as prior single-node works [13,14,21].

8 Related Work

Multi-Node FHE Accelerators. Multi-node FHE accelerators predominantly employ coarse-grained ciphertext-wise parallelism. FAB-2 [2] introduces the first multi-FPGA FHE accelerator. HEAP [1] proposes a hybrid scheme-switching method to parallelize bootstrapping. Cinnamon [12] optimizes the key-switching algorithm to reduce inter-chip communication. Hydra [26] targets secure inference for large CNNs and LLMs. Additional works explore multi-GPU acceleration [4,23]. Thunder distinguishes itself by migrating BConv computation directly into the fabric to reduce communication overhead. Furthermore, Thunder's architecture integrates seamlessly into HEAP, improving its overall performance by 1.45× and 1.42× on HELR and ResNet-20, respectively.

In-Transit Computation. In-transit computation offloads communication-intensive tasks to network devices to reduce data traffic. Grossman et al. [11] accumulate intermediate results within routers. SwitchML [22] executes floating-point accumulation within switches to minimize cross-node traffic during machine learning training. In contrast, Thunder deploys dedicated BConv units within the fabric, eliminating broadcast operations and minimizing communication overhead through algorithm-architecture co-design.

9 Conclusion

In this paper, we propose Thunder, an efficient multi-node FHE acceleration framework. Thunder leverages in-transit computation to reduce communication overhead in fine-grained limb-wise parallelism, thereby improving FHE performance. Specifically, we propose a streaming BConv algorithm to hide communication latency. We migrate BConv computation from individual nodes to the fabric, eliminating global data synchronization and reducing inter-node data traffic. These optimizations reduce communication overhead by up to 92.7%, delivering up to 10.05× speedup over single-node accelerators and up to 2.92× over state-of-the-art multi-node accelerators.

Acknowledgments. This work is supported by the National Key R&D Program of China (Grant Nos. 2023YFB4503200 and 2023YFB4503201), the Strategic Priority Research Program of Chinese Academy of Sciences (Grant No. XDB0690100), the National Natural Science Foundation of China for Distinguished Young Scholars (Grant No. 62125208), and National Natural Science Foundation of China (Grant No. 62427809). Lutan Zhao is the corresponding author.

Disclosure of Interests. The authors have no competing interests to declare that are relevant to the content of this article.

References

1. Agrawal, R., Chandrakasan, A., Joshi, A.: Heap: A fully homomorphic encryption accelerator with parallelized bootstrapping. In: ISCA2024. IEEE (2024).
2. Agrawal, R., et al.: Fab: An fpga-based accelerator for bootstrappable fully homomorphic encryption. In: HPCA2023, pp. 882–895 (2023)
3. Agrawal, R., et al.: High-precision rns-ckks on fixed but smaller word-size architectures: theory and application. In: WAHC, pp. 23–34. New York, NY, USA (2023)
4. Badawi, A., A.: Multi-gpu design and performance evaluation of homomorphic encryption on gpu clusters. TPDS **32**(2) (2021)
5. Ant-research: Ant-ace (2025). https://github.com/ant-research/ace-compiler
6. Bossuat, J.-P., Mouchet, C., Troncoso-Pastoriza, J., Hubaux, J.-P.: Efficient Bootstrapping for Approximate Homomorphic Encryption with Non-sparse Keys. In: Canteaut, A., Standaert, F.-X. (eds.) EUROCRYPT 2021. LNCS, vol. 12696, pp. 587–617. Springer, Cham (2021). https://doi.org/10.1007/978-3-030-77870-5_21
7. Cheon, J.H., Kim, A., Kim, M., Song, Y.: Homomorphic Encryption for Arithmetic of Approximate Numbers. In: Takagi, T., Peyrin, T. (eds.) Advances in Cryptology – ASIACRYPT 2017. ASIACRYPT 2017. Lecture Notes in Computer Science, vol. 10624. Springer, Cham (2017). https://doi.org/10.1007/978-3-319-70694-8_15
8. Ebel, A., et al.: Orion: A fully homomorphic encryption framework for deep learning. In: ASPLOS, pp. 734–749. ASPLOS '25, New York, NY, USA (2025)
9. Fan, S., Wang, Z., Xu, W., Hou, R., Meng, D., Zhang, M.: Tensorfhe: Achieving practical computation on encrypted data using gpgpu. In: HPCA (2023)
10. Fan, S., et al.: Fast: An fhe accelerator for scalable-parallelism with tunable-bit. In: ISCA, pp. 92–106. ISCA '25, New York, NY, USA (2025)
11. Grossman, J.: Filtering, reductions and synchronization in the anton 2 network. In: IPDPS 2015, pp. 860–870 (2015)
12. Jayashankar, S., et al.: Cinnamon: A framework for scale-out encrypted ai. In: ASPLOS, pp. 133–150. ASPLOS '25, New York, NY, USA (2025)
13. Kim, J.: Ark: Fully homomorphic encryption accelerator with runtime data generation and inter-operation key reuse. arXiv preprint arXiv:2205.00922 (2022)
14. Kim, J.: Sharp: A short-word hierarchical accelerator for robust and practical fully homomorphic encryption. In: ISCA (2023)
15. Kim, S., et al.: Bts: an accelerator for bootstrappable fully homomorphic encryption. In: ISCA, pp. 711–725. ISCA '22, New York, NY, USA (2022)

16. Kim, S., et al.: CiFHER: A Chiplet-Based FHE Accelerator with a Resizable Structure . In: SEED. pp. 119–130. Los Alamitos, CA, USA (May 2024)
17. Lee, E.: Low-complexity deep convolutional neural networks on fully homomorphic encryption using multiplexed parallel convolutions. In: ICML (2022)
18. Podschwadt, R., Takabi, D.: Classification of encrypted word embeddings using recurrent neural networks. In: PrivateNLP@ WSDM, pp. 27–31 (2020)
19. Quah, I.: Logistic regression training examples using openfhe (2023). https://github.com/openfheorg/openfhe-logreg-training-examples, openfhe.org
20. Samardzic, N.: F1: A fast and programmable accelerator for fully homomorphic encryption. In: MICRO-54, pp. 238–252 (2021)
21. Samardzic, N.: Craterlake: a hardware accelerator for efficient unbounded computation on encrypted data. In: ISCA (2022)
22. Sapio, A.: Scaling distributed machine learning with In-Network aggregation. In: NSDI 21, pp. 785–808. USENIX Association (2021)
23. Wang, Z.: He-booster: An efficient polynomial arithmetic acceleration on gpus for fully homomorphic encryption. TPDS **34**(4) (2023)
24. Xu, Z.: Fast: Fpga acceleration of fully homomorphic encryption with efficient bootstrapping. In: FPGA. FPGA '25, New York, NY, USA (2025)
25. Yang, Y., Zhang, H., Fan, S., Lu, H., Zhang, M., Li, X.: Poseidon: Practical homomorphic encryption accelerator. In: HPCA, pp. 870–881 (2023)
26. Yang, Y.: Hydra: Scale-out fhe accelerator architecture for secure deep learning on fpga. In: HPCA, pp. 1174–1186 (2025)
27. Zhou, X., et al.: Accelerating stencil computation with fully homomorphic encryption using gpu. In: Euro-Par 2024, pp. 212–224 (2024)

TAIN: Scalable Tensor-Aware Acceleration for Quantum Chemistry on Heterogeneous Architectures

Wenhao Liang[1,2], Lianhua He[1], Runfeng Jin[1,2], Yingqi Tian[3], Yidong Chen[4], Yingjin Ma[1(✉)], and Zhong Jin[1]

[1] Computer Network Information Center, Chinese Academy of Sciences, Beijing, China
{liangwenhao,jinrunfeng}@cnic.cn, {helh,yingjin.ma,zjin}@sccas.cn
[2] University of Chinese Academy of Sciences, Beijing, China
[3] Institute of Computing Technology, Chinese Academy of Sciences, Beijing, China
tianyingqi@ict.ac.cn
[4] Tsinghua University, Beijing, China
chenyidong@tsinghua.edu.cn

Abstract. Accurately computing dynamic correlation energy (DCE) is critical for characterizing strongly correlated systems in quantum chemistry simulations. However, DCE calculations involve massive tensor contractions that incur prohibitive computational costs and form the dominant bottleneck. Although modern heterogeneous architectures provide high-throughput low-precision tensor units, DCE workloads struggle to benefit from these hardware gains due to strict precision requirements, irregular computation patterns, and limited scalability. In this work, we propose TAIN, a novel tensor-aware solver for efficient DCE computation. TAIN leverages 1) an indices-aware tensor compression algorithm to identify and approximate over 80% of non-critical tensor contractions while preserving chemical accuracy; 2) a neural-network-based heterogeneous scheduling strategy to retain communication-bound contractions on CPUs and batch other tensor contractions on GPUs; 3) pipelined execution and a hierarchical task partitioning strategy to reduce redundant work and achieve efficient load balancing. Experiments show that TAIN achieves up to 17.8× speedup over the state-of-the-art library. TAIN reaches 97% strong and 97.7% weak scaling on 4,000 nodes, reducing the time-to-solution for the bioluminescence system from days to a single hour.

Keywords: Tensor Contractions · Quantum Chemistry Simulation · Heterogeneous Architectures

1 Introduction

The simulation of dynamic correlation is a fundamental research problem in quantum chemistry, particularly in the study of strongly correlated systems.

M. Torquati et al. (Eds.): Euro-Par 2026, LNCS 16781, pp. 481–494, 2027.
https://doi.org/10.1007/978-3-032-35248-4_33

These systems are central to a wide range of physical and chemical phenomena, including high-temperature superconductivity [19], transition-metal catalysis [16], and organic light emission [12]. Accurate computation of dynamic correlation energy is therefore essential for understanding their electronic structure and for reliably predicting their properties.

In recent years, the n-electron valence second-order perturbation theory (NEV PT2) [1] has emerged as a popular approach for computing DCE due to its excellent accuracy and numerical stability. However, the extremely high computational cost of this method severely limits its practical applicability. For instance, when calculating the typical excited states reactions with a few dozen orbitals, such as bioluminescence systems, the computation can take several days. The primary bottleneck lies in the intensive tensor contractions, which account for more than 95% of the total runtime. These tensor computations have a computational complexity of $\mathcal{O}(L^9M^2)$, where L is the number of orbitals in the system and M is the tensor dimension. For large systems, the required computational resources become prohibitive, severely limiting scalability.

With the development of modern computing hardware, especially the introduction of tensor units, heterogeneous accelerators can achieve a tens-of-fold speedup over double-precision implementations on dense and regular computation patterns. However, like many scientific applications [8,15], the calculations of strongly correlated systems have struggled to benefit from these hardware capabilities. This gap is driven by three core limitations:

Strict Accuracy Requirements. Quantum chemistry calculations are highly sensitive to numerical accuracy, particularly in strongly correlated systems where many electronic states are nearly degenerate. However, approximation techniques such as low-precision arithmetic or aggressive tensor compression often introduce numerical errors that are unacceptable in accuracy-critical workloads. As a result, achieving both high precision and reduced computational cost remains challenging, which limits the applicability of low-precision computation in strongly correlated electronic-structure calculations.

Irregular Workloads. Tensor operators in DCE computing exhibit highly irregular patterns, which lead to irregular computation and memory-access behavior. These characteristics conflict with the dense and regular execution paradigms for which modern accelerators (e.g., GPUs) are specifically optimized, resulting in low hardware utilization. As a result, even when executed on GPUs, many tensor contractions fail to reach high throughput or sustain efficient execution.

Limited Scalability. The computational complexity of tensor contractions is $\mathcal{O}(L^9M^2)$, leading to an enormous number of floating-point operations even for moderately sized systems. As the number of orbitals L increases, the tensor computations and memory requirements grow extremely quickly. This make the overall computation prohibitively expensive, preventing current methods from scaling to large systems and limiting the applicability of DCE in realistic scientific simulations.

To address these limitations, we propose TAIN, a novel tensor-aware solver for efficient quantum chemistry simulations on heterogeneous architectures. Our main contributions are:

- We present an indices-aware tensor compression algorithm to enable low-rank computation, while low-precision quantization techniques are used to effectively exploit GPU tensor units without compromising accuracy.
- We propose a neural-network (NN)-based heterogeneous scheduling strategy that schedules communication-bound tensor operators on CPUs to reduce data movement overhead and achieves high hardware utilization via batched execution on GPUs.
- We propose a pipeline optimization scheme and a hierarchical task partitioning strategy to achieve load balancing across multiple nodes.
- We achieve speedups of up to 17.8× and 10.4× over the state-of-the-art library on one NVIDIA GPU and one AMD GPU, and strong and weak scaling of 97% and 97.7% on 4,000 nodes, reducing the time for bioluminescence computation from days to within one hour.

2 Background and Challenges

2.1 Tensor Contractions in Quantum Chemistry

In quantum chemistry, multireference (MR) methods are widely used for accurately describing strongly correlated systems. Among these methods, NEVPT2 has emerged as a prominent multireference perturbation theory approach due to its high accuracy and numerical stability, particularly for challenging near-degenerate systems. In the NEVPT2 method, reduced density matrices (RDMs) serve as the central quantities for capturing dynamic correlation effects. In particular, the fourth-order RDM (4-RDM) play a critical role in enabling high-accuracy calculations, which can be written as

$$\Gamma_{ijklmnpq} = \langle \Psi | a_i^\dagger a_j^\dagger a_k^\dagger a_l^\dagger a_m a_n a_p a_q | \Psi \rangle, \tag{1}$$

here Ψ is a wavefunction with L orbitals, $i, j, k, l, m, n, p, q \in \{0, 1, ..., L-1\}$, $|\rangle$ denotes the Dirac notation, $a_i^\dagger$ and a_j represent the creation and annihilation operators on orbitals i and j, respectively.

Because the wavefunction grows exponentially with system size, practical computations represent both the wavefunction and operators in tensor form, namely matrix product states (MPS) and matrix product operators (MPO). Under this representation, the 4-RDM can be rewritten as

$$\Gamma_{ijklmnpq} = \langle \text{MPS} | \text{MPO}(i, j, k, l, m, n, p, q) | \text{MPS} \rangle. \tag{2}$$

Thus, each 4-RDM element can be computed as a tensor network contraction, as illustrated in Fig. 1(a). Due to quantum-number symmetries [13], these tensors exhibit block-sparse structure, as shown in Fig. 1(b). Blocks of different colors correspond to distinct quantum numbers and exhibit highly irregular sizes. In practice, this results in a mixture of large dense matrices and numerous small matrix blocks, leading to highly irregular workloads. Because the 4-RDM contains eight indices, which requires $\mathcal{O}(L^8)$ tensor network contractions. Each contraction has a computational cost of $\mathcal{O}(LM^2)$, leading to an overall complexity of $\mathcal{O}(L^9M^2)$, where M is the max dimension of MPS.

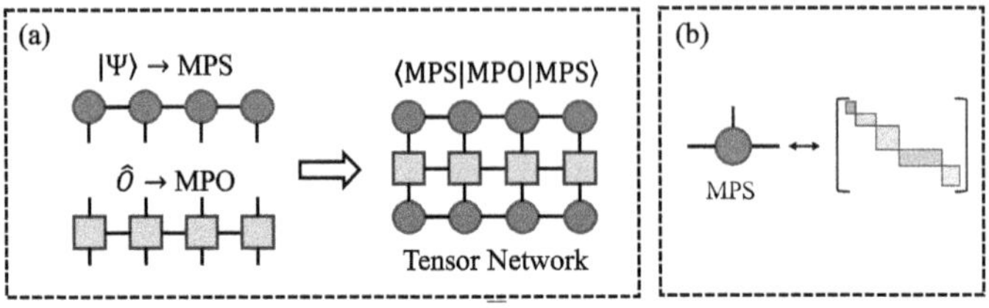

Fig. 1. (a) Representation of MPS and MPO in graphical notation. Blue circles and yellow squares represent tensors in MPS and MPO, respectively. (b) Each tensor is composed of a series of matrices with different sizes. (Color figure online)

2.2 Mismatch Between Quantum Chemistry and Heterogeneous Architectures

Modern heterogeneous architectures, especially GPU-accelerated systems, derive most of their computational throughput from low-precision tensor units, which are highly efficient for dense and regular matrix operations. However, NEVPT2 tensor contractions do not naturally match these assumptions. They require high numerical accuracy, exhibit highly irregular tensor structures, and involve fine-grained dependencies, making it difficult to directly exploit the performance potential of heterogeneous accelerators. This mismatch gives rise to three major challenges.

Maintaining Accuracy Under Tensor Approximation. Low-rank approximation and mixed-precision arithmetic are promising for reducing the cost of tensor contractions, but they can introduce numerical errors that violate chemical accuracy [5]. In strongly correlated systems, mhartree-level energy differences must be resolved reliably, while FP32 provides only 6–7 decimal digits of precision. As rounding errors accumulate across long contraction chains, existing approximation strategies struggle to guarantee accuracy.

Executing Irregular Tensors Efficiently on Accelerators. Tensor contractions in NEVPT2 vary widely in block size, sparsity pattern, and contraction dimension, leading to large fluctuations in compute intensity and memory-access behavior. GPUs are well suited for large and compute-intensive contractions, whereas CPUs often perform better on small or communication-bound operations. Without workload-aware scheduling, heterogeneous platforms cannot exploit these irregular contractions efficiently.

High Complexity Limits System Scalability. The overall cost of NEVPT2 tensor contractions scales as $\mathcal{O}(L^9M^2)$, where L is the number of orbitals and M is the bond dimension. As system size grows, this cost quickly becomes prohibitive. In addition, tensor transpositions, memory movement, and irregular task sizes introduce substantial overheads, while conventional index-based partitioning often leads to severe load imbalance in distributed execution. These factors together limit scalability to large strongly correlated systems.

3 Related Work

Prior work has reduced 4-RDM cost through density-matrix approximation and tensor compression. Colmenero et al. [2] introduced low-order RDMs in contracted Schrödinger equation methods, and Zgid et al. [18] used 1-RDM and 2-RDM information to approximate the 3-RDM and 4-RDM in NEVPT2. However, such approximations may introduce intruder-state problems or compromise accuracy. Tensor compression methods [4] further reduce cost with smaller tensor representations, but reliable accuracy guarantees remain difficult.

Parallel optimization has also been widely explored. Quantum chemistry packages [6,14,17] commonly adopt MPS-based representations because they map well to Level-3 BLAS operations, but most remain CPU-oriented. Recent efforts exploit heterogeneous accelerators in tensor-network and electronic-structure calculations, including ITensor [3], large-scale DFT [11], and strongly correlated methods [7].

4 TAIN Design

TAIN is designed to address the challenges of efficient DCE computation on heterogeneous architectures. It consists of three key components: 1) an indices-aware tensor compression algorithm that identifies and approximates non-critical tensor contractions while preserving chemical accuracy; 2) a NN-based heterogeneity scheduling strategy that retains communication-bound contractions on CPUs and batches other tensor contractions on GPUs; 3) pipelined execution and a hierarchical task partitioning strategy to reduce redundant work and achieve efficient load balancing across multiple nodes. as illustrated in Fig. 2.

4.1 Indices-Aware Tensor Compression Algorithm

We observe that RDM elements are not equally important. In particular, for high-order RDMs, only a small subset of elements are dominant and contribute far more to the accuracy of the final results than others. Preserving these dominant elements from approximation helps mitigate the accuracy loss introduced by approximation, as shown in Fig 3. To realize this idea, we require a criterion for identifying dominant elements. By analyzing the relationship between the magnitudes of RDM elements and their corresponding indices, we reveal a key

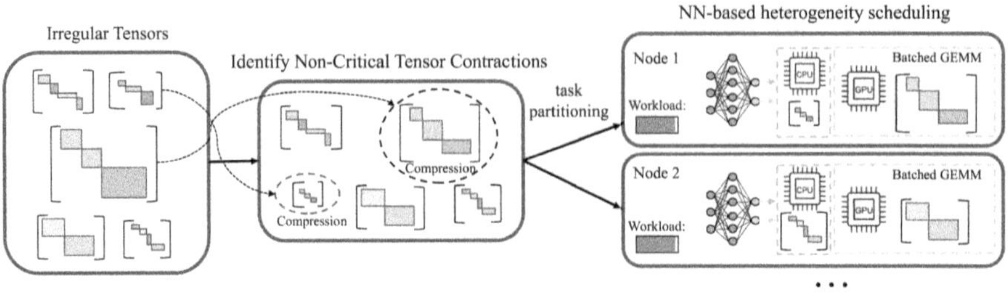

Fig. 2. The overview of TAIN. A tensor enclosed by an elliptical dashed line indicates that it has been selected and compressed.

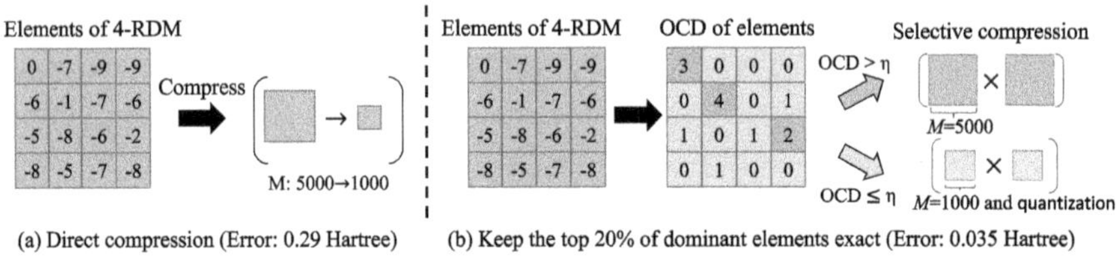

Fig. 3. Comparison between direct compression and TAIN on the Cr_2 molecule with 12 orbitals and 12 electrons. Keeping the top 20% of dominant elements exact significantly reduces the accuracy loss (from 0.29 Hartree in (a) to 0.035 Hartree in (b)).

insight: the importance of an RDM element is closely related to the arrangement of its indices.

Based on this insight, we propose an indices-aware tensor compression algorithm with two stages, as shown in Algorithm 1:

Stage 1. Prior to tensor contractions, we quantify the importance of each RDM element via a heuristic scoring mechanism based on its index pattern. Taking the 4-RDM as an example, each element is associated with eight indices (i, j, k, l, m, n, p, q). We separately count the occurrence frequencies of indices in the first and second halves, each containing four indices, and store them in two frequency maps, `first_half` and `second_half`. The importance score is then defined as the total number of matched indices between the two halves, computed by summing the minimum occurrence count of each shared index.

Stage 2. To enable controlled approximation, we introduce a threshold parameter η. When the importance score of an RDM element is less than or equal to η, the element is classified as non-critical, and compression is applied to the MPS tensors. The threshold controls the accuracy-performance trade-off: a larger η compresses more contractions but may increase numerical error, whereas a smaller η retains more exact contractions at higher cost. We choose η through a small calibration run under the chemical-accuracy constraint and use $\eta = 1$ in our experiments, which compresses about 80% of contractions for the evalu-

Algorithm 1: Indices-Aware Tensor Compression Algorithm

```
Input: M_min, η, indices, MPS, MPO
Output: RDM
Stage 1:
Initialize two empty maps: first_half and second_half;
for i ← 0 to 3 do
    first_half[indices[i]] ← first_half[indices[i]] + 1;
for i ← 4 to 7 do
    second_half[indices[i]] ← second_half[indices[i]] + 1;
importance ← 0;
foreach (key, count) ∈ first_half do
    if key ∈ second_half then
        importance ← importance + min(count, second_half[key]);
Stage 2:
if importance ≤ η then
    MPS ← Compression(MPS, M_min);
RDM ← Contraction(MPS, MPO);
return RDM;
```

ated systems. The compression schemes include reducing the tensor dimension to $M_{\min}$ and quantizing the tensors to the TF32 format. Finally, the RDM element is computed through tensor contractions between the MPS and MPO tensors.

This importance check is a constant-time operation ($O(1)$) that does not scale with the system size. Accordingly, TAIN leverages this lightweight indices-based evaluation to identify and retain critical tensor contractions for accuracy preservation. Meanwhile, it applies a controlled compression scheme to non-critical contractions and supports low-precision quantization, effectively harnessing the high-throughput tensor units of modern heterogeneous accelerators to achieve substantial speedups.

4.2 NN-Based Heterogeneous Scheduling Strategy

We analyze the irregularity of tensor structures and find that over 30% of tensor blocks are small (dimension < 100), many even below 10. These small tensors are communication-bound and better suited for CPUs than GPUs. Accurate tensor size prediction before contraction is thus critical for efficient workload placement. Further analysis reveals that tensor shapes are nearly uniform across different contractions, since MPS and MPO dimensions remain fixed. Tensor sizes in early contractions can therefore reliably predict those in later steps. Using this property, we only need to sample a small number of contractions to predict all tensor sizes in the full DCE computation. Based on the above observation, we propose an NN-based heterogeneous scheduling strategy with three phases:

Phase 1: Dataset construction. We first execute a small number of tensor network contractions on CPUs and GPUs to collect typical tensor features (e.g., block dimensions and count). Using these observed ranges, we generate numerous synthetic matrix blocks with varied sizes and data types, and perform comprehensive GEMM benchmarks. We record execution time including CPU-GPU data transfer to build a performance dataset for model training. The dataset is machine-dependent because it reflects the CPU/GPU performance and transfer cost of a specific platform.

Phase 2: Offline learning. We use a lightweight multilayer perceptron (MLP) to predict the execution cost on CPUs and GPUs from GEMM dimensions (M, N, and K) and data type. The MLP is chosen because these low-dimensional features do not require a deep model, while an MLP can still capture nonlinear effects from block size and CPU-GPU transfer cost. Thus, it provides a practical trade-off among prediction accuracy, generalization, and low online scheduling overhead. In our implementation, the MLP has two hidden layers with 128 neurons each and is trained with the Adam optimizer (batch size=32) on more than 10k synthetic GEMM performance samples. The offline profiling and training process completes within one hour on each evaluated platform. On held-out validation samples, the trained model achieves over 95% accuracy in predicting the faster device. After training, we obtain a compact model that can be reused across DCE calculations on the same platform, amortizing the training cost.

Phase 3: Online prediction. At runtime, the trained model estimates the execution cost of each tensor contraction and dynamically selects the best device. This neural-network-based scheduler efficiently handles irregular small-matrix workloads, reduces redundant data transfer, and improves overall performance.

Following task scheduling, many irregular tensor operations still execute on GPUs. To improve utilization, we batch compatible matrix multiplications while preserving quantum-number constraints. Specifically, we track dependencies introduced by *InsertBlock* and *AddBlock* operations, reorder tensor blocks according to quantum labels, execute compatible GEMMs in batches, and then accumulate intermediate results according to the recorded dependencies. This preserves the contraction semantics while exposing GPU batch parallelism.

4.3 Pipeline Optimizations

TAIN also applies two implementation-level pipeline optimizations to reduce redundant work and memory usage. Since the MPS tensors remain invariant during RDM evaluation, TAIN caches their transposed form once and reuses it across contractions, avoiding repeated memory-bound transpositions at an additional storage cost of $O(LM^2)$. In addition, TAIN groups 4-RDM elements by the first four indices and writes each completed group back immediately, reducing peak memory usage from $O(L^8)$ to $O(L^4)$.

4.4 Hierarchical Task Partitioning Strategy

Fundamental principles of quantum mechanics dictate that a large fraction of RDM elements are identically zero and can be pruned. Specifically, in a 4-RDM,

Algorithm 2: Hierarchical Task Partitioning Strategy

Input: L, P (number of compute nodes)
Output: Balanced task assignment

parallel for each $(i, j, k, l) \in [0, L)^4$ **do**
  `workload`$(i, j, k, l) \leftarrow 0$;
  foreach $(m, n, p, q) \in [0, L)^4$ **do**
    `workload`$(i, j, k, l) \leftarrow$ `workload`$(i, j, k, l) +$ `Prescan`(i, j, k, l, m, n, p, q);

`tasks` $\leftarrow$ `BuildTaskPool`$([0, L)^4,$ `workload`$)$;
`assignment` $\leftarrow$ `PartitionByLoad`$($`tasks`$, P)$;
parallel for each *node* $r \in \{0, \ldots, P-1\}$ **do**
  Execute `assignment`$[r]$ on node r;

the last four indices (m, n, p, q) correspond to annihilation operators. According to the Pauli exclusion principle, an orbital can accommodate at most two electrons with opposite spins; thus, any element where more than two of these indices are identical must vanish. While traditional index-based partitioning assumes that tasks with similar index ranges incur comparable computational costs, this assumption is violated after pruning. Since the density of non-zero elements varies drastically across index groups, uniform partitioning based on outer-loop indices (i, j, k, l) inevitably leads to severe load imbalance.

To address this issue, we propose a hierarchical task partitioning strategy, as detailed in Algorithm 2. The key idea is to decouple the workload estimation from the actual tensor network contractions, enabling a load-aware distribution of computational tasks. The strategy proceeds in three distinct phases. First, we perform a lightweight parallel prescan over the 4-RDM index space. For each outer-loop index combination (i, j, k, l), we aggregate the number of valid non-zero elements into a `workload` value. Second, these values are used to construct a global task pool, where each task is characterized by its actual computational weight rather than its index range. Finally, we employ a load-based partitioning algorithm (e.g., Karmarkar-Karp algorithm) to distribute these tasks across P compute nodes. By prioritizing load-balancing based on the actual number of non-zero contractions, this approach ensures nearly uniform workload distribution, enhancing the parallel efficiency on large-scale heterogeneous clusters.

5 Evaluation

5.1 Evaluation Setup

Testbeds. The experiments are performed on two platforms: 1) NVIDIA Platform: A server featuring an AMD EPYC-7452 32-core CPU and one NVIDIA A100 GPU. The software stack includes Ubuntu 24.04, CUDA 12.7. Batched GEMM are implemented using *cublasXgemmGroupedBatched* from cuBLAS [10]. 2) AMD Platform: A cluster comprising 4,000 nodes. Each node is equipped with a Hygon C86 32-core CPU and four AMD MI50 GPUs, and 128 GB of DDR4 memory. The nodes are interconnected via 200Gbps InfiniBand. The software stack includes Centos 7.6, ROCm 4.3, and HPC-X 2.11.0. Batched GEMM are implemented using *xgemm_vbatched* from MAGMA [9].

Benchmark. We select Cr_2, and the 1,2-Dioxetanon (DIO) as benchmark molecular systems. These molecular systems are typical strongly correlated systems and hold significant research value. The Cr_2 molecule contains 12 orbitals and 12 electrons, and the chosen basis set is ANO-RCC-VTZP. The DIO molecule plays a central role in bioluminescence. It contains 18 electrons and 15 orbitals, and the basis set used is ANO-RCC-VDZP. The default maximum bond dimension is set to 5,000 for DIO and 1,000 for Cr_2. The M_{min} is set to 2,000 for DIO and 250 for Cr_2. We set $\eta = 1$ based on the calibration described in Sect. 4.1, which approximates about 80% of tensor contractions while preserving chemical accuracy.

Baseline. We use *OpenMolcas* as our baseline, which is state-of-the-art library for DCE computing. The results of *OpenMolcas* are obtained using 32 CPU threads with double-precision (FP64).

Table 1. Accuracy Verification of TAIN

Molecule	Direct compression	TAIN(FP64)	TAIN(TF32)
Cr_2, Energy	3.386E-2	1.469E-4	4.452E-4
DIO, S_1-S_0 gaps	4.781E-3	5.262E-4	9.329E-4

5.2 Accuracy Verification of TAIN

Table 1 shows the accuracy verification of TAIN, with baseline results obtained from *OpenMolcas*. We evaluate numerical accuracy by comparing the absolute errors of different methods relative to the baseline. For the Cr_2 molecule, accuracy is evaluated using total energies, whereas for the DIO molecule, we examine the energy differences between two degenerate states (S_1-S_0). The results show that direct compression introduces energy errors of 3.386×10^{-2} Hartree for Cr_2 and 4.781×10^{-3} Hartree for DIO, both of which exceed the threshold of chemical accuracy (1 mHartree). In contrast, TAIN achieves substantially smaller errors of 4.452×10^{-4} and 9.329×10^{-4} under TF32 precision, both of which remain well within the threshold of chemical accuracy. These results demonstrate that the indices-aware tensor compression effectively reduces computational cost while preserving the numerical fidelity required for accurate DCE calculations.

5.3 Ablation Study

To demonstrate the effectiveness of each optimization, we perform an ablation study using *OpenMolcas* as the baseline, as shown in Fig. 4. Specifically, *GPU* denotes GPU acceleration with double-precision computation and pipeline optimization. *Compression* represents the indices-aware tensor compression technique. *TAIN* represents our end-to-end optimized system that integrates tensor compression, heterogeneous scheduling, and batched execution. We report scheduling and batched execution as one stage because the two optimizations are tightly coupled: the scheduler determines which contractions are offloaded to GPUs, while batched execution determines how these offloaded contractions are executed efficiently.

On the NVIDIA platform, the indices-aware tensor compression achieves speedups of 6.5× and 12.6× over the baseline. Meanwhile, the end-to-end performance reaches 8.1× and 17.8× speedups relative to *OpenMolcas*. On the AMD platform, the results are similar to those on the NVIDIA platform. The index-aware tensor compression achieves speedups of 3.8× and 6.3× over the baseline. Ultimately, TAIN achieves end-to-end speedups of 4.7× and 10.4× compared with *OpenMolcas*. The largest gain comes from indices-aware compression, while heterogeneous scheduling and batched execution provide additional gains by improving hardware utilization on irregular small-block workloads. Notably, the performance gains become more pronounced as the system size increases (e.g., the DIO system), demonstrating that our tensor optimization strategies effectively mitigate the computational bottlenecks associated with larger system simulations.

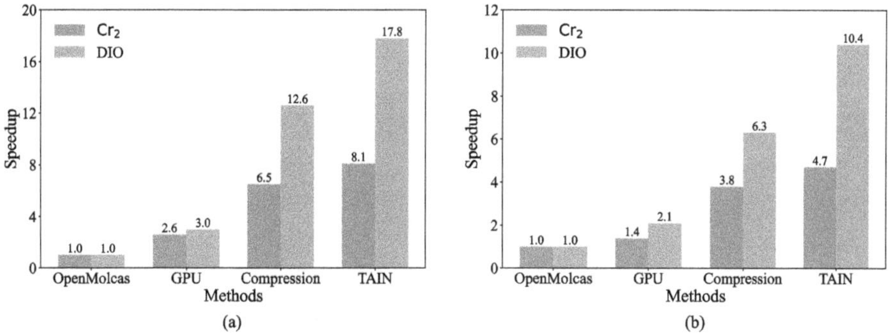

Fig. 4. Performance comparison of optimization methods on a single NVIDIA GPU (a) and a single AMD GPU (b).

5.4 Large-Scale Evaluation

In this section, we evaluate the load balancing optimization and scalability of TAIN on the AMD platform. The benchmark is the DIO molecule. We adopt the MPI+OpenMP+ROCm hybrid programming model for heterogeneous acceleration: MPI handles inter-node communication over 200Gbps InfiniBand with RDMA enabled, OpenMP parallelizes CPU computations with 8 threads per process, and ROCm accelerates GPU tensor contractions. Inter-process communication is optimized with non-blocking MPI calls to hide communication latency.

Load Balance Evaluation. To evaluate the effectiveness of the load-balancing strategy, we measure the maximum load $L_{\max}$ and the average load L_{avg} across all computational nodes. We define the load-balance metric $\gamma = L_{\max}/L_{\text{avg}}$, where values closer to 1 indicate more balanced task partitioning and approach the ideal case of $L_{\max} \approx L_{\text{avg}}$. This metric captures the extent to which the slowest node deviates from the average workload and directly reflects the impact of load imbalance on parallel efficiency.

Figure 5 compares the load-balance metric γ for the baseline sequential index-based partitioning (denoted as *no balance*) and TAIN (denoted as *balance*) on 512, 1,024, 2,048, and 4,000 nodes. Under the baseline approach, γ remains as high as 2.3, indicating that some nodes are assigned more than twice the average workload, which leads to load imbalance and limits scalability. In contrast, TAIN consistently reduces γ to values close to 1 across all evaluated scales, demonstrating near-optimal load distribution.

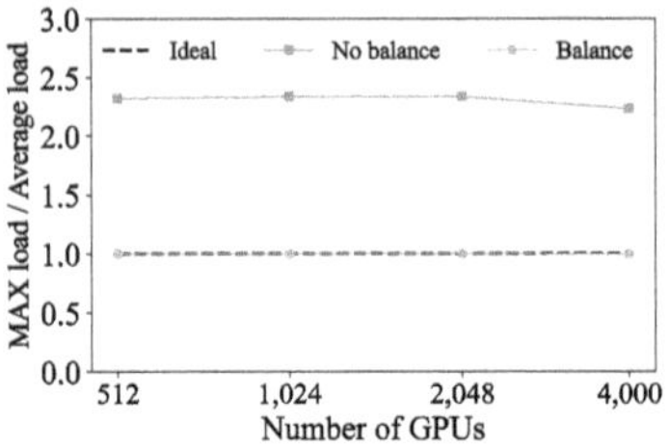

Fig. 5. Comparison of load balancing across nodes.

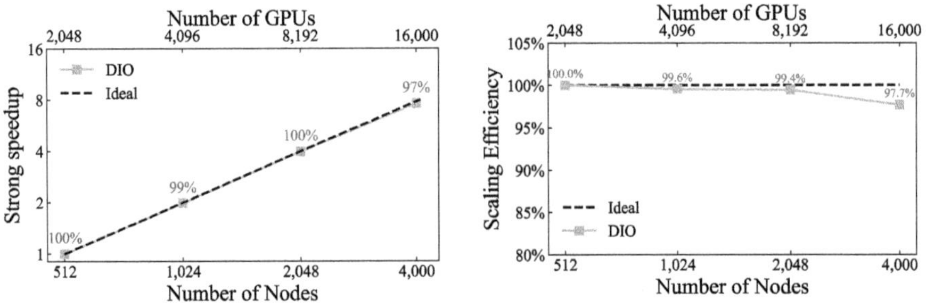

(a) strong scaling (b) weak scaling

Fig. 6. Strong and weak scaling of TAIN.

Strong Scaling. Figure 6(a) presents the strong scaling of TAIN. TAIN achieves a 7.6× speedup when scaling from 512 to 4,000 nodes, maintaining a strong scaling efficiency consistently above 97%, which reduces the time-to-solution for the bioluminescence system from days to a single hour. As the number of compute nodes increases for a fixed problem size, the diminishing granularity of local tasks leads to a relative rise in task management and scheduling overhead, which accounts for the marginal decline in parallel efficiency. Overall, these results demonstrate that TAIN delivers near-linear strong scalability, proving its capability for extreme-scale quantum chemistry simulations.

Weak Scaling. Figure 6(b) presents the weak scaling performance of TAIN. To evaluate weak scalability, we design experiments in which the total computational workload increases proportionally with the number of nodes, thereby keeping the workload per node approximately constant. When the system scales from 512 nodes to 4,000 nodes, the total workload increases by approximately eight times, resulting in a weak scaling efficiency of 97.7%. These results demonstrate that TAIN effectively sustains near-ideal weak scaling across large node counts. The high weak scaling efficiency confirms that the scheduling and load-balancing strategies effectively alleviate distributed execution overheads, allowing TAIN to maintain stable per-node performance with system scaling.

6 Conclusion

This work presents TAIN, a scalable tensor-aware solver for quantum chemistry on heterogeneous architectures. TAIN combines indices-aware tensor compression with heterogeneity-aware scheduling to reduce computational cost while preserving chemical accuracy and to efficiently exploit heterogeneous resources. Pipeline and load-balancing optimizations further improve scalability for large-scale executions. Experimental results show that TAIN achieves up to 17.8× speedup over state-of-the-art libraries and attains 97% strong scaling and 97.7% weak scaling on 4,000 nodes.

Acknowledgments. This work was supported by Strategic Priority Research Program (XDB0500101), National Natural Science Foundation of China (No.22173114, 22333003), Youth Innovation Promotion Association (No.2022168), and Project of Ganjiang Innovation Academy (E455F001) of Chinese Academy of Sciences. Most of the computational experiments were implemented in the "ORISE" HPC clusters, we are also highly appreciated the helps from the supporting team.

Disclosure of Interests. The authors have no competing interests to declare that are relevant to the content of this article.

References

1. Angeli, C., Cimiraglia, R., Evangelisti, S., Leininger, T., Malrieu, J.P.: Introduction of n-electron valence states for multireference perturbation theory. J. Chem. Phys. **114**(23), 10252–10264 (2001)
2. Colmenero, F., Valdemoro, C.: Approximating q-order reduced density matrices in terms of the lower-order ones. II. Appl. Phys. Rev. A **47**(2), 979–985 (1993). https://doi.org/10.1103/PhysRevA.47.979
3. Fishman, M., White, S.R., Stoudenmire, E.M.: The ITensor Software Library for Tensor Network Calculations. SciPost Phys. Codebases, p. 4 (2022)

4. Guo, S., Watson, M.A., Hu, W., Sun, Q., Chan, G.K.L.: N-electron valence state perturbation theory based on a density matrix renormalization group reference function, with applications to the chromium dimer and a trimer model of poly (p-phenylenevinylene). J. Chem. Theory Comput. **12**(4), 1583–1591 (2016)
5. Guo, Y., Sivalingam, K., Neese, F.: Approximations of density matrices in N-electron valence state second-order perturbation theory (NEVPT2). I. Revisiting the NEVPT2 construction. J. Chem. Phys. **154**(21), 214111 (2021). https://doi.org/10.1063/5.0051211
6. Manni, L., et al.: The openmolcas web: A community-driven approach to advancing computational chemistry. J. Chem. Theory Comput. **19**(20), 6933–6991 (2023)
7. Liang, W., Jin, R., Tian, Y., Ma, Y., Jin, Z.: Efficient Computing for Reduced Density Matrix on GPUs. In: 2023 IEEE International Conference on High Performance Computing & Communications, Data Science & Systems, Smart City & Dependability in Sensor, Cloud & Big Data Systems & Application (HPCC/DSS/SmartCity/DependSys), pp. 146–153. IEEE, Melbourne, Australia (2023). https://doi.org/10.1109/HPCC-DSS-SmartCity-DependSys60770.2023.00029
8. Michalakes, J.: HPC for Weather Forecasting. In: Grama, A., Sameh, A.H. (eds.) Parallel Algorithms in Computational Science and Engineering. MSSET, pp. 297–323. Springer, Cham (2020). https://doi.org/10.1007/978-3-030-43736-7_10
9. Nath, R., Tomov, S., Dongarra, J.: An improved magma gemm for fermi graphics processing units. Int. J. High Perf. Comput. Appl. **24**(4), 511–515 (2010)
10. NVIDIA: Nvidia cuda documentation (2025). https://docs.nvidia.com/cuda/cublas/index.html
11. Shang, H., et al.: Large-scale simulation of quantum computational chemistry on a new sunway supercomputer. In: SC22: International Conference for High Performance Computing, Networking, Storage and Analysis, pp. 1–14. IEEE (2022)
12. Shuai, Z., Peng, Q.: Excited states structure and processes: Understanding organic light-emitting diodes at the molecular level. Phys. Rep. **537**(4), 123–156 (2014)
13. Singh, S., Pfeifer, R.N., Vidal, G.: Tensor network states and algorithms in the presence of a global u (1) symmetry. Phys. Rev. B—Condensed Matter and Mater. Phys. **83**(11), 115125 (2011)
14. Sun, Q., et al.: Pyscf: the python-based simulations of chemistry framework. Wiley Interdisc. Rev. Comput. Mol. Sci. **8**(1), e1340 (2018)
15. Tu, J., Yeoh, G.H., Liu, C., Tao, Y.: Computational fluid dynamics: a practical approach, Elsevier (2023)
16. Vogiatzis, K.D., et al.: Computational approach to molecular catalysis by 3d transition metals: challenges and opportunities. Chem. Rev. **119**(4), 2453–2523 (2018)
17. Xie, Z., et al.: Kylin 1.0: An ab-initio density matrix renormalization group quantum chemistry program. J. Comput. Chem. **44**(13), 1316–1328 (2023)
18. Zgid, D., Ghosh, D., Neuscamman, E., Chan, K.L.: A study of cumulant approximations to n-electron valence multireference perturbation theory. J. Chem. Phys. **130**(19), 194107 (2009)
19. Zhou, X., Lee, W.S., Imada, M., Trivedi, N., Phillips, P., Kee, H.Y., Törmä, P., Eremets, M.: High-temperature superconductivity. Nat. Rev. Phys. **3**(7), 462–465 (2021)

Performance Evaluation of a CPU-GPU Coprocessing-Based Simulation Software on Converged Computing Architectures

Romain Gallé[1,2](✉), Jonathan Rouzaud-Cornabas[1,2], and Thierry Gautier[3]

[1] BioTiC Team, Inria de Lyon, Villeurbanne, France
{romain.galle,jonathan.rouzaud-cornabas}@inria.fr
[2] INSA Lyon, Inria, CITI, UR3720, Villeurbanne 69621, France
[3] Ctrl-A Team, Univ. Grenoble Alpes, Inria, CNRS, Grenoble INP, LIG, Grenoble 38000, France

Abstract. Converged computing architectures like AMD's MI300A Accelerated Processing Unit (APU) and Nvidia's Grace Hopper Superchip (GH200) are now featured in world's most powerful supercomputers. On these architectures, both CPU and GPU are on the same chip. However, fundamental design choices separate MI300A and GH200: the first comes with a single physically unified memory for the CPU and GPU cores, while the other has two separate memories, but with the ability for compute units to fetch information from both, through NVLink-C2C. Heterogeneous compute applications (*i.e.* with latency and/or throughput sensitive tasks) are expected to get the most out of these new chips, without the CPU-GPU communication bottleneck of PCIe-based architectures. In this paper, we study how the different design choices in GH200 and MI300A can impact the performance of a balanced latency-and-throughput-sensitive simulation software. We also evaluate how converged architectures can reduce memory transfer costs. Finally, we suggest options to get the most out of these architectures based on our performance measurements.

Our findings show that, depending on the balance of latency-bound and throughput-bound tasks in simulation software, some converged architectures will be more suited than others for executing these codes, with differences in speed of up to 2.78× in our case.

Keywords: Heterogeneous computing · Converged computing · Unified memory · CPU-GPU co-processing · GH200 · MI300A

1 Introduction

Converged memory architectures like Nvidia's Grace Hopper Superchip [2], and AMD's MI300A Accelerated Processing Unit (APU) [23] are now equipping the most powerful supercomputers in the world. In 2025, 3 of the top 10 supercomputers from Top500 [3], and 7 of the top 10 from Green500 [1] are equipped

M. Torquati et al. (Eds.): Euro-Par 2026, LNCS 16781, pp. 495–508, 2027.
https://doi.org/10.1007/978-3-032-35248-4_34

with these chips. They stand out by their hardware architecture, having both CPU and GPU on the same silicon board, with the promise of greatly reduced communication costs between chips. This paves the way to efficient managed memory APIs, lowering the implementation costs of heterogeneous computing applications. Making them closer can also enable better collaboration between the CPU and GPU, allowing repartition of tasks by computing affinity where communication costs would have been prohibitive before.

Even though both platforms can be called "converged architectures", they still diverge in nature (see Table 1). The Grace Hopper Superchips (GH200) comes with two separate on-chip memories, LPDDR5X ($\leq$ 500 GB/s bandwidth) for the Grace CPU, and HBM3 (4 to 4.8 TB/s bandwidth) for the Hopper GPU (more details provided in [2]). The two compute units can then communicate through an NVLink-C2C interconnect (900 GB/s bandwidth), allowing both CPU and GPU to read from each other's memory. Cache-coherency is maintained on both chips, and the interconnect allows access at the cache line granularity. The System Memory Management Unit (SMMU), keeps track of allocations system-wide, making it a global page table [20].

On the other hand, the MI300A APU has only one HBM3 memory, and both CPU (CCD) and GPU (XCD) can access it directly (5.3 TB/s bandwidth, more details in [26]). They also share the last level "Infinity Cache", which is a memory-side cache aimed at reducing off-chip memory accesses and increasing local bandwidth [26] (up to 17.2 TB/s). However, as opposed to GH200, the CPU and GPU both have their own page table, and the GPU cannot read from the CPU table - which induces page table synchronizations and transfers to allow the GPU to access CPU-owned memory. APIs allow this synchronization to happen up-front or on-demand [26].

Table 1. Main differences between GH200 and MI300A

Chip	GH200	MI300A
CPU memory	480 GiB LPDDR5X ($\leq$ 500 GB/s)	Shared with GPU
GPU memory	96 GiB HBM3 (4 to 4.8 TB/s)	128 GiB HBM3 (5.3 TB/s)
Inter-memory comm.	NVLink-C2C (900 GB/s)	256 MiB Infinity Cache (17.2 TB/s)
CPU cores	72 Arm Neoverse V2	24 x86 Zen 4
Power budget	Up to 1000W	Up to 720W

Although both architectures are similar in their CPU-GPU communication costs reduction, their differences in core counts and memory layouts raise questions on the ways to efficiently leverage them for performance. Recent works (see Sect. 2) show that sometimes one or the other performs best on applicative use-cases, depending on various non-trivial criteria like power budget [6] or memory access patterns [24].

Comparative studies of MI300A and GH200 performance exist [5,14,29], however they generally either focus on GPU-only performance, or on portability of kernels (*e.g.* using RAJA or Kokkos [14,29]) between the CPU and GPU. Instead, we want to address the gap in comparatives studies for CPU-GPU co-processing, meaning in cases where significant parts of the compute load have a strong affinity with either the CPU or the GPU, forcing collaboration between both chips to achieve better performance. Indeed, despite the strong push towards GPU-porting, many simulators still need to run partially on the CPU, because of the porting complexity induced by the structure of their simulation model [13,28].

Aevol, an evolution simulation software [16] is one of those: work that is bandwidth-sensitive has been ported to the GPU, and sequential, latency-sensitive processes are still executed on the CPU. Both chips compute significant amounts of the workload. Until now, performance was greatly impacted by CPU-GPU transfer costs. With new converged memory architectures, we expect to get a significant improvement. From a programmer's perspective, the unified memories on both systems are also expected to provide easier memory management.

In this paper, we first present the current state of the art for benchmarks and comparative works on Grace Hopper and MI300A in Sect. 2. We then give context and details on the Aevol benchmark in Sect. 3. We evaluated its performance on MI300A and GH200. We compared various logically unified memory systems on GH200, against shared memory system like MI300A, and traditional PCIe-based architectures. We present our results in Sect. 4, showing significant improvements in performance using converged computing architectures, while underlining the necessity of balancing GPU performance with powerful CPUs, to ensure efficient execution of co-processed computations.

2 Related Works

In this section, we focus on the current state-of-the-art on performance characterization and comparative studies for GH200 and MI300A.

Grace Hopper System Characterization. [20] made a detailed study of GH200's memory management system. They compared the performance of applications using the new integrated CPU-GPU system page table with NVLink-C2C, against the managed memory system, and traditional manual CPU-GPU copies. In most cases, C2C outperformed other approaches, paving the way for simpler implementation and fast execution of heterogeneous computing codes. [18] came to the same conclusions. [9] focused on intra-node and inter-nodes memory operations. They provide both upper bounds for bandwidth and latency with micro-benchmarks, but also define expectations for application performance. They show that despite the significant improvements to development and performance of heterogeneous applications, data locality in nodes is still key to fast execution. [13,25] propose methods for taking advantage of both chips on GH200, for linear algebra and Partial Differential Equations solvers.

MI300A System Characterization. [26] focuses on characterizing the unified physical memory system in MI300A. They show that shared memory offer good performance over managed memory using separate memories, and allow important gains in memory costs as it prevents traditional CPU-GPU memory duplication. [15,19,21] on the other hand, focuses on inter-node communication in MI300A and MI250X. Their benchmarks show that careful choice of communication interface can lead to important speedups in multi-APU HPC simulations, and provide guidelines for optimization.

[4,24] focus on the partitioning system in MI300A, allowing to expose the 6 XCD units and the respective memory in HBM and Infinity Cache as 1, 3 or 6 NUMA nodes. [4] show a 30% improvement with 6 nodes over 1, depending on the workload. [24] looks at cache hierarchies, and show that partitioning reduces latency and interconnect traversals by improving data locality. They also show that in some cases, it might be better to distribute large buffers across several processes. Finally, [12] mixes partitioning with MPI, evaluating bandwidth and latency in intra-node and inter-node asymmetrical NUMA effects, and offering optimization strategies in such contexts.

Several papers are more generally evaluating performance on MI300A [7,8,17,22], comparing either CPU vs GPU performance, unified memory over traditional copies, and demonstrating the use performance portability frameworks like Kokkos in such contexts.

Comparative Works for MI300A and GH200. Papers like [5,6] focus on energy consumption and power caps. The former presents a precise energy model, able to attribute application energy by execution unit (FPU, tensor core, integer ALU) and memory level (L1, L2, HBM), but also to control and datapath. The latter proposes an extension of the roofline model to include systems like GH200 and MI300A and their power consumption thresholds. They also provide architectural trends for both chips, suggesting the GH200 overtakes MI300A for CPU performance, but under-performs on the GPU. It also suggests that, although MI300A has better maximum specifications than GH200 on paper, it is severely hindered by its max thermal budget of 550W (720W with water cooling) compared to GH200's maximum of 1000W.

[29] extends the works from [4] by comparing performance on GH200 and MI300A with the RAJA Performance Suite. Their focus is on kernel portability, but they seem to achieve better performance on GH200. [14] use Kokkos to port the LAMMPS molecular dynamics code on GH200 and MI300A. Their GPU-focused benchmark show significantly better performance on GH200, as [27]. They demonstrate good scalability on 4x setups with both platforms. [11] gets better performance on MI300A's GPU than on H100.

Summary. None of these papers study GH200 and MI300A performance in co-processing cases such as ours, with different tasks executed on the CPU and GPU part, but focus more on performance portability. They also do not try to compare their unified memory systems. Moreover, the performance metrics they study sometimes show better behavior in one or the other. Thus, it is likely that GH200 and MI300A might be best suited for different types of workloads. In this paper, we study a simulation software greatly impacted by memory transfer costs, with both bandwidth-sensitive and latency-sensitive tasks, and try to analyze the impacts of these architectures on execution performance.

3 Methodology for the Benchmark

3.1 Applicative Context: the Aevol Model

Aevol is an evolution simulation software [16], in which a population of individuals (*i.e.* agents), represented as strings, evolve over time. Strings are transformed at each step by mutations (insert, delete, update). Mutated individuals then need to be processed to assign a fitness to a given string, this is called evaluation. During each simulation step, many individuals undergo mutations, and are then re-evaluated. Each simulation counts thousands of individuals. Global synchronizations occur at each step, because of the reproduction part, during which the best individuals can replace their neighbors[1].

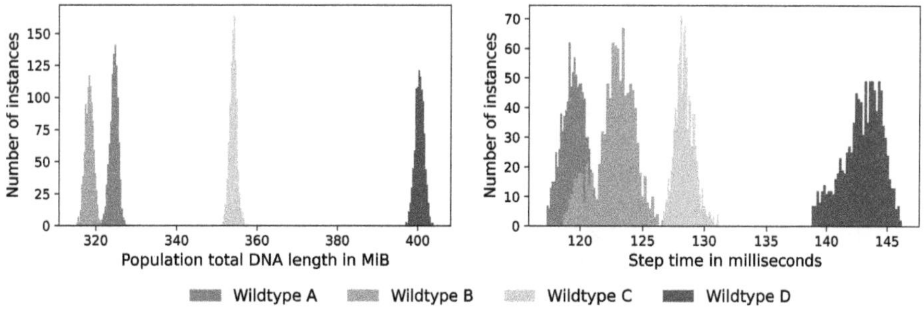

Fig. 1. Distribution of population total DNA length at each step (left) and step compute time (right) for 4 different input populations and the same experimental parameters (seed, population size, mutation rate) for 1000 steps each. Execution time varies a lot over steps even in the same simulation. It is not always correlated to population size (see Wildtypes A and B). Total population size also changes during a simulation, with individual sizes varying even more (not shown here).

In terms of computing, two different tasks take up most of the computing time: a sequential, stateful traversal of irregular-sized strings on one part, and a parallel, multiple-pattern matching task on the other part. The first task is associated with the evaluation, while the second with the mutation part. These tasks are executed for each individual, and evaluation is parallel at the individual level, while the second is parallel up to the character level (in the processed strings). Because of the irregularity of data, its high branching rate and its

[1] Full model description at https://www.aevol.fr/model-description/

sequential construction, the evaluation is more latency-bound, with affinity to CPUs. On the other hand the mutation task has none of these constraints, and thus is throughput-bound, with affinity to GPUs. An example for time and data irregularity is shown in Fig. 1.

The tasks that are of interest to this paper are implemented in 4 phases: memory management, GPU work, GPU-to-CPU transfer, and CPU work (see Fig. 2).

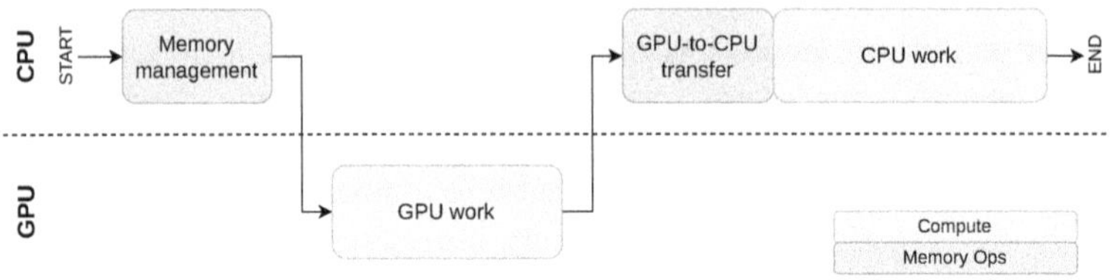

Fig. 2. The 4 main phases in a step and their context of execution.

Memory management encapsulates buffer extensions on the GPU and CPU (very rare), computing of future individuals offsets in the destination buffer (most of the compute time), and future grid creation (trivial). Unique individuals - as opposed to the population, which can contain clones - are handled using double-buffering, meaning one buffer is used for the current individuals, and another one for the next individuals.

GPU work is the multiple-pattern matching phase. Each individual is submitted as a thread block (or workgroup for AMD hardware) with 256 threads (to handle 10^5 to 10^6 elements). It also updates the strings according to the mutations that occurred as a side effect. It strictly uses integer operations, with very few branches. GPU-to-CPU transfer consists of copying back the identified-pattern sequences to the CPU, to be evaluated. Finally, CPU work is the evaluation part, with the stateful traversal of irregular strings. During this step, each individual is evaluated in parallel, using as many threads as made available.

3.2 Experimental Setup

Hardware Description. This benchmark was run both on converged computing architectures, but also more traditional CPU-GPU setups. The traditional setups were selected out of a balance of access constraint, and the fact they both had GPUs of the previous generation respective to MI300A and GH200. With the extra criterion that their CPUs had enough cores to compare to GH200's 72-core ARM CPU. The two selected platforms were as follows: 2 AMD EPYC 7453 (Zen 3), x86 CPUs with 28 cores each, with Nvidia A100 GPUs in their 80 GiB variant. And 1 AMD EPYC Trento x86 CPU with 64 cores, and MI250X GPUs with 128 GiB memory. Both architectures feature a PCIe 4.0 16x interconnect (32 GB/s bandwidth), with HBM2e memory for the GPU. Each time, only one

GPU was used. For the two converged architectures, we used one Grace Hopper Superchip, with 96 GiB HBM3 memory on the Hopper GPU, and an 72-core ARM CPU with 480 GiB LPDDR5X memory. The MI300A were assembled in groups of 4 nodes, but we only used one at a time (with bindings). Each node had 24 CPU cores and 6 XCD (228 compute units), with 128 GiB of HBM3 shared memory.

On both traditional setups, a manual memory management implementation was run, where copies are executed as presented in Sect. 3.1. On MI300A, the same system was used, except that there was no copy, because of the shared memory between the CPU and GPU units. However on GH200, we tested several options: the same manual version as for the traditional setups, two versions using the CUDA managed memory system - one only relying on the automatic runtime, and the other using hints. The hints allowed to indicate the system to use a read-only view on the CPU side, as data was never written on this side. This avoided taking ownership of data, and thus unnecessary copies when executing the GPU work phase again, as there was no need to fetch unmodified data from the CPU. This is implemented by using `cudaMemAdvise`, with the `setReadMostly` hint before starting to read data, and `unsetReadMostly` after being done. We also tried using the `setPreferredLocation` hint, and explicit prefetches with `cudaMemPrefetchAsync`, without much success on improving performance. We then tested one of GH200's newest feature, that allows the GPU to read directly from the CPU memory using the NVLink-C2C interconnect, up to the cache line level [20]. Implementation-wise, it simply consists in replacing `cudaMallocManaged` with `malloc`.

Metrics Used in the Benchmark. Real simulations run for millions of steps, and the first thousands steps answer to really particular dynamics inherent to the model. Thus, we want to study the other regime, that happens after a few tens of thousands of steps. To achieve this, we reuse "stable" populations, that we call Wildtypes. A run in this benchmark consists of loading a Wildtype population, running the evolution for 1100 steps and keeping the last thousand steps, as the first hundred is considered to be a warm-up (especially since the first GPU allocations are costly but executed very rarely). When extracting data, outliers are filtered out by culling the outmost 1% percentiles.

For each step, the durations of each phase described in Sect. 3.1 are recorded using the `steady_clock` of the C++ `std::chrono` API. They are then saved at the end of each run to avoid potential I/O latency during a run.

Application Parameters. Since simulation instances behaves differently - in particular in regards to the number of mutant individuals and the amount of characters changed per step, several combinations of simulation parameters have been tested out. We chose parameters in the commonly used ranges by the users of this software. Mutation rates (expressed in chance per character) were 5×10^{-5} and 5×10^{-6}. We used the following population sizes: 1024, 4096, 16384, 65536, 131044. We were not able to benchmark larger sizes because of memory capacity limitations: generating the source population takes significant amounts of memory, because population size explodes during initial stages of the evolution. Later stages require around 100× less memory, but constitutes most of the total run time, hence making it our focus. Due to the stochastic nature of this model [16], we tested out 4 different seeds per run. We also used 8 different input populations, because variability in execution time is very sensitive to the properties of the input population (see Fig. 1).

4 Results

Figure 3 depicts the detailed median execution times per phase depending on the system used. We can observe that the A100 platform gets the worst results, while the C2C implementation on GH200 is the fastest. Numbers above bars are medians, which can divert significantly from the mean as explained in the following sections. Black lines on top of bars represent the standard deviation. The following sections and figures focus on more specific aspects of the same data for comparison, but this figure can be used as a reference for analysis to come back to for a global vision.

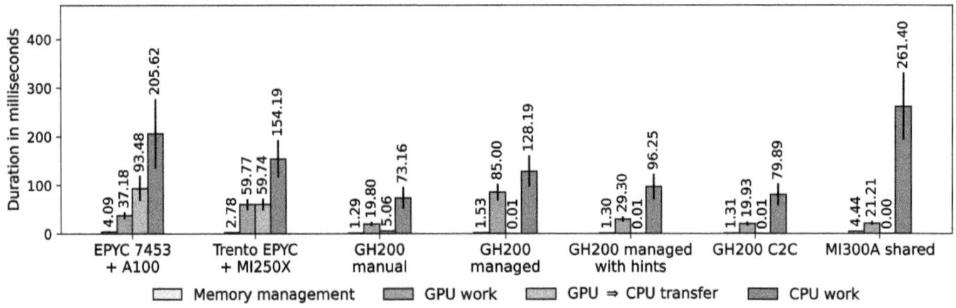

Fig. 3. Median duration and standard deviation for each step phase, depending on system of execution.

4.1 Scaling with Problem Size

Figure 4 depicts the execution time scaling relative to problem size for the CPU work and GPU work phases. The results show that as problem size increases to reach 131k individuals, median duration increases linearly, both for CPU and GPU work. The steepness of the time increase is however very variable depending on the architecture used, with a ≈ 5× speedup between GH200 and MI300A on the CPU part, and a ≈ 3× speedup between GH200 and MI250X on the GPU.

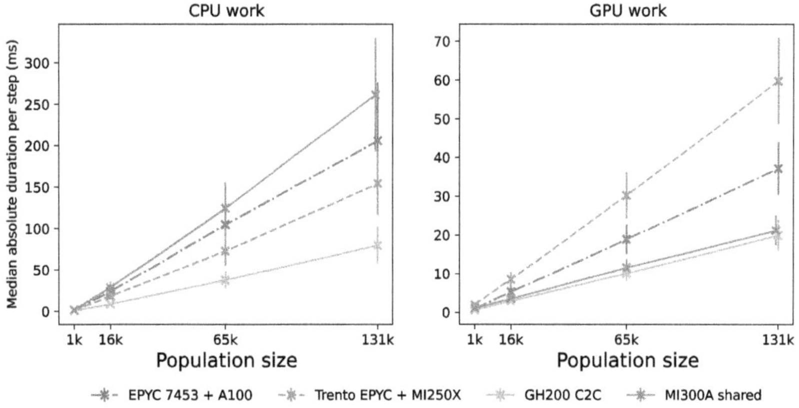

Fig. 4. Scaling on problem size on the 4 studied architectures for the CPU work and GPU work phases.

4.2 Compute Performance

CPU and GPU timings between the different GH200 versions are discussed in Sect. 4.3. In this section, when referring to GH200, we implicitly refer to the manual memory version executed on GH200.

GPU work on A100 is twice as fast as on MI250X, which is expected as publicly-stated data on INT8 OPS performance for A100 is around two times higher than on MI250X - we mainly use INT32 operations, but no data is available for this type of operations. GPU performance between GH200 and MI300A is also different - the mean is close to the median here, with 19.9 ms for GH200 and 21.63 ms for MI300A, giving an 8% advantage to GH200's GPU on average. Official sources state similar INT8 OPS capabilities between both, without giving much more details. The timings difference could come from various micro-architectural details, including the different power budget.

On the CPU part, to our surprise, MI300A hardly performs better than previous-gen CPUs, with a mean time of 233 ms, against 201 ms for EPYC 7453 and 136 ms for Trento EPYC. However, MI300A only features 24 CPU cores, against 56 for the EPYC 7453 and 64 for the Trento EPYC, giving a better per-core throughput. The major execution time difference with GH200 can then be attributed to its 72 CPU cores. When normalizing the values per-core, the performance difference would be closer to 1.14×. However, when executing the same code on 24 cores on GH200, mean time for the CPU part is 143.9 ms, so still 1.62× faster than on MI300A!

Although we cannot provide a strongly conclusive explanation for this difference, we suspect CPU memory bandwidth saturation, as it is supposedly higher (around 2×) on GH200. Specifically, measurements from [6] show a maximum bandwidth of ≈ 200 GB/s on MI300A's CPU, while we attain a 297 GB/s throughput on GH200 when transferring data from the GPU to CPU - making it close to the 1.62× speedup we observe. Micro-architectural profiling on a median

24-core simulation 1.6× faster on GH200 did not give strong differences between both platforms (using AMD Prof and Nsight Systems). Energy measurements are also very similar, with an average of 263 ± 38W on GH200 versus 270 ± 13W on MI300A. The same simulation with 72 threads used about 346 ± 61W on GH200, thus we can exclude the different power budget as a potential limiter in our case.

This CPU-GPU imbalance issue on MI300A severely hinders performance in our type of scenario, making GH200 more suited for efficient execution.

4.3 Managed Memory System Performance

Table 2. Median and mean step durations for the versions executed on GH200. Relative mean is computed with respect to the manual version.

Variant name	Median step	Mean	Relative mean
GH200 manual	112.22 ± 27.9 ms	104.2 ms	1.00
GH200 managed auto	224.80 ± 50.9 ms	204.9 ms	1.97
GH200 managed with hints	144.85 ± 34.2 ms	130.3 ms	1.25
GH200 C2C	114.67 ± 28.2 ms	100.2 ms	0.96

Table 2 presents the total median and mean step times for each version executed on GH200, along with relative mean speedup compared to the manual version.

From this table, we can observe the performance of the automatically managed memory version is very degraded compared to manual management. This can be explained by the high penalty induced by data transfers: memory is constantly brought back on either the CPU or GPU as required, wasting resources as the compute unit has to wait in the meantime. But, in our case, memory access patterns are pretty simple: on the GPU, individuals are scheduled by the default runtime in the form of thread blocks (one individual per block), but then buffer reads for each block are sequential (with striding). On the CPU, scheduling of individuals is based on their size, but each core treats one individual at a time, again with sequential buffer reads. Thus, we would expect the automatic system to behave better.

This performance penalty can be explained in the light of the hint-based version timings, which only suffers from a 25% speed decrease compared to the manual version. Most of the speedup comes from the GPU work phase (see Fig. 3), whose median time has been cut by three fold compared to the automatic version. The CPU work phase also runs 25% faster. When profiling simulations, the number of page faults stays roughly similar with the automatic version. However the total migrated data size from the CPU to the GPU falls to almost zero, while the previous version had the same amount as GPU to CPU transfers.

It suggests the read-only view worked as intended in our case, as data sent to the CPU is discarded instead of being copied back to the GPU after use. Hence the major GPU work time reduction.

Thus, it seems that in our case, the number of page faults is not the most important factor at play, but the volume of data transfers is. Even with GH200's fast interconnect, the automatic managed memory system does not seem to keep up in this scenario.

Although a 25% performance cost can be acceptable with respect to the ease of development induced by the managed memory system, GH200's C2C supersedes it both in performance and ease of use. Indeed, in our benchmark, the C2C version performed even better than the manual version, by about 4% on average. This improvement can clearly be attributed to the removal of explicit GPU-to-CPU transfers. It appears the C2C system is able to cope with the demand on the CPU: when looking at the average duration of the CPU phase, it is 1.3% slower than the manual version (68.15 vs 69 ms), while having similar spread (22.1 vs 22.55 ms deviation), but different medians (73.2 vs 79.9 ms). The difference in medians can be explained by the rugged distribution of data points, more than a major difference in execution times. Thus, C2C succeeded in completely hiding memory transfer costs in our type of scenario.

To conclude, performance of managed memory is a bit disappointing, for a simple use case such as ours (see Fig. 2) and with such a powerful interconnect as GH200's, we still get up to 2× slowdowns. C2C offers a new, hardware-based and better performing approach, without changing much to the unified memory paradigm.

4.4 Memory Transfers Performance

Table 3. Median and mean transfer times, with relative mean (rel. mean) to the slowest platform (A100). GH200 offers a 16× speedup relative to A100 on PCIe, and 11.8× relative to MI250X also on PCIe. Mean effective bandwidth (BW) is also included, GH200 and MI250X have an almost zero standard deviation, while the A100 platform has a 27% variability (5.26 GB/s deviation), explaining the speed difference with MI250X.

Variant name	Median transfer	Mean	Rel. mean	Mean BW
A100 platform	93.48 ± 25.9 ms	87.77 ms	1.00	19 GB/s
MI250X platform	59.74 ± 11.9 ms	61.83 ms	0.70	25 GB/s
GH200 manual	5.06 ± 1.0 ms	5.24 ms	0.06	297 GB/s

The CPU-GPU transfer phase (see Table 3), which amounts to about 25% of mean step time on the A100 platform, gets reduced by 16× on GH200, only representing 5% of the mean step time. For MI250X, transfer time represents 23% of mean step time, and gets reduced by a 11.8 factor on GH200. This clearly demonstrates the expected gains in bandwidth between the CPU and GPU, promised by converged computing architectures. As discussed in Sect. 4.3, C2C performs even better by hiding memory transfer costs. This metric has no point on MI300A, which does not require explicit transfers. As a reminder, maximum theoretical bandwidth with PCIe 4.0 (16x) is 32 GB/s, against 900 GB/s for NVLink-C2C (1:28 ratio), meaning we reached 33% of the theoretical bandwidth for GH200. The difference in transfer time between MI250X and A100 is due to bandwidth stability, as its bandwidth regularly drops to 15 GB/s for unknown reasons, giving an average bandwidth of 19 GB/s.

5 Conclusion

In this paper, we evaluated the performance of Nvidia's Grace Hopper superchip, against AMD's MI300A APU, with a simulation software using CPU-GPU co-processing. In this scenario where CPU performance matters as much as GPU performance, we demonstrated that GH200's Grace CPU makes it more suited for co-processing than MI300A: its higher number of cores, along with a more important memory throughput makes a significative difference. MI300A seems more specialized for GPU-only operation, with minimum work dedicated to the CPU, like task orchestration or *in situ* post-processing - but not for significant compute tasks. This resulted in a global mean step time 2.78× higher than on GH200, with about 84% of it being CPU compute, against 69% on Grace Hopper.

However, both chips succeeded in their original promise of drastically cutting memory transfer costs between the CPU and GPU. While MI300A completely suppresses the need for applicative transfers, GH200 cuts it by 16-fold. Additionally, in our case, GH200's C2C system, allowing the GPU to read from CPU chip memory, also completely hides applicative memory transfers. Conforming to [20]'s results, Nvidia's C2C system is also a very good proposition to replace the canonical managed memory system on its Superchips, as it performed much better, with the same beneficial impacts on ease of programming.

In the future, we will continue working on irregular co-processing and a dynamic online scheduling algorithm for execution on large scale converged memory platforms, with hundreds of nodes. Also, we did not leverage their ability to perfectly interleave CPU and GPU work. Indeed, C2C for GH200 and MI300A's architecture suppresses the need to set up complex batching processes. Finally, a deeper micro-architectural comparison between MI300A and GH200 could be required, to give more insight on some of the results of this paper.

Acknowledgments and Artifact Availability.. This project was provided with computing HPC and storage resources by GENCI at CINES thanks to the grant 2025-AD010616625 on the supercomputer Adastra's MI250x and MI300 partitions. Experiments on the A100 and GH200 platforms presented in this paper were carried out using the Grid'5000 testbed, supported by a scientific interest group hosted by Inria and including CNRS, RENATER and several Universities as well as other organizations (see https://www.grid5000.fr.) The artifact (containing sources and data to reproduce experiments from this paper) is available in the Zenodo repository [10].

Disclosure of Interests. The authors have no competing interests to declare that are relevant to the content of this article.

References

1. Green500 November 2025 (Feb 2026). https://top500.org/lists/green500/2025/11/
2. NVIDIA GH200 Grace Hopper Superchip Architecture Whitepaper (Feb 2026). https://nvdam.widen.net/s/c9lts6msjj/nvidia-grace-hopper-superchip-architecture-whitepaper
3. Top500 November 2025 (Feb 2026). https://top500.org/lists/top500/2025/11/
4. Abouelmagd, A., et al.: GPU Partitioning, Power, and Performance of the AMD MI300A, SCA/HPCAsia 2026, pp. 215–227. ACM (Jan 2026). https://doi.org/10.1145/3773656.3773680
5. Antepara, O., Oliker, L., Williams, S.: Roofline analysis of tightly-coupled CPU-GPU superchips: a study on MI300A and GH200, SC workshops 2025, pp. 1205–1216. ACM (Nov 2025). https://doi.org/10.1145/3731599.3767497
6. Antepara, O., et al.: Benchmark-driven models for energy analysis and attribution of GPU-accelerated supercomputing. SC **25**, 888–904 (2025). https://doi.org/10.1145/3712285.3759815 ACM
7. Bertolli, C., et al.: Performance analysis of runtime handling of zero-copy for OpenMP Programs on MI300A APUs. In: SC-W 2024, pp. 1420–1429. IEEE Press (Feb 2025). https://doi.org/10.1109/SCW63240.2024.00183
8. Dickmann, D., et al.: Evaluating AMD Instinct™ MI300A APU: performance insights on LLM training via knowledge distillation. In: CUG 2025, pp. 115–126. ACM (Nov 2025). https://doi.org/10.1145/3757348.3757361
9. Fusco, L., Khalilov, M., Chrapek, M., Chukkapalli, G., Schulthess, T., Hoefler, T.: Understanding Data Movement in Tightly Coupled Heterogeneous Systems: A Case Study with the Grace Hopper Superchip (Aug 2024). https://doi.org/10.48550/arXiv.2408.11556
10. Gallé, R., Rouzaud-Cornabas, J., Gautier, T.: Artifact of the paper: performance evaluation of a cpu-gpu coprocessing-based simulation software on converged computing architectures (2026). https://doi.org/10.5281/zenodo.20511304
11. Godoy, W., et al.: Mojo: MLIR-based performance-portable HPC science kernels on GPUs for the python ecosystem. In: SC Workshops 2025, pp. 2114–2128. ACM (Nov 2025). https://doi.org/10.1145/3731599.3767573
12. Garcia de Gonzalo, S., Gatram, A., Saravanakumar, A.: Micro-benchmarking communications libraries on the MI300A compute partitioning modes. In: SCA/HPCAsiaWS 2026, pp. 312–322. ACM (Jan 2026). https://doi.org/10.1145/3784828.3785238
13. Ichimura, T., et al.: Heterogeneous computing in a strongly-connected CPU-GPU environment: fast multiple time-evolution equation-based modeling accelerated using data-driven approach. In: SC Workshops 2024, pp. 1967–1978 (2024). https://doi.org/10.1109/SCW63240.2024.00246
14. Johansson, A., Weinberg, E., Trott, C., McCarthy, M., Moore, S.: LAMMPS-KOKKOS: performance portable molecular dynamics across exascale architectures. In: SC Workshops 2025, pp. 1217–1232. ACM (Nov 2025). https://doi.org/10.1145/3731599.3767498

15. Kuncham, G.K.R., Zhang, S., Mohammad, S., Chen, C.C., Panda, D.K.: MPI Communication performance on AMD MI300A: microbenchmarks and applications. In: SC Workshops 2025, pp. 977–984. ACM (Nov 2025). https://doi.org/10.1145/3731599.3767462
16. Luiselli, J., Parsons, D.P., Gallé, R., Banse, P., Rouzaud-Cornabas, J., Beslon, G.: Aevol-9: a simulation platform to decipher the evolution of genome architecture (2025). https://doi.org/10.1101/2025.04.10.648095
17. Malaboeuf, E., Obrejan, K., Peybernes, M., Bigot, J., Bourne, E., Grandgirard, V.: Porting a Fortran plasma simulation to Exascale on AMD GPUs using both OpenMP and Kokkos. In: SC Workshops, vol. 25, pp. 2051–2067. ACM (2025). https://doi.org/10.1145/3731599.3768148
18. Ohshima, S., Ida, A., Kawai, M., Fukaya, T., Yokota, R.: A Study on the performance and usability of managed memory and unified memory for accelerating numerical calculation program. MCSoC **25**, 41–48 (2025). https://doi.org/10.1109/MCSoC67473.2025.00017
19. Schieffer, G., Shi, R., Markidis, S., Herten, A., Faj, J., Peng, I.: Understanding data movement in AMD Multi-GPU systems with infinity fabric. In: SC-W 2024, pp. 567–576. IEEE Press (Feb 2025). https://doi.org/10.1109/SCW63240.2024.00079
20. Schieffer, G., Wahlgren, J., Ren, J., Faj, J., Peng, I.: Harnessing Integrated CPU-GPU system memory for HPC: a first look into Grace Hopper. In: ICPP 2024, pp. 199–209. ACM (Aug 2024). https://doi.org/10.1145/3673038.3673110
21. Schieffer, G., et al.: Inter-APU communication on AMD MI300A Systems via Infinity Fabric: a Deep Dive (Aug 2025). https://doi.org/10.48550/arXiv.2508.11298
22. Sfiligoi, I.: Comparing CPU and GPU compute of PERMANOVA on MI300A. PEARC **25**, 1–3 (2025). https://doi.org/10.1145/3708035.3736040
23. Smith, A., et al.: Realizing the AMD exascale heterogeneous processor vision. In: ISCA 2024, pp. 876–889. IEEE Press (Jul 2025). https://doi.org/10.1109/ISCA59077.2024.00068
24. Tee, A., Curtis, N., Wolfe, N., Wong, D.: The MALL is Open: exploring shared caches and latency in AMD CDNA™ 3 GPUs. In: SC Workshops, vol. 25, pp. 1110–1116 (2025). https://doi.org/10.1145/3731599.3767487
25. Tsai, Y.H., Bode, M., Anzt, H.: What will the grace hopper-powered jupiter supercomputer bring for sparse linear algebra? In: SCA/HPCAsia 2026, pp. 228–235. ACM (2026). https://doi.org/10.1145/3773656.3773691
26. Wahlgren, J., et al.: Dissecting CPU-GPU unified physical memory on AMD MI300A APUs. In: IISWC 2025, pp. 368–380 (Oct 2025). https://doi.org/10.1109/IISWC66894.2025.00038
27. Wilfong, B., Radhakrishnan, A., Le Berre, H., Prathi, T., Abbott, S., Bryngelson, S.H.: Testing and benchmarking emerging supercomputers via the MFC flow solver. In: SC Workshops **25**, 669–677. ACM (2025). https://doi.org/10.1145/3731599.3767424
28. Wilkinson, F., Cockrean, A., Lin, W.C., McIntosh-Smith, S., Deakin, T.: Assessing the GPU offload threshold of GEMM and GEMV kernels on modern heterogeneous HPC systems. In: SC-W 2024, pp. 1481–1495. IEEE Press (Feb 2025). https://doi.org/10.1109/SCW63240.2024.00188
29. Yokelson, D., et al.: Cross-architecture performance analysis using the RAJA performance suite. In: ICPP 2025, pp. 617–626. ACM (Dec 2025). https://doi.org/10.1145/3754598.3754668

AtSpMV: Model-Guided Adaptive Tiling and Load Balancing for SpMV on GPUs

Jiajun Cheng[1], Junshi Chen[1,2](✉), Qi Li[1], Longsheng Song[1], Yang Zhao[1], Jun Shi[1], Xiaoyu Hao[1], and Hong An[1,2]

[1] University of Science and Technology of China, Hefei 230026, China
{chengjiajun,liqi123,sls_ustc,yang_zhao,hxy2018}@mail.ustc.edu.cn, {cjuns,shijun18,han}@ustc.edu.cn

[2] Laoshan Laboratory, Qingdao, Shandong, China

Abstract. Sparse Matrix-Vector Multiplication (SpMV) performance on modern GPUs is frequently bottlenecked by the inherent mismatch between sparse data irregularity and regular hardware parallelism. Existing libraries typically rely on rigid "one-size-fits-all" configurations, struggling to adapt to diverse sparsity patterns. Moreover, they often neglect preprocessing efficiency, leading to severe overheads that negate kernel-level optimizations. To address these limitations, we introduce AtSpMV, an adaptive framework driven by a dual-stage performance model. It combines offline hardware profiling with a low-overhead online phase. By integrating the offline hardware model with the specific features of the incoming matrix, AtSpMV dynamically determines optimal parameters such as tile shape and load distribution. Furthermore, it features a GPU-accelerated, load-balanced preprocessing workflow to drastically reduce matrix preparation time. Comprehensive evaluations on NVIDIA A100 and H100 GPUs across 2,798 matrices demonstrate that AtSpMV achieves average speedups of 1.28× to 5.45× over state-of-the-art libraries, including cuSPARSE, CSR5, DASP, and amgT. In real-world PageRank applications, AtSpMV delivers up to a 4.18× end-to-end speedup.

Keywords: Blocked sparse matrix · Sparse matrix-vector multiplication · Parallel algorithm · Performance modeling

1 Introduction

Sparse matrix operations form the backbone of scientific computing, underpinning critical applications in linear system solving, finite element analysis, and graph analytics [1,4,9]. Among these, Sparse Matrix-Vector Multiplication (SpMV) presents a fundamental paradox: while modern GPUs excel at regular, dense parallelism, sparse matrices are inherently irregular, characterized by poor memory locality and unbalanced loads. To bridge this gap, the community has seen a surge in innovations—from novel storage formats [12–14,21] to dynamic code generation [2,7,19] and Tensor Core utilization [15,16,23].

M. Torquati et al. (Eds.): Euro-Par 2026, LNCS 16781, pp. 509–522, 2027.
https://doi.org/10.1007/978-3-032-35248-4_35

Despite these advances, a critical disconnect remains: recent state-of-the-art implementations effectively force all matrices into a "**one-size-fits-all**" strategy [6,8,14–16,19]. For example, DASP [15] processes rows within specific length ranges using a fixed 1×32 tile shape, while amgT [16] employs a rigid 4×8 configuration. As shown in Fig. 1, when the matrix row lengths do not align well with these pre-determined tile shapes—a condition we refer to as *mismatch*—redundant computations and padding overheads arise, leading to significant performance degradation.

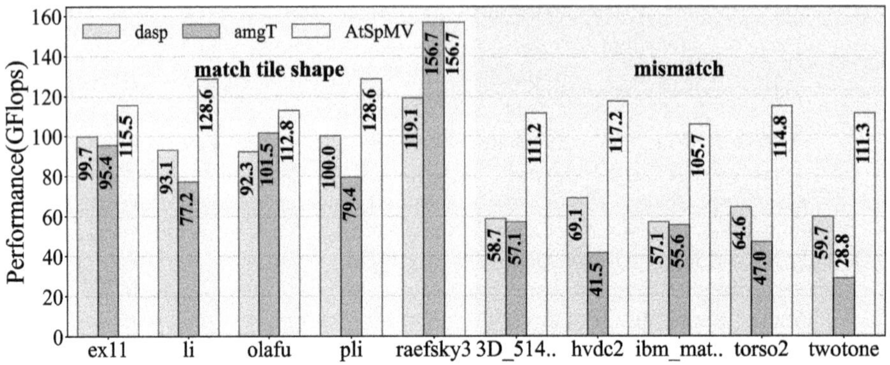

Fig. 1. Performance impact of matrix-tile mismatch on the fixed tiling (DASP, amgT) vs. adaptive tiling (AtSpMV) methods, evaluated on matrices with similar nonzero counts on an NVIDIA A100 GPU.

The "one-size-fits-all" limitation similarly hampers load balancing. Existing methodologies typically enforce uniform workload parameters, such as static warp-level tile quotas, across matrices with highly divergent non-zero distributions [14–16,19]. Such hardware-agnostic rigidity fails to account for dynamic Streaming Multiprocessor (SM) scheduling and resource contention, preventing the workload from aligning with the underlying GPU microarchitecture. Consequently, these static approaches inherently cap SpMV throughput by neglecting the complex interplay between matrix sparsity and hardware resource availability.

Furthermore, while existing frameworks heavily optimize the SpMV kernel, they often neglect load-balancing in prerequisite stages like format conversion [14–16]. This static preprocessing suffers from severe performance degradation when handling matrices with irregular data distributions. For instance, on an NVIDIA A100, amgT [16] requires 16.89× more preprocessing time for the highly skewed *Boyd2* matrix compared to the uniformly distributed *Landmark* matrix of similar size. Such disproportionate overhead completely negates downstream kernel optimizations, bottlenecking end-to-end deployment.

Motivated by these observations, we propose two core principles for optimizing SpMV. First, rather than relying on a rigid "one-size-fits-all" paradigm, the selection of tile shapes, load-balancing strategies, and other tunable algorithmic parameters must adapt dynamically to both the inherent data characteristics of the sparse matrix and the specific hardware architecture. Second, to guarantee genuine end-to-end performance gains, the matrix preprocessing phase must also be fully accelerated on the GPU, with a strict emphasis on maintaining load balance to mitigate the overhead caused by irregular sparsity patterns.

We evaluate AtSpMV on NVIDIA A100 and H100 GPUs using 2,798 matrices from the SuiteSparse collection, which spans diverse scientific domains. AtSpMV achieves average speedups of 1.43x, 5.00x, 1.65x, 1.60x, and 1.06x over cuSPARSE-CSR, cuSPARSE-BSR, DASP, amgT, and CSR5 on the A100, respectively. On the H100, it delivers average speedups of 1.28x, 5.46x, 1.60x, 1.72x, and 1.38x.

2 Background and Related Work

2.1 SpMV and Storage Formats

Sparse Matrix-Vector Multiplication (SpMV, $Y = A \cdot X$) is a foundational operation in scientific computing. While standard representations like the Compressed Sparse Row (CSR) format are widely adopted, their rigid structures inherently trigger severe load imbalance and irregular memory accesses on parallel architectures like GPUs, particularly for matrices with skewed non-zero distributions. To mitigate these bottlenecks, a diverse range of specialized formats [3,12,14,21] and adaptive block-level strategies (e.g., TileSpMV [19]) have been developed. However, these works typically focus solely on the computational efficiency of these formats, neglecting the substantial preprocessing time required to generate them. Consequently, this excessive overhead often negates the speedups achieved during the iterative phase.

2.2 Load Balancing Strategies in SpMV

Load imbalance, driven by the highly skewed, power-law distribution of non-zeros, remains a primary bottleneck in GPU-accelerated SpMV. To mitigate this, existing strategies broadly partition workloads based on rows, non-zeros (e.g., CVR [24], CVB [18], CSR5 [14]), a hybrid of both to account for write-back overheads (e.g., Merge-based SpMV [17]), or cache-line capacities to align memory accesses (e.g., CAMLB-SpMV [8]).

However, these static paradigms suffer from a rigid "one-size-fits-all" limitation that severely degrades GPU occupancy by applying uniform parameters across diverse matrices. Paradoxically, allocating finer-grained workloads (i.e., fewer elements per warp) often yields higher occupancy and parallel efficiency. Furthermore, as shown in Fig. 2, exceptionally long rows do not strictly constitute performance bottlenecks. Governed by Streaming Multiprocessor (SM) scheduling policies, while long rows continuously occupy specific SMs, other SMs dynamically fetch and process numerous shorter rows, inherently balancing the global execution time. By neglecting such hardware-specific dynamics, existing

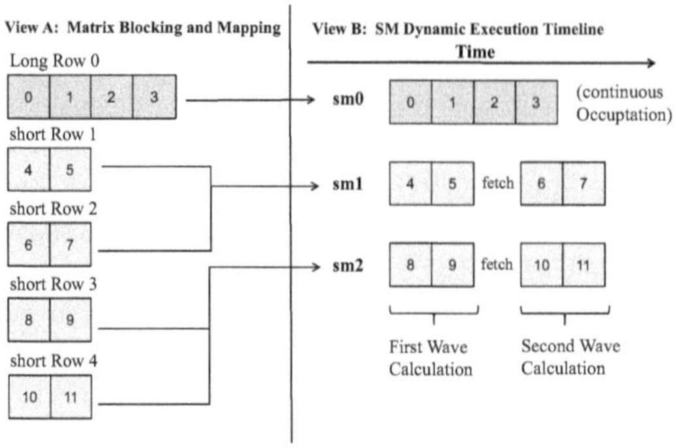

Fig. 2. Illustration of spatial workload mapping and temporal SM dynamic scheduling for irregular SpMV.

methods fail to optimally map irregular workloads, leaving substantial performance untapped.

2.3 AI-Automated SpMV Frameworks

The complexity of modern hardware has catalyzed the adoption of automated compilers like TVM [5] and Triton [22]. In the SpMV domain, AlphaSparse [7] utilizes an AI-driven Operator Graph to autonomously design matrix formats and kernels, achieving up to 3.2× speedup over manual baselines.

However, this search-based paradigm is often incompatible with the latency-sensitive requirements of scientific computing. While individual SpMV executions span microseconds, AlphaSparse's prohibitive search process can last hours. This disproportionate preprocessing overhead negates its gains in dynamic or time-critical scenarios where "time-to-solution" is the paramount metric.

Existing SpMV optimizations (Table 1) thus present a clear dichotomy: traditional libraries rely on rigid tiling and static load-balancing that fail to adapt to irregular sparsity, while AI-generated solutions offer adaptability at the cost of impractical offline overheads. To bridge this gap, we propose **AtSpMV**, a framework that reconciles these conflicting goals. By integrating model-guided adaptive tiling with hardware-aware dynamic load balancing and a fully GPU-accelerated preprocessing pipeline, AtSpMV achieves superior adaptability without compromising online efficiency.

3 Design of AtSpMV

The architecture of AtSpMV bridges offline hardware profiling with a highly optimized online preprocessing pipeline. First, an **offline performance model** extracts baseline execution metrics directly from the underlying hardware. During the **online preprocessing phase**, a lightweight **performance model** initially fuses these hardware profiles with the input matrix's dynamic features

Table 1. Qualitative comparison of state-of-the-art SpMV frameworks.

Framework	Tiling Strategy	Load Balancing	Preprocessing	Search/Prep. Overhead
cuSPARSE-CSR	unknown	unknown	GPU	Low
cuSPARSE-BSR	Fixed Block	unknown	GPU	Low
DASP	Fixed (1×32)	Static	CPU	Medium
amgT	Fixed (4×8)	Static	GPU	Low
csr5	Hardware-aware	Static	CPU	Medium
tileSpMV	Fixed(16×16)	Static	CPU	Medium
AlphaSparse	AI-Generated	Format-dependent	GPU	Prohibitive (Hours)
AtSpMV (Ours)	**Adaptive**	**Adaptive**	**GPU(Load balance)**	**Low(stable)**

to autonomously dictate the optimal tile shape and load-balancing strategy. This decision seamlessly drives a **GPU-accelerated, load-balanced format conversion workflow**, drastically reducing setup overhead and ensuring strict end-to-end performance gains for real-world applications.

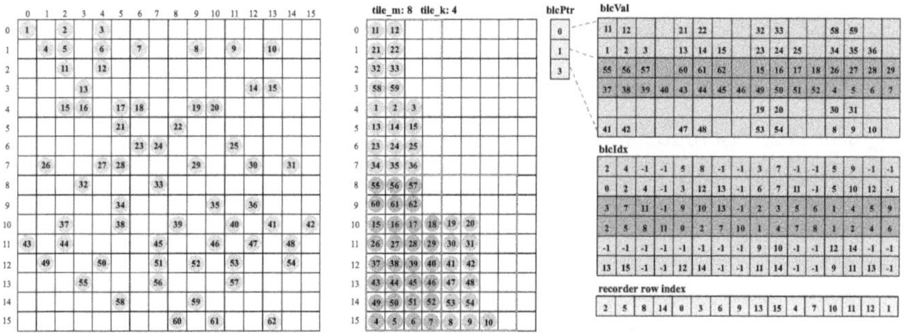

(a) An example sparse Matrix A (b) recorder the rows and tiled with 8x4 shape (c) The representation of matrix data with AtBSR format

Fig. 3. The workflow of constructing the AtBSR format: (a) original matrix A; (b) row-recorded and tiled (8×4) matrix; (c) its AtBSR memory layout.

3.1 Storage Format

AtSpMV employs a selection mechanism to choose a storage format based on matrix characteristics. Specifically, conventional sparse formats such as CSR or ELL are selected for small-scale matrices with uniformly distributed non-zeros; otherwise, the proposed AtBSR format is employed.

We propose a compressed block storage format named AtBSR. Figure 3 illustrates its construction process: the matrix rows are first reordered according to their number of non-zero elements, then compressed into blocks based on a specified tile shape, finally producing the following components: (1) blcVal: stores all elements within a tile, including both non-zeros and padded zeros; (2) blcIdx: stores the column indices for all elements in the tile, with the same number of elements as blcVal; (3) recorder row index: preserves the mapping between original and reordered row indices; (4) blcPtr: marks the starting position of each row block.

By sorting rows according to their length and compressing their elements, AtBSR achieves higher storage density and also makes load-balanced matrix processing more straightforward.

3.2 Performance Modeling Mechanism

Algorithm 1. AtSpMV: Adaptive SpMV kernel (per-warp execution)

```
Require: Sparse matrix A (tile_m × tile_k), vector X, threshold K, flag LB_EN
Ensure: Result vector Y
  // Phase 1: Adaptive Workload Mapping
  warp_id ← GetGlobalWarpIndex()
  row ← GetAssignedRow(warp_id)
  if LB_EN then                                   ▷ Scenario A: Load-Balanced Mode
      assigned_blocks ← GetPartitionedTask(warp_id, K) ▷ Process max K blocks
  else                                            ▷ Scenario B: Unbalanced Mode
      assigned_blocks ← GetAllBlocksInRow(row)    ▷ Process entire row exclusively
  end if
  // Phase 2: Computation
  sum_partial ← 0
  for each block b ∈ assigned_blocks do
      sum_partial ← sum_partial + BlockDotProduct(b, X)
  end for
  // Phase 3: Write-back Strategy
  if ¬LB_EN then                                  ▷ Unbalanced: Direct write-out
      Y[row] ← sum_partial                        ▷ Guaranteed single-warp ownership
  else                                ▷ Load-Balanced: Uniformly use Atomic Add
      atomicAdd(&Y[row], sum_partial)    ▷ Handles both short and long rows via
  atomics
  end if
```

We formalize the SpMV computation paradigm as a tunable execution flow (Algorithm 1). The sparse matrix A is first partitioned into blocks of dimension $tile\_m \times tile\_k$. Unlike static tiling, this spatial configuration is a dynamic parameter in our performance model. The workload mapping is then governed by a capacity threshold K, which dictates the distribution of row-blocks across warps through two distinct modes:

- **Workload Mapping Modes:** When load balancing is enabled (LB_EN), a warp processes at most K blocks per row, effectively fragmenting long rows to increase parallelism. In unbalanced mode, the capacity cap is bypassed, granting a single warp exclusive ownership of an entire row regardless of its length.

- **Hybrid Write-back Strategy:** The framework switches its write-back mechanism based on the mapping mode to balance synchronization costs and latency.
  - *Direct Write:* In unbalanced mode, the warp performs *intra-warp accumulation* and writes the result directly to Y. This avoids atomic contention but may suffer from row-length skew.
  - *Atomic Reduction:* In load-balanced mode, since a row may span multiple warps, *inter-warp reduction* is enforced via atomic additions to ensure correctness.

By parameterizing the block dimensions ($tile\_m, tile\_k$) and the threshold K, we transform the kernel execution time into a mathematically tractable function. This enables our model to predict performance by analyzing the trade-off between workload symmetry and the overhead of global atomic reductions.

Offline Hardware Profiling. Hardware heterogeneity—encompassing divergent SM counts, memory hierarchies, and instruction latencies—causes identical operations to perform differently across GPU generations. To systematically address this without incurring runtime overhead, we introduce an offline profiling phase. We parameterize hardware performance at the single Streaming Multiprocessor (SM) level to model intra-SM scheduling and dynamic fetching behaviors. By applying linear fitting to offline data, we construct shape-specific empirical cost functions that map the execution time of a single thread block (CTA) to its assigned sparse blocks (B_{CTA}). Notably, these shape-specific cost functions implicitly account for the latency variations resulting from memory access alignment and coalescing across different tile configurations. Formally, the execution time function for a single CTA under tile shape $\mathcal{S}$, denoted as $\mathcal{C}_{\text{CTA}}(\mathcal{S}, B_{\text{CTA}}, \mathcal{P})$, is defined as:

$$\mathcal{C}_{\text{CTA}}(\mathcal{S}, B_{\text{CTA}}, \mathcal{P}) = \begin{cases} f_{\text{unbal}}(\mathcal{S}, B_{\text{CTA}}) & \text{if } \mathcal{P} = \text{Unbalanced} \\ f_{\text{bal}}(\mathcal{S}, B_{\text{CTA}}) & \text{if } \mathcal{P} = \text{Balanced} \end{cases} \quad (1)$$

By capturing these intrinsic hardware mapping functions offline, we provide the foundational constants required for our lightweight runtime evaluation model, ensuring accurate performance predictions across diverse GPU architectures.

Online Adaptive Modeling. AtSpMV employs a lightweight analytical cost model to instantaneously map an unseen matrix to an optimal configuration $\langle \mathcal{S}^*, \theta^* \rangle$ from a search space of $6 \times 4 = 24$ candidates (6 tile shapes $\times$ 4 partitioning modes: $\{\text{Unbalanced}, \theta = 4, 8, 16\}$). The model predicts the end-to-end execution time by simulating the GPU's wave-based scheduling mechanism.

Unbalanced Time Prediction (Wave-Heavy Simulation). The **Unbalanced** strategy is bottlenecked by the distribution of row lengths. We sort all CTA workloads in descending order $[b_1, b_2, \ldots, b_M]$. The total time T_{unbal} is simulated across W waves on N_{SM} multiprocessors:

$$T_{\text{unbal}} = T_{\text{first}}(\mathcal{S}, b_{\text{heavy}}) + \sum_{w=2}^{W} T_{\text{steady}}(\mathcal{S}, b_{w,\text{heavy}}) \tag{2}$$

where T_{first} accounts for the launch overhead and execution of the heaviest CTA in the first wave, while subsequent waves follow the steady-state throughput of the remaining bottleneck CTAs.

Balanced Time Prediction (Bottleneck-Aware Simulation). The **Balanced** strategy partitions the workload into N warps with a capacity cap θ. Given the total blocks and the resulting CTA count, the model derives an average workload b_{char}. The predicted time T_{bal} is calculated as:

$$T_{\text{bal}} = T_{\text{first}}(\mathcal{S}, \min(b_{\max}, \theta)) + (W - 1) \times T_{\text{steady}}(\mathcal{S}, b_{\text{char}}) \tag{3}$$

This formulation explicitly balances the initial latency of the bottleneck warp (constrained by θ) against the averaged steady-state throughput across remaining waves.

Optimal Selection. For each unseen matrix, AtSpMV evaluates all 24 configurations and selects the one that minimizes the predicted time:

$$\langle \mathcal{S}^*, \theta^* \rangle = \arg\min_{\mathcal{S},\theta} \{T_{\text{unbal}}(\mathcal{S}), T_{\text{bal}}(\mathcal{S}, \theta)\} \tag{4}$$

This heuristic identifies the optimal configuration with marginal overhead, maximizing GPU throughput while bypassing prohibitive empirical tuning costs.

3.3 GPU-Accelerated Load-Balanced Matrix Preprocessing

Matrix preprocessing typically incurs substantial overhead, predominantly driven by the format conversion stage (e.g., transforming CSR into our AtBSR format). Unlike other lightweight preprocessing steps, format conversion must traverse all non-zero entries. Consequently, the irregular distribution of non-zeros (i.e., row-length skew) severely bottlenecks the execution, as threads processing exceptionally long rows dominate the overall time.

To mitigate this, we introduce a GPU-accelerated, load-balanced format conversion scheme that reuses the SpMV kernel's workload distribution strategy. For highly skewed matrices, the conversion workload of long rows is partitioned across multiple warps. Threads write directly to memory locations perfectly aligned for subsequent SpMV execution, ensuring optimal data locality.

4 Evaluation

4.1 Experiment Setup

Experiments are conducted on NVIDIA A100 and H100 GPUs (CUDA v12.4). We perform all evaluations in FP64, aligning with scientific computing standards, while our design remains adaptable to other precisions. We compare AtSpMV against several state-of-the-art SpMV implementations: cuSPARSE `cusparseSpMV` (CSR and BSR), the 2D-tiling based CSR5 [14], the Tensor Core-accelerated DASP [15], and amgT [16] (omitting TileSpMV due to modern CUDA compatibility issues).

We evaluate our framework on 2,798 diverse matrices from the SuiteSparse Collection [10]. Exhibiting extreme structural variety, dimensions range from 190 to 2.26×10^8 rows (median 40.4K) and up to 5.79×10^9 non-zeros (median 489K). To highlight severe load imbalances, 66.1% of matrices average short rows (< 10 NNZ), whereas 3.3% feature exceptionally dense rows (≥ 100, up to 43,800 NNZ/row). Furthermore, 76.6% are square and 41.3% symmetric. Table 2 summarizes hardware and baseline details.

Table 2. The two GPUs and six algorithms evaluated

Two NVIDIA GPUs	Algorithms
A100 (Ampere) PCIe	(1) cuSPARSE-CSR
– FP64 (CUDA/Tensor Core): 9.7/19.5 TFLOPS	(2) cuSPARSE-BSR
– Memory: 40 GB	(3) DASP
– Bandwidth: 1555 GB/s	(4) amgT
H100 (Hopper) PCIe	(5) CSR5
– FP64 (CUDA/Tensor Core): 30/60 TFLOPS	(6) **AtSpMV (this work)**
– Memory: 80 GB	
– Bandwidth: 2048 GB/s	

4.2 Performance Comparison

Figure 4 presents the FP64 precision performance comparison across the evaluated matrices. Our method achieves superior performance on the vast majority of matrices on the A100 and H100 platform. Specifically, AtSpMV outperforms cuSPARSE-CSR on 2,731 matrices, cuSPARSE-BSR on 2,772 matrices, DASP on 2,526 matrices, amgT on 2,589 matrices, and CSR5 on 2,404 matrices. On the A100 platform, it delivers average speedups of 1.43×, 5.00×, 1.65×, 1.60×, and 1.06× over these baselines. On the H100 platform, the average speedups are 1.28×, 5.46×, 1.60×, 1.72×, and 1.38×.

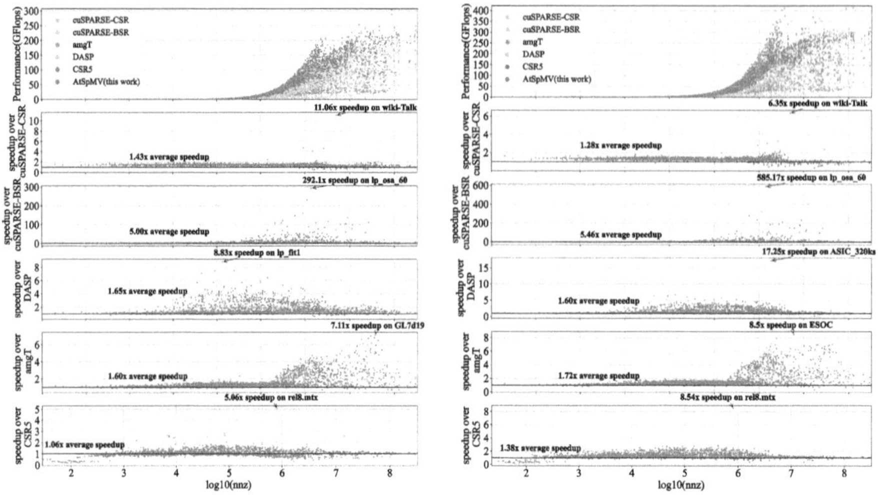

(a) NVIDIA A100 (b) NVIDIA H100

Fig. 4. Performance comparison of AtSpMV against state-of-the-art methods on A100 and H100 GPUs in FP64 precision

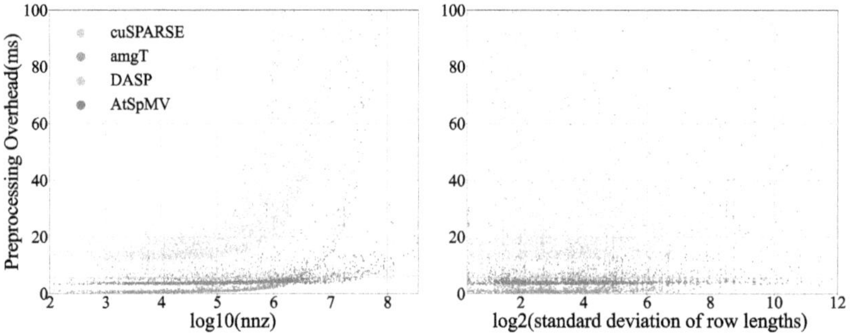

(a) (b)

Fig. 5. Preprocessing overhead comparison of AtSpMV against state-of-the-art methods on the A100 GPU.

4.3 Preprocessing Overhead Comparison

As introduced in Sect. 3.3, we evaluate the one-time preprocessing overhead of format conversion and workload partitioning, excluding disk I/O and AtSpMV's specific offline profiling. Notably, this hardware profiling is a one-time offline task that requires only $\sim$11 s on an H100 GPU, and the resulting profiles can be reused for all subsequent matrix executions on the same architecture. Even for schemes that utilize the standard CSR format, preprocessing steps such as workload partitioning remain essential. On an NVIDIA A100 GPU, AtSpMV achieves significant speedups, outperforming cuSPARSE-CSR, DASP, and amgT by an average of 1.43×, 11.85×, and 2.15×, respectively.

More importantly, AtSpMV demonstrates exceptional robustness against workload irregularity. As illustrated in Fig. 5a and Fig. 5b, AtSpMV's preprocessing efficiency remains highly stable despite increasing matrix sizes and extreme row-wise imbalance (measured by the standard deviation of non-zeros per row). While other state-of-the-art methods suffer from significant performance degradation under such challenging conditions, our load-balanced design consistently mitigates these overheads. This consistent execution time across diverse matrices underscores AtSpMV's viability for practical, large-scale deployment.

4.4 Integrated Performance Evaluation

To validate AtSpMV's practical impact, we evaluate its end-to-end performance using PageRank [20], a graph analytics workload dominated by iterative SpMV operations. Since each iteration requires one SpMV, the total runtime is highly sensitive to the balance between preprocessing efficiency and kernel throughput.

As shown in Fig. 6, we benchmark various real-world graphs from the SNAP dataset [11] on an NVIDIA A100 GPU. AtSpMV consistently outperforms cuSPARSE-CSR, achieving an end-to-end speedup of 1.27× to 4.18×. Notably, this end-to-end execution time encompasses both the one-time preprocessing overhead (i.e., format conversion and workload partitioning) and the cumulative time of all iterations. These improvements stem from our dual-optimization strategy: the load-balanced preprocessing prunes setup latency, while adaptive tiling accelerates per-iteration computation. By reconciling these often-conflicting goals, AtSpMV demonstrates superior scalability for iterative graph algorithms on large-scale datasets.

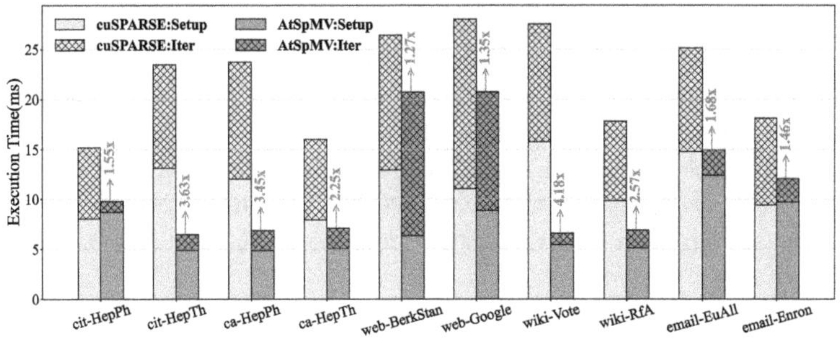

Fig. 6. PageRank end-to-end performance: AtSpMV vs. cuSPARSE-CSR on NVIDIA A100 GPU.

4.5 Performance Analysis

Evaluating AtSpMV on 2,798 SuiteSparse matrices reveals that adaptive routing directs 71.7% of matrices to the AtBSR format for irregular sparsity. Despite introducing structural padding, the NNZ-weighted padding ratio is merely 4.65%, effectively marginalizing overhead in compute-heavy matrices. Ultimately, AtSpMV bridges the gap between theoretical and practical performance: it achieves a 75.7% hit rate (yielding throughput within 5% of the exhaustive-search optimal). Furthermore, 89.9% of matrices show <10% performance loss, with a median loss of just 2.1% (mean 3.5%).

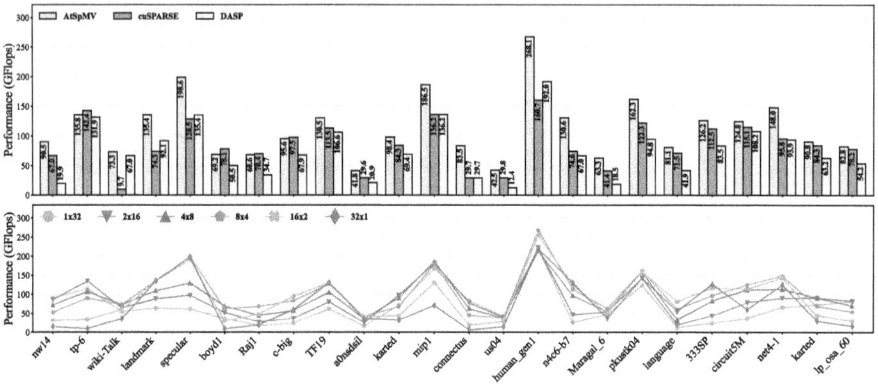

Fig. 7. Performance comparison of AtSpMV across six candidate tile shapes on A100 GPU.

As Fig. 7 illustrates, SpMV throughput is extremely sensitive to tile shapes, precluding static configurations. No single shape dominates: *specular* heavily favors 4x8, while *human_gen1* peaks at 1x32.

With a low median prediction error of 6.1%, AtSpMV's analytical model successfully captures these dynamics. For the highly irregular *wiki-Talk* matrix, dynamic shape selection achieves 73.3 GFlops, outperforming cuSPARSE by over 7.5x. These findings confirm that reconciling matrix-specific sparsity with hardware-aware simulation is critical for maximizing GPU utilization.

5 Conclusion

This paper presents **AtSpMV**, an adaptive SpMV framework driven by a dual-stage model that decouples offline hardware characterization from online parameter selection. By enforcing a divergence-free warp-level execution model and providing a fully GPU-accelerated, load-balanced preprocessing workflow, AtSpMV eliminates traditional bottlenecks. Evaluations on A100 and H100 GPUs across 2,798 matrices demonstrate AtSpMV outperforms cuSPARSE, CSR5, DASP, and amgT by 1.28x–5.45x on average. Finally, end-to-end PageRank benchmarks confirm its practical viability with up to a 4.18x application speedup.

Acknowledgements. This work was supported by the Strategic Priority Research Program of Chinese Academy of Sciences (Grant No. XDB0500102) and Laoshan Laboratory (No. LSKJ202300305). We also thank the anonymous reviewers for their constructive comments.

Disclosure of Interests. The authors have no competing interests to declare that are relevant to the content of this article.

References

1. Ahamed, A.K.C., Magoules, F.: Iterative methods for sparse linear systems on graphics processing unit. In: 2012 IEEE 14th International Conference on High Performance Computing and Communication & 2012 IEEE 9th International Conference on Embedded Software and Systems, pp. 836–842. IEEE (2012)
2. Ashoury, M., Loni, M., Khunjush, F., Daneshtalab, M.: Auto-SpMV: automated optimizing SpMV kernels on GPU. arXiv preprint arXiv:2302.05662 (2023)
3. Bell, N., Garland, M.: Implementing sparse matrix-vector multiplication on throughput-oriented processors. In: SC 2009, pp. 18:1–18:11 (2009)
4. Brin, S., Page, L.: The anatomy of a large-scale hypertextual web search engine. Comput. Netw. ISDN Syst. **30**(1–7), 107–117 (1998). https://doi.org/10.1016/S0169-7552(98)00110-X
5. Chen, T., et al.: {TVM}: an automated {End-to-End} optimizing compiler for deep learning. In: 13th USENIX Symposium on Operating Systems Design and Implementation (OSDI 2018), pp. 578–594 (2018)
6. Cong, X., Sun, F., Chen, Y., Xie, C., Liu, Y., Qian, D.: CB-SpMV: a data aggregating and balance algorithm for for cache-friendly block-based SPMV on GPUs. In: Proceedings of the 39th ACM International Conference on Supercomputing, pp. 149–160 (2025)
7. Du, Z., Li, J., Wang, Y., Li, X., Tan, G., Sun, N.: Alphasparse: generating high performance SpMV codes directly from sparse matrices. In: SC22: International Conference for High Performance Computing, Networking, Storage and Analysis, pp. 1–15. IEEE (2022)
8. Guo, J., Xia, R., Liu, J., Zhu, X., Zhang, X.: CAMLB-SpMV: an efficient cache-aware memory load-balancing SPMV on CPU. In: Proceedings of the 53rd International Conference on Parallel Processing, pp. 640–649 (2024)
9. Kepner, J., Bader, D., Buluç, A., Gilbert, J., Mattson, T., Meyerhenke, H.: Graphs, matrices, and the graphblas: seven good reasons. Procedia Comput. Sci. **51**, 2453–2462 (2015). https://doi.org/10.1016/j.procs.2015.05.353. international Conference On Computational Science, ICCS 2015
10. Kolodziej, S.P., et al.: The suitesparse matrix collection website interface. J. Open Source Softw. **4**(35), 1244 (2019)
11. Leskovec, J., Sosič, R.: Snap: a general-purpose network analysis and graph-mining library. ACM Trans. Intell. Syst. Technol. (TIST) **8**(1), 1–20 (2016)
12. Li, J., Sun, J., Vuduc, R.: HiCOO: hierarchical storage of sparse tensors. In: SC18: International Conference for High Performance Computing, Networking, Storage and Analysis, pp. 238–252 (2018). https://doi.org/10.1109/SC.2018.00022

13. Liu, L., Liu, M., Wang, C., Wang, J.: LSRB-CSR: a low overhead storage format for SpMV on the GPU systems. In: 2015 IEEE 21st International Conference on Parallel and Distributed Systems (ICPADS), pp. 733–741. IEEE (2015)
14. Liu, W., Vinter, B.: CSR5: an efficient storage format for cross-platform sparse matrix-vector multiplication. In: Proceedings of the 29th ACM on International Conference on Supercomputing, pp. 339–350 (2015)
15. Lu, Y., Liu, W.: DASP: specific dense matrix multiply-accumulate units accelerated general sparse matrix-vector multiplication. In: Proceedings of the International Conference for High Performance Computing, Networking, Storage and Analysis, pp. 1–14 (2023)
16. Lu, Y., et al.: Amgt: algebraic multigrid solver on tensor cores. In: SC24: International Conference for High Performance Computing, Networking, Storage and Analysis, pp. 1–16. IEEE (2024)
17. Merrill, D., Garland, M.: Merge-based parallel sparse matrix-vector multiplication. In: SC'16: Proceedings of the International Conference for High Performance Computing, Networking, Storage and Analysis, pp. 678–689. IEEE (2016)
18. Namashivavam, N., Mehta, S., Yew, P.C.: Variable-sized blocks for locality-aware SpMV. In: 2021 IEEE/ACM International Symposium on Code Generation and Optimization (CGO), pp. 211–221. IEEE (2021)
19. Niu, Y., Lu, Z., Dong, M., Jin, Z., Liu, W., Tan, G.: Tilespmv: a tiled algorithm for sparse matrix-vector multiplication on GPUs. In: 2021 IEEE International Parallel and Distributed Processing Symposium (IPDPS), pp. 68–78. IEEE (2021)
20. Page, L., Brin, S., Motwani, R., Winograd, T.: The pagerank citation ranking: bringing order to the web. Technical report, Stanford infolab (1999)
21. Rice, J.R., Boisvert, R.F.: Solving Elliptic Problems Using ELLPACK. Springer, Heidelberg (1985)
22. Tillet, P., Kung, H.T., Cox, D.: Triton: an intermediate language and compiler for tiled neural network computations. In: Proceedings of the 3rd ACM SIGPLAN International Workshop on Machine Learning and Programming Languages, MAPL 2019, pp. 10–19. Association for Computing Machinery, New York, NY, USA (2019). https://doi.org/10.1145/3315508.3329973
23. Wildgrube, F., et al.: GPUs all grown-up: fully device-driven SpMV using GPU work graphs. In: Proceedings of the 52nd Annual International Symposium on Computer Architecture, pp. 1777–1791 (2025)
24. Xie, B., et al.: CVR: efficient vectorization of SpMV on x86 processors. In: Proceedings of the 2018 International Symposium on Code Generation and Optimization, pp. 149–162 (2018)

X-BQSR: Holistic Acceleration of Base Quality Recalibration for Scalable Genomic Analysis

Eugenio Marinelli, Ivan Donchev Kabadzhov(✉), and Raja Appuswamy

EURECOM, Biot, France
ivan.kabadzhov@eurecom.fr

Abstract. With the continued decline in sequencing costs, genomics-based precision medicine is gaining increasing importance. The Genome Analysis Toolkit (GATK) is the standard framework for converting raw genomic data into actionable variants, but one of its most expensive steps is base quality score recalibration (BQSR), which corrects systematic sequencing errors. Despite significant work on accelerating other parts of the variant calling pipeline, BQSR has not been systematically explored on GPUs.

In this work, we analyze BQSR to identify computational and I/O bottlenecks and show that simply offloading key stages to an accelerator is insufficient to achieve overall gains. We then present X-BQSR, a holistic redesign of the entire BQSR pipeline, including I/O, compression, and kernel execution, to better leverage GPU parallelism. We implement X-BQSR using portable SYCL kernels for NVIDIA, AMD, and Intel GPUs, along with native CUDA and HIP backends for comparison, and we evaluate its performance against previous FPGA work. Our evaluation shows up to 141.7× acceleration compared to single-threaded GATK and 8.7× acceleration compared to a proprietary GPU-accelerated solution.

Keywords: base quality recalibration · genomics · GPU acceleration · high-performance computing

1 Introduction

Over the last two decades, the cost of DNA sequencing has dropped faster than Moore's law, from over $1,000,000 in 2001 to well under $1,000 today [10]. As we move into the era of $100 sequencing, genomics-driven precision medicine efforts have become widespread in both research and clinical practice. Germline genomic analysis, or the task of studying mutations that are inherited and present in every cell, is of vital importance as it has several applications, from clinical diagnosis of rare diseases in humans, to population-genomics studies that map genetic diversity in other organisms. The gold standard computational pipeline used

M. Torquati et al. (Eds.): Euro-Par 2026, LNCS 16781, pp. 523–538, 2027.
https://doi.org/10.1007/978-3-032-35248-4_36

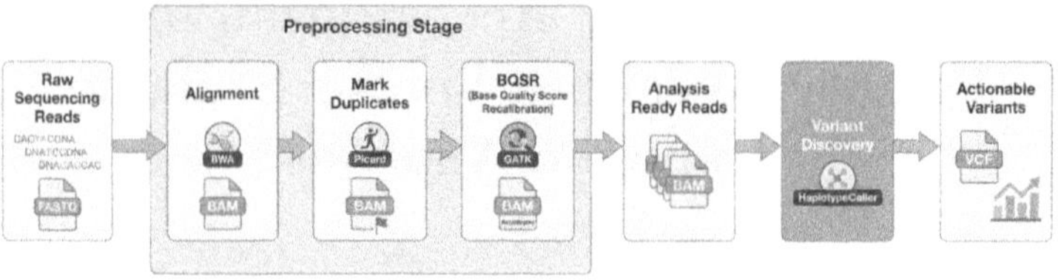

Fig. 1. GATK germline variant calling pipeline.

for germline genomic analysis is the Genome Analysis Toolkit (GATK) [1,4,9] germline variant calling pipeline shown in Fig. 1.

It is well known that the GATK pipeline is computationally intensive. For instance, an evaluation by Intel [12] showed that the pipeline took 1.5 days to run the pipeline for a whole-genome sequencing dataset at 30× coverage on a 36-core CPU. This naturally makes the pipeline a key bottleneck in any genomic analysis that processes multiple such sequences, and hence, a key optimization target for hardware-accelerated solutions from both industry and academia. As shown in Fig. 1, Base Quality Score Recalibration (BQSR) is the final preprocessing step that recalibrates systematic errors to ensure variant discovery receives high-fidelity, analysis-ready reads. While prior research has accelerated alignment and discovery using optimized CPU threading (e.g., elPrep [3]), GPUs (e.g., CUSHAW [7]), and FPGAs [2], BQSR remains a bottleneck. To our knowledge, the BQSR stage has been the focus of only one academic study, which proposed an algorithm-hardware co-optimization strategy using FPGA by Lo et al. [8]. While that work demonstrated the potential of hardware acceleration, it only targeted the BaseRecalibrator phase of BQSR, neglected the ApplyBQSR phase, and did not perform end-to-end integration within the full GATK pipeline. On the other hand, NVIDIA Parabricks library [11] provides a closed-source solution for BQSR acceleration targeting NVIDIA GPUs. But their CUDA implementation is closed source, and not portable to multi-vendor GPUs and accelerators, like Intel Flex or AMD MI250.

In this work, we bridge this gap by making several contributions. First, we present an in-depth analysis of BQSR to identify various computational and I/O bottlenecks in the CPU-based implementation and to identify GPU-offload targets for an accelerated redesign. Second, we present **X-BQSR**, a redesign of the core BQSR algorithms to unlock the massive SIMT parallelism of GPUs. In doing so, we not only develop optimized GPU kernels for performing the core computation but also perform a holistic redesign of all other aspects of BQSR including I/O, compression, memory management, and data transfers, to ensure that the improvement unlocked by GPU acceleration is not overshadowed by other hidden overheads. Third, we implement three variants of **X-BQSR** using CUDA, HIP, and SYCL. Our SYCL **X-BQSR** implementation is the first, portable, vendor-neutral, open-source implementation of BQSR that can

E. Marinelli and I. D. Kabadzhov—These authors contributed equally to this work.

run on multicore CPUs, integrated GPUs, and multi-vendor discrete GPUs using a single code base. Finally, we present a rigorous evaluation comparing **X-BQSR** with the original single-threaded GATK BQSR, Spark-enabled multi-threaded GATK BQSR, FPGA BQSR from Lo et al., and NVIDIA Parabricks BQSR. In doing so, we show that: (i) **X-BQSR** can outperform NVIDIA Parabricks by 3.6× to 8.7× across varying dataset scales; (ii) SYCL **X-BQSR** matches or exceeds the performance of its CUDA counterpart while remaining portable across NVIDIA, AMD, and Intel GPUs; and (iii) unlike FPGA implementations that require external data pre-formatting, our implementation serves as a drop-in replacement in the GATK germline pipeline, providing up to a 141.7× speedup at the BQSR level and a 2.7× speedup for the GATK preprocessing stage as a whole compared to optimized multithread CPU workflows. We plan to make our code fully open source together with the camera-ready version of our manuscript.

Table 1. Pipeline and BQSR breakdown for HG004 (NovaSeq)

Stage	Time (min)	Share (%)
Alignment (bwa-mem2)	156.0	18.9
GATK Sort / Markdup	219.0	26.5
BQSR model build (`BaseRecalibrator`)	223.8	27.1
BQSR apply (`ApplyBQSR`)	226.8	27.5

(a) Pipeline-level breakdown

Component	Time (min)	Share (%)
Input Processing	**68.46**	**32.3**
Parsing	62.71	29.6
Decompression	5.56	2.6
Computation	**58.14**	**27.4**
`BaseRecalibrator`	38.63	18.2
`ApplyBQSR`	19.51	9.2
Output Processing	**85.50**	**40.3**
Formatting	27.50	13.0
Compression	56.98	26.8

(b) BQSR workflow breakdown

2 Design

Modern high-throughput sequencing (HTS) instruments read DNA one base at a time and assign a quality score to each base call that is intended to approximate the probability that the predicted base is incorrect. While instrument calibration provides a reasonable initial estimate, systematic biases commonly remain that lead to errors in estimates. These errors may depend on sequencing context (e.g., local k-mer patterns), cycle (position within the read), and lane-specific effects. Since downstream variant callers weight evidence using base qualities, miscalibration can translate into misweighted observations at scale, affecting the accuracy of variant calls [4,5]. BQSR calibrates base-quality scores by estimating empirical error rates conditioned on covariates while excluding known-variant loci. The workflow consists of two stages: (1) model construction (`BaseRecalibrator`), which takes as input a binary alignment map (BAM) file containing aligned reads and builds recalibration statistics, and (2) score application (`ApplyBQSR`), which writes a new BAM file with corrected quality scores based on the learned model.

To motivate the need for holistic acceleration of BQSR, Table 1a reports an end-to-end breakdown of the GATK preprocessing pipeline on a whole-genome sequencing (WGS) dataset (D4 from Sect. 3). As can be seen, the two BQSR phases together account for 54.6% of the total preprocessing time, making BQSR a high-leverage target for reducing overall workflow latency. Following Amdahl's Law, this establishes a maximum theoretical speedup of approximately 2.2× for the entire pipeline if BQSR execution time were reduced to zero.

Table 1b further decomposes the total runtime of the algorithm into (i) input processing (disk I/O, BGZF decompression, and parsing), (ii) core BQSR computation, and (iii) output processing (formatting, BGZF compression, and writing). The latter is valid only for `ApplyBQSR`, as `BaseRecalibrator` does not write out a new BAM file but only a text file containing the recalibration tables, whose I/O cost is negligible, as the tables span only a few KB. The results show that end-to-end performance is constrained not only by compute but also by input/output processing (parsing and (de)compression); `BaseRecalibrator` is dominated by input handling, whereas `ApplyBQSR` is dominated by output formatting and compression.

These measurements motivate the holistic redesign adopted by **X-BQSR**, where we designed optimized GPU kernels to handle the complex computation of various stages of BQSR (as described in Sect. 2.1), and wrapped these kernels in a scalable pipeline that efficiently parallelizes serialization/compression and overlaps computation with I/O to eliminate bottlenecks in the data path (as described in Sect. 2.2).

2.1 GPU Kernel Design

X-BQSR implements the BQSR pipeline as a three-stage SIMT-optimized architecture: (1) **Sequence Clipping** via metadata transformations, (2) **Feature Derivation** using base-parallel flattening for balanced workload distribution, and (3) **Table Aggregation** via a two-level atomic strategy. This section details how these kernels resolve the sequential bottlenecks and memory contention inherent in the original CPU algorithms.

`BaseRecalibrator` **Sequence Clipping.** Unlike traditional CPU-based implementations that process genomic reads as individual objects, X-BQSR utilizes a Structure-of-Arrays (SoA) layout. Each field (CIGAR, sequence, quality) is stored in a large flat vector, with strings from different reads placed contiguously. We parallelize at the read level, assigning one thread to scan the CIGAR field and identify adapter regions. By using the SoA format, we implement clipping as a simple metadata update to a *span vector* that stores the starting position and length, avoiding expensive string manipulation or memory copies. This design ensures coalesced memory access and explains why the Clip stage accounts for a negligible fraction of the total runtime in our evaluation (Fig. 4c).

`BaseRecalibrator` Feature Detection. This stage computes two per-base binary vectors. The first (`isSNP`) marks sequencing error events by comparing each aligned read to the reference genome. This involves scanning the CIGAR string, advancing read and reference pointers according to edit operators (M, I, D) [6] and marking each aligned mismatch as an observed error event. The second (`skip mask`) indicates bases that must be excluded from training. This includes positions that (i) overlap known variant sites, (ii) contain ambiguous nucleotides, or (iii) lie outside the post-clipping span. Skip mask is generated by intersecting the read's reference alignment interval with known-site intervals and mapping the resulting locations back to read coordinates.

There are two potential parallelization strategies that can be adopted for computing these two binary vectors on the GPU, namely, a one-thread-per-read mapping or a one-thread-per-base mapping.

With one-thread-per-read mapping, each thread processes a single read and performs three steps. First, it determines the interval of the reference genome covered by the clipped alignment. Second, it intersects this interval with the list of known variant sites to identify which reference coordinates must be ignored during recalibration. Third, the thread walks the CIGAR operations to translate those reference coordinates into the corresponding read indices. Whenever a reference position associated with a known site maps to a base in the read, the kernel marks that position in the per-read skip mask. SNP events detection is computed similarly, with each thread traversing both read and reference based on the CIGAR and comparing the bases: if they differ, a mismatch is marked in a `SNP vector`.

The base-parallel design, in contrast, is based on the key idea that a CIGAR string encodes the alignment as a sequence of pairs $< length, operation >$, where the operation can be I (insertion), D (deletion), M (match/mismatch), H (hard clip), and so on. For example, a CIGAR such as $(10M2D5M)$ describes ten aligned bases, followed by two deletions and five additional aligned bases. Thus, one possible transformation is to expand this representation so that each operation is repeated per base. In the previous example this would produce a vector such as $MMMMMMMMMMDDMMMMM$. By computing a prefix sum over this expanded vector (reset at the beginning of each read), threads can directly derive the corresponding read and reference coordinates without sequentially walking the CIGAR. This removes the intra-read dependency and produces a more uniform workload across GPU threads.

In **X-BQSR**, we implemented both these approaches. In our early evaluation, we found read-level parallelism to outperform base-level one as the transformation requires materializing additional vectors and performing a prefix scan, increasing global memory traffic. Thus, we retained the read-level implementation for this stage.

`BaseRecalibrator` **Table Aggregation.** Once eligible bases are identified in the previous step, `BaseRecalibrator` computes the covariates associated with each position. Covariates are discrete features that capture systematic biases in sequencing output. In the `BaseRecalibrator` formulation, the covariate tuple for base i includes:

- Reported quality score Q_i: directly extracted from the Phred-encoded quality string; its cardinality is bounded (typically < 100).
- Cycle covariate $\texttt{cycle}_i$: the base index within the read, computed in a strand-aware manner such that comparable sequencing cycles map to similar values; cardinality is proportional to the maximum read length.
- Context covariate $\texttt{context}_i$: a strand-corrected k-mer centered at the base (commonly $k = 2$ or 3), encoded in a compact 2-bit representation per base; cardinality is at most $4^k + 1$ (including an invalid sentinel).

Concretely, after clipping, masking, and mismatch detection, `BaseRecalibrator` uses various vectors produced in these stages to compute the covariate tuples, for example, $(RG, Q, cycle, context)$. These tuples represent multidimensional indexes that are used to update tables recording the number of times each covariate appears and the number of mismatches with respect to the reference genome for that base quality.

In the CPU-based GATK `BaseRecalibrator` implementation, covariate construction is naturally implemented as a single pass where (i) the covariate keys are derived from the eligible bases and (ii) the tables are updated directly. As default GATK `BaseRecalibrator` is single-threaded, there is no contention when updating the tables. However, when parallelized on the GPU, the tables will be updated simultaneously for thousands of bases. Consequently, updates must be protected with atomics and might experience significant contention. To avoid performance issues, we implemented this stage of `BaseRecalibrator` using two distinct kernels rather than one.

Covariate Emission (Base-Parallel). The first kernel in **X-BQSR** for this stage just computes covariate indices.

Because this step has no intra-read dependencies, we parallelize it at the base level rather than at the read level. To do so, we flatten all reads into a single list of bases. Rather than assigning one thread per read, we partition this flattened list into nearly equal contiguous segments that are processed by GPU threads (or groups of threads). Each thread therefore receives approximately the same number of bases to process, independent of the original read boundaries. To determine which read a given base belongs to, we precompute a prefix-sum array over the read lengths. This array stores, for each read, the starting offset of that read in the flattened base list. Given a global base index, a thread performs a search over this prefix array to identify the corresponding read and the offset within that read. Once this mapping is known, the thread can access the appropriate entries in the previously computed vectors (skip mask, mismatch flags, context keys, and quality scores) and compute the covariate indices for that base. This strategy effectively converts the irregular workload caused by variable-length reads into a balanced distribution of work across GPU threads. As a result, threads within a warp tend to execute a similar amount of work, improving overall GPU utilization.

Scalable Table Aggregation (Contention-Aware). Once the covariate indices and the corresponding per-base SNP information have been computed, the second kernel in **X-BQSR** updates the covariate tables. Each update consists of indexing the tables with the covariate index and incrementing two values stored at that entry: (i) a counter representing how many times that covariate appears and (ii) a counter tracking the number of mismatches observed for that base. Since the tables are relatively small and the number of updates is extremely large (billions of bases), concurrent updates on the GPU would result in a very large number of atomic operations that must be serialized due to contention, drastically hurting performance. To mitigate this issue, we adopt a two-level histogram update strategy. As all tables fit in the GPU shared memory, each thread block first updates a local copy of the tables. Atomic operations within a block are significantly faster than atomics in global memory. Then, a single thread per block merges the local histogram into the global table, greatly reducing global memory contention.

ApplyBQSR. Having discussed the design of **X-BQSR**'s `BaseRecalibrator` phase, we now focus on the `ApplyBQSR` phase which rewrites the quality score of each base by evaluating a hierarchical Bayesian model built using the covariate tables computed in the previous phase. Similar to the covariate-emission in the Feature Detection stage, we use base-level parallelism for redesigning `ApplyBQSR`. In particular, for each base, a thread reconstructs the covariate tuple $(\text{readGroup}, \text{qual}, \text{cycle}, \text{context})$, similar to what is done in the `BaseRecalibrator` algorithm. This tuple is used to retrieve the empirical statistics needed to evaluate the Bayesian model and obtain the recalibrated quality score. The resulting quality score is then quantized into the final integer Phred value.

A key observation in this kernel is that many bases may share the same combination of covariates, for example when they have the same quality score, cycle, and context. As a result, the recalibrated quality score may be recomputed repeatedly for identical covariate tuples. To avoid this redundancy, we introduce a device-wide lookup table that stores the result of the computation for each unique covariate combination. The table is implemented as a flattened multidimensional array over the covariate domains (read group, quality score, context, and cycle). The table size is bounded: up to 94 quality values, roughly 1,000 context values, and up to 1,000 cycle values (500 positions across two strands). Since each entry stores a 1-byte quantized score, the table occupies about 1 MB. Because BQSR models covariates independently for each read group, the table must be replicated per read group. In practice, however, samples usually contain only 110 read groups, so the overall memory footprint remains small. During execution, each thread computes the covariate indexes and checks whether the recalibrated value is already present in the table. If so, it reuses the cached value directly. Otherwise, it computes the value and atomically updates the table.

2.2 Pipeline Optimizations

Having presented the design of GPU kernels in **X-BQSR**, we now describe various pipeline optimizations that ensure that the acceleration achieved by kernel offload to GPUs is not overshadowed by overheads in the input–output I/O path.

Optimizing BAM Input. As shown in Table 1b, BAM parsing in input processing was a major overhead for `BaseRecalibrator`. The primary obstacle to scaling BAM reading is record boundary discovery; after BGZF decompression, the BAM byte stream is a concatenation of variable-length records, and identifying record starts requires a sequential scan. We address this issue by leveraging the `.bai` index that typically accompanies coordinate-sorted BAM files in best-practice workflows. The BAI linear index provides BGZF virtual offsets that correspond to valid BAM record starts. We extract and deduplicate these virtual offsets and use them as candidate slice boundaries. Because a virtual offset encodes both a compressed block position and an uncompressed offset within the block, it represents a safe restart point for BGZF inflation, enabling deterministic search and decoding.

To balance slices, we build a lightweight BGZF block index recording block offsets and `ISIZE` values, which lets us estimate decoded slice size and choose the furthest boundary within a target budget. A final tail slice covers all remaining records.

Finally, once the slices are defined, ingestion proceeds via an asynchronous, double-buffered pipeline. Batches correspond to work units transferred to the GPU, which are fixed-size slices that fit within the device's memory. While a batch is parsed and converted to our SoA-based in-memory representation, a separate thread simultaneously reads and decompresses the next batch. This overlap hides the disk I/O and BGZF decompression latency behind the CPU-side parsing and packing work, allowing for sustained throughput to be fed to GPUs.

Optimizing BAM Output. While the `BaseRecalibrator` algorithm only generates and writes to disk a small file containing the recalibration tables computed, `ApplyBQSR` in addition to input and compute stages, must also write a BAM file containing the updated quality score values for each read. The output of a large BAM file can be significant, and it can dominate the end-to-end time of the entire pipeline. This is because it involves several steps: (1) serialization of the BAM record as a BAM record in a flat byte stream; (2) compression of the byte stream in blocks of at most 64 KB; (3) writing the compressed byte blocks (BGZF blocks) to a file.

In order to optimize the BAM output, we exploit multithread CPU parallelism. Each CPU thread serializes a batch coming from the GPU after quality score recalibration and enqueues the serialized byte buffer (containing the BAM records) for a writer thread to process. It is important to note that the batch can come out-of-order due to different GPUs' processing speeds; therefore, the writer is in charge of processing those batches in order. Once the correct serialized batch arrives, the writer splits it into chunks of 64 KB and assigns each chunk to different threads to be compressed. After compression, each chunk is enqueued to be written on disk.

Pipelining Computation and I/O. Since the pipeline end-to-end throughput is heavily impacted by input and output paths, in order to minimize the latency of the different stages, we built a pipeline where the full input path, the GPU processing stages, and the output path overlap: readers prepare batches asynchronously, GPU worker threads submit them for execution, and completed batches are returned to the host for output processing. While one batch is executing on the GPU, the next batch is prepared concurrently to keep the device busy. When the algorithm requires writing a BAM file (as in the case of `ApplyBQSR`), the batch goes through the output stage: the batches are serialized, compressed in parallel, and written on disk.

3 Evaluation

In this section, we present the results from our evaluation of **X-BQSR**.

Software Setup. We developed X-BQSR in SYCL to provide a high-performance, vendor-neutral solution for the entire BQSR pipeline. To evaluate the portability of our design, we also implemented CUDA and HIP versions of the `BaseRecalibrator` stage. We compare **X-BQSR** against single-threaded GATK and multi-threaded GATK-Spark v4.6.2.0, NVIDIA Parabricks v4.6.0-1, and an FPGA-accelerated `BaseRecalibrator` from prior work. All `X-BQSR` kernels are compiled using the Intel oneAPI DPC++ Compiler v2025.1.0. The CUDA and HIP implementations utilize the CUDA Toolkit (nvcc) v12.6 for NVIDIA hardware and HIP v6.3.4 (ROCm v6.3.3) for AMD hardware.

Hardware Setup. Benchmarks were performed on a dual-socket Intel Xeon Platinum 8454H server (128 logical cores) with 1 TB of RAM. For accelerated workloads, we utilize an NVIDIA L40S (48 GB), an AMD Instinct MI210 (64 GB), and an Intel Flex 170 (16 GB), all via PCIe 4.0. FPGA comparisons utilize a Xilinx VCU118 platform clocked at 100 MHz, connected via PCIe 3.0.

Datasets. We use six dataset samples from GIAB individuals (Table 2): the NA12878 (HG001) and three members of the Ashkenazi trio (HG002, HG003, and HG004). We use the GRCh38 reference for all experiments. After alignment, we process the reads following the GATK Best Practices workflow [1]. Because GATK BQSR is designed for error profiles of short-read data, true long-read datasets are outside the scope of this work. The output of this duplicate-marking step serves as the input for our evaluation. Across all datasets, **X-BQSR** and

NVIDIA Parabricks maintain bit-perfect parity to the gold-standard single-core GATK.

In all experiments, input and output data reside on local NVMe storage to ensure consistent I/O performance. All experiments were conducted 10 times to ensure statistical rigor; the reported values represent the average of these runs, and because the results exhibited a negligible deviation of less than 5%, error bars are omitted from the figures.

Table 2. Datasets used for validation

Dataset	Name	#Reads	Read Len
D0	HG001-HiSeq2500	168.544.418	100
D1	HG001-HiSeq4000	88.774.172	150
D2	HG002-HiSeqX	777.447.412	150
D3	HG003-HiSeqX	1.001.580.652	150
D4	HG004-NovaSeq	1.166.740.818	150
D5	HG002-HiSeq2500	898.865.538	250

3.1 Comparison with State-of-the-Art

We start the evaluation by benchmarking `X-BQSR` against the standard single-threaded GATK implementation. The results for the `BaseRecalibrator` and `ApplyBQSR` stages (Fig. 2) clearly show the performance gap between traditional CPU methods and accelerated implementations. The single-threaded GATK baseline serves as the upper bound for execution time, requiring over 5 h (18,134 s) for the D5 dataset. Across the production-scale datasets (D2–D5), **X-BQSR** `BaseRecalibrator` achieves speedups over the GATK gold standard of 125.0× (D2), 129.0× (D3), 141.7× (D4), and 136.3× (D5). For `ApplyBQSR`, **X-BQSR** achieves improvement ranging from 75.2× to 84.3× over single-threaded CPU execution.

We compare **X-BQSR** with the proprietary NVIDIA Parabricks-BQSR tool. In `BaseRecalibrator`, **X-BQSR** consistently outperforms Parabricks with speedups ranging from 6.1× to 8.7× for the larger datasets (D2D5). For instance, on the D4 dataset, **X-BQSR** completes the stage in 95 s compared to 830 s for Parabricks. For `ApplyBQSR`, **X-BQSR** exhibits a consistent 3.6× to 3.9× speedup over Parabricks across the D2D5 datasets. Specifically, **X-BQSR** processes the 1.16 billion reads of D4 in 162 s (vs. 616 s for Parabricks) and the 898 million reads of D5 in 205 s (vs. 743 s for Parabricks). As Parabricks is provided as a precompiled binary within a Docker container, its optimization strategies and kernel configurations are opaque. Thus, it is not possible for us to identify the specific causes of the performance gap with Parabricks. We ensure a fair comparison by using the latest stable version (v4.6.0-1) and following the vendor's recommended settings. In any case, these results demonstrate that our open, standards-based solution outperforms state-of-the-art proprietary ones.

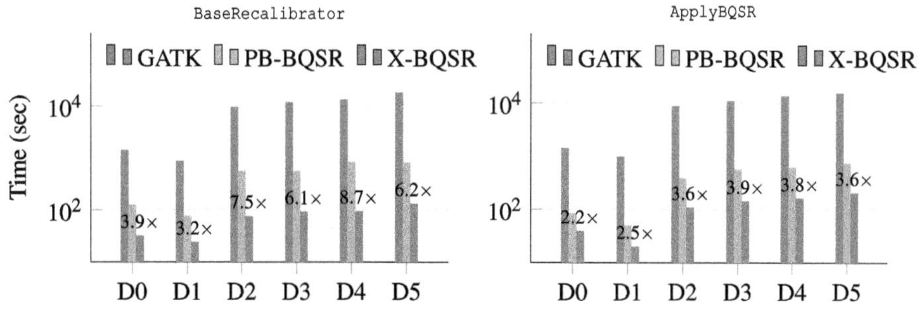

Fig. 2. Execution time comparison of **X-BQSR** against GATK and NVIDIA Parabricks (D0–D5). Speedup values (×) are relative to NVIDIA Parabricks.

3.2 Multi-GPU and CPU Scalability

Beyond single-device performance, we evaluate the scalability of our implementation by distributing the BQSR workload across multiple accelerators using dataset D5. Each GPU operates as an independent worker in an asynchronous, double-buffered pipeline. As shown in Figs. 3a and 3b, **X-BQSR** demonstrates superior scaling compared to Parabricks. In `BaseRecalibrator`, **X-BQSR** reduces execution time from 220 s to 134 s when moving from one to two GPUs, achieving 1.64× speedup. In contrast, Parabricks shows almost no improvement (815 s vs. 813 s). In the `ApplyBQSR` stage, achieving linear scaling is more difficult due to the requirement of a single-threaded writer process that must serialize data to disk in a specific order to maintain GATK compatibility. As the number of GPUs increases, the computational portion of the workload is reduced, but this ordering requirement leads to output I/O becoming a dominating time sink, effectively capping the maximum achievable speedup.

While our SYCL implementation is technically portable to CPU architectures, **X-BQSR** is architecturally optimized for the massive parallelism and memory hierarchy of GPUs. GATK-Spark provides a multi-threaded CPU baseline via Apache Spark. We excluded it from our primary end-to-end comparison in Fig. 2 because GATK-Spark is currently designated as a BETA tool by Broad Institute and is not recommended for production benchmarking. However, we show the scaling results here for completeness. Figure 3c illustrates the scalability of GATK-Spark from 2 to 128 threads on the D5 dataset. While GATK-Spark shows consistent speedup as thread counts increase, reaching a 20.66× speedup for `BaseRecalibrator` and 14.12× for `ApplyBQSR` at 128 threads relative to the 2-thread baseline, it still falls significantly short of "ideal" linear scaling. More importantly, even when utilizing all 128 threads of the dual-socket server, the CPU-based Spark implementation remains significantly slower than a single GPU running X-BQSR. Specifically, the GATK-Spark `BaseRecalibrator` stage is 3.1× slower (411 s vs. 133 s) and the `ApplyBQSR` stage is 6.0× slower (1,226 s vs. 205 s) than a single NVIDIA L40S running **X-BQSR**.

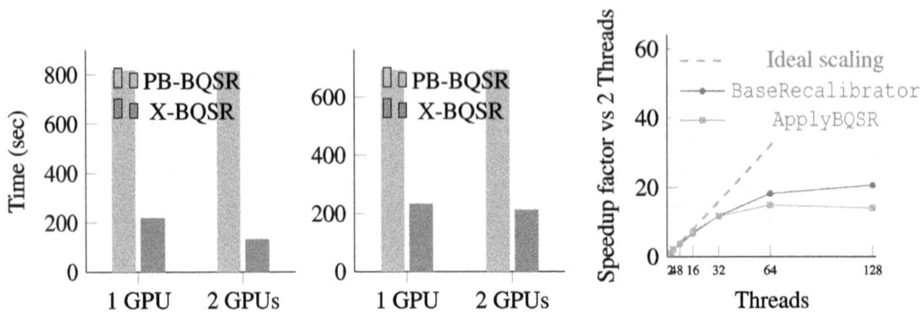

(a) GPU `BaseRecalibrator` (b) GPU `ApplyBQSR` (c) GATK-Spark Scalability

Fig. 3. Scaling D5 dataset across GPU (**X-BQSR**, Parabricks) and CPU (GATK-Spark).

3.3 Kernel Performance and Cross-Architecture Portability

In this section, we present a study of performance portability of **X-BQSR** kernels on multi-vendor GPUs. By focusing on kernel-only execution time (Fig. 4a and 4b), we isolate the algorithmic performance from host-side I/O and driver overhead. As can be seen, the SYCL-based **X-BQSR** kernels are highly competitive with native toolchains. On the D5 dataset, our `BaseRecalibrator` kernels on the NVIDIA backend outperform optimized native CUDA kernels by approximately 2.8% (76.78 s vs. 78.99 s). For AMD hardware, while our initial SYCL port demonstrated portability, the native HIP implementation provides a measurable speedup, reducing the total `BaseRecalibrator` kernel time for D5 from 195.98 s to 191.35 s. This native implementation leverages AMD-specific compiler optimizations and avoids the intermediate abstraction layers of the SYCL runtime. In the `ApplyBQSR` phase, the performance hierarchy aligns with raw hardware specifications, with the NVIDIA L40S leading, followed by the Intel Flex 170 and the AMD MI210.

Figure 4c presents the breakdown of execution time across various stages of **X-BQSR** to identify specific architectural bottlenecks. In `BaseRecalibrator`, the **Feature Detection** stage, which encompasses skip-masking, SNP detection, and context covariate emission, is the primary execution driver on AMD hardware. While we ensure high GPU occupancy, the complex instruction mix and address generation required for context emission become compute-limited on the CDNA2 SIMD units.

Conversely, the **Table Aggregation** stage highlights the efficacy of our two-level aggregation strategy. By utilizing shared-memory histograms to minimize global atomic contention, architectures with high L2-cache atomic resolution, like the AMD MI210, remain highly competitive. Intel, however, shows significant overhead in this stage, as the Xe-HPG architecture resolves atomics with higher latency, confirming that while our design successfully mitigates hardware contention, performance remains bounded by the underlying atomic throughput of the GPU.

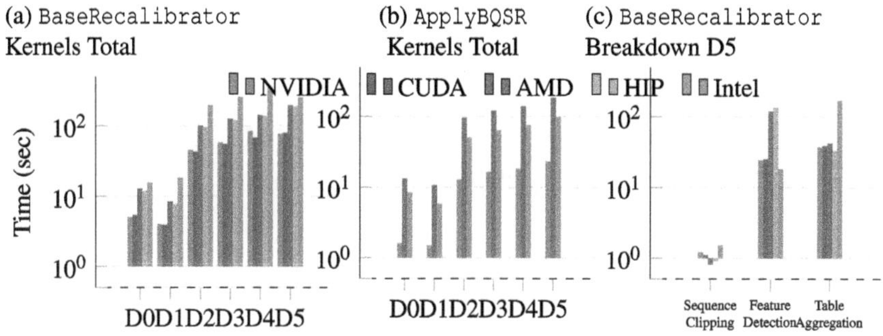

Fig. 4. Cross-architecture kernel performance comparison.

To further understand the architectural drivers behind the performance trends observed across multi-vendor GPUs, we use two SYCL microbenchmarks to isolate the hardware limits of BQSR: (i) the contended atomics benchmark (mimicking **Table Aggregation**) and (ii) the STREAM triad benchmark (mimicking the `ApplyBQSR` phase streaming pattern). The contended-atomics benchmark performs R `fetch_add` operations into a global table of 94 bins using `sycl::atomic_ref`. The 94-bin size is chosen to match the **Cycle** covariate, which is the primary source of atomic contention in `BaseRecalibrator`. The STREAM triad benchmark measures steady-state device bandwidth, mirroring the memory-access pattern of the `ApplyBQSR` phase.

Table 3. Atomic update throughput (Gop/s) and sustained device bandwidth (GB/s)

Device	Contended Atomics (Gop/s)	STREAM (GB/s)
NVIDIA L40S	3.09	689
AMD MI210	11.37	1302
Intel Flex 170	0.90	344

Table 3 presents the results from these benchmarks. The AMD MI210 reaches 11.37 Gop/s on atomics, 4× higher than the NVIDIA L40S. Hardware counters showed that >99% of these operations are resolved within the MI210's L2 cache. This explains why AMD remains highly competitive in the **Table Aggregation** stage despite having lower raw compute clock speeds than the L40S. For memory bandwidth, the MI210 sustains 1302 GB/s, while the L40S sustains 689 GB/s. Despite this 1.9× bandwidth advantage, the `ApplyBQSR` phase is substantially slower on AMD. Profiling shows high VALU utilization on the MI210, suggesting that the SYCL instruction mix for address generation and hierarchical Bayesian calculation becomes compute-limited on the CDNA2 SIMD units, preventing the kernels from saturating the available HBM2e bandwidth. The Intel Flex 170 sustains 344 GB/s but is limited by its lower atomic throughput (0.90 Gop/s), which is consistent with its longer **Table Aggregation** times. A quantitative analysis confirms the predictive value of these metrics; while atomic throughput successfully predicts aggregation rankings, the `ApplyBQSR` performance on AMD highlights the critical importance of compiler-level instruction scheduling in cross-architecture SYCL deployments.

3.4 FPGA Comparison

To further contextualize our performance, we compare **X-BQSR** against a state-of-the-art FPGA redesign of BQSR by Lo et al. [8], which provides a solution for accelerating only the `BaseRecalibrator` stage of BQSR. They do not focus on the second phase of BQSR (`ApplyBQSR`). We present a comparison of our GPU-accelerated `BaseRecalibrator` in **X-BQSR** with Lo et al.'s FPGA solution for completeness. With the FPGA accelerator architecture, the host partitions the dataset into read chunks of size 100,000 and sends them to the FPGA sequentially for writing into SDRAM. Due to limited FPGA resources, we cannot process all 100,000 reads in a single iteration. Only 16 processing elements are implemented on the FPGA, so all 100,000 reads are processed across 6,250 iterations. Upon completing a chunk of reads, the BQSR accelerator asserts an interrupt to notify the host to send the next chunk. To maximize throughput, the host transfers the next chunk of reads to DRAM concurrently while the FPGA processes the previous chunk.

Unlike our GPU implementation, the FPGA architecture requires data to be preformatted into a specific binary structure. Consequently, an end-to-end FPGA workflow necessitates two additional pre-processing phases: (i) the extraction of bases, quality scores, and error metadata from the input BAM file, and (ii) the construction of the FPGA-specific data structures. Table 4 summarizes the execution times for the three phases of the FPGA workflow alongside the GATK baseline. While the standalone FPGA-BQSR compute kernel achieves a speedup of up to 24.6× over GATK, this is lower than the 40× speedup reported in the original study. Our profiling indicates that the discrepancy stems from memory latency: the Load stage (fetching data from FPGA DRAM) requires 865 clock cycles in our environment, compared to the 534 cycles reported by Lo et al. using a 4-channel DRAM configuration. At 100 MHz, this results in a BQSR execution time of approximately 0.054 s per 100,000 reads ($865 \times 6,250 \times 10 \times 10^{-9} \approx 0.054$ s).

Table 4. BQSR execution time and speedup relative to the GATK single-core baseline

Data	GATK (s)	Extract (s)	Construct (s)	FPGA-BQSR (s/Speedup)	X-BQSR FPGA (s/Speedup)	X-BQSR GPU (s/Speedup)
1M	16.20	50.77	22.68	0.70/23.2×	12.80/1.27×	0.05/341.3×
2M	30.00	82.57	43.54	1.33/23.5×	13.12/2.29×	0.10/300.0×
4M	60.00	163.09	85.95	2.60/23.1×	12.91/4.65×	0.21/292.5×
8M	126.00	336.77	494.99	5.11/24.6×	13.77/9.15×	0.42/303.6×
16M	246.00	721.07	1,133.82	10.15/24.2×	15.12/16.3×	0.83/295.3×

The primary limitation of the FPGA approach is revealed when considering end-to-end integration. The required pre-processing phases (Extract and Construct) take 4× to 7× longer than the entire single-threaded GATK execution, effectively negating the gains of the hardware accelerator. In contrast, our **X-BQSR** implementation provides a holistic redesign that accelerates both I/O and computation. By eliminating hidden pre-computation overheads, **X-BQSR** serves as a seamless drop-in replacement for GATK, providing true end-to-end acceleration for germline variant calling pipelines.

4 Conclusion

In this work, we focused on BQSR, one of the most time-consuming steps of the widely used GATK germline variant calling pipeline. We motivated the need for hardware acceleration of BQSR and showed how focusing only on GPU acceleration of the computational part, as done by prior work, will only yield marginal improvement in overall time due to I/O bottlenecks. We presented **X-BQSR**, our holistic redesign with several I/O and compute optimizations, and showed how **X-BQSR** can provide up to 141.7× improvement over GATK and up to 8.7× improvement over closed-source solutions while being vendor-agnostic, open source[1], and performance portable. In future work, we first plan to integrate **X-BQSR** with other preprocessing stages (alignment, sorting and mark duplicates) and then with downstream variant callers to develop a fully open, standards-based, GPU-accelerated solution for scaling genomic data analysis.

Acknowledgments. This work was supported by the European Union Horizon 2020 programme [101136962]; UK Research and Innovation (UKRI) under the UK Government's Horizon Europe funding guarantee [10098097, 10104323] and the Swiss State Secretariat for Education, Research and Innovation (SERI). Additional support was provided by the Horizon Europe Project "SYCLOPS", funded by the European Union HE Research and Innovation programme under grant agreement No. 10109287.

Disclosure of Interests. The authors have no competing interests to declare that are relevant to the content of this article.

References

1. Broad Institute: Genome analysis toolkit (GATK) 4 (2019)

[1] https://gitlab.eurecom.fr/dislab/bqsr.

2. Chen, Y., Schmidt, B., Maskell, D.L.: A hybrid short read mapping accelerator. BMC Bioinform. (2013)
3. Decap, D., Fostier, J., Reumers, J., Costanza, P., Herzeel, C.: elPrep: high-performance preparation of sequence alignment/map files for variant calling. PLoS ONE (2015)
4. DePristo, M.A., et al.: A framework for variation discovery and genotyping using next-generation DNA sequencing data. Nat. Genet. (2011)
5. Ewing, B., Hillier, L., Wendl, M.C., Green, P.: Base-calling of automated sequencer traces using phred. I. accuracy assessment. Genome Res. (1998)
6. Li, H., et al.: The sequence alignment/map format and SAMtools. Bioinformatics (2009)
7. Liu, Y., Schmidt, B., Maskell, D.L.: CUSHAW: a CUDA compatible short read aligner to large genomes based on the burrows-wheeler transform. Bioinformatics (2012)
8. Lo, M., Fang, Z., Wang, J., Zhou, P., Chang, M.C.F., Cong, J.: Algorithm-hardware co-design for BQSR acceleration in genome analysis toolkit. In: FCCM (2020)
9. McKenna, A., et al.: The genome analysis toolkit: a mapreduce framework for analyzing next-generation DNA sequencing data. Genome Res. (2010)
10. NHGRI: The cost of sequencing a human genome (2019)
11. NVIDIA Corporation: Nvidia parabricks (2020)
12. Prabhakaran, A., Gururaj, K., Naik, M., Gopalan, S., Shargorodskiy, A., Brau, E.: Accelerate genomics research with the broad-intel genomics. Intel/Broad Genomics (2017)

Hierarchical Parallel Computing for Optimal Qubit Mapping in NISQ Systems

Jean-Philippe Valois(✉), Guillaume Helbecque, and Nouredine Melab

Univ. Lille, CNRS, Inria, Centrale Lille, UMR 9189 CRIStAL, F-59000 Lille, Lille, France
{jean-philippe.valois,guillaume.helbecque,nouredine.melab}@univ-lille.fr

Abstract. Qubit mapping is a crucial step in quantum compilation for noisy intermediate-scale quantum (NISQ) hardware, where abstract quantum circuits must be adapted to physically constrained devices. We present a massively parallel branch-and-bound algorithm for the exact resolution of qubit mapping—formulated as an NP-hard combinatorial optimization problem—designed to address the inherent exponential complexity of this task. Our approach leverages both intra-node and inter-node parallelism, combining asynchronous exploration of independent subproblems with a dynamic and hierarchical work stealing mechanism across thousands of concurrent processes. Extensive experiments on a modern supercomputer demonstrate near-linear strong scaling at the intra-node level, and substantial strong scaling across compute nodes in distributed settings. Leveraging these capabilities, together with an appropriate bounding operator and guiding heuristics, we achieve state-of-the-art performance and compute reference optimal solutions for benchmark circuits of sizes exceeding previously solved instances. These results establish efficient large-scale parallelization as a practical enabler for exact qubit mapping, while paving the way for future extensions to GPU-accelerated HPC platforms.

Keywords: Qubit Mapping · Parallel Branch-and-Bound · Combinatorial Optimization · High-Performance Computing · Hierarchical Parallel Computing · Quantum Computing · NISQ Systems

1 Introduction

Quantum computing holds the promise of addressing problems that are intractable for classical machines, by exploiting the distinctive principles of quantum mechanics to accelerate certain classes of computations. Despite this potential, current hardware remains constrained to Noisy Intermediate-Scale Quantum (NISQ) devices, which are limited both in their size, and in their operational reliability [15]. As in classical computing, quantum algorithms must undergo a

M. Torquati et al. (Eds.): Euro-Par 2026, LNCS 16781, pp. 539–552, 2027.
https://doi.org/10.1007/978-3-032-35248-4_37

compilation stage before execution. In the quantum context, this process includes the qubit mapping step, which has a direct impact on the error rate of the executed circuits [14]. In this work, we frame the qubit mapping task as a Quadratic Assignment Problem (QAP), a well-known NP-hard combinatorial optimization problem. We address this formulation using a massively parallel Branch-and-Bound (B&B) algorithm, enabling the computation of optimal solutions. Our goal is to extend the scalability limitations of this approach by exploiting efficient hierarchical parallelization.

The main contributions of this work are summarized as follows.

- We propose a parallel B&B algorithm for exact qubit mapping that leverages both intra-node and inter-node parallelism, combined with an effective bounding procedure and guiding heuristics.
- We investigate the scalability and computational efficiency of the proposed approach. The resulting parallel B&B implementation achieves state-of-the-art execution times for this formulation of the qubit mapping problem, and enables the computation of optimal solutions for benchmark circuits larger than those previously addressed.

The remainder of this paper is organized as follows. Section 2 introduces the qubit mapping problem along with its mathematical problem formulation, and reviews related works. Section 3 describes the proposed B&B algorithm, including its operators and parallelization strategy. Section 4 reports an extensive experimental evaluation on representative qubit mapping benchmarks. Finally, Sect. 5 concludes the study and outlines directions for future research.

2 Problem Statement and Related Works

Quantum circuits constitute the standard computational model for quantum algorithms. In this representation, horizontal lines correspond to qubits—commonly referred to as *logical qubits*—while quantum gates are applied sequentially from left to right. These operations may involve either a single qubit (*e.g.*, the Hadamard gate) or two qubits (*e.g.*, the CNOT gate). Figure 1a depicts a simple three-qubit circuit composed of Hadamard and CNOT operations.

When executed on real machines, such circuits must comply with the architectural constraints of NISQ devices, which characterize the current generation of quantum hardware. These systems typically provide a limited number of noise-prone *physical qubits* and support only restricted qubit–qubit interactions, defined by the device coupling graph (*cf.* Fig. 5). Interactions between qubits that are not directly connected must therefore be mediated by inserting additional SWAP gates. These gates exchange the quantum states of adjacent qubits, increasing both the circuit depth and the overall error probability.

These constraints define the overall adaptation process of mapping an abstract circuit to physical hardware. This process is typically decomposed into two phases: (i) *qubit mapping*, which assigns logical qubits to physical ones, and (ii) *circuit routing*, which inserts SWAP operations to enable two-qubit gates.

The present work focuses on the qubit mapping stage, whose objective is to determine an initial assignment of logical to physical qubits that minimizes the number of SWAP operations required during routing. Since the circuit depth (*i.e.*, the maximum number of sequential gates applied on any qubit) directly impacts the vulnerability of the computation to decoherence and noise, an effective qubit mapping is essential to preserve the fidelity of the execution. Figure 1 illustrates this effect by showing how different mappings of the same three-qubit circuit can lead to markedly different hardware-compliant implementations: one requiring an additional SWAP gate, and another avoiding such overhead entirely.

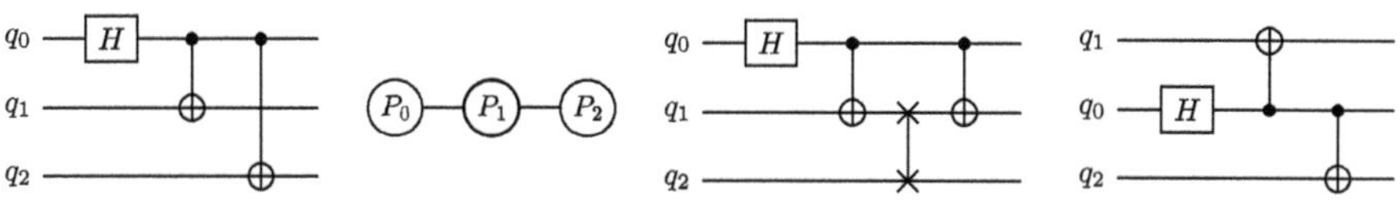

(a) Circuit (b) Coupling (c) Mapping $\{0, 1, 2\}$ (d) Mapping $\{1, 0, 2\}$

Fig. 1. Illustration of the qubit mapping problem and its impact on circuit reliability. (a) Example quantum circuit. (b) Topology of the target device. (c) Mapping $\{0, 1, 2\}$ requires the insertion of an additional SWAP gate, increasing the circuit depth. (d) Mapping $\{1, 0, 2\}$ leads to a more efficient implementation.

In this work, we model the qubit mapping problem as a permutation-based combinatorial optimization problem and aim to solve it exactly using a parallel B&B algorithm. More specifically, we adopt the QAP formulation employed in [18]. This model relies on two matrices: the circuit frequency matrix F, which describes interaction frequencies between logical qubits, and the device distance matrix D, which captures the connectivity structure of the target hardware. Together, these matrices define an NP-hard QAP whose search space grows exponentially with the number of qubits.

Definition 1 (QAP for qubit mapping). *Consider a quantum circuit involving n logical qubits, described by an $n \times n$ frequency matrix $F = (f_{ij})$, and a target quantum device with $N \geqslant n$ physical qubits, represented by an $N \times N$ distance matrix $D = (d_{ij})$. The qubit mapping problem consists of finding an injective mapping π from logical to physical qubits that minimizes the overall routing cost:*

$$\min_{\pi \in \mathcal{S}_n^N} RC(\pi). \tag{1}$$

The set $\mathcal{S}_n^N$ denotes the collection of all mappings from n logical qubits to N physical qubits, whose cardinality is $N!/(N-n)!$. The routing cost function RC is defined as

$$RC(\pi) = \sum_{i=1}^{n} \sum_{j=1}^{n} f_{ij} d_{\pi(i)\pi(j)}, \tag{2}$$

where the term $f_{ij} d_{\pi(i)\pi(j)}$ provides an estimate of the number of SWAP operations required to implement the interactions between logical qubits q_i and q_j.

The qubit mapping problem has received considerable attention in the literature, with most existing approaches relying on heuristic strategies to cope with its high computational complexity [10,11,16]. Although such heuristics are essential for handling large circuits, exact methods play an important complementary role. They provide optimal reference solutions, offer structural insights into the problem, and establish rigorous performance bounds that can guide the development and evaluation of heuristic techniques. Among these exact approaches, Zulehner *et al.* [21] proposed an A* search-based method tailored to linear quantum architectures. Later, Zhu *et al.* [20] introduced the QAP formulation for qubit mapping and addressed it using a B&B algorithm. However, these methods remain fundamentally sequential, which severely limits their scalability as the size of the search space grows exponentially. More recently, Valois *et al.* [18] addressed this limitation by extending the work of Zhu *et al.* [20] with a scalable parallel B&B framework. Their approach demonstrated that exploiting modern High-Performance Computing (HPC) infrastructures makes it possible to optimally solve significantly larger qubit mapping instances. Building on this line of work, the objective of the present study is to design a parallel B&B solver for qubit mapping that improves upon the operators used in [18], with the goal of achieving enhanced computational performance.

3 Parallel Branch-and-Bound Algorithm

3.1 Branch-and-Bound for Qubit Mapping

We now describe the B&B tree-search framework adapted to address the qubit mapping problem defined in Eq. (1). The search space is organized as a permutation tree in which each node represents a partial assignment of logical qubits to physical qubits. *Terminal* nodes correspond to complete assignments of the n logical qubits and are evaluated using the objective function RC defined in (2).

Throughout the exploration, the algorithm maintains the best solution identified so far, whose cost is denoted by UB (for "upper bound"). Internal nodes are expanded by assigning an additional logical qubit, thereby generating child nodes that extend the current partial mapping. For each node, a bounding procedure computes a lower bound on the routing cost achievable by any completion of the partial assignment. Nodes whose bound is greater than UB are discarded, whereas the remaining nodes are kept for further exploration.

The search process terminates once all nodes have either been explored or pruned, at which point the algorithm returns the set of qubit mappings that achieve the minimal routing cost UB. Figure 2 illustrates a B&B permutation tree for a small instance with $n = N = 3$.

3.2 Bounding Operator

In our qubit mapping context, the bounding phase consists of computing lower-bound estimates of the routing cost function RC defined in (2). To this end, we employ the Gilmore–Lawler Bound (GLB), a classical bounding method for the

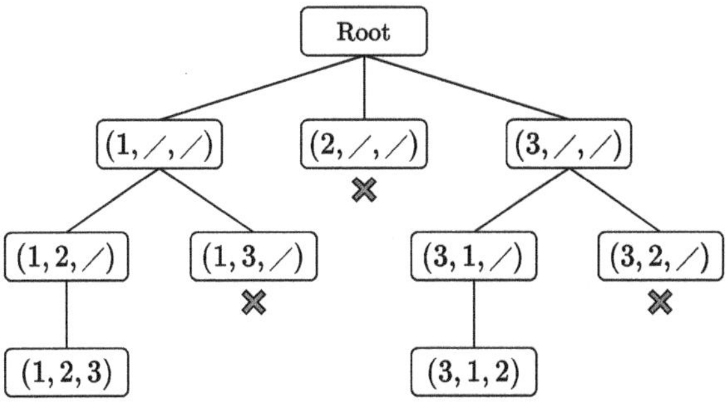

Fig. 2. Example of a B&B permutation search tree for an instance of size 3.

QAP [6]. Computing the GLB ultimately reduces to solving a linear assignment problem, which can be efficiently addressed using the Hungarian algorithm [13].

This choice differs from the approaches proposed by Zhu *et al.* [20] and Valois *et al.* [18], which rely on the Dual Procedure (DP) bounding operator introduced by Hahn and Grant [7]. Although the DP generally produces tighter lower bounds, it incurs a significantly higher computational cost, with a time complexity of $\mathcal{O}(n^5)$ compared to $\mathcal{O}(n^3)$ for the GLB [22]. Furthermore, the DP requires maintaining large auxiliary matrices at each node of the search tree, while the GLB does not introduce comparable memory overhead.

This difference has important implications for scalability. As the number of explored nodes increases, the memory requirements of the DP can quickly become prohibitive for larger instances. In parallel B&B implementations, this limitation is even more pronounced, since frequent node exchanges for load balancing further increase both memory consumption and communication overhead.

3.3 Guiding Heuristics

To further improve the computational performance of the proposed B&B algorithm, we incorporate three guiding heuristics designed to improve the efficiency of the search.

- **Greedy initialization.** Before starting the B&B search, an initial solution π_0 is generated using the greedy heuristic proposed in [20]. The corresponding routing cost $RC(\pi_0)$ provides an initial value for UB. This early bound enables the algorithm to discard subproblems whose lower bound already exceeds this value, thus promoting early pruning.
- **Logical qubit prioritization.** Logical qubits are ordered according to their interaction activity, defined as the total number of two-qubit gates in which a qubit participates. Qubits with the highest activity are assigned earlier in the mapping process, so that their placement more rapidly influences the lower-bound computations. This ordering typically strengthens bounds earlier in the search and increases the chances of pruning unpromising branches.

- **Physical qubit prioritization.** Physical qubits are prioritized based on their connectivity within the coupling graph of the target NISQ device, *i.e.*, the number of edges incident to each qubit. Highly connected physical qubits are therefore considered first when assigning a new logical qubit. Combined with the previous heuristic, this strategy tends to place strongly interacting logical qubits onto well-connected physical qubits, which facilitates the early discovery of high-quality mappings and encourages more effective pruning.

3.4 Parallel Design

The design of parallel B&B algorithms has been extensively studied [5]. A widely adopted and effective approach is the parallel tree exploration model, in which multiple disjoint subtrees of the search space are explored concurrently and asynchronously across different computing threads. This model leverages the inherently recursive nature of B&B algorithms, which makes them naturally suited for parallelization. However, asynchronous execution of independent workers introduces challenges such as irregular workloads, unpredictable communication patterns, and the need for efficient load balancing and global termination detection mechanisms. Consequently, achieving high parallel efficiency requires both an appropriate data structure for managing the distributed workload and an effective management policy. In the following, we detail these key components: (1) the decentralized data structure used to store and organize the search space, (2) the load balancing strategy enabling dynamic redistribution of work among threads and compute nodes, and (3) the hierarchical termination detection mechanism ensuring correct and efficient completion of the parallel B&B algorithm.

Decentralized Pool-Based Data Structure. In this work, the B&B tree nodes are managed through a decentralized, pool-based data structure [8], where the data are distributed across computing resources, as illustrated in Fig. 3. This design accounts for the Non-Uniform Memory Access characteristics of large-scale, multi-core systems, in which storing data close to the processing unit reduces memory latency. Specifically, each compute node maintains several pools, typically one per computing thread.

Each pool is implemented as a non-blocking split deque [4]. A pool is logically divided into a private and a shared region, separated by an atomic split pointer, as illustrated in Fig. 4. This organization isolates local operations from potentially concurrent external accesses—such as those arising from load balancing—allowing lock-free manipulation of the private region while enabling controlled external access to the shared region. The atomic split pointer dynamically adjusts the boundary between the two regions without data copying, maintaining high local performance while supporting safe and efficient concurrent interactions.

Dynamic Load Balancing. We adopt a locality-aware dynamic Work-Stealing (WS) mechanism to maintain balanced workloads and high resource utilization.

The objective is to minimize idle time by dynamically redistributing pending tree nodes among threads and compute nodes.

The WS mechanism operates in two stages. At the intra-node level, an idle thread first attempts to steal work from other threads on the same compute node. It locks the shared region of a potential victim's pool and checks whether it contains enough elements (tree nodes) to steal. If so, one element is taken. Otherwise, the thief may request the targeted thread to enlarge its shared region for future attempts before selecting another thread as a potential victim. This fine-grained approach favors low-overhead local balancing while preserving memory locality.

If no work is found locally, the inter-node stage is triggered. In this case, the idle thread targets pools on remote compute nodes. Instead of stealing only one element, the initiator thread retrieves a larger batch—typically half of the shared region—from a victim. This coarser-grained transfer limits inter-node communication while ensuring that the thief thread receives enough work to supply its sibling threads on the same compute node.

Both intra- and inter-node stages rely on the same random victim selection policy, where targets (threads or compute nodes) are chosen uniformly at random [2], ensuring even distribution of stealing attempts without centralized coordination. The granularity policy adapts to the memory hierarchy: single-element steals within a compute node and multi-element steals across compute nodes.

By combining hierarchical locality-awareness, randomized victim selection, and adaptive granularity, the WS mechanism achieves efficient parallel exploration of the B&B tree with minimal synchronization and communication overhead.

Termination Detection. In asynchronous environments, where computing units operate independently and at varying speeds, detecting global termination remains a major challenge [12]. In this work, a hierarchical consensus-based algorithm is employed to detect completion across distributed processes. The method maintains a record of active threads and their states to determine whether any computations are still in progress. Each thread holds a local state variable, set to either BUSY or IDLE, while each compute node maintains a node-level state, marked BUSY if at least one of its threads is busy and IDLE otherwise. The detection process is initiated when a thread becomes idle, that is, when its local work pool is empty and all WS attempts fail. The initiator first sets its own state to IDLE and then checks the states of other threads within the same node. If any thread remains busy, the detection process stops and the B&B algorithm resumes. If all threads within the node are idle, the node's state is updated to IDLE, and an inter-node verification phase is triggered. When all nodes are confirmed idle, the algorithm concludes global termination. This hierarchical design minimizes inter-node communication by performing intra-node checks first, ensuring efficient and scalable termination detection.

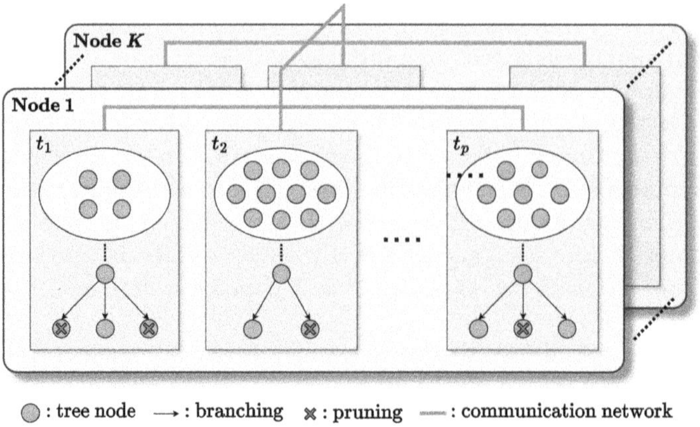

Fig. 3. Overall workflow of the parallel B&B algorithm in a distributed setting across K compute nodes, each leveraging p CPU cores. Each computing thread t_i maintains a private pool of tree nodes and concurrently performs branching and pruning operations. Intra-node and inter-node communication mechanisms used for dynamic load balancing and information sharing are also illustrated.

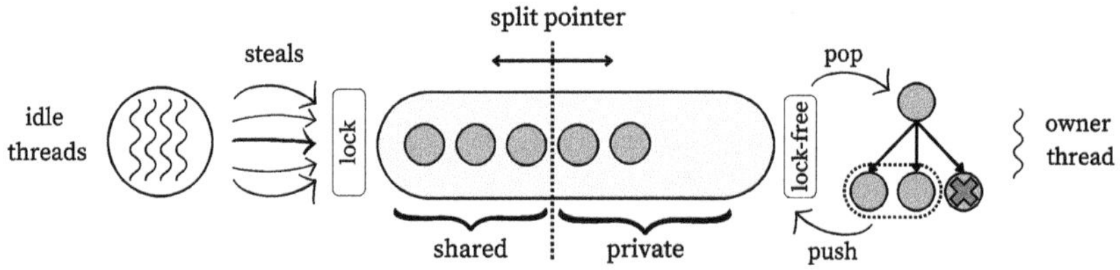

Fig. 4. Simplified view of a split double-ended pool. The double-ended pool is partitioned into private and shared regions by a pointer. In the private region, the pool management thread performs non-blocking operations such as inserting and removing nodes for B&B exploration. In the shared region, other threads access the pool in a synchronized manner to perform task stealing.

4 Experimental Results

4.1 Experimental Protocol and Setup

The parallel tree search algorithm proposed in this study is implemented using the `P3D-DFS` framework [9], developed in the Chapel programming language. This framework enables the implementation and execution of parallel B&B algorithms on CPU-based architectures, ranging from single-node systems to large-scale supercomputers. The complete source code used in this study is publicly available at https://github.com/Guillaume-Helbecque/P3D-DFS.

All experiments are conducted on the TOP500 Joliot-Curie supercomputer [17], whose compute nodes are equipped with two 64-core AMD Epyc ROME 7H12 @ 2.6 GHz CPUs and 256 GB of RAM. The nodes are interconnected *via* a fast InfiniBand HDR100 network configured in a Dragonfly+

topology. The B&B implementation relies on Chapel 2.7.0 in a fine-tuned configuration environment, using GCC 14.2.0 as the back-end compiler.

The experimental evaluation first investigates the strong-scaling behavior of the proposed approach at both intra-node and inter-node levels. We then compare its computational performance against the state-of-the-art on a set of representative benchmark instances. Reported execution times all correspond to averages over five independent runs.

4.2 Scalability and Performance Evaluation

We begin by evaluating the strong-scaling behavior of the proposed parallel algorithm, referred to as **PBB-QM**. The experiments use benchmark circuits from RevLib [19] with sizes ranging from $n = 17$ to 27, targeting the 27-qubit IBM Cairo architecture whose coupling graph is shown in Fig. 5. The scalability of PBB-QM is assessed at two complementary levels: (1) intra-node scaling, which evaluates multi-core parallelism within a single compute node, and (2) inter-node scaling, which evaluates distributed parallelism across multiple compute nodes.

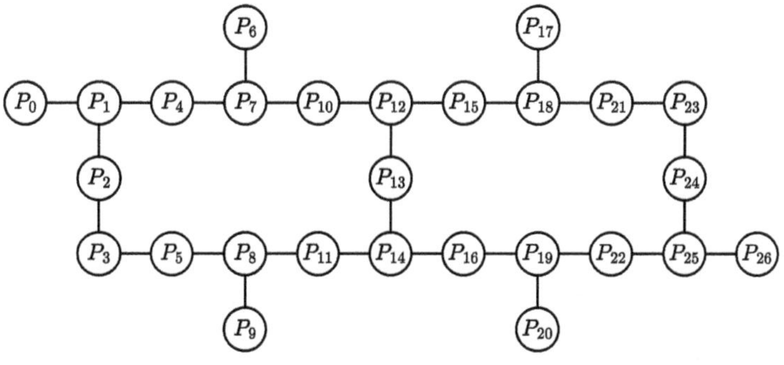

Fig. 5. Coupling graph of the IBM Cairo quantum device [3].

Figure 6a presents the intra-node strong-scaling results for three representative benchmarks: `5xp1_194`, `cmb_214`, and `cu_219`, using up to 128 CPU cores. These circuits were selected as representative moderately challenging problem instances. As shown in Fig. 6a, PBB-QM exhibits nearly ideal intra-node scalability, maintaining linear speedup up to 32 CPU cores and closely approaching it as the number of cores increases further. When utilizing the full capacity of a compute node (128 cores), the algorithm attains between 75% and 87% of the linear speedup for every considered problem instance, highlighting the efficiency of the proposed intra-node parallelization scheme and the low overhead of local task scheduling and synchronization mechanisms.

Figure 6b reports the inter-node strong-scaling results for three additional representative benchmarks: `rd73_312`, `sym9_317`, and `arb8_323`. These circuits were chosen as representative challenging problem instances. Experiments use up to 64 compute nodes (each providing 128 CPU cores), and speedups are measured relative to the intra-node multi-core baseline with 128 cores. The results shown in Fig. 6b indicate that PBB-QM maintains substantial scalability across compute nodes, although with more pronounced limitations than in the intra-node setting. In particular, the speedup curves tend to plateau beyond 32 compute nodes, an effect that is more visible for the rd73_312 instance. This behavior arises because, as the number of computational resources increases, the remaining workload becomes insufficient to fully offset communication overhead and the sequential initialization phase of the algorithm. As a result, the scalability of PBB-QM does not continue to grow proportionally with additional nodes. In the best case, the achieved speedup reaches 59% of the ideal linear scaling when using the full capacity of 64 nodes.

Figure 7 provides additional insight into the inter-node scalability trends observed in Fig. 6b. For the rd73_312 instance, it reports the fraction of the total runtime spent on the main parts of the parallel B&B algorithm as the number of compute nodes increases. The profiling results show that sequential and synchronized operations—primarily initialization and work stealing—account for an increasingly large portion of the execution time as more nodes are used. In contrast, only the core computational operators of the B&B algorithm (branching and bounding) effectively benefit from parallelization, as their workload is distributed across processes. Consequently, scalability becomes progressively limited as the number of compute nodes grows for instances of this size. In particular, Fig. 7 shows that the parallelizable fraction of the program represents only about 41% of the total runtime when using 64 nodes. This observation is consistent with the results in Fig. 6b, where the achieved speedup for the rd73_312 instance reaches roughly 39% of the ideal linear scaling, remaining below the theoretical bound imposed by the parallelizable workload, in accordance with Amdahl's law [1]. These results explain the scaling plateau observed beyond 32 nodes and highlight the main scalability bottlenecks encountered by PBB-QM on the considered computation-bound benchmark instances.

Finally, we compare the performance of PBB-QM with the parallel B&B approach proposed by Valois *et al.* [18] on a broader set of RevLib [19] benchmark circuits. This benchmark set corresponds to the one used in [18] for their large-scale experiments, augmented here with an additional circuit, sym9_317, featuring 27 qubits and thus matching the size of the target IBM Cairo NISQ device (*cf.* Fig. 5). Table 1 reports, for each circuit, the optimal routing cost together with a comparison of the number of explored tree nodes and execution times obtained by PBB-QM and the baseline implementation of [18]. The corresponding speedups achieved by PBB-QM are also reported. Both algorithms were executed on the same cluster in distributed mode using 64 compute nodes. The results show that PBB-QM consistently outperforms the approach of [18], yielding significant speedups across all benchmark circuits, reaching up to ×39. By effectively exploiting the available computing resources, most instances are solved in less than 10 s. Moreover, PBB-QM enables the optimal solution of the additional instance sym9_317, which could not be solved using the implementation of [18]. The DP-based bounding operator—although significantly reducing the size of the explored B&B tree—induces substantial memory overhead (as discussed in Sect. 3.2), ultimately exceeding the available memory on this instance. Overall, these results highlight the computational efficiency of PBB-QM for solving challenging qubit mapping instances optimally, and confirm the suitability of the GLB bounding procedure in a massively parallel setting.

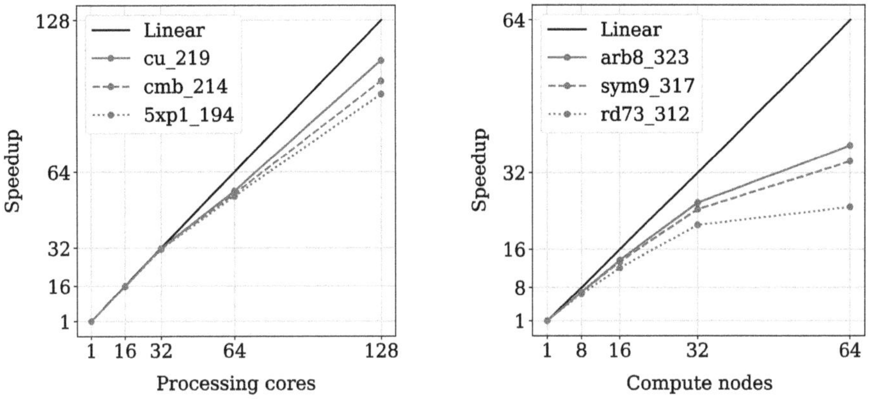

(a) Intra-node.

(b) Inter-node.

Fig. 6. Strong-scaling evaluation of the parallel B&B algorithm PBB-QM considering both levels of parallelism: (a) intra-node scaling, and (b) inter-node scaling.

In general, the experimental results indicate that the hierarchical parallel approach is not yet exploited to its full potential. Although the proposed method extends the reach of exact resolution—yielding optimal solutions for benchmark circuits with up to 27 qubits within relatively short execution times (*cf.* Table 1)—the considered instances remain too small to fully leverage large-scale supercomputers (*cf.* Fig. 6 and Fig. 7). Future work could therefore consider benchmark circuits targeting larger NISQ devices than the IBM Cairo architecture (Fig. 5) used in this study. Assuming IBM hardware, the next larger NISQ processor after IBM Cairo would be the IBM Rochester device [3], featuring 53 qubits and thus representing a substantial increase in computational complexity for optimal qubit mapping.

5 Conclusions

In this study, we introduced a massively parallel B&B framework for the exact resolution of the qubit mapping problem, formulated as a permutation-based QAP. Building upon prior work on this formulation, the proposed approach addresses the scalability challenges inherent to this NP-hard problem by leveraging hierarchical parallelism. Combined with efficient operators and guiding

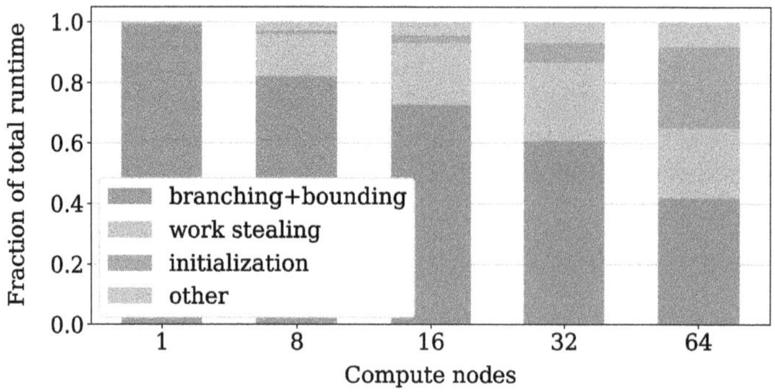

Fig. 7. Normalized breakdown of execution time components for the `rd73_312` instance across different numbers of compute nodes. Each stacked bar shows the proportion of time spent in branching and bounding, work stealing, initialization, and other operations.

Table 1. Results of PBB-QM on RevLib benchmark circuits targeting the 27-qubit IBM Cairo architecture (*cf.* Fig. 5). For each instance, the optimal cost, number of visited nodes, and runtime (in seconds) are reported. Results are compared against the baseline algorithm of Valois *et al.* [18].

circuit	n	optimal	tree size ($\times 10^3$)		time (s)		speedup
			[18]	PBB-QM	[18]	PBB-QM	
5xp1_194	17	3034	377	4432	29.9	5.9	×5.1
ryy6_256	17	14 942	2127	332 223	108.4	22.5	×4.8
alu3_200	18	8306	1057	78 723	59.1	6.8	×8.7
sqrt6_259	18	2222	113	215	25.6	5.4	×4.7
add6_196	19	15 408	234	653	20.7	5.8	×3.6
cmb_214	20	4428	2133	12 802	59.2	5.4	×11.0
ex1010_230	20	224 476	143	301	22.3	6.2	×3.6
decod_217	21	3644	336	282	14.3	6.9	×2.1
dk17_224	21	3600	574	1820	26.7	6.1	×4.4
apla_203	22	8004	495	33 374	35.0	6.2	×5.6
cm105a_210	22	1780	3434	16 089	48.4	5.9	×8.2
plus63mod4096	23	52	38 065	4782	134.5	5.1	×26.4
arb8_323	24	1880	132 412	2 349 769	1423.1	122.0	×11.7
cu_219	25	2652	10 237	195 920	328.4	16.6	×19.8
rd73_312	25	654	1 110 113	3 678 732	6455.3	165.7	×39.0
in0_235	26	44 912	1856	510 496	65.6	36.6	×1.8
sym9_317	27	598	—	4 597 186	OOM[a]	210.3	—

[a]OOM = Out-of-memory

heuristics, the resulting implementation was evaluated through extensive experiments on a TOP500 supercomputer. The results demonstrate substantial strong scaling at both the intra-node and inter-node levels. In addition, the method achieves state-of-the-art computational performance on realistic benchmark circuits while extending the range of instances that can be solved optimally. These findings highlight the potential of HPC and carefully designed parallel algorithms to meet the growing computational demands of quantum compilation.

As discussed in the experimental section, while the computational performance of the proposed B&B algorithm has been thoroughly demonstrated, fully exploiting large-scale supercomputers with this approach would require the consideration of more demanding problem instances targeting larger NISQ devices. Another promising direction is the development of GPU-accelerated B&B variants capable of exploiting heterogeneous multi-GPU architectures, which could further improve scalability. Finally, future work could investigate more sophisticated problem formulations beyond the QAP statement considered here, including problem-specific models that incorporate additional criteria such as error-aware qubit mapping.

Acknowledgments. This research was funded by the Agence Nationale de la Recherche (ANR) under the EquipEx+ MesoNET project [grant number ANR-21-ESRE-0051] and the UltraBO project [grant number ANR-22-CE46-0011]. This project was provided with computing HPC and storage resources by GENCI at TGCC thanks to the grant 2025-AD010616819 on the supercomputer Joliot Curie's ROME partition.

Disclosure of Interests. The authors have no competing interests to declare that are relevant to the content of this article.

References

1. Amdahl, G.M.: Validity of the single processor approach to achieving large scale computing capabilities. In: Proceedings of the 18–20 April 1967, Spring Joint Computer Conference, pp. 483–485. Association for Computing Machinery, New York, NY, USA (1967)
2. Blumofe, R.D., Leiserson, C.E.: Scheduling multithreaded computations by work stealing. J. ACM **46**(5), 720–748 (1999)
3. Bozzo-Rey, M., Loredo, R.: Introduction to the IBM Q experience and quantum computing. In: Proceedings of the 28th Annual International Conference on Computer Science and Software Engineering, pp. 410–412 (2018)
4. van Dijk, T., van de Pol, J.C.: Lace: non-blocking split deque for work-stealing. In: Euro-Par 2014: Parallel Processing Workshops, pp. 206–217 (2014)
5. Gendron, B., Crainic, T.G.: Parallel branch-and-bound algorithms: survey and synthesis. Oper. Res. **42**(6), 1042–1066 (1994)
6. Gilmore, P.C.: Optimal and suboptimal algorithms for the quadratic assignment problem. J. Soc. Ind. Appl. Math. **10**(2), 305–313 (1962)
7. Hahn, P., Grant, T.: Lower bounds for the quadratic assignment problem based upon a dual formulation. Oper. Res. **46**(6), 912–922 (1998)

8. Helbecque, G., Carneiro, T., Melab, N., Gmys, J., Bouvry, P.: PGAS data structure for unbalanced tree-based algorithms at scale. In: Computational Science - ICCS 2024, pp. 103–111 (2024)
9. Helbecque, G., Gmys, J., Melab, N., Carneiro, T., Bouvry, P.: Parallel distributed productivity-aware tree search using Chapel. Concurr. Comput. Pract. Exp. **35**(27), e7874 (2023)
10. Li, G., Ding, Y., Xie, Y.: Tackling the qubit mapping problem for NISQ-era quantum devices. In: Proceedings of the Twenty-Fourth International Conference on Architectural Support for Programming Languages and Operating Systems, pp. 1001–1014 (2019)
11. Liu, J., Li, P., Zhou, H.: Not all SWAPs have the same cost: a case for optimization-aware qubit routing. In: 2022 IEEE International Symposium on High-Performance Computer Architecture (HPCA), pp. 709–725 (2022)
12. Matocha, J., Camp, T.: A taxonomy of distributed termination detection algorithms. J. Syst. Softw. **43**(3), 207–221 (1998)
13. Munkres, J.: Algorithms for the assignment and transportation problems. J. Soc. Ind. Appl. Math. **5**(1), 32–38 (1957)
14. Murali, P., Baker, J.M., Javadi-Abhari, A., Chong, F.T., Martonosi, M.: Noise-adaptive compiler mappings for noisy intermediate-scale quantum computers. In: Proceedings of the Twenty-Fourth International Conference on Architectural Support for Programming Languages and Operating Systems, pp. 1015–1029 (2019)
15. Preskill, J.: Quantum computing in the NISQ era and beyond. Quantum **2**, 79 (2018)
16. Rouzé, J., Melab, N., Gmys, J., Tuyttens, D.: A parallel memetic algorithm for qubit mapping on noisy intermediate-scale quantum machines. Eng. Appl. Artif. Intell. **161**, 112081 (2025)
17. TOP500.org: TOP500 The List (2025). https://www.top500.org/lists/top500/2025/11/
18. Valois, J.P., Helbecque, G., Melab, N.: Efficient and scalable branch-and-bound algorithm for exact qubit allocation. Futur. Gener. Comput. Syst. **179**, 108342 (2026)
19. Wille, R., Große, D., Teuber, L., Dueck, G.W., Drechsler, R.: RevLib: an online resource for reversible functions and reversible circuits. In: Proceedings of the 38th International Symposium on Multiple Valued Logic, pp. 220–225 (2008)
20. Zhu, P., Cheng, X., Guan, Z.: An exact qubit allocation approach for NISQ architectures. In: Quantum Information Processing, p. 19 (2020)
21. Zulehner, A., Gasser, S., Wille, R.: Exact global reordering for nearest neighbor quantum circuits using A*. In: Reversible Computation, pp. 185–201 (2017)
22. Çela, E.: The Quadratic Assignment Problem. Springer, New York (1998)

G-STAR: GPU-Accelerated Statistical Static Timing Analysis Using Level-by-Level Replication

Boyang Zhang, Chih-Chun Chang, Yi-Hua Chung, Che Chang, Cheng-Hsiang Chiu, Aditya Das Sarma, and Tsung-Wei Huang(✉)

University of Wisconsin-Madison, Madison, WI, USA
{bzhang523,chih-chun.chang,yihua.chung,cchang289,chenghsiang.chiu, adassarma,tsung-wei.huang}@wisc.edu

Abstract. Statistical static timing analysis (SSTA) is a critical component of modern Electronic Design Automation (EDA) flows for modeling on-chip process variations. Among various SSTA methods, *first-order block-based SSTA* (FB-SSTA) supports efficient level-by-level timing propagation with high data parallelism, making it particularly suitable for GPU acceleration. However, existing GPU-based FB-SSTA solutions assume that the entire timing graph and data fit in GPU memory, an assumption that breaks down as circuit size increases. To overcome this challenge, we propose G-STAR, a GPU-accelerated FB-SSTA algorithm designed for memory-constrained FB-SSTA workloads. G-STAR enables efficient levelized FB-SSTA via level-by-level replication, combined with a replicated-pin scheduler that reuses GPU memory and avoids redundant phase propagation. Compared to a state-of-the-art GPU solution, G-STAR achieves up to 9.24× speedup on large designs and successfully completes FB-SSTA on multi-million-pin circuits where the baseline fails due to GPU *out-of-memory* errors.

1 Introduction

Statistical static timing analysis (SSTA) is a critical stage in Electronic Design Automation (EDA). Compared to traditional static timing analysis (STA), it enables more accurate delay estimation by modeling on-chip process variation (OCV) as random variables [3]. Among existing SSTA solutions, *Monte Carlo-based* SSTA (MC-SSTA) has been widely explored. For example, [8] introduces an MC-SSTA framework that uses QMC sampling and Karhunen-Loéve expansion to reduce dimensionality. Although MC-SSTA achieves high accuracy, the reliance on extensive sampling often leads to very long runtime (e.g., hours for million-gate designs [7]), limiting its practical use in industrial settings.

To overcome this runtime limitation, [9] introduces *first-order block-based SSTA* (FB-SSTA), a *level-by-level* timing-propagation method that approximates timing distributions by linearly propagating statistical moments. Unlike MC-SSTA, FB-SSTA computes first-order sensitivities of all timing quantities to

M. Torquati et al. (Eds.): Euro-Par 2026, LNCS 16781, pp. 553–567, 2027.
https://doi.org/10.1007/978-3-032-35248-4_38

each variation source, so it does not require any time-consuming sampling processes. Figure 1(a) illustrates the FB-SSTA process on a circuit of two gates [7]. In the circuit, each pin stores multiple *phases* of timing quantities, such as delay (d), voltage fluctuation ($\varDelta V$), temperature shift ($\varDelta T$), and others projected to one PVT (Process, Voltage, Temperature) condition. In this example, we show three phases, so each pin stores three phases of timing quantities. In real designs, there can be hundreds or even thousands of phases [4]. To perform FB-SSTA on this circuit, a common solution is to construct its level list, as shown in Fig. 1(b), and then propagate the timing quantities level by level from primary input (PI) pins to primary output (PO) pins through the circuit network.

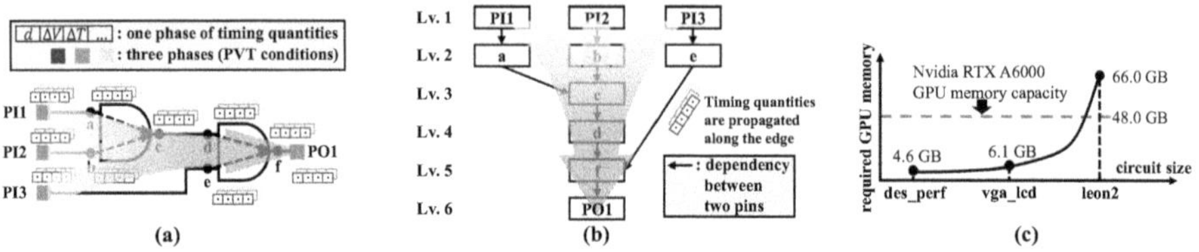

Fig. 1. (a) Illustration of first-order block-based SSTA (FB-SSTA) on a circuit of two gates. (b) Timing quantities are propagated level by level from primary inputs (PIs) to primary outputs (POs). (c) Required GPU memory of existing level-by-level FB-SSTA algorithms can exceed the available capacity when the phase count is large (e.g., 1024).

The level-by-level propagation in FB-SSTA, together with the massive data parallelism that appears as circuits grow in size and complexity, makes FB-SSTA well-suited for GPU acceleration. To this end, [6] presents a GPU-accelerated FB-SSTA framework that parallelizes levelized timing propagation while explicitly handling spatial correlations through principal component analysis. More recently, [5] proposes a GPU-accelerated FB-SSTA engine that models statistical timing propagation in a differentiable form to support downstream physical design optimization. Despite runtime improvement via GPU, nearly all existing GPU-based FB-SSTA solutions assume that the entire timing graph and its data, i.e., the level list and phase data in Fig. 1(b) fit in GPU memory. In other words, they overlook a practical challenge, one we encountered when working with a major EDA vendor, the ever-increasing phase complexity and circuit size cannot easily be accommodated within GPU memory. For example, as shown in Fig. 1(c), under 1024 phases, performing level-by-level FB-SSTA on leon2 (4.3M pins) requires 66.0 GB of GPU memory. This exceeds the 48.0 GB available on Nvidia RTX A6000, which is already large for modern GPUs.

To address this memory challenge, [1] proposes G-STP, a GPU-accelerated FB-SSTA algorithm designed specifically for memory-constrained SSTA workloads. G-STP models an FB-SSTA workload as a *task graph*, where each task represents the propagation of timing quantities at a pin and each edge represents the dependency between two tasks. It then pre-allocates the maximum available GPU memory and uses a job queue to schedule these propagation tasks pin by pin. This scheduling process is GPU memory–aware coupled with a heuristic to minimize the GPU memory footprint during execution. However, G-STP has two major drawbacks. First, it relies on a job queue to decide which pin to process next, which can introduce significant CPU scheduling overhead as the circuit size grows. For example, under a circuit with 397.8K pins, this overhead can reach 26.46% of the total runtime (discussed later in Fig. 7). Second, based on its scheduling strategy, G-STP launches kernels and data transfers pin by pin, leading to excessive kernel and data transfer launches when the circuit size grows. Since each launch only handles the timing propagation of a single pin, these small, frequent launches underutilize the GPU's parallel resources and become highly inefficient.

Consequently, we propose G-STAR, a GPU-accelerated SSTA engine that performs fast levelized timing propagation through a level-by-level replication strategy. To enable correct levelization of timing quantities under limited GPU memory, G-STAR inserts replicated pins on selected levels. It also introduces a replicated-pin scheduler that reuses GPU memory locations to reduce memory usage after replication, together with an efficient GPU kernel that minimizes unnecessary computation and memory accesses on replicated pins. We evaluate G-STAR on ten industrial circuits generated by OpenTimer and compare it with G-STP. Experimental results show that G-STAR achieves up to 9.24× speedup in overall SSTA performance on large designs, and successfully completes SSTA on several circuits with more than 3M pins where G-STP fails due to GPU out-of-memory (OOM) errors.

2 Background

2.1 Problem Formulation

G-STAR is inspired by the memory-constrained SSTA problem introduced by G-STP [1], as well as our collaboration with a major EDA vendor to retarget their FB-SSTA tool to GPUs. For simplicity, we hereafter use the term SSTA to denote the FB-SSTA paradigm. As illustrated in Fig. 2, consider the two-phase case: in (a), each circuit pin stores two phases of timing quantities, where each phase contains one min delay (d^{min}) and one max delay (d^{max}). On the GPU, these delays are organized into a min phase vector (P_{min}) and a max phase vector (P_{max}), as shown in (b). The length of both P_{min} and P_{max} equals the phase count, which is two in this example. We refer to these two vectors collectively as *phase data*. With these organizations, the goal is to propagate phase data from PIs to POs of the circuit, a process we refer to as *phase propagation*. Phase propagation becomes more expensive as the number of phases increases, since each pin must store a longer phase vector in memory. In practice, the phase count often reaches the thousands, resulting in substantial storage demands [4,7]. Following the G-STP formulation and current industrial practice [1], we focus on circuits whose phase data fit in CPU memory but cannot be fully accommodated in GPU memory as the phase count increases. Although CUDA Unified Memory could be used in this case, it is not ideal for high-performance SSTA kernels with predictable access patterns, since automatic CPU–GPU migration may trigger unnecessary page faults and degrade performance. Therefore, we manage memory transfers explicitly to maintain predictable performance.

Figure 2(c) illustrates the phase propagation process from pins $PI1$ and $PI2$ to pin c through gate $AND1$. Here, P^imin and P^imax represent the min and max phase vectors of pin i. The phase vectors from $PI1$ and $PI2$ first propagate to a and b by adding the edge delays (d_{edge}), and are then combined at $AND1$ using `min` and `max` operations. These operations are guided by a per-gate permutation vector (π), whose length equals the phase count (two in this example). In SSTA, π aligns random-variable coefficients so timing operations can be computed correctly [1]. It defines how the input phase vectors are combined to produce the output phase vectors, as described in Eq. 1. If a gate has multiple outputs, the same permutation vector is shared across all outputs.

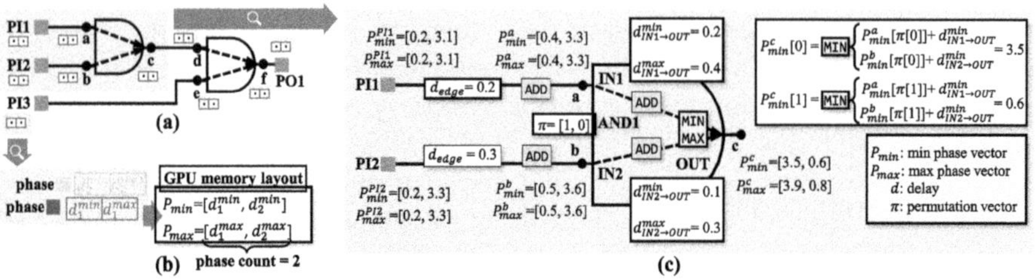

Fig. 2. (a) Illustration of SSTA on the circuit in Fig. 1. (b) Under two phases, each pin carries two sets containing one min delay (d^{min}) and one max delay (d^{max}), arranged in one min phase vector (P_{min}) and one max phase vector (P_{max}) on GPU. (c) Phase vector (P_{min} and P_{max}) propagation from $PI1$ and $PI2$ to pin c through gate $AND1$.

$$P^c_{min}[i] = \mathtt{min}(P^a_{min}[\pi[i]] + d^{min}_{IN1\to OUT}, P^b_{min}[\pi[i]] + d^{min}_{IN2\to OUT}) \qquad (1)$$

Equation 1 shows how the min phase vector of pin c (P^c_{min}) is computed. For each entry i in P^c_{min}, we use the permutation vector π to select the corresponding entries from P^a_{min} and P^b_{min}. We then add the appropriate edge delays and take the `min` of the two resulting values. This produces the result for entry i in P^c_{min}. The max phase vector of c (P^c_{max}) is computed in the same way, except that the `min` operation is replaced with `max`.

2.2 Limitations of State-of-the-Art Methods

Recent GPU-accelerated SSTA frameworks [2,5,6] improve performance by exploiting the large amount of data parallelism in SSTA, but they assume that the entire timing graph and all phase data fit in GPU memory. This assumption becomes impractical as circuit size and phase count grow. To address this issue, G-STP [1] introduces a GPU-parallel approach for memory-constrained

SSTA workloads. As shown in Fig. 3(a), G-STP models phase propagation as a task graph, where each task performs phase propagation for a single pin, including CPU-GPU data transfers and GPU kernel execution. During execution, the scheduler maintains a job queue to decide which pin to process next, and transfers only the required phase data into pre-allocated GPU memory, as illustrated in Fig. 3(b). This pin-by-pin scheduling strategy reduces GPU memory usage through a memory-aware scheduling heuristic.

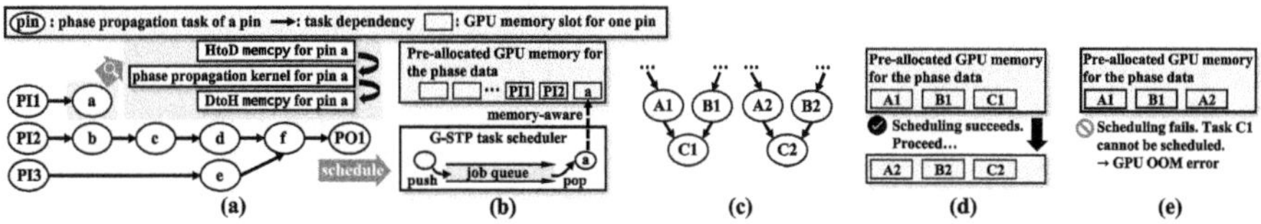

Fig. 3. (a)–(b) illustrate SSTA in G-STP. (a) The task graph representation of the circuit in Fig. 1. (b) The task graph is scheduled on G-STP's task scheduler to perform SSTA. (c)–(e) demonstrate the OOM issue in G-STP. (c) An example task graph assuming the GPU can store phase data for three pins. (d) A successful scheduling of the task graph. (e) A failed scheduling where G-STP encounters a GPU OOM error.

Although G-STP can perform SSTA under limited GPU memory, its pin-by-pin scheduling strategy introduces two major drawbacks. First, it incurs high CPU scheduling overhead and many small GPU operations, including frequent kernel launches and `memcpy`s, which reduces GPU utilization. Second, the scheduler can still fail with GPU out-of-memory (OOM) errors because task execution depends on the order in which ready tasks are selected. This behavior is shown in Fig. 3(c)–(e). In this example task graph (c), we assume that after tasks A1 and B1 are scheduled, both tasks C1 and A2 become ready. In (d), if the scheduler happens to pick C1 next, then tasks A1, B1, and C1 can finish and free their memory slots for the remaining tasks, and the schedule succeeds. However, in (e), if the scheduler instead picks A2 first, then A2 occupies the memory slot that C1 needs. Once A2's phase data are loaded, all three memory slots become full, leaving no free slot for C1's phase data. Because C1 cannot be scheduled for phase propagation, G-STP reaches a dead end and encounters a GPU OOM error, meaning the GPU has no available memory to load the phase data for the next required pin.

To reduce CPU scheduling overhead and better utilize GPU parallelism, many existing works [5–7,9] use *levelized* phase propagation, which processes phase data level by level in batches. However, this approach becomes increasingly limited by GPU memory capacity as circuit size and phase count grow. Existing implementations often store the entire levelized structure and all associated phase data on the GPU, which can exceed available GPU memory for large circuits with millions of pins, as illustrated in Fig. 1(c).

3 G-STAR

As a consequence, we introduce G-STAR, a GPU-accelerated SSTA algorithm based on the levelized approach. To enable levelized phase propagation under the GPU memory constraint, we first identify the minimum amount of phase data that needs to be stored on the GPU at once. In levelized propagation, phase data can be propagated between adjacent levels as long as no multi-level (i.e., > 2) dependencies exist. In this scenario, we try to store only two consecutive levels of phase data, a previous level (*prev*) and a current level (*cur*), to reduce the GPU memory requirement, as shown in Fig. 4. Specifically, we pre-allocate one *prev* buffer and one *cur* buffer on the GPU, each large enough to hold the phase data of the largest level in the circuit (three pins in this example). During phase propagation, we first transfer the phase data of the previous level from the CPU to *prev*, and then launch a kernel that propagates the entire level of phase data from *prev* to *cur*. After the kernel finishes, we transfer the results in *cur* back to the CPU. Finally, we perform a pointer swap between *prev* and *cur* so that, in the next level, the kernel can again read from *prev* and write to *cur* without extra `memcpy` overhead. This full process is illustrated in Fig. 4(b).

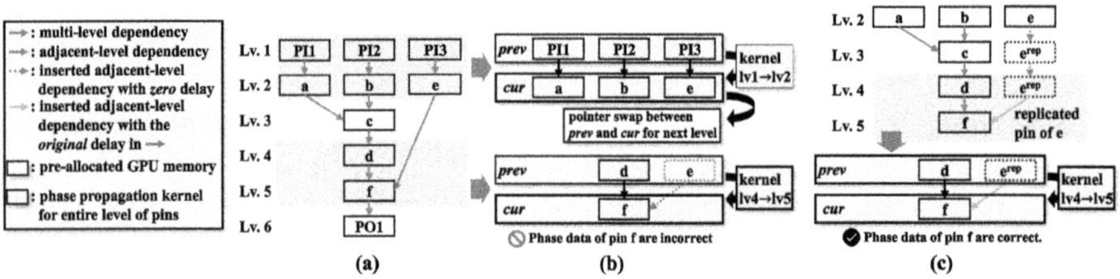

Fig. 4. Illustration of levelized phase propagation on GPU when only two consecutive levels (*prev* and *cur*) of phase data are stored. (a) Level list from Fig. 1. (b) Incorrect propagation caused by a multi-level dependency. (c) We replicate pin e twice to remove its multi-level dependency so that the phase data propagate correctly from e to f.

However, while this method only requires storing two consecutive levels of phase data, it can produce incorrect phase results, as illustrated in Fig. 4(b). After the kernel propagates the phase data from level 4 to level 5, the phase data of pin f are incorrect because the phase data of its dependent, pin e, never get propagated to level 4 due to the multi-level dependency between e and f.

To address this problem, the key idea behind G-STAR is to reconstruct the level list by inserting replicated pins in selected levels to replace all multi-level dependencies with adjacent-level dependencies. In G-STAR, we first apply a level-by-level replication algorithm to insert replicated pins where necessary, ensuring that phase data are propagated correctly. We then apply a replicated-pin scheduler to reuse GPU memory locations for replicated pins and reduce the memory overhead introduced by replication. Finally, G-STAR performs levelized phase propagation with an efficient GPU kernel.

Algorithm 1: Level-by-level replication

```
1  // L: original level list
2  // pq: fanout pins ordered by level (descending)
3  foreach l ∈ L do
4      foreach cur_p ∈ l do
5          push fanouts with multi-level dependencies into pq;
6          f_largest ← pq.pop();
7          insert replicated pins between cur_p and f_largest;
8          add adjacent-level dependencies (original + zero delay);
9          while pq not empty
10             f ← pq.pop(); connect f to its replicated pin with original delay;
```

3.1 Level-by-Level Replication Algorithm

G-STAR replaces all multi-level dependencies with adjacent-level dependencies in the level list through a level-by-level replication algorithm, as shown in Fig. 4(c). To remove the multi-level dependency from pin e to pin f (marked in red in (a)), we insert two replicated pins of e in levels 3 and 4 and connect them with adjacent-level dependencies. Because phase data must accumulate edge delays as they propagate, the final inserted dependency from the replicated pin in level 4 to f (marked in orange) must preserve the *original delay* of the multi-level dependency it replaces, while the remaining inserted dependencies (dashed) have zero delay. With these replicated pins in place, the phase data of e are correctly propagated to level 4 and appear in *prev*, allowing us to compute the phase data of f correctly.

Algorithm 1 details this strategy. For each pin *cur_p* in each level, we examine its fanout pins and push those with multi-level dependencies into a priority queue ordered by descending pin level (lines 3–5). We then pop the fanout pin with the largest level $f_{largest}$, and insert the necessary replicated pins between *cur_p* and $f_{largest}$, adding adjacent-level dependencies with the appropriate original or zero delay (lines 6–8). Next, we pop the remaining fanout pins from the queue and link each to its corresponding replicated pin using one dependency edge that preserves the original delay, without introducing extra replicated pins.

3.2 Replicated-Pin Scheduler

Although the level-by-level replication algorithm enables correct phase propagation, it can still introduce a large number of replicated pins into the reconstructed level list. This is because modern circuits contain many multi-level dependencies, and these dependencies often span many levels. To replace such long-range dependencies with adjacent-level dependencies, a pin may need to be replicated multiple times across multiple intermediate levels. For example, as illustrated in Fig. 5(a)–(b), removing only three multi-level dependencies requires adding eight replicated pins, even though the original level list contains only seven pins. To mitigate this issue, we design a replicated-pin scheduler for G-STAR that

Algorithm 2: Replicated-pin scheduler

```
1  // lifetime_rep: a vector of [p_rep, first_level, last_level]
2  // slots: a list of [slot_index, free_level]
3  foreach p_rep ∈ L_rep
4  |  [first_level, last_level] ← get_lifetime(p_rep);
5  |  lifetime_rep.push(p_rep, first_level, last_level);
6  sort lifetime_rep by first_level (ascending);
7  foreach [p_rep, first_level, last_level] ∈ lifetime_rep
8  |  assign ← false;
9  |  foreach [slot_index, free_level] ∈ slots
10 |  |  if free_level ≤ first_level
11 |  |  |  p_rep.slot_index ← slot_index;
12 |  |  |  free_level ← last_level + 2;
13 |  |  |  assign ← true;   break;
14 |  if !assign
15 |  |  slot_index_new ← slots.size();
16 |  |  free_level_new ← last_level + 2;
17 |  |  p_rep.slot_index ← slot_index_new;
18 |  |  slots.push(slot_index_new, free_level_new);
```

reuses GPU memory locations (*slots*) to reduce the memory requirement after replication.

As part of this design, we pre-allocate a standalone *rep* buffer on the GPU to store phase data exclusively for replicated pins, and use the scheduler to assign each replicated pin to a memory slot in *rep* for its phase data. Because the phase data of replicated pins reside entirely in *rep*, they are reused across levels without being transferred back to the CPU, avoiding additional CPU–GPU data transfer overhead. Algorithm 2 details this scheduler design. The scheduler first computes the lifetime of each replicated pin p_{rep}, defined by the first and last levels at which the pin appears (lines 3–5). A replicated pin's phase data are written only once at its first level (*first_level*) and read only once at its last level (*last_level*). Within this lifetime, no additional phase computation or data transfer is required. The scheduler then sorts replicated pins by their *first_level* and assigns them to slots in *rep* using a greedy reuse strategy: if an existing slot becomes free before this pin's lifetime begins, that slot is reused (lines 9–13); otherwise, a new slot is allocated (lines 14–18). To ensure correctness, a slot is marked as free only after *last_level* + 2 rather than *last_level* + 1. This additional one-level delay prevents the slot from being reused while the phase data of the replicated pin are still being read at *last_level*, a situation that can lead to incorrect results.

Figure 5(a)–(b) illustrates Algorithm 2, with explanation outlined in the caption. By reusing slots whose phase data are no longer needed, the scheduler minimizes the number of slots required in *rep* while maintaining correctness. More importantly, this clear lifetime management of replicated-pin phase data enables an efficient kernel design. In the next section, we show how this design avoids

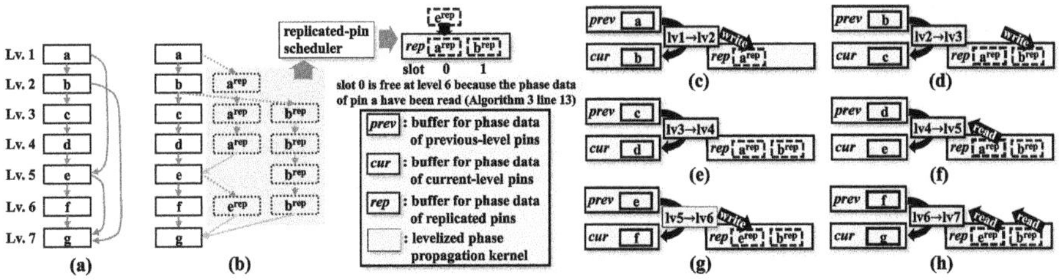

Fig. 5. (a)–(b) Example of applying the replicated-pin scheduler to a level list, where eight replicated pins are added to remove three multi-level dependencies (marked in red). The scheduler reuses memory slots in *rep*, allowing the phase data of all eight replicated pins to be stored using only two slots. Because the last level of replicated pin a^{rep} is 4, its slot is released at level 6, allowing replicated pin e^{rep} to reuse slot 0 (Algorithm 2, line 13). (c)–(h) Levelized execution of the phase propagation kernel guided by the replicated-pin scheduler.

redundant phase propagation for replicated pins during levelized execution. It is also worth noting that both Algorithm 1 and Algorithm 2 are performed only once during initialization before SSTA execution. The reconstructed level list can then be reused for all subsequent SSTA iterations, making the replication cost a one-time preprocessing overhead.

3.3 Levelized Phase Propagation Kernel

Building on the replicated-pin scheduler (Algorithm 2), we design a levelized phase propagation kernel that avoids redundant phase propagation for replicated pins. Algorithm 3 presents the kernel design. In this kernel, the phase data of each pin are handled by T GPU threads, where each thread handles a subset of phases with a stride size of T. For each pin, the kernel first checks whether it is a replicated pin. If the pin is replicated and its phase data have already been written to the *rep* buffer in its first level, the kernel immediately skips further computation for that pin (lines 4–6). This early-exit mechanism ensures that each replicated pin's phase data are written to *rep* only once, thereby avoiding redundant phase propagation across levels. After this check, the kernel determines the destination buffer for storing the results: original pins write their phase data to *cur*, while replicated pins write to their assigned slots in *rep*. During phase propagation, the kernel reads input phase data from either *prev* or *rep*, depending on whether a fanin pin is original or replicated. For gate output pins, the kernel aggregates phase data across all fanins using `min` and `max` operations (lines 11–20). For non-gate pins, which have only a single fanin, the kernel directly propagates the phase data by adding the corresponding delay (lines 21–25). Figure 5(c)–(h) visualizes this levelized kernel execution process.

With the replicated-pin scheduler, the kernel knows exactly when to access each replicated pin's phase data, eliminating unnecessary accesses. More importantly, since the kernel executes level by level, the scheduling overhead is bounded

Algorithm 3: Levelized phase propagation kernel

```
// p: pin (id) handled by this thread; phase_offset: first phase handled by this
   thread (stride = T); T: number of threads per pin; π: permutation vector;
   N_phases: phase count; d: edge delay; src_min/max, dst_min/max: input/output
   phase data (min/max delays)
parallel for each thread tid
    p ← tid / T;
    if p.is_replicated and p.first_level < current level
        // skip replicated pins already written to rep
        return;
    phase_offset ← tid % T;
    π ← p.gate_permutation;
    dst ← p.is_replicated ? rep : cur;
    for phase ← phase_offset to N_phases − 1 step T
        if p.is_gate_output_pin
            min_val ← +∞;   max_val ← −∞;
            foreach fanin pin f ∈ p.fanins
                src ← fanin_p.is_replicated ? rep : prev;
                min_tmp ← src_min[f][π[phase]] + d_min^fanin;
                max_tmp ← src_max[f][π[phase]] + d_max^fanin;
                min_val ← min(min_val, min_tmp);
                max_val ← max(max_val, max_tmp);
            dst_min[p][phase] ← min_val;
            dst_max[p][phase] ← max_val;
        else
            f ← p.fanin;
            src ← fanin_p.is_replicated ? rep : prev;
            dst_min[p][phase] ← src_min[f][phase]+d_min^fanin;
            dst_max[p][phase] ← src_max[f][phase]+d_max^fanin;
```

by the maximum number of levels rather than the size of the circuit graph, as in G-STP.

4 Experimental Results

We implemented G-STAR in C++ and CUDA and compiled it using nvcc v12.2 with -O2 and -std=c++17 enabled. We performed experiments on a 2.0 GHz 64-bit Linux machine equipped with an Intel Xeon Gold 6138 CPU with 182 GB RAM, and an Nvidia Tesla V100 GPU of 32 GB global memory. We consider G-STP [1] as our baseline since it represents the state-of-the-art GPU-accelerated SSTA algorithm designed for memory-constrained SSTA workload. We compare the performance of G-STAR and G-STP on ten industrial circuits. These circuits, generated using the widely-used open-source timer OpenTimer [4], are configured by default with 1024 phases to accommodate various statistical corners. Note that 1024 phases is also the configuration used to generate the golden reference for result validation. Later, we will evaluate G-STAR's performance under different phase counts. Circuit statistics are given in Table 1, where #pins and #edges only count the pins and edges in the original circuit before adding replicated pins, and each result is the average of 10 independent runs.

4.1 Overall Performance Comparison

Table 1 compares the overall performance between G-STP and G-STAR. The value under the mem_{CPU} column shows the total CPU memory required to store all phases of the entire circuit. Note that mem_{CPU} includes only the phases of original pins. The phases of replicated pins are stored in the GPU and managed by the replicated-pin scheduler, which will be discussed in Section ??. The value under the $\text{mem}_{GPU}^{G-STAR}$ column represents the GPU memory required by G-STAR to perform correct SSTA, including the memory required to store phases for original pins (mem_{orig}) and additional memory required for replicated pins (mem_{rep}). We do not report the required GPU memory for G-STP because its allocation is dynamic and depends on the available memory at runtime.

In terms of total SSTA runtime, G-STAR consistently outperforms G-STP across all circuits. For small circuits with 13.1K to 66.8K pins, G-STAR achieves 7.06×–8.30× speedups over G-STP. For medium circuits with 303.7K to 397.8K pins, the speedups further increase to 8.62×–9.24×, with the highest value observed on des_perf. For large circuits with 2.4M to 4.3M pins, the advantages of G-STAR become even more pronounced. Specifically, G-STAR can successfully complete all large circuits, while G-STP fails on many (leon3mp, netcard, and leon2) due to out-of-memory (OOM) errors. The only large circuit that G-STP can complete is usb_phy_ispd, for which G-STAR is 8.41× faster.

We attribute the performance advantage of G-STAR over G-STP to our efficient levelized phase propagation, which avoids the complex task graph–based propagation used in G-STP. This levelized approach minimizes CPU-side overhead during SSTA and supports more efficient data transfers. Further details will be discussed in Sect. 4.3.

4.2 Performance Under Different Phase Counts

Figure 6 shows the speedup of G-STAR over G-STP under different phase counts for des_perf and vga_lcd. We focus on these two circuits because they are the largest ones that both G-STP and G-STAR can complete within our chosen range of phase counts. Overall, the speedup of G-STAR over G-STP gradually decreases as the phase count increases, since larger phase counts result in longer kernel execution times and reduce the relative contribution of CPU scheduling. The highest speedup appears at 256 phases, where G-STAR achieves 19.89× on des_perf and 22.48× on vga_lcd over G-STP. This trend is expected because G-STP performs kernel execution and memory transfers pin by pin, while G-STAR operates level by level. As the phase count increases, the pin-by-pin execution strategy in G-STP becomes relatively more efficient because each pin carries a larger workload. However, for larger circuits, such as leon3mp, netcard, and

Table 1. Comparison of overall performance between G-STP [1] and G-STAR on ten industrial circuits generated by OpenTimer [4] under 1024 phases.

circuit	#pins	#edges	mem_{CPU} (GB)	$\text{mem}_{GPU}^{G-STAR}$ (GB)		total SSTA runtime (ms)	
				mem_{orig}	mem_{rep}	G-STP	G-STAR
wb_dma	13.1K	16.5K	0.2	0.01	0.02	236.26	31.62 (7.47×)
tv80	17.0K	23.0K	0.26	0.01	0.04	265.15	37.51 (7.06×)
ac97_ctrl	42.4K	53.5K	0.65	0.03	0.07	660.09	84.72 (7.79×)
aes_core	66.8K	86.4K	1.02	0.05	0.12	1078.77	129.84 (8.30×)
des_perf	303.7K	387.3K	4.63	0.2	0.44	5367.41	580.50 (9.24×)
vga_lcd	397.8K	489.9K	6.07	0.5	0.88	6483.45	752.08 (8.62×)
usb_phy_ispd	2.4M	2.9M	37.33	3.08	4.65	41848.44	4973.78 (8.41×)
leon3mp	3.4M	4.1M	51.52	1.23	5.32	OOM	6901.37
netcard	4.0M	4.9M	61.02	2.59	7.2	OOM	7833.23
leon2	4.3M	5.3M	66.04	3.65	7.08	OOM	8499.19

#pins, #edges: total number of pins and edges in the original circuit before adding replicated pins; mem_{CPU}: total CPU memory to store all phases of the entire circuit (without replicated pins); mem_{orig}, mem_{rep}: required GPU memory in G-STAR to store phases for original and replicated pins; OOM: GPU out-of-memory error

leon2, G-STP cannot exploit this advantage because its algorithm encounters GPU OOM failures.

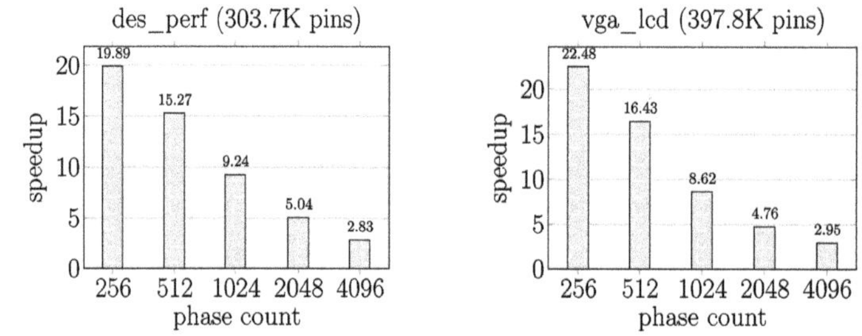

Fig. 6. Speedup of G-STAR over G-STP under different phase counts.

4.3 Runtime Breakdown

In this section, we first break down the total SSTA runtime of G-STAR and G-STP into two parts: *CPU scheduling* and *GPU execution*. CPU scheduling includes kernel launches, data transfer (`memcpy`) launches, and task-graph scheduling (used only in G-STP). GPU execution includes kernel execution and data transfers, including host-to-device (HtoD) and device-to-host (DtoH) `memcpy`. We then examine the GPU execution time in percentage terms.

Total SSTA Runtime Breakdown. Figure 7(a)–(b) show the total SSTA runtime breakdown in terms of CPU scheduling and GPU execution for vga_lcd under 4096 phases. We choose vga_lcd for this experiment because it is the largest one that can support 4096 phases without overflowing the CPU memory on our machine. In G-STP, GPU execution accounts for 73.54% of the total runtime, leaving a substantial 26.46% spent on CPU scheduling. In contrast, G-STAR achieves nearly 100% GPU execution time with only minimal CPU scheduling overhead. The higher CPU scheduling cost in G-STP comes from its task-graph execution model, which relies on a job queue to decide which pin to process next during SSTA execution and launches kernels and `memcpy` operations on a per-pin basis. These runtime scheduling decisions and frequent launches introduce significant CPU overhead. In contrast, G-STAR adopts a level-by-level replication strategy that enables a simpler and more efficient levelized phase-propagation model without an expensive runtime scheduler involved. The replication process (Algorithms 1 and 2) is performed once before SSTA execution and reused across iterations, incurring little CPU scheduling overhead. Moreover, the levelized model allows kernels and `memcpy` operations to be launched on a per-level basis, largely reducing the number of launches compared to G-STP.

GPU Runtime Breakdown. Figure 7(c)–(d) compares the GPU runtime breakdown of G-STP and G-STAR. A key difference lies in kernel execution time: in G-STP, kernels take 2003.5 ms (29.99%), whereas in G-STAR they take only 97.5 ms (3.01%). This reflects the higher kernel efficiency enabled by G-STAR's per-level kernel launches, compared to the per-pin launches used in G-STP. Despite this improvement, GPU runtime in both methods is still dominated by data transfer, accounting for 70.01% of the GPU runtime in G-STP and 96.99% in G-STAR. These transfers include both HtoD and DtoH `memcpy`. HtoD `memcpy` occurs only during initialization to transfer metadata (e.g., circuit topology) and input phase data to the GPU. As a result, most of the transfer time comes from DtoH `memcpy`, which moves the computed phase results back to the CPU and accounts for more than 99% of the total transfer time in this benchmark. However, this HtoD `memcpy` is necessary because the resulting phase data must be returned to the CPU for downstream SSTA applications to use, such as timing-driven optimization [7]. Note that the phase data of replicated pins do not contribute to this overhead, since they remain in the GPU *rep* buffer and are reused across levels without being transferred back to the CPU.

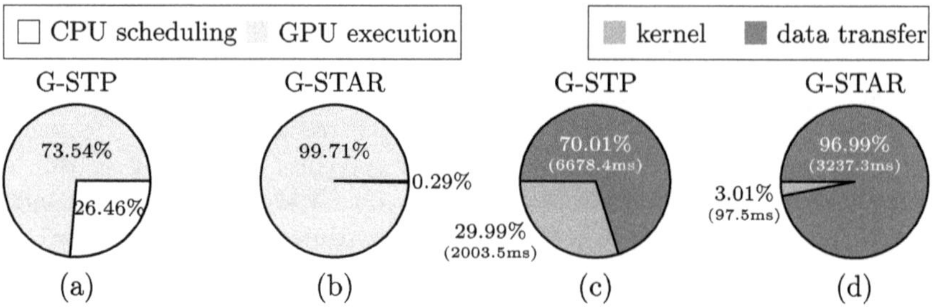

Fig. 7. Runtime breakdown comparison between G-STP and G-STAR for vga_lcd with 4096 cases. (a)–(b) show the total runtime breakdown. (c)–(d) show the GPU runtime breakdown with the actual runtime values shown below the percentages. Data transfer includes both HtoD and DtoH `memcpy` operations.

5 Conclusion

In this paper, we have proposed G-STAR, a GPU-accelerated FB-SSTA engine designed for memory-constrained FB-SSTA workloads. G-STAR enables efficient levelized FB-SSTA via level-by-level replication, combined with a replicated-pin scheduler that reuses GPU memory and an efficient kernel that avoids redundant phase propagation. Compared to a state-of-the-art GPU solution, G-STAR achieves up to 9.24× speedup on large designs and successfully completes FB-SSTA on multi-million-pin circuits where the baseline fails due to GPU OOM errors. This project is supported by NSF grants 2235276, 2349144, 2349143, 2349582, and 2349141. The authors would like to also thank reviewers for their constructive feedback in improving this paper.

Disclosure of Interests. The authors have no competing interests to declare that are relevant to the content of this article.

References

1. Chang, C.C., Huang, T.W.: Statistical timing graph scheduling algorithm for GPU computation. In: ACM/IEEE Design Automation Conference (DAC) (2025)
2. Chiu, C.H., Morchdi, C., Chang, C.C., Yu, C., Zhou, Y., Huang, T.W.: Optimizing CUDA graph scheduling with reinforcement learning-a case study in SSTA propagation. In: 2025 ACM/IEEE 7th Symposium on Machine Learning for CAD (MLCAD), pp. 1–8. IEEE (2025)
3. Forzan, C., Pandini, D.: Statistical static timing analysis: a survey. Integration **42**(3), 409–435 (2009)
4. Huang, T.W., Guo, G., Lin, C.X., Wong, M.D.: Opentimer v2: a new parallel incremental timing analysis engine. IEEE Trans. Comput. Aided Des. Integr. Circuits Syst. **40**(4), 776–789 (2020)
5. Lu, Y.C., Guo, Z., Kunal, K., Liang, R., Ren, H.: Insta: an ultra-fast, differentiable, statistical static timing analysis engine for industrial physical design applications.

In: 2025 62nd ACM/IEEE Design Automation Conference (DAC), pp. 1–7. IEEE (2025)
6. Shen, Y., Hu, J.: GPU acceleration for PCA-based statistical static timing analysis. In: 33rd IEEE International Conference on Computer Design (ICCD), pp. 674–679. IEEE (2015)
7. Sinha, D., Guerra e Silva, L., Wang, J., Raghunathan, S., Netrabile, D., Shebaita, A.: Tau 2013 variation aware timing analysis contest. In: Proceedings of the 2013 ACM International Symposium on Physical Design, pp. 171–178 (2013)
8. Veetil, V., Sylvester, D., Blaauw, D.: Efficient Monte Carlo based incremental statistical timing analysis. In: Proceedings of the 45th Annual Design Automation Conference, pp. 676–681 (2008)
9. Visweswariah, C., Ravindran, K., Kalafala, K., Walker, S.G., Narayan, S.: First-order incremental block-based statistical timing analysis. In: Proceedings of the 41st Annual Design Automation Conference, pp. 331–336 (2004)

A Task Parallel Algorithm For Fast Hybridized PDE Solvers

Joseph McLaughlin(✉), Brittany Erickson, and Jee Choi

University of Oregon, Eugene, OR, USA
{jmclaug2,bae,jeec}@uoregon.edu

Abstract. Earthquake-cycle simulations require solving a large sparse elliptic system at every timestep, making repeated linear solves the dominant cost. We present a task-parallel hybridized finite-difference solver for multi-core CPUs based on SBP-SAT discretizations. SBP-SAT hybridization preserves sparse stencil operators within each subproblem, making subproblem size a tunable parameter. We exploit this to develop a dependency-aware task-parallel algorithm that overlaps subproblem solves with global trace assembly, reducing bulk-synchronous barriers and improving cache reuse, and a Roofline-based performance model that selects the subproblem size minimizing end-to-end solve time. On 64-core Sapphire Rapids and 104-core Ice Lake systems, our solver achieves up to 9.1× speedup over a baseline hybridized solver, up to 4.7× over IC(0)-preconditioned CG, and up to 12× over sparse multifrontal QR. Model-guided sizing achieves up to 31× speedup over commonly used fixed sizes, substantially reducing per-solve costs for earthquake-cycle simulations.

Keywords: Hybridized methods · task-parallel solvers · multi-core CPUs · earthquake-cycle simulations · PDEs

1 Introduction

A primary challenge when solving partial differential equations (PDEs) is their reliance on low arithmetic intensity operations, where memory accesses dominate compute, leaving processing units idle. Techniques such as cache-obvious algorithms [2], sparse matrix formats [1,6], specialized preconditioners [5,22], address this constraint at different levels of the solver stack. In contrast, hybridization is a technique that reduces the degrees-of-freedom (DOFs) required to represent the underlying system of linear equations when solving elliptic PDEs [11]. Hybridization decomposes the problem into independent *subproblems* connected at interfaces, which define a smaller *global trace system*. We exploit two key properties of hybridization—data-independent subproblems and reduced memory footprint—that directly address the memory and parallelism constraints of modern architectures to develop a new parallel algorithm for solving PDEs on multi-core CPUs.

M. Torquati et al. (Eds.): Euro-Par 2026, LNCS 16781, pp. 568–582, 2027.
https://doi.org/10.1007/978-3-032-35248-4_39

Our approach relies on a key distinction between hybridized finite differences (FD) and finite element methods (FEM). In hybridized FEM, such as hybridizable discontinuous Galerkin (HDG) [15], subproblem interiors are typically represented by dense local matrices, so local factorization and solve costs increase rapidly with subproblem size. Consequently, large subproblems are often unattractive in practice. In contrast, our hybridized SBP-SAT finite-difference formulation preserves sparse, stencil-structured operators within each subproblem. This makes the subproblem size a flexible tuning parameter, allowing it to grow without incurring the dense-local algebra penalty and enabling a principled trade-off between local work and the cost of the global trace solve.

We target earthquake-cycle simulations, which model multi-scale deformation of the Earth over hundreds of years [8]. These simulations require implicit time integration, solving a large sparse system at every timestep, often requiring hundreds of thousands of solves per simulation. In solve-dominant workloads, even modest per-solve speedups translate directly to reduced wall-clock time.

1.1 Contributions

We make three key contributions towards improving the performance of hybridized PDE solvers.

1. We develop a task-based parallel algorithm that captures data dependencies across subproblems and global problem assembly, reducing bulk-synchronous barriers and improving cache reuse (Sect. 2.3). On 64-core Sapphire Rapids and 104-core Ice Lake systems, this achieves up to 9.1× speedup over a baseline parallel hybridized solver (Sect. 4.2).
2. We develop a Roofline-derived model that predicts the optimal subproblem size by balancing local solve costs against global trace solve costs (Sect. 3). Our model selects the optimal parameter in 87.7% of cases, with average performance within 1.7% of an exhaustive search (Sect. 4.3).
3. We compare against widely-deployed *non-hybridized* commercial solvers, IC(0)-preconditioned CG and multi-frontal QR from Intel MKL, achieving up to 4.7× and 12× speedup, respectively (Sect. 4.6).

1.2 Related Work

The existing literature on hybridization for solving PDEs largely focuses on its use as a memory reduction technique, leaving its potential as a performance optimization strategy largely underexplored. Work prioritizing memory reduction increases subproblem density (i.e., number of subproblems), making each subproblem as small as possible [3,9,13]. This grows the size of the global trace system, motivating preconditioner research [7,20] for faster convergence. Low-density approaches [10] use larger subproblems to shrink the trace system but provide no guidance on optimal sizing. One study [14] compared three densities and observed that performance degrades at extremes, but did not provide guidance on selecting the optimal density. Our work explicitly models this trade-off.

Hybridization is distinct from algebraic domain decomposition and bordered block-diagonal (BBD) methods. In BBD formulations, the global matrix is partitioned after discretization, producing a border that couples subproblems; this border is typically dense and partition-dependent. Classical substructuring methods similarly operate algebraically and often solve interface coupling implicitly. In contrast, hybridization introduces trace unknowns during discretization, ensuring the global system is sparse and structured by the mesh layout. This explicit sparse structure is what enables our task-parallel algorithm and performance model.

Task parallelism has been applied throughout PDE solver workflows, including factorization [4,25] and preconditioning [26]. However, these efforts target solver and assembly phases, not the numerical method itself. Hybridized methods naturally decompose into independent subproblems coupled through a sparse trace system, making them well-suited to task-based execution. Yet, existing implementations largely rely on bulk-synchronous models. We show that task-based execution improves cache reuse and reduces synchronization overhead.

2 Parallel Hybridized PDE Solver

We solve a version of the 2D anti-plane shear deformation problem [18] with *variable* coefficients:

$$-\left(\frac{\partial}{\partial x}+\frac{\partial}{\partial y}\right)\cdot\left(\mu(x,y)\left(\frac{\partial}{\partial x}+\frac{\partial}{\partial y}\right)u(x,y)\right)=f(x,y) \tag{1a}$$

on the unit square $0 \leq x, y \leq 1$ with mixed Dirichlet/Neumann boundary conditions. This problem arises in earthquake-cycle simulations, where implicit time integration requires solving a linear system at every timestep. Because matrix factors are reused across timesteps, the dominant cost is the solve phase.

2.1 Hybridized Scheme

We discretize using the summation-by-parts finite difference method with simultaneous approximation terms (SBP-SAT) [17,19,24], which provides high-order accuracy and provable energy stability within a stenciled kernel [16]. Throughout this work we use a second-order accurate SBP-SAT discretization. Hybridization decomposes the domain into sub-domains coupled at interfaces (Fig. 1a-b),

$$\begin{bmatrix}\mathbf{M} & \mathbf{F}\\ \mathbf{F}^{\mathsf{T}} & \mathbf{D}\end{bmatrix}\begin{pmatrix}\mathbf{u}\\ \boldsymbol{\lambda}\end{pmatrix}=\begin{pmatrix}\bar{\mathbf{g}}\\ \bar{\mathbf{g}}_{\delta}\end{pmatrix}. \tag{2}$$

Here, $\mathbf{M}$ is block-diagonal with each block encoding a subproblem, $\mathbf{F}$ encodes interface conditions, $\mathbf{D}$ is a sparse diagonal matrix, and $\boldsymbol{\lambda}$ contains trace variables on internal interfaces. Vectors $\bar{\mathbf{g}}$ and $\bar{\mathbf{g}}_{\delta}$ contain the source data for the external boundaries and internal interfaces. The solution is obtained using the Schur complement,

$$\boldsymbol{\Lambda}_{\mathbf{A}} = \mathbf{D} - \mathbf{F}^{\mathsf{T}}\mathbf{M}^{-1}\mathbf{F}, \tag{3a}$$

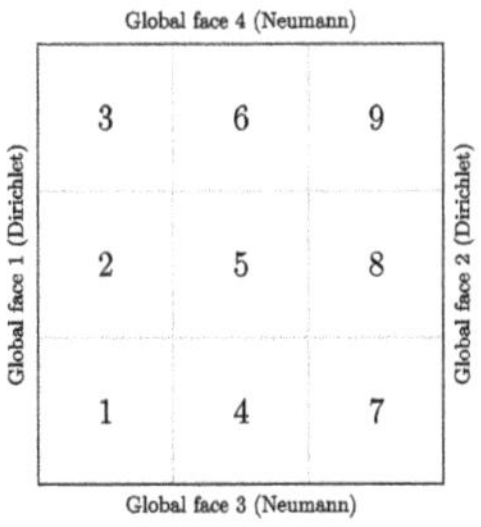

(a) Division of the global domain into subproblems.

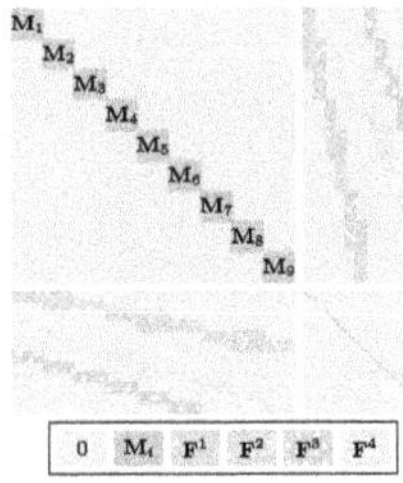

(b) Nonzero pattern of the computational domain.

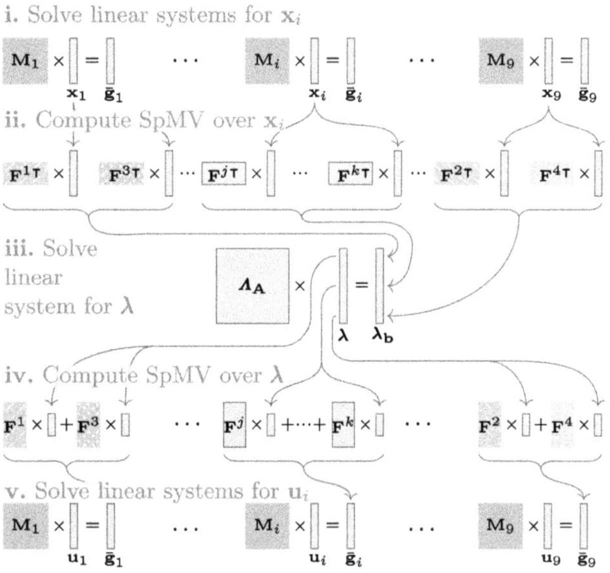

(c) Task graph of the hybridized method. Note that steps **i–v** are conventionally computed with a barrier after each step.

Fig. 1. Visualizations of the **(a)** global domain, **(b)** computational domain, and **(c)** task graph for a 3×3 decomposition of the hybridized problem specified in Eq. 2. Submatrices of $\mathbf{F}$ are shaded in the same color/pattern if they have the same nonzero pattern.

$$\boldsymbol{\lambda}_{\mathbf{b}} = \bar{\mathbf{g}}_{\delta} - \mathbf{F}^{\mathsf{T}}\mathbf{M}^{-1}\bar{\mathbf{g}}, \tag{3b}$$

$$\boldsymbol{\Lambda}_{\mathbf{A}}\boldsymbol{\lambda} = \boldsymbol{\lambda}_{\mathbf{b}}, \tag{3c}$$

$$\mathbf{M}\mathbf{u} = (\bar{\mathbf{g}} - \mathbf{F}\boldsymbol{\lambda}). \tag{3d}$$

Equations 3b and 3d decompose into independent subproblem solves; Eq. 3c is the global trace solve. The trace operator $\boldsymbol{\Lambda}_{\mathbf{A}}$ is computed once and reused across timesteps; nonlinear or time-varying coefficients would require periodic refactorization (Fig. 2).

2.2 Problem Configuration

We use square subproblems of uniform size for simplicity, though extending the problem to non-uniform decomposition is straightforward. The total number of subproblems is ℓ^2, each containing n^2 grid points, giving a global problem size of $\bar{n}^2 = (n\ell)^2$. The number of internal interfaces is $r = 2\ell^2 - 2\ell$. Figure 1a illustrates a 3×3 decomposition with $\ell^2 = 9$ and $r = 12$ interfaces. We strictly consider the 2D anti-plane shear problem, a standard benchmark problem in earthquake-cycle simulation.

Algorithm 1: Naively parallel.

1 **parallel for** $i \in 1 \cdots \ell^2$
2   Solve $\mathbf{M}_i \mathbf{x}_i = \mathbf{g}_i$
3 $\mathbf{x} = \mathbf{x}_1 \oplus \cdots \oplus \mathbf{x}_n$
4 $\boldsymbol{\lambda}_\mathbf{b} = \mathbf{F}^\mathsf{T} \mathbf{x}$

Algorithm 2: Bulk synchronous parallel.

1 **parallel for** $i \in 1 \cdots \ell^2$
2   Solve $\mathbf{M}_i \mathbf{x}_i = \mathbf{g}_i$
3 **parallel for** $i \in 1 \cdots \ell^2$
    `// First set of subproblems`
4   **if** $i/n \quad mod\ (2 - n \quad mod\ 2) \neq 1$ **then**
5   **parallel for** $j \in 1 \cdots r$
6   Retrieve sub-matrix $\mathbf{F}_{ij}$
7   **if** $\mathbf{F}_{ij}$ *exists* **then**
8                 $\boldsymbol{\lambda}_{\mathbf{b}j} = \mathbf{F}_{ij}^\mathsf{T} \mathbf{x}_i$
9 **parallel for** $i \in 1 \cdots \ell^2$
    `// Second set of subproblems`
10   **if** $i/n \quad mod\ (2 - n \quad mod\ 2) \neq 0$ **then**
11   **parallel for** $j \in 1 \cdots r$
12   Retrieve sub-matrix $\mathbf{F}_{ij}$
13   **if** $\mathbf{F}_{ij}$ *exists* **then**
14                 $\boldsymbol{\lambda}_{\mathbf{b}j} = \mathbf{F}_{ij}^\mathsf{T} \mathbf{x}_i$

Algorithm 3: Task parallel.

1 **for** $i \in 1 \cdots \ell^2$
2   **Task A: out($\mathbf{x}_i$)**
3   Solve $\mathbf{M}_i \mathbf{x}_i = \mathbf{g}_i$
4   **for** $j \in 1 \cdots r$
5   Retrieve sub-matrix $\mathbf{F}_{ij}$
6   **if** $\mathbf{F}_{ij}$ *exists* **then**
7   **Task B: in($\mathbf{x}_i$), mtx($\boldsymbol{\lambda}_{\mathbf{b}j}$)**
8                 $\boldsymbol{\lambda}_{\mathbf{b}j} = \mathbf{F}_{ij}^\mathsf{T} \mathbf{x}_i$

Fig. 2. Three methods of computing stages **i** & **ii** from the task graph in Fig. 1c: using a naively parallel, single-kernel method (Algorithm 1), a bulk-synchronous parallel method (Algorithm 2) and a task-parallel method (Algorithm 3). The task-parallel method prioritizes temporal locality, improving the likelihood that intermediate data ($\mathbf{x}_i$) will remain in cache for subsequent tasks.

2.3 Task-Parallel Algorithm

General Schur complement reductions are typically computed using large single-kernel methods (Alg. 1) because they often lack guarantees about the matrix structure. In contrast, the non-zero structure of the hybridized SBP-SAT method allows us to break this work into fine-grained computations, as shown in Fig. 1c, where the work is broken into five stages (**i**–**v**), each with multiple computational tasks.

There are read-after-write (RAW) dependencies between tasks in stages **i** and **ii** (over $\mathbf{x}_i$), tasks in stages **iii** and **iv** (over $\boldsymbol{\lambda}$), and tasks in stages **iv** and **v** (over $\mathbf{g}_i$). There is also a write-after-write (WAW) dependency between tasks in stage **ii** and the global solve in stage **iii** (over $\boldsymbol{\lambda}_b$). Conventional bulk synchronous parallelism (BSP) would require global synchronization between stages to address the RAW dependencies, as well as additional inter-task synchronization (in stage **ii**), mutex locks, or thread-private buffers with global reduction, to address the WAW dependency.

Algorithm 2 describes a BSP algorithm for stages **i** and **ii**. Instead of using mutex locks or thread-private buffers with global reduction, both of which are computationally more expensive, we use a global barrier (between line 2 and 3) to eliminate the WAW dependency. The second barrier (between line 8 and

9), in particular, divides the computation into sets of non-adjacent subproblems (i.e., subproblems that do not share an interface with others in the same set), eliminating write conflicts to $\boldsymbol{\lambda}_\mathbf{b}$ when subproblems are computed in parallel. For the example in Fig. 1a, these would be even and odd-numbered (*i.e.*, two-colored) subproblem sets.

The BSP model requires more synchronization than is absolutely necessary so we analyze the dependencies between tasks across all five stages to construct a task graph, as shown by the arrows in Fig. 1c. This allows us to use task-parallelism to execute more tasks asynchronously, which reduces the synchronization overhead and increase temporal locality of intermediate data. Additionally, some intermediate data computed in one stage (*e.g.*, $\mathbf{x}_5$ in stage **i**) is consumed by more tasks in the subsequent stage (*e.g.*, stage **ii**) compared to other intermediate data (*e.g.*, $\mathbf{x}_1$), due to having more internal interfaces (*e.g.*, subproblem 5 has four interfaces, whereas subproblem 1 only has two). We further exploit this dependency structure by prioritizing tasks whose intermediate results are consumed by a greater number of downstream tasks. Because these tasks are memory-bandwidth bound, executing them before others improves temporal locality and reduces evictions of frequently reused data.

Our task-parallel algorithm for stages **i**, **ii** is described in Algorithm 3. We omit the algorithm for stages **iv**, **v**, as it is similar but constructed from the edge-reversed graph of the former. We implement these routines using OpenMP's task constructs. We use the `depend` clause to assign dependencies on the intermediate data, the `mutexinoutset` clause to serialize writes to the same memory location, and the `priority` clause to prioritize the execution of tasks that generate more frequently consumed intermediate data.

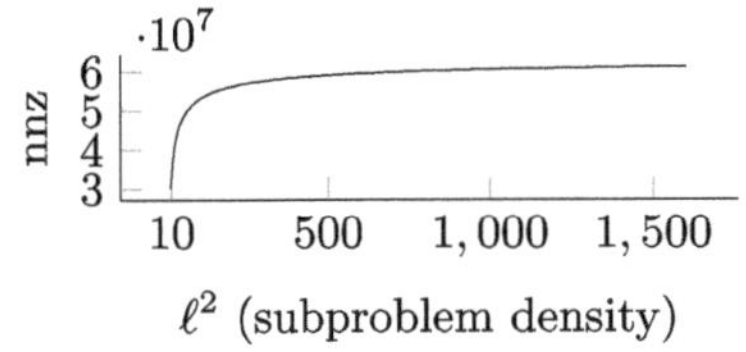

(a) The number of nonzero elements in $\boldsymbol{\Lambda}_\mathbf{A}$ as given by Eq. 5.

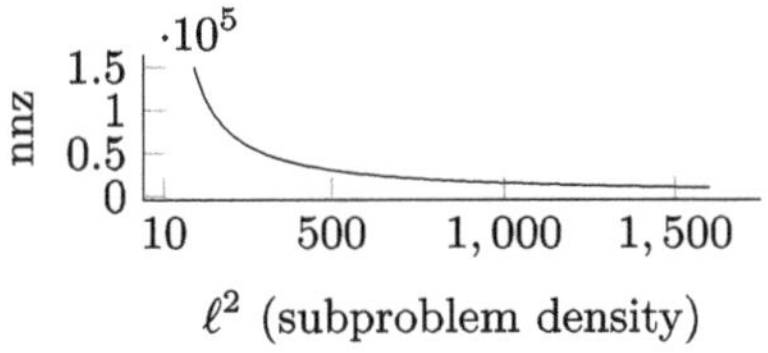

(b) The number of nonzero elements in $\mathbf{M}_i$ as given by Eq. 6.

Fig. 3. The number of nonzero elements in **(a)** $\boldsymbol{\Lambda}_\mathbf{A}$ and **(b)** $\mathbf{M}_i$ as a function of the subproblem density (ℓ^2) for a constant global volume of $\bar{n}^2 = 1e6$.

3 Performance Model

A key parameter in hybridized PDE solvers is the subproblem density (*i.e.*, the number of subproblems for a given total DOFs), which significantly impacts performance [14]. However, prior work has only explored it heuristically or for a small set of values, without guidance on optimal selection. To address this, we develop a performance model that selects the optimal subproblem density for a given global volume size and processor. Our model derives from the Roofline model [27], which predicts performance based on arithmetic intensity and peak compute and memory throughput. Our model first derives the number of nonzero elements (nnz) in $\mathbf{\Lambda_A}$ (global problem) and $\mathbf{M}$ (subproblems) as functions of ℓ^2, which are then used to compute the number of arithmetic operations and bytes accessed by Eqs. 3b, 3c, and 3d. Our model then predicts execution times, which we balance between the subproblems and the global problem to identify the subproblem density that minimizes total execution time.

3.1 Deriving the Number of Nonzero Elements

To compute $\mathbf{\Lambda_A}$, we solve the sparse system $\mathbf{Mx} = \mathbf{F}$ in 3a, storing each $\mathbf{F}^i$ boundary as a $n^2 \times n$ matrix. The number of unique submatrices is $p \leq \ell^2$ (with $p = \ell^2$ for variable-coefficient problems), and the number of interfaces is $r = 2\ell^2 - 2\ell$. Solving this system yields $(p \cdot n \cdot 2r)$ vectors $\mathbf{y}$ of length n^2, and since $n = \bar{n}/\ell$, increasing the subproblem density ℓ^2 decreases each subproblem size n^2 for fixed $\bar{n}^2$. Each $\mathbf{y}$ is used in the product $\mathbf{F}^{i\mathsf{T}}\mathbf{y}$, yielding $\mathbf{\Lambda_A} \in \mathbb{R}^{rn \times rn}$. The nnz in $\mathbf{\Lambda_A}$ is given by

$$\text{nnz}_{\mathbf{\Lambda}} = n^2 \sum_{i=1}^{\ell^2} (\phi_i^2), \tag{4a}$$

where $\phi \in \mathbb{Z}^{\ell^2}$ encodes the number of interfaces for each subproblem,

$$\phi = \left[\underbrace{2, 2, 2, 2}_{4}, \underbrace{3 \cdots 3}_{4\ell-8}, \underbrace{4 \cdots 4}_{(\ell-2)^2} \right], \tag{4b}$$

corresponding to corner (4), boundary ($4\ell - 8$), and interior ($(\ell - 2)^2$) subproblems, respectively. Substituting Eq. 4b into Eq. 4a gives

$$\text{nnz}_{\mathbf{\Lambda}}(\ell) = (\bar{n}^2/\ell^2)(16\ell^2 - 28\ell + 8). \tag{5}$$

Similarly, the second-order SBP-SAT discretization of Eq. 1a yields five nonzeros per row, so nnz in $\mathbf{M}$ is given by

$$\text{nnz}_{\mathbf{M}}(\ell) = 5\bar{n}^2/\ell^2. \tag{6}$$

As shown in Fig. 3, $\text{nnz}_{\mathbf{\Lambda}}$ grows with ℓ^2 while $\text{nnz}_{\mathbf{M}}$ decreases, illustrating the cost trade-off between the global and subproblems.

3.2 Deriving the Execution Time Model

We use $\text{nnz}_{\mathbf{\Lambda}}$ and $\text{nnz}_{\mathbf{M}}$ to derive execution time models for the global problem (Eq. 3c) and subproblems (Eq. 3d), then minimize their sum to find the optimal subproblem density. This is possible since any weighted sum of $\text{nnz}_{\mathbf{\Lambda}}$ and $\text{nnz}_{\mathbf{M}}$ is bounded by a second-degree polynomial, and is thus convex with a unique global minimum.

The global problem is modeled as memory-bound, giving

$$T_{\mathbf{\Lambda}} = \frac{\text{bytes}_{\mathbf{\Lambda}}}{\beta_{\text{peak}}}, \tag{7}$$

where $\text{bytes}_{\mathbf{\Lambda}}$ depends on the storage scheme: $(rn)^2$ or $(rn)^2/2$ for dense LU or Cholesky, and $2 \cdot \text{nnz}_{\mathbf{\Lambda}}$ for sparse methods. The subproblem execution time is modeled as

$$T_{\mathbf{M}} = \frac{\text{bytes}_{\mathbf{M}}^{(1+\varepsilon)}}{\beta_{\text{peak}}}, \tag{8}$$

where ε is a parallel penalty term capturing solver implementation overheads, and $\text{bytes}_{\mathbf{M}}$ is $(n)^2$, $(n)^2/2$, or $2 \cdot \text{nnz}_{\mathbf{M}}$ for LU, Cholesky, or sparse storage, respectively. The optimal subproblem size is then

$$\tau(n) = \arg\min_{n} \{T_{\mathbf{\Lambda}} + 2T_{\mathbf{M}}\}. \tag{9}$$

This model has a unique global minimum because $T_{\mathbf{M}}$ and $T_{\mathbf{\Lambda}}$ trade off with ℓ: as subproblem density increases, each subproblem shrinks, with total subproblem cost scaling as $\ell^{-2\varepsilon}$ (decreasing for $\varepsilon > 0$), while $T_{\mathbf{\Lambda}}$ grows since more interfaces enlarge the global problem. The parameter ε scales cleanly with $\bar{n}^2$, allowing it to be measured offline once and reused across problem sizes.

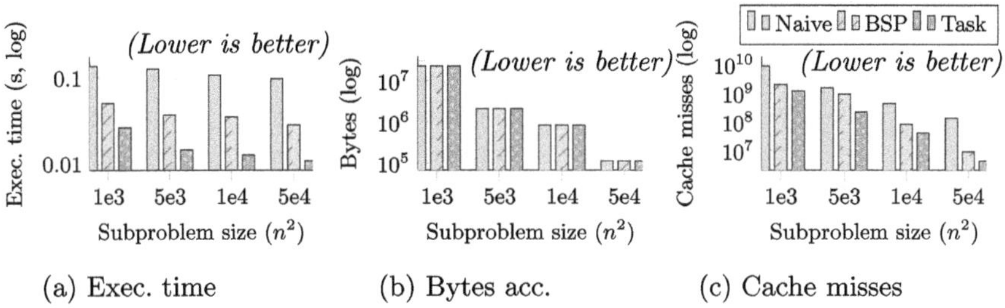

Fig. 4. Comparison of three variants of our parallel hybridized PDE solver for a global volume of $\bar{n}^2 = 1\text{e}6$ grid points. Naive (Alg. 1) stores the interface matrix $\mathbf{F}$ in CSR and performs a single SpMV to compute $\mathbf{F}^\mathsf{T}\mathbf{x}$; BSP stores $\mathbf{F}$ as multiple submatrices and computes multiple SpMVs; Task eliminates implicit barriers via task-based parallelism. Figure **(a)** shows execution time improves significantly with both optimizations, with the lowest time at the largest subproblem size due to fewer total bytes accessed, as shown in Fig. **(b)**. Figure **(c)** confirms that L3 cache misses also decrease with each optimization.

3.3 Model Analysis

The primary role of this model is to identify subproblem sizes that balance local and global costs without exhaustive empirical tuning. Equation 9 has a unique global minimum because T_{M} and T_{Λ} trade off with ℓ so the total subproblem cost scales as $\ell^{-2\varepsilon}$ (decreasing for $\varepsilon > 0$), since each subproblem shrinks faster than their number grows, while T_{Λ} increases with ℓ as each additional subproblem introduces new interfaces, growing the global problem as ℓ^2 for dense factorizations.

4 Experimental Results

We evaluate the bulk-synchronous (Algorithm 2) and task-based (Algorithm 3) methods across subproblem sizes (Sect. 4.2), the accuracy of our performance model across solvers, volume sizes, platforms, and core counts (Sect. 4.3), and our solver against prior hybridized work (Sect. 4.5) and non-hybridized CG and multi-frontal QR baselines (Sect. 4.6).

4.1 Experimental Setup

We evaluate on two Intel CPU platforms, each configured with one thread per core and fixed clock frequency. All measurements are averaged over 10 runs and collected using PAPI [12]. Code was compiled with the Intel OneAPI compiler (release 2024.1.0) and Intel OpenMP library, using the `-O3` and `-fiopenmp` flags, with `OMP_NUM_THREADS=64` and `104` for the Sapphire Rapids and Ice Lake platforms, respectively, and `OMP_PLACES= ''cores''` and `OMP_PROC_BIND= ''close''` for thread placement. This configuration outperformed thread spreading, as the largely independent subproblems favor locality-preserving access patterns with limited cross-socket traffic. All linear algebra operations use Intel MKL routines, including dense Cholesky, CG, and multi-frontal QR solvers. We evaluate global volume sizes from $\bar{n}^2 = 1e6$ to $\bar{n}^2 = 3.2e7$; larger sizes are excluded due to excessive runtime and/or memory requirements of competing methods. Throughout, we report subproblem *size* (n^2) rather than subproblem *density* (ℓ^2) for clarity, where $n^2 = \frac{\bar{n}^2}{\ell^2}$ for a fixed global domain.

4.2 Impact of Task-Based Parallelism

We evaluate the bulk-synchronous (Algorithm 2) and task-parallel (Algorithm 3) methods against a naive parallel baseline for a global volume of $\bar{n}^2 = 1e6$ grid points and $\ell^2 = 64$ subproblems; sufficient to fully occupy the Sapphire Rapids cores. Other global volume sizes show similar trends and are omitted. As shown in Fig. 4a, both methods improve performance over the baseline, with task parallel achieving the lowest execution time across all subproblem sizes. The largest subproblem size yields the best performance, with 3.4× and 9.1× speedups for BSP and task parallel, respectively, consistent with the reduction in total bytes accessed as shown in Fig. 4b. Figure 4c confirms that task parallelism incurs the fewest cache misses, confirming that prioritizing intermediate data reuse improves temporal locality and cache utilization.

4.3 Performance Model Accuracy

We evaluate our model by comparing predicted subproblem sizes against those found by exhaustive empirical search (oracle), across global volume sizes, solver algorithms, CPU platforms, and core counts. Exhaustive search is infeasible at the largest volumes due to varying memory footprints, so we restrict comparison to regimes where sufficient empirical data can be collected. We test two contrasting solvers, dense Cholesky (smaller problems) and sparse multi-frontal QR (larger problems), to demonstrate that the model generalizes across algorithms. Overall, our model matches the oracle in 79 of 90 cases (87.7%). Mismatches arise from projecting a continuous model onto discrete subproblem sizes that evenly divide the global volume. Even in incorrect cases, the execution time penalty is minimal and amounts to an average slowdown of 4.8% for mispredictions, and 1.7% across all cases.

Table 1. Comparison of predicted (Model) and empirically determined optimal subproblem sizes for the Sapphire Rapids (SPR) and Ice Lake (ICX) platforms, using maximum available cores of 64 and 104, respectively. In two cases (highlighted in gray), the predicted optimal size differs from the empirically determined optimal, but only by one valid step size.

Dense Cholesky

$\bar{n}^2$	Model	SPR	Model	ICX
1e6	91	91	77	77
2e6	100	100	85	85

Sparse multi-frontal QR

$\bar{n}^2$	Model	SPR	Model	ICX
1e6	200	200	142	142
2e6	218	218	172	172
4e6	246	282	200	200

Sparse multi-frontal QR

$\bar{n}^2$	Model	SPR	Model	ICX
8e6	282	312	258	258
1.6e7	340	340	300	300
3.2e7	400	400	360	360

Table 1 shows a subset of the optimal subproblem sizes predicted by our model compared to the empirically determined optimal sizes across the Sapphire Rapids and Ice Lake platforms when *using all available cores*. For Cholesky, our model selects the correct subproblem sizes on both systems for global volume sizes of $\bar{n}^2 = 1e6$ and $2e6$. For multi-frontal QR, our model selects the correct subproblem sizes in 10 out of 12 cases across both platforms. The two incorrect predictions occur on Sapphire Rapids and the predictions differ by only a single discrete step from the oracle due to rounding and divisibility constraints on subproblem sizes. These results demonstrate that our performance model is both accurate and robust. Notably, performance is relatively insensitive to small deviations from the model-predicted optimum, with neighboring subproblem sizes exhibiting comparable execution times.

4.4 Performance Model Parameters

Our model uses two theoretically derived machine parameters, α_{peak} and β_{peak}, computed directly from hardware specifications (8.2 Tflops/s and 562 GB/s for Sapphire Rapids; 5.3 Tflops/s and 762 GB/s for Ice Lake), and one empirically derived parallel penalty ε, which captures implementation-dependent solver inefficiencies. We find $\varepsilon = 1.2$ for dense Cholesky and $\varepsilon = 1.1$ for multi-frontal QR, consistent with Cholesky exposing less parallelism. Notably, ε is stable across global volume sizes and platforms, so only a single offline measurement is needed.

4.5 Comparison Against Prior Hybridized Solvers

To isolate the contribution of subproblem-size selection from implementation differences, we re-implemented the test problems from two prior hybridized-solver studies [21,23] (logically Cartesian "rectilinear" meshes for second-order 2D Poisson) within our own solver framework, then ran each problem at both the author-reported subproblem size and the size selected by our model. All other components (*e.g.*, linear algebra library, threading, task graph) are held fixed. The model prediction in Fig. 5 is reported as additional validation against the directly measured speedup. We also include an Intel Broadwell platform, as these studies predate our hardware. For the 1.5e6-point problem from [23] ($n^2 = 36$), our model predicts up to 3× speedup on Sapphire Rapids using the optimal subproblem size; our analogous implementation achieves up to 4.9×. For the 1.7e6-point problem from [21] ($n^2 = 53$), our model predicts up to 30× speedup, and our implementation achieves up to 31×. These results are shown in Fig. 5.

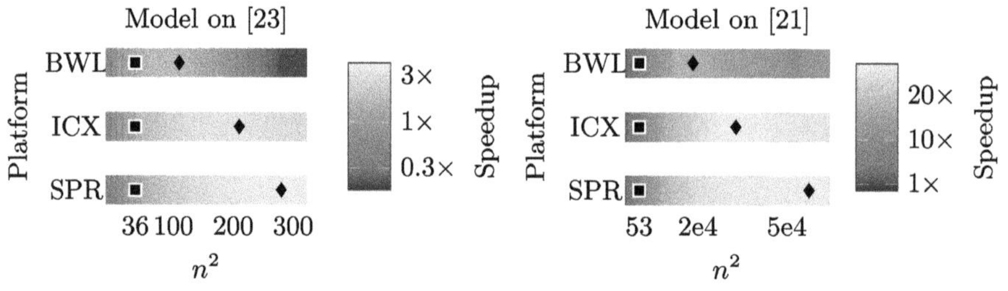

Fig. 5. Our performance model applied to the 1.5e6 problem from [23] and the 1.7e6 problem from [21]. We plot the performance of the subproblem size chosen by our model (◇) in contrast to the subproblem size used by the authors (□). This is plotted for Intel Broadwell (BWL), Ice Lake (ICX), and Sapphire Rapids (SPR) CPU platforms.

4.6 Performance Against Other Sparse Solvers

Finally, we compare our hybridized PDE solver against alternative *non-hybridized* PDE solvers to demonstrate the effectiveness of hybridization as a performance optimization strategy. We compare against both an iterative method,

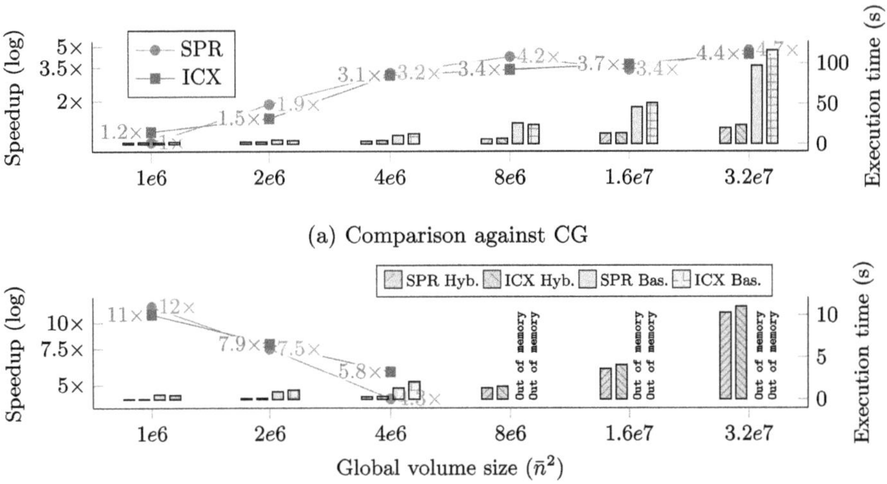

Fig. 6. Speedup of our parallel hybridized PDE solver (Hyb.) against baseline (Bas.) non-hybridized CG and sparse multi-frontal QR solvers (Intel MKL) on the Sapphire Rapids and Ice Lake platforms using 64 and 104 cores, respectively. The sparse QR solver ran out of memory at $\bar{n}^2 \geq 8e6$ and could not be compared. Our optimally configured hybridized solver is significantly faster than both competing methods, even at large global volume sizes.

CG, and a sparse direct method, multi-frontal QR. When comparing each solver, we use the same method to solve the subproblems and the global problem in our hybridized method to make the comparison as fair as possible.

Figure 6 shows the speedup achieved by our parallel hybridized PDE solver against IC(0) preconditioned CG (Fig. 6a) and multi-frontal QR (Fig. 6b) methods, for global volume sizes ranging from $\bar{n}^2 = 1e6$ to $3.2e7$, on our two test platforms. Against CG, our parallel hybridized PDE solver achieves speedup up to 4.7× on the Sapphire Rapids platform, and up to 4.4× on the Ice Lake platform, demonstrating significantly better performance. IC(0) preconditioning is a strong baseline for structured-grid Poisson problems, typically reducing iteration counts by $3 - 5\times$ compared to diagonal preconditioning while maintaining good parallel scalability. The fact that our hybridized solver outperforms this well-tuned iterative method demonstrates the effectiveness of our method.

Against multi-frontal QR, our parallel algorithm achieves speedup ranging from 4.3× to 12× on the Sapphire Rapids platform, and speedup ranging from 5.8× to 11× on the Ice Lake platform. Speedup over sparse direct decreases with problem size, but for large problems direct methods hit a memory wall and become impossible to factorize without large amounts of memory. This is shown in Fig. 6b, where we see that multi-front QR runs out of memory during factorization (256 GB) for $\bar{n}^2 \geq 8e6$.

The ability of this method to scale up to larger problems beyond $\bar{n}^2 \geq 8e6$ is unique to hybridized SBP-SAT, as the subproblem interiors remain as sparse finite difference operators. Conventional HDG, with dense subproblem interiors, hits a scaling limit as the dense problem requires a larger global problem that becomes a majority of the cost at these scales.

5 Summary

This work presents the first analytical study of sparse interior hybridized methods (hybridized SBP-SAT). Unlike dense interior methods (e.g., HDG), sparse interior methods preserve sparsity within subproblems, enabling scaling to larger problem sizes without prohibitive memory costs. Building on this, we develop a performance optimization strategy and a novel task-parallel algorithm for multi-core CPUs that eliminates bulk-synchronous barriers and overlaps subproblem solves with trace assembly, achieving up to 9.1× speedup over a baseline hybridized solver. We also develop a performance model that predicts the optimal subproblem size, matching an oracle in 87.7% of cases with only 1.7% average execution time overhead. Using this optimal size, our algorithm achieves up to 4.7× speedup over preconditioned CG and up to 12× over multi-frontal QR, while requiring less memory. These results establish hybridized SBP-SAT as an effective strategy for sparse PDE solvers, remaining practical where sparse direct methods exhaust memory, and well-suited to high-order discretizations and time-dependent simulations such as earthquake cycle modeling. Future work will target GPUs, distributed-memory systems, and extensions to 3D and anisotropic problems.

Disclosure of Interests. The authors have no competing interests to declare that are relevant to the content of this article.

References

1. Bian, H., Huang, J., Dong, R., Liu, L., Wang, X.: Csr2: a new format for simd-accelerated spmv. In: 2020 20th IEEE/ACM International Symposium on Cluster, Cloud and Internet Computing (CCGRID), pp. 350–359 (2020)
2. Blelloch, G.E., Gibbons, P.B., Simhadri, H.V.: Low depth cache-oblivious algorithms. In: Proceedings of the Twenty-Second Annual ACM Symposium on Parallelism in Algorithms and Architectures, SPAA 2010, pp. 189–199. Association for Computing Machinery (2010)
3. Bonnasse-Gahot, M., Calandra, H., Diaz, J., Lanteri, S.: Hybridizable discontinuous galerkin method for the 2-d frequency-domain elastic wave equations. Geophys. J. Int. **213**(1), 637–659 (2018)
4. Bouteiller, A., Herault, T., Cao, Q., Schuchart, J., Bosilca, G.: Parsec: Scalability, flexibility, and hybrid architecture support for task-based applications in ecp. Inter. J. High Perform. Comput. Appli. **39**(1), 147–166 (2025)
5. Chen, A., Erickson, B.A., Kozdon, J.E., Choi, J.: Matrix-free sbp-sat finite difference methods and the multigrid preconditioner on gpus. In: Proceedings of the 38th ACM International Conference on Supercomputing, pp. 400–412 (2024)

6. Choi, J.W., Singh, A., Vuduc, R.W.: Model-driven autotuning of sparse matrix-vector multiply on gpus. In: Proceedings of the 15th ACM SIGPLAN Symposium on Principles and Practice of Parallel Programming,. PPoPP 2010, pp. 115–126. Association for Computing Machinery (2010)
7. Dobrev, V., Kolev, T., Lee, C.S., Tomov, V., Vassilevski, P.S.: Algebraic hybridization and static condensation with application to scalable h(div) preconditioning. SIAM J. Sci. Comput. **41**(3), B425–B447 (2019)
8. Erickson, B.A., et al.: The community code verification exercise for simulating sequences of earthquakes and aseismic slip (seas). Seismol. Res. Lett. **91**(2A), 874–890 (2020)
9. Fernandez, P., Nguyen, N.C., Peraire, J.: The hybridized discontinuous galerkin method for implicit large-eddy simulation of transitional turbulent flows. J. Comput. Phys. **336**, 308–329 (2017)
10. Frigo, M., Castelletto, N., Ferronato, M., White, J.A.: Efficient solvers for hybridized three-field mixed finite element coupled poromechanics. Comput. Math. Appli. **91**, 36–52 (2021)
11. Guyan, R.J.: Reduction of stiffness and mass matrices. AIAA J. **3**(2), 380–380 (1965)
12. Jagode, H., Danalis, A., Anzt, H., Dongarra, J.: Papi software-defined events for in-depth performance analysis. Inter. J. High Performance Comput. Appli. **33**(6), 1113–1127 (2019)
13. Jaust, A., Schütz, J., Aizinger, V.: An efficient linear solver for the hybridized discontinuous galerkin method. PAMM **16**(1), 845–846 (2016)
14. King, J., Yakovlev, S., Fu, Z., Kirby, R.M., Sherwin, S.J.: Exploiting batch processing on streaming architectures to solve 2d elliptic finite element problems: a hybridized discontinuous galerkin (hdg) case study. J. Sci. Comput. **60**, 457–482 (2014)
15. Kirby, R.M., Sherwin, S.J., Cockburn, B.: To cg or to hdg: a comparative study. J. Sci. Comput. **51**(1), 183–212 (2012)
16. Kozdon, J.E., Erickson, B.A., Wilcox, L.C.: Hybridized summation-by-parts finite difference methods. J. Sci. Comput. **87**(3), 85 (2021)
17. Kreiss, H.O., Scherer, G.: Finite element and finite difference methods for hyperbolic partial differential equations. In: Mathematical Aspects of Finite Elements in Partial Differential Equations, pp. 195–212. Elsevier (1974)
18. Lubarda, M.V., Lubarda, V.A.: Intermediate Solid Mechanics. Cambridge University Press (2020)
19. Mattsson, K., Nordström, J.: Summation by parts operators for finite difference approximations of second derivatives. J. Comput. Phys. **199**(2), 503–540 (2004)
20. Muralikrishnan, S., Bui-Thanh, T., Shadid, J.N.: A multilevel approach for trace system in hdg discretizations. J. Comput. Phys. **407**, 109240 (2020)
21. Rhebergen, S., Wells, G.N.: Preconditioning for a pressure-robust hdg discretization of the stokes equations. SIAM J. Sci. Comput. **44**(1), A583–A604 (2022)
22. Saad, Y.: Iterative Methods for Sparse Linear Systems, 2nd edn. SIAM, Philadelphia, PA (2003)
23. Sevilla, R., Giacomini, M., Huerta, A.: A face-centred finite volume method for second-order elliptic problems. Int. J. Numer. Meth. Eng. **115**(8), 986–1014 (2018)
24. Svärd, M., Nordström, J.: Review of summation-by-parts schemes for initial-boundary-value problems. J. Comput. Phys. **268**, 17–38 (2014)
25. Trott, C.R., et al.: Kokkos 3: programming model extensions for the exascale era. IEEE Trans. Parallel Distrib. Syst. **33**(4), 805–817 (2021)

26. Vu, N.L., et al.: A scalable elliptic solver with task-based parallelism for the spectre numerical relativity code. Phys. Rev. D **105**(8), 084027 (2022)
27. Williams, S., Waterman, A., Patterson, D.: Roofline: an insightful visual performance model for multicore architectures. Commun. ACM **52**(4), 65–76 (2009)

GWBP: Accelerating Weighted Back-Projection for Image Reconstruction via Efficient GPU Parallel Optimization

Hongbo Miao[1] and Haodong Bian[1,2(✉)]

[1] School of Computer Technology and Applications, Qinghai University, Xining 810016, China
[2] Intelligent Computing and Applications Laboratory of Qinghai Province, Qinghai University, Xining 810016, China
hpc_bhd@163.com

Abstract. Weighted Back-Projection (WBP) is a classical and widely used reconstruction method in tomography and cryo-electron tomography (cryo-ET). Given a tilt series acquired at different angles, WBP forms a 3D volume by applying weighting and accumulating geometry-dependent back-projection contributions across all tilts, making it attractive for its simplicity and robustness. However, modern cryo-ET datasets continue to grow in tilt count, volume size, and resolution, and often incorporate costly three-dimensional CTF correction (3D-CTF correction). As a result, WBP increasingly dominates end-to-end runtime, while conventional CPU pipelines suffer from insufficient throughput and limited scalability. **We propose GWBP, a highly optimized GPU implementation of the WBP parallel algorithm.** First, GWBP performs kernelization of per-tilt operators and maintains persistent residency of intermediate data on the GPU. This design bypasses redundant correction steps on the host and minimizes host-device communication. Next, to enhance computational efficiency, we propose fragmentation-aware task batching and temporal buffer reuse. This synergistic approach effectively minimizes memory access. Finally, a stream-oriented scheduling scheme is introduced to overlap communication with computation, thereby eliminating pipeline bubbles and enhancing overall throughput. Compared to the state-of-the-art multi-core CPU implementation, GWBP reduces end-to-end runtime from 3.131 s to 0.655 s, achieving up to a 4.78× speedup.

Keywords: Weighted Back-Projection · GPU acceleration · Cryo-ET · 3D-CTF · Pipeline optimization

1 Introduction

Cryo-electron tomography (cryo-ET) has become an important tool for visualizing macromolecular structures by reconstructing three-dimensional volumes from

M. Torquati et al. (Eds.): Euro-Par 2026, LNCS 16781, pp. 583–597, 2027.
https://doi.org/10.1007/978-3-032-35248-4_40

a tilt series acquired at multiple viewing angles [15]. At the core of this modality is Weighted Back-Projection (WBP), a classical direct reconstruction method that forms a 3D volume by weighting and back-projecting the tilt images [13]. Due to its simplicity, robustness, and compatibility with established processing workflows, WBP remains a common choice in electron tomography and cryo-ET pipelines, where it is often coupled with weighting and contrast-transfer-function (CTF) related corrections [16].

Historically, efforts have focused on the theoretical refinement of WBP to reconcile its performance with Fourier-based methods [14]. Subsequent innovations have sought to optimize the projection operators themselves; for instance, Zhou et al. leveraged cross-correlation-based back-projection to suppress artifacts in GPR imaging [20], while Long et al., in X-ray CT reconstruction, proposed separable footprint (SF) forward and back-projection methods to improve the accuracy and efficiency of 3D cone-beam projection, which improves reconstruction accuracy for large-cone-angle rays, but also introduces higher computational cost due to the more complex trapezoidal approximation in the axial direction [10].

Challenges. While significant efforts have been dedicated to algorithmic refinement, the burgeoning scale of dataset resolution, tilt count, and reconstruction volume has increasingly exacerbated computational overhead. Our analysis identifies CPU-based implementations of back-projection as a critical limiting factor in overall throughput. This inefficiency is twofold: first, the repetitive accumulation of voxel values across numerous projections creates redundant write operations; second, the geometry-driven interpolation induces irregular memory access, which collectively strains the cache hierarchy and impede memory throughput [19]. Furthermore, end-to-end performance is frequently bottlenecked by pipeline inefficiencies, including the complex orchestration of weighting, 3D-CTF correction, and accumulation, alongside the latency penalties of redundant resource allocation and high-volume I/O for MRC output [4]. The computational burden is further amplified when 3D-CTF correction is enabled, as the requirement to process multiple depth-dependent layers for each tilt significantly scales the total runtime [9].

Key Insights. In response to these challenges, we propose GWBP, a highly-optimized GPU implementation of the WBP parallel algorithm. GWBP overcomes CPU-side throughput limitations by mapping the WBP algorithm onto the high-density compute resources of the GPU, utilizing an optimized streaming execution model to saturate device bandwidth. Its primary advantages are threefold: ❶ kernelizes each skewed operator and maintains data residency on the device to minimize host-to-device overhead; ❷ introduces a fragmentation-aware task batching strategy and a temporal buffer reuse mechanism to effectively reduce memory access latency and overhead; and ❸ by strategically scheduling kernel execution through stream operations, the system overlaps communication with computation (including transmission, rectification, and accumulation), thereby minimizing pipeline bubbles and maximizing overall throughput.

Contributions. The main contributions of this work are as follows:

- **Persistent Residency.** At the heart of our approach is the kernelization of per-tilt operators and the persistent residency of intermediate data on the GPU; this design bypasses redundant correction steps on the host and minimizes host-device communication.
- **Task Batching and Resource Reuse.** To enhance computational efficiency, we propose fragmentation-aware task batching and temporal buffer reuse. This synergistic approach effectively minimizes memory access.
- **Efficient Stream-Based Scheduling.** A stream-oriented scheduling scheme is introduced to overlap communication with computation (transfer, correction, and accumulation), thereby eliminating pipeline bubbles and enhancing overall throughput.

2 Background and Related Work

2.1 Weighted Back-Projection with 3D-CTF

Given a tilt series $\{I_n\}_{n=1}^{N}$ with angles $\{\theta_n\}$ and per-tilt weights $\{w_n\}$, the baseline computes, for each voxel (x, z, y), a detector coordinate u_n via a rigid rotation around (x_0, z_0):

$$u_n(x, z) = (x - x_0)\cos\theta_n - (z - z_0)\sin\theta_n + x_0. \tag{1}$$

The reconstruction accumulates contributions from all tilts:

$$V(x, z, y) = \sum_{n=1}^{N} w_n \cdot \hat{I}_n(u_n(x, z), y), \tag{2}$$

where $\hat{I}_n$ denotes the tilt image after weighting and 3D-CTF correction. Sampling on non-integer u follows the baseline linear interpolation:

$$\hat{I}_n(u, y) = (1 - \alpha)\,\hat{I}_n(t, y) + \alpha\,\hat{I}_n(t + 1, y), \quad t = \lfloor u \rfloor,\ \alpha = u - t. \tag{3}$$

When 3D-CTF correction is enabled, the baseline applies a depth-sliced correction. For each voxel location and tilt, a slice index is selected by discretizing the tilt-dependent depth coordinate with step Δz and an offset h:

$$n_z = \left\lfloor \frac{z_n(x, z) + h}{\Delta z} \right\rfloor. \tag{4}$$

2.2 Related Work

Algorithmic and CPU-Level Optimizations. A substantial body of work has focused on improving the performance of WBP-based reconstruction at the algorithmic and CPU-system levels. Widely used software such as IMOD provides an end-to-end tomography workflow [8]. On multi-core CPUs, Tomo3D and its subsequent versions accelerate reconstruction through parallelization and low-level optimizations, including vectorization and careful handling of disk access [1,2]. These efforts demonstrate that even for classical algorithms, production-scale datasets and integrated pipelines demand coordinated optimization across computation mapping, data organization, synchronization, and write-back.

GPU-Accelerated Optimizations. GPU acceleration has been widely explored for tomography and reconstruction. Toolboxes such as ASTRA provide GPU implementations of projection and back-projection operators and support a range of reconstruction algorithms [12]. AreTomo integrates marker-free alignment and reconstruction in a GPU-accelerated workflow [18]; Tomo Live enables on-the-fly alignment and reconstruction during acquisition [5]; and RELION-5 extends electron tomography processing within a standardized framework [3]. From a performance-engineering perspective, TiltRec further highlights renewed interest in high-throughput classical reconstruction on both CPUs and GPUs [7]. Overall, these efforts suggest that practical performance depends increasingly on end-to-end coordination across correction, reconstruction, and I/O, rather than on a single accelerated kernel alone.

3 Motivation

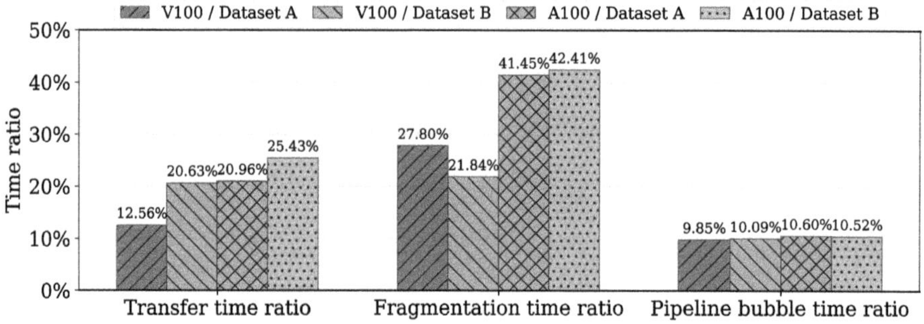

Fig. 1. WBP algorithm hotspot overhead analysis on NVIDIA V100 and A100.

To deeply understand the performance landscape of the WBP algorithm, we conduct a comprehensive profiling across diverse hardware architectures (NVIDIA V100 and A100 GPUs) and representative datasets. As illustrated in Fig. 1, we identify three critical bottlenecks that impede the execution efficiency of the WBP algorithm:

- **Excessive Host to Device Data Transfer.** Our breakdown analysis shows that data movement between the Host and Device consumes 12.56% to 25.43% of the total execution time. This overhead stems from the high-frequency synchronization necessitated by WBP computational characteristics. (Motivation 1)
- **Task Fragmentation.** The most prominent bottleneck lies in fragmented task execution, accounting for 21.84% to 42.41% of the runtime. This phenomenon is characterized by a massive number of small-scale kernels processing granular data. (Motivation 2)

- **Pipeline Bubbles.** We observe persistent pipeline bubbles during sequential kernel execution, which stagnate the GPU for 9.85% to 10.52% of the total wall-clock time. (Motivation 3)

Motivation 1

The excessive host-device interaction indicates that current methods fail to maintain intermediate data persistence on the device, thereby failing to mitigate the significant latency incurred by frequent data transfers.

Motivation 2

Such fragmentation results in diminished computational intensity and suboptimal data reusability, highlighting the need for fragmentation-aware task batching and resource recycling to bolster execution efficiency.

Motivation 3

Rigid dependency chains that hinder overlapping computation and memory access. To reclaim these lost cycles, it is imperative to achieve asynchronous execution by leveraging multi-stream concurrency.

4 Method

4.1 Overview

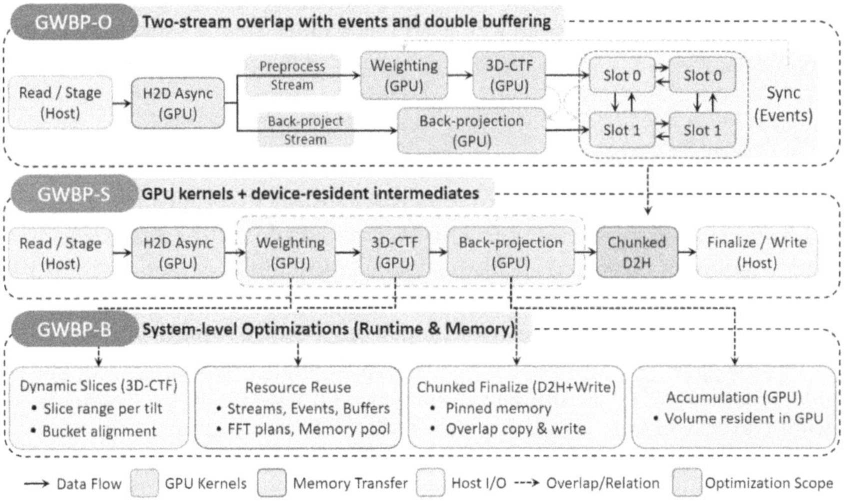

Fig. 2. End-to-end workflow and where each GWBP stage applies.

GWBP keeps the same geometric mapping, interpolation rule, weighting operator, and 3D-CTF correction model as the baseline. Figure 2 summarizes the end-to-end workflow and shows where the three cumulative optimization stages apply: GWBP-S for GPU kernelization with persistent residency, GWBP-B for task batching and resource reuse, and GWBP-O for efficient stream-based scheduling. The core principle is to optimize the *pipeline* rather than a single kernel: keep intermediate data on device, avoid unnecessary 3D-CTF work, reduce host coordination and write-back stalls, and overlap preprocessing with back-projection.

This definition is preserved in GWBP; our optimizations only change how efficiently the corresponding corrected slices are produced, transferred, and consumed.

4.2 GWBP-S: GPU Kernelization with Persistent Residency

GWBP-S targets the dominant per-tilt computation path. Its core idea is to move weighting, 3D-CTF correction, and back-projection to GPU kernels and connect them through persistent device buffers, so that large intermediates no longer need to be materialized on the host between stages. In this way, GWBP-S bypasses redundant host-side correction steps and minimizes host-device communication along the critical path.

GPU Weighting. The first optimization is to offload the baseline 1D weighting step to the GPU while preserving its original filtering rule. For each tilt, the input micrograph is copied to a device buffer, and weighting is applied there by batched row-wise cuFFT. Each row is linearly padded to the enlarged FFT length, transformed by a batched R2C FFT, multiplied by the same radial/Gaussian weighting rule as in the CPU baseline, and transformed back in place. This design preserves the original weighting behavior, exposes row-level parallelism, and removes host-side FFT processing from the per-tilt critical path.

GPU 3D-CTF Correction with Device-Resident Corrected Stacks. The second optimization is to keep the full 3D-CTF stage on the GPU and avoid host-side staging of corrected slices. Instead of recomputing a full forward FFT for every corrected slice, GWBP-S performs one forward 2D FFT for the current tilt, expands the base spectrum across all required depth offsets on the GPU, and reconstructs the corrected stack by a single batched inverse cuFFT. The slice-dependent phase-flip rule remains identical to the baseline, but the resulting corrected stack is stored persistently in device memory and consumed immediately by the next stage. In this way, GWBP-S bypasses redundant correction steps and removes intermediate device-to-host transfers from the weighting–CTF–back-projection chain.

GPU Back-Projection with Per-tilt Lookup Reuse. The third optimization is to simplify the innermost accumulation path. For a fixed tilt, the mapping from reconstruction coordinates (i, k) in the xz plane to detector coordinates and slice indices is independent of y. GWBP-S therefore precomputes, once per tilt, an xz lookup map containing the left interpolation index, interpolation coefficient, and slice index. During accumulation, one thread is assigned to one output voxel in the flattened volume layout. Each thread reuses the precomputed mapping, reads two neighboring samples from the corrected stack, performs the same linear interpolation as the baseline, and accumulates directly into the persistent device volume. This removes repeated coordinate transforms and index evaluation from the innermost loop while preserving the numerical semantics of the original formulation.

Overall, GWBP-S converts the original host-coordinated WBP pipeline into a device-resident execution path. The main benefit is not only kernel acceleration itself, but also the elimination of unnecessary intermediate transfers between weighting, 3D-CTF correction, and back-projection, thereby minimizing host-device communication.

4.3 GWBP-B: Task Batching and Resource Reuse

After kernelization, end-to-end runtime is no longer dominated solely by arithmetic throughput. In practice, the remaining bottlenecks come from three sources: unnecessary 3D-CTF work, repeated per-tilt resource setup, and output-stage finalize/write-back overhead. GWBP-B addresses these costs through fragmentation-aware task batching and temporal resource reuse at the system level, thereby reducing unnecessary memory access and coordination overhead.

Fragmentation-Aware Task Batching. The first optimization is a fragmentation-aware batching strategy that avoids correcting slices never referenced by the current tilt geometry. Correcting the full depth range for every tilt is wasteful because only a subset of slices is actually used by Eq. (4). For each tilt n, GWBP-B computes a conservative valid slice interval over the reconstruction domain and corrects only that range:

$$k \in [k_{\min}^{(n)}, k_{\max}^{(n)}], \quad k_{\min}^{(n)} = \left\lfloor \frac{z_{\min}^{(n)} - z_0}{\Delta z} \right\rfloor, \quad k_{\max}^{(n)} = \left\lceil \frac{z_{\max}^{(n)} - z_0}{\Delta z} \right\rceil, \tag{5}$$

where $z_{\min}^{(n)}$ and $z_{\max}^{(n)}$ are the minimum and maximum transformed depth coordinates attained by all voxels under tilt n.

To preserve baseline indexing, GWBP-B shifts the slice lookup into the reduced local stack. Let n_z^{base} denote the baseline slice index from Eq. (4). The local index is

$$n_z^{\text{local}} = n_z^{\text{base}} - k_{\min}^{(n)}, \tag{6}$$

so that the compact range $\{0, \ldots, k_{\max}^{(n)} - k_{\min}^{(n)}\}$ remains numerically equivalent to the original discretization over the valid window.

To avoid highly irregular small FFT batches, we optionally align the slice count to a bucket size B:

$$L^{(n)} = k_{\max}^{(n)} - k_{\min}^{(n)} + 1, \qquad \tilde{L}^{(n)} = \left\lceil \frac{L^{(n)}}{B} \right\rceil \cdot B. \tag{7}$$

When needed, the corrected range is conservatively extended to length $\tilde{L}^{(n)}$. This improves batched FFT regularity, stabilizes performance across tilts with different valid slice counts, and avoids unnecessary memory access beyond the valid slice range.

Resource Reuse Across the Tilt Loop. The second optimization is to eliminate repeated setup costs that remain after kernelization. GWBP-B therefore reuses long-lived GPU resources across the full tilt loop. In our implementation, the input image buffer, corrected-stack buffer, depth-offset array, and persistent reconstruction volume are allocated once and reused for all tilts. In the 3D-CTF stage, geometry-dependent resources for a fixed image size are also reused across tilts, while batch-dependent buffers and inverse cuFFT plans are expanded lazily and cached by batch size. This reduces repeated device allocation, plan creation, and auxiliary preprocessing overhead when consecutive tilts share the same geometry, while also minimizing memory access effectively.

Output-Stage I/O Optimization. The third optimization is a batched output strategy that reduces finalize/write-back stalls. Once the reconstruction size is known, GWBP-B creates the output MRC container and preallocates the full file extent before bulk data are written:

$$S_{\text{file}} = 1024 + S_{\text{sym}} + N_x \cdot N_y \cdot N_z \cdot \text{sizeof(float)}, \tag{8}$$

where 1024 is the MRC header size and S_{sym} is the symmetry-data region. GWBP-B then attaches a large fully buffered I/O stream to the output file, so that the final volume write is serviced by fewer, larger host-side flushes rather than many small writes. In practice, this reduces file-growth and metadata-management overhead during finalization and improves sustained output throughput for large reconstructed volumes.

For output compatibility, GWBP-B also computes reconstruction statistics directly from the device-resident volume:

$$v_{\min} = \min_{p\in\Omega} V(p), \quad v_{\max} = \max_{p\in\Omega} V(p), \quad \mu = \frac{1}{|\Omega|}\sum_{p\in\Omega} V(p), \tag{9}$$

and writes them into the MRC header without an additional full-volume host scan. Together, these optimizations reduce per-tilt coordination overhead, unnecessary memory access, and output-stage waiting in the end-to-end pipeline.

4.4 GWBP-O: Efficient Stream-Based Scheduling

After GWBP-B reduces unnecessary work and setup overhead, the main remaining inefficiency is the pipeline bubble between preprocessing and accumulation. In a serialized schedule, weighting and 3D-CTF correction for tilt n must complete before its back-projection can begin, and preprocessing for tilt $n+1$ is delayed by the accumulation of tilt n. GWBP-O addresses this bottleneck by overlapping the two phases.

Two-Stream Overlapped Schedule. The primary optimization in GWBP-O is to decouple preprocessing from accumulation with two non-blocking CUDA streams, as illustrated in Fig. 3. A *preprocess stream* is used for host-to-device transfer, optional weighting, and 3D-CTF correction, while a *back-projection stream* is used for accumulation into the persistent reconstruction volume V. After warm-up, preprocessing of tilt $n+1$ can proceed concurrently with back-projection of tilt n, thereby overlapping communication with computation and reducing idle time between stages.

Double-Buffered Device Slots. To enable overlap safely, GWBP-O uses two device slots indexed by

$$s(n) = n \bmod 2.$$

Each slot $s \in \{0,1\}$ contains a pinned host input buffer H_s, a device image buffer D_s^{img}, and a corrected-stack buffer D_s^{ctf}. Tilt n is therefore preprocessed into slot $s(n)$, while the back-projection stream may simultaneously consume the corrected stack from the other slot. This double-buffered organization allows the two streams to overlap without overwriting in-flight data.

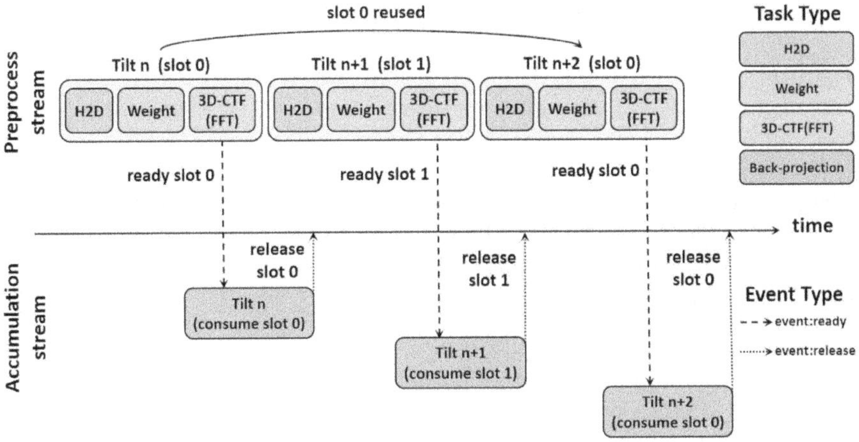

Fig. 3. Two-stream overlap between preprocessing and back-projection in GWBP-O.

Correctness-Preserving Event Synchronization. GWBP-O changes the inter-tilt execution schedule, but not the numerical semantics of WBP. Correctness is preserved by event-based synchronization. After preprocessing finishes for a slot, a ready event is recorded; the back-projection stream waits on this event before consuming the corrected stack. After accumulation completes, a release event is recorded; the preprocess stream waits on this event before reusing the slot. Since all updates to V are issued on the same back-projection stream, accumulation remains serialized and race-free. Thus, GWBP-O improves throughput by removing scheduling bubbles, while keeping the reconstruction behavior equivalent to the baseline.

5 Evaluation

5.1 Experimental Setup

Platforms. We conduct experiments on two systems. Platform 1 runs Ubuntu 22.04.5 on a dual-socket Intel Xeon Gold 6542Y CPU with 48 physical cores (96 threads) and four NVIDIA Tesla V100-PCIE-32GB GPUs. Platform 2 runs Ubuntu 24.04.3 on a dual-socket Intel Xeon Gold 6530 CPU with 64 physical cores (128 threads) and two NVIDIA A100-SXM4-40GB GPUs. Although both platforms contain multiple GPUs, all reported GPU experiments use a single GPU per run. The CPU baseline is derived from prior work on parallel WBP on multi-CPU systems [17], uses OpenMP parallelism, and is executed without explicit CPU affinity restrictions. The software environment includes GCC 10.5.0, Intel ICC 2021.1 Beta, Intel MKL 2021.0 Update 1, and CUDA Toolkit 12.6.

Baseline. The CPU baseline runtimes differ across platforms because the two systems vary in CPU microarchitecture, memory/NUMA behavior, and I/O stack, all of which can noticeably affect a bandwidth- and I/O-sensitive WBP pipeline. In contrast, GWBP reduces sensitivity to host-side variability by minimizing repeated resource creation, staging output to fast local storage when enabled, and performing chunked write-back with overlapped execution. As a result, while absolute runtimes may change between platforms, the relative GPU speedup trend remains consistent.

Datasets. We evaluate on two proteasome datasets, which were obtained from the Electron Microscopy Public Image Archive (EMPIAR) [6]. All runs use identical reconstruction parameters, so that runtime comparisons reflect implementation differences rather than parameter changes.

Validation. We compute the Relative Mean Error (RME) reported by the baseline validation script, and deem a run correct if $RME < 0.001$ under identical reconstruction parameters. Because floating-point operations are not strictly associative and shared clusters exhibit performance jitter, repeated runs may yield slightly different runtimes, whereas the numerical discrepancies remain within the tolerance specified above.

5.2 Results

We compare the CPU baseline with three cumulative GPU variants that represent successive optimization stages in Sect. 4: GWBP-S, GWBP-B, and GWBP-O. Our results are organized in two parts. We first present a bottleneck breakdown for the CPU baseline and the best (GWBP-O) to identify where time is spent and how each optimization takes effect. We then report the speedup progression and summarize runtime and speedup across platforms and datasets.

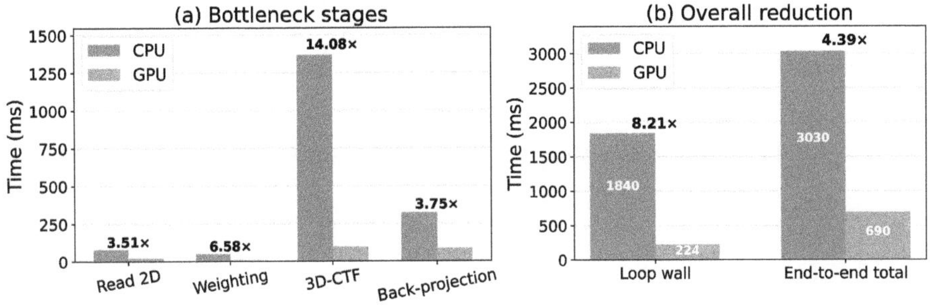

Fig. 4. Stage-level time breakdown comparing the CPU baseline and the best GPU pipeline on the NVIDIA A100 platform with Dataset A.

Bottleneck Breakdown. To attribute performance gains to concrete pipeline components, we instrument both the CPU baseline and GWBP-O with lightweight timing around the major pipeline components. In Fig. 4, we report the stage-level costs for CPU-side read/staging (*Read 2D*), weighting, 3D-CTF correction, and back-projection, together with the loop wall time and the end-to-end total runtime. It shows that the CPU baseline is dominated by 3D-CTF correction (1368 ms), followed by back-projection (324 ms), so the loop wall time is largely determined by these compute-heavy stages. After optimization, 3D-CTF achieves the largest reduction at 14.08×, while weighting and back-projection are reduced by 6.58× and 3.75×, respectively. As a result, the loop wall time drops by 8.21× and end-to-end gain remains substantial at 4.39×, showing that GPU kernelization, device-resident execution, and reduced in-loop coordination are effective in removing the critical bottlenecks.

Ablation Study. Guided by the bottleneck analysis, we next evaluate how performance improves when optimizations are introduced in a cumulative manner. Figure 5 summarizes the progression from the CPU baseline to GWBP-S, GWBP-B, and GWBP-O on both platforms.

The first stage, *GPU kernelization with persistent residency* (GWBP-S), already provides clear gains: on Proteasome-A, it achieves 1.60× speedup on

V100 and 1.79× on A100, while on Proteasome-B the gains are 1.17× and 1.35×, respectively.

Adding *task batching and resource reuse* (GWBP-B) yields the largest improvement, raising the speedup to 3.99× and 4.64× on Proteasome-A, and to 2.95× and 3.24× on Proteasome-B. This confirms that, beyond kernel acceleration itself, reducing unnecessary work and system-level overhead is the dominant factor for end-to-end performance.

Finally, *efficient stream-based scheduling* (GWBP-O) further improves the runtime to 4.38× and 4.78× on Proteasome-A, and to 3.16× and 3.33× on Proteasome-B. The additional gain at this stage is smaller, because after the main bottlenecks have been removed, the remaining costs are less overlappable and increasingly bounded by fixed pipeline overheads.

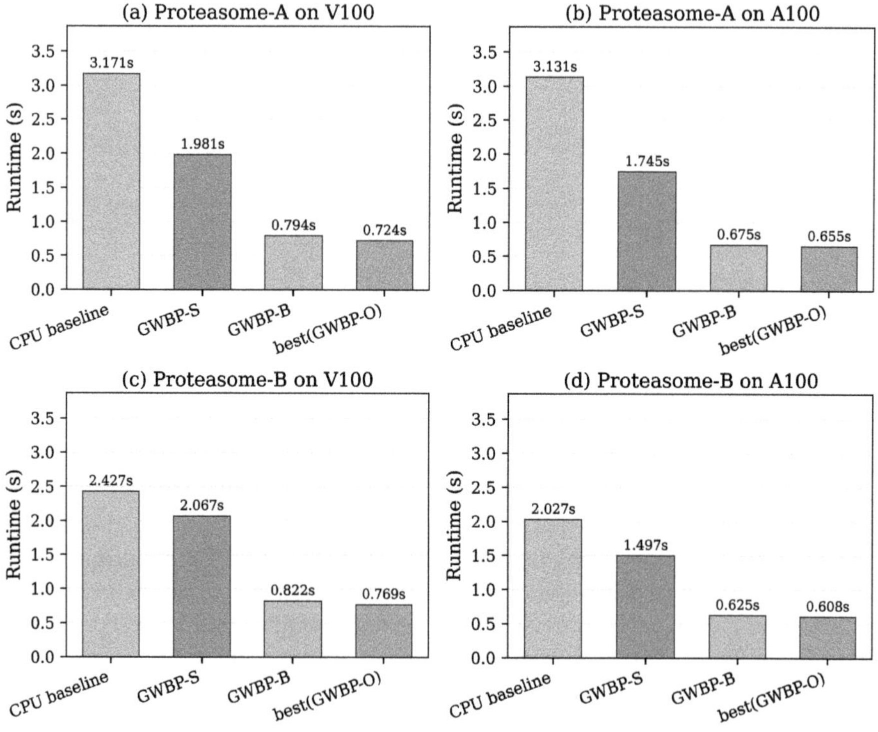

Fig. 5. Speedup progression across optimization stages on two platforms.

End-to-End Runtime and Speedup. Table 1 summarizes end-to-end runtime and speedup over the CPU baseline on both platforms and both datasets. Compared to the state-of-the-art multi-core CPU implementation, GWBP reduces end-to-end runtime from 3.131 s to 0.655 s on Proteasome-A with A100, achieving the best observed result of 4.78× speedup. During single-GPU execution, NVIDIA-SMI sampling shows that the peak GPU memory consumption of GWBP-O is 2.63/1.81 GiB on Proteasome-A/B on V100 and 2.75/1.93 GiB on Proteasome-A/B on A100.

Table 1. End-to-end runtime and speedup on two platforms.

Dataset	Method	Platform 1 (V100)		Platform 2 (A100)	
		Runtime (s)	Speedup	Runtime (s)	Speedup
Proteasome-A	CPU baseline	3.171	1.00×	3.131	1.00×
	GWBP-S	1.981	1.60×	1.745	1.79×
	GWBP-B	0.794	3.99×	0.675	4.64×
	best(GWBP-O)	0.724	4.38×	0.655	4.78×
Proteasome-B	CPU baseline	2.427	1.00×	2.027	1.00×
	GWBP-S	2.067	1.17×	1.497	1.35×
	GWBP-B	0.822	2.95×	0.625	3.24×
	best(GWBP-O)	0.769	3.16×	0.608	3.33×

6 Conclusion

This paper presented GWBP, a highly optimized GPU implementation of WBP for cryo-ET reconstruction. GWBP accelerates the complete reconstruction pipeline rather than a single kernel: it kernelizes per-tilt operators and maintains persistent residency of intermediate data on the GPU, applies fragmentation-aware task batching and temporal buffer reuse to improve computational efficiency, and introduces a stream-oriented scheduling scheme to overlap communication with computation. Together, these optimizations reduce bottlenecks across weighting, 3D-CTF correction, and back-projection while improving overall throughput. Compared to the state-of-the-art multi-core CPU implementation, GWBP reduces end-to-end runtime from 3.131 s to 0.655 s, achieving up to a 4.78× speedup.

Acknowledgments and Artifact Availability. This study was funded by the National Key Research and Development Program of China (No. 2023YFB3002404), the Guanghe Foundation (No. Ghfund202407010052). The artifact is available in the Zenodo repository [11]. The development version of GWBP is hosted on GitHub (https://github.com/OptiYouth-Lab/GWBP). We are committed to the long-term maintenance of the project.

Disclosure of Interests. The authors have no competing interests to declare that are relevant to the content of this article.

References

1. Agulleiro, J.I., Fernandez, J.J.: Fast tomographic reconstruction on multi-core computers. Bioinformatics **27**(4), 582–583 (2011). https://doi.org/10.1093/bioinformatics/btq692
2. Agulleiro, J.I., Fernandez, J.J.: Tomo3D 2.0—exploitation of advanced vector extensions (AVX) for 3D reconstruction. J. Struct. Biol. **189**(2), 147–152 (2015). https://doi.org/10.1016/j.jsb.2014.11.009
3. Burt, A., et al.: An image processing pipeline for electron cryo-tomography in Relion-5. FEBS Open Bio **14**(11), 1788–1804 (2024). https://febs.onlinelibrary.wiley.com/doi/abs/10.1002/2211-5463.13873
4. Cheng, A., et al.: MRC2014: extensions to the MRC format header for electron cryo-microscopy and tomography. J. Struct. Biol. **192**(2), 146–150 (2015). https://doi.org/10.1016/j.jsb.2015.04.002, recent Advances in Detector Technologies and Applications for Molecular TEM
5. Comet, M., et al.: Tomo Live: an on-the-fly reconstruction pipeline to judge data quality for cryo-electron tomography workflows. Acta Crystallographica Section D (2024). https://journals.iucr.org/d/issues/2024/04/00/qv5004/
6. Iudin, A., et al.: EMPIAR: the electron microscopy public image archive. Nucleic Acids Res. **51**(D1), D1503–D1511 (2022). https://doi.org/10.1093/nar/gkac1062
7. Jiao, Y., et al.: TiltRec: an ultra-fast and open-source toolkit for cryo-electron tomographic reconstruction. Bioinformatics **41**(3) (2025). https://academic.oup.com/bioinformatics/article/41/3/btaf068/8015615
8. Kremer, J.R., Mastronarde, D.N., McIntosh, J.: Computer visualization of three-dimensional image data using IMOD. J. Struct. Biol. **116**(1), 71–76 (1996). https://doi.org/10.1006/jsbi.1996.0013
9. Kunz, M., Frangakis, A.S.: Three-dimensional CTF correction improves the resolution of electron tomograms. J. Struct. Biol. **197**(2), 114–122 (2017). https://doi.org/10.1016/j.jsb.2016.06.016, electron Tomography
10. Long, Y., Fessler, J.A., Balter, J.M.: 3D forward and back-projection for X-Ray CT using separable footprints. IEEE Trans. Med. Imaging **29**(11), 1839–1850 (2010). https://doi.org/10.1109/TMI.2010.2050898
11. Miao, H., Bian, H.: Artifact of the paper:gwbp: Accelerating weighted back-projection for image reconstruction via efficient GPU parallel optimization (2026). https://doi.org/10.5281/zenodo.20506358
12. Palenstijn, W.J., Bédorf, J., Sijbers, J., Batenburg, K.J.: A distributed ASTRA toolbox. Adv. Struct. Chem. Imaging **2**(1), 1–13 (2016). https://doi.org/10.1186/s40679-016-0032-z
13. Radermacher, M.: Weighted Back-Projection Methods, pp. 91–115. Springer US, Boston, MA (1992). https://doi.org/10.1007/978-1-4757-2163-8_5
14. Radermacher, M.: Weighted Back-projection Methods, pp. 245–273. Springer New York, New York, NY (2006). https://doi.org/10.1007/978-0-387-69008-7_9
15. Wang, Z., Zhang, Q., Mim, C.: Coming of age: cryo-electron tomography as a versatile tool to generate high-resolution structures at cellular/biological interfaces. Int. J. Mol. Sci. **22**(12) (2021). https://doi.org/10.3390/ijms22126177
16. Zhang, K.: Gctf: real-time CTF determination and correction. J. Struct. Biol. **193**(1), 1–12 (2016). https://doi.org/10.1016/j.jsb.2015.11.003

17. Zheng, K., Wu, K., Yao, Y., Bian, H., Huang, J., Wang, X.: Research on parallel weighted back-projection algorithm on multi-CPU. In: Advanced Intelligent Computing Technology and Applications - 21st International Conference, ICIC 2025, Ningbo, China, July 26-29, 2025, Proceedings, Part XIV. Lecture Notes in Computer Science, vol. 15855, pp. 193–204. Springer (2025). https://doi.org/10.1007/978-981-96-9908-7_16
18. Zheng, S., et al.: AreTomo: an integrated software package for automated marker-free, motion-corrected cryo-electron tomographic alignment and reconstruction. J. Struct. Biol. X **6**, 100068 (2022). https://doi.org/10.1016/j.yjsbx.2022.100068
19. Zheng, Z., Mueller, K.: Cache-aware GPU memory scheduling scheme for CT back-projection. In: IEEE Nuclear Science Symposium & Medical Imaging Conference, pp. 2248–2251 (2010). https://doi.org/10.1109/NSSMIC.2010.5874183
20. Zhou, L., Huang, C., Su, Y.: A fast back-projection algorithm based on cross correlation for GPR imaging. IEEE Geosci. Remote Sens. Lett. **9**(2), 228–232 (2012). https://doi.org/10.1109/LGRS.2011.2165523

JAX vs Kokkos Performance Comparison: A Magnetohydrodynamic Solver Case Study

Thierry Antoun[1(✉)], Rémi Bourgeois[2], Pascal Tremblin[1], Samuel Kokh[1], and Jérôme Bobin[3]

[1] Université Paris-Saclay, UVSQ, Inria, CNRS, CEA, Maison de la Simulation, 91191 Gif-sur-Yvette, France
{thierry.antoun,pascal.tremblin,samuel.kokh}@cea.fr
[2] Université Paris-Saclay, CEA, Service de Génie Logiciel pour la Simulation, 91191 Gif-sur-Yvette, France
remi.bourgeois@cea.fr
[3] Université Paris-Saclay, CEA, IRFU, 91191 Gif-sur-Yvette, France
jerome.bobin@cea.fr

Abstract. Python-based array computation frameworks such as JAX are now considered viable alternative GPU programming approaches alongside established C++ portability frameworks. This work presents a comparative study of two single-GPU implementations of a three-dimensional second-order magnetohydrodynamics (MHD) solver with MUSCL–Hancock reconstruction: one developed in C++/Kokkos and one using JAX. The C++ implementation serves as a pre-existing, optimized reference code and provides a performance baseline for comparison with the JAX version. Both implementations are evaluated on multiple GPU architectures, including NVIDIA V100, A100, and H100, as well as AMD MI250X and MI300A. The analysis focuses on two main key performance indicators: Million Cell Update per second and peak memory usage, complemented by performance observations on JAX's just-in-time compilation behavior. The impact of JAX-specific optimization techniques—such as array concatenation and compiler fusion effects is examined. The results highlight differences in JAX performance across hardware architectures and variations in memory requirements. Overall, JAX demonstrates promising computational performance for kernels on structured data, approaching Kokkos levels after targeted optimizations. This study provides a quantitative basis for understanding trade-offs between programming models when targeting modern GPU platforms for scientific HPC workloads.

Keywords: GPU computing · high-performance computing · performance portability · magnetohydrodynamics (MHD) · JAX · Kokkos · XLA · numerical simulation

M. Torquati et al. (Eds.): Euro-Par 2026, LNCS 16781, pp. 598–611, 2027.
https://doi.org/10.1007/978-3-032-35248-4_41

1 Introduction

Magnetohydrodynamics (MHD) and, more broadly, compressible fluid dynamics simulations are central to modeling many physical phenomena. These simulations involve solving hyperbolic systems of partial differential equations using finite-volume discretizations, resulting in stencil-based computational patterns operating over structured grids. Such workloads impose demanding requirements on memory bandwidth, data locality, and arithmetic throughput, making them representative benchmarks for evaluating modern HPC architectures.

GPU accelerators have become a dominant platform for these applications. A variety of programming models have emerged to address performance portability and developer productivity across heterogeneous systems. C++-based frameworks such as Kokkos [9] provide abstractions for expressing parallel computation independently of the target hardware. JAX [1] represents a distinct approach by combining array programming with just-in-time compilation through the XLA [8] compiler, enabling execution on multiple hardware backends including NVIDIA and AMD GPUs.

A practical question for the HPC community is whether Python-based frameworks such as JAX can deliver competitive performance against mature, production-grade C++ codes, and at what development cost. This work addresses this question by comparing two implementations of a three-dimensional second-order MHD solver with MUSCL–Hancock [10] reconstruction: one in C++/Kokkos serving as a production-grade baseline, and one in JAX progressively optimized using JAX-specific strategies. Both are evaluated on NVIDIA V100, A100, H100 and AMD MI250X, MI300A GPUs, using Million Cell Updates per second and peak memory usage as key performance indicators.

Although prior work has compared JAX with other programming models in HPC contexts [13,14], a direct comparison with C++/Kokkos for the same scientific algorithm remains unexplored. This study fills this gap by benchmarking identical MHD solver implementations in JAX and C++/Kokkos.

2 Programming in JAX

JAX is a numerical computing framework designed for high-performance scientific simulations on modern accelerators. It reproduces most of the NumPy [15] application programming interface, allowing developers to express vectorized numerical algorithms in concise and familiar Python syntax, similar in spirit to CuPy [16], which also mirrors NumPy for GPU acceleration. Unlike CuPy, JAX provides device portability: computations written with JAX arrays can be executed on CPU, GPU, or TPU without modification by selecting the desired backend. JAX also offers composable transformations essential for scientific workloads, including automatic differentiation (`jax.grad`), function vectorization (`jax.vmap`), and data parallelism (`jax.pmap`).

A key aspect of JAX performance lies in just-in-time compilation [20] through the `@jax.jit` transformation [21]. When first invoked, a function is traced to produce a symbolic representation called JAXPR, which is lowered to High-Level Optimizer (HLO) IR and compiled by XLA [8]. The compiler performs kernel fusion and memory optimization. The effectiveness of a given optimization in JAX therefore depends on whether XLA is able to fuse the corresponding operations efficiently.

These benefits require pure functions [17] operating on immutable arrays [18]. Because arrays cannot be modified in place, each update creates a new array, which may increase memory consumption if intermediate results are not efficiently fused. These constraints, however, promote optimized execution and controlled memory traffic.

3 Numerical Model and Reference HPC Baseline

3.1 Governing Equations and Discretization

To evaluate performance and portability on modern GPU architectures, we consider a three-dimensional magnetohydrodynamics (MHD) solver for the ideal MHD equations [29]. The solver relies on a second-order MUSCL–Hancock finite-volume discretization on a structured Cartesian grid [10]. Spatial indices are denoted by i, j, and k, and time integration is indexed by n. The conservative variables

$$(\rho,\ \rho\mathbf{u},\ \rho E,\ \mathbf{B}),$$

representing eight fields in total, are denoted by $\mathbf{U}_{i,j,k}$. The update of the conserved variables follows the standard finite-volume scheme:

$$\begin{aligned}\mathbf{U}^{n+1}_{i,j,k} = \mathbf{U}^{n}_{i,j,k} &- \frac{\Delta t}{\Delta x}\left(\mathbf{F}^{n}_{i+\frac{1}{2},j,k} - \mathbf{F}^{n}_{i-\frac{1}{2},j,k}\right)\\ &- \frac{\Delta t}{\Delta y}\left(\mathbf{G}^{n}_{i,j+\frac{1}{2},k} - \mathbf{G}^{n}_{i,j-\frac{1}{2},k}\right)\\ &- \frac{\Delta t}{\Delta z}\left(\mathbf{H}^{n}_{i,j,k+\frac{1}{2}} - \mathbf{H}^{n}_{i,j,k-\frac{1}{2}}\right),\end{aligned} \tag{1}$$

where $\mathbf{F}$, $\mathbf{G}$, and $\mathbf{H}$ denote the MHD fluxes. The timestep Δt is computed according to the Courant–Friedrichs–Lewy (CFL) condition [30], given spatial steps Δx, Δy, and Δz. Full details of the flux computation and numerical formulation are provided in [7].

3.2 Ark-2-Mhd: Production-Grade Reference Solver

The JAX implementation is compared against ark-2-mhd [6], a C++/Kokkos solver that serves as a production-grade reference baseline [7]. The code implements a multi-dimensional, cell-centered finite-volume scheme for the ideal MHD equations, described in [31]. This new solver has been shown to achieve up to approximately 3.5× higher performance than constrained-transport MHD solvers, as reported in [32]. Its kernels were implemented using

`Kokkos::parallel_for` with an `MDRangePolicy` [28], enabling portable multi-dimensional parallel execution across architectures. Its largest kernels reach 56 to 66% of the GPU memory bandwidth on H100, indicating a memory-bound behavior with high usage of the DRAM and low usage of the SM computational throughput (see Table 1 that comes from [7]). The ark-2-mhd solver builds upon earlier developments in hydrodynamics, in particular the scheme introduced in [33], which has been benchmarked and validated. The MHD extension therefore inherits a previously tested and validated hydrodynamic core.

The JAX MHD solver was developed following the same numerical scheme as `ark-2-mhd`, using the hydrodynamic solver by Mocz [2] as a structural reference for the JAX implementation. It reproduces exactly the same flux evaluation procedure, time integration strategy, and update formulation as `ark-2-mhd`, without any modification of the algorithmic structure. To ensure correctness, the JAX implementation was systematically compared with `ark-2-mhd` during development by cross-checking timestep evolution and field quantities. Once agreement was established, the solver was further validated using standard MHD and hydrodynamics benchmarks [5] [3].

Throughout this study, all simulations are performed in double precision using the 3D Orszag-Tang vortex [4] setup: uniform initial density $\rho = \frac{25}{36\pi}$ and pressure $p = \frac{5}{12\pi}$, with an initial periodic magnetic field:

$$B_x = -\sin\left(\frac{2\pi y}{\sqrt{4\pi}}\right), \qquad B_y = \sin\left(\frac{4\pi x}{\sqrt{4\pi}}\right), \qquad B_z = 0, \tag{2}$$

and an initial periodic velocity field:

$$v_x = -\sin(2\pi y), \qquad v_y = \sin(2\pi x), \qquad v_z = 0. \tag{3}$$

Table 1. GPU resource utilization per kernel measured on an NVIDIA H100, showing that `ark-2-mhd` operates in a memory-bound regime.

Kernel	DRAM %	**SM %**
`FluxesAndUpdateKernel`	66%	30%
`wrapped_negate`	57%	17%

3.3 Limitation

Two aspects of the experimental setup may affect the generality of the results. The periodic boundary conditions of the Orszag-Tang vortex structurally favor JAX, as neighboring cell access relies on `jnp.roll`, an XLA-native operation that fuses efficiently. Performance presented in this paper may differ for non-periodic configurations. Additionally, due to memory constraints, simulations were performed on a 256^3 grid on the V100 and MI250X architectures, and on a $512 \times 256 \times 256$ grid on the A100, H100, and MI300A systems, reflecting the different memory capacities available across these platforms.

3.4 Key Performance Indicator

In this study, two main performance indicators were used: the **Million Cell Updates per Second (MCUPS)** and the **GPU memory peak**. The first metric is defined as:

$$\text{MCUPS} = \frac{N_x \times N_y \times N_z \times N_{step}}{t_{\text{exec}} \times 10^6}, \tag{4}$$

where N_x, N_y, and N_z are the grid dimensions, N_{step} the number of simulation steps and t_{exec} is the total wall-clock time of the simulation. A higher MCUPS value reflects better utilization of the hardware. The second indicator, the **memory usage peak**, measures the maximum GPU memory footprint observed during execution. This metric is essential for evaluating *scalability* across architectures. Together, these criteria provide a balanced view of both raw performance, resource efficiency, and implementation complexity, enabling meaningful comparisons between JAX and C++/Kokkos across different hardware platforms.

The present study relies on JAXPR [19], Perfetto [27], and HLO [25] for program and trace analysis, Nsight Compute [12] and Rocprof [24] for dominant GPU kernel profiling, and Kokkos-tools [22] for C++/Kokkos memory peak measurement.

4 Results

4.1 Code Optimisations

Based on the numerical scheme of `ark-2-mhd`, a first JAX-based MHD implementation was developed and its performance compared to the Kokkos reference. For this implementation, performance varies significantly across architectures. On Nvidia platforms, the C++/Kokkos implementation clearly dominates JAX performance: it is approximately 2.5× faster on A100 and up to 3.5× faster on V100 and H100. In contrast, results on AMD systems are comparatively more favorable to JAX, with Kokkos being only ≈ 1.5–1.7× faster on MI300A and MI250X respectively. The goal of this study is to investigate whether JAX-specific optimizations can narrow this performance gap, and at what cost.

First Optimization: Python and JAX Loop. Python `while` and `for-loops` generally lead to poor performance in JAX [23], which provides efficient alternatives for iterative computations. In our case, the `for-loop` in the first implementation has been replaced by a `jax.lax.scan` operation, to which the number of time steps, known at compile time, is provided. Knowing this number allows JAX to trace and compile the loop body once as a single computation block, which is then executed efficiently in one pass. As shown in Table 2, replacing the explicit `for`-loop with `jax.lax.scan` leads to heterogeneous performance across architectures. While performance remains essentially unchanged on V100,

Table 2. MCUPS for `for-loop` vs `lax.scan` across architectures.

Architecture	for-loop	lax.scan
V100	90	94
A100	293	406
H100	500	490
MI250X	189	289
MI300A	925	955

MI300A and H100, noticeable improvements are observed on A100 and MI250X, indicating that some architectures benefit more from loop transformation.

By profiling the JAX implementation using Perfetto (Fig. 1), we observe that the `for-loop` re-enters the Python interpreter at every iteration, causing alternating CPU/GPU idle periods. In contrast, `lax.scan` compiles the update function once and executes all timesteps as a single fused XLA computation, eliminating Python overhead. On A100, this reduces kernel dispatch from 297 to $\sim$27 per iteration, yielding a $\sim$1.4$\times$ speedup. On H100 however, XLA already performs kernel fusion with the `for-loop` (23 kernels per iteration), explaining why `lax.scan` yields no additional benefit on this architecture. Same result was observed on V100 and MI300A.

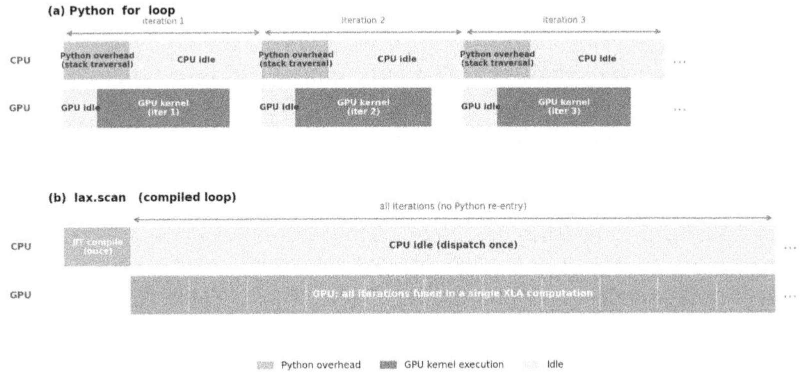

Fig. 1. Perfetto profiling showing execution timeline for a Python `for-loop` (a) and `jax.lax.scan` (b). In the Python loop, the CPU re-enters the runtime at each iteration to dispatch the next GPU kernel, causing alternating idle periods on both CPU and GPU. With lax.scan, the loop is compiled once by XLA and all iterations are fused into a single GPU computation, eliminating Python overhead entirely.

Second Optimization: Gather the Operations. In our initial `for-loop` implementation, spatial gradients were computed *variable by variable*, as shown in Fig. 2.

```
@jax.jit
def get_gradient(f):
    f_dx = minmod_1D(
        jnp.roll(f,  1, axis=0),
        f,
        jnp.roll(f, -1, axis=0))
    f_dy = ...
    f_dz = ...
    return f_dx, f_dy, f_dz
```

```
rho_dx, rho_dy, rho_dz = get_gradient(rho)
P_dx,   P_dy,   P_dz   = get_gradient(P)
vx_dx,  vx_dy,  vx_dz  = get_gradient(vx)
vy_dx,  vy_dy,  vy_dz  = get_gradient(vy)
vz_dx,  vz_dy,  vz_dz  = get_gradient(vz)
Bx_dx,  Bx_dy,  Bx_dz  = get_gradient(Bx)
By_dx,  By_dy,  By_dz  = get_gradient(By)
Bz_dx,  Bz_dy,  Bz_dz  = get_gradient(Bz)
```

Fig. 2. Gradient computation using `get_gradient`.

This formulation triggers eight independent calls to `get_gradient`, each requiring six `jnp.roll` operations to fetch neighboring values and three element-wise operations implementing the minmod limiter [11]. To guide the XLA compilation to perform better fusion, all physical variables can be stacked into a single array:

$$\mathbf{U} = \text{stack}[\rho, P, v_x, v_y, v_z, B_x, B_y, B_z],$$

and the gradient computation applied once to this unified tensor. This strategy led to new results shown in Fig. 3. Again, the impact of this optimization varies across architectures. Substantial speedups are observed on H100 and V100, where execution time is nearly halved, while only modest improvements are seen on MI300A. In contrast, performance remains largely unchanged on A100, and a slight performance degradation is observed on the MI250X. Profiling on the H100 shows that XLA reduces the number of GPU kernels from 27 to 11 per iteration. As shown in Table 3, the three dominant kernels are each invoked once per iteration, indicating complete fusion across all primitive variables by XLA. However, on the A100, XLA does not achieve additional kernel fusion with the `concatenate` implementation, resulting in no performance gain over the `scan-loop`.

Analysis of MI250X Performance Degradation for the Concatenation Strategy. Table 4 reports the dominant GPU kernels for both the `scan` and `scan+concatenation` implementations on MI250X, measured with `rocprof`. With concatenation, the two dominant kernels are `loop_slice_subtract_fusion` and `loop_add_multiply_slice_subtract_fusion`, whose names suggest slice-based operations absent in the scan-only version. To understand this, we compared the optimized HLO generated by XLA on MI250X and MI300A. On MI300A, XLA fuses operations directly on the concatenated tensor `[8,256,256,256]` as a unified block. On MI250X however, XLA decomposes

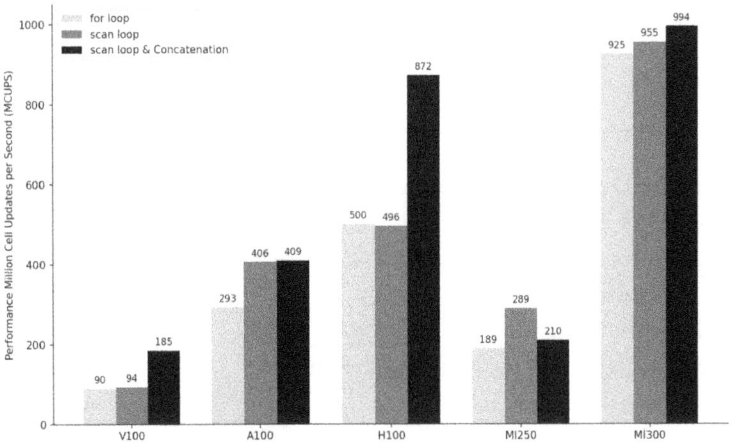

Fig. 3. Performance comparison between previous optimizations and the concatenation. This modification produced notable performance improvements on the V100 and H100 GPUs, where MCUPS effectively doubled. In contrast, results on the A100 and MI300A architectures show a slight increase in performance, while the MI250X exhibits a decrease. Higher values indicate better performance.

Table 3. Dominant GPU kernels for the stacked implementation on H100 (~1423 iterations). Each kernel is called exactly once per iteration, indicating complete XLA fusion across all primitive variables. Kernel names are assigned by XLA and do not directly correspond to user-level code.

Kernel	Count	Total time	Avg per call
`loop_select_fusion`	1423	23.88 s	16.78 ms
`loop_multiply_fusion`	1423	6.43 s	4.52 ms
`loop_subtract_fusion`	1423	6.18 s	4.34 ms

it into per-variable slices `[1,256,256,256]`, resulting in kernels that read from a large number of separate memory buffers. This behavior is consistent with the less mature XLA/ROCm backend for MI250X. To quantify the memory impact, we collected high bandwidth memory (HBM) access counters using `rocprof` (Table 5). The dominant kernel with concatenation generates 1.8× more HBM memory requests than its equivalent without concatenation, confirming that XLA's per-variable slicing strategy increases memory traffic and directly explains the observed performance degradation on MI250X.

4.2 JAX HPC Code Performance

Profiling JAX with traditional HPC tools is challenging since XLA dynamically fuses and renames GPU kernels at each execution, making roofline analysis

Table 4. Dominant GPU kernels on MI250X for scan and scan+concatenation implementations. Kernel names are assigned by XLA and do not directly correspond to user-level code.

Kernel	Avg duration (ms)	% total time
scan only		
`loop_add_multiply_select_subtract_fusion`	13.0	22.2%
`loop_multiply_subtract_fusion`	10.3	17.6%
`loop_add_select_fusion`	8.5	14.5%
scan + concatenation		
`loop_slice_subtract_fusion`	27.0	33.8%
`loop_add_multiply_slice_subtract_fusion`	17.1	21.5%
`loop_add_select_fusion`	6.7	8.4%

Table 5. Average HBM memory requests per call for the dominant kernel on MI250X, measured with AMD hardware counters.

	scan only	scan + concat
HBM read requests	115M	318M
HBM write requests	71M	23M
Total	**186M**	**341M**

non-trivial. Nevertheless, by filtering initialization kernels and directly targeting dominant compute kernels in Nsight Compute, we find that the workload is memory-bound across all JAX implementations and architectures, with DRAM utilization reaching 80–82 % of peak on H100 indicating that the implementation is close to the hardware memory bandwidth limit. (Table 6).

Table 6. GPU resource utilization per kernel measured on an NVIDIA H100. Kernel names are assigned by XLA and do not directly correspond to user-level code. DRAM % measures memory bandwidth utilization and SM % the compute throughput. All kernels are *memory-bound*, with high DRAM utilization (81–82 %).

Kernel	DRAM %	SM %
loop_multiply_fusion	81%	6%
wrapped_negate	81%	5%
loop_divide_fusion	82%	5%

4.3 JAX Compilation Time Cost

JAX compiles functions just-in-time upon first invocation, a cost that can be persisted across runs via a compilation cache [26]. For this reason, compilation time was excluded from the performance results above. However, since the cache is invalidated when array shapes or JAX versions change, we report it here for completeness. C++/Kokkos incurs no such overhead as it compiles ahead-of-time.

As shown in Fig. 4, compiling the full `lax.scan` loop takes a similar amount of time as compiling a single `update` step across all architectures. This may seem counterintuitive, but unlike a Python `for-loop` which unrolls all N iterations during tracing and produces a computation graph of size $O(N)$, `lax.scan` traces the loop body only once and introduces a symbolic loop primitive, keeping the graph size $O(1)$ with respect to N. The compilation cost is therefore dominated by the `update` body itself, with negligible overhead from the loop structure.

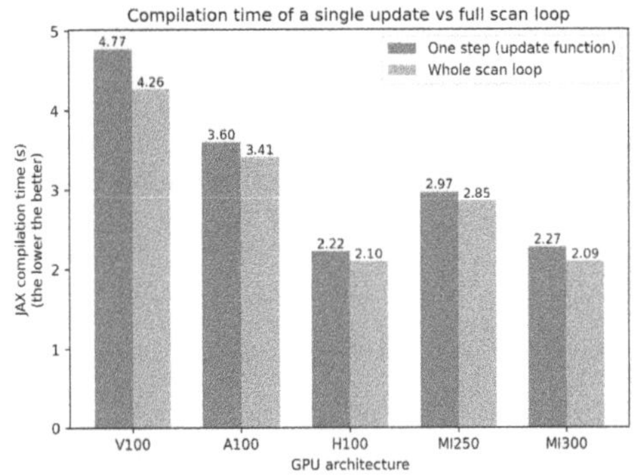

Fig. 4. JAX compilation time comparison between a single `update` step and the full `lax.scan` loop across five GPU architectures. Compiling the complete time-stepping loop is consistently cheaper than compiling a standalone step, demonstrating that XLA performs an optimized fusion of the loop body rather than replicating compilation for each iteration. Lower values indicate better performance.

5 JAX vs Kokkos Performance

Once these optimizations were completed, the computational and memory performance of JAX were compared to that of Kokkos `ark-2-mhd`. Note that no specific optimization was applied to the Kokkos implementation, which is used as a mature production reference.

5.1 Compute Performance

Figure 5 compares the best JAX performance against Kokkos `ark-2-mhd`. Optimization reduces the gap on all architectures: the Kokkos/JAX ratio drops from 3.84× to 1.87× on V100, from 3.05× to 1.75× on H100, and reaches 1.13× and 1.42× on MI250X and MI300A respectively, showing that JAX can approach Kokkos performance with targeted optimization.

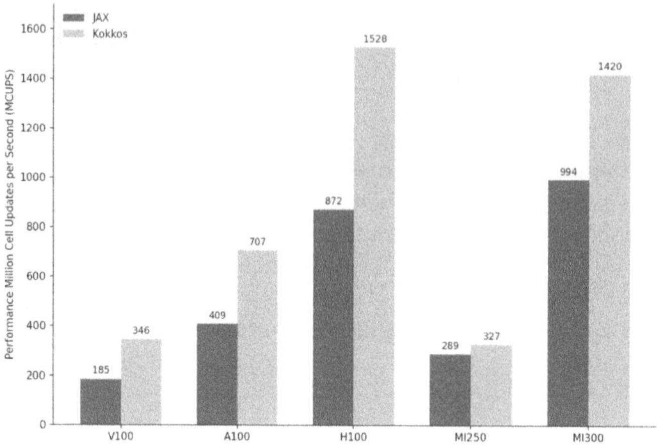

Fig. 5. Final performance comparison between the JAX and C++/Kokkos implementations. The results reported for JAX correspond to the best performance configuration identified throughout this study. Higher values indicate better performance.

5.2 Memory Usage Performance

As shown in Fig. 6, Kokkos memory usage remains stable at 9 GB on 256^3 grids and 18 GB on $512 \times 256 \times 256$ grids, regardless of architecture. JAX exhibits a significantly larger and architecture-dependent footprint: 26–37 GB for the initial version and 34–38 GB after concatenation. This overhead originates from array

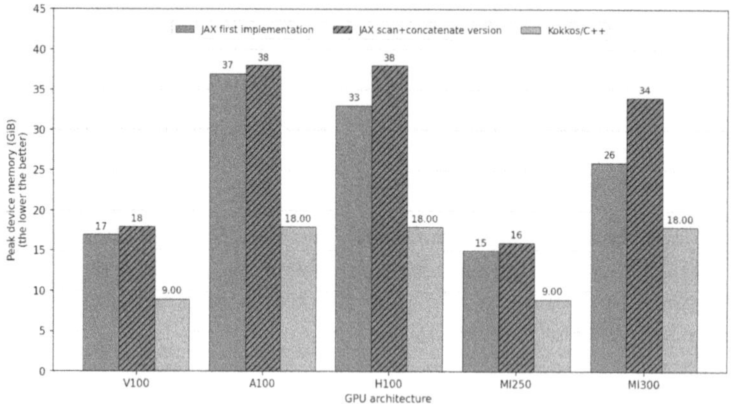

Fig. 6. Measured peak device memory usage for three solver implementations—JAX (first version), JAX (optimized with scan + concatenation), and C++/Kokkos ark-2-mhd implementation. Note that simulations are performed on a uniform 256^3 grid on the MI250X and V100 architectures, whereas a $512 \times 256 \times 256$ grid is used on the other systems.

immutability, which forces the creation of intermediate buffers that XLA cannot fully eliminate

6 Conclusion

This study presented a comparison between two GPU implementations of a three-dimensional second-order MHD solver with MUSCL-Hancock reconstruction: one written in C++/Kokkos and the other using JAX. Both versions were run on five different architectures and were evaluated based on their computational capacity and maximum device memory usage. The study also explored the impact of specific JAX implementation choices.

The experimental results show that C++/Kokkos delivers higher computational performance across all tested architectures. However, using optimization strategies, the JAX implementation approaches this performance level. The primary trade-off is memory: JAX exhibits a larger peak memory footprint due to programming constraints such as array immutability and the creation of intermediate buffers. This work represents a novel contribution by providing a quantitative basis for understanding the trade-offs between JAX and C++/Kokkos for GPU-based MHD solvers: after targeted optimizations, JAX achieves promising computational performance while offering a potentially lower entry barrier for scientists accustomed to NumPy-style programming. However, reaching these performance levels still requires a solid understanding of XLA compilation behavior and JAX-specific optimization strategies. Possible directions for further work include extending the study to multi-GPU configurations or to solvers based on unstructured meshes.

Disclosure of Interests. The authors have no competing interests to declare.

Artifact Availability. The artifact is available in the Zenodo repository [34].

References

1. Google Research, "JAX: Autograd and XLA for High-Performance Numerical Computing," 2025. GitHub repository. https://github.com/google/jax
2. P. Mocz, "jax-euler benchmark," 2024. GitHub repository. [Online]. Available: https://github.com/pmocz/jax-euler-benchmarks
3. Brio, M., Wu, C.C.: An upwind differencing scheme for the equations of ideal magnetohydrodynamics. J. Comput. Phys. **75**, 400–422 (1988). https://doi.org/10.1016/0021-9991(88)90120-9
4. Orszag, S.A., Tang, C.-M.: Small-scale structure of two-dimensional magnetohydrodynamic turbulence. J. Fluid Mech. **90**(1), 129–143 (1979). https://doi.org/10.1017/S002211207900210X
5. Taylor, G.I.: The formation of a blast wave by a very intense explosion. Proc. Roy. Soc. Lond. A **201**(1065), 159–174 (1950)
6. Padioleau, T., Bourgeois, R.: "ARK-2-MHD: A High-Order Magnetohydrodynamics Solver," 2024. GitLab repository. https://gitlab.erc-atmo.eu/remi.bourgeois/ark-2-mhd

7. Bourgeois, R.:Contributions to the study of MHD convection, Ph.D. dissertation, Univ. Paris-Saclay, Gif-sur-Yvette, France (July 2024). https://theses.fr/2024UPASP044
8. Leary, C., Wang, T.: "XLA: TensorFlow, compiled," TensorFlow Dev Summit, 2017. https://openxla.org/xla
9. Carter Edwards, H., Trott, C.R., Sunderland, D.:"Kokkos: Enabling manycore performance portability through polymorphic memory access patterns," Available: https://doi.org/10.1016/j.jpdc.2014.07.003
10. Toro, E.F.: Riemann Solvers and Numerical Methods for Fluid Dynamics (1997) Springer
11. Sweby, P.K.: High resolution schemes using flux limiters for hyperbolic conservation laws. SIAM J. Numer. Anal. **21**(5), 995–1011 (1984)
12. NVIDIA Corporation, "NVIDIA Nsight Compute," NVIDIA Developer Tools. https://developer.nvidia.com/nsight-compute
13. Demeure, N., Kisner, T., Keskitalo, R., Thomas, R., Borrill, J., Bhimji, W.: Porting a large cosmology code to GPU: a case study examining JAX and OpenMP, Technical Report, Lawrence Berkeley National Laboratory (2023). [Online]. Available: https://cug.org/proceedings/cug2023_proceedings/includes/files/pap107s2-file1.pdf
14. Tchakoute, R.N., Tadonki, C., Dokladal, P., Mesri, Y.:"Benchmark-based Study of CPU/GPU Power-Related Features through JAX and TensorFlow," arXiv preprint (May 2025). https://arxiv.org/abs/2505.03398
15. Harris, C.R., Millman, K.J., van der Walt, S.J., Gommers, R., et al.: Array programming with NumPy. Nature **585**(7825), 357–362 (2020)
16. Okuta, R., et al.: CuPy: A NumPy-Compatible Library for NVIDIA GPU Calculations. In: Proceedings of the Workshop on Machine Learning Systems (LearningSys) – NIPS (2017). https://github.com/cupy/cupy
17. JAX Developers, "Stateful computations," JAX documentation. https://docs.jax.dev/en/latest/stateful-computations.html
18. JAX Developers, "The sharp bites," JAX documentation. https://docs.jax.dev/en/latest/notebooks/Common_Gotchas_in_JAX.html
19. JAX Developers, "JAX internals: The jaxpr language," JAX documentation. https://docs.jax.dev/en/latest/jaxpr.html
20. JAX Developers, "Ahead-of-time lowering and compilation," JAX documentation. https://docs.jax.dev/en/latest/aot.html
21. JAX Developers, "Just-in-time compilation," JAX documentation. https://docs.jax.dev/en/latest/jit-compilation.html
22. Kokkos Team, "Kokkos-Tools: Profiling and Debugging Utilities for Kokkos," GitHub Repository (2025). https://github.com/kokkos/kokkos-tools
23. JAX Developers, "Frequently Asked Question," JAX documentation. https://docs.jax.dev/en/latest/faq.html
24. AMD, "ROCm profiling tools - rocprof," ROCm documentation. https://rocm.docs.amd.com/projects/rocprofiler/en/docs-5.5.1/rocprof.html
25. Google, "XLA HLO: High Level Optimizer Operations," XLA documentation. https://openxla.org/xla/operation_semantics
26. JAX Developers, "persistent compilation cache," JAX documentation. https://docs.jax.dev/en/latest/persistent_compilation_cache.html
27. JAX Developers, "Profiling computation," JAX documentation. https://docs.jax.dev/en/latest/profiling.html
28. Kokkos Developers, "Kokkos documentation," https://kokkos.org/kokkos-core-wiki/

29. Storcks and Leonard, "astronomix – differentiable MHD in JAX," Zenodo (2025)
30. Courant, R., Friedrichs, K., Lewy, H.: Über die partiellen Differenzengleichungen der mathematischen Physik, Mathematische Annalen, vol. 100, pp. 32–74 (1928). https://doi.org/10.1007/BF01448839
31. Tremblin, R. et al.: A multi-dimensional, robust, and cell-centered finite-volume scheme for the ideal MHD equations. J. Comput. Phys. **519** 113455 (Dec 2024). https://doi.org/10.1016/j.jcp.2024.113455
32. Lesur, G.R.J., Baghdadi, S., Wafflard-Fernandez, G., Mauxion, J., Robert, C.M.T., Van den Bossche, M.: IDEFIX: a versatile performance-portable Godunov code for astrophysical flows. Astronomy & Astrophysics **677**, art. A9 (2023). https://doi.org/10.1051/0004-6361/202346005:contentReference[oaicite:0]index=0
33. Padioleau, T., Tremblin, P., Audit, E., Kestener, P., Kokh, S.: A high-performance and portable all-Mach regime flow solver code with well-balanced gravity. Application to compressible convection," Astrophys. J. **875**(2), 28 (2019). https://doi.org/10.3847/1538-4357/ab0f2c:contentReference[oaicite:0]index=0
34. Antoun, T., Bourgeois, R., Tremblin, P., Kokh, S., Bobin, J.: Artifact of the paper: JAX vs Kokkos Performance Comparison: A Magnetohydrodynamic Solver Case Study. In: Proceedings of the 32nd International European Conference on Parallel and Distributed Computing (Euro-Par 2026), Pisa, Italy (2026). Zenodo. https://doi.org/10.5281/zenodo.20528641

A Novel Parallel Strategy for Monte Carlo Simulations in Heterogeneous Distributed Systems

Fernanda G. O. Passos[1(✉)], Bernardo Lopo Silva[1], Diego Passos[1], and Vinod E. F. Rebello[2]

[1] Instituto Superior de Engenharia de Lisboa, Instituto Politécnico de Lisboa, R. Conselheiro Emídio Navarro 1, 1959-007 Lisbon, Portugal
bernardomls2004@hotmail.com
{fernanda.passos,diego.passos}@isel.pt
[2] Instituto de Computação, Universidade Federal Fluminense, Niterói, Brazil
vinod@ic.uff.br

Abstract. The Monte Carlo Method (MCM) is an invaluable tool for modeling and analyzing complex systems across multiple domains. For most applications, the MCM is massively parallelizable since the domain can be decomposed independently. However, as processing capacities continue to rise, this paper demonstrates that the common parallelization approach can exhibit a poorer than expected scalability, yielding diminishing efficiency gains as more processors are used. We propose an alternative approach based on task-based parallelism and the concepts of autonomic computing to address the root causes: load imbalance, synchronization, performance heterogeneity, and resource sharing. Our proposal leverages fine-grained tasks, dynamic scheduling, and the hierarchical management of the EasyGrid AMS middleware to achieve better scalability, sustaining efficiencies of more than 90% in both dedicated and heterogeneous computing scenarios when running an MCM simulation of thermal dispersion in porous media on an on-premises cluster. Additional evaluations on AWS EC2 cloud infrastructure further validate the scalability of our proposal.

Keywords: Parallel Monte Carlo Method · EasyGrid AMS middleware · Distributed Systems · Heterogeneous Systems

1 Introduction

The Monte Carlo Method (MCM) [12,17] is a statistical tool still commonly used to simulate phenomena modeled by stochastic processes across various disciplines, including engineering [16], physics [18], and medicine [8]. The specific methodology can vary depending on the problem being addressed. Generally, the approach involves repeatedly using random inputs sampled from a defined

M. Torquati et al. (Eds.): Euro-Par 2026, LNCS 16781, pp. 612–625, 2027.
https://doi.org/10.1007/978-3-032-35248-4_42

domain for the system being studied, which operates on these inputs in a deterministic manner. The results of these iterations are then aggregated to estimate key characteristics of the system.

The MCM is generally employed when the alternative – *e.g.*, the deterministic modeling of the system – is prohibitively complex. However, the accuracy of MCM is directly associated with the number and/or duration of repetitions performed or, from another perspective, the number of samples taken from the domain. Specifically, MCMs typically require a minimum number of samples to converge and can therefore require significant computational effort depending on the application. In these cases, parallelization is a valuable tool for reducing response times and enabling the practical use of the method.

Most MCM algorithms comprise a set of massively parallel scientific applications in which the problem can be decomposed into subdomains with no dependencies between them. This allows multiple independent instances of the MCM to run on different processors and requires only that the different partial results be aggregated into a final solution. In principle, with more available processors, more subdivisions can be created in the domain and more independent instances executed, reducing the convergence time. In practice, however, the aggregation process can become a bottleneck, limiting the application's parallel efficiency.

The contribution of this paper is the proposal of an alternative approach based on the *1PTask* model [14] and a comparison of its parallel efficiency with that of the traditional parallel MCM. The core idea is to create a degree of parallelism that scales with problem size rather than with the dimensionality of the computing infrastructure on which the application runs. Traditional approaches [9,22] typically rely on an *1PProc* model, in which each processing core executes a coarse-grained process for the duration of the application's execution. In this case, the work to be processed is generally divided into P chunks, where P is the number of available processors. Under an *1Ptask* model, the work is divided into $t >> P$ chunks, called *tasks*, all with a finer granularity.

As a case study, we use the MCM application *Thermions* [21], which investigates thermal dispersion in porous media. We compare the performance of traditional parallelization with that of the proposed approach in dedicated, heterogeneous, and shared distributed environments. Our analysis helps understand the behavior of these parallel approaches in the face of characteristics of current distributed infrastructures, such as clusters, clouds, or grids.

The remainder of this paper is organized as follows. Section 2 reviews some of the literature on MCM parallelization, particularly highlighting the most traditional approaches. Section 3 presents the proposed alternative approach for MCM together with an application-centric middleware called the EasyGrid AMS. Sections 4 and 5 describe the experiments performed to evaluate our proposal and the traditional approach on an on-premises cluster and in AWS EC2. Finally, Sect. 6 concludes the paper and presents some future directions.

2 Parallel Monte Carlo Simulations

Monte Carlo Methods (MCMs) are naturally parallelizable because many samples are independent, making them especially suitable for high-performance computing or GPU acceleration [1]. Brockwell [4] distinguishes two MCM parallelization approaches: parallelizing each instance/iteration of the Monte Carlo simulation and parallelizing several independent instances, each executed by a different processor. The author focuses on the first approach, with special attention to systems represented by Markov Chains. Brockwell argues that this approach is particularly interesting when the space of chain-states of the system is very large. In such cases, the sequential execution of a single instance of the Monte Carlo simulation can already be prohibitively complex.

Camarasu-Pop *et al.* [5,6] propose a *framework* for MCM in computational grid infrastructures using a moldable parallel master-worker implementation. In the first article [5], the authors address scheduling processes or *jobs* in computational grids, which can be costly due to communication latencies being higher than those between nodes in a cluster. The authors use the master-worker model and classify their parallel solution as moldable, since the granularity of instance *jobs* is adjusted according to the processing time of each worker. Follow-up work proposed a fault-tolerant incremental solution [6].

Others have taken a more practical perspective, presenting or describing concrete implementations of MCM parallelization methods. For example, in [19], the authors describe a library called *ParaMonte* for several programming languages, including C/C++, Fortran, MATLAB, Python, and R. The library implements sequential and parallel functionalities for Monte Carlo simulations. Analogously to the classification proposed by Brockwell [4], the library supports two parallelism modes: 1) multiple independent instances of the Monte Carlo simulation are executed by different processors; 2) each instance is partitioned among the specified processors. Although there are not many details about the first mode, called *Perfect Parallelism*, the text suggests that it follows an *1PProc* model: each processor receives and runs a complete instance of the simulation, and then the result is sent to a single central process that checks the problem convergence.

Similarly, [2] presents a set of *scripts* for parallelizing programs that implement Monte Carlo simulations. It is yet another example of parallelization based on *1PProc*. In this case, the implementation relies on *scripts* that establish remote *shell* connections to machines by copying the program, running instances, and downloading the results back to a master process that combines them.

On the other hand, other efforts consider the specific characteristics of certain applications. In [7], the authors propose a strategy for the "hybrid" parallelization of a method called *Particle in Cell Monte Carlo Collision* for low-temperature plasma simulation. The authors classify their parallelization strategy as "hybrid" because it harnesses parallelism at both the *thread* level (using OpenMP) and the node level using the *Message Passing Interface* (MPI). At the MPI level, parallelization is achieved by statically distributing the particles to be simulated among the nodes at the start of execution. Due to the possibility of particle interactions and their effects on particle motion, this particular application of the MCM requires a high degree of communication and synchronization among the processes, thereby reducing the efficiency of this form of parallelism.

Another aspect commonly discussed in the literature related to the parallelization of MCM is the generation of random numbers. For parallelization not to negatively affect the accuracy of these methods – especially in strategies in which completely independent instances of the Monte Carlo simulation are distributed over several processors –, processors must generate independent sequences of random numbers. Otherwise, convergence issues may arise, reducing the effectiveness of parallel solutions [2].

2.1 Parallel Monte Carlo Thermions

The *Thermions* application considers the displacement of N particles through a porous medium at each discretized-time increment. This displacement is subject to the random action inherent in the MCM. The method can be executed across the P available processors, with each one responsible for simulating the movement of a fraction of the total number N of *thermions*. After all N displacements have been calculated, a single processor aggregates the results to obtain the final distribution of thermions.

Souto *et al.* [21] proposed a parallel MPI solution for the *Thermions* application that simply divides the simulation domain D into P equal parts and assigns them to each homogeneous processor. In a heterogeneous or shared environment, this partitioning approach may be ineffective, as faster processors would remain idle while slower ones continue to work. To mitigate this issue, load balancing techniques [10] are frequently considered to redistribute unprocessed work (thermions) to idle resources. We will refer to this solution as the *traditional solution*, as it aligns with MCM approaches commonly found in the literature.

This traditional solution initially creates a *pool* of tasks, each task being responsible for simulating the thermal dispersion of a single *thermion* particle, in the master process for later, on-demand, distribution to worker nodes. The master at first distributes a set of particles to each of the P worker processes. As workers terminate, they each return their solution and request new particles from the master's *pool.*

The algorithm in Fig. 1a represents the execution steps of the master process in the traditional MPI version of the Monte Carlo simulation. The inputs are N, the number of partitions in the simulation domain D, and P, the total number of worker processes. In the *Thermions* application, the domain corresponds to the universe of simulated particles with $N = |D|$, *i.e.*, each *thermion* is a partition/task. The master process partitions the domain D into N tasks and places them in the set T. Each task will eventually be distributed among the P worker processes, each executing on one of the P processors. When a worker p_i (with $0 \leq i < P$) completes task j (with $0 \leq j < N$), its solution is sent to the master via message passing. Each time a solution arrives, the master checks if any unprocessed tasks remain and sends a new task back to p_i. The solution of task j is then integrated into the final solution through a reduction operation. When all tasks have been processed, the master sends a termination message to all worker processes. The algorithm in Fig. 1b describes the corresponding worker processes that receive a task t from the master, simulate the particle's motion, and send their solution back to the master. This repeats until the stop message is received. The random components are generated by the master and incorporated into task t for reception by the worker process at each iteration.

Require: N - number of partitions;
D - domain; P - number of workers.
Ensure: sol_{final} - final solution.
$T \leftarrow partition(D, N)$
for $i \leftarrow 0$ to $P - 1$ **do**
remove task j from T, send to p_i
end for
while $T \neq \varnothing$ **do**
receive $solution_j$ from p_i
remove task j from T, send to p_i
reduce $solution_j$ in sol_{final}
end while
receive last P solutions and reduce
send *finished* to all P processes

(a) Master.

receive *message* from master
while *message* $\neq$ *finished* **do**
get task t from *message*
calculate MC simulation of t
send solution to the master
receive new *message* from master
end while

(b) Worker.

Fig. 1. Example Master and Worker algorithms for the traditional parallel MCM.

3 MCM-1PTask: A Novel Parallel Strategy for MCM

Scaling this traditional approach to parallelize MCM to harness many processors faces several issues: (i) in large scale systems, the centralized master process may become a bottleneck when aggregating simulation results from worker processes and sending new tasks; (ii) the absence of a dynamic task scheduler makes it hard to cope efficiently with the capacity heterogeneity between available processors and varying MCM task execution times; and (iii) even with dynamic scheduling, the coarse granularity of worker processes hamper efforts to fully utilize the available computational resources. In summary, the traditional parallelized version of MCM tends to scale out inefficiently.

To address these limitations, an alternative MCM parallelization strategy is proposed here, namely MCM-1PTask, which is based on two pillars: transitioning the partitioning model from *1PProc* to *1PTask* (see Sect. 3.2) and integrating the application with the EasyGrid AMS middleware (see Sect. 3.1).

3.1 The EasyGrid AMS Middleware

EasyGrid AMS [3] is an *application management system* (AMS) that offers a framework capable of transparently – or with minor modifications – managing the execution of parallel MPI applications across large-scale heterogeneous infrastructures. The integration is achieved at compile time, with developers only having to reformulate their MPI processes as smaller-grained tasks, in line with the *1Ptask* model [14]. Calls to the MPI library are intercepted by the AMS middleware to provide enhanced functionality and additional features. In the context of the *Thermions* application, N MPI processes will be created (in a controlled manner) to each execute a single task independent of the value of P, while, under the 1Pproc model, each of the P MPI processes may execute one or more tasks depending on the distribution.

EasyGrid AMS employs a three-level tree-like hierarchy of distributed controllers: a global manager, site managers, and host managers. Each host manager's objective is to schedule their application's processes on their host machine within the distributed infrastructure (such as a cluster, grid, or cloud), subjecting their execution to the policy of the local operating system. Each site manager performs proactive load balancing of application processes across the machines associated with that cluster or geographical location, with the global manager performing the same action across different sites [3]. To minimize host idle time, tasks are not distributed on demand but a priori to host managers, where they are queued and wait until CPU resources become available. The load balancers at the site and global levels move tasks between queues to keep the predicted total execution times of all queues similar [13]. Each task, when initiated, becomes a dynamically created MPI process. When and where each process is created is controlled by the host and site managers, respectively. Furthermore, the controllers are responsible for routing communications (messages) between MPI processes and for holding messages for processes that may not yet be executing. Another important feature is a fault-tolerant mechanism that leverages the 1PTask model and the dynamic scheduler to simply re-run failed tasks, rather than deal with the overhead and complexity of checkpoints [20]. In addition, the framework provides an application programming interface (API) that allows the developer to obtain runtime information about the application's execution [15] and implement self-configuring capabilities.

3.2 Defining the Tasks

The MCM-1PTask strategy also uses a master process that performs domain partitioning, distributes tasks, and collects solutions from the distributed processes. The algorithm in Fig. 2a describes the steps that involve partitioning the domain D into N tasks at the beginning to generate the set T. Each task $j \in T$ is sent to worker process p_j, given $0 < j \leq N$, rather than just one of P workers in the traditional version. Given that N is typically much larger than P, the number of processors, multiple tasks may be allocated to the same processor. The master process waits for each task's solution and reduces them to generate the final result.

The algorithm for the worker processes is a simple, non-iterative version of the traditional implementation as shown in Fig. 2b. Each process receives the initial data, performs the independent simulation (the intensive processing phase), sends the solution back to the master, and terminates. These MCM-1PTask algorithms are simpler than those in Fig. 1 for a programmer, as they decouple workload distribution from the application logic with the help of wrappers around the standard MPI calls. EasyGrid AMS managers intercept all application tasks, distribute them hierarchically among managers (see Sect. 3.1) and execute one task at a time on each available processor as it becomes ready.

Require: N - number of partitions; D - domain.
Ensure: sol_{final} - found solution.

$T \leftarrow partition(D, N)$
for all $j \in T$ **do**
  send task j to worker process p_j
end for
for $i \leftarrow 0$ to $N-1$ **do**
  receive $solution_j$
  reduce $solution_j$ in sol_{final}
end for

(a) Master.

receive task t from master
calculate MC simulation of t
send *solution* to the master

(b) Worker.

Fig. 2. Algorithms for the proposed MCM-1PTask.

3.3 Reduction Operation

Like the traditional implementation, MCM-1Ptask also employs a reduction operation on the results produced by the tasks. Given the EasyGrid AMS intercepts calls to the MPI library, including *MPI_Reduce*, this allows an opportunity to provide enhancements to such operations, in this case, the function *AMS_Reduce*. This function has the same arguments as *MPI_Reduce*, except for an additional fifth argument that can be used to specify the required user-defined operation to be carried out, similar to the *MPI_Op_create* function[1].

Once the user specifies the operation to be performed on the received solution messages via the API, EasyGrid AMS performs the corresponding reduction operations hierarchically through its managers. Each host manager performs the user-defined reduction operation for the tasks allocated to it and sends the result to the manager directly above it in the hierarchy. This reduces the potential for bottlenecks since the master process will receive solutions that have already been partially reduced by its distributed managers below it.

4 On-Premises Experimental Evaluation

To evaluate the proposed parallelization strategy, experiments were conducted on an on-premises computational *cluster*. We used 16 machines with 2 quad-core

[1] https://www.mpi-forum.org/docs/mpi-5.0/mpi50-report.pdf.

Intel Xeon 2.00 GHz processors (128 cores in total), 16 GB of main memory each, and hyper-threading disabled. All nodes are interconnected by Gigabit Ethernet switches. The operating system was CentOS Linux with Network File System (NFS) and OpenMPI version 4.0.1.

Both MPI implementations of the *Thermions* application used in the following experiments were based on the approach presented in [21], with the traditional solution being referred to as the *traditional MPI version* and the MCM-1PTask solution as the *EasyGrid AMS version*. The test instance of the problem has 10,000 *thermions*, and simulating each *thermion* takes around 4 s of processing time on the machines used. In the EasyGrid AMS version, this value roughly represents the execution of each MPI worker process.

4.1 Parallel Scenario Description

Experiments were performed varying the number of machines H according to the set {2,4,6,8,10,12,14,16}. As each machine has 8 cores, the total number of processing units P in each experiment was $8 \times H$. In Scenario 1, all H machines are dedicated to the application, enabling an evaluation of the *speed-ups* and the efficiency under "ideal" conditions. Scenario 2 simulates a heterogeneous (non-uniform) compute environment or a shared static computing infrastructure by using 8 external loads (corresponding to the number of cores per processor) that compete for processors on each of the $\frac{H}{2}$ machines. This external load behaves like a CPU-intensive process during execution. External loads in Scenario 2 are statically allocated and remain on the same machines throughout the test application's execution. Scenario 3 represents a more dynamic compute environment where the external loads move around. The same 8 loads run for 10 s on each of the $\frac{H}{2}$ machines; then migrated and run for another 10 s on the other $\frac{H}{2}$ machines. This is repeated every 10 s until the end of the experiment.

4.2 Results

Figure 3 presents a comparison of the performances for the traditional MPI and EasyGrid AMS implementations in Scenario 1. For each version, the two graphs show the total number of processing units P used, the average execution time, with 96% confidence intervals, and the *speed-up* relative to the average sequential execution time of 41311.23 s. The *speed-up* plot also shows a reference line for linear *speed-up*, allowing an easy visualization of the efficiency (defined as the ratio between the obtained and ideal *speed-up*, P times the average CPU capacity available to the MC simulations) of each parallelization strategy.

The results in Fig. 3 show that the EasyGrid AMS version consistently achieves lower execution times than the traditional MPI version in the dedicated environment. In addition, with 64 or more processors, the difference between the execution times of the two strategies tends to increase. This result is more evident in the *speed-up* graph of the traditional MPI version, which shows increasing inefficiency, whereas the EasyGrid AMS version maintains efficiencies above 90% despite executing 10000 MPI worker processes, illustrating a scalability problem

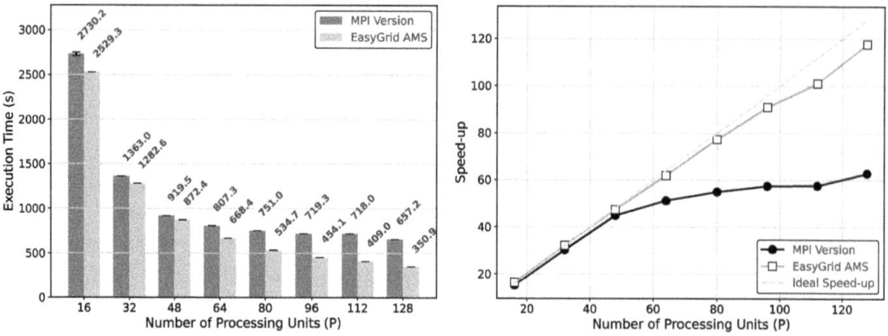

Fig. 3. A comparison of execution times and speed-ups for Scenario 1.

with the traditional approach. This is due to the centralized task management by the master process, which becomes a bottleneck. On the other hand, executions with EasyGrid AMS do not manifest this problem since its management structure is distributed, even though, from the developer's perspective, the application still implements the same master-worker model. Even when the reduction bottleneck does not affect execution (with 16, 32, and 48 CPUs), the EasyGrid AMS version is slightly more efficient because the proactive dynamic scheduler can adjust task allocations in response to varying task processing rates, thus minimizing worker idle times while waiting for new tasks.

Scenario 2 simulates an unbalanced processing environment, with half of the hosts in the experiment only able to provide 50% of their total capacity. While this should not affect the traditional version, which allocates tasks on demand, the EasyGrid version will need to make significant changes by moving some allocated tasks from slower processing hosts to faster ones. Will this adversely impact performance? Fig. 4 presents the measured percentage of CPU usage by the static load processes during tests with the traditional and EasyGrid AMS versions for $P = 16$. With the traditional MPI version, as expected, the extra loads typically account for 50% of the machine's CPU utilization. However, with the EasyGrid AMS version, the average CPU usage for the extra loads is around 45%. This is because the operating system scheduler (Linux kernel 2.6.18) tends to penalize long, CPU-intensive processes [11], such as the static loads in Scenario 2. Conversely, as the tasks in the EasyGrid AMS version follow the 1PTask model, the processes tend to be shorter-running and therefore benefit slightly from a higher scheduling priority, getting around 55% of the CPU. Note that this difference is less noticeable in Scenario 3, since the external loads run for only 10 s before being moved to other hosts, and thus the lifetimes of the two programs' processes are similar.

Figure 5 presents the results of the experiments in Scenario 2. Note that the ideal speed-up reference line was calculated as $0.75 \times P$, since application tasks are expected to get, on average, 75% of the total available processing capacity – 100% of $\frac{P}{2}$ processors and 50% of the other $\frac{P}{2}$ processors. Additionally, to

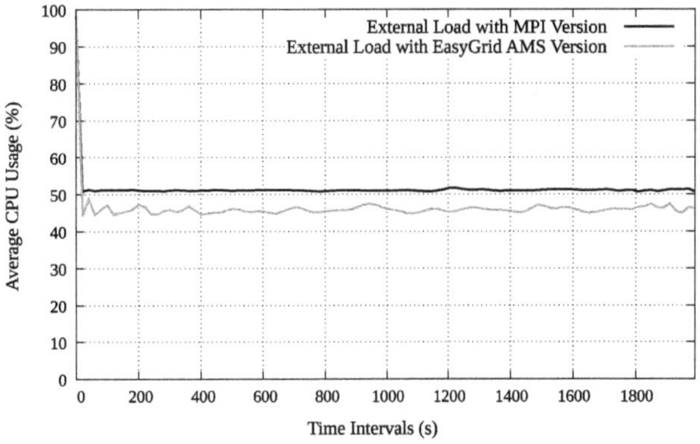

Fig. 4. Average CPU utilization of 8 static external loads executing concurrently with the traditional MPI and EasyGrid AMS versions, respectively.

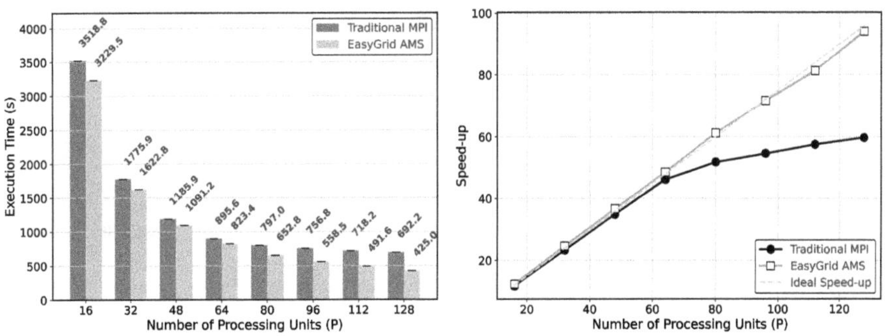

Fig. 5. A comparison of execution times and speed-ups for Scenario 2.

provide a fair comparison and account for the fact that the EasyGrid AMS version obtained a higher than expected CPU utilization, as illustrated in Fig. 4, the EasyGrid *speed-ups* have been multiplied by a normalization factor of $\frac{0.75}{0.775}$.

As expected, the execution times, while slower, and *speed-ups* follow a trend similar to Scenario 1. The EasyGrid AMS version is always faster, and the difference increases as the number of available processors grows. The EasyGrid AMS version exhibited efficiencies close to 100% regardless of the value of P, even super-linear *speed-ups* at times. Better resource utilization and lower parallelization overheads than the traditional MPI version help achieve good near-linear scalability. On the other hand, the traditional version shows good efficiency with $P \leq 64$ (about 97%), but with 80 or more processors, there is significant degradation, culminating in an efficiency of just 62% with 128 CPUs.

The efficiency degradation of the traditional MPI version in this scenario was lower than that recorded in Scenario 1. First, this version is not adversely affected by the external loads, aside from the expected slowdown. When fewer computing resources are available, the bottleneck during the reduction phase is somewhat mitigated. As task execution times increase, the reduction phase becomes proportionally less significant and, consequently, has a smaller negative effect on efficiency. In addition, the machines with external loads process tasks more slowly, which tends to desynchronize the arrival times of workers' simulation results at the master process. Nevertheless, these graphs continue to highlight the traditional MPI version's scalability deficiencies: while performance is competitive with few computing resources, as more become available, it fails to effectively take full advantage.

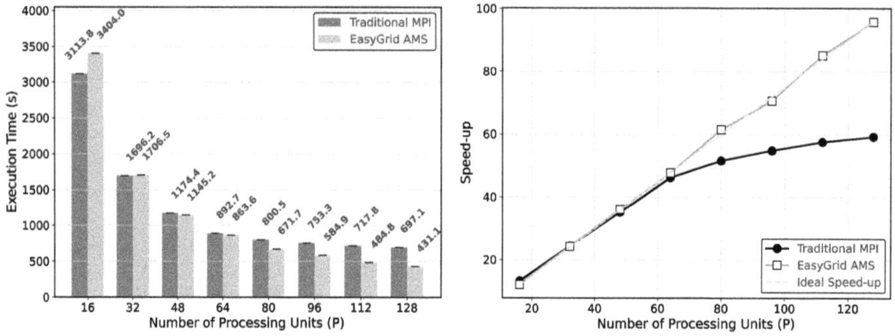

Fig. 6. A comparison of execution times and speed-ups for Scenario 3.

Figure 6 illustrates the results for the volatile Scenario 3, where the computing capacity of a node available to the MC simulations oscillates over time. Surprisingly, the MPI version frequently obtains faster execution times than its corresponding executions in Scenario 2. On the other hand, the performance of the EasyGrid AMS version was slightly, but consistently, worse in Scenario 3 than in Scenario 2. The explanation lies in the interaction between the scheduling of tasks – performed proactively by EasyGrid AMS, and on demand by the traditional version – and the behavior of the external loads. Previously, the dynamic schedulers in the EasyGrid AMS quickly determined the relative performances of the nodes and, within a few iterations, rebalanced the application load accordingly. Here, Scenario 3 was designed to confuse the dynamic scheduler. The locations of the external loads change every 10 s, which is roughly the time it takes to execute a task on a loaded node. The scheduler uses this task's performance to predict the next and decide if rebalancing is required. However, with loads migrating, the performance prediction will be incorrect. The aim is to discover how sensitive the performance of the EasyGrid AMS version is to a misbehaving dynamic scheduler.

Even in this scenario, the EasyGrid AMS version remains superior in terms of scalability. Note that, for $P = 16$, the average execution time of the traditional version was better compared to the EasyGrid AMS version, and, for $P = 32$, both performed similarly. For $P \geq 48$, however, the results are reversed, and the EasyGrid AMS version has shorter execution times. In fact, the efficiency of the EasyGrid AMS version remains around 100% regardless of the value of P. The same, however, cannot be said for the traditional MPI version, which again suffers significant efficiency losses at higher processor counts.

5 Experimental Evaluation in the Cloud

Experiments were also conducted on Amazon EC2 to evaluate both the traditional MPI and EasyGrid AMS versions in the on-demand market. Two types of experiments were performed using similar general-purpose instances under two distinct configurations: (i) up to 16 `m4.2xlarge` instances with 32 GiB RAM, 4 Intel CPUs, and Hyper-threading (HT) enabled (8 vCPUs), and (ii) up to 16 `m4.4xlarge` instances with 64 GiB, 8 CPUs, and HT disabled. The cluster was configured with OpenMPI version 4.0.1 on an Ubuntu Linux image with NFS. We used clusters with 2, 8, 12, and 16 instances and focused on Scenario 1 – *i.e.*, without external loads. The executions of the traditional MPI and EasyGrid AMS versions were alternated to minimize interference from external co-tenanted cloud applications and allow a fair comparison. We also performed preliminary experiments to measure the sequential execution time with HT disabled (13,794.15 s) to compute the *speed-ups*.

Analyzing the results where HT is disabled, Fig. 7 demonstrates that the EasyGrid AMS version achieves performance near, or in some cases slightly above, the ideal. The traditional MPI approach plateaus at a speed-up of approximately 82 for $P = 96$ and $P = 128$, again underperforming compared to the proposed approach. With HT enabled, both approaches suffer from reduced efficiency, limited to a maximum of 65.53% (but above 50%), because on Intel processor-based cloud instances, two logical vCPUs share the same physical core. Despite this, EasyGrid AMS still offers greater scalability than the traditional MPI version, achieving significantly higher *speed-up* with $P = 96$ and $P = 128$.

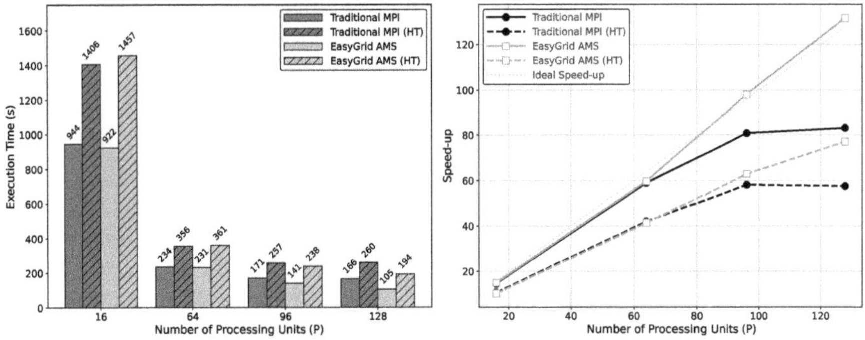

Fig. 7. Execution times and speed-up comparisons on Amazon EC2 general-purpose instances, with HT enabled and disabled.

6 Conclusion and Future Directions

MCM is widely employed in stochastic processes to simulate problems in several areas, such as engineering, biology, and finance. While MCM is massively parallel – especially when there is no communication between partitions – traditional approaches often rely on a master-worker paradigm, which can lead to performance bottlenecks at scale. Moreover, implementations tend to lack adaptability to execute effectively in heterogeneous or shared environments. In this paper, we adopted the same master-worker approach but modified it to use the 1Ptask model together with the EasyGrid AMS, demonstrating that this approach yields better efficiency for this kind of application.

For this purpose, an experimental evaluation was conducted using a real application called *Thermions*. The results showed good efficiency (constantly above 90%) for the EasyGrid AMS version in a dedicated environment, combined with good scalability—*i.e.*, the ability to maintain high efficiency as more processors are used. In this same scenario, the traditional version exhibited lower efficiencies and, in particular, poor scalability. In heterogeneous scenarios, the EasyGrid AMS version also demonstrated adaptability through dynamic scheduling, thereby maintaining very high efficiencies. The EasyGrid AMS version was also more efficient than the traditional approach when executed in the cloud.

In future work, we aim to study the efficiency of our proposal at an even larger scales to understand the limits of the implementation and its practical application. In addition, some results indicate super-linear speed-ups, suggesting an investigation into cache memory usage and other factors that may explain this. In highly dynamic environments, we will seek to identify techniques to reduce the overhead caused by the dynamic scheduler's behavior.

Acknowledgments. This work was supported partially by computational resources from FCT I.P., approved under the Project 2024.18373.CPCA. The authors also acknowledge the financial support of CNPq (Brazil) through the project CNPq/AWS 421828/2022-6.

Disclosure of Interests. The authors have no competing interests to declare that are relevant to the content of this article.

References

1. Anderson, J.A., Jankowski, E., Grubb, T.L., Engel, M., Glotzer, S.C.: Massively parallel Monte Carlo for many-particle simulations on GPUs. J. Comput. Phys. **254**, 27–38 (2013). https://doi.org/10.1016/j.jcp.2013.07.023
2. Badal, A., Sempau, J.: A package of Linux scripts for the parallelization of Monte Carlo simulations. Comput. Phys. Commun. **175**(6), 440–450 (2006)
3. Boeres, C., Rebello, V.E.F.: EasyGrid: Towards a framework for the automatic grid enabling of legacy MPI applications. Concurr. Comput.: Pract. Exper. **16**(5), 425–432 (2004)
4. Brockwell, A.E.: Parallel Markov chain Monte Carlo simulation by pre-fetching. J. Comput. Graph. Stat. **15**(1), 246–261 (2006)

5. Camarasu-Pop, S., et al.: Dynamic partitioning of GATE Monte-Carlo simulations on EGEE. J. Grid Comput. **8**(2), 241–259 (2010)
6. Camarasu-Pop, S., et al.: Monte Carlo simulation on heterogeneous distributed systems: A computing framework with parallel merging and checkpointing strategies. Futur. Gener. Comput. Syst. **29**(3), 728–738 (2013)
7. Chaudhury, B., et al.: Hybrid Parallelization of Particle in Cell Monte Carlo Collision (PIC-MCC) algorithm for simulation of low temperature plasmas. In: Majumdar, A., Arora, R. (eds.) SCEC 2018. CCIS, vol. 964, pp. 32–53. Springer, Singapore (2019). https://doi.org/10.1007/978-981-13-7729-7_3
8. Constantin, M.A., Schuurman, N.K., Vermunt, J.K.: A General Monte Carlo Method for Sample Size Analysis in the Context Of Network Models. Psychol, Methods (2023)
9. Esselink, K., Loyens, L.D.J.C., Smit, B.: Parallel Monte Carlo simulations. Phys. Rev. E **51**, 1560–1568 (1995)
10. Jiang, Y.: A survey of task allocation and load balancing in distributed systems. IEEE Trans. Parallel Distrib. Syst. **27**(2), 585–599 (2016)
11. Jose, J., Sujisha, O., Gilesh, M., Bindima, T.: On the fairness of Linux O(1) scheduler. In: 5th International Conference on Intelligent Systems, Modelling and Simulation, pp. 668–674 (2014)
12. Metropolis, N., Ulam, S.: The Monte Carlo method. J. Am. Stat. Assoc. **44**(247), 335–341 (1949)
13. Nascimento, A., Sena, A., Boeres, C., Rebello, V.E.F.: Distributed and dynamic self-scheduling of parallel MPI grid applications. Concurr. Comput.: Pract. Exper. **19**(14), 1955–1974 (2007)
14. Nascimento, A., Sena, A., da Silva, J., Vianna, D.Q.C., Boeres, C., Rebello, V.E.F.: On the advantages of an alternative MPI execution model for grids. In: CCGRID '07: Proceedings of the 7th IEEE International Symposium on Cluster Computing and the Grid, pp. 575–582. IEEE Computer Society, Rio de Janeiro, Brazil (2007)
15. Passos, F.G.O., Rebello, V.E.F.: An autonomic parallel strategy for the projection of ecological niche models in heterogeneous computational environments. In: Euro-Par 2016: Parallel Processing, pp. 363–375. Springer Int. Publ, Cham (2016)
16. Rioux-Lavoie, D., Sugimoto, R., Özdemir, T., Shimada, N.H., Batty, C., Nowrouzezahrai, D., Hachisuka, T.: A Monte Carlo method for fluid simulation. ACM Trans. Graph **41**(6), (2022)
17. Rubinstein, R.Y., Kroese, D.P.: Simulation and the Monte Carlo Method. John Wiley & Sons (2016)
18. Saunders, W.R., Grant, J., Müller, E.H.: A new algorithm for electrostatic interactions in Monte Carlo simulations of charged particles. J. Comput. Phys. **430**, 110099 (2021)
19. Shahmoradi, A., Bagheri, F.: ParaMonte: A high-performance serial/parallel Monte Carlo simulation library for C, C++, Fortran. J. Open Source Softw. **6**(61), 2741 (2021). https://doi.org/10.21105/joss.02741
20. Silva, J., Rebello, V.E.F.: Low cost self-healing in MPI applications. In: Recent Advances in Parallel Virtual Machine and Message Passing Interface, 14th European PVM/MPI User's Group Meeting, pp. 144–152. Springer (2007)
21. Souto, H.P.A., da Silveira, O.T., Moyne, C., Didierjean, S.: Thermal dispersion in porous media: computations by the random walk method. Comput. Appl. Math. **21**, 513–544 (2002)
22. Stokes-Ress, I., Baude, F., Doan, V.D., Bossy, M.: Managing parallel and distributed Monte Carlo simulations for computational finance in a grid environment. In: Lin, S., Yen, E. (eds.) Grid Computing, pp. 183–204. Springer, US (2009)

Sparsh: Breaking the Communication Bottleneck in Sequence Parallel Video Diffusion Inference with Predictive Sparse Communication

Huimin Liu, Haozhe Li, Zhenyi Zheng, Jiangsu Du(✉), and Nong Xiao

Sun Yat-sen University, Guangzhou, China
{liuhm59,zhengzhy37}@mail2.sysu.edu.cn,
{dujiangsu,xiaon6}@mail.sysu.edu.cn

Abstract. Sequence Parallelism (SP), such as DeepSpeed-Ulysses, has emerged as the de facto standard for scaling high-resolution video generation for its superior memory efficiency in handling long contexts and reduced communication. However, the bandwidth-intensive All-to-All communication inherent in SP still becomes a critical bottleneck, severely limiting scaling efficiency. We propose Sparsh, a distributed video diffusion inference framework with predictive sparse communication. Unlike standard Ulysses-style sequence parallelism which indiscriminately transmits attention tensors in all diffusion steps, Sparsh eliminates the transmission of Key and Value tensors entirely in most steps by exploiting their temporal redundancy. Particularly, instead of remotely fetching KV tensors via All-to-All communication, Sparsh introduces a fidelity-aware predictive synthesis mechanism that reconstructs remote KV states locally. Further, Sparsh employs an online adaptive controller that dynamically adjusts prediction strategies based on real-time error feedback, ensuring that the communication reduction does not compromise generation quality. Experiments on multiple models demonstrate that Sparsh reduces communication cost by 50% in predictive steps and by 28% overall compared to state-of-the-art Ulysses baselines, offering a scalable solution for distributed high-resolution video generation.

Keywords: DiT · Sequence Parallelism · Efficient Communication

1 Introduction

The advent of Transformer-based diffusion and flow matching architectures, exemplified by Sora [2] and further advanced by state-of-the-art models such as Wan [19] and CogvideoX [20], has revolutionized video generation. However, scaling these models to high resolutions and long durations creates immense memory and computational demands. To address this, Sequence Parallelism partitions the sequence dimension across multiple GPUs to enable distributed inference. Representative implementations include Ulysses Attention [10].

M. Torquati et al. (Eds.): Euro-Par 2026, LNCS 16781, pp. 626–640, 2027.
https://doi.org/10.1007/978-3-032-35248-4_43

However, this scalability comes at a non-negligible cost. The Ulysses architecture necessitates two rounds of All-to-All communication at each attention layer: the first to transpose the sequence-parallel Q, K, and V tensors into head-parallel layout before the attention computation, and the second to redistribute the attention output back to sequence-parallel layout. Even though attention computation inherently scales quadratically ($O(N^2)$), highly optimized kernels like FlashAttention have drastically reduced its execution time. Paradoxically, the linear communication overhead ($O(N)$) can account for up to 30% of the total time within an attention layer. This substantial communication cost imposes a severe bandwidth wall that restricts scalability in multi-node clusters.

Recent research [13] has identified significant temporal redundancy in attention outputs across consecutive denoising steps. Building on this insight, we further discover that such temporal coherence is deeply rooted in the underlying Key and Value tensors. However, in distributed inference settings like the Ulysses architecture, these KV tensors—which constitute the dominant share of the communication volume—are still transmitted fully at every step.

To address this bottleneck, we propose a communication-efficient attention framework that operates at an intra-layer granularity. We leverage the observed coherence to eliminate redundant KV transmission by predicting their states from historical data. Meanwhile, we maintain the standard All-to-All communication for the Query to preserve the structural integrity of the attention operation. To ensure high fidelity, we introduce an asynchronous adaptive mechanism that transmits ground-truth KV data overlapping with the main computation to monitor errors and update prediction coefficients dynamically. This design allows the system to adapt to distribution shifts without stalling the main inference stream. By specifically targeting the data movement overhead, our method effectively mitigates the network bottleneck in sequence parallelism. In summary, we make the following contributions:

- We identify that KV tensors constitute the dominant share of All-to-All communication overhead in Ulysses-based sequence parallelism, and that their strong temporal coherence across denoising steps represents an untapped opportunity for communication reduction.
- We propose a KV prediction framework that replaces KV All-to-All communication with polynomial extrapolation from historical states, coupled with an asynchronous error-correction mechanism that dynamically governs prediction parameters without stalling the main inference stream.
- We evaluate our framework on Wan series and CogVideo models, demonstrating consistent reductions in communication overhead and inference latency with negligible impact on generation quality.

2 Background

2.1 Diffusion Transformers

Diffusion Transformers (DiTs) [17] generate high-fidelity video by iteratively reversing a noise process. Starting from Gaussian noise $\mathbf{z}_T \sim \mathcal{N}(\mathbf{0}, \mathbf{I})$, the model reconstructs the clean latent $\mathbf{z}_0$ through a discrete denoising chain [6,18] conditioned on context $\mathbf{c}$ (e.g., prompts). At each step t, the network ϵ_θ predicts the noise field to update the state:

$$\mathbf{z}_{t-1} \leftarrow \text{Solver}\left(\mathbf{z}_t, \epsilon_\theta(\mathbf{z}_t, t, \mathbf{c})\right), \quad t = T, \ldots, 1 \tag{1}$$

Unlike pixel-space UNets, DiTs operate on a flattened latent sequence. The input video is first compressed by a VAE into latent space (downsampled by factors k_s, k_t) and then tokenized. Importantly, DiTs flatten the entire 3D spatiotemporal video volume into a single 1D sequence. For a video of resolution $H \times W \times F$, the resulting sequence length N—which represents the total number of patches across all frames—is:

$$N = \frac{H \cdot W \cdot F}{(k_s \cdot p)^2 \cdot k_t} \tag{2}$$

where p is the patch size. Despite latent compression, N scales linearly with video quality. For high-resolution generation (e.g., $N > 100\text{k}$), the $O(N^2)$ complexity of Self-Attention creates prohibitive memory and compute bottlenecks on single devices, necessitating distributed strategies like Sequence Parallelism.

2.2 Sequence Parallelism

For DiT inference parallelism, minimal batch sizes (e.g., $B = 1$ or 2) make Pipeline Parallelism (PP) suboptimal, favoring intra-layer methods like Tensor Parallelism (TP) and Sequence Parallelism (SP).

Further, SP has become the de facto standard, outperforming TP in two key aspects (Fig. 1). First, while TP partitions model parameters, SP partitions the input sequence across devices. Because DiTs process extremely long sequences with moderate parameter counts, SP better minimizes the dominant activation memory footprint. Second, TP requires frequent All-Reduce synchronizations after every linear projection. In contrast, SP restricts communication solely to the self-attention module, allowing token-wise operations (e.g., LayerNorm, MLPs) to execute independently with zero inter-device communication.

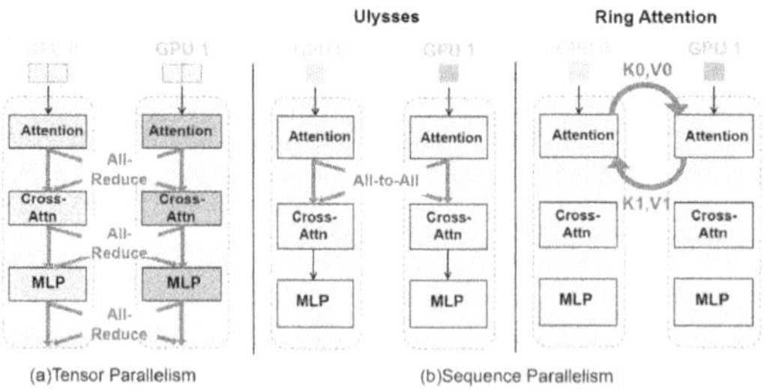

Fig. 1. Comparison of Tensor Parallelism and Sequence Parallelism.

Among SP variants, we adopt DeepSpeed-Ulysses [10] over Ring Attention [14] as our baseline for its superior kernel integrity. Instead of iteratively streaming KV blocks, Ulysses aggregates the full sequence via All-to-All communication to execute a unified attention kernel, maximizing arithmetic intensity. Specifically, given input tensors $Q_i, K_i, V_i \in \mathbb{R}^{\frac{N}{P} \times H \times D}$ on device i, an initial All-to-All reshuffles them to gather the full sequence while splitting the head dimension, yielding $\tilde{Q}_i, \tilde{K}_i, \tilde{V}_i \in \mathbb{R}^{N \times \frac{H}{P} \times D}$ with $O(N \cdot H \cdot D)$ communication volume. Following local attention computation $\tilde{O}_i = \text{Softmax}(\tilde{Q}_i \tilde{K}_i^\top / \sqrt{D})\tilde{V}_i$, a second All-to-All restores the original sequence partitioning $O_i \in \mathbb{R}^{\frac{N}{P} \times H \times D}$ for subsequent layers.

2.3 The Communication Bottleneck Analysis

To quantify Ulysses Parallelism overhead, we profiled a single forward pass across three representative DiT models on an 8-GPU RTX 5090 node equipped with PCIe interconnects (Fig. 2). The Self-Attention mechanism consistently dominates the workload. Crucially, strictly within these attention blocks, the All-to-All communication creates a severe bottleneck, consuming roughly 20% to 34% of the total forward pass time across the evaluated models. In extreme cases, communication accounts for over half of the attention layer's execution time, highlighting the critical need to optimize data transfer in bandwidth-constrained environments.

This bottleneck structurally worsens as GPU compute capabilities outpace interconnect bandwidth growth. Following Amdahl's Law [1], serialized All-to-All communication imposes a theoretical ceiling on achievable speedups. This limitation is severely amplified in multi-node scale-out deployments required for long-context video generation. Therefore, mitigating this communication overhead is a critical necessity for scalable inference.

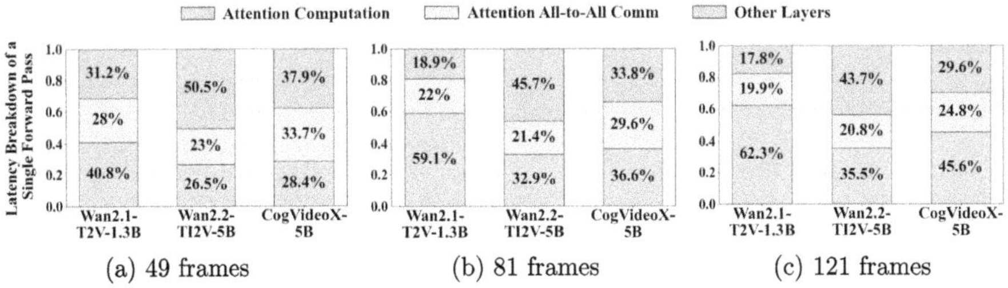

Fig. 2. Latency breakdown of a single forward pass across different models under varying frame settings.

3 Motivation: Empirical Analysis of Key-Value Evolution

3.1 Temporal Coherence in Denoising Trajectories

Our framework is grounded in a key empirical discovery: Key (K) and Value (V) states in diffusion models evolve along continuous and differentiable trajectories, making them highly predictable via local polynomial approximations. This geometric regularity suggests that we can extrapolate future states from historical derivatives, effectively replacing expensive All-to-All communication with low-cost local computation.

To validate this observation, we employ Principal Component Analysis to project the high-dimensional attention tensor trajectories from the Wan2.2-TI2V-5B model into a lower-dimensional space. Figure 3 illustrates this denoising process through two complementary views of the same trajectory: Fig. 3a captures the full sequence ($t = 0$ to 49), while Fig. 3b provides a zoomed-in perspective of the stable regime ($t = 10$ to 49). While both K and V tensors exhibit similar properties, we focus on the K trajectory for clarity.

The global view in Fig. 3a highlights a dramatic scale disparity between the initial and subsequent generation steps. Specifically, the states within the first 8 steps ($t \leq 8$) exhibit massive variance, occupying a value range distinct from the rest of the generation trajectory. This erratic behavior indicates the model undergoes rapid, non-linear state transitions during initialization, where historical data provides little predictive value for the immediate future. Consequently, this phase strictly requires communication to synchronize global context.

Once the initialization chaos subsides, the latent states settle into a well-behaved and coherent path. As revealed in the localized view (Fig. 3b), the trajectory from $t = 13$ to $t = 46$ traces a remarkably smooth curvilinear path. This geometric regularity indicates KV state evolution is governed by consistent local dynamics and underlying continuity. Consequently, state transitions within this window are highly amenable to mathematical modeling. Leveraging this inherent predictability, we can extrapolate future KV states to eliminate redundant communication, without sacrificing the structural integrity of the attention mechanism.

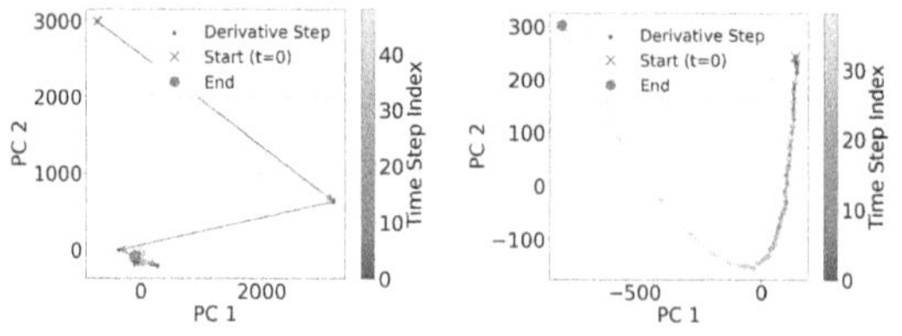

(a) Global Trajectory ($t = 0 \sim 49$)

(b) Local Trajectory ($t = 10 \sim 49$)

Fig. 3. PCA visualization of Key (K) states.

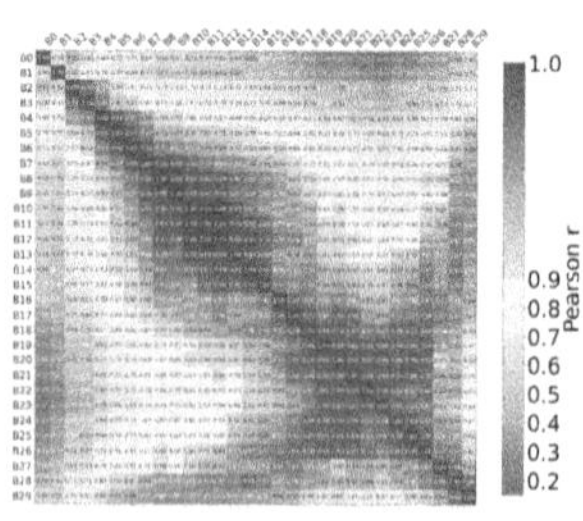

Fig. 4. Epsilon Correlation Across Blocks.

3.2 Motivating the Hermite Basis

To accurately extrapolate future KV states, selecting an appropriate mathematical approximation basis is critical. We discover that the step-to-step differences (ΔK, ΔV) inherently follow a zero-centered, leptokurtic (peaked Gaussian-like) distribution. This statistical prior makes Hermite polynomials the optimal basis for modeling their temporal evolution.

To validate this, we examine the element-wise differences $\Delta K_t = K_t - K_{t-1}$ at representative timesteps within the stable denoising phase. As ΔK and ΔV exhibit nearly identical statistical characteristics, we use ΔK for visualization in our plots. As illustrated in Fig. 5, two consistent statistical properties emerge across the generation process: (1) all distributions are strictly zero-centered ($\mu \approx 10^{-4}$), confirming that KV tensors evolve smoothly without systematic directional drift; and (2) all distributions exhibit strictly positive excess kurtosis, forming a leptokurtic profile that is significantly more peaked with heavier tails than a standard Gaussian distribution [3].

This leptokurtic structure directly motivates our choice of approximation basis [9]. By the Gram-Charlier expansion, any zero-centered leptokurtic distribution decomposes naturally as:

$$p(x) = \phi(x) \left[1 + \frac{\kappa_3}{6} H_3(x) + \frac{\kappa_4}{24} H_4(x) + \cdots \right], \tag{3}$$

where $\phi(x)$ is the Gaussian density and $H_n(x)$ the n-th Hermite polynomial. Crucially, Hermite polynomials form a canonical basis that is orthogonal with respect to the Gaussian weight function $w(x) = e^{-x^2/2}$, satisfying the condition:

$$\int_{-\infty}^{+\infty} H_n(x) H_m(x) e^{-x^2/2} dx = \sqrt{2\pi} n! \cdot \delta_{nm}, \tag{4}$$

where δ_{nm} is the Kronecker delta. This orthogonal property ensures that each higher-order term independently captures a specific mode of deviation from the Gaussian ideal, directly motivating their adoption in Sparsh.

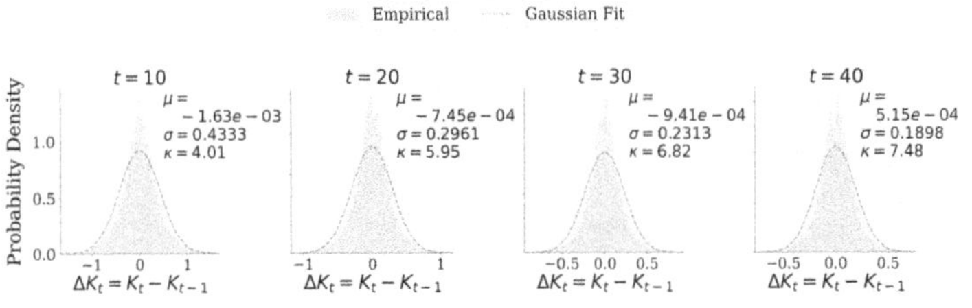

Fig. 5. Statistical Properties of KV state differences ($\Delta K/\Delta V$) in Wan2.2.

4 Design

Driven by the analysis in Sect. 3, we propose a KV predicting framework. It comprises a Hermite-based Predictive Model (Sect. 4.1) for KV approximation and an Adaptive Hybrid Policy (Sect. 4.2) for dynamic control.

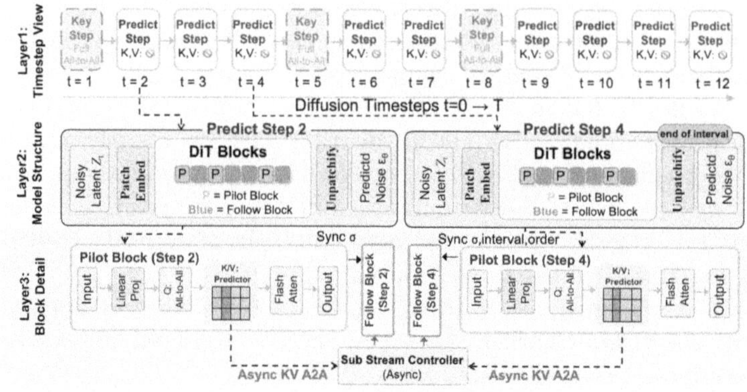

Fig. 6. Sparsh Overview.

4.1 Hermite-Based Predictive KV Estimation

We formulate a lightweight predictive model grounded in Hermite interpolation to approximate the evolution of KV states during the stable denoising phase. While Eq. 3 identifies Hermite polynomials as the canonical basis for describing static feature distributions, we leverage them here as a temporal basis to extrapolate future states. For either tensor $T \in \{K, V\}$, the general prediction at step t is expansion-based around a synchronized key step t_{anc} (i.e., the step where full communication occurred). To bridge the gap between continuous Hermite basis and discrete denoising steps, we define Δt as the synchronization interval between consecutive key steps. Let P_i denote the KV state cached at the i-th most recent key step, such that $P_0 = T_{t_{key}}$ corresponds to the most recently synchronized state. We then formulate the prediction as:

$$\widehat{T}_t = P_0 + \sum_{n=1}^{N} \frac{\Delta^{(n)} P_0}{n!} \cdot \tilde{H}_n(x) \tag{5}$$

where $\Delta^{(n)} P_0$ represents the n-th order forward difference (e.g., $\Delta^{(1)} P_0 = P_0 - P_1$, $\Delta^{(2)} P_0 = P_0 - 2P_1 + P_2$), serving as a discrete proxy for the continuous n-th order derivatives [16]. To ensure numerical stability during this extrapolation, we map the relative prediction horizon to a normalized coordinate $x = \frac{t - t_{key}}{\Delta t} \cdot \sigma$, where $\sigma \in (0, 1)$ acts as a contraction factor that scales down the evaluation coordinate x, bounding the magnitude of higher-order Hermite terms and thereby limiting error amplification during extrapolation—a known challenge in high-order trajectory extrapolation [11]. An initial σ is determined via offline profiling before inference, and subsequently refined online by the adaptive policy in Sect. 4.2. Within this contracted space, $\tilde{H}_1(x) = 2x$ and $\tilde{H}_2(x) = 4x^2 - 2$ capture the local velocity and acceleration of the KV trajectory.

4.2 Adaptive Hybrid Scheduling Policy

While the KV trajectory is smooth, relying solely on open-loop extrapolation entails risks: small approximation errors can accumulate over long sequences, causing the predicted state to drift from the ground truth. To prevent this, we propose an adaptive closed-loop system (Fig. 6) that dynamically tunes prediction parameters (prediction interval Δt, contraction factor σ, and polynomial order N) based on real-time feedback.

Offline Calibration and Initialization. Before deployment, Sparsh performs lightweight offline profiling to initialize a robust configuration via three consecutive steps: temporal window identification, structural block grouping, and controller parameter calibration.

First, we profile KV differences across all timesteps to identify the stable temporal interval $[T_{start}, T_{end}]$, typically excluding the chaotic initial steps and the final refinement steps, within which the prediction is activated. As the transition from chaotic structural formation to stable denoising is primarily governed by the pre-trained diffusion scheduler's SNR evolution, this temporal window remains highly consistent across diverse prompts.

Second, to enable lightweight online control, we partition the L transformer blocks based on inter-layer prediction error similarity. Observing a strong diagonal block structure in the Pearson correlation matrix (Fig. 4), we sequentially assign blocks into groups. A new Pilot Block is anchored whenever its error correlation with the current Pilot drops below $\rho = 0.9$. Remaining Follower Blocks are assigned to their most correlated adjacent Pilot. This yields K disjoint groups ($K \ll L$), where one Pilot reliably represents the error dynamics for its entire follower group.

Third, using the stable temporal window and block grouping above, we perform a final calibration pass with prediction enabled to set the initial prediction interval Δt, contraction factor σ, and sensitivity thresholds (ϵ_{safe}, ϵ_{danger}). Thresholds are defined as relative quantiles of the profiled error distribution. We empirically anchor ϵ_{safe} at P_{20} and ϵ_{danger} at P_{80}.

Asynchronous Online Controller. While offline calibration provides a solid foundation, relying solely on static values during inference remains insufficient. The generative process of Diffusion Transformers is inherently dynamic. Different input prompts and random seeds create varying trajectory complexities that deviate from the calibrated profile. Furthermore, prediction errors naturally

Algorithm 1: Pilot-Guided Adaptive Control Policy

Input: Current step t, prediction start step T_{start}, current params $(\sigma, N, \Delta t)$

$\mathbf{v}_t \leftarrow K_t - K_{t-1}, \quad \mathbf{a}_t \leftarrow \mathbf{v}_t - \mathbf{v}_{t-1}$;

$\varepsilon \leftarrow \max\left(\frac{\|\widehat{K}-K_{gt}\|}{\|K_{gt}\|}, \frac{\|\widehat{V}-V_{gt}\|}{\|V_{gt}\|}\right)$; /* prediction error */

$\rho \leftarrow \|\mathbf{a}_t\|/(\|\mathbf{v}_t\| + \delta)$; /* curvature ratio */

/* Every predict step: update σ */

if $\varepsilon > \epsilon_{danger}$ **then** $\sigma \leftarrow \sigma \times \alpha$;

/* Every key step: update N and Δt */

if $(t - T_{start}) \bmod \Delta t = 0$ **then**

  if $\varepsilon > \epsilon_{danger}$ ***and*** $\rho > \rho^*$ **then**

    $N \leftarrow 2, \quad \sigma \leftarrow \sigma \times \alpha, \quad \Delta t \leftarrow \Delta t_{init}$;

  else if $\varepsilon > \epsilon_{danger}$ **then**

    $N \leftarrow 1, \quad \sigma \leftarrow \sigma \times \alpha^{-1}, \quad \Delta t \leftarrow \Delta t_{init}$;

  else if $\varepsilon < \epsilon_{safe}$ **then**

    $\Delta t \leftarrow \Delta t + 1$;

  Broadcast $(\sigma, N, \Delta t)$ to Follower Blocks;

return $(\sigma, N, \Delta t)$;

accumulate during iterative denoising steps and propagate through the network depth. Without real-time correction, fixed configurations risk being either too conservative, limiting speedup, or too aggressive, introducing visual artifacts. Therefore, we introduce an online, closed-loop, and crucially asynchronous feedback mechanism.

Leveraging the established Pilot-Follower structure, the runtime workflow operates as a continuous cycle detailed in Algorithm 1. Immediately after a Pilot Block's prediction, the system launches non-blocking All-to-All communication on a dedicated CUDA stream to retrieve the ground-truth KV, allowing the GPU to proceed with attention computation without stalling. Upon completion of communication, a lightweight CPU worker thread asynchronously quantifies the relative prediction error and trajectory curvature to assess generation quality.

Based on these two metrics, the controller employs a hierarchical adaptation policy. First, as an immediate safety mechanism, the contraction factor σ tightens whenever the error exceeds a danger threshold (ϵ_{danger}), preventing divergence in subsequent steps. Second, at synchronization steps, the controller adjusts structural parameters ($\Delta t, N$) according to trajectory complexity. When high error coincides with high curvature ($\rho > \rho^*$), indicating a non-linear manifold transition, the controller uses higher-order prediction, resets Δt, and recalibrates σ to a smaller value. Crucially, we cap $N = 2$ to avoid overfitting transient spikes, because per-step KV transitions exhibit a leptokurtic distribution ($\kappa \gg 3$) sensitive to high-order terms (Fig. 5). Meanwhile, the local trajectory remains smooth (Fig. 3b), confirming low-order polynomials suffice to capture underlying dynamics. When error is high but curvature is low (linear drift), the controller reverts to linear prediction ($N = 1$), resets Δt, and recalibrates σ to a larger value. Finally, when error falls below the safety margin ϵ_{safe}, indicating a stable regime, the controller incrementally extends Δt to maximize efficiency.

These updated parameters are broadcast to all Follower Blocks in the same group and carried over by the Pilot Block for its next timestep. This ensures the entire group adapts synchronously to the current generation difficulty without incurring communication overhead for follower layers.

5 Evaluation

5.1 Experimental Setup

Testbed. We evaluate on a node with 8 × NVIDIA RTX 5090 GPUs via PCIe 5.0 (41 GB/s unidirectional, no P2P). For multi-node scalability, we use a 2-node cluster (4 × H200 GPUs per node) with intra-node NVLink (900 GB/s bidirectional) and 200 Gbps inter-node RoCE.

Models and Workloads. We evaluate Sparsh on three representative video generation models (Table 1). We focus on the 1.3B to 5B parameter range as it represents the standard deployment target for commodity clusters, effectively balancing generation quality against memory constraints.

Baseline Setting. We implement Sparsh upon DeepSpeed-Ulysses, sharing identical attention kernels and communication primitives across all baselines. We set the sequence parallelism size (P) to the maximum divisor of the attention head count (H) that does not exceed the total number of GPUs. This maximizes the degree of parallelism while strictly satisfying the partition constraint ($H \pmod{P} = 0$).

Table 1. Model configurations used in evaluation.

Model	Params	Resolution	Frames	Seq Length	Head Config ($H \times D$)
Wan2.1-1.3B	1.3B	832 × 480	81	32760	12 × 128
Wan2.2-5B	5B	1280 × 704	121	27280	24 × 128
CogVideoX-5B	5B	720 × 480	49	19360	48 × 64

5.2 Overall Performance

We evaluate Sparsh on generation efficiency and quality against the standard Ulysses baseline. Efficiency is measured by end-to-end latency speedup and communication time speedup. For quality, we adopt VBench [7] and report PSNR, SSIM, and LPIPS to quantify frame-level fidelity against baseline outputs. We curate a subset of 295 VBench prompts, utilizing Gemini 3 Pro to enrich them with intricate motion, dynamic lighting, and high-frequency textures (e.g., fur and fluid spray). This expansion ensures our evaluation captures complex Q-KV interactions across chaotic trajectories rather than simple static scenes. This setup provides a comprehensive assessment of our system's robustness and its ability to maintain temporal dependencies across varied generative intensities.

Generation Efficiency. As illustrated in Fig. 7, Sparsh significantly optimizes the critical path by reducing the All-to-All communication time by up to 1.38× compared to the Ulysses baseline. This efficiency is driven by our adaptive controller, which successfully skips redundant data transfers based on real-time feature redundancy. Quantitatively, Table 2 confirms that Sparsh consistently elevates end-to-end throughput across all workloads, increasing the total speedup from 4.47× to 4.84× on CogVideo-5B, while maintaining a steady 5%–8% marginal gain on the Wan2.x series.

By effectively alleviating the communication bottleneck, Sparsh provides immediate gains on our PCIe testbed. Furthermore, this reduction in data movement is decisive for bandwidth-limited environments, inherently ensuring superior scaling potential. To verify multi-node scalability, we evaluate CogVideoX-5B ($P = 8$) on a 2-node cluster equipped with 8 NVIDIA H200 GPUs. In this distributed setting, where overall communication accounts for ~25% of total generation latency, Sparsh compresses communication time to 74% of the baseline. This yields a 1.07× end-to-end speedup, aligning with our single-node observations and confirming the framework's robustness.

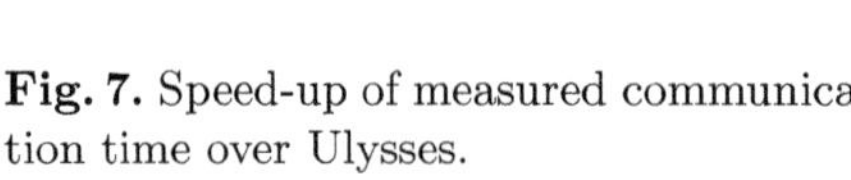

Fig. 7. Speed-up of measured communication time over Ulysses.

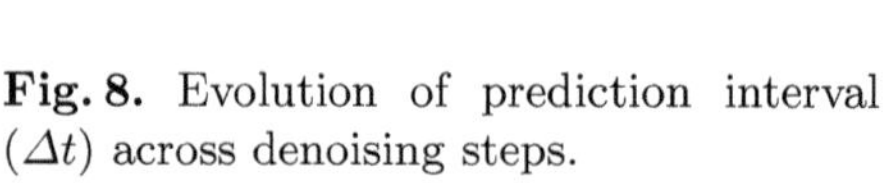

Fig. 8. Evolution of prediction interval (Δt) across denoising steps.

Generation Quality. As shown in Table 2, pixel-level similarity metrics (LPIPS, PSNR, SSIM) confirm that Sparsh outputs remain highly faithful to the baseline across all three models. Furthermore, on Wan2.2-TI2V-5B, the highest-quality model among our testbed and thus the most demanding for detecting perceptual degradation, Sparsh achieves a VBench total score of 84.41 versus the baseline's 85.69, a deviation of less than 1.5%. These results demonstrate that the efficiency gains of Sparsh come with negligible impact on visual fidelity.

Table 2. Comparison of inference speedup (relative to single-GPU) and generation quality. Sparsh†: static variant. Sparsh: full adaptive variant.

Model	Method	E2E Speedup ↑	Generation Quality		
			LPIPS ↓	PSNR ↑	SSIM ↑
Wan2.2-5B	Ulysses	3.12×	–	–	–
	Sparsh†	3.27×	0.142	22.01	0.792
	Sparsh **(Ours)**	3.30×	0.080	24.50	0.862
Wan2.1-1.3B	Ulysses	3.84×	–	–	–
	Sparsh†	4.04×	0.148	20.87	0.781
	Sparsh **(Ours)**	4.07×	0.085	24.23	0.868
CogVideo-5B	Ulysses	4.47×	–	–	–
	Sparsh†	4.79×	0.203	20.39	0.836
	Sparsh **(Ours)**	4.84×	0.102	23.78	0.903

5.3 Asynchronous Control Evaluation

Control Dynamics and Stability. Figure 8 illustrates the controller real-time prediction interval Δt evolution during $[T_{start}, T_{end}]$ for two contrasting Wan2.2-5B prompts. For low-variance static scenes (e.g., a green chair), it rapidly expands Δt to maximize throughput. Conversely, under highly chaotic dynamics (e.g., lions fighting), a fail-safe mechanism dynamically contracts Δt whenever prediction error ϵ breaches ϵ_{danger} from abrupt feature shifts.

Quantitatively (Table 2), this content-aware policy improves both efficiency and visual fidelity. Compared to the static baseline Sparsh† (e.g., fixed $\Delta t = 3$ for Wan2.2-5B), our adaptive approach achieves higher end-to-end speedup and boosts generation quality (PSNR: 24.50 vs. 22.01). Our asynchronous update mechanism drives this benefit by dynamically optimizing the Hermite parameter (σ) and prediction interval (Δt).

Overhead Hiding of Asynchronous Control. Decoupling control logic from the critical path via CPU multi-threading and GPU sub-streams is our key design advantage. Profiling confirms that even on CogVideo-5B, where one Transformer block only takes 14.7ms, the entire 4ms control pipeline (2ms asynchronous KV transfer, 2ms policy computation) is fully hidden within block execution. Measuring end-to-end latency of Sparsh† with and without the controller (fixing Δt) shows negligible throughput degradation ($< 0.1\%$). This proves primary computation entirely overlaps controller operations, yielding adaptive gains with zero latency penalty.

5.4 Memory Overhead and Hardware Implications

While Sparsh introduces a space-for-time trade-off by caching historical KV states, this overhead is largely inconsequential at the system level. As Table 3

Table 3. Peak memory overhead analysis per GPU.

Model	Config.	Denoise (GB)	M_{extra} (GB)	Overall (GB)
Wan2.2-Ti2V (1.3B)	Ulysses	16.83	–	24.07
	Sparsh (BF16)	22.46	+5.63	24.07
	Sparsh (FP8)	19.65	+2.82	24.07
Wan2.2-Ti2V (5B)*	Ulysses	15.07	–	23.05
	Sparsh (BF16)	22.33	+7.26	23.05
	Sparsh (FP8)	18.81	+3.74	23.05
CogVideoX (5B)	Ulysses	20.45	–	23.48
	Sparsh (BF16)	26.52	+6.07	26.52
	Sparsh (FP8)	23.50	+3.05	23.50

shows, in end-to-end pipelines, the VAE decoding phase typically dictates the peak memory footprint. Consequently, the additional denoising memory required by Sparsh is effectively masked, resulting in zero increase to the overall pipeline peak memory. For scenarios where denoising memory does bottleneck the system (e.g., CogVideoX), we introduce an FP8 KV cache optimization. Storing historical states in FP8 reduces the extra memory footprint by ~50% with no noticeable qualitative visual degradation, though rigorous quantitative benchmarking is deferred to future work.

6 Related Work

Communication Optimizations in Sequence Parallelism. To alleviate the communication wall in distributed sequence parallelism, existing system-level optimizations, including Ring Attention [14], LightSeq [12], and USP [4], hide latency via computation-communication overlapping or optimized routing. However, these methods still transmit full KV tensors, and in practice the fragmented computation across devices often fails to perfectly overlap with this sheer data volume. In contrast, Sparsh takes an orthogonal approach by reducing the data payload itself via Hermite polynomial forecasting, breaking the bandwidth wall while preserving the standard attention execution graph.

Temporal Redundancy in Diffusion Models. Recent works exploit temporal coherence across denoising steps via two paradigms: block-skipping (TeaCache [13], PAB [21]) and feature prediction (HiCache [5], TaylorSeer [15]). However, both paradigms are primarily optimized for single-GPU execution and require global synchronization across blocks in distributed settings, introducing significant consensus overhead. Furthermore, approximating final outputs severs the semantic interaction between the dynamic Query and its context. Sparsh targets communication-level redundancy with a unified execution flow, ensuring native compatibility with large-scale parallel systems.

7 Conclusion

We presented Sparsh, a KV prediction system that accelerates Diffusion Transformer inference under Ulysses sequence parallelism by reducing KV communication overhead. Leveraging the smooth evolution of KV states in the stable denoising phase, we employ Hermite-based extrapolation to predict future KVs without communication. To handle dynamic generation conditions, an adaptive Pilot-Follower controller continuously monitors prediction errors and adjusts extrapolation parameters at runtime. Experiments demonstrate that Sparsh effectively reduces communication cost while preserving generation quality, with pronounced benefits in bandwidth-constrained deployment scenarios.

Acknowledgements and Artifact Availability. This research is supported by the National Key R&D Program of China under Grant No.2025YFB3003501, the National Natural Science Foundation of China under Grant No.62402534, the GuangDong Basic and Applied Basic Research Foundation under Grant No.2023A1515110117, the Yunnan Provincial Major Science and Technology Special Plan Projects under Grant No.202502AD080009, the Pazhou Lab Research Project No. PZL2023KF0001, and the Alibaba Innovative Research. The artifact associated with this paper is available in the Zenodo repository. [8]

Disclosure of Interests. The authors have no competing interests to declare that are relevant to the content of this article.

References

1. Amdahl, G.M.: Validity of the single processor approach to achieving large scale computing capabilities. In: AFIPS SJCC, pp. 483–485 (1967)
2. Brooks, T.: Video generation models as world simulators. OpenAI (2024)
3. DeCarlo, L.T.: On the meaning and use of kurtosis. Psychol. Methods **2**, 292 (1997)
4. Fang, J., Zhao, S.: USP: A unified sequence parallelism approach for long context generative AI. arXiv preprint arXiv:2405.07719 (2024)
5. Feng, L.: HiCache: Training-free acceleration of diffusion models via Hermite polynomial-based feature caching. arXiv preprint arXiv:2508.16984 (2025)
6. Ho, J., Jain, A., Abbeel, P.: Denoising diffusion probabilistic models. Adv. Neural. Inf. Process. Syst. **33**, 6840–6851 (2020)
7. Huang, Z.: VBench: Comprehensive benchmark suite for video generative models, pp. 21807–21818. CVPR (2024)
8. Huimin, L., et al.: Sparsh: breaking the communication bottleneck in sequence parallel video diffusion inference with predictive sparse communication. Zenodo (2026). https://doi.org/10.5281/zenodo.20521419
9. Hyvärinen, A., Oja, E.: Independent component analysis: algorithms and applications. Neural Netw. **13**(4–5), 411–430 (2000)
10. Jacobs, S.A.: DeepSpeed Ulysses: System optimizations for enabling training of extreme long sequence transformer models (2023). arXiv:2309.14509
11. Karras, T.: Analyzing and improving the training dynamics of diffusion models, pp. 24174–24184. CVPR (2024)

12. Li, D.: LightSeq: Sequence level parallelism for distributed training of long context transformers. arXiv preprint arXiv:2310.03262 (2023)
13. Liu, F.: Timestep embedding tells: It's time to cache for video diffusion model. arXiv preprint arXiv:2411.19108 (2025)
14. Liu, H., Zaharia, M., Abbeel, P.: Ring attention with Blockwise transformers for near-infinite context. arXiv preprint arXiv:2310.01889 (2023)
15. Liu, J., et al.: From reusing to forecasting: accelerating diffusion models with TaylorSeers. In: ICCV, pp. 15853–15863 (2025)
16. Lu, C.: DPM-solver: A fast ode solver for diffusion probabilistic model sampling in around 10 steps. arXiv preprint arXiv:2206.00927 (2022)
17. Peebles, W., Xie, S.: Scalable diffusion models with transformers. In: ICCV, pp. 4195–4205 (2023)
18. Song, J., Meng, C., Ermon, S.: Denoising diffusion implicit models. arXiv preprint arXiv:2010.02502 (2020)
19. Team, W.: Wan: Open and advanced large-scale video generative models. arXiv preprint arXiv:2503.20314 (2025)
20. Yang, Z.: CogVideoX: Text-to-video diffusion models with an expert transformer. arXiv preprint arXiv:2408.06072 (2024)
21. Zhao, X., Jin, X., Wang, K., You, Y.: Real-time video generation with pyramid attention broadcast. arXiv preprint arXiv:2408.12588 (2024)

Privacy-Preserving Data Center Demand Response Using Multi-party Computation

Seyda Nur Guzelhan(✉), Fatih Acun, Can Hankendi, Ayse K. Coskun, and Ajay Joshi

Boston University, Boston, MA 02215, USA
{seyda,acun,hankendi,acoskun,joshi}@bu.edu

Abstract. The rapid growth of AI has significantly increased data center energy demand, placing increasing pressure on power grids. Demand Response (DR) programs utilize the flexibility of power consumers, such as data centers, to help balance the supply and demand in power grids. In collaborative data center DR participation, multiple data centers share information with an external coordinator for improved power dispatch and quality of service for their workloads. However, disclosing sensitive information such as power usage and workload performance to an untrusted third party raises significant privacy concerns. To address this, we use Multi-Party Computation (MPC) to perform secure power dispatch without revealing sensitive inputs. Standard MPC has heavy communication overhead, which challenges real-time DR requirements. To meet real-time DR requirements, we optimize our system by tailoring fixed-point bitwidths and substituting expensive divisions with polynomial approximations and Newton-Raphson iterations. Evaluated using the MP-SPDZ library, our optimizations yield up to 33× fewer communication rounds and a 45× speedup, delivering sub-second latency for up to 16 data centers while matching the power dispatch accuracy of the baseline.

Keywords: Collaborative Data Center Demand Response · Privacy · Multi-Party Computation

1 Introduction

The rapid rise of artificial intelligence (AI) and cloud computing applications has driven a sharp increase in both the number and the scale of data centers [15]. Being large-scale electricity consumers with unique power consumption profiles, data center loads create new operational challenges for power grids [26]. However, with their real-time workload modulation capabilities, data centers are uniquely suited to support power grids by dynamically adjusting their power consumption through participation in the demand response (DR) programs. Independent System Operators (ISOs) run DR programs to coordinate with flexible electricity users, requesting increases or decreases in power consumption to balance the

M. Torquati et al. (Eds.): Euro-Par 2026, LNCS 16781, pp. 641–655, 2027.
https://doi.org/10.1007/978-3-032-35248-4_44

grid supply and demand. Prior work on data center DR (DCDR) participation employs methods such as hardware power capping and workload scheduling to modulate data center power consumption while satisfying workloads' quality-of-service (QoS) requirements [16,30]. To further reduce the risk of QoS violations and increase compatibility with DR requirements, collaborative DCDR enables workload migration across data centers that are owned by the same company [29]. Recent frameworks introduce collaboration across data centers without needing workload migration: a third-party aggregates real-time metrics from multiple data centers to determine power targets that respect each facility's QoS requirements [2], as illustrated in Fig. 1a. However, this approach creates a fundamental tension between coordination and privacy. To participate, data centers may need to share operational information, such as power usage and workload latency, with the coordinating entity. Such data can be commercially sensitive, as power consumption patterns may reflect aspects of facility utilization and operational scale, while QoS-related metrics can provide insight into service-level objectives and system performance margins. These concerns are not hypothetical: industry surveys identify privacy as a primary barrier to inter-operator coordination in energy markets [15]. Thus, the reluctance to share operational details is a key barrier to broader adoption of collaborative DCDR.

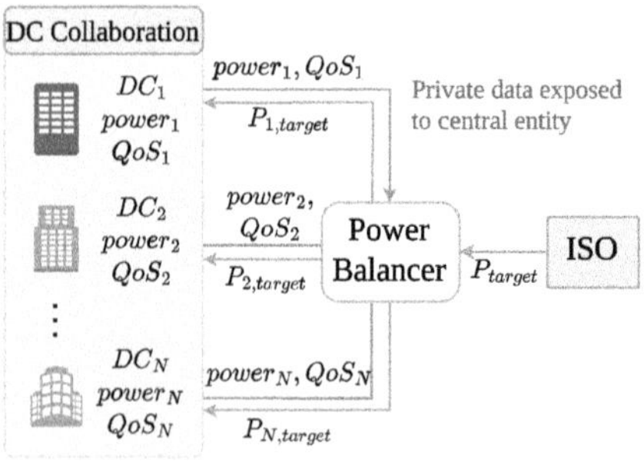

(a) Plain collaborative DCDR.

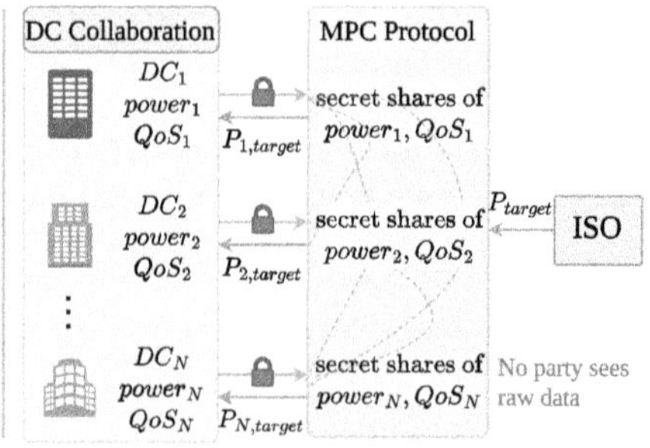

(b) Proposed secure collaborative DCDR.

Fig. 1. Overview of the plain and secure collaborative DCDR frameworks. In the plain setting, data centers reveal some of their operational constraints to a third-party aggregator. In the secure setting, data centers secret-share their constraints, and the aggregator computes the power allocation without accessing raw data.

In addition to the privacy problem, DR programs like Regulation Service Reserves (RSR) are latency-sensitive, leaving little margin for secure computation overhead. Differential Privacy injects noise that degrades dispatch quality at small coalition sizes [10], and Homomorphic Encryption incurs costs orders of magnitude above plaintext, making real-time deployment infeasible [11]. Multiparty computation (MPC) is a natural fit: multiple parties jointly evaluate a function over private inputs without revealing them [12]. MPC produces exact outputs, preserving the correctness of the power dispatch, and its overhead is dominated by communication rounds rather than computation, which can be optimized for the specific operations in the target formula. We therefore focus on MPC in this paper.

In this work, we design a *secure collaborative DCDR system* that replaces the untrusted third-party coordinator with an efficient MPC-based protocol (Fig. 1b). Each participant secret-shares its power consumption and QoS parameters, and the coordinating party executes the allocation entirely over the shares, producing optimal power targets without ever accessing the underlying data. However, directly evaluating the allocation formula under MPC is prohibitively expensive due to two sources of overhead. First, the default 64-bit fixed-point representation allocates precision far beyond what physical power sensors provide; since communication volume scales linearly with bitwidth, the excess precision directly inflates message sizes. Second, each secure division on 64-bit operands costs roughly 40 sequential communication rounds, compared to 2 rounds for a multiplication, making divisions the dominant cost driver: at a 5 ms round trip time, a single division alone incurs over 200 ms of network-induced latency. To address these, we tailor the fixed-point bitwidth to the range of power and QoS values, which is publicly known from hardware specifications and service-level agreements, and we replace the costly secure divisions with a two-stage reciprocal method that uses iterative multiplications [5,25].

We demonstrate the efficacy of our design using a recent collaborative DCDR framework, Conductor [2], which coordinates participation in the RSR program by dynamically allocating the ISO's aggregate power target across data centers in a QoS- and power-aware manner. We choose Conductor because it does not require inter–data center workload migration and relies only on plaintext information sharing for power allocation, leaving room for stronger privacy enhancements. We implement the secure power allocation in MP-SPDZ [17], a highly optimized multi-protocol MPC library, and benchmark performance across different security settings. Our contributions are as follows:

- We design and evaluate an MPC-based secure collaborative DCDR system that eliminates the need to disclose private data to any coordinating entity.
- We optimize our system by introducing tailored fixed-point representations for secure arithmetic and by replacing costly secure division operations with a two-stage Chebyshev–Newton–Raphson reciprocal method.
- We provide a comprehensive empirical evaluation along four axes: (1) security settings spanning semi-honest to malicious adversaries, (2) scalability up to 64 data centers, (3) arithmetic precision sensitivity of the power dispatch, and (4) MPC communication costs under local- and wide-area networks.

Our optimizations yield up to a 33× reduction in communication rounds and a 45× reduction in end-to-end latency compared to a naïve MPC implementation using default MP-SPDZ arithmetic. As a result, our framework delivers sub-second execution for up to 16 data centers and sub-minute execution for 64 data centers, while matching the power dispatch accuracy of the plaintext Conductor.

The rest of the paper is as follows: Sect. 2 reviews related work on DCDR and privacy-preserving smart grid protocols. Section 3 provides preliminaries on collaborative DCDR and MPC. Section 4 presents our MPC-based DCDR method. Section 5 evaluates the framework across security models, arithmetic precisions, and network conditions. Section 6 concludes the paper.

2 Related Work

Securing collaborative DCDR sits at the intersection of two lines of research: mechanisms for DCDR programs, and privacy-preserving protocols for smart grid applications. We survey each and identify the gap that motivates our work.

Data Center Demand Response. Data centers have been widely studied as candidates for participation in DR programs, including emergency DR and RSR [6,13]. Prior work proposes a range of mechanisms to modulate data center power draw in accordance with program requirements, such as hardware power capping, job co-location, and temporal workload shifting [16,20]. An important challenge in these approaches is preserving workload QoS requirements while enforcing power constraints. To mitigate QoS degradation, QoS-aware techniques proactively meet service targets by allocating compute resources according to application-level requirements [30]. Prior work considers collaborative DCDR to further improve QoS and enhance DR performance by migrating workloads between data centers [29]. Complementary studies consider collaboration across data centers without migrating workloads, instead coordinating DR participation by dynamically redistributing power budgets across data centers to meet a shared target [2]. Similar to multi-data-center collaboration, tenant-level collaboration has been explored in multi-tenant data centers via game-theoretic and market-based frameworks for DR participation [7].

Privacy-Preserving Protocols in Smart Power Grids. MPC has seen growing adoption in the smart grid [9]. However, the computational profile of existing MPC deployments differs fundamentally from what DCDR requires. Privacy-preserving smart metering protocols [22] aggregate integer-valued power readings over billing intervals, where both the input domain and the update frequency are modest enough that MPC's communication overhead remains manageable. Peer-to-peer energy trading extends MPC to market-clearing mechanisms [28], but the computation is triggered once per auction round, so latency pressure is limited. Power flow studies using MPC [14] demonstrate that richer numerical workloads are feasible in principle; however, these analyses solve a single static snapshot offline and do not contend with repeated, time-critical updates. Tian et al. [27] propose a private multi-area economic dispatch under a semi-honest threat model, demonstrating that MPC can handle real-valued grid optimizations, but their framework solves a single optimization problem without real-time latency requirements and does not analyze stronger adversary models. What is missing from this body of work is an MPC pipeline that meets collaborative DCDR requirements: real-valued inputs, sub-second re-execution, and robustness across threat models.

3 Preliminaries

In this section, we provide the background for the collaborative DCDR setting and the sensitive data problem (Sect. 3.1), and the MPC primitives that enable a secure evaluation (Sect. 3.2).

3.1 Collaborative Data Center Demand Response

Data centers can effectively engage in DR programs by utilizing hardware power capping and power-aware scheduling to modulate their power consumption [16]. They can adjust their power consumption rapidly and provide seconds-granularity DR, as required in RSR programs [23]. In the RSR program, participants declare their average power consumption, $\bar{P}$, and reserve capacity, R, before program execution. During execution, the participant is required to track a power target, updated every few seconds (e.g., 2 s), calculated as follows:

$$P_{\text{target}}(t) = \bar{P} + y(t)R, \tag{1}$$

where $y(t) \in [-1, 1]$ denotes the regulation signal. Accordingly, the target power ranges from $\bar{P} - R$ to $\bar{P} + R$. Performance on power tracking (tracking error) is measured as the absolute distance between the power target and the consumption (P_{consumed}) normalized by the provided reserve, $|P_{\text{target}}(t) - P_{\text{consumed}}(t)|/R$.

In collaborative RSR participation, multiple data centers form a coalition and interact with the grid as a single aggregated resource. The coalition receives a single power target, $P_{\text{target}}(t)$, which is then distributed among the participating data centers as individual targets, $P_{i,\text{target}}(t)$. This collaborative setting is motivated by the observation that aggregate DR targets can often be satisfied more effectively through coordinated power allocation across sites than by enforcing identical power constraints independently at each data center. By accounting for differences in workload QoS sensitivity across data centers, such coordination can reduce QoS violations while improving tracking of the aggregate DR target. Prior work, Conductor [2], has demonstrated the potential of this collaborative approach for mitigating QoS violations in data centers and improving the power tracking capability as a collaboration. Our implementation for the baseline collaborative DCDR follows the design introduced in Conductor, in which each data center provides real-time operational signals, such as QoS-related metrics, to a power balancer, which determines QoS-aware per-data-center power targets. The power balancer calculates the individual power target by distributing the collaborative power target based on proportional allocation with respect to the real-time QoS (Q_i^R) and the average power consumption ($\bar{P}_i$) of each data center, denoted by subscript i, as follows:

$$P_{\text{i,target}}(t) = P_{\text{target}}(t) \left(\tau \frac{Q_i^R(t)}{\sum_{k=1}^{N} Q_k^R(t)} + \phi \frac{\bar{P}_i}{\sum_{k=1}^{N} \bar{P}_k} \right), \tag{2}$$

where $P_{\text{target}}(t)$ is the total power target for data center collaboration at time t, $P_{\text{i,target}}(t)$ is the power budget assigned by the power balancer to a data center, τ and ϕ are parameters to balance the impact of Q^R and $\bar{P}$ on power allocations, and N is the total number of data centers in the collaboration.

In this collaborative DCDR setting, data centers currently exchange information with the power balancer in plaintext. However, both QoS and power consumption can be commercially sensitive, especially when data centers belong to different organizations. To address this confidentiality gap, we use MPC to compute QoS-aware power allocations without learning any individual data center's raw QoS metrics or power consumption.

3.2 Multi-party Computation (MPC)

MPC enables N mutually distrusting parties to jointly evaluate a function f while guaranteeing two properties: 1) correctness, such that the output matches the result of computing f on plaintext inputs, and 2) privacy, such that no coalition of corrupted parties learns anything beyond what can be inferred from their own inputs and the output [12]. In our setting, the function f is the power allocation in Eq. 2, and each data center's QoS metric and power consumption serve as private inputs.

Threat Models. MPC security guarantees depend on assumptions about the adversary's behavior and reach. A *semi-honest* adversary follows the protocol but tries to infer private information from observed messages, while a *malicious* adversary may deviate arbitrarily to learn private data or corrupt the output [12]. The corruption threshold t specifies how many of the N parties the adversary may control: protocols with $t < N/2$ operate in the *honest-majority* setting, while those tolerating $t \geq N/2$ assume *dishonest majority* and require heavier cryptographic primitives such as oblivious transfer [18,19]. Stronger threat models provide broader protection but at higher communication cost, a trade-off we quantify across four protocol families in Sect. 5.

Cost of Secure Arithmetic. MPC protocols split each private input into secret shares distributed across all parties, such that any subset below the corruption threshold learns nothing about the original value [24]. Local arithmetic on these shares is lightweight, but any operation that combines values held by different parties requires all parties to exchange messages and wait for a full network round-trip time (RTT) before the protocol can proceed. It is this communication that dominates MPC cost, as total latency grows linearly with the number of sequential communication rounds.

The number of required rounds and the amount of data that must be exchanged depend on the operation. Addition of shared values is non-interactive: each party simply adds its local shares. Multiplication requires 2 rounds to consume a precomputed triple [4], with message size scaling with operand bitwidth. Division is far more expensive on both counts: MPC provides no native inverse for encoded real numbers, so a single secure division on 64-bit operands costs roughly 40 sequential rounds, compared to 2 rounds for a multiplication [5,17]. For parties connected over a wide-area network with an RTT of 5 ms, this means a single division alone incurs at least $40 \times 5 = 200$ ms of network-induced latency, independent of compute power, while a multiplication adds only 5–10 ms. Division is therefore the primary cost driver in secure collaborative DCDR, and the main target for the optimizations presented in Sect. 4.

Fixed-Point Arithmetic. MPC protocols natively operate over finite fields or rings, not real numbers [8]. To handle the real-valued quantities in Eq. 2, values are encoded in fixed-point representation with ℓ bits of precision, with each multiplication incurring an additional truncation round [5]. The choice of ℓ directly affects both accuracy and cost: too few bits introduce numerical errors, while too many inflate the field size and increase communication [5,21]. When input values are bounded to a known range, as is the case for power and QoS metrics, the bitwidth can be tailored accordingly rather than set conservatively. We exploit this in Sect. 4.

Online and Offline Phases. The offline phase precomputes the cryptographic material needed for secure multiplications (e.g., multiplication triples) independently of the inputs, and can therefore be amortized or pipelined across control intervals. The online phase begins once parties provide their inputs and consume this precomputed material to evaluate the target function. For latency-sensitive applications such as DR, where allocations must be computed every few seconds, the online phase is the binding constraint when offline preprocessing is enabled.

4 MPC-Based Collaborative DCDR

Our goal is to design a collaborative DCDR system to efficiently compute individual power targets for each data center without exposing any participant's private data. The core idea is as follows: every data center secret-shares its private inputs (power and QoS), the MPC protocol performs the balancing arithmetic on these shares, and each data center receives shares belonging only to its own target to reconstruct the output. Algorithm 1 summarizes the end-to-end procedure. Two practical challenges arise when moving from this conceptual protocol to an efficient implementation: (1) choosing the right number representation for secure arithmetic, and (2) eliminating expensive secure division operations. We address each challenge below.

Algorithm 1. Secure Multi-Data-Center Power Balancing via MPC

Require: Secret shares $\langle \bar{P}_i \rangle$, $\langle Q_i^R \rangle$ of each DC_i, $i \in \{1, \ldots, N\}$; collaborative power target P_{target} from ISO; balancing factors τ, ϕ
Ensure: Individual power target $P_{i,\text{target}}$ revealed only to DC_i

```
for i = 1 to N do
    Secret-share ⟨P̄_i⟩ and ⟨Q_i^R⟩ to all parties          ▷ Send private inputs
        – sync –
    ⟨P_{i,target}⟩ ← P_target · (τ ⟨Q_i^R⟩/⟨Q_sum^R⟩ + φ ⟨P̄_i⟩/⟨P̄_sum⟩)   ▷ Secure power balancing
        – sync –
    Reconstruct P_{i,target} from ⟨P_{i,target}⟩           ▷ Receive private outputs
end for
return P_{i,target}
```

Line 4: $\langle P_{i,\text{target}} \rangle \leftarrow P_{\text{target}} \cdot \left(\tau \frac{\langle Q_i^R \rangle}{\langle Q_{\text{sum}}^R \rangle} + \phi \frac{\langle \bar{P}_i \rangle}{\langle \bar{P}_{\text{sum}} \rangle} \right)$

4.1 Secure Arithmetic Representation

The MP-SPDZ library offers two ways to represent real numbers inside a secure protocol: secure fixed-point (`sfix`) and secure floating-point (`sfloat`) [17]. The choice matters because it directly affects both computational cost and numerical range. MPC arithmetic is emulated over large prime fields (or integer rings) to maintain security guarantees, so traditional hardware floating-point units, which complete an operation in a single clock cycle, cannot be used [17]. Secure fixed-point is the cheaper format for the operations in our protocol. Addition is a free local operation (0 rounds), and multiplication requires 2 communication rounds (one field multiplication plus one truncation) [5]. The corresponding secure floating-point operations are far more expensive: sfloat addition requires tens of rounds (the exact value depends on the security setting and parameters) due to exponent alignment and renormalization, and sfloat multiplication requires roughly 10 rounds [3]. Plaintext hardware arithmetic, of course, requires no communication at all. The trade-off is a limited dynamic range, determined by the chosen bit-width. The bit-width must be set conservatively to prevent overflow across all possible inputs, which means a fixed-point type often reserves a larger range than most values actually need.

The default `sfix` implementations use 53 precision bits to match the IEEE fp64 precision. In a DCDR setting, however, inputs originate from physical sensors and actuators whose own measurement precision is typically well below 53 bits. Allocating precision that the input data does not need wastes communication and compute in every secure operation. We therefore define custom fixed-point types, denoted $\widetilde{\texttt{sfix}}$, whose bit-widths are tailored to the DCDR value range, and evaluate both 64-bit and 32-bit variants. Reducing from 64 to 32 bits has two direct effects. First, every message exchanged between parties shrinks proportionally, cutting total communication volume by roughly half. Second, field-arithmetic operations on smaller elements are faster, reducing per-operation compute time. The round count for basic multiplications is unchanged, but sub-operations whose depth scales with bit-width, such as post-multiply truncation,

Algorithm 2. Division-Free Power Balancing via Newton–Raphson Iterations

Require: Secret-shared sums $\langle Q^R_{\text{sum}}\rangle$, $\langle \bar{P}_{\text{sum}}\rangle$; Newton–Raphson iterations K
Ensure: $\langle 1/Q^R_{\text{sum}}\rangle$, $\langle 1/\bar{P}_{\text{sum}}\rangle$ (secret-shared reciprocals)

```
for each denominator ⟨x⟩ ∈ {⟨Q^R_sum⟩, ⟨P̄_sum⟩} do
    ⟨w⟩ ← PolyApprox_{1/x}(⟨x⟩)                    ▷ Chebyshev approximation of 1/x
    for k = 1 to K do
        ⟨w⟩ ← ⟨w⟩ · (2 − ⟨x⟩ · ⟨w⟩)                ▷ Newton–Raphson refinement
    end for
end for
Replace each division in Alg. 1 with multiplication by the corresponding ⟨w⟩
```

require fewer rounds at 32 bits, an efficiency gain we quantify against the loss in numerical precision in Sect. 5.

4.2 Replacing Secure Division with Multiplication

Algorithm 1 requires division to compute each data center's power target. In plaintext arithmetic, this is trivial, but inside an MPC protocol using fixed-point arithmetic, a single division requires approximately 40 communication rounds (dominated by normalization and iterative reciprocal computation), compared to just 2 rounds for a multiplication [5], a difference of over 20×. Since communication latency dominates MPC runtime (over wide-area links), eliminating divisions can cut protocol time dramatically. Our approach follows the strategy of von der Heyden et al. [14], who use iterative methods to replace costly inverse operations in secure power-flow computations. The core idea is to compute secret-shared reciprocals in two stages, summarized in Algorithm 2.

Stage 1: Chebyshev Initial Estimate. The Newton–Raphson iteration for reciprocals converges only when the initial guess w_0 is close enough to the true value; specifically, convergence is guaranteed when $w_0 \in (0,\ 2/x)$ [25]. In a plaintext setting, one could simply inspect x and pick a reasonable starting point, but in MPC the input is secret-shared and cannot be examined. We solve this by fitting a degree-m Chebyshev polynomial to the function $1/x$ over a bounded input range. Evaluating this polynomial on a secret-shared input requires only secure multiplications and additions, producing an estimate $w_0 \approx 1/x$ that falls within the convergence range. In practice, a small degree $m \in [3, 7]$ is sufficient.

Stage 2: Newton–Raphson Refinement. Starting from the Chebyshev estimate w_0, we iteratively refine the approximation to $\frac{1}{x}$ with the Newton–Raphson update for division [25]: $w_{k+1} = w_k\,(2 - x\,w_k)$, where k denotes the iteration number. Each iteration doubles the number of correct digits (quadratic convergence) and costs only two secure multiplications and one subtraction from the public constant 2. In practice, 3 to 5 iterations suffice to reach full fixed-point precision. Once the secret-shared reciprocals $\langle 1/Q^R_{\text{sum}}\rangle$ and $\langle 1/\bar{P}_{\text{sum}}\rangle$ are available, every division in Algorithm 1 is replaced by a multiplication, yielding a large reduction in total communication rounds and wall-clock protocol time.

5 Experimental Evaluation

Table 1. Experimental evaluation axes: security setting and corresponding MPC protocol, number of parties, arithmetic methods, and network conditions. SH: Semi-honest, Mal: Malicious, HM: Honest majority, DM: Dishonest majority.

MPC Protocol	Number of Parties	Arithmetic	Network
SH-HM: Shamir [8]	2–16 (Case Studies 5.1)	`sfloat`	LAN (1 ms)
SH-DM: Temi [19]	2–64 (Scalability 5.2)	$\widetilde{\texttt{sfix}}_{64}$, $\widetilde{\texttt{sfix}}_{32}$	WAN (5 ms)
Mal-HM: Mal-Shamir [8]		NR_{64}, NR_{32}	WAN (10 ms)
Mal-DM: MASCOT [18]			

We evaluate the secure power-balancing protocol to answer two questions: how much error, if any, does MPC introduce relative to a plaintext baseline and is that error acceptable, and can the optimized protocol scale to realistic multi-data-center deployments? We evaluate along four axes, summarized in Table 1: MPC protocol, i.e., security setting (four protocols spanning honest/dishonest majority and semi-honest/malicious corruption), scalability (2–64 parties), arithmetic precision (64- and 32-bit fixed-point versus floating-point), and network type (LAN and WAN with up to 10 ms RTT). All experiments run on a single node with an Intel Xeon Gold 6242 CPU at 2.80 GHz with 32 cores. We model and execute experiments using FlexDC-Sim [1], an open-source data center DR simulator, with the data center configurations and workloads from prior work [2]. Each data center is driven by CPU- or GPU-based workload traces [1,2].

5.1 Case Studies

The goal of this subsection is to verify that our secure protocol preserves the correctness of the plaintext power allocation. We measure this by tracking performance: the normalized distance between the power target and actual consumption, $|P_{\text{target}} - P_{\text{consumed}}|/R$, across five collaboration scenarios with 2 to 16 data centers. $\widetilde{\texttt{sfix}}$ denotes tailored fixed-point representation (Sect. 4.1) while NR denotes the division-free variant (Sect. 4.2). We group our arithmetic methods into two precision tiers: 1) The 64-bit tier ($\widetilde{\texttt{sfix}}_{64}$ and NR_{64}) matches the numerical precision of the plaintext IEEE fp64 baseline, producing identical power tracking with no increase in mean error; and 2) The 32-bit tier ($\widetilde{\texttt{sfix}}_{32}$ and NR_{32}) halves the bitwidth to reduce communication cost, at the expense of

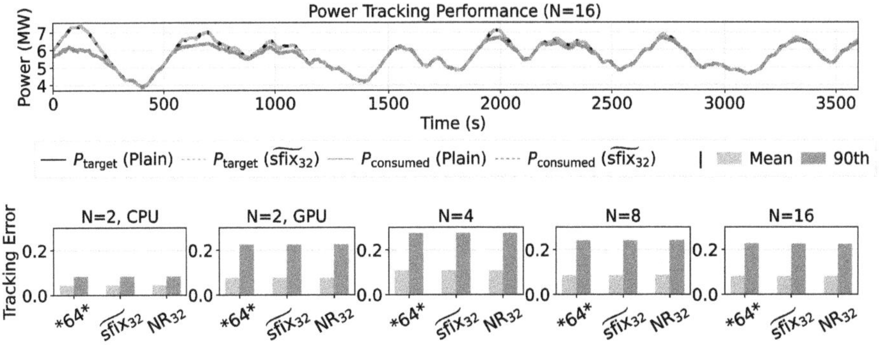

Fig. 2. Power tracking performance (N = number of data centers). **Top:** Aggregate power target (P_{target}) versus consumed power (P_{consumed}) for $N = 16$. The 64-bit MPC traces are identical to the plaintext baseline and thus omitted; the 32-bit traces closely track plaintext with minor deviations. **Bottom:** Mean and 90th-percentile tracking error ($|P_{\text{target}} - P_{\text{consumed}}|/R$) across plaintext and MPC optimized methods from Sect. 4. 64-bit variants match the plaintext exactly, and 32-bit variants introduce negligible error.

small rounding errors from the reduced fractional precision. We do not consider 16-bit arithmetic because it introduces notable deviations in power tracking, even in plaintext. Since MPC matches the requested bit precision exactly, this error is purely a numerical precision issue, not an MPC artifact. Overall, 32 bits is the lowest practical bitwidth for this application.

Figure 2 shows the power tracking accuracy of the secure protocol across all five scenarios. The top panel plots the aggregate power target against consumed power for $N = 16$ over one hour. The 64-bit tier produces outputs identical to the plaintext baseline and is omitted while 32-bit tier tracks the target with only minor deviations. These confirm that MPC adds zero accuracy penalty when the bitwidth preserves the full precision of the original computation. The bottom panel quantifies this across all N: The 64-bit tier matches the plaintext mean and 90th-percentile error exactly, while the 32-bit tier introduces only a small additional error that remains comparable to the plaintext baseline across all N, making it a viable choice when the communication savings from halved bitwidth (Sect. 5.2) outweigh the marginal accuracy cost.

5.2 Scalability Analysis

MPC protocols are communication-bound: latency is largely determined by the number of sequential communication rounds and the round-trip time (RTT) between parties (Sect. 3). To isolate the impact of these two factors, we benchmark every protocol–N–arithmetic combination listed in Table 1 under three network settings that reflect realistic data center interconnection scenarios: LAN with 1 ms RTT, representing co-located parties with minimal network delay; WAN with 5 ms RTT, representing geographically distributed parties within the

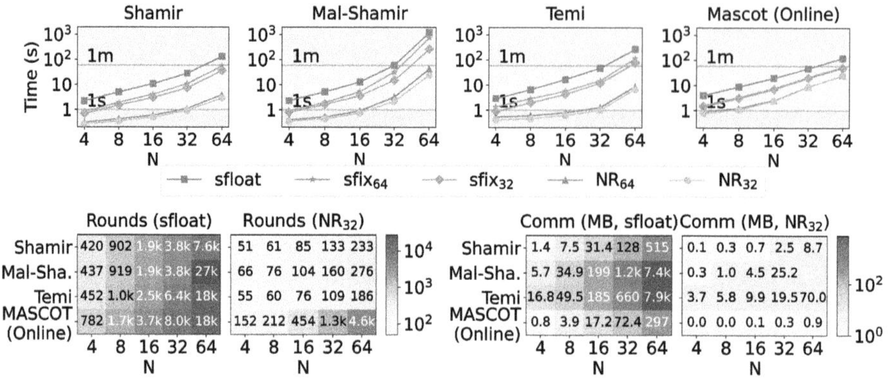

Fig. 3. Execution time (top) and communication cost (bottom) of the secure power-balancing protocol as a function of the number of data centers $N \in \{4, 8, 16, 32, 64\}$, across four security settings. Green and red bands mark sub-second and over-one-minute execution times.

same region/city; and WAN with 10 ms RTT, representing parties spread across distant regions. We simulate these conditions by injecting one-way latency into the MP-SPDZ networking layer: for a target RTT of r, each party receives incoming messages with a delay of r. Because protocol runtime scales roughly linearly with both the round count and the RTT, even modest reductions in the number of communication rounds translate into proportionally large time savings. This is precisely why the optimizations in Sect. 4 matter: replacing `sfloat` with `sfix` and then reducing the precision, and the subsequent move to the NR variant reduces both compute and communication costs.

We present our results of scalability benchmarks in Fig. 3. The top row shows that each successive optimization reduces execution time up to an order of magnitude. For Shamir at $N = 16$, `sfloat` takes over 30 s, $\texttt{sfix}_{64}$ brings this down to a few seconds, and NR_{64} completes in under 1 s. This pattern holds across all four protocols: the NR variants reach the sub-second region for up to $N = 16$ across all threat models. The bottom row explains where these savings come from. The round count heatmaps show that NR_{32} reduces rounds by 8 to 33 times compared to `sfloat` for honest majority protocols (e.g., Shamir drops from 1862 to 85 rounds at $N = 16$). Communication volume follows a similar pattern: Shamir at $N = 16$ transmits 31.4 MB under `sfloat` versus 0.7 MB under NR_{32}, a 45 times reduction. We note that the reported latency for protocols Shamir, Temi, and malicious Shamir correspond to the total (online + offline); however, our analysis of MASCOT focuses strictly on its online phase. This is because MASCOT (with no preprocessing optimizations) fails to meet the latency constraints of second-scale data exchange even at minimal network sizes (e.g., N = 4). Furthermore, networks larger than N = 16 result in memory exhaustion errors across several fixed-point precision configurations. However, Keller et al. [18] propose a series of optimizations that amortize the cost of

MASCOT by reusing the cryptographic metadata created in the preprocessing phase. Thus, we assume that data centers can execute this offline phase prior to the actual computations [18].

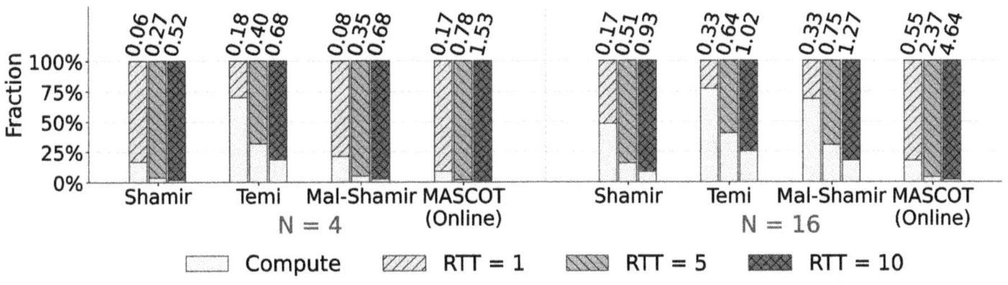

Fig. 4. The impact of network delays on total execution time (in seconds) for $N \in \{4, 16\}$ data centers using the NR_{32} variant. Bars are broken down by base computation time versus network latency penalties under LAN (RTT = 1 ms) and WAN (RTT = 5 and 10 ms) conditions. Numbers above each bar indicate total execution time in seconds. Network latency dominates total execution time.

To isolate the effect of network latency, we compared execution times across the three simulated environments (Fig. 4). In a localized LAN setting (1 ms RTT), the baseline execution times remain naturally low; however, moving to geographically distributed WAN settings (5 ms and 10 ms RTT) fundamentally exacerbates the communication bottleneck. In these scenarios, the severe penalty of sequential communication exposes the fragility of traditional protocols. Consequently, the aggressive round reduction achieved by our NR variants transforms from a mere optimization into the primary driver of performance, ensuring total execution times remain strictly under the one-second threshold up to 5 ms network delays.

6 Conclusion

In this work, we present an MPC-based system for secure collaborative DCDR. By tailoring fixed-point representations and replacing secure divisions with a Chebyshev–Newton–Raphson reciprocal method, we reduce the communication rounds by up to 33× and execution time by up to 45×. Our evaluation shows that the optimized protocol satisfies the DCDR constraints: completing at sub-second latency for up to 16 parties under WAN conditions, with negligible impact on power tracking error. These results hold across protocol settings spanning semi-honest and malicious adversary models. While we use Conductor as a concrete case study, our optimizations apply to any power dispatch setting where participants share real-valued inputs and the allocation involves division, offering a practical path to privacy-preserving collaborative DR as data center coalitions continue to grow.

Acknowledgments. We thank the Rafik B. Hariri Institute for Computing and Computational Science and Engineering (Focused Research Program award #2024-07-003). We thank Connor Wagaman, Palak Jain, and Prof. Adam Smith for valuable discussions on privacy-preserving algorithms. This work has been partially funded by the National Science Foundation DESC program under Award No. 2450111.

Disclosure of Interests. The authors have no competing interests to declare that are relevant to the content of this article.

LLM Usage Considerations. We used LLMs to assist with text editing. All ideas, experiments, and results presented in this work are entirely the authors' own.

References

1. Acun, F., Hankendi, C., Levine, E., Reynolds, H., Bardwick, J., Coskun, A.K.: Investigating power consumption flexibility of ai data centers for demand response participation. In: Proceedings of the 17th ACM International Conference on Future and Sustainable Energy Systems, p. 5. E-Energy '26, ACM (2026)
2. Acun, F., Paschalidis, I.C., Coskun, A.K.: Conductor: a collaboration framework for multi-data-center demand response. In: 2024 IEEE 15th International Green and Sustainable Computing Conference (IGSC), pp. 22–28. IEEE (2024)
3. Aliasgari, M., Blanton, M., Zhang, Y., Steele, A.: Secure computation on floating point numbers. Netw. Distrib. Syst. Secur. Symp. 405 (2013)
4. Beaver, D.: Efficient multiparty protocols using circuit randomization. In: Advances in Cryptology — CRYPTO '91, pp. 420–432. Springer (1991)
5. Catrina, O., Saxena, A.: Secure computation with fixed-point numbers. In: Financial Cryptography and Data Security, pp. 35–50. Springer (2010)
6. Chen, H., Zhang, Y., Caramanis, M.C., Coskun, A.K.: EnergyQARE: QoS-aware data center participation in smart grid regulation service reserve provision. ACM Trans. Model. Perform. Eval. Comput. Syst **4**(1) (2019)
7. Chen, N., Ren, X., Ren, S., Wierman, A.: Greening multi-tenant data center demand response. SIGMETRICS Perform. Eval. Rev. **43**(2), 36–38 (2015)
8. Cramer, R., Damgård, I.B., Nielsen, J.B.: Secure Multiparty Computation and Secret Sharing, Cambridge University Press (2015)
9. Deokar, P., Arora, S.: Multiparty computation for privacy-preserving communication in the smart grid. In: Smart Trends in Computing and Communications, pp. 299–309. Springer Nature, Singapore (2026)
10. Dwork, C., McSherry, F., Nissim, K., Smith, A.: Calibrating noise to sensitivity in private data analysis. In: Proceedings of Third Conference on Theory of Cryptography, pp. 265–284. Springer (2006)
11. Gentry, C.: Fully homomorphic encryption using ideal lattices. In: Proceedings of 41st ACM Symposium on Theory of Computing, pp. 169–178 (2009)
12. Goldreich, O., Micali, S., Wigderson, A.: How to play any mental game. In: Proceedings of 19th ACM Symposium on Theory of Computing, pp. 218–229 (1987)
13. Guo, Y., Li, H., Pan, M.: Colocation data center demand response using Nash bargaining theory. IEEE Trans. Smart Grid **9**(5), 4017–4026 (2018)
14. von der Heyden, J., et al.: Privacy-preserving power flow analysis via secure multiparty computation. IEEE Trans. Smart Grid **16**(1), 344–355 (2025)

15. International Energy Agency (IEA): Energy and AI (2025). https://www.iea.org/reports/energy-and-ai, licence: CC BY 4.0
16. Jahanshahi, A., Yu, N., Wong, D.: PowerMorph: QoS-aware server power reshaping for data center regulation service. ACM Trans. Archit. Code Optim. **19**(3) (2022)
17. Keller, M.: MP-SPDZ: a versatile framework for multi-party computation. In: Proceedings of ACM SIGSAC Conference on Computer and Communications Security (2020)
18. Keller, M., Orsini, E., Scholl, P.: MASCOT: faster malicious arithmetic secure computation with oblivious transfer. In: Proceedings of ACM SIGSAC Conference on Computer and Communications Security, pp. 830–842 (2016)
19. Keller, M., Sun, K.: Secure quantized training for deep learning. In: International Conference on Machine Learning, pp. 10912–10938. PMLR (2022)
20. Liu, Z., Wierman, A., Chen, Y., Razon, B., Chen, N.: Data center demand response: avoiding the coincident peak via workload shifting and local generation. SIGMETRICS Perform. Eval. Rev. **41**(1), 341–342 (2013)
21. Mohassel, P., Zhang, Y.: SecureML: a system for scalable privacy-preserving machine learning. In: IEEE Symposium on Security and Privacy, pp. 19–38 (2017)
22. Mustafa, M.A., Cleemput, S., Aly, A., Abidin, A.: A secure and privacy-preserving protocol for smart metering operational data collection. IEEE Trans. Smart Grid **10**(6), 6481–6490 (2019)
23. PJM Interconnection: PJM Manual 12: Balancing Operations, Revision 44. https://www.pjm.com/-/media/DotCom/documents/manuals/archive/m12/m12v44-balancing-operations-03-01-2022.pdf (2022)
24. Shamir, A.: How to share a secret. Commun. ACM **22**(11), 612–613 (1979)
25. Stoer, J., Bulirsch, R.: Introduction to Numerical Analysis, Springer (2002)
26. The Wall Street Journal: A new threat to power grids: Data centers unplugging at once (2026). https://www.wsj.com/business/energy-oil/a-new-threat-to-power-grids-data-centers-unplugging-at-once-741f1bda
27. Tian, N., Guo, Q., Sun, H., Zhou, X.: Fully privacy-preserving distributed optimization in power systems based on secret sharing. iEnergy **1**(3), 351–362 (2022)
28. Wang, B., Xu, L., Wang, J.: A privacy-preserving trading strategy for blockchain-based P2P electricity transactions. Appl. Energy **335**, 120664 (2023)
29. Zhang, Y., Tsiligkaridis, A., Paschalidis, I.C., Coskun, A.K.: Data center and load aggregator coordination towards electricity demand response. Sustain. Comput. Inform. Syst. **42**, 100957 (2024)
30. Zhang, Y., Wilson, D.C., Paschalidis, I.C., Coskun, A.K.: HPC data center participation in demand response: an adaptive policy with QoS assurance. IEEE Trans. Sustain. Comput. **7**(1), 157–171 (2022)

Accelerating Multi-agent Reinforcement Learning on Heterogeneous Platforms

Samuel Wiggins[1](✉), Grace Zgheib[2], Mahesh A. Iyer[2], and Viktor Prasanna[1]

[1] University of Southern California, Los Angeles, CA, USA
{wigginss,prasanna}@usc.edu
[2] Altera Corporation, San Jose, CA, USA
{grace.zgheib,mahesh.iyer}@altera.com

Abstract. Multi-Agent Reinforcement Learning (MARL) enables multiple agents to learn coordinated behaviors through interaction with a shared environment, but its training process is computationally intensive and difficult to scale efficiently across heterogeneous hardware platforms. We present a hardware-agnostic MARL training protocol that accelerates MARL training on systems composed of diverse computing devices, including CPUs, GPUs, etc. Our protocol systematically coordinates training tasks across devices, manages workload partitioning, and ensures efficient synchronization to maximize hardware utilization across various MARL algorithm classes while preserving algorithm semantics. To adapt to performance variability across heterogeneous resources, we incorporate a Runtime Load Balancer that dynamically distributes training workload based on device execution characteristics during runtime. We evaluate our approach using representative MARL algorithms spanning decentralized and centralized training paradigms across multiple benchmarks and heterogeneous platforms. Our implementations achieve up to 10.37× speedup over state-of-the-art baselines. We open-source our work at https://github.com/SamWiggz/Hetero_MARL.

Keywords: Multi-Agent Reinforcement Learning · Heterogeneous Computing

1 Introduction

Multi-**A**gent **R**einforcement **L**earning (MARL) is an emerging technology that has seen success in various applications such as power distribution networks [20], UAV swarm [26], traffic signal control [3], etc. In MARL, multiple agents learn and interact within a shared environment, each aiming to maximize its reward while accounting for others' actions. Compared to **S**ingle-**A**gent **R**einforcement **L**earning (SARL), where the environment remains static during learning, MARL introduces non-stationarity as agents simultaneously adapt and influence a shared environment [5]. This creates a dynamic landscape where each agent

M. Torquati et al. (Eds.): Euro-Par 2026, LNCS 16781, pp. 656–669, 2027.
https://doi.org/10.1007/978-3-032-35248-4_45

must adjust to both the environment and the changing behaviors of other agents. Many novel algorithms introduce coordination and communication mechanisms to address this non-stationarity challenge.

Because of the introduced complexity involved with enabling efficient inter-agent communication to combat non-stationarity, training a MARL system is becoming a more time-consuming process over time [22]. Heterogeneous platforms composed of CPUs and accelerators (i.e., GPUs, etc.), combining different types of computational resources, are often employed. CPU devices have traditionally been used to run application-specific environments, providing a plug-and-play solution for MARL researchers looking to test their novel algorithms across various scenarios. Accelerator devices are increasingly utilized to handle the intensive computations required for training deep learning models [27,28], which is an integral part of MARL training.

We conduct a comprehensive analysis of state-of-the-art MARL libraries and implementations and observe several limitations and inefficiencies. *(1) Underutilization of System Resources:* the Standard Training Protocol (shown in Fig. 1) used in popular MARL frameworks [6,8,17] and implementations [7,9,12,14] usually partitions the entire simulation and training phases on different devices, performing each phase (discussed in Sect. 2.1) sequentially, effectively under-utilizing heterogeneous compute resources. Such a task allocation can be sub-optimal, given that state-of-the-art CPUs show comparable performance in many MARL training works to GPUs [24]. *(2) Lack of Semantic Preservation:* few MARL frameworks [23] apply techniques such as asynchronous updates or parameter sharing to accelerate end-to-end training time. These mechanisms break training semantics, which is a necessity for MARL researchers when comparing against novel algorithms. However, achieving semantically correct results requires careful orchestration and task management among training processes. *(3) Limited range of supported MARL algorithms:* there are many classes that constitute a broad range of MARL algorithms (discussed in Sect. 2.3). Current state-of-the-art libraries only support a subset of these classes.

In this work, we address the challenges and limitations of current libraries by developing an open-source training protocol for high-throughput MARL training on heterogeneous systems. Our main contributions are:

- We conduct a detailed analysis of the state-of-the-art training protocol used for training MARL systems, identifying limitations and inefficiencies.
- We propose a Hardware-agnostic MARL Training Protocol that enables collaborative CPU and accelerator training, along with the ability to use multiple learners across multiple heterogeneous devices.
- We develop a Runtime Load Balancer that distributes the workload among multiple heterogeneous devices during end-to-end MARL training.
- We evaluate our work on various MARL algorithms and benchmarks on multiple platforms. Our implementations speed up MARL training by up to 10.37× against state-of-the-art implementations by enabling CPU-(multi) accelerator collaborative training.
- We open-source[1] our work with example algorithms across MARL classes.

[1] https://github.com/SamWiggz/Hetero_MARL.

2 Background

2.1 Multi-agent Reinforcement Learning

Multi-Agent Reinforcement Learning considers an $N-$agent partially observable Markov Game [11] composed of a state space $\mathcal{S}$, an action space for each agent $\mathcal{A}_i$ $(i \in 1...N)$, a reward function for each agent $R_i : \mathcal{S} \times \mathcal{A} \mapsto \mathbb{R}$, and transition probability $\mathcal{T} : \mathcal{S} \times \mathcal{A} \mapsto P(\mathcal{S})$ which defines the probability for agents to transition to other states given their current states and actions taken. For agent i, we denote its policy as a probability distribution over its action space $\pi_i : \mathcal{S} \rightarrow P(\mathcal{A}_i)$. Each agent i aims to find an optimal policy that maximizes its own expected cumulative reward until terminal time step T: $R_i = \sum_{t=0}^{T} \gamma^i r_i^t$, where γ is a discount factor. Agent policy networks are usually represented by **D**eep **N**eural **N**etworks (DNNs). Methods for training an agent's policy network (discussed in Sect. 2.3) are a key research focus for the MARL community due to the challenges introduced by non-stationarity and partial observability [5].

The training of MARL systems can be broken down into two phases as: **(1) Data Collection:** multiple actors, each holding an agent's policy network, interact with the environment(s) to collect data points used for training. These data points (a tuple consisting of observation, action, reward, and next observation) are called experiences and are stored in a replay buffer for later use during the next phase. Multiple environment simulations can be launched, denoted as the number of rollouts R. **(2) Model Update:** a learner samples a batch of experiences from the replay buffer to train agent policy networks using optimization algorithms such as **S**tochastic **G**radient **D**escent (SGD) and Adam [16]. Updated policy network parameters are then sent back to the actors to use during the next Data Collection phase.

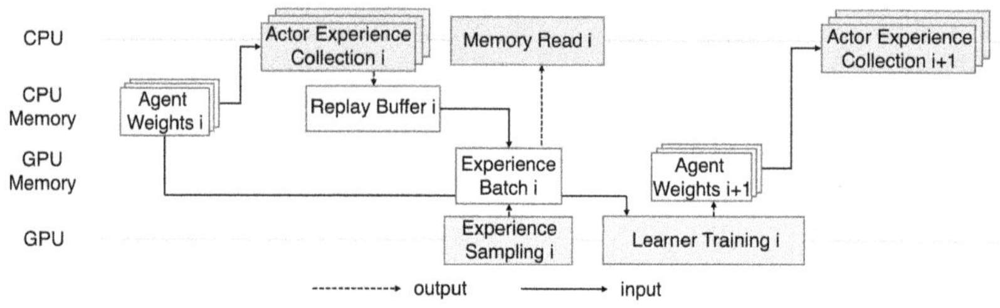

Fig. 1. Standard Training Protocol used in the state-of-the-art MARL libraries and implementations [6,8,17].

2.2 Standard Training Protocol

The Standard Training Protocol, illustrated in Fig. 1, is commonly employed by most state-of-the-art MARL libraries and implementations [6,12,17]. For simplicity, we show a system that uses a CPU for the Data Collection phase and a GPU for the Model Update phase. While the assignment of these tasks to specific devices can vary across MARL libraries or implementations, this task mapping is typically used automatically when a GPU is available. The protocol operates sequentially, with each phase executed one after the other, where the completion of both phases constitutes a single training iteration.

To highlight the inefficiencies inherent in the Standard Training Protocol, we present profiling results from an example MARL algorithm, **M**ulti-**A**gent **D**eep **D**eterministic **P**olicy **G**radient (MADDPG) [12], varying the problem size by adjusting the number of agents for a single training iteration, shown in Fig. 2. As the problem size increases, the proportion of time spent on the Data Collection phase decreases, leaving the CPU increasingly idle during the Model Update phase on the GPU. CPUs have become increasingly powerful over the years, demonstrating comparable performance to GPUs in various Deep Learning tasks [1,10,30] (discussed in Sect. 3.2). Additionally, the Standard Training Protocol is limited to a single learner, which trains all agents' policy networks on a CPU or a single accelerator, hindering scalability and leaving additional platform resources underutilized. Leveraging multiple accelerators for large problem sizes (i.e., large models, batch sizes, number of agents, etc.) could vastly improve a MARL system's training throughput, as shown in previous (multi-agent) Reinforcement Learning works [8,18].

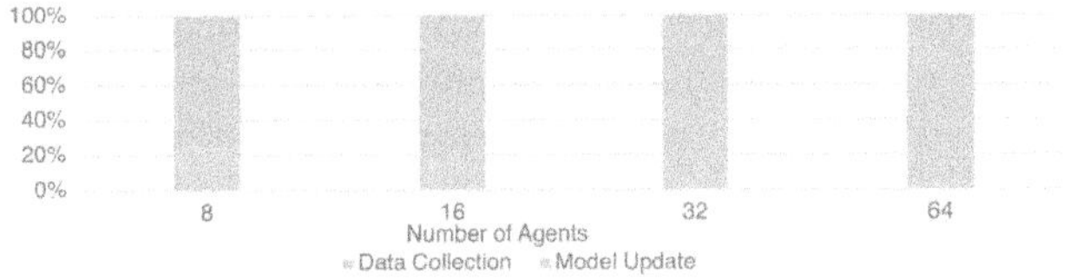

Fig. 2. Training iteration breakdown using the Standard Training Protocol.

2.3 Taxonomy of MARL Algorithms

MARL researchers propose various methods of inter-agent communication, which vary widely across algorithms [29]. Based on computation characteristics, a broad range of MARL algorithms can be categorized across two dimensions as shown in the taxonomy in Fig. 3 [24]. **(1) Training Scheme** can be broken down into two categories. In *Centralized* Training, a learner is responsible for coordinating the training of all agent policy networks. This learner has global knowledge of all agents' experiences. In *Decentralized* Training, each agent does not have access

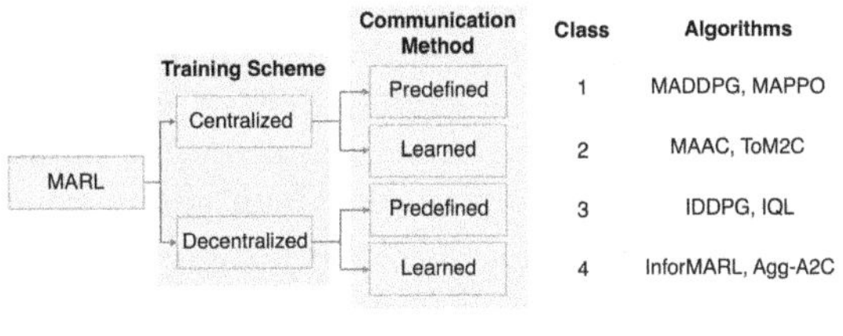

Fig. 3. Taxonomy of MARL

to the experiences of other agents, and it has to heavily rely on inter-agent communication whenever possible to gain such global knowledge about other agents. **(2) Communication Method** can be broken down into two categories. *Predefined* communication refers to a fixed communication method that remains unchanged throughout end-to-end training. In *Learned* communication, messages and connections between agents evolve over time. Figure 3 includes example MARL algorithms [4,7,9,12,14,19,21] from each of the four classes across both dimensions.

3 Related Work and Challenges

3.1 Related Work

There are limited works that focus on high-performance MARL training.

`RLlib` [8] is a popular open-source library for reinforcement learning built on the Ray framework [13]. It has been successful in producing highly optimized SARL implementations on distributed platforms. However, there is limited support for state-of-the-art MARL algorithms (only Class 3 from Fig. 3), with most being decentralized extensions of SARL algorithms without inter-agent communication. Multi-GPU training is only applicable to SARL algorithms.

`MARLlib` [6], based on `RLlib`, primarily focuses on MARL. It incorporates the largest collection of algorithms and environments compared to other libraries. Despite its large number of supported algorithms, it is limited to centralized and decentralized training with predefined communication MARL algorithms (Classes 1 and 3). `MARLlib` is built on an older version of Ray compared to `RLlib`, having no support for multi-GPU training.

`JaxMARL` [17] is a library that introduces GPU-enabled environment simulations using the JAX framework [2]. However, it suffers from underutilization of CPU resources since the Data Collection and Model Update phases are always mapped to the GPU. Multi-core CPU devices have become quite powerful for MARL training and should be used to fully exploit the compute power of heterogeneous resources [24]. `JaxMARL` does not support multi-GPU training and only few types of algorithms (Classes 1 and 3).

`MARLess` [23] is a serverless computing work that dynamically enables parameter sharing between agents' policies during training to reduce the number of active learners while launching a varying number of actors to balance training quality with cost efficiency. These adaptations cause a *(2) Lack of Semantic Preservation*, which may be acceptable for production settings but is a strict requirement for fair algorithm comparisons needed by MARL researchers.

3.2 Challenges

The Standard Training Protocol, illustrated in Fig. 1, is commonly employed by most state-of-the-art MARL libraries and implementations, including `RLlib`, `MARLlib`, and `JaxMARL`. It uses a single learner to update all agents' policy models on either a CPU or a GPU. This single device limitation causes an *(1) Underutilization of System Resources* provided by multi-core CPUs and multi-accelerator systems, significantly prolonging the time-consuming training process [22], especially with complex communication mechanisms and problem sizes that support larger numbers of agents, agent model sizes, and batch sizes. A new training protocol (Sect. 4) is needed to extend the Standard Training Protocol, which introduces its own set of challenges, including a *(2) Lack of Semantic Preservation* in many works. Coordinating multiple learners across CPU and accelerator devices requires careful synchronization and shared memory for both model parameters and the replay buffer. Load balancing across heterogeneous learners (Sect. 5) must preserve the original training semantics to ensure consistent reward convergence, a priority for MARL researchers.

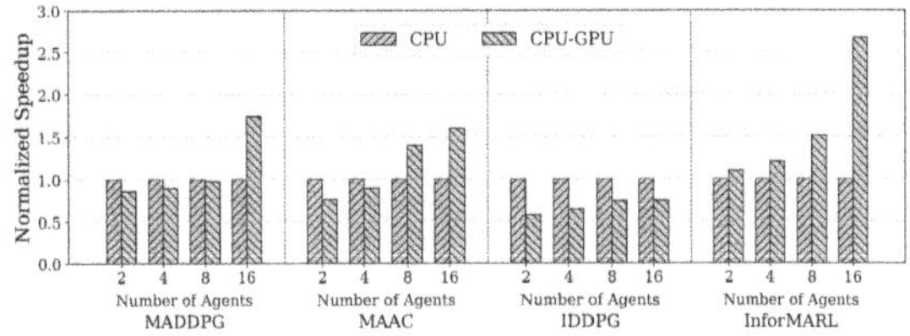

Fig. 4. CPU and CPU-GPU MARL Training

Many MARL libraries and implementations feature accelerator-enabled MARL training, where the Standard Training Protocol defaults to using a GPU if detected in the user's system. However, as shown in Fig. 4, the normalized performance (normalizing CPU training performance to 1) comparison between CPU and CPU-GPU platforms (64-core Intel Xeon CPU and an NVIDIA RTX 6000 Ada GPU) across different problem sizes (varying the number of agents) and the same four algorithms shows that CPU platforms can outperform CPU-GPU platforms due to additional PCIe latency and kernel overheads associated with GPU training. Again, each MARL algorithm exhibits different compute and memory characteristics, resulting in varying degrees of performance benefit (if any) from using accelerators depending on the algorithm and problem size.

Additionally, the *(3) Limited Range of Supported MARL Algorithms* in current libraries [6,8,17] restricts researchers' ability to experiment with different approaches. As the complexity of algorithms continues to increase, it is crucial to provide accessible tools that enable researchers to optimize their implementations, reduce training time, and facilitate experimentation with novel algorithms across different MARL classes. A more scalable training protocol than the Standard Training Protocol is needed to enable the effective use of multiple devices across heterogeneous platforms. Such a protocol does not currently exist, leaving MARL researchers without the tools to efficiently utilize their heterogeneous resources while experimenting with various algorithmic approaches.

4 Hardware-Agnostic MARL Training Protocol

To address the challenge of the *(1) Underutilization of System Resources* stemming from the Standard Training Protocol, we introduce a Hardware-agnostic MARL Training Protocol, shown in Fig. 5. The CPU platform includes three

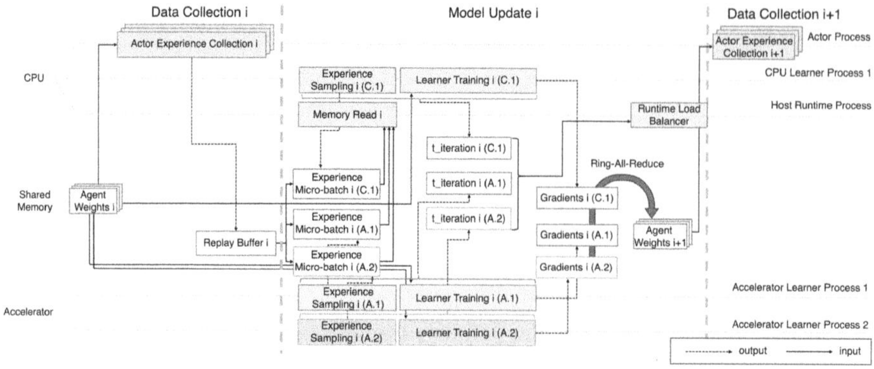

Fig. 5. The Hardware-agnostic MARL Training Protocol enables multi-device training. The letter in parentheses (C or A) indicates the device (CPU or accelerator), while the number refers to the device number (i.e., accelerator 1, CPU 1). For example, "Learner Training i (A.1)" represents the learner training at iteration i on accelerator 1.

types of processes: the actor process, CPU learner processes, and the Host Runtime process. The actor process is responsible for the Data Collection phase, where agent policy models interact with environment simulations to generate experiences. These experiences are stored in a replay buffer created in a shared memory space accessible to all processes. The actor appends experiences to this shared replay buffer, while the learner processes sample batches of experiences to perform policy network updates using optimization algorithms such as SGD and Adam. The Host Runtime process initiates all other processes (actor and learner processes), ensures proper synchronization by setting barriers, and is responsible for the Runtime Load Balancer that distributes the workload to the learner processes. Learner processes perform the agent policy training. Accelerator devices are associated only with learner processes.

Unlike the Standard Training Protocol, our protocol can deploy multiple learner processes agnostic of the capabilities of each device, which includes enabling CPU and accelerator collaborative training. The Hardware-agnostic MARL Training Protocol uses the DDP training paradigm [15] to efficiently distribute model updates across multiple devices while maintaining synchronization between them. When training with multiple learners, each learner processes a micro-batch (a subset of the original full-batch) of experiences. For example, if training with two accelerators of equal capability and a batch size of 1000, a possible distribution would be a micro-batch of 500 experiences per accelerator. Gradients are synchronized and accumulated using a Ring-All-Reduce mechanism [15], which allows gradient computation to overlap with synchronization during the DNN optimization step (e.g., SGD or Adam), ensuring efficient device utilization. Updated policy weights are sent back to the actor process for the next training iteration. Because it is hard to determine the optimal micro-batch size per device, the Host Runtime process gathers learner runtime information from each device, which the Runtime Load Balancer (Sect. 5) uses to reduce potential workload imbalance.

Importantly, the Hardware-agnostic MARL Training Protocol alleviates the *(2) Lack of Semantic Preservation* in prior acceleration works [23]. All learner processes operate on a consistent model state and participate in synchronous gradient aggregation at the end of every training iteration. Micro-batches are partitioned from a single logical full-batch sampled from the shared replay buffer, and gradients are aggregated via Ring-All-Reduce before any optimizer step is applied. As a result, the effective parameter update is equivalent to computing the gradient on the entire full-batch in a sequential execution. Our protocol does not use stale gradients, asynchronous parameter updates, or delayed weight propagation, unlike other works. The Host Runtime process further enforces iteration-level barriers between actor and learner processes to ensure that experience collection, gradient aggregation, and policy model updates occur in a semantically preserving order.

5 Runtime Load Balancer

Our Hardware-agnostic MARL Training Protocol enables multi-learner training using multiple CPU and accelerator devices, where each learner trains on a subset of the full-batch called a micro-batch. When using multiple devices, a naive strategy would be to evenly assign each learner the same micro-batch size. This approach fails to account for the heterogeneity in device capabilities, such as differences in hardware parallelism, memory bandwidth, and frequency, which can result in faster devices sitting idle while waiting for slower ones to complete their training tasks. Another method to achieve load balancing is to distribute the load based on each device's relative performance. This can be done by recording the full-batch Model Update execution time on each device individually and then distributing the batch based on the profiling results. However, we show that this may not result in a balanced system using an example in Fig. 6 with a batch size of 1000 on a single CPU and GPU system (a 64-core Intel Xeon CPU and an NVIDIA RTX 6000 Ada GPU). We normalized the Model Update execution time for all plots with respect to the CPU with a batch size of 1000 (left-most bar plot), where the full-batch performance difference between a CPU and GPU learner is 1.1×. The right two bar plots in the figure show the normalized execution time for the CPU and GPU learners with assigned micro-batch sizes of 550 and 450, respectively, based on their relative performance when processing a batch of 1000. The performance difference with the new micro-batch assignment has increased to 1.2×. This one-time calculation of micro-batch size based on device performance is suboptimal.

The Runtime Load Balancer dynamically determines how the global batch should be divided between the L_c CPU learners and L_a accelerator learners. During each training iteration, the Host Runtime records, for every learner i of device type $k \in \{c, a\}$ (CPU or accelerator), its Model Update execution time $T_{MU}^{(i,k)}$ and its synchronization time $T_{\text{sync}}^{(i,k)}$, defined as the portion of the Model Update time spent in communication (i.e., Ring-All-Reduce operations). The

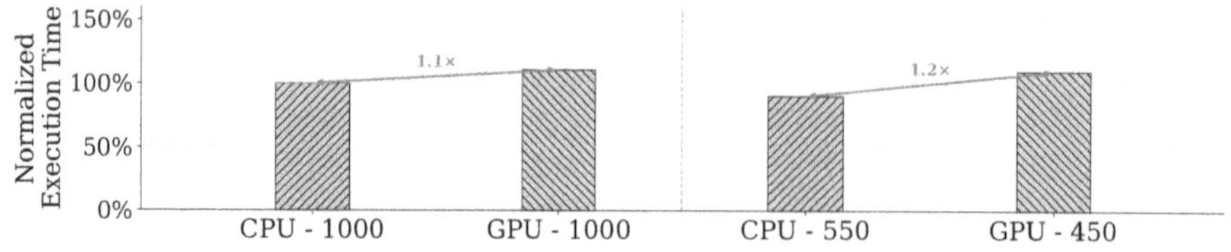

Fig. 6. Normalized execution time comparison between CPU and GPU devices with varying batch sizes. The x-axis is formatted: device - batch size.

effective compute time for each device type is then computed as

$$\widehat{T}_k = \frac{1}{L_k}\sum_{i=1}^{L_k}\left(T_{MU}^{(i,k)} - T_{\text{sync}}^{(i,k)}\right), \qquad k \in \{c, a\}. \tag{1}$$

We denote ρ_c and ρ_a as the fractions of the global batch assigned to CPU and accelerator learners, where $\rho_c + \rho_a = 1$. Using the effective compute times, the Runtime Load Balancer updates the batch fractions proportionally to the inferred throughput of each device type:

$$\rho_k^{\text{new}} = \frac{w_k}{\sum_{j\in\{c,a\}} w_j}, \qquad w_k = \frac{\rho_k}{\widehat{T}_k}, \qquad k \in \{c, a\}. \tag{2}$$

This enables configurations where, for example, accelerator learners measured to be 3× faster than CPU learners naturally receive approximately 3/4 of the workload. By continuously adjusting the batch fractions, the Runtime Load Balancer ensures that faster devices are not idle while waiting for slower ones, thereby reducing iteration-time bottlenecks and improving overall system performance.

6 Experiments

6.1 Experimental Setup

Evaluation Environment: We conduct our experiments on three different platforms. The first platform, *Server C1*, consists of two Intel Xeon Gold 6530 processors (totaling 64 cores, 2.1 GHz each) with 1 TB of system memory. The second platform, *Server CG2*, has two Intel Xeon Gold 6326 processors (totaling 32 cores, 2.9 GHz each), 256 GB of system memory, and two NVIDIA RTX 3090 GPUs (24 GB memory each) connected through PCIe. The third platform, *Server CG4*, consists of two Intel Xeon Gold 6530 processors, 1 TB of system memory, and four NVIDIA RTX 6000 Ada GPUs (48 GB memory each) connected via PCIe. Note that the NVIDIA RTX 6000 Ada has more compute power (91.1 vs. 19.5 peak FP32 TFLOPS) than the NVIDIA A100 GPU. These platforms range from homogeneous CPU-only systems and commodity heterogeneous setups commonly used in MARL research to more capable multi-accelerator systems, demonstrating the generalizability of our protocol beyond conventional configurations. We implement our designs using PyTorch v2.6.0, CUDA v12.6, and Python v3.10.16.

Table 1. Algorithms used covering all Taxonomy Classes

Class	Algorithm	Communicated Message
1	MADDPG [12]	Observations and Actions
2	MAAC [7]	Contribution embedding via Multi-Head Attention Mechanism
3	IDDPG [9]	No inter-agent communication
4	InforMARL [14]	Aggregated neighbor node information via Graph Neural Network

MARL Algorithms and Environments: Our open-source repository includes example implementations across all classes of MARL algorithms from the taxonomy in Fig. 3, demonstrating its generality across various communication mechanisms. The algorithms used and their communication message specifications for four algorithms encompassing the four distinct classes of the taxonomy are shown in Table 1. We will refer to these algorithms by the class they correspond to (e.g., Class 1 refers to MADDPG). We assess our protocol using multiple environment simulations from the **M**ulti-Agent **P**article **E**nvironment (MPE) [12] along with custom environments [7,14] used to evaluate the algorithms in Table 1. The environments encompass cooperative and competitive scenarios, and their specifications are consistent with their original open-source implementations. While we demonstrate our protocol with these specific MARL algorithms and environments, it is adaptable and can be extended to incorporate other algorithms and simulation environments.

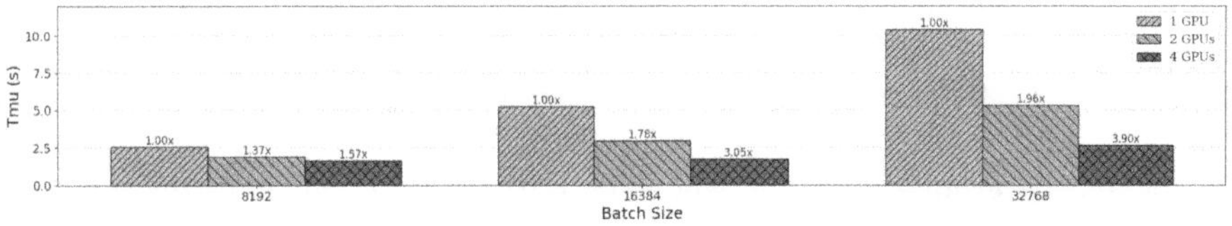

Fig. 7. Hardware-agnostic MARL Training Protocol scalability across various batch sizes and number of GPU devices. The numeric labels above each bar show the speedup relative to the 1-GPU baseline for the same batch size.

6.2 Hardware-Agnostic MARL Training Protocol Scalability

We evaluate the scalability of our Hardware-agnostic MARL Training Protocol by measuring the Model Update execution time (T_{MU}) while varying the number of GPU devices on *Server CG4* in an 8-agent Cooperative Navigation MADDPG experiment, as shown in Fig. 7. We vary the batch size to control the problem size, splitting the batch into even micro-batches that can be distributed across each NVIDIA RTX 6000 Ada GPU. The results show that scalability depends strongly on the problem scale: when the batch size is small (e.g., 8192), each GPU receives a micro-batch that is too small to saturate its data-parallel resources, so distributing computation across multiple GPUs yields only modest gains. As the batch size increases, each micro-batch is large enough to efficiently utilize the available GPUs. For example, at a batch size of 32768, our

Hardware-Agnostic MARL Training Protocol reduces T_{MU} from 10.38 s on 1 GPU to 5.30 s on 2 GPUs and 2.66 s on 4 GPUs, approaching near-linear scaling. These results demonstrate that larger problem sizes benefit substantially from multi-accelerator execution using our training protocol.

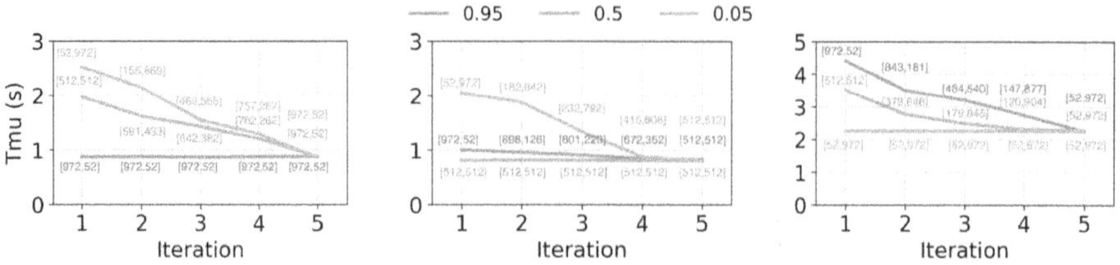

Fig. 8. Model Update execution time (T_{MU}) under different micro-batch initialization across problems with increasing batch sizes (from left to right: 1024, 2048, 4096). Value above plots: [micro-batch on CPU, micro-batch on GPU].

6.3 Runtime Load Balancer Evaluation

We evaluate the effectiveness of our Runtime Load Balancer on *Server CG2*, balancing the workload between a CPU learner and an accelerator learner (RTX 3090) in an MADDPG experiment. Figure 8 reports the Model Update execution time (T_{MU}) over multiple iterations for varying batch sizes. Each line graph corresponds to a different initial micro-batch assignment between the two learners. For instance, an initialization of 0.95 indicates that 95% of the batch is initially allocated to the CPU learner and 5% to the accelerator learner. The optimal assignments for each problem size are 0.95, 0.5, and 0.05 (from left to right), as indicated by a horizontal line when the initial assignment matches the optimal batch assignment. Regardless of initialization or problem scale, the Runtime Load Balancer consistently converges to an optimal distribution within just a few iterations. The overhead of the balancer is negligible, contributing only 5–20 ms per training iteration across the experiments reported in the next section (Sect. 6.4), where the corresponding single-iteration execution times ($T_{iteration}$) range from 0.2 s to 9.5 s. Even in the smallest problem setting, this overhead represents at most 2.5% of the iteration time, and for larger workloads it falls below 1%, making it orders of magnitude smaller than the dominant computation performed during each iteration.

6.4 Overall Performance

We evaluate the overall performance of end-to-end training using our protocol compared to a baseline using the Standard Training Protocol. **Standard**: This baseline is representative of MARL libraries such as `MARLlib`, `RLlib`, etc. Training is offloaded to an accelerator if detected in a user's underlying system. For CPU-based training (no detected accelerator), a single CPU learner uses the system's maximum core count. The overall training time on each of the three platforms is shown in Fig. 9.

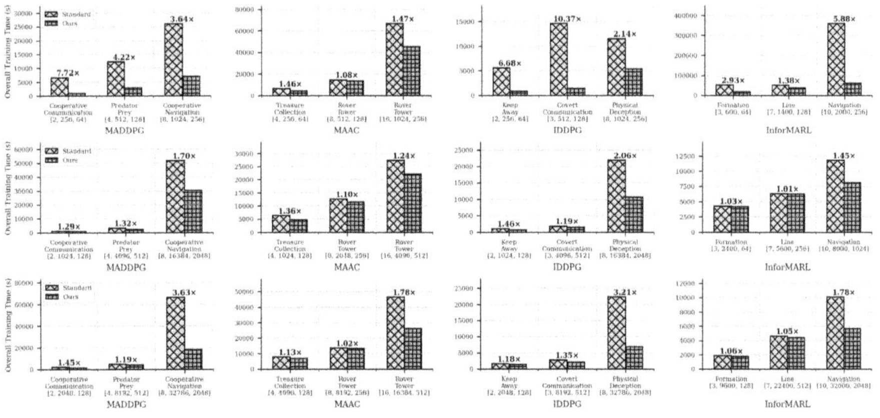

Fig. 9. Overall training time comparison between Standard and our protocol across three platforms. Results are shown for *Server C1* (top), *Server CG2* (middle), and *Server CG4* (bottom). The x-axis displays the MARL algorithm, environment simulation, and problem size (brackets read as: [number of agents, batch size, model size]).

On the multi-core CPU platform *Server C1*, the Hardware-agnostic MARL Training Protocol improves performance by launching multiple learner processes, each assigned a subset of CPU cores, rather than statically binding a single learner to all available cores as in the Standard Training Protocol. The Standard approach maximizes core utilization within a single process, but when the per-core computational workload is small, especially for less intensive MARL algorithms (Class 1 and 3), this leads to excessive inter-core communication and synchronization overhead, ultimately limiting scalability. By partitioning cores across multiple learners, our protocol reduces contention within each learner while maintaining synchronous updates across learners, especially in smaller problem sizes or less computationally intensive MARL algorithms (Class 1 and 3), resulting in up to 10.37× training speedup. For Class 2 and 4 algorithms, which involve more computationally intensive tasks such as attention mechanisms and GNN-based inter-agent communication, the benefit of using our protocol is still notable, achieving a speedup of up to 5.88×, turning an over 4-day experiment into one that takes only 17 h.

On accelerator platforms *Server CG2* and *Server CG4*, we observe significant gains, with up to a 2.06× and 3.63× overall training time speedup on larger problem sizes, respectively. As noted in Sect. 6.2, performance is highly dependent on the problem scale and underlying algorithm, thus making these performance improvements directly tied to the higher computational demands introduced by larger batch sizes, number of agents, and DNN models. As these factors grow, the demand for more efficient resource allocation and workload balancing of heterogeneous resources becomes critical.

7 Conclusion

We developed an open-source, Hardware-agnostic MARL Training Protocol that enables high-throughput MARL on heterogeneous devices. Our experiments demonstrated performance gains across multiple classes of MARL algorithms, environment simulations, problem sizes, and heterogeneous and homogeneous platforms, all without altering the underlying algorithm semantics. While our protocol provides the abstraction for multi-node training, future work will model inter-node latency and bandwidth costs, as well as explore primitive placement strategies that map learners, actors, and replay buffers across nodes.

Acknowledgments and Artifact Availability. This work was supported by Intel Corporation and the National Science Foundation under grant OAC-2411446. The artifact is available in the Zenodo repository [25].

Disclosure of Interests. The authors have no competing interests to declare that are relevant to the content of this article.

References

1. Awan, A.A., Subramoni, H., Panda, D.K.: An in-depth performance characterization of CPU-and GPU-based DNN training on modern architectures. In: Proceedings of the Machine Learning on HPC Environments, pp. 1–8 (2017)
2. Bradbury, J., et al.: JAX: composable transformations of Python+NumPy programs (2018). http://github.com/google/jax
3. Chu, T., Wang, J., Codecà, L., Li, Z.: Multi-agent deep reinforcement learning for large-scale traffic signal control. IEEE Trans. Intell. Transp. Syst. **21**(3), 1086–1095 (2019)
4. Witt, D., et al.: Is independent learning all you need in the StarCraft multi-agent challenge? arXiv preprint arXiv:2011.09533 (2020)
5. Hernandez-Leal, P., Kaisers, M., Baarslag, T., De Cote, E.M.: A survey of learning in multiagent environments: Dealing with non-stationarity. arXiv preprint arXiv:1707.09183 (2017)
6. Hu, S., et al.: MARLlib: a scalable and efficient multi-agent reinforcement learning library. J. Mach. Learn. Res. **24**(315), 1–23 (2023)
7. Iqbal, S., Sha, F.: Actor-attention-critic for multi-agent reinforcement learning. In: International Conference on Machine Learning, pp. 2961–2970. PMLR (2019)
8. Liang, E., et al.: RLlib: abstractions for distributed reinforcement learning. In: International Conference on Machine Learning, pp. 3053–3062. PMLR (2018)
9. Lillicrap, T.: Continuous control with deep reinforcement learning. arXiv preprint arXiv:1509.02971 (2015)
10. Lin, Y.C., Deng, G., Prasanna, V.: A unified CPU-GPU protocol for GNN training. In: Proceedings of the 21st ACM International Conference on Computing Frontiers, pp. 155–163 (2024)
11. Littman, M.L.: Markov games as a framework for multi-agent reinforcement learning. In: Machine Learning Proceedings, pp. 157–163. Elsevier (1994)
12. Lowe, R., Wu, Y.I., Tamar, A., Harb, J., Pieter Abbeel, O., Mordatch, I.: Multi-agent actor-critic for mixed cooperative-competitive environments. Adv. Neural Inf. Process. Syst. 30 (2017)

13. Moritz, P., et al.: Ray: A distributed framework for emerging AI applications. In: 13th USENIX Symposium on Operating Systems Design and Implementation (OSDI 18), pp. 561–577 (2018)
14. Nayak, S., Choi, K., Ding, W., Dolan, S., Gopalakrishnan, K., Balakrishnan, H.: Scalable multi-agent reinforcement learning through intelligent information aggregation. In: International Conference on Machine Learning, pp. 25817–25833. PMLR (2023)
15. Paszke, A., et al.: PyTorch: an imperative style, high-performance deep learning library. Adv. Neural. Inf. Process. Syst. 32 (2019)
16. Ruder, S.: An overview of gradient descent optimization algorithms. arXiv preprint arXiv:1609.04747 (2016)
17. Rutherford, A., et al.: JaxMARL: multi-agent RL environments and algorithms in JAX. In: Proceedings of the 23rd International Conference on Autonomous Agents and Multiagent Systems, pp. 2444–2446 (2024)
18. Stooke, A., Abbeel, P.: Accelerated methods for deep reinforcement learning. arXiv preprint arXiv:1803.02811 (2018)
19. Tesauro, G.: Extending Q-learning to general adaptive multi-agent systems. Adv. Neural. Inf. Process. Syst. **16** (2003)
20. Wang, J., Xu, W., Gu, Y., Song, W., Green, T.C.: Multi-agent reinforcement learning for active voltage control on power distribution networks. Adv. Neural. Inf. Process. Syst. **34**, 3271–3284 (2021)
21. Wang, Y., Zhong, F., Xu, J., Wang, Y.: ToM2C: Target-oriented multi-agent communication and cooperation with theory of mind. arXiv preprint arXiv:2111.09189 (2021)
22. Wang, Z., Hong, T.: Reinforcement learning for building controls: the opportunities and challenges. Appl. Energy **269**, 115036 (2020)
23. Wei, R., et al.: Multi-agent reinforcement learning with serverless computing. In: Proceedings of the 2025 ACM Symposium on Cloud Computing, pp. 225–239 (2025)
24. Wiggins., S., Meng., Y., Kannan., R., Prasanna., V.: Characterizing speed performance of multi-agent reinforcement learning. In: Proceedings of the 12th International Conference on Data Science, Technology and Applications - DATA, pp. 327–334. INSTICC, SciTePress (2023). https://doi.org/10.5220/0012082200003541
25. Wiggins, S., Zgheib, G., Iyer, M.A., Prasanna, V.: Artifact of the paper: Accelerating Multi-Agent Reinforcement Learning on Heterogeneous Platforms (2026). https://doi.org/10.5281/zenodo.20500249
26. Xia, Z., et al.: Multi-agent reinforcement learning aided intelligent UAV swarm for target tracking. IEEE Trans. Veh. Technol. **71**(1), 931–945 (2021)
27. Zhao, X., Wu, C.: Large-scale machine learning cluster scheduling via multi-agent graph reinforcement learning. IEEE Trans. Netw. Serv. Manage. **19**(4), 4962–4974 (2021)
28. Zhou, M., et al.: MALib: a parallel framework for population-based multi-agent reinforcement learning. J. Mach. Learn. Res. **24**(150), 1–12 (2023)
29. Zhu, C., Dastani, M., Wang, S.: A survey of multi-agent reinforcement learning with communication. arXiv preprint arXiv:2203.08975 (2022)
30. Zhu, Z., Xu, S., Tang, J., Qu, M.: GraphVite: a high-performance CPU-GPU hybrid system for node embedding. In: The World Wide Web Conference, pp. 2494–2504 (2019)

Author Index

M. Torquati et al. (Eds.): Euro-Par 2026, LNCS 16781, pp. 671–673, 2027.
https://doi.org/10.1007/978-3-032-35248-4